648978

B ✓

33  ...LIAMS
...ERS.

D1577585

Wandsworth

BASEMENT STOCK

08.92 EAST SUSSEX BEDFORDSHIRE			
09.92 +2m 53.66	28/11/58 +2m 30 NOV 98		
LAMBETH 25.06.99 +2y 398396	2 months 1011228 BUCKS		
13.08. 33	07 APR 00 +2 1812155		

West Hill Library
West Hill London SW18 1RZ
Telephone 01-871 6386

THIS BOOK SHOULD BE RETURNED ON OR BEFORE
THE LATEST DATE SHOWN ON THIS LABEL.

Basement

THE DERBYSHIRE MINERS

A STUDY IN INDUSTRIAL AND SOCIAL HISTORY

THE DERBYSHIRE MINERS

A STUDY IN INDUSTRIAL AND SOCIAL HISTORY

BY

J. E. WILLIAMS
M.A., PH.D.

Lecturer in Economic History
in the University of Leeds

GEORGE ALLEN AND UNWIN LTD
RUSKIN HOUSE · MUSEUM STREET · LONDON

PRINTED IN GREAT BRITAIN
in 11 on 12-pt. Plantin type by
UNWIN BROTHERS LIMITED
WOKING AND LONDON

PREFACE

When the Derbyshire Area of the National Union of Mineworkers asked me to write its official history it was anxious that the task should not be narrowly conceived and that industrial, social and political developments should be fully discussed. Apart from this major directive and an injunction from the Area Secretary that I was not to write a eulogy, both of which I welcomed, I was given a free hand.

With labour movement historiography still in its infancy the regional historian is faced with the problem of relating his own findings to an account of national events which is still incomplete and, in large part, still the subject of controversy. Little can be taken for granted. Moreover, trade union records are notoriously fugitive and it will no doubt be many years before the history of the Derbyshire miners is rewritten, if at all. For these reasons I have thought it desirable to deal with events in a fair amount of detail, quoting extensively from the available documents.

The union has been extremely generous in the facilities and financial support it has provided for the research and I should like to express my thanks for the unfailing encouragement I have received. The bulk of the work was completed during my tenure of the Douglas Knoop Research Fellowship in Economic History in the University of Sheffield. In this connection I record my gratitude to Professors G. P. Jones, J. C. Gilbert and D. C. Hague for the kindliness and consideration they showed at various stages in the project.

Helpful advice and criticism have come from many sources. I am very much indebted to my former colleague, Dr. Sidney Pollard, and to Mr. H. W. Wynn, the Area Secretary, for reading the whole of the initial draft. I have benefited greatly from the comments of Professor W. H. B. Court and Mr. John Saville who read the work in thesis form. My discussions with Mr. Saville have taken up much of his time and have helped to clarify many points. Professor W. H. G. Armytage and Dr. Royden Harrison have also been of great assistance with some of the earlier chapters. Dr. Henry Pelling made some valuable suggestions on Chapter XII before it was originally published as an article in the *International Review of Social History*. Mr. Brian McCormick has very kindly provided me with some useful references and statistics. The blemishes which still remain are entirely my responsibility.

My thanks are also due to Mr. P. J. Stevenson for allowing me to read his unpublished work on the early history of trade unionism among the Derbyshire miners; to Mr. Morton H. Edmunds for permission to examine the files of the *Derbyshire Times*; to Mr. F. Collindridge, Secretary of the Yorkshire Area of the National Union of Mineworkers, for access to the records of the South Yorkshire Miners' Association; to Mrs. F. Wilson for lending me the papers of Thomas Spencer; to Mr. A. R. Griffin for providing me with a copy of the minutes of the Nottinghamshire and District Miners' Industrial Union; to Mr. Arthur Horner for sending a leaflet issued by the United Society of Brushmakers; to officials of the National Coal Board for allowing me to inspect colliery records; to the staff of the Chesterfield Public Library for their unfailing help and courtesy; and to Mr. Walkland and Mr. Hallam, of the Department of Geography, the University of Sheffield, for their work in preparing a map of the Derbyshire coalfield.

Mrs. C. J. Millard was my secretary for the whole of the period of my research and writing. She assisted in the collection of the material, the statistical calculations and the drawing of the graphs. I am extremely grateful for her loyal and efficient co-operation which made my work so much easier. We were both thankful for the help of Mrs. D. C. Hague when the pressure of typing the final draft became too great.

J. E. WILLIAMS

Windermere
December, 1959

CONTENTS

A*

ABBREVIATIONS

The following abbreviations are used in the footnotes:

D.M.A. Minutes of the Derbyshire Miners' Association

S.Y.M.A. Minutes of the South Yorkshire Miners' Association

M.F.G.B. Minutes of the Miners' Federation of Great Britain

Throughout the tables the symbol — is used for 'figures not available'.

ILLUSTRATIONS

DIAGRAMS

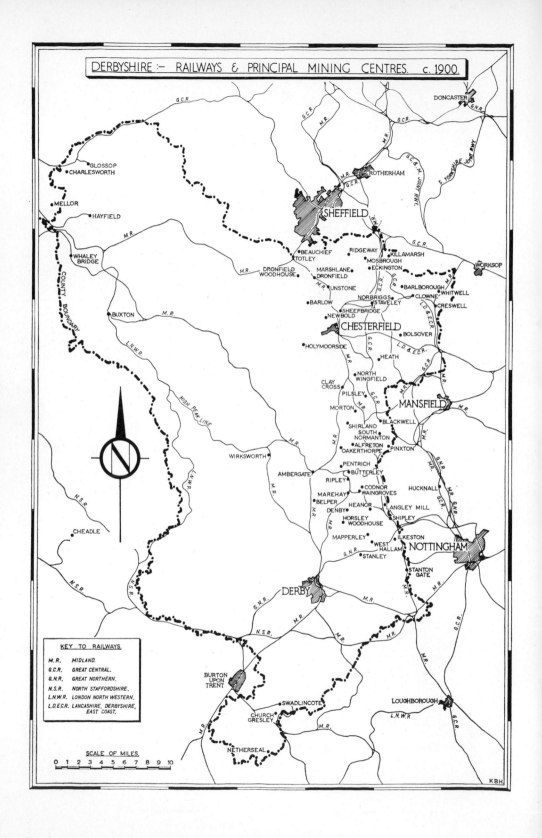

DERBYSHIRE:— RAILWAYS & PRINCIPAL MINING CENTRES. c. 1900.

DONCASTER

GLOSSOP
CHARLESWORTH

MELLOR

HAYFIELD

ROTHERHAM

WORKSOP

SHEFFIELD

WHALEY BRIDGE

BEAUCHIEF
TOTLEY
RIDGEWAY
KILLAMARSH
MOSBROUGH
ECKINGTON
MARSHLANE
DRONFIELD
WOODHOUSE
DRONFIELD
BARLBOROUGH
WHITWELL
UNSTONE
NORBRIGGS
STAVELEY
CLOWNE
CRESWELL
BARLOW
SHEEPBRIDGE
NEWBOLD

BUXTON

CHESTERFIELD

HOLYMOORSIDE
BOLSOVER

HEATH

NORTH WINGFIELD

CLAY CROSS

PILSLEY

MANSFIELD

MORTON

WIRKSWORTH

SHIRLAND
SOUTH NORMANTON
ALFRETON
OAKERTHORPE
PINXTON

BLACKWELL

PENTRICH
BUTTERLEY

AMBERGATE
RIPLEY

CODNOR
WAINGROVES

HUCKNALL

MAREHAY
BELPER
DENBY

HEANOR
HORSLEY WOODHOUSE
LANGLEY MILL
SHIPLEY

MAPPERLEY

ILKESTON
WEST HALLAM

NOTTINGHAM

STANLEY

CHEADLE

STANTON GATE

DERBY

BURTON UPON TRENT

SWADLINCOTE

CHURCH GRESLEY

LOUGHBOROUGH

NETHERSEAL

HIGH PEAK LINE

COUNTY BOUNDARY

KEY TO RAILWAYS.

M.R.   MIDLAND.
G.C.R.   GREAT CENTRAL.
G.N.R.   GREAT NORTHERN.
N.S.R.   NORTH STAFFORDSHIRE.
L.N.W.R. LONDON NORTH WESTERN.
L.D.&E.C.R. LANCASHIRE, DERBYSHIRE, EAST COAST.

SCALE OF MILES.

0 1 2 3 4 5 6 7 8 9 10

K.B.H.

PROLOGUE

PROLOGUE

I. THE RISE OF THE COAL INDUSTRY IN DERBYSHIRE

A detailed study of the rise of the British coal industry in the period before the industrial revolution has led Professor Nef to remark: 'Conditions of coal-mining were such as to produce within the industry itself a sharper cleavage between the owners of capital and the manual workers than had hitherto existed, to bring into being an industrial and financial organization for production more nearly approaching that of modern times and to give a greater power to capital while weakening the position of the manual worker and making him a wage-earner, frequently in a large industrial unit.'[1] As a result of Professor Nef's researches, the factors which combined to produce these changes during the sixteenth and seventeenth centuries are now well known. The dissolution of the monasteries resulted in a considerable transference of coal-bearing lands from ecclesiastical authorities, who were often conservative in their attitude towards commercial development, to laymen, who were prepared to invest large amounts of capital, or to allow others to do so, in order to exploit the mineral resources which lay beneath their estates. The incentive for these early industrial capitalists was provided by the growing demand for coal. Deforestation led to a remarkable rise in the price of timber, and coal was substituted for wood as industrial fuel wherever the appropriate technique could be developed.

Before these changes took place coal had been mined only on a very small scale. In Derbyshire we first hear of coal being worked in 1256 in the forest of Duffield Frith.[2] There are also references to the digging of coal at Denby, Breaston, Wingerworth and in the wapentakes of Scarsdale and Repton before the close of the thirteenth century. During the following century there appears to have been a considerable amount of mining on the eastern side of the county, particularly around Belper, and there is evidence that coal was being dug at Stanton, Hanley, Morley Park, Birdenser and Duckmanton during the fourteenth and fifteenth centuries. Even before 1430 there was a proleptic echo of the famous Butterley Company at Codnor where John, Lord de Grey had a coal-mine valued after his death at 33s. 4d.[3]

During the Middle Ages coal was not much used. A small amount was required for domestic purposes and for one or two specialized trades

[1] J. U. Nef, *The Rise of the British Coal Industry*, (London), 1932, II, pp. 196–7.
[2] *V.C.H. Derbyshire*, II, p. 349.
[3] *Ibid.* p. 351; R. H. Mottram and C. Coote, *Through Five Generations*, (London), 1950, p. 34.

such as lime-burning and smithery. In the building account of
Melbourne Hall in 1402 a payment of 4d. is mentioned for a horse-load
of coals, bought for burning the plaster.[1] Similarly, coal was used for
burning lime for agricultural purposes. The demand was small and the
price was low. Indeed, coal was sometimes taken freely by the tenants
as part of their perquisites, like peat or underwood. The customary of
Bolsover contained a clause stating that it was 'lawful for sokemen to
dig for seacoal . . . and to their proper uses, without the view and delivery
of the bailiff of foresters'.[2] Otherwise, leases were granted for the digging
of coal, the royalty being sometimes determined by the number of
picks at work and the consequent output of coal. William de
Semondslegh, the receiver of the Belper ward, accounting for the year
1315–16, mentions such leases.[3]

By the sixteenth century a number of important developments were
taking place. The coal-bearing lands which were controlled by Darley
Abbey, Dale Abbey and Beauchief Abbey all changed hands at the time
of the dissolution of the religious houses.[4] Some of the mines in Derbyshire began to be leased by the Crown. In 1537 Henry Parker was
granted the lease of a mine at Swanwick at an annual rent of £4, in
1570 Thomas Henshaw acquired a mine at Oakerthorpe at an annual
rent of £2 and in 1636 George Turner was granted mines at Alfreton
at an annual rent of £4. Capital was becoming increasingly important
and mines began to be worked by partnerships. As early as 1433
Richard Milner and his partnership were granted a mine at Morley
Park at an annual rent of £7 6s. 8d. until it should be worked out. From
the reign of Elizabeth I there are several instances, in north Derbyshire,
of small coalmines owned by partnerships.[5]

These changes coincided with a rapid increase in the price of timber.
Between 1451 and 1642 the general level of prices increased threefold
but the price of wood rose more than sevenfold. The land was becoming
almost denuded of its trees, and it became essential to replace wood by
some other fuel. Writing in the seventeenth century, Kynder remarks:
'Trees I doe acknowledge are soe few, in ye Peake espetially . . . but
these are supply'd with pitt-coale, Peate & Turff.'[6] The problem was
widespread and throughout the country attempts were being made to
substitute coal for wood or charcoal in various industrial processes.
In come cases it was found that coke could be used more easily than
coal. Coke was made in Derbyshire from the middle of the seventeenth

---

[1] W. D. Fane, 'Melbourne Castle and Park', *J. Derbys. Arch. Soc.* XI, (1889), p. 137.
[2] *V.C.H. Derbyshire*, II, p. 350. For a full discussion of the origin of the word
'seacoal' see Nef, *op. cit.* II, pp. 452–3.   [3] *Ibid.* p. 350.
[4] Nef, *op. cit.* II, p. 438   [5] *Ibid.* p. 51.
[6] P. Kynder, 'Historie of Derbyshire', *The Reliquary* (Old Ser.), XXII, (1881–2),
p. 23.

century and possibly even earlier.[1] Previously straw had been used as fuel by Derbyshire maltsters but henceforth nearly all beer brewed in Derbyshire was made from malt dried with coke, which, until the end of the seventeenth century, was obtained almost exclusively from a special grade of hard coal dug near the town of Derby.[2] So successful proved the new process that Derbyshire beer was actually preferred to other brews, and became famous throughout England.[3] There is no evidence that Derbyshire participated in the numerous attempts to smelt iron with coal although, according to Galloway, the project was entertained in the county earlier than anywhere else.[4]

Professor Nef considers that coalmining first became an important industry in Derbyshire during the period between 1550 and 1615 when he finds references to numerous collieries, most of which appear to have been recently started. At this time there were mines at Bolsover, Eckington, Wingerworth, Tibshelf, Sutton-in-Ashfield, Totley, Chesterfield and Shuttlewood. Further south there were mines at Heanor, Langley, Stanley, Butterley, Duffield Chase, Ripley and many other places.[5] Some idea of the scale of these enterprises can be gleaned from the fact that two collieries at Woodseats and Eckington had sometimes as many as four or five hundred wainloads awaiting sale at the 'bank' or shaft head.[6] The development appears to have continued throughout the seventeenth century, though it is improbable that the rate of increase in output was as great after 1625 as in the reigns of Elizabeth I and James I. When Celia Fiennes visited Chesterfield in 1697 she observed 'the Coale pitts and quarraes of stone are all about even just at the town end'.[7] The principal mines in the seventeenth century appear to have been at Smalley, Heanor and Denby, all lying within nine miles of Derby. These districts obtained their barley in exchange for coal, carried overland into Leicestershire and Northamptonshire, but most of the output was absorbed in the local industries of malting, soap-boiling, lime-burning and, later, iron-founding.[8]

The markets which were served by Derbyshire at this time were necessarily restricted by the difficulties of transport. Derbyshire, with the rest of the great Midland coalfields, was remote from the sea and unable to ship its coal to London like the North-Eastern coalfield or to Ireland like the Welsh, Lancashire and Cumberland coalfields. Over the

[1] R. L. Galloway, *Annals of Coalmining*, (London), 1898, I, p. 186.
[2] Nef, *op. cit.* I, pp. 215–16.
[3] John Houghton, *A Collection for the Improvement of Husbandry and Trade*, ed. R. Bradley, (London), 1727, I, p. 109; *V.C.H. Derbyshire*, II, p. 354.
[4] Galloway, *op. cit.* I, p. 184.
[5] Nef, *op. cit.* I, p. 57.   [6] *Ibid.* I, p. 58.
[7] C. Morris, ed. *The Journeys of Celia Fiennes*, (London), 1947, p. 96.
[8] T. S. Ashton and J. Sykes, *The Coal Industry of the Eighteenth Century*, (Manchester), 1929, p. 232; Houghton, *op. cit.* I, p. 105.

border in Nottinghamshire, Bilborough, Wollaton and Strelley were within reasonable haulage distance of the Trent, but, in Derbyshire, places such as Butterley, Ripley, Heanor, Langley, Denby and Codnor were all too far even from the Derwent to serve any but local needs, and are placed by Professor Nef in the class of those producing under 10,000 tons a year.[1] There were no conveniently situated navigable rivers and the age of canals, improved roads and railways had not yet arrived. 'Here', said Kynder, in 1663, 'is no highwaies or post-waies. . . .'[2]

If Derbyshire was denied access to the wider markets, the local demand for coal in the sixteenth and seventeenth centuries was sufficient to provide a stimulus for the mining industry. By the eighteenth century coalmining was becoming firmly established in the county and there was already emerging a pattern of ownership and control which, despite the great economic changes of the industrial revolution and the growth of the joint stock company, remained in existence until the nationalization of the industry in 1947.

Throughout the county the great landowners were working their minerals directly or through salaried agents or letting out part of them to entrepreneurs. Generally speaking, as in earlier times, the coal was worked by lessees. Writing in 1811, Farey states that the only consider- able landowners in both Derbyshire and Nottinghamshire who worked coal on their own account were the Duke of Devonshire, Lord Middleton, Earl Manvers, Edward Miller Mundy, William Drury Lowe, Henry Case Morewood and D'Ewes Coke, 'except it be in a small way, for their own and neighbours' consumption'.[3] The Dukes of Devonshire had mines near Chatsworth Park and at Whittington near Chesterfield.[4] They also leased parts of their estates for mining purposes.[5] The Morewood family began their connection with coalmining in 1789 when George Morewood, lord of the manor of Alfreton, acquired a Crown lease for the ancient mine at Swanwick which had been in the hands of the Turner family or their trustees since 1636. He eventually purchased the mineral rights from the Turner trustees and in 1822, for the sum of £1,500 his successor, Henry Case More- wood, bought the minerals at Swanwick Delves from the Commissioners of H.M. Woods, Forests and Land Revenues.[6] The Drury Lowe family and the Miller Mundy family were lords of the manors of Denby and Shipley respectively. Both were operating extensive collieries in the nineteenth century.

---

[1] Nef, op. cit. I, map facing p. 57.   [2] Kynder, loc. cit. p. 200.
[3] J. Farey, General View of the Agriculture and Minerals of Derbyshire, (London), 1811–17, I, p. 182.
[4] Ashton and Sykes, op. cit. p. 26.   [5] Ibid. p. 184.
[6] R. Johnson, 'An Ancient Swanwick Coal Mine', J. Derbys. Arch. Soc. LXXIII, (1953), pp. 118–20.

Similarly, in 1790, Benjamin Outram of Butterley Hall entered into a partnership with William Jessop, John Wright and Francis Beresford to establish an iron-works and to develop the ancient coal workings on the Butterley Hall estate.[1] This was the beginning of Benjamin Outram and Company (later known as the Butterley Company), a precursor of the vertically integrated firms which were to play such a prominent part in the development of the Derbyshire coalfield in the nineteenth century.[2] John Wright, the son of a Nottingham ironmaster and banker, eventually bought out the Beresford and Outram interests and in 1815 a new partnership agreement gave William Jessop the younger one-third of a capital of £30,000. John Wright had the remaining two-thirds, and, in addition, he bought the Butterley Park estate on his own account, and the Butterley Hall estate (formerly a partnership asset) either on his own account or in trust for the new company.[3] The Wright family maintained its association with coalmining until 1947 when there were four Wrights on the board of directors of the Butterley Company.[4]

But not all of these early industrial capitalists were able to acquire ownership of the land they worked for coal. Sometimes the lessees of mines were humble yeomen and leasehold farmers who required coal for lime-burning and sank pits which supplied the domestic and industrial needs of themselves and their neighbours. Thus John Barnes of Barlow, the son of a tenant farmer, and himself, after 1756, the freeholder of some 70 acres at Ashgate, obtained in 1763, of the trustees of the Earl of Oxford, the lease of a small colliery at Barlow, in the parish of Staveley.[5] From these small beginnings developed the Grassmoor Company which continued to be guided and controlled by the Barnes family until quite recent times.

During the eighteenth century the demand for coal was still increasing and Derbyshire began to feel the impact of the industrial revolution. The introduction of machinery, the growth of the factory system and the consequent development of the iron trade all stimulated the demand for coal. Before the introduction of coke for the smelting of iron, there were only four blast-furnaces in Derbyshire with an aggregate production of 800 tons of pig-iron annually. In 1788 only one charcoal blast-furnace remained but there were seven coke-fired blast-furnaces with an aggregate annual production of 4,500 tons of pig-iron. By 1796 there were ten blast-furnaces producing 7,650 tons of pig-iron.[6]

Moreover, the market for Derbyshire coal was considerably widened

---

[1] Mottram and Coote, op. cit. pp. 39–40.   [2] See Chapter I, pp. 35–41.
[3] Mottram and Coote, op. cit. pp. 47–48.   [4] Ibid. p. 175.
[5] Barlow MSS. Cited in Ashton and Sykes, op. cit. p. 3.
[6] Stephen Glover, A History of the County of Derby, (Derby), 1829, I, p. 230.

by the rapid development of improved means of transport. During the eighteenth and early nineteenth centuries many excellent turnpike roads were made connecting Derby by various routes with Manchester, Sheffield, Huddersfield and other large towns in the neighbourhood.[1] There is not a great deal of evidence to show the extent to which the coal trade gave an impetus to the construction of turnpike roads in Derbyshire although specially easy rates were allowed for coal by several trusts in Nottinghamshire.[2] However, an examination of the map of Derbyshire in Glover's *History of the County of Derby* (1829), shows a network of turnpike roads covering the colliery districts.

More important than the roads were the canals. The first of these, the Grand Trunk Canal, linking the rivers Trent and Mersey, was planned by Brindley, and was begun in 1776.[3] It brought Derbyshire into connection with the rapidly growing industrial area of south Lancashire and became particularly important for the carriage of coal. The Chesterfield canal was also projected by Brindley. The Act of Parliament, authorizing the Company to raise £100,000 in shares of £100 each, was obtained in 1770, and the canal was finished about seven years later.[4] It ran from the Trent near Gainsborough to Chesterfield, through parts of Nottinghamshire, Yorkshire and Derbyshire, taking a route almost 45 miles in length. Again coal provided the bulk of the traffic. The Erewash canal had its origin in the desire of the owners of extensive mines on the borders of Nottinghamshire to find an outlet for their coal. It was begun in 1777, the engineer being William Jessop, one of the original partners of Benjamin Outram and Company. The canal followed the course of the Erewash valley for about 11 miles from Langley Bridge to the Trent, near Sawley.[5] The Cromford canal continued from Langley Bridge to Cromford. The Act of Parliament authorizing its construction was passed in 1789. Again, the engineer was William Jessop. The Cromford canal played a vital part in the birth of the Butterley Company and by 1828, out of 325,000 tons of commodities carried on this canal, 230,000 tons were coal.[6] Another important route for coal, the Peak Forest canal, connecting the north of Derbyshire with the Ashton-under-Lyne canal, was completed in 1803. In connection with these main waterways a number of subsidiary canals were developed.[7]

Many of the Acts of Parliament relating to canals also authorized the

[1] Stephen Glover, *A History of the County of Derby*, (Derby), 1829, I, pp. 255–6.
[2] H. Green, 'The Southern Portion of Nottinghamshire and Derbyshire coalfield and the Development of Transport before 1850', *J. Derbys. Arch. Soc.* LVI, (1935), p. 66.
[3] Glover, *op. cit.* I, pp. 261–2.
[4] *Ibid.* I, pp. 263–4.
[5] *Ibid.* I, pp. 264–5.
[6] *Ibid.* I, p. 268.
[7] *Ibid.* I, p. 265, 269; Green, *loc. cit.* p. 67.

construction of 'rail-ways'. It is not known when railways were first used in and around Derbyshire collieries, although John Curr of Sheffield, mineral agent to the Duke of Norfolk's collieries, writes in 1797: 'About twenty-one years ago I introduced rail-ways and corves at the Sheffield colliery. . . .'[1] This would be in 1776, and the rails were probably of wood. Later he speaks of laying cast-iron roads, of which he could claim seven years' experience at the time of writing, which dates these as 1789. The Act of Parliament of 1793, for the making of a canal from the Trent through Derby to Little Eaton, included the making and maintaining of a rail or wagon way from Little Eaton to Smithy Houses in the parish of Denby, a wagon way to Smalley Mill, and also, if required, for the sole use of the Earl of Chesterfield, the making of a branch wagon way to Horseley Colliery.[2] The branches were not constructed but the main route, which was largely the work of Benjamin Outram, was used by horse-drawn trams until 1908. Similarly, the Act for the Nottingham canal in 1792 authorized the construction of railways leading to the canal; and Edward Miller Mundy had a railway from his colliery to Shipley wharf, about half a mile away.

Most of the early railways were comparatively short, and were intended to convey coal from the mines to the nearby canals but at the beginning of the nineteenth century two railways were completed with the object of taking coal to markets considerable distances away overland. The Pinxton to Mansfield Railway, completed about 1819, and the Cromford and High Peak Railway, opened in 1830, joined the Cromford canal at opposite ends and thus formed a continuous route from Mansfield to Whaley Bridge and beyond.[3] From Pinxton wharf iron wagons were drawn by horses as far as Kirkby Summit, and thence by their own weight they travelled down to Mansfield, horses afterwards pulling the returning wagons to the summit again. According to Glover 294,697 tons were conveyed along this railway from 1819 to 1826, and of these 227,692 tons were coal.[4] The Cromford and High Peak Railway was a combination of inclined planes up which wagons were pulled by stationary steam engines, and level stretches upon which locomotives or horses could be used. In connection with the Manchester and Liverpool Railway it eventually provided a direct link between Liverpool and the counties of Derbyshire and Nottinghamshire.

The improved methods of transport had a profound influence upon the trade of the inland colliery districts. Evidence presented to the Committee on the Coal Trade in 1830 shows that the monopoly

[1] John Curr, *The Coal Viewer and Engine Builder's Practical Companion*, (Sheffield), 1797, p. 5.
[2] Eric Potter, 'Through the Butterley Country in Search of Outram's Railway', *Ad Rem*, (House Magazine of the Butterley Company), No. 5, (1953), p. 4.
[3] Green, *loc. cit.* p. 67. [4] Glover, *op. cit.* I, p. 268.

formerly possessed by sea-borne coal was rapidly being broken. Districts which had once been supplied by the coastal coalfields were now obtaining their fuel from the Midlands by way of the canals. In 1816 some 355,554 chaldrons of Derbyshire coal were conveyed by canals and railways.[1] Farey states:

Vast quantities of Coals are annually sent out of the Counties of Derby and Nottingham southward, by means of the Cromford, Derby, Erewash, Grantham, Leicester, Melton Mowbray, Nottingham, Nutbrook, and Trent Canals. . . .[2]

Pilkington writes in 1789:

It is scarcely possible to ascertain the exact quantity of coal, which is got in Derbyshire every year. But it is certainly very large. For besides what is consumed in the neighbouring country, a considerable quantity is conveyed by the Erewash canal into Leicestershire.[3]

In the twelve months ending 30 June, 1808, coal and coke to the value of £122,838 passed through the Cromford, Erewash and Nottingham canals alone.[4]

Carriage by canal was much cheaper than by road but not cheaper than by sea. The carriage of coal between Chesterfield and the Trent cost only one-fifth of that by road.[5] However, no duties were levied upon inland coal and the new areas supplied by the canals obtained fuel at a much lower price than did London and other places supplied by sea. In 1800 London prices ranged from 43s. to 50s. a ton. Seven years earlier the price of land-sale coal at Derby was 5s. 10d. a ton.[6] Similarly, with the railways; after the opening of the Pinxton to Mansfield railway the price of coal per ton fell from 10s. or 13s. to about 8s. or 8s. 6d.[7]

Thus, by the end of the eighteenth century, the Derbyshire coalfield was making considerable progress. An enormous geographical extension of its markets had taken place and an increasing demand for coal was being created by a rapidly expanding industrial system. The final phase of expansion, the capturing of the London market, had to await the further development of the railways and the introduction of the locomotive.

[1] S.C. on the State of the Coal Trade, (1830), Evidence of Buddle, p. 59.
[2] Farey, op. cit. I, p. 182.
[3] James Pilkington, A View of the Present State of Derbyshire, (Derby), 1789, I, pp. 145–6.   [4] Farey, op. cit. I, p. 185.
[5] Gentleman's Magazine, XLVII, p. 124, cited in G. Cadbury and S. P. Dobbs, Canals and Inland Waterways, (London), 1929, p. 23.
[6] Ashton and Sykes, op. cit. pp. 235–6.
[7] Green, loc. cit. p. 68.

2. METHODS OF MINING

The great North Midland coalfield lies to the east of the Pennines, within the counties of Yorkshire, Derbyshire, Nottinghamshire and Lincolnshire, with a small extension into Leicestershire. It consists of an 'exposed coalfield' in the west, where the measures crop out over an area of about 900 square miles, and a 'concealed coalfield' in the east, where they continue beneath unconformable Permo-Triassic and later rocks, and are now known to cover about 2,000 square miles. The area is richest in first-class industrial and house coals, since all the seams contain beds of bright coal, which have low ash and sulphur contents and are unsuitable for coking. Second in importance is the hard steam coal found in the Top Hard seam (or 'Barnsley bed') and supplemented by the Deep Hard seam in the west and south of the area. Gas and coking coals are present in the west and north of the field, mainly in seams lower than the Deep Hard.[1]

Early mining was confined to the exposed coalfield, which stretches from Nottingham northwards past Sheffield to Leeds, a distance of just over 60 miles, and increases in width from about 8 miles in the south to 20 miles in the north. In the Middle Ages most of the coal that was needed could be obtained by the opencast working of seams near the surface. At Denby, for example, William Rosel complained in 1307 that Hugh de la Grene of Darley and two others had cut down a thousand of his oaks in order to dig coal.[2] Another method of obtaining coal and ironstone was that of sinking what are known as 'bell' or 'beehive' pits, remains of which have been found in Derbyshire.[3]

These early mines were shaped rather like an inverted funnel with a narrow shaft of small diameter widening out considerably underground. Coal would be hauled up the shaft in corves on the end of a rope. Gradually such refinements as windlasses were added and later these were driven by horses. Celia Fiennes describes the mines about Chesterfield, in 1697, as follows:

> They make their mines at the Entrance like a well and so till they come to the Coale, then they digg all the ground about where there is Coale and set pillars to support it and so bring it to the well, where by a basket like a hand-barrow by cords they pull it up, so they let down and up the miners with a cord.[4]

[1] For more detailed accounts of the geology of the Derbyshire coalfield see Ministry of Fuel and Power, *North Midland Coalfield Regional Survey Report*, (1945); Sir Arthur Trueman, ed. *The Coalfields of Great Britain*, (London), 1954, pp. 167–96; Walcot Gibson, *Coal in Great Britain*, (London), edn. of 1927, pp. 181–207.

[2] *V.C.H. Derbyshire*, II, p. 350.   [3] Galloway, *op. cit.* I, pp. 32–34.

[4] C. Morris, ed. *The Journeys of Celia Fiennes*, (London), 1947, p. 96.

Further south, at Denby and Smalley, where the demand for coal was greater, mining techniques appear to have been more elaborate. John Houghton, writing in 1693, describes how the coals at Denby were drawn up by a horse, 'as in a malt mill, where there is a barrel, on which a rope winds, so that while one end winds up, the other goes down through the pulley and so contrary . . .'. He continues:

At Smaley, my friend went down the pit 20 fathom, by ladders of twelve staves each, set across the pit one by another; when he was so deep, he went underground (he believes as far as from my house to St. Paul's Church, which is near half a mile) in a mine or vein which was about six foot, where were coals over head and under ground, the workmen knew not how thick: from this place he was led 20 yards through a narrow passage, upon hands and feet, till he came to a large space which was the head of a sough which laid all the pits dry that were on that land and presently he came to a pit 20 yards deeper than before, out of which they drew water brought from another pit 20 yards deeper with two vessels, which would hold about 60 gallons each; they were hoopt with iron and biggest in the midst: when one of these came to the top a boy with a hoop drew them to him, and easily did throw the water down, which in that concave made a noise like thunder.[1]

Derbyshire pits were originally worked by the bord and pillar method. In 1811 a colliery near Chatsworth Park was still worked by this method; and a surveyor's account of another colliery at Whittington shows that pillar working was practised as late as 1821, and that eight-ninths of the coal was being removed from the earth.[2] Longwall working originated in Shropshire, it is thought, in the early or middle seventeenth century and its introduction into other coalfields represented a considerable technical advance. Its use in parts of Derbyshire soon after the middle of the eighteenth century is shown by various references in the account book of Barlow colliery.[3]

Under the bord and pillar system each hewer worked in his own stall, sometimes alone, sometimes accompanied by a single helper. The new method required a greater division of labour and the co-operation of several workers in a single task. The unit of employment became the gang or company of working colliers. The differentiation of function among the colliers became more marked as time went on. By 1815 it could be seen quite clearly even in relatively small mines: at Norbrigg Pit, near Killamarsh, the pit crew consisted of five holers, one hammerer, one river (or rembler), two loaders, two trammers or hurriers (putters), one hanger-on, and one banksman.[4]

---

[1] Houghton, *op. cit.* I, p. 105.   [2] Ashton and Sykes, *op. cit.* p. 26.
[3] Barlow MSS. cited in Ashton and Sykes, *op. cit.* p. 30.
[4] Ashton and Sykes, *op. cit.* p. 29.

Farey gives the following account of longwall working in Derbyshire:

The working . . . commences, by a set of Colliers called Holers, who begin in the night, and hole or undermine all the bank or face of the Coal, by a channel or neck from 20 to 30 inches back, and 4 to 6 inches high in front, pecking out the holeing-stuff with a light sharp tool called a pick, hack or maundrel: and placing short strutts of wood in such places where the coal seems likely to fall, in consequence of being so undermined. . . .[1]

When the Holers have finished their operations through the whole length of the Bank, or Banks, and cut a vertical nick at one or each end of the Bank, called the cutting-end, and have retired, a new set of Men called Hammermen, or Drivers, enter the works, and fell the Coal, by means of long and sharp iron wedges, set into the face of the Coal at top or near it . . . which they drive by large Hammers, till the Coal is forced down, and falls in large blocks, often many yards in length: . . . a man called the Rembler next follows, and with a hammer-pick breaks the blocks of Coal into sizeable pieces: and the drawing apparatus being ready, the loaders fill the Coals into the Corves or Trams. . . .

A new set of Men now enter the Pit, called Punchers or Timberers, taking with them a number of stout posts of wood, cut or sawed off to a certain length, from very old Underwood or the thinnings of Plantations, or the straight arms of trees. These puncheons they set up in a row, in front of and almost touching the new face of the Coal, applying a small flat piece of wood, or templet, at top of each, unless the roof which they punch-to, as it is called, be very hard. . . . The work is now ready for the Holers to return, and after another day's work as above described, the Punchers return, and in pretty good roof they take down the puncheons in succession and remove them forwards almost to the face of the Coal as before.[2]

Coalmining has always been a dangerous occupation and some of the hazards faced by the Derbyshire miner, even in the Middle Ages, have been placed on record. In 1291 we hear that Henry Fitz-Jocelin was dragging coals in a corf out of a 'colepyt' at Denby, and that the corf fell from his hands on the head of Henry Ryling of Kilburn, 'who died thereof after making his confession'.[3] There are also various references to fatal casualties in the pits through miners being buried by falls of the roof when using their picks. Early in the fourteenth century, Nicholas, son of John 'Le Grobber', and Richard 'Le Grobber' were crushed to death in a pit at Stanton. In 1313, at Hanley, Goddard of Kilburn was killed while attempting to descend into a 'colepyt' by a rope which broke. At Wingerworth, in the same year, a beggar woman named Maud Webster was gathering coal when a great mass of earth fell upon her.[4] Apart from such fatalities, the twin enemies of

---

[1] Farey, op. cit. I, p. 343.
[3] V.C.H. Derbyshire, II, p. 350.
[2] Ibid. I, pp. 344–51.
[4] Ibid. p. 351.

the coalminer, gas and water, were ever present. As early as 1322 Emma, the daughter of William Culhare, was killed by choke-damp at Morley as she was drawing water from a 'colepyt'.

In more recent times, when mines were being driven to a greater depth, choke-damp and fire-damp became a source of serious danger in the ill-ventilated workings. A writer in 1675 states that the usual remedy for victims of choke-damp was to 'dig a hole in the earth and lay them on their bellies with their mouths in it'. And he continues: 'If that fail they tun them full of good ale; but if that fail they conclude them desperate.'[1] As to fire-damp, he mentions that 'at Wingerworth, two miles beyond Chesterfield, within this month or five weeks, a coal-pit of Sir F. Humblock's hath been fired four times by this vapour and hath hurt four several men'.[2]

For a long time the occurrence of such explosions was regarded as inevitable but at a later stage attempts were made to remove fire-damp either by producing a deliberate explosion or by ventilation. In Staffordshire and Leicestershire a primitive device was used for exploding the gas. By means of a system of hooks and a loop of wire a lighted candle was drawn from a position of relative safety to the part of the mine where the gas had concentrated.[3] In Derbyshire, at the beginning of the nineteenth century, Joseph Butler of Killamarsh used an elaboration of this method. Farey tells how 'he lays a slight tram-road along the bottom of the heading, and keeps a pulley fixed in or near the forefield, over which a rope passes, so that when the accumulation of damp is suspected on the Men's return to work, the tram can be drawn into the further end of the thurl, carrying a lighted Candle to explode the gas . . . '.[4]

There were various methods of ventilation in use in Derbyshire. One of the simplest methods, which was practised even in the early years of the nineteenth century, was to make a fan of gorse or furze, which was lowered into the shaft and moved up and down rapidly several times.[5] Where mines were driven horizontally into the hill-side, a floor of timber would be constructed, along which the miners could draw their sledges and beneath which water could flow from the workings and fresh air could enter, the hot and impure air flowing out beneath the roof.[6] The vertical shaft was often divided by boards: one side was then used for pumping and down this the fresh air descended; the other was used for winding and up this the used air ascended to the surface.[7] Sometimes fires were kept burning at the foot of the shaft or

[1] *Philosophic Transactions of the Royal Society*, (1675), No. 117, p. 391, quoted in Galloway, *op. cit.* I, pp. 186–7.

[2] *Ibid.*

[4] Farey, *op. cit.* I, p. 336.

[6] Ashton and Sykes, *op. cit.* p. 46.

[3] Ashton and Sykes, *op. cit.* p. 45.

[5] *Ibid.*

[7] Farey, *op. cit.* I, p. 333.

suspended in baskets in ventilating shafts. At Killamarsh, Joseph
Butler used to sink a shaft of small diameter a short distance from his
air shaft, with which it was connected by a narrow tunnel, two yards
below the surface. The air shaft itself was bricked over at the top and the
fire-basket was suspended in the small shaft. In this way a stronger
flow of air was produced.[1]

It has been said that coalmining did not pass through an industrial
revolution.[2] Although, from an economic standpoint, the industry was
profoundly affected by the technical changes which were taking place
in other industries, when practically every other industry was being
mechanized there seemed to be little scope for more machinery in
coalmining. The industry continued to use methods of working which
were not substantially different from those which were adopted when the
increased demand for coal made deep mining a necessity.

There were, of course, improvements in drainage and winding gear.
Farey gives a list of thirty-three water-courses, some of them two to
three miles in length, which drained the coalpits and lead-mines of
Derbyshire, 'lasting Monuments of the spirit and perseverance of the
Miners in this district'.[3] Pumps were also used for ridding mines of
water. The earliest were the churn pumps, 'a series of inclined wooden
Pumps, each of which was worked by a Man, who sat and pulled up the
bucket by means of a cross handle'. Later came the chain or rag pumps
'worked by a great number of Men in succession'. Rag pumps were
still in use at Whittington Moor at the beginning of the nineteenth
century. At Barlow Colliery and other places the pumps were worked
by cranks driven by waterwheels.

The first steam engine for pumping was erected at Yate Stoop
lead-mine during the 1730's. The colliery proprietors soon followed suit
and a large number of such engines were installed throughout the
county. The first steam winding-engine was erected at Oakthorpe
Colliery, in Measham, in 1790. By the beginning of the nineteenth
century Farey was able to write: 'Great numbers of the larger Collieries
have now Pumping Steam-Engines, some of which are of great power.'
Winding-engines were by that time so common that Farey noticed more
than fifty in Derbyshire and Nottinghamshire alone.[4]

Underground the methods of working changed very little during the
period of the industrial revolution and it was not until later in the nineteenth century, when economic conditions were much less favourable,
that the coal-owners began seriously to explore the possibilities of
mechanization.

[1] Farey, op. cit. I, p. 334.   [2] Ashton and Sykes, op. cit. p. 174.
[3] Farey, op. cit. I, pp. 328–31.   [4] Ibid. I, p. 338.

3. WAGES AND CONDITIONS

Combinations of workmen are at least as old as the fourteenth century. The ravages of the Black Death in the early part of that century led to such a shortage of labour that the workers were able to demand much higher wages than had been customary. There is evidence to show that the 'coliers' and 'grovers' of Derbyshire took advantage of these circumstances.[1] But at this point the State intervened with the Statutes of Labourers[2] which provided for the fixing of wages by the justices of the peace. Despite this legislation, it appears that Derbyshire workers were able to obtain increases in wages. In 1358 there were 120 persons presented in the Morleston wapentake alone for having taken excessive wages and for charging excessive prices for ale, bread and corn. They included agricultural labourers, smiths and colliers. Many of them were heavily fined.[3]

By the eighteenth century the system of wage regulation by the justices of the peace was rapidly falling into desuetude but the laws forbidding workmen to combine were still enforced. It is not surprising, therefore, that wages continued to exhibit a marked rigidity. The earnings of colliers generally during the early years of the century have been estimated at between 12d. and 18d. a day.[4] The colliery book of John Barnes for the pits at Barlow shows a normal day wage for hewers between 1744 and 1776 of 1s. 6d. and the same rate was paid for driving underground ways.[5]

However, apart from the bad harvests of 1727-8, 1740, and 1756-7, when the price of food was high and real wages were correspondingly low, the trend of general prices from 1715 to 1765 was downward. From about 1775 two factors combined to produce increases in miners' wages. The outbreak of the American War led to a general rise of prices with currency inflation and wage rates became more flexible. This occurred at a time when the Derbyshire coalfield, in common with the other inland areas, was entering upon a period of prosperity as a result of improved methods of transport and the growing use of coal for smelting iron. Thus from 1776 to 1779 there is a tendency for the rate at Barlow to rise from 1s. 6d. to 1s. 8d. a day. At Butterley, in 1790, sinkers received a day-wage of 2s. 2d. and in the following year eight sinkers received 2s. 3d., three 2s. and eight 1s. 6d., while five labourers

[1] V.C.H. Derbyshire, II, p. 351.
[2] 23 Edw. III (1349), cc. 1-8; 25 Edw. III (1351), st. II; 34 Edw. III (1360), cc. 9-11.
[3] V.C.H. Derbyshire, II, p. 167.
[4] T. S. Ashton, 'The Coalminers of the Eighteenth Century', Economic History, I, (1928), p. 314.
[5] G. W. Daniels and T. S. Ashton, 'The Records of a Derbyshire Colliery, 1763-1779', Economic History Review, II, (1929), pp. 126-7.

were given 2s. a day each. In 1795 wages of underground workers were 2s. 4d. and 2s. 6d.[1]

The upward trend of prices was given an impetus by the Napoleonic wars and reached its zenith in 1813. Particulars of miners' wages are insufficient to allow of any close correlation with retail prices. Professor Ashton, putting the general wage in 1780 at 1s. 8d. as it was at Barlow, and the general wage in 1813 at 3s. 4d. as it was in Durham, suggests that wages had more than kept pace with prices, but had advanced slightly less than the cost of living as expressed in Silberling's index.[2]

Not all workers were paid at the normal day rate. Some of the miners employed by John Barnes at Barlow for driving levels were paid by the piece which probably enabled them to increase their earnings. Moreover, additional payments, either in kind or in money, were invariably given for work of a difficult or disagreeable nature. Thus, at Barlow, ale was issued as a compensation for work in wet or inconvenient places. More frequently, the payment was made in money.[3]

A common method of payment was for the employer to give the miners a weekly or fortnightly 'subsistence' which did not bear any strict relation to the earnings of the period. At intervals the account of each man was reckoned and the balance handed over. This system offered certain advantages to both worker and employer. For the worker, it provided a minimum below which his weekly income could not fall and prevented undue fluctuations in his standard of living. For the employer, it was a means of deferring part of his wages bill until such time as he found himself with sufficient ready cash.[4] The provision of money to meet the wages bill was not always easy, especially in times of financial crisis. In 1793, when war was declared on France, the proprietor of Hasland Colliery had to obtain coin of small denomination from local tradespeople.[5]

The eighteenth century saw the beginnings of truck and the butty system which, with all their attendant evils, were to cause so much misery in the nineteenth century. There seems to be no evidence of truck at Barlow in the eighteenth century but at Hasland (the forerunner of the Grassmoor Colliery), the proprietor, John Brocksopp, also owned a farm. In the Hasland Colliery Book Professor Ashton finds numerous references to colliers being paid with farm produce. Some of the colliers with families appear to have laid down supplies of beef for the winter out of their autumn wages, for between 18 September and 27 November, 1793, no less than £53 2s. 5d., and between 17 September and 7 December, 1794, £66 2s. was paid to them in the form of beef. From

[1] Ashton, *loc. cit.* p. 317. [2] *Ibid.* p. 320.
[3] Daniels and Ashton, *loc. cit.* p. 126. [4] Ashton, *loc. cit.* p. 322.
[5] Hasland Colliery Book, cited in Ashton, *loc. cit.* p. 322.

1805 Brocksopp began to buy up from neighbouring farmers barren cows which were probably used as food for the colliers.[1]

The butty system had its origins in the collective contract or charter system of which Ashton and Sykes have provided several examples in Derbyshire. Thus, at Barlow, the task of sinking the shaft in 1763 was undertaken by members of a family named Booker, who contracted for work at a collective piece-wage. Similarly, the working of the coal was the subject of a bargain with a company of colliers. During the year 1764, George Bramwell and Company were regularly paid to 'get, draw, and sale' coal at 2s. 1d. a load; a rate that persisted till after 1767, when 2s. 2d. became the regular contract price.[2] John Barnes, the proprietor, supplied the miners with pit-props and candles and paid the workers who maintained the underground ways and attended to the pumps.

Another example is provided by Benjamin Outram and Company. Here, when bargains for cutting coal were concluded, a small payment was at once made by way 'of earnest'; thereafter round sums were paid as 'subsistence' each fortnight; and a final balance was struck on the completion of the work. According to a statement for the period 21 March to 3 April, 1795, three companies of colliers were paid an aggregate of £50 16s. in wages.[3]

A similar system of engagement was in operation at Hasland at the end of the eighteenth century. At Tibshelf, Norbriggs, Tupton, Woodthorpe and Wingfield, in the early years of the nineteenth century, the charter men had to pay the cost of punching the pit, of raising the coal, including the wages of one of the two banksmen and, at least at Norbriggs, of delivering the coal in iron corves at the canal.[4]

Ashton and Sykes have shown that these companies of working colliers originally enjoyed equality of status but, they comment: 'By a process for which there are parallels in the fourteenth and probably in all succeeding centuries, the more powerful personalities among the workers, having acquired a little capital, ceased to be simply leaders and became masters, intervening between the men of property and the working colliers. The more or less democratic co-partnery of earlier times, it would seem, had as its degenerate offspring the hated butty system of the nineteenth century.'[5]

[1] Ashton, loc. cit. pp. 322–3.
[2] Ashton and Sykes, op. cit. p. 104. The writers comment: 'The phrase "get, draw and sale", which is the formula used throughout the record is probably not in this case to be taken as implying that the coal was actually delivered to the customer by the working colliers: the word "sale" is evidently used here . . . with the meaning "expose for sale", and the task of the gang of colliers was complete when they had stacked the coal on the pit bank.'
[3] Ibid. p. 106.   [4] Ibid. p. 105.   [5] Ibid. pp. 113–14.

The butty system is generally considered to have been at its worst and most persistent in Staffordshire and Derbyshire.[1] Here, there remained, until the advent of the railways widened enormously the market for coal from inland mines, a number of small collieries. In 1842 the Children's Employment Commission reported that the coalmines in Derbyshire 'are wrought by butties who hire all the workpeople'.[2] In the mining districts which had access to navigable water every increase in the scale of mining tended to eliminate the foremen who participated in colliery financing. Neither truck nor the butty system ever obtained a firm hold in the large-scale mining concerns of Northumberland and Durham. Professor Ashton writes: 'Like the butty system, truck developed in response to a real economic need. The two sprang up in the same soil; both were the product of a relatively early stage of capitalism. . . . When . . . they ceased to be necessary and had become problems, the evils of truck shop and butties were found to be inextricably intertwined.'[3]

[1] R. N. Boyd, *Coal Pits and Pitmen*, (London), 1892, p. 15; J. L. and B. Hammond, *The Town Labourer*, (London), 1917, pp. 9n, 174. But see S. M. Hardy, 'The Development of Coal Mining in a North Derbyshire Village, 1635–1860', *University of Birmingham Historical Journal*, V, (1957), pp. 147–66.

[2] *Children's Employment Commission*, 1842, First Report, No. 177, p. 40.

[3] Ashton, *loc. cit.* pp. 324–5.

AN EIGHTEENTH-CENTURY COLLIERY VENTILATION SHAFT
Unearthed at Shirland Delves, near Alfreton, in 1957
By courtesy of the Derbyshire Times

PART I: THE DERBYSHIRE MINERS
1800–1880

CHAPTER I

THE DEVELOPMENT OF THE
COAL INDUSTRY

I

The growth of industry, the canals and the pre-locomotive railways gave a continued impetus to the development of the Derbyshire coalfield in the early decades of the nineteenth century. Thus, in 1835, Edward Miller Mundy was sending coal by the Grand Junction canal and its connections to Newport Pagnell, Buckingham and London. In 1824 his four pits at Shipley were producing about 45,000 tons of coal a year. The six-monthly turnover was more than £11,000 and, after paying all the working expenses of the pits, £5,733 was regarded as clear profit for the year. The average rate of profit was 2s. 6d. per ton of coal. By 1835 the annual turnover had decreased to less than £15,000 and Mundy's margin of profit appears to have been reduced, for in that year he made only £2,513. The contract prices which were paid to the butties ranged between 2s. 2d. and 4s. 3d. a ton in 1824 and between 2s. 2d. and 7s. 0d. in 1835. Selling prices, which varied according to the quality of the coal and its destination, had not increased to the same extent as wage rates. In 1824 prices ranged between 4s. 6d. and 10s. 0d. a ton; in 1835 between 4s. 0d. and 16s. 0d.[1]

The inevitable combination of coal and iron, which provided the basis for the industrial revolution, rapidly became an important feature of Derbyshire's economy. The revolutionary changes in the technique of iron production as a result of Henry Cort's discoveries had already led to the construction of ten blast-furnaces in Derbyshire before the end of the eighteenth century. After 1800 the number of blast-furnaces and the production of pig-iron continued to increase as shown by the following table:

[1] Records of the Shipley Collieries.

Production of Pig-Iron in Derbyshire, 1806–1848[1]

	Number of blast-furnaces		Estimated annual production of pig-iron Tons
1806	11		10,000
1823	—		14,038
1825	14		19,100
1827	15		20,800
1828	—		22,360
1830	—		17,999
	In blast	Out of blast	
1847	20	10	95,160
1848	20	10	78,000

The ironstone beds at Codnor Park, Morley Park, Somercotes, Chesterfield and Staveley were the most valuable in the county and their presence encouraged the growth of a number of important firms combining successive stages of production in the coal and iron trades under single control.

The Butterley Company has already been mentioned as a precursor of these vertically integrated firms. The Company was originally formed to exploit the iron-ore deposits in the Codnor district but it soon proved easily practicable and economically advantageous for the same concern to mine both iron and coal. By 1829, the Butterley Company controlled furnaces, a foundry and a steam-engine manufactory at Butterley; furnaces, a foundry and bar-iron works at Codnor; the Ormonde, Portland and Heanor collieries; the Crich limestone quarries and lime-works, and the Codnor Park lime-works. In March, 1829, the two furnaces in blast at Butterley and the two at Codnor Park were each producing on an average 35 tons of pig-iron per week. The Company employed some 1,500 men, of whom half were employed in the mines.[2]

The expansion of the Butterley Company continued during the subsequent decades. In 1815 the total capital had been £30,000: by 1858 it was £436,000, of which Francis Wright owned £350,000 and William Jessop the rest.[3] By 1848 the Company had six furnaces in blast out of a total of twenty for all Derbyshire, producing nearly 21,000 tons of pig-iron.[4] Fourteen years later there were still only twenty-three furnaces in blast in the whole of Derbyshire, producing an aggregate of 126,000 tons of pig-iron.[5] Of those, the Butterley Company owned five and

---

[1] The table is based on figures given by Glover, *op. cit.* I, p. 230; G. R. Porter, *The Progress of the Nation*, (London), ed. F. W. Hirst, 1912, pp. 238, 240.

[2] Glover, *op. cit.* p. 231.

[3] Mottram and Coote, *op. cit.* p. 77.   [4] *Ibid.* p. 76.

[5] *The Derbyshire Red Book*, (Derby), 1862, quoted in *Derbyshire Times*, 11 January, 1862.

manufactured their produce into 'superior bar iron, boiler plates, sheets, and large girders for armour-plated vessels, and other purposes'.[1]

The increasing demand for iron necessarily involved the Company in greater efforts to produce coal. By 1862 it was raising between 700,000 and 800,000 tons annually from fourteen shafts.[2] Eight years later it owned the Codnor Park, Butterley Park, Forty Horse, Hartshay, Langley, Loscoe, Newlands, New Main, Ripley, Upper Birchwood, and Brand's collieries, all in the Alfreton district; Marehay, Whiteley and Watergate collieries in the Ripley district; and Granby Colliery, near Ilkeston. The Butterley Company was then employing about 8,000 men.[3]

Another early example of this type of organization, on a much smaller scale, is provided by the Alfreton Iron Works. In 1806 James Oakes and Company had a blast-furnace at Somercotes which produced 1,450 tons of pig-iron. By 1829 the Company owned two iron-ore mines, three collieries, two blast-furnaces and an extensive foundry. The collieries, besides supplying the iron-works, sent a considerable proportion of their output to various parts of the Midland counties. About 500 men were employed, of whom 350 worked in the iron-ore mines and the collieries.[4]

At Staveley, in 1786, Ward and Barrow had a blast-furnace which, in 1806, produced 596 tons of pig-iron.[5] From these small beginnings developed the great Staveley Coal and Iron Company. By the 1840's G. Hodgkinson Barrow was the proprietor of extensive iron-foundries and collieries at Staveley. In July, 1840, he was planning to erect two large furnaces; to construct a canal, a mile and a quarter in length, across the Norbriggs road; to open collieries along its banks and to put down a pumping engine of 80 horse-power.[6] The Hopewell Colliery was started in 1845 and the Speedwell Colliery soon afterwards. A piece of coal weighing 24 tons (20 tons when shaped) was sent from Speedwell to the Great Exhibition in 1851. Campbell Colliery was sunk in 1853, followed two years later by New Hollingwood Colliery and Seymour Colliery.[7]

On the death of G. H. Barrow this extensive industrial plant passed to his son, Richard, who in 1862 was the owner of the largest collieries in Derbyshire. They were then capable of raising 800,000 tons of coal annually from five shafts, one of which had raised more than 1,100 tons in a twelve-hour day. Richard Barrow used the iron made by his

---

[1] *The Derbyshire Red Book*, (Derby), 1862, quoted in *Derbyshire Times*, 11 January, 1862.   [2] *Ibid.*
[3] *Derbyshire Times*, 3 December, 1870.
[4] Glover, *op. cit.* I, pp. 83, 232.   [5] *Ibid.* p. 83.
[6] *Derbyshire Chronicle*, 11 July, 1840.
[7] *The Staveley Story*, (published by the Staveley Company), n.d. p. 23.

own two furnaces, as well as that from two other furnaces in the county, for castings of every description. More than 4,000 tons of girders and columns, for the Exhibition building of 1862, were turned out in three months without interfering with the ordinary work of the foundries.[1]

II

Organizations such as this were ripe for conversion into limited liability companies. The process had been facilitated by the company legislation of 1855–6 and 1862. Richard Barrow was advancing in years and wished to be relieved from a considerable amount of the care and responsibility which were inseparable from the sole proprietorship of so large a concern. Accordingly, in December, 1863, he sold out to a joint-stock company, the Staveley Coal and Iron Company (Limited).[2] A total capital of £600,000 was subscribed in two or three days without any prospectus or circular being issued. Richard Barrow remained at Ringwood Hall to act as chairman of the Company and held a very large number of the shares. At this time, the Staveley works were among the most extensive in the country, employing over 3,000 workers. Each year the collieries were raising 1,000,000 tons of coal and the furnaces and iron-foundries were producing 20,000 tons of castings.[3]

Richard Barrow died in April, 1865, leaving £500,000 personalty[4] but the newly formed Company continued the tradition of industrial development at Staveley. One of the prime movers was Henry Davis Pochin who played a prominent part in the financing of colliery and engineering enterprises in Derbyshire. He was born at Woodstone, Leicestershire, in 1824 and eventually began business in Manchester as a manufacturing chemist. He discovered a means of completely decomposing china clay by sulphuric acid which he patented in 1855. Soon afterwards he introduced the material, known as 'Aluminas Cake', into the paper-making trade where it was very widely used. He also succeeded in producing a distilled resin which remained undecomposed and free from colour and became the foundation of almost all toilet soaps.[5]

Thus, by the early 'sixties, the business of H. D. Pochin and Company began to earn substantial profits and more funds became available for investment. Henry Pochin, with some friends of his in Manchester, started to buy up various coal and iron firms then in private hands,

[1] The Derbyshire Red Book, 1862, loc. cit.
[2] Cf. J. H. Clapham, Economic History of Modern Britain, (Cambridge), 1932, II, p. 138.
[3] Derbyshire Times, 19 December, 1863.   [4] Ibid. 8 April, 1865.
[5] Sir Allan Grant, Steel and Ships, The History of John Brown's, (London), 1950, p. 26.

forming them into public companies in which he and his friends took between them the bulk of the capital.[1]

This was the age of the 'ironclad' naval vessel and, as a result of Bessemer's discoveries, the beginning of the age of steel. Pochin and his friends were behind the creation of the Staveley Company and planned to introduce rolling mills for the manufacture of every description of iron and the Bessemer process on a large scale for steelmaking.[2] A few months later, in March, 1864, the same group acquired a controlling interest in the Sheffield steel and armour plate firm, John Brown and Company, which, like the Staveley Company, became a limited liability company.[3]

On the creation of the Staveley Company, Charles Markham became the managing director. The Markhams were an old Northamptonshire family, chiefly associated with the legal profession. Charles Markham broke with this tradition for, after being educated at Oundle and Edinburgh University, he devoted his studies to engineering. He became partner and manager of the Marquise Iron and Rolling Mills near Calais and returned to England after the revolution of 1848. After devoting a year to the study of chemistry he joined the engineering staff of the South-Eastern Railway and eventually became Assistant Locomotive Superintendent to the Midland Railway at Derby. Here he perfected a device which enabled the Midland engines to be fired by coal instead of coke, at an annual saving of £50,000 to the Company.[4]

It was at Derby that Markham made friends with Richard Barrow and one of the conditions attached to the conversion of his business to a limited liability company was that Markham should serve as managing director for at least five years. Thus began the long association of the Markham family with the Staveley Company.[5]

Under the energetic direction of Charles Markham the Company continued to expand rapidly. In April, 1865, the *Derbyshire Times* reported:

The Staveley Coal and Iron Company stands at the head of all the Limited Liability Companies of recent formation. The Company have just declared a dividend at the rate of 25 per cent per annum. It is said by eminent mineral men that though the valuation of these extensive works amounts to £600,000 they have been almost given away at that price.[6]

By 1878 the Company had a paid-up capital of £1,326,000.[7]

[1] Sir Allan Grant, *Steel and Ships, The History of John Brown's*, (London), 1950, p. 27.
[2] *Derbyshire Times*, 19 December, 1863.
[3] Grant, *op. cit.* p. 27; *Derbyshire Times*, 5 March, 1864.
[4] *The Staveley Story*, p. 11.   [5] *Ibid.*
[6] *Derbyshire Times*, 29 April, 1865.   [7] *Ibid.* 9 February, 1878.

Another company which was launched by H. D. Pochin and his friends was the Sheepbridge Coal and Iron Company. In 1857 William Fowler with his father took on lease a large area of land between Chesterfield and Whittington Moor and began working coal. Subsequently Hankey, a London banker, joined the partnership. Part of the coalfield was sublet to other companies.[1] By 1862 W. Fowler and Company had established the Sheepbridge Iron Works with three blast furnaces. John Brown and Company, of Sheffield, used Sheepbridge mild and hot blast iron for the manufacture of armour plate which, in a test at Portsmouth on 22 November, 1861, was said to 'exceed every test heretofore made'.[2] The Sheepbridge Coal and Iron Company was formed in 1864 with William Fowler as chairman and managing director. In 1868 J. Stores Smith became managing director, Fowler retaining the chairmanship.[3] Charles McLaren later joined the board of this company and eventually became the chairman. Sheepbridge, which in 1854 was a 'mere plain', became 'a thriving little town' within ten years of the formation of the Company and the population of Whittington increased rapidly to 2,863 in 1861 and to 5,779 in 1871.[4]

As the sub-leases lapsed, the Sheepbridge Company began to take over the working of more collieries. By 1871 four collieries were being worked by the Company: the Sheepbridge Colliery, sunk in the centre of the works, producing 250 tons of coal a day; the Dunston Colliery, rather more than a mile from the works, yielding 250 tons a day; Nesfield Colliery, two miles from the works, near the village of Barlow, with 250 tons a day; and Norwood Colliery, at Killamarsh, nine miles from the works, with 700–800 tons a day. The total quantity of coal raised was about 10,000 tons weekly, of which 3,000 tons were used on the works, 6,000 tons were sold in the various markets and 1,000 tons were converted into coke. Some 2,000 men and boys were employed at the works and collieries.[5] In 1873 the Company began to work, jointly with the Staveley Company, the large bed of coal on the Newstead Abbey estate: a reflection of the financial relationship between the two firms.[6]

As well as having financial interests in John Brown and Company, the Staveley Company and the Sheepbridge Company, Henry Pochin had shares in similar companies in other parts of the country. These included Palmer's Shipbuilding and Iron Company; Bolckow Vaughan Company, the ironmakers of Middlesbrough; and the Tredegar Iron and Coal Company. He became a director of all these companies, and was deputy chairman of many of them. His son-in-law, Charles

[1] *Derbyshire Times*, 27 May, 1871.
[2] *Derbyshire Red Book*, 1862, *loc. cit.*
[3] *Derbyshire Times*, 29 May, 1871.
[4] *Ibid.* 10 June, 1874; 27 May, 1871.
[5] *Ibid.* 27 May, 1871.
[6] *Ibid.* 6 September, 1873.

McLaren, in addition to becoming chairman of the Sheepbridge Company also became chairman of the Tredegar Iron and Coal Company and later became the first Baron Aberconway.[1]

III

Apart from the iron trade, the other important factor which influenced the development of the Derbyshire coal industry in this period was the coming of the railways. Ever since the construction of the canals the coal-owners of the Erewash Valley had monopolized the Leicestershire markets.[2] John Ellis, of Leicester, succeeded in interesting George Stephenson in a projected line from Swannington to Leicester, which was begun towards the end of 1830 and opened on 17 July, 1832. The monopoly enjoyed by the coalmasters of the Erewash Valley was thus broken. George Stephenson had opened his new pits at Snibston and was delivering coal at Leicester at less than 10s. a ton. The Derbyshire and Nottinghamshire coal-owners were obliged to seek a reduction of 3s. 6d. a ton on the canal rates in an attempt to compete with the Leicestershire coal but the committees of the Erewash, the Soar, and the Leicester canals would not agree to this.[3]

Eventually, at a meeting at the Sun Inn, Eastwood, on 16 August, 1832, the leading coal-owners of the Erewash Valley resolved that 'there was no other plan for their adoption than to attempt to lay a railway from these collieries to the town of Leicester'.[4] The new line was to run from Pinxton to Leicester and amongst those who promised subscriptions were Barber and Walker, Edward Miller Mundy, John Wright, Francis Wright, James Oakes, the Duke of Portland, Henry Case Morewood and D'Ewes Coke.[5] This proposal eventually became merged with a wider scheme for the Midland Counties Railway which, it was stated in 1833, was 'intended to connect the towns of Leicester, Nottingham and Derby, with each other and with London: a junction for this latter object being designed with the London and Birmingham Railway near Rugby. A branch would also extend to the Derbyshire and Nottinghamshire collieries, and to the termination of the Mansfield Railway at Pinxton.'[6] Among the directors were T. E. Dicey, Matthew Babington, William Jessop, E. M. Mundy and J. Oakes.[7]

The Midland Counties Railway Bill met with opposition in the House of Lords from the canal interests and also from the North Midland Railway which was at that time planning to construct a line from Derby

---

[1] Grant, *op. cit.* pp. 27–28.
[2] F. S. Williams, *The Midland Railway*, (London), edn. of 1878, pp. 3–4.
[3] *Ibid.* pp. 5–8.
[4] *Ibid.* p. 8.
[5] *Ibid.* p. 9.
[6] *Ibid.* p. 13.
[7] *Ibid.* p. 18.

B*

to Leeds. The Midland Counties Company had spoken of extending their Erewash line up the valley, over the ridge near Clay Cross and on to Chesterfield; and in this scheme the North Midland Company saw a serious rival.[1] The moneyed men of the North, the 'Liverpool party', who had given their support to the Midland Counties Company because they were anxious to secure a through route to the South, were not prepared to sacrifice the Midland Counties Bill in the interests of a few coal-owners in a remote Nottinghamshire valley and eventually the Bill was carried without the Erewash extension. 'Oakes and Jessop', said Vignoles, the engineer, 'were disgusted and angry; but they could not help themselves. Their line and themselves were left out in the cold.'[2]

The complications of railway politics resulted in the coal-owners of the Erewash Valley being responsible for the initiation of a great project from which they derived little immediate benefit. The Midland Counties Railway later became part of the Midland Railway and it was not until 1847 that the Erewash Valley line was finally opened by the Midland Railway Company.

Meanwhile, George Stephenson was at work on the construction of the North Midland line: a circumstance which is closely linked with the development of the Clay Cross Collieries. Remembering his experiences in Leicestershire, Stephenson saw in the North Midland Railway and its connections great possibilities of opening up new markets for the abundant supplies of coal in the district through which the new line passed. At a time when everybody else was sceptical about the possibility of coal being carried from the Midland Counties, and sold in London at a price to compete with the sea-borne coal of the Newcastle Vend, he declared his firm conviction that the time was fast approaching when the London market would be regularly supplied with north-country coal carried by rail.[3]

In 1837 several seams of coal were cut through during the construction of the Clay Cross tunnel and Stephenson immediately saw the possibilities of developing collieries in the district and, eventually, sending coal by rail to London. He communicated with his friends, the 'Liverpool party', who, acting on his advice, joined him in a lease of land at Clay Cross.[4] The original partners in the firm George Stephenson and Company were Robert Stephenson, George Carr Glyn (afterwards Lord Wolverton), William Jackson, M.P., Joshua Walmsley, M.P., George Hudson ('The Railway King'), S. Morton Peto, M.P., Joseph Sandars and E. L. Betts. All of these men were famous in their day as

---

[1] Williams, op. cit. pp. 23–24. [2] Ibid. p. 25.
[3] S. Smiles, Life of George Stephenson, (London), edn. of 1858, p. 375.
[4] C. E. Stretton, History of the Midland Railway, (London), 1901, p. 51.

pioneers of railway construction and industrial development. Glyn was on the original directorate of the North Midland Railway; Jackson and Peto were partners in the firm of Peto, Brassey, Betts and Jackson, who built the Canadian Grand Trunk Railway and many other great railways. Charles Binns, who was Walmsley's son-in-law and Stephenson's private secretary, became General Manager of the Company.[1] Clay Cross coal was first sent to London in 1840, by rail to Rugby and thence by canal. The Company also had the distinction of being the first to send coal to London direct by the London and Birmingham line in 1845,[2] when 'so far from creditable was it considered to carry the black diamonds by that means that the trucks were covered with tarpauling to hide them from the public gaze'.[3]

George Stephenson and Company grew steadily in size and importance. A number of coke ovens were built at a cost of £3,000 to provide fuel for the locomotives on the new railway[4] and in 1838 the Company started to work the Crich Limestone Quarries and Limeworks at Ambergate. In 1841 Stephenson entered upon a contract with the owners of land at Tapton, Brimington and Newbold and began mining operations there on an extensive scale.[5] In order to use the coal that could not be sold profitably in the markets, the Company turned its attention to the production of iron in 1846. It possessed at least two seams of iron ore in the district known as the Black Rake and the Brown Rake. The working of these was discontinued when the Midland Railway Company, in making their line to London, found iron ore in Northamptonshire and sold it to the Clay Cross Company. Two blast-furnaces were erected in 1847 at a cost of £24,000; a third and an iron-foundry were added in 1854.[6]

When Stephenson died in 1848 his son Robert succeeded him as the largest share proprietor in the Clay Cross Company. Soon afterwards Robert Stephenson severed his connection with the firm, and Peto, Walmsley and Jackson became the three proprietors.[7] In 1871 the now Sir William Jackson, M.P., acquired the whole of the Company's interests and became the sole proprietor. The Clay Cross Company was one of the few such concerns in Derbyshire which continued to be a private one during the age of limited liability. It did not become a limited liability company until 1913 and even then the first directors were all members of the Jackson family.[8]

[1] A Hundred Years of Enterprise, (published by the Clay Cross Company), 1937, p. 13.   [2] Ibid. pp. 14–15.
[3] Derbyshire Times, 8 November, 1873.   [4] Williams, op. cit. p. 438.
[5] Derbyshire Chronicle, 13 March, 1841; Smiles, op. cit. p. 415.
[6] A Hundred Years of Enterprise, p. 25.
[7] Williams, op. cit. pp. 439–40.
[8] A Hundred Years of Enterprise, p. 33.

George Stephenson's work completed, and demonstrated the full possibilities of, the revolution in transport which had been begun by the canals. In 1861 it was stated: 'The celebrated Main Coal of Clay Cross has attained such a decided position in the London market that the supply from the collieries is going to London, and until that market is satisfied no other can be supplied.'[1] By 1854 four pits had been sunk at Clay Cross; Nos. 5 and 6 were sunk at Morton in 1865 and 1874; No. 7, Parkhouse, at Danesmoor in 1867; and No. 9, Avenue, at Wingerworth in 1881.[2] Clay Cross, which had been a small hamlet of some five or six cottages in 1837, became a busy, thriving community of between 6,000 and 7,000 inhabitants in 1865. By 1876 over 2,000 men were employed underground.[3]

The amount of coal sent by rail from Clay Cross to London increased steadily. In 1862, of a total of 4,977,251 tons supplied to the metropolis, Clay Cross contributed 186,051 tons.[4] By 1870, Clay Cross was sending 385,632 tons, one-tenth of all the coal entering London by railway.[5] Other companies, such as the Butterley Company, the Staveley Company and Barber and Walker, began to follow suit and during the 'sixties and 'seventies there were at least thirty-four centres in Derbyshire and Nottinghamshire sending considerable amounts of coal direct to London by rail.[6]

IV

The entry of inland coal into the London market in 1845 coincided with, but did not cause, the breakdown of the 'limitation of the vend' of North Country coal, the most conspicuous output and price-controlling combination of the early nineteenth century.[7] Thereafter there was no possibility of reviving the combination although the attempt was made in 1850 when G. R. Porter commented: 'The facilities for competition on the part of the owners of inland coal-fields are far greater now than

[1] *Derbyshire Times*, 23 November, 1861.
[2] *A Hundred Years of Enterprise*, p. 34.
[3] *Derbyshire Times*, 27 August, 1864; 8 July, 1865; 16 July, 1876.
[4] *Ibid.* 17 January, 1863.   [5] *Ibid.* 7 January, 1871.
[6] Clay Cross, Codnor Park, Riddings, Eckington, Pinxton, Langley Mill, Staveley, West Birchwood, Hucknall, Shipley, Sheepbridge, Pilsley, Tibshelf, Grassmoor, Swanwick, Unstone, Dronfield, Cotmanhay, Birley, New Birchwood, Swadlincote, Oakerthorpe, Renishaw Park, Shirland, Whittington, Doe Hill, Heanor, Snobstone, Ripley, Tapton, Alma, Babbington, Selston, Annesley.
[7] For a full discussion of the 'limitation of the vend' and the reasons for its breakdown see P. M. Sweezy, *Monopoly and Competition in the English Coal Trade, 1550–1850*, (Harvard), 1938.

they were in 1845, while through the extension of railways these facilities are being continually augmented.'[1] Thus, in 1850 only 55,000 tons of coal were carried to London by rail, in 1860 the figure was 1,500,000; in 1870, 3,500,000; and in 1880 as much as 6,200,000. The seaborne supply, which was 3,500,000 tons in 1850 and 3,600,000 in 1860, fell to a minimum of 2,500,000 in 1872, rising again to 4,740,000 in 1886.[2] After the breakdown of the North-East Coast monopoly it was 'practically an open fighting trade'[3] with free and unrestricted competition. If local associations of owners gave price rulings they 'had no means of enforcing the rules at all', so that they were not 'in fact carried out . . . at least . . . not entirely'.[4] As a result there were changes in the organization of the London trade. Coal was no longer carried to London to the order of the merchants but sold to them on the London Coal Exchange by factors acting for the owners.[5]

The following table shows the amounts of coal sent by rail to London from some of the principal Derbyshire forwarding centres between 1862 and 1872:

Coal sent by rail to London, 1862–1872[6]

	1862 Tons	1868 Tons	1869 Tons	1870 Tons	1871 Tons	1872 Tons
Clay Cross	186,051	292,325	357,275	385,632	377,234	352,835
Codnor Park	50,460	70,400	96,713	94,760	—	—
Riddings	—	100,799	101,765	98,466	—	—
Eckington	—	89,792	99,863	100,229	—	—
Pinxton	—	94,501	88,134	93,007	—	—
Langley Mill	—	68,195	85,032	138,172	163,241	178,985
Staveley	—	55,847	69,066	62,446	74,180	70,390
Shipley	—	—	—	41,305	72,840	91,888
Sheepbridge	—	—	—	55,045	83,793	85,390
Pilsley	—	—	—	14,861	64,435	69,785
Tibshelf	—	—	—	10,796	56,095	94,290
Grassmoor	—	—	—	29,343	45,640	46,023
Swanwick	—	—	—	35,883	46,374	45,261
Unstone	—	—	—	3,011	21,102	40,994
Dronfield	—	—	—	5,107	11,747	13,301

As time went on various new branch lines were developed which gave increasing numbers of collieries access to the main railway routes.

---

[1] G. R. Porter, *Progress of the Nation*, (London), edn. of 1851, pp. 283–4.
[2] Clapham, *op. cit.* II, p. 301.
[3] *S.C. on the Causes of the Present Dearness and Scarcity of Coal*, 1873, Evidence of George Elliot, Q. 7518.
[4] *Ibid.* Evidence of R. Tennant, Q. 2657.   [5] Clapham, *op. cit.* II, p. 301.
[6] The table is based on figures taken from the *Derbyshire Times*, 1862–73.

More important was the construction of the Chesterfield and Sheffield line, a distance of about twelve miles, at a cost of £465,954.[1] The line was opened on 2 February, 1870, and almost immediately led to an intensive development of the coalfield in the Unstone and Dronfield districts. Starting with a modest 3,011 tons in 1870, Unstone was sending 40,994 tons of coal by rail to London in 1872. It was estimated, in 1869, that when all the collieries in this district were opened out something like half a million tons of coal would be carried annually by the new line.[2]

The increasing number of collieries sending coal to London resulted in a division of the trade and this is reflected in the monthly returns of the coal traffic to London in 1871 and 1872.[3] Clay Cross continued to maintain the ascendancy and was no doubt helped to do so by the extensive marketing organization which it had created with agents in London and many other places.[4] It will, however, be observed from Chart 1 that there is a marked falling off in the trade of Clay Cross from 1870 at a time when the trade of other centres was, on the whole, increasing. Nevertheless, the Langley Mill area was the only other colliery district which came anywhere near to being of the importance of Clay Cross in the London trade.[5]

Although Derbyshire, and Clay Cross in particular, for some time had a virtual monopoly of the London inland coal trade over the Midland route, the construction of new lines in other parts of the country eventually destroyed that monopoly in much the same way as the canals and railways had compelled the coalfields of Northumberland and Durham to share their trade with the inland areas.

During the 'sixties there was increasing competition from the South Yorkshire collieries which began sending their coal to London by the Great Northern Railway. Samuel Plimsoll, who was later to become a popular figure among the Derbyshire miners, was one of the pioneers of this development. As early as 1850, when he was a brewer's young clerk in Sheffield, his active mind turned to the problem.[6] Unlike the Midland Railway which carried coals as freight, the Great Northern bought the coals at the pit-head and disposed of them in London through a single merchant, Herbert Clarke, whose brother, Seymour Clarke, was the manager of the Great Northern.[7] Plimsoll, with the small amount of capital at his disposal, tried to break this monopoly

[1] *Derbyshire Times*, 26 June, 1869.   [2] *Ibid.* 20 November, 1869.
[3] *Ibid.* 12 August, 1871; 14 September, 1872.
[4] *Ibid.* 3 March, 1873; *A Hundred Years of Enterprise*, p. 15.
[5] Langley Mill, a rail and canal junction, was an important collecting and forwarding centre.
[6] D. Masters, *The Plimsoll Line*, (London), 1955, p. 38.
[7] *Ibid.* p. 42.

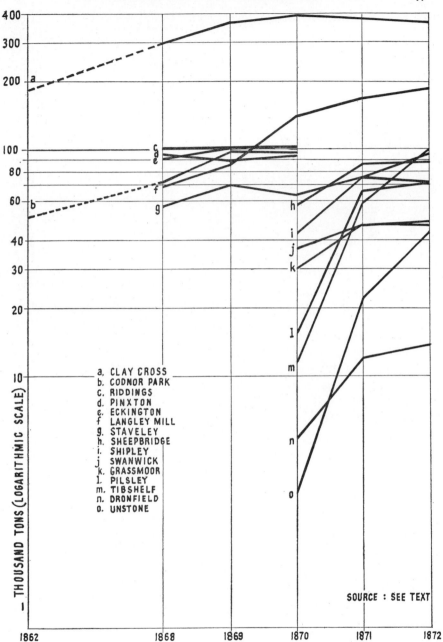

Chart 1.—Coal sent by rail to London, 1862–72.

and almost ruined himself in the process. It was not until he married Eliza Ann Railton, who was related to both the Newtons and the Chambers of the Yorkshire firm of mine-owners and iron-founders, that he was able to bring his earlier plans to fruition. In 1860 he signed an agreement with the Great Northern Railway which gave him the use of coal sidings at King's Cross in return for which he undertook to load 400,000 tons of coal a year from Doncaster or Retford over the Great Northern.[1]

The entry of South Yorkshire into the London coal trade was the signal for the beginning of a rate war between the Midland Railway and the Great Northern Railway. This resulted in such uncertainty as to the rates that coal-owners refused to undertake new contracts or to sink new pits. The coal trade suffered and so did the railways.[2] The dispute between the railway companies reached a climax in 1871 when both of them had cut their rates to such an extent that they lost more than £100,000 within six months.[3] Thereafter they decided to charge an economic price, which meant that the Derbyshire and Nottinghamshire coal-owners enjoyed lower rates than those of South Yorkshire. The Midland Railway Company succeeded in preserving a differential rate of about 8d. a ton in favour of the Derbyshire collieries which are, on an average, about 34 miles nearer to London than those of South Yorkshire. Thus, if the Derbyshire collieries were compelled to share some of the expanding London trade with South Yorkshire, by reason of their geographical position they retained their ascendancy. In 1872 nearly half of all the coal entering London by railway came from the Derbyshire field, extending from Dronfield by way of Unstone, Chesterfield and Clay Cross and along the entire length of the Erewash Valley line to Nottingham.[4] By 1875, Yorkshire had one-eighth of the trade and Derbyshire fully two-fifths.[5]

The struggle between the Great Northern and the Midland now took on a different form. The Great Northern resolved to construct a line from Nottingham to Derby in an attempt to capture some of the London coal traffic from Derbyshire. The Midland Company was loyally supported by the coalmasters of the Erewash Valley who regarded the Great Northern as the friend of the South Yorkshire coal-owners.[6] Nevertheless the Great Northern Company's Bills for a line into Derbyshire were sanctioned by Parliament in 1872. The line was opened in 1875 and became particularly important as an additional route for coal from Ilkeston, Pinxton and Langley Mill.[7]

---

[1] D. Masters, *The Plimsoll Line*, (London), 1955, p. 65.
[2] Williams, *op. cit.* pp. 268–71.   [3] *Derbyshire Times*, 15 July, 1871.
[4] *Ibid.* 14 February, 1872.   [5] *Ibid.* 22 May, 1875.
[6] Williams, *op. cit.* pp. 277–8.   [7] *Derbyshire Times*, 12 June, 1875.

V

The rate war between the Midland and the Great Northern was merely a manifestation of the economic trends which were affecting the coal industry during the 'sixties and the 'seventies. The period between 1860 and 1873 was one of rapid and almost continuous economic advance. The large overseas demand for rails and machines, the victory of the iron steamship and the general expansion of trade ushered in a period of rising prices and a steadily increasing demand for coal.

In 1861 the market for Derbyshire coal was such that it was found impossible, in many districts, to meet the orders which were pouring in from all sides. Hard coal, for steam purposes, was in particularly great demand despite the fact that its production during the past few years had been doubled.[1] Each day, at Staveley, fifteen trains of coal were being despatched and the Seymour pit alone was turning out more than 700 tons of best locomotive coal.[2]

There was a temporary setback in the following year as a result of the depression in the Lancashire cotton trade. The outbreak of the American Civil War in 1861 had led to a cotton famine and many of the Lancashire mills, some of which used Derbyshire coal, had to close down. At Clay Cross, in June, 1862, the depression 'had never been known to be so bad'. Many of the pits were not working more than four or five days a fortnight.[3] Towards the end of the year, however, the coal trade began to improve. By 1863 it had returned to its former level of activity and some of the larger firms, led by Richard Barrow of Staveley, were increasing the wages of colliers by 10 per cent. without being asked.[4]

The upward trend continued throughout the 'sixties and new colliery enterprises were being developed on every hand. In 1861 the Wallsend Coal Company was sinking into the Black Shale bed at Newbold, the Pierces opened their Foxley Oaks pit at Whittington and Knowles and Company opened a new colliery at Belper.[5] Several new companies were floated. The Chesterfield and Midland Silkstone Colliery Company was projected in 1861, with a capital of £40,000, to establish a colliery at Sheepbridge and within a month the minimum capital was subscribed. In the following year was launched the Hasland Colliery Company with a capital of £5,000 and, in 1863, the Whittington Freehold Colliery Company with a capital of £135,000. In 1864 Nicholls and Fletcher sold their colliery at Brampton to a limited liability company which planned to extend it considerably, and another company was formed to

---

[1] *Derbyshire Times*, 24 August, 1861; 19 January, 1861.
[2] *Ibid.* 17 May, 1861.   [3] *Ibid.* 14 June, 1862.
[4] *Ibid.* 12 December, 1863.   [5] *Ibid.* 1 June, 1861; 15 June, 1861.

work a large acreage of coal between Hallgate and Alfreton. The Winger-worth Coal Company opened its Holmewood Colliery in 1868.[1]

The growth of the coal trade was marked by a corresponding growth of the iron trade. It will be seen from the following table that the production of pig-iron in Derbyshire reached a peak in 1866:—

Production of Pig-iron in Derbyshire, 1860–1869[2]

	Furnaces	Tons
1860	23	126,000
1863	31	170,000
1866	33	200,000
1867	30	160,000
1868	28	159,000
1869	31	188,000

The decline in the latter half of the 'sixties was due to the fact that the argillaceous ironstone of Derbyshire was too costly, except where high quality was essential, and furnaces began to depend increasingly for their supplies on Northamptonshire where large deposits of ore were being opened out. Nevertheless, by 1870 the amount of coal raised in the county had reached 5,102,267 tons and some 16,405 persons were employed in mining.[3]

From 1871 to 1873 were the boom years and also the period when the railway rate war was at its height. Prices began to rise sharply and reached their peak in 1873. The initial demand was for coal for manufacturing purposes and for the use of merchant steamers and in May, 1872, large quantities of steam coal were being sent to Blackwall, Poplar and other depots.[4] Later, when the coal panic had reached its height, merchants were frantically stocking all types of coal in an attempt to forestall the rapidly increasing prices.[5] The price of best Silkstone coal in London at the end of 1870, one of the most unprofitable years then known to the trade, was 22s. a ton.[6] By March, 1873, it was being delivered at 49s. or 50s. a ton, although the pit-head prices were then between 16s. 6d. and 22s. a ton.[7]

Conditions in 1872 gave rise to the sort of comments which have been a familiar feature of the inflationary years since 1945:

We have food at famine prices, coal and iron doubled in value in six months, and an incurment of inflated trade. What does it mean? Are we to have a general rise in prices, or are we to have the balance of society upset, and the

[1] *Derbyshire Times*, 25 January, 1868.
[2] The table is based on figures in *Derbyshire Times*, 8 July, 1871.
[3] *Reports of H.M. Inspectors of Mines and Quarries*, 1870. See Appendix I to this chapter.
[4] *Derbyshire Times*, 11 May, 1872.
[5] *Ibid.* 22 March, 1873.
[6] *Ibid.* 22 December, 1877.
[7] *Ibid.* 22 March, 1873.

so-called working classes rising above those who have hitherto been known as middle class? At present we see that coal has risen cent per cent and iron even more, that wages are rapidly rising and that the sudden influx of prosperity limits production by inducing habits of idleness among our labouring classes. Meanwhile the middle class is getting daily poorer. . . . The lawyer must raise his fees, and the doctor his charges, the salaried manager or clerk must obtain a higher payment for his work, and in short the change going on all round must become universal.[1]

Scapegoats were sought on all sides. It was suggested that the high wages paid to the colliers operated adversely on the situation in two ways: they discouraged the colliers from working more than was necessary to meet their immediate needs and they added to the cost of production.[2] The first argument is one which will be discussed later.[3] In answer to the second, the *Derbyshire Times* stated: 'So far as we know the coal and iron masters have taken very great care that for every extra sixpence they have paid their men, they have charged the public an additional shilling, and herein lies another reason why the price of coal cannot long remain as it is.'[4] Elsewhere it was remarked: 'At the present time the great mine owners of this district must be reaping fortunes which will compensate them for years of disappointment in the past and will also enable them to provide against a possible rainy day.'[5]

Apart from the coal-owners and the miners, a third group who came in for criticism were the London merchants. The wide disparity between the pit-head price and the market price was accounted for partly by the costs of transport and partly by the 'City Dues', a tax which had been levied on all coal entering London ever since the Lord Mayor was granted an impost of 1s. per chaldron for rebuilding the city after the great fire of 1666. The rest went to the merchants. By the 'seventies the organization of the London inland coal trade was changing, consignment for sale was declining, purchase direct from the pit was increasing all the time and 'the air was full of rumours about an unscrupulous group of inland coal-dealers, described as the Forty Thieves'.[6] In 1873 the Government set up a Select Committee under the chairmanship of Ayrton to inquire into the reasons for the dearness and scarcity of coal. The Committee was unable to find any evidence of rings or combinations either on the coalfields or among the London merchants.[7] 'The Forty Thieves if they existed were individualistic bandits', remarks Clapham.[8] But not everyone was convinced. Much disgust was generally expressed

[1] *Derbyshire Times*, 27 July, 1872.   [2] *Ibid.* 3 August, 1872.
[3] See Chapter II, pp. 60–1.   [4] *Derbyshire Times*, 27 July, 1872.
[5] *Ibid.* 3 August, 1872.   [6] Clapham, *op. cit.* II, p. 302.
[7] *S.C. on the Causes of the Present Dearness and Scarcity of Coal*, 1873, Report, p. x.
[8] Clapham, *op. cit.* II, p. 302.

'at the failure of the Coal Committee to saddle the right horses with the responsibility for the dearness of coals'.[1]

The boom ended in 1873 and the course of prices turned downward. Between 1873 and 1896 wholesale prices, measured by Sauerbeck's index, fell by 45 per cent. By 1879, a year of economic depression, the price of coal on the London Market had fallen to 21s. a ton,[2] a shilling less than it had been in the unprofitable year of 1870. The falling off was more gradual than the increase of 1870 to 1873 as can be seen from Chart 2.[3]

The tonnage of coal carried by rail to London in July, 1872, had been the largest ever known as a result of the scramble to beat the rising prices. As soon as prices began to fall a similar phenomenon was observed. Despite the seasonal nature of the coal trade, in July, 1873, when the thermometer stood at 100° and the actual consumption for gas and household purposes must have been at its lowest, more coal was sent to London than during any former period of the year. The effects of the panic among the London consumers in the early part of the year had not entirely passed away and merchants, fearing that there might be a great advance in price towards the close of the year, were stocking for winter consumption.[4] At this time, the pit-head price of coal near Chesterfield was 12s. a ton. With carriage and dues it was delivered in London at 24s. a ton but sold to consumers at 32s. 'so there is a good margin of profit for some persons, independent of what is made by the colliery owner'.[5]

Although the merchants might retain their margin they were powerless to resist the general decline in the demand for coal which, with minor seasonal variations, persisted down to 1880. The trouble lay not in London, where the consumption of coal had increased from 6,759,101 tons in 1870 to 10,058,811 tons in 1879,[6] but in Britain's changing economic position. She was losing her world predominance and for the first time in the nineteenth century encountering serious foreign competition. Agriculture, shipping, and the iron and steel trades all suffered after the world-wide commercial collapse of 1873-4. British exports of iron and steel tumbled from nearly 3,500,000 tons in 1872 to less than 2,500,000 tons in 1878.[7]

The recession in the iron trade had disastrous effects upon the Derbyshire coal industry. The vertically integrated firms were unable to absorb the usual amount of their coal production in their blast-furnaces and foundries: thus, by 1878, the Sheepbridge Company was paying no

[1] *Derbyshire Times*, 12 July, 1873.   [2] *Ibid*, 18 October, 1879.
[3] See Chapter IV, p. 147.   [4] *Derbyshire Times*, 16 August, 1873.
[5] *Ibid*. 6 September, 1873.   [6] *Ibid*. 10 January, 1880.
[7] Clapham, *op. cit.* II, p. 227.

dividend and calling for further capital.[1] Similarly, the furnaces and works of the North of England and South Wales were using much less fuel. The consequence was a glut of coal which tended to be thrown on to the London market thereby making that trade increasingly competitive.

The problem was aggravated by the growing potential production of the coal industry.[2] Many large collieries were being opened out both on the continent and in this country. An Inspector of Mines reported that in 1873, in Yorkshire alone, thirty collieries had been opened out and were in production. In the same year he had received notice of a further ninety-seven that were about to be sunk and up to May, 1874, he had received notice of eighteen more which made the total number of collieries then being sunk in Yorkshire well over 100. It was estimated that many of these new concerns would produce a daily average of 1,000 tons.[3]

As Clapham has pointed out, the generation which had been accustomed to years of rising prices naturally confused the after effects of the crisis of 1873 with the early stages of the great price fall of the late nineteenth century.[4] As early as September, 1872, Charles Binns, the manager of the Clay Cross Company, spoke of the 'bubble character' of the inflation of the coal market[5] and in 1876, when there were vast numbers of loaded waggons standing in the sidings of London depots, the *Derbyshire Times* confessed: 'We have evidently over-built and over-produced and over-supplied, and even over-charged in the past few years of enormous prosperity, and we are now face to face with an absolute dearth of demand.'[6] On another occasion readers were told: 'The greatness of our so-called prosperity in 1873 seems to have necessitated a correspondingly deep depression. . . .'[7]

By 1877 many collieries were working only three or four days a week and the owners were saying that they were working without profit and were just able to make both sides of their accounts balance.[8] Some gave up the unequal struggle. Among the smaller men there were failures and bankruptcies. The larger organizations were able to cut their losses by closing some of their pits. Messrs. J. and G. Wells, for example, decided in May, 1878, to close two of their pits at Renishaw Park and to work only their Hornthorpe Pit at Eckington and Nos. 2 and 4 at Renishaw Park. This resulted in about 600 men being thrown out of employment in an area which, until then, had been considered a fortunate one.[9]

[1] *Derbyshire Times*, 5 October, 1878.
[2] *R.C. on Depression of Trade*, 1886, Evidence of J. D. Ellis, QQ. 3002–16.
[3] *Reports of H.M. Inspectors of Mines and Quarries*, 1873; *Derbyshire Times*, 6 June, 1874. [4] Clapham, *op. cit.* II, p. 383. [5] *Derbyshire Times*, 28 September, 1872.
[6] *Ibid.* 15 April, 1876. [7] *Ibid.* 5 October, 1876.
[8] *Ibid.* 11 August, 1877. [9] *Ibid.* 11 May, 1878.

VI

The economic condition of the British coal industry down to 1880 was such that there were no revolutionary changes in the technique of mining. A few thoughtful pioneers turned their attention to the possibilities of cutting coal by means of machinery in the early years of the prosperous 'sixties and again in the years following 1873 when it was suggested that 'coal getting machinery will . . . take an important part in the cutting and raising of coal and so tend to bring prices down'.[1] The first practicable coal-cutting machine was patented in 1861 by Donisthorpe, Firth and Ridley. It was driven by compressed air and was of the percussion type in which a piston instead of a human arm drove the pick. In the following year the machine was demonstrated at the West Ardsley Colliery, Leeds, and shortly afterwards it was introduced into a few pits in the neighbourhood of Chesterfield.[2] In the 'seventies there were experiments with rotary cutters, in which the work was done by a toothed wheel placed parallel and close to the floor. But none of these machines had any great impact upon the coal industry. There were difficulties in using them, especially where the strata were tilted, faulted or irregular. Even where they worked well they represented a useful but by no means revolutionary saving in manpower. Thus, in 1872, one of the patentees of the earliest machine claimed that forty-eight men with the machine could do the work of sixty without it.[3] 'There was no risk of coal imports,' writes Clapham, 'and very little competition with British coal in overseas markets as yet. The upshot was that only some very tiny fraction of that coal was cut by machinery in the 'eighties. No important part was so cut even forty years later.'[4]

There were, of course, important innovations as a result of the increased scale of mining. The Act of 1850 marked the beginning of the inspection of mines and, urged on by inspectors and the law, engineers were obliged to pay more attention to ventilation in their ever-deepening mines. As late as 1849 the best method of ventilation in Derbyshire was the double shaft, sometimes aided by a furnace.[5] By this time the Belgians were experimenting with the use of fans and the idea was already being followed in South Wales. Fans were in use at the Earl Fitzwilliam's collieries in South Yorkshire in 1852 and at Twisdale Colliery, Durham, in 1860. It was not, however, until after 1862, when

---

[1] *Derbyshire Times*, 13 November, 1875.   [2] *Ibid.* 7 June, 1862; 20 June, 1863.
[3] H. F. Bulman and R. A. S. Redmayne, *Colliery Working and Management*, (London), edn. of 1906, p. 119.
[4] Clapham, *op. cit.* II, p. 103.   [5] *V.C.H. Derbyshire*, II, pp. 354–5.

Guibal of Mons patented his fan, that fan ventilation became widespread in this country. The four collieries belonging to the Sheepbridge Company were all ventilated by furnaces until 1871.[1] Fans became more usual during the 'seventies. A Guibal fan ventilator was installed at the Albert Colliery of the Derbyshire Silkstone Coal Company in 1875 at a cost of several thousand pounds. The ventilator was 40 feet in diameter and was capable of driving 200,000 cubic feet of air per minute through the mine.[2]

Deeper pits also needed improved methods of winding. In 1877 the Staveley Company installed at the Ireland New Colliery a pair of winding engines which were the largest they had ever had. The cylinders were 36 inches in diameter with a 72 inch stroke; the diameter of the drum was 21 feet. These engines were expected to raise 1,000 tons of coal a day from a depth of over 900 feet.[3] There were also, during the 'sixties and 'seventies, various inventions designed to prevent accidents resulting from over-winding, or the breakage of pit-ropes. John King, of Pinxton, one of the pioneers in the provision of safe winding, invented a patent hook in 1866[4] and two years later Calow's Patent Safety Catch was demonstrated at Clay Cross.[5]

Other changes which came in during this period were the use of iron supports in some places instead of timbering, and the use of iron tubbings in sinking the shaft through water-bearing strata. The use of young boys and donkeys for taking the corves of coal from the workings to the bottom of the shaft was discontinued almost entirely by about 1875 and replaced, at least on the main 'roads', by mechanical methods of haulage.[6]

[1] *Derbyshire Times*, 27 May, 1871.
[2] *Ibid.* 11 September, 1875.   [3] *Ibid.* 17 February, 1877.
[4] *Transactions of the Chesterfield and Derbyshire Institute of Mining, Civil and Mechanical Engineers*, III, (London), 1875, p. 291.
[5] *Derbyshire Times*, 30 May, 1868.   [6] *V.C.H. Derbyshire*, II, p. 355

APPENDIX I

Output and Manpower, 1856–1880

	Midland District[1]		Derbyshire	
	Output Tons	Numbers employed	Output Tons	Numbers employed
1856	4,500,000	—	—	—
1857	4,750,000	—	—	—
1858	5,060,000	—	—	—
1859	5,460,000	—	—	—
1860	6,215,000	—	—	—
1861	6,503,319	23,434	—	—
1862	6,647,000	—	—	—
1863	7,000,000	26,600	—	—
1864	7,300,000	—	—	—
1865	7,575,000	20,000	—	—
1866	7,600,000	27,000	—	—
1867	7,600,000	27,000	—	—
1868	7,699,000	28,000	4,957,879	16,240
1869	8,100,000	—	5,092,000	16,300
1870	8,366,000	—	5,102,267	16,405
1871	9,252,900	—	5,360,000	18,000
1872	10,657,100	—	—	—
1873	11,533,307	—	—	28,123
1874	12,232,296	52,397	7,152,944	30,480
1875	12,430,600	52,477	7,190,921	30,097
1876	12,500,055	52,448	6,959,101	29,586
1877	13,071,566	50,285	7,054,091	28,085
1878	13,575,320	49,354	7,289,380	26,975
1879	14,144,265	50,000	7,561,235	27,859
1880	14,633,260	49,330	7,903,834	27,256

Source: *Reports of H.M. Inspectors of Mines*, 1856–1880.

[1] The Midland inspection district included Derbyshire, Nottinghamshire, Leicestershire and Warwickshire.

CHAPTER II

THE CONDITION OF THE MINERS

I

The changes in the coal industry during the industrial revolution were having increasing effects upon the lives of the miners. Coal was becoming one of the basic industries and was growing more sensitive to cyclical fluctuations in trade. To the miner, perhaps more than to any other worker, the phrases 'good times' and 'bad times' were acquiring a special significance.

Before the advent of improved transport the miners employed at the smaller, inland collieries enjoyed an advantage in that they had a greater opportunity to supplement their earnings during lean years, or lean seasons, by labour in some by-employment. In Derbyshire, for example, the miners often found it easy to obtain work as farm-hands but, as Professor Nef has shown, in Durham and Northumberland, and in the Firth of Forth district, where coalmining had come to engage a large portion of the local population, it must have been impossible to absorb temporarily any considerable number of colliers in by-employments.[1]

Similarly, Professor Ashton has shown how the miners of Wales and the Midlands conformed less closely than those of Scotland and the north of England to the ideal 'non-competing group' of economic theory. For, in the eighteenth century, labour in the pits of these coalfields was less specialized than in the larger and deeper pits of the north.[2] This state of affairs persisted in Derbyshire until the early part of the nineteenth century. A document relating to Poor Law Settlement examinants at Staveley between 1822 and 1828 gives details of the industrial careers of forty-seven individuals.[3] Of these, fifteen had worked as colliers at one time or another, but only three stated definitely that they had worked in the pits all their lives.

[1] Nef, *op. cit.* II, p. 184.
[2] T. S. Ashton, 'The Coal Miners of the Eighteenth Century', *Economic Journal, Economic History Supplement*, no. iii, (1928), p. 333.
[3] Jackson Collection, Sheffield Municipal Reference Library; cited in Ashton, *loc. cit.* p. 333.

The development of coalmining in Derbyshire during the nineteenth century resulted in an increasing proportion of the population entering the industry and an increasing specialization of labour until it was no longer possible for large numbers of unemployed colliers to find alternative employment in times of bad trade. By the 'sixties and the 'seventies a depression in the coal trade was a serious matter for the mining areas of Derbyshire. The closing of a pit had become a major disaster for those who depended upon it for their livelihood. During the depression of 1862 the distress was such that a soup kitchen had to be opened in Chesterfield.[1] At Clay Cross, where many of the pits were not working above four or six days a fortnight, Whitsuntide was 'a time of gloom'.[2]

More serious was the depression of the late 'seventies. As various pits were closed miners began to tour the district in search of work, depending upon workhouses for their nightly shelter.[3] In Chesterfield the Relief Fund Committee reported that they found 'many families huddled together, pining for the bare necessities of life, yet quietly submitting to their fate'.[4] At Ripley, many of the men discharged by the Butterley Company were unable to find work elsewhere and a soup kitchen had to be established.[5] By the end of 1878 the poverty was such that a representative of the Vegetarian Society took the opportunity of calling the attention of the public to a diet which would enable them to live on sixpence a day.[6]

The thought occurred frequently to contemporary observers, as it has done to present-day critics, that the colliers saved little or nothing when times were good. The *Derbyshire Times* commented in 1861:

It is to be regretted that the mining population generally do not, in these times of prosperity, carefully husband a portion of their earnings, to be laid by to fall back on in adverse times.[7]

Again, in 1872, when some miners were earning more than 10s. a day, they were advised to save:

We should like to see miners possess their own houses and gardens wherever possible; and where this cannot be there is no reason why they might not have a little nest egg in the bank which would be available in sickness or old age, and which would at any rate save them from the degradation of parish relief.[8]

There was, no doubt, a streak of Epicureanism in the miner's philosophy, which has not altogether disappeared. Never knowing

---

[1] *Derbyshire Times*, 6 December, 1862.   [2] *Ibid.* 14 June, 1862.
[3] *Ibid.* 26 January, 1878.   [4] *Ibid.* 3 March, 1877.
[5] *Ibid.* 19 January, 1878.   [6] *Ibid.* 21 January, 1878.
[7] *Ibid.* 2 February, 1861.   [8] *Ibid.* 17 February, 1872.

when bad times, or even fatal accident, would befall him, he tended to enjoy himself whilst he could. In this there was no selfishness. He was always prepared to help the less fortunate. Liberal subscriptions were sent to relieve the distress in Lancashire in 1862.[1] In 1874, when Joseph Arch visited Clay Cross to seek support for the locked out agricultural workers, the miners of the district resolved to establish a local relief fund to which each man would contribute sixpence a week.[2]

Any special occasion was an excuse for a celebration in the most lavish style that funds would permit. At a collier's wedding in Chester-field, in 1841, a party of thirty-seven demolished 'the greater part of 36 lb. beef, 3 couple of fowls, and a leg and a shoulder of mutton, 4 plum puddings, 2 gallon of gin, 2 gallon rum, and a load of malt brewed for the occasion. Two houses were filled upstairs and down to suffocation. The entertainments were fiddling, dancing, singing, etc. The party broke up at 5 o'clock the following morning, with their faces blackened and minus their hats.'[3]

A study of the newspapers of this period gives the impression that the collier's favourite pursuits included drinking, gambling, poaching, cock-fighting and brawling, but in a predominantly mining community one would expect a considerable proportion of those appearing in the police courts to be miners and it is unsafe to conclude that the incidence of prosecutions for such offences as drunkenness and brawling was greater among the miners than amongst other sections of the population in Derbyshire. On the other hand, figures for the year ending 20 September, 1864, show that the incidence of convictions for drunkenness in five Midland mining counties was higher than in a group of agricultural counties:

Drunkenness in Mining Districts (Year ending 20 September, 1864)[4]

County	No. proceeded against	No. convicted	No. proceeded against (per thousand)	No. convicted (per thousand)
Derbyshire	690	625	2·4	2·1
Nottinghamshire	706	576	3·4	2·7
Staffordshire	3,306	2,656	5·2	4·2
Warwickshire	410	348	2·1	1·8
Leicestershire	518	349	2·0	1·4
		Averages	3·0	2·4
Averages in a group of agricultural counties			1·9	1·7

[1] *Derbyshire Times*, 13 December, 1862; 20 December, 1862.
[2] *Ibid.* 4 April, 1874.
[3] *Derbyshire Chronicle*, 30 January, 1841.
[4] The table is based on figures taken from the *Mining Journal*, quoted in *Derbyshire Times*, 8 July, 1865.

The question of the miner's inability to save is linked with his propensity to 'play'. In 1862 the old practice of colliers failing to appear for work on the Monday was so prevalent that some employers began to take action under the unequal law of Master and Servant.[1] Within the space of a week the proprietors of the West Staveley Colliery prosecuted no fewer than seven men for leaving their work without notice. Some of them were sentenced to fourteen days' hard labour whilst others were ordered to return to work and allow the costs to be deducted from their wages.[2] Richard Barrow, the proprietor of the Springwell Colliery, tried to tackle the problem in a different way. In November, 1863, he gave notice that 'he will, during the winter months, give an allowance of wages' to the coal hewers on condition that 'work is not neglected on Mondays and Tuesdays'. Those who neglected their work were not to receive the advance.[3] During the prosperous year of 1872 there were many complaints about the effects of the behaviour of the collier upon the price of coal. 'The colliery or foundry hand finds that in four days a week or less he can earn as much as he can spend', stated the *Derbyshire Times*, 'and consequently, he will not work more, although the whole country is crying out for coal. . . . The output is checked and diminished because the collier is not a saving man, and must therefore occupy his time by spending what he has earned, instead of working to earn more.'[4] Elsewhere it was stated: 'We must see less worship of St. Monday, fewer scores at the beer-house and greater moderation in dress and expenditure.'[5]

The same views were expressed by witnesses before the Coal Committee in 1873. Booth maintained that the men earning high wages were worse off than they were before because of their unthrifty habits.[6] Woodhouse stated: 'I think that they have directed their attention principally to increased sources of enjoyment.'[7] On the other hand, Evans, the inspector of mines for Derbyshire, believed that a large number of men were saving[8] and William Pickard, the Lancashire miners' leader, considered that the increased rate of wages had led to a

---

[1] For a full account of the operation of the law of Master and Servant see Daphne Simon, 'Master and Servant' in *Democracy and the Labour Movement*, ed. J. Saville, (London), 1954, pp. 160–200.   [2] *Derbyshire Times*, 6 December, 1862.

[3] *Ibid.* 28 November, 1863.   [4] *Ibid.* 3 August, 1872.

[5] *Ibid.* 17 February, 1872. For further references to 'St. Monday' see T. S. Ashton, *An Economic History of England: The Eighteenth Century*, (London), 1955, p. 204; W. H. B. Court, *The Rise of the Midland Industries, 1600–1838*, (Oxford), 1938, p. 206; T. C. Barker and J. R. Harris, *A Merseyside Town in the Industrial Revolution: St. Helens, 1750–1900*, (Liverpool), 1954, p. 287; S. Pollard, *A History of Labour in Sheffield*, (Liverpool), 1959, p. 61.

[6] *S.C. on the Present Dearness and Scarcity of Coal*, 1873, Evidence of Booth, QQ. 2175–2177, 2291–2293, 2349–2356.

[7] *Ibid.* Evidence of Woodhouse, Q. 3772.

[8] *Ibid.* Evidence of Evans, QQ. 951, 967.

general improvement in the social conditions of the miners and that the stories of miners drinking champagne and feeding their dogs on legs of mutton had been greatly exaggerated.[1]

The explanation of the miner's attitude to his work probably lies in Professor Chapman's analysis of the movement for shorter hours in the 'fifties and early 'sixties. He concludes that once the worker has attained a subsistence level 'the first step towards improvement of welfare is not in the direction of goods, food or clothing, but towards leisure; and that until men are seduced by various events or methods towards higher consumption, they will remain at their earlier level, until at least their desire for rest has been secured'.[2] The basic needs of the miner and his family were easily satisfied in the 'sixties. His pint of beer was comparatively cheap and beyond that his pleasures were few and simple. Pigeon-flying and rabbit-coursing were popular pastimes among the Derbyshire miners. The Coal Committee reported:

In general the condition of the workmen has been much improved, and . . . the rise in the rate of wages has not, under the exceptional circumstances, been unreasonable, nor been unattended with considerable benefit to the workmen; indeed in some cases the workmen have preferred improving the conditions under which they work to increasing the amount of their wages in money.[3]

II

A familiar concomitant of living at the subsistence level was debt, encouraged by the truck system. Its beginnings in Derbyshire can be seen in the Butterley Cash Book for 1790–6, which shows that the men received their monthly pay partly in vouchers on the local tradesmen which were redeemed by the employer at stated periods.[4] Despite the Truck Act of 1831[5] the system lingered on, especially in the country districts where the law was more easily evaded. The Commissioners appointed to inquire into the employment of children in mines reported in 1842 one clear instance of the payment of wages in truck in Derbyshire. The mother of two boys stated:

They are paid once a month, and [she] is quite sure if she wanted any money between times she could not have it otherwise than by a ticket for Hoseley's tommy-shop. Has never been obliged to sell her goods purchased there, but

[1] S.C. on the Present Dearness and Scarcity of Coal, Evidence of Pickard, QQ. 4029–4031, 4103, 4194–4198.
[2] G. Chapman, Culture and Survival, (London), 1940, p. 99.
[3] S.C. on the Present Dearness and Scarcity of Coal, 1873, Report, p. xi.
[4] Butterley Cash Book, 1790–6, cited in Mottram and Coote, op. cit. p. 54.
[5] 1 & 2 Will. IV, c. 36.

has bought of others; they sell bacon, cheese, potatoes, flour, bread, groceries, flannels and worsted. Twice a year they are paid only once in six weeks; they then call it the Tommy Fair. Has known those who had money to go to Belper save 1s. out of 3s. by buying their goods there.[1]

Similarly, the truck system was in operation until 1844 at Haslam's colliery at Pentrich.[2]

The truck system and the butty system were closely interrelated. A witness told one of the Commissioners: 'They take a ticket from the butties, who are always ready to give it, as they may receive so much in the shilling for themselves.'[3] The methods used by the butties in their payment of the labourers, and by overlookers in the payment of the butties, are thus described by J. M. Fellows, the Sub-Commissioner for Derbyshire:

In most coal fields the butties are paid every other Saturday night; at others only once a month, and they are allowed to draw subsistence money weekly. On the butty receiving the money he appoints the colliers and children to meet him, either at his own or some beer-shop he has an interest in, and generally keeps them waiting until he considers it has answered his purpose well enough, when the landlord produces the change and his bill. By this stratagem and system the colliers and the children are not only compelled to wait, but consider themselves lucky if they get home before midnight; being moreover driven to the necessity of making all their market on a Sunday morning. At some fields the butties are only settled with once a month or six weeks, and no subsistence is allowed them, except from a tommy-shop belonging to the overlooker of the works.[4]

As late as 1897 a Brimington stallman, Joshua Handford, was prosecuted under the Truck Act and a second summons was taken out against him in his capacity as agent of the employers, the Boythorpe Colliery Company. Henry Hawkins, a filler, stated in evidence that he and his brother-in-law were told that they could buy goods at Handford's shop cheaper than elsewhere. Every week deductions were made from their wages for goods bought at the shop and on other occasions tickets were given to them authorizing the purchase of boots at a Chesterfield shop for which deductions of 1s. a week were made from their wages. Handford was fined £2 with costs and Barnes, the chairman of the bench, himself a colliery proprietor, expressed the view that the

---

[1] *Children's Employment Commission (Mines)*, 1842, Evidence of J. M. Fellows, No. 363, App. Pt. II, p. 342, l.45.
[2] F. Engels, *The Condition of the Working Class in England in 1844*, (London), 1892, p. 255.
[3] *Children's Employment Commission*, 1842, Evidence of J. M. Fellows, No. 355, App. Pt. II, p. 341, l.33.
[4] *Ibid.* Report of J. M. Fellows, ss. 38–40, App. Pt. II, p. 255.

Boythorpe Company was liable for Hawkins's wages and ought never to have allowed the case to continue.[1]

The butties were compelled by the agreements they made with the coal-owners to be stern taskmasters and invariably struck a hard bargain.[2] The *Derbyshire Times* commented: 'As is too often the case, the working man is not the most liberal of employers and is apt to grind those who are, unfortunately, placed in his power.'[3] This was a fruitful source of discontent and the men were sometimes obliged to seek redress in the courts.[4] They were not always successful. In March, 1862, Isaac Tagg summoned John Hodkin, a contractor at the Sheepbridge colliery, for non-payment of 5s. wages. Hodkin stated that the manager had reduced Tagg's wages because he had lost three tubs of coal for which he should have been paid at 8d. each.[5]

III

In addition to such irritations, the working conditions of the miners in the early part of the nineteenth century, as described by the Children's Employment Commission in 1842, were far from pleasant. Ventilation was grossly inadequate and the pits abounded with fire-damp and black-damp. The only instance of furnace ventilation, then the most efficient method, found in Derbyshire in 1842, was at Clay Cross,[6] yet even here there was an explosion of fire-damp in 1840 in which a workman, John Young, was badly burnt.[7] Safety lamps were rarely used and fatal explosions occurred frequently. The presence of large quantities of carbonic acid gas and the heat of the pits caused much discomfort to the miners and added greatly to their fatigue. James Davis, a holer employed in Lord Middleton's colliery, stated:

There is not a good ventilation; they are very much put about by the black-damp; are prevented working for a day or two together; never has had the wildfire since he worked there; never use the Davy lamp; the pit is always tried by a man going with a naked candle; the butties are on the look out to see all is right.[8]

John Beasley, a pitman at Shipley, said that he had sometimes found the pit 'as hot as a stove'.[9]

---

[1] *Derbyshire Times*, 15 May, 1897. [2] See Appendix I to this chapter.
[3] *Derbyshire Times*, 7 February, 1872.
[4] *Ibid.* 22 August, 1863; 7 February, 1872.
[5] *Ibid.* 8 March, 1862.
[6] *Children's Employment Commission*, 1842, J. M. Fellows, Report, s. 30: App. Pt. II, p. 254. [7] *Derbyshire Chronicle*, 13 June, 1840.
[8] *Children's Employment Commission*, 1842, J. M. Fellows, Evidence, No. 12: App. Pt. II, p. 266, l.57. [9] *Ibid.* No. 40: p. 290, l.49.

Still less attention was paid to drainage. It was stated by all classes of witnesses that some pits in Derbyshire were dry and comfortable, but 'very many were so wet that people had to work all day over their shoes in water, at the same time that water was constantly dripping upon them from the roof'.[1]

The hours of work were long, being anything from thirteen to sixteen a day. At the Butterley Company's Hard Coal Pit, men and boys alike went down at 6 a.m. and seldom came up before 9 p.m.[2] Agents, overlookers and enginemen in general stated that one hour was allowed for meals but the Commission found that in practice, in the majority of pits, the time allowed was only half an hour, twenty minutes or even a quarter of an hour. In many pits no time whatever was allowed for meals.[3] The only recognized holidays were Christmas Day, Good Friday and a day or two at Whitsuntide.[4]

Working under such conditions the colliers had a short expectation of life. Most of them, by the age of forty, if they had not a confirmed asthma, suffered from difficult breathing[5] and had a look of premature old age.[6] The loaders, who had great weights to lift and breathed a worse atmosphere than any other in the pit, were prematurely aged at twenty-eight or thirty.[7] One witness described them as being 'old men before they are young ones'.[8]

No women or girls were employed in the Derbyshire pits[9] but the employment of boys was universal. Many of these unfortunate children started work at the age of five or six. Few began work in the pits at a later age than eight.[10] They were obliged to endure the same dreadful conditions underground as the miner and to work the same hours. William Ghent, aged seven, who had worked in the pit for two years, told one of the Commissioners that he 'has to work nearly up to his knees in sludge all day; his legs are cold, but other parts are very warm. He had rather get coal than head; it is so wet, and he cannot stand up; it makes his neck ache. He is so tired, dirty and wet when he gets home, that he undresses, gets his supper, and is glad when he is in bed.'[11] The Sub-Commissioner for Derbyshire stated:

I have met with pits where it rained so as to wet the Children to the skin in a few minutes, and at the same time so hot that they could scarcely bear their clothes on to work in, and in this wet state they had to continue fourteen

---

[1] *Children's Employment Commission*, 1842, First Report, p. 50, s. 231.
[2] *Ibid.* J. M. Fellows, Evidence, No. 180, App. Pt. II, p. 311, l.35.
[3] *Ibid.* First Report, p. 119, s. 464.
[4] *Ibid.* J. M. Fellows, Report, App. Pt. II, p. 255, s. 37.
[5] *Ibid.* p. 256, s. 57.   [6] *Ibid.* s. 49.   [7] *Ibid.* s. 57.
[8] *Ibid.* J. M. Fellows, Evidence, App. Ptd. II, No. 105, p. 292, 1.48.
[9] *Ibid.* First Report, s. 154, p. 36.   [10] *Ibid.* First Report, ss. 59–62, p. 11.
[11] *Ibid.* J. M. Fellows, Evidence, App. Pt. II, No. 195, p. 315, ll.10, 14.

AN ATMOSPHERIC ENGINE (1791)
From Pentrich Colliery, Derbyshire
Crown Copyright, Science Museum, London

hours, and perhaps had to walk a mile or two at night without changing or drying their clothes.[1]

The youngest children were employed for the first six or twelve months in attending to the wind-doors. At seven years old they 'drove between'. This task is described in detail by the Commissioners:

The corve without wheels, with from eight hundredweight to nearly a ton, is drawn the length of the bank (mostly about 200 yards) by three asses. The 'between driver' is placed behind the second ass and has to attend to the two first: the last is driven by the ass lad, who is often not more than twelve years of age. The elder boy wears a dog-belt . . . but not to draw with continuously, the descent being frequently sufficient, or even more than sufficient, for the corve to run without much drawing: the elder boy walks backwards, and has at the same time to urge the last ass on, and by his belt prevent the corve running against the side of the bank. When the corve reaches the waggon-road it is placed on wheels, and left to the care of two other boys (one perhaps about thirteen, the other eight or nine years old); the elder one wears the dog-belt, and occasionally draws by it, or in some pits, when the descent is good, he merely uses the 'crop-stick'; in returning, the youngest boy goes before the waggon, and the elder pushes behind. Until a boy gets accustomed to the dog-belt it frequently produces soreness on the hips, and otherwise injures him.[2]

One or two boys were also employed to follow the loader (i.e. to place the small coal on the corve, and to keep the floor of the bank level) as well as one about twelve years old to assist in hanging the corves on the chain so that it could be drawn up the shaft.[3]

The whole of the children in the pit, with the exception of the hanger-on, were working in a stooping posture throughout the day. In the pits around Brampton the seams were so thin that several had only a two-foot headway to all the workings. These were worked entirely by boys. 'In Mr. Barnes's pit', reported the Sub-Commissioner, 'these poor boys have to drag the barrows, with 1 cwt. of coal or slack, 60 times a day 60 yards, and the empty barrows back, without once straightening their backs, unless they choose to stand under the shaft, and run the risk of having their heads broken by a coal falling.'[4] The coal from these pits was retailed both in Brampton and Chesterfield at 3s. a ton.[5]

With very few exceptions the proprietors and their agents took no charge whatever of the children but left them to the mercy of the butties neither knowing nor caring how they were treated. In the vast majority of pits the butty bargained for, dismissed and used the child

---

[1] *Children's Employment Commission*, 1842, J. M. Fellows, Report, App. Pt. II, s. 24, p. 254.
[2] *Ibid*. First Report, s. 301, pp. 69–70.
[3] *Ibid*. s. 302, p. 70.
[4] *Ibid*. Report, App. Pt. II, s. 26, p. 254.
[5] *Ibid*. s. 28, p. 254.

C

just as he wished.[1] Beating with the ass-stick, ear- and hair-pulling, kicking and even throttling were common punishments. John Beasley, of Shipley, told the Sub-Commissioner:

When he was a boy they were beaten most unmercifully by the corporals, who were complete blackguards; they mostly used the ass-stick, about as thick as your thumb; they often kicked them, and sometimes used the fist; has seen them throttle the boys, but never so bad but what they soon recovered; has been himself so punished that he was obliged to leave the pit. . . .[2]

In the few instances where the proprietors did interfere the treatment of the children was better. John Hayne, of Staveley, said that 'on Mr. Barrow's fields both men and children are as well-treated as at any field. He used to work at Heanor; there and at Shipley and that neighbourhood they are worked and used shameful.'[3]

The practice of employing very young children as engineers to let down and draw up the workpeople increased the number of fatal accidents. The Sub-Commissioner for Derbyshire reported:

Met with more than one instance of Children only ten years old having the lives of the colliers left to their mercy, and have seen others so inattentive to their duty as to let the corve be drawn over the pulley, and half a ton of coals thrown the distance of a hundred yards or more down the shaft; but notwithstanding these accidents occurring in the immediate neighbourhood, the practice of appointing Children to this responsible post still continues in the most respectable fields.[4]

An engineman employed at Morewood's collieries said that at Swanwick and Somercotes the motive for employing boys instead of men was merely because boys could be had at less wages.[5]

If the children were not maimed or killed by some serious accident they suffered in other ways. Witnesses of every class, children, young persons, colliers, underground stewards, agents, parents, teachers, and ministers of religion gave evidence which convinced the Commissioners that something must be done. Long hours, hasty meals, unhealthy atmospheres, exposure to heat and water, excessively heavy work and frequent beatings all took their toll. Most of the children employed in the Derbyshire pits from an early age were bow-legged and not so well formed, if even of the same family, as those who worked above ground. Long hours virtually deprived them of daylight, giving them a sallow complexion. Insufficient sleep resulted in dullness and stunted

[1] *Children's Employment Commission*, 1842, First Report, s. 506, p. 126.
[2] *Ibid*. J. M. Fellows, Evidence, No. 40, p. 274, l. 12.
[3] *Ibid*. No. 440, p. 253, l. 13.   [4] *Ibid*. Report, App. Pt. II, ss. 34–36, p. 255.
[5] *Ibid*. Evidence, No. 327, p. 366, l. 49.

growth. Most of these children arrived home at the end of a day's work with aching limbs and in need of rest. Some of them had to be led home by their parents. Their lives were spent either at work or in bed. One lad had 'been a week together and never seen daylight, but on Sunday, and not much then, he was so sleepy'.[1] A medical witness stated that when a collier had worked from childhood, and became forty, he looked much older than those of the same age above ground.[2]

Such a life left little opportunity for education. In any case the facilities were few. There were, in Derbyshire, some National and Free schools from which the collier children were excluded by the rules of the schools. The constant reply of the coal-owners and agents was 'No school, no reading room, no club, or anything of the sort connected with these coal works'.[3] The only other means of instruction for the children employed in the mines, if they were not too tired to attend, were the Sunday schools. The physical condition of the children and the inadequacy of the instruction they received prevented them from deriving any real benefit from attendance at these schools. The Sub-Commissioner reported:

I, as well as the schoolmaster, have found a dullness about these children not in other boys; with one striking exception, namely the Chesterfield Union, in which it is the custom to work only ten hours a day; here the children look much happier, and without the dullness so apparent in them in other parts of the district.[4]

Elsewhere in the county witnesses were unanimous in their views on the education of collier children:

They appear more tired and do not attend so early; and the parents when applied to often say they come home so wearied that they cannot get them to school in time. When the boys have been beaten, knocked about, and covered with sludge, all the week, they want to be in bed all day to rest on Sunday.[5]

Of the inefficiency of the Sunday schools, the Sub-Commissioner gives a number of practical illustrations. One child, who had been at such a school for three years, could not 'say his A.B.C.'. Another, who had attended a Baptist Sunday School for four or five years could not spell 'horse' or 'cow' and was 'otherwise very ignorant'. A child who had been at the Methodists' Sunday School at Ripley for five years

---

[1] *Children's Employment Commission*, 1842, J. M. Fellows, Evidence, No. 271, p. 326, l. 45.
[2] *Ibid.* No. 10, p. 266, l. 8.
[3] *Ibid.* Report, ss. 69 *et seq.* p. 257, Evidence, pp. 275 *et seq.* Nos. 45, 60, 66, 109, 125.
[4] *Ibid.* p. 258, s. 87.   [5] *Ibid.* Evidence, p. 266, l. 33.

'cannot spell in the least; cannot tell what d - o - g spells—he says "gun" '.[1]

The moral condition of the children and young persons employed in the mines depended much upon the character of the butty and the overlooker. Some of these men were class teachers among the Methodists and would not allow a bad example to be set for the children. Others were profane and immoral, encouraging in the children swearing and every other kind of vice.[2] After his examination of the district the Sub-Commissioner entertained 'a much higher opinion of the colliers, both men and children, than he did from hearsay'. He was, however, perturbed by the indifference of the parents to the children's education. He stated that the sole wish of the parents examined by him seemed in general 'to make all they could out of their children at as early an age as possible without regarding their future welfare'; and that 'he has not only heard of, but has witnessed the anxiety of the father and mother that their coming off-spring may be a boy; both uniting in lamenting their fate should it happen to be a girl, because in that case they could not send it so early to labour'.[3]

In other respects the children appear to have been well cared for by their parents:

Their food, generally speaking, is full as ample and good as those who are labouring above ground . . . , their clothing consists of a coarse flannel shirt or jacket, and trousers mostly of the same material. . . . As to cleanliness during work, it is impossible; but at the same time I was much pleased at the particularly neat and clean appearance of the collier children I met with at the various Sunday-schools. Those cottages I visited belonging to the colliers varied very much in different parts of the district; at Ilkistone [Ilkeston] and its neighbourhood they were decidedly much more neat and comfortable than any of their neighbours who were engaged either in lace-making, stocking-making, or agriculture; but at South Normanton and Kirkby they were the picture of dirt and wretchedness. I observed in all parts, if there was but little furniture, every collier's cottage had a blazing fire; this they get free of any expense, and certainly it is a set-off against some of their deprivations.[4]

IV

On 7 June, 1842, soon after the publication of the report of the Royal Commissioners on the employment of women and children in mines, Lord Ashley introduced his measure prohibiting the employment of

---

[1] *Children's Employment Commission*, 1842, J. M. Fellows, Evidence, p. 295, l. 35; p. 294, l. 1; p. 315, l. 18.   [2] *Ibid.* Report, p. 257, ss. 60 *et seq.*
[3] *Ibid.* p. 258, s. 88.   [4] *Ibid.* p. 256, ss. 50–55.

women underground, restricting the labour of boys, and making it an offence for wages to be paid at or near a public-house. Despite opposition from the colliery proprietors, and notably from the Marquis of Londonderry, the Bill became law on 10 August, 1842.[1] There followed a stream of colliery legislation, much of which had to be fought for by trade union action. An Act for the inspection of coalmines was passed in 1850.[2] Inspection was continued for a further period of five years by the Act of 1855,[3] which specified seven general rules to be observed at all collieries and provided for special rules to be framed and put in force at every colliery subject to the approval of a principal Secretary of State. The Act was, however, received with great dissatisfaction by the miners. It appeared to them inequitable that they should be liable to imprisonment for an offence, while the masters could only be fined. On the other hand, by the introduction of general, and the enforcement of special, rules the responsibility of management became more clearly defined, and the owners became accountable in the courts of law for keeping their pits in a safe condition.

The Act of 1855 had to be renewed in 1860 and on this occasion Parliament decided to legislate in a more permanent form. The most important feature of the act of 1860[4] from the point of view of safety was that boys under eighteen were forbidden to act as enginemen. There was also the important clause enabling the men to appoint a checkweighman at their own expense. Two years later, after the Hartley Colliery disaster in Northumberland in which 204 men lost their lives, another Act laid down that every mine should have at least two entrance shafts.[5] The Coal Mines Act of 1872[6] went even further towards providing safe conditions of work by giving the men employed at a colliery power to inspect the workings from time to time. It also required that every mine should be under the control of a registered manager, holding a certificate of competency, and introduced a number of clauses regulating the examination of candidates and the granting of certificates. The age limit for boys employed in mines remained at ten years but the hours of work were reduced to ten a day. The hours for attendance at school, between the ages of ten and thirteen, were fixed at twenty a fortnight. A long-standing grievance of the miner was remedied by the provision that in all but very exceptional cases he was to be paid for his coal by weight and not by measure.

The general effect of this legislation from 1842 onwards was to provide safer working conditions and the gradual reduction of the amount of child labour employed in the pits. Accidents, however, continued to happen, emphasizing the need for yet greater care on the

---

[1] 5 & 6 Vict., c. 99.   [2] 13 & 14 Vict., c. 100.   [3] 18 & 19 Vict., c. 108.
[4] 23 & 24 Vict., c. 151.   [5] 25 & 26 Vict., c. 79.   [6] 35 & 36 Vict., c. 76.

part of men and employers alike. The Clay Cross disaster of 11 June, 1861, in which twenty-three lives were lost, was the worst in Derbyshire until 1882 when forty-five men were killed, again at Clay Cross. The accident of 1861 originated at the end of the colliery which lay near the old workings of the Black Shale No. 1 pit. Nathaniel Dawes, working at the face, noticed that the coal was coming more freely than usual and was further alarmed by the issue of a stream of water between the dirt and the coal.[1] Within a short time a large part of the mine was flooded.[2]

In 1856 the loss of life in the Midland district (i.e. Derbyshire, Leicestershire, Nottinghamshire and Warwickshire) was one to every 97,000 tons of coal raised. By 1880 the output of coal in the district had been more than trebled but the fatal accident rate was only one to every 245,780 tons.[3] The inspector of mines for the district was able to state in 1877: 'Most people will, I feel sure, be satisfied with the result of the working of the Mines Act so far as the prevention of accidents is concerned.' At the same time he pointed out that the character of mining in the area had completely changed since 1860. The small shallow pits had been worked out and there were now deep sinkings which, because of their cost, necessitated pits of large area, a factor which added greatly to the difficulties of ventilation and to the general problems of safe and economical working.[4]

The commonest cause of accidents was falls of roof. In 1875 the inspector of mines commented:

Many of them may be classed amongst preventable accidents; such, for instance, as 'holing' without 'sprags'; working under a roof after being cautioned that it was dangerous, in consequence of the want of timber to support it; trying to pass in front of coal which had already been 'holed', and the 'sprags' knocked out; and going into working places after a shot had been fired without properly examining the roof.[5]

There were also numerous accidents with tubs. Evans, the inspector, stated that this was due to the 'dangerous practice which prevails in many collieries of allowing boys to place themselves before loaded tubs for the purpose of bringing them down steep places'.[6]

Accidents in shafts caused the deaths of seventeen persons in the Midland District in 1875.[7] During the 'sixties and the 'seventies, however, a number of changes were introduced which helped to minimize such accidents. In 1863 Barton, of Alfreton, invented an apparatus to prevent men on the bank from falling down the shaft, which was approved by the inspector of mines.[8] The gradual raising of the age-limit

[1] *Derbyshire Times*, 15 June, 1861.   [2] *Ibid.* 27 July, 1861.
[3] See Appendix II to this chapter.
[4] *Reports of H.M. Inspectors of Mines*, 1877.
[5] *Ibid.* 1875.   [6] *Ibid.*   [7] *Ibid.*
[8] *Derbyshire Times*, 1 August, 1863.

for enginemen, and such inventions as Calow's safety catch and King's safety hook[1] tended to reduce the number of cases of over-winding with the result that during the ten years from 1860 to 1870 there were only two such cases in the whole of the Midland counties.[2] During 1861 Hedley, the district inspector, paid particular attention to shafts, suggesting the use of fencing and pointing out the dangers of brattices.[3] As a result of his representations, of the ten collieries with bratticed shafts in the district, three had provided second shafts during the year and four others were in the process of doing so.[4] After the Hartley pit accident, when double shafts became compulsory, bratticed shafts disappeared completely, but such reforms took time. The double shaft system was sometimes established by the construction of a communicating drift between two pits. This was done at Staveley in September, 1863, between the Farewell and Dowell pits.[5]

Improvements in ventilation, and particularly the introduction of fan ventilation in the 'seventies, helped to make conditions in the mines more tolerable and to reduce the number of explosions but, until the use of safety lamps became widespread, accidents were numerous. One of the more serious was the explosion at the Renishaw Park Colliery, belonging to J. and G. Wells, on 10 January, 1871, when twenty-five men and two boys were killed and twelve others were injured. In 1877 W. E. Teale, of Worsley, deplored the use of naked lights in mines but blamed the miners for its continuance. He wrote:

In fact, so wedded are they to candles that they prefer to pay for their own in preference to using safety lamps 'supplied and paid for by the owners' . . . . Many managers have said to me 'I wish it was made compulsory that no naked lights should be allowed in a pit'.[6]

The men's resistance, as will be shown, was based partly on economic and partly on health grounds.[7] Belgium was one of the pioneers in making the use of safety lamps compulsory and specifying the type of lamp to be used but although the use of safety lamps increased steadily in this country nothing was done to define exactly the conditions under which they must be used until 1911.

The operation of the general and special rules presented problems for both employers and workers. The coal-owners desired to see such general rules adopted as would not interfere with the economical working of collieries. They also sought, in the special rules, to throw the

---

[1] See Chapter I, p. 55.
[2] *Reports of H.M. Inspectors of Mines*, 1860–70.
[3] The brattice was the wooden partition which was used to divide single shafts. See Prologue, p. 26.
[4] *Derbyshire Times*, 11 October, 1862. [5] *Ibid.* 12 September, 1863.
[6] *Ibid.* 17 February, 1877. [7] See pp. 277, 374, 478–80.

responsibility as much as possible on the miners, and hence much wrangling ensued between the proprietors and the government inspectors with regard to the framing of these rules. Employers were frequently prosecuted by the inspectors for breaking the law[1] and after the passing of the Act of 1872 the responsibility imposed upon colliery officials was considerable. Herein lay the origin of the National Colliery Managers', Deputies' and Underviewers' Association, a branch of which was formed at Ripley in 1877 for the protection of the officials in the district.[2] Workmen were frequently fined in the courts for such offences as smoking in the pits, negligently 'gobbing' (i.e. burying) tools, neglecting to support the roof properly, not drawing the props in accordance with the rules, riding on tubs, over-loading cages and leaving the colliery without giving proper notice.[3] On the controversial subject of supporting the roof a deputation in 1873 waited on Bruce, the Home Secretary, who ruled that timbering 'should be done under the supervision and responsibility of the manager'.[4]

Cases arising out of breaches of mines legislation were usually heard before the local magistrates, many of whom were colliery proprietors. Sometimes they retired from the bench whilst the case was being heard,[5] but not invariably. The composition of the magisterial bench became one of the grievances of the miners, who felt that consciously or unconsciously the magistrates favoured the owners rather than the workmen.[6] The colliery proprietor was a powerful figure who, in addition to controlling their working lives, appeared to have the law on his side.

V

Indeed, as the scale of operations in the coal industry increased, the employers began to exercise a growing influence upon many aspects of the lives of the miner and his family. When a large colliery was opened out it was usually necessary for the owners to provide housing for their workers and so developed the drab, featureless colliery villages. As early as 1841 George Stephenson and Company had built 130 cottages at Clay Cross[7] and in 1865 invited tenders for the erection of a further sixty-

---

[1] E.g. *Derbyshire Times*, 21 September, 1861, 8 July, 1865, 27 November, 1875, etc.
[2] *Derbyshire Times*, 17 August, 1878.
[3] E.g. *Derbyshire Times*, 26 January, 1861; 20 April, 1861; 21 January, 1871; 4 December, 1872; 22 July, 1874; 18 November, 1874, etc.
[4] R. N. Boyd, *Coal Pits and Pitmen*, (London), 1892, p. 187.
[5] E.g. *Derbyshire Times*, 27 November, 1875; 4 December, 1872.
[6] Cf. R. Kidd, *The Harworth Colliery Strike: A Report to the Executive Committee of the National Council for Civil Liberties*, (London), 1937, pp. 9–10.
[7] *Derbyshire Chronicle*, 14 August, 1841.

four at Morton.[1] In 1868 the same Company was building some eighty houses at Danesmoor in connection with the new colliery there.[2] Similarly, the Monkwood Colliery Company built about sixty houses in the Unstone district when the collieries were being opened out there in 1870.[3] Wright and Jessop, the proprietors of the Butterley Works, built a large village known as Ironville which, in 1870, had a population of some 1,500.[4] The Sheepbridge Company, in the following year, had seventy houses and cottages for officials and workpeople.[5] This kind of development resulted in most of the large colliery concerns becoming considerable landlords. The powerful weapon of eviction was placed in their hands and, as will be shown, some of them did not scruple to use it in times of industrial strife.[6]

In addition to housing, the employers frequently provided amenities such as schools, churches, chapels and institutes for their colliery villages. Charles Binns announced the intention of his Company to erect a school at Clay Cross in 1841: 'The Company feel deeply for the interests of the rising generation at Clay Cross, and it is their wish that they shall be properly educated and made to understand the relative duties of life.'[7] This was not accomplished until 1855 when schools were opened for boys, girls and infants at a cost of £3,000 to £4,000. The building consisted of a public room with the infant school and a library on one side and the boys' and girls' schools on the other. Outside were a pleasure ground and a recreation ground to which the Company's employees had free access. The schools were self-supporting, each man or boy employed on the works contributing 1d. a week towards them.[8] In 1847 the Company established a society for the encouragement of cottage gardening and in connection with this there was an annual show.[9] When Danesmoor was being developed, the Company gave a plot of land to the New Connexion Friends for the erection of a chapel and promised further support.[10]

In 1865 the Staveley Company set aside £1,000 for religious and educational purposes[11] and four years later granted £400 for the building of a Primitive Methodist chapel and Sunday School, £1,200 towards a church and £600 towards the erection of a girls' school at Staveley. In addition, J. Barrow, the chairman of the Company, contributed privately £500.[12] In the dining hall established by Richard Barrow at the

[1] *Derbyshire Times*, 23 December, 1865.   [2] *Ibid.* 10 October, 1868.
[3] *Ibid.* 2 April, 1870.   [4] *Ibid.* 3 December, 1870.
[5] *Ibid.* 27 May, 1871.   [6] See Chapter III, pp. 106, 111.
[7] *Derbyshire Chronicle*, 14 August, 1841.
[8] *White's History, Gazetteer and Directory of the County of Derby*, (Sheffield), 1857, p. 792.
[9] *Derbyshire Times*, 27 September, 1862.   [10] *Ibid.* 10 October, 1868.
[11] *Ibid.* 8 September, 1866.   [12] *Ibid.* 27 October, 1869.

C*

Staveley works it was possible to have 'a bowl of broth or soup for 1d., a plate of potatoes, 1d., lemonade 1½d., cup of tea or coffee, 1d., bread and butter, 1d., all articles being of the best quality. . . . A breakfast can be obtained for 2d., and a capital dinner, with hot meat and bread, for 4½d.'[1] Richard Barrow was also responsible for establishing what was probably the first workmen's train ever to be run in this country, familiar to the Derbyshire miners as the 'Paddy Mail'. Barrow obtained permission from the Midland Railway Company in 1854 to run a workmen's train in the early morning from Chesterfield to Staveley, and back at night. Barrow provided the engine and coaches and handed over the whole of the receipts to the Midland Company. The charge made to the workmen was 6d. a week or about ⅐d. a mile and yielded a profit of more than 50 per cent.[2] In 1871, when trade was good, the Staveley Company established a building society.[3]

Many of the colliery companies began to run sick clubs or 'field clubs' as they were commonly called. The operation of these clubs caused much dissatisfaction. In 1866 James Cutts, a miner, brought an action in the Queen's Bench division against the proprietors of the Wingerworth colliery for the recovery of club money of 1s. a week which was deducted from his wages fortnightly. Membership of the club was compulsory and Cutts objected to these and other deductions under the Truck Act. He stated that he was a member of the Ancient Order of Foresters in which for 10½d. a fortnight, 'he had great benefits', whilst for the shilling stopped by the employer he got 'nothing but what they chose to give him'. In the course of his evidence, Cutts remarked: 'If every miner in the United Kingdom paid his shilling into his own society, duly registered, it would be thousands of pounds a year to the good.' The judge ruled that such stoppages were illegal.[4]

As time went on the rules of some of these clubs were modified in order to allow the workmen to play a greater part in their management. At Staveley, in 1868, the Sick and Accident Fund came under the control of a committee consisting of Charles Markham, the principal officers of the Staveley Company and eleven working men elected annually by their fellow workmen.[5] As late as 1877, however, a miner wrote:

There are collieries in Derbyshire where the employers consider themselves the sole managers of the colliery club; balance sheets are never heard of, the financial position of the club being a matter of conjecture. No matter how wisely the funds are administered the system is wrong. Those who pay have a right to the management. If the employers contribute to the funds of the

[1] *Derbyshire Times*, 28 May, 1864.   [2] *Ibid.* 19 September, 1874.
[3] *Ibid.* 6 May, 1871.   [4] *Ibid.* 18 August, 1866.
[5] *Ibid.* 10 October, 1868.

club they have a right to assist in its management. If the workmen subscribe the whole of the funds they have a right to the whole of the management. . . . I think the time has arrived when no intelligent person will care to subscribe to the funds of any unregistered friendly society or club, their management generally being capricious and unsatisfactory.[1]

The annual 'feast' or the 'treat' in celebration of the winning of a new seam provided an occasion for the employers to display their generosity and to inculcate appropriate virtues in their workmen. Typical of such celebrations is a treat given by George Stephenson and Company in the grounds of Tupton Hall, the residence of Charles Binns, during the Clay Cross feast week of 1841. A contemporary account of the proceedings is worth quoting at some length:

At one side near the table was a recess to contain 'All Allsopp and Sons Burton Mild' in very portly-looking 'fifty-fours'. Above the head of the table appeared a transparency with the words 'Industry and Sobriety produce Comfort and Competence'. The preparations for the occasion had been going on since the preceding week; near 800 lb. of beef and mutton, of the best quality, had been provided, also a liberal quantity of ingredients for that invaluable accompaniment to roast beef, good plum pudding, together with bread and vegetables in abundance. . . .

About half past twelve the marshalling of the forces commenced. First and foremost came the wives and female children of the workmen, to whom precedence in the procession was granted; next to whom, and immediately preceding the band, came the clerks of the establishment, accompanied by a flag emblematical of universal charity and love, bearing the representation of an Indian and a Turk succouring a Christian, with the motto 'Love to All', 'Go thou and do likewise' [sic], then followed, in order, four abreast, the carpenters, sawyers, smiths, fitters, masons and bricklayers; next came a numerous body of miners, then the coke burners, the colliery loaders and banksmen, and lastly the carters, labourers, etc. etc.[2]

At the end of the meal, 'when the plates, etc. had been cleared away, and the glasses were filled to the brim with Burton stingo', Charles Binns mounted the table and proposed the health of the Queen and announced various benefactions. 'No man', he said, 'had a deeper feeling for the welfare of the working man than Mr. Stephenson. . . . If the Company prospered they would prosper; if the Company fell they must fall.'[3]

Similarly, in 1861, the Pierces of Whittington gave a treat to their workmen and their friends to celebrate the sinking of the Foxley Oaks Pit. 'A novel feature was introduced into the proceedings of the day by the voluntary attendance of the workmen and a number of their families at Church, where a very useful and practical sermon was preached by

---

[1] *Derbyshire Times*, 3 November, 1877.
[2] *Derbyshire Chronicle*, 14 August, 1841.   [3] *Ibid.*

the Rev. W. Wheeler. . . .'[1] Samuel Beale and Company used to give an annual supper to the miners of the Newbold Colliery at the Nag's Head.[2] J. Barrow gave a treat to fifty of his workmen in celebration of the completion of a tunnel at the Springwell Colliery in 1862.[3] Further instances are too numerous to mention. The practice was universal and the pattern was familiar: a hearty meal, followed by pious exhortations.

VI

The influence of religion, and particularly Primitive Methodism, upon the miners during this period was very great. The mid-nineteenth century was an intensely religious age and Puritanism and Evangelicalism permeated all aspects of life. Employers and trade union leaders alike spoke to the miners in a manner which, today, would be regarded as more appropriate to the pulpit. Biblical texts were quoted on every possible occasion. Hymns and prayers were an essential feature of both trade union meetings and employers' treats. When the annual tea meeting was held at Springwell Colliery in 1863 there were addresses during the day by workmen who were local preachers among the Wesleyans, Free Church and Primitive Methodists. 'After tea', we are told, 'the Love-Feast was held in a tent.'[4] One of the earliest recorded public meetings of miners in Chesterfield began with singing and prayer[5] and on some occasions special miners' hymns were sung.[6] Trade union meetings were frequently held in chapels (or public houses) and the Derbyshire Miners' Association banner, with its biblical text 'Bear ye one another's burdens', which adorned the Council Chamber until 1955, bears witness to the continuing influence of religion until comparatively recent times.

The Hammonds have called attention to the way in which the miners were particularly given to Methodism and have suggested that its attraction lay in 'the very special and miraculous sense of protection, just as the belief in the miraculous salvation of religion is particularly strong among the deep-sea fishermen of Brittany'.[7] They see, also,

---

[1] *Derbyshire Times*, 1 June, 1861.

[2] *Ibid.* 18 June, 1862.   [3] *Ibid.* 6 September, 1862.

[4] *Ibid.* 29 August, 1863. The Love-Feast (the Agape) in the early Christian church was a meal on the analogy of the Last Supper followed by the Eucharist. Later the meal became separated from the Eucharist, and, as the Agape or Love-Feast, continued to exist as a symbol of fellowship or a means of charity. (C. Gore (ed.) *A New Commentary on Holy Scripture*, (London), 1937, pp. 336–7.)

[5] *Ibid.* 3 December, 1864.   [6] *Ibid.* 15 September, 1866.

[7] J. L. and B. Hammond, *The Town Labourer, 1760–1832*, (London), 1917, p. 272. Cf. Pierre Loti, *Pêcheur d'Islande*.

another element in the new religion suggested by a passage from Gilbert Murray's discussion of Greek religion:[1] 'The Methodists told the miners what Seneca told the unhappy rich in the Claudian Terror, or Epictetus had told an age seeking for new reconciliations amid the ruins of the old religions, or St. Augustine had told the distracted peoples of Europe after the sack of Rome, that every man carried with him his own fate, and that the sovereign happiness of all, the happiness of faith and resignation, was not the prize of wealth or power or learning or conquest, but of a state of mind and heart that poor could attain as readily as rich; the slave as readily as his master. . . . "Whom the Lord loveth He chasteneth", was the message of Wesley.'[2] More recently Dr. Hobsbawm has suggested that the evangelistic technique, doctrine and organization of the Primitive Methodists were generally suitable to working-class groups such as miners and farm-labourers living in the villages of an early, relatively undeveloped industrialism but he also remarks: 'If we did not know how close the connection between the Primitives and organized labour was, we should not easily guess it from an inspection of their doctrines and organization.'[3]

Methodism has been praised for saving the country from revolution as well as for inspiring the struggle of the working classes. The apparent conflict between these two views is nicely reconciled by the Hammonds: 'The teaching of Methodism was unfavourable to working-class movements; its leaders were hostile and its ideals perhaps increasingly hostile; but by the life and energy and awakening that it brought to this oppressed society it must, in spite of itself, have made many men better citizens, and some even better rebels.'[4] In the early part of the nineteenth century, as Dr. Wearmouth has shown, Methodism was staunch in its Toryism, fearful of Radical agitation and warned its people to keep clear of all political entanglements.[5] So much so that Cobbett wrote in 1824:

The bitterest foes of freedom in England have been, and are, the Methodists. Rail they do . . . against the West Indian slave-holders; but not a word do you ever hear from them against the slave-holders in Lancashire and in Ireland. On the contrary, they are continually telling the people here that they ought to thank the Lord not for a bellyful and a warm back, but for that abundant grace of which they are the bearers, and for which they charge them only one penny per week each.[6]

[1] Gilbert Murray, *Four Stages of Greek Religion*, (New York), 1912, p. 103.
[2] J. L. and B. Hammond, *op. cit.* p. 276.
[3] E. J. Hobsbawm, *Primitive Rebels*, (Manchester), 1959, pp. 137–40.
[4] J. L. and B. Hammond, *op. cit.* p. 287.
[5] R. F. Wearmouth, *Methodism and the Struggle of the Working Classes, 1850–1900*, (Leicester), 1954, pp. 210–11.
[6] *Political Register*, 3 January, 1824.

Similarly, the attitude of Methodism towards trade unionism, although not so clearly defined, was equally unsympathetic.[1] The intense spiritual individualism of Methodism was directly opposed to the spirit of the trade union movement of the time, yet by the end of the nineteenth century its attitude became much less rigid in trade union affairs and in politics.[2]

Methodism won many of its adherents among the poorer classes, it taught them to read and write, it gave them certain spiritual values, it even allowed them to become preachers. 'The Methodist, whatever his shortcomings, became a man of earnestness, sobriety, industry, and regularity of conduct.'[3] Such men were respected and soon found themselves in positions of trust and responsibility in the trade union movement. Dr. Hobsbawm writes of the Primitive Methodists: 'It is not too much to think of them as primarily a sect of trade union cadres.'[4]

Despite its rebellious tone Methodism undoubtedly had a pacific effect upon the Derbyshire miners. Most of their early leaders were Primitive Methodists who constantly urged them, in times of crisis, to be orderly and not to resort to violence.[5] Even the strike weapon was used with great reluctance and only in times of extreme difficulty or provocation. Moreover, the fervour which was aroused by speeches containing scriptural allusions enabled the leaders to appeal to the emotions rather than to the intellects of their members. An Anglican clergyman, who spent the last thirty years of the nineteenth century among the Derbyshire miners and who shows little sympathy with Dissenters, writes:

Their leaders are to be found in Co-operative Societies, or Hospital Committees, among Chapel Trustees, and Deacons, in Teetotal Societies, members of Parish Councils, School Boards, and a variety of other places. No-one can do anything but themselves. If they could rule, earth would be a paradise, and, because they cannot, injustice and misery are the consequence. . . . These people you meet wherever you go, but in these colliery districts they stand out more prominently than anywhere else as they are men who have studied well the science of knowing what to say to catch the average collier's ear. The moment the collier begins to think for himself their power is gone for ever.[6]

[1] Wearmouth, op. cit. p. 171.   [2] Ibid. pp. 173, 213.
[3] Sidney Webb, The Story of the Durham Miners, (London), 1921, p. 23.
[4] Hobsbawm, op. cit. p. 138.
[5] In order to make the point that the influence of Primitive Methodism was 'by no means necessarily moderate' in character Dr. Hobsbawm cites an example from the twentieth century, that of Arthur Horner, who presumably abandoned his Methodism when he became 'a revolutionary' (op. cit. p. 149). Henry Hicken presents a parallel twentieth-century case in Derbyshire (see Chapter XV, pp. 583-4.) but he was an exception. Most of the Derbyshire leaders of the nineteenth century (and even later) were Primitive Methodists and remained so. They were also moderates.
[6] F. J. Metcalfe, Collieries and I; or Thirty Years' Work among Derbyshire Colliers, (Manchester), 1903, pp. 23–25.

A pamphlet published in 1864, signed by 'Seven Aged Colliers', complained that the Methodists ('but . . . not the Wesleyans') were consistently favoured by the management of the Pinxton Colliery and were enabled to prosper at the expense of other workmen.[1]

VII

Religion, particularly Dissent, was one of the few influences upon the mind of the Derbyshire miner at this period. Such other moral and intellectual guidance as he received came mainly from the politicians. There is little evidence to show the extent of the influence of Chartism upon the Derbyshire miners although it is improbable that it was great. In the southern part of the county, however, where the miners came into contact with the frame-work knitters, it is possible that some of them attended Chartist meetings. The stockingmakers of Pentrich and Belper were extremely militant and joined in the wave of Luddism which swept through Nottinghamshire and Leicestershire during the latter years of the Napoleonic wars and the first years of peace. Machines were destroyed at Pentrich in 1811[2] and the stockingers of Belper were on strike for higher wages in 1817.[3] In the same year occurred the so-called 'Pentrich Revolution' when a group of discontented agricultural workers, led by a certain Jeremiah Brandreth, known as the 'Nottingham Captain', planned to march on London and overthrow Liverpool's government. There was an abortive raid on the Butterley works and the rioters were eventually dispersed by a troop of the 15th Hussars from Nottingham. Fifty were arrested and tried at the next Derby assizes. Brandreth and two others were executed, twenty were sentenced to transportation and the rest were pardoned.[4]

It is not, therefore, surprising to find Jonathan Rembrandt Hall Bairstow addressing Chartist meetings in Belper market place in 1841.[5] 'He did not confine himself to abusing the great ones of the land', we are told, 'but came nearer home, and tried his hand on the Belper tradesmen and shopkeepers.' On a Sunday evening he delivered a sermon, preceded by singing and prayer, to a large audience gathered from Belper, Milford, Holbrook, Bargate, Duffield, and surrounding districts. Taking as his text the first six verses of the fifth chapter of

---

[1] *Management of Collieries: Colliers, Their Oppression and Complaints, How are they to be remedied?* (Lincoln), 1864. [2] H.O. 42/118. [3] H.O. 42/170.
[4] J. B. Firth, *Highways and Byways in Derbyshire*, (London), 1908, pp. 432–6. The executions were witnessed by Shelley who wrote a violent pamphlet on the subject under the name of 'The Hermit of Marlow'.
[5] See Julius West, *A History of the Chartist Movement*, (London), 1920, pp. 166, 191, 203, for further information about the activities of Bairstow.

James,[1] and in a manner reminiscent of the Levellers, he attempted to show how the ancestors of the owners of land and property had obtained their possessions, and argued that the retention of this property was as much robbery as it was at the time of the Norman Conquest.[2] He went still further than this, and declared 'that no possessions, property or effects of any description whatever could rightfully appertain to any man but that which he had worked for by his own hands and that any manufactory that employed any workman and by that means gained a living, was in fact a robber and a tyrant, and as a finale, he boldly shouted forth that he had not devised one word that could not be borne out by the precepts of the Bible'.[3]

Another figure who played a prominent part in arousing the political consciousness of the Derbyshire miners was J. Charles Cox, landowner, colliery proprietor, magistrate, son of a clergyman, and later a clergyman himself. He lived for a time in the Belper district and is now perhaps best known for his antiquarian and topographical writings on Derbyshire. Cox became interested in the work of Joseph Arch among the agricultural workers and through his influence became convinced of the necessity for the extension of the county franchise.[4] This was a problem which affected the agricultural labourers and the miners more than any other workers because most of them lived outside the boroughs where the household franchise was granted in 1867. Cox was largely responsible for bringing these matters to the notice of the Derbyshire miners and for gaining their support for the agricultural workers. Joseph Arch, who was a Primitive Methodist preacher, frequently spoke and preached in the Clay Cross district.

In 1874, Cox delivered a lecture in the market hall at Clay Cross urging the necessity of extending the franchise to all householders[5] and J. M. Gavan, of Durham, addressed a meeting on the same subject at Somercotes. Another speaker at this meeting was a delegate from the Lincolnshire Labour League.[6] John Catchpole, one of the early leaders of the Derbyshire miners, became secretary of the Chesterfield Municipal and Parliamentary Electoral Association but he appears to have been

[1] Go to now, ye rich men, weep and howl for your miseries that shall come upon you. Your riches are corrupted, and your garments are motheaten. Your gold and silver is cankered; and the rust of them shall be a witness against you, and shall eat your flesh as it were fire. Ye have heaped treasures together for the last days. Behold, the hire of the labourers who have reaped down your fields, which is of you kept back by fraud, crieth: and the cries of them which have reaped are entered into the ears of the Lord of sabaoth. Ye have lived in pleasure on the earth, and been wanton; ye have nourished your hearts, as in a day of slaughter. Ye have condemned and killed the just; and he doth not resist you.

[2] See Christopher Hill, 'The Norman Yoke', in *Democracy and The Labour Movement*, ed. J. Saville, (London), 1954, pp. 11–66.

[3] *Derbyshire Chronicle*, 2 October, 1841.   [4] Wearmouth, *op. cit.* pp. 234–5.

[5] *Derbyshire Times*, 14 March, 1874.   [6] *Ibid.* 10 October, 1874.

extremely inefficient. In October, 1877 he was censured 'for neglecting his duty in not attending the meetings with that regularity consistent with the office he held'. It was reported that the meetings of the association had often been called and members had assembled, but had been obliged to disperse again without transacting business because the secretary was not present. It was also alleged that he had failed to take minutes of the meetings when he did attend. In the face of this indictment Catchpole resigned.[1]

Apart from religion and politics, which were closely intertwined, the only other cultural influence to which the miner appears to have been subjected were the 'Penny Readings' which began to be organized in the 'sixties by some of the colliery firms. These consisted of readings, recitations and music. Typical of such entertainments is one given by the Wingerworth Coal Company in their reading room at North Wingfield on 10 February, 1866, and presided over by J. Charles Cox. The programme was as follows:[2]

March by the Band.
Reading—A chapter on fools—Rev. B. Mandale.
Song—The B's—H. Fletcher.
Recitation—The dish, with cover—Miss Crofts.
Fantasia—Home Sweet Home!—Miss Cutler.
Recitation—English Oak—V. Eyre.
Song—The Mistletoe Bough (new version)—Mr. Cox.
Duet (violins)—Messrs. Gascoyne and White.
Song—Sweet Spirit Hear My Prayer—Miss E. Ward.
Recitation—The Razor Seller—Mr. Ward.
Song—Sunshine and Cloud—Mr. Todd.
Recitation—The Miller's Maid—Mr. Hawkins.
Song—The Spider and the Fly—Master Ward.
Reading—The Barrel Organ—Mr. Morley.
Song—Nelly Blythe—W. Todd.
Recitation—The Marriage on Trust—G. Hall.
General Jackson's Quadrille—the Band.
Song—A Hundred Years Ago—Mr. Cox.

There was little opportunity for the miner to improve himself by education although he was constantly being urged to do so by his leaders. The work of the Science and Art Department made possible a certain amount of technical education. Classes of this kind, with small fees and held in the evening to facilitate the attendance of working men, were started at Chesterfield, Clay Cross and Staveley in October, 1869.[3] The

[1] *Derbyshire Times*, 6 October, 1877.　　[2] *Ibid*. 17 February, 1866.
[3] *Ibid*. 9 October, 1869.

colliery proprietors became interested in this work. Charles Markham of Staveley, Charles Binns of Clay Cross and others contributed towards the establishment of schools. The matter was taken up by the coal-owners and ironmasters of the Erewash Valley. A meeting at the Ironville Institute in 1869 resolved that a guarantee fund should be raised in order to secure the services of a properly qualified teacher in mining, drawing, mechanics, and chemistry; and classes were started at Alfreton, Riddings, Codnor Park, Butterley and Ilkeston.[1]

During the 'seventies the Cambridge University Extension Movement became active in Derbyshire. James Stuart, its pioneer, spoke about higher education at the first annual meeting of the Chesterfield and Derbyshire Institute of Mining, Mechanical and Civil Engineers in May, 1872. The tone of the meeting was set by a lengthy paper on 'The Future of Mining Institutes' prepared by G. H. Wright and R. F. Martin, of the Babbington Collieries, in which they expressed the pious hope that 'True Education will never encourage men to change their state of life, either as workmen or professional men, as patriots or Christians; but to do their duty in that state of life in the which it has pleased God to call them'.[2] Stuart urged the desirability of co-operation between the universities and such institutes 'to carry on a sort of missionary work in education' and attributed the failure of the attempts at higher scientific education to the absence of qualified teachers. For the provision of these teachers, some central institution was essential. 'The great majority of people cannot go to education, but must have it brought to them, and whatever education is to be successful must be catholic in its spirit, and must include all classes.'[3] Stuart concluded by appealing for financial support. Something like £40,000 would be needed to put his scheme into operation and local funds would be required to flow in and supplement the efforts of the universities. He also suggested that suitable teachers could be provided if the universities would allow Fellows to retain their stipends when engaged in educational work outside the walls of the university.

The Cambridge University Extension Movement began its work in Chesterfield with a meeting held in the Municipal Hall on 23 November, 1874. The Rev. Lawrence explained that it was quite optional for those who attended the classes to write papers or answer questions, or simply to go as listeners. The great result they aimed at was to teach thoroughly, 'and this without any ultimate end'. He regarded this as a point of great importance in securing the attendance of working men, 'for they found they were not lectured in order that they might become trades unionists

[1] *Derbyshire Times*, 11 September, 1869.
[2] *Transactions of the Chesterfield and Derbyshire Institute of Mining, Mechanical and Civil Engineers*, I, (London), 1873, p. 162.   [3] *Ibid.* pp. 163–4.

or capitalists, whigs or tories, or anything else. The lecturers gave them the facts only, and left them to form their own opinions from them. They were very careful not to allow the lectures to be propaganda for anything.'[1] Catchpole, the miners' leader, was present and seconded the resolution to form a local committee to which he was elected. Those who are familiar with the difficulties of organizing adult classes will find some consolation in his words:

He craved the indulgence of the meeting, not being accustomed to take such subjects in hand, but felt encouraged to give the opinion of a working man. He had much pleasure in supporting the movement, and from the kind expression and very liberal opinions expressed by the promoters he thought the working men of the district ought to encourage the scheme to the utmost of their power—and no doubt they would. The subject had been named at the working men's club on Friday last, when they saw articles in the local papers, and ten or twelve expressed their readiness to embrace every opportunity. With regard to the miners there had not yet been an opportunity of bringing the matter before any of their meetings, the time being so short, but considering the steps they had taken to improve themselves there was no doubt a large number of them would take it up.[2]

Despite Catchpole's glib assurances, the university extension movement appears to have had little impact upon the Derbyshire miners of this period. Professor Peers has described some of the reasons for the failure of the extension movement to meet the educational needs of the working classes. They were primarily economic. The cost of providing the courses of lectures was necessarily high and it was difficult for working-class people to pay the comparatively heavy fees which had to be charged. 'Arrangements were usually made to admit artisans at a lower fee, but that smacked of patronage.'[3] Thus, in 1880, six years after the inauguration of the scheme, a writer to the *Derbyshire Times* remarked 'how really few working people attended', and this after the class fee had been reduced to two shillings. Yet, we are told, 'the lecturer uses very simple, homely words. In truth a child could understand him.'[4] At the annual meeting in September, 1887, it was reported that the classes 'had not been so numerously attended . . . as in former years' although the committee had again brought down the price of admission so that it was within the reach of the working man in the town.[5] Professor Peers writes: 'University Extension courses began to appeal more and more to comfortable members of the middle classes —to people of leisure, rather than to working men. The necessity for attracting large audiences, in order to meet the cost, led to the emphasis

[1] *Derbyshire Times*, 28 November, 1874.   [2] *Ibid.*
[3] R. Peers, *Adult Education in Practice*, (London), 1934, p. 31.
[4] *Derbyshire Times*, 7 February, 1880.   [5] *Ibid.* 1 October, 1887.

being placed on attractive lectures rather than serious class work, and the keen student found the courses stimulating but not very satisfying.'[1] Moreover, the subjects chosen became increasingly irrelevant to the political, social and economic problems which were being faced by active trade unionists. By 1889 lectures were being delivered in Chesterfield on 'The Principles of Chemistry'. The Mayor explained that chemistry had been chosen in preference to other subjects 'because there was so much to be ascertained, and so many experiments to be made, for he felt that unless they could interest the students in some practical manner—unless they could practise before them all experiments which would prevent them from going to sleep—they would not have been able to get a class together'.[2]

Suitable educational facilities would doubtless have helped the Derbyshire miners in their efforts to organize a trade union. Their abortive attempts of the 'forties, 'sixties and 'seventies, which must now be described, were largely prompted by outsiders and by a few local leaders. The growth of trade unionism in this period was at once encouraged and hindered by the conditions under which the miners lived and worked. On the one hand the men had many grievances; on the other, their restricted outlook and the power and influence of the coal-owners discouraged them from seeking change. Much of the conservatism of the Derbyshire miners must be attributed to the tardy development of large-scale production in the coalfield. Relations between employer and worker in the smaller units of production tended to be more personal, more like those between the squire and the agricultural labourer, than they were elsewhere. For the minority who sought to foster trade unionism the struggle was therefore to be long and at times bitter until, in 1880, the Derbyshire Miners' Association was finally established.

[1] Peers, *op. cit.* p. 31.   [2] *Derbyshire Times*, 12 October, 1889.

APPENDIX I

Copy of an Agreement Between The Hard Coal Company of Colliers and
E. M. Mundy, Esq., November, 1824

Conditions of an AGREEMENT made and entered into this nineteenth day of November one thousand eight hundred and twenty four, between J. A. Twigg on the part of E.M.M., Esq., on the one part, and Joseph Clay, John Smith, Samuel Abbott & Theophilus Brown on the other, as follows.

We the above named company of workmen, do agree for ourselves with the before named J. A. Twigg, to get, take down, and send out of the Hard Coal Pit called or known by the name of the Pit No. 1; situate at Shipley Colliery in the parish of Shipley and County of Derby: upon the following conditions.

1st. That we the aforesaid company of Colliers will gather up at our own expence all runnings in, in the Benks or works at the said Pit, and keep the underground gates to the said Benks or works clean and in good repair.

2nd. We agree to find all kinds of Timber for the support of the said Benks or Gates at our own cost and charge, also all Carfs, Garlands and Boxes, that are used for the purpose of sending out Coals and Slack, Spoil or Dirt out of the said Pit and also to find at our own cost and charge all kinds of working tools, waggons, etc. used for underground purposes; and also all Gearing used for underground purposes to asses or Horses employed in the said Pit either in leather or Iron that may be used from time to time during the period of this bargain—and also will well and sufficiently pack all the said Gates or Gateroads in a proper and workmanlike manner according to the directions of the underground agents employed at the said Colliery for the time being—also all the air-gates or windings free of expence to E.M.M., Esq.

3rd. We agree to find a proportionate share of the Slack used for the Engines employed at the said Colliery for the purpose of pumping water according to the present usage or custom established at the said Colliery: and also agree to furnish and supply free of expence all the Coal or Slack, used at the said Colliery for the purpose of working the Whimsey for winding Coals at the said Pit.

4th. We the above named Company of Colliers agree to work as many days per week, as the agents at the said Colliery shall require; and shall keep the shaft in good repair and examine it at least once a week. And we the before-named company of colliers do hereby agree to work the beforenamed Pit in a regular peaceable and workmanlike manner, according to the directions of the Agents employed by and for the beforesaid E.M.M., Esq. and in default thereof bind ourselves to forfeit and pay unto the said E.M.M., Esq. the sum of one Guinea per day; for every day that we neglect to work the beforenamed Pit in a manner as beforesaid. And we the said company also agree to Load at our own expence the said Coals, Cobbles, or Slack into the Waggons at the Pit mouth that shall be raised from time to time from the said Pit, during the period of this agreement, except such as are used for the purpose of working the Engines. And this agreement shall stand good and in full force for twelve Calendar months from the date hereof at least until the face of the present Coal workings shall be removed or wrought in a workmanlike manner to the full space and end of 30 Yards from the present face of the workings, unless the Agents employed by the said E.M.M., Esq. for the time being shall see proper to direct to the contrary.

And we the above named company of colliers do hereby agree to receive as a full compensation for Getting the coal as beforesaid from the beforenamed E.M.M., Esq. the sum of Three Shillings and Eightpence per ton for every ton of marketable Coal raised from the said Pit, each and every ton to contain 23 cwt. to the ton and 120 lbs. to each cwt. that shall be got out of the said Pit within the compass of what is called a Waggon stint or 43 Yards from the face of the present workings; but as there are now three Gate-roads in the said Pit and in all probability some parts of the wall or workings may shift faster than the other, it is mutually agreed that the average length of the said Gate-roads shall be taken prior to any extra advance of price or Charter taking place, and when such advance does become due it shall be paid in the following proportions. Viz. For the first 43 Yards from the face of the present workings the sum of 3s. 8d. per ton and one penny per ton in addition to the above price for every 43 Yards afterwards up to the length of one hundred and thirty Yards.

And we the above named Company of Colliers do hereby bind ourselves to lay on regular loading at the said Pit that is to say that we will not lay on more than one ton at one draught but will do our utmost endeavour to prevent all inconvenience (in that respect) to the workmen employed at the No. 2 Pit and do also bind ourselves not to employ any workman or workmen (man or boy) employed or that shall hereafter be employed at Shipley Colliery by any other Butty or Butties at the said place.

Signed.

Wm. Beardsley,
  Witness.

APPENDIX II

Fatal Accident Rates, Midland District, 1856–1880

	Output Tons	Tons raised per death
1856	4,500,000	97,000
1857	4,750,000	86,000
1858	5,060,000	121,000
1859	5,460,000	136,500
1860	6,215,000	124,000
1861	6,503,319	94,000
1862	6,647,000	154,000
1863	7,000,000	134,000
1864	7,300,000	110,000
1865	7,575,000	92,383
1866	7,600,000	131,034
1867	7,600,000	118,750
1868	7,699,000	128,317
1869	8,100,000	103,846
1870	8,366,000	167,320
1871	9,252,900	99,494
1872	10,657,100	134,900
1873	11,533,307	147,837
1874	12,232,296	222,405
1875	12,430,600	191,240
1876	12,331,546	160,150
1877	12,903,886	222,481
1878	13,440,184	244,367
1879	14,036,242	298,643
1880	14,500,995	245,780

Source: *Reports of H.M. Inspectors of Mines and Quarries, 1856–1880.*

CHAPTER III

EARLY ATTEMPTS AT
TRADE UNION ORGANIZATION

I

It has been said that for the student of labour organization in the coal industry the eighteenth century belongs to pre-history.[1] Such combinations of workmen as existed operated in conditions of great secrecy, very often under the guise of friendly societies and sick and burial clubs which were beginning to appear in the colliery villages towards the end of the eighteenth century. It is unlikely that many records were kept of the industrial activities of such societies. Certainly none have survived in Derbyshire.

Despite the law there were, of course, strikes among the miners and after the legislation of 1825,[2] although trade union activity was hedged with many restrictions, the need for absolute secrecy had disappeared. It was some time before the miners, held in virtual serfdom by the truck system and the custom of yearly hirings, were able to progress beyond ephemeral strike organizations. Indeed, such was the lack of unity among them that Hepburn's attempt to build up a union in the Northumberland and Durham coalfield was crushed in 1832, with the aid of non-union labour from Derbyshire.[3] When delegates from the north-east visited Alfreton they were stripped, beaten and dragged through the village horse-pond.[4] On the other hand, 'thousands of colliers' in Derbyshire were persuaded by delegates from Lancashire to join Doherty's National Association for the Protection of Labour in 1831.[5]

Whatever part the Derbyshire miners may have played in this and

---

[1] Ashton and Sykes, *op. cit.* p. 133.   [2] 6 Geo. IV, c. 129.
[3] E. Welbourne, *The Miners' Unions of Northumberland and Durham*, (Cambridge), 1923, p. 39.
[4] *Durham Chronicle*, 6 June, 1832, cited in Welbourne, *op. cit.* pp. 38–39.
[5] H.O. 44/25, cited in S. and B. Webb, *History of Trade Unionism*, (London) edn. of 1920, p. 123.

similar organizations the various attempts at 'General Union' between 1818 and 1834 ended in failure[1] and it was left to miners in other parts of the country to develop an industrial union. Strong county unions grew up in Northumberland, Durham, Lancashire and Yorkshire, leading to the formation at Wakefield in 1841 of the Miners' Association of Great Britain and Ireland. Under the leadership of Martin Jude, it developed an extensive propagandist activity, at one time employing no less than fifty-three organizers, who visited every coalfield in the country.[2]

At this time unrest among the colliers of Derbyshire was growing. In 1841 a number of the men employed by Stephenson and Company at Clay Cross turned out for an increase in wages and seven of the leaders, tried by William Milnes and P. Morewood under the Master and Servant laws, were committed to Derby gaol for fourteen days each, for leaving their employment without proper notice. This appears to have had the desired effect for on the following day most of the colliers returned to work.[3] There was a more serious dispute in South Derbyshire in the following year, described somewhat vaguely by a witness before the Royal Commission of 1867 as being 'mixed up altogether with a rise in wages, and the people's charter as it was called, and beer'.[4] Apparently it was the custom in South Derbyshire and in Staffordshire to supply beer for the colliers in stores at the pit-head. The employers found that this encouraged the men to drink and had the effect of sending them off to the public house in search of more beer. 'There were lots of instances of persons never going to their homes at all, but stopping fuddling all day and night in public houses and coming to work at the collieries next morning.'[5] The attempts of the employers to put an end to this practice, coupled with other grievances, led to a strike which lasted for two or three months but trade was bad and the men were eventually defeated. The dispute was extremely bitter and the leaders of the movement were severely punished.[6]

In February, 1844, two delegates from the Miners' Association appeared in the Chesterfield district 'endeavouring to unsettle the minds of the colliers'.[7] This was not a difficult task. Within a week of their arrival they were 'succeeding to an alarming extent'. Those who had already joined the union were using 'all possible means to entice others' to do so.[8] A printed circular was distributed among colliery agents in the neighbourhood of Chesterfield signed by 'the members of the Miners'

---

[1] G. D. H. Cole, *Attempts at General Union, 1818–1834*, (London), 1953, p. 155.
[2] S. and B. Webb, *op. cit.* pp. 181–2.
[3] *Derbyshire Chronicle*, 20 March, 1841.
[4] *R.C. to enquire into Trades Unions and Other Associations*, 1867–9, Q. 11,906.
[5] *Ibid.*   [6] *Derbyshire Courier*, 24 February, 1844.
[7] *Ibid.* 17 February, 1844.   [8] *Ibid.* 24 February, 1844.

Association'.[1] It announced that the object of the combination was to better the conditions of the members and disclaimed all wish to strike, preferring 'an amicable adjustment of differences'. Their 'specific and simple plan' was 'that each colliery-owner shall be furnished with a copy of such prices as shall be thought necessary and reasonable, and in which it is intended to go on the principle of making the cost price, as far as labour is concerned, equal or nearly so on every colliery in the trade, and to such uniformity of cost price the masters to add what they may deem a proper and reasonable return for their capital'. The circular went on to condemn the spirit of competition between masters and the 'contentious war of strikes and stagnations' which they produced: 'The moral and physical consequences of contentious warfare between capital and labour does appear to us to be fully illustrated by the fable of two noble animals combating or fighting for a choice piece of prey, and while the combat was going on, another animal of diminutive size and strength [i.e. the public] came and carried off the prey; while neither of the two, such was their state of exhaustion, could prevent it.' Despite these protestations, by the end of March, 1844, the colliers in many parts of Derbyshire, along with those of Nottinghamshire, Staffordshire and Yorkshire, had ceased work.[2]

The leaders of the movement, in addition to Mycroft, one of the paid organizers,[3] were Thomas Vernon of Somercotes, Samuel Smith of Radford, Nottinghamshire, and a man by the name of Clarke, who were described as being 'mostly ranter preachers'.[4] At a meeting in Chesterfield market place, early in April, Vernon complained that although they had been called 'turn-outs' they had in fact been turned out by the masters who had refused to permit them to work any longer unless they abandoned the union.[5] This was the principal issue as far as the employers were concerned. About the middle of April there was a large meeting of influential coalmasters from Derbyshire, Nottinghamshire and Leicestershire at which it was decided not to employ any colliers who were in the union, 'and to put it down previous to entertaining the question of any regulation in wages or the price of coal'.[6] Charles Binns stated 'that every man who has resumed work at Clay Cross has abandoned the union entirely and has signed a declaration to that effect; and moreover, that Messrs. G. Stephenson and Company have no intention of employing any man who is a member of any such union'.[7] Similarly, at Staveley, Shipley, Denby and West Hallam the proprietors refused to employ union men.[8]

---

[1] *Derbyshire Courier*, 2 March, 1844.   [2] *Ibid*. 30 March, 1844.
[3] *Ibid*. 27 April, 1844.   [4] *Ibid*. 6 April, 1844.
[5] *Ibid*. 13 April, 1844.   [6] *Ibid*. 20 April, 1844.
[7] *Ibid*. 27 April, 1844.   [8] *Ibid*. 30 March, 20 April, 27 April, 1844.

The miners had many grievances. Wages and hours, truck, the butty system, methods of weighing coal and working conditions in the mines all came to be involved in the dispute. Samuel Smith, speaking at a meeting on Brimington Common, said:

It was impossible for a miner to procure at his present wages food and furniture to support life. The masters made rules that the cottages should be kept clean and the children cleanly and decently dressed but how was it possible when the miners' wives had in many cases to go to bed because they were pined and had not clothing to look after the children who were running wild like something turned out of a wood.

According to Thomas Vernon, 'The masters wanted to work twelve hours for 3s'.[1]

This statement is corroborated by the report of the Children's Employment Commission which gave the wage of an adult collier in Derbyshire as 3s. a day.[2] In the Chesterfield Union 12 hours was considered to be a day's work but elsewhere in the county colliers were working between 13 and 16 hours a day.[3] Glover states that the average wage of colliers employed by the Butterley Company in 1829 was between 15s. and 20s. a week.[4] If this can be taken as typical of the rate prevailing throughout the county it would appear, from the scanty evidence available, that there was little change in money wages in Derbyshire between 1829 and 1842. Movements in real wages, however, were quite considerable. Taking the average of 1828–32 as a basis, the cost of living, as measured by Silberling's index, dropped 2 per cent. in 1833–7 and rose 8 per cent. above the basis in 1838–42. Thereafter the trend was downward but the years between 1838 and 1842, with their widespread unemployment and low wages, were a period of great hardship for the working classes generally.

By 1844 the cost of living was falling and so was the price of coal. Barrow, in his statement issued to the Staveley colliers, wrote: 'You admit that only 10 per cent. and 5 per cent. have been taken off your wages, when you know, and the *Public* know, that iron and coal have been reduced in much greater proportion—the former product 100 per cent. instead of only 15.'[5] But the miners appear to have been interested in their wages primarily in relation to the number of hours they had to work. Thus at one colliery, near Dronfield, they were offered an increased rate which they refused to accept without a reduction in hours.[6]

[1] *Derbyshire Courier*, 6 April, 1844.
[2] *Children's Employment Commission* (*Mines*), 1842, First Report, p. 154, ss. 642–3.
[3] *Ibid*. pp. 107–8, ss. 411–12.
[4] Glover, *op. cit.* II, p. 231.
[5] *Derbyshire Courier*, 11 May, 1844.
[6] *Ibid.* 27 April, 1844.

II

The policy of the Miners' Association, as shown by the circular which was issued at the beginning of the dispute in Derbyshire, was to secure some measure of uniformity in wages throughout the country. The colliers of Northumberland and Durham were able to earn about 4s. a day of eight to ten hours but towards the end of 1843 they obeyed the call of the Executive Council of the Association to limit their earnings to 3s. a day.[1] The object of this was to restrict, as far as possible, the supply of coal to the current demand without allowing the coal-owners to accumulate a surplus quantity to meet the demand which might be made during a strike on the termination of the annual contract on 5 April, 1844.

Early in April the Miners' Association held its national conference at Glasgow. Delegates representing 70,000 men voted, by 28,042 to 23,357, in favour of striking against their grievances, and the Northumberland and Durham men, numbering some 30,000, who for the past six months had been preparing for action, entered on 5 April into a prolonged and bitter struggle for more equitable terms of hiring and payment.[2] On the following day, Mycroft, who had just returned from the Glasgow conference, was addressing a meeting of miners on Brimington Common.[3] Thus the Derbyshire miners, already locked out for joining the union, were now part of a wider struggle of which they scarcely realized the full significance.

The importance of the incursion of the Miners' Association into Derbyshire, from the point of view of trade union organization, was that it provided, for the first time, a focus for the various local grievances which existed in the coalfield. In the minds of many, the movement became vaguely linked with Chartism. At one meeting Thomas Vernon stated that 'the masters were afraid that if the men got their object now, they would next strike for the Charter, but this was ridiculous'.[4] But local committees, which were established at the pits, began to demand changes which went far beyond those originally contemplated in the circular issued by the Association. It was this aspect of the movement which caused the employers so much anxiety. Charles Markham told the Royal Commission of 1867: 'We understood from what transpired that they wished to become dictators of our property,

[1] *Derbyshire Courier*, 13 April, 1844. Welbourne, *op. cit.* p. 64, writes: 'To discover how much the fall in wage—in 1843 some 15 per cent.—was due to the action of the men is now impossible.'
[2] S. and B. Webb, *op. cit.* p. 186.
[3] *Derbyshire Courier*, 6 April, 1844.   [4] *Ibid.*

and to manage our works in their own kind of way.'[1] Another employer informed his men that the question of wages was 'only a secondary one' and that he was much more concerned about 'the interference of the Union'.

'You are aware', he wrote, 'that at first I made no objection to the Union, made no enquiries as to who were Unionists and who were not—latterly, however, the leaders of the Union usurped the place of the masters, giving yourselves how long you were to work, on what days, whose boats were to fill and whose were not, consequently the works were stopped and you have been playing the last three weeks.'[2]

Typical of the demands made by the local committees are those made at Brimington:[3]

Resolutions past at a Committee held at Brimington
April 15th, 1844.

Resolved

1st That the average wage for Pickmen be 4s. Per day for 8 hours. . . . 2nd that the Banksmen Loaders and Trammers be Paid in proportion. . . . 3rd that we receive our Wage Weekly, and that we allow no more than two days to be kept in hand. . . . 4th that we get no more than 20 cwt. to the ton Providing we engage by the Bargain. . . . 5th that we be Paid no longer in Truck. . . . 6th that should the Master take away any advantage of any Particular Persons the whole shall stand out till he Complys.

We're agreed to give you till the 20th of this Month for Consideration.

Yours the Members of the
Miners Association of the
Westwood and Bower Ironstone
Companies.

P.S. Please to send an answer as soon as Possible Direct as followers. For the Secretary of the Miners Association Care of John Dronfield, Red Lion Inn, Brimington.

A similar document was drawn up by 'the Members of the Miners Benefit Society, Pinxton Lodge', in which they demanded the dismissal of all black-legs and refused to work under the two butties, William Harvey and W. Pepper.[4] After receiving a reply from the employer, the committee agreed 'that the clause of our former statement was wrong with taking that power from our Masters wich we had no right therefore wee consider ourselves as being in a fault'. They refused, however, to withdraw their demands for increased wages nor would they withdraw from the union and sign 'the Document'. The main grievance appeared

---

[1] R.C. to enquire into Trades Unions and Other Associations, 1867–9, Sixth Report, Evidence of Charles Markham, Q. 11,491.
[2] Derbyshire Courier, 4 May, 1844.   [3] Ibid. 20 April, 1844.
[4] See Appendix I to this chapter.

to be the butty system which had been largely responsible for the reduction of the men's wages.

'We as working men consider the Buttie sistem a very great evil amongst the colliers,' stated the committee, 'for when a reduction must come all these men takes the advantage of us and lays more upon us than is legal, we can prove that the men represented had laid work upon us to great excess that we cannot bear and they all four were not doing more than two men.'[1]

At Clay Cross prices were the principal issue. Leaflets were circulated stating that prices were considerably below those of 1841 but according to the proprietor of the *Derbyshire Courier* who was invited to inspect the Company's books, the union's handbills were complete misrepresentations.[2] The men at Clay Cross were said to average about 4s. a day of eight hours and in some cases, during certain periods of the year, they were paid as much as 6s. a day.[3] Similarly, at Staveley, another large and prosperous concern, wages had been higher than at some of the neighbouring collieries from which the Miners' Association had taken examples for its handbills.[4] Barrow, the proprietor, claimed that it had been proved before magistrates that his men could earn '3s. and upwards for nine hours of labour'.[5] The butty system caused much of the trouble at Staveley and eventually Barrow announced:

'Arrangements are now making for those men now at work, and for fresh hands who are daily coming to work, to receive *a fair Day's pay for a fair Day's Work*, without the money going through the hands of the Butty.'[6]

By the middle of April most of the Nottinghamshire and several of the Derbyshire collieries were doing very little work, although the coal-owners' policy of excluding trade union labour was beginning to bear fruit in the neighbourhood of Derby. Shipley and West Hallam had resumed work and the men had abandoned the union; at Kilburn there had been no stoppage at all; and the men were beginning to drift back to work at Denby. Only Marehay and Morley Park were standing firm.[7] A week later some sixty men left the union and resumed work at Clay Cross but the colliers in the Sheffield district and at Dronfield and Eckington were continuing the struggle.[8] Swanwick, Pentrich and Ripley collieries were fully manned by the beginning of May and at Staveley, where there had been a number of cases of eviction, non-union labour began to arrive from Staffordshire towards the end of the month.[9]

In this way the union was broken and the men were gradually induced

[1] See Appendix I to this chapter.
[3] *Ibid.*
[5] *Ibid.* 30 March, 1844.
[7] *Ibid.* 20 April, 1844.
[9] *Ibid.* 4 May, 1 June, 13 April, 1844.

[2] *Derbyshire Courier*, 4 May, 1844.
[4] *Ibid.* 11 May, 1844.
[6] *Ibid.* 11 May, 1844.
[8] *Ibid.* 27 April, 1844.

to return to work. Trade was depressed and others were ready to fill their places. The strike pay which had been promised by the leaders was not forthcoming.[1] At most pits the men won minor concessions. The majority of employers were willing to give some consideration to the men's grievances provided they abandoned the union. The men at Clay Cross, for example, agreed to leave their union and resume work in return for a slight advance on the price for large coal.[2] There had never been any real unity of action. Negotiations had been handled almost entirely by the local committees which were working in isolation. The Miners' Association had merely succeeded in creating sporadic and unco-ordinated action throughout the county which, in a period when there was a surplus of labour, was easily resisted by the employers.

III

The dispute was accompanied by a certain amount of violence and disorder. There was the inevitable friction between unionists and black-legs. Mary Hall, who 'had been active in saluting the "black-legs" with the music of tea trays and a stick', as they were going to and returning from work, was assaulted by one of them, Charles Hague. The magistrates dismissed the case, observing that the woman had brought the assault upon herself by her conduct.[3] In contrast to this Leonard Stevenson and Joseph Taylor, colliers of Dronfield, were committed to hard labour for one month, 'for attempting to force George Searston from attending to his employment'.[4] Whilst the law could be lenient in the case of non-unionists, the provisions of the Act of 1825 were stringently enforced. Two women at Staveley were charged with assaulting William Buxton, collier, the bench being of the opinion that an assault had been committed by the women taking hold of the coat of the complainant. Maynard, the chairman of the bench, remarked:

> There are a great many men here today from Staveley, and they will understand that even if men choose to work for 6d. a day, and 16 hours a day, they have a perfect right to do so; and that those who interfere, whether they be women or men, must take the consequences. . . .[5]

There were, of course, some cases of actual physical violence. The brothers John and Thomas Jarvis were charged with having assaulted

---

[1] *R.C. on Trades Unions*, 1867–9, Sixth Report, Q. 13,726, Eighth Report, Q. 16,354.
[2] *Derbyshire Courier*, 11 May, 1844. In 1867 a man by the name of Marriott addressed a meeting at Clay Cross on the advantages gained by the strike of 1844. He is reported as saying 'his wages were raised 2s. to 2s. 6d. and two hours per day less' but this statement must be treated with reserve. (*Ilkeston Pioneer*, 17 January, 1867.)
[3] *Ibid*. 13 April, 1844.   [4] *Ibid*. 11 May, 1844.   [5] *Ibid*. 6 May, 1844.

Matthew Robinson, 'by striking him on the head and body, and knocking and throwing him down'. There was a second charge that this was done 'for the purpose of forcing and inducing the said Matthew Robinson to belong to a certain club or association at the Nag's Head Inn, Staveley, being an association of miners and colliers'.[1] The worst disorders appear to have been in the Killamarsh and Dronfield districts where the men held out for longer than elsewhere. At Killamarsh, the unionists equipped themselves with a drum, fifes, whistles, kettles, pots and pans, for the purpose of escorting the 'knobsticks' (i.e. black-legs) from the pits. Two of these unfortunate men, George Taylor and George Bowskell were met, on one occasion, by about 100 men, women and children, 'who struck up the well-known air "March in Good Order", seconded by yells, hoots and groans of the most furious description'. Bowskell's wife poured a bucket of boiling water over the heads of the mob when they arrived at her home and on the following evening 'she sallied forth with a large dust-shovel full of burning hot embers, which she scattered like Jupiter's thunderbolts on the assembled multitude'. On another occasion the unionists and their families entered Bowskell's garden and destroyed all his fruit trees.[2]

These demonstrations, apparently begun in a semi-jocular spirit, took a more serious turn towards the end of June. A mob of from 200 to 300 men, women and children, armed with bludgeons and bearing flags and drums, assembled near the Cottam Colliery and later the windows of a number of non-unionists were broken and their gardens devastated. A few days later, when Bowskell's house was put under police protection, it was visited 'by nearly 100 men armed with guns, dirks, swords, bludgeons, etc.' who dared the police to make their appearance and said 'they would do for them'. The police, we are told, 'very prudently declined sallying from their lodgement until the following morning'. During the night the men marched off to the brick kilns belonging to Appleby, Walker and Company and destroyed many thousands of unfinished bricks and tiles. At this point the police stated that no more protection could be given and recommended the employers to apply to the county magistrates for military forces.[3]

At Dronfield the men employed by Booker and Company were even more violent. On 20 May an attempt was made to blow up the house of William Hattersley, manager of the Oxclose Colliery. A powerful explosion was produced by a home-made bomb consisting of a pipe, about a foot long and three or four inches in diameter, filled with gunpowder and plugged at each end.[4] A few nights later a canister of powder, with a fuse attached, was thrown through the bedroom window

[1] *Derbyshire Courier*, 30 March, 1844.   [2] *Ibid*. 18 May, 1844.
[3] *Ibid*. 29 June, 1844.   [4] *Ibid*. 25 May, 1844.

of the house of John Ward, of Stubley, who was employed as a watchman at the Oxclose Colliery.[1]

The litigation arising out of the dispute of 1844 was perhaps its most successful aspect. Evictions, truck and the subtleties of the law relating to masters and servants were matters upon which the miners needed professional advice and in 1843 the Northumberland and Durham union had already taken the initiative in engaging W. P. Roberts, an able Chartist lawyer, with strong labour sympathies, to fight every case in the local courts.[2] The Miners' Association of Great Britain and Ireland followed this example by appointing Roberts their standing legal adviser at a salary of £1,000 a year in 1844.[3] Roberts came to Derbyshire as a result of a resolution passed at the Glasgow conference condemning the conduct of the Chesterfield magistrates 'who had sent four men to Derby gaol without suffering them to speak for themselves and who wanted to put all the witnesses out of that which ought to be an open court'.[4] Roberts was particularly active against the truck system which was, by that time, illegal. In a case at Derby he offered to abandon the proceedings if the coalmasters would give up the truck system. His object was not to extract money, he said, but to put down the system.[5] His arrival in the district alarmed many of the coal-owners and had the salutary effect of causing the proprietors of the Pentrich Colliery to publish the following notice:

The Messrs. Haslam think it necessary, in order to prevent all mistakes, to announce that all persons employed in their colliery will receive their wages wholly in cash, and may expend them when and as they choose to do. If they purchase goods in the shops of Messrs. Haslam they will receive them as heretofore at wholesale prices, but they are not expected to make their purchases there, and work and wages will be continued as usual whether purchases are made in these shops or elsewhere.[6]

IV

The strike of the Northumberland and Durham men dragged on until August, 1844, ending in complete failure.[7] Thereafter the Miners' Association of Great Britain and Ireland gradually declined in importance until by 1848 it had, for all practical purposes, ceased to exist.[8] After the collapse of the Miners' Association there was no serious attempt

[1] *Derbyshire Courier*, 1 June, 1844.   [2] Welbourne, *op. cit.* pp. 66–67.
[3] S. and B. Webb, *op. cit.* pp. 182–3.   [4] *Derbyshire Courier*, 6 April, 1844.
[5] *Sheffield Independent*, 15 June, 1844.   [6] Quoted in Engels, *op. cit.* p. 255.
[7] Welbourne, *op. cit.* pp. 78–79; *Derbyshire Courier*, 24 August, 1844.
[8] S. and B. Webb, *op. cit.* p. 186.

at trade union organization among the Derbyshire miners until the 'sixties.[1] This is probably explained by the fact that the men were not subjected during this period to any serious economic pressure. Following the depression of the years 1847 and 1848 there were reductions in miners' wages generally, resulting in a fall of just over 3 per cent. between 1840 and 1850.[2] The cost of living, however, had fallen more than that during the same period.[3] Thereafter, during the prosperous 'fifties, miners' wages began to rise although there is a serious discrepancy in the statistical conclusions of Bowley and Wood as to the extent of the increase.[4] A Derbyshire witness before the Royal Commission of 1867 estimated that miners' wages had gradually risen 'to be pretty nearly double what they were' in 1842.[5] Similarly, no complete or scientifically accurate cost-of-living index for industrial wage earners during the 'fifties has yet been constructed, although it is generally agreed that whilst wholesale prices rose fairly sharply the increase in the cost of living was not very great.[6] Thus, comparatively modest wage increases were sufficient to secure a rise in the standard of living.

On the other hand, many of the old grievances of 1844 still remained. Truck, although decreasing in importance, lingered on, causing Jeremiah Briggs to write in 1858:

In my opinion the cause of all human misery arises from the stoppage of wages. The system of stoppages is bad; and in the hands of unprincipled employers destructive of all remunerative employment and deterring to the earnings of all labour. . . . Who is to blame? Not so much the employers as the shopkeepers, for it is their duty to unite against an 'oppression on the earnings of labour' and by legislative enactment obtain a law that every workman shall have what he earns, and lay it out as he likes, and not be stopped of it in bondage by the masters.[7]

[1] R.C. on Trades Unions, 1867–9, Sixth Report, Evidence of Charles Markham, Q. 11,487; Evidence of J. T. Woodhouse, Q. 11,904. Henshaw, Q. 13,727, refers to an unsuccessful strike led by Yorkshire delegates when he worked at Wingerworth in 1857.
[2] A. L. Bowley, Wages in the United Kingdom, (London), 1900, p. 109.
[3] Clapham (op. cit. I, p. 559) puts it rather optimistically at 'perhaps 30 per cent'. Dr. Hobsbawm writes: 'Few would deny that things improved rapidly in Britain (though not in Ireland) from the earlier forties on, the crisis of 1847 interrupting a period of progress rather than initiating it.' (E. J. Hobsbawm, 'The British Standard of Living, 1790–1850', Economic History Review, X, (1957), p. 48n.)
[4] Ibid. II, p. 452. For the period 1850–86 Wood's calculation gives the miners a rise of only 8 per cent. Bowley's figures show a rise of 20 per cent.
[5] R.C. on Trades Unions, 1867, Sixth Report, Evidence of J. T. Woodhouse, Q. 11,904.   [6] Clapham, op. cit. II, p. 460.
[7] Ilkeston Pioneer, 8 April, 1858. Jeremiah Briggs (1804–75) was born in Leicester and was for many years in practice as a solicitor at Derby. He was well known for his unwearying advocacy of paying wages without stoppages. Through his efforts the Truck Act was passed and he also brought forward a scheme for taking votes by ballot which was not adopted. (Derbyshire Times, 6 March, 1875.)

There were also grievances arising from the weighing of coal. The system in operation at Staveley in 1844 was described by Barrow as follows:

You are paid *subsist* by the usual measure—which is estimated to contain a certain weight—and if the actual weight over the Machine should exceed that estimate, you receive the balance—but that very rarely happens. You are in no way imposed upon. You are paid by the usual long weight of 22 cwt. to the ton, under the same that the owners of the Royalty are paid—whose agents regularly inspect the books and weights, and which are also open to you, as well as to the carriers, in case of any supposed error.[1]

At some collieries, however, the men were getting as much as 120 lb. to the hundredweight and 29 cwt. to the ton.[2] Moreover, the practice of confiscation, whereby the men received no payment at all for a tub which contained even a small amount of dirt or slack, caused a great deal of discontent.[3] The miners demanded payment for the full amount of coal sent up and for 20 cwt. to the ton but the *Derbyshire Times*, as late as 1869, posed the problem quite simply: 'If they get only 20 cwt. to the ton they will simply be paid so much less.'[4] Last, and most important of all, was the question of hours. Many of the pits were working twelve or more hours a day.[5] The men were still demanding the eight-hour day which they had failed to secure in 1844.

With the revival of unionism in the 'sixties these were the issues which came to the fore, showing that it is unrealistic to discuss movements in miners' real wages in this period without considering the conditions under which they were earned. All these questions were, of course, related to wages and affected the earning capacity of the miner but it is interesting to note that he chose to approach the problem in this indirect way rather than to demand increased payment. He was anxious to maintain his wages but at the same time wanted more leisure.

v

The work of Alexander Macdonald, in the late 'fifties, culminated in the formation of the Miners' National Union at Leeds in 1863 which was to be an important federal organization for remedying the miners' grievances. Prominent in the Miners' National Union in the early days was the South Yorkshire Miners' Association which came into being on

---

[1] *Derbyshire Courier*, 11 May, 1844.
[2] *R.C. on Trades Unions*, Eighth Report, Evidence of William Brown, Q. 16,406.
[3] *Ibid*. Brown, QQ. 16,409, 16,431, 16,460.
[4] *Derbyshire Times*, 31 March, 1869.
[5] *R.C. on Trades Unions*, Sixth Report, Evidence of Charles Markham, Q. 11,608; Eighth Report, Evidence of William Brown, Q. 16,457.

10 April, 1858, following an arbitrary lock-out of several thousand men. The formation of this compact district association enabled Macdonald, in the same year, to call a national conference at Ashton-under-Lyne, at which, however, only 4,000 men were represented.[1] It was the South Yorkshire Miners' Association which first demanded the right to have a representative of the men at the pit-bank to check the weighing of the coal. During 1859 there were many bitter disputes and the employers at several collieries were forced to agree to the men's request. The South Yorkshire Association then determined to secure legislation on the matter and with the help of Macdonald obtained an amendment of the Mines Regulation Bill of 1860 which empowered the miners of each pit to appoint a checkweigher, but confined their choice to men actually in employment at the particular mine.[2] The employers attempted to evade this clause in various ways. At Barnsley, John Normansell, appointed checkweigher, was promptly dismissed from employment and refused access to the pit's mouth. He was eventually reinstated after a costly legal battle which lasted for two years. In 1864 Normansell was elected secretary to the South Yorkshire Miners' Association.[3]

In all of this the Derbyshire miners appear to have played but little part. In April, 1861, however, when the coal trade was brisk, the coalowners in the Chesterfield district, which had always enjoyed shorter hours than other parts of the county, decided to introduce a working day of eleven hours instead of nine and a half hours in order to increase production. This aroused the Derbyshire miners to action and South Yorkshire seized the opportunity to encourage them.[4] The men employed at the Speight Hill pits, belonging to the Wingerworth Iron Company, took the lead by striking and calling a meeting of the colliers of the district in the market place at Chesterfield.[5] About 1,000 men, including strikers from Wingerworth, the Glasshouse Colliery, near Eckington, and Appleby's colliery, assembled to hear a speech by Richard Davies of Attercliffe, near Sheffield, who had been brought there to tell them about the advantage of having a union similar to that in Yorkshire.

Davies urged the desirability of having a union in Chesterfield and hoped that 'if there was any person present who was oppressing the working man and endeavouring to stay him from having his fair share of remuneration he would take into consideration the recommendation contained in the Bible to sympathize with a workman's just claims. . . . The true English weight was 20 cwt. to the ton but the masters demanded from the collier 30 cwt. to 34 cwt. to the ton.' He went on to describe

[1] S. and B. Webb. *op. cit.* pp. 301–2.
[2] Mines Regulation Act, 1860, Section 29.
[3] S. and B. Webb, *op. cit.* pp. 304–5.
[4] *Derbyshire Times,* 6 April, 1861.   [5] *Ibid.* 13 April, 1861.

conditions in Yorkshire where the men used to work twelve hours a day and send up 34 cwt. to the ton. They now worked eight hours and had 'a just weight' and could earn as much in eight hours as they used to in twelve.

'Miners can by such work begin to improve themselves,' said Davies. 'They were considered the most ignorant class in the Kingdom by some; but they could by that short time begin to study. They had time to act and think for themselves. They might now, by their own perseverance, be rescued from the bondage of slavery. They ought to think about the future instead of indulging at the card table or the domino board.'[1]

At the end of the meeting Davies retired to the Three Tuns Inn with a large number of miners 'to form a union . . . in conjunction with Yorkshire'. In this task he was assisted by Mannifield, also of Attercliffe.[2] This was one of the earliest of numerous attempts by the South Yorkshire Miners' Association to extend its influence into Derbyshire. A successful branch appears to have been established at Chesterfield and large meetings were held at the Three Tuns Inn during 1861.[3] The South Yorkshire Association also had a lodge at Grassmoor at this period, for it is recorded in the Association's minutes as having subscribed 13s. 4d. during the South Yorkshire lock-out of 1864. There are also references to delegates who visited Eckington, Clay Cross and other parts of Derbyshire.[4]

In November, 1863, the Miners' National Union held its first conference in the People's Co-operative Hall at Leeds. Here the policy of the union was clearly stated. The importance of securing an adequate standard of living by means of legislative regulation of conditions of work was emphasized in the numerous resolutions of the conference.

'Overtoil,' says the report, 'produces over-supply; low prices and low wages follow; bad habits and bad health follow, of course; and then diminished production and profits are inevitable. Reduction of toil, and consequent improved bodily health, increases production in the sense of profit; and limits it so as to avoid overstocking; better wages induce better habits, and economy of working follows. . . . The evil of overtoil and over-supply upon wages, and upon the labourer, is therefore a fair subject for complaint; and, we submit, as far as these are human by conventional arrangements, are a fair and proper subject for regulation. Regulations must, of course, be twofold. Part can be legislated for by compulsory laws; but the principle [sic] must be the subject of voluntary agreement.'[5]

[1] *Derbyshire Times*, 20 April, 1961.   [2] *Ibid.*   [3] *Ibid.* 10 August, 1861.
[4] *Minutes of the South Yorkshire Miners' Association* (subsequently referred to as *S.Y.M.A.*), 9 May, 27 June, 11 July, 1864; *Derbyshire Times*, 3 October, 1863; 9 July, 23 July, 1864.
[5] *Transactions and Results of the National Association of Coal, Lime and Ironstone Miners of Great Britain*, held at Leeds, 9, 10, 11, 12, 13 and 14 November, 1863, p. 14; quoted in S. and B. Webb, *op. cit.* p. 303.

The restriction of labour in mines to a maximum of eight hours a day was strongly urged; but at Macdonald's instance it was resolved not to ask for a legal regulation of the hours of adult men, but to confine the parliamentary proposal to a Bill for boys.

VI

During this period another union, the Practical Miners,[1] was also attempting to win the support of the Derbyshire miners. In December, 1864, it held its national conference at Chesterfield and John Catchpole, who was to become an important figure in mining trade unionism in Derbyshire, was elected to the credential committee.[2] There are no other references to the activities of the Practical Miners in Derbyshire and it is unlikely that they attracted a wide following.

Catchpole, however, who was then employed at the Staveley Company's Springwell Colliery, was one of the founders of a local association within Macdonald's federation. The men at Catchpole's pit had many grievances. They were obliged to send up 28 cwt. to the ton and if a tub were as little as 2 lb. short of a hundredweight they were not paid for the other 110 lb. They were also dissatisfied with the records which were kept of the amount of coal sent up. In November, 1865, they threatened to strike but the Company conceded payment for half-hundredweights and allowed the men to have checkweighmen.[3] The first to be appointed were Catchpole and Straw.[4]

In the same month Catchpole and others subscribed sufficient money to send Joseph Edwards, of Woodhouse, near Sheffield, to the annual conference of the Miners' National Union at Newcastle.[5] Edwards, who had worked in Derbyshire and Nottinghamshire pits for 26 years and remembered the days when men were getting 30 cwt. to 40 cwt. to the ton and working 14 to 16 hours a day,[6] was impressed by what he saw and heard at Newcastle. When he returned home and told his friends what had transpired at the conference they were fired with enthusiasm and decided at once to form a local association. The Derbyshire and Nottinghamshire Miners' Association, as it was eventually called, came into being on 23 December, 1865, at the George Inn,

[1] Little is known about this national union which appears to have been set up in opposition to Macdonald's federation after various disputes about the way in which union funds should be expended.

[2] *Derbyshire Times*, 31 December, 1864.

[3] *Ibid.* 4 November, 1865; *Ilkeston Pioneer*, 2 November, 1865.

[4] *Ibid.* 8 November, 1866.

[5] *R.C. on Trades Unions*, 1867–9, Eighth Report, Evidence of Brown, Q. 16,402.

[6] *Derbyshire Times*, 7 April, 1866.

Southgate, Eckington. The officers were William Ball, president; John Hadfield, treasurer; John Catchpole, secretary; Joseph Edwards, agent.[1]

At the Newcastle conference Edwards had struck up a friendship with William Brown, who soon became the principal leader of the movement in Derbyshire and Nottinghamshire.[2] Brown's family had worked for seventy years at Fenton's Thorp Hall Colliery, near Leeds, and Brown himself had been a working miner for twenty-five years. He had been on strike for seventeen weeks in 1844 and had received only $7\frac{1}{2}$d. strike pay during the whole of the period. Eventually he was dismissed for his trade union activities and moved to Bower's Pepper Lane Colliery at Hunslet, also near Leeds. He worked there for ten weeks and during that time was given three notices to leave. Later he took a small shop next to Bower's glue works and started a green-grocery business. He continued to take an active part in trade unionism and at length became agent for the miners in the Leeds and Methley district.[3]

Edwards sent pressing invitations to Brown to speak at various meetings in Derbyshire and Nottinghamshire. These caused Brown some embarrassment. He wanted to do as much as he could for the Derbyshire and Nottinghamshire men but, at the same time, he could not neglect his duties in Yorkshire. In his evidence before the Royal Commission of 1867 he described his difficulties. Saturday was his free day when he could go where he liked but on other days he had to obtain the permission of his committee before going into Derbyshire. On one occasion, when he was already billed to speak at Barnsley, he was stung to seek Normansell's permission to abandon the meeting by Catchpole's remark: 'I suppose you think that because you are more respected in the Barnsley district you will sell a few more books among the colliers there than in the Staveley district, and that is the reason you cannot come.'[4] Brown, in his evidence before the Royal Commission, tended to minimize his activities in Derbyshire and Nottinghamshire. He was, in fact, a frequent visitor to the area in the early days of the Association and became a full-time agent on 22 October, 1866.[5]

Meanwhile Edwards was arranging a series of meetings in various centres to gain support for the newly established association. One of the earliest was held in February, 1866, at the Dusty Miller, North Whittington, the principal speakers being Brown and Edwards. Catchpole, who was in the chair, said that the objects of the union were to seek an advance in wages and a shortening of the hours of labour which

[1] R.C. on Trades Unions, 1867–9, Eighth Report, Evidence of Brown, Q. 16,402.
[2] Ibid.   [3] Ibid. QQ. 16,354–16,387.
[4] Ibid. Q. 16,424.   [5] Ibid. Q. 16,418.

were 'so protracted that few men could work for six continuous days'. Although they earned a good wage for one day they could not do so for the week. According to Edwards, this was because they had not asked for an advance. 'He hoped they would not think of having strikes: but if anything was wrong to let them send for the agent to go with a deputation to the masters.'[1]

A meeting at the New Inn, Whittington, resulted in the formation of a lodge for the men employed at the Sheepbridge and neighbouring works.[2] Songs in praise of trade unions opened a meeting of about 200 miners at the Nag's Head Inn, Staveley. It was addressed by J. Fitz-George, Secretary of the Hardeners' Branch of the Sheffield filemakers, who appealed for assistance for his members who were locked out and urged the advantages of trade unionism. Edwards denounced the hours of work for miners and criticized the weighing and butty systems. He condemned the practice of allowing young boys to work in the pits and urged the miners to secure for themselves, through the union, 7s. a day for seven hours' work.[3]

By July, 1866, the movement was gathering a considerable amount of support and several mass meetings were arranged. About 4,000 coal and ironstone miners on Selston Common pledged themselves to support the Miners' National Association and further resolved: 'That in the opinion of this meeting eight hours per day are sufficient for a miner to work in the pit and we are also of the opinion that miners should be paid by the checkweighman's note for the future: and we, the miners of Nottinghamshire and Derbyshire will use our best endeavours to carry out the same.' The meeting, which opened with a hymn, was brought to a close 'by the singing of the doxology and the chairman pronouncing the benediction'.[4]

William Brown and William Ball were present at a similar meeting of 1,000 miners at Chesterfield in August. Again the meeting opened with a hymn, 'God never made a slave'. Andrew Hall, of Old Basford, took the chair and said that the miners' union had been started so many times and in so many places and it had always failed because the leading men, who had been put in a place of trust and should have set an example, had deceived their fellow men and had made off with the funds.

'The union of the present,' he continued, 'is more safely constructed, and I am happy to tell you that this Association is a glorious object—for instance, when we read the word of Holy Truth what does it teach us?—that union is strength and strength is love, and love is the very essence of God himself. Therefore the failure of unions in the past has been for the want of union, of

---

[1] *Derbyshire Times*, 24 February, 1866.   [2] *Ibid.* 26 March, 1866.
[3] *Ibid.* 31 March, 1866, 7 April, 1866.   [4] *Ibid.* 14 July, 1866.

love, of kind action, and men who can prove themselves to be men. . . . Respect yourselves and try to raise yourselves and if you do the world will keep you.'

Brown, who was received 'with hearty cheers', said that there were men in Nottinghamshire and Derbyshire who did not know what weight they got from one six months' end to another.[1]

In the same month another large meeting was held in a field adjoining the Three Tuns Inn, at Hill Top, near Eastwood. The miners brought their wives and sweethearts to enjoy tea, cricket and other pastimes, and then assembled in a large marquee under the presidency of Sisson, of Cotmanhay, to hear an address by Brown. They heard from him that within the last four months they had added another 3,000 members to their ranks. 'What could be done in Yorkshire might be done there', he said. 'It was only a matter of pounds, shillings and pence, combined with honesty and straightforwardness. . . . They did not want any strikes or lock-outs; they wanted fair play, and nothing more.' John Holmes, of Leeds, and John Normansell then spoke about the eight-hour day for which the meeting pledged its support.[2]

As the movement gathered force, meetings were held in an increasing number of centres. Towards the end of August, Brown, Ball and Daniel Green addressed a series of meetings at Swanwick, Somercotes, Morton, Hucknall, Ripley and Selston. The increase in the membership was very large, varying between 20 and 130 at each meeting.[3] The pattern was everywhere the same: the singing of a hymn and a demand for improved wages and conditions coupled with advice to show a conciliatory spirit in trying to obtain the desired concessions. Brown, who appears to have been something of a singer, would sometimes delight his audience with a favourite ballad.[4]

VII

By now the crisis was near at hand. It was precipitated by the action of Charles Markham, managing director of the Staveley Company. On 6 September he called together a large number of colliers from various pits belonging to the Company, pointed out that their wages had improved since the firm became a limited liability company, and warned them to pause before joining the union, 'and reflect upon the loss and misery which might result, not only to themselves, but to their wives and families'.[5] Markham was, in many ways, one of the more enlightened employers and most of the minor grievances about weighing had already

---

[1] *Ilkeston Pioneer*, 9 August, 1866. [2] *Ibid.*
[3] *Derbyshire Times*, 1 September, 1866; *Ilkeston Pioneer*, 30 August, 1866.
[4] *Ilkeston Pioneer*, 27 September, 1866.
[5] *Derbyshire Times*, 15 September, 1866.

D*

been settled. Checkweighmen had been conceded and the Company paid a representative of the men 24s. a week to decide when tubs should be disallowed for payment because they contained too much dirt. Markham was, however, very firmly opposed to trade unionism and also to the union's main economic objectives. He informed the men that 'no alteration in the present arrangement would result in any advantage to them, as a reduction in the quantity upon which they were at present paid, would cost an equivalent reduction in the price paid'.[1]

The Clay Cross Company followed Markham's lead and during September, 1866, both at Staveley and at Clay Cross, men who were known to have joined the union began to receive a month's notice to leave their work and their houses. At the end of one week as many as 100 of the colliers at the Springwell pit and between 70 and 100 who lived in the Staveley Company's houses at Barrow Hill were given notice to leave.[2]

The colliers and their wives were determined to hold out. As the notices expired they showed no signs of leaving their houses but calmly awaited a magistrate's order. A meeting was held at which it was resolved to support those who had been dismissed and to keep them in the district so that they would not help to reduce the rate of wages by removing to other collieries. A few non-unionists arrived from Staffordshire but they were by no means sufficient to fill all the vacancies. One of the leaders of the union suggested that a number of tents should be hired and erected in the neighbourhood to accommodate the families who were evicted. 'So strongly do some of the women feel on the matter that we heard of one who is near her confinement expressing perfect willingness to undergo the hardships of camp life for a time', stated the *Derbyshire Times*.[3]

By the beginning of October the breach between masters and men at Staveley was daily growing wider. The whole of the miners employed at the Hopewell pit, with one exception, were given a month's notice to leave their work.[4] As men were dismissed on account of their trade union activity, the Association began to appoint more paid agents. Joseph Lee, a local preacher, who had been dismissed from Springwell Colliery, was a case in point.[5] Presiding over a meeting of 600 men and women at the Nag's Head Inn, Staveley, he told them that since he had received his notice he was 'warming to the work, and liked the union all the better'.[6]

On this occasion the spiritual guidance was provided by Richard

---

[1] *Derbyshire Times*, 15 September, 1866.   [2] *Ibid.* 29 September, 1866.
[3] *Ibid.*   [4] *Ilkeston Pioneer*, 18 October, 1866.
[5] *R.C. on Trades Unions*, 1867–9, Sixth Report, Evidence of J. T. Woodhouse, Q. 12,418.   [6] *Ilkeston Pioneer*, 18 October, 1866.

Bunting, of Ilkeston, who also became a full-time agent employed by the union.[1] Their object in uniting, he said, was 'to obtain their own freedom to the benefit of society and to the glory of God. . . .' After expounding several scriptural texts he asserted:

But the union was in unison with the scriptures, for they declared 'it was pleasant for brethren to dwell together in unity'. Those who worked in a pit were brethren, or members of the Church. . . . At Airdrie the colliers had tried the 'friendly touch' as he hoped the miners of Staveley would try to do. They tried all means in their power in order to avoid a strike, but they were vain efforts; and after a strike the masters yielded to the terms of the men. Now the men earned 6s. a day. . . . The union had already done Derbyshire much good. . . . He hoped all would join, especially the Christians. The duty was enjoined upon them by High Heaven.[2]

William Brown, who had advised the leaders against taking strike action on the grounds that they would be unable to support all their members, referred to their reluctance to fight but said that they were prepared to do their duty if necessary; even if the fight lasted for four months. 'The miners must pray for strength to go to their employers as men. For whatever was gained was given to them by High Heaven.' Ending on a more practical note he stated that two of their representatives, Herring and Ball, who had gone into Staffordshire, had sent a report saying that as the men there were joining the union 'there was no need to fear that many of them would come and take their work and homes'.[3]

At Clay Cross feeling ran equally high. Many of those who had received notices to leave their work and houses exhibited them proudly in their windows.[4] Over 3,000 miners, with their wives and friends, attended an open-air meeting presided over by H. Clarke, of South Wingfield, another paid agent of the movement.[5] Joseph Lee told them that the Staveley lodge had more than 1,000 members. 'He did not know how the miners of Clay Cross "stood it", but he had been given to understand that they had got started and he hoped that they would go on and on until every miner who worked in the locality would be a union man in money matters, and an honest man at heart'. Brown's announcement that the union now had 7,500 members in Derbyshire and Nottinghamshire was greeted with loud cheers.[6]

By this time the South Yorkshire Association was beginning to take a more active interest in the Derbyshire struggle. Philip Casey, a Barnsley checkweighman, was present at the Clay Cross meeting and told his

---

[1] *R.C. on Trades Unions*, 1867–9, Sixth Report, Evidence of J. T. Woodhouse, Q. 12,418.   [2] *Ilkeston Pioneer*, 18 October, 1866.
[3] *R.C. on Trades Unions*, 1867–9 Eighth Report, Evidence of Brown, Q. 16,433; *Ilkeston Pioneer*, 18 October, 1866.   [4] *Ilkeston Pioneer*, 18 October, 1866.
[5] *R.C. on Trades Unions*, 1867–9, Sixth Report, Evidence of Woodhouse, Q. 12,418.
[6] *Ilkeston Pioneer*, 18 October, 1866.

audience frankly that the miners of Derbyshire had had a bad name among the miners of Yorkshire for a considerable number of years:

Whilst the men of Yorkshire were striving to better their conditions by working shorter hours, etc. they in Derbyshire had been working all hours, feeding up the markets and taking their chance away. . . . When they now asked for an advance in Yorkshire they were told that in Derbyshire the men were working 12 or 13 hours per day, and that the masters were underselling them. It was time the men of Derbyshire began to bestir themselves and to strive to better their condition. They had told him in Yorkshire to encourage the men of Derbyshire all he could, and if anything were wanting, if it lay in their power to grant it, it would be forthcoming.[1]

True to its word, the South Yorkshire Association resolved, on 29 October, 1866: 'That some practical and experienced person should be at once sent and stationed at the head-quarters in Derbyshire, to advise and to give every information necessary to the carrying out of their association and to use his utmost endeavours with leading officers of the district to bring the present dispute to a successful termination.' Accordingly, Casey was dispatched to Derbyshire for a period of three weeks with a weekly wage of £2 10s. 0d. and an allowance for travelling expenses.[2] He stayed with John Hadfield, the Derbyshire and Nottinghamshire Association's treasurer, in Beetwell Street, Chesterfield.[3] The Yorkshire delegates to the national conference were instructed to give all possible support to the Derbyshire miners and to raise the question of placing an agent in Derbyshire for a few months at the expense of the national association. Normansell, the Yorkshire secretary, pointed out that the battle must be brought to a successful conclusion 'or the Derbyshire men will for ever remain slaves and a drag upon the energies of all miners of progress'.[4]

A month later it was reported to the Council of the South Yorkshire Association that the national conference had voted £200 to buy tents for the evicted families to live in during the struggle, and the conference had also imposed a levy of 3d. a week upon all districts connected with the national association for the support of the Derbyshire men and some of the Lancashire men who were at that time facing a similar situation.[5]

The intervention of the South Yorkshire Association gave rise to the impression that the Derbyshire men were merely part of that organization.[6] Brown, however, had already denied the assertion that they were connected with South Yorkshire and proudly asserted that 'the Derbyshire man had a union of his own and the miners of South Yorkshire had nothing to do with it except if they got into difficulties

[1] *Ilkeston Pioneer*, 18 October, 1866.   [2] *S.Y.M.A.* 29 October, 1866.
[3] *Ilkeston Pioneer*, 18 October, 1866; 29 October, 1866.
[4] *S.Y.M.A.* 29 October, 1866.   [5] *Ibid.* 26 November, 1866.
[6] *The Times*, 10 November, 1866; *Ilkeston Pioneer*, 22 November, 1866.

by their masters locking them out, and if they should thus become short of anything to support them the South Yorkshire men would tender them any assistance in their power. . . . William Brown did not come into Derbyshire until he was sent for. The men had said they dare not go before the masters to complain because if they did there was "the poke" [dismissal] staring them in the face'.[1] On another occasion, a speaker at New Whittington said that there were 160 union men at Springwell pit before Brown ever came into the district.[2]

VIII

The situation in Derbyshire was discussed at length by the national conference at Nottingham in November. Catchpole, one of the Derbyshire delegates, said that the districts of Staveley, Butterley and Clay Cross were in a state of turmoil. According to Barker, also from Derbyshire, as soon as the men in these districts took action, they were immediately dismissed. They now had more 'victims' on their hands than they could support. The men were being evicted and as the Butterley Company had about 700 houses it was a difficult matter to find them lodgings. Philip Casey then read a detailed report on the situation in Derbyshire and Nottinghamshire. Within little more than three months the membership of the union had increased from 300 to 7,300. Of these, 2,800 members were in Nottinghamshire, 1,800 at Staveley, 700 at Clay Cross and 2,000 in various other parts of Derbyshire. More than 200 men had been thrown out of work in Nottinghamshire, 70 men had been discharged at Clay Cross and nearly 100 men had been dismissed and turned out of their homes by the Staveley Company. Ordinary contributions amounted to £350 a fortnight. The object of the Association had been to raise a permanent fund for the protection of its members but the fortnightly liabilities, which now exceeded the income by £190, were as follows:

	£	s.	d.
Hucknall Torkard	220	0	0
Staveley lock-out	100	0	0
Clay Cross lock-out	70	0	0
Victims at various other places	60	0	0
Incidental allowances to members	70	0	0
Delegates wages and rail to Council meetings	10	0	0
Printing and post	10	0	0
	£540	0	0

---

[1] *Ilkeston Pioneer*, 25 October, 1866. [2] *Ibid.* 13 December, 1866.

Thus the payment to the men who were on strike or locked out amounted to £1 each every fortnight and to meet these heavy expenses an additional levy had to be paid by those in work.[1]

The financial position of the Association was made more serious by the turn of events at Staveley. On 3 November, 600 men employed at the Springwell Colliery gave in their notices and plans were being made to bring out the whole of the Staveley men numbering about 2,600. The Staveley contract rules were a source of great discontent, particularly the following:

Rule 3. Stallmen shall do their work themselves and not by deputy, but shall be bound to accept the assistance of such labourers as the owner or his viewer and underviewer may provide.

Rule 5. Every stallman or labourer may, from time to time *without notice*, be removed by the owner from his pit or stall, for any other work necessary to be performed at these collieries, and coal and iron mines and works, and he shall not object to such removal, but shall perform the work required.

Rule 14. All stallmen and labourers engaged on the day shift in getting or loading coal, shall be down in the pit before 6 o'clock in the morning and shall not leave their place of work before half-past 5 o'clock in the afternoon, except on half-days, when they shall not leave before 12 o'clock noon. They shall be allowed on full days half an hour for dinner, beginning at 12 o'clock noon.

Rule 30. Any stallman or labourer disobeying any of these general, special, or contractual rules, obligatory to him, shall be liable for each offence to forfeit a sum not exceeding 20s.

Rule 31. Every stallman or labourer who shall neglect or absent himself from his work without leave or *lawful* excuse for any day, or part of a day, shall forfeit for each offence, a sum not exceeding 5s.

Rule 32. All fines made payable by these rules and regulations shall be *assessed* and *imposed* by the viewer or underviewer, who will also give the orders of dismissal for breach or neglect of duty.[2]

The colliers objected to the injustice of compelling a man to accept the services of any person the owner or viewer might think proper to force upon him and argued that if a stallman was compelled to pay a deputy, it ought to be one of his own choice. Stallmen, working by contract, were aggrieved at the prospect of being removed from their places without notice lest the change should take place at a time when conditions were improving, after a period of hard, unrewarding work. Robert Rowarth was sentenced to twenty-eight days' hard labour for refusing to work in a different part of the pit because the place belonged to a union man who had been dismissed.[3] Rule 14 was universally

---

[1] *Ilkeston Pioneer*, 22 November, 1866.
[2] *Ibid.*   [3] *Ibid.* 13 December, 1866.

objected to because it implied a period of twelve hours underground for men and boys. Rules 30, 31 and 32, were considered unfair because the Company set up a court of justice in which they and their agents were the sole arbiters.[1]

The national conference was told by Macdonald that he had received a letter from the Clay Cross men stating that Charles Binns had offered to grant them ten hours a day and a small advance in wages or tonnage on condition that the union was broken up. Macdonald roundly condemned the conduct of Binns and said of J. G. Jackson, one of the proprietors and a Liberal M.P. for North Derbyshire, that 'he was a Liberal in public but not in private'. The conference declared its resolve 'To assist the men and frustrate the intention of the Company to extinguish the Association'.[2]

By the end of November most of the men had ceased work at Staveley, some were being taken before the courts for refusing to leave their houses and others were actually being ejected. Groups of men, yoked to waggons, could be seen helping each other to move their few possessions from Barrow Hill to Whittington where tents had been erected in a field.[3] Non-unionists were moving into the empty houses and there were some minor disturbances, although Brown said that he had never seen a strike or lock-out in Yorkshire or Staffordshire which had been conducted so peaceably as the one at Staveley. Many of the unemployed men and boys turned their leisure time to advantage by buying books out of their meagre strike pay and starting schools for mutual instruction.[4] The union executive made preparations to erect, if necessary, a sufficient number of huts to house the homeless families.[5] William Pickard, of the Lancashire miners, came to Derbyshire with money from the national association to buy cottages and timber for the building of huts.[6]

IX

Meanwhile attempts were being made to break the union. The coalmasters of Derbyshire subscribed towards a fighting fund of £100,000[7] and Charles Markham, who denied before the Royal Commission of 1867 that the Staveley Company belonged to any such association,[8] set to work to organize his Free Labour Society as a

[1] *Ilkeston Pioneer*, 22 November, 1866.   [2] *Ibid.*
[3] *Ibid.* 22 November, 1866; 29 November, 1866; 17 January, 1867.
[4] *Ibid.* 29 November, 1866; 10 January, 1867.   [5] *Ibid.* 29 November, 1866.
[6] *Ibid.*   [7] *Ibid.* 6 December, 1866.
[8] *R.C. on Trades Unions*, 1867–9, Sixth Report, Evidence of Markham, Q. 11,600.

counter-blast to the efforts of the unionists.[1] His task was made easier by the sufferings and deprivations of the strikers. Picked men were sent to various collieries to organize non-unionist meetings. At the first meeting at New Hollingwood, on 22 November, George Martin described the misery and destitution which strikes had brought to the homes of the men, paralysing the well-meant efforts of masters and capitalists and setting the workmen and employers at loggerheads: 'He had always prided himself on being a God-fearing man; and he could not help reflecting that the suffering to which he had been reduced through strikes was God's righteous judgment on him. God was whipping him for flying in the face of providence.'[2] (God was evidently on the side of unionists and non-unionists alike!) Another speaker remarked that 'Mr. Markham had always been known as a friend of the working man, and if he was allowed he would always remain so'. A resolution was passed unanimously pledging all present to keep out of the union. Similar meetings were held at other places accompanied by the inevitable hymns and prayers. A meeting at Barrow Hill was attended by non-unionists from the Seymour and Speedwell collieries who were brought up by a special workman's train sent by the Company.[3] Charles Markham addressed some of the meetings, declaring, 'in a spirit of fairness', that the Company could do more for the men than the union.[4]

The movement spread to Clay Cross. A man named Thelwall presided at the first meeting which resolved: 'That this meeting is of opinion that it is desirable to form an association for the protection of miners and others, being non-unionists.' It was also decided 'that the Clay Cross Company be respectfully requested to grant the use of the public hall for the meetings of the society'.[5] Some members of the union attended one of these meetings and created a disturbance but this was deprecated by several speakers at a subsequent union meeting.[6] The unionists were inclined to underestimate the activities of their rivals and Joseph Lee dismissed the movement as consisting of 'only a few of the deputies, the lamp men, and the pilot-cloth persons, with others present from mere curiosity'.[7]

The non-unionists adopted various devices to win over the strikers, one of the most successful being the appeal to hunger. Early in January, 1867, the non-unionists at Staveley roasted a bullock, provided by their

[1] For a full account of the Staveley Free Labour Society see *Reports of Non-Union Meetings held by Workpeople employed by the Staveley Coal and Iron Company in vindication of the Freedom and Liberty of Labour*, (Chesterfield), 1867, (Manchester Municipal Reference Library).   [2] *Ilkeston Pioneer*, 29 November, 1866.
[3] *Ibid.* 6 December, 1866.   [4] *Ibid.* 13 December, 1866; 24 January, 1867.
[5] *Ibid.* 6 December, 1866.   [6] *Ibid.* 13 December, 1866.
[7] *Ibid.* 6 December, 1866.

employers, and burned Brown's effigy.[1] Henshaw, one of the men picked out by agents of the Staveley Company to give evidence before the Royal Commission of 1867, described the scene: '300 or 400 men that had been sticking to the union, and who were going with empty stomachs, when they saw this beef were ready to swallow it whole if they could, and they all flocked in and had a share of it, and went to work the next morning.'[2] Soon afterwards the unionists also roasted a bullock for themselves, subscribed for by the public of Whittington, Staveley and neighbourhood, but the damage had been done. The men were becoming dispirited. At one meeting Bunting expressed his hope that they would not be depressed because Brown had been unable to come:

They had suffered long and hard; they had suffered from loss of benefits which ought to have gone into their families. . . . When the union ship set sail they did not expect the sad affair which had happened at Barnsley [i.e. the disaster at the Oaks Pit] or that 1,500 or 1,700 men would be thrown upon the funds in Lancashire. Still, the men at these places were paying more money than they were, and had sent them more relief this fortnight than they had contributed themselves. They must be alive to their own interests, and keep in compliance with their lodges.[3]

There were now about 1,500 men out in Derbyshire and 1,300 in Lancashire, requiring something like £3,000 a fortnight in strike pay. An additional fortnightly levy of 6d. had been imposed upon its members by the South Yorkshire Association but even so the available funds were inadequate. The Yorkshire miners were therefore urged to do all they possibly could to collect funds in addition to the levy.[4] For the fortnight ending 7 January, 1867, the South Yorkshire Association, in addition to forwarding a levy of £150 to the national association, also 'lent' £260 to the Derbyshire men.[5] By 4 February there was 'so much confusion and desertion' among the Derbyshire miners that the South Yorkshire Association recommended all lodges receiving clearances from Derbyshire 'not to enter such members in the lodge books, but the lodge secretaries must forward all such clearances to the offices, Nelson Street, Barnsley, in order that enquiries may be made by the district secretary as to whether or not such clearances be genuine'.[6] A fortnight later it was decided that no more grants or loans should be voted to the Derbyshire men and the 6d. levy was discontinued.[7] On 18 March payment of the levy to the national association

[1] *Ilkeston Pioneer*, 10 January, 1867.
[2] *R.C. on Trades Unions*, 1867–9, Sixth Report, Evidence of Thomas Henshaw, Q. 13,801.
[3] *Ilkeston Pioneer*, 10 January, 1867. [4] *S.Y.M.A.* 10 December, 1866.
[5] *Ibid.* 7 January, 1867. [6] *Ibid.* 4 February, 1867.
[7] *Ibid.* 18 February, 1867.

for the support of the Lancashire and Derbyshire men was also discontinued.[1]

Meanwhile the Derbyshire men were attempting to raise funds from other sources. A deputation consisting of Thomas Hill and Charles Barber waited upon the London Trades Council at their meeting in the Bell Inn, Old Bailey, on 12 January. After some discussion, credentials were given to the deputation entitling them to apply to the London trade unions for assistance.[2] The records of the Brushmakers contain the following entry: 'January 30th, 1867. . . . A Deputation from the Miners of Derbyshire applied for assistance for their members who are Locked Out because they have joined a Trade Society. Proposed by Mr. Nuttall Seconded by T. Platt "That Ten pounds be granted to them from the General Trade Fund". Ordered to be sent round for the votes by Two Men out of work.'[3]

The leaders of the union, however, were unable to prevent the men from drifting back to work and renouncing their association. By the end of January 2,123 men had been enrolled in the Staveley Non-union Society.[4] At the Seymour, Speedwell and Farewell pits unionism was all but extinct. Dowell and Old Hollingwood were fast regaining their men. At Springwell only 20 of the 500 strikers had returned to work but their places were rapidly being filled by men brought from Staffordshire.[5] This had the effect of causing the Springwell men to abandon the union and by the end of the month one of the deputies was able to report that 'they are coming in as fast as they can sign their names'.[6] The union was crushed but the dispute was not entirely without benefit to the men. Markham told the Royal Commission of 1867:

The pits used to draw coal formerly 12 hours a day, and when the question was discussed after the union was all broken up I sent for a deputation of the men, and we talked the matter over, and we thought that we could do the work in 10½ hours. . . . Everybody was paid by the ton, so it made very little difference to us either one way or the other.[7]

The weakening of the strikers' position was largely due to the inadequacy of the union's funds. The Derbyshire men who were in work had neglected to contribute their levies in support of the strikers

[1] S.Y.M.A. 18 March, 1867.

[2] Ilkeston Pioneer, 17 January, 1867. Cf. G. Tate, London Trades Council, 1860–1950, (London), 1950, pp. 23–24.

[3] W. Kiddier, The Old Trade Unions from Unprinted Records of the Brushmakers, (London), 1930, p. 47. See also Appendix II to this chapter.

[4] Reports of Non-Union Meetings held by Workpeople employed by the Staveley Coal and Iron Company, p. 98.

[5] Ilkeston Pioneer, 24 January, 1867.   [6] Ibid. 31 January, 1867.

[7] R.C. on Trades Unions, 1867–9, Sixth Report, Evidence of Markham, Q. 11,608.

who had eventually been reduced to half pay.[1] Brown was bitterly disappointed. At Clay Cross, where the men had likewise seceded from the union, he said that the Derbyshire men were the worst of all the men with whom he had been associated:

Had they paid as they ought to have done, all the victimized men would have had their money, and they would now have about £1,000 in hand. . . . They could not work at a more suitable place than Clay Cross, for they were like clay, and could be shaped into any mould. The Council at Barnsley had sent them £24 a fortnight but they had done nothing for themselves. They had not been dealt with half hard enough. However, if those who had seceded from the union would come back, the past this time would be overlooked.[2]

A Derbyshire miner who had gone to work in Yorkshire commented:

I, as one of the Yorkshirebites, can go to work at six in the morning and come out at two in the afternoon, with 7s. But what did I get in Derbyshire? Why 3s. 6d. and worked harder too. I am happy I have come here; they stuck to me like glue; there is no falling from the union here by men being bribed by the masters, as is done by some in Derbyshire. . . .[3]

In one or two places the men showed a stronger determination to resist the employers, particularly in the Whittington district and at Pinxton where two publicans were forbidden by the magistrates to allow union meetings on their premises.[4] A fire in one of the pits of Coke and Company, of Pinxton, which appeared to have been started deliberately, was attributed to the unionists but this they vehemently denied.[5] However, by the end of January the movement in North Derbyshire was virtually extinct and in the following June it was announced at the miners' national conference at Bolton that there were only 500 members in the northern part of the county but the union continued to be active in South Derbyshire and in Nottinghamshire where there were still 1,400 members.[6]

X

Early in February, Brown turned his attention to the colliery districts near Burton-upon-Trent and with the aid of Lee, Ackroyd, of Dudley Hill, near Bradford, and Dickson, also from the West Riding, he set to work to organize the miners at Church Gresley, Swadlincote and Newhall. From the outset the coal-owners adopted a policy of opposition and by the middle of May about 200 miners had been dismissed and

[1] *Ilkeston Pioneer*, 31 January, 1867.   [2] *Ibid.* 14 March, 1867.
[3] *Ibid.* 24 January, 1867.   [4] *Ibid.* 17 January, 1867.
[5] *Ibid.* 10 January, 1867, 17 January, 1867.   [6] *Ibid.* 4 July, 1867.

many others were under notice for joining the union. Feeling began to run very high, meetings were held weekly and extra police were drafted into the district.[1] Church Gresley became the centre for a long and bitter struggle. On 24 May, the locked-out miners, with their wives and children, assembled in front of the People's Hall and headed, appropriately enough, by the Swadlincote Garibaldi Band, marched through Gresley to Swadlincote market place to hear the speeches. They then returned to Gresley where, after an address had been delivered by the Rev. Thomas Kent, over 200 children each received a 4 lb. loaf.[2]

Brown appealed to the South Yorkshire Association for assistance but this time it was not so readily forthcoming. On 3 June, Normansell was authorized to accompany two others as a deputation from the United Trades Alliance, of which South Yorkshire was a member, to Nottingham, for the purpose of investigating the position of the Church Gresley men.[3] It was decided that they had a just claim and, according to the rules of the Alliance, were each entitled to receive 5s. a week.[4] Normansell also raised the matter at the miners' national conference at Bolton and proposed that a loan of £350 should be granted for the support of the Church Gresley men. This was strongly opposed on the ground that if the principle of granting loans in such cases were conceded Wigan, Farnworth, Kearsley, and other districts would make claims, and there would be no end to applications. The motion was eventually carried, with the addition that a deputation should be sent into the district to endeavour to settle the dispute.[5] Towards the end of July a deputation from the United Trades Alliance and the Miners' Association had an interview with some of the employers but no agreement was reached.[6]

The struggle in South Derbyshire aroused a great deal of interest in the trade union world. Tom Halliday, from Lancashire, visited Church Gresley to address the locked-out miners,[7] the Working Men's Association convened a meeting of the trades of London to hear a statement from a deputation of the men, and George Potter's *Beehive* asked: 'Do they [the employers] suppose that the artisans of England can ever allow their brethren to be thus treated'?[8] The South Yorkshire Association resolved, on 16 September: 'That the Gresley lock-out should be managed and supported by the Association . . . as it is of the greatest importance to this district that "union" should be established in Derbyshire, which in a strong possession of the coal owners can only

[1] *Ilkeston Pioneer*, 23 May, 1867.   [2] *Ibid.* 30 May, 1867.
[3] *S.Y.M.A.* 3 June, 1867. The United Kingdom Alliance of Organized Trades was formed to support the members of any trade who should find themselves locked out by their employers. (S. and B. Webb, *op. cit.* pp. 258–9.)
[4] *Ibid.* 10 June, 1867.   [5] *Ilkeston Pioneer*, 4 July, 1867.
[6] *Ibid.* 25 July, 1867.   [7] *Ibid.* 1 August, 1867.
[8] *The Beehive*, 30 November, 1867.

be done by the aid of the South Yorkshire and similar associations.'[1] The Gresley miners were to be supported 'to the utmost extent of all pecuniary means the Council can command'.[2] At the same time, South Yorkshire was dissatisfied with the attitude of the delegates to the national conference and condemned 'the cold manner in which the various districts . . . are supporting the Gresley men and . . . the anti-union spirit exhibited towards their fellow men in South Yorkshire on the Gresley question'.[3] The Yorkshire men agreed to pay a 6d. levy and coal was sent for the use of the locked-out miners.[4] Bass, the Member of Parliament for Derby, attempted to bring the dispute to an end but the agent of the Earl of Chesterfield refused to treat with him, whereupon he decided to provide each miner with an allowance of beef for Christmas, giving away some 2,380 lb.[5]

The dispute did not end until March, 1868, by which time some of the men had been locked out for over a year. To the end they kept up their weekly demonstrations with bands playing. As men began to drift back to work and non-union labour arrived from Staffordshire there was a certain amount of violence and disorder. Windows were broken and the roads leading to the pits were picketed. Many of the non-union men were roughly handled and on 19 November, 1867, ten men were sentenced to terms of imprisonment ranging from one to three months on charges of assault, threatening and intimidation. On one occasion the non-unionists going to and from their work were followed by crowds of men, women and children, 'performing on fire shovels, frying pans, tea trays, kettles, and other tin instruments, interluded with foul imprecations and dangerous threatenings and occasionally accompanied with stones and other missiles'.[6]

The main issue in dispute was, again, the men's right to join the union. William Johnson, Lord Chesterfield's manager at Bretby Colliery, maintained that the worst collier he had could earn 4s. 6d. in eight hours and that a good one could make 6s. in that time. The *Ilkeston Pioneer* commented: 'The ground upon which a lock-out was resorted to showed that the masters knew the evils resulting from the principles of the union which is an attempt on the part of the delegates and leaders to manage the collieries and say who shall and who shall not be employed and upon what system the collieries shall be worked.'[7] The men's attempt to gain recognition for their union failed completely. The dullness of the coal trade; the influx of strangers into the district who were ready to take the places of those locked out; and the refusal of

[1] *S.Y.M.A.* 16 September, 1867.   [2] *Ibid.* 30 September, 1867.
[3] *Ibid.* 11 November, 1867.
[4] *Ibid.* 25 November, 1867; 23 December, 1867.
[5] *Ilkeston Pioneer*, 2 January, 1868.
[6] *Ibid.* 21 November, 1867.   [7] *Ibid.* 11 January, 1868.

those who were at work to contribute towards the support of those who were unemployed; all helped to bring about the collapse of the movement.[1] Brown told the defeated men that if they had been more united, the Yorkshire, Northumberland and Lancashire miners would have stood by them but a great struggle was pending in Lancashire, many men were out in Yorkshire and consequently no more assistance could be expected from those districts. 'Under existing circumstances', said Brown, 'a ship-load of gold could not establish a union in this district.'[2]

XI

The failure of 'Billy Brown's Union' as it was called, put an end to any further attempts to organize an independent association for a number of years. The Derbyshire men as a whole were not yet ready for trade unionism. Many of them were suspicious of the leadership. In describing the advantage of organization Brown said at one meeting: 'To get this, they must, to a man, join the union and not say: "I joined the union once 16 years ago and because a man ran away with 4s. 6d. won't join any more." '[3] One miner commented: 'I know the colliers don't like placing their money in the hands of unknown men. I should like to know what Mr. Brown, Mr. Ball and other pit agents get for running about the country to manage other people's affairs.'[4] Another replied: 'His insidious endeavours will certainly cause a more narrow examination of the Association's policy and manner of working; but of this I am certain, that the examination will result in a hearty approval, and of course an accession of members.'[5] There were also rumours that Brown owned a number of houses, which he had to deny publicly: 'He had worked in the pit for 25 years; held a good standing in society; had always endeavoured to pay his way, and if he was balanced that day he had not a shilling of his own. He had only 7s. 6d. a day and a wife and seven children to keep out of it.'[6] Whatever the extent of

[1] *S.Y.M.A.* 16 March, 1868.   [2] *Ilkeston Pioneer*, 21 March, 1868.
[3] *Derbyshire Times*, 1 September, 1866.
[4] *Ilkeston Pioneer*, 9 August, 1866.   [5] *Ibid.* 30 August, 1866.
[6] *Ibid.* 18 October, 1866. The accuracy of this report was subsequently denied, the writer stating that Brown said his payment was 5s. 6d. a day (*Ilkeston Pioneer*, 25 October, 1866). This is corroborated by Brown's evidence before the Royal Commission of 1867, (Sixth Report, Q. 16,405). Payments made to Brown, Clarke, Bunting, Lee, Ball and Ward for three fortnights in January and February, 1867, were as follows: Fortnight ending 31 January, 1867, William Ball, £3 19s. 0½d.; R. Bunting, £4 13s. 0d.; H. Clarke £4 1s. 3d.; William Brown, £6 19s. 7½d. Fortnight ending 14 February, 1867, H. Clarke, £4 7s. 0d.; W. Ball, £4 3s. 9d.; J. Lee (omitted last time), £3 19s. 11d.; J. Lee, £4 1s. 11d.; R. Bunting, £4 5s. 9d.; W. Brown (on account) £3 3s. 7d. Fortnight ending 28 February, 1867, J. Lee, £4 3s. 10d.; W. Ball, £4 0s. 2d.; R. Bunting, £3 16s. 3d.; H. Clarke, £4 5s. 10d.; W. Ward, £8 6s. 5d.; W. Brown, £9 2s. 4d. (*R.C. on Trades Unions*, Sixth Report, Evidence of A. Higginson, Q. 12,418.)

Brown's wealth the collapse of the union left him in a difficult situation. In May, 1868, he applied to the South Yorkshire Association for financial assistance and a grant of £25 was made to help him to start a small business.[1] A further application for a loan of £30 was rejected in April, 1870,[2] but soon afterwards Brown became agent for the North Staffordshire miners.[3]

If the movement had been a failure it had at least helped to train some local leaders. Men like Lee, Catchpole, Bunting, Clarke and many others were schooled in an organization which was forthright in its demands, inspired by religious fervour, opposed to all violence, and very much concerned with the moral improvement of its members.

The rules of the Association, as stated by Bunting, were severely practical:

1. To raise from time to time, by contributions among members, a fund for mutual support.
2. To assist its members in striving to obtain better legislation for the efficient management of the mines, whereby the lives and health of the miners may be protected, and a better remuneration for their labour.
3. Compensation for accidents whereby the employers are liable.
4. To assist members who have been unjustly dealt with by their employers or agents.
5. A weekly allowance to members injured while following their employment.
6. A weekly allowance to members locked out, victimized, or driven into a strike.
7. To shorten the hours of labour and also to infuse steadier habits of working among its members.
8. To secure the true weight of the miners' material at the pit banks, thus giving to both employers and employed their legitimate due.
9. To extend the Association's principles to our less fortunate brethren by aiding all other similar associations that have for their object the emancipation of their fellow men from the grasp of capital.[4]

The moral and religious aspects of the union were to be seen in its organization and its leadership. Shortly before the defection of the North Derbyshire men, in January, 1867, the union had 'two ministers and five lecturers' which Beardsley, one of the local leaders, thought 'was not too many, for they wanted stirring up a little at times like their religious friends. When a revivalist came their members flocked to his side, but as he went again they soon began to weary of well-doing, and lecturers were equally necessary in the miners' case. . . . Every association incurred expenses, and those who grumbled didn't understand

[1] S.Y.M.A. 25 May, 1868, 8 June, 1868.   [2] Ibid. 25 April, 1870.
[3] Derbyshire Times, 6 September, 1873.
[4] Ilkeston Pioneer, 1 November, 1866.

their affairs.'[1] The religious influence exercised by the union will be evident from the meetings which have already been described. One of the union leaders said that there were 'hundreds of local preachers' working in the pits.[2] Woodhouse referred to Brown's 'preaching' before the Royal Commission of 1867. He was questioned further: 'When you say "preaching", do you mean religious preaching?—*Quasi* religion, giving out a text and shouting from it.'[3] Returning to this subject later in his evidence Woodhouse continued: 'He took a text and preached the same as itinerant preachers do, but in so doing I have no doubt he appealed to their feelings, and working people are very excitable, and when their feelings were up they would say, "Let us join the union". '[4] Similarly, the singing of hymns was so much a part of union business that a special miners' hymnbook was provided for members.[5]

With religion went pacifism. Bunting complained that when he had applied for the use of a room at Ilkeston he had been questioned about the matter 'as if something was wrong, and they were about to revolutionize the place'. In reply he stated that 'they would sing, pray and speak, and the Committee must judge whether they were wrong'.[6] When the checkweighman at Springwell Colliery was under notice, Brown advised the miners not to make his dismissal a reason for ceasing work, but to carry on as usual, until the Executive Council had decided upon the course to be taken.[7] On another occasion he said that 'he would walk twenty miles' to find the perpetrator of one of the Sheffield outrages. 'He saw no favour in intimidation nor in resorting to anything which might have any violence about it, nor could he give the slightest encouragement to anything in the shape of outrage.'[8]

The efforts of the union leaders to uplift the miner both morally and socially were unceasing. 'If there were amongst the mining population certain people who were pigeon flyers or drunkards, should that be any impediment to an honest man?' asked Brown.[9] On other occasions he urged the advantages of education but recognized that the men were incapable of further exertion at the end of a long day's work.[10] According to Bunting the colliers were 'the worst educated class of operatives in the United Kingdom'.[11] The object of the union, said Clarke, was to make the miner a more thoughtful and moral man.[12]

Here was the pattern for future development. The characteristics of Brown's union were to be the dominating features of unionism among the Derbyshire miners for the remainder of the nineteenth

[1] *Ilkeston Pioneer*, 10 January, 1867.   [2] *Ibid.* 22 November, 1866.
[3] *R.C. on Trades Unions*, 1867–9, Sixth Report, Woodhouse, Q. 11,909.
[4] *Ibid.* Q. 11,990.   [5] *Ilkeston Pioneer*, 10 January, 1867.
[6] *Ibid.* 18 October, 1866.   [7] Ibid. 25 October, 1866.   [8] *Ibid.*
[9] *Ibid.*   [10] *Ibid.* 30 August, 1866.
[11] *Ibid.* 10 January, 1867.   [12] *Ibid.*

century. The leadership remained in the hands of men who were ardent Methodists. As late as 1893 it was reported that Methodism of various kinds was very strong among the Derbyshire miners 'and it is a remarkable fact that nearly all the members of the Council of the Derbyshire Miners' Association are either local preachers or class leaders'.[1] Such men were forthright in demanding an improvement in the economic position of the miner, yet avoided violence, disorder and industrial strife whenever possible and worked constantly to educate and improve the union's membership in accordance with their own standards of good conduct.

[1] *Daily Chronicle*, 28 July, 1893.

APPENDIX I

Miners' Petitions, 1844

1. *The Pinxton Miners*

From the members of the Miners Benifit Soceity
to Mr.————— agent to —————

Sir.

This is a statement of the conditions which we the men of No. 3 & 4 will come to work.

1. We will not work wile any Blackleg is pemited.

2. That we will not work aney more at aney price for William Harvey & W. Pepper.

3. That John Slater Be Butie at No. 4 on condition of goining our Benifit Society. We will not work under him without or aney other person.

4. That John Knowles be Butie or over man at No. 3. We men of that pit pledg ourselves to work for no other person.

5. That all other persons goining our Benefit Society ave their own plases and where not we will stand to a man except aney person ath done something worthy of punishment or discharged.

6. That we have a written agreement whensomever we commence work and no more hands imployed then there is a days work for every day the pit draws.

7. That a Gate Hend be 4s. per web.

8. That wooding be 4s. per side 36 or 28 yards.

9. That hooling be 10d. per stint 2 yards long 2 foot 5 inch $\frac{1}{2}$ deep.

10. That day work be 4s. for 8 Hours.

11. That looding be 6d. per hour.

12. That Banking be 3s. 6d. per day for a decent man and not an idle drone.

13. That all boys be raised according to their abilaty.

14. That the turn shall not exceed 10 hours and one from that for dinner except there be too sets of men.

15. That we be alowed to see that we ave our rights of coals every month which ath itherto been a very great evil amongst us.

This statement we the members of the miners Benefit Society consider at gust and right Neither do we mean to deviate from it in any point whatever.

Writen By the order of the Committee of the Miners Benefit Society. Pinxton Lodge.

(*Derbyshire Courier*, 27 April, 1844)

2. *The Pinxton Miners*

To ————— Esquire.

Sir.

We the men late working at No. 3 & 4 wish to lay before you our past grievances, that your honour will not be surprised at the men of these pits coming to such illegal and hasty conclusions respecting the Butties at these Pits.

We as working men consider the Buttie sistem a very great evil amongst the colliers, for when a reduction must come all these men takes the advantage of us and lays more upon us than is legal, we can prove that the men represented had laid work upon us to great excess that we cannot bear and they all four were not doing more than two men, we do not know what may be the wages they was receiving, but this we do know.

> Wile they could laugh us men to scorn
> Our hearts with grief did sigh and mourn.
> As they from house to house did drink
> Caused us poor working men to think,
> and as we thought, this was our mind
> That drink did not come from the wind.

Consequently we have taken it into consideration that the clause of our former statment was wrong with taking that power from our Masters wich we had no right therefore wee consider ourselves as being in a fault. But wee wish to inform you that the wage wee ask for wee do not intend to deviate from and as regards our Union wee will not sign your Documents on any account whatever.

We the undersigned are the Committee.

George Hordy	John Smith
George Ellis	Wm. Lee
James Tupman	John Straw
Matthew Knowles	John Wetson
John Hayes	

Your humble servants the Members of the Miners' Association.

(*Derbyshire Courier*, 4 May, 1844)

3. *The Intake Miners*

To Mr. William Newbould, Esq., Intake Colliery.

Sir, It is with all that degree of deference to you that we your servants do wish to present a statement of Sundry Prices which we consider is nothing but right that you our Master should give and likewise that we your servants should receive that we and our wives and children may live and pay our way whilst in this World below for we are Commanded in God our Creator's word to owe no man anything but to provide things honest in the sight of all men and Sir you know as well as we do that we cannot provide these things unless we have the means therefore. Sir we hope that you will coincide with every part of our Statement with very little hesitation, and likewise as inculcated in God's most holy word That it is better to give than to receive and where much is given much is required and we your servants only wish to live and let others live for Sir we know that we must all soon die and return to the dust from whence we sprang and our Spirits return to God who gave them no more to return, therefore Sir we hope you will consider the home connected with you our Master behaving well to us your servants as we have both a command given in Scripture to act with becoming deference to each other as regards our respective Connexions in the Offices of this life. For this was a declaration left upon record by Our Lord and Master and there is another golden rule that Commands us to do unto others as we would that they should do unto us and we hope Sir that rule will be put into practical operation with both Master and Servants and Sir we only want a fair remuneration for our Labour which we hope you will be ready to give as soon as you see our requests and as your servants will be ever ready to do our duty in the Bowels of the Earth and by so doing both Masters and Servants will feel the benefit and I hope a better feeling will exist and when we have done with this life we may meet in a better World.

For Intake Colliery

April 8, 1844.   A Statement of Sundry Prices.

		s.	d.	
For new gates and levels		3	6	per yard
Board hards first 3 yards		2	8	per yard
Board remaind 9 ft. wide		2	6	per yard
Board gates		2	8	per yard
Deep and Basset Slits [?]		3	0	per yard
Ripping		6	6	per yard
For a new Benk open 60 yards		Two pounds		
Hard coals		6	6	per waggon
Sales coals		4	4	per waggon
Tolly coals		3	10	per waggon
Recovering		2	0	per yard
Getting metals		1	6	per pair
Knocking woods		1	0	per score
For datalling		4	2	per day
For hanging on in the pit bottom		3	8	per day
Hostling py		3	0	per week
Horse drivers		1	3	per day
Trappers			8	per day

And when the Benk is 16 yards from the Horse gate You must allow 4d. per day a man as Jenny money and You must advance the coals 2d. per waggon over 50 yards. And we must have 13 corves of Good Coals per quarter and single men must have the same or 6s. 6d. per quarter. And No One will be allowed to work in the Pits for the future but Colliers and their Sons. This is All we want and we hope you will comply with our wishes.

(*Derbyshire Times*, 8 June, 1901.)

APPENDIX II

Leaflet Issued by The United Society of Brushmakers, 1867

To the Members of the United Society of Brush Makers
Baptist's Head, St. John's Lane, Clerkenwell,
February 9th, 1867.

Gentlemen,

A Deputation from the Miners of Derbyshire and Nottinghamshire having waited upon this Society and solicited help for their members who have

been dismissed from their work, and ejected from their homes for the crime?
of joining a Trade Society, we have resolved to request your support to the
following proposition:—

Proposed—"That ten pounds be granted from the General Trade Funds to
the Miners now locked out by their former Employers for joining a Trade
Society." Our votes are 189 for and 80 against. The following is the Miners'
own statement.

The Miners' Appeal to the various Trades in England.

Gentlemen,

We take the liberty of appealing to you through the medium of our Agents
who are Members of the Derbyshire and Nottinghamshire Miners'
Association.

The Miners of the two Counties have united together in order to get some
of the grievances under which they are labouring redressed. The Masters
having become aware of their ultimate object, have combined to destroy
the Association in its infancy; hence the present struggle.

Two large Firms have Locked Out about 1,200 hands, for no other cause
than joining the Miners' Union, and many smaller Firms have followed their
example and thrown hundreds more upon our Funds. We have at the present
time 1,500 hands upon our funds, most of whom have been ejected from
their houses, and are now compelled (in many instances) at present to live
two and three families in one small cottage.

The men have not asked for any Advance of Wages, nor anything else, but
simply joined the Miners' Association, which they have a perfect right to do
if they think proper according to the Laws of the Country; but the Masters
will not allow them that privilege.

We appeal for your sympathy and assistance (under these circumstances),
to enable us to break off the chains of Tyranny and Oppression which has
so long held us down. Hoping our appeal will be responded to, and that the
Trades generally will assist us in our struggle against Despotic Powers.

We remain,

Yours respectfully,

On behalf of the Derbyshire and Nottinghamshire Miners' Association,

J. HADFIELD, Treasurer.

W. HERRING, Secretary.

Miners' Office, Chesterfield, Jan. 14th, 1867.

CHAPTER IV

THE SOUTH YORKSHIRE ASSOCIATION
AND THE DERBYSHIRE
AND NOTTINGHAMSHIRE ASSOCIATION

I

Although the Derbyshire miners lacked any effective organization after the crushing defeats of the 'sixties they appear to have retained some of the spirit of trade unionism. During the early 'seventies, when the coal trade was entering a boom period, they began to combine, at the colliery level, to obtain a number of concessions. Their principal objective was the nine-hour day and coupled with this were demands for weekly instead of fortnightly payment, improvements in prices and the right to have checkweighmen.

At most collieries these requests were agreed to and a friendly atmosphere prevailed. In November, 1871, the men employed by the Staveley Company were granted a nine-hour day and weekly payment, both taking effect from 1 January, 1872. 'Soon after', we are told, 'the bells of Staveley church rang out a merry peal.'[1] Similar concessions were granted by James Oakes and Company to the men at the Cowper Colliery, Riddings, who showed their gratitude by marching in procession, headed by the Codnor Brass Band, to Riddings House, the residence of T. H. Oakes.[2] The Sheepbridge Coal and Iron Company agreed to introduce the nine hours' system if the other large employers in the district would do the same.[3] At Renishaw the men were granted the nine-hour day and advances of 4d. a ton on hard coal and 2d. a ton on slack with the result that their rate of wages varied from 5s. to 8s. a day.[4]

At other collieries the men were involved in strikes. The Butterley Company offered some resistance until 2,000 of the colliers in the Ripley

[1] *Derbyshire Times*, 4 November, 1871.   [2] *Ibid.* 13 January, 1872.
[3] *Ibid.* 4 November, 1872.   [4] *Ibid.* 13 and 17 January, 1872.

district abandoned their work. Their demands for the nine-hour day, and the right to have checkweighmen were conceded and, as a compromise, they agreed to accept an advance of 2d. a ton instead of the 3d. they were seeking.[1] The men employed at Morewood's collieries, near Alfreton, were also on strike for the nine-hour day and weekly payments.[2]

There is little information about the way in which the nine hours' system was implemented. At Clay Cross, however, work in the pit was begun at 6 a.m. and ceased at 4 p.m. except on Saturday, when work stopped at 12.30 p.m. On all days except Saturday a period of half an hour was allowed for a meal, thereby making a working week of 54 hours.[3]

No sooner had the men won the nine hours' system than they began to demand further increases in wages. By 1872 the price of coal was beginning to rise fairly sharply and those firms which had reduced wages two years previously on the understanding that wages would be increased when trade improved were asked to fulfil their promise. In January there were strikes among the men employed by the Sheepbridge Company, the Dronfield Silkstone Coal and Coke Company and the Pilsley Colliery Company.[4] The Sheepbridge Company prosecuted 100 of the coal getters at the Norwood Colliery for breach of contract. William Fowler, one of the principal partners in the Company, sat on the Bench at the Eckington petty sessions 'but took no part in the proceedings'. W. J. Clegg, of Sheffield, who was to become the legal adviser to the Derbyshire Miners' Association,[5] appeared on behalf of the majority of the men. Only one miner was proceeded against, the magistrates assessing the damages at £3. The other cases were adjourned for a month to give the men an opportunity of returning to their work if they chose.[6]

The Butterley Company was faced with a strike of about 3,000 colliers at Ripley, Selston, Loscoe and other places which lasted for four days. All these men were non-unionists and for a long time had been receiving much lower wages than those paid in South Yorkshire. Late in 1871 they had obtained an advance of 2d. a ton, which was speedily followed by another successful agitation for a further 2d. a ton. In January, 1872, the men, who had been getting 125 lb. to the hundredweight, demanded 112 lb. The Company agreed to this but sought to reduce the recently gained 4d. advance to 2d. The dispute was eventually settled by the men agreeing to a reduction of 1d. a ton.[7]

[1] *Derbyshire Times*, 9 December, 1871.   [2] *Ibid.* 13 January, 1872.
[3] *Ibid.*   [4] *Ibid.* 13, 17 and 20 January, 1872.
[5] See Chapter VI.   [6] *Derbyshire Times*, 20 January, 1872.
[7] *Ibid.* 27 January, 1872; *Ilkeston Pioneer*, 1 February, 1872.

II

By this time the South Yorkshire Miners' Association was again becoming interested in events in Derbyshire. In February it was reported to the Executive that two new lodges which had been formed in the neighbourhood of Unstone wished to join the Association and that the miners of Killamarsh were also anxious to join the South Yorkshire district.[1] Normansell attended meetings of the Unstone and Killamarsh men on 4 and 5 March and on 11 March the men employed at the Rosa and Unstone collieries were formally admitted to the Association by the Council as members of the Rosa, New Whittington and Unstone lodges.[2] By 25 March the Killamarsh miners had found a sufficient number of men to pay the entrance fee and the Killamarsh lodge was established with G. Wardley as secretary.[3] In the following month the Swallow Nest lodge was formed and the Association's fortnightly balance sheet for 8 April, 1872, gives the following particulars of membership and contributions:[4]

	£	s.	d.
Rosa, 32 members	1	8	1
New Whittington, 25 members	2	1	$7\frac{1}{2}$
Unstone, 20 members	2	17	9
Killamarsh, 77 members	—		
Swallow Nest, 29 members	13	10	$3\frac{1}{2}$

This revival of trade union activity was noticed by the *Derbyshire Times* which reminded its readers of the events at Staveley six years previously and remarked: 'There is no doubt but what the men have taken advantage of the prosperous state of trade, but it is by no means plain that the coal-owners will quietly acquiesce in the matter.'[5] However, in a period of rapidly increasing demand and rising prices, the employers were not inclined to oppose the growth of the union. By 21 October, 1872, there were 17 lodges in Derbyshire with 1,311 members. In the following January there were 21 lodges with 2,134 members and by 30 November, 1874, there were 38 lodges and membership had reached the peak figure of 7,018.[6]

Meanwhile, attempts were also being made to revive the idea of an independent association. On 12 August, 1872, a demonstration of miners was held at Clay Cross in support of the eight hours' system, and also for the purpose of forming a union, to be called the Derbyshire

---

[1] *S.Y.M.A.* 26 February, 1872.   [2] *Ibid.* 11 March, 1872.
[3] *Ibid.* 25 March, 1872.   [4] *Ibid.* 8 April, 1872.
[5] *Derbyshire Times*, 23 March, 1872.   [6] See Appendix I to this chapter.

and Nottinghamshire Miners' Association. Thomas Shore, check-weighman at No. 1 pit, Clay Cross, presided and addresses were delivered by a number of representatives from the Butterley, Morton, Devonshire Silkstone, Grassmoor, Lings and Clay Cross collieries.[1] The chairman advised those present to join the proposed union 'as a means of reducing their working hours to the number already adopted in the adjoining county [i.e. Yorkshire], and also as a safeguard against poverty and dependence in time of sickness'. George Utteridge complained that the miners were not receiving a fair proportion of the recent increase in the price of coal. The coalmasters, he said, were receiving greatly increased profits, whilst the increase in the colliers' wages had been comparatively small.

The inspirers of this movement, the miners of Clay Cross, were later to join the South Yorkshire Association but from the original lodges of Clay Cross, Ripley and Selston the Derbyshire and Nottinghamshire Association spread southwards until, in 1873, it covered an area extending from Hasland to Ilkeston and from Kilburn to Pinxton. It then had 22 lodges, a total membership of 3,000 and a reserve fund of £1,500.[2] A year later the membership had reached a peak of 5,000 and there were 44 lodges.[3] William Peach, of Selston, was the general secretary of the Association and other active leaders were George Brown, of Heage; John and Thomas Purdy, of Ripley; Thomas Wheeldon, of Codnor; Edward Potter, of Ilkeston; and John Statham, of Ripley.

Both organizations were members of Macdonald's federation and there was little rivalry between them. Their spheres of influence were largely determined by geographical considerations, the South Yorkshire Association operating in the north-eastern part of the county and the Derbyshire and Nottinghamshire Association mainly in the south. Only at Clay Cross does there appear to have been any serious discussion of the relative merits of the two associations. In September, 1872, at a meeting for the furtherance of the Derbyshire and Nottinghamshire

[1] *Derbyshire Times*, 17 August, 1872. Among the speakers were George Utteridge, Clay Cross; Joseph Straight, Devonshire Silkstone Colliery; William Allen, Tapton Colliery; Thomas Wheeldon, Butterley Colliery; Samuel Hancock, Morton Colliery; Joseph Hawley, Morton Colliery; Samuel Smith, Clay Cross; John Statham, Butterley Colliery; George Radford, Clay Cross; Thomas Hopkinson, Staveley.

[2] *Ilkeston Pioneer*, 4 September, 1873; *Derbyshire Times*, 6 September, 22 October, 1873. The lodges were Somercotes, Ripley, Green Hillock, Heage, Codnor, Selston, Greenhill Lane, Swanwick, Normanton, Stonyford, Grassmoor, Lea Brooks, Alfreton, Birchwood, Hasland, Pinxton, Pinxton Wharf, Calow, Westwood, Ilkeston, Shipley and Cotmanhay.

[3] *Derbyshire Times*, 19 August, 1874. The new lodges were Bagthorpe, Normanton No. 2, Loscoe, Marlpool, Heanor, Langley Mill, Ilkeston Nos. 2 and 3, Kilburn, Somercotes Nos. 2 and 3 in Derbyshire and Kimberley, Kirkby, Annesley Nos. 1, 2 and 3, Hucknall Torkard, Old Brinsley, Clifton, Underwood, Old Radford and Bulwell in Nottinghamshire.

E

Association, Samuel Hancock, of Morton Colliery, denounced it as being 'rotten at the core' and argued that it 'would never develop itself for the masters could take it off at any time if they were so minded'. Another speaker, Rodgers, also described the Derbyshire and Nottinghamshire Association as 'a rotten one' and stated that 'in joining the South Yorkshire they would be doing the best for themselves'. One of the chief objections to the South Yorkshire Association was its refusal to admit men over 55 years of age because of its superannuation scheme.[1] In June, 1873, the Secretaries of the South Yorkshire Association were instructed 'to make every enquiry into the so-called Derbyshire and Nottinghamshire Miners' Association' and to present a report to the next Council meeting but no further action was taken.[2] It has been impossible to trace any official records of the Derbyshire and Nottinghamshire Association which went out of existence by the end of the decade but there is little doubt that it modelled itself, both in organization and in policy, on the older and more firmly established South Yorkshire Association.

III

The fortunes of both unions were intimately linked with the changing conditions in the coal trade during the 'seventies and fluctuations both in wages and in membership followed closely movements in the price of coal. It is difficult to generalize about miners' wages in this period, even in a fairly restricted area. The two unions were negotiating with employers in three counties: Yorkshire, Derbyshire and Nottinghamshire. Price lists, hours of work, deductions, methods of weighing, house rents, allowances of coal, free medical attention and various other concessions were all factors which entered into local wage negotiations and varied considerably from colliery to colliery. Moreover, when the unions resolved to demand an increase or resist a reduction in wages it was not always possible to achieve the same result at every colliery. The decisions which were taken at Barnsley by the Council of the South Yorkshire Association on increases to be demanded and reductions to be accepted can be taken as the norm which was enforced with varying degrees of success in the union's remote outposts in Derbyshire. The Derbyshire and Nottinghamshire Association appears to have kept its wages policy in step with that of the South Yorkshire Association although there were probably more local variations.

[1] *Derbyshire Times*, 21 September, 1872.   [2] *S.Y.M.A.* 16 June, 1873.

In the spring of 1868 wages in South Yorkshire stood at the rate at which they had been fixed in 1865, when the employers conceded a 5 per cent. increase with weekly payments. In April, 1868, when trade was falling off, the men submitted to a reduction of 5 per cent.[1] Over three years elapsed before the wages question was raised again in a general form, although disputes were rife at several collieries and particularly violent at Thorncliffe in January, 1870, when thirty houses were sacked by rioting colliers and several persons were seriously injured in a conflict with armed police.[2] The price of coal began to rise sharply in 1871 and in September of that year the employers conceded the 5 per cent. taken off in 1868 and advanced the price of coal on 1 October. Thus 1871 came to be regarded as the base year for all further wage negotiations during the 'seventies. The success of the South Yorkshire miners and the example set by the engineers in securing the nine-hour day no doubt encouraged the Derbyshire miners, particularly those employed by firms with large numbers of engineers and foundry workers, to demand the concessions which they did in the latter half of 1871.[3]

In 1872 the flood tide of advances set in, and in seeking their share of them the miners of Derbyshire began to join one or other of the unions. By August of that year the Clay Cross Company's men at the Clay Cross, North Wingfield, Pilsley and Morton collieries had been granted three advances amounting to about 10 per cent. each on wages paid before 4 October, 1871.[4] The men also demanded checkweighmen, 21 cwt. to the ton and no deductions. The Company agreed to these changes and also to the men forming their own accident, sick and funeral fund in conjunction with the South Yorkshire Association. Similar agreements were reached at Brampton, Whittington, Barlow, Dunston, Nesfield, Hasland, Boythorpe, Wingfield, Lings, Grassmoor, Williamthorpe, Parkhouse, Holmewood, Harstoft, Holmewood Top, and Shirland collieries. At the New Staveley, Old Staveley, Dronfield Silkstone, Sheepbridge and other collieries the only outstanding question was that of 'long weight' which was to remain in force until the Mines Regulation Act became fully operative on 1 January, 1873.[5] The Tibshelf and New Birchwood collieries, and the Babbington, Cinder Hill and Bulwell collieries in Nottinghamshire provided cottages, gardens, pig styes, gas, water, rates, medical attention and coal (except for cartage) and a weekly payment during sickness, all for a

---

[1] *Derbyshire Times*, 1 January, 1869.   [2] *Ibid.* 29 January, 1870.

[3] See S. and B. Webb, *op. cit.* pp. 313–17.

[4] *Derbyshire Times*, 31 July, 10 August, 1872; *Ilkeston Pioneer*, 8 August, 1872.

[5] The change involved not only the use of weight instead of measure but also the substitution of the imperial ton for the long ton, hitherto in use, which varied from district to district.

weekly occupancy rent of 2s. 6d. The tonnage men worked by individual contract and were getting 25 cwt. to the ton.[1]

At other collieries relations between management and men were not so smooth. The men at the Butterley Company's collieries, in August, 1872, demanded to have their coal weighed at 21 cwt. to the ton in the presence of checkweighmen and an advance of 6d. a ton together with 15 per cent. on all day work. They had already joined the Derbyshire and Nottinghamshire Association and threatened to strike unless their demands were conceded. Similarly, the colliers at the fifteen pits of the Alfreton Iron and Coal Company abandoned their work and passed a series of resolutions demanding that all coal should be weighed at 22 cwt. to the ton in the presence of a checkweighman, that wages should be advanced 6d. a ton on stall and 15 per cent. on day and other work 'as a share in the rise in the price for coals during July and August', and that they should be allowed to organize their own sick, accident and funeral funds in accordance with the rules of their union. These demands were soon conceded and the men returned to work. There were also strikes at the South Normanton, Hill Top, Pinxton, Langton and Carnfield collieries for shorter hours, increased tonnage rates, and the right to employ checkweighmen.[2]

Towards the end of August, 1872, there were further wage demands. The Staveley colliers asked for an increase of 25 per cent. The men employed by the Dronfield Silkstone Coal Company demanded an increase of 1s. a ton and an allowance of 18 hundredweight of coal a month. Other colliery proprietors in the Dronfield district were asked to make similar concessions. A mass meeting held at Dronfield revealed that some of the employers had granted small increases without being asked and others had given part of the amount demanded but the men were still dissatisfied and agreed to form a lodge in conjunction with the South Yorkshire Association.[3]

The coming into operation of the Mines Regulation Act produced a further crop of strikes in January, 1873. A re-arrangement of working hours by Barber, Walker and Company to comply with the limitations imposed upon the labour of boys between 12 and 16 years of age led to strikes at the Moor Green and Eastwood collieries for the eight-hour day. The Company's train, which conveyed men living at Langley, Heanor and Ilkeston from Langley Mill station to the pits, was attacked by the strikers; the house of Hutton, an underviewer, was damaged and his windows were broken.[4] At Alfreton and Swanwick there was a strike of nearly 600 men and boys at Morewood's collieries which appeared to be occasioned by the new Act but which was also concerned

[1] *Derbyshire Times*, 17 August, 1872.   [2] *Ibid.*
[3] *Ibid.* 31 August, 1872.   [4] *Ibid.* 18 January, 1873.

with tonnage rates.[1] It lasted a fortnight and the local shopkeepers displayed great sympathy with the men and offered to give them unusual credit.[2]

In March of the same year there were further disputes in the Dronfield district. By that time most of the men in the locality were members of the South Yorkshire Association and were demanding the increases which had been agreed upon at Barnsley. On 21 March Normansell and Casey, the secretaries of the Association, had secured from representatives of the coal-owners a further advance of 20 per cent. upon the wages paid before 4 October, 1871.[3] Eventually, most of the employers in the Dronfield and Unstone district agreed to pay the increases.[4] There were also demands for increased wages from banksmen and enginemen.[5] In November, 1873, a large meeting of carpenters, smiths, banksmen, engineers, firemen and labourers, employed at the collieries in the Dronfield and Unstone district, was held at the Horse and Jockey Inn, Unstone, to form a branch of the South Yorkshire Coal Operatives' Association.[6]

This remarkable series of wage concessions reached its zenith in 1873 when the price of coal was also at its highest. As far as the official claims of the South Yorkshire Association were concerned, the increases amounted to $57\frac{1}{2}$ per cent. on the wages paid before 4 October, 1871.[7] In some parts of Derbyshire the advances in wages were probably rather less; in other parts considerably more. When the colliery owners in the Dronfield district were called upon to pay the last of the series of increases negotiated by the South Yorkshire Association in March, 1873, they argued that they 'were already paying for getting greatly in advance of what was required by the Committee of the Miners' Association; that they had already raised the price of getting, taking all matters into account, 100 per cent., whereas they should, according to the circular, be paying only $57\frac{1}{2}$ per cent., and that, so far from raising the price at present given they were, in point of fact, entitled to make a reduction'.[8] The *Ilkeston Pioneer* estimated in January, 1874, that miners' wages in the past year had been increased about 50 per cent. and in some instances more: 'It is evident from the scarcity of men, that machinery will have to be adopted.'[9]

The effects of high wages upon the social conditions of the colliers and the relation between wages and the price of coal have been discussed in previous chapters.[10] The policies of the two unions on these matters

[1] *Derbyshire Times*, 18 January, 1873.   [2] *Ibid.*
[3] *Ibid.* 26 March, 1873.   [4] *Ibid.* 16 and 19 April, 1873.
[5] *Ibid.* 16 April, 3 and 17 May, 1873.   [6] *Ibid.* 12 November, 1873.
[7] *Ibid.* 26 March, 1873; 11 and 15 July, 1874; 30 March, 1878; *S.Y.M.A* 15 January, 29 May, 23 September, 1872; 10 March, 1873.   [8] *Ibid.* 26 March, 1873.
[9] *Ilkeston Pioneer*, 8 January, 1874.   [10] See pp. 51-2, 60-1.

were clearly expounded by a number of speakers. The theory that high wages were responsible for the high price of coal was not accepted. J. C. Cox was of the opinion that 'the price of coal was raised before the wages. It was the result of legitimate trade.'[1] Thomas Purdy told members of the Derbyshire and Nottinghamshire Association at Ilkeston in October, 1873, that 'coal was selling at 8s. per ton in 1871 and was now sold at £1. Out of the 12s. per ton advance labour had only 2s., therefore capital had the remainder.'[2] Hedward, another of the leaders of the Derbyshire and Nottinghamshire Association blamed the agents for taking advantage of the situation when the men asked for an advance of wages and increasing the price of coal 'most unjustly'.[3] On the other hand, some of the union leaders were prepared to agree that many of the miners were squandering their enhanced earnings. According to John Purdy, one miner's wages had risen from 3s. 6d. a day to £5 a week 'and still his wife and family, as well as himself, were none the better, either in personal appearance or comfort at home'.[4] William Brown, who was now organizing the Staffordshire miners, 'was sorry to have to admit that about fifteen per cent. of the mining population of the present day drank too freely, gambled too much, and neglected their work, causing their families to suffer; but whilst they found pigeon-fliers, dog-runners and such like amongst them they would find more Sunday school teachers, more local preachers, more tract distributors, more Good Templars, and those who were trying to do good to their fellows than in any other operative class they could name'.[5]

IV

Both unions strove unceasingly to shorten the hours of work. The inaugural meeting of the Derbyshire and Nottinghamshire Association had been largely devoted to this question and the demand for a uniform eight-hour day, similar to that which prevailed in Yorkshire, was to become an inevitable feature in the policy of most of the miners' unions for the remainder of the century. It rested on the assumption that as more coal had been raised in nine hours than in ten or twelve, the sequence would continue. This the great majority of employers were not prepared to believe. In August, 1872, the colliers in the Ripley

[1] *Derbyshire Times*, 4 September, 1872.
[2] *Ibid.* 22 October, 1873. These are presumably pit-head prices.
[3] *Ilkeston Pioneer*, 9 April, 1874.   [4] *Derbyshire Times*, 16 April, 1873.
[5] *Ilkeston Pioneer*, 6 March, 1873.

district joined the Derbyshire and Nottinghamshire Association and demanded an eight-hour day but they were not successful.[1] It was argued in evidence before the Coal Commission of 1873 that the Mines Regulation Act, by limiting the hours of labour of boys between twelve and sixteen years of age, in practice shortened the working day for adults as well. This diminished the output of coal and caused an increase in the cost of production of 1s. 4d. to 1s. 8d. a ton. Other witnesses, however, including a government inspector, estimated the increase at 8d. a ton or less. In any case, the Mines Regulation Act was exonerated because there was strong evidence to show that the shortening of the working day was more attributable to the eight hours' movement, which had begun before the passing of the Act.[2] The strikes in Derbyshire, occasioned by the new legislation, caused some concern at Barnsley. 'The entire county' was described as being 'in a perfect state of excitement' and members were 'strongly advised to be very careful in the action they may take in the matter, and wherever the short hours may be adopted to bring the change gradually and peaceably, and in such manner as will prevent injury from being inflicted on any member'. The Secretaries pointed out that at one colliery alone the shorter working day made a difference of 96 tons of coal or an average of 2 tons of coal a man. Where the fillers were paid by the day and claimed the same money as they received before the change the collieries were, in many instances, losing 4s. a day on each man.[3]

The movement for shorter hours was probably most successful in the Chesterfield district, where hours of work had always been less than in other parts of the county. A deputation of workmen, including John Catchpole, who was by now active in the South Yorkshire Association, met the managers of the collieries in the district in February, 1873, and agreed upon the following terms:

1. The lamps to be given out at 6 o'clock every morning and not before except by permission of the underviewer in urgent special cases, and no lamps to be given out to the men after 6.20 a.m.
2. All hands to be down the pit by 6.30 a.m., and coal drawing to commence at that time and to cease at 3.30 p.m. each day, except Saturday, when it shall cease at 12.30 p.m.
3. The following mealtimes to be observed, viz.:—11 to 11.30 a.m. each day, except Saturday, when it shall be from 9.30 to 9.45 a.m.

It will be seen that this was not an eight hours 'from bank to bank' such as the Yorkshire miners enjoyed, but Catchpole and his associates

---

[1] *Derbyshire Times*, 21 August, 1872.
[2] *S.C. on the Causes of the Present Dearness and Scarcity of Coal, passim.*
[3] *S.Y.M.A.* 10 January, 1873.

were sufficiently pleased with the arrangement to express their satisfaction in a resolution:

> In consideration of the managers of the district having conceded the eight hours' system unsolicited, the deputation here present pledge themselves and promise to use their influence with their fellow workmen to make the best possible use of the reduced hours, that the output may not be reduced, and that the managers may have no cause to regret the step they have taken.[1]

Soon afterwards the Dronfield employers and their workmen reached a similar agreement.[2]

The Mines Regulation Act was regarded by the South Yorkshire Association as one of the many advantages which the Derbyshire men enjoyed but for which they had never fought and they were urged to join the union as a means of enforcing the Act.[3] At some collieries the discussions between the masters and the men about the framing of the special rules caused dissension. In March, 1873, the secretaries were instructed to meet a few members of the Derbyshire lodges to assist them in examining the special rules and preparing any objections which might be considered necessary.[4] The men at Shirland threatened to strike until the rules were amended to their satisfaction.[5] The union attached particular importance to the clauses relating to the appointment of certificated managers which affected the safety of the mines. Normansell told a meeting at Wakefield:

> The legislature never intended that one man should have the management of a dozen collieries, for he could not come from Derbyshire to South Yorkshire and be said to have a deal of supervision of a mine. Several persons . . . had been put down as managers who were in fact consulting engineers, and as such acted for several collieries.[6]

On the other hand, the miners employed at Pilsley Colliery held a meeting to discuss the reason for a certificate of service being withheld from John Tomlinson who had been acting manager for T. Holdsworth for about fifteen years. 'It is as though Parliament had said to colliers: "Thus far shalt thou go and no farther" ', commented a Pilsley miner. 'Not a very pleasant thought when a collier has tried to raise himself, by perseverance and study, above the common herd, to find himself thus put down by the laws of the country.'[7] The clause which gave to the workmen the right of inspection[8] does not appear to have been acted upon at many collieries.[9]

[1] *Derbyshire Times*, 5 February, 1873.   [2] *Ibid*. 15 February, 1873.
[3] *Ibid*. 4 December, 1872; 5 February, 1873.   [4] *S.Y.M.A.* 24 March, 1873.
[5] *Ilkeston Pioneer*, 7 August, 1873; *Derbyshire Times*, 9 August, 1873.
[6] *Derbyshire Times*, 19 February, 1873.   [7] *Ibid*. 17 May, 1873; 24 May, 1873.
[8] Mines Regulation Act, 1872, Clause 50, section 30.
[9] E.g. *Derbyshire Times*, 6 December, 1873.

V

In addition to industrial activities the unions had other responsibilities. According to J. C. Cox, who was a popular speaker with members of the Derbyshire and Nottinghamshire Association, a trade union had two great functions to perform: 'First, a friendly society or benefit club; and second, combination for the purpose of forcing certain regulations for the men and the masters.'[1] Financial benefits giving security against poverty in times of sickness, death and unemployment, played a much more prominent part in trade union affairs at this time than they do today. Normansell gave full particulars of the benefits paid by the South Yorkshire Association in his evidence before the Royal Commission on Labour Laws. The sick were paid 8s. a week, widows 5s. and a shilling for each child under twelve not at work, and superannuation varied from 5s. to 9s. a week according to the length of membership. Strike payment was the same as for the sick, with extra for children. Grants were made from the funds for funeral expenses and for the permanently disabled. Such benefits required high contributions. Each member paid 10s. entrance fee, a shilling a week, and married men an extra shilling a quarter.[2] 'The principles of union', said Catchpole, 'will certainly give workmen a position they cannot otherwise occupy; and thus provide for times of distress and bereavement to which no class are more liable.'[3]

The social position of the miner could also be improved by political action and during the 'seventies both unions were becoming increasingly conscious of the part their members might play in the affairs of the nation. The extension of the franchise was the obvious starting point. J. C. Cox, who had become interested in this question as a result of his connection with the agricultural workers, gave a number of lectures to lodges of the Derbyshire and Nottinghamshire Association. To a meeting at Ripley, which he was unable to attend, he wrote:

I trust that you will not forget to add your voice to that of the working classes of the north and of the agricultural workers in the demand for manhood suffrage which is the ultimate and only just solution of the question of representation. By the leave of an extended suffrage we should soon sweep away such gross instances of class legislation as the Criminal Law Amendment Act, and should be able, by restoring the people to the soil, to avoid the sad necessity of driving the finest of our labourers out of the country to seek a subsistence in America and our colonies.[4]

[1] *Derbyshire Times*, 4 September, 1872.
[2] *R.C. on the Master and Servant Act, 1867, and the Criminal Law Amendment Act, 1871*, First Report, (1874), Evidence of Normansell, p. 76.
[3] *Derbyshire Times*, 20 February, 1875.   [4] *Ibid.* 6 September, 1873.

E*

The extension of the franchise appeared to be the key to the solution of these problems but until manhood suffrage was achieved the miners had to content themselves with passing resolutions[1] and giving help and encouragement to others who were less fortunate than themselves. Joseph Arch, and Banks and Bradbury, leaders of the Lincolnshire and Neighbouring Counties Labour League, spoke frequently at lodge meetings and demonstrations of the Derbyshire and Nottinghamshire Association, sometimes appealing for funds, and in 1874 a number of locked-out agricultural workers joined in the miners' demonstration at Ilkeston, proudly bearing their banners.[2]

Other popular figures with the Derbyshire miners during the 'seventies were their national leaders, Burt and Macdonald, together with such men as Lloyd Jones, Samuel Plimsoll and A. J. Mundella. Lloyd Jones, the one-time Owenite, had by this time been elected to the Co-operative Central Board, which developed into the Co-operative Union, the co-ordinating body for propaganda and education.[3] In 1874, at the annual demonstration of the Derbyshire and Nottinghamshire Association at Ilkeston, he criticized the 'Wages Fund' theory and secured the adoption of a resolution:

That in the opinion of this meeting, the full emancipation of labour, and the protection of wealth, can best be secured by adopting principles of co-operation; and this meeting would urge upon members of the association the advisability of having collieries of their own in order to secure the capitalist labourer in the channels of industry.[4]

Plimsoll, the brewer's clerk turned wealthy coal merchant by marriage, was a close friend of John Normansell, despite the lengthy and violent dispute at Thorncliffe between his father-in-law, John Chambers, and the South Yorkshire Miners' Association.[5] His unceasing efforts to improve the lot of the merchant seamen captured the imagination of the South Yorkshire miners and when, in 1873, he faced a costly libel action arising out of the publication of his book, *Our Seamen*, they voted £1,000 towards his defence fund.[6] From his speech at the South Yorkshire Association's demonstration at Chesterfield in 1873 the *Derbyshire Times* drew the conclusion:

And perhaps also the beautiful words of Madame de Staël quoted by Mr. Plimsoll that 'to understand is to forgive' may not be without their force here.

---

[1] *Derbyshire Times*, 16 August, 6 September, 1873; 9 August, 1874; 21 August, 1875; *Ilkeston Pioneer*, 4 September, 1873.   [2] *Ibid.* 19 August, 1874.
[3] G. D. H. Cole and Raymond Postgate, *The Common People*, (London), edn. of 1949, p. 383.   [4] *Derbyshire Times*, 19 August, 1874.
[5] D. Masters, *The Plimsoll Mark*, (London), 1955, p. 66. About 800 colliers were locked out at the Newton Chambers pits from 24 March, 1869, to 17 August, 1870, because they demanded weekly payment and 20 cwt. to the ton. The dispute cost the Association £17,000 in strike payments.   [6] *Derbyshire Times*, 26 April, 1874.

So long as unions do not mean strikes, or intimidations, or bitter antagonism between capital and labour, the public are not likely to complain if the collier does get a good day's wage for a shorter day's work.[1]

VI

Mundella, the Nottingham hosiery manufacturer, was perhaps more closely connected with the South Yorkshire Miners' Association than any of the others, particularly after his election as Member of Parliament for Sheffield in 1868. He was one of the pioneers of industrial arbitration and in evidence before the Royal Commission on Trade Unions described how he had introduced the system among the Nottingham hosiery workers.[2] The idea was inspired by the *Conseils des prud'hommes* in France and Belgium but Mundella was always careful to distinguish between the continental system and his own:

Some stupid people keep writing about the *Conseils des prud'hommes*, and identifying them with Courts of Arbitration. There is no resemblance between the two. The former are merely third parties constituted a Court to settle disputes that have arisen out of past transactions. The latter consist of the parties themselves not merely settling past questions but arranging the rates of labour and all questions arising therefrom for the *future*. They are *preventive*. *Conseils des prud'hommes* do not prevent strikes or violence, and France has to go through the same experience as ourselves.[3]

Elsewhere he wrote of the *Conseils des prud'hommes*: 'They are of no practical advantage in any country where the right of combination exists, and the best proof is what is transpiring in Belgium at this moment'.[4] Mundella's indefatigable efforts to promote a system of industrial arbitration which fully recognized the existence of trade unions won the support of many union leaders at a time when the whole trade union movement was being carefully scrutinized by a Royal Commission. The rival schemes of Lord St. Leonards, Judge Kettle and others were all examined by the Commission, which eventually recommended the adoption of Mundella's plan.[5]

Meanwhile Mundella had been addressing meetings in Sheffield, Nottingham and other places on the advantages of arbitration and in 1868 provided a striking practical illustration by his successful intervention in the bitter mining dispute in South Lancashire. John

[1] *Derbyshire Times*, 16 August, 1873.
[2] *R.C. to enquire into Trade Unions and Other Associations*, 1867–9, 10th Report, (1868), Evidence of A. J. Mundella, QQ. 19343–19347.
[3] Mundella-Leader Correspondence, 3 September, 1868.
[4] *Ibid.* 1 April, 1869. For a full account of the *Conseils des prud'hommes* see *R.C. on Trade Unions*, Eleventh & Final Report, 1869, Vol. II, Appendix, p. 149.
[5] *R.C. on Trade Unions, Final Report*, Vol. I, p. xxvii, ss. 98–100.

Normansell, with other prominent trade union leaders, became an apostle of arbitration and soon after the publication of the report of the Royal Commission on Trade Unions he received a letter from Mundella urging him to follow up the recommendations of the Commission and press for the establishment of a court of arbitration.[1] In April of that year Mundella explained to his friend Leader the reasons for his anxiety to establish the system:

> My only desire is that employers will have the sense to adopt what is good in my plan and to seize the present state of trade as a favourable opportunity of doing it; otherwise I fear, when trade revives, they will reap the bitter fruits of their present obstinacy and folly. Should trade revive next year, as there is every reason to hope, there will be terrible retribution. . . . I fear Normansell and all his societies will be involved in temporary ruin, and when prosperity returns they will not be in so tractable a frame of mind as at present.[2]

Within a few months of writing this, Mundella achieved some measure of success with Normansell, who invited him to intervene in a lock-out at the Denaby Main Colliery.[3]

Resolutions in favour of the principle of arbitration were adopted at the annual demonstrations of both the South Yorkshire and the Derbyshire and Nottinghamshire associations in 1873. Two years later Macdonald supported a similar resolution at Ripley and was able to say, elsewhere:

> Twenty-five years ago when we proposed the adoption of the principle of arbitration, we were then laughed to scorn by the employing interests. But no movement has ever spread so rapidly or taken deeper root than that which we then set on foot. Look at the glorious state of things in England and Wales. In Northumberland the men now meet with their employers around the common board. . . . In Durhamshire a Board of Arbitration and Conciliation has also been formed; and 75,000 men repose with perfect confidence on the decisions of the Board. There are 40,000 men in Yorkshire in the same position.[4]

Macdonald, whom Mundella believed to be working for the great Scottish coal-owner, Lord Elcho, and described as 'a dishonest but clever and unscrupulous miners' agent . . . this bad fellow *who is Elcho's Limited*', was evidently in full agreement with Mundella on the virtues of arbitration.[5]

[1] W. H. G. Armytage, *A. J. Mundella, 1825-1897: The Liberal Background to the Labour Movement*, (London), 1951, pp. 53, 69.
[2] Mundella-Leader Correspondence, 1 April, 1869.
[3] Armytage, *op. cit.* p. 318.
[4] *Capital and Labour*, 16 June, 1875. Quoted in S. and B. Webb, *op. cit.* p. 338.
[5] Mundella-Leader Correspondence, 18 June, 1872.

It does not appear to be necessary to resort to a Marxian interpretation of history, as Professor Armytage has implied,[1] to be critical of Mundella's influence upon the trade unions which, as will be shown later, tended to create difficulties for the officials of the South Yorkshire Association. Indeed both the Webbs and Jevons have pointed out that although the establishment, from 1869 onwards, of joint boards and joint committees marked the complete recognition of the trade unions by the great employers, this notable victory brought results which largely neutralized its advantages: 'The men gained their point at the cost of adopting the intellectual position of their opponents. When the representatives of the employers and the delegates of the men began to meet to discuss the future table of wages, we see the sturdy leaders of many Trade Union battles gradually and insensibly accepting the capitalists' axiom that wages must necessarily fluctuate according to the capitalists' profits, and even with every variation of market prices.'[2] Lloyd Jones, who had spoken in support of arbitration at Chesterfield in 1873, was quick to see its implications. In the following year he warned working men of 'the danger there is in a principle, that wages should be regulated by market prices, accepted and acted on, and therefore presumably approved of by Trade Unions. These bodies, it is to be regretted, permit it in arbitration, accept it in negotiations with their employers, and thus give the highest sanction they can to a mode of action most detrimental to the cause of labour.'[3] Jones went on to advocate the establishment of a minimum wage but this was something for which the miners had to fight many years later, after some of them had experienced the vicissitudes of the sliding scale.

J. C. Cox, speaking at Ripley in 1872, said that he believed, with Auberon Herbert, that the trade unions had saved the country from revolution.[4] There is probably little justification for this sweeping assertion but there is no doubt that the readiness with which the South Yorkshire and the Derbyshire and Nottinghamshire Associations

---

[1] Armytage, op. cit. p. 318.

[2] S. and B. Webb, op. cit. pp. 338–9; H. S. Jevons, The British Coal Trade, (London), 1915, p. 461. The Webbs comment: 'The course of prices after 1870 demonstrates how disastrously this principle would have operated for the wage-earners had it been universally adopted. Between 1870 and 1894 the Index Number compiled by the Economist, representing the average level of market prices, fell steadily from 2996 to 2082, irrespective of the goodness of trade or the amount of the employers' profits. Any exact correspondence between wages and the price of the product would exclude the wage-earners, as such, from all share in the advantages of improvements in production, cheapening of carriage, and the fall in the rate of interest, which might otherwise be turned to account in an advance in the workman's Standard of Life.' It is only when factors other than the price of the commodity are taken into account that arbitration becomes acceptable to the trade unions.

[3] The Beehive, 18 July, 1874, quoted in S. and B. Webb, op. cit. pp. 340–1.

[4] Derbyshire Times, 4 September, 1872.

accepted the principles of conciliation and arbitration was a reflection of the leaders' desire for industrial peace. New lodges in Derbyshire were only admitted to the South Yorkshire Association if they were at peace with their employers and the secretaries were of the opinion that they 'must be dealt with very cautiously, or we may have "wars and rumours of wars" before the men can all become members of this association, and having a little experience of the past opposition to unions in that district, our advice to the men is keep quiet and peaceable but yet firm, and determine to become thoroughly united and organized to a man when every grievance will gradually pass away, without either strikes or lock outs taking place'.[1] In 1873 lodges were reminded by their leaders at Barnsley 'to keep more at Peace with their Employers and Managers and among themselves than they have hitherto done'.[2] The story is told that Normansell, exasperated by the pertinacity of a checkweighman over trivial incidents, wrote to him: 'Send a deputation to the Railway Hotel, Royston, on Saturday next, at half-past one p.m. and make sure that you send the greatest fools you have at the colliery, not forgetting to include yourself.'[3]

The Association's first demonstration at Chesterfield in 1873 again shows the conciliatory attitude of the officials at Barnsley. J. Stores Smith, the Managing Director of the Sheepbridge Company, later to become active in local Liberal politics, was invited to take the chair. He explained his presence thus:

When Mr. Normansell called upon me to say that it was the desire of the Committee that I should preside on this occasion, that they particularly wished that a coalmaster should occupy the position of your president today because this great assembly was called together as much as anything to celebrate and culture a friendly relationship which happily exists between employers and employed all over the important district covered by your union, and to endeavour to perpetuate these feelings, deepen and extend them; and that masters and men might rejoice together over the good times we have latterly enjoyed—my whole heart went out to him and you, and I longed to say at once an unhesitating 'yes'.

He went on to acknowledge 'the temperate and wise counsel' that had made their demands reasonable, 'the conciliatory manner in which they had been preferred', and concluded:

But if . . . you should allow rash counsel and passionate selfishness to rise up to the top of your demands and grow blindly savage and restlessly unreasonable you will find that neither numbers, nor friends, nor enthusiasm will aid you, and the God of right and truth will be against you and in the end you will be discomfited.[4]

¹ *S.Y.M.A.* 7 October, 1872.   ² *Ibid.* 17 July, 1873.
³ *Derbyshire Times*, 6 December, 1873.   ⁴ *Ibid.* 13 August, 1873.

VII

Much of the success of both unions in recruiting members in Derbyshire can be attributed to the direct appeal which they made to the miner's love of demonstrations and social gatherings. Casey, speaking at the Chesterfield demonstration in 1873, estimated that it would cost £2,400 'but it would come back in new members, in peace between employer and employed, and in showing people what they were and what they did'.[1] Moreover, the annual demonstrations provided an important platform for the expounding of policy: an occasion for the great national figures, and local employers with Liberal sympathies, such as J. C. Cox and J. Stores Smith, to air their views along with the local union leaders. Mundella was invited to address the Chesterfield demonstration in 1873 but made the excuse that he had another meeting.[2] He confided in Leader, however, that he did not like being on the platform with Plimsoll: 'His wretched vanity and reckless talk render it painful and undesirable to be associated with him.'[3] Burt, Macdonald, Lloyd Jones, Joseph Arch and Plimsoll, unworried by such personal antipathies, were frequent attenders.

The South Yorkshire Association was the first of the miners' unions to hold an annual demonstration but by 1873 similar demonstrations were being held in every organized mining district in the country. As early as 1866, when the South Yorkshire miners were arranging their first demonstration, there was a proposal to hold it in Chesterfield.[4] A similar proposal in 1873 was criticized by the Secretaries who asked: 'How is it possible to take twenty thousand members in and out of a small place like Chesterfield in one day?' It was eventually decided to hold two demonstrations, one at Barnsley and the other at Chesterfield.[5]

The Chesterfield demonstration, which is said to have added more than 500 members to the union, was a great success.[6] The officials of the South Yorkshire Association were anxious to ensure that their new members followed the best tradition: 'As your Committee are aware that great efforts have been made by the members at every such gathering to *excel* their South Yorkshire friends in good *order* and appearance, all Lodges and members are particularly requested to carry out the

[1] *Derbyshire Times*, 13 August, 1873.
[2] Mundella-Leader Correspondence, 5 August, 5 October, 1873.
[3] *Ibid.* 20 June, 1873. Mundella believed that Plimsoll was working for Roebuck, his political rival in Sheffield.
[4] *S.Y.M.A.* 23 July, 14 August, 1866.
[5] *Ibid.* 16 and 30 June, 1873.   [6] *Ilkeston Pioneer*, 28 August, 1873.

Programme and all other instructions which will be issued.'[1] These instructions called for an almost military precision:

1. Let us see every member respectably dressed and particularly the half members.

2. Have a nice White Rosette, or a neat star, but by all means don't have a Rosette the size of a dinner plate, the same as we have seen at some of the Demonstrations of late. (Have nothing gaudy.)

3. Keep in perfect order, four abreast, while in procession.

4. Do not smoke while in procession, or when falling in on the Church Field.

5. Keep the females out of the procession, and do not allow any of the spectators to get between the bands or members while passing through the streets in procession.

6. Every lodge to go to its own billet, and leave a good name behind as before.

7. Every member to be in procession, and not on the footpath and among the general public, as we have seen some on previous occasions, *which looks bad.*[2]

As a further precaution, two members from each of the Derbyshire lodges were to attend the Barnsley demonstration so that they could more effectively assist with the arrangements at Chesterfield.[3]

Soon after 8 o'clock on Monday, 11 August, 1873, the special trains began to arrive at Chesterfield bringing the miners and their families. Many others arrived on foot. It was estimated that there were almost 30,000 visitors in the town. All the Derbyshire lodges were represented, together with many from South Yorkshire. The huge procession mustered at 12 o'clock on the new recreation ground and, with banners flying, marched to the Drill Field accompanied by some thirty brass bands.

'It presented', we are told, 'a most animate appearance, the new silken banners with their mottoes and devices looking exceedingly well. The New Whittington Lodge, headed by the Hallamshire Rifle Band, were specially commented upon for their neatness, all the members wearing white cotton gloves and beautiful silken rosettes. . . . The crowd was remarkably well dressed and the colours of the different uniforms of the bands intermixed with the banners and the showy dresses of the crowd had a motley and curious appearance. The procession was one of the most extraordinary spectacles ever witnessed in Chesterfield and such were the numbers that it occupied

[1] *S.Y.M.A.* 4 July, 1873.   [2] *Ibid.* 4 and 17 July, 1873.
[3] *Ibid.* 14 July, 1873.

over an hour to traverse the road from the new recreation ground to the Drill Field.'[1]

Three weeks later, on 1 September, the Derbyshire and Nottingham-shire Association also held its first annual demonstration at Ripley. It was not so impressive as the Chesterfield demonstration but there were eight bands and the procession was nearly a mile in length. 'The members of the lodges', it was reported, 'were decorated with different coloured rosettes.'[2] In the following year the demonstration was held at Ilkeston and new banners were bought specially for the occasion. Some of them were beautifully designed and cost as much as £32. Somercotes Lodge No. 1 rejoiced in a banner bearing the inscription 'Love thy neighbour as thyself' with a representation of the good Samaritan. A branch of the same lodge was known by a banner which showed a widow before the Board of Guardians applying for relief and saying that because her husband had joined the miners' association there was no need for her to obey 'the dictator' here when he ordered her to 'sell off her furniture'. Annesley Lodge had a banner on which was represented the miserable condition of the miner 'before the union' and the felicity he enjoyed 'after the union'.[3] At the Ripley demonstration, in 1875, the miners wore 'white cotton gloves and "flashy" waistcoats' in honour of the occasion.[4]

Behind these elaborate displays lay a considerable degree of local organization which encouraged the miners and their families to participate in the affairs of the unions. Lodges would frequently arrange teas and entertainments after which addresses would be given by local leaders.[5] At a public tea held at New Whittington in May, 1873, 300 miners, wives and sweethearts subscribed £21 10s. towards a new banner for the lodge.[6] In July, 1874, the miners of Clay Cross paraded through the streets headed by a band to 'inaugurate' their new banner, which was made in London at a cost of £60.[7] Similarly, at a public tea held at Heage by the Derbyshire and Nottinghamshire Association in the same year, £11 3s. 6d. was collected towards the cost of a banner for the lodge.[8] Sometimes, as at Codnor in February, 1874, as many as 600 people would be present at such gatherings.[9]

The annual demonstrations of 1873 and 1874 marked the height of the success of both unions. The price of coal, wages and membership

---

[1] *Derbyshire Times*, 13 August, 1873.
[2] *Ibid.* 6 September, 1873; *Ilkeston Pioneer*, 4 September, 1873.
[3] *Derbyshire Times*, 19 August, 1874.   [4] *Ibid.* 21 August, 1875.
[5] One of the earliest miscellaneous documents in the possession of the Derbyshire Area is a receipt, dated 22 October, 1886, for £1 1s. 4½d. in payment for a ham.
[6] *Derbyshire Times*, 31 May, 1873.
[7] *Ibid.* 4 July, 1874.   [8] *Ibid.* 21 March, 1874.
[9] *Ibid.* 28 February, 1874.

had all reached their maximum.[1] Thereafter the doctrines of arbitration and co-operation, which had been preached in the years of prosperity, seemed to offer little protection against falling prices and wage reductions, and the miners either abandoned their unions in disappointment, or wrecked them with internal strife.

VIII

In the boom years the miners' thoughts, no doubt influenced by the activities of Lloyd Jones, had turned to the possibility of applying the co-operative principle to coalmining and in the period of falling prices both the South Yorkshire and the Derbyshire and Nottinghamshire Associations, in common with miners' unions in other districts, embarked unwisely upon schemes of colliery ownership. 'Unfortunately', remarks Sidney Webb, eager to point out the advantages of consumers' co-operation, 'they did not then realise that the essential feature of their successful Co-operative Stores was not the combination of workmen, nor the aggregation of small savings, but the conduct of business without the lure of profit-making, for use instead of for exchange, under the control, not of associated producers, or associated capitalists, but of associated consumers.'[2] Nor could these experiments be described as true producers' co-operatives. In 1874-5 the Durham Miners' Association formed an ordinary joint-stock company to buy the Monkwood colliery, near Chesterfield. 'It was called the Co-operative Mining Company', says Webb, 'and the title seems to have been the only thing co-operative about it.'[3]

The Shirland Colliery Company, Ltd., launched by the South Yorkshire Association in 1875, with a nominal capital of £150,000, was not even co-operative in name, although it has often been cited as an example of co-operative enterprise which failed.[4] The capital required to buy the colliery amounted to £76,500. Of this, the South Yorkshire Association had, by 19 August, 1875, subscribed £31,500 of which £25,000 went to the vendor, £5,000 towards the working capital and £1,500 to a guarantee fund.[5] 'This will have the effect of exhausting their capital and preventing a strike', said the *Derbyshire Times*, 'which the Executive, in all probability, had in view in purchasing the colliery.'[6] The vendors agreed to accept the remaining £45,000 in debenture bonds, repayable every six months for a period of 21 years, on condition

---

[1] See Chart 2 and Appendix II to this chapter.
[2] S. Webb, *The Story of the Durham Miners*, (London), 1921, p. 119.
[3] *Ibid.* p. 120.
[4] E.g. Jevons, *op. cit.* pp. 459–60; *Derbyshire Times*, 31 July, 1875.
[5] *S.Y.M.A.* 19 August, 1875. [6] *Derbyshire Times*, 10 June, 1874.

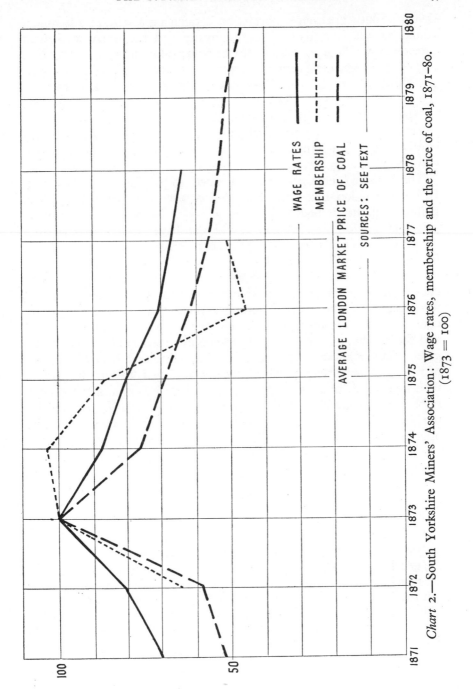

Chart 2.—South Yorkshire Miners' Association: Wage rates, membership and the price of coal, 1871–80. (1873 = 100)

that the South Yorkshire Association became a registered trade union. Mundella was chairman of the Company and the other non-union directors were Thomas Moore, of Sheffield; John Holmes, of Methley; and W. J. Clegg, the Sheffield lawyer. John Normansell, Philip Casey, D. Moulson and Samuel Broadhead, who also acted as treasurer, represented the South Yorkshire Miners' Association. At a meeting in August, 1875, the directors appointed Casey managing director and secretary of the Company at a salary of £250 for the first twelve months and set up a sub-committee to appoint 'a duly and well qualified certificated manager'.[1]

The Shirland enterprise was doomed to failure from the start. Before the union had taken the colliery over the *Derbyshire Times* pointed out that it had never been a paying concern, 'otherwise the principal vendor, Mr. Baillie, would not have been a mortgagee'.[2] There were long delays in arranging the transfer of ownership which lasted from June, 1874 until July, 1875, when a committee of five, including J. J. Barlow, of Tibshelf, was appointed to manage the colliery until the directors were able to take control. Whilst negotiations were going on, the owners were prevented from entering into any contracts, with the result that the colliery was virtually at a standstill and the miners, who were unable to support their families, had to be given 'victim allowances' by the union.[3] Added to this was the difficulty of raising sufficient capital and lodges were urged 'to take up Shares with their local funds, as well as individual members and the general public'.[4] A suggestion from the Shirland lodge that each member of the Association should pay a 5s. levy was not acted upon.[5] Despite opposition in the Council, sufficient money was somehow scraped together to complete the purchase to which the Association was already firmly committed and from which there could be no retreat without costly litigation and the forfeiture of the money already paid. But the colliery was running at a loss and early in 1876 it became apparent that further capital would have to be found. To this end, John Holmes, one of the directors, addressed a series of meetings throughout the district.[6] Members of the union were told by their officials:

The Shirland question is of vital importance to us as an association and we need have no fear as to the ultimate success of the transaction, if our members will take the matter up as they ought. FAILURE is not on the face of it, without our members intend it to be so. . . . If our members will pay a levy of 6d. per week, that will amount to over £800 per fortnight, which will make Shirland to float and to become a successful undertaking. . . . The working class could move mightily if once they have the will, because they have the

---

[1] *S.Y.M.A.* 19 August, 1875.   [2] *Derbyshire Times*, 31 July, 1875.
[3] *S.Y.M.A.* 31 December, 1874; 21 July, 1875. [4] *Ibid.* 3 May, 1875.
[5] *Ibid.* 28 July, 1875.   [6] *Ibid.* 10 February, 1876.

power in their hands, and we ought, and we must, be the first association that has ever succeeded in such an undertaking.[1]

In March, 1876, Council was confronted with a resolution from the directors 'that the South Yorkshire Miners' Association be and they are, hereby required to subscribe for 20,000 additional shares and to pay thereon 6d. per week per member until they are fully paid up, if they be desirous of keeping the present directors on the board, and making the undertaking a success'.[2]

Shirland had been intended to demonstrate that good wages and a reasonable profit were not incompatible, but it had been bought at an absurdly high price and in addition to facing a series of delays and difficulties it had to compete on the open market.[3] With the colliery running at a loss and the price of coal falling, wage reductions were inevitable and Casey, the union leader turned colliery manager, became involved in bitter disputes with the men, which eventually led to his resignation. The final blow came towards the end of 1876 when it was discovered that the colliery was likely to be flooded and the Association decided to invest no further money in it. The Company went into liquidation and the colliery was bought by Benton and Woodiwiss, railway contractors, for £11,000, the union losing the whole of its invested capital.[4] The colliery was completely flooded in the rains and gales of January, 1877, soon after it changed hands.[5]

A similar experiment on a smaller scale was carried out by the Derbyshire and Nottinghamshire Association. In 1874 the Derbyshire Co-operative Mining Society was formed at Ripley to start a colliery on the Stanley Lodge estate, near Ilkeston. The Society acquired about 104 acres of freehold land for £25,000 and began to work the coal beneath. By March, 1875, over 3,000 shares had been taken up, many by colliers. The Society did not long survive the increasing economic difficulties of the 'seventies and finally collapsed in January, 1878.[6] One of the Derbyshire miners' leaders later attributed the colliery's failure to the opposition of the landowner: 'The thing might have been different, I think, only it happened to be taken up by a body of working men called the co-operators. . . . [It] certainly went to the dogs because they were refused—it was not a question of cost—they were absolutely refused the right to pass over about two fields in order to get to the Great Northern Railway to reach the Derby market.'[7]

[1] *S.Y.M.A.* 23 March, 1876.   [2] *Ibid.* 6 March, 1876.
[3] Cf. W. W. Rostow, *British Economy of the Nineteenth Century*, (Oxford), 1948, p. 217.   [4] *Ilkeston Pioneer*, 1 March, 1877.
[5] *Derbyshire Times*, 13 January, 1877.
[6] *Ibid.* 6 March, 1875; *Ilkeston Pioneer*, 10 January, 1878.
[7] *R.C. on Mining Royalties* Second Report, 1891, Evidence of James Haslam, QQ. 8158–8161.

IX

The failure of these enterprises, the reaction against arbitration and the gradual decline of both unions are inextricably interwoven with the succession of wage reductions which started early in 1874. By this time a joint committee had been established for negotiations between the South Yorkshire Association and the colliery proprietors of South Yorkshire and North Derbyshire and it had been agreed that alterations in wages should be uniform and should take place simultaneously. There were, however, many colliery proprietors in both Derbyshire and Yorkshire who argued that it was difficult for them to act together because they were not all circumstanced alike and that it would be better for each district to adopt its own course.[1] Thus, the picture of wage reductions in this period is complicated by the fact that many employers refused to conform to the general pattern which was agreed upon by the joint committee. Mundella had confidently asserted in 1868 that he would not have much difficulty in showing Charles Markham that 'it is to the interest of respectable firms like the Staveley Company that wages should be equalized in a given district',[2] but not all the Derbyshire employers were prepared to accept this doctrine.

In March, 1874, when the employers' side of the joint committee met in Leeds and resolved to give notice of a general reduction of 25 per cent. on the wages of 1871, many colliery proprietors in Derbyshire were already attempting to reduce wages by 15 per cent. The colliers employed by the Clay Cross Company had submitted to such a reduction; the men at Tupton were on strike; and at Eckington the matter was still being discussed.[3] Early in May, delegates representing over 23,000 miners at Barnsley resolved:

That in the opinion of this meeting the time for a reduction of miners' wages has not yet arrived; but this meeting requests the Secretaries to issue a circular stating their views, and that the coal owners in the meantime be requested to allow the matter to remain in abeyance for another week.

The coal-owners, fearing that in the event of the reduction not being accepted a general lock-out would take place, acceded to the resolution on the understanding that the matter should not be adjourned for more than a week.[4] When Normansell met the coal-owners again he informed them of a further resolution:

That in the opinion of the members of this Council a reduction of coal miners' wages in South Yorkshire and North Derbyshire is inevitable:

[1] *Derbyshire Times*, 28 March, 1874.
[2] Mundella-Leader Correspondence, 4 September, 1868.
[3] *Derbyshire Times*, 21 and 28 March, 1874.   [4] *Ibid.* 16 May, 1874.

but before the amount of reduction can be agreed upon, the question be again laid before the members of every lodge connected with the Association, between now and Thursday evening next, the 21st instant, so that all delegates may be sent to the special Council meeting, on Friday 22nd instant, prepared to agree to reduction, and thereby finally settling the matter, with the understanding that whatever may be the amount agreed to, the same to commence from the 20th instant or on the first day of the 'pay' in the present week, as the case may be.[1]

The colliery proprietors had by now moderated their demands and were asking for a reduction of 12½ per cent. on the gross earnings of the men or 20 per cent. on the wages of 1871. The meeting of the Council of the South Yorkshire Miners' Association decided to recommend the men to accept a reduction of 10 per cent. on the wages of 1871. The masters then proposed a reduction of 10 per cent. on gross earnings. There was great division of opinion in the Council on this proposal. The officials read letters from Burt, Halliday and others, stating that the condition of trade in the mining districts in all parts of the country was not such as would warrant striking. A resolution accepting the employers' proposal was defeated and the Council adhered to its original decision to submit to a reduction of 10 per cent. on the wages of 1871.[2] The coal-owners then decided to give notice throughout the whole district that a reduction of 12½ per cent. would be made on the gross earnings of the colliers.

The cleavage within the ranks of the South Yorkshire Association became more pronounced. Whilst many of the South Yorkshire men were urging strike action the majority of the Derbyshire men appeared to be more willing to accept the proposed 10 per cent. reduction on gross earnings. Normansell, Catchpole and other leaders were exercising all their powers of diplomacy to preserve industrial peace and managed to secure the Council's acceptance of a resolution submitting to the 10 per cent. reduction on gross earnings which had previously been offered by the employers. On 6 July, two days before the employers' notices were due to expire, Normansell informed them of Council's latest decision to accept the 10 per cent. reduction on gross earnings provided that wages were not again interfered with for a period of three months from July 8.[3]

Whilst these negotiations were going on, the union leaders were attempting to justify their policy to the dissentients within the Association. At an open air meeting at Barnsley, Catchpole was greeted with cries of 'Go back to Derbyshire' when he urged the acceptance of the resolution submitting to a reduction of 10 per cent. on gross earnings.

[1] Derbyshire Times, 30 May, 1874.　　　　　[2] Ibid. 1 July, 1874.
[3] Ibid. 11 July, 1874.

Normansell, who said that with 24,000 miners on strike they could spend all the money they had in the course of a few days, was asked: 'Where's the money gone?' Casey's speech urging moderation and good sense caused an uproar. 'You've got our money' shouted the miners and, amid great excitement, J. Wood proposed: 'That Messrs. Normansell and Casey be suspended from their office at once and receive three months' wages instead of notice.' Catchpole, who was in the chair, ruled the motion out of order and the meeting broke up in great confusion. One of the principal objections to a percentage deduction from gross earnings was that it was difficult for the men to judge how it would affect their earnings and for the public to understand their case properly.[1]

In the face of such disunity the employers took a stronger line. They declined to abandon their demand for a $12\frac{1}{2}$ per cent. reduction on gross earnings and stated that if this was not accepted by 16 July the offer would be withdrawn and they would consider themselves 'at liberty to demand a larger reduction'. They also resolved to form a coal-owners' association 'for the purpose of securing the masters against strikes, and promoting a more harmonious feeling in the settlement of disputes between employers and employed'.[2] Within a few days Robert Baxter, of London, a large colliery proprietor, had drawn up the articles of the South Yorkshire and North Derbyshire Coal-Owners' Association which had a capital of £200,000. The Association claimed the right of full control of wages and working hours and, in return, insured colliery proprietors against losses arising out of strikes or lock-outs.[3]

At many of the Derbyshire collieries the men accepted a 10 per cent. reduction on gross earnings but at most of the large South Yorkshire pits and at Staveley, Sheepbridge and other places in Derbyshire, the employers demanded a $12\frac{1}{2}$ per cent. reduction or even more.[4] Eventually the Executive agreed with the employers to accept an immediate reduction of 10 per cent. on the gross earnings and to submit the remaining $2\frac{1}{2}$ per cent. to arbitration. Two thousand colliers assembled in a field near the Crown Inn, Staveley, to hear an explanation of their position by Normansell and Macdonald. Amidst cries of 'It's a shame' and 'Where the devil has the money gone?' Normansell advised the men to accept arbitration and in reply to those who opposed it and urged the sale of the Shirland colliery he argued that if the union sold all its property there would only be about three weeks' strike pay for them. 'If the workman got a fair share of the advance when trade was good', said Macdonald, 'he was bound to submit to reduction when

[1] *Derbyshire Times*, 11 July, 1874.   [2] *Ibid.* 15 July, 1874.
[3] *Ibid.* 18 July, 1874. See Appendix III to this chapter.
[4] *Ibid.* 18 July, 1874.

prices came down.' He asked them 'to look at the trade of the country, to look at their homes and families, and say "These we will protect, our funds we will save; on the advice of our friends we will wait patiently for better times" '. But the men were far from being convinced and regarded their leaders with a considerable amount of suspicion. Enoch Boden, of the Cottam Colliery, paid tribute to the work which Normansell had done in the past but considered that 'in this instance he had gone a little too far. When he saw from the newspapers that the executive committee had arranged with the masters to accept arbitration on the $2\frac{1}{2}$ per cent., he considered that was taking the men by the throat. They were the most deceitful, dishonest, and "Judas-like" men that walked about the two counties.'[1]

The Yorkshire miners were equally hostile. The majority of them repudiated the terms agreed upon between their Executive and the colliery proprietors and felt that the money which was locked up in the Shirland Colliery should have been available for supporting a strike. The Executive, on the other hand, maintained that the men were not entitled to receive strike payments because they had refused to resume work on the terms which had been agreed with the employers. At an open-air meeting at Barnsley one of the Yorkshire colliers condemned the behaviour of their secretaries 'who had treated those who paid them with marked disrespect' and another demanded 'that every book and document belonging to the Secretaries and the Treasurer should be examined since the beginning of 1871 by a qualified person' on the ground that there had never been any audit except by their own officials. 'What with frequent meetings, for attending which each delegate received 11s. and his railway fare, as well as other lavish expenditure in various ways,' said E. Jones, of Monk Bretton lodge, 'their money had been sent to the four winds of heaven.' Samuel Woffenden, of Elsecar, considered that the men had been abandoned by their two leaders whom they had made into gentlemen and 'raised from clogs to carriages'. A vote of censure on the Secretaries and the Executive was carried and those present were urged to attend their lodge meetings and send delegates to Council upon whom they could depend.[2]

Despite such violent opposition, the official policy of the union prevailed. Burt and Macdonald were chosen as arbitrators by the South Yorkshire Association and the men began to return to work.[3] The decision of the arbitrators was in favour of the employers and there was a general reduction of $12\frac{1}{2}$ per cent. on gross earnings. Normansell estimated that the dispute lost the district £80,000 in wages and cost the Association £22,000 in three weeks. He was particularly critical of the part which had been played by Woffenden and praised the North

---

[1] *Derbyshire Times*, 25 July, 1874.   [2] *Ibid.*   [3] *Ibid.* 1 August, 1874.

Derbyshire men for their moderation in comparison with some of the old established lodges in Yorkshire. But the reduction in wages and the general discontent with the conduct of the union leaders and the delegates led to a rapid fall in membership.[1] During September, Normansell and Casey were busy trying to salvage what they could from the wreckage of the Association by addressing meetings throughout the district. At Clay Cross the men, who were discontented because they had not received strike payments, were told by Normansell that 'every penny' which had been paid at Tupton and Morton was 'illegal'. He advised them to look to their local organization and attend their meetings regularly.

'There are now 150 checkweighmen connected with our Association,' said Normansell, 'some very good ones—yet when they have a good one someone else wants his place, and he agitates, calls a meeting, and gets the man removed, very often to put a worse in his place. There are checkweighmen who cannot add up their accounts, and some never have been added up for three years, but have been copied from the masters' accounts, and some of these are Good Templars, and go out on Sunday preaching. It is the same also with secretaries.'[2]

But already the Derbyshire men were beginning to think in terms of secession from the South Yorkshire Association. In September, 1874, Barlborough lodge discussed the possibility of organizing an association for North Derbyshire, each lodge controlling its own funds and contributing towards the management of the association, but eventually decided to re-join the South Yorkshire Association.[3]

X

Early in 1875 Normansell threatened to resign because, he said, 'there is no peace of mind or satisfaction given to the great bulk of the men, and when this is the case after nearly seventeen years' service, it is high time a change took place'.[4] He was, however, persuaded to continue in office. Similarly, Catchpole talked of resignation in February, but remained active as a delegate until the establishment of an independent union in Derbyshire.[5] In addition to these difficulties, wages continued to fall. In March, 1875, Normansell, Casey, Woffenden, Catchpole,

[1] *S.Y.M.A.* 18 August, 1875: 'There is a great deal said about members falling off, or in other words ceasing to contribute to the Association, which we believe to a certain extent is quite true. . . .'
[2] *Ilkeston Pioneer*, 10 September, 1874; *Derbyshire Times*, 12 September, 1874.
[3] *Derbyshire Times*, 23 September, 1874.
[4] *S.Y.M.A.* 11 January, 19 April, 1875.
[5] *Derbyshire Times*, 20 February, 1875.

Haigh and Tuke met Charles Markham, the president of the Coal-Owners' Association, and agreed to accept a reduction of 10 per cent. on the 1871 wages on condition that no further reductions should be made for four months from the second pay day in April when the 10 per cent. reduction would take effect.[1]

By the autumn the Association was in a parlous state. In October a special meeting was told by Isaac Haigh, one of the district auditors, that there had been a great falling off both in members and finances since Christmas and unless they did something 'to stir up the district' they would not be in existence in six months' time. A deficiency of £4,553 18s. 5d. had been discovered and this was attributed to the failure of lodge secretaries to fill in the pay sheets accurately during the strike of 1874. The Council had been prepared to overlook the matter but the special meeting passed a vote of no confidence in the Secretaries, Normansell and Casey. Catchpole moved a further resolution:

That this meeting deeply regrets the very rapid downward course of the Association in members and finances, and strongly urges upon all miners of the district to rally firmly round the principles of union, and pledges itself not to rest satisfied until the Association is placed upon a sounder basis than at present, and one that will be an honour to the members and all others connected with it.

Normansell defended himself by recalling that he had, years ago, wanted the Treasurer to attend at the offices two days a week and pay all claims so that the Secretaries would not need to handle money and that he had also asked for an audit in 1874. He declared that he had never had any peace since the agitation of 1874 set in.[2] Within three months he died from inflammation of the brain.[3]

When nominations were received for the secretaryship in January, 1876, they included Casey; Woffenden, of Elsecar, who had been prominent in the unofficial movement of 1874; and J. Barlow, of Tibshelf, who had been associated with the beginnings of the Shirland enterprise.[4] John Frith, of Parkgate, near Rotherham, who had been acting secretary since the death of Normansell, was elected Secretary in February, 1876.[5]

Almost immediately after his election Frith was faced with a demand by the Coal-Owners' Association for a further reduction of 15 per cent. on the gross wages.[6] Notices were issued by many of the Derbyshire colliery proprietors announcing that the reduction would take effect in March.[7] The men employed by the Clay Cross Company were among

---

[1] *Derbyshire Times*, 20 March, 1875.   [2] *Ibid.* 23 October, 1875.
[3] *Ibid.* 1 January, 1876.   [4] *Ibid.* 22 January, 1876.
[5] *S.Y.M.A.* 21 February, 1876.   [6] *Derbyshire Times*, 11 March, 1876.
[7] *Ibid.* 18 March, 1876.

the first to strike but others soon followed their example.[1] By the beginning of April most of the Derbyshire collieries were at a standstill or seriously undermanned. There were the usual conflicts between unionists and non-unionists. At the B Winning Colliery of the Blackwell Company between 200 and 300 men and women besieged the pit bank and dealt severely with some of the non-unionists. Two or three were seriously injured and the police were called in from Alfreton and surrounding places.[2] At Clay Cross the non-union men were prevailed upon to throw in their lot with the strikers who, by means of a collection, provided them with 'strike pay' amounting to 1s. 9d. for married men and 1s. for single men.[3]

On this occasion the South Yorkshire Association adopted a much firmer attitude. Membership had already fallen from about 24,000 to about 17,000 since the strike of 1874 and there was considerable dissatisfaction among those who remained within the union. A deputation met the representatives of the coal-owners and asked them to agree to a reduction of $7\frac{1}{2}$ per cent. on the 1871 wages instead of the 15 per cent. on the gross wages. The majority of the delegates to Council were in favour of this course, although many of them were opposed to accepting any reduction at all.[4] The employers were equally determined to have their 15 per cent. Frith, realizing that a conflict was likely, did his best to dispel rumours that there was no money in the union to support a strike of all its members. 'The money', he said, 'will be forthcoming at the proper time.'[5]

In asserting the unreasonableness of the employers' demands the union was very largely supported by public opinion. Even the *Derbyshire Times*, which was not notable for its sympathy with the miners' unions, remarked:

The reduction now proposed by the masters will reduce the wages of the colliers to about 8 per cent. higher than the price of 1871, and it is a serious question whether the masters are justified in proposing so large a reduction. The colliers must live, and under the present prices of food the lowering of wages to the extent of 3s. in the pound is by no means a small alteration in the income of these men. We know that it is alleged by the masters that at the present trade is so bad that they cannot conduct their business to a profit, but this plea must be taken with a grain of salt, because the price of coal has certainly not fallen to anything like the extent that it is now proposed to reduce the wages, and we should like to see some clear explanation as to the justification of the present proposal.[6]

Charles Binns was quick to point out that, until the strike, the wages at Clay Cross, with the exception of one pit, were 34 per cent. above the

[1] *Derbyshire Times*, 1 April, 1876. [2] *Ibid.* 8 April, 1876.
[3] *Ibid.* 15 April, 1876. [4] *Ibid.* 8 April, 1876.
[5] *Ibid.* 15 April, 1876. [6] *Ibid.* 1 April, 1876.

wages of 1871, and that a reduction of 15 per cent. would leave 19 per cent above 1871.[1] John Catchpole, however, accused Binns of evading the real issue:

We say that we did not follow the coal owners up to the extent the coals rose in the market, and therefore should not be asked to go down in front of them. Coals rose from 6s. 8d. to 20s. at the pit mouth per ton; colliers' wages from 20s. to 31s. 6d. in the pound, therefore a good margin was left for the owners. Colliers have, as a rule, given back 6s. of the 11s. 6d., retaining 5s. 6d. A proposed reduction would take 4s. more, leaving about 1s. 6d. Will the coal owners sell as much coal now for 21s. 6d. as they sold in 1870 for 20s.? Of course, I mean all counties taken into consideration. Colliers are now asked to perform the same amount of labour for 21s. 6d. as they did for 20s. prior to October, 1871.[2]

An East Derbyshire colliery proprietor maintained that the state of trade did not warrant a greater reduction than 10 per cent:

The masters may in this instance be able to insist on greater reductions, but if they are so foolish they are only laying up in store further trouble for themselves. The men will be almost more than human if they do not insist on a still larger share of the profits than they have hitherto had.[3]

Towards the middle of April the Executive, searching for a compromise, recommended the Council to vote for the acceptance of a reduction of 10 per cent. on the 1871 wages but this was rejected.[4] Macdonald, Burt and Crawford attended a meeting of the Council soon afterwards and strongly advised the delegates, in view of the depressed state of trade, to offer to accept the reduction of 10 per cent. This course was also urged by William Chappell, the new agent to the Association, at a meeting of miners at Worksop.[5] Early in May Chappell attended a meeting consisting of members of the committees and representatives of ten of the largest lodges in the South Yorkshire district in order to convince them of the desirability of accepting the 10 per cent. reduction. He told them that the Coal Owners' Association had shifted from its original proposal of a 15 per cent. reduction on gross earnings and that the door was now open for further negotiations.[6] After much work on the part of the officials the policy of the Executive began to gain support. The men at Clay Cross agreed to the Executive's proposal and at the Dronfield Silkstone Collieries the employers allowed the men to resume work at a reduction of 10 per cent. on the 1871 wages.[7] It was not very long before a small majority of the lodges was obtained in favour of the Executive's proposal and the coal-owners were approached at once. The coal-owners were by this time less amenable. They now proposed a

[1] *Derbyshire Times*, 8 April, 1876.   [2] *Ibid.* 15 April, 1876.
[3] *Ibid.* 22 April, 1876.   [4] *Ibid.* 15 April, 1876.
[5] *Ibid.* 6 May, 1876.   [6] *Ibid.* 10 May, 1876.   [7] *Ibid.*

12½ per cent. reduction on gross wages, which was equivalent to a reduction of 15 per cent. on the wages of 1871. Alternatively, the men could resume work at 10 per cent. reduction on gross wages provided they would allow the remaining 5 per cent. to go to arbitration.

The union deputation protested strongly against these proposals saying that they thought it rather strange that arbitration should be suggested at this stage, since their own offer of arbitration had been refused by the coal-owners at a previous interview. They further stated that they were willing to offer a 7½ per cent. reduction and to let the whole question of the reduction be decided by arbitration, the difference between the 7½ per cent. and the final award taking effect from the date of settlement. This was declined. The deputation then retired for consultation among themselves and returned to offer a 10 per cent. reduction on gross earnings, which was equivalent to a reduction of approximately 12½ per cent. on the 1871 wages. This offer was also refused, and the union representatives were reminded that the men had already returned to work at a few collieries with a reduction of 15 per cent. on gross earnings. The deputation argued that the men had resumed work on these terms pending a settlement.[1]

But the truth of the matter was that the men were gradually returning to work under whatever arrangement they could reach with their employers. At Renishaw Park, Beighton, Barlborough, Tapton and Dronfield, and at many places in South Yorkshire, terms were being made varying from 7½ to 10 per cent. reduction on gross wages.[2] By the middle of May the majority of the men were back at work, after a struggle which lasted nearly two months, at reductions on gross wages varying from 10 to 12½ per cent.[3] One of the principal reasons for their defeat was the failure of the union, despite Frith's assurances at the outset, to provide adequate strike payments. The men at Staveley received only one week's pay during the whole period of the dispute and had to return to work at the coal-owners' official reduction of 12½ per cent. on gross wages.[4]

'Mr. Cox and many of his trades union friends', wrote Charles Markham, 'believe that wages can be advanced by combination, but I am thoroughly convinced that trades unions have not the slightest permanent power to accomplish such objects beyond slightly accelerating or retarding the alterations of wages, and I am profoundly impressed with the conviction that trades unions are detrimental to the interests of society.'[5]

In the eyes of the union members, and particularly those employed at the Shirland Colliery, the dispute of 1876 was a testing time for the

[1] *Derbyshire Times*, 17 May, 1876.   [2] *Ibid.*
[3] *Ibid.* 20 May, 1876.   [4] *Ibid.* 10 May, 1876.
[5] *Ibid.* 3 June, 1876.

new co-operative venture. There had already been disagreements between Casey and the men which resulted, in February, in a deputation being sent from Barnsley to inquire into the matter.[1] In April, when the Shirland men received notices of a reduction of 15 per cent. in the same way as the men at the neighbouring collieries, they were not, we are told, 'sparing in their remarks on the managers of the "Union's own colliery" '.[2] Casey, who had been working under difficulties for a long time, resigned his position as secretary and commercial manager to the company and was succeeded by John Holmes.[3] The men complained that for nearly two years they had not worked full time and that they were not provided with copies of the balance sheets as were the other lodges. They could not understand why the colliery was running at a loss nor where the money had gone, although one speaker confidently asserted: 'It was spent on carriages and dinners at the hotel.'[4] When the men ceased work the Executive of the South Yorkshire Association strongly advised the directors of the Shirland colliery to allow the men to continue working at a $7\frac{1}{2}$ per cent. reduction on the 1871 wages and recommended that the whole question should go to arbitration.[5] Work was not resumed until June when the men returned to the colliery expecting the standard $12\frac{1}{2}$ per cent. reduction on gross earnings. To their amazement they were confronted with new price lists which entailed a reduction of about 30 per cent. for most workers. A further strike ensued and there was much bitterness. The men who decided to remain at work were escorted to and from the pit by the police, six summonses were issued for intimidation and all the strikers living in the Company's houses were ordered to leave.[6] When the dispute was over, representatives of the local lodges resolved: 'That the Shirland Colliery is not likely to pay whilst its officials offer a premium for non-unionism by employing non-unionists in preference to good and tried members of the Association.'[7] A Shirland miner complained:

The men at the colliery at present will never instil it into the minds of the Shirland people that they have a co-operative principle in them, as I think the head of the concern had his own interests more at heart than the colliery.[8]

XI

Whether Shirland would have succeeded under different management is a matter for speculation but there is no doubt that its failure and the

[1] S.Y.M.A. 24 February, 1876.
[2] Ilkeston Pioneer, 13 April, 1876; Derbyshire Times, 15 April, 1876.
[3] Derbyshire Times, 15 April, 1876.   [4] Ibid. 22 April, 1876.
[5] S.Y.M.A. 20 April, 1876.   [6] Derbyshire Times, 28 June, 1876.
[7] South Yorkshire Miners' Association, Minutes of Meeting of No. 18 Panel, 28 September, 1876.   [8] Derbyshire Times, 8 July, 1876.

larger failure of the union to prevent a general reduction of wages added to the growing discontent among the miners. Other unions were facing the same problem. Ben Pickard, the secretary of the West Yorkshire Association, had already written to all his lodges telling them 'that we are on the eve of a terrible crisis and that there is not to be a strike but that terms are to be made somehow'.[1] William Brown, who had been leading the Staffordshire miners, was criticized to such an extent that he resigned.[2] Between July and October, 1876, the membership of the South Yorkshire Association dropped from 15,696 to 9,295½.[3]

The Derbyshire men were becoming increasingly dissatisfied with the South Yorkshire Association. One of the main difficulties was the remoteness of Barnsley. Delegates from Derbyshire were not always able to attend Council meetings or were obliged to leave before the business was completed. Thus, as early as October, 1872, we find Clay Cross and Killamarsh delegates being granted permission to leave a Council meeting at 12 o'clock (noon) by request of their lodges, 'but in consequence of asking leave of absence having become of late too much practised, this Council recommend all lodges and delegates to avoid it as much as possible, and stay at the Council until the business be finished'.[4] The Derbyshire men also felt that they were inadequately represented at Barnsley and in June, 1873, the Secretaries had been instructed 'to arrange the Association into "panels", in order to enable the Council to appoint the District Committee from various localities, so as to give a more equal representation than has hitherto been the case'.[5] In March, 1876, there were proposals from Morton and several other Derbyshire lodges that the union should be re-named the 'South Yorkshire and North Derbyshire Miners' Association' and this was eventually accepted.[6]

After the wage reduction of 1876 there was much criticism of the union leaders but it was agreed by the Council that their action in settling this dispute was, 'when we take all things into consideration, the best thing that could be done in the circumstances, inasmuch as a considerable portion of the members were working at 12½ per cent. reduction and there seemed no possible chance of effecting a settlement on any better terms . . .'. It was also resolved that 'the question of separating South Yorkshire from North Derbyshire be swept from the board and that all parties endeavour to work together in the future on the best possible terms for the mutual benefit of all concerned'.[7] There

[1] *Derbyshire Times*, 21 June, 1876.   [2] *Ibid.* 24 June, 1876.
[3] *S.Y.M.A.* 10 July, 30 October, 1876. Boys were counted as half members.
[4] *S.Y.M.A.* 21 October, 1872.   [5] *Ibid.* 16 June, 1873.
[6] *Ibid.* 1 March, 1876.   [7] *Ibid.* 12 June, 1876.

was, at the same time, a further re-arrangement of the union's structure. The old District Committee was superseded by a Central Board which, instead of being elected by the Council, was elected directly by the lodges, divided into nineteen panels. 'The appointment of a Central Board', members were told, 'is to economise, and also to work more effectively the varied machinery connected with this Association, and at the same time to give a more equal representation to the various lodges comprising the district.'[1]

But the Derbyshire men were by now losing interest in the subtleties of the union's machinery of government. They were greatly dissatisfied with the deficiencies in the funds of the South Yorkshire Association and the absence of adequate strike pay and on 20 June, 1876, a meeting was held in Chesterfield to consider the desirability of establishing a separate union. The meeting was attended by delegates from 21 Derbyshire lodges, representing about 2,500 men. Nine of the lodges, numbering 1,241 members, voted for a separate union; 7 others, numbering 802 members, were in favour of trying the new constitution, and keeping all the money in the lodge funds, except the levy for the working expenses of the union; 3 lodges, numbering 163 members, were neutral; and 2, with 268 members, were in favour of remaining in the South Yorkshire Association.[2] The question was referred back to the lodges for further consideration and on 30 November rules for the new association were formally adopted. It was decided to make a vigorous canvass among the miners who had formerly belonged to the South Yorkshire and North Derbyshire Association and the first delegate meeting was held on 7 December at the Freemason's Arms, Newbold Road, Chesterfield.[3]

The decline in membership created further problems for the South Yorkshire Association. When the union had 16,000 members, a quarter of its income had been sufficient to meet the requirements of the widows and children, superannuated and permanently disabled members but by the end of 1876 a much larger proportion of the union's total income was required for these purposes, leaving a smaller amount for industrial activities.[4] Thus, when the employers demanded a reduction of wages amounting to $6\frac{1}{2}$ per cent. in February, 1877, the union was obliged to acquiesce.[5] In the following month the existing benefit schemes were wound up and some £3,000, which was all that was available, was distributed among the widows. An attempt was made to establish new benefit schemes on a sounder financial basis. Actuaries were consulted and proper trustees were appointed to ensure that money belonging to

---

[1] *S.Y.M.A.* 15 June, 1876. [2] *Derbyshire Times,* 24 June, 1876.
[3] *Ibid.* 2 December, 1876. [4] *S.Y.M.A.* 11 December, 1876.
[5] *Ibid.* 19 February, 1877; *Derbyshire Times,* 17 and 24 February, 1877.

F

the benefit funds was not used for other purposes. Members were left free to decide whether they would subscribe to these funds or not and, in order to encourage new members, the entrance fee for the association was suspended for a period of three months.[1] The newly formed East Derbyshire Association met under the presidency of John Catchpole to consider these developments and decided unanimously not to re-join the South Yorkshire Association but to hold meetings throughout the district to develop its own organization.[2]

In August, 1877, came yet another demand for a reduction in wages.[3] The Council of the South Yorkshire Association resolved unanimously not to concede the demand nor to accept the masters' offer of arbitration.[4] Negotiations dragged on until the following March, by which time Chappell had persuaded members of the union that, in their present situation, a reduction of 5 per cent. was inevitable.[5] He eventually concluded an agreement with the employers: 'That the reduction of 5 per cent. as proposed by the deputation from the men be accepted, but that it is not to be considered a final reduction. . . .'[6] By this time the men had forfeited the whole of the $57\frac{1}{2}$ per cent. which they had gained between 1871 and 1874 and their wages were back to the 1868 level.[7]

This further reduction in wages aggravated the difficulties of the South Yorkshire Association. On 27 May, the Council received representatives from Derbyshire who suggested that it would be for the benefit of their district if they could secure agreement on separation and receive a portion of the Widows' Fund according to the number of members paying into it. The Derbyshire men said that they had 'laboured hard to keep the spark of union burning, but in vain, but if they had a self-acting district of their own, with their headquarters at Chesterfield, then they might regenerate the dead bonds of unionism in their locality, but still retain the tie of friendship which ought to exist between the two districts'. The leaders of the South Yorkshire Association pointed out: 'They think as we are now going on we are no better than if we had no union at all, but they are willing to hear any suggestion from this district and will hope that we shall give the question our earnest consideration, as they are now convinced that it will be the best and only means of establishing a state of unionism in Derbyshire.'[8] But the financial situation of the South Yorkshire Association was such that there was little prospect of any money being handed over to Derbyshire. Many of the Derbyshire lodges were ceasing to send contributions to Barnsley and in July, 1878, the Central Board

[1] *Derbyshire Times*, 10 March, 1877.
[2] *Ilkeston Pioneer*, 5 April, 1877; *Derbyshire Times*, 4 April, 1877.
[3] *Derbyshire Times*, 25 August, 1877.   [4] *Ibid.* 5 September, 1877.
[5] *Ibid.* 2 March, 1878.   [6] *Ibid.* 30 March, 1878.
[7] *Ibid.*   [8] *S.Y.M.A.* 27 March, 1878.

had to consider whether to sell or mortgage the offices.[1] It was eventually decided to ask Clegg, the union's legal adviser, to lend £2,000 and accept the deeds of the Association as a security.[2]

In December, 1878, the coal-owners proposed a further reduction in wages. They argued that the men were earning more than workers in other trades and one representative stated that if the reduction were conceded the miners would still be better paid than agricultural labourers. The employers wished to show that the men were making 6s. to 7s. 6d. a day, but this was strenuously denied by the union representatives who pointed out that some of the masters averaged the wages upon the gross returns, without allowing for deductions of any kind. They further stated that there were hundreds of men who were not earning more than 12s. to 16s. a week and that, far from conceding a reduction, the men considered they were entitled to a 12½ per cent. advance in view of the improvement in the trade and the increase in the price of coal.[3]

The union made determined efforts to resist the proposed reduction. In collaboration with the West Yorkshire Association it was agreed that the unions should be thrown open for all miners to join free of charge 'so that we may be unanimous in opposing the inexcusable demand now being made by the coal-owners of this district'.[4] Members of the union were advised to reject arbitration unless the owners were willing to submit their accounts to inspection by a qualified accountant[5] and the men agreed to this by a large majority.[6] Chappell and Frith then went to Sheffield to seek the advice of Mundella and eventually the union proposed that a comparison should be made between the prices of coal and wages between 1868 and 1879. The arbitrator was Thomas Ellison, Judge of the Sheffield County Court, who reported: 'It appears to me that the wages now received by the miners are barely sufficient to afford a decent maintenance of themselves and families.' He awarded that there should be no reduction in wages: 'Provided always that this award is not intended, and shall not be construed, to restrict or in any way interfere with the right of the owners to close at their discretion all or any of the collieries within the said area.'[7] The arbitrator had indicated to the employers an escape route which they were not slow to follow. George Lees and John Caroline, the Association's auditors, reported: 'Our Employers are finding all sorts of pretexts to break through the late Arbitration Award—such as setting down part or whole of their collieries to compel men to accept work on their terms. They

[1] S.Y.M.A. 22 July, 1878.   [2] Ibid. 30 September, 1878.
[3] Derbyshire Times, 1 January, 1879.   [4] S.Y.M.A. 6 January, 1879.
[5] Ibid. 15 January, 1879.   [6] Ibid. 27 January, 1879.
[7] Ibid. 26 May, 1879. Cf. S. and B. Webb, Industrial Democracy, (London), edn. of 1911, p. 229, for an appraisal of this decision.

treat Arbitration with contempt, and what more they will do, if not checked in their course, is far more easy to imagine than describe.'[1]

After this failure the South Yorkshire Association continued to lose its Derbyshire members. By December, 1879, there were only 250 members in the county.[2] Meanwhile the Derbyshire men, under the leadership of James Jones, were advocating a 10 per cent. advance in wages. Chappell was frequently present at their meetings to advocate caution. 'Why', he asked at Stonebroom, 'should they go in for a 10 per cent. advance when the state of trade would not justify it? . . . If they went in for 10 per cent. increase it would mean 3s. per ton increase to the manufacturers, but it would only be 1s. increase to the householders, and it would be generally detrimental to the interests of the coal trade.'[3] However, during June and July, 1879, there were strikes against reductions in wages at Lings, Boythorpe and Staveley. At Eckington some 400 men and boys were locked out for nine weeks until Chappell succeeded in bringing the dispute to an end. At Clay Cross, in September, the men decided to accept a reduction of 5 per cent.[4]

Somewhat belatedly the South Yorkshire Association decided, on 29 September, to ask for an advance of 10 per cent. 'with a view to putting a stop to the unjust demands of the employers',[5] but by this time the union was well on the way to disintegration. For some time there had been friction between Chappell and his colleagues over the question of the restriction of output. In September Macdonald had sent out a letter urging the necessity of this policy. Both Frith and Pickard, of West Yorkshire, were in agreement with it but Chappell was opposed to it. In December, 1879, came the final catastrophe. A resolution was adopted dispensing with Chappell's services and some of the wealthiest lodges seceded from the union in his support.[6] Another group seceded under the leadership of Casey, whose services had ceased to be recognized by the Central Board in September, 1878.[7] This split in the South Yorkshire Association marks the end of a period in the history of mining trade unionism in Derbyshire. Thereafter the two counties went their separate ways and from 1880 the Derbyshire men redoubled their efforts to build up a strong and independent organization.

The Derbyshire and Nottinghamshire Association suffered the same

---

[1] South Yorkshire Miners' Association, *Auditors' Report and Balance Sheet for the Quarter ending 23 December, 1878 and the four months ending 16 April, 1879.*

[2] *S.Y.M.A.* 22 December, 1879. These members were formed into nine lodges —Swallow Nest, North Staveley, Beighton, Killamarsh, New Whittington, Morton, Clay Cross, Parkhouse and Renishaw Park.

[3] *Derbyshire Times*, 14 June, 1879.   [4] *Ibid.* 13 September, 1879.

[5] *S.Y.M.A.* 29 September, 1879.

[6] *Ibid.* 9 September, 1879; *Derbyshire Times*, 27 December, 1879.

[7] *S.Y.M.A.* 2 September, 1878.

fate as the South Yorkshire Association when the price of coal began to fall. In March, 1874, the Butterley Company began to alter the price lists without notice and introduced at the Britain pit a new screen of much wider gauge which, the men claimed, robbed them of one hundredweight in the ton. The great strike of miners in Staffordshire and Worcestershire brought these grievances to a head. On 3 April the men at Ripley, Selston, Loscoe, Heanor, Langley Mill and other places refused to load trucks from Cannock Chase. The union secretary wrote to Sir John Alleyne, the general manager of the Company, who declined to negotiate through the conciliation board which, the men argued, had been set up at his request. The union arranged a public meeting in Codnor market place which was addressed by one of the colliery managers. After some discussion it was decided to break up the conciliation board, resume work and leave all disputes in the hands of the union council for settlement, but when the men returned to their pits they found themselves locked out. Sir John Alleyne argued that the men had requested the setting up of the conciliation board and had violated their agreement by striking before the matter could be discussed. As a result of the strike a great deal of trade had been lost and Sir John 'did not see the justice of putting those miners who had not broken their contracts, and remained at work, on short time for the benefit of those who had struck'. The men eventually decided to resume work and the matters in dispute were submitted to arbitration.[1]

The Derbyshire and Nottinghamshire Association had to face the same series of reductions in wages as the South Yorkshire Association, although, for a time, it appears to have been more successful in resisting them. In October, 1875, the South Yorkshire Association refused to give financial assistance to the Derbyshire and Nottinghamshire Association on the ground that the latter was then resisting a 10 per cent. reduction in wages which Yorkshire had submitted to five months previously.[2] By 1878 the Derbyshire and Nottinghamshire Association was virtually extinct. At a meeting held at South Normanton in January, one of the last to be reported in the newspapers, members were told by Edward Smith, of Pinxton Wharf, that the men had not been so united as they should have been, and consequently the masters had taken advantage of them.[3]

XII

The decline of both unions left the Derbyshire miners without any organization apart from the rudimentary county association which

[1] *Derbyshire Times*, 2 May, 1874.   [2] *S.Y.M.A.* 8 October, 1875.
[3] *Ilkeston Pioneer*, 10 January, 1878.

Catchpole and Jones were attempting to form. Neverthelcss, the events of the 'seventies did not represent complete failure. Wage advances had been lost but the shorter working day, fewer hundredweights to the ton and the recognition of checkweighmen were considerable gains. Perhaps more important than any of these was the changed attitude of the employers towards trade unionism.

This may not have been apparent to the miners who lived through these years. The employers continued to use most of their traditional weapons against the unions, including vitimization, eviction and the withdrawal of concessions. In 1872, Charles Binns announced that 'if a union was established to dictate to the masters the terms of agreement between them and the men, he would at once withdraw all the assistance the Company gives to the schools, chapels, social institutes and so forth that flourish so much in Clay Cross under the paternal rule of Sir William Jackson and partners, and would cut off all the allowance coal to the men'.[1] The miners of Dronfield who met, in the same year, to discuss the possibility of joining the South Yorkshire Association were so afraid of victimization that they requested newspaper reporters not to publish the names of speakers.[2] The men on strike at Morewood's collieries in October, 1875, were given notice to leave their cottages and some of them were told that they would not be employed again under any circumstances.[3] At Clay Cross, in 1878, it was alleged that a man had been dismissed because of the part he had taken in elections for the Local Board and the Board of Guardians.[4] At Butterley, after the strike of 1874, eleven members of the Derbyshire and Nottinghamshire Miners' Association were dismissed and were unable ever again to secure employment at a colliery.[5] The process of black-listing by the employers was sometimes carried out by clipping a man's leaving certificate at the corner. One man, with such a certificate, was said to have been refused work at 128 places.[6]

Often the unions could do little more than register ineffectual protests. The miners employed by the Butterley Company sent the following petition to the management:

This humble petition of the miners in the Company's employ shows that eleven of their fellow workmen, all of them respected, are not allowed to

---

[1] *Derbyshire Times*, 28 September, 1872.
[2] *Ibid.* 31 August, 1872.   [3] *Ibid.* 2 October, 1875.
[4] *Ibid.* 27 April, 1878. See J. E. Williams, 'Paternalism in Local Government in the Nineteenth Century', *Public Administration*, XXXIII, (1955), pp. 439–46 for further instances of the influence of landowners and industrialists upon local government.
[5] *Ibid.* 19 August, 16 September, 1874; 15 September, 1875. Their names were S. Shooter, G. Brown, S. Cox, G. Taylor, T. Vickers, J. Statham, J. Seal, W. Purdy, T. Wheeldon, J. Wright, T. Purdy.   [6] *Ilkeston Pioneer*, 9 April, 1874.

resume work under the Company, through the unfortunate misunderstanding which took place some time ago; and yet these men were not the only or the chief leaders in the affair, and several of them had nothing whatever to do with the matter; and further, the great body of the men resumed work with the distinct pledge that there should be no marked men. Now this proceeding has caused much and general dissatisfaction amongst the Company's workmen, and if not satisfactorily adjusted it is likely to lead to serious complications. Your petitioners therefore pray that a full investigation of the matter may take place, and that the men may be dealt with in harmony with the golden rule, 'As ye would that men should do unto you, do ye even so to them', and your petitioners will ever pray.

Although the petition was signed by 1,100 men, no satisfactory reply was given.[1] Occasionally, as at Morewood's collieries in 1872, the men were able to secure reinstatement by further strike action.[2]

Beneath these petty irritations, however, there was a fundamental change. J. Stores Smith, the Managing Director of the Sheepbridge Company, speaking at the Chesterfield demonstration in 1873, told the miners: 'You are here—a great fact—strong in number, strong in union, strong in funds, and strong in enthusiasm, and we must accept the fact and endeavour to co-operate with you in making the best of it.'[3] During the 'sixties the coal-owners had refused to recognize unionism and the movement was completely crushed. During the early 'seventies, against a background of expanding trade, they were prepared to negotiate with the unions and this tacit recognition, once accorded, was not easily withdrawn in the period of falling prices and wages which followed. Indeed, the establishment of joint committees and other machinery for conciliation and arbitration tended to institutionalize, and the creation of the Coal-Owners' Association facilitated, the whole process of collective bargaining. The way was now open to establish a miners' union in Derbyshire on a firmer footing than had ever previously been possible.

[1] *Derbyshire Times*, 16 September, 1874.
[2] *Ibid.* 26 September, 1872.   [3] *Ibid.* 13 August, 1873.

APPENDIX I

Membership of the South Yorkshire Miners' Association in Derbyshire[1]

Lodge	21 October 1872	13 January 1873	30 November 1874	4 April 1876	Withdrawal
Rosa	100	122	144	75	—
New Whittington	99	141	350	200	—
Unstone	87	125	424	300	May, 1877
Killamarsh	136	189	371	234	—
Swallow Nest	192	269	200	100	—
Beighton	33	41	67	$33\frac{1}{2}$*	—
Old Hollingwood	70	140	400	200	December, 1879
Devonshire Silkstone	69	100	180	130	June, 1878
Dunston	42	71	219	135	August, 1878
Foxley Oaks	19	29	159	60	August, 1878
Tapton	51	53	306	240	January, 1879
Dronfield Silkstone	69	82	261	120	December, 1879
Morton	139	139	170	172	—
Renishaw Park	50	158	408	242	—
Clay Cross	66	95	560	210	October, 1879
Wingerworth	20	30	152	64	December, 1876
Barlborough	69	121	68	31	December, 1876
Staveley	—	57	235	190	January, 1878
Pilsley	—	71	152	111	January, 1878
Tibshelf	—	53	240	180	January, 1878
Tupton	—	48	180	93	December, 1879
Shireoaks	—	—	514	416	July, 1876
Mosborough	—	—	91	38	July, 1876
Brimington	—	—	49	23	July, 1876
Seymour	—	—	130	112	July, 1876
Hucknall Huthwaite	—	—	67	45	July, 1876
Barlow	—	—	120	53	July, 1876
South Normanton	—	—	47	40	July, 1876
Renishaw	—	—	59	40	August, 1878
Lings	—	—	100	75	December, 1879
Cutthorpe	—	—	55	55	June, 1878
Brampton	—	—	70	33	December, 1876
South Wingfield	—	—	80	83	December, 1876
Shirland	—	—	85	104	December, 1876
Silver Hill	—	—	60	56	January, 1879
North Staveley	—	—	133	111	—
Parkhouse	—	—	182	65	—
Total	1,311	2,134	7,018	$4,789\frac{1}{2}$*	
Approx. total membership of S.Y.M.A.	11,000	13,000	20,000	16,000	

*Boys were counted as half members.

[1] Compiled by Mr. P. J. Stevenson from the balance sheets of the South Yorkshire Miners' Association.

APPENDIX II

South Yorkshire Miners' Association
Wage Rates, Membership and the Price of Coal, 1871–1880

	Wage Rates (October, 1871 = 100)	Membership	Average London Market Price of Coal (Per ton) s. d.
1871	110.5	—	16 8 (estimated)
1872	127.5	12,773	18 11 (estimated)
1873	157.5	20,144	31 0
1874	137.5	20,791	23 8
1875	126.5	17,263	21 8
1876	111.5	9,213	19 1
1877	105	10,250	17 5
1878	100	—	16 4
1879	—	—	15 11
1880	—	—	14 10

Sources: *South Yorkshire Collieries Arbitration, April and May, 1879, Printed from the Shorthand Notes of the Official Reporters*, (Sheffield), 1879, p. 44.
South Yorkshire Miners' Association, *Balance Sheets*, 1872–1877.
Mines and Quarries: General Report, with Statistics, 1913, (Cd. 7741), p. 226.
Derbyshire Times, 1871–1880.

APPENDIX III

The South Yorkshire and North Derbyshire
Coal-Owners' Association, 1874

'The articles of association have been drafted by Robert Baxter, Esq., of London who is a large colliery owner. The name of the Company is the South Yorkshire and North Derbyshire Coal-Owners' Association and the capital £200,000, dividing into 20,000 shares of £10 each. The articles of association provide that—Before any firm be admitted as a member of the association they shall subscribe two shares in respect of every 1,000 tons of coal annually raised from their pits, and deposit a promissory note, amounting to 10 per cent. of the total sum in respect of profits assured in each year, payable to the association. Such promissory notes shall form a guarantee fund, and the board shall demand thereon to meet calls or liabilities; but if any member desire to pay the amount in cash in lieu of giving a promissory note he shall be at liberty to do so and the money shall be invested in Consols, and the interest thereon paid to the depositor. Any master may retire from the association on giving six months' notice and paying up his proportion of the liabilities and share of the actions that have been inaugurated by any colliery that is on strike. With regard to assurance and compensation, the articles state that each firm

F*

shall assure its profits at such a rate, not being less than 1s. nor exceeding 2s. 6d. per ton, as may be agreed upon with the finance committee after considering the special circumstances of the colliery. The assurance payments to be made in each case by the association in respect of profits shall be based upon the quantity of coal actually being worked at the time when the pit was put on strike or restriction, taken on the average workings during the previous three months, such average not to exceed the rate at which the colliery is assured. The contribution from each firm shall be based on the last returns of tonnage, and as to assurances on the amount of notes given, and calls will from time to time, as required, be made on each firm in due proportion after the rate. Each firm will be allowed to amend its returns—the intention of the association being that each pit should be assured as closely as possible upon the actual workings.

'The association claims the right of full control of wages, working hours— if any advance in the rate of wages payable to workmen, any concession or variation in the terms of their contracts, occasioning any additional payment to them, or an advantage in the rate of wages, or alteration in the number of their hours, shall be made, or agreed to be made except in the case of growing boys. . . . One of the concluding rules is "That no member of this association shall hold out any pecuniary inducement to any workman to enter into his service beyond the original wages paid at the colliery. Nor employ any workman on strike or locked out at any colliery belonging to the association." In fact the masters are taking a leaf out of the book of the men and forming a trade union of their own.'

(*Derbyshire Times*, 18 July, 1874.)

PART II
THE DERBYSHIRE MINERS' ASSOCIATION
1880–1914

CHAPTER V

THE COAL INDUSTRY

I

Until the outbreak of the First World War the British coal industry continued to enjoy a period of almost uninterrupted expansion. The annual output, which is estimated to have been about 10 million tons at the beginning of the nineteenth century, rose to 64 million tons in 1855, to 147 in 1880, to 225 in 1900, and to 287 in 1913.[1] This rapid development was first stimulated by the industrialization of Great Britain and most of the increased production was consumed at home. In the second half of the nineteenth century, however, the industrialization of Europe and improvements in shipping led to a growing export trade in coal. The quantity of coal exported in 1855 was about 5 million tons, or $7 \cdot 7$ per cent. of the country's total production. By 1913 we were sending overseas nearly 98 million tons, or 34 per cent. of our total output. In the same period the percentage value of coal to total exports rose from $2 \cdot 5$ to $10 \cdot 4$.[2]

On the other hand, the yearly output of coal in Great Britain per head of all persons employed in mining was falling. In the five years 1879–83 it averaged 319 tons per head; ten years later, in 1889–93, it was 282 tons; twenty years later still, in 1909–13, it was 257 tons.[3] These and similar figures, to which a great deal of publicity was given, readily suggested that, since the output of each person employed in mining was falling so rapidly, individual miners had been progressively and deliberately restricting their output or otherwise declining in personal efficiency. The notion that the difficulties of the coal industry were, in part at least, due to a growing practice of 'ca'canny' was dismissed by the Samuel Commission:

The miner is only one factor in the production of coal; his output in any given time depends, not on himself alone, but on two other factors of at least

[1] *Coal Industry Commission*, 1919, III, Appendix, (Cmd. 361), p. 29; Jevons, *op. cit.* p. 676.
[2] Jevons, *op. cit.* p. 676. These figures include bunker coal from 1873 onwards.
[3] *R.C. on the Coal Industry*, 1925, Report, I, (Cmd. 2600), p. 127.

equal importance and often of greater importance—the physical conditions of the mine and the efficiency of management.[1]

The fundamental problem of the industry was one of rising costs of production. Once the more easily accessible coal had been taken, it was necessary to sink deeper shafts and to work more difficult seams in many areas. Moreover, as the workings became more extensive, more men were occupied in keeping roadways open, in haulage and repair, and proportionately fewer in the productive work of getting coal.[2] Similarly, the introduction or extension of new processes, such as screening and washing, led to an increase in the proportion of surface workers. It has been estimated that whereas the capacity for production increased by about 60 per cent. between 1889 and 1913, the numbers which had to be employed underground to obtain that production increased by more than 90 per cent. In the same period the number of surface workers increased no less than about 185 per cent.[3] These rising costs might, for a time, have been offset by improvements in organization and technique. Mechanization is the most obvious example, yet in 1901 only $1\frac{1}{2}$ per cent. of the total output of coal in Great Britain was cut by machinery as compared with 25 per cent. in America.[4]

Thus, during the period 1884 to 1913, the British coal industry presents a contradictory picture of rapid expansion accompanied by rising costs of production. Without any reorganization of the industry this situation was only possible under two conditions: an increase in prices or a reduction in wages and profits. Professor Allen has shown that between 1880–4 and 1900–4 the price of coal rose relatively to general prices, and that the increased value more than compensated for the fall in output per head. Between 1900–4 and 1910–13, however, the rise in coal prices was less than the increase in the general level. This meant that while the real value of the miners' yearly output rose from the middle 'eighties to the opening years of the present century, during the ten years before 1914 it was falling. At the same time there was a tendency for profits per ton and real wages to increase until 1904 and thereafter to decline. 'In other words, up to 1900–4 the increased effort required to produce a ton of coal was paid for by customers; after then part of the increased effort was made without additional payment.'[5] By 1914 the industry appears to have been approaching the limit of its expansion and whether it would have adapted itself to the trends which

---

[1] R.C. on the Coal Industry, 1925, Report, I, (Cmd. 2600), p. 116.
[2] Ibid. pp. 123–5.
[3] J. W. F. Rowe, Wages in the Coal Industry, (London), 1923, pp. 13–15.
[4] R.C. on the Coal Industry, 1925, Report, I, (Cmd. 2600), p. 122.
[5] G. C. Allen, British Industries and Their Organization, (London), edn. of 1952, p. 48.

set in during the early years of the present century, in the absence of war, is a matter for speculation.[1] The First World War ruled out the possibility of any such adaptation and, as will be shown later, created many new problems.[2]

Against the general background of the British coal industry, developments in Derbyshire during the period 1880–1914 can be seen in perspective. The rate of growth was not equal in all districts. Of the bigger districts, South Wales and Yorkshire show large increases in annual production, while in Durham, and particularly in Lancashire, there was a comparatively slow rate of expansion. Of the medium-sized districts, Nottinghamshire and Derbyshire show a more than average increase while Lanarkshire shows considerably less. Warwickshire and Leicestershire show the largest expansion of all, but these are quite small districts, and the effect is largely neutralized by the stagnation of production in Staffordshire, and also, to a less extent, in most other small coalfields.[3] Thus, while the national output rose from 147 million tons in 1880 to 287 million in 1913 the production of the Derbyshire coalfield increased from nearly 8 million tons to about 18 million. Between 1880 and 1913 Derbyshire's output increased by 125 per cent. and its share in the national production increased from 5·4 per cent. to 6·9 per cent. In the same period the labour force employed underground in Derbyshire increased by 129 per cent.[4]

This unevenness in development was due to the age and geological condition of the various coalfields and to the character of their markets. The Derbyshire coal trade owed its great expansion, in the early nineteenth century, to the local demand created by a rapidly developing iron industry and, later, to the opening of the London and other markets, which followed the advent of the railways. The Derbyshire 'Brights' had established a reputation as one of the best house coals in Great Britain and in the early 'eighties Derbyshire was still producing mainly house and gas coal. The county's trade was therefore partly seasonal but became considerably less so when the valuable 'Top Hard' seam of good steam coal began to be exploited. The year 1876 had seen the sinking of the first pit in the Leen Valley, in Nottinghamshire, to work this seam and for many years it was not worked in any other district. The Sheepbridge Company reached the same seam at a depth of 285 yards at their Glapwell sinking in July, 1883,[5] but it was not until the early 'nineties that the 'Top Hard' began to be developed extensively in Derbyshire and on the borders of Nottinghamshire, particularly in the Mansfield district.

[1] Cf. J. H. Jones, G. Cartwright and P. H. Guénault, *The Coal-Mining Industry*, (London), 1939, p. 5.   [2] See Chapters XIII and XIV.   [3] Rowe, *op. cit.* p. 15.
[4] See Appendix I to this chapter.   [5] *Derbyshire Times*, 7 July, 1883.

One of the pioneers was Emerson Bainbridge[1] who, in 1888, acquired from the Duke of Portland the lease of the Bolsover and Creswell coalfield. This area was at that time 'unproved' and many colliery owners in the county were inclined to believe that the enterprise would be a failure. But by the beginning of 1890 the whole of the capital for the Bolsover Colliery Company had been subscribed and J. P. Houfton became its general manager. Sinking operations at Bolsover began in June, 1890, and in September of the following year coal was found at a depth of 365 yards. In 1894 plans were made for sinking another pit at Creswell, work began in 1896 and coal was reached two years later.[2] In 1905 there were further sinking operations at Crown Farm, in the parish of Mansfield Woodhouse.[3] In connection with these collieries 'model villages' were built at Bolsover and Creswell and 'Forest Town' was created.

Other companies began to follow suit. In 1895 the Staveley Company reached the top-hard coal at the Warsop Main Colliery, midway between the villages of Warsop and Shirebrook,[4] and in the following year decided to sink two further shafts: one near Shirebrook station and the other, the Markham Colliery, between Chesterfield and Bolsover.[5] In 1896 the Shirebrook Colliery Company began sinking two shafts, each 18 feet in diameter, at Shirebrook under the direction of Arnold Lupton, a professor of mining. Coal was reached a year later at a depth of about 600 yards[6] and between 1891 and 1901 the population of Shirebrook increased from 567 to 6,200.[7] A. B. (afterwards Sir Arthur) Markham obtained a lease from the Duke of Devonshire and invited tenders for sinking two shafts to the top-hard coal at Oxcroft in June, 1900, work was begun on a branch line from Staveley to serve the new colliery in April, 1901, and in the following month the Oxcroft Colliery Company was formed with a capital of £40,000 and with A. B. Markham and his brother, C. P. Markham, as directors.[8] Similarly, in 1892, the

---

[1] Emerson Muschamp Bainbridge, 1845–1911, founder and managing director of the Bolsover Colliery Company, Limited. Member of a North of England family claiming a distant relationship with Ralph Waldo Emerson. Educated at Edenfield House, Doncaster, and afterwards articled to mining engineering with the Marquis of Londonderry and studying at the University of Durham. Manager of the Sheffield and Tinsley Collieries in 1870 and later of the Duke of Norfolk's Nunnery Colliery, of which he became managing director with a controlling interest in 1874. Other directorships included the Lancashire, Derbyshire and East Coast Railway, the Sheffield District Railway, Hardy Patent Pick Company, New Hucknall Colliery, Yorkshire Engine Company, Wharncliffe Silkstone Colliery, etc. M.P. for the Gainsborough division, 1895–1900.　　　　　　　　　　　[2] *Derbyshire Times*, 20 May, 1911.

[3] *Ibid.* 3 June, 1905.　　　[4] *Ibid.* 5 October, 1895.　　　[5] *Ibid.* 22 February, 1896.

[6] *Ibid.* 20 February, 1897.　　　　　　　　　　　[7] Census figures, 1891–1901.

[8] *Derbyshire Times*, 28 June, 1900; 13 April, 1901; 11 May, 1901. Charles Paxton Markham, 1865–1926, the son of Charles Markham, was elected to the board of the Staveley Coal and Iron Company on the death of his father in 1888. He was chairman of the Company from 1903–26. His younger brother, A. B. (later Sir Arthur) Markham, 1866–1916, was Liberal M.P. for the Mansfield Division 1900–16, and interested in various colliery enterprises.

South Normanton Colliery Company was formed by a group of Durham colliery financiers to exploit the top-hard seam.[1] The Spinkhill Colliery Company, with a capital of £25,000, was another company which was formed to work the top-hard coal, this time at Park Hill, in the parish of Barlborough.[2] By 1913 fully 25 per cent. of the Derbyshire production was top-hard.[3]

In most of the new pits production was made cheaper by easier natural conditions, a larger scale of operations and the introduction of modern equipment. By 1905 there was no firm raising so much coal from so few collieries as the Bolsover Company, which was winding an average of 3,000 to 3,200 tons a day at Creswell and about 2,850 tons a day at Bolsover. Since the opening of the two collieries they had together produced almost 15 million tons of coal. Houfton, the general manager, estimated that the Mansfield Colliery would add another million tons of coal a year to the Company's output, making it the largest producer of top-hard coal in the county.[4] For a time the Creswell Colliery held a world's record for an output of 3,800 tons in a single day but this was surpassed by the Warsop Main Colliery, which, in January, 1908, turned 3,920 tons of coal in 11 hours and 20 minutes.[5] In July, 1910, the Bolsover Company created another record at its Mansfield Colliery by raising an average of 4,469 tons in 7 hours and 42 minutes' winding over a period of $5\frac{1}{2}$ days.[6]

As these large new collieries with the latest equipment were developed, many of the older and smaller collieries began to close down because they were either uneconomic or worked out. The problem was particularly acute in the Dronfield and Unstone districts. In 1895 the Unstone Main Company ceased operations and a drift mine was closed at Dronfield.[7] Within a decade there was little mining left. 'Unstone used to be a beautiful village', said a member of the Chesterfield Board of Guardians in 1906, 'but the mineral people came, and polluted their streams and took their water. . . . The coal went quickly, and today it left them dirt heaps, dead and decrepit men.'[8] The general effect of these changes was to shift the centre of gravity of the Derbyshire coalfield to the area east of Chesterfield.

During the opening years of the present century it was feared that Chesterfield would be robbed of its main source of prosperity. A. B. Markham estimated that with the exception of one pit, the top-hard coal

[1] *Derbyshire Times*, 5 September, 1903; 23 January, 1904.

[2] *Ibid.* 17 January, 1903. The directors were John Soar, Bolsover; Joseph Wragg, Shuttlewood; William Reaney, Bolsover; William Watkinson, Bolsover; James Kirk, Bolsover; John Williamson, Bolsover.

[3] Rowe, *op. cit.* p. 25.   [4] *Derbyshire Times*, 3 June, 1905.
[5] *Ibid.* 18 January, 1908.   [6] *Ibid.* 23 January, 1911.
[7] *Ibid.* 26 January, 22 June, 25 June, 1895.   [8] *Ibid.* 3 March, 1906.

on the Chesterfield side would be exhausted within fifteen or twenty years and that the same would be true of the Erewash and Leen valleys. Because of this he considered that the future for industrial development, possibly in the iron and steel trades, lay with the Mansfield district.[1] On the other hand, W. B. M. Jackson, of the Clay Cross Company, pointed out that the larger pits in the neighbourhood would not be worked out for many years to come.[2] The fact that neither of these coal-owners foresaw the growing importance of by-product coke ovens is illustrative of the backwardness of the British coal industry in this field. In 1923, Charles Markham, speaking to Chesterfield businessmen, recalled the statements which had been made twenty years previously about the trade of the county drifting towards Mansfield. 'Little did he realise at that time the . . . possibilities of the coke ovens and the by-products. The advent of the coke ovens, which he looked upon as being only in their infancy, would have a wonderful effect upon this part of the county, because they had no end of good coking coals in the immediate neighbourhood.'[3]

The exploitation of the 'Top Hard' seam led to a further widening of the market for Derbyshire coal. In addition to providing coal for household purposes and for the manufacture of gas, Derbyshire began to produce an increasing amount of steam coal. The gas and steam coals were largely absorbed by the gas and railway companies who placed contracts annually with the various colliery companies. The contracts, for monthly deliveries at a fixed price, were usually entered into during June or July when coal was cheap. In times of rising prices it was important for the colliery owners to allow themselves a sufficient margin to meet any increases in costs which were likely to arise before the contracts expired.[4] The miners' leaders, as will be shown later, believed that the system was partly responsible for preventing the miners from improving their wages. The railway contracts were said to 'rule the markets' in that they tended to fix the price of steam coal for shipping and for the general markets.[5] On the other hand, large contracts extending over two years, such as the Grassmoor Company secured from a gas company in 1895, provided the miners with an assurance that they would have regular work regardless of the state of trade.[6]

The savings on contracts could be quite considerable. The Earl of Wharncliffe, himself a coal-owner and chairman of the Manchester, Sheffield and Lincolnshire Railway Company, told the shareholders in the depression year of 1895 that the low price of coal would enable them

[1] *Derbyshire Times*, 2 May, 1903.   [2] *Ibid.* 13 December, 1902.
[3] *Ibid.* 6 January, 1923.   [4] *Ibid.* 31 October, 1885; 2 June, 1894.
[5] *Ibid.* 17 May, 1902; 10 December, 1904. See Chapters VII and VIII.
[6] *Ibid.* 15 June, 1895.

to reduce their fuel bill for the coming year by £20,000.[1] In the boom year of 1900 the railway companies delayed making their contracts until September in the hope that there would be a fall in prices.[2] Emerson Bainbridge denied the accusations of the railway companies that the price of coal was attributable to a coal-owners' 'ring'[3] but three years later A. B. Markham admitted that 'there was ... an understanding between certain large collieries—and he did not mind saying he took part in the plunder—to charge certain prices and sell only to certain agents. The companies squeezed the agents, and the agents squeezed the general public, and high prices resulted.'[4]

Steam coal was in great demand for export and Derbyshire had for some time done a certain amount of trade with the Baltic by way of the Humber ports.[5] By 1893 this had virtually ceased but the increasing supplies of steam coal produced by the new top-hard collieries and the improvement in trade after 1896 encouraged the colliery proprietors to develop their exports once again.[6] Nevertheless, the difficulties of securing cheap carriage to suitable ports tended to restrict the amount of inland coal which found its way overseas.[7] As late as 1905 it was estimated by Sir Charles McLaren, of the Sheepbridge Company, that of the 24 million tons of coal raised annually in North Derbyshire and Nottinghamshire not 5 per cent. was sent abroad.[8] At this time the Bolsover Company was shipping about 300,000 tons a year from its Bolsover Colliery under contract to the coal exporters Pyman, Bell and Company.[9] In 1909 the Shirebrook Colliery Company was exporting coal to Russia, Italy, Spain, Germany, Norway and Sweden and had been sending about 30,000 tons annually to France until that trade was captured by Germany.[10] By 1912 considerable quantities of coal were being sent to Hull for export from the Staveley, Mansfield, Clay Cross, Glapwell, Grassmoor, Hardwick, Langwith, Pilsley and Shirebrook collieries.[11] The amount of coal exported from the Humber ports rose from 6,264,063 tons in 1911 to 8,883,353 tons in 1913.[12]

London continued to be the county's most important market and as late as 1886 nearly two-fifths of all coal sent by rail to London came from Derbyshire.[13] But this trade had certain disadvantages. It has already been noted that a fall in the demand for iron meant that increased quantities of coal were sent to London not only from Derbyshire

[1] Derbyshire Times, 3 August, 1895.
[2] Ibid. 11 August, 1900.
[3] Ibid.
[4] Ibid. 2 May, 1903.
[5] Ibid. 16 May, 1885.
[6] Ibid. 22 April, 1893, 7 April, 1900.
[7] See below, pp. 181–7.
[8] The Times Engineering Supplement, 31 May, 1905.
[9] Derbyshire Times, 31 March, 1906.
[10] Ibid. 23 October, 1909.
[11] Ibid. 24 August, 1912.
[12] Lord Aberconway, The Basic Industries of Great Britain, (London), 1927, p. 370.
[13] Derbyshire Times, 22 January, 1887.

but also from the other iron-producing areas, which had the effect of reducing the price.[1] The problem was aggravated by the organization of the market. The seaborne coal, sent to London from the North of England, was in the hands of agents who were paid by commission and subject, in most cases, to an agreement fixing the prices to be charged for the various qualities of coal. The inland coal, however, was disposed of by merchants who were free to obtain their own prices from the consumers.[2] Moreover, it was the custom to send coal to London without its being ordered, with the result that heavier tonnages were sometimes sent than were necessary to meet the ordinary requirements of the market.[3] Thus the colliery owners had little or no control over the supply and were unable to engage in any restrictive practices to maintain the price of coal. The merchants, on the other hand, were accused of manipulating their prices to the consumers according to demand, regardless of the stocks of coal in their yards and sidings.[4] To prevent this, several colliery owners, including the Marquis of Londonderry, began to sell direct to the consumer. The Clay Cross Company had for a long time maintained its own marketing organization in London[5] and during the 'eighties the Staveley, Pinxton, Eckington and Grassmoor collieries all followed its example.[6]

In March, 1884, the Pinxton Colliery was selling coal at 2s. a ton below the merchants' rates but the number of companies selling direct to the consumer was insufficient to have much influence upon the general level of coal prices and the London market continued to be controlled by the merchants.[7] The worst offenders were the small dealers who bought from the principals at the wharf or in the railway yard and 'took the coals home to their own places and sold . . . as little as 14 lbs. sometimes'.[8] These men frequented the yards more than the wharves, for the poor consumed chiefly the inland coal from Derbyshire and Nottinghamshire rather than the 'best Wallsend', with its older reputation and higher price.[9] In February, 1900, when the price of coal was rising sharply, best coal in London was being quoted at 40s. a ton and 'seconds' at 32s. But in the poorer neighbourhoods, where people bought in small quantities, the dealers were charging 2s. 4d. a cwt. and 'causing much misery and suffering'.[10]

Another feature of the London market was the ancient tax—the

---

[1] *Derbyshire Times*, 17 April, 1880. See also Chapter I, p. 53
[2] *Ibid.* 16 February, 1884.   [3] *Ibid.* 15 May, 1880.
[4] *Ibid.* 22 October, 1881.   [5] See Chapter I, p. 46.
[6] *Derbyshire Times*, 22 January, 1887.
[7] *Ibid.* 15 March, 1884; 31 October, 1885.
[8] *S.C. on the Causes of the Present Dearness and Scarcity of Coal*, 1873, Evidence of R. Cory, Q. 7136.
[9] *Ibid.* Q. 7150.   [10] *Daily Telegraph*, 5 February, 1900.

'City Dues'—levied upon all coal brought into the metropolis.[1] This was used for financing public works in London and had persisted in various forms ever since the sixteenth century. During the Napoleonic wars it had risen to the extent of 12s. 6d. a chaldron and had last been regulated in 1832 when a duty of 1s. 1d. a ton was imposed.[2] The tax, which affected inland and seaborne coal alike, was due to expire in 1889 and the colliery owners of the north of England, as well as the inland districts, decided to oppose any attempt to renew it. In 1881 the coal dues realized £571,867, of which about two-thirds was paid by the inland coal-owners, Derbyshire and Nottinghamshire alone contributing more than £150,000.[3] As a result of the agitation started by the coal-owners and several chambers of commerce the dues were reduced to 4d. a ton in July, 1889, and finally abolished on 12 July, 1890.[4]

II

The Derbyshire coal trade owed much of its expansion to the coming of the railways and continued to remain peculiarly sensitive to railway charges which presented many problems in this period. The process of amalgamation gave the railway companies a monopolistic position which enabled them to offer preference either to individuals or to certain districts in the shape of lower rates or better facilities. In the coastal areas, however, there was competition from shipping and the railway companies offered very low rates to consignments which otherwise might have gone by sea. It was estimated that freight charges from three-fifths of the stations in the country were affected by the competition of transport by sea.[5] This inevitably aroused strong protests from the inland manufacturers and traders. By the early 'eighties they were becoming extremely critical of the railways. General prices had been falling for years and the great depression made the high rates charged during the good years seem excessive. The railway companies, on the other hand, had enlarged their stations and terminal facilities and were proposing to increase their charges.

The railway rate war of the 'seventies had left the Derbyshire colliery owners in a more advantageous position than those of South Yorkshire.[6] Since that time the rates had slowly risen until they were slightly above the 1870 level but the Midland Railway Company had succeeded in

---

[1] See Chapter I, p. 51.   [2] 1 and 2 William IV, c. 76.
[3] *Derbyshire Times*, 29 April, 1882.   [4] *Ibid.* 24 August, 1889; 19 July, 1890.
[5] *S.C. on Railway Companies' Amalgamations*, 1872, Report, p. xix.
[6] See Chapter I, p. 48.

maintaining a difference of 1s. to 1s. 2d. a ton in favour of Derbyshire.[1] Before the rate war began, the cost of sending a ton of coal from Derbyshire to London had been about 7s. 8d. This had fallen as low as 5s. 6d. in the summer of 1871 but rose to 6s. 4d. in 1872 and 7s. 9d. in 1880.[2] But even Derbyshire's favourable rates were considerably higher than the cost of sending coal by sea from the Tyne to the Thames, which was estimated in 1880 at about 5s. a ton.[3] If Derbyshire was dissatisfied, Yorkshire was doubly so, and the colliery owners of both counties attempted to solve their problems by breaking the monopoly of the railway companies which served their districts. Thus, while the colliery proprietors of South Yorkshire were doing all they could to secure a line independent of the Great Northern, those of Derbyshire were inviting the Great Northern to extend its system as a counter to the Midland.

Neither Derbyshire nor Yorkshire met with any immediate success in their attempts to find a cheaper route for sending coal to London. Moreover, colliery proprietors were unable to follow the example set by some iron, steel and engineering firms in moving to the coast. In September, 1881, it was reported that Wilson, Cammell and Company, of Dronfield, were removing their large steel works to Workington on the Cumberland coast, where, in 1865, the Lonsdale Dock had been opened.[4] This firm controlled haematite mines in Cumberland and by moving to Workington had ready access not only to the raw materials but also to a port for shipment of the finished product.[5] The saving in railway charges is estimated to have been £60,000 a year.[6] Meanwhile, for almost two years, the question of railway rates and fares had been considered by a Select Committee on which the coal interest was well represented by Alfred Barnes, Member of Parliament for the Chesterfield division of Derbyshire and part proprietor of the Grassmoor Colliery.[7] The Committee investigated most of the old problems—the need for a uniform classification of goods; the supposed evils of railway control of canals; the desirability of recognized and published terminal charges—but its main wish was to see the Railway and Canal

---

[1] *Derbyshire Times*, 24 December, 1881; 15 April, 1882.
[2] *Ibid.* 14 and 28 July, 1880.   [3] *Ibid.* 14 July, 1880.
[4] *Ibid.* 7 September, 1881. Industrialists in other inland areas were doing likewise. In 1884 it was reported that six important firms in South Staffordshire were migrating to the coastal districts in order to save transport costs. (G. C. Allen, *The Industrial Development of Birmingham and the Black Country, 1860–1927*, (London), 1929, p. 234.) Cf. *R.C. on Depression of Trade and Industry*, Second Report, 1886, Evidence of J. D. Ellis, Q. 3204.
[5] Clapham, *op. cit.* III, p. 261.
[6] J. H. Stainton, *The Making of Sheffield*, (Sheffield), 1924, p. 269.
[7] Alfred Barnes played a prominent part in forming the Mining Association of Great Britain and was its president in 1881 and 1888.

Commission strengthened and made permanent.[1] Nothing was done: but the publication of the evidence presented to the Committee provided further ammunition for the colliery owners.

Allport, the general manager of the Midland Railway Company, had stated that the cost of conveying coal over a long distance was 0·20d. per ton per mile and it was argued that since the Company charged 0·43d. per ton per mile it could afford to make a reduction of 10d. per ton in the rate from Derbyshire to London. It was estimated that such a reduction would make a difference of £10,000 a year to Clay Cross; £7,000 to Eckington and Grassmoor; and fully £5,000 to Blackwell, Pilsley, and several other collieries in Derbyshire.[2]

Towards the end of 1881 a Colliery Owners' League was formed to campaign for the carrying of coal from Derbyshire, Nottinghamshire and South Yorkshire at ¼d. per ton per mile and 6d. per ton for wagon hire with the abolition of all terminal charges.[3] The League met with no success[4] but by 1885 the position of the colliery owners began to look more hopeful. The opening of the Hull and Barnsley line, in June, provided an alternative route for Yorkshire coal. The rate from Cudworth by way of Hull and thence by sea to London, with all incidental charges, was 7s. 1d. a ton, whereas the charge by rail amounted to 8s. 1d.[5] In the same year, the Great Northern announced that its large new dock at Boston would soon be completed. It was expected that coal would be taken by the Great Northern from Nottingham to Boston and thence by sea to London at a lower rate than that charged for direct rail transport.[6]

Meanwhile there were signs that Parliament was about to intervene. In 1884 Chamberlain tabled his Bill to extend the powers of the Railway and Canal Commissioners but its only effect was to stimulate the creation of a Railway Companies' Association to fight it.[7] Gladstone's second ministry fell in June, 1885, and no further attempts were made to deal with the railways until he returned in the following February, with Mundella as President of the Board of Trade. Mundella's Bill, which was a modification of Chamberlain's, aroused tremendous opposition from the railway interest and contributed to the fall of the government in August, 1886.[8] Eventually, in 1888, Parliament dealt with the problem by the Railway and Canal Traffic Act.[9] Every railway company was

[1] S.C. on Railway Rates and Fares, 1882, Report.
[2] Derbyshire Times, 24 December, 1881; 17 June, 1882.
[3] Ibid. 24 December, 1881.   [4] Ibid. 22 July, 1882.
[5] Ibid. 28 August, 1886.   [6] Ibid. 21 February, 22 August, 1885.
[7] See C. H. Grinling, The Great Northern Railway, (London), 1898, p. 369.
[8] See W. H. G. Armytage, 'The Railway Rates Question and the Fall of the Third Gladstone Ministry', English Historical Review, LXV, (1950), pp. 18–51.
[9] 51 and 52 Vict. c. 25.

called upon to submit a revised classification of merchandise traffic, and a revised schedule of maximum rates and charges, including the much discussed terminal charges, which were then to be approved by Parliament. The effect of these changes, so far as Derbyshire was concerned, was that coal going to London, an average distance of 140 miles, could now be charged at 7s. 7½d. per ton, an increase of 1s. 0½d.[1] An increase in terminal charges was a further source of discontent.[2]

The revised rates came into operation on 1 January, 1893, when the railways raised all rates to the maximum allowed by the Board of Trade to recoup themselves for the loss on reductions. The coal-owners of Derbyshire, Nottinghamshire and Leicestershire met to consider the situation and decided that 'during the present state of trade and general depression it was not the proper time to increase rates, but very much the reverse. . . .'[3] A deputation met the directors of the Midland Railway with the object of inducing them to re-consider the new railway rates for coal and on 17 February the Company agreed to modify many of their charges retrospectively from 1 January, 1893. The outcry which followed the introduction of the new rates led to the setting up of yet another parliamentary committee in May, 1893.[4] In his evidence before the Committee, Alfred Barnes, president of the Derbyshire, Nottinghamshire and Leicestershire Coal-Owners' Association, referred to a ring of about nine railway companies, including the London and North-Western, the Great Northern, the Midland and the Great Western, which had combined for many purposes: 'Upon the one point of rates they are decided, and so the public have no chance with them.'[5] The inquiry resulted in a further Act of Parliament in 1894 which stated that if the railways raised their rates above the level of 1892 they had to prove that such an increase was reasonable. The test that was to be taken by the Railway and Canal Commission was that there must be some permanent increase in the cost of service.[6]

The railway companies began to increase their charges by indirect methods such as the withdrawal of allowances for wastage in transit. Several test cases, brought before the Commissioners by Derbyshire and other colliery proprietors, were only partially successful.[7] On 29 June, 1896, at Sheffield, there was a large meeting of coal-owners from Yorkshire, Derbyshire, Nottinghamshire and Leicestershire. They agreed unanimously to resist in every possible way what they regarded as the arbitrary action of the railway companies and resolved that they would neither sell nor consign coal except at the existing scale, nor

[1] *Derbyshire Times*, 25 July, 1891.   [2] *Ibid.* 2 May, 1891.
[3] *Ibid.* 25 February, 1893.   [4] *S.C. on Railway Rates and Charges*, 1893–4.
[5] *Derbyshire Times*, 8 July, 1893.   [6] 57 and 58 Vict. c. 54.
[7] *Derbyshire Times*, 10 August, 21 December, 1895; 4 July, 1896.

accept any settlement with the companies which did not provide for a reduction of those rates which had been directly or indirectly increased since 1892.[1]

The colliery proprietors were unsuccessful in their attempts to return to the *status quo* of 1892 but the railway companies, on their side, were extremely chary of increasing their rates directly. Moreover, by 1896 general prices were at last beginning to rise and traders, manufacturers and colliery owners found the indirect increases which had been made since 1892 less irksome. Lord Claud Hamilton, the chairman of the Great Eastern Railway Company, was able to tell the Chesterfield Chamber of Commerce in 1900 that 'the railway rates, which were grumbled at in times of depression, but not now, were low, or at all events for most articles carried, not unduly high. . . . The time had arrived when the great railway companies would have to consider whether they might make a slight advance in the rates of certain goods.'[2]

In addition to parliamentary and legal action the colliery owners adopted economic sanctions against the railway companies and continued their policy of introducing new lines to the coalfields. C. H. Parkes, the chairman of the Great Eastern, stated at the Company's half-yearly meeting in 1889 that a great proportion of their fuel came from Derbyshire and Yorkshire and when the contracts ended on 30th June 'they found that a sort of combination had been made amongst the coal owners in these counties and had raised the price to one uniform level—viz. 8s. 6d. or 2s. 6d. more than in the previous year. Fortunately they had 30,000 tons in hand, and they only bought the best of the dear coal, feeling sure that the syndicate would break up. It had now done so and they had contracted for 20,000 tons a year at 7s. 3d.' At the same time the Company was also experimenting with the use of liquid fuel (oil and tar).[3] But not all the railway companies were in a position to resist the higher prices and some of them had to face an increase of more than 40 per cent. on their fuel costs in 1889.[4] In the following year, when the average selling value per ton of all coal was 8s. 3d. a ton at the pit-head, it was estimated that the railway companies were paying from 70 to 80 per cent. more for their fuel than they were eighteen months or two years previously.[5]

There were various proposals to provide Derbyshire coal with a cheaper outlet by rail. In 1888 the Manchester, Sheffield and Lincolnshire Company proposed a line from Beighton to Chesterfield giving a direct connection with Grimsby, which was already an important coal shipping port.[6] This line was extended to Annesley and eventually

[1] *Derbyshire Times*, 4 July, 1896.   [2] *Ibid.* 10 March, 1900.
[3] *Ibid.* 3 August, 1889.   [4] *Ibid.* 25 January, 1890.
[5] *Ibid.* 21 June, 1890.   [6] *Ibid.* 4 August, 1888; 17 January, 1891.

became part of the much bigger scheme of Sir Ernest Watkin, the chairman of the Manchester, Sheffield and Lincolnshire Company, to establish a direct route to London terminating at Marylebone.[1] The extension was sanctioned by Parliament in 1893, the Company changed its name to the Great Central in 1897, and ran its first train into Marylebone Station in March, 1899.[2] The new line provided a third route from the Derbyshire and Nottinghamshire coalfields to London in competition with the existing facilities offered by the Midland and the Great Northern.

Another proposed line of the 'nineties, now almost forgotten, was the Lancashire, Derbyshire and East Coast Railway running from Warrington by way of Macclesfield, to Chesterfield and thence to Lincoln and Sutton-on-Sea where it was planned to construct large docks.[3] The railway was promoted by the landowners in Derbyshire and Lincolnshire, particularly by the mining interest.[4] Emerson Bainbridge, who had recently begun to develop his colliery at Bolsover, stated that the railway 'would provide new markets for the produce of the whole neighbourhood. . . . The effect would be also to tap all the various lines which were crossed and to carry coal from these railways, whether from north or south . . . to the docks at Sutton-on-Sea.'[5]

The railway was to have its headquarters at Chesterfield and work on the Chesterfield to Lincoln section was begun on 7 June, 1892, with the ceremony of cutting the first sod. On that occasion the prospects of the company were summed up by Sir William Lang:

The new line would touch and serve Cheshire's salt mines and chemical works; Staffordshire's potteries; Macclesfield's silk works; Warrington's big breweries; the mills of that crowded hive of industry, Lancashire; Staveley's and Sheepbridge's blast furnaces and mineral fields; Penistone's breezy heights; Baslow's sheltered glade; Lincolnshire's beds of iron ore; Lincoln's agricultural implement works; and the far reaching tract of agricultural land served by the Great Eastern network of railways.[6]

In 1892 this picture was fully accepted as the almost certain future of the concern, but as the work progressed it was found that the section from Chesterfield to the west presented greater engineering difficulties than the Company could face, and in 1895 Parliament authorized the abandoning of this part of the original scheme. The line from Chesterfield to Lincoln was constituted as a separate undertaking and, instead

[1] *Derbyshire Times*, 28 January, 1893.   [2] Clapham, *op. cit.* III, p. 345.
[3] The proposed route was Warrington, Knutsford, Macclesfield, Buxton, Chesterfield, Tuxford, Lincoln, Alford and Sutton-on-Sea.
[4] W. Arkwright, of Sutton Scarsdale, A. W. Byron (then Arkwright's agent) and Dixon H. Davies (later solicitor to the Great Central Railway) were largely responsible for carrying the Bill through Parliament.
[5] *Derbyshire Times*, 21 February, 1891.   [6] *Ibid.* 18 November, 1905.

of constructing a dock at Sutton-on-Sea with a direct line from Lincoln, the directors of the Company decided to make Boston their place of export. The mileage by this route was less than by the proposed line to Sutton-on-Sea and both the Great Northern Company and the Boston Town Council agreed to the scheme.[1] Two years later, the Lancashire, Derbyshire and East Coast Company decided to sell all its powers to construct a railway from Lincoln to Sutton-on-Sea to a new company, the Lincoln and East Coast Railway and Dock Company.[2] Although the Lancashire, Derbyshire and East Coast Railway never extended beyond Chesterfield and Lincoln it served as an important outlet for coal from large collieries owned by the Staveley, Sheepbridge, Shirebrook and Bolsover Companies and from many other smaller concerns.[3] In 1905 it became part of the Great Central system.[4]

Addressing the Chesterfield Chamber of Commerce in 1901, Alexander Henderson commented on the manner in which 'the commercial men of Chesterfield had forced the railway companies to allow them to establish a good inland trade' but even then they were not satisfied. In the first decade of the present century they turned their attention increasingly to the export trade. Boston was soon considered to be inadequate as a coal dock and the Chamber of Commerce, backed by such powerful figures as Markham, Deacon, Bainbridge and Westlake began to press the Great Central to provide new docks at Grimsby 'which would be equal to dealing with large quantities of coal, and be second to none in the country'.[5] The Great Central, which had already done much to improve the existing docks at Grimsby, responded nobly with its great new dock system of 45 acres at Immingham, which was finished just in time to be laid idle by the First World War.[6]

III

In addition to its special problems of reaching the markets the Derbyshire coal industry had, of course, to cope with the more general movements in trade. After the boom of 1873 general prices were falling until

[1] *Derbyshire Times*, 9 and 16 November, 1895.
[2] *Ibid.* 16 January, 1897. Among the directors of the new company were Emerson Bainbridge, Percy Graham and Buchanan Westmacott. They also acquired the North Sea Fisheries (East Lincolnshire) Harbour and Dock Company which the Lancashire, Derbyshire and East Coast Railway Company were authorized by Parliament to purchase in 1892.   [3] *Ibid.* 3 July, 1897.   [4] *Ibid.* 18 November, 1905.
[5] *Ibid.* 15 June, 1901. Henry Westlake was at this time managing director of the Staveley Company, a director of the Newstead Coal Company, Limited, and joint managing director of the Wagon Finance Corporation, Limited. In 1908 he was appointed a director of Cammell, Laird and Company, Limited. Maurice Deacon became general manager of the Sheepbridge Coal and Iron Company in 1897 and managing director in 1900.   [6] Clapham, *op. cit.* III, pp. 348, 384.

1896 and rising until the outbreak of war in 1914. These trends were deflected at times by the upward and downward movements of economic activity. For coal the troughs occurred in 1879, 1886, 1896, 1905 and 1909, and the peaks in 1883, 1890, 1900, 1907 and 1913.[1] Unlike general prices, however, the secular turning point for coal was 1886. The explanations of the so-called 'Great Depression' have been many and various. The Royal Commission on the Depression of Trade, which reported in 1886, enumerated overproduction, the scarcity and appreciation of precious metals, commercial restrictions, excessive speculation, changes in wealth-distribution and agricultural depression among its causes. Mr. H. L. Beales, however, has emphasized the extent to which the term 'Great Depression' is a misnomer by standards of output and real wages and has called attention to the increasing productive efficiency of industry and the increasing competitive efficiency of other countries.[2] Professor Rostow has taken the analysis a stage further by linking the supply–demand explanation with a monetary explanation, the relative cessation of foreign lending. In particular he has pointed to the decisive importance of the end of railway-building and the resultant movement of savings into less profitable channels: 'The expectations of 1871–3 had encouraged great expansion of plant. Cheap money, new invention, and the need to reduce costs carried on the process in the decade that followed. The expected marginal efficiency of capital declined.'[3]

More recently Mr. D. J. Coppock has shown that the rate of growth of industrial productivity in the British economy was checked in the 1870's by a decline in the rate of growth of industrial capital per head. This was caused partly by an exogenous decline in the rate of export growth, which reduced the incentive to invest, and partly by the ending of a period of technical innovation based on the inventions making use of steam and iron. These factors may have been reinforced by a decline in entrepreneurial efficiency in certain industries.[4]

The outward signs of the depression were nowhere more apparent than in the coal industry. The brief recovery of 1880–3, which depended largely upon rail-iron orders and the British ship-building boom,

[1] See Chart 3 and Appendix II to this chapter.
[2] H. L. Beales, 'The "Great Depression" in Industry and Trade', *Economic History Review*, V, No. 1, (1934), pp. 65–75.
[3] W. W. Rostow, *British Economy of the Nineteenth Century*, (Oxford), 1948, pp. 88–89.
[4] D. J. Coppock, 'The Climacteric of the 1890's: A Critical Note', *The Manchester School of Economic and Social Studies*, XXIV, (1956), pp. 1–31; E. H. Phelps Brown and S. J. Handfield-Jones, 'The Climacteric of the 1890's: A Study in the Expanding Economy', *Oxford Economic Papers*, IV (1952), pp. 266–307; A. E. Musson, 'The Great Depression in Britain, 1873–1896', *Journal of Economic History*, XIX, (1959), pp. 199–228.

was characterized in Derbyshire by renewed activity in the great iron-works towards the close of 1879. This led to a rapid and extra-ordinary advance in the value of local shares. In January, 1880, the shares of the Sheepbridge Company, which four months previously had been quoted at 50 per cent. discount, rose to a fractional premium.

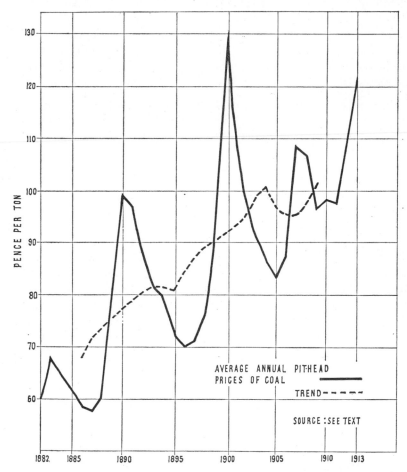

Chart 3.—Average annual pit-head prices of coal and trend, 1882–1913.

In the same period the Staveley Company's shares rose from 5 to 28 or 30 per cent. premium and those of John Brown and Company, Sheffield, rose from 35 per cent. discount to par or above. During the week ending 17 January alone there was an average increase of 5 to 10 per cent. for most shares of this kind.[1] The joint stock boom proved to be short-lived

[1] *Derbyshire Times,* 17 January, 1880.

and had little or no effect on the coal trade. The price of best Silkstone coal in London fell from 21s. a ton in January to 20s. in April, the lowest since 1870.[1] During the next two or three years there was little sign of improvement although strikes and rumours of strikes among the miners created shortages and panics among consumers which, coupled with the manipulations of the market by the merchants, had the effect of artificially and temporarily increasing prices.[2]

Miners and coal-owners alike were baffled by what appeared to be an insoluble problem. Prices were falling, profits were diminishing, short time was widespread and wages were low. The *Derbyshire Times* commented:

> The masters are selling their coal far too cheaply, and the men are getting far too small wages, and the result is that the whole district is suffering from hard times, notwithstanding the fact that more coal is produced than at any previous time in the history of the Derbyshire coalfield.[3]

Despite falling prices, production in Derbyshire increased from 7,903,834 to 9,231,536 tons between 1880 and 1885. Only in 1886, the year of lowest prices, was there a reduction in output to 8,908,865 tons.[4]

The truth was that coalmining was entering a period of increasing costs. For this reason the miners' proposals to restrict output were not attractive to their employers who, in addition to facing decreasing returns, were already beginning to feel the first cold draughts of foreign competition. As early as 1882 it was argued that the increase in the price of coal resulting from an advance in miners' wages had given an advantage to the German and other continental owners of coalmines.[5] 'This is a depression in the true sense of the term', remarked the *Derbyshire Times* in 1885, 'for whilst capital is unproductive and wages low, producers go on even at a loss in expectation of a change for the better.'[6] With wages representing a high proportion of total costs, the payment of low wages was a short-term solution for the coal-owners. For the larger concerns with a sufficient command of capital the long-term solution was to sink new pits and install the most modern equipment.

The period of expansion from 1886 to 1890 had two distinct phases. It began with a revived export trade to both North and South America and was followed in 1889–90 by further exports and long-term loans to South America.[7] These developments led to renewed activity in the

---

[1] *Derbyshire Times*, 17 April, 1880.
[2] *Ibid.* 26 February, 22 October, 1881; 21 October, 30 December, 1882; 3 March, 1883; 3 May, 1884; 4 April, 18 July, 1885.
[3] *Ibid.* 1 April, 1882.   [4] See Appendix I to this chapter.
[5] *Derbyshire Times*, 30 December, 1882.
[6] *Ibid.* 31 October, 1885.   [7] Rostow, *op. cit.* p. 85.

engineering, iron and steel trades,[1] which soon had its effects upon the coal trade. By March, 1886, most of the Derbyshire collieries were working full time and the loaded wagons which had occupied the sidings along the Erewash Valley during the period of recession rapidly gave way to empty ones.[2] Towards the end of the year the price of best Silkstone coal rose to 23s. a ton in London and 8s. at the pit-head.[3] In the summer of 1887 the seasonal decline in demand resulted in more short time and lower prices and the recovery in the following winter was by no means complete, orders being plentiful but prices remaining low.[4] The output of coal which had declined to 8,908,865 tons in 1886 rose to 9,063,407 in 1887.[5] By 1889 the second phase of the recovery had set in and the coal trade began to improve. The railway companies found that they had to pay an increase of 40 per cent. or more for their locomotive coal on the contracts of the previous year.[6] Coal was in great demand in the early part of 1890 and the price was higher than at any period since 1875. Best inland or Black Shale coal was selling in London at 28s. a ton in January, falling to 25s. in March.[7] By the middle of the year, when the railway contracts were being made, the railway companies were paying as much as 80 per cent. more for their coal than they did in 1888.[8]

The boom of 1886-90 did not have the same effect upon prices as that of 1868-73. In the later period general prices rose by about 4 per cent. whereas in the earlier they rose by over 12 per cent. The smallness of the increase in general prices for the period 1886-90 has been attributed very largely to the amount of cost-reducing investment which had taken place in industry since 1873.[9] In the iron industry, for example, technical improvements and better transport facilities assisted in lowering costs with the result that Cleveland No. 3 pig-iron, which until 1886 was controlled by a local price-fixing association, rose from 33s. a ton in 1885 to only 37s. in 1890, an increase of about 12 per cent.[10] The average pit-head price of coal, however, rose from 4s. 10d. in 1887 to 8s. 3d. in 1890, an increase of about 70 per cent.[11] The coal boom of 1889-90 was not on the extraordinary scale of 1871-3 but for the first time since the early 'seventies fairly serious inelasticities in supply appeared in the industry.

Early in 1891 the depression returned and continued, unabated,

[1] *Derbyshire Times*, 30 October, 1886; 1 January, 17 December, 1887; 28 January, 21 July, 1888.
[2] *Ibid.* 20 March, 1886.   [3] *Ibid.* 22 January, 1887.
[4] *Ibid.* 16 July, 10 December, 1887.   [5] See Appendix I to this chapter.
[6] *Derbyshire Times*, 25 January, 1890.   [7] *Ibid.* 1 March, 1890.
[8] *Ibid.* 21 June, 1890.   [9] Rostow, *op. cit.* p. 86.
[10] T. H. Burnham and G. O. Hoskins, *Iron and Steel in Britain, 1870-1930*, (London), 1943, p. 137; H. W. Macrosty, *The Trust Movement in British Industry*, (London), 1907, pp. 57-60.   [11] See Appendix II to this chapter.

until 1896. It was felt initially in the iron trade. Shareholders were told, at the annual meeting of the Staveley Company, that 'pig iron could not be made at a profit'.[1] By April, 1893, the coal trade was beginning to feel the full weight of the depression.

'The crisis which we alluded to months ago is almost upon us', proclaimed the *Derbyshire Times*. 'Masters have striven against the adverse tide as best they could, but they have not been managing to hold their own. Prices have fallen and are falling, and unfortunately dark as the prospect is at present, they have not yet reached their bottom figure. . . . Wages are as they were in 1891. Prices are 4s. per ton lower. . . . Our Baltic trade has left us and we cannot compete with other parts of the country.'[2]

Wages, railway rates and increasing competition from other coalfields were all factors which were adding to the difficulties of the Midland coal-owners during this period of general depression. The miners of Northumberland and Durham, who had agreed to adopt sliding scales in the late 'seventies, were driven, not without protest, to accept reductions in wages of 15 per cent. or more between 1891 and early 1893.[3] Lower wages, together with cheaper transport by sea, gave the northern coal-owners a considerable advantage over their competitors in other districts. In some cases the coal-owners of Northumberland and Durham were accepting large gas coal contracts at as low a price as 5s. 6d. a ton at the pit-head.[4] 'The private firm, the fighting trade, capitalism according to Karl Marx, were still the notes of the coal industry as the nineteenth century ran out', writes Clapham.[5]

Moreover, the rapidly falling prices after 1890—from 8s. 3d. to 6s. 10d.—were directly responsible for the industrial strife of 1893. This much Charles McLaren admitted to the shareholders of the Sheepbridge Company but he placed the onus upon the consumers:

He hoped, as a result of the strike, that the railway companies and the great corporations who bought gas coal would see that it was not to their interest to screw down, as they had been inclined to do in recent years, owners to the very lowest price for the coal they supplied. . . . To a large extent that had been the cause of the strike.[6]

A year later, however, he said:

They ought to recognize the powers the men now possessed, and instead of trying to undersell each other in order to gain a paltry advantage over a trade rival they ought to endeavour as far as they could to settle prices together in concert, if necessary, with the leaders of the Miners' Federation, on a basis

[1] *Derbyshire Times*, 3 October, 1896.   [2] *Ibid.* 22 April, 1893.
[3] Welbourne, *op. cit.* pp. 181, 185, 284, 290–1.
[4] *Derbyshire Times*, 29 April, 1893.   [5] Clapham, *op. cit.* III, p. 264.
[6] *Derbyshire Times*, 25 November, 1893.

which would be remunerative to all parties. . . . The men complained, and perhaps justly, that while they were trying to keep up prices the owners did not assist them in the effort.[1]

Competition among the owners had played its part in lowering prices whereas the miners had shown the extent of the strength which lay in combination. Thus, at a time when business men generally were resorting to associations and other devices as an escape from falling profit margins and increasingly severe competition, it is not surprising that a proposal emerged for the immediate formation of a coal trust for the United Kingdom.[2]

Sir George Elliot, who had started life as a coalminer and had become one of the greatest of coal-owners with interests in more than one coalfield, propounded his famous scheme in a letter to *The Times* of 20 September, 1893.[3] His ideas were no doubt influenced by the formation of the Rhenish-Westphalian Coal Syndicate in Germany. They also foreshadowed some of the minority proposals of the Sankey Commission.[4] Elliot called attention to the wasteful lay-out of coal workings underground due to the divisions of property at the surface; wasteful methods of extraction; wasteful customs of competitive sale; waste of labour and goodwill of the miners. He advocated the creation of a semi-public giant coal company and estimated that the venture would require a capital of £110,000,000, one-third in 5 per cent. debentures.

Elliot sent out about 2,000 circulars advocating the plan but the replies were unfavourable. Clapham remarks: 'The British coal industry of 1893, with its thousands of distinct stiff-necked and often suspicious units and its stubborn geographic diversities, was not nearly ready for a grand scheme of public utility national organization. Besides, the money could not have been raised.'[5] In October, 1895, Emerson Bainbridge, in his presidential address to the Chesterfield and Midland Counties Institution of Mining Engineers, discussed the impracticability of Elliot's scheme. 'Its magnitude was such', he said, 'that there was little hope of bringing it into workable shape.'[6] He also voiced the growing fears of many business men that their most serious problem was foreign competition. 'It is questionable', he said, 'whether any combination which endeavours to maintain the price of a commodity so universally needed as coal could ever be maintained without serious prejudice to the general welfare of the country.'[7]

---

[1] *Derbyshire Times*, 29 September, 1894.
[2] Cf. Rostow, *op. cit.* p. 89. [3] Cf. Macrosty, *op. cit.* pp. 86–88.
[4] *R.C. on the Coal Industry*, 1919, Report, II, pp. xxii-xxviii.
[5] Clapham, *op. cit.* III, p. 220.
[6] *Derbyshire Times*, 19 October, 1895. [7] *Ibid.*

G

The depression continued in Derbyshire until 1896. Some iron-works were closed down; none was working to full capacity. At the annual meeting of the Sheepbridge Company in 1894 it was stated that only three of eight furnaces were in blast.[1] Short-time working was the rule at most Derbyshire collieries.[2] By June, 1895, many of the pits were working only one day a week. 'The outlook in the Derbyshire coalfield is very dark', reported the *Derbyshire Times*. 'There is absolutely no market and there is no likelihood at present of a change for the better.'[3] While many large modern collieries were being developed in an attempt to reduce costs, many others were being closed. The Pinxton Coal Company closed its No. 1 pit in May, 1896, and its No. 3 pit a few weeks later.[4] In August the Grassmoor Colliery Company decided to close half of the Tupton pits, throwing over 1,000 men out of work.[5] By this time the average price of coal at the pit-head had reached its lowest point: 5s. 10d. a ton.[6]

Thereafter conditions in the coal trade began to improve. By the beginning of 1899 orders for coal were plentiful and all the collieries were working full time.[7] In April the price of house coal was increased by 1s. a ton and Derbyshire was described as 'sharing to the full in the national prosperity'.[8] The boom was artificially prolonged and heightened by the South African War which caused a sharp rise in prices.[9] Between mid-December, 1899, and mid-January, 1900, the pit-head prices of Derbyshire coal rose by 7s. a ton to a level which had never previously been surpassed except during the great lock-out of 1893. Some collieries had thousands of tons on order.[10] The year was one of export coal values, and of general coal prices, such as had never been known. Before 1899 the highest coal export year had been 1890, with £17,802,000. In 1896 the figure had fallen to £14,380,000. By 1899 it had risen to £21,690,000. In 1900 it was £36,410,000.[11] Between 1896 and 1900 the average price of coal at the pit-head had risen from 5s. 10d. to 10s. 10d. a ton.[12]

The boom was short-lived. At the first meeting of the newly formed Iron Trades Consultative Council, in August, 1900, Sir Benjamin Hingley, the president, said:

'Prices had been of late unduly forced owing to the cost of raw materials, fuel and consequently labour, and something in the nature of a slump had

---

[1] *Derbyshire Times*, 29 September, 1894.   [2] *Ibid.* 15 December, 1894.
[3] *Ibid.* 8 June, 1895.   [4] *Ibid.* 13 June, 1896.
[5] *Ibid.* 1 August, 1896.   [6] See Appendix II to this chapter.
[7] *Derbyshire Times*, 21 January, 1899.   [8] *Ibid.* 1 April, 1899.
[9] Clapham, *op. cit.* III, p. 18.   [10] *Derbyshire Times*, 27 January, 1900.
[11] Finlay A. Gibson, *A Compilation of Statistics of the Coal Mining Industry of the United Kingdom*, (Cardiff), 1922, p. 158.   [12] See Appendix II to this chapter.

resulted. . . . Though himself largely interested in collieries, he had no hesitation in saying that coalmasters had gone to great extremes, and that trade had suffered in consequence.'

Another speaker, Ebenezer Parks, complained that costs had tended to check the boom in the iron and steel trades.[1] Similarly, Lord Claud Hamilton, the chairman of the Great Eastern Railway, told members of the Chesterfield Chamber of Commerce that 'the colliery proprietors were making very large profits'.[2] By August the railway and gas companies had still not yet made their contracts and this was taken as an indication that prices would fall before the end of September.[3] By holding back, the railway companies secured a reduction of 2s. a ton. Moreover, they entered into short term contracts only in the expectation of further reductions in prices within the year.[4] The *Derbyshire Times* commented:

We are on the eve of bad, and, I fear, troublous times in the iron trade. . . . Poor prices and lack of orders in the iron trade presage bad times for the coal industry. By those best able to judge it is believed that we have seen the last of good trade for some time to come, and that a terrible slump will shortly be experienced.[5]

By March, 1901, coal prices were falling rapidly and Derbyshire owners were accepting railway contracts as low as 8s. 6d. a ton.

The revival of protectionist policies and the necessity of financing the South African War created further problems for the coal-owners. In 1901 the Chancellor of the Exchequer, Sir Michael Hicks-Beach, resorted to an export duty of 1s. a ton on coal. He argued that it was not an ordinary indirect tax burdensome to British consumers because, thanks to Britain's semi-monopolistic position, the foreign consumer would pay it.[6] There was an immediate outcry from the coal-owners, many of whom were Liberals and Free Traders. In Chesterfield they joined forces with Liberal politicians and miners' leaders to condemn the new tax at a public meeting, which was presided over by the mayor, W. Spooner. Maurice Deacon, of the Sheepbridge Company, moved a resolution:

That this meeting of the inhabitants of Chesterfield and district desires to enter a strong protest against the proposal of the Chancellor of the Exchequer to place an export duty of 1s. per ton on coal, being firmly convinced that such a duty would be partial and unfair in its incidence, and cannot fail to have a prejudicial effect not only on the coal industry, but on the trade of the country generally, and calls upon the Chancellor of the Exchequer to withdraw at the earliest possible moment so ill-timed, ill-starred, and ill-advised a scheme.[7]

[1] *Derbyshire Times*, 25 August, 1900.
[2] *Ibid.* 10 March, 1900.
[3] *Ibid.* 11 August, 1900.
[4] *Ibid.* 22 December, 1900.
[5] *Ibid.* 2 February, 1901.
[6] 92 H. C. Deb. 4s. cc. 640–6.
[7] *Derbyshire Times*, 27 April, 1901.

The agitation became closely linked with the question of the wages of the miners who, at one point, threatened to strike if the tax was not repealed. The discussion raged in various forms until 1906 when the coal export duty was finally abolished by Asquith.

Meanwhile the price of coal continued to fall. During 1901 the price of the Sheepbridge Company's coal was reduced by about 5s. a ton.[1] By 1902 the prevailing price for railway contracts had fallen from as much as 16s. od. in 1900 to about 9s. 3d. a ton.[2] Two years later it was down to 8s.[3] Once again pits were closed and miners thrown out of employment. In June, 1904, two pits at Pinxton and the Clay Cross Company's No. 2 pit were closed. In the following month the Alma Colliery Company announced its intention of closing the Hard Coal and Tupton seams at North Wingfield and the Staveley Company decided to close its Hartington Silkstone pit.[4] In August all but one of the pits at Grassmoor were closed.[5] Where pits were not closed they were mostly working short time.

'The depression in the coal trade', said the *Derbyshire Times*, 'is greater than at any period during the last ten years and speaks forcibly of the terrible stagnation that exists in the general trade of the country. . . . Times are hard, and when collieries are closed, as many in Derbyshire are, or only working one, two or three days a week, the wonder is how the miners are able to support themselves and their families.'[6]

The average pit-head price of coal had fallen from 10s. 10d. a ton in 1900 to 6s. 11d. in 1905 but towards the end of that year there were signs of improvement.[7] There was a slight increase in the price of coal during 1906 and a minor boom in 1907 when the average pit-head price rose to 9s. od. a ton.[8] This was attributed by Sir Charles McLaren, of the Sheepbridge Company, to growing demands from the United States for iron and from Germany for iron and coal.[9]

The directors of the Sheepbridge Company reported that the demand for pig-iron, bars and castings fell away after June, 1907, and continued to decrease in 1908. The decline was accompanied by lower prices but the reduction in the cost of raw material did not follow in proportion. The selling prices of coal were well maintained during the latter part of 1907 but in 1908 they too declined materially although contracts in operation at the higher prices assisted in upholding the average realized prices.[10] The fall continued into 1909 and by June of that year prices

[1] *Derbyshire Times*, 5 October, 1901.
[2] *Ibid.* 17 May, 1902.   [3] *Ibid.* 11 June, 1904.
[4] *Ibid.* 2 July, 1904.   [5] *Ibid.* 20 August, 1904.
[6] *Ibid.* 10 September, 1904.   [7] *Ibid.* 16 December, 1905.
[8] See Appendix II to this chapter.   [9] *Derbyshire Times*, 28 September, 1907.
[10] *Annual Report of the Sheepbridge Coal and Iron Company for the year ending 30 June, 1908.*

had reached their lowest point since 1906.[1] Within two years there had been a reduction of about 4s. a ton.[2]

Conditions in the coal trade remained uncertain until 1911. Prices were almost stationary. In 1909, 1910 and 1911 the average pit-head prices were 8s. 1d., 8s. 2d. and 8s. 2d. respectively.[3] There were many complaints about German competition and it was suggested that the Midland coalfield was losing ground to the North-Eastern coalfields in the scramble for exports. Derbyshire coal prices had been largely maintained but not increased by securing favourable railway and gas contracts.[4] In the latter half of 1911, however, contracts were being renewed at lower prices. J. and G. Wells, the owners of the Eckington collieries, stated: 'The profit made has been adversely affected by the reduction in the price of gas coal during the latter half of the year. . . .' The directors of the Hardwick Colliery Company reported a deficit of over £11,000: 'Owing to the abnormal summer the collieries were only partially employed, which, coupled with the low prices at which gas contracts were renewed, resulted in the loss previously stated.'[5]

Towards the end of 1911, however, there was a distinct improvement in the iron trade[6] and early in the following year the price of coal on the London market increased by 3s. to 4s. a ton.[7] Derbyshire's export trade also began to revive and during July alone over 33,000 tons of coal were sent to Hull for shipment.[8] The boom continued well into 1913 when the average pit-head price of coal rose to 10s. 2d. a ton.[9]

IV

During this period the British iron and steel industry was rapidly losing its supremacy. Output was increasing at a much slower rate than in the United States and Germany.[10] The production of pig-iron in Derbyshire, which had risen from 366,760 tons in 1880 to 650,000 in 1890 and 770,000 in 1900, fell to 610,000 in 1904.[11] The Derbyshire ironmasters, in common with other industrialists, became increasingly alarmed by foreign competition. J. A. Longden, the managing director of the Stanton Ironworks Company, visited America with the commission sent by the British Iron and Steel Association and saw at

[1] *Annual Report of the Sheepbridge Coal and Iron Company for the year ending 30 June, 1909.*   [2] *Derbyshire Times,* 2 October, 1909.
[3] See Appendix II to this chapter.   [4] *Derbyshire Times,* 30 September, 1911.
[5] *Ibid.* 23 March, 1912.   [6] *Ibid.* 18 November, 1911.
[7] *Ibid.* 20 January, 1912.   [8] *Ibid.* 24 August, 1912.
[9] See Appendix II to this chapter.
[10] Burnham and Hoskins, *op. cit.* pp. 25–32.
[11] Lord Aberconway, *The Basic Industries of Great Britain,* (London), 1929, p. 41.

Pittsburgh nine of the Edgar Thompson furnaces in blast, each turning out as much iron as all their nine furnaces at Stanton, with 30 men doing the work of 300 in Britain. 'Generally speaking', he said, 'they had nothing to fear from American competition as regards pipe making; but as to the manufacture of pig iron, unless they were prepared to dynamite all their furnaces and start afresh, they must go on as they were.'[1] Maurice Deacon, of the Sheepbridge Company, stated in 1902 that a protective tariff against German manufactured steel would have been preferable to the export duty on coal.[2] Two years later the *Derbyshire Times* argued that there was no greater enemy of the coal-miner than the iron dumper.[3]

Of the principal iron-making firms, the Staveley, Sheepbridge, Butterley, Clay Cross, Stanton,[4] Renishaw and Denby companies, all except the last two were large colliery owners. Their works consisted, in the main, of blast-furnaces, rolling-mills, pipe and other foundries, together with wagon shops and departments connected with the upkeep of their collieries and works. Their chief products were forge and foundry pig-iron, merchant bars and common castings, whilst several of them became important makers of cast-iron pipes for water and gas mains, iron tubbing for colliery shafts and, with the development of the London underground railways, iron shields and tubbing for tunnelling. The large profits derived from enterprises of this kind were unlikely to repeat themselves. In 1886, despite the depression in trade, the Staveley Company secured a contract for pipes worth £120,000 in connection with Manchester's scheme for obtaining water from Thirlmere[5] and, in 1901, a further contract for the cast-iron pipes required for the Derwent Valley water project.[6] 'In more than one instance', writes Lord Aberconway, 'the ironmaster financed, at great profit to himself, the undertaking which gave him its orders.'[7]

Like Derbyshire coal, most of the pig and finished iron made in the Derbyshire works was consumed at home and was not directly dependent upon foreign trade. The pig-iron was sent to Yorkshire, Birmingham, Wolverhampton, Lancashire and the Eastern Counties and there was, in addition, a very large local consumption. The finished products of the rolling mills and foundries were absorbed not only in the local collieries and other trades, but also in the Midlands, in London and in the south, where, however, they came into competition with the seaborne products of Middlesbrough and the Tees.[8] The pipe

[1] *Derbyshire Times*, 14 December, 1901.   [2] *Ibid.* 18 January, 1902.
[3] *Ibid.* 10 September, 1904.   [4] Formerly James Oakes and Company.
[5] *Derbyshire Times*, 20 January, 1886.   [6] *Ibid.* 9 February, 1901.
[7] Aberconway, *op. cit.* pp. 41–42.
[8] *The Times Engineering Supplement*, 31 May, 1905.

foundries were particularly susceptible to keen competition from Middlesbrough, Scotland and the Birmingham district, and, so far as business on the south coast was concerned, even from France. The situation was made worse by a disastrous policy of price-cutting which the Derbyshire companies pursued among themselves.[1] Moreover, iron was giving way to steel for constructional purposes of all kinds and the output of bar iron was not finding the ready market it did in former days, when the well-known iron-bridge makers and engineering firms of the Midlands, such as Andrew Handyside and Company, of Derby, were large consumers of angle iron in the work which made them famous.[2]

Originally designed, before the advent of railways, to meet a small local demand, and at a time when labour was cheap, the Derbyshire iron-works were finding it difficult to bring themselves into line with the modern plants which had been laid down at Middlesbrough and in the United States. This was the period when the districts with old-fashioned furnaces were rapidly losing their economic advantages.[3] Not all the Derbyshire iron-works were prepared to adopt the newest methods. It was argued by some of those responsible for their management that the class of iron made in their furnaces would gain nothing in quality or cheapness by the use of the larger furnaces of the north and that their existing furnaces were the best adapted to the trade they served.[4]

The larger firms, however, installed modern equipment when their resources permitted. In 1896 the Sheepbridge Company introduced Whitwell stoves to improve the efficiency of their blast-furnaces[5] and five years later Charles McLaren[6] described the Company's new, automatically charged furnaces as 'one of the most beautiful pieces of mechanical ingenuity to be seen anywhere. It represented the very latest development of American electric power, so that it reduced the labour cost to a minimum. There was not another furnace of the kind in Europe.'[7] Similarly, in 1889, the Staveley Company blew in eight new blast-furnaces[8] and decided, in 1905, to erect three large modern furnaces the output of which would be greater than that from the whole of the eight furnaces then in operation.[9]

If the Derbyshire iron industry was not entirely a dying one, it at least appeared that it was incapable of any considerable expansion. In times of depression in the iron trade, the Derbyshire coal and iron firms sold an increased quantity of coal and even in the boom year of

[1] Aberconway, *op. cit.* p. 43.   [2] *Ibid.*
[3] Burnham and Hoskins, *op. cit.* p. 143.   [4] Aberconway, *op. cit.* p. 42.
[5] *Derbyshire Times*, 19 September, 1896.   [6] Afterwards Lord Aberconway.
[7] *Derbyshire Times*, 5 October, 1901.   [8] *Ibid.* 28 September, 1889.
[9] *Ibid.* 18 November, 1905; 17 February, 1906.

1900, when pig-iron was selling at over 70s. a ton, it was stated by Charles McLaren, of the Sheepbridge Company:

They did not anticipate that iron would ever be their leading profit-making branch, but they had inherited ironworks and worked to maintain them, and make them as reasonably profitable as they could. . . . They were beginning . . . a new chapter in the life and development of the Company. They had closed, so to speak, the iron improvements. They had spent a great deal of money in bringing them up . . . to the highest point of perfection that the business of the Company would prudently permit, and now they were embarking on a policy of extending their colliery property in a direction which he hoped would make the Company a valuable investment for years to come.

He explained that although they might suffer from competition with America in iron it was extremely unlikely that they would do so in coal.[1]

Thus the relative preponderance of backward over forward integration in times of depression, which at first sight appears to run counter to the accepted view, is largely explained by the fact that coal was not only a raw material but also a commodity which could be marketed with profit. In 1881 the Secretary of the Sheepbridge Company announced:

The directors are of opinion that the entering upon the Glapwell coalfield and the vigorously carrying on of all the works necessary to establishing a colliery, cannot in the interests of the Company be postponed any longer. . . . A considerable outlay will also be required at Newstead, in order to meet the continually increasing demand for that coal.[2]

The 'Top Hard' seam was won at the Glapwell sinking in July, 1883, and in the same year the Company secured an additional lease of Silkstone coal, thereby prolonging the life of the Nesfield Colliery.[3] In 1896 some small pieces of land were bought in order to consolidate the Blackwell coalfield.[4] During the twenty years 1878 to 1898 the Company's output of coal increased from 384,000 to 1,120,000 tons whereas the production of iron rose from 41,000 to only 81,000.[5]

Similarly, in 1882, the directors of the Staveley Company arranged a lease for sixty-three years of the coal on the Sutton and Duckmanton estates of W. Arkwright, covering an area of over 5,000 acres.[6] By 1885 the new colliery on the Sutton estate was in full operation[7] and in

---

[1] Burnham and Hoskins, op. cit. p. 137; Derbyshire Times, 29 September, 1900.
[2] Derbyshire Times, 15 January, 1881.
[3] Annual Report of the Sheepbridge Company for the year ending 30 June, 1883.
[4] Derbyshire Times, 19 September, 1896.   [5] Ibid. 1 October, 1898.
[6] Annual Report of the Staveley Company for the year ending 30 June, 1882. Arkwright was a descendant of Richard Arkwright, the textile manufacturer.
[7] Annual Report of the Staveley Company for the year ending 30 June, 1885.

the following year work began on the sinking of a second colliery, Markham No. 2.[1] In 1895, because their supply of house coal was limited, the Company obtained a further lease from Arkwright which led to the development of the Bond Colliery, near Temple Normanton.[2] By 1898 the Company was raising 3,500,000 tons of coal a year.[3]

The Butterley Company pursued a similar policy, turning its attention increasingly, during the last quarter of the nineteenth century, to coal-mining. In 1876 the Denby Hall property was leased, and in 1887 the Kirkby property. The Kirkby shafts were the first to tap the concealed coalfield lying under the 'New Red Sandstone' and became one of the most important of the Company's mines.[4] At the turn of the century the Butterley Company owned nineteen pits producing just over a million tons of coal a year but some of these were losing money, and even in the newest—Upper Hartshay and Plumtre—the equipment was obsolete. After the appointment of Eustace Mitton as the Company's general manager, in 1905, certain economies were made. Seven pits were closed, and improved methods were introduced at the remainder, with the result that twelve pits were producing 2,750,000 tons of coal a year as compared with only a million tons from the previous nineteen.[5]

In the early years of the present century both the Staveley and the Sheepbridge companies continued to increase their control over coal-fields and began to create subsidiary companies. In 1905 the Staveley Company entered into an agreement with the Hickleton Main Colliery Company, of which A. B. Markham was a director, for jointly sinking and equipping two deep mines in the Doncaster district.[6] To carry out this plan the Brodsworth Main Colliery Company was formed, with a nominal capital of £300,000 to be provided by the associated companies in equal proportions.[7] By 1908 the Brodsworth Colliery, within two years of turning the first sod, was producing 6,000 tons of coal weekly and the Company was planning to develop another large colliery of between 6,000 and 10,000 acres at Edlington, near Doncaster.[8] In the following year land was acquired at Palterton for the sinking of a colliery to work the 'Top Hard' seam lying beneath the Sutton estate.[9] By 1913 the Staveley Company had leased 27,400 acres of coal, excluding joint holdings at Newstead and Brodsworth, as compared with only 4,000 acres in 1864. In the same period the royalties paid had increased

[1] Derbyshire Times, 20 January, 1886; Annual Report of the Staveley Company for the year ending 30 June, 1886.
[2] Annual Report of the Staveley Company for the year ending 30 June, 1896.
[3] Derbyshire Times, 25 June, 1898.
[4] Mottram and Coote, op. cit. p. 95.   [5] Ibid. pp. 113–14.
[6] Derbyshire Times, 26 August, 1905.
[7] Annual Report of the Staveley Company for the year ending 30 June, 1905.
[8] Derbyshire Times, 3 October, 1908.   [9] Ibid. 25 December, 1909.

G*

from £9,074 to £53,998 and the production of coal from 751,800 to 2,345,000 tons.[1]

Similarly the Sheepbridge Company, in 1900, acquired an interest in the Dinnington Main Coal Company, which was formed to work the coalfield north of Kiveton Park, near Sheffield.[2] In 1902 another coalfield at Maltby, in Yorkshire, was leased from the Earl of Scarbrough and in 1906 the Maltby Main Colliery Company was formed with a capital of £350,000 of which the Sheepbridge Company held £200,000.[3] In 1912 the Company, in conjunction with John Brown and Company, created yet another subsidiary, the Rossington Main Colliery Company, to sink a new colliery at Rossington, in Yorkshire.[4] Finally, the year 1914 saw the acquisition of a controlling interest in another large coalfield contiguous with the Dinnington area and the formation of the Firbeck Main Colliery Company.[5] By 1913 the total output of the Sheepbridge Company's pits, together with the subsidiary collieries in which it was interested, amounted to nearly 2,500,000 tons a year.[6]

The increasing emphasis upon coalmining led the coal and iron companies to turn their attention towards by-products which were to be of great importance during the First World War. In 1911 the Staveley Company installed fifty new coke ovens at the Devonshire Works, and additional plants for the production of tar, sulphate of ammonia, sulphuric acid and benzol.[7] A year later a large soap factory was erected.[8] The Sheepbridge Company, in 1907, created another subsidiary, the Power Gas Corporation, to undertake the recovery of ammonia and tar from the slack produced at the Langwith Colliery.[9] In the same year a by-product plant was also laid down at Dinnington.[10]

New plant and machinery, new collieries and ironstone mines, and additional housing and railway facilities all required large sums of money but there was little inflation of capital. In the main, the revenue earned in good years provided the means for these extensions and yet allowed substantial dividends to be paid. During the depression years of the 'eighties dividends on ordinary share capital paid by the Sheepbridge Company never exceeded 2 per cent. and for several years there was no dividend at all. The dividends paid by the Staveley Company in the same period fluctuated between $2\frac{1}{2}$ and $4\frac{1}{6}$ per cent. until 1889 when a dividend of $7\frac{1}{2}$ per cent. was declared. In the boom year, 1890,

---

[1] *Derbyshire Times*, 27 September, 1913.

[2] *Annual Reports of the Sheepbridge Company for the years ending 30 June, 1900; 30 June 1901.*

[3] *Annual Report of the Sheepbridge Company for the year ending 30 June, 1906.*

[4] *Ibid. 1912.*   [5] *Derbyshire Times*, 2 May, 1914.

[6] *Ibid.* 4 October, 1913.   [7] *Ibid.* 30 September, 1911.   [8] *Ibid.* 11 May, 1912.

[9] *Annual Report of the Sheepbridge Company for the year ending 30 June, 1907.*

[10] *Derbyshire Times*, 3 October, 1908.

the Sheepbridge Company was able to pay $7\frac{1}{2}$ per cent. and the Staveley Company, 15 per cent. Thereafter the Sheepbridge dividends gradually fell to $2\frac{1}{2}$ per cent., rising steeply between 1898 and 1901 from 5 per cent. to 20 per cent. The Staveley dividends fell to $4\frac{7}{12}$ per cent. in 1898 and rose to a peak of $33\frac{1}{3}$ per cent. in 1900. The dividends of both companies fell to $7\frac{1}{2}$ per cent. in 1904 and then began to rise. In 1912 the Sheepbridge Company was paying 20 per cent. and the Staveley Company 25 per cent.[1]

In 1902, after a period of rapid expansion, the nominal capital of the Staveley Company was no higher than it had been ten years previously, when it stood at £1,326,000.[2] The Company's contribution of £150,000 towards the financing of the Brodsworth Main Colliery started with an appropriation of £20,000 from the profits of 1905–6. It was estimated that the opening out of the new colliery would take from four to five years and that the Company would be able to finance the development out of profits as the work proceeded.[3]

The formation of the subsidiary companies gave rise to some uneasiness among the shareholders of the Sheepbridge Company. The policy was defended by Maurice Deacon, the managing director, in 1906 on the grounds that it minimized risks and enabled the Sheepbridge Company 'to control a large area and the selling of the coal in the market'.[4] For the Dinnington, Maltby and Rossington enterprises the Company had to provide £618,978. Some £430,000 was reserved from profits and written off the capital account but by 1914 there was still £188,978 to be found. In addition, the Company had subscribed £150,000, out of a total capital of £300,000, to the Firbeck Main Colliery Company. Since 1892 there had been no increases of the Sheepbridge Company's capital yet further capital was needed for the subsidiary concerns until, as in the case of Dinnington, they were able to provide adequate capital for themselves. The company therefore increased its capital to £1,250,000 by the issue of 450,300 new ordinary shares of £1 each. Lord Aberconway told a meeting of shareholders that this was the logical outcome of their policy of acquiring new coalfields to take the place of those that were becoming exhausted:

Therefore they took these large areas in South Yorkshire, but as they did not want to put all their eggs into one basket, knowing that new collieries must be more or less speculation, while retaining the absolute control of these

[1] Figures compiled from the annual reports of the Staveley and Sheepbridge Companies.
[2] *Annual Report of the Staveley Company for the year ending 30 June, 1892*; *Derbyshire Times*, 27 September, 1902.
[3] *Annual Report of the Staveley Company for the year ending 30 June, 1905.*
[4] *Derbyshire Times*, 29 September, 1906.

new undertakings they admitted other shareholders to participate. In other words, they found the majority of the capital, so really their risks were spread over a considerable area.[1]

V

The depression years of the 'eighties were a testing time for the Derbyshire collieries. Many of the smaller, uneconomic concerns had to close down. The Swadlincote Colliery Company went into liquidation in 1880.[2] The following year the Monkwood Coal Company failed, with liabilities amounting to £33,000.[3] In 1885 two collieries were closed at Heanor and T. H. and G. Small, the proprietors of the Stanley and South Normanton collieries, filed a petition for liquidation with liabilities of between £20,000 and £30,000.[4] The Westfield Colliery Company, Hasland, and the Boythorpe Coal Company, Chesterfield, were both wound up in 1887.[5]

The larger and older established firms were able to survive, mainly by ploughing back the profits which they had accumulated in the good years. The Grassmoor Colliery Company is a good example. The Barnes family had been interested in coalmining ever since the eighteenth century.[6] Alfred Barnes studied engineering at Robert Stephenson's works in Newcastle but the long hours and close work caused his health to break down. He was then apprenticed to Tod, Maylor and Company, a Liverpool firm with a large shipping and mercantile trade, and during his four years there he gained a considerable amount of commercial knowledge. When he returned to Chesterfield in 1846 he was told by his father, who owned some land at Grassmoor, that he was to start a colliery there. A lease was arranged with the Duke of Devonshire and Grassmoor was started with three small shafts. According to Barnes, 'the first load of coal was taken away by old Mrs. Hopkinson . . . on her donkey cart'.[7] They then sank two pits which cost them £40,000 and left them with only £28 in the bank. Barnes claimed to have foreseen the great trade boom of the early 'seventies and, although he was derided by other coal-owners and had no money, he bought 350 wagons on credit and, for some time, kept them idle in his sidings:

He was prepared for the demand, others were not, and he made a very large sum of money—he would not say how much, but he sold 120,000 tons of coal, and made by it more money than Grassmoor would ever make again

---

[1] *Derbyshire Times*, 2 May, 1914.
[2] *Ibid.* 25 December, 1880.   [3] *Ibid.* 9 February, 1881.
[4] *Ibid.* 13 June, 22 August, 19 December, 1885.
[5] *Ibid.* 22 January, 5 March, 1887.   [6] See Prologue, p. 19.
[7] *Derbyshire Times*, 28 November, 1896.

in one year. The whole of that money he invested in the pits. They sank to the Black Shale: everything that had been made out of the colliery had been kept in the district, and although they had been near bankruptcy in theory many times, they had always had the colliery.[1]

It was, perhaps, a sign of the times that the Grassmoor Company sought limited liability in 1884. The nominal capital then stood at £200,000. With the exception of G. Leach, the Company's cashier, the subscribers were all members of the Barnes family.[2] Large-scale working, requiring considerable capital investment, was the secret of survival. By 1896 the Grassmoor Company controlled a great group of collieries capable of producing 24,000 tons of coal a week. There were 60 miles of underground workings, six of which were at the face.[3]

Similarly, the new enterprises which were started during this period were on a much larger scale than their predecessors. Reference has already been made to the extensive collieries which were developed to exploit the Top Hard seam. Those working other seams were on an equally large scale. The Hardwick Coal Company, with a share capital of £350,000, was formed in 1900 to purchase as a going concern the Holmewood and other collieries, which had been successfully worked by a private partnership since 1839, and to establish a new colliery at Williamthorpe capable of raising 4,000 tons of coal a day. The three pits at Holmewood, which were producing about 680,000 tons a year, were to be fully developed underground so as to increase their output to 1,000,000 tons a year.[4] The coal bed to which the new shaft was sunk at Williamthorpe lay 550 yards beneath the surface and in 1905 it was the deepest colliery in the Midland district.[5]

Mining engineering of this order was aided by the use of new techniques. At Williamthorpe sinking operations began in October, 1901, but such great quantities of water were encountered that two years later a depth of only 180 yards had been reached. Workings connected with the disused Lings colliery had to be passed through, and as these were full of water the old colliery had to be almost completely drained before any further progress could be made. There were great difficulties in the construction of the shaft, which was 19 feet in diameter. For 180 yards it had to be tubbed and, although the ground yielded $2\frac{1}{2}$ tons of water a minute and the pressure of water near the bottom of the tubbing was from 600 to 700 lb. per square inch, the iron plates were so tightly wedged together that the shaft was perfectly dry.[6] At the Bolsover

[1] *Derbyshire Times*, 28 November, 1896, (report of a speech by Barnes).
[2] *Ibid*. 6 December, 1884.   [3] *Ibid*. 28 November, 1896.
[4] *Ibid*. 11 July, 1903. The directors were Captain Chambers Didham, Tibshelf; C. J. Didham, Hasland House, near Chesterfield; M. H. Humble, Walton House, near Chesterfield; Mrs. Ward, Heath, near Chesterfield.
[5] *Ibid*. 7 January, 1905.   [6] *Ibid*.

Company's Creswell Colliery the shaft was 445 yards deep, 18 feet in diameter, and lined with tubbing to a depth of 125 yards. The Staveley Company's Warsop Main Colliery had shafts 528 yards deep and 19 feet in diameter.[1]

Wider and deeper shafts called for improvements in winding. At Grassmoor, where a shaft descended 1,350 feet to the Black Shale seam, a horizontal winding engine with two 36-inch cylinders and a 6-foot stroke was used.[2] The winding engine for Williamthorpe, made by Markham's of Chesterfield, had cylinders 42 inches in diameter and a 7-foot stroke.[3] In 1887 the Shireoaks Colliery Company put down a pair of new winding engines, made by James Farrer, of Barnsley, at the Southgate Colliery. The shaft and crank of these engines weighed over 7 tons.[4] At Creswell the two winding engines had 40-inch cylinders and a 7-foot stroke.[5]

Cages also increased in size and capacity. At Grassmoor in 1896 double-decked cages were in use, carrying two tubs on each deck.[6] The double-decked cages at Creswell and Warsop were each able to carry six tubs of 12 cwt. and eight tubs of 11 cwt. respectively.[7] At Williamthorpe it was decided to install triple-decked cages capable of carrying twelve trams, or 7 tons of coal, to the surface every 45 seconds.[8] By such methods as these the new collieries were able to bring their increased output to the surface with great speed and vied with each other to create records. The downcast shafts at both Warsop and Williamthorpe were equipped to wind 3,000 tons of coal in a working day of $8\frac{1}{2}$ hours.[9]

Trade unionists and colliery managers alike, however, became aware of the dangers of high-speed winding. In 1907 the Midland branch of the National Association of Colliery Managers met at Nottingham to consider the use of band brakes. R. Laverick told his colleagues that the subject was of the utmost importance because several accidents had occurred in the district as a result of cages going down pits too rapidly.[10] Meanwhile various safety devices were being introduced. In 1882 John King's safety hook, for the prevention of over-winding, was tested by the Pinxton Colliery Company. The *Derbyshire Times* reported: 'The two-decked cage loaded with coals weighing upwards of two tons was drawn up into the headgear where Mr. King's plate was fixed for disengaging the hook, and in an instant the rope went flying over the pulley, leaving the cage safely suspended on the hook.'[11] Another

[1] *Derbyshire Times*, 27 July, 1907.
[2] *Ibid.* 28 November, 1896.
[3] *Ibid.* 7 January, 1905.
[4] *Ibid.* 12 March, 1887.
[5] *Ibid.* 27 July, 1907.
[6] *Ibid.* 28 November, 1896.
[7] *Ibid.* 27 July, 1907.
[8] *Ibid.* 7 January, 1905.
[9] *Ibid.* 7 January, 1905; 21 July, 1907.
[10] *Ibid.* 14 December, 1907.
[11] *Ibid.* 7 October, 1882. See pp. 55, 71.

invention to achieve the same end was introduced by C. Sebastian Smith at the Shipley Colliery in 1896. He argued that the speed at which the cage was run up to the wheel was sometimes so great that, before the rope was detached by the safety hook, the cage rose the full length of the suspending chains and then dropped with so much force that the suspending tackle broke away from the detaching hook and allowed the cage to fall down the shaft. To prevent this he devised a system of props in the headgear to catch the cage.[1] Accidents were also caused by ropes breaking and in 1868 T. Calow, of Staveley, had invented a safety catch which gripped the wooden slides then widely used for guiding the cage down the shaft. The introduction of wire or rail slides necessitated a modification of this device which Calow demonstrated at Staveley and at the Newcastle upon Tyne Engineering and Industrial Exhibition in 1887.[2] In 1908 S. G. Bennett, a Chesterfield electrician, patented a safety cage which attracted much attention among miners and colliery owners. It employed a ratchet apparatus and was installed at one of the pits of the Pilsley Colliery Company where it operated successfully.[3] Two years later Bennett patented a disengaging gear which was installed at the Butterley Company's Ormonde Colliery, near Heanor.[4] In the same year another safety device for arresting the fall of cages was patented by Henry Claytor, of Clay Cross.[5]

Underground also there were some important advances in mining techniques. The necessity of reducing cost caused many colliery owners to consider the introduction of coal-cutting machinery. In 1897 Charles Latham, the Director of Mining Instruction at University College, Nottingham, told a meeting of Midland colliery managers:

The depressed condition of the coal trade had made the mining engineer turn his attention in the direction of any appliance which might, no matter in how small a degree, tend to lessen the cost of production, without in any way increasing the risk to life or limb of those employed underground, and consequently the question of coal getting by mechanical means was one which at the present time was occupying, and he thought rightly too, a foremost place in the thoughts of all classes of the mining community.[6]

Various difficulties stood in the way of mechanization. Many coal-cutting machines had been invented but, until the early years of the present century, none was entirely successful. Some were too cumber-

---

[1] C. Sebastian Smith, 'Safety Props for supporting Cages in the headgear of Pits in Cases of Overwinding', *Transactions of the Chesterfield and Midland Counties Institute of Mining Engineers*, 1896.
[2] *Derbyshire Times*, 16 April, 1887. See pp. 55, 71.
[3] *Ibid.* 8 August, 19 December, 1908; 27 November, 1909.
[4] *Ibid.* 4 June, 1910.   [5] *Ibid.* 22 October, 1910.
[6] *Ibid.* 17 April, 1897.

some, others were too expensive, whilst the majority produced too much small coal. Moreover, many of the seams in Derbyshire were so difficult to work that the use of machinery was completely precluded.

By 1903, F. W. Hardwick, Professor of Mining at Firth College, Sheffield, was able to tell Derbyshire undermanagers and deputies that most of the mechanical difficulties of getting coal by machinery had been removed and the question then before them was the extent to which it was economical to use such machines. He was of the opinion that 'the larger employment of the cutting machines in the United States was attributable mainly to the inferior class of labour employed in the American pits'.[1] Nevertheless, some colliery proprietors were doubtful about the ability of the British miner, whatever his superiority, to compete with his pick against foreign machinery.[2] By 1897 the whole of the undercutting in Pope and Pearson's collieries, at Normanton, Yorkshire, was being done by machinery.[3] In 1894 a Rigg and Meikle-john coal-cutting machine was introduced into one of the Staveley Company's pits. It was driven by compressed air and worked by four men, one controlling the machine, two laying rails and setting props, and another following the machine, clearing out the cut to let the coal drop. In a trial at the Springbank Colliery, Airdrie, the machine had made an undercut of 3 feet for a distance of 70 yards in 90 minutes.[4] But the introduction of such machinery was slow in Derbyshire as elsewhere. By 1900 there were only 58 machines in the county which holed 645,685 tons of coal, and 13 small machines, which headed about 11,847 yards, getting out about 24,926 tons. In 1902 there were 19 more holing machines, accounting for an additional 151,775 tons of coal. The heading machines had increased to 16 but they drove only 7,209 yards of heading and yielded 14,672 tons of coal. The total amount of coal raised in Derbyshire in 1902 was 15,519,964 tons.[5] Thus the percentage of machine-cut coal in Derbyshire in that year was 4·6, or 3·2 per cent. above the aggregate for the whole country.[6]

Increasing attention was also paid to the lighting of mines. Where candles were no longer used, illumination was provided by the miners' oil lamp, which was neither safe nor efficient. Various attempts were made to perfect an electric lamp but it was found difficult to produce one which combined cheapness, portability, safety and intensity of light. Some progress was made. At the Creswell Colliery, in 1907, there were 1,500 lamps in use worked by secondary batteries, which were charged by a small dynamo.[7] Such lamps were not good by

[1] *Derbyshire Times*, 10 January, 1903.   [2] *Ibid.* 17 January, 1897.
[3] *Ibid.* 17 April, 1897.   [4] *Ibid.* 3 November, 1894.
[5] *Reports of H.M. Inspectors of Mines*, 1902.
[6] *Derbyshire Times*, 10 January, 1903.   [7] *Ibid.* 27 July, 1907.

modern standards for, in the same year, a Derbyshire colliery manager stated:

There were reasons why safety and intensity of light could not go hand in hand. At some time they felt that they ought to have a better light than they had at present to work by, and he hoped before many years had elapsed a lamp would be invented capable of producing a light equal to 6–10 candlepower.[1]

Although it was not easy to provide the miner with a satisfactory source of light at the coal face, electricity began to be used for lighting other parts of mines. Swan's incandescent lamp was demonstrated at a meeting of the Society of Telegraph Engineers in 1880 and, in the discussion which followed, Professor Tyndall suggested that it might be adapted for use in collieries. Trials were carried out by R. E. Crompton and Company, in co-operation with Swan's Electric Lighting Company, at the Pleasley Colliery in Derbyshire and also by the proprietor of the Earnock Colliery, near Glasgow. These may have been the first collieries in the world to be lighted by electricity.[2] The developments were discussed in 1881 by the Mechanical Section of the British Association, meeting at York, under the presidency of Siemens.[3] But progress was slow, and as late as 1896 the Grassmoor Colliery was still lit by gas jets.[4] Electric lights were in use at the Butterley Company's Britain Colliery in 1902, at Williamthorpe in 1905 and at Warsop Main in 1907.[5]

The increasing use of electricity meant that power supplies had to be improved. The chairman of the South Normanton Colliery Company said, in 1904: 'They had turned their old-fashioned lighting arrangement into a modern construction, and their 100 horsepower electric plant supplied light, he believed, as good as any in the country, even as good as that supplied to the King.'[6] By changing over from direct to alternating current generators the Butterley Company, in 1905, was able to install power lines connecting all its Nottinghamshire pits in one group and all its Derbyshire pits in another.[7] In 1901 the Clay Cross Company installed a blowing engine of 450 horsepower driven by blast-furnace gas. In addition to providing blast to the furnaces it also generated electricity for the works and collieries within a radius of several miles.[8]

---

[1] *Derbyshire Times*, 23 November, 1907.
[2] *Ibid.* 10 September, 1881. Clapham, (*op. cit.* II, p. 109) has it that the Earnock Colliery 'is believed to have been the first in the world to be lighted by electricity' but makes no mention of the Pleasley Colliery.
[3] *Ibid.*   [4] *Ibid.* 28 November, 1896.
[5] Mottram and Coote, *op. cit.* p. 114; *Derbyshire Times*, 7 January, 1905; 27 July, 1907.   [6] *Derbyshire Times*, 23 January, 1904.
[7] Mottram and Coote, *op. cit.* p. 114.
[8] *Derbyshire Times*, 21 December, 1901.

Other colliery companies gave encouragement to the formation of electricity companies. In 1898 both Maurice Deacon and Charles Markham gave evidence before a Committee of the House of Lords in support of the Bill for the General Power Distributing Company. Deacon stated that it would be to the advantage of collieries to have electric power without having to bear the capital outlay for the installation of generating plant and that the production from a large installation would be very much better than the production of small installations at individual collieries.[1]

The use of electricity for lighting was the first step towards its use for other purposes underground. Emerson Bainbridge told the Institute of Mechanical Engineers in 1890 that the development was 'in its infancy' and had in few places got beyond the lighting and pumping of the first experiments but that it was 'already . . . successfully applied' for underground haulage in some South Yorkshire pits.[2] Deacon proposed to use electric power for haulage in 1898. C. R. Morgan, the general manager of the Hardwick and Wingerworth collieries, went further and said that his Company would use it for haulage and also for coal-cutting and pumping. 'It would also be of use to them for tools in their workshops, and also for the use of lathes, drilling machines, and so forth.'[3] At Bolsover, in 1905, an electrical plant of 700 horsepower was installed and provision was made for doubling its capacity if necessary. It was intended to provide the whole of the power for the colliery with the exception of winding and ventilation.[4] But the use of electricity for power made even slower progress than its use for lighting. The coal-owners agreed with Robert Smillie, speaking for the miners, that electric cutters were dangerous in a fiery mine. Indeed, A. B. Markham would have had the use of electricity prohibited altogether in such mines.[5] Similarly, J. P. Houfton, the general manager of the Bolsover Company, told the Midland Counties Institute of Mining and Mechanical Engineers as late as 1911 that he did not believe in the electric motor at the coal face at all.[6]

Perhaps the most revolutionary technical changes of all in this period occurred not underground but in the handling of the coal at the pit-head. Before the great price-fall and the advent of foreign competition, British coal producers paid little attention to economy and grading apart from a certain amount of hand picking and hand sorting. As a

[1] *Derbyshire Times*, 25 June, 1898.
[2] *Transactions of the Institute of Mechanical Engineers*, 1890, pp. 383–4.
[3] *Derbyshire Times*, 25 June, 1898.   [4] *Ibid*. 3 June, 1905.
[5] *Departmental Committee on Electricity in Mines*, 1904, Evidence of Robert Smillie, Q. 3184; Evidence of A. B. Markham, Q. 4273.
[6] *Transactions of the Midland Counties Institute of Mining and Mechanical Engineers*, March, 1911.

result Britain was, in 1914, 'far behind the continental countries' in preparing coal for market.[1] In 1905, on the other hand, the Germans were said to be selling on guaranteed chemical analysis and guaranteed percentage of error in the sizes of the coals they supplied.[2] In the words of the historians of the Butterley Company: 'Customers were now becoming very choosy. Coal was no longer just coal but known by different names for its different sizes and qualities.'[3] This situation led most of the important colliery companies to install machinery at the pit-head for screening, sizing, sorting and washing the coal before it was sent to the consumer. At Grassmoor the picking bands for sorting the coal, the screens and the weighing apparatus were said, in 1896, to be 'all models of their kind'.[4] The picking band at No. 2 Pit, travelling at the rate of 70 feet a minute, was capable of handling 1,200 tons of coal and slack in $8\frac{1}{2}$ hours. In the same year a new picking band was being erected at a cost of £6,000.[5] At the Creswell and Warsop collieries there were extensive screening plants. The large coal passed on belts direct to the wagons and the smaller coal was automatically conveyed to the jigging screens where it was sorted into four grades. It was then hand picked by boys as it passed along separate belts to the wagons.[6] It was not until after the First World War that washeries became widely used. Rheolaveur washeries were introduced by the Butterley Company in 1922.[7]

Many colliery companies also began to develop by-products and ancillary activities such as brickmaking. The Grassmoor Colliery Company had two Schofield machines and two Fawcett presses which produced from 12,000 to 14,000 bricks a day. The semi-plastic bricks were then burnt in ordinary open-topped kilns.[8] Before 1914 the Butterley Company was also making its own bricks from its own brickfields.[9] Beehive coke ovens, which wasted both heat and by-products, were used at most collieries in Derbyshire until the turn of the century. There were 180 of them at Grassmoor in 1896.[10] The Clay Cross Company continued to use the type of oven which had been installed in 1840 to provide coke for the Midland Railway Company's locomotives.[11] In developing by-product coke ovens, as in other matters, the Continental countries had taken the lead and in 1905 the Clay Cross Company introduced Simplex by-product ovens from Belgium.[12] Fifty modern

[1] Jevons, op. cit. p. 230.
[2] R.C. on Coal Supplies, 1905, p. 8.
[3] Mottram and Coote, op. cit. p. 114.
[4] Derbyshire Times, 28 November, 1896.
[5] Ibid.
[6] Ibid. 27 July, 1907.
[7] Mottram and Coote, op. cit. p. 114.
[8] Derbyshire Times, 28 November, 1896.
[9] Mottram and Coote, op. cit. p. 114.
[10] Derbyshire Times, 28 November, 1896.
[11] See Chapter I, p. 43.
[12] Derbyshire Times, 11 November, 1905.

coke ovens were erected at the Hardwick Colliery in 1911.[1] A year later the *Derbyshire Times* reported:

The by-product plants covered by the various collieries in Derbyshire have proved so profitable that we hear of large extensions to the existing plants being undertaken by two large companies in the district. . . . There is undoubtedly a very considerable revenue to be obtained by scientific development of by-product plant, and Derbyshire colliery owners have not been slow to appreciate the fact.[2]

[1] *Derbyshire Times*, 27 May, 1911.   [2] *Ibid*. 27 January, 1912.

APPENDIX I

Output, Employment and Productivity in Derbyshire, 1880–1913

| | Output Tons | Number of Persons Employed | | | Output per Person Employed | |
		Under ground	Above ground	Total	Under ground Tons	Under and above ground Tons
1880	7,903,834	21,183	6,073	27,256	373	289
1881	8,508,923	21,322	6,100	27,422	399	310
1882	8,358,936	21,269	6,090	27,359	393	305
1883	8,787,967	21,765	6,139	27,904	403	314
1884	8,581,001	22,846	6,211	29,057	387	304
1885	9,231,536	23,636	6,288	29,924	390	308
1886	8,908,865	23,801	6,217	30,018	374	296
1887	9,063,407	23,512	6,225	29,737	385	304
1888	9,409,592	24,654	6,514	31,168	381	301
1889	10,093,222	25,678	6,607	32,285	393	312
1890	10,455,974	28,193	6,955	35,148	370	297
1891	11,039,536	30,587	7,575	38,162	360	289
1892	11,141,152	32,193	7,987	40,180	346	277
1893	7,882,779	32,714	7,669	40,383	240	195
1894	11,472,579	33,963	8,221	42,184	337	271
1895	11,295,786	33,585	8,847	42,432	336	266
1896	11,774,639	33,438	9,054	42,492	352	277
1897	12,648,419	33,797	9,127	42,924	374	294
1898	13,573,754	34,085	8,843	42,928	398	316
1899	14,594,424	35,191	8,850	44,041	414	331
1900	15,243,031	37,384	9,404	46,788	407	325
1901	14,907,344	39,934	9,979	49,913	373	298
1902	15,519,964	40,576	10,196	50,772	382	305
1903	15,145,710	41,433	10,263	51,696	365	292
1904	15,078,680	41,421	10,215	51,636	364	292
1905	15,683,476	40,833	10,398	51,231	384	306
1906	16,567,209	41,321	10,583	51,904	400	319
1907	18,083,016	44,350	10,949	55,299	407	327
1908	16,958,155	44,407	11,249	55,656	381	304
1909	16,869,347	45,469	10,753	56,222	371	300
1910	17,276,941	46,164	10,824	56,988	374	303
1911	17,164,490	46,609	11,176	57,785	368	297
1912	16,567,927	47,577	11,373	58,950	348	281
1913	18,129,424	48,486	11,883	60,369	373	300

Source: *Reports of H.M. Inspectors of Mines, 1880–1913.*

APPENDIX II

Average Annual Pit-head Prices of Coal, 1882–1913

| | Midlands | United Kingdom | |
	Average price per ton in pence	Average price per ton in pence	Trend (Nine years' moving average)
1882	83·88	60·00	—
1883	71·88	68·00	—
1884	72·24	65·00	—
1885	69·00	62·00	—
1886	66·36	58·50	67·46
1887	67·80	57·87	71·46
1888	65·64	60·60	73·57
1889	78·72	76·20	75·41
1890	90·36	99·00	77·35
1891	89·16	96·00	78·89
1892	87·84	87·00	80·27
1893	91·56	81·51	81·42
1894	81·84	79·43	81·43
1895	73·56	72·42	80·54
1896	69·84	70·26	84·28
1897	72·00	71·00	87·09
1898	74·00	76·22	89·02
1899	83·05	91·03	90·41
1900	122·76	129·66	91·98
1901	109·78	112·29	93·44
1902	96·72	98·84	95·27
1903	90·86	91·93	98·88
1904	86·67	86·59	100·66
1905	82·26	83·39	96·96
1906	72·23	87·50	95·41
1907	103·77	108·70	95·29
1908	98·89	107·00	97·15
1909	91·33	96·37	101·04
1910	86·34	98·37	—
1911	86·73	97·79	—
1912	98·27	108·68	—
1913	106·37	121·52	—

Source: Finlay A. Gibson, *A Compilation of Statistics of the Coal Mining Industry of the United Kingdom*, (Cardiff), 1922, p. 157.

CHAPTER VI

TRADE UNION ORGANIZATION AND FINANCE

I. THE OFFICIALS AND THE EXECUTIVE COMMITTEE

The precise details of the founding of the Derbyshire Miners' Association are not known. From 1876 the dissatisfaction with the policy pursued by the South Yorkshire Association led to a number of meetings in Derbyshire at which the possibility of secession was discussed. The split in the South Yorkshire Association at the end of 1879 created a situation which was favourable to the establishment of a separate organization in Derbyshire and no doubt those who had been most active in advocating secession were quick to seize their opportunity. In February, 1880, it was reported:

> After several weeks' deliberation amongst the representatives of over 10,000 miners in Derbyshire, they have decided to form an Association, under the title of the 'Derbyshire Miners' Association', and whose headquarters are to be at Chesterfield. . . . These new steps, it is expected, will reduce the number of lodges permanently contributing to the South Yorkshire and North Derbyshire Miners' Association as most, if not all, lodges in East Derbyshire will join their own County Association.[1]

In September, 1889, W. E. Harvey stated that the union 'was formed some ten years ago by five men who met at the Sun Inn, Chesterfield, and decided to form, if possible, an association. These five persons were Messrs. Haslam, Harvey, J. Catchpole, John Smith and R. Bunting.'[2] There are no records of this meeting. No doubt there were many such gatherings before the Derbyshire Miners' Association was formally constituted. The earliest extant record of the Derbyshire Miners' Association is a printed account of income and expenditure for the period from 4 January to 19 February, 1880, which is probably the union's first financial statement for it includes in the expenditure account an item: 'To John Briggs Bell—Printing Circulars—Initiary Meeting—

---

[1] *Derbyshire Times*, 21 February, 1880.   [2] *Ibid.* 14 September, 1889.

5s. 6d.' The name of James Haslam appears as 'Secretary *Pro Tem.*' and the accounts were audited by J. Catchpole and J. Smith.

References to 'J. Catchpole' are apt to be confusing at this period. There were two Catchpoles, John and Jonathan, but it is not known whether they were related. John Catchpole was born at Thrandestone, in Norfolk, in 1843, and came to Chesterfield at the age of 9. He had been a prominent miners' leader ever since the 'sixties, had taken an active part in the South Yorkshire Association and had been a strong supporter of the movement for secession. In 1865 he had become checkweighman, the first in Derbyshire, at the Staveley Company's Springwell Colliery, and was later checkweighman at the Ballarat Colliery, New Whittington, and the Lockoford Colliery, near Chesterfield. He was also a Primitive Methodist local preacher for over forty years. John Catchpole was certainly one of the founders of the Association but, beyond speaking at one or two meetings and writing an occasional letter to the press, he appears to have taken no leading part in the movement after 1880. Like many trade union leaders of his day who became weary of the constant insecurity arising from the threat of victimization, he started 'a small business' as newsagent, stationer and sub-postmaster at Holywell Cross, Chesterfield, which he carried on until his death in 1919.[1] Little is heard of Jonathan Catchpole before 1880 but he too had been active in the movement for secession and along with James Haslam, W. E. Harvey, Richard Bunting and John Smith, drafted and signed the first rules of the Association.

Whoever may have played a part in the founding of the union, these were the five men who guided it during the early years of its existence. Like John Catchpole, Richard Bunting, of Ilkeston, was a local preacher, had been a prominent trade union leader since the 'sixties and was, by now, one of the *éminences grises* of the movement. John Smith, of Danesmoor, who was then 47 years of age, was a close friend of Haslam and, as a member of the Clay Cross lodge of the South Yorkshire Association, had served as a delegate to Barnsley during the early 'sixties.[2] But it was Haslam and Harvey, both younger men, who were to be the twin pillars of the Association for the next thirty years.

James Haslam was born at Clay Cross in 1842. His father was a shoemaker, and he was the youngest of a family of ten children. He received a rudimentary education at the old Stable School at Clay Cross and at an early age went to work on the pit brow, earning 10d. for a working day of twelve hours. At the age of 16 he began to work in the pit and subsequently passed through all the different

---

[1] *Derbyshire Times*, 2 August, 1919.
[2] South Yorkshire Miners' Association, Clay Cross Lodge, Receipt Book; *Derbyshire Times*, 2 April, 1910.

branches of the miner's trade.[1] Like many of the miners' leaders of this period he was a Primitive Methodist and remembered with pride the days when the so-called 'Ranters' used to sing and shout through the streets of Clay Cross.[2] Haslam became Secretary of the Clay Cross lodge of the South Yorkshire Association in October, 1875, in succession to Thomas Shore. He continued in office until 11 October, 1879, when the lodge sent its delegate bearing financial contributions to Barnsley for the last time. During Haslam's tenure of the secretaryship the number of financial members in the Clay Cross lodge fell from 350 to 17, and the fortnightly contributions to the South Yorkshire Association from £16 3s. 10d. to 10s. 6d.[3] Thus it is not surprising that Haslam was among those who saw the necessity for the organization of an independent county association.

William Edwin Harvey had a similar background. He was born at Hasland, near Chesterfield, in 1852, being the youngest of five children. His father died when he was still a child and his mother had to eke out a living by baking bread. Harvey was educated at the village church school until he was 10 years of age and then had to go to the pit. At the age of 17 he heard a lecture on trade unionism which induced him to join the Hasland lodge of the South Yorkshire Association. He soon began to take an active and prominent part in the work of his lodge and when he was only 21 years old he was elected delegate to the Council meetings at Barnsley. This led to his dismissal from the colliery and, like many another earnest trade unionist, he found himself blacklisted and refused employment at every other colliery in the neighbourhood. He therefore moved to Sheepbridge where, after about six years, he again suffered because of his trade union activity and was obliged to move to Morton to obtain employment. Harvey was converted to Primitive Methodism and by the time of the formation of the Derbyshire Miners' Association he had been a local preacher for several years.[4]

When the union was first formed Haslam was Secretary, Harvey Treasurer and Bunting President. Smith and Catchpole, in addition to acting as auditors were described as 'Committee men'. At this time the slender financial resources of the Association did not permit the employment of full-time officials and Haslam and Harvey and their colleagues had to carry out their trade union duties after a full day in the pit. For these services the Secretary was paid £1 a month and the Treasurer, 6s. 8d. The President received no payment other than 5s.

---

[1] William Hallam, *Miners' Leaders*, (London), 1894, p. 37.
[2] *Derbyshire Times*, 17 April, 1909.
[3] South Yorkshire Miners' Association, Clay Cross Lodge, Receipt Book.
[4] Hallam, *op. cit.* p. 41; *Derbyshire Times*, 2 May, 1914.

for each attendance at a Council meeting. The Secretary and Treasurer were paid 2s. and 1s. 9d. respectively for such attendances and the two auditors each received 3s. for the periodical inspections of the accounts. In addition, if it was necessary for the officials to attend meetings or serve on deputations during working hours they were compensated for loss of wages and their travelling expenses were refunded. When Haslam attended the Sliding Scale Conference at Birmingham, in October, 1881, he was paid 12s. 6d. a day for wages and personal expenses.[1]

According to the 1880 rules the President was nominated from the lodges and elected or re-elected by the Council every six months. The General Secretary was elected by a majority of the members throughout the Association. He was subject to the control of the Council and was not allowed to vote at Council meetings but the Council had no power to dismiss him without the sanction of the lodges. The Secretary's wages were determined by the Council and paid by the Treasurer weekly. The General Treasurer was elected by the delegates at a Council meeting, each delegate's voting power depending upon the numbers in his lodge. The Treasurer's wages, railway fares and expenses were determined by the Council and his tenure of office was subject to the same conditions as that of the Secretary. Provision was also made for the election of a District Committee which was to be 'always in existence'. It consisted of not less than nine 'experienced' members, including the President, Secretary and Treasurer. Each had a vote at all District Committee meetings and received the same expenses for attendance as the delegates to the Council. Various fines were imposed upon members of the executive for dereliction of duty.

Victimization was a constant danger which had to be faced by members of the executive and by local officials alike. Haslam once recalled how, when the union was first formed, it was difficult to persuade anyone to take the chair at their public meetings. When Harvey and he went to a village to address the miners they had to turn to the fireplace and say 'Mr. Chairman'.[2] In 1881 it was stated by the officials:

We are well aware that it is very dangerous for the men at many of the Collieries to advocate Unionism, but it will have to be done by somebody, and we most earnestly trust that every available opportunity will be seized to advance our cause.[3]

Within a year of the founding of the union, Richard Bunting, the President, was dismissed from the Cottam Colliery. He managed to

---

[1] *Minutes of the Derbyshire Miners' Association* (subsequently referred to as *D.M.A.*), 15 October, 1881.
[2] *Derbyshire Times*, 17 April, 1909.   [3] *D.M.A.* 3 September, 1881.

obtain employment at the Shireoaks Colliery and asked the Council to excuse him from addressing various public meetings on the grounds that 'it would have been very injudicious to have lost time to attend the Meetings, when doing so very likely would have imperilled his position at the new place of work, especially if the reason for his absence had been known'.[1] On 14 May, 1881, Bunting was again dismissed because of trade union sympathies and a friend who tried to obtain employment for him at the Staveley Colliery was told that Bunting was unacceptable and that 'anyone else would have to go if they urged their plea to the extent that he (Bunting's friend) had done'. Bunting was granted 'Victim Pay' and was to use his enforced leisure to extend and improve the union's organization. His position was described by the Council as being 'sufficiently unpleasant . . . for a man to stand in who has done nothing amiss (beyond speaking in the interests of his fellow-men and himself), but made doubly unpleasant by the extreme indifference of the men for whose welfare he has incurred the enmity of men whose will is good enough to make Outcasts and Social Pariahs of all who dare to expose their unjust systems, or gainsay their autocratic will'.[2] Bunting eventually found work at Langwith and was succeeded by John T. Humphries, of Stonebroom, as President at some time between October, 1881 and August, 1882.[3]

W. E. Harvey found himself in a dilemma of a different kind. In May, 1881, he notified the Council that he would be unable to attend future meetings. Haslam explained that Harvey was a member of his colliery cricket club, that the manager of the colliery, who was himself a player, was very much interested in the game, and that a number of matches had been arranged for Saturdays during the summer months. Harvey was expected to take part in these, 'being a prominent member of the club', and he could not, 'without causing grave offence and utterly disrupting affairs, be absent on those occasions'. He offered to resign the treasurership but, as he was not a delegate, the Council decided that Joseph Windle, the delegate from his lodge, should act for him in his absence.[4] During the following cricket season Harvey was succeeded by Windle as General Treasurer.

Jonathan Catchpole was another of the union's early leaders who suffered victimization. In 1883 he was still serving on the District Committee and acting as auditor when he was dismissed by his employers.[5] Catchpole was not entirely dependent upon his victimization payment for he was agent for the sale of rubber stamps, a business which must have become rather more lucrative after he was authorized

---

[1] D.M.A. 22 January, 1881.
[3] The records are incomplete here.
[5] Ibid. 3 February, 19 February, 1883.

[2] Ibid. 3 September, 1881.
[4] D.M.A. 28 May, 1881.

by the Council to supply them to the lodges at 4s. each, 'Ink, Pad and Box complete'.[1]

The only satisfactory solution to such problems was the appointment of full-time officials. In October, 1881, the Council resolved: 'That the General Secretary commence as soon as he can get liberty from his employment, to work for the Association, and that he be paid from the General Fund.' He was to receive £1 13s. a week for the first three months together with travelling and other 'unavoidable' expenses.[2] In November, 1882, Haslam's wage was raised to £1 17s. a week and, at the same time, the question of appointing a full-time Assistant Secretary was referred to the lodges.[3] The proposal was eventually accepted and nominations had to be made by 17 February, 1883. Each lodge had one vote for every fifty members on its books and votes were transferable.[4]

The candidates were Jonathan Catchpole (Derbyshire Silkstone lodge), W. E. Harvey (Morton lodge), William Hallam (Staveley lodge), Henry Jarvis (Old Hollingwood lodge) and Richard Bunting (Clay Cross lodge). They were given opportunities of addressing meetings at different centres before the election took place on 17 March.[5] Two years later, playing in colliery cricket teams or brass bands was to be condemned as 'flunkeyism'[6] but in 1883 W. E. Harvey, despite his addiction to playing cricket with his colliery manager, was elected Assistant Secretary. His position was confirmed at the next meeting of the Council which also decided that his wages should be £1 15s. a week. Haslam, as General Secretary, was to have, along with the Treasurer, the complete financial control of the union and to be responsible for all accounts and business transactions.[7]

Two of the unsuccessful candidates who had done so much to establish the union disappeared from the scene into comparative obscurity. Despite his victimization and resignation from the presidency Bunting had maintained his connection with the Association as a member of the Clay Cross lodge but after his failure to secure election to the assistant secretaryship he ceased to play a prominent part in the movement. Jonathan Catchpole, still unemployed, tried to establish himself as a machine agent but found that he was unable to make a living. In June, 1883, the Council granted him £1 16s. towards the cost of removing his furniture to Awsworth, near Ilkeston, where he hoped to obtain work once again as a collier.[8]

Henry Jarvis was also having great difficulty in finding employment.

[1] *D.M.A.* 19 February, 3 March, 1883. [2] *Ibid.* 29 October, 1881.
[3] *Ibid.* 25 November, 1882. [4] *Ibid.* 3 February, 1883.
[5] *Ibid.* 17 February, 1883. [6] *Ibid.* 20 January, 1885.
[7] *Ibid.* 31 March, 1883. [8] *Ibid.* 12 June, 1883.

Born at Staveley in 1839, Jarvis had worked at various collieries in Derbyshire and Yorkshire since the age of 12. He was first involved in an industrial dispute in 1854 when there was a lock-out of miners at Pilley Green, near Barnsley. In 1866 he was discharged from the Staveley Hollingwood Colliery and also, soon afterwards, from the Aldwarke Main Colliery, because of his trade union activities.[1] By 1883 Jarvis was once again in trouble as a result of his efforts to establish the new Association. In June of that year he was receiving victimization payment and was 'morally certain' that he would not succeed in obtaining employment where he was known. He therefore decided to try his fortune in tea-hawking and asked for a grant from the Council to set him up in business. He pointed out that he would always be willing to hold meetings in the interests of the miners when he was on his rounds. The Council agreed to this proposal, and allowed him £5.[2]

Jarvis was supported by the union until September, 1883, when he reported to the Council that his financial position was satisfactory and expressed the hope 'that the support given to him, in his trade, may be continued and extended'.[3] Although he no longer worked in a mine Jarvis continued to organize meetings for the union, for which he received his expenses, and in 1884 he was elected President. Jarvis combined the presidency with his tea-hawking until 1887. In that year, for reasons unspecified in the minutes, the Council decided to terminate the appointment of Joseph Windle as Treasurer.[4] Jarvis was then elected to this more remunerative position.[5]

The new President, in succession to Jarvis, was R. P. Carter. He had worked as a miner for many years at Clay Cross and had been a prominent member of the Baptist sect. A few years before his election as President he had left Clay Cross to live at St. Helens, in Lancashire, but later returned to Derbyshire.[6] Carter held office until 1890 when he had a serious accident which resulted in the loss of a leg.[7] A fund was opened to help Carter who had to undergo a second operation but, in May, 1891, he died.[8] It was during Carter's tenure of the presidency that elections to that office became annual instead of six-monthly.

Meanwhile the work of the Treasurer was growing rapidly. The improvement in trade during the late 'eighties and the wage concessions which followed led to a great increase in membership. In January, 1890,

[1] Hallam, op. cit. p. 45.   [2] D.M.A. 12 June, 1883.
[3] Ibid. 7 August, 4 September, 1883.
[4] Ibid. 30 August, 1887. Windle later became an under-manager at one of the Sheepbridge Company's pits. He died in March, 1930, at the age of 80. (Derbyshire Times, 29 March, 1930.)   [5] Ibid. 20 December, 1887.
[6] Derbyshire Times, 1 September, 5 October, 12 October, 1889.
[7] D.M.A. 8 April, 1890.
[8] Ibid. 29 July, 23 September, 16 December, 1890; 5 May, 1891.

the lodges were asked to consider the question of raising the Treasurer's 'salary', as it was now called, 'seeing that there is a great deal more money, more work, and more responsibility than formerly'. Jarvis argued that his salary should be double that of the previous Treasurer because the Association's income had increased more than fourfold.[1] He had already received, with the other officials, various percentage increases, which followed the wage concessions obtained for the miners. The Council had granted the officials increases of 10 per cent. in October, 1888, and 5 per cent. in July, 1889. Soon after the second increase it was resolved 'That in future no officials' salaries be increased until the same has been before the lodges' but, a month later, this decision was reversed as far as the Secretaries were concerned and it was decided that their salaries should 'be advanced by percentage as received by the men'.[2] Jarvis, however, in February, 1890, was granted an increase of 5s. a month, making his salary £2, 'without percentage up or down'.[3]

In addition, Jarvis continued to receive additional allowances for time spent on union business at the rate received by delegates to Council. Frequently he would be employed for a day and sometimes for a much longer period. In January, 1890, he was authorized by the Council to undertake 'a week's missioning' in the Ilkeston district with Benjamin Gregory, one of the union's stalwarts in that area. For this he received £2 3s. 6d.[4] Two months later the Treasurer was provided with a safe and allowed a day's wages and expenses 'to attend at Clay Cross to settle up the day after Council or Executive Meetings'. Haslam explained: 'The work has now grown to such an extent, that the Accounts cannot be entered even by staying to the last train.'[5] These additional payments to Jarvis aroused some criticism in the Council. 'This theme', wrote Haslam, 'takes up a good deal of time and is getting tiresome.' In order to allay this 'constantly recurring irritation' the lodges were asked to review the whole question of the Treasurer's position.[6]

In the following November the lodges were asked to consider the question of appointing Jarvis as a full-time official.[7] Only 20 of the 69 lodges voted on this issue. Of these, 14 were in favour of appointing Jarvis, and six against. Some delegates thought that Jarvis had been given undue preference and it was decided to ask the lodges to consider the general principle of appointing another official without naming Jarvis. 'Your Secretaries always recognize the Members' absolute right to decide all such matters. . . .', stated the Executive Committee.

[1] D.M.A. 16 January, 1890.
[2] Ibid. 20 October, 1888; 1 July, 30 July, 27 August, 1889.
[3] Ibid. 11 February, 1890.
[4] Ibid. 16 January, 11 February, 1890.   [5] Ibid. 8 April, 1890.
[6] Ibid. 6 May, 1890.   [7] Ibid. 18 November, 1890.

'Now make up your minds to a majority ruling one way or the other, and let us have no bother afterwards.'[1] Eventually, it was decided by 123 votes to 109 that no extra official should be appointed but that Jarvis should be employed when necessary at a salary of £2 a week.[2]

The great lock-out of 1893 revealed the inadequacy of this arrangement. It was reported to the Council that Jarvis had been at the office daily during the whole of the dispute, returning borrowed money, making out pay sheets and answering communications, while the Secretaries had been attending meetings. Indeed, the demand for meetings had been so great that the Secretaries had been obliged to send Jarvis to many of them.[3] In December, 1893, the question of appointing a full-time Treasurer was raised again. It was argued that Jarvis, during the previous five months, had been fully occupied, that it had been impossible to do the work without him and that additional help had also been required.[4] A month later it was decided, by 240 votes to 128, to appoint a permanent Treasurer.[5] Jarvis was elected by an overwhelming majority and it was agreed that he should be paid £2 5s. a week, 'which shall include office cleaning, the wages to rise and fall according to the district'.[6]

After the appointment of Jarvis as Treasurer there were no changes in the three permanent officials until 1906. William Hallam became 'President, pro tem.' after Carter's accident, was elected to the presidency in November, 1890, at the age of 35, and remained in office until 1898. He had been elected checkweighman at the Markham Colliery in 1883 and later became a delegate to the Council. Unlike many of the other union leaders he was an Anglican. He was a member of the Staveley parish church choir and clerk to the parish council.[7] He is best remembered today by historians of the labour movement for his *Miners' Leaders*, which he published in 1894. In commenting upon the keen intellect, sturdy common sense, courage and self-sacrifice of the miners he wrote:

It would be surprising, indeed, if a body of Englishmen possessing such qualities as these, did not find itself able at all times to produce leaders of no ordinary calibre. We are not astonished, therefore, to find that the officers of the miners' unions have been men, generally of exceptional, and often of quite remarkable abilities.[8]

During the latter years of Hallam's long tenure of the presidency, Barnet Kenyon was running a close second in the annual elections and in 1898 he was at last successful. Born at Anston, near Worksop, in

[1] *D.M.A.* 16 December, 1890.   [2] *Ibid.* 13 January, 1891.
[3] *Ibid.* 17 October, 1893.   [4] *Ibid.* 11 December, 1893.
[5] *Ibid.* 9 January, 1894.   [6] *Ibid.* 6 March, 1894.
[7] *Ibid.* 8 April, 18 November, 1890; *Derbyshire Times*, 12 April, 1902.
[8] Hallam, *op. cit.* p. viii.

1850, he began work at the age of 10 in a quarry. He afterwards became a farm labourer and later became a miner in the South Yorkshire coalfield. In 1876 he moved to Clowne and, after two years' work at the Barlborough Colliery, was elected checkweighman at the nearby Southgate Colliery. Kenyon played a prominent part in public life and is said to have won popularity by 'his general courtesy and able and thoughtful speeches'. He was a Primitive Methodist, became a local preacher in 1882 and a class leader in 1886. When the Clowne Co-operative Society was formed in 1889 he became its President and in 1895 he became a member of the Worksop Board of Guardians and the Clowne Rural District Council.[1] Kenyon held the presidency of the Association until 1906 although his position was closely contested by Hallam until the latter's premature death from a heart attack in July, 1902, at the age of 46.[2] In 1901 both Kenyon and Hallam offered to withdraw their nominations if James Martin would accept the presidency but he declined.[3]

In January, 1903, the Council decided to create a new office of Vice-President which would be filled by annual elections.[4] The first Vice-President was Frederick Bonsall, of Somercotes. Born in 1856 he had spent the whole of his working life, since the age of 10, at the Birchwood Colliery of the Babbington Company. He was the President of his lodge and had served as a delegate and a member of the Executive Committee for many years. In 1886 he became a local preacher and, later, one of the senior superintendents of the Birchwood Free Church. In 1896 he was elected to the Alfreton Urban District Council.[5] James Martin succeeded Bonsall as Vice-President in 1904 but Bonsall regained the office in 1906.[6] In April of that year, however, he resigned on his appointment as General Secretary of the Midland Counties Miners' Permanent Relief Fund.[7]

There were other and more important changes in 1906. James Haslam was elected to Parliament and, even if he continued to be an official of the union, it was obvious that another appointment would have to be made to carry on the bulk of his work. With over £200,000 invested and a membership of nearly 30,000 this did not present a serious problem for the Association. 'The general body of members', reported the *Derbyshire Times*, 'were quite of opinion that whatever expenditure is necessary in regard to the new official is justified in their own interests.' It was decided that Haslam should continue as General Secretary, Harvey should be Financial and Corresponding

---

[1] *Derbyshire Times*, 17 February, 1906.
[2] *Ibid.* 12 July, 1902.   [3] *Ibid.* 16 November, 1901.
[4] *Ibid.* 31 January, 1903.   [5] *Ibid.* 17 February, 1906.
[6] *Ibid.* 5 December, 1903; 30 December, 1905.   [7] *Ibid.* 21 April, 1906.

JAMES HASLAM

Secretary and that nominations should be sent in for the vacant position of Assistant Secretary.[1] By March, Barnet Kenyon had been elected and the office of President had now to be filled.[2]

In May, James Martin was elected President.[3] He had contested the office on previous occasions and had a long record of union work and public service. Martin was born at Basford, Nottingham, in 1850 and went to Staveley at the age of 8. In the following year he began work at the Speedwell pit as a door-trapper and later became a driver. Eventually he obtained work at the coal face at the Ireland Colliery. He had taken a leading part in trade unionism ever since the days of Brown's union in 1866–7. In 1874 he was elected delegate for the Staveley lodge to the Council of the South Yorkshire Association and had been Secretary of his lodge ever since the strike of 1876. On 13 February, 1882, he was elected checkweighman at Ireland Colliery. Martin received his only formal education at a night school which he attended regularly, 'becoming most enthusiastic and a close reader'.[4]

In late 1906 Jarvis, who had long wanted a house in Chesterfield, moved into one of the two built by the Association in Tennyson Avenue. He lived there for about six months, suffering greatly from bronchitis, and died in May, 1907.[5] Frank Hall, who had received 4,250 votes to Martin's 16,250 in the contest for the presidency and was now Vice-President, succeeded Jarvis as Treasurer, a position for which there were seventeen nominations.[6] There was a suggestion, during this election, that a 'practical man' should be chosen but one member pointed out:

The catch phrase 'practical man' is directed against the checkweighmen who, for the purposes of this election, are to be looked upon as 'non-practical men'. . . . Some talk of the phrase in question in ignorance, not knowing what 'practical man' means; others do so to restrict the area of appointment so as to secure to themselves a better prospect of being appointed than they otherwise would have.[7]

But this was only the beginning of the agitation against the domination of the union by checkweighmen.[8] Meanwhile Harvey had been elected to Parliament in January, 1907, but this led to no further changes in the officials.

Frank Hall was born near Sheffield in 1862. While he was quite young his parents removed to Derby, and afterwards to Trentham, in Staffordshire, where his father was butler to the chaplain of the Duke of Sutherland. When Hall was 9 years of age his father entered the

---

[1] *Derbyshire Times*, 17 February, 1906.   [2] *Ibid.* 3 March, 21 April, 1906.
[3] *Ibid.* 19 May, 1906.   [4] *Ibid.* 21 April, 1906.
[5] *Ibid.* 18 May, 1907.   [6] *Ibid.* 19 May, 1906; 15 June, 13 July, 1907.
[7] *Ibid.* 1 June, 1907.   [8] See below, pp. 264–6.

H

service of Hugh Wood, of Swanwick Hall. The Halls were unable to pay the 6d. a week required for their son's education and, at the age of 11, Frank Hall went to work at the Swanwick Collieries. Later he received night-school education, being a regular attender at the science and art classes at Ripley from their inception. He studied mining and other subjects but when, at the age of 20, it was suggested to him that he should study for a mine manager's certificate 'he felt that it would not give him the opportunity he desired of doing something to improve the position of his fellow men'. Hall eventually became a checkweighman at the Alfreton Colliery and began to take an active part in the affairs of the Association. Much of his reputation was based upon his handling of the lengthy disputes and intricate legal and arbitration proceedings which went on for several years at the Alfreton Colliery before his election. He held various public offices including the chairmanship of the Alfreton Urban District Council. He was also engaged in friendly society work and was one of the auditors of the Ripley Co-operative Society.[1]

Hall was succeeded by William Sewell as Vice-President and there were no further changes in the officials until 1913. Meanwhile, Haslam's health was failing. In March, 1907, he became seriously ill and had to abandon his parliamentary duties completely.[2] In the following May he had an operation from which he recovered sufficiently to enable him to attend a meeting of the Council in July and to make his first public speech since his illness in November.[3] His protracted illness kept him out of parliamentary life for almost a year. The death of his youngest son, from pneumonia, in April, 1910, and of his wife in May, 1911, came as a great shock to him.[4] In the following year his health deteriorated and he was advised by his doctor not to stand for re-election to Parliament.[5] In December he was so seriously ill that his life was in danger.[6] The Council expressed its hope that 'he may soon be better and back at his old work that he loves so well' but Haslam never sat in the Council chamber again.[7] At 10.25 on the evening of 31 July, 1913, he died with his family and Harvey at his bedside.[8]

Haslam's death severed an important link with the past. He had, by now, become a national figure and the tributes which were paid to him called attention to his dislike of extreme militancy. 'Mr. Haslam', said *The Times*, 'was a typical trades unionist of the old school and was more akin in character and personality to Mr. Burt than to any other

[1] *Derbyshire Times*, 15 June, 1907.   [2] *Ibid.* 16 March, 1907.
[3] *Ibid.* 18 May, 13 July, 23 November, 1907.
[4] *Ibid.* 23 April, 1910; 20 May, 1911. Haslam had twelve children of whom three had died by May, 1911.
[5] *Ibid.* 23 November, 1912.   [6] *Ibid.* 4 January, 1913; *D.M.A.* 4 January, 1913.
[7] *D.M.A.* 11 January, 1913.   [8] *Derbyshire Times*, 2 August, 1913.

Labour representative in the House, and he was as much respected among the colliery officials and employers in Derbyshire as among the miners.'[1] Most of the national daily papers pointed out that Haslam had been opposed to the 1912 strike and that when he was committed to it he laboured unceasingly for industrial peace. The *Daily Chronicle* commented:

Mr. Haslam, like his friend and colleague the late Enoch Edwards, was a victim of the national coal strike of last year. For the whole six months of the negotiations connected with that strike Mr. Haslam was taking part in meetings almost daily, sitting far into the night and resuming early next morning, in spite of failing health and the doctors' warning of the consequences. When his colleagues appealed to him to rest, the reply came, 'No, no; I cannot desert my people in this crisis'.[2]

But some of Haslam's people felt deserted not only by him but also by the other officials after the 1912 strike. More than once it was proposed that the officials should be called upon to resign and there is little doubt that the opposition to the union's leadership which began to develop, as part of the general tide of industrial unrest, from about 1909, was one of the factors which helped to hasten Haslam's death.[3]

Extremist criticism did not prevent the union from contemplating the passing away of one of its founders with suitable awe and respect. The Council placed on record:

its high appreciation of the long and valuable services of Mr. James Haslam, M.P., the General Secretary, who to their deep grief and sorrow has now joined the great majority. We recognize the early struggles, the antipathy and open aversion to Trades Unions, which he had to contend with, how manfully he endured the scorn and calumny in the infant days of the Association, how incessantly he proclaimed the principles of betterment and freedom for the miners, and laid down the foundations in this County of one of the best Trade Unions in Britain. He accomplished much, did a good day's work, fought great battles, and won great victories. He was a faithful and honest servant but today we mourn his loss: his seat is vacant. The world and Derbyshire in particular is all the poorer, and we all pay our tribute to so useful and beneficial a life but the greatest tribute we could pay to him would be to emulate his example by not living alone for self but for the uplift of others. . . .[4]

Haslam was buried with full honours. In the cortège were represent-atives from all the national and local organizations with which he had been associated, Members of Parliament and delegates from the lodges. Harvey delivered a stirring panegyric at the graveside and laid a wreath on behalf of the Association. A few months later the Council decided to

[1] *The Times*, 1 August, 1913. [2] *Daily Chronicle*, 1 August, 1913.
[3] See below, pp. 264-6. [4] *D.M.A.* 2 August, 1913.

commission an oil painting of Haslam for the Chesterfield Town Hall and, following the example of Yorkshire and Durham, to erect a statue in honour of its late leader in front of the union's offices.[1]

Harvey, who was to have unveiled the statue, became ill on 22 April, 1914, whilst he was in London attending Parliament. Despite his doctor's advice he insisted on voting on the Welsh Disestablishment Bill, a subject on which he had very strong views, before returning to Chesterfield at his usual time at the end of the week. The day after his return he was found to be suffering from pneumonia and died on 28 April. Shortly before his death he wrote the inscription for his tombstone: 'He served his day and generation and then fell asleep.'[2] His health had been unsatisfactory for some years and the death of Haslam, the additional work resulting from it, his parliamentary duties and the adverse criticism which he had to face after the 1912 strike all contributed to Harvey's decline. The final blow came in November, 1913, with the death of his wife. Harvey was accorded the same honours as Haslam and a second statue was commissioned.[3]

'Associated, as he was, with Mr. Haslam in the inception of our own organization,' declared the Council, 'he was an eloquent advocate of its claims and defender of its rights, was justly watchful of the position it had attained in the industrial world, and keenly watchful lest anything should sully its reputation or lessen its power.'[4]

After Haslam's death Harvey became General and Financial Secretary, Hall the General Corresponding Secretary and Treasurer and Kenyon, who had succeeded Haslam as Member of Parliament for the Chesterfield division, the agent.[5] Nominations were requested for the position of Assistant Secretary and Compensation Agent and in January, 1914, Frank Lee was declared elected.[6] Lee was born at Pinxton in 1867 and moved to Tibshelf with his parents in 1878. He began work in the pit at the age of 13 and became a checkweighman in 1896. He was treasurer of the Tibshelf No. 1 lodge, a delegate to the Council and acted as minute clerk to the Council and Executive Committee from 1908. Like most of his colleagues he was a local preacher and held a variety of public offices. 'There will be no violent or disruptive exertions on the part of the new agent', the *Derbyshire Times* assured its readers.

[1] *D.M.A.* 8 September, 20 September, 1913. The Association declined the Chesterfield Corporation's offer of a site for Haslam's statue in the centre of the town. (*Derbyshire Times*, 18 October, 1913.)

[2] *Derbyshire Times*, 2 May, 1914. Harvey left estate to the gross value of £5,052. (*Derbyshire Times*, 11 July, 1914.)

[3] *D.M.A.* 29 April, 6 July, 25 July, 1914. The statues were unveiled by Kenyon on 26 June, 1915, and still stand outside the union's offices. Harvey's son presented a portrait of his father to the Chesterfield Town Council to hang beside that of Haslam. (*Derbyshire Times*, 13 June, 1914.)   [4] *Ibid* 29 April, 1914.

[5] *Ibid.* 20 September, 1913.   [6] *Ibid.* 10 January, 1914.

'He is the type of leader who will carry on the traditions of the Derbyshire Labour movement—allied to the Liberal party.'[1] On the death of Harvey there was another rearrangement of the duties of the officials but no new official was appointed. Kenyon became the General Agent, Hall the General Corresponding and Financial Secretary and Lee the Treasurer and Compensation Agent.[2] In June, 1914, the word 'Corresponding' was deleted from Hall's title by order of the Council.[3]

By 1914 the salaries of the officials had risen considerably as a result of the various increases in miners' wages to which they were linked. The officials who were also Members of Parliament received £8 a month with a percentage addition of £2 as well as their parliamentary salaries. The other full-time officials received £11 a month with a percentage addition of £7 3s. od.

During the period 1880–1914 the Executive Committee increased in size and importance. Although the original rules of the Association provided for a Committee of not less than nine, the revised rules of 1883 stipulated 'not less than five or more than nine'. There were at that time seven members of the Committee, including the President, Secretary and Treasurer, but in December, 1888, the Council resolved: 'That the Executive be increased to the number of nine and further, that a note be added to the effect that the Executive be selected, as far as possible, from the different points of the compass.'[4] This was the first indication of the desire for a panel system. The attractions of representing the Association at the growing number of national and international conferences brought the matter to a head. In March, 1891, the question of arranging panels was referred to the lodges. The officials explained:

It is thought that to prevent dissatisfaction among Lodges and Members, that [sic] it might be a good plan and largely save the time of the Council, if, say, about nine panels were formed, and that when one or more men were required to attend a Conference, audit the accounts, or what not, that one of the panels should be asked to appoint suitable men of their own choice, this to go in rotation until all the panels had been gone through. . . .[5]

In June there were further discussions on the proposed panel system and economy was urged by the officials: 'It should be remembered that there is no intention to again reproduce a system like the old and costly Yorkshire one.'[6]

Eventually the lodges were arranged in nine panels, each of which elected one member to the Executive Committee. The revised rules of 25 August, 1910, provided for an Executive Committee of 'not less than

[1] *Derbyshire Times*, 17 January, 1914.   [2] *D.M.A.* 30 May, 1914.
[3] *Ibid.* 27 June, 1914.   [4] *Ibid.* 18 December, 1888.
[5] *Ibid.* 10 March, 1891.   [6] *Ibid.* 30 June, 1891.

five or more than twelve experienced financial members, in addition to the President, Vice-President, Secretaries, and Treasurer'. The lodges were then re-arranged in twelve panels and the Executive increased to twelve members.[1]

2. THE COUNCIL AND THE LODGES

The supreme government of the Association was vested in the Council which, according to the 1880 rules, consisted of 'a President, Secretary or Secretaries, Treasurer, and one experienced member duly elected (as Delegate), by and from each of the financial Lodges composing the Association . . .'. Each lodge having fifty members or under had one vote with additional votes for every other clear fifty members. No delegate was allowed to abstain from voting on any of the questions which came before the Council. There was to be an ordinary Council meeting at least once in three months. Delegates who failed to be in their places at 10 o'clock on the days appointed for Council meetings were liable to a fine of 6d.

In the early days of the Association the workings of the Council caused a great deal of discussion. Teething troubles were inevitable in a new organization of this kind. The men who were creating it were learning by experience the art of trade union government and the pitfalls of bureaucracy. The volume of important work which the union had to carry out was steadily growing but, at the outset, the machinery was barely capable of dealing with it. Administrative traditions had to be built up and much valuable time was spent in discussing *minutiae*. In 1882 Haslam had to remind delegates: 'It is highly desirable that the Council should begin promptly, as there is but little time to discuss some of the important matters that are continually to the front; let everyone try to be there to the minute, as the Rule must be carried out, otherwise, and that will be very unpleasant.'[2] Eventually, in November, 1882, it was decided to hold Council meetings fortnightly, instead of monthly as they had been since 1880, but not all the extra time appears to have been used profitably.[3] In February, 1883, there was a discussion on the question of smoking at Council meetings which resulted in a resolution forbidding it.[4] The delegates also spent a great deal of time discussing the details of the rubber stamps to be supplied to the lodges and whether they should be ordered from Jonathan Catchpole.[5] Most

---

[1] *D.M.A.* 22 October, 1910.   [2] *Ibid.* 5 August, 1882.
[3] *Ibid.* 25 November, 1882.   [4] *Ibid.* 3 February, 1883.
[5] *Ibid.* 19 February, 3 March, 1883. Two stamps were to be purchased for the District Secretary, 'the one to have two hands clasped, symbolical of Unity as the District Stamp; the other and smaller one, for the purpose of stamping the flap of envelopes, &c.'

time of all was wasted in questioning the officials about trivial items of expenditure.[1]

The 1880 rules provided that: 'The Delegates attending regular Council Meetings shall be paid at such rate of wages, railway fares and expenses, as may from time to time be agreed upon by the Council, with the sanction of the majority of the Lodges. . . .' Initially the delegates received 2s. for each attendance and were paid by the lodges. The holding of fortnightly Council meetings was therefore an additional financial burden upon the lodges and made it impossible for them to increase the amount paid to their delegates. In June, 1883, the Council reverted to monthly meetings and in the following month it was resolved: 'That all Delegates to Council (whole days) receive 5s. 6d. for wages, expenses 1s. 6d. and railway fare at the rate of 1d. per mile.'[2] At the same time, the question of a movable Council was referred to the lodges. It was felt by lodges in the south of the county that they were bearing an unfair burden of travelling expenses and that every other Council meeting should be held at Ilkeston.[3] There was another proposal that the northern and southern halves of the county should meet alternately each fortnight but Haslam quickly pointed out: 'That will never do, as one Council would simply undo what the other had done.'[4]

During the serious strike in the Ilkeston district in 1885 the Council departed from its usual practice of meeting at Chesterfield and held a meeting at Ilkeston but beyond that there was no further attempt to establish a movable Council.[5] Instead, the problem of travelling expenses was given further consideration. The Old Hollingwood lodge proposed: 'That all Lodges stop their Delegates' Money (Railway Fare) from the amount paid to Council, thus equalizing the cost.'[6] Nothing was done until 1885 when, after the centralization of the Association's funds, the delegates' expenses were paid by the General Treasurer but Council meetings were still costly affairs. The union's financial reserves were sadly depleted by the Ilkeston strike and in August, 1885, the question of the Council's meeting only once in two months was raised. Haslam balanced economy against democracy: 'The Lodges must give the matter their serious attention, as there is a good deal to be said both ways. With the small lodges we have, Monthly Councils become very expensive, while on the other hand, Monthly

---

[1] See below, p. 262.
[2] *D.M.A.* 28 April, 10 July, 1883. The remuneration of delegates remained unchanged until 1910 when a percentage addition was made. (*D.M.A.* 17 December, 1910.)
[3] This would have benefited such lodges as Manners, Oakwell, Cossall, West Hallam, Stanley, Peacock, Shipley and Ripley.   [4] *D.M.A.* 10 July, 1883.
[5] *Ibid.* 4 August, 1885.   [6] *Ibid.* 7 August, 1883.

Meetings enable Delegates to hear how matters are going on at other places.'[1] It was decided that no lodge of less than twenty members should be entitled to send a delegate to the Council.[2] In the following month the decision was taken to hold Council meetings once in two months but the Secretaries were given the right to call special meetings whenever necessary.[3] By 1905 the Association was again holding monthly Council meetings but there was still some opposition. In November of that year, at a meeting of the Southgate lodge, with Barnet Kenyon in the chair, it was decided to object to monthly Council meetings.[4]

In 1895 Beatrice Webb, who was then collecting material for *Industrial Democracy*, attended a meeting of the Council to study its procedure but, unfortunately, the Webbs make no comment upon it in their finished work.[5] There were many discussions on the number of times a delegate should be allowed to speak and the amount of notice required before a subject could be debated. Eventually, in July, 1906, the following standing orders were agreed upon:

1. The Chairman shall call the roll of Delegates at 9 a.m.

2. The Chairman shall call out Minutes by their numbers and any Delegate who has been instructed by his Lodge to ask a question on the same shall cry 'tick'.

3. The Chairman shall ask the Secretaries to answer questions that have been sent to them with reference to expenses from the Lodges, the same to be sent in at least one day before the Council Meeting. The object of this is to enable the Secretaries to have their answers ready, and we beg to say that unless this is done it makes it most difficult to give a detailed answer to any question of expense, as in many cases these items of expense have been incurred seven or eight weeks before this. So we ask the Lodge Secretaries to send their questions in writing on separate sheets to Mr. Kenyon at least one day preceding Council Meetings.

4. The Chairman shall then go back to the ticks on the Minutes until they have been disposed of.

5. The Council shall then proceed to deal with questions on the agenda, arranged by the Secretaries, and no other business shall be introduced at the Council Meeting but what appears on the agenda, which business must have been sent in officially at least two days preceding the Council Meeting. If the Secretaries of the Lodges will attend to this we can prepare a printed or typed agenda for every Delegate at each Council Meeting.

6. No Delegate shall be allowed to speak more than once on a question, subject, or resolution.

7. A mover of a resolution shall have the right of reply.

[1] *D.M.A.* 4 August, 1885.   [2] *Ibid.*
[3] *Ibid.* 1 September, 1885.   [4] *Derbyshire Times*, 25 November, 1905.
[5] *D.M.A.* 17 September, 1895; Sidney and Beatrice Webb, *Industrial Democracy*, (London), 1897. For Beatrice Webb's private comments on the Derbyshire leaders see Chapter XII, pp. 484–5.

8. No Delegate will be allowed to leave the Council Meeting before its close without the consent of Council, and no Delegate's wages shall be paid until the meeting is closed only on the signature of the Chairman.

9. The Council shall meet at 9 a.m. and close at 1 p.m. unless important business has been unconsidered, when the Standing Orders may be suspended or the business relegated to the Executive Committee.[1]

The activities of the lodges were carefully regulated by the Council. The 1880 rules laid down that no new lodge could be formed without the sanction of the Council and lodges were not permitted to strike until the facts of a dispute had been considered by the Council or the District Committee and referred to the other lodges. If a majority of the members were in favour of a lodge striking, the full members (i.e. those over 16 years of age) were to receive 8s. a week and 1s. for each child under 13 years of age who was not at work. Half members received 4s. a week. Members who were locked out or victimized received similar benefits but the rules stated clearly:

No member or members will be supported as victims who may have been discharged from their employment for neglecting their work, swearing or using abusive language to their owners, managers or other officers, violating the Special and General Rules, stealing or hiding his fellow-workmen's tools, or refusing to do his work according to bargain, or otherwise being guilty of acts calculated to endanger the safety of the Colliery in which he may be employed.

If, after four weeks, a man who had been victimized was still unable to find employment, the continuance of his support was left to the discretion of the Council or the District Committee.

For these benefits members were required to pay an entrance fee of 1s. 6d., or 9d. in the case of half members. To encourage recruitment the entrance fee was payable in three fortnightly instalments and whilst it was being paid, members were exempt from paying contributions and levies. Otherwise, the regular contribution for all full members was 6d. a fortnight and for half members 3d. In addition, the Council was empowered, with the consent of the lodges, to impose levies or reduce benefits if at any time the Association's funds became inadequate to meet all the claims of the members. Any member who allowed his contributions, levies or fines to fall into arrears to the extent of 1s. 6d. (or 9d. in the case of half members) was deemed 'unfinancial' and was not entitled to any benefits until a month after he had reduced his arrears to less than 1s. 6d. Members were required to obtain clearance certificates from their old lodges before joining other lodges or forming new ones.

All lodges held fortnightly a general meeting which was arranged to

---

[1] *Derbyshire Times*, 14 July, 1906; *D.M.A.* 21 September, 1912.

H*

precede the meetings of the Council or the District Committee. The lodge presidents were elected or re-elected every six months by a majority of the members of the lodge.[1] The lodge secretaries were elected every twelve months. They were paid for their services according to a scale which ran from 6s. a quarter for lodges with less than 35 members to 37s. 6d. for lodges of 600 or more. Lodge treasurers were similarly elected or re-elected every twelve months. Their scale of payments was on the same basis as that for the secretaries and ran from 4s. to 22s. 6d. a quarter. Except in the case of new lodges, treasurers were required to have been financial members of the Association for at least twelve consecutive months before their election.

All lodges had a committee of not less than five nor more than nine financial members, the president, secretary and treasurer being members *ex officio*. The size of the committee depended upon the size of the lodge. Committees met monthly to investigate all grievances and complaints of members and to watch over the interests of the Association generally. Members were allowed sixpence for attendance at Committee meetings but, in 1884, it was pointed out 'that the allowance to Committee-men is intended to be spent for the good of the house at which the Meetings are held, and the Treasurer of each Lodge is expected to pay the amount to the Landlord for Refreshments for the Committees, and get a Bill for each payment, the same to be produced at the audit'.[2] The lodges were supplied by the Association with contribution books, cash books, lodge seals and stamps, and all the necessary documents. The expenses of the renting, lighting and heating of lodge rooms and of stationery were also borne by the Association.

There were the usual fines for violation of the rules, absence and unpunctuality. The lodge presidents, secretaries, treasurers, delegates and committee members were all liable to fines of sixpence for being late at or not attending meetings. In addition there were various fines designed to raise the moral tone of the Association to the high standards which were thought desirable by its Nonconformist leaders. Any member swearing or using other abusive language in meetings was to be fined 1s. Members attending meetings when drunk and disturbing business were to be removed from the room and fined 2s. 6d. Any member 'taunting or upbraiding another with receiving any benefits' of the Association was also to be fined 2s. 6d. A similar fine was imposed upon 'any member boasting of his independence towards his employers or managers, on account of being a member of the Association'.

In the early years of the union there was a great deal of discussion about the remuneration of the lodge officials, which was thought by many members to be excessive. In March, 1881, the matter was

[1] Elections later became annual.   [2] *D.M.A.* 23 December, 1884.

referred to the lodges for consideration.[1] There were further discussions
on the subject in September, 1882, when the wages of local officials
were contrasted with the smallness of the gross receipts and Haslam
was instructed to issue 'a suggestive note' to the lodges.

'We believe', he wrote, 'the scale is not too high, always supposing a man
does his duty fairly. If Local Officials will earnestly strive to improve our
position as a Society, taking every opportunity of urging on the men the
necessity of organization, attend the Meetings regularly, and advise and guide
the men in the right direction, practically carrying out that work they were
elected for, their pay would be a mere acknowledgment, and this most
certainly should and must be done, if ever we are to rise to a position worthy
of the name of an Association. . . .'[2]

As the union became more prosperous the payments made to local
officials were increased. By 1910 lodge presidents were being paid 5s. a
quarter, the scales for the secretaries of lodges ranged from 6s. 6d. a
quarter for those with less than 35 members to 125s. 6d. for those
with a membership of between 1,900 and 2,000, and for treasurers from
4s. 6d. to 83s. 6d. Committee members received 1s. for attendance at
each meeting. These basic scales were linked to the miners' wages and
supplemented by the current percentage additions.[3]

Apathy, which is sometimes thought to be a problem of recent origin
in the trade union world,[4] was singled out by Haslam, in 1886, as the
principal cause of inefficiency on the part of lodge secretaries:

There is far too much apathy and indifference exhibited by many of our
Secretaries, which is no doubt accounted for largely by the indifference of the
Members generally. . . . It is said the men do not attend, and that is why
full meetings are not had, but if only a few came, there would be a more
general knowledge of the business of the Association than there can be by
Committee Meetings only, and the Committee and Officials should try to
infuse some life into the proceedings; anyway, the duties of the Secretaries
and others are clearly defined in the Rules, and men who are paid a salary
for their work are bound to carry them out.[5]

This was only one of the many criticisms of local officials for dereliction
of duty. In the early days the fear of victimization was undoubtedly a
strong deterrent to active participation in the affairs of the Association
but the failings of local officials continued to be a cause for complaint
long after the union had become firmly established. Haslam's emphasis

[1] *D.M.A.* 19 March, 1881.   [2] *Ibid.* 2 September, 1882.
[3] *Rules of the Derbyshire Miners' Association*, (1910) Paras. 68, 70, 73, 79.
[4] Cf. J. Goldstein, *The Government of British Trade Unions*, (London) 1952, pp.
60–66; V. L. Allen, *Power in Trade Unions*, (London), 1954, pp. 4–5. Both writers show
that apathy is not new but Dr. Goldstein regards it as a serious problem whereas
Dr. Allen does not.   [5] *D.M.A.* 16 March, 1886.

upon the remuneration of the officials overlooks the fact that it was so small that they were, in effect, voluntary workers, with all the merits and defects of their species. They neglected to send in monthly returns, failed to return ballot papers, and were late in submitting their lodge books for the annual audit. In March, 1894, the Council called the attention of the lodges to these matters: 'We look to the Committee and Lodge officials to render us all the support they can in the proper management of the Association business.'[1] As late as 1913 local officials were rebuked because some of them expected additional payment for dealing with old-age benefits despite the fact that their remuneration had recently been increased.[2]

The expense of sending delegates from small lodges to the Council continued to cause much discussion.[3] In 1891 the officials complained: 'Six Lodges send in amongst them £16 2s. 9d.; the six Delegates take to pay them £3 1s. 10d. and there is not a case for any one of them. Men, try to be reasonable, you know it is wrong to spend money in that way.'[4] The whole question of the small lodges became linked with that of non-unionism after the wage advances, amounting to 40 per cent., gained in 1888–90. The clouds were already gathering for the great storm of 1893 and unity seemed essential if the wage concessions were to be retained in the face of falling prices. In September, 1892, the delegates came to the Council prepared to advocate drastic measures such as compelling all men to pay union subscriptions through the checkweigh fund, or collecting the money at the pit gate and thereby obliging all men to join the lodge at the colliery where they worked. This would have meant the abolition of some of the small lodges which were not based upon any particular colliery. After a lengthy discussion it was decided to leave matters as they were.[5]

The problem became acute in 1895 when the current wage agreement under the conciliation scheme was nearing its end. Many non-unionists who did not live near their place of work were practising the deception of saying that they were members of lodges in Chesterfield or in the village where they lived. Again there was a demand for the abolition of the 'pick up' lodges, as the small lodges were called. Eventually the Council decided to allow them to continue for the purpose of members discussing the business of the Association but the secretaries of such lodges were required to supply their members with stamped notes, to take to their collieries every month, so that the checkweighman and union officials there would know who were financial members and would be able to press non-unionists to join the lodge at the pit.[6] It

[1] D.M.A. 6 March, 1894.   [2] Ibid. 11 January, 1913.
[3] Ibid. 1 July, 1890.   [4] Ibid. 13 January, 1891.
[5] Ibid. 20 September, 1892.   [6] Ibid. 23 July, 1895.

was not until May, 1903, that all lodges not connected with collieries were abolished.[1] This decision was re-affirmed in October, 1908, when it was ruled by the Council that all men must pay their contributions at the colliery where they worked and secretaries of lodges were instructed not to accept contributions from men working at pits other than their own.[2]

3. FINANCE AND MEMBERSHIP

It is clear from the 1880 rules of the Association that the constitution was drafted in the hope of avoiding what were regarded as the more objectionable features of the South Yorkshire Association. The Executive Committee prefaced the rules with the following remarks:

> In issuing the present Code of Rules your Committee feel that they are only supplying a desideratum that has been felt to be a decided necessity for the men of Derbyshire. The Association, we think, has taken a wise course in adopting rules that have for their object the regulation of wages and the protection of labour only. As [sic] your Committee are of opinion from the experience they have had that Widows' and Orphans' Sick and Accident Funds are best apart, and cannot be interfered with if not mixed up with Labour Funds, which is a great temptation in times of dire necessity. The reduction too, of the entrance fee and contributions, and the system of Lodges banking their own money will go a long way towards establishing that confidence which past events have severely shaken. Your Committee are of opinion that it is not so much the amount of money at the bankers, as the moral power that will be infused into the men by meeting together, that will give us a prestige with our employers, as well as with our fellow-Unionists throughout the country.[3]

The object of the founders of the Association was to ensure that the bulk of the funds should remain in the hands of the lodges but the 1880 rules were not sufficiently explicit. There were discussions about the amounts which ought to be contributed to the district funds by the lodges and what levies ought to be paid to support members who had been victimized.[4] In November, 1882, it was decided that one penny for each member should be contributed to the district funds each week. 'A good few look askance at one-third being paid to the District', wrote Haslam. 'Men be generous; watch how your money is expended, but do not cripple the Movement by undue parsimony.'[5] It was also

---

[1] *Derbyshire Times*, 23 May, 1903.   [2] *D.M.A.* 24 October, 1908.
[3] *Rules of the Derbyshire Miners' Association*, 1880, Cf. *Derbyshire Times*, 21 February, 1880.
[4] *D.M.A.* 3 September, 1881.   [5] *Ibid.* 25 November, 1882.

reported, at the same meeting, that important points needed to be added to the rules in order to make clear the principle on which each lodge banked its own funds.[1] In the following year it was felt that the agreement which had been signed by the Treasurer and duly sealed with a 2s. 6d. inland revenue stamp was perhaps not sufficient to safeguard the Association's funds and it was decided to consult a lawyer. 'We could not spoil the ship for a pennyworth of tar', wrote Haslam.[2]

In April, 1883, the Council empowered Barnet Kenyon, of the Clowne lodge, and Laurence Kilroy, of the Old Hollingwood lodge, to revise the rules of the Association. The new rules, approved by the Council on 10 July, 1883, give a much clearer picture of the way in which the decentralization of the funds was intended to operate. The General Fund was 'for the protection of labour, and to pay a weekly allowance to members locked out, on strike, or victimized by their employers' or for such other objects as might be decided by the Council with the sanction of the lodges. Each lodge banked its own funds. Lodges were required to choose 'about three good business men' as a Banking Committee. As the Association was still unregistered, members of these committees were required to sign a standard form of bond laid down in the rules. It bound them to handle the funds in accordance with the rules and gave the lodge or the Association the power to prosecute them if they departed from the agreement. No money was to be withdrawn from the bank for any purpose without a resolution signed by the Chairman of the Council and the Banking Committee of the lodge and details of this arrangement were to be deposited with the bank for its guidance. Each lodge was to contribute its proper share, according to the number of its members, to all members of the Association who were authorized to receive benefits.

In addition to the General Fund there was a District Fund to meet the working expenses of the Association. This was provided by the lodges at a rate for each member which was decided by the Council with the sanction of the lodges. The District Treasurer was required to supply the Secretaries with detailed accounts each week and had to obtain the sanction of the Council for all items of expenditure. He was also required to sign a standard form of bond which had to be witnessed by the President and the General Secretary. It bound him to handle the funds in accordance with the rules and the decisions of the Council, and gave the President, officers and members of the Council the power to prosecute him if he defaulted. The District books and accounts were to be audited every three months (or as often as required), and the result of the audit was to be submitted to the Council. The auditors were to be appointed in accordance with the Trade Union

[1] *D.M.A.* 25 November, 1882.   [2] *Ibid.* 17 February, 1883.

Act of 1871,[1] if the Association decided to register, and they received the same remuneration as delegates to Council meetings. The District Fund was to be allowed to accumulate to £200 and was to be invested in the names of four Trustees, one of whom was to be the Treasurer. The Trustees were nominated by the lodges and elected or removed by a majority of the votes of the Council. They, too, were paid at the same rates as the delegates to Council meetings. The District Treasurer was required to render accounts in January and July of each year, and on other occasions if it was thought necessary by the Trustees, showing details of the total income and expenditure of the Association together with the amount of funds in hand. These accounts were to be supplied to each lodge.

The burdens of office have been known to modify the most radical minds and the leaders of the Derbyshire Miners' Association were no exception. Having organized a secession movement from the South Yorkshire Association on the grounds that the centralization of funds was dangerous and unwise, they soon found, as District officials, that it was perhaps safer, after all, to have the funds in their own hands. Within a year of the introduction of the revised rules they issued a circular pointing out the disadvantages of the existing financial arrangements:

The present Association, at its commencement, for the purpose of establishing confidence among the Miners of Derbyshire, adopted the principle of every lodge Banking its own Funds. Documents of every description that was thought to be necessary for the protection of those funds were provided, and it only required that the officials and members of the lodges should take an earnest, and honest, interest in their Society for the whole machinery to work with thorough satisfaction. But what are the facts of the case? We find Treasurers who have not signed the Bonds: Lodges whose Funds are not Banked according to Rule; and an amount of insecurity that is a danger always. There is also, an unwillingness on the part of the lodges to part with their Funds at the Council's bidding for the support of members, according to Rule; and a very evident conservatism at a number of Lodges, so far as the Funds are concerned, inasmuch, as although the moneys obviously belong to every member of the Union, there is a feeling that if we part with our Funds for the support of those who may require them, there will be nothing for us if we should require assistance.

. . . If the Funds banked, wherever they may be, belong to each Lodge exclusively, then we are but a number of Federated Lodges, each Lodge managing its own business in its own way, but conforming to the Council's decrees so far as to pay honourably any demands that may be made upon them, for Rule purposes. There is no such intention in our present Rules, and to

[1] 34 & 35 Vict. c. 31, s. 11. '. . . which account the said trustees shall cause to be audited by some fit and proper person or persons by them to be appointed.'

admit it as a principle would, in our opinion, be to undermine the foundations of our Society. We are not without examples where Lodges have shared their money up. Other moneys are lying in Banks where Lodges have broken up, and through the obstinacy of the sometime Trustees, and for want of a connecting link whereby the Council can step in, the money is lost to us. We think from the foregoing you will perceive that from indifference, narrow-mindedness, and a want of that honesty that was known at the first would be required, our present system is anything but perfect. We therefore recommend to your *serious consideration* the desirability of the Funds of our Society being centralized in future.[1]

The officials went on to advance powerful arguments against the existing system. It was more costly because a great deal was spent in stamps and stationery when transferring the moneys and receipts and in paying the trustees. It was difficult to know the true financial position of the Association because the lodges either refused or neglected to send in proper accounts. The method of raising money from the lodges, necessitating the signature of trustees, was slow and cumbrous. With the funds centralized so that their real value could appear on each balance sheet the members would be encouraged and the Association strengthened. In conclusion, the officials urged the necessity for increased subscriptions:

During the calls that have been made, Lodges, some of them have been in existence from the first, have exhausted their funds, and the members have had to pay Levies out of their pockets. This has been in consequence of their having but few members. But it is very discouraging that men who have struggled on for years should have to pay 1s. 3d. per week, whilst other members, simply because they have a larger Lodge, have only to pay 3d. Centralizing would obviate that. . . . The recent demands upon our funds have shown that 3d. per week, when all costs are taken out does not allow you to save a great deal. We, therefore, respectfully urge upon you the desirability of paying 6d. per week, so that there may be funds when a rainy day overtakes us.[2]

In 1885 the plan of centralizing the funds was adopted and, almost immediately, there was a demand that the Banking Account should appear on all future balance sheets. 'It was an accidental omission', explained the officials.[3] The proposal to increase contributions to 6d. a week was not accepted although the expenses of lodge meetings and Council meetings continued to drain the Association's funds. In January, 1885, the Ilkeston lodges were requested to find cheaper accommodation and the officials proposed that lodges should meet their local expenses by an increased contribution from the members. They

---

[1] Derbyshire Miners' Association, Circular, 24 May, 1884.
[2] *Ibid.*   [3] *D.M.A.* 20 January, 1885.

pointed out that the Durham Miners' Association had such a scheme:
'Durham owes her success very largely to this, and it is undeniable she
stands in the fore-front of Miners' Unions.'[1] In the following year
the contribution was raised to 4d. a week and, after the great lock-out of
1893, to 6d.[2]

There were also various changes in the benefits payable to financial
members. The experiences of the struggle of 1893 led the Waleswood
lodge and others near the Yorkshire border to demand that strike payment should be increased to bring them into line with the Yorkshire
Association. They also proposed the introduction of a death benefit as
operated in Yorkshire.[3] After the matter had been discussed by the
lodges it was decided not to introduce a death benefit but to increase
strike and victimization payments to 10s. a week. The Secretaries
commented: 'The decision the Lodges have given proves they intend
the Association to exist for labour purposes only.'[4] A similar problem
arose in 1899 when the Nottinghamshire and Derbyshire Associations
had to set up a joint committee to consider the question of paying
uniform benefits to members of lodges on the borders of the two counties.[5] The proposal to introduce death benefits was revived by the
Markham lodge in 1908 but the traditional opposition of the Association to friendly society functions prevailed.[6] In 1909 it was decided to
introduce progressive scales of payment for members taking part in
local strikes. After four weeks they were to receive 12s. a week and
after eight weeks, 14s. These increased payments did not apply to
general disputes.[7]

Shortly before the 1893 dispute unemployment was growing rapidly,
particularly in the Ilkeston, Monkwood, Awsworth and Bolsover districts
where collieries had either closed or reverted to single shift working.
There was no provision in the rules for men who were unemployed
for such reasons to receive any payment from the Association but
in May, 1893, the lodges decided that £500 should be paid to the
unemployed at the rate of 7s. a week for married and 5s. for single men.[8]
A further £500 was voted in July but the scheme was discontinued
during the lock-out.[9] By April, 1895, the Association felt that its
finances were sufficiently sound to re-introduce 'out-of-work' payments
and £200 was voted for payment to men who had been unemployed for
28 days or more.[10] A further grant of £100 in the following month met
with opposition. Some lodges argued that the payments were illegal

[1] D.M.A. 20 January, 1885.
[2] Ibid. 26 October, 1886; 9 November, 11 December, 1893; 6 March, 1894.
[3] Ibid. 1 May, 1894.   [4] Ibid. 26 June, 1894.
[5] Derbyshire Times, 1 April, 1899.   [6] D.M.A. 29 August, 1908.
[7] Ibid. 10 July, 1909.   [8] Ibid. 2 and 30 May, 1893.
[9] Ibid. 3 July, 1893.   [10] Ibid. 30 April, 1895.

but it was pointed out that the rules provided, with the consent of the members, for the making of grants.[1] In July the unemployed members of the Association were exempted from paying contributions and the qualifying period for receiving benefit was reduced to fourteen days.[2]

The union continued to make grants to the fund but in January, 1896, it was reported that the fund was becoming 'burdened with old men' and it was proposed that no member should be allowed more than three months' unemployment benefit in any one year. 'It must clearly be understood this Fund was not established as an Old-Age Pension Fund', said the officials.[3] The limit of three months was imposed in March, except in cases where whole collieries were closed.[4] In the following October it was laid down that members receiving unemployment payments must obtain, at least twice a week, the signature of a checkweighman at some colliery at which they had been refused work.[5] An unofficial strike of pit boys in 1902, causing large numbers of men to be unemployed, led the Council to decide that in such cases men should be eligible for payment after six days.[6] Benefits such as these were of considerable importance to miners before the introduction of a national scheme of unemployment insurance. In the depression year of 1905 W. E. Harvey said that the Derbyshire Miners' Association had 'saved the rates thousands of pounds'. During three of the summer months the union had distributed £17,000, £11,000 and £13,000 in unemployment benefits.[7]

Similarly, in the absence of governmental action, the Association turned to the provision of old-age pensions. As early as 1899 Haslam said that he saw no likelihood of any practical scheme being evolved which did not call upon the working classes for contributions to its funds:

They heard a great deal of talk about capturing royalty rents and about disestablishing the Church as a means of the establishment of such a fund. But such talk was cheap; and in his opinion the common sense of the people of this country would, for many a day yet to come, allow men to reap the benefit from their own property.[8]

Barnet Kenyon expressed a similar view at the union's annual demonstration in the following year.[9] Harvey took a more radical line than his colleagues. In 1908 he said:

When they came to speak of the question of old-age pensions and the sources from which provision for them could be made, he and his colleagues would

---

[1] *D.M.A.* 28 May, 1895.   [2] *Ibid.* 23 July, 1895.
[3] *Ibid.* 7 January, 1896. Cf. R. V. Sires, 'The Beginnings of British Legislation for Old-Age Pensions', *Journal of Economic History*, XIV, (1954), pp. 237–8.
[4] *Ibid.* 3 March, 1896.   [5] *Ibid.* 13 October, 1896.
[6] *Derbyshire Times*, 2 August, 1902.   [7] *Ibid.* 11 November, 1905.
[8] *Ibid.* 29 July, 1899.   [9] *Ibid.* 14 July, 1900.

have something to say with regard to royalties and to the land which was really stolen property.[1]

In 1905 the Association made a grant of £5 in support of the London Trades Council's campaign for old-age pensions but the Old-Age Pension Act did not come until 1908 and meanwhile the Association decided to do something about establishing its own pension scheme.[2] From 1 July, 1906, every financial member who had been in the union for 15 years was to receive a pension of 5s. a week for life at the age of 60 if he was unable to work. No additional contributions were required.[3] At the annual demonstration, in the following August, members of the Association were told by Enoch Edwards, President of the Miners' Federation of Great Britain:

It is a thousand times the better policy that you should spend your funds on old-age pensions and building workmen's homes than to spend it on strikes. Industrial peace is the best for every miner and for his master as well.[4]

There were few changes in the general financial arrangements after the centralization of the funds in 1885. During the prosperous years down to 1890 the reserves accumulated rapidly and the officials, unaccustomed to handling large sums of money, became somewhat apprehensive. The Association began by depositing its funds with Crompton and Evans' Union Bank, Ltd., Chesterfield, but when the account was nearing £5,000, in 1890, it was decided that it might be safer to open a new account with the Sheffield Banking Company.[5] In July, 1890, the officials reported to the Council: 'It has been mooted that certain Directors of Banks, where our funds are invested, are large Shareholders both in Collieries and Ironworks, and that it is not to our best interests for our funds to remain where there is the least possibility of danger.'[6] After being reassured by their legal adviser, however, the officials recommended that the existing arrangements should continue.[7]

Thereafter the Association continued to pursue a policy of seeking safe investments and spreading its risks, real or imagined. By January, 1891, the account with the Sheffield Bank had also reached £5,000 and the officials suggested: 'If we could put the whole of the £10,000 in, say, the Bank of England, it would be a good thing, and start saving again on the small nucleus remaining.'[8] After making inquiries at the Bank, Haslam and Harvey reported: 'We are clearly of opinion that the

[1] *Derbyshire Times*, 9 May, 1908.   [2] *Ibid.* 25 March, 30 December, 1905.
[3] *Ibid.* 23 June, 1906. The qualifying period was later reduced to 12 years. (*Rules of the Derbyshire Miners' Association*, 1910.)   [4] *Ibid.* 11 August, 1906.
[5] *D.M.A.* 8 April, 6 May, 1890.   [6] *Ibid.* 1 July, 1890.
[7] *Ibid.* 29 July, 1890.   [8] *Ibid.* 13 January, 1891.

. . . conditions do not in any way meet our requirements.'[1] Soon afterwards an attempt was made to persuade the officials to invest the
Association's funds in the proposed Lancashire, Derbyshire and East
Coast Railway.[2] In April, 1891, Haslam gave evidence before the
parliamentary committee which considered the Bill and Rickards,
counsel for the Manchester, Sheffield and Lincolnshire Railway Company, stated: 'It was not at all improbable that the miners' associations
would take shares in the new railway.'[3] But the Executive Committee
had already decided to recommend to the lodges that the Association's
funds should continue to be banked with Crompton and Evans' and the
Sheffield Company and this was accepted.[4]

Until the dispute of 1893 the funds continued to be evenly distributed
between the two banks, savings being diverted from the one to the other
after the accumulation of each additional £5,000. Crompton and
Evans' paid $2\frac{1}{2}$ per cent. interest on deposits up to £5,000 and 3 per
cent. on any further investments but the Sheffield Company paid a
flat rate of only 2 per cent. In 1893 the whole of the union's reserves
had to be withdrawn from the banks. For this service Crompton and
Evans' made no charge but the Sheffield Company charged £21 1s. 6d.[5]
The Council felt aggrieved at such treatment and when the funds began
to accumulate again, after the dispute was over, it was decided to close
the account with the Sheffield Bank, to deposit up to £15,000 with
Crompton and Evans' and then open an account with the Nottingham
and District Bank.[6] Crompton and Evans' continued to be the Association's principal bankers and eventually it was written into the rules that
the funds should be 'invested with Messrs. Crompton & Evans' Union
Bank, Limited, at Chesterfield, or some other recognized Bank in
England'.[7]

In 1909 Harvey and Hall reported to the Council that they had
arranged with Crompton and Evans' 'that in future all our moneys
invested in that Bank should bear 3 per cent. Interest, besides which
the Manager undertakes to collect all the moneys paid into their
Branches in other Towns and all moneys paid to them (through any
Bank whatever) belonging to this Association free of charge, which
means a considerable saving of our Funds. It is therefore thought that
the above-named considerations claim from us substantial recognition
in the form of a large amount of money being invested in Crompton and
Evans' Bank.'[8] This did not prevent the Association from patronizing
other banks to ensure that their deposits with Crompton and Evans'

[1] *D.M.A.* 10 February, 1891.   [2] *Ibid.* 10 March, 1891.
[3] *Derbyshire Times*, 25 April, 1891.   [4] *D.M.A.* 7 April, 5 May, 1891.
[5] *Ibid.* 5 January, 1895.   [6] *Ibid.* 6 February, 1895.
[7] *Rules of the Derbyshire Miners' Association*, 1910.
[8] *D.M.A.* 16 January, 1909.

did not become excessive. At various times new accounts were opened with the London City and Midland Bank, the York City and County Banking Company, the London Joint Stock Bank, the Sheffield Banking Company, the Sheffield Union Bank, the Sheffield and Hallamshire Bank, the United Counties Banking Company, Williams Deacon's Bank and others. The new accounts were generally opened by transferring £10,000, £15,000 or £20,000 from Crompton and Evans' or from some bank where it had been decided to close the Association's account. The factors which determined the opening and closing of accounts were the services, charges and interest rates which prevailed at the different banks. In 1909 there was a move by some of the delegates to Council to secure the opening of an account with the Co-operative Wholesale Banking Society but they were unsuccessful.

As the liquid assets of the Association grew it became more prepared to enter into long-term investments in the form of loans to local government authorities. The arrangements for the Association's loans were invariably made by Samuel Edward Short, a Chesterfield accountant, who was recognized as a public auditor under the Industrial and Provident Societies Act, 1893. Short had audited the Association's accounts since 1894 and, at the time of his death in May, 1914, was described as the union's 'financial adviser'.[1] He was also one of Chesterfield's aldermen and, not unnaturally, invested much of the Association's money with the Chesterfield Corporation. The tramway system, the gas and water board and various other public utilities in the town were partly financed by the Derbyshire Miners' Association. Smaller sums were lent to the Ilkeston Corporation, but, despite innumerable appeals from other local authorities throughout the country, no loans were made outside Derbyshire. These investments generally carried a rather higher rate of interest than could be obtained from the banks. The Chesterfield Corporation was prepared to pay up to $3\frac{3}{4}$ or 4 per cent. and to repay the principal by yearly or half-yearly instalments. Ilkeston preferred to pay only 3 per cent. and to repay the whole of the principal at the end of a stated period. In both cases, as much as three months' notice was required before the money could be withdrawn. By August, 1914, loans to local authorities accounted for almost 60 per cent. of the Association's funds, the remainder being deposited in the banks.[2]

[1] *D.M.A.* 5 June, 1895; *Derbyshire Times*, 9 May, 1914. S. E. Short was Chairman of the Eckington coal company, J. and G. Wells, Ltd. He was also a director of various firms including F. W. Spridgeon, Ltd., lace manufacturers, of Long Eaton; the Trent Motor Traction Company, Ltd.; S. E. Redfern, Ltd., Chesterfield; and the Chesterfield Estates. He was auditor to the Bolsover, Oxcroft, Bullcroft, and Hatfield Main colliery companies and secretary to the Chesterfield and District Hides and Skin Company; Ashover Hydro, Ltd.; Cavendish Motors, Ltd.; the Derbyshire and South Yorkshire Billposting Company and the Richmond Building Society.
[2] *Ibid.* 22 August, 1914.

The progress of the Association between 1880 and 1914 can be measured by its growing membership and financial reserves. Until the funds were centralized not even the officials knew how much money was in the General Fund which was held by the lodges, but for the first month of the union's existence a total of £17 16s. 10d. was sent to Chesterfield from 28 lodges. After paying the expenses of the officials and committee-men and various bills for stationery and printing, the Treasurer was left with a balance of a little over £3 in hand.[1] When an attempt was made, in May, 1881, to present a general statement of the number of members and the amount of money available in the General Fund, the number of lodges had decreased to 14. Of these, one neglected to report the number of its members and two refused to disclose details of their banking accounts. The total reported membership was then 696 and there was at least £97 18s. 4½d. in hand or in the bank, in addition to the £14 5s. 2d. held by the General Treasurer.[2] In January, 1885, after the centralization of the funds, there was an income of £32 0s. 3½d. from 32 lodges with about 1,000 members and £210 had been banked.[3] By December, 1914, there was an income of £3,094 for the month from 90 lodges with a membership of 42,403 and investments amounting to £311,926. Between 1881 and 1914 investments per head increased more than fifty-fold from 2s. 10d. to nearly £8.[4]

The accumulation of these reserves was not achieved without setbacks. Membership rose from 696 in May, 1881, to a peak of 2,837 in May, 1883, after some wage concessions had been gained. The number of lodges, which had dwindled from 28 in 1880 to 14 in May, 1881, rose to 42 in May, 1883. Thereafter, in the face of declining trade and wage reductions the membership fell to just above 1,000 but the organization remained intact, the number of lodges never again falling below 32. The Association's funds, which had risen to £242 in March, 1885, fell to £100 after the strike in the Ilkeston district in the following August but by January, 1887, there were 38 lodges and £395 in the bank. The formation of the Miners' Federation of Great Britain in 1889, and the increases in wages which it was able to obtain as trade improved towards the end of the decade, led to a spectacular advance both in membership and in financial reserves. In January, 1890, there were already 60 lodges with a membership of 9,680 and a reserve fund of £3,243 but by the end of that prosperous year there were 69 lodges, over 12,000 members, and over £10,000 in the banks.

On the eve of the dispute of 1893 the Association had assets of over £30,000 and a membership of over 18,000 in 76 lodges. Lock-out

[1] D.M.A. 19 February, 1880.   [2] Ibid. 28 May, 11 June, 1881.
[3] Ibid. 20 January, 1885.   [4] See Chart 4 and Appendix I to this chapter.

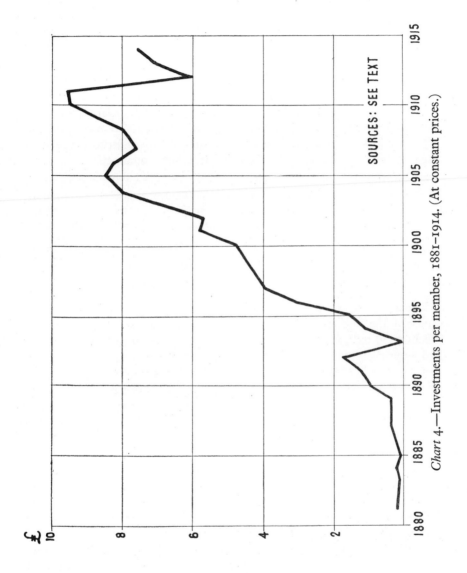

Chart 4.—Investments per member, 1881–1914. (At constant prices.)

SOURCES: SEE TEXT

payments began on 18 August and, within a month, the funds had dwindled to £829 9s. 4d.[1] It was then resolved by the Council: 'That the President and Secretaries wait upon the Members of Parliament for this County and try to borrow money to pay at least two weeks' pay, and that Local Lodges seek amongst their friends and see if there are any persons willing to lend the Association money, and if there are, they borrow and forward the same to the General Secretary.' At the same time it was decided to pay 5 per cent. on all borrowed money.[2] The refusal of Thomas Bayley, Liberal Member of Parliament for Chester-field and a partner in the Digby and Manners Colliery Companies, to lend money to the Association, enabled his opponents to make political capital out of the situation. Bayley had allowed his men to go back to work at the old rates and the *Derbyshire Times* exclaimed:

On his own showing he is a traitor to those to whom he pledged his word. He, with other colliery owners in the midland counties, agreed that a reduc-tion was necessary. . . . His miners started without even the sanction of the Derbyshire agents, Messrs. Haslam and Harvey, and what was the result? Some newspapers put Mr. Bayley's profits at £1,000 a day. . . . Mr. Haslam approached Mr. Bayley. Derbyshire miners were starving. The men in the Chesterfield division required assistance. But Mr. Bayley was at once poor. He could not let them have a little bit of his tremendous wealth.[3]

Nevertheless, by various means, the Association managed to carry on until the end of the struggle. About £3,000 was borrowed, the offices were mortgaged for £2,000, and one or two of the lodges, which had been accumulating funds, sent sums of as much as £400 or £500 to Chesterfield.[4] As the men began to resume work they paid a levy of 1s. a day to support those who were still locked out but by the time there was a general resumption of work the Association was in debt to the tune of £7,000.[5] 'There were only three trustees who stood for that £7,000,' said Harvey, some years later, 'and they could have been bought up for £20.'[6]

At the end of the lock-out the Association had only 12,500 financial members but numbers were rapidly increased by the suspension of the entrance fee. The raising of the weekly contribution to sixpence, to-gether with a sixpenny levy, enabled the Association to achieve solvency very quickly.[7] By 9 January, 1894, the mortgage on the offices had been paid off and other debts to lodges and individuals were gradually being repaid.[8] In September, with over £12,000 in reserve, the Council resolved: 'That the persons who lent money to this Association during

---

[1] *D.M.A.* 25 July, 19 September, 1893.   [2] *Ibid.* 19 September, 1893.
[3] *Derbyshire Times*, 7 October, 1893.   [4] *Ibid.*
[5] *D.M.A.* 17 October, 1893.   [6] *Derbyshire Times*, 10 November, 1906.
[7] *D.M.A.* 11 December, 1893.   [8] *Ibid.* 9 January, 1894.

the lock-out of 1893 be written to, asking them to withdraw the same with the interest due at the expiration of the year from the time of its being lent.'[1]

Although the 1893 dispute caused a temporary reduction in membership the union's organization remained intact. The number of lodges continued to increase steadily, reaching 80 in 1905, and 90 in 1908. Membership followed the course of trade and wages, dwindling from 19,675 in 1895 to 16,323 in 1898 and then rising to 27,972 in 1902. There were minor reverses in 1903 and 1904 but by 1906 there were 29,480 members, increasing to 38,475 in 1908 and, after slight reductions in 1909 and 1910, rising to 42,130 in 1912. After the strike of that year membership fell to 40,747, rising to 42,403 in 1914. The union's funds increased steadily after 1893, totalling £345,529 in 1911. Thus it was able to face the dispute of 1912 with confidence and the inroads made upon its reserves, although serious, were by no means so disastrous as they had been in 1893. The Association was paying out about £20,000 a week during the 1912 strike but it finished the year with £244,022 in hand, and, by the outbreak of war in 1914, this had risen to £294,534.

4. RELATIONS WITH OTHER UNIONS

When the Derbyshire Miners' Association was formed, in 1880, Macdonald's National Union was still in existence. Its objects, laid down in 1863, were 'to consider, provide for, and execute as far as possible, all public and general business as relating to the interests of operative miners, as regards legislation for the inspection of mines, and for compensation for accidents; but they are not expected to interfere with any local trade disputes'. There had been various attempts to widen the activities of the National Union but they had met with little success. In 1877 William Crawford, the Secretary of the Durham Miners' Association, became Secretary of the National Union. Four years later Thomas Burt, the Northumberland miners' M.P., succeeded to the presidency on the death of Macdonald and the control of the national organization passed almost entirely into the hands of men who were adherents to the principle of the sliding scale and opponents of the Eight Hours' Bill.[2]

Unlike South Wales, Northumberland and Durham, the coalfields of Yorkshire, Nottinghamshire, Derbyshire, Lancashire, Cheshire, Staffordshire and North Wales had either not experienced or were

---

[1] *D.M.A.* 18 September, 1894.
[2] S. and B. Webb, *op. cit.* pp. 393–4; R. P. Arnot, *The Miners*, (London), 1949, p. 82.

rapidly abandoning sliding scales, their markets were mainly inland, their working conditions and pit customs were broadly similar and they were geographically close to one another. It was the miners of these central coalfields, led by Yorkshire and Lancashire, who were most active in demanding a national federation which would deal with wage questions. Unable to work through the Miners' National Union, they began to work together as an independent group, and out of this wages movement, which grew rapidly between 1885 and 1888, there developed a new organization, the Miners' Federation of Great Britain, which was formally constituted in 1889.[1]

In 1880 the Derbyshire Miners' Association was not affiliated with the Miners' National Union but, from the outset, it was represented at most of the major conferences whether called by the National Union or by the leaders of the central coalfields. In January, 1881, delegates were sent to the national conference at Manchester with instructions to protest against 'the strenuous efforts that are being made to induce, and compel, workmen to contract out of the Employers' Liability Bill'.[2] After the conference the Council pledged itself 'to take hold of any means that may be extended from the National, together with using all our endeavours individually, to promote and extend, to the uttermost, the much desired organization'.[3] In April, 1881, Haslam and Harvey represented the Association at the conference at Birmingham which was called by Crawford to discuss the general question of sliding scales.[4] 'Each district can send any number of men they choose', he explained. 'The Meeting will be purely deliberative, and will, therefore, be more of a conversational character. Be sure to send some from your District.'[5] The Council decided to send one representative to a further conference on sliding scales at Birmingham in October, 1881.[6]

But sliding scales were of no great interest to the Derbyshire miners who heard with approval Haslam's report of the Birmingham conference of December, 1881, at which it had been proposed that the rules of the National Union should be altered so as to permit the calling of conferences on general wages questions.[7] The Association had yet another illustration of the value of an effective national organization in 1882 when it was faced with several costly legal cases. The officials were urged by Crawford to publish a circular explaining their difficulties.[8] The campaign resulted in a handsome contribution from the Durham Miners' Association.[9] In July, 1883, a proposal that the Association

[1] S. and B. Webb, *op. cit.* pp. 393–4; Arnot, *op. cit.* pp. 80–87.
[2] *D.M.A.* 24 December, 1880.
[3] *Ibid.* 22 January, 1881.   [4] *Ibid.* 19 March, 1881.
[5] Miners' National Union, Circular, 9 March, 1881.
[6] *D.M.A.* 15 October, 1881.   [7] *Derbyshire Times*, 24 December, 1881.
[8] *D.M.A.* 5 August, 1882.   [9] *Ibid.* 2 September, 1882.

should join the National Union was rejected by the Council after the officials had pointed out: 'The Terms are ½d. per Member per month, about £5 for our present Membership. The objects are purely political, no financial assistance being granted.'[1] In December, 1884, however, it was decided to impose a levy of a halfpenny a month on each member 'so that we may at once join the Miners' National Union'.[2] Thereafter the Association was represented at all the national conferences and Haslam and Harvey began to serve on deputations seeking changes in the law relating to coalmining.

These growing activities with the National Union did not prevent the Derbyshire Miners' Association from taking part in the general wages movements of the central coalfields. In 1883 Haslam and Harvey attended conferences at Manchester and Birmingham to discuss the restriction of output.[3] Of the Manchester conference held on 27 July, the officials said: 'It will be necessary for someone to go . . . but the funds are low, and Delegates cannot go without money.'[4] As wages improved and membership increased, the expense of attending conferences ceased to be a serious impediment and the Derbyshire miners soon came to realize the advantages of co-operation with other counties. Nevertheless, the union was not represented at the special inaugural conference of the Miners' Federation of Great Britain which met at Newport on 26 November and 29 November, 1889, although Haslam was present at the miners' general conference on hours and wages which was held on the intervening days.[5] He had attended the Birmingham conference of 8 October at which a small committee had been appointed to draft proposals for the establishment of the Federation but he did not raise the question of joining the new organization until his Executive Committee meeting of 19 November, seven days before the opening of the inaugural conference. The matter had then to be referred to the lodges and on 17 December the Council resolved: 'That we do not join the Federation.'[6]

Haslam, as a member of the Central Board of the Miners' National Union, would have little liking for the Federation, with 'its aggressive policy and its semi-Socialistic principles of a minimum wage and a legal day',[7] but, in February, 1890, when the Federation was demanding a wage increase of 10 per cent., there was an overwhelming majority of members in favour of affiliation. The Council resolved: 'That Derbyshire join the National Federation of Great Britain' but also placed on record 'its belief in, and desire that conciliatory measures be resorted

[1] *D.M.A.* 10 July, 7 August, 1883.   [2] *Ibid.* 23 December, 1884.
[3] *Ibid.* 31 March, 28 April, 1883.   [4] *Ibid.* 3 February, 1883.
[5] Arnot, *op. cit.* pp. 101–2, 104; *D.M.A.* 22 October, 1889.
[6] *D.M.A.* 24 September, 19 November, 17 December, 1889.
[7] S. and B. Webb, *op. cit.* p. 394.

to'.[1] It was not until May, 1890, that the Association formally severed its connection with the National Union and Haslam resigned his seat on the Central Board. 'The Association was on with the new love before it was off with the old', the officials explained, 'and had not passed a formal Resolution to leave, but joining the other had implied that, hence Mr. Haslam's action in sending to Mr. Crawford.'[2]

Once committed to the Federation the Association began to play its part. At the Nottingham conference in April, 1890, Derbyshire was offered a seat on the Executive, which was taken by Harvey until the end of the year, and Haslam was appointed to give evidence before the Royal Commission on Mining Royalties.[3] In December, 1890, the Association decided to nominate Haslam for the vice-presidency of the Federation but he was not elected. Harvey was nominated for the Executive and was successful.[4] Thereafter, one or other of the Secretaries, and sometimes both, represented Derbyshire on the Executive of the M.F.G.B. Harvey was elected in January, 1891, 1893, 1895–7, 1899, October, 1900, 1901–2, 1904, 1906, 1908 and 1910; Haslam in January, 1892, 1894–6, 1898, October, 1900, 1901, 1903, 1905, 1907, 1909 and 1911. Barnet Kenyon served on the Executive in 1912, and in 1913 Frank Hall began his thirty years of service broken only by one year, 1922. Haslam and Harvey missed any opportunity they might have had of becoming national officials by not taking an active part in the establishment of the Federation in 1889. The turnover of national officials was low, generally depending upon death or infirmity, and there were no changes at all until the death of Pickard in 1904. Haslam never became a national official but Harvey, with his superior powers of oratory, made sufficient impression upon members of the Federation to secure his election to the vice-presidency, by 369 votes to 220, at the Swansea conference in October, 1912.[5] He held this position until his death in 1914.

At a time when foreign competition was becoming a major problem, the international activities of the Federation helped to widen the horizons of the Derbyshire leaders. The Miners' National Conference of October, 1889, had affirmed that 'an International Miners' Congress has become an absolute necessity when we consider the immensely increased powers of production which have taken place in every country and the easy and cheap means of transit from nation to nation'[6] and out of this arose the International Miners' Conference at Jolimont, in 1890. Haslam and Harvey were authorized by the Council to represent

---

[1] *D.M.A.* 11 February, 1890. See Chapter VII, pp.297–8.

[2] *Ibid.* 6 May, 1890.   [3] *Ibid.* 8 April, 1890.   [4] *Ibid.* 16 December, 1890.

[5] *Minutes of the Miners' Federation of Great Britain* (subsequently referred to as *M.F.G.B.*), 4 October, 1912.

[6] *Minutes of the Miners' National Union*, 9 October, 1889.

Derbyshire and Harvey distinguished himself by moving a resolution expressing 'profound sympathy with the German miners and their representatives attending this Congress in being subject to such arbitrary and unconstitutional laws . . .'.[1] Thereafter the Association was represented at most of the international conferences, at first by one or two of the officials, and later by two members from the lodges as well. In addition, one of the Derbyshire officials would sometimes attend an international conference on behalf of the Federation. The German congress of 1907 was attended by Harvey, Kenyon and two representatives of the lodges, with Haslam as a delegate from the Federation.[2]

Similarly, the Association became increasingly active at the Trades Union Congresses. It began in the 'eighties by sending one delegate and a small subscription of three guineas but, in 1890, Haslam was appointed to represent the Federation at the Liverpool Congress and Harvey represented the Association.[3] It then became the practice for at least two of the officials to attend the Congresses, one representing the Association and the other the Federation. In 1893, when the Federation undertook to pay affiliation fees to the T.U.C. for all its constituent associations, Derbyshire decided to discontinue its annual contribution on the ground that it was no longer necessary.[4] By 1905 the Association was sending to Congress two representatives from the lodges in addition to the two officials and in 1909, three years after his election to Parliament, Haslam became chairman of the Parliamentary Committee of the T.U.C.[5]

Amidst the general industrial unrest of 1910 Haslam presided at the Trades Union Congress. In his address he protested against indiscipline and stressed its injury to collective bargaining: 'We must urge upon our members the absolute need for loyalty and the essential discipline which must be granted to us if our word, and our bond, and our agreements are to be respected.'[6] The Congress was held at Sheffield and the presence of the Lord Mayor, the Earl Fitzwilliam, at the opening ceremony, led to a disturbance. There was at the time a dispute between Fitzwilliam and the miners employed at his Elsecar Collieries and before Haslam could utter a word the coalowner's presence was sharply challenged from the floor of the Congress by Stokes, of the London Glassblowers, and Chandler, of the Railway Clerks' Association, who left the hall in protest, followed by half-a-dozen sympathizers. When order had been restored Haslam said: 'I want you to understand, first of all, that I am getting an old man, and have not a strong voice. Let me

[1] Arnot, *op. cit.* p. 157. Some of the German miners had been prohibited from collecting subscriptions for the purpose of sending delegates to the Conference.
[2] *Derbyshire Times*, 23 March, 1907.
[3] *D.M.A.* 4 August, 1885; 8 April, 29 July, 1890.   [4] *Ibid.* 21 August, 1893.
[5] *Ibid.* 23 October, 1909.   [6] *T.U.C. Report*, 1910, p. 48.

say with regard to the complaint of Mr. Stokes that the arrangements made with his lordship were acceptable to the Yorkshire Miners, and that ought to satisfy everyone.'[1]

At the local level the Association participated in the formation of a Trades Council in Chesterfield, in 1893. The Secretaries were instructed by their Council to supply R. O. Hornagold, the initiator of the scheme, with a list of lodge secretaries living in and around Chesterfield, and to attend the inaugural meeting.[2] This was held at the Queen's Head on 9 June, with Plumber, Vice-Chairman of the Chesterfield and District Amalgamated Society of Railway Servants, in the chair. Hornagold referred to the importance of securing working-men magistrates and the need for unanimity of action amongst trade unionists in the town. 'The Trades Council', he said, 'would become the "boss of the show" instead of the Town Council.' Haslam and Harvey, who were both present, gave their blessing to the venture. Harvey observed that 'the formation of a Trades Council meant the bringing together of all the toilers of the borough for purposes that would benefit them'.[3] The newly formed Trades Council did much useful relief work during the 1893 lock-out but, as the Webbs have shown, it was more and more on the political side that the Trades Councils succeeded in uniting the energies of the trade unions of a particular town, a trend which was probably reinforced by their exclusion from the T.U.C. in 1895.[4] From the outset Haslam and Harvey were much more interested in using the new organization for securing the municipalization of the Chesterfield gas and water undertakings than they were in arranging joint industrial activities with other trade unions in the town.[5]

Within the coal industry itself, in Derbyshire, the Association was concerned with three other groups of workers: the enginemen and firemen, the banksmen and the deputies. As early as 1872 the Durham colliery engineers had seceded from the miners' association and had formed the Durham County Colliery Enginemen and Boilerminders' Association.[6] Out of this movement arose the National Federation of Colliery Enginemen and Boilermen which, by 1913, had 10,000 members.[7] On 4 November, 1891, a meeting was held at the Old Angel Hotel, Chesterfield, presided over by Samuel Rowarth, of Clay Cross, and Henry Bonsall, of Chesterfield. Among those present were W. H. Lamberton, secretary of the Durham Colliery Enginemen's Association and of the National Federation, T. Weighall, secretary of the Northumberland Association, and P. Bosson, of Stoke-on-Trent. It was decided

[1] T.U.C. Report, 1910, p. 42. [2] D.M.A. 30 May, 1893.
[3] Derbyshire Times, 17 June, 1893.
[4] Ibid. 16 September, 1893; S. and B. Webb, op. cit. p. 557.
[5] Derbyshire Times, 17 June, 1893.
[6] Arnot, op. cit. p. 65. [7] T.U.C. Report, 1913.

to call upon all colliery enginemen and firemen in Derbyshire to form a union.[1] Already, in 1890, both the Amalgamated Society of Enginemen, Cranemen, Boilermen and Firemen and the Derbyshire Miners' Association had made overtures to the Derbyshire enginemen but, as Rowarth pointed out, although these unions had done some useful work their leaders did not fully understand the problems of the enginemen and neither of the unions went 'far enough for the colliery enginemen and firemen of Derbyshire today', who wanted advances in wages and legislation to ensure safety by regulating their hours of work and requiring certificates of efficiency.[2] The Derbyshire Enginemen's and Firemen's Union was founded on 22 February, 1892, with Hosea Marriott as President and Rowarth as Secretary. It then had 48 members. Rowarth, with untiring energy and slender resources, steadily built up the organization in Derbyshire and brought in the Nottinghamshire enginemen as well. By 1911 the Derbyshire and Nottinghamshire Enginemen's and Firemen's Union had a membership of 1,400 in 23 branches and was able to open new offices in Mansfield.[3]

From the outset Rowarth had made it plain that he wished men to leave the Derbyshire and Nottinghamshire Miners' Associations and join the new union which, he hoped, would eventually affiliate with the miners' unions.[4] The miners' leaders were in favour of the development but it was fiercely resisted by the delegates to Council, the checkweighmen and others.[5] The result was that the Derbyshire Miners' Association pursued a policy of seeking concessions for the enginemen in the hope of retaining their membership.[6] In April, 1892, the Council resolved: 'That we cannot entertain the Enginemen's application for help to enable them to form a separate Association.'[7] Whilst favouring a separate union, however, the enginemen never lost sight of the value of co-operation with the larger organizations. In 1894 they sent a deputation to the Derbyshire Miners' Association to propose federation on the lines which had been adopted in the north-eastern coalfields.[8] In March, 1894, the principle was accepted and a committee of five was appointed to meet a committee of enginemen to draw up rules.[9] The Nottinghamshire Miners' Association also came into the scheme and a joint board was established. It was, however, carefully laid down in the rules that nothing contained therein should 'in any way interfere with any Association in the management of its own local affairs or government'.[10]

[1] *Derbyshire Times*, 7 November, 1891.
[2] *Ibid.* 25 October, 1890; 29 October, 1892; *D.M.A.* 23 September, 1890.
[3] *Derbyshire Times*, 21 October, 2 December, 1911.
[4] *Ibid.* 28 May, 1892.   [5] *Ibid.* 28 October, 1892.
[6] *D.M.A.* 11 January, 9 February, 1892.
[7] *Ibid.* 5 April, 1892.   [8] *Ibid.* 6 February, 1894.
[9] *Ibid.* 6 March, 1894.   [10] *D.M.A.* 7 May, 1910.

The three organizations co-operated fairly well on a wide range of industrial matters in which they had a common interest.[1]

The banksmen presented similar problems. Although they worked in the same industry and many of them were in the same union as the underground workers, the banksmen were creatures apart. Their wages were not covered by the general agreements negotiated by the Association and their special difficulties were catered for by the calling of banksmen's conferences when the need arose. The Association looked after their interests to the best of its abilities but there came a time when the banksmen were engulfed by the waves of the 'new unionism' and separate organizations, which promised to guard their interests more closely, were created. In November, 1908, there was a conference at which A. J. Bailey, of the National Amalgamated Union of Labour, met the officials of the Derbyshire Miners' Association. It was agreed that there was little hope of improving the wages and conditions of the banksmen as long as they were divided between the two unions and that the men should be asked to decide, by means of a ballot, which union they favoured.[2] The result was inconclusive, only 56 out of 88 lodges voted and there were 1,021 votes in favour of the N.A.U.L. as against 1,018 for the D.M.A.[3] There were further discussions with Bailey and it was decided to seek the establishment of a county price list for the banksmen in co-operation with the N.A.U.L.[4] The 1912 strike revealed the need for more than informal co-operation between the two organizations. Members of the D.M.A. were prevented from returning to work because the N.A.U.L. was still unable to reach an agreement with the employers.[5] This impasse resulted at last in the conclusion of a working agreement between the two unions which provided for consultations before taking strike action and for the transference of members between the unions without loss of benefits.[6] By entering into this agreement the D.M.A. pledged itself to secure for the N.A.U.L. recognition by the employers.[7]

Another group who felt the need for organization were the deputies. In 1908 the National Association of Colliery Deputies established a branch in Derbyshire, under the presidency of James Hibberd, of Alfreton.[8] Their relations with the Derbyshire Miners' Association were cordial. At their annual dinner in 1909, Frank Hall said: 'In the event of any trouble with the management he did not think that men

---

[1] The Nottinghamshire Miners' Association withdrew from the joint board in 1913 after various disputes with the enginemen's union. (A. R. Griffin, *The Miners of Nottinghamshire*, (Nottingham), 1956, pp. 172–3.)

[2] *D.M.A.* 28 November, 1908.

[3] *Ibid.* 8 May, 1909.   [4] *Ibid.* 25 September, 1909.

[5] *Ibid.* 13 April, 4 May, 1912.   [6] *Ibid.* 18 May, 1912.

[7] *Ibid.* 15 February, 1913.   [8] *Derbyshire Times*, 8 August, 1908.

WILLIAM EDWIN HARVEY

from the Derbyshire Miners' Association would take their places. . . .
The deputies were the pick of the men, and, in his opinion, they should
be paid the best wages possible.'[1] Some of the deputies were in favour of
affiliation with the Derbyshire Miners' Association and in July, 1911,
the Council was asked whether it could agree to transference of
membership between the two unions but the proposal was rejected.[2]

5. A PERIOD OF TRANSITION

The Association was born and came to maturity during a period of
transition in the trade union movement and, whilst some of the developments which took place were markedly influenced by the past, others
pointed to the future. The old traditions of the 'sixties and the 'seventies, the dislike of violent methods, the religious fervour, the love of
display, the co-operation with the Liberal politicians and advisers, the
hostility to professional trade union leaders and the domination of the
union by checkweighmen, all lingered on, but with diminishing force.
On the other hand, the impact of the 'new unionism', syndicalism
and Socialism, was leading to a growth of militancy, a refusal to work
with non-unionists, and the rejection of Liberalism both industrially
and politically. The link between the old and the new was the conversion
of the movement into an institution with officials firmly entrenched
amidst a growing paraphernalia of bureaucracy. This development was
made possible by the rapidly increasing membership and financial
resources, and necessary by the union's ever-widening range of activities
and interests. It pointed forward to the *beau idéal* of the modern trade
union, as strongly rooted in society as the Church of England and
almost as respectable. It prolonged the influence of the past, however,
as most institutions do, and made it more difficult for the advocates of
change to put their theories into operation.

In the early years the officials were full of fervour and Derbyshire's
failure, in the past, to create an independent miners' union, was used
as a goad to sting the men into activity. The preface to the 1880 rules
referred to 'the stigma that has clung to us up to the present, viz.
"There is no one to inspire confidence in the men to carry out Union
in Derbyshire", without being connected with parties outside. Your
Committee say—Arouse ye men, and prove the falsity of the libellous
scandal, by making your Association not only more gigantic in numbers
than your predecessors, but of greater moral and financial strength,
which shall be exercised in relieving and eventually, we trust, in

[1] *Derbyshire Times*, 17 July, 1909.   [2] *D.M.A.* 1 July, 31 July, 26 August, 1911.

I

preventing many of the evils under which we now suffer.' Similarly, Haslam pointed out in 1881:

It is . . . highly desirable that all Local Officials should exert themselves to some extent to keep alive our Organization, as, unless this is done, the Society will continue to be at its best a poor, consumptive, delicate article, utterly unfitted to cope with the great questions that are continually coming to the front, and of very little use indeed, as an instrument whereby to elevate its Members and the Miners of this locality generally, either financially or socially.[1]

Again, in the following year, he wrote: 'Strong efforts must be made to get good meetings, and try to improve our Union, otherwise we shall still be, as we have been too long, a drag on the better organized districts.'[2]

Demonstrations continued to be important instruments for stirring the weary and apathetic into activity. As early as May, 1881, when the Association was struggling for its very existence, it was thought worth while to contribute two guineas towards the expenses of the Stephenson centenary celebration and, in addition, to collect money at the pits to pay for a band to lead the miners' part of the procession through the streets of Chesterfield. 'It was considered, under the present depression of trade,' wrote Haslam, 'that one penny per man would be as much as could reasonably be expected.'[3] There were demonstrations at Ilkeston and Chesterfield in September, 1883, with such speakers as Lloyd Jones, Charles Bradlaugh, Ben Pickard, John Wilson and William Brown.[4]

But it was not until the revival of trade, towards the close of the 'eighties, that the Association was able to contemplate a county demonstration on the lines of those held at Chesterfield in the 'seventies by the South Yorkshire Association. The first large-scale demonstration was held on the Recreation Ground, Chesterfield, in 1889. There was a procession of fifty-one lodges with fifteen bands and it was estimated that between 20,000 and 30,000 people were present. Already there were signs of change:

The proceedings were opened by the singing of 'Praise ye the Lord, 'tis good to raise', in order, as explained by Mr. Norburn, to let others see that they were not all heathens, but it was evident that many of those present considered it a somewhat novel way in which to open a meeting and the well known hymn did not meet with the reception one would have expected. . . . A large portion of the miners assembled round the rostrum, but a good many

[1] D.M.A. 3 September, 1881.
[2] Ibid. 5 August, 1882.   [3] Ibid. 28 May, 1881.
[4] Derbyshire Times, 25 August, 8 September, 1883. Pickard, Wilson and Brown were the leaders of the Yorkshire, Durham and Staffordshire miners respectively.

of them betook themselves to the swingboats, shooting galleries, Aunt Sallies, and other like amusements, which had been erected in the grounds and not a few found the refreshment booth far more interesting than the speeches.[1]

Thereafter, the demonstrations themselves became an institution. They were held annually, except when trade was particularly bad, and provided a platform for national leaders such as Ben Pickard and Enoch Edwards, and for the Liberal manufacturers and industrialists such as J. A. Jacoby, T. Bayley, T. D. Bolton and Sir Walter Foster, who represented the Derbyshire mining constituencies in Parliament. As the years went by the demonstrations became more elaborate. From 1890 there were two platforms in order to accommodate the growing number of dignitaries and to allow for more speeches to be made, the miners choosing between tweedledum and tweedledee. In 1891 it was said of the officials: 'These gentlemen wore handsome gilt badges, upon which was inscribed the motto, "United we stand, divided we fall". The members of the Executive wore red sashes, and each lodge was headed by its banner.'[2] New faces began to appear on the platforms: in 1892, Sir Charles Dilke; in 1894, John Burns; in 1898, W. M. Thompson, the editor of *Reynolds's Newspaper*; in 1901, William Brace, deputizing for 'Mabon', the Welsh miners' leader; in 1904, Will Crooks and Richard Bell.

The 1908 demonstration reached a peak of splendour: 'At least two bands appeared in such gorgeous array that even an admiral in all the glory of his blue and gold must needs have hid his diminished head.'[3] But it marked the end of an epoch. The sharp recession in trade of 1909 prompted the Association to hold only small local demonstrations and in 1911, under the shadow of the Osborne judgment and the Fisher injunction, a meeting of the Trustees resolved, after taking legal advice: 'That we cannot consent to any payment being made for railway fares to a Demonstration, or any other expenses connected with a Demonstration. We therefore recommend that no Demonstration be held this year.'[4] The strike of 1912, the death of Haslam in 1913 and of Harvey in 1914, and the First World War, helped to complete the break with an old tradition.

In building up a powerful and growing organization it was natural that Haslam should find it necessary to establish a permanent head-quarters for the Association. The earliest meetings of the Executive and the Council were held at the Sun Inn, West Bars, Chesterfield, where the landlord, Blanksby, allowed the union to use his rooms free

[1] *Derbyshire Times*, 14 September, 1889.
[2] *Ibid.* 5 September, 1891.   [3] *Ibid.* 8 August, 1908.
[4] *D.M.A.* 10 June, 1911. See Chapter XII, p. 502, for the Fisher injunction.

of charge, no doubt relying upon the propensity of the miners' delegates to consume beer as a means of compensation.[1] Towards the end of 1889, however, when the Council was rapidly increasing in size, the Secretaries were instructed to speak to Blanksby 'about making the large room more comfortable for the winter Council meetings', but these negotiations were evidently not satisfactory for, in the following month, Haslam and two members of the Council were deputed to find better accommodation.[2] This they found at the Falcon Temperance Café, in Low Pavement, Chesterfield, at a rent of £10 a year, and Blanksby and his wife were presented with a silver tea and coffee service and duly thanked for helping to rear the lusty infant which had now outgrown its original home.[3]

The removal to the Falcon Café was, however, only a temporary measure. It had been envisaged, from the outset, that the union would one day have its own premises. The 1880 rules had stated quite clearly: 'The General Business of the Association shall be carried on at Chester-field, in the County of Derby, where there shall be offices for that purpose.' The decision to appoint a full-time Assistant Secretary led Haslam, in March, 1883, to advise that they would 'do well to take into consideration the Question of having an office where the Books, &c. can be kept, and where the Secretaries can do their Business'.[4]

In May, 1889, the Council decided to establish a building fund and the lodges were asked to form committees for collecting money.[5] There was not much response and in February, 1890, the Council recommended a levy of a shilling per member. In an attempt to reassure those who viewed the project with suspicion, Haslam argued: 'Surely it will be better to have the Home, if we can get it; it would be an ornament and a pride to the Association, and once built, could not possibly be a burthen, as the rents for the Secretaries' houses would, reasonably speaking, meet Taxes and Repairs.'[6] Again, in June, a further appeal was issued: 'What is it you fear? there is no intention of using any of the Union Funds. . . . We only want fairly sized WORKING-MEN'S HOUSES, and a Room in which to meet on Council days, with Offices beneath the Room. Look at it generously men, we are paying £10 rent now.'[7] By April, 1891, only £120 had been raised and a further appeal was made. Lodges were urged to hold teas, bazaars and concerts.[8]

The land was bought in November, 1891, at a cost of about £400 and the Secretaries and the Trustees of the Building Fund were in-structed 'to secure an architect and get on with the building of the

[1] *D.M.A.* 16 January, 1890.   [2] *Ibid.* 19 November, 17 December, 1889.
[3] *Ibid.* 16 January, 1890; *Derbyshire Times*, 7 June, 1890.
[4] *D.M.A.* 3 March, 1883.
[5] *Ibid.* 7 May, 1889.   [6] *Ibid.* 11 February, 1890.
[7] *Ibid.* 3 June, 1890.   [8] *Ibid.* 7 April, 1891.

Offices at the earliest opportunity'. Haslam commented: 'We shall have to borrow a good sum of money, which will be a burden. This will be heavier or lighter, according as we get ill or well supported by our Members and others.'[1] By April, 1892, however, despairing of raising enough capital by subscription, the Council decided that any money required for building purposes should be drawn from the Association's funds but that the Building Fund should continue. Haslam was instructed to obtain tenders for building, and the contract was given to William Maule of Nottingham. The work was to be completed by the following March for the sum of £2,675.[2]

The new building, planned in more prosperous times, was formally opened on Saturday, 24 June, 1893, shortly before the great lock-out of that year. The ceremony was combined with the annual demonstration and the Liberal politicians were there in force. Rollinson, the architect, handed to the Member for Chesterfield a silver key bearing the inscription: 'This key was presented to Mr. Thomas Bayley, M.P. wherewith to open the hall and offices of the Derbyshire Miners' Association, 24 June, 1893.'[3] On the following Tuesday the Council met for the first time in the new building and congratulated the officials and members of the Association 'on the successful rearing and opening of these beautiful and commodious premises' and expressed the hope that they would be 'a rallying place for a very many years; for an earnest and honest effort to further improve the condition of the Miners of this County, a centre of influence and power to uphold the right and stamp out the wrong, a light house to shed its benign rays where unionism is scarce and dark ...'.[4]

The building of the offices brought forth a great deal of ill-informed criticism. One member recalled the purchase of the Shirland Colliery by the South Yorkshire Association in the 'seventies. 'Are we going to witness a repetition of the tactics which have overthrown the unions of the past?' he asked. 'Once begin to dabble with the union funds and confidence will be lost and the men will leave the union as fast as they have been induced to join it.'[5] The rather ugly little Victorian building with, until recently, its half-tiled walls and drab paintwork, known to generations of Derbyshire miners as 'Saltergate', was depicted by the opponents of the union as a veritable palace, costing anything up to £6,000, in which the miners' leaders would live in luxury and idleness, free of charge and with innumerable perquisites, while the miners were starving. The expression of such views in the local Press and at public meetings appealed to the latent suspicion of trade union officials which

---

[1] D.M.A. 17 November, 1891.
[2] Ibid. 5 April, 31 May, 1892.   [3] Derbyshire Times, 1 July, 1893.
[4] D.M.A. 27 June, 1893.   [5] Derbyshire Times, 28 November, 1891.

still existed in the minds of many of the miners after their unfortunate experiences of the 'seventies.

The same attitude can be seen in the treatment of the officials over the matter of their expenses. In the early days of the Union the Council examined their personal expenditure minutely and in a most hostile fashion. 'There is a great deal of carping continually about the expenses,' complained the officials in 1883, 'but the circumstances, when explained, invariably give satisfaction. We would like to see a more generous spirit prevail amongst our Members, as from appearances, it would seem that Lodge Meetings are chiefly confined to the stale task of fault finding.'[1] A fortnight later Haslam protested:

It becomes very irksome to be continually baited and badgered about Six-pence here and Threepence there. The Council has been repeatedly told, by the Secretary, that he spends considerable of his own money besides what he charges them, and if Members think that a man can attend Meetings at Public Houses and stand to his own Expenses, we fancy it is more than any of them would like to do.[2]

Such criticism gradually diminished as the men became accustomed to the idea of a full-time salaried leadership but as late as 1912 Kenyon's expenditure on 'refreshments' was queried. The Council expressed its view that 'it is high time such petty spite as this complaint embodies should surely now cease'.[3]

Even with full-time officials the need for professional advice on finan-cial, legal and medical matters became more pressing as the work of the union developed. The regular advice given by S. E. Short on financial matters has already been noted. As early as March, 1883, after the Association had been involved in a number of lawsuits, the question of engaging a legal adviser was raised.[4] The Association never went so far as to appoint a full-time legal officer but a steady connection was maintained with Clegg and Sons, of Sheffield, who conducted most of the union's business. William Johnson Clegg, the founder of the partner-ship, had acted as legal adviser to the South Yorkshire Association in the 'seventies and had been associated with the Shirland Colliery experiment as a director. He was a self-made man, beginning life as a solicitor's clerk and later becoming Collector of Rates for Sheffield and then an accountant. The turning point in his career came when he decided to become a solicitor. Stainton writes:

It was no easy step which he took, for he had a wife and many children dependent upon him, but he left them in Sheffield and, going to London, took two small rooms there, and joined the staff of a firm of solicitors. He

---

[1] D.M.A. 14 April, 1883.   [2] Ibid. 28 April, 1883.
[3] Ibid. 16 November, 1912.   [4] Ibid. 3 March, 1883.

sacrificed himself entirely to his ambition. He rose at five in the morning, and studied until it was breakfast time, then he spent the day at business, condensed his dinner, tea and supper into one meal, and again devoted himself to study. So in 1868 he passed his examination when 42 years old and began life afresh in the town of his birth.[1]

In 1883, on the passing of the Bankruptcy Act, Clegg became Sheffield's first Official Receiver, and by that time his sons were able to take charge of the business which he had built up in Figtree Lane. Most of the Association's litigation was in the hands of William E. Clegg who became active in local Liberal politics and was knighted in November, 1906.[2]

The union's medical adviser was Josiah Court, of Staveley. Born at Warwick in 1841, the son of a chemist, he went to work in a shipping office at Liverpool at the age of 14. There he made friends with John Brunner who worked in the same office and was later to become the founder of the great chemical firm, Brunner, Mond and Company. But it was his friendship with a young doctor named Lowndes which finally determined his career. After some persuasion Court's father agreed to allow him to study medicine at the General Hospital, Birmingham, and at Guy's Hospital, London. Court began to practise as a surgeon at Staveley in 1864 and remained there for the rest of his life. He had a strong missionary zeal: until the age of 91, we are told, 'he was to be seen week after week attending the open-air services of the Salvation Army in the main street of Staveley'. His research work on miners' nystagmus, which will be discussed later, earned him the gratitude of the Derbyshire miners and led to his being admitted to honorary membership of the union. In politics, unlike most of the union's advisers, Court was a Conservative but although his activities on the political platform ran counter to those of the Association they did not destroy his close personal relationship with it.[3] On more than one occasion he appeared as a speaker at the union's demonstrations.[4]

In addition to its regular advisers the Association was sometimes able to make use of the services of the Liberal Members of Parliament who owed their seats largely to the support of the miners. It was Thomas Dolling Bolton, the member for North-East Derbyshire, who arranged, free of charge, the conveyance of the land for the new building in 1891, and who advised the Association to register under the Trade Union Act, 1871, so that it could legally hold the property.[5]

[1] J. H. Stainton, *The Making of Sheffield*, (Sheffield), 1924, p. 305.
[2] *Derbyshire Times*, 10 November, 1906.
[3] Hallam, *op. cit.* p. 1; *British Medical Journal*, I, (1938), pp. 424–6; *Derbyshire Times*, 2 August, 9 August, 1924. Court was knighted in 1920.
[4] *Derbyshire Times*, 7 May, 1898; 20 July, 1909.
[5] *D.M.A.* 15 December, 1891; 31 May, 1892.

Humbler assistance was also enlisted in the shape of a shorthand clerk. In June, 1912, the officials pointed out: 'It is now time the Lodges considered the advisability of appointing a clerk who can take down from dictation letters in shorthand and type them up, also give some general assistance in the office.'[1] The proposal was approved and an examiner from the Chesterfield Commercial School was appointed. It was stipulated: 'Abilities being equal, a working miner will be given the preference. The son of one of our members, not a working miner, will be given preference over an outsider. Canvassing Delegates or interviewing Central Officials is strictly forbidden, and will be a disqualification.'[2] Joseph Lynch, of New Whittington, was appointed. He was described by the examiner as 'a young man of good address, and his application is supported by a business experience which, quite apart from his educational ability, qualifies him in a marked degree, for the position he is seeking to fill'.[3] The appointment of Lynch is interesting because he eventually became an official of the Association, an example of the new type of trade union leader who was able to come up through the administration rather than from the pit or the shop-floor. The bureaucracy was already beginning to reproduce itself.

If the twentieth century brought security and external acceptance for the Association it also brought criticism from within. As Max Beer has pointed out, the first symptoms of syndicalism were to be seen, from 1908 onwards, in the rebellion of many trade unionists against their leaders, a 'revolt against . . . official-ridden and petty trade unionism'.[4] During these years all aspects of the union's organization and, as will be seen later, its industrial and political policies, were sharply criticized. In 1909 a writer called attention to the results of apathy among the members of the Association:

Persons are elected on some committees who have no reputation for intelligence, and in such instances such men are elected delegates to the miners' council because they get good wages for four hours, to start at 9 and give over at one, and give the delegates and officials the opportunity to attend cricket and football matches at the expense of the Association. When the business is not finished the Executive are called together to have another easy day and a good day's wage. . . . It will be interesting to know how many masters' favourites are regular officials of the Association. . . . Some time ago one of the delegates had such a trouncing in the Council for his unmanly tactics for doing work under price and other things, that he told the delegates that he would not go again to Council. . . .[5]

[1] D.M.A. 1 June, 1912.
[2] Ibid. 29 June, 1912.   [3] Ibid. 24 August, 1912.
[4] M. Beer, A History of British Socialism, (London), edn. of 1940, II, p. 357.
[5] Derbyshire Times, 3 July, 1909.

In the same month the Council deprecated 'the somewhat common practice of writing to the press, airing supposed or real grievances in connection with this Association' and appealed to all members 'to uphold the prestige and dignity of the Association' but this did not prevent further criticism.[1]

Two years later another member alleged: 'I can give instances where sycophants are delegates to Council, and the officials at Chesterfield know it to be true.'[2] The chief targets for the attack were the check-weighmen, many of whom were alleged to be in league with the employers. In August, 1911, an attempt was made by the Ireland lodge to carry a resolution that delegates should be elected only from the coal face but this was rejected 'seeing that all men who are members of our lodges are eligible for election as Delegates'.[3] In the following September the Executive registered a formal protest 'against the statements frequently made about the seething discontent which is said to pervade our membership, believing, as we do, that the men as a whole are intensely loyal to the Association'.[4] Nevertheless, there appears to have been some substance in the criticisms which were levelled against the composition of the Council for in November, 1911, the Eckington delegate was asked to withdraw 'he neither being a miner or a checkweigher, but an insurance agent'.[5]

Nor were the officials and their advisers immune from attack. As early as 1905 Haslam and Harvey, with the backing of Council, felt it advisable to institute proceedings for slander against Thomas Priestley, a publican and former butler to C. P. Markham, who was alleged to have accused them of receiving £100 each from Markham for settling a strike at the Seymour Colliery in 1891–2. Priestley denied that he had made such statements and was awarded costs, and Haslam and Harvey, who had made great play of the necessity of vindicating their honour, retired from the fray with diminished prestige.[6] By 1912 there was a mounting opposition to the union's officials which manifested itself in a variety of ways. They were accused of not visiting the lodges sufficiently and of neglecting their duties because of parliamentary work. There were complaints about their salaries and expenses and about the presentation of the monthly balance sheet. The Bolsover Lodge demanded to inspect the Association's accounts and was refused, by the Council, on the ground that the accounts were open for inspection only by individual members and not by lodges.[7]

The general unrest led to a resolution to dispense with the services of

[1] D.M.A. 31 July, 1909.   [2] Derbyshire Times, 29 July, 1911.
[3] D.M.A. 26 August, 1911.   [4] Ibid. 30 September, 1911.
[5] Ibid. 11 November, 1911.   [6] Derbyshire Times, 23 December, 1905.
[7] Ibid. 3 and 17 August, 7 September, 1912.

I*

Short in October, 1911, because of his connections with various collieries, but the officials protested that the firm of Short Brothers had audited the accounts for many years and during that time had made many valuable suggestions:

We are quite aware they are and have been interested in certain Collieries, but this matters nothing to us, as there is nothing in our Accounts the firm could tell the owners (even if they were disposed to do so, and which, of course, would be a grave breach of professional etiquette) that would be detrimental to us.[1]

In April, 1912, after the strike of that year, there was a move to bring about the resignation of the officials, which was defeated by 64 votes to 9.[2] The matter came before the Council again in the following month when it was pointed out:

We can assure you that these resolutions are doing your cause a great amount of harm and weakening the officials' influence with the Employers in many ways, and we sincerely hope that you will not, for the sake of the interest of our 38,000 members, make this a question for the Press. . . .[3]

The Press, however, was well aware of the discontent within the union. The *Derbyshire Times* commented:

The unrest which is characterizing the whole of the Labour world today is permeating trade unions also. Men are beginning to think for themselves and form their own opinions, where in the past they were content to let their leaders think and act for them. If the change is to take place without a disruption of the present associations, the machinery must be sufficiently elastic to allow for this evolution. The miners of Derbyshire should be the best judges of whether their Association fulfils these conditions.[4]

But the evolutionary process had little time to work itself out. Within the next two years Haslam and Harvey had passed from the scene and the Association, with the rest of the trade union movement, was thrown into the melting pot of the First World War.

---

[1] *D.M.A.* 23 October, 1911. See also Chapter XII, pp. 507-8.
[2] *Ibid.* 13 April, 1912.   [3] *Ibid.* 14 May, 1912.
[4] *Derbyshire Times*, 7 September, 1912.

APPENDIX I

Membership and Funds, 1881–1914

Year	Membership	Total Investments £	Investments per head £	Investments per head at constant prices £ (at 1881 prices)
1881	696	97	·14	·14
1882	1,000 *	120 *	·12	·12
1883	2,837	300 *	·11	·11
1884	1,296	210	·17	·18
1885	2,000 *	170	·09	·10
1886	2,500 *	395	·16	·18
1887	2,500 *	800 *	·32	·38
1888	3,000 *	1,000 *	·33	·39
1889	9,680	3,243	·34	·37
1890	12,677	10,038	·79	·92
1891	18,728	19,241	1·02	1·19
1892	17,847	27,221	1·53	1·75
1893	18,968	−2,836	Nil	Nil
1894	17,908	16,747	·94	1·14
1895	19,675	25,915	1·31	1·64
1896	15,142	38,312	2·53	3·16
1897	15,268	49,979	3·27	3·99
1898	16,323	59,844	3·67	4·31
1899	20,329	78,396	3·86	4·65
1900	24,330	100,317	4·12	4·69
1901	24,286	124,204	5·07	5·83
1902	27,972	137,782	4·92	5·66
1903	27,199	160,732	5·91	6·72
1904	24,429	175,809	7·2	8·09
1905	26,188	195,602	7·5	8·42
1906	29,480	218,288	7·4	8·22
1907	36,087	249,599	6·92	7·52
1908	38,475	275,808	7·17	7·86
1909	37,944	294,554	7·76	8·53
1910	37,428	326,087	8·72	9·37
1911	38,928	345,529	8·88	9·44
1912	42,130	244,022	5·79	5·97
1913	40,747	281,077	6·9	6·97
1914	42,403	311,926	7·36	7·58

*Estimates.

Sources: Derbyshire Miners' Association, Account Books and Balance Sheets.
Board of Trade (Labour Department), *Reports on Trade Unions*, 1896–1910, (C. 8644, C.9013, C.9443, Cd.422, Cd. 773, Cd.1348, Cd.2838, Cd.4651, Cd.6109).
Annual Returns submitted to the Chief Registrar of Friendly Societies, 1912–1914.
Cost-of-Living Index: A. L. Bowley, *Wages and Income in the United Kingdom since 1860*, (Cambridge), 1937, p. 30.

CHAPTER VII

WAGES, DISPUTES
AND INDUSTRIAL POLICY, 1880–93

I

After the splitting up of the South Yorkshire Association the miners of Derbyshire were as weak and disunited as ever. In the extreme north-eastern part of the county lodges such as New Whittington, Kiveton Park, North Staveley and Killamarsh had helped to form the Sheffield and Rotherham District of the South Yorkshire and North Derbyshire Association under the leadership of Chappell who was already approaching the coal-owners with proposals for the adoption of a sliding scale.[1] In the south the disappearance of the Derbyshire and Nottinghamshire Association had left the men completely unorganized. The new Derbyshire Association, based on Chesterfield, with 28 lodges in an area bounded by Unstone and Seymour in the north, and Blackwell and New Hucknall in the south, had the formidable task of consolidating its position there and spreading its influence over the rest of the county.[2]

The boom in the iron and steel trades in the early months of 1880 inspired the newly formed Association to propose that the Derbyshire miners should ask for a wage increase of 10 per cent. A ballot was taken in January and, of the 4,482 papers issued, 4,000 were in favour of giving in notices for the rise, 419 were not returned and only 63 were against. Reports from collieries to which ballot papers had not been sent, showed that the miners there were also in sympathy with the movement. Nevertheless, the Council hesitated on the ground that other districts might be prepared to join in the application and the result was that nothing

---

[1] *Derbyshire Times*, 17 January, 1880.
[2] *D.M.A.* 19 February, 1880. The lodges were: Ireland Colliery; Unstone Little Pit; Foxley Oakes, Dunston; Rangeley; Derbyshire Silkstone; Rhodes' Colliery; Hornthorpe; Unstone Main; Clay Cross, No. 2, Main; Clay Cross, No. 3, Tupton; Clay Cross, No. 4, Main; Clay Cross, No. 7, Main; Morton Hard Coal; Morton Blackshale; Dowell; Cottam; Brampton; Boythorpe; Nesfield; Holmewood; Blackwell, A Winnings; Blackwell, B Winnings; Renishaw Park; New Hucknall; Pilsley; Seymour; Hundall.

was done.[1] The Executive Committee issued a leaflet attributing the failure of the scheme to the disorganization of the miners. 'The circular asks the men', reported the *Derbyshire Times*, 'how long they intend to remain dormant, and urges them to at once arouse themselves.'[2]

During the following summer the true state of the coal trade became apparent. In May there was much unemployment in the Unstone and Dronfield districts due to the closure of collieries there.[3] In June the miners employed at the Monkwood Colliery, who were earning from 12s. to 10s. a week and in many cases even less, had an unsuccessful strike.[4] Nor did the winter bring much improvement. In November the Swadlincote Colliery Company dismissed the whole of its 200 employees.[5] When Chappell attempted to secure a wage increase of $7\frac{1}{2}$ per cent. for the men at the Norwood and Eckington collieries in December he met with a blank refusal, although J. Stores Smith, the managing director of the Norwood Colliery, showed some interest in the adoption of a sliding scale.[6]

By the end of the year the Derbyshire Association had only ten lodges and was virtually powerless. Early in 1881 the Yorkshire Association decided to abandon the sliding scale and demand a 10 per cent. increase in wages but the Derbyshire Association was unable to follow suit.[7] Instead it had to content itself with a resolution passed at the February Council meeting: 'That Mass Meetings be held at all the chief Mining Centres within the reach of our organization, at the earliest possible moment, to agitate for an advance of wages and extend the Association.'[8] The plan met with a small measure of success. During the month of March the number of members increased by 652, mainly in the Clay Cross district, and wage increases of between $2\frac{1}{2}$ and 5 per cent. were conceded at Cottam, Holmewood, Lings, Grassmoor, Pilsley, Dunston, Derbyshire Silkstone, Clay Cross, and the Staveley and Sheepbridge collieries.[9]

Meanwhile, in those parts of the county which were still unorganized, the position of the men was rapidly deteriorating. A thousand Ilkeston miners employed at E. M. Mundy's collieries came out on strike in February in an unsuccessful attempt to resist an increase in working hours.[10] At Brampton Colliery, where the majority of the men were non-unionists, there was an unsuccessful strike over a reduction in prices in June. In such cases, where the union men were in a minority, they were supported by the Association despite the fact that the strike

[1] *Derbyshire Times*, 17 and 31 January, 21 February, 1880.
[2] *Ibid.* 21 February, 1880.   [3] *Ibid.* 19 May, 1880.
[4] *Ibid.* 19 and 26 June, 1880.   [5] *Ibid.* 24 November, 1880.
[6] *Ibid.* 11 and 18 December, 1880.   [7] *Ibid.* 8 January, 5 March, 1881.
[8] *D.M.A.* 19 February, 1881.   [9] *Ibid.* 19 March, 1881.
[10] *Derbyshire Times*, 5 February, 1881.

was unauthorized by the Council.[1] At other collieries some of the concessions which had been gained were already being taken away because of the seasonal decline in trade. At Clay Cross pit-head notices were posted stating that the advance of a penny a ton which had been given in March would be discontinued on 19 May.[2] In the following month the officials asserted: 'We shall evidently gravitate back into serfdom, (we have already arrived at penury,) if we do not as one man push forward our claims to a living wage, and our independency, as citizens of a free country.'[3]

At the same time, the Association was having to fight for recognition. The manager of the Grassmoor Colliery told some of the miners there, in May, that they would have to leave their employment if they continued to be members of the union. A letter was sent to Alfred Barnes, the owner of the colliery, who was also the Liberal Member for Chesterfield, and the Council resolved that Burt and Macdonald should be informed if the reply was unsatisfactory. Barnes, who was in Guernsey, stated that he had received no letters from home.

'This, it will be perceived, was tantamount to no reply at all', wrote Haslam. 'There seems a disposition on the part of the Liberal M.P. to shuffle out of the business. . . . This, however, must not be allowed. A man of such pronounced and advanced *Liberal Opinions*, must be induced or *compelled* to express a direct opinion of the justice, or otherwise, of the action taken against the workmen at his Collieries.'[4]

Towards the end of 1881 Haslam attended the M.N.U. conference, at Birmingham, at which some important decisions were taken. Burt pronounced that the improvement in trade was such as to warrant the men asking for an increase in wages, and a deputation of twelve county leaders, which included Haslam, was appointed to meet representatives of the Mining Association of Great Britain. On the strength of this, the Derbyshire Association decided to take no further action until after the joint meeting. The Mining Association, however, replied that 'the wages question was outside the scope and province of the National Mining Association, and therefore such a meeting could not take place'.[5]

During 1882 the grievances of the Derbyshire miners continued to increase. Some of the checkweighmen were meeting with hostility

[1] D.M.A. 11 June, 1881. Rule 44 stated: 'That at any Colliery where the workmen in the Association are in a minority, the Councilor District Committee shall not be at liberty to authorise a strike nor shall the members of the Lodge or Lodge officials injudiciously imperil their position, whilst the majority are apathetic and indifferent, but should the majority (non members) decide to strike, the Association will support its members until such dispute is settled, or they have obtained work elsewhere.'

[2] *Derbyshire Times*, 14 May, 1881.

[3] D.M.A. 11 June, 1881.   [4] *Ibid.* 28 May, 11 June, 1881.

[5] *Derbyshire Times*, 24 December, 1881; Arnot, *op. cit.* pp. 66–67.

from the employers. In July Michael Straw, the manager of the Boy-thorpe Colliery, was fined 10s. with £2 1s. 6d. costs, for contravening section 18 of the Coal Mines Regulation Act, 1872, by not affording facilities to Patrick McDermott for performing his duties as checkweigh-man. The case was subsequently heard in the Queen's Bench division and involved the Association in much costly litigation. Haslam, with unusual violence, stated at a Chesterfield meeting: 'That if Mr. Straw was where Pat McDermott came from he would get his head blown off. Many a man had got shot for less than he had done.' This outburst resulted in Haslam's appearance in the Chesterfield police court where he was charged with using threatening language and bound over to keep the peace. He appealed successfully against this decision and was awarded costs by Mr. Justice Field and Mr. Justice Stephen in the Queen's Bench division.[1] Similarly, at the Brampton Colliery, after an unsuccess-ful strike against a reduction of a penny a ton, George Henshaw, the checkweighman, was told to leave. This led the Council to resolve: 'We view the power of Employers to discharge Checkweighmen without taking them before the Magistrates, according to the Mines Regulation Act, as being most scandalously unjust, and as pointing most conclusively to the need of amendment in that section of the Act applying to Checkweighmen.'[2]

II

The failure to secure any improvement in wages caused the men to turn their attention increasingly to the possibilities of restricting output. As Mr. Rowe has pointed out, the economics of the coal industry were such that employers and workmen were bound to have entirely different attitudes to this question. Inter-regional competition was the principal characteristic of the British coal trade in the nineteenth century and even later. The great differences in the costs of production between regions and even between collieries prevented any tendency to resort to output limitation and price maintenance. Mr. Rowe writes: 'The coal-owner is always aiming at the maximum output per shift, in good times that he may make more profit, and in bad times that the cost of pro-duction per ton may be kept down to the minimum. But the miners' outlook was quite different. When trade was good . . . prices rose and wages followed, with the result that after a time the miner might feel that he would rather work less than earn more money, and he might also think that it was after all a pity "to spoil the market". . . . Again, in

[1] D.M.A. 5 August, 1882; Derbyshire Times, 9 and 23 December, 1882.
[2] D.M.A. 5 August, 1882.

times of bad trade the miner might reckon it preferable to work three days a week at good wages, than six days a week at lower rates. In times of good trade the cost of production did not concern him, for it meant an addition to profits, while in times of bad trade he was only interested in so far as a decreased cost of production might mean more employment.'[1] In March, 1882, after William Crawford had addressed a large gathering of miners at Chesterfield, Harvey moved a resolution condemning 'the keen competition which is everywhere seen in our coal trade as wrong in principle and ruinous in practice, producing comparative want amongst the employed and disaster among the employers' and 'the power of the owners to flood the markets by overproduction of coal, the result being that prices are kept down and a rate of wages continued which will not support in decency, much less comparative comfort, the working men and their families'.[2]

These difficulties were not peculiar to Derbyshire, and a succession of miners' conferences at which they were discussed gave some encouragement to the Derbyshire leaders.[3] The Manchester conference of delegates from the central coalfields, held in September, carried a Yorkshire resolution recommending that a vigorous effort should be made, by all districts not tied to the sliding scales, to obtain an increase in wages of 15 per cent. by 1 October and, if that should fail, that there should be a strike. There were also proposals for the restriction of output but each district was left to deal with the matter in its own way.[4]

A circular, signed by Haslam, was issued by the Association to the whole of the collieries of Derbyshire whether members of the union or not. It recommended that the men at each colliery should discuss the question of a wage increase and send one or more delegates to a conference at the Sun Inn, at 4 p.m., on 23 September, and that all the miners should have a holiday at a date to be agreed upon by the conference, to enable them to make a final decision on their course of action at a mass meeting. This was the beginning of the policy of holding 'Pit Set' conferences, at which non-unionists were able to express their views on the Association's proposals. It arose out of the weakness of the organization and the impossibility of its achieving anything alone. 'Knowing the disorganized state of Derbyshire', wrote Haslam, 'and the torpid, almost fossilized, apathy into which the men have sunk, we are induced to issue the present circular. . . .'[5] Some forty or fifty delegates, representing between 20,000 and 25,000 Derbyshire and Nottinghamshire miners, attended the conference at the

---

[1] Rowe, op. cit. pp. 137–8. Cf. R.C. on Depression of Trade and Industry, Second Report, 1886, Appendix, Part I, p. 420.
[2] Derbyshire Times, 25 March, 1882.   [3] D.M.A. 5 August, 1882.
[4] Ibid. 2 September, 1882; Derbyshire Times, 9 September, 1882.
[5] Derbyshire Miners' Association, Circular, 15 September, 1882.

Sun Inn and resolved to ask for a wage increase of 15 per cent. Some of the delegates were appointed to meet the colliery owners and to report to another conference on 27 September before the mass meeting which was arranged for 4 October.[1]

The results of the negotiations were disappointing. Nowhere was 15 per cent. conceded. Several of the larger collieries offered increases ranging from 5 to 10 per cent. Some promised further increases when trade improved.[2] The mass meeting at Chesterfield was well attended. Haslam had asked the employers to release their men and most of them had agreed to do so. Large contingents walked from Clay Cross, Danes-moor and Tupton because the Midland Railway Company had declined to grant any reduction in fares for miners travelling to the meeting. A great procession assembled in the market place and, with banners flying and bands playing, marched to a nearby field to hear speeches by Ben Pickard and John Frith, from Yorkshire; William Brown, from Staffordshire; and the Derbyshire leaders. Haslam moved, and Thomas Whyman seconded, a resolution condemning 'undue competition', demanding an advance of 15 per cent. and supporting, if necessary, 'a restriction of labour'.[3] A meeting at Heanor pledged itself to the same policy. Charles Markham commented:

I have always contended that trade combinations may accelerate an advance or retard a reduction in the rate of wages, but that they have power to do anything more is a fallacy, which will be proved if a great industrial struggle should arise. . . . It is quite certain that, if wages were at once advanced 15 per cent. it would lead to an introduction of a great number of additional hands. If the delegates could induce 50,000 or 100,000 men to retire from the coal trade, the demand would at once exceed the power of production, and prices would immediately rise until the balance was again restored by the introduction of fresh hands. If the price of food could be reduced by mass meetings and expensive bands and banners, they would be numerous enough.[4]

On 13 October the delegates from the central coalfields met once again in Manchester and agreed that strike notices, taking effect from the first pay day after 16 October, should be sent to the employers.[5] Another conference of delegates was held at the Sun Inn on Saturday, 21 October, at which it was reported that the 15 per cent. increase was being paid at a few pits. It was agreed that the men who were working should contribute 1s. weekly, together with the whole of the increase they had obtained, towards the support of those who were still on strike. Of the various offers made in Derbyshire and Nottinghamshire, ranging

---

[1] *Derbyshire Times*, 27 September, 1882.
[2] *Ibid.* 4 October, 1882. [3] *Ibid.*
[4] *Ibid.* 11 October, 1882. [5] *Ibid.* 18 October, 1882.

from 5 to 15 per cent., the mode was 10 per cent. The South Yorkshire coal-owners proposed an increase of 5 per cent. and the adoption of a sliding scale. The West Yorkshire owners, seeing what was happening in neighbouring counties, offered a 10 per cent. increase and promptly raised the price of their coal.[1] The result was that the adjourned conference at Manchester, on 27 October, decided to accept an advance of 10 per cent. 'as a compromise'.[2]

Derbyshire adopted this recommendation and within a very short time most of the men were receiving the 10 per cent. increase in wages. But the question of the restriction of output remained unsettled. The *Derbyshire Times* reminded its readers of the absenteeism among the miners and the 'famine price' of coal in 1873:

The result of keeping St. Monday and St. Tuesday and even St. Wednesday was to force up the price of coal to an unnatural extent, and also it is true that the miners then reaped large wages. They have lost since far more than they gained, in the prolonged depression which directly resulted from the wild inflation of those days. Let us therefore have no limitation of output, but cheap coal and plenty of it.[3]

Nevertheless, Ben Pickard, the Yorkshire miners' secretary and unofficial leader of the central coalfields, issued a circular on 6 November in which he reported that 114,674 men in North Wales and the Midlands had voted in favour of the restriction of output.[4]

Meanwhile the wage concession which had been gained was helping to swell the ranks of the Derbyshire Miners' Association. During October and November nine new lodges joined the union and others at Staveley, Beighton and Unstone were about to join. In the distant and poorly organized Ilkeston area, lodges were being formed at the Cossall and Manners collieries.[5] At a 'pit set' conference Haslam reported that the wage increase of 10 per cent. had been granted throughout the whole of the district covered by the Association. Only at the Springwell, Hartington, Old Hollingwood and Ireland pits, which belonged to the Staveley Company, had there been strikes. About 795 men and 82 boys had been out for seven days. In Lancashire there were 508 men on strike; in Yorkshire 632 men and 150 boys; in Nottinghamshire, 815 men and 152 boys; and in North Wales, 45 men. After some discussion it was agreed to impose a levy of 6d. a man for the support of the strikers.[6]

Towards the end of 1882 the question of restriction of output was much discussed. The employers were already complaining that the

[1] *Derbyshire Times*, 1 and 11 November, 1882.   [2] *Ibid.* 1 November, 1882.
[3] *Ibid.* 4 November, 1882. For 'St. Monday' see Chapter II, p. 60.
[4] *Ibid.* 11 November, 1882.
[5] *D.M.A.* 25 November, 1882.   [6] *Derbyshire Times*, 27 November, 1882.

10 per cent. wage increase was producing stagnation in trade and were threatening to discontinue the additional payment. Haslam told the New Whittington miners: 'If 4d. per ton advance was sufficient to produce such stagnation, then it would be well to let the country go to ruin. A better plan would be to produce less coal, by competent workmen doing less hours.'[1] A national conference, held at Leeds on 19–21 December, 1882, passed a resolution in favour of restriction of output and agreed that the eight-hour day and the five-day week, or its equivalent, should be brought into operation on 1 February, 1883.[2] This proved to be as impossible in Derbyshire as it was in the other coalfields. Haslam, who was at the Leeds conference, addressed innumerable meetings on the restriction of output. At Stonebroom he described it as 'the question of the hour' and called attention to the fate of the miners in the Forest of Dean who were already facing a 10 per cent. reduction in wages. He also attacked the system whereby the railway and gas companies were able to make their yearly contracts during the summer months when coal was at the lowest possible price. He complained that the railway rates were excessive and that the companies were 'able to get coal at prices fixed by themselves'.[3] Towards the end of March about 19,000 circulars and ballot papers were sent out, asking the men to indicate whether they were in favour of the eight-hour shift and the five-day week. It was explained:

What is meant by 'eight hours from bank to bank' is that the men who commence to descend the shaft at six in the morning should begin to ascend again at two; or commence going down at seven in the morning and begin to ascend at three; either way, the principle is for the men to descend and ascend within the eight hours.[4]

About half the ballot papers were returned. Of these, 8,445 were in favour of restriction, 28 against and 1,198 neutral. Haslam and Harvey were appointed delegates to the national conference at Birmingham which met on 9–10 April to consider the possibilities of implementing the Leeds resolutions. It was decided to discuss the matter with the coal-owners, and Crawford and Ashton were instructed to write to the Mining Association of Great Britain asking them to hold a joint conference. As in 1881 the Mining Association declined to enter into any negotiations and a national conference of miners at Manchester, on 29 May, had to content itself with expressing regret that the employers had refused to meet the workmen's representatives.[5] The truth was that the miners' unions were not yet sufficiently strong to attempt to enforce their wishes. After this rebuff they continued to pursue the chimera of

[1] *Derbyshire Times*, 16 December, 1882.   [2] Arnot, *op. cit.* pp. 68–69.
[3] *Derbyshire Times*, 31 March, 1883.   [4] *Ibid.* 14 April, 1883.
[5] *Ibid.* 14 April, 1883; Arnot, *op. cit.* p. 69.

restriction but it did not become a matter of practical politics until after the formation of the Miners' Federation of Great Britain.

The arguments against restriction of output in this period generally ignored the question of foreign competition and considered the proposition within a closed economy. A writer in *Chambers's Journal*, in 1883, argued that if prices and wages were artificially raised additional capital and labour would be attracted to the industry and restriction would 'vanish into thin air'.[1] The miners could do little to control the influx of capital but they envisaged a system of apprenticeship as a means of restricting the supply of labour. Lloyd Jones, speaking at Ilkeston in 1883, compared 'the present unnatural system of overproduction' with the trade practices of two or three hundred years previously, 'when a man was not accredited as a tradesman unless he had served a proper apprenticeship, and when supply was not allowed to shoot so far ahead of demand'.[2]

III

Whilst the agitation for restriction of output was going on, the Association was also concerned with problems of more local interest. In March, 1883, Haslam declared:

Brethren, the process of organizing is disclosing, to a frightful extent, the innumerable evils that we have allowed to come upon us during the last few years. At every Colliery new and pernicious systems have been brought about; regulations and conditions of a character that reduces the men to the position of a serf. Confiscation and Robbery are rampant, and Physical Humanity compelled to toil like machines.

To remedy these evils Haslam preferred the use of moral power to strikes.

Rather let each, and every one, of us try to perfect our Society, educate the more ignorant and refractory of our Miners to a more correct knowledge of the laws of economy; and if we are up to our duty, pursuing the same zealously and earnestly, and at the same time quietly, we shall be enabled to wield a moral power that will go far to obviate the necessity for Strikes that, however beneficial in the past, have always reacted damagingly on the Unions taking part in the same.[3]

Nevertheless, strikes occurred, generally at the collieries where the union organization was weak or virtually non-existent. On 30 April, 1883, there was a strike at the Grassmoor Colliery because the men were asked to work half an hour more each day and an hour and three-

---

[1] *Chambers's Journal*, May, 1883.
[2] *Derbyshire Times*, 12 September, 1883.   [3] *D.M.A.* 3 March, 1883.

quarters less on Saturday, which meant that they lost three-quarters of an hour in six days.[1] After about a fortnight the strike collapsed and some of the ringleaders were dismissed. The refusal of their employers to pay them wages which were still outstanding led to legal action being taken by the Association.[2] The Company entered a successful counter-claim for damages arising from the miners leaving their work without giving proper notice.[3] An attempt to reduce the wages of the men at the Mapperley Colliery resulted in a strike which lasted about four months. The lodges were reluctant to part with their funds but £430 14s. 3d. was raised by subscription and eventually the Mapperley men went back to work at their former rate of wages.[4]

There were also disputes about the use of safety lamps which was becoming more widespread after the explosion at the Parkhouse Colliery, near Danesmoor. At the Cotes Park Colliery, near Somercotes, the men argued that the feeble light given by their primitive lamps so impeded their work that their earnings were reduced. They demanded an increase of 4d. a ton as compensation, refused to comply with the manager's proposal that they should bear half the cost of the lamps, and complained that their eyesight was affected.[5] At Grassmoor, where the miners had previously provided their own candles, the owners bore the entire cost of the safety lamps but the men still claimed an increase of 3d. a ton.[6] Safety lamps became a major issue and, at a demonstration held in Chesterfield, the action of the employers in enforcing their use without additional payment was condemned as being 'arbitrary and unfair' in a resolution moved by James Martin. He was supported by Ben Pickard and also by Joseph Windle who said: 'It was ridiculous to think that the men could earn as much with safety lamps as they could with naked lights.'[7] Some miners said that they would rather work for 6d. a day less with a candle than work with a safety lamp.[8] The controversy, once begun, continued in both its aspects, medical and economic, for something like twenty years and, as will be shown later, led to Court's investigations into miners' nystagmus and an important arbitration case in 1901.[9]

IV

With the seasonal recovery of trade in the autumn of 1883 the union felt able to take part in the movement for a further wage increase

[1] *Derbyshire Times*, 12 May, 1883. [2] *D.M.A.* 12 June, 1883.
[3] *Derbyshire Times*, 7 July, 1883. [4] *D.M.A.* 12 June, 2 October, 1883.
[5] *Derbyshire Times*, 6 January, 1883. [6] *Ibid.* 12 May, 1883.
[7] *Ibid.* 12 September, 1883. [8] *Ibid.* 4 August, 1883.
[9] See pp. 374, 478-80.

decided upon at a conference of miners' leaders from the central coal-fields held in Manchester. At a meeting of delegates representing over 20,000 miners, on 29 September, at the Sun Inn, Chesterfield, it was resolved: 'That the miners of Derbyshire make an application for an advance of 15 per cent. and that they unite with Yorkshire and other counties in an attempt to secure a general advance of a similar amount.'[1] Haslam and Harvey were authorized to issue circulars to the employers informing them of the decision and asking them to receive deputations.[2] Meanwhile there had been meetings of coal-owners at Derby and Sheffield at which it was emphatically decided to give no increase whatever in wages.[3] Charles Markham, of the Staveley Company, issued a circular to his workmen in which he stated:

The working classes are powerless to regulate the price of food and other necessaries of life, which entirely depends on supply and demand, and the same principle applies to every trade and industry. . . . I have always admitted that combination might accelerate or retard the rise or fall in the price of labour, but it must ultimately depend on supply and demand. Whenever a substantial advance takes place in the price of coal, no one will be more delighted than the Staveley Company to advance wages.[4]

The miners in other counties met with similar refusals and when their leaders re-assembled at Manchester on 2 November, it was decided to send out strike notices expiring in the first week of December. Most of the employers stood firm. Charles Seely's colliers at Tibshelf, Birch-wood and Cinder Hill, however, were persuaded not to send in notices, on the understanding that they would receive the same advance as the rest of the district. The miners employed by the Pinxton, Blackwell and Butterley Companies entered into a similar agreement. Such manoeuvres had the effect of creating disunity but large numbers of Derbyshire miners handed in their notices in accordance with the Manchester resolution. By 24 November, Haslam was able to announce that 8,667 notices had already been sent in and that within the next few days the number would be greatly increased.[5] However, when the delegates from the various coalfields met at Sheffield on 3–4 December for their adjourned conference there were considerable differences of opinion. Eventually it was decided to postpone the strike 'until all notices in every district and county can terminate at one and the same time'.[6]

A meeting of Derbyshire delegates re-affirmed their opinion that they

[1] *Derbyshire Times*, 3 October, 1883.
[2] Arnot, *op. cit.* p. 70, states incorrectly: 'In no county, however, were the employers willing to meet deputations to consider the question of an advance.' Cf. *Derbyshire Times*, 27 October, 1883.
[3] *Derbyshire Times*, 17 and 20 October, 1883.   [4] *Ibid.* 10 November, 1883.
[5] *Ibid.* 28 November, 1883.   [6] *Ibid.* 5 December, 1883.

were entitled to an increase in wages and authorized Haslam, Harvey, Jarvis and Gregory to attend the adjourned conference at Manchester on 27 December 'to support the representatives of Yorkshire in endeavouring to secure an advance of 10 per cent'.[1] The reduced demand of 10 per cent. was adopted by the adjourned conference and it was decided that each district should negotiate separately. At a further conference on 24 January, 1884, when it was apparent that not even the 10 per cent. would be conceded, it was resolved: 'That we cannot agree to take any immediate general action on the wages question, and therefore recommend districts to take what action is necessary; but if any district or county is attacked a conference be called to decide what action shall be taken in such case.' Because of declining trade and the intransigence of the coal-owners the joint wages movement, like the movement for the restriction of output, had to come to a standstill.

The only gain, as far as Derbyshire was concerned, was the organization of a number of collieries at which trade unionism had been at a low ebb. The men employed at the Manners Colliery, Ilkeston, were given an increase of $7\frac{1}{2}$ per cent. The Butterley Company's miners obtained a similar concession but this was later withdrawn when it became apparent that there would be no strike.[2] Harvey and others had also visited a number of collieries on the borders of the county around Burton-on-Trent.[3] In this area Church Gresley had been the centre of the bitter struggle in the 'sixties and the miners were so poorly organized that they had continued to work during the 1882 strike. When they joined in the 1883 agitation the men employed at the Netherseal, Granville's, Church Gresley, Lady Chesterfield's and Bretby and Hall's collieries, received the 10 per cent. increase which they had to forgo in 1882.[4] But this small area, virtually a self-contained geographical and economic unit, was too remote from Chesterfield ever to be effectively organized by the Derbyshire Miners' Association and eventually, in 1883, a separate union, the South Derbyshire Amalgamated Miners' Association, was formed under the leadership of William Buckley.

The miners' unions now had to turn from the offensive to the defensive. By 1884 the coal trade was plunging to the depths of its depression. With the coming of the spring and the seasonal decline in trade the employers began to make inroads on the wages and conditions of the miners. At Trowell Moor Colliery, near Ilkeston, the men were locked out because they refused to get more than 20 cwt. of coal to the ton.[5] In the Dronfield and Unstone district some collieries were closed because they were running at a loss and large numbers of miners

[1] *Derbyshire Times*, 26 December, 1883.
[2] *Ibid.* 26 December, 1883; 2 and 16 January, 1884.   [3] *Ibid.* 31 October, 1883.
[4] *Ibid.* 26 December, 1883; 2 January, 1884.   [5] *Ibid.* 26 March, 1884.

were locked out because they were unwilling to accept a reduction in wages.[1] By May they had accepted a reduction of 10 per cent.[2] In the same month 1,500 miners employed by Crompton and Company at the Butcher Wood, Stanton Hill, and Pleasley collieries came out on strike because their employers sought to raise their rent by threepence a week, increase their subscriptions to the colliery 'field clubs' by a penny a week, and discontinue their free allowance of coal. The men asserted that these changes would be equivalent to a reduction in wages of 2s. a week but, after five weeks, they had to accept their masters' terms.[3]

When wages and conditions deteriorated in this way it was very often the union men who suffered most. Because of their unpopularity with their employers they were sent to the most difficult and unremunerative working places. Such injustices had long been avoided in the north-eastern coalfields where, four times a year, lots were drawn to determine the place in which each hewer should work.[4] The desirability of adopting this practice, known as 'cavilling', was considered by the Derbyshire lodges early in 1885. The officials stated:

> It is a fact that there are certain men at almost every Colliery who can have the best jobs etcetera regularly, because they act unmanly. Some carry tales, some play cricket or band instruments. In fact, there are a variety of ways in which the connection is maintained. These men will never be union men while the system exists.[5]

But cavilling was never adopted in Derbyshire and favouritism continued to be an important instrument of colliery management.[6]

V

The nibblings of 1884 were but the prelude to a more general attack on miners' wages in 1885. Towards the end of March the coal-owners of Yorkshire, Staffordshire and Scotland all decided to make reductions.[7] Derbyshire soon followed their example. A meeting of coal-owners at Chesterfield, on 21 March, resolved unanimously: 'That owing to the present low prices of coal and the great depression in the trade, the advance given to the men in October, 1882, must be taken off the present wages.'[8] On the same day a conference of Derbyshire miners'

---

[1] *Derbyshire Times*, 19 March, 5 and 12 April, 1884.
[2] *Ibid.* 3 May, 1884.   [3] *Ibid.* 14 May, 14 June, 1884.
[4] Welbourne, *op. cit.* p. 12.   [5] *D.M.A.* 20 January, 1885.
[6] The writer was told by a former colliery official that it was the practice, until quite recent times, for men at certain collieries to receive additions to their wages for reporting to the management what transpired at union meetings.
[7] *Derbyshire Times*, 21 March, 1885.   [8] *Ibid.* 25 March, 1885.

delegates, in the presence of Cowey, the President of the Yorkshire Miners' Association, resolved: 'That this meeting believes the present attempt to reduce the wages of miners in Yorkshire and Derbyshire is altogether unnecessary, and we therefore determine to the best of our ability, by every legal means in our power, to prevent such a reduction.'[1]

On 30 March the men employed on the night shift at the Wharncliffe, Silkstone, Rockingham, High Green, and other large collieries, brought out their tools and the great strike of the South Yorkshire miners had begun.[2] The dispute spread rapidly throughout the district and there was much distress at Denaby, near Mexborough, where the Denaby Main Colliery Company evicted miners from their cottages whilst order was maintained by a special draft of 200 West Riding policemen.[3] Meanwhile the Derbyshire miners were negotiating with their own employers who were already issuing notices for the 10 per cent. reduction in wages. By 18 April, at all but two of the Derbyshire collieries, Southgate and Kiveton Park, the notices had been withdrawn at the request of the men on the understanding that their wages would be determined by the result of the South Yorkshire dispute.[4] Weekly collections were made to support the men on strike. £167 was collected during the week ending 18 April and £240 during the following week.[5]

Towards the end of the month the Yorkshire miners began to drift back to work on the owners' terms. The men employed by Newton Chambers and Company, at the Tankersley Collieries, were among the first to resume work. 'The action taken by the Derbyshire miners', it was reported, 'has caused dissatisfaction here, as it is thought that all ought to be either in or out together.'[6] By the middle of May the Yorkshire strike had completely collapsed after a struggle lasting seven weeks. The Derbyshire men, who had enjoyed a period of comparative prosperity during the strike, had now to face the realities of the situation and honour their agreement to accept the 10 per cent. reduction along with Yorkshire.[7]

Some of the Derbyshire coal-owners had already imposed, or were attempting to impose, direct or indirect reductions in wages in addition to the agreed 10 per cent. and this caused a number of strikes in various parts of the county.[8] The most serious dispute occurred in the Ilkeston district where the men employed at the Oakwell, Manners, Cossall and Stapleford collieries refused to accept the general reduction because the full value of the increase given in 1882 had been taken from them in various ways.[9] The strike started at Oakwell, Manners and Stapleford

[1] *Derbyshire Times*, 25 March, 1885.   [2] *Ibid.* 4 April, 1885.
[3] *Ibid.* 15 April, 1885.   [4] *Ibid.* 25 April, 1885.
[5] *Ibid.* 6 May, 1885.   [6] *Ibid.* 29 April, 1885.
[7] *Ibid.* 27 and 30 May, 6 June, 1885.   [8] *Ibid.* 13 and 20 June, 1885.
[9] *D.M.A.* 4 August, 1885; *Derbyshire Times*, 8 August, 1885.

on 15 July and at Cossall on 21 July, and lasted six weeks. Although most of the 1,600 men involved were non-unionists, Harvey and the Nottinghamshire leader, Joseph Hopkin, were called in to advise them.[1] The employers at first demanded a reduction of 3d. a ton but later said that they would be satisfied with 2d. The men then suggested a reduction of 1d. a ton and eventually both sides agreed to 1½d.[2]

The dispute was marked by the worst violence and disorder which had been experienced in the coalfield since 1866. On 5 August a hostile crowd of over 1,000 men and women assembled at the Cossall Colliery to molest a well-known non-unionist, Francis Newton. On discovering that he had already left the pit, the crowd surged towards his house in Station Road, Ilkeston. Stones were thrown, windows were broken and one woman tied to a fence in front of Newton's house a wooden gallows with a black stocking dangling from it. The mob later visited the house of William Holding, the colliery manager, and smashed down the doors, demolished a greenhouse and a garden wall, and killed a pig and a number of hens. Holding retaliated with his shot gun and nine of the rioters were wounded. Extra police were brought into the town from Nottingham, Derby, Mansfield, Langley Mill, Alfreton and Chesterfield, and thirteen men and youths were arrested.[3] It was stated in their defence that Holding fired before any stones were thrown or any damage was done.[4] The prisoners, whose ages ranged from 11 to 21, were bound over because of their youth and the fact that they were not regarded as the ringleaders of the riot.[5]

The six-week strike caused much distress in the town. Some families, in addition to being unemployed and having relatives imprisoned, were having county court orders served on them for debt. Many of the Ilkeston tradesmen organized soup kitchens and gave breakfasts to the children.[6]

During the autumn of 1885 an attempt was made to recover some of the lost ground. On 24 September delegates representing the miners of Yorkshire, Lancashire, North and South Staffordshire, East Worcestershire, Derbyshire and Nottinghamshire, met at Nottingham under the presidency of Enoch Edwards, of Staffordshire. The conference discussed reports from the delegates on the state of the coal trade and the rates of wages prevailing in their respective districts. The reports were generally to the effect that trade was gradually improving and that wages were inadequate. It was therefore decided to ask for 15 per cent. increase in wages.[7]

[1] *Ilkeston Pioneer*, 30 July, 1885.
[2] *Derbyshire Times*, 29 August, 5 September, 1885.
[3] *Ilkeston Pioneer*, 13 August, 1885; *Derbyshire Times*, 8 August, 1885.
[4] *Derbyshire Times*, 15 August, 1885.
[5] *Ibid.* 19 August, 1885.   [6] *Ibid.* 15 and 29 August, 1885.
[7] *D.M.A.* 1 September, 1885; *Derbyshire Times*, 30 September, 1885.

To implement this decision Haslam and Harvey were instructed by their Executive Committee to arrange meetings throughout the county.[1] At every meeting the miners pledged themselves to support the movement for a 15 per cent. increase. 'But for trade unions', said Harvey, at Alfreton, 'the advance of 1882 would not have been made, and, but for non-trade unionists it would never have been taken away.'[2] As if to illustrate his point, the Pinxton Colliery Company announced, a few days later, that it intended to grant an immediate wage increase of 10 per cent.[3] On Saturday, 10 October, the Derbyshire delegates assembled at the Sun Inn, Chesterfield, to discuss the situation. Most of the collieries in the county were represented and the attendance was larger than at any similar gathering during the previous two years. Many of the delegates reported that the 15 per cent. increase had been refused and it was decided that Derbyshire should support strike action and restriction of output if these policies were adopted by the other counties.[4]

When the adjourned miners' conference assembled at Manchester on 22 October it was apparent that the coal-owners were nowhere willing to concede an increase in wages of 15 per cent. and it was decided to take a ballot vote of the districts represented, asking the men to state whether they were willing to strike in November.[5] The voting was in favour of strike action but when the delegates re-assembled in Manchester on 5 November they moderated their demands. It was resolved: 'That seeing 26,000 miners of Lancashire, Derbyshire and Leicestershire, have received an advance on the present rate of wages of 10 per cent., and that 7,400 have not suffered a reduction in Nottinghamshire and Staffordshire, we hereby agree that a notice for a 10 per cent. advance be given on the third making-up day in November, and, if the owners refuse to concede an advance, the men be advised to bring out their tools.'[6] In Derbyshire, the Clay Cross men took the lead, about 1,000 of them handing in their notices, but the response generally was poor.[7] On 24 November the Executive Committee resolved: 'That in the event of the majority not having given in their Notices, our Secretaries advise those who have given Notice to withdraw them.'[8] In other counties the story was the same. In the whole of Nottinghamshire only 200 men handed in notices and when they discovered that others had not done so they quickly withdrew them.[9] Within a short time the wages movement had collapsed.

[1] *D.M.A.* 29 September, 1885.
[2] *Derbyshire Times*, 7 October, 1885.
[3] *Ibid.* 10 October, 1885.
[4] *Ibid.* 14 October, 1885.
[5] *Ibid.* 24 October, 1885.
[6] *Ibid.* 7 November, 1885.
[7] *Ibid.* 21 November, 1885.
[8] *D.M.A.* 24 November, 1885.
[9] A. R. Griffin, *The Miners of Nottinghamshire*, (Nottingham), 1957, p. 42.

VI

The failure of the 1885 strike was to be expected. The coal trade was in the throes of depression and union membership was declining. In common with other districts Derbyshire had to face a most difficult period during which many of the coal-owners were whittling away wages, introducing new and irksome regulations, and refusing to employ trade unionists.[1] By 1887 the union leaders were almost driven to despair by the petty depredations of the employers. In February they reported:

We are having abundant evidence just now of the very one-sided and unfair Contract Rules in use at many of our Collieries, whereby men agree that confiscations, fines, dismissals, and low wages, may occur at the whim and will of the Manager or Under-Official; on the other hand, the men seem to have little or no rights at all. Shall we ever be in a position to demand fair play, we wonder?[2]

One of the most serious disputes occurred at the Clay Cross Company's Morton Colliery, in April, 1887. The men were locked out for five weeks and eventually the owners threatened to close the pit if their terms were not accepted. The trouble arose because the Company wished to introduce a device which had the comforting but deceptive name of 'Billy Fairplay'. It was an automatic machine which separated the hard coal from the slack and indicated the weight of each, so that the men could be paid at different rates for the different qualities.[3] 'Billy Fairplay' had already appeared in Yorkshire and at the Netherseal Colliery on the southernmost borders of Derbyshire, but this was his first incursion into the heart of the county. Jackson, the general manager of the Clay Cross Collieries, proposed to pay 1s. 6d. a ton for slack, which was equivalent to a reduction of about 33 per cent. on all coal rejected by the machine, without paying any more for the coal that stood the test. Haslam commented: 'The coal is already filled by riddle; and we hope that every miner in Derbyshire will help the Morton men to resist so undesirable a scourge as Billy being introduced among us.' The men found that they were unable to obtain employment at neighbouring pits and eventually had to accept 2s. a ton for hard coal and 1s. 4d. for slack, which amounted to a reduction in wages of about 5 per cent.[4]

---

[1] *Derbyshire Times*, 28 October, 1885; 27 March, 1886; *D.M.A.* 27 October, 24 November, 1885.   [2] *D.M.A.* 15 February, 1887.
[3] Cf. Welbourne, *op. cit.* p. 179, Arnot, *op. cit.* p. 283.
[4] *D.M.A.* 18 January, 1887; *Derbyshire Times*, 14 and 21 May, 11 June, 1887.

Difficulties of this kind kept the officials busy but did not prevent them from dealing with the wider issues of industrial policy. The specific problems of the Derbyshire coal trade naturally claimed much of their attention and here the Association was prepared to make common cause with the employers. In October, 1886, the Council resolved: 'That we do all we can to assist in repealing the Coal Tax, called City Dues, in London, by getting up a petition, &c. upon the subject.'[1] Two months later Haslam was authorized to join the deputation to the Chancellor of the Exchequer to discuss the City Dues.[2] Their abolition became the subject of a resolution which was carried at many gatherings of Derbyshire miners: 'That this meeting regards the London coal tax as an unjust impost upon our trade, as tending to cripple its scope; while its incidence is unfair in its application to the metropolitan area.' Harvey proposed a similar resolution at the annual demonstration of the Nottinghamshire miners in April, 1888.[3] High railway freight charges were likewise condemned by the Association and in July, 1888, Haslam presided over a meeting of the inhabitants of Clay Cross in support of the proposed new line of the Manchester, Sheffield and Lincolnshire Railway from Beighton to Chesterfield.[4] Matters of more general interest such as the restriction of output and the abolition of mining royalties also inspired many resolutions.

The Association showed great interest in the new Mines Bill and Haslam was empowered to give evidence before the commission of inquiry.[5] The Bill became law as the Coal Mines Regulation Act of 1887, which, amongst other things, provided for the inspection twice yearly of all weights and measures in use at collieries and thereby helped to eliminate many of the grievances arising from the weighing of coal. The earliest inspections in Derbyshire disclosed a number of iniquities, particularly at the smaller collieries. J. E. Morris, addressing a conference of inspectors of weights and measures at Derby in June, 1888, described how butty colliers who had saved sufficient capital frequently took over pits nearly worked out, employed four or five men, 'and were sometimes capable of anything'. He quoted an instance of finding what was called a yardstick which was one-and-a-half yards long.[6] Some colliery proprietors were prosecuted for the technical offence of using defective weighing machines because adjustments had been made, with the consent of the men, allowing for dirt or the weight of the tub.[7] In some cases the men claimed that they could earn more when their coal was weighed by these methods.[8]

[1] *D.M.A.* 26 October, 1886.
[2] *Ibid.* 21 December, 1886.
[3] Griffin, *op. cit.* p. 52.
[4] *Derbyshire Times*, 4 August, 1888.
[5] *D.M.A.* 13 April, 1886.
[6] *Derbyshire Times*, 30 June, 1888.
[7] *Ibid.* 21 April, 18 August, 1888.
[8] *Ibid.* 21 April, 12 May, 1888.

VII

The Edinburgh conference of October, 1887, at which the unions decided to ask for a 10 per cent. increase in wages and to take action to secure some restriction of output, was the last of the succession of failures and disappointments which marked the years of depression. Haslam issued a circular in which he stated:

The Edinburgh Conference has now been held, and the following among other things agreed to:

(a) That eight hours in 24 be a maximum day's work for all persons employed underground when single shifts are worked, and seven hours where a double shift is worked; the time to be reckoned from bank to bank.
(b) That a general holiday be observed each week, the day to be fixed by each district (locally) and strictly observed, even though men have been idle on any or all preceding days that week.
(c) A week or longer general holiday, if necessary, is to be taken to clear off stocks and secure an advance of 10 per cent.
All districts in the United Kingdom to play the same week.
(d) The House of Commons is to be asked to fix by law the working day at not more than eight hours in any 24.
(e) The whole of the miners to be balloted and their opinions ascertained on any or all of the above points, and another national conference to carry any or all of the programme out.

Haslam concluded with a characteristic plea for action:

Make one gigantic effort for your cause, and if you do, and act wisely afterwards, you will raise your wages in more ways than one (there is too much work done without pay today); stop a good deal of the robbery that is going on; ensure an amount of civility that you do not now receive; reduce your working hours to a reasonable number, and place yourselves, once for all, in a position to make something like fair contracts at your work. Let all do their part manfully, honestly, intelligently, and we shall succeed.[1]

The Edinburgh programme was given an enthusiastic reception at innumerable meetings of Derbyshire miners. The Association issued ballot papers to 10,966 underground workers over 18. The voting was as follows:

	For	Against
1. Shall eight hours per day of 24 hours be adopted?	9,519	336
2. Shall we have a holiday in each week?	8,051	647
3. Play one week or longer once in each year?	8,583	990
4. Shall Parliament fix the working hours?	9,226	407

[1] *Derbyshire Times*, 5 November, 1887.

On 19 November delegates from 64 collieries assembled at the Sun Inn, Chesterfield, and resolved: 'That this conference is glad to learn that the result of the ballot is, so far, encouraging, and hereby empowers its delegates to the Newcastle conference to fall in with any well-considered schemes for accomplishing the objects of the resolutions as speedily as possible.'[1]

But when Haslam and Harvey attended the Newcastle conference, on 22 November, they found that there were no representatives from Durham or South Wales. In response to a telegram Abraham, the Welsh leader, explained that the South Wales delegates would not come because the Miners' National Union was not represented. Durham did not even reply to the telegram. Both Northumberland and Durham had opposed the eight-hour day at the Edinburgh conference, but whilst Burt and Fenwick, the Northumberland leaders, temporized, it was obvious that Wilson and Crawford, the Durham leaders, were thoroughly opposed to any further action. The cleavage between the supporters of the sliding scale who dominated the Miners' National Union, and the more militant unions of the central coalfields, was now clearly revealed. The attempts which were made to win the co-operation of Durham and South Wales ended in complete failure and the national movement for improved wages and conditions once again came to a standstill.[2]

VIII

During 1888 it became increasingly apparent that the coal trade was improving and there were various isolated attempts to obtain wage increases. In Derbyshire, for example, as early as December, 1887, the men employed at three collieries in the Ilkeston district handed in strike notices but later withdrew them.[3] It was not until the summer, however, that any concerted attempt was made to obtain a general wage increase throughout the central coalfields. The proposal appears to have been first mooted by Lancashire[4] but Derbyshire cannot have been far behind. In July it was resolved: 'That this Council is in favour of joining with other Counties for an advance of 10 per cent. and that a pit set conference be called.'[5] Circulars were issued and the conference of colliery delegates, which met at the Sun Inn on 18 August, endorsed the policy advocated by the Council.[6] Meetings were held throughout the

[1] Derbyshire Miners' Conference Minute Book, 19 November, 1887; *Derbyshire Times*, 26 November, 1887.
[2] Arnot, *op. cit.* pp. 85–86.   [3] *Derbyshire Times*, 24 December, 1887.
[4] Arnot, *op. cit.* p. 92.   [5] *D.M.A.* 31 July, 1888.
[6] Derbyshire Miners' Conference Minute Book, 18 August, 1888; *Derbyshire Times*, 25 August, 1888.

county to explain the situation to the miners. At Alfreton, Harvey stated that Derbyshire had agreed to discuss the possibilities of joint action with Yorkshire and the other Midland counties.[1] The campaign went well and on 22 September, at a further meeting at the Sun Inn, the delegates expressed their approval.[2]

Meanwhile Ben Pickard, the Yorkshire miners' leader, was arranging for joint action to be taken. On 10 September, 1888, he sent out a circular inviting 'all miners now free from sliding scales' to attend a conference which would consider the best means of securing a 10 per cent. increase in wages. With the exception of those from Stirlingshire, the delegates who assembled at Manchester on 25 September, in response to Pickard's invitation, were inevitably from the central coalfields: Lancashire, North Wales, Yorkshire, Derbyshire, Nottinghamshire, Leicestershire and five of the smaller district unions in the Midlands.[3] Two resolutions were carried unanimously:

1. That seeing that the conference is agreed upon notice to be given for an advance of wages, it is hereby agreed that all notices shall be given so as to terminate in the week ending 27 October.

2. That in the case of any colliery or district represented at this conference being offered any advance less than that decided upon at this conference— namely 10 per cent.—they shall still carry out the resolution by lodging notices demanding the full amount agreed upon. Further that no district shall accept 10 per cent. on such condition that it shall lose it in the event of any other district represented at this conference not obtaining it.[4]

After the Manchester conference, meetings were again held throughout Derbyshire. At Staveley a large open-air meeting was addressed by Harvey and Pickard in tones reminiscent of the 'sixties.

'According to Bible law', said Harvey, 'those who did not work ought not to eat; but somehow they seemed to get the best of the joints. . . . A man who inquired into the state of trade, who had a knowledge of the Board of Trade returns, and understood the inspection report, was too much of a disturber to be allowed to stay and he was accordingly discharged. Employers would sooner have men who could drink, fly pigeons, and who took dogs out with a string.'

Pickard spoke in a similar strain:

Our greatest of teachers, as they learned from the Bible, was one of the greatest of communists. He never taught the doctrine that the poor were better without bread, but he taught the doctrine that the hungry should be fed and the naked clothed, and today that doctrine was taught in every church and chapel. Was it acted upon? (Cries of 'No!')[5]

[1] *Derbyshire Times*, 8 September, 1888.
[2] Derbyshire Miners' Conference Minute Book, 22 September, 1888.
[3] Arnot, *op. cit.* p. 92.
[4] *Derbyshire Times*, 29 September, 1888.   [5] *Ibid.* 6 October, 1888.

THE DERBYSHIRE MINERS' ANNUAL DEMONSTRATION, 1906

There were many such meetings and, at each one, the miners pledged themselves to carry out the Manchester resolutions.

On 6 October, Haslam and Harvey addressed a conference of delegates at the Sun Inn. Haslam discussed the charge that the union leaders were arousing an ignorant populace to an action which they did not understand. 'It is doubtless quite possible', he said, 'that in some cases the men might have remained acquiescent.' In 'one of the most downtrodden districts in the county'—he referred to Grassmoor—he was told by an old lady that 'the men were so screwed and pinched that every bit of courage had left them'. He also criticized sliding scales which gave the employers 'a kind of guarantee that for a period they were free from any eruption among the miners'. On the subject of freedom of contract he used the same arguments as those which had been advanced eight years previously by T. H. Green in his famous lecture on *Liberal Legislation and Freedom of Contract*: 'He had never discovered that a bargain could be fairly made where there was not something like equality of power.'[1] Harvey confined his remarks to the more immediate problems: 'District strikes, it was now well understood, were of no use whatever. . . . It was not from foreign competition that they had so much to fear—it was the unfair competition and the sharp tricks in trade among employers that affected them more.'[2]

During the following week the men began to hand in their notices for the 10 per cent. wage increase. At most collieries the employers refused to give way. They argued that the supply of coal exceeded the demand and that they were so tied down by contracts that they could not recoup themselves by raising the price of coal.[3] In Derbyshire the increase was conceded only at the Boythorpe, Pilsley, Alma, Cossall, Manners, Oakwell, West Hallam and Shipley collieries. At most of the other collieries over 20,000 strike notices were due to expire on 27 October. The notices at Blackwell, Alfreton and a few other places were due to expire rather later because the men were on monthly contracts.

The attempt of Clegg, who was then Mayor of Sheffield, to mediate was received with little enthusiasm. Henry Jarvis described Pickard's reply to Clegg's letter as 'just the reply he expected'. 'The day of arbitration is gone by', he continued, 'until we have got the 10 per cent. advance and are thus lifted from the bottom rung of the ladder.'[4] Harvey recalled the occasion, in 1879, when Judge Ellison had been called upon to arbitrate. It will be remembered that Ellison had given his award in the manner of the Delphic oracle but Harvey interpreted it as an award in favour of the men.[5] 'The employers', he said, 'refused

---

[1] *Derbyshire Times*, 13 October, 1888. Cf. R. L. Nettleship, ed., *Works of Thomas Hill Green*, (London), 1911, III, pp. 365–86. [2] *Ibid*. 13 October, 1888.
[3] *Ibid*. 27 October, 1888. [4] *Ibid*. [5] See Chapter IV, pp.163–4.

K

to grant the advance which the arbitrator declared to be due, and that had caused him to lose confidence in arbitration.'[1]

The publication of Charles Markham's will added fuel to the fire. Haslam spoke at Ripley of the struggles which had occurred at the Staveley Collieries, 'and yet Mr. Markham had died possessed of a personal estate worth £230,000. There was nothing in the sliding scale that could arrest the thieving propensities of the officials of the collieries. They were continually playing the men off one against another, trading on their helplessness and weakness, and reducing their wages in a manner unknown to the general public.' John Catchpole, in a letter to the Press, wrote:

> The men can scarcely be expected to accept a statement that mining pro-perty never yields profit nor declares dividends, when they read of an owner dying leaving a quarter of a million of personalty. Whatever may be the explanation, the men will connect this wealth with the result of their labour.[2]

When the delegates from the central coalfields met at Derby on 29 October, it was reported that the advance had been conceded un-conditionally in all the counties with the exception of Derbyshire and Yorkshire. In Derbyshire, 6,000 men had been granted the increase and 6,000 were on strike. In Yorkshire, 10,000 men had received the advance, 30,000 were on strike, and a further 7,000 were working out their notices. The conference pledged itself to support the men out on strike by a levy of 1s. a week, to be increased to 2s. if need be; and appointed a committee of seven to receive and distribute the levy.[3]

Events in Derbyshire and Yorkshire were watched with interest by the other coalfields. In Derbyshire it was the larger firms, the Grassmoor, Clay Cross, Staveley and Sheepbridge companies which remained obdurate, thereby encouraging some of the smaller ones to follow their example.[4] But the strike was short-lived. By the afternoon of Saturday, 27 October, the Grassmoor Company had conceded the advance and the men resumed work on the following Monday. The Clay Cross and Staveley companies capitulated on the Tuesday, and the Sheepbridge Company on the Wednesday. The *Derbyshire Times* commented: 'It will be impossible now that the four largest companies have given in for the small concerns to maintain the fight.'[5]

On 3 November the officials were able to announce to a 'pit set' conference at Chesterfield that with the exception of one or two isolated instances, a wage increase of 10 per cent. had been granted at all the Derbyshire collieries. Amidst cheering the delegates carried a

---

[1] *Derbyshire Times*, 13 October, 1888.   [2] *Ibid*. 20 October, 1888.
[3] Arnot, *op. cit.* p. 93; *Derbyshire Times*, 3 November, 1888.
[4] *Derbyshire Times*, 27 October, 1888.   [5] *Ibid*. 3 November, 1888.

resolution thanking Haslam and Harvey, 'for the able manner in which they have conducted the campaign'. It was decided that the men working at pits where 28 days' notice was required should ask their employers to reduce the period to 14 days so that future strikes could begin uniformly.[1]

IX

The success of 1888 and the continued rise in the price of coal encouraged the unions to press for further increases in wages in 1889. Towards the end of February, 1889, Lancashire suggested a conference to discuss another advance of 10 per cent. and to 'agree upon some uniform system of restriction'. On 26 March Haslam attended a miners' conference at Birmingham which represented every important district except Durham and resolved to ask for the 10 per cent. advance.[2] A conference of Derbyshire colliery delegates decided to join with the other counties in the wages movement and appointed Haslam, Harvey, Kenyon and Martin to attend a further national conference at Nottingham on 24 April.[3] At the Nottingham conference the reports of delegates indicated that the employers were generally unwilling to concede the advance and it was decided to hand in strike notices which would expire on 29 June. This decision was endorsed by a further conference of Derbyshire delegates on 7 May and the Secretaries were authorized to arrange meetings throughout the county.[4]

During the campaign which followed, Harvey propounded the theory of a minimum wage. His principal objection to sliding scales was that they had 'no bottom in them'. 'No collier', he said, 'ought to work for less than £2 a week.' At Whittington Moor he strongly urged the men not to air their grievances at street corners or to 'throw their money away on handicaps, horse races, dog races and pigeon flying' but to join the union.[5] At New Whittington he attacked the railway and gas contracts: 'It was an injustice to make contracts when men were working short time and when they were powerless to resist. This time, however, they had given their employers plenty of notice, so that where contracts were formed the colliers might be taken into consideration as well as the masters.'[6]

[1] Derbyshire Miners' Conference Minute Book, 3 November, 1888; *Derbyshire Times*, 10 November, 1888.
[2] *D.M.A.* 12 March, 1889; *Derbyshire Times*, 30 March, 1889; Arnot, *op. cit.* p. 96.
[3] Derbyshire Miners' Conference Minute Book, 13 April, 1889. *Derbyshire Times*, 20 April, 1889.
[4] Derbyshire Miners' Conference Minute Book, 7 May, 1889.
[5] *Derbyshire Times*, 11 May, 1889.   [6] *Ibid.* 18 May, 1889.

Meanwhile the Yorkshire coal-owners had made a final offer of a 5 per cent. advance in wages to be given on 1 July and another 5 per cent. advance on 1 October, on condition that wages were to remain settled until July, 1890. At the request of the Yorkshire miners a special conference met at Manchester on 28 May to consider the new situation. Many of the Derbyshire employers were willing to offer the Yorkshire terms but Haslam and Harvey were sent to Manchester with instructions 'to abide by the decisions of previous conferences', and to fall in with the wishes of the majority. They were, however, 'to oppose the binding for twelve months'.[1] With prices rising sharply this proved to be a crucial issue and there were lively discussions at the conference. Eventually, on Yorkshire's own proposal, the delegates agreed that Yorkshire should accept the terms which had been offered if they could be obtained unconditionally and that other districts should be prepared to accept similar terms. Where these conditions could not be obtained the men were to strike on 29 June for the full 10 per cent. increase in wages.

By the first week in June many of the Derbyshire collieries had agreed to give the 10 per cent. increase in two instalments.[2] Meetings were held to enlist support for the men who were still fighting for the increase. Joseph Marriott described the man who had got the advance but did not pay his sixpenny levy as 'one of the greatest blacklegs there was in existence'.[3] It was stated at the national conference which assembled at Birmingham, on 8 October, that £11,870 6s. 6d. had been paid in support of the men on strike in Somerset, Lancashire, Yorkshire, Shropshire, North Staffordshire and Derbyshire. Most of the districts had by that time gained the 10 per cent. advance, generally in two instalments. But Haslam reported that some underground workers at many collieries in Derbyshire were still underpaid: 'There were some places where they had not got the utmost fraction of the previous advance; but the men intended to demand the remainder, and that would then complete the full 20 per cent. asked for since October, 1888.'[4]

The refusal of the Pilsley Coal Company to grant the 10 per cent. wage increase to the banksmen led to a strike which was joined by the under-ground workers. Haslam stated that the average wages of the pit banks-men of the county did not exceed 12s. 6d. or 13s. a week: 'In the name of common sense, how could a man live respectably upon it with a family? How could he pay rent and be a decent citizen on a wage like that?'[5] The strike ended when the employers agreed to increase the banksmen's wages from 3s. to 3s. 2d. a day.[6] At the new Alfreton pit, belonging to

[1] Derbyshire Miners' Conference Minute Book, 25 May, 1889.
[2] *Derbyshire Times*, 8 June, 1889.
[3] *Ibid.* 22 June, 1889.   [4] *Ibid.* 12 October, 1889.
[5] *Ibid.* 16 November, 1889.   [6] *Ibid.* 28 November, 1889.

the Blackwell Colliery Company, there was a strike over the victimization of Benjamin Gregory, an active trade unionist who had served on
the Executive Committee in the early days of the Association.[1] The
Company also refused to pay the full 10 per cent. increase or to allow
the miners payment for any coal in their tubs weighing less than ½ cwt.
The dispute was successfully handled by Frank Hall who was then
checkweighman at Alfreton.[2]

X

The Newport conference, at which the Miners' Federation of Great
Britain was formally constituted, brought the Derbyshire delegates into
open conflict with the new organization. For some time there had been
an undercurrent of criticism of Derbyshire because its organization was
so weak and because the practice of holding 'pit set' conferences meant
that the Derbyshire Association's representatives were speaking for
unionists and non-unionists alike. Added to this was Haslam's reluctance
to sever connections with the Miners' National Union and its leaders
whom he admired so much.[3]

The first clash with the newly formed Federation arose over the eight
hours' question. There was a division of opinion between those who
wished to achieve the eight-hour day by strike action and those who
wished to achieve it by legislation. Harvey moved and Haslam seconded
a resolution in favour of strike action.[4] In a rousing speech Harvey
declared: 'There would, no doubt, be a great deal said as to securing
the eight hours' day by Act of Parliament, but if they waited until it was
obtained by legislation, the grass would grow over the graves of some of
them. . . . If the whole of the counties represented would tender
notices, they would secure the eight hours' day in 1890.'[5] In Derbyshire
12,233 ballot papers had been issued. Of these, 8,641 were returned in
favour of a strike, 556 were against, and 1,649 were neutral. Trouble
arose over the ballot papers which were unaccounted for and also over
the fact that non-unionists had participated in the ballot. The conference
felt that Derbyshire would prove to be unreliable if a strike materialized
and eventually, by 100 to 20, an amendment was carried in favour of
referring the question back to the districts and pressing for
parliamentary action.[6]

[1] Gregory enjoyed the unique distinction of having a lodge named after him:
'B. Gregory's Lodge.' It was not based upon any colliery but upon his own house-to-
house collections in the Ilkeston district.

[2] *Derbyshire Times*, 28 November, 1889.   [3] See Chapter VI, pp. 251–2.

[4] *Derbyshire Times*, 30 November, 1889.   [5] Quoted in Arnot, *op. cit.* p. 136.

[6] *Sheffield Independent*, 4 December, 1889.

The second clash occurred over the decision to demand a further wage increase of 10 per cent. Samuel Woods, the Lancashire leader, proposed: 'That as it has now been decided that notices shall be given to demand an advance in wages, we agree that notices be not withdrawn unless the advance is given; that any men who may have to strike for the advance be supported by the districts represented at this conference; and that a proportionate levy be called for from each district by the secretary of this conference.' Pickard was on the point of taking the vote when Harvey tried to speak. After a brief altercation with the chairman he was allowed to raise an objection to the proposal on the grounds that the proportionate levy was a procedure which had not been adopted on previous occasions. He was interrupted by Cowey, the Yorkshire leader, who charged him with being 'of the non-union element'. Harvey replied that 'if the matter was to depend on trades unions only it would come to nothing'. The conference decided that the vote should be taken without further interruption. The resolution was carried with Derbyshire dissenting.[1] Haslam and Harvey explained later:

Our sole reason for voting against Mr. Woods' resolution was because its provisions for support are for union men only, and we believe, to be successful, that we need the same general understanding and the same wide effort both in giving in notice and in raising levies for whoever might be out, as we did last July. Nevertheless we are prepared, and we are going in with the rest.[2]

These disputes merely served to underline Derbyshire's refusal to join the Federation. In his presidential address to the Birmingham conference in January, 1890, Ben Pickard dealt with the matter at some length:

One of the members at the Newport Conference, a leader in Derbyshire, made, he thought, some very extravagant statements about the Federation rage, and because he spoke so strongly he was placed upon the Rules Committee, and that committee fully believed that Derbyshire would join the Federation; and from the statements made by Mr. Harvey there was no fear felt of his not joining. Until the very last meeting this opinion was held; then some doubts were thrown out as to Derbyshire's joining at all. There was a lot of talk about Derbyshire fighting their own battle now, bossing their own show, and paddling their own canoe in the future. He hoped the men would ask why this was being done, and why they were being put into a false position. Let them ask whether they considered when that Federation secured another advance of wages, they, too, would be able to secure a similar advance without the support of men whose efforts had obtained grand advantages for them.[3]

[1] *Sheffield Independent*, 30 November, 1889.
[2] *Ibid.* 2 December, 1889.   [3] *Ibid.* 28 January, 1890.

Harvey subsequently denied that he had been on a committee formed for the purpose of drafting rules:

> He was re-elected on the Strike Committee, which was elected not in the Conference hours, but at a private meeting which excluded Northumberland and Durham, to draft questions for the Federation, but not rules. Mr. Pickard asked them to draft rules for the Federation, and he objected, but there was not another man to join him in his objection, and he proceeded to draft rules. He said that they were not appointed to draft rules, but only questions to be put before the lodges.[1]

On another occasion he said:

> It was possible in inaugurating a movement to adopt such tactics as did not commend themselves to men who desired to discuss and understand questions by embracing them. He believed that it was a right thing done in a hurry. There was no feeling on his part in the matter, and he believed the county would eventually join the Federation, but the men thought they had a right to be consulted and treated with the courtesy they were prepared to extend to others.[2]

Harvey appears to have been saving his face. Cowey, the Yorkshire leader, asserted that Harvey not only served on the Rules Committee but had also been paid for doing so and was well aware of the implications of his position. 'The fact was', he explained, 'Mr. Harvey made certain promises which Mr. Haslam could not accept; and the result was Mr. Harvey went back to his men and took another view of the matter.'[3] This is consistent with Haslam's attitude to the proposed Federation from the outset: an attitude which stemmed from his innate conservatism, his dislike of aggressive policies and his close attachment to the old Miners' National Union. His delaying tactics in connection with the Newport conference have already been noted, although he denied later that he had in any way kept the information about the new organization from the men.[4] But the fact that the men had not been consulted provided him with a powerful argument for restraining Harvey from plunging wholeheartedly into the Federation.

As Haslam and Harvey had promised, Derbyshire went in for the 10 per cent. wage increase at the same time as the other counties. The Lancashire and Yorkshire employers tried to bind the men to forgo any further increases for a period of six months. The Derbyshire leaders were in an isolated position because of their failure to join the Federation. If they were confronted with a similar offer what action would they take? With whom would they consult? By their own actions the

[1] *Sheffield Independent*, 24 January, 1890.   [2] *Ibid.* 27 January, 1890.
[3] *Ibid.* 29 January, 1890.   [4] *Ibid.* 30 January, 1890. See Chapter VI, pp. 251–2.

Derbyshire leaders had placed themselves in this dilemma but Haslam, at a meeting at Clay Cross on 6 December, chose to blame Pickard:

> Owing to a somewhat unnecessary display of temper on the part of the chairman of the Newport conference the important business as to the wages question was only half dealt with. He believed that before the end of December there would be a conference called, where the offers that might be made to any counties could be talked over and an agreement arrived at.[1]

Three days later a 'pit set' conference resolved: 'That the Secretary write Thomas Ashton, the Secretary of the National Conference, asking if another conference can be called to come to some common understanding as early as possible.'[2]

Ashton replied tersely that 'the old kind of wages conference ended at Newport'. By so doing he showed the Derbyshire men that the only way they could participate in future wages movements was through the Association and the Federation. Ashton's letter was described by a further conference of colliery delegates as being 'very unsatisfactory'. Their resolution continued:

> We think we have fair grounds for complaint that such action should be taken in the absence of Derbyshire who has always been represented at and supported all such movements for the past ten years and we believe that the arbitrary action of the Federation Board in attempting to boycott colleagues will be conducive to harm instead of good to the cause of miners generally.

As a further gesture of defiance it was resolved: 'That in the opinion of this Conference the time *has not* come when pit set conferences in Derbyshire shall cease.'[3]

The cleavage between Derbyshire and the Federation was widened by Haslam's reluctance to advocate striking. At Clay Cross he said:

> He would like the question of fighting to be discussed. It was a question, to his mind, which arose in connection with the wave of prosperity they were experiencing, whether something could not be done all over the country in the way of arrangements to test the selling price of coal, and give all men their fair share of the advance without the bother and turmoil they now experienced being arrived at. . . . He had no desire to see coal at famine prices. If that was done capital would be brought into the field that was not required, and they knew from past experience what the result would be.[4]

At Eckington he suggested that 'now they had reached a wage on which a miner could reasonably live, a board of conciliation consisting of masters and workmen should be formed'.[5] Haslam's advocacy of these policies

[1] *Derbyshire Times*, 14 December, 1889.
[2] Derbyshire Miners' Conference Minute Book, 9 December, 1889.
[3] *Ibid.* 11 January, 1890.
[4] *Derbyshire Times*, 14 December, 1889.   [5] *Ibid.*

of restraint culminated in a resolution which was carried by a 'pit set' conference at Chesterfield on 9 December:

That this Conference, believing that it is undesirable to create unnecessary alarm and panic in commercial circles and among the public generally, thinks the time has come when the employers and workmen of all counties by delegation should meet together and agree to a policy that while giving their workmen their fair share of any future advance in the price of coal will not unnecessarily push the present advantageous opportunity to the ultimate injury of trade and wages.[1]

According to Cowey there was a rumour that Derbyshire was on the verge of adopting a sliding scale.[2]

Fortunately for Haslam and Harvey there was little difficulty over the wage claim. Once the Yorkshire coal-owners had agreed to an unconditional advance of 10 per cent. there was not much doubt that the Derbyshire employers would do the same. By the middle of December the increase had been granted at most collieries.[3] Many of the Derbyshire employers, however, declined to accept the proposal of a 'pit set' conference that the banksmen should share in the advance.[4] On 17 December the Council of the Derbyshire Miners' Association instructed Haslam to send a circular to all employers requesting an increase in all banksmen's wages of 20 per cent. on the rates prevailing up to July, 1889.[5] At most collieries small increases were given but a banksmen's conference on 25 January, 1890, expressed its dissatisfaction with the advances received and resolved to continue the agitation for the full 20 per cent.[6]

XI

The public controversies between Haslam and Harvey and the Federation were not sufficient to keep Derbyshire out of the new organization for long. It was the members of the Derbyshire Miners' Association, as Haslam and Harvey constantly reiterated, who had the final word in this matter. With the price of coal still rising and the possibility of securing yet another increase in wages they very soon decided to throw in their lot with the national movement. Derbyshire was not represented at the first annual conference of the Federation, held at Birmingham on 22-24 January, 1890, at which a demand was put forward for an increase

---

[1] Derbyshire Miners' Conference Minute Book, 9 December, 1889.
[2] *Sheffield Independent*, 29 January, 1890.
[3] *Derbyshire Times*, 21 December, 1889.
[4] Derbyshire Miners' Conference Minute Book, 9 December, 1889.
[5] D.M.A. 17 December, 1889.
[6] Derbyshire Miners' Conference Minute Book, 25 January, 1890.

K*

of 10 per cent. on the wages of all underground workers. On 11 February, however, the Council of the Derbyshire Miners' Association, after a lengthy discussion, resolved: 'That Derbyshire join the National Federation of Great Britain.' A note following this minute states: 'There was an overwhelming majority for this course to be taken, and Mr. Haslam wrote to Mr. Ashton at once.'[1] It was also resolved:

That we join in the effort to secure 10 per cent. along with the Federation as speedily as possible. Nevertheless, we believe in, and desire that conciliatory measures be resorted to, for securing the same and would welcome any fair arrangement whereby matters of this kind could be amicably settled between employers and workmen on a National or semi-National scale.[2]

The Derbyshire coal-owners proved to be less reluctant than the leaders of their workmen to recognize the values of combination. Alfred Barnes, the Liberal M.P. for Chesterfield and a partner in the Grassmoor Colliery Company, took the lead in establishing a powerful coal-owners' federation which included all the coalfields in the country, except the sliding scale districts of South Wales, Northumberland and Durham. Presiding over a meeting at the Westminster Palace Hotel in London, he spoke of the necessity for combination on the part of the employers because of the recently established Miners' Federation against which individual owners, or even districts, 'must be powerless'. The coal-owners denied that they were making anything like the increased profits which the miners' leaders were suggesting. They asserted that after meeting the higher prices of timber and metal, and increases in other charges, together with the advances given to surface-men following the rise of miners' wages, their share of the increase in the market prices of coal was exceedingly small and quite insufficient to enable them to meet the further advances demanded at the Birmingham conference.[3]

Harvey was cautious. 'We ought to be sure of our ground before making the demand', he said.[4] The Miners' Federation, however, at a conference held in London, on 15 February, decided that notices demanding the 10 per cent. increase should be handed in so as to expire on the nearest 'making-up day' (i.e. pay day) to 15 March. The employers had meanwhile adopted a unanimous resolution that the demand 'should be resisted to the utmost'.[5]

In the negotiations which followed, Derbyshire played an important part in helping to bring about a peaceful settlement. On 22 February representatives of the Association met representatives of the Derbyshire coal-owners at the Station Hotel, Chesterfield, and both sides agreed to

---

[1] *D.M.A.* 11 February, 1890.   [2] *Ibid.*
[3] *Derbyshire Times*, 8 February, 1890.
[4] *Ibid.*   [5] *Ibid.* 15 February, 1890.

urge their respective national federations to arrange a joint meeting at an early date.[1] A conference between representatives of the Coal-Owners' Federation and delegates of the Miners' Federation met on 4 March, at the Westminster Palace Hotel, with Alfred Barnes in the chair. The miners' delegates, led by Ben Pickard, argued that the price of coal was continuing to rise and that another shilling a ton had been imposed as a result of the demand for a wage increase and the likelihood of a strike. Barnes said:

> He had not got a single sixpence at his colliery for the three years ending June last. Taking into consideration their business, he would like to ask why the coal-owners were not entitled to recoup themselves for the three years during which they had no profit whatever. The prices which had been quoted as for the London market were such as he had never heard of. . . .

In reply to a request from Haslam for a comparison of prices, E. Parker Rhodes, the coal-owners' secretary, stated that the average prices for coal at one of the largest Derbyshire collieries were, for the four months ending 31 October, 1888, 5s. 5·53d.; for the eight months ending 30 September, 1889, 6s. 0d.; and for the three months ending 31 December, 1889, 6s. 9·60d.[2]

No agreement was reached at this conference but the miners' representatives met in Manchester on 13 March and decided to seek a compromise. They informed the owners that they would accept an immediate increase of 5 per cent. and a further 5 per cent. on 1 July. The owners postponed their reply until after their meeting on 17 March. Meanwhile the strike notices expired and the men ceased work on 15 March. At their meeting on 17 March the owners refused to accept the miners' proposal but offered to meet their representatives again 'with the object of endeavouring to come to some arrangement whereby the matter in dispute may be amicably arranged if possible'. At a joint meeting on 20 March, after some discussion, the owners agreed to pay an immediate increase of 5 per cent. and a further 5 per cent. in the first week of August. The short strike had come to an end.

Haslam's part in these negotiations had inevitably been a prominent one because Barnes, the principal spokesman of the owners who presided at all the joint conferences, was supported by representatives of the Staveley and Sheepbridge Companies. The *Derbyshire Times* commented: 'The miners of this county, it must be said, have not been unfortunate enough to be led by a fiery fanatic, and even Mr. Haslam's opponents concede that throughout the dispute he has asked the men to conduct themselves creditably and has himself avoided violence in

---

[1] *D.M.A.* 11 February, 1890; *Derbyshire Times*, 1 March, 1890.
[2] *Derbyshire Times*, 8 March, 1889.

either speech or demeanour.'[1] But Haslam was criticized by some of the men who believed that he was largely responsible for the division of the 10 per cent. into two instalments. Joseph Marriott, presiding over a meeting at Whittington Moor, remarked:

Mr. Haslam had occasionally given expression to views he did not concur in, and he had written to Mr. Halsam to that effect, but, although some might think that Mr. Haslam might occasionally put more fight into his speeches, Mr. Haslam acted honestly and was entitled to his opinions.[2]

Haslam had, in fact, spoken strongly in favour of the compromise, as he admitted later:

If what he had said had tended to ease the friction between the masters and the men he had nothing to regret. . . . Was it worth while to strike for a month or two for a comparatively small concession? He had his own opinion, and thought they had every reason to congratulate themselves on the almost bloodless victory.[3]

Since 1888 the nominal wages of miners in the federated districts had increased by 40 per cent. but the settlement of 1890 was the last of this remarkable series of wage concessions. Neither the owners nor the miners believed that the price of coal could continue to rise indefinitely and, indeed, it was freely reported after the 1890 settlement 'that the miners' representatives and masters have come to a tacit understanding that the question will not be re-opened for some considerable time'.[4] The return of falling prices early in 1891 ensured that the owners would be obliged to make the next move. Meanwhile the miners turned their attention to a number of outstanding problems which had accumulated during the prolonged wages agitation.

XII

The Federation's refusal to have any dealings with non-unionists led to a much clearer demarcation in Derbyshire between those who were officially participating in the various wages movements and those who were not. The old 'pit set' conferences were reluctantly abandoned and Haslam and Harvey, realizing that they must have the backing of a strong union membership if their opinions were to be taken seriously in the deliberations of the Federation, set out to swell the ranks of the Association. Before Derbyshire joined the Federation, in December, 1889, Harvey spoke with moderation on the subject of trade union membership: 'They would be more able to win non-union men over

---

[1] *Derbyshire Times*, 22 March, 1890.   [2] *Ibid.* 26 April, 1890.
[3] *Ibid.* Cf. *D.M.A.* 11 March, 1890.   [4] *Derbyshire Times*, 22 March, 1890.

by kindness and persuasion than by treating them as lepers.'[1] By the following April, however, union policy had changed to such an extent that Haslam told members of the Association: 'They had a right to treat a man who receded from the union and to butt him as a social pariah, for such a man not only jeopardized himself but also his fellow workmen day by day.'[2]

As early as June, 1889, the Council had decided to order 6,000 medals, to be sold at a penny each to those lodges whose members wished to wear them. 'The ensign upon them', continued the maladroitly worded resolution, 'shall be grasping hands, and the inscription be the "Derbyshire Miners' Association".'[3] The scheme eventually became more elaborate. Smaller medals of varying shapes, bearing particulars of the months they covered, were issued quarterly to the men who were not in arrears with their contributions. In May, 1891, the officials wrote: 'All members are desired to wear the Medals as the surest way to detect those unprincipled men who profess to be in the Union here or there, but in reality are nowhere. We have a lot of these men about, and this is one way to detect them.'[4] Two months later the Executive Committee recommended members of the Association 'where the majority are Union men, to use every legal effort to induce the others to join, and failing this we advise our Members neither to work or ride with them, but that due Notice of their intention to take such action be given to the Management in each case before being put into practice'. Members were warned, however: 'Approach your Managers respectfully and point out your reasons for the above steps being taken, and see whether they can or will help you. We do not want to cause any Company inconvenience or difficulty, but feel bound to safeguard our Association's position.'[5]

The first attempt to enforce union membership was made at the Pilsley Colliery in September, 1891. Haslam wrote to T. Houldsworth, the proprietor, asking him to bring pressure to bear on a few non-unionists to join the Association. This he refused to do. 'We profess to live in a free country', he replied, 'but the tone of your letter ignores freedom altogether and proposes to set up in its stead coercion in its strictest form.'[6] But the miners had the last word. By striking they brought the colliery to a standstill and the non-unionists decided that enforced membership of the Association was preferable to unemployment. The *Derbyshire Times* commented: 'Mr. Haslam may equivocate but he cannot deny that up to a short time ago he was opposed to the coercive and boycotting tactics which have now been determined

---

[1] *Derbyshire Times*, 14 December, 1889. [2] *Ibid.* 26 April, 1890.
[3] *D.M.A.* 4 June, 1889. [4] *Ibid.* 5 May, 1891.
[5] *Ibid.* 28 July, 1891. Not '1892' as stated in S. and B. Webb, *Industrial Democracy*, (edn. of 1911), p. 214. [6] *Derbyshire Times*, 31 October, 1891.

upon by the miners' union.'[1] The policy of the Federation had prevailed. During the years which followed, the Association tackled the non-union question at one colliery after another, achieving its objective by gradual means rather than by embarking upon a costly county-wide dispute.

Another matter which caused much dissension in the Derbyshire coalfield at this time was the absence of price lists at most collieries. The issue became important soon after the wage increase of 1888. 'The colliers', said Harvey, 'were no better off with the 10 per cent. than they were before, because of masters having reduced prices for various work of which the outside world knew nothing. If the men were better organized they would be able to fight against this kind of thing, and to demand a fixed price for certain work.'[2] The adoption of 1888 as a base year for the purpose of calculating percentage wage increases and decreases implied that there was a standard wage which could easily be ascertained. But, as Mr. Rowe has shown, such 'standards are illusory even with the use of price lists'.[3] When there were no agreed prices for specific tasks the situation was much worse. A percentage increase could be reduced by re-adjusting the basic price or the nature of the task and there was no redress for the miner other than to refuse to work under the new conditions.

To overcome these difficulties the Association began a campaign for the introduction, at every colliery, of agreed price lists which would become part of the contract of employment and could, if necessary, be enforced in the courts. A meeting of colliery delegates on 9 November, 1889, resolved: 'That this conference is pleased to learn that price lists are being accepted and established at collieries in Derbyshire and hopes every effort will be made to make them general.'[4] Progress was inevitably slow but at one colliery after another the owners were obliged to admit the Association's officials to their offices and sign an agreed schedule of prices. A typical example is that for the Morton Colliery 'agreed by W. B. M. Jackson, Esq. (Manager), pro. the Clay Cross Co. and Deputation, consisting of Wm. E. Harvey, Miners' Agent; Samuel Rodgers, Elijah Moore, Thomas Davis, Richard Jarvis'. It came into force on 13 February, 1891 and stated clearly: '30 per cent. advance to be paid on all the above prices, to be increased or reduced according to the District.'[5] By January, 1892, Harvey was able to say that the principle of a price list had been accepted at every colliery.[6]

The Association also became involved in the great issues which were being taken up nationally by the Federation. The influx of unskilled

[1] *Derbyshire Times*, 24 October, 1891.   [2] *Ibid.* 18 May, 1889.
[3] Rowe, *op. cit.* p. 49.
[4] Derbyshire Miners' Conference Minute Book, 9 November, 1889.
[5] *Clay Cross Collieries, No. 5 Main, Schedule of Prices* (see Appendix I to this chapter).   [6] *Derbyshire Times*, 9 January, 1892.

labour into the pits during the years of prosperity continued to threaten both the economic position and the safety of the miner. The first annual conference of the M.F.G.B. in January, 1890, decided to agitate for an amendment of the Mines Act, 1887, which laid down that no man should be allowed to work as a coal-getter without two years' experience under skilled supervision. The Federation advocated that no one should be employed at the coal face who had not entered the mine before the age of sixteen. The proposal never became law but it was the subject of many speeches and resolutions in Derbyshire as elsewhere. Haslam and Harvey constantly urged the men 'to make their calling a trade'. Most of the un-skilled labour came from the land, and the agricultural labourer, 'the plough boy' as he was called, received a great deal of attention from the miners' leaders. At Clay Cross in November, 1890 Haslam advocated 'a re-form of our land laws, so that men in rural districts might be able to remain on the land, and not be compelled to compete with the colliers and the artisans of our towns'.[1] The various proposals for land reform which were being put forward in this period aroused much interest among the miners.

The long-standing agitation about mining royalties turned out to be a damp squib. In 1889 the miners' national conference at Birmingham had welcomed the setting up of the Royal Commission and expressed the hope 'that the outcome of its labours may be the full and complete restoration of the mineral to the State'.[2] But several of the miners' representatives who gave evidence before the Commission were opposed to the nationalization of minerals. Haslam stated: 'I do not think the nationalization of minerals is at all practicable or likely to come about; that is what I am prepared to say.'[3] In reply to a further question about compensation he said: 'I want my friend to remember this, that there are men, working men even, who buy little plots of land, sometimes to build upon, sometimes for agricultural purposes. Those men, anywhere near mining districts, have bought them subject to the mineral—they have bought them at a price subject to that—and I should not think it right to take away those men's minerals and not pay them for the minerals.'[4] Although he was not an abolitionist, Haslam suggested that a reduction in royalties would alleviate foreign competition: 'I think, if 2d. per ton in wages would make all the difference in competition with foreign competitors, that 2d. per ton in royalties would have the same effect.'[5]

The Federation agreed that royalties were harmful to the coal trade but had no unanimous proposals for dealing with them. The Commis-sion noted that most of the miners' representatives and all the lessees' representatives disapproved of nationalization: 'In these circumstances,

[1] *Derbyshire Times*, 29 November, 1890.   [2] Quoted in Arnot, *op. cit.* p. 98.
[3] *R.C. on Mining Royalties, Second Report*, 1891, Q. 8213.
[4] *Ibid.* Q. 8216.   [5] *Ibid.* Q. 8164.

and as the nationalization of minerals is only a portion of the larger question of the nationalization of land, we do not consider that it is necessary for us to discuss it further.'[1] The result was that the Commission recommended no fundamental changes. The purely economic arguments against royalties were weak. According to information put in by Alfred Barnes, who was a member of the Commission, coal royalties in Derbyshire averaged about 4¾d. a ton.[2] On the basis of this calculation and with the caution that ' "average prices" are not, as a rule, "true averages" ', the Commission compared the percentage of royalty to price for the years 1888 and 1889:[3]

	Derbyshire Average Price	Percentage of Royalty to Price
1888	5s. 6d.	7·57
1889	7s. 9d.	5·37

On the other hand, miners' wages, which tended to rise with the price of coal, accounted for about 60 per cent. of the costs of production.[4]

XIII

The most important issue during the wage truce was the eight-hour day. There is little doubt that the Derbyshire miners had good reason to be dissatisfied with the length of their working day. A parliamentary paper published in July, 1890 gave the following particulars of the hours worked in Derbyshire collieries:[5]

	Number of persons	Average number of hours per day from bank to bank	Average intervals for meals per day (hours)	Average number of hours actually worked at face	Usual number of days worked per week
Men and boys engaged in getting minerals	17,470	9·28	0·47	7·88	5·11
Men and boys engaged in conveying minerals from face to pit bottom	5,393	9·25	0·47	—	5·2
All other underground workers	2,815	9·35	0·52	—	5·25
		Average number of hours per day exclusive of meal times			
Persons employed on the surface	6,607	8·70	0·72	—	5·25
Total	32,285				

[1] R.C. on Mining Royalties, Final Report, 1893, para. 224, p. 47.
[2] Ibid. Appendix III, p. 84.   [3] Ibid. Appendix V, p. 96.
[4] Ibid. Appendix VI, p. 98.
[5] Return showing the Average Number of Hours and Days Daily and Weekly worked by Men and Boys from Bank to Bank, and otherwise, in and about Mines in the United Kingdom, July, 1890, Accounts and Papers, LXVIII, 284. For a full discussion of the eight-hour day see B. McCormick and J. E. Williams, 'The Miners and the Eight-Hour Day, 1863–1910', Economic History Review, XII, (1959), pp. 222–38.

Only in Leicestershire, Gloucestershire, Nottinghamshire and parts of Lancashire and Wales, with averages ranging between 8 and 8·42, were the hours worked at the coal face greater than those in Derbyshire. In Northumberland and Durham, on the other hand, where two shifts were worked, the averages were 6·07 and 5·66 respectively. Another report in the same year showed that the average number of hours worked weekly, at various collieries in Derbyshire, had changed little since the reduction of hours in 1872.[1] In the Alfreton district the miners generally were working an average of 51·5 hours in an average week of five days. At Staveley the weekly average was 54 hours and in the Chesterfield district, where working hours had always tended to be fewer, the average was 48. Of the districts mentioned, Clay Cross was the only one in which any change was reported: a reduction from 54 hours to 48 between 1880 and 1890.

An independent inquiry conducted by the M.F.G.B. in October, 1890, gave detailed information of hours of work collected from 69 Derbyshire collieries.[2] There were considerable variations in the hours worked at the coal face and the times taken for meals and travelling to and from the face. At Church Gresley, where trade unionism had been so effectively crushed during the 'sixties, the men were working 10 hours at the face compared with only 7 hours at the Grassmoor No. 4 Colliery. Travelling time varied between 90 minutes at the Norwood and Grassmoor No. 4 collieries and 10 minutes at the Grassmoor No. 2 Colliery. At the Boythorpe, Pleasley, Mapperley and Stanton collieries no time at all was allowed for meals: at others such as the Ireland and Hartington collieries as much as 40 minutes was allowed. These are the extremes. An analysis of the statistics gives the following results:

	Average	Median	Mode
Hours worked at coal face	8·47	8·5	8·5
Time taken in travelling (mins.)	40·9	40·0	40·0
Stoppage for meals (mins.)	23·6	30·0	30·0

There is no significant correlation between the hours worked at the coal face and the time taken in travelling or the time allowed for meals, which seems to indicate that the length of the working day was a measure of the strength of local trade union bargaining power or the generosity of the employer.

[1] *Return showing the Average Number of Hours worked as a Week's Work in the Chief Trade Centres . . . in the years 1850, 1860, 1870, 1880 and 1890 . . .*, August, 1890, *Accounts and Papers*, LXVIII, 375.

[2] Miners' Federation of Great Britain. *Statistical Report of the Hours worked at Collieries in every Mining District in Great Britain, except Durham, Northumberland and Cleveland*, October, 1890.

The agitation for the eight-hour day began to gather momentum in 1890 after the Federation had successfully tested the strength of its organization on the issue of increased wages. The miners had been unable to decide whether to attempt to secure the eight-hour day by industrial or by political action but at various stages in the struggle both methods were used. The Federation also worked for support from the Trades Union Congress and the International Miners' Federation. At the first annual conference in January, 1890, at which Derbyshire was not represented, the Federation at last decided to take parliamentary action and to adopt the Bill which had been prepared by R. B. Cunninghame Graham in the previous year.[1]

The immediate reactions of both the employers and the Government were discouraging. According to the newly formed coal-owners' federation the concession of the eight-hour day would have meant a reduction in the country's total output of not less than 20 million tons, and would have increased the price of coal to the consumer by something like 5s. a ton.[2] On 17 February a deputation from the M.F.G.B. saw Henry Matthews, the Home Secretary. After Pickard, Cunninghame Graham, Haslam and Jones, the North Wales leader, had spoken in favour of the eight hours' movement the Home Secretary expressed doubt that time could be found for Cunninghame Graham's Bill and held out no hope that the Government would support 'any legislation which had for its object to impose restrictions upon the freedom of adult males in the disposal and management of their own labour'.[3]

The issue of the eight-hour day was bedevilled by the conflict which was raging within the T.U.C. between the older unions, led by Henry Broadhurst, and the 'new' unions, strongly influenced by Keir Hardie and Socialism. The new unionists, with their demand for a compulsory eight-hour day for all workers, had been routed at the 1889 Congress held in Dundee but the miners' leaders, who were not convinced of the need for a general eight-hour day, had secured a resolution supporting an Eight Hours' Bill for miners on the ground that theirs was an exceptional case. The parliamentary committee of the T.U.C. was also instructed to prepare a Bill but did not do so. Nevertheless, the miners' own Bill appeared on the order paper of the House of Commons on 23 April, 1890. Lack of time prevented the Commons from dealing with the matter and it soon became apparent that no further progress would be made during the remainder of the parliamentary session. Harvey told the Shirland lodge, on 3 May: 'He was not so afraid

---

[1] Arnot, op. cit. p. 139. R. B. Cunninghame Graham, 1852–1936; elected Liberal M.P. for North Lanarkshire, 1886; championed the cause of the miners.
[2] Derbyshire Times, 8 February, 1890.
[3] Ibid. 22 February, 1890.

personally of the capitalists and some Members of the House as he was of men such as Mr. Broadhurst and Mr. Bradlaugh.'[1]

The failure of the parliamentary committee of the T.U.C. to draft an Eight Hours' Bill for the miners led to a vote of censure by the M.F.G.B. conference at Nottingham, on 11 April, 1890. It was decided to affiliate with the T.U.C., to send a delegation consisting of Pickard, Woods, Cowey, Haslam and Whitefield to the next congress, and to do everything possible to secure the election of a parliamentary committee which would be in sympathy with the miners' Eight Hours' Bill. When the T.U.C. met at Liverpool on 1 September, 1890, the miners found themselves outmanoeuvred. The general eight-hour day came first on the agenda and its opponents moved an amendment which would have prevented any further discussion of the miners' eight-hour day. The Federation delegates, who were pledged to an eight-hour day for miners, found themselves supporting an eight-hour day for all. Haslam was afraid 'that in the general argument they would have suffered by the vote at Liverpool and by the alarm it might have created'.[2] He believed that an eight-hour day would lead to a temporary reduction in wages and that many workers would not want it but argued: 'A pennyworth of ease is worth a penny.'[3]

A special conference of the M.F.G.B. held at Bristol on 11 November, 1890, discussed the whole question of electoral tactics in the campaign and decided to recommend members to support candidates who promised to vote for an Eight Hours' Bill. Harvey, in seconding the motion, asserted: 'Radical as I am, I will advise the support of a Tory who would support the Eight Hours rather than a Radical who is opposed to it.' The conference also decided to ask the Coal-Owners' Association to convene a joint meeting to discuss the Eight Hours' Bill and 'to try to agree mutually upon an eight hours' day from bank to bank; and if that is agreed to, the same to be made a special rule under the Coal Mines Regulation Act, 1887'.[4]

A joint conference of the coal-owners and the miners' leaders from the Federated districts, South Wales and Scotland, was held on 21 January, 1891, at the Westminster Palace Hotel, with Alfred Barnes presiding. Harvey was present as a member of the Executive of the M.F.G.B. and the Association was represented by Haslam, Kenyon and Hallam.[5] The coal-owners did not commit themselves but asked for a further meeting on 11 February at which they stated that it was impossible to agree to the miners' proposals.

[1] *Derbyshire Times*, 10 May, 1890. Charles Bradlaugh had argued against the statutory regulation of hours in an article in *The Reformer*.
[2] *Ibid.* 20 September, 1890.   [3] *Ibid.* 29 November, 1890.
[4] *M.F.G.B.* 11 November, 1890.   [5] *D.M.A.* 13 January, 1891.

The matter was next discussed internationally. Keir Hardie had proposed a European strike of miners for the eight-hour day at the Jolimont conference in 1890 but further consideration had been postponed for a year as a result of Cowey's intervention. On 13 January, 1891, before the joint meeting with the employers the Derbyshire miners' Council had resolved: 'That failing a settlement with the owners on the Eight Hours' question, or by Act of Parliament, that our men be balloted as to whether they are in favour, or not of going on Strike along with the Continental Miners to secure the same.'[1] There is no record of the result of this ballot but one of the sensations of the miners' international conference at Paris, in March–April, 1891, was Haslam's statement that 95 per cent. of the Derbyshire miners were in favour of an international strike. Defuisseaux, a Belgian delegate, mistaking this for a national ballot, delivered a fiery speech. 'Let them look to the miners of England', he said. 'Let them look at them to the extent of 95 per cent. sat in their homes before their firesides, surrounded by their children, and governed only by their consciences, filling up those ballot papers in favour of a strike.' But the Federation ballot had only a two to one majority in favour of a strike, the French and the German delegates were hesitant, and eventually the Belgian motion for a general strike was withdrawn.[2]

XIV

Shortage of time again prevented the House of Commons from dealing with the miners' Eight Hours' Bill on 18 March, 1891, and W. H. Smith, the leader of the House, subsequently decided that it would not be necessary to set apart a day for discussion on the Bill because the government had appointed a Royal Commission on Labour. According to Thomas Bayley, the Nottingham coal-owner, who was then the Gladstonian Liberal candidate for the Chesterfield division, it 'was meant to shelve the questions affecting the working classes'.[3] The composition of the Commission, with the Marquis of Hartington[4] as its chairman, has been described as being 'significantly weighted against the wage-earners'.[5]

By 112 votes to 34 the Federation decided to boycott the Commission and the result was, as far as Derbyshire was concerned, that well-known critics of trade unionism such as Benjamin Morris, a deputy at the

[1] D.M.A. 13 January, 1891.
[2] Miners' Federation of Great Britain, *Report of International Miners' Conference at Paris*, 1891.   [3] *Derbyshire Times*, 3 May, 1891.
[4] Became 8th Duke of Devonshire in December, 1891.
[5] S. and B. Webb, *History of Trade Unionism*, (edn. of 1920), p. 595.

Blackwell Colliery, were called upon to give evidence. One of the Federation's objections to the inquiry had been that the miners' representatives on the Commission, Burt and Abraham, were chosen from Northumberland and South Wales. Nevertheless, Abraham was careful to establish that the Derbyshire witnesses spoke only for themselves and not for the Derbyshire Miners' Association. In reply to Abraham's questions, John Bennett, a stallman at the Swanwick Colliery, stated that he had not communicated with the Commission asking to be called but had received an invitation from the Secretary. He could not explain how the Secretary obtained his name.[1] Haslam was greeted with laughter when he told the miners at Ripley: 'They had some very good representatives indeed sent out of that locality to make up for the absence of the Derbyshire leaders.'[2]

In the evidence given by the Derbyshire witnesses, Benjamin Morris's plea for the formation of boards of conciliation and arbitration and the adoption of a sliding scale was the only digression from the great question of the day, the Eight Hours' Bill, which, for the miners, overshadowed everything else including the Royal Commission itself. William Kerry, a contractor at Swanwick, John Bennett and Benjamin Morris, were all thoroughly opposed to any legislative interference with the hours of labour, and all believed that the Association's ballot on the question had not been conducted fairly.[3] In reply to such allegations Haslam asked: 'What interest would Haslam and Harvey have in wanting the colliers to work less hours if the colliers did not want to work less hours?'[4]

The agitation for the eight-hour day continued throughout 1891. At the T.U.C. a resolution instructing the parliamentary committee 'to use all legitimate means in its power to secure the passage of the Miners' Eight Hours' Bill in the House of Commons' was carried despite strenuous opposition from Northumberland and Durham. Preparations were also made for dealing with the eight hours' question at the Federation's annual conference at Hanley in January, 1892. At a special meeting of the Derbyshire Executive Committee on 21 November, 1891, the agenda for the conference was considered in detail and three of the resolutions were:

(1) That we are in favour of soliciting the support of other trades to help us to secure an Eight Hours' Day, and we believe this can best be done by someone meeting the various Trades Councils, and inducing them, if possible, to send up petitions, numerously signed, from their Trades, in favour of the same.

[1] *R.C. on Labour*, (1892), Minutes of Evidence, I, QQ. 8818–8824.
[2] *Derbyshire Times*, 9 January, 1892.
[3] *R.C. on Labour*, (1892), Minutes of Evidence, I, QQ. 8599, 8603, 8723–8735, 8901.
[4] *Derbyshire Times*, 9 January, 1892.

(2) That we hold Public Meetings at our Collieries and send up resolutions to our Members in favour of an Eight Hours' Day.

(3) That failing to get an Eight Hours' Bill this Session, we favour an International strike to secure the same.[1]

The annual conference reached similar decisions except on the issue of the international strike. Sir Charles Dilke, an active supporter of the Eight Hours' Bill, delivered a speech to the conference in which he warned the miners of the dangers of such a policy and the motion calling for a general strike if the Bill were not passed in the next session of Parliament was defeated by 103 votes to 74.

The parliamentary campaign of 1892 resulted in the Bill reaching the second reading where it was defeated by 272 votes to 160. Alfred Barnes, the Liberal Unionist member for Chesterfield, described it as 'totally impracticable and unworkable'.[2] But the agitation continued. Dilke spoke at the Derbyshire miners' annual demonstration in support of a resolution: 'That this meeting endorses the action taken by those Members of Parliament who have introduced the Eight Hours' Bill, and those Members of Parliament who supported the Bill on its second reading during the last session of Parliament, and hereby determines to leave no stone unturned until the same is passed in law. . . .'[3] In the general election of 1892 Barnes was ousted from the Chesterfield division by the Gladstonian Liberal candidate, Thomas Bayley, who was pledged to support the Eight Hours' Bill, and Salisbury's administration gave way to Gladstone's.[4]

After further rebuffs in the autumn at the T.U.C., the Federation decided to have a full discussion of the eight hours' question. It called a 'National Conference of Miners' Representatives of England, Scotland and Wales' to be held at the Hen and Chickens Hotel, Birmingham, on 9–12 January, 1893. Derbyshire was represented by Haslam and two delegates from the Clay Cross No. 1 and Danesmoor branches, W. Butler and John Houseley. Harvey attended as a member of the Executive of the M.F.G.B.[5] The debate, which lasted for two days, turned upon Cowey's resolution calling for legislative enactment, which was opposed by the delegates from Northumberland and Durham who favoured direct negotiations between employers and the workmen.

'We have not had the method of shortening hours in our hands for long', said Harvey. 'The great bulk of the miners in this country have not been admitted into the pale of citizenship very long. Now, I am glad to say, the bulk of them believe that it will be better to use the machinery that is put into their hands and obtain it by law, thus making it sure, than to revert to the

---

[1] *D.M.A.* 21 November, 1891.
[2] *Derbyshire Times*, 9 April, 1892.   [3] *Ibid.* 23 July, 1892.
[3] See Chapter XII, p. 493.   [5] *D.M.A.* 15 November, 1892.

dislocation of trade and to the great strikes such as those which have taken place in the past.'[1]

Haslam called attention to the competition which existed between the colliery districts:

Having learned the lesson that the best thing we could do was to seize upon the existing position and try to put every employer in comparatively the same position as far as we were able in a monetary sense, we have an idea that we ought to put our employers in the same position with regard to the working hours of the miners throughout the country.[2]

Cowey's resolution was carried 'by an overwhelming majority' and, at the annual conference of the Federation, which followed the conference on the eight hours' question, it was resolved: 'That we press the Eight Hours' Bill upon the new Government with unabated vigour; that, as in the past, every means be used for petitioning Parliament, writing and seeing members, deputations, &c., until the Bill becomes law.'[3] On 3 March a large deputation of miners' representatives, including Haslam and Harvey, and members of the parliamentary committee of the T.U.C. met Gladstone who told them:

Until there is a very near approach to unanimity, to what they call moral unanimity, I think Mr. Asquith will agree with me, among the miners themselves you will not be able to get a compulsory Bill; and I do not think that any large minority ought to be put down by force in such a matter.[4]

Despite this discouragement the Federation persisted with its Bill and, on 3 May, 1893, the day of the second reading, Haslam and Harvey joined the other miners' leaders in lobbying the members at the House of Commons.[5] Inevitably, in the debate, the Derbyshire evidence before the Royal Commission on Labour was mentioned. Dilke was quick to reply: 'It was the evidence of one of those persons who is called a "butty man", who went and gave evidence against the Union. But the opinion of Derbyshire is not to be gathered from the evidence of a butty man who gave evidence before the Royal Commission. The opinion of Derbyshire is to be gathered from the votes of the Derbyshire members.'[6] None of the Derbyshire members had an opportunity of speaking, but Foster, Bayley, Bolton and Jacoby, the Liberal members for the four mining constituencies, all voted in favour of the Bill, which passed its second reading by 280 votes to 201. Unfortunately for the miners, the Government was unable to find time for any further discussion of the Bill and the great issue once again fell into abeyance.

---

[1] *M.F.G.B.* 10 January, 1893.   [2] *Ibid.* 11 January, 1893.
[3] *Ibid.* 13 January, 1893. See Appendix II to this chapter.
[4] *Ibid.* 3 March, 1893.   [5] *D.M.A.* 4 April, 1893.
[6] 11 H.C. Deb. 4s., c. 1892; Miners' Federation of Great Britain, *Report of Debate on Second Reading of the Mines Eight Hours' Bill*, 3 May, 1893.

APPENDIX I

A Colliery Price List, 1891

Clay Cross Collieries, No. 5 Main, Morton, Schedule of prices agreed to by W. B. M. Jackson, Esq. (Manager), pro the Clay Cross Co., and Deputation, consisting of Wm. E. Harvey, Miners' Agent, Samuel Rodgers, Elijah Moore, Thomas Davis, Richard Jarvis.

1.—On and after Wednesday, 18th day of February, 1891, the following prices shall be paid for the undermentioned classes of work at this Colliery, in all cases subject to such advances and deductions as may from time to time rule the district.

	s.	d.
2.—Getting coal	2	2
3.—Getting Slack	1	6
4.—Cutting for leading stalls per yard	3	6
5.—Turning new gate, building wood pack, and ripping as before	18	0
6.—Ripping in gates, half-yard thick, per yard	1	10
7.—Ripping in gates, one yard thick, per yard	3	8
8.—Ripping in cross-gates, 2 feet thick	4	5
9.—Ripping in cross-gates, 3 feet thick	5	6

10.—All ripping above 3 feet thick to be paid by bargain.

11.—Where ripping is ordered to be discontinued, packers shall be provided the Stallman to enable him to build gate-end packs within suitable distance, so that reloading of packers shall not be necessary.

12.—Heading end	3	8
13.—Face, per yard	3	6

14.—Any Stallman being called out to do odd work to be paid at the

rate of per day	4	10

15.—Any Loader being called out to do odd work to be paid at the

rate of per day	4	4

16.—If at any time in any stall it is prohibited to fire shots on account of gas or other cause, the Company will provide the Stallman with a safety explosive at the cost of powder, and if no shots of any kind can be allowed, and it is considered that extra labour is entailed an allowance will be granted.

17.—Where a Stallman meets with a fault or other trouble (except such trouble is caused by the men's negligence) remuneration shall be made to him by the Company, the amount to be decided upon by the Under-manager and the Stallman, or where necessary by the Manager and the Stallman.

30 per cent. advance to be paid on all the above prices, to be increased or reduced according to the District.

This Price List to come into operation on February the 18th, 1891.

APPENDIX II

An Eight Hours' Petition, 1893

To the Honourable the Commons of Great Britain and Ireland, in Parliament assembled.

The Humble Petition of the miners of   in public meeting assembled and held this   day of   1893. Sheweth that your Petitioners pray your Honourable House to pass into Law this Session, the Miners' Eight Hours' Bill, brought into the House by Mr. Storey, Mr. Pickard, Mr. Wood, Mr. Abraham, and other Members.

And your Petitioners as in duty bound, will ever pray etc.

Signed on behalf of the meeting.

Chairman.

CHAPTER VIII

THE GREAT LOCK-OUT OF 1893

I

Whilst the agitation for the eight-hour day was in progress the average selling value of coal per ton at the pit-head was falling from 8s. 3d. in 1890 to 6s. 10d. in 1893, and the employers were already attempting to reduce wages. The first symptoms of the renewed malaise of the coal industry began to appear in 1891. On 11 May Harvey, speaking to the Eckington miners, referred to rumours in the Press that the coal-owners' association had decided on a $7\frac{1}{2}$ per cent. reduction in wages and that the first move was to be made in the Forest of Dean.[1] It was reported to the Executive of the M.F.G.B. in the following December that the Durham coal-owners had attempted a reduction of 10 per cent. and that the South Wales employers were demanding a new sliding scale which would entail a reduction in wages. At the annual conference at Hanley, a few weeks later, delegates heard that South Wales had accepted the new scale and that Northumberland had agreed to a reduction of 5 per cent. They thereupon passed a resolution expressing the opinion 'that wages in the coal trade are not too high at the present time' and the determination to 'do all we can to resist any reduction in wages, no matter what price the employers think proper to dispose of their coal'.[2]

A special conference at Manchester was called for 11 February, 1892, to consider 'the advisability of laying the whole of the pits in the nation idle for two or more weeks with a view to clearing away the surplus coal in the markets and thus maintain the miners' wages'. Haslam and Harvey and two other delegates were authorized to represent Derbyshire and 'to support any scheme the Federation may adopt to stop the downward tendency of wages'.[3] Durham, Northumberland and South Wales declined to send any delegates and Scotland sent only one, so the conference was virtually confined to the Federation. It was decided to cease work on 12 March and to resume at a date to be settled by the adjourned conference on 16 March.

[1] *Derbyshire Times*, 16 May, 1891.
[2] *M.F.G.B.* 12–16 January, 1892.
[3] *D.M.A.* 9 February, 1892.

This was no ordinary trade dispute. The Federation believed that by restricting the supply of coal they were helping the coal-owners as well as the miners. Haslam said: 'His aim was to bring the employer and the workman together, to prevent the old cut-throat policy which acted so detrimentally to the interests of both.'[1] The Derbyshire employers, on the whole, maintained a passive attitude and in some cases approved the action of the men to the extent of waiving their right to receive legal notices.[2] According to Haslam, some of the colliery owners 'seemed to treat the movement as a general holiday'.[3] Harvey told the Alfreton miners: 'He had not an unkind word to say about one employer in Derbyshire. He believed that the great majority of employers were with them.'[4] But the restrictionist policy inevitably became linked with the eight hours' agitation. Haslam told the Kilburn miners:

At Staveley, Clay Cross, Grassmoor and Blackwell, where he was known, the firms told him it would have been better to work four days per week rather than stop a whole week. But that had not been mentioned until the stop was announced. Why not have six days a week of eight hours from bank to bank?[5]

For a whole week the collieries in the Federation area were at a standstill. When the adjourned conference assembled at the Westminster Palace Hotel, on Thursday, 17 March, it was unanimously agreed that the object of the stoppage had been achieved, and the miners were advised to resume work on the following Monday.[6]

The results of the stoppage are difficult to assess. Its beginning, on 12 March, coincided with the locking-out of the Durham miners who were resisting a 10 per cent. reduction in wages.[7] The attempts to import Belgian coal to London were frustrated by the refusal of the coal porters, who had recently been admitted to the Federation, to unload it.[8] There was a temporary increase in coal prices but the general decline was not arrested. The activities of the merchants were once again sharply criticized. Pickard wrote from his sick-bed to the adjourned conference:

The 'Week's Stop' has also shown that the selling of coal is not regulated by the much-abused laws of political economy—supply and demand. The middleman, the coal merchant, and those who rig the market, have deliberately set such old-fashioned and obsolete laws at defiance.[9]

The Economist argued that although the miners might blame the 'grasping intermediaries' who were 'profiting by the distress', the policy

[1] *Derbyshire Times*, 27 February, 1892.
[2] *Ibid.* 5 March, 1892.
[3] *Ibid.* 27 February, 1892.
[4] *Ibid.* 5 March, 1892.
[5] *Ibid.* 12 March, 1892.
M.F.G.B. 17 March, 1892.
[7] Welbourne, *op. cit.* p. 272.
[8] *Derbyshire Times*, 12 March, 1892.
[9] *M.F.G.B.* 16–18 March, 1892.

of alternate spells of work and idleness, at irregular and unknown intervals, was playing into the hands of the middlemen by keeping the market 'in a continual state of unsettlement and apprehension'.[1] But in the following January, J. O'Connor, the Secretary of the Coal Porters' Union, told the annual conference of the Federation 'that the so-called middlemen in the coal trade were the employers or colliery proprietors themselves. There were not 40 coal merchants in London, who were not colliery proprietors.'[2]

On one result of the stoppage there was unanimous agreement. It had been a remarkable display of strength and solidarity. Pickard wrote: 'By the action of the Federation, ocular demonstration has been provided for those doubters as to the ability to put Rule 20 into operation.'[3] Arguing against the introduction of an eight-hour day by legal enactment Alfred Barnes said: 'If the Federation are able to call out 400,000 for a week's stoppage, surely they are able to make a reasonable arrangement as to hours.'[4]

The conference which ended the week's stoppage also marked the beginning of the Federation's next essay in restrictionism. It recommended that the men should work only five days a week from 1 April, with Monday as a general 'play-day'. The Derbyshire colliery proprietors immediately suggested that the Association should appoint a deputation to meet a similar number of owners.[5] The meeting was held at the Station Hotel, Chesterfield, on 29 March, with Alfred Barnes in the chair. Most of the larger concerns, including the Clay Cross, Sheepbridge, Blackwell, Staveley, Eckington and Grassmoor companies, sent representatives to meet Haslam, Harvey and several other local union leaders.[6] The Derbyshire miners were then working half an hour extra each day so that they could finish work earlier on Saturdays, and the employers were not slow to realize the possibilities of closing the pits on Saturdays instead of Mondays.[7] The miners' leaders, who were committed to the Federation decision, were unable to make any concessions.

The proposal for closing the pits on Saturdays was not received with favour in most parts of the county, and the lodges sent their delegates to the Council on 5 April with instructions to oppose it unless the employers agreed to shorten the other working days by half an hour,

[1] *The Economist*, 5 March, 1892.   [2] *M.F.G.B.* 11 January, 1893.
[3] *Ibid.* 16–18 March, 1892. Rule 20 stated: 'That whenever any County, Federation, or District is attacked on a wage question, or any action taken by a general Conference, all members connected with the Society shall tender a notice to terminate their contracts—if approved by a Conference called to consider the advisability of such joint action being taken.'
[4] *Derbyshire Times*, 9 April, 1892.   [5] *Ibid.* 26 March, 1892.
[6] *Ibid.* 2 April, 1892.   [7] *Ibid.* 9 April, 1892.

making the 'holiday' a full sixth of the working week in accordance with the recommendation of the Federation. Haslam and Harvey were instructed to support this policy at the forthcoming conference of the Federation at Derby, on 7 April, and it was also resolved: 'That we loyally abide by the decision of the Federation with regard to the stop-day.'[1] The Derby conference decided in favour of the Saturday stop-day but Haslam's proposal that the remaining five working days should each be shortened by half an hour was defeated by moving a previous question.[2] However, a resolution was unanimously carried that the extra half hours should be paid for. 'We are hopeful', wrote Haslam, 'by the present action to administer a severe blow at the old fossilized custom of working Friday and again at night, and are inaugurating a movement that will eventually dispose of double shifts once and for all.'[3]

The stop-day was not easy to enforce.[4] On 31 May the Council expressed astonishment 'that men in this County have been threatened unless they work Friday nights, or Saturday when required, they will be summoned, which is contrary to the understanding come to at the meeting with the Coal-Owners at Chesterfield on April 2nd'. A resolution was carried, authorizing all members of the Association to refuse to work on Friday nights or Saturdays, except in cases of extreme emergency. The officials appealed to the men to be 'honourable and straightforward' in the matter:

Until there is an alteration or change agreed upon by the Federation, every Union man at least should strictly adhere to the arrangement come to, and not go sneaking in on Friday nights as some are doing, for by so doing they are betraying their fellow men, shaking the confidence of the Leaders, upholding abominable customs, and doing harm to the general cause. This may appear strong language, but if the reports of some of the Delegates are true, there is need for reproof and correction.[5]

The difficulties of enforcing the five-day week and its failure to stem the tide of depression led the Federation to abandon the policy on 27 August. The *Derbyshire Times* called the attention of the miners to a statement made by the Duke of Devonshire, 'far-seeing, plain, and practical business man as he is', at the annual meeting of the Furness Railway Company:

It appears to me altogether a mistake to suppose there is an unlimited consumption for articles such as coal, coke, and manufactured iron and steel. There is a demand for them at certain prices, but at certain states of the industries of the world, and of this country in particular, there is no demand for them at prices exceeding a certain level.[6]

[1] *D.M.A.* 5 April, 1892; *Derbyshire Times*, 9 April, 1892.
[2] *D.M.A.* 5 April, 1892.   [3] *Ibid.*   [4] *Ibid.* 3 May, 1892.
[5] *Ibid.* 31 May, 1892.   [6] *Derbyshire Times*, 3 September, 1892.

II

Meanwhile the Federation was beginning to prepare for what looked like being a desperate struggle to maintain wages in the face of falling prices. During 1892 there were wage reductions in Scotland, South Wales and Northumberland. The Durham miners, who had been locked out on 15 March, received considerable financial support from the Federation. Derbyshire alone was contributing £400 a week despite the reluctance of members to pay the sixpenny levy, and Haslam visited Durham with Woods and Cowey to deliver the Federation's first contribution to the strike fund which amounted to £3,700.[1] Nevertheless, after twelve weeks' privation, the Durham miners had to accept a reduction of 10 per cent.

Only in the Federated districts did wages remain intact. Haslam was able to tell the Alfreton miners: 'He was glad to say that in Derbyshire they had comparative quietude, but there were all kinds of private troubles which required attention.'[2] These included the Association's campaigns for recruiting non-unionists and for securing price lists and weekly pay days at all Derbyshire collieries. Another grievance was the inadequate payment of the boys: 'It was a scandalous thing', said Haslam, 'that a boy should be badly paid because he belonged to a class of labour for which no definite price list had been made.'[3] The Association was then collecting information about boys' wages and had in mind the introduction of a basic wage of 1s. 6d. a day, with an annual increase of 4d. a day, but, as the Executive Committee pointed out: 'This is not a time for demanding advances in wages, or making aggression, but a time for defence.'[4] In November, 1892, Harvey, speaking at New Whittington, said: 'There were forebodings on every hand ... with regard to the coal trade. . . . He believed they were on the verge of a crisis the world had never yet realized.'[5]

During the early months of 1893 the Federation made a determined attempt to extend its influence to every coalfield in the country. Against the wishes of their leaders, the Durham miners had decided to join the Federation after the lock-out of 1892. The Northumberland miners were moving in the same direction and in March, 1893, Harvey, Cowey and Bailey were appointed by the Executive Committee of the Federation to address meetings in the county in order to counter statements which had been made at a meeting of the Northumberland miners'

[1] D.M.A. 31 May, 1892; Arnot, op. cit. p. 214.
[2] Derbyshire Times, 5 November, 1892.   [3] Ibid.
[4] D.M.A. 18 October, 1892; Derbyshire Times, 21 May, 1892.
[5] Derbyshire Times, 12 November, 1892.

Council and reported in the Newcastle papers.[1] The Northumberland leaders were as hostile to this delegation as the Durham leaders had been to the one on which Haslam had served in the previous year. Nevertheless, Northumberland was formally admitted to the Federation in the following June.[2] The leaders of Northumberland and Durham were perpetually in opposition to the policies of the Federation both before and after becoming members of it. South Wales was sympathetic but still tied to the sliding scale, and Scotland was poorly organized. The Federation's wages policy and the eight hours' question continued to prevent national unanimity.

Like the other counties, Derbyshire soon began to feel the effects of falling prices. On 7 February, 1893, the Executive Committee of the Association resolved: 'That the question of this Association appealing to the Federation to consider the advisability of a stop day, or two days, per week, go before the Lodges for their consideration.'[3] Three days later, at a meeting of the Executive Committee of the Federation, 'there was a general complaint in almost all Districts of Pits closing through men objecting to accept reduction'. In South Wales the latest ascertainment of the retail prices of coal called for a further reduction in wages of $7\frac{1}{2}$ per cent. in accordance with the sliding scale. The Executive Committee therefore decided to work for the twin objectives of restriction of output and action on a national scale by recommending 'that the Miners in all Mining Districts take a General Holiday, commencing on such date as a Conference called for the purpose may determine'.[4] The special national conference, which was held at Birmingham on 28 February to 1 March, was unable to agree on the desirability of taking a 'general holiday'. Haslam, who advocated a shorter working week, moved: 'That the recommendation of the Executive Board for a General Holiday, be not accepted by this Conference.' The resolution was carried by 133 votes to 117 but when Haslam attempted to gain support for Derbyshire's policy of having a weekly 'stop-day' he was defeated by 182 votes to 47. The matter was then referred to the Executive Committee and thus ended the Federation's last attempt at a concerted restriction of output.[5]

The position of the Derbyshire miners deteriorated rapidly during the first half of 1893. Although there was no formal reduction of wage rates many collieries were closed, short time was almost universal and attempts were made to reduce the cost of labour by various indirect methods. In February the Low Main seam at the Manners Colliery, Ilkeston, was closed, throwing about 70 men and boys out of work.[6]

[1] *M.F.G.B.* 16 March, 1893.   [2] *Ibid.* 29 June, 1893.
[3] *D.M.A.* 7 February, 1893.   [4] *M.F.G.B.* 10 February, 1893.
[5] *Ibid.* 1 March, 1893.   [6] *Derbyshire Times*, 18 February, 1893.

At Clay Cross, where the management wished to withdraw an allowance of 3d. a ton which had been granted to men working 'under the tops' at No. 4 Tupton pit, Haslam told the miners: 'He did not think they had much to fear with regard to reductions, except those made in an insidious manner outside public knowledge. . . . He would have liked the position better had an attempt been made upon the direct tonnage rate of the coal.'[1] The miners employed by the Pinxton Colliery Company emerged successfully from a dispute only to find that during the Whitsuntide holiday the management had erected two 'Billy Fairplay' machines, which made a difference of 1s. a day to the wages of face workers.[2] In June, J. and G. Wells, Ltd., informed the Eckington miners that they could not go on working their collieries unless there was a revision of wages.[3]

On 10 June, Harvey reviewed the situation in Derbyshire at a mass meeting of the Eckington miners. 'At the present time', he said, 'they had differences with almost every company in the county.'[4] The colliers were, in the words of the *Derbyshire Times*, 'on the verge of starvation'.[5] A correspondent of the *Clarion*, who visited Chesterfield, wrote:

There is a very large number of miners in Derbyshire—some say 25,000 or 30,000. There are, I was informed, about 15,000 in what may be called the Chesterfield district. Of these, about 9,000 are on two days' work a week. The remainder have no work at all. These simple facts speak with an eloquence of their own.[6]

There was much discussion about the remedies which should be adopted. The coal-owners believed that by reducing wage costs they would be able to regain some of their lost trade. They expressed views similar to those of Emerson Bainbridge who told his workmen at the New Hucknall Colliery: 'He did not grudge them their fair share in advances when trade was prosperous, but when it was declining it was but reasonable that they should also take part in the loss such decline caused.'[7] They argued that the reductions which had been accepted in Northumberland, Durham, South Wales and Scotland had attracted trade to those areas at the expense of the inland coalfields, which were already at a disadvantage because of high railway freight charges. The miners' leaders were blamed for this situation. 'What nonsense it is', said the *Derbyshire Times*, 'to boast that the men here are still in receipt of the full 40 per cent. advance. So they are! But at what a sacrifice.'[8] Both Josiah Court and Thomas Bayley dwelt upon the disadvantages

[1] *Derbyshire Times*, 29 April, 1893.
[2] *Ibid.* 10 June, 1893.
[3] *Ibid.* 17 June, 1893.
[4] *Ibid.*
[5] *Ibid.* 27 May, 1893.
[6] *Clarion*, 3 June, 1893.
[7] *Derbyshire Times*, 11 February, 1893.
[8] *Ibid.* 24 June, 1893.

THE UNVEILING OF THE MEMORIALS TO JAMES HASLAM AND W. E. HARVEY
at the Union's Headquarters, 26 June, 1915

suffered by the inland coalfields when they spoke at the miners' annual demonstration in 1893.[1]

The miners, on the other hand, were no longer prepared to accept the doctrine that wages should follow prices. They asserted that the wages which they had received in 1888 had been grossly inadequate and that there could be no question of their returning to that low level even if prices fell to the 1888 level.

'If low wages produced good trade', said Harvey, 'why didn't they have it in 1886–7, when wages were 40 per cent. lower than at present? . . . He did not feel justified in going to the employers and saying that they would accept less money with the hope that they would rob somebody else of a day's work who had already suffered a reduction. . . . To the employers they would say: "You may cut your own throats if you like, but you are not going to cut ours." '[2]

Similarly, Haslam argued that if a reduction in wages meant an increase in trade for Derbyshire 'it would simply mean taking it from somebody else, who again would have to undersell to recover it. It would be a bad game of beggar-my-neighbour till everybody got down to the bottom again.'[3] At a meeting at Brampton he told the miners: 'The Federation was gradually moving on to the time when those who produced the coal would have the fixing of the price. If, however, they broke their ranks, they left themselves open to attack.'[4] Harvey said:

He looked forward to a time when colliers would have fixity of tenure. By that he meant they could not be subjected to spasmodic changes, fluctuations, as they had been. He believed they had been the creatures of thimble-riggers and manipulators of the market. They had been made to believe they could go up and down according to the seasons, and so forth. He wished to get to the point to which the Federation was bringing them every day nearer when a ton of coal would be worth so much, and summer or winter the miners would be paid that so much for it.[5]

III

These theories were soon to be put to the test. On 23 June, at the request of the coal-owners, representatives of the Federation met representatives of the employers at the Westminster Palace Hotel to discuss the advisability of reducing wages. The meeting was adjourned until 30 June when A. M. Chambers, a Yorkshire coal-owner, stated the case for the employers and presented a formal demand for a 25 per cent.

[1] *Derbyshire Times*, 1 July, 1893.   [2] *Ibid.* 17 June, 1893.
[3] *Ibid.*   [4] *Ibid.*   [5] *Ibid.*

L

reduction in wages. (1893 = 140 per cent.) After giving innumerable examples of declining prices he concluded:

Wages were advanced on account of the improvement of trade, on account of the increase of prices, and now that prices have gone back in the way in which they have, we can only ask you to meet us by recommending your constituents to give us a substantial reduction on the present rate of wages to enable us to keep what little trade we have in the outside districts, and give relief to the manufacturers and others in the districts, so that we may see the end of bad trade reached and have some revival of trade.[1]

Alfred Hewlett, a Lancashire coal-owner, pointed out that whereas the average selling price of coal had fallen by 35 per cent., the employers were demanding only a 25 per cent. reduction in wages.

Pickard said that it would be necessary to refer the matter to the districts and then to a special conference, which would mean that about a month would elapse before a final reply from the men could be given. The employers thereupon agreed that their notices to terminate contracts should not expire until about 25 July. They also offered to submit the question to arbitration but Pickard showed little enthusiasm. 'The miners did not get any of the advances by arbitration', he said. When the miners' leaders were again reminded of the arbitration proposal by Fitzherbert Wright, of the Butterley Company, Thomas Ashton replied: 'Of course that would have to be laid before the men like the other questions.'[2]

Immediately after this meeting the Executive Committee of the Federation decided that it could not recommend the miners to accept any reduction in wages. The owners' offer of arbitration was ignored and the districts were recommended to deal with the wages question as soon as possible and to send delegates to a special conference at Birmingham on 18 July 'to say "yes" or "no" to the Owners' demand for a reduction in wages of 25 per cent.'.[3] Three days later a special meeting of the Council of the Derbyshire Miners' Association resolved: 'That we ballot all men working in the Collieries in Derbyshire as to whether they will accept the Employers' demand for a 25 per cent. reduction, or resist it.'[4]

The results of the ballot are not recorded in the Association's minutes, but according to the *Derbyshire Times* 19,864 of the 25,000 ballot papers issued were in favour of resisting the reduction. The newspaper was highly critical of the way in which the ballot was conducted:

Balloting paper! What a travesty of the name!... In Derbyshire there are 40,000 employed in and about collieries. The ballot papers were only issued

---

[1] *M.F.G.B.* 30 June, 1893.   [2] *Ibid.*
[3] *Ibid.*   [4] *D.M.A.* 3 July, 1893.

to coal getters, numbering 25,000. Of these, 19,864 voted against any reduction. Owing to the way the ballot papers were drawn up they could do no other, but these 19,864 miners have voted for the whole of the 40,000 men.

Arbitration was advocated as the ideal policy.[1] At a meeting of the Butterley Company's miners at Ripley Harvey affirmed his acceptance of arbitration 'rightly carried out' but criticized it 'when they had sold that which ought to be arbitrated upon'. He continued:

If the employers had met the leaders of the men and arbitration had taken place as to what price the coal should be sold at to gas companies, railway companies, and large consumers, and fixed the price to give the men a living wage, and the employers a fair return, he would have accepted that. . . . They had had a little of arbitration. He remembered one taking place, with regard to wages, in Sheffield, and the umpire was Judge Ellison. . . . A good deal was said about the disloyalty of the men, but what about the employers? On that occasion they kicked over the traces, and although the umpire said 'no reduction' they forced one right through the Midland counties. . . . Mr. Fitzherbert Wright had said 'and don't forget arbitration'. They hadn't.[2]

At a special conference on 19–20 July at Birmingham the delegates from Yorkshire, Lancashire, Cheshire, the Midland Federation, Derbyshire, South Derbyshire, Nottinghamshire, Leicestershire, North Wales and Cumberland all voted against accepting the proposed reduction in wages. The Durham miners were in favour of arbitration and were unable to give any assurance that they would be governed by the decisions of the conference. Northumberland was also opposed to resistance and was not prepared to pay any levy in support of those who might be locked out. A resolution 'to submit to no reduction in wages' was carried by a large majority despite Durham's amendment in favour of arbitration. Harvey, seconded by Cowey, then moved:

That this conference is of opinion that those districts who have suffered reductions in wages and who are now members of the Federation, should take a ballot vote within fourteen days, with a view to giving notice for an advance in wages equal to the reductions suffered during the last two years; and any district failing to comply with this resolution shall not hereafter be considered members of this Federation.

The resolution was carried by 199 votes to 50.[3] The attitude of Derbyshire towards Northumberland and Durham was also clearly expressed by Haslam at a meeting at Somercotes: 'If the northern men did desert them he knew what would happen. They would have to go out of the Federation. They could not keep a man in their lodge if he blacklegged in a strike.'[4]

[1] Derbyshire Times, 22 July, 1893.   [2] Ibid.
[3] M.F.G.B. 19 July, 1893.   [4] Derbyshire Times, 22 July, 1893.

On 21 July the miners' leaders again met the coal-owners' representatives and Pickard reported the Federation's decision.[1] The owners
could do little except renew their offer of arbitration. 'The owners have
thrown down the gauntlet', said Pickard, 'and placed us in an awkward
position. . . . Yes, war is declared.'[2] Four days later the Council of the
Derbyshire Miners' Association met at nine o'clock in the morning and
sat until five o'clock in the evening dealing with some forty resolutions,
many of which concerned the arrangements for the impending lock-out.
It was decided that men who were already on strike, locked out,
victimized or unemployed, should continue to be paid during the first
fortnight of the stoppage. Otherwise, strike payments were not to begin
until 18 August. Applications had been received from various collieries
asking to be allowed to continue working stone drifts and headings, and
repairing shafts, but it was resolved: 'That we carry out the resolutions
of the Birmingham Conference, and allow no man to go to work during
the stoppage, only to feed horses, get out water, put out gob fires, but in
no case must coal be turned.' The enginemen were recommended 'to
abide by the decision of the Federation, and accept no reduction in
wages'.[3]

On 25 July F. Parker Rhodes and T. Ratcliffe Ellis, the joint secretaries to the coal-owners' federation, issued a manifesto stating the case
of the employers. The first part of this document covered familiar ground.
It set forth the arguments which had been used by the chairman,
A. M. Chambers, at the meeting with the miners' representatives on
30 June. It showed that coal prices had fallen considerably since the
last increase was given and argued that the reduction in wages in Scotland, South Wales, Northumberland and Durham had put the coal-
owners of the federated districts at a disadvantage. As proof of this it was
stated that during the previous year the output of Scotland had increased
by 1,750,000 tons, of South Wales by 1,000,000, and of Northumberland
and Durham by 1,000,000.

The Derbyshire miners were, of course, well aware of this situation
but believed that the disadvantageous position of the inland coalfields
ought to be remedied by reducing railway rates rather than wages.
They had supported the coal-owners in their campaigns for lower
freight charges and better railway facilities for the county and at the
height of the 1893 crisis a mass meeting of the Clay Cross men assembled
to hear J. H. Watson, the secretary of the Railway Reform Association,
advocate the nationalization of the railways. He told them that the
carriage of coal by rail was often greater than the contract price of the
coal itself. From this he drew the conclusion that the miners appeared
to be working for the railways and advised them to boycott the railway

[1] M.F.G.B. 21 July, 1893.   [2] Ibid.   [3] D.M.A. 25 July, 1893.

companies by walking whenever possible. The meeting passed a lengthy resolution calling for a reduction in railway freight charges.[1]

Other points in the coal-owners' manifesto were effectively dealt with by Ashton, the Secretary of the M.F.G.B.:

The second paragraph stated that selling prices which were at their lowest point about July, 1888, began to improve, and an advance in wages of 10 per cent. was conceded. The facts are that no advance was given at that time, until all conciliatory means had failed, and a general demand was made by the miners, and notices given to cease contracts, and even then 30,000 miners in Yorkshire, and 6,000 in Derbyshire were on strike a week for the advance.

Miners' wages at that time were much too low, and their organization was powerless to act in their isolated state, to improve their position, and it was only by several counties uniting together that forced the Employers in 1888 to concede the advance of 10 per cent.

The second and third advances in 1889–90 were obtained with less friction, but when the fourth was asked for, and then demanded, the miners were met with strong opposition, and it was not until after near 200,000 miners had been on strike four or five days, the advance was conceded. . . .

When the last advance of wages was received in 1890, selling prices were not at the highest point, as Districts whose wages were regulated by a Sliding Scale proved. . . . The Federation of Great Britain were content for wages to remain at the rate then obtained and never asked for any further advance. The present rate is considered fair, and the Federation will fight hard to keep it. . . . The workmen's case is simple and clear. They did not reap their share of the profits on the high selling prices. They never asked for that. They struggled to establish a fair, just, and reasonable rate of wages, and having accomplished that, will fight campaign after campaign if needs be to keep it.[2]

IV

Mutual recriminations of this kind did not prevent the great lock-out from beginning in the last week of July, 1893. About 300,000 men were involved in the dispute. At a meeting of the Executive Committee of the Federation on 2 August, Harvey reported that 'all of the pits in Derbyshire were stopped except three, and these were under notice'. Similar stories came in from most of the other districts. Monmouth had not carried out the decisions of the Birmingham conference and was suspended from the Federation pending an explanation. A resolution was carried asking the Northumberland and Durham miners to seek advances in wages equal to the reductions which they had suffered during

[1] *Derbyshire Times*, 5 August, 1893.
[2] *M.F.G.B.* Note added to Minutes of Executive Committee Meeting, 21 July, 1893.

the previous two years. 'Now we know of a surety that prices have risen in London and other markets to the extent of 6s. per ton', stated the Executive Committee, 'and we are of opinion that if the men in these counties insist upon the advances they are certain to obtain the same'.[1]

The most surprising news heard by the Committee was the offer of several employers to pay the old rates of wages if work were resumed. The Midland coal-owners proposed that notices should be withdrawn on the understanding 'that no increase in wages should be asked for until prices came back to the 1891 level'. It was decided that these proposals should be considered at a conference on 23 August.[2]

The Derbyshire miners were opposed to any partial resumption of work. At a meeting of the Council, on 21 August, it was moved by Derbyshire Silkstone lodge and seconded by B Winnings lodge: 'That no pits in connection with this Federation be allowed to resume work, until a general settlement is made for all to commence work at the same time, and that our representatives support this policy at the Conference.'[3] Thomas Bayley, the Liberal Member of Parliament for the Chesterfield division, torn between his dual loyalties to the coal-owners and the miners, described the situation as 'a double lock-out'. He told a meeting of miners:

He understood that if he wanted to start his collieries at the old price to-morrow, he would not be able to get a man to go in. That was why he called it a double lock-out for a definite, clear purpose, which purpose was to clear the markets of the stock of coal, so that both masters and men might do better in the future. Colliery owners and colliers had, and ought to have, unity of interest.

But the comment of the Conservative *Derbyshire Times* was: 'To run with the hare and hunt with the hounds is always a difficult task.'[4]

Reports presented to the Federation conference on 22–23 August showed that all the collieries were still idle except for a few small, non-union pits which were difficult to control.[5] In Derbyshire, for example, the men employed at the Top Drift Colliery, at Stanley, continued to work on the understanding that their wages would not be reduced 'at least before the spring'.[6] The general picture, however, with the exception of Northumberland and Durham, was one of solidarity. Ralph Young, the secretary of the Northumberland miners, wrote to say that 6,943 members had voted in favour of handing in strike notices and 7,994 against. When the Durham representatives were asked what action they had taken to carry out the decisions of the Birmingham

[1] *M.F.G.B.* 2 August, 1893.   [2] *Ibid.*
[3] *D.M.A.* 21 August, 1893.   [4] *Derbyshire Times*, 19 August, 1893.
[5] *M.F.G.B.* 22 August, 1893.   [6] *Derbyshire Times*, 5 August, 1893.

conference, 'no clear answer was given'. After some discussion Harvey moved, and J. Walsh (Yorkshire) seconded: 'That we, the Representatives of this Federation, cannot allow the Durham Delegates to sit in this Conference, seeing this District, through their Officials, have not carried out the Birmingham Conference Resolutions.' The resolution was carried by 172 votes to 10 and Durham was thereby expelled from the Federation. A resolution calling for a delegation to be sent to Northumberland and Durham to 'explain the real position of the wage question' was moved by Haslam, seconded by T. Greenall (Lancashire) and carried unanimously. The conference re-affirmed its decision to accept no reduction in wages but agreed that if the coal-owners would withdraw their notices for a 25 per cent. reduction in wages, they would resume work immediately and not ask for an advance until prices had reached the 1890 level.[1]

There was a prolonged and lively discussion on the desirability of a partial resumption of work where the old rates were being offered. This policy was popular in Nottinghamshire, South Derbyshire and Staffordshire, where the union funds were running out and where many of the coal-owners were prepared to withdraw their notices for the 25 per cent. reduction, but with the Yorkshire, Lancashire and Derbyshire delegates committed to support the continuance of the general stoppage, the result was a foregone conclusion. By 120 votes to 64 it was decided: 'That no pit in this Federation be allowed to recommence work until a general settlement is made for all to commence at one and the same time.'[2]

The employers were unwilling to accept the proposals of the Federation for a general resumption of work at the old rates until prices reached the 1890 level and a meeting of the Executive Committee, on 1 September, decided to ascertain the feelings of the districts by asking them to take a ballot. The men were asked the following questions:

(1) Will you agree to 25 per cent. Reduction in wages, or any part thereof?
(2) Will you accept the Employers' offer of arbitration?
(3) Shall all men resume work who can do so at the old rate of wages?

The first two questions were based on the offers made by the employers. The third was a proposal of the Executive Committee.[3]

A special conference of the Federation was held at Nottingham on 14–15 September to consider the results of the ballot. The voting was overwhelmingly against accepting either a reduction or arbitration but more evenly divided on the third question: 61,923 were in favour of

---

[1] *M.F.G.B.* 22–23 August, 1893.
[2] *Ibid.* 22–23 August, 1893; *Derbyshire Times*, 26 August, 1893; *D.M.A.* 21 August, 1893.   [3] *M.F.G.B.* 1 September, 1893.

a partial resumption of work, and 91,369 against. In Derbyshire, however, there were only 1,604 votes in favour of this policy and 17,474 against. Some 16,510 miners in the Midland Federation (Staffordshire, Shropshire, the Forest of Dean, Somerset, Warwickshire, Gloucestershire) and in Cumberland were already back at work, and W. Whitefield, of the Midland Federation, seconded by A. Sharp, of Cumberland, moved: 'That where no reduction is asked for the men be allowed to return to work, providing that all men working for any Company, or at any colliery, return at once so far as the conditions of the pit or pits will allow.' This was defeated by the combined forces of Yorkshire, Lancashire and Derbyshire. Harvey then proposed, and J. Murray (Yorkshire) seconded, a resolution which was carried unanimously:

This Conference, after hearing reports from the Districts and recognizing this question has been decided by the ballot of the men, we advise the men to remain firm, as we still believe the 25 per cent. reduction is unwarrantable and uncalled for. At the same time we are prepared to return to work at the old rate of wages, and will meet the Owners to discuss in the interests of trade, the necessity of their demand being withdrawn.[1]

A copy of this resolution was sent to the coal-owners who replied that they were 'not prepared to encourage false hopes by accepting a meeting on such a basis', but at the same time they were 'quite willing to meet the Miners' representatives to discuss the proposed reduction'.[2] A special conference of the Federation assembled at the recently opened headquarters of the Derbyshire Miners' Association in Chesterfield, on 29 September, to consider this reply. On a motion by W. Parrott (Yorkshire), seconded by Haslam, it was decided not to meet the owners to discuss a reduction in wages 'so that no false hopes may be held out'. This was coupled with a renewal of the offer to return to work at the old rates of wages with a pledge not to seek any further increase 'until 1890 and 1891 prices are realized'.[3]

v

On the issue of the reduction in wages the opposing parties had reached a deadlock but there had been important changes on the question of a partial resumption of work. In Derbyshire a difference of opinion had developed between Haslam and Harvey. Haslam continued to favour the general stoppage and defended the policy until it became a lost cause. At a great open air meeting of miners at Alfreton he criticized Bailey, the Nottinghamshire leader, for holding mass meetings and advising the

[1] M.F.G.B. 14–15 September, 1893.
[2] Ibid. 29 September, 1893.　　　　　　　　　　[3] Ibid.

men to return to work at the old rates of wages where they could. 'They would', he said, 'by adopting this course, lose control over their forces and they would be unable to get that control back again if the policy were found to be unwise.'[1]

Harvey, on the other hand, began to speak in favour of a partial resumption of work. As a result of this he was misrepresented and misunderstood. One lodge secretary was reported to have said: 'If this is not a case of quick conversion, I don't know what is. . . . What is the Federation going to do with these districts who have violated the 20th rule?'[2] Harvey's *volte face* was later explained as follows:

Mr. Harvey has expressed himself favourable to this policy now that the Markets are empty and Works are stopping for want of fuel, believing it would either break up the Coal-Owners' Compact or cause a joint Meeting with Owners and make them more amenable to reason; but has always said this could not [*sic*] be done only by consent of the Federation who received the Mandate from the men, and whoever has put any other construction upon his utterances with regard to this subject has misrepresented him entirely. For as late as Council Meeting, September 19th, he protested against men working at small Pits near Chesterfield, it being contrary to Council and Federation Resolution.[3]

Nevertheless, the will of Haslam prevailed and, at the Chesterfield conference of the Federation, the Derbyshire delegates were able to report that they had held no meetings and would stand by their previous ballot. No other district was prepared to support the continuance of the general stoppage and it was then unanimously resolved: 'That where no reduction is asked for, the men be allowed to return to work, providing that all men working for any Company, or at any Colliery can return at once, so far as the conditions of the pit or pits will allow.' It was also decided that the men who resumed work should pay a levy of 1s. a day or 5s. a week for the support of those who continued to be locked out. Harvey then moved, and J. Murray (Yorkshire) seconded: 'That all levies paid by men who are working at the old rate of wages, grants from other societies, and subscriptions sent in to the Secretary, shall be equally distributed amongst the members of the Federation who are resisting the 25 per cent. reduction.' This was carried unanimously.[4]

Meanwhile the distress among the miners and their families was increasing daily. Even before the lock-out, poverty had been growing as a result of short-time working and the closure of many pits. In May it was reported: 'Trade, locally, is stagnant and amongst the colliers there is much distress.' Haslam and Harvey were criticized for enjoying 'a delightful Whitsuntide continental holiday' at the international

[1] *Derbyshire Times*, 23 September, 1893.   [2] *Ibid.*
[3] *D.M.A.* 19 September, 1893.   [4] *M.F.G.B.* 29 September, 1893.

L*

conference in Brussels and for spending excessive amounts of money on the new offices and houses whilst the miners were 'starving'. The Association was already then considering the possibility of making unemployment payments and the first grant of £500 was approved on 30 May.[1] The distress was intensified by the lock-out, and soup kitchens and relief funds were established in most of the mining centres. In the Chesterfield district alone, 9,150 free breakfasts were given to needy children during the second week in September.[2] At Tibshelf, Colonel Seely ordered the distribution of soup to his workmen's children.[3] The Langwith miners were provided with hares and rabbits by the Duke of Portland, the lessor of the colliery in which they worked.[4] The Bishop of Southwell wrote:

> The distress caused by the strike is extreme, and reaches far beyond those personally engaged in the strike itself, falling as it does on the workers in the other trades that require coal, but still more upon the smaller shopkeepers in the towns and villages, who not only lose their trade, but are constrained to give to those on strike, goods for which, in many cases, they will not be able even to pay themselves.[5]

The *Derbyshire Times* commented: 'Something is being done to keep the people from starving, but after all this, help can only be slight.'[6]

With hunger went disorder. Early in September disturbances began to be reported in most of the counties where the miners were locked out. The well-known Featherstone riot in which two men were killed and sixteen wounded by the military, on 7 September, added fuel to the fire and is still remembered with feeling even today.[7]

In Derbyshire the first outbreak of violence occurred at Killamarsh, on 28 August. At 6.30 a.m. a gang of labourers, drawn mainly from the non-union men of various collieries in the district, were set to work to fill waggons at the Holbrook Colliery of J. and G. Wells, Ltd. By 10 o'clock a crowd of 600 or 700 people was hooting and jeering at the unfortunate non-unionists and began to throw stones. About 300 of the demonstrators then marched upon the workmen who fled, twelve of them taking refuge in the engine shed. At this point police reinforcements arrived from Sheffield, Chesterfield and Dronfield, and the crowd was driven away from the colliery. Later, as six constables were escorting Lawrence Bell, a non-unionist, to his home, they were stoned. Haslam, who had recently become a magistrate, was called in to restore order: 'He deprecated violent conduct, and asked the colliers to behave

---

[1] *Derbyshire Times*, 27 May, 10 and 24 June, 1893; *D.M.A.* 2 and 30 May, 1893.
[2] *Derbyshire Times*, 16 September, 1893.   [3] *Ibid.*
[4] *Ibid.*   [5] *Ibid.*   [6] *Ibid.* 9 September, 1893.
[7] Arnot, *op. cit.* pp. 236–41; N. Dennis, F. Henriques and C. Slaughter, *Coal is Our Life*, (London), 1956, pp. 82–3.

as men. Their cause was a just one, and if they could not win by constitutional methods, they could not by violent ones.' At the same time he criticized the management for provoking the men.[1]

There were further disturbances in the Eckington district on 30 August. Again they centred round one of Wells's collieries. About 150 or 200 miners, armed with stones and heavy sticks, marched on the Hornthorpe Colliery, opened the points to the railway sidings, and sent two wagons, filled with slack, careering down a gradient of one in twenty and on to the main line. Three sets of gates at level crossings were destroyed and the main line was blocked. The prompt action of a railway signalman prevented an excursion train from crashing into the obstruction. An express train which was following closely behind, and a goods train which was due to pass in the opposite direction, were both stopped just in time to avert a serious accident. Meanwhile, the saboteurs had gone off to deal with ten more wagons in a similar fashion but when they realized that they had been observed by a colliery official they replied with a volley of stones and withdrew. 'The district', it was reported, 'is in a state of terror, and bands of men are patrolling the lanes after nightfall.'[2] At a meeting at Swanwick Harvey deplored the action of the men but, like Haslam, criticized the colliery company concerned:

It was such companies as these that were at the root of this disturbance and that started conflict. . . . Mr. Wells, of Eckington, some time ago, cut out of the *Derbyshire Times* a leading article and had it printed in circular form and distributed to his men as they came out of the pit. And why? Because it was an attack on himself and his colleague, and on the Association.[3]

On the same day as the Eckington riot there was a disturbance at Bolsover. A crowd of men gathered in a field near the colliery and demanded that the 'blacklegs' should be sent out. Despite assurances from J. P. Houfton, the manager, and Enoch Overton, the checkweigh-man, that there were no non-unionists at work, the crowd refused to disperse. Later a banksman was pursued by the men and saved from being roughly handled only by the intervention of the police and the local union leaders. Houfton subsequently admitted:

A little slack that was at the bottom has been loaded up. It is understood between myself, on behalf of the colliery, and the union officials, that this might be done without friction. . . . Then there has been some dissatisfaction for some days over our employing about 30 men in the pits repairing roads and finishing work at the bottom. This is a new colliery and there was a bit of work that we were bound to finish.

[1] *Derbyshire Times*, 2 September, 1893.   [2] *Ibid*.   [3] *Ibid*.

The men were not pacified until Overton led a deputation to Houfton and obtained an undertaking that all such work should cease.[1] On the following day there were further disorders. Tubs were overturned, windows were broken and a crowd of more than a thousand miners, headed by a man carrying a red flag, marched into the colliery yard. They were closely followed by the police but refused to disperse until six of the Bolsover workmen and six others had been allowed to descend the shaft and inspect the colliery.[2]

There were even more violent demonstrations in the southern part of the county. On 5 September there were serious disturbances in the Alfreton district. A crowd of several hundred men assembled at South Normanton, headed by the customary flag bearer. However, unlike the flag in North East Derbyshire, the colour was not the Socialist's red but black. The men marched towards Alfreton.

'In the main,' we are told, 'the bands were composed of irresponsible young fellows. . . . They stopped traps and demanded assistance from the occupants. . . . Many persons were frightened and intimidated into rendering monetary assistance which was soon disposed of in gallons of beer. This certainly had not a quietening effect. Finding themselves unmolested they practically took possession of public houses *en route*, demanding gallon after gallon of beer which was devoured in a speedily gluttonous manner.'

After creating an uproar in Alfreton they inspected a small horse-gin pit at Oakerthorpe and moved on to Shirland Colliery where other demonstrators joined them until about 3,500 people had assembled. The fillers who were at work there fled in all directions and one was roughly handled. Nine men then insisted on inspecting the pit and demanded that the manager should have two men employed at the pumps as the work was too much for one, and that a man who was employed 'spragging' should be brought out. These conditions were accepted by the manager and the crowd began to disperse when police reinforcements arrived from Alfreton. This had the effect of angering the men, many of whom were armed with sticks, stones, pieces of iron and even crow-bars.[3]

Meanwhile the Chief Constable of Derbyshire had asked for military assistance and within half an hour a detachment of the Royal Dublin Fusiliers had arrived from Sheffield, accompanied by C. P. Markham who came prepared to read the Riot Act. This duty was eventually performed by a local magistrate, Christopher Wood, of Swanwick, who was already on the scene, and the crowd began to melt away. On the evening of the following day a large gathering of miners at the Angel Inn, Alfreton, resolved:

That this meeting condemns the action of the authorities in drafting extra police and military forces into this town, believing that they contribute to

[1] *Derbyshire Times*, 2 September, 1893.   [2] *Ibid.*   [3] *Ibid.* 9 September, 1893.

disorder and riot, and calls on the authorities to withdraw them, and asks at the same time all miners to remain peaceable and orderly.[1]

Similar disturbances were reported from other parts of the county. At Ilkeston miners were said to be marching about armed with sticks and threatening violence to men who were working at the West Hallam Collieries. At Unstone and Dronfield men with blackened faces formed a procession, sang songs, drank and fought among themselves. A mob of about 200 men from Hucknall Huthwaite descended upon one of the Babbington Company's new pits at Tibshelf and carried off in triumph four men who had been assisting the sinkers.[2]

Gradually, more police and troops were drafted into the mining centres. Contingents of police from Sheffield, Leicester and the Derbyshire county constabulary arrived in Chesterfield within a few days of the first outbreaks of disorder. The Sheffield and Leicester police were quartered in the Market Hall where they played cards and read newspapers whilst their less fortunate Derbyshire colleagues passed their time by drilling at the Skating Rink.

'So far as can be learned', said the *Derbyshire Times*, 'there is no reason to anticipate a disturbance in the Borough of Chesterfield, though foolish rumours are flying about. . . . The miners are behaving in a most orderly manner, and if there is any outbreak it is believed it will be due to the rougher and thriftless element to be found in all towns, men who are not colliers or following any other occupation regularly.'[3]

A fortnight later the arrival from the Chippenham district of Wiltshire of a contingent of policemen wearing cutlasses caused some consternation but the Deputy Chief Constable of Chesterfield had the wisdom to order that these old police weapons should be stored away until the men went home.[4] In some areas the police reinforcements occupied their time by giving concerts in aid of the miners' relief funds.[5]

The troops stationed in the Alfreton area were reinforced by a company of the Second Dragoon Guards who were brought by special train from London.[6] Troops were also drafted into Chesterfield. The scene is vividly described by the *Westminster Gazette*:

A charming picture meets your eye the moment you leave the station. Down on a green plateau, sloping towards a clear little stream, a number of red-coats have pitched their camp. Seen from the square in front of the station, in an atmosphere which looks unnaturally clear after Sheffield, Rotherham, and the adjoining districts, you can hardly imagine a more idyllic scene of martial life. The white tents in the background, camp fires burning on the

[1] *Derbyshire Times*, 9 September, 1893.　　[2] *Ibid.* 2 and 9 September, 1893.
[3] *Ibid.* 2 September, 1893.　　[4] *Ibid.* 16 September, 1893.
[5] *Ibid.* 21 October, 1893.　　[6] *Ibid.* 16 September, 1893.

green, and chefs (for there seem to be a good many cooks engaged in preparing the soldiers' broth) passing among big lumps of raw meat and other foodstuff; the horses grazing or running according, apparently, to their own sweet wills; and groups of soldiers standing about everywhere, laughing, gossiping and enjoying their ease. It is a scene that would do credit to any London stage. Presently your eyes roam further, and you note that there is a curioūs background to the picture, for over the wall which separates the camp from the road hang a large number of men and boys. They form a striking contrast to the well-fed, warmly dressed soldiery. Their faces are pinched with cold and want of food; their eyes hang hungrily on the provisions in the camp, and they keep on changing their positions in order to keep their limbs from getting numbed with cold. These are the strikers, of course, and after you have watched them awhile you cease to think the animated camp scene pretty. On the contrary, it becomes a depressing outward and peaceable sign of the tragedy called a miners' strike. . . . Two hungry, white-faced men stand by the roadside, guarding a large basket. A board leans against the collecting box with this inscription—'Chesterfield Trades and Labour Council collection in aid of the miners'.[1]

The influx of troops and additional police forces aroused much indignation. Whilst condemning all forms of violence the miners' leaders argued that what had taken place had been greatly exaggerated in the Press, provoked by the employers, and exacerbated by the presence of the troops and the police. The Council of the Derbyshire Miners' Association resolved:

That the persons who are mainly to blame are the employers, through their unreasonable demands, for a reduction of 25 per cent. on wages, and also by breaking through the implied engagement that no men should be employed except to feed cattle, put out fires, and deal with water.[2]

J. A. (afterwards Sir Alfred) Jacoby, the Liberal Member of Parliament for Mid-Derbyshire, addressed the Pilsley miners on the Featherstone riot and condemned the presence in the county of 'a great many blue-coated gentlemen and some red-coats'. He thought 'it was a matter of congratulation in Derbyshire that there was little attempt at anything like violence'.[3]

VI

By the end of September the funds of the Derbyshire Miners' Association were rapidly dwindling and arrangements were made to borrow money and to mortgage the union's offices.[4] The decisions taken

---

[1] *Westminster Gazette*, quoted in *Derbyshire Times*, 30 September, 1893.
[2] *Derbyshire Times*, 16 September, 1893.
[3] *Ibid.* 23 September, 1893. [4] See Chapter VI, p. 248.

at the Chesterfield conference of the Federation resulted in very few men returning to work in Derbyshire. The Manners Colliery, Ilkeston, owned by Thomas Bayley, resumed work at the old rates before the Federation had reached any decision on the matter and the owners of the Salterwood, Denby, Ford's, Ripley and West Hallam collieries were all anxious to have the men back at the old rates as soon as possible.[1] The Butterley Company, on the other hand, was prepared to pay the old rates at its Staffordshire collieries but not in Derbyshire.[2] By the beginning of October only five or six collieries in Derbyshire had resumed work[3] but the resumption of work in other districts, and the levies which were paid in support of those who were still locked out, meant that a small amount of money came into Derbyshire to enable the struggle to continue.

Various attempts were made to end the dispute. The Bishop of Southwell, preaching a special sermon in Holy Trinity Church, Ilkeston, dwelt upon the widespread distress and suffering:

> He hoped that they would get some terms for resuming work now that the deadlock was doing harm and not good. He knew that they had put these things into the hands of the districts and great bodies could not be easily moved; but they were all reasonable. If they thought the strike was not for good, it was their duty to say so and to say upon what terms they would, as Englishmen, agree to a settlement.[4]

On 2 October the Mayors of Sheffield, Leeds, Bradford, Nottingham, Derby and Barnsley held a conference at Sheffield and decided to invite three representatives of the coal-owners and three representatives of the miners, with their respective secretaries, to meet them on 9 October 'when the Mayors named will be glad to lay before the said joint meeting such suggestions as it is hoped will form a basis of a just and satisfactory settlement'.[5] The Mayors proposed that the men should return to work at the old rates of wages, that they should submit to a 10 per cent. reduction six weeks later, and that a 'Tribunal of Conciliation' should be established to deal with future wage disputes. Neither the miners nor the owners were prepared to agree to these terms.[6]

Soon afterwards, a Federation conference was held at Birmingham on 12–13 October. The delegates re-affirmed their offer to return to work at the old rate of wages and not to seek any increase until the 1890–1 prices were realized. They also expressed their willingness, immediately after resuming work, 'to meet the coal-owners to try and devise means whereby dislocations of trade may not occur, such as are

[1] *Derbyshire Times*, 30 September, 1893.   [2] *Ibid.* 7 October, 1893.
[3] *Ibid.*
[4] *Ibid.* 16 September, 1893.
[5] *Ibid.* 7 October, 1893.   [6] *Ibid.* 14 October, 1893.

now in existence'.[1] It was reported that 59,974 men had returned to work and 255,687 were still locked out. Because of this situation Harvey again moved: 'That all men who resume work pay a levy of 1s. per day for each day worked during the continuance of the lock-out.'[2]

Harvey was firmly convinced that the partial resumption of work could have only beneficial results. He told the miners at Alfreton:

> Selfishness would, after all, lead them to victory, for the masters would not be prepared to stand by and see trade and prices disappear. . . . They had at present 70,000 miners at work at the old rate of wages and he was confident that the coal owners would still further become divided.[3]

Haslam, on the other hand, feared that the drift back to work might extend to those collieries where a reduction was still being insisted upon. The most dangerous defections from the coal-owners' associations were, in Haslam's eyes, those employers who offered to compromise by taking the men back at a smaller reduction than the 25 per cent. originally demanded. The Blackwell Company, for example, was prepared to allow its men to return to work at a 15 per cent. reduction. A similar offer was made at Bolsover where, it was reported, 'a strong force of Shropshire police are in charge of the colliery, and the management will give proper protection to any miners who agree to go to work at a 15 per cent. reduction'.[4] Haslam described such offers as 'a direct inducement to blacklegism'.[5] The *Derbyshire Times* was equally critical of this policy, but for different reasons:

> The infidelity of certain owners to the Coal-Owners' Association has been due to a desire to take advantage of the present famine rates in the coal trade, heedless of the almost absolute certainty of a rapid drop in prices as soon as the supply once more exceeds the demand.[6]

By the end of October, however, the coal-owners' association had officially moderated its demands and was prepared to accept a reduction of 15 per cent. This aroused much criticism. If the coal-owners were justified in asking for 25 per cent. at first, it was asked, why were they now going to be satisfied with 15 per cent.? A. M. Chambers, the Yorkshire coal-owner, later explained to representatives of the Federation that such criticism was 'based on a misunderstanding' and called attention to a subsequent coal-owners' resolution in which they re-affirmed their conviction that the state of trade entitled them to the 25 per cent. reduction and that the prevailing prices of coal were 'entirely artificial' but made their offer of a 15 per cent. reduction 'with a desire to end the present widespread distress and dislocation of trade,

---

[1] *M.F.G.B.* 13 October, 1893.
[2] *Ibid.*
[3] *Derbyshire Times*, 21 October, 1893.
[4] *Ibid.*
[5] *Ibid.* 14 October, 1893.
[6] *Ibid.*

and in deference to the appeals made to them, as contained in the suggestions of the Mayors'.[1]

But Thomas Bayley, himself a coal-owner, gave a different explanation. 'The fact is,' he said, 'the coal-owners who have entered into these big contracts have sold the men's labour before they have bought, and that is where they have made a mistake.' He pointed out that the coal-owner's liability to supply coal according to contract ceased on the day a strike or lock-out began and he regarded the initial demand for a 25 per cent. reduction with suspicion:

There has never been anything like it before. When the men come to us for increases they never ask for more than 10 per cent. at a time. . . . As it is, the big men and companies, especially those in Yorkshire, who are the ring-leaders in the movement, had only to bring this tremendous reduction upon the Federation to free themselves from their contract liabilities for the time being and clear off their accumulation of coal at a very handsome figure. . . . You must understand that it is not customary to dispose of more than from 50 per cent. to 75 per cent. of your output by contract, the rest goes into the open market. When prices reach a certain level, the coal-owners can recoup themselves out of the public for what they lose on the contract.[2]

This equilibrium had presumably been reached and it was now going to be more profitable for the owners to make concessions. Their representatives met the miners' leaders at the Westminster Palace Hotel on 3–4 November 'to debate the wages question without prejudice'. The coal-owners proposed a meeting of 'an equal number of Coal-owners' and Miners' Representatives, with the General Secretary of each body as *ex-officio* members, and three other persons to act as Conciliators'. The conciliators were to be agreed upon between the coal-owners' and the miners' representatives or, if no agreement were possible, to be nominated by 'a person in high authority'. They were to endeavour to bring about a settlement 'by arrangement or conciliation' but if this failed, the terms of the settlement were to be decided 'by a majority of the Conciliation Board including the Conciliators'. Pending the final settlement the men were to resume work on the following terms:

(1) The 15 per cent. off the advances now in dispute shall not be retained by the Employers or paid to the workmen, but shall be paid by each Coal-owner who is a party to this agreement each week into a separate account at the bank, to the joint credit of the Conciliators, to abide the decision of the Conciliation Board.

(2) When the final settlement of the present dispute has been arrived at, the amounts so paid into the bank with any accretions shall be distributed to the employers or the workmen in accordance with the terms of settlement.[3]

[1] *M.F.G.B.* 3 November, 1893.   [2] *Derbyshire Times*, 14 October, 1893.
[3] *M.F.G.B.* 3 November, 1893.

Following an adjournment for the miners' leaders to consider these proposals, Pickard explained to the employers the reasons for the Federation's refusal to accept them:

In the first place it presupposes, however lightly it may be put, a fifteen per cent. reduction. It may be said that if it is paid into the bank it will not be a reduction, but the admission of a fifteen per cent. being deducted from the workmen's wages further presupposes that the men believed a deduction should be taken to that extent.[1]

He then put forward the Federation's proposals which stipulated that the men should resume work at the old rate of wages until 1 April, 1894; that the minimum or standard rate of wages should be 30 per cent. above the wages rate of 1 January, 1888; and that a board of conciliation should be set up to deal with wage questions from 1 April, 1894.[2]

The employers were not prepared to accept the principle of a minimum wage.

'With regard to the very strong arguments which you have used about the living rate of wages,' said Chambers, 'I may remind you that we have offered facilities, and we offer those facilities again for testing whether your statements on that subject, or the statements which have been put forward on your behalf on the subject, are correct or whether the statements which we have put forward are correct.'

He then proposed the setting up of a 'Board of Conciliation' with an independent chairman to decide the rate of wages at which the men should return to work. Pickard argued that this was not conciliation but arbitration, and the joint meeting adjourned.[3]

The Federation delegates decided that the employers' offer to have the dispute settled by arbitration should be placed before the men as soon as possible.[4] Circulars, signed by Pickard and Ashton, were sent to all the districts. They set forth the employers' and the Federation's proposals and the employers' counter-proposals for submitting the dispute to arbitration. They concluded:

We cannot advise you to accept the Employers' terms of settling the dispute. We have been fighting for a living wage, and therefore, before coming to a final vote, we strongly urge you to read to your members the verbatim report of the proceedings of the Joint Conference in London. . . .[5]

The various proposals and counter-proposals for settling the dispute were considered by the Council of the Derbyshire Miners' Association on 9 November. Resolutions were carried regretting the proposals of the owners and accepting those of the Federation.[6]

[1] M.F.G.B. Reprint from Daily Chronicle, 5 November, 1893.
[2] M.F.G.B. 3 November, 1893.
[3] Ibid. Reprint from Daily Chronicle, 6 November, 1893.
[4] M.F.G.B. 4 November, 1893.
[5] Miners' Federation of Great Britain, Circular, n.d.   [6] D.M.A. 9 November, 1893.

VII

When the Federation conference assembled at Manchester, on 15 November, the delegates were unanimous in their rejection of the coal-owners' proposals but there was an important new development. Ashton reported that he had received a letter from the Prime Minister that morning. 'Her Majesty's Government', wrote Gladstone, 'have felt it their duty to make an effort to bring about a resumption of negotiations between employers and the employed, under conditions which they hope may lead to a satisfactory result.' He proposed a joint meeting of coal-owners' and miners' representatives under the chairmanship of Lord Rosebery, the Foreign Secretary.

'In discharging this duty', he continued, 'it is not proposed that Lord Rosebery should assume the position of an arbitrator or umpire, or himself vote in the proceedings, but that he should confine his action to offering his good offices in order to assist the parties in arriving between themselves at a friendly settlement of the question in dispute.'[1]

The invitation was promptly accepted and the conference embodied its future policy in the following resolution:

1. That all men, as far as possible, resume work at the old rate of wages until 1 April, 1894.
2. That a Board of Conciliation be formed to deal with the following questions:
 (a) To deal with the 30 per cent. minimum rate of wages.
 (b) Whether the difference in the standard rate of wages, namely, 40 per cent. on the 1888 rate shall be dealt with on the rates ruling prior to the stoppage or from the time work is resumed until 1 April, 1894.[2]

On 17 November the miners' and coal-owners' representatives assembled at the Foreign Office with Rosebery in the chair. Eventually a compromise was reached. The men were to return to work immediately, at the old rate of wages until 1 February, 1894, and a Board of Conciliation was to be established for the determination of the rate of wages after that date. The Board was to consist of fourteen representatives from each side and to elect its own independent chairman, or, in the event of disagreement, to ask the Speaker of the House of Commons to nominate one. The chairman was to have a casting vote.[3] On the following day, on a motion by J. Murray (Yorkshire), seconded by Haslam, the Federation conference, which had now moved to London, ratified the terms of the agreement.[4]

[1] M.F.G.B. 15 November, 1893. [2] Ibid.
[3] Ibid. 18 November, 1893. [4] Ibid.

The settlement was regarded by the miners' leaders with optimism. Haslam told the Tibshelf miners:

He looked to conciliation to do much. He was not going to say dogmatically, stupidly, that there might not come a phase of trade which would require some consideration in easing off the cost of production, but what had they been fighting? Not the German at Gibraltar, not the foreigner in any foreign part, but the men at home, who had been cutting one another's throat. They had been fighting the Midland Railway Company, the gas and other companies, and in his opinion a conciliation board would so stiffen the position and put backbone into the employers, that neither the Midland nor any other company would ever keep coal at the price they had had it, and by that basis wages would be able to be maintained. . . . It had been said, he believed, that the men had lost something like 15 per cent. for three years, but what had they gained? Like the battle between France and Prussia, it was the settling battle of the century, and a long while afterwards, he trusted.[1]

The employers took a different view of the outcome of the dispute. H. D. Pochin, the chairman of the Sheepbridge Coal and Iron Company, described the settlement as 'a senseless termination to a senseless strike'. He estimated the cost to the Company at more than £11,000 and told the shareholders: 'The prices of coal were likely to be maintained for some weeks—how many neither he nor anyone else could form a probable estimate—but he did not think they could expect prices to last much longer than the beginning of February, and then would come the struggle again.' He advised coal-owners to think about contributing to 'a sort of insurance fund' which would enable them to resist future strikes.[2] The *Derbyshire Times* regarded the 'minimum wage' as the 'crucial point' of the dispute: 'If the men adhere to their determination of the present wage as a minimum, it is useless for the Board of Conciliation to meet, for this stumbling block will be in the way of any agreement being come to.'[3]

The 1893 settlement can best be assessed by considering the extent to which the contending parties were successful in achieving their initial objectives. Mr. Page Arnot has represented it as a great victory for the Federation.[4] It is true that after a long and desperate struggle the men had gone back to work, for a time, at the old rates but, with coal at high prices because of the lock-out, this was to be expected. It is also true that the Board of Conciliation worked fairly well in so far as the Federated districts were able to maintain a minimum wage of 30 per cent. above the 1888 level whilst in other coalfields there were successive reductions. The Federation had shown its strength and the employers were not likely to enter lightly into a similar struggle in the future.

[1] *Derbyshire Times*, 25 November, 1893.   [2] *Ibid.*
[3] *Ibid.*   [4] Arnot, *op. cit.* pp. 252–8.

Nevertheless, the Federation had proclaimed two important principles at the outset of the dispute, both of which were ignored in the final settlement. The first was the right of the miners to have some control over the selling price of coal which, as Mr. Arnot himself has shown, was successfully challenged by the coal-owners when the rules of procedure for the Board of Conciliation were being drafted.[1] The second was the right to a minimum wage which the employers resisted at their meeting with the miners' leaders on 4 November. 'I am not aware', said Chambers, 'that this principle of a living wage has ever been applied to any other trade, at least not for centuries.'[2]

By the settlement, as Mr. Rowe has pointed out, 'the principle that wages must in the main follow prices had been reasserted'.[3] This was implicit in the establishment of the Board of Conciliation and its subsequent operations. Fortunately for the Federation, the trend of prices from 1887 to 1914 was upward and there was never any necessity for the coal-owners to demand a return to the 1888 level of wages. But the retention of the additional 30 per cent. was to become an achievement of diminishing importance as the price of coal and the cost of living continued to rise, and the issue of the minimum wage was again to come sharply to the forefront in the great dispute of 1912.

[1] *Ibid.* p. 253.
[2] *M.F.G.B.* Reprint from *Daily Chronicle*, 6 November, 1893.
[3] Rowe, *op. cit.* p. 36.

APPENDIX I

A Plea for the Locked-Out Colliers

The sailor on the stormy wave,
May find perchance a watery grave.
The soldier, too, at duty's call,
May on the field of battle fall,
But on the wave or in the strife,
The better chances are of life
Than his, who in some darksome mine,
Where sun, nor moon, nor star doth shine
But unseen death, and danger lurk,
To strike the miner at his work.
A spark, a flame, a whirlwind's sweep,
May thunder through those caverns deep,
And scorch or rend him limb from limb,
Till scarce a trace is left of him.
Or should he 'scape the flash and flame,
The deadly damp remains to claim
Its victims, and in slumber deep
Their senses seal in death's last sleep.
The Sailor ocean's peril braves,
Regardless of its winds and waves.
The soldier sentinel doth stand,
As guardian of our native land.
The ploughman ploughs the furrows deep.
The peaceful shepherd tends the sheep.
The rustic home the cattle brings.
His scythe the mower blithely swings.
The workers at the forge and mill
Their daily task of work fulfil.
But if the miner ceased his toil
To win from earth its buried spoil,
The mighty vessel, steam propelled,
Would as a captive bird be held.
No monster gun from turret's height
Would thunder forth old England's might.
The forge's blast no more would burn,
The whirling wheels would cease to turn,
And England's glory fade,
And vanish all her boasted trade.
If such the locked-out miners be,
Shall we stand by and tamely see
Their wives and famished children cry
For bread, and them the boon deny.

Nor aid in the unequal fight
Of labour 'gainst both wealth and might.
Hunger is sharp and hard to bear,
And victory won by want, despair,
Can never make a lasting peace
Nor labour's cry for justice cease.
Since then so much to them we owe,
The stream of charity should flow,
With pity, tenderness, imbued
To mark a nation's gratitude,
And help them in this hour of need,
By kindly word and generous deed,
Their rightful wages to maintain
And all they ask in justice gain.

                                    T. C.

Belper, 9 October, 1893.

[Probably written by Titus Cartwright (1844–1918), of Belper, a local preacher and miners' leader.]

CHAPTER IX

WAGES, DISPUTES
AND INDUSTRIAL POLICY, 1894-1910

I

Soon after the signing of the Rosebery agreement the miners' leaders turned their attention to the establishment of the Board of Conciliation. It was decided that the fourteen delegates who had attended the Rosebery conference should continue to represent the Federation until it held its annual conference in January, 1894.[1] As a result, both Haslam and Harvey attended the first meeting of the Board, at the Westminster Palace Hotel, on 13 December, 1893. At the annual conference, however, it was decided that the Federation should be represented by the Executive Committee and one other delegate. Haslam was elected to the Executive Committee but Harvey failed to secure election as the additional delegate.[2] The Derbyshire coal-owners were represented on the Board by Maurice Deacon and Arthur Barnes.

The main business of the first meeting was to appoint an independent chairman. Four names were submitted by the coal-owners and one by the miners, but it proved impossible to reach agreement.[3] It was agreed that the names of those suggested should not be divulged and they are not mentioned in the official records, but Harvey stated later:

It was a fact that at the Foreign Office, Lord Rosebery wanted to discuss the minimum wage question, and had time permitted his opinion on that question, it would have been settled then. That was the reason the employers objected to Lord Rosebery as chairman of the Board of Conciliation.[4]

In accordance with the terms of the Rosebery agreement the matter was then referred to the Speaker of the House of Commons.

Whilst the Speaker was deliberating, a second meeting was held, at which the miners submitted their draft rules of procedure. Their most

---

[1] *M.F.G.B.* 9 December, 1893. [2] *Ibid.* 19 January, 1894.
[3] *Ibid.* 13 December, 1893. [4] *Derbyshire Times*, 14 April, 1894.

important proposal was that there should be a 'standard rate of wages', which would be 30 per cent. above the 1888 level, and that the Board should have power only to deal with wages above the standard rate. They also proposed that the Board should have power 'to deal with the selling prices to be charged to Householders, Railways, Gas Companies, and Manufacturers' and 'to demand the books in order to ascertain selling rates, profits, and cost of production'. The employers were not prepared to accept the proposals.[1]

On 25 January, 1894, A. W. Peel, the Speaker of the House of Commons, wrote to T. Ratcliffe Ellis and Thomas Ashton, the joint secretaries of the Conciliation Board, informing them that he had nominated Lord Shand to be the chairman. At the third meeting of the Board, on 14 February, it was agreed that the appointment of Shand should be 'cordially accepted' and that the whole code of rules should be brought before him at the next meeting.[2] Thus it was not until the fourth meeting, on 3 April, that the Board was fully constituted and its rules of procedure adopted.[3] Shand swept aside all the contentious proposals which had been made by the miners and, in doing so, incurred great unpopularity. His most outspoken critic was William Bailey, the Nottinghamshire leader, who described him as 'a biased partisan and unfitted to occupy such a responsible position'.[4] Bailey contended that Shand 'ought not to have been in so big a hurry to strike out all the miners wanted and leave in everything the owners wanted'.[5] It was, however, the official policy of the Federation that the Rosebery settlement was a great victory and, on 17 April, the Conciliation Committee, which consisted of the Executive Committee and J. Wadsworth (Yorkshire), censured Bailey and accepted his assurance 'that he had no intention of casting any reflection upon Mr. Pickard or any of the Miners' representatives of the Conciliation Board in the statements he has made'.[6]

The Derbyshire leaders were much more cautious than Bailey in their comments on the situation. Haslam told the Alfreton men:

He was very sorry that a colleague (Mr. Bailey) had used the language he had done with regard to Lord Shand. . . . He must admit that although disappointed—and every one of the miners' delegates must have been disappointed at not getting all they asked for—he was not surprised that there should have been objections to incorporating in the rules of procedure the points to which they attached so much importance. . . . He thought reasonable men would deprecate the unwisdom of provoking a quarrel simply over the rules which were to govern the proceedings of their meeting.[7]

[1] *M.F.G.B.* 8 December, 1893; *Derbyshire Times,* 20 January, 1894.
[2] *M.F.G.B.* 14 February, 1894.   [3] See Appendix I to this chapter.
[4] Griffin, *op. cit.* p. 105.   [5] *Derbyshire Times,* 14 April, 1894.
[6] *M.F.G.B.* 17 April, 1894.   [7] *Derbyshire Times,* 14 April, 1894.

Harvey, addressing a meeting at Ripley, said that others might condemn the action of Lord Shand in refusing to accept the minimum wage as one of the rules of the Conciliation Board but he advised the men 'to wait patiently for developments'.[1]

They did not have to wait long. By the end of May the effects of the shortage of coal caused by the lock-out had completely disappeared and prices had resumed the precipitous decline which had set in after the boom of 1890. The Scottish miners, who had not been involved in the 1893 lock-out but had joined the Federation in large numbers soon afterwards, were all facing reductions in wages after a long and bitter strike. The miners of Cumberland and Somerset were also being asked to accept reductions. At the Federation conference held at the County Hotel, Carlisle, on 29–30 May, every district reported that trade was bad. In Derbyshire there were 200 men out of work and the pits were working about three days a week. It was resolved: 'That all Districts belonging to this Federation, where reductions in wages have recently taken place, be requested to give a proper notice for the same to be returned, and we are favourable to a levy being made to support them.'[2] Haslam and W. Parrott (Yorkshire) were later sent by the Executive Committee to Somerset to stiffen resistance there but were unable to prevent the acceptance of a 10 per cent. reduction.[3]

On 30 May the coal-owners asked for a meeting of the Conciliation Board 'to consider an application for an alteration in the rate of wages'. The Executive Committee of the Federation refused to agree to this request on the grounds that it was not in accordance with Rule 9 which stated: 'The application for the meeting shall state clearly the object of the meeting.'[4] Pickard argued that the coal-owners should specify the amount of the proposed reduction. His refusal to act jointly with Ratcliffe Ellis in calling a meeting of the Board led Ellis to act alone. There were two meetings of the Board, on 19 June and 3 July, which the miners' representatives did not attend. Ellis then suggested that an informal meeting should be held on 6 July to end the deadlock over the rules of procedure. After a lengthy discussion the employers agreed to amend their request for a meeting of the Board by stating that they wished 'to reduce the present rate of wages by taking off the last two advances of 5 per cent. each, as given in each District'.[5]

The meeting then considered the question of the minimum wage. After a series of separate discussions, with deputations passing from room to room, the following suggested terms of settlement were drawn up, without prejudice to either side:

[1] *Derbyshire Times*, 14 April, 1894.
[2] *M.F.G.B.* 29–30 May, 1894.
[3] *Ibid.* 6 June, 16 June, 1894.
[4] *Ibid.* 6 June, 1894.
[5] *Ibid.* 6 July, 1894.

1. That the present rate of wages be reduced, as from the 1st August, 1894, by taking off the last two advances of 5 per cent. each, and that the wages remain at that rate until the 1st January, 1896.

2. That for a period of two years from the 1st August, 1894, the rate of wages shall not be below 30 per cent. above the rate of wages of 1888, nor more than 45 per cent. above the rate of wages of 1888.

3. That from the 1st January, 1896, to the 1st August, 1896, the rate of wages shall be determined by the Conciliation Board, within the above named limits.

4. That the Conciliation Board shall be continued for this purpose, for two years from 1st August, 1894.[1]

Haslam spoke strongly in favour of the proposals at Clay Cross:

He believed that last year men would have thrown up their hats at the suggested arrangement the employers now gave them the opportunity of accepting. If the men agreed, all well and good; if not, they would be taken before Lord Shand, and the employers would get what they could. The offer of a minimum wage would be withdrawn, and at the end of November they could if they cared, go back into the old arena of quarrel and fight.[2]

But the Derbyshire miners were not convinced. When ballot papers were sent to all members of the Association, only 9,488 were returned. Of these, 4,907 were in favour of the proposed settlement, and 4,581 against. Nevertheless, at the Federation conference, in London, on 18 July, Haslam wielded his voting power of 18,000 in favour of accepting the proposals. The conference itself was by no means unanimous: the settlement was approved by 99,500 votes to 57,500. Yorkshire, the Midland Federation, Derbyshire and North Wales voted for the proposed terms: Lancashire and Cheshire, Nottinghamshire, Leicestershire and South Derbyshire voted against.[3]

On 19 July the Board of Conciliation met to deal with the matter formally, and the coal-owners, as they had promised, presented their case for the proposed wage reduction of 10 per cent. For each district they provided the average selling price of coal at a number of representative collieries for the three months ending 30 November, 1890, after the last increase was granted; and for the three months ending 31 July, 1893, the period immediately before the lock-out. They also provided the average selling price for the month of May, 1894. For twenty companies in Derbyshire and Nottinghamshire the average prices were 7s. 3·9d., 6s. 0·15d. and 5s. 9·62d. respectively. The coal-owners also argued that the volume of trade had contracted. Thus, the average number of days worked per week in Derbyshire and Nottinghamshire had fallen from 4·96 in November, 1890, to 3·23 in May, 1894.

[1] *M.F.G.B.* 6 July, 1894. [2] *Derbyshire Times*, 14 July, 1894.
[3] *M.F.G.B.* 18 July, 1894.

It will be noted that no allowance was made, in these comparisons, for the seasonal decline in trade and the miners' leaders were rightly suspicious of the periods which had been chosen. The employers argued that they were entitled to a much greater reduction than the 10 per cent. they were claiming and urged the necessity of a compromise. Eventually the miners' leaders agreed to accept the proposals which had been drawn up at the informal meeting on 6 July.[1]

Twenty-one owners in Derbyshire had expressed their willingness to abide by the decisions of the Conciliation Board[2] but the Staveley Company was a notable exception. The following exchange took place between Haslam and Chambers:

Haslam: Might I ask if you read out the Staveley Company in Derbyshire?
The President: No, it was not read. The Sheepbridge Company was read out, and they have nearly the same Directors you know.
Haslam: But still Sheepbridge is not Staveley.
The President: No, it is not.
Haslam: I was only asking the question for information. I do not want to go away with a wrong impression.

Eventually it was decided that the agreed terms should apply to all firms whose names were handed to Ashton by Ellis on or before 31 July.[3]

This was the real settlement of the 1893 dispute. It was welcomed by the Executive Committee of the Derbyshire Miners' Association as a breathing space: 'We trust our members will accept the settlement as being the best possible under the circumstances, and remain true to the Union, thereby strengthening the exchequer of the Association, and so prepare themselves for any emergency that may happen in the future.'[4] Haslam commented:

The unrest caused by the wage question being re-opened during the last few weeks, has been a most anxious time . . . and we are not surprised at the

---

[1] *M.F.G.B.* 19 July, 1894. The information was obtained from the Blackwell Colliery, Grassmoor, Clay Cross, Netherseal, Wingerworth, Hardwick, New Hucknall, Stanton Ironworks Company, Butterley Company, Sheepbridge Coal and Iron Company, Pinxton Colliery, Riddings Colliery, J. and G. Wells, Ltd., Albert Colliery, Coppice and Woodside Collieries, Pentrich Colliery, Oakwell, Norwell Colliery, Glapwell Colliery and Langwith Colliery.

[2] W. C. Haslam (Pentrich Colliery), James Oakes and Company (Riddings Collieries), J. and N. Nadin and Company (Stanton Colliery), Brewis Brothers (Boythorpe Colliery), Clay Cross Company, C. R. Palmer Morewood (Swanwick Colliery), Blackwell Colliery Company, Sheepbridge Coal and Iron Company, Wingerworth Coal Company, Grassmoor Company, Hardwick Colliery Company, Coke and Company (Pinxton Collieries), Stanton Ironworks Company, Joseph Springthorpe (Calow Colliery), Diminsdale Colliery Company, Butterley Company, Mapperley Colliery Company, J. and G. Wells, Ltd. (Eckington Collieries), Ashmore and Sons (Holme Close Colliery), Derbyshire Silkstone Company (Albert Colliery), Derby Kilburn Colliery Company (Stanley Kilburn Colliery).

[3] *M.F.G.B.* 19 July, 1894.   [4] *D.M.A.* 25 July, 1894.

uneasiness manifested amongst our Members. As to the settlement, no one likes reduction in wages. Still, we believe the right thing has been done in accepting a reduction of 10 per cent., with a minimum of 30 per cent. on 1888 prices for two years. It is the first time in the history of Trades Unions that a minimum wage has been obtained.[1]

The gains derived from this settlement were of doubtful value. The important principle of the minimum wage had been conceded by the employers, but only for two years. Unfortunately for the miners they were years of deepening depression, and the artificially high wage rates which they had managed to maintain were more than counter-balanced by short-time working. Thomas Bayley stated in the House of Commons, in April, 1894, that the miners of Derbyshire and Notting-hamshire were only working 4 or 4½ days a week.[2] Another estimate was: 'I wish this were so. It would be nearer to say only 1 or 1½, as an average.'[3] The problem was particularly acute at the Grassmoor Collieries. Haslam alleged that the men were being kept on short time as a punishment for not returning their employer to Parliament but Alfred Barnes stated:

We have refused large orders at ruinous rates, simply because we were determined to maintain prices and have in consequence had to work less time. . . . Because we are genuinely endeavouring to maintain prices, we are abused by the very men who, a short time ago, were advising us to do this very thing.[4]

The final settlement of July, 1894, merely intensified the problem of maintaining prices. By removing the incentive to speculative buying it led to an even greater stagnation in the coal trade. On 4 August it was reported: 'On the London Coal Exchange the effects were very marked . . . the business done was extremely light, only hand to mouth orders being given.'[5] By the summer of 1895 short-time working was even more serious than it had been in the previous year. The following figures, taken from the wage sheets of one of the largest collieries in Derbyshire, give some indication of the decline in miners' earnings during the period:

	Average number of days worked per week	Total wage bill (1892–3 = 100)
1892–3	4·00	100
1893–4	2·26	64
1894–5	2·16	43

At another large colliery the miners were working five days a week at

[1] D.M.A. 25 July, 1894.
[3] Derbyshire Times, 28 April, 1894.
[5] Ibid. 4 August, 1896.
[2] 23 H.C. Deb. 4s. 1349.
[4] Ibid. 7 April, 1894.

7s. 6d. or 8s. a day in 1892 compared with one or two days a week at 6s. 9d. or 7s. 6d. a day in 1895.[1] Haslam told the New Tupton miners:

Since 1893 the great bulk of the men near that locality had had very little steady employment, and there was, therefore, a good deal of excuse for the remissness of the men in keeping up their connection with the union. . . . They ought, however, to bear in mind the fact that if they had any large falling off in membership, they had a disease of a very contagious character.[2]

Nevertheless, membership was to decline from 18,968 in 1893, to 15,142 in 1896.

One of the principal issues, so far as Derbyshire was concerned, was the competition from the northern coalfields where the miners had accepted substantial reductions in wages. The employers maintained that if the Derbyshire miners would accept similar reductions they would be able to compete more effectively for the available trade, and short-time working would be considerably reduced. 'According to the masters' theory', said Harvey, 'the men of the Midlands ought to fight those of the North by competition, until, like the Kilkenny cats, they had eaten each other.'[3] The *Derbyshire Times* commented:

It is absurd for the local colliers to continue cutting their own throats, whilst their brethren in the North are mulcting the spoils. . . . If the miners' union of the country is not strong enough to prevent men in one district accepting lower wages than those of another, no wonder the men locally are growing disgusted at paying money into an organization whose *raison d'être* ought to be universal unity of action, by which alone the men obtain equal wages.[4]

The situation was complicated by the failure of the miners' leaders to realize the necessity of developing new and more economic collieries. They assumed that because output was steadily increasing and more pits were being sunk, the coal-owners were deceiving them when they said that trade was bad and collieries were running at a loss. In 1894, Haslam, referring to the developments being carried out by Emerson Bainbridge, said:

He could not understand why employers, who were publishing the importance of selling coals remuneratively, were at the same time always scheming for additions to their plant and extending their operations. . . . Sinking pits at such times, and thus overstocking the market, was not the way to keep up prices.[5]

In the following year Harvey said:

[1] *Derbyshire Times*, 13 July, 1895.   [2] *Ibid.* 7 September, 1895.
[3] *Ibid.* 26 October, 1895.   *Ibid.* 21 September, 1895.
[5] *Ibid.* 7 April, 1894.

There was no outlook—if speculation was anything to go by—that was so bright as the coal trade. If it was a game in which hope had been lost, how was it that they found Emerson Bainbridge, the Staveley Company, and the whole lot of them spying out the minerals as fast as they could, and laying down large plants. . . . The great families of Derbyshire could get houses and hunting studs, and the family that used to have one family house could now have several. There was no firm in Derbyshire other than limited liability companies—and they had been working on borrowed money—that had failed during the last thirty years.[1]

II

After 1 January, 1896, the Federation was free to demand an increase in wages but, as wages were then on the agreed minimum, the coal-owners were unable to demand a reduction until the termination of the agreement on 1 August, 1896. On 11 November, 1895, the Council of the Derbyshire Miners' Association passed a resolution recommending the annual conference of the Federation 'to ask the Employers for the 10 per cent. conceded in 1894, and make the 40 per cent. upon 1888 prices the minimum rate of wages for a time, to be agreed upon by the Conference'.[2] In the same month, however, the Executive Committee of the Federation decided to recommend that the existing wages arrangement should not be disturbed, although it was reported that everywhere the output of coal was greater than it had been in the past.[3]

Soon afterwards there were negotiations with the coal-owners on the future of the Conciliation Board. The owners proposed that it should continue in accordance with the Rosebery agreement but they were not prepared to recognize the existing minimum wage, demanding instead a further reduction of 10 per cent. Haslam and Harvey were, at this time, both members of the Executive Committee of the Federation and therefore members of the Board. They both expressed the view that, without the minimum wage, having the Board would be no better than having a sliding scale.

'They were not', said Haslam, 'going to agree to any Conciliation Board with an independent chairman. Why? The inevitable result would be a $2\frac{1}{2}$ or a 5 per cent. reduction. . . . If they came to that position, the sooner they established a sliding scale the better. What he objected to was this—that in these days of competition the wages of working men should be decided by men underselling each other in the coal trade.'[4]

[1] *Derbyshire Times*, 12 October, 1894. [2] *D.M.A.* 11 November, 1895.
[3] *M.F.G.B.* 20 November, 1895. [4] *Derbyshire Times*, 18 April, 1896.

Harvey described the owners' proposal as 'nothing more nor less than accepting the principle of a sliding scale, and one without any bottom, as in ninety cases out of a hundred, whoever might be chairman, he would take the selling prices on the Exchange and contracts made for gas, iron and railway companies as a basis on which to found his decision'.[1]

After several meetings of the Conciliation Board, at which no agreement was reached, the negotiations broke down. The joint agreement governing the Conciliation Board came to an end on 31 July, 1896, but the employers made no attempt to secure their proposed reduction in wages. According to Mr. Page Arnot, 'No joint meeting took place for two years. But during that two years wage rates remained steady.'[2] After their experiences of 1893 the employers were not prepared to enter into a full scale conflict with the Federation on the formal matter of wage rates. Harvey told the Grassmoor miners: 'There might be sectional fighting now that the Conciliation Board was at an end but, granted a united body of men, he promised any employer in the country who tried it on a very warm time of it.'[3] Nevertheless, prices were still falling and the employers tried to reduce their costs in a variety of ways. In Derbyshire, 1897 was a year of local strikes. In the words of Harvey: 'It appeared that there was a determination on the part of the owners of Derbyshire to nibble wherever they could.'[4] Towards the end of the year, however, prices began to rise and in the spring of 1898 the Federation claimed an increase in wages of 10 per cent.

On 6 July the owners' representatives met the miners' representatives and offered to increase wages by $2\frac{1}{2}$ per cent. from 1 October if the miners would agree to the establishment of a new Conciliation Board. It was to come into existence on 1 January, 1899, for a period of two years. During that time wage rates were not to be less than 30 per cent., nor more than 45 per cent., above the 1888 levels.[5] The scheme was warmly commended by Haslam, Harvey and Jarvis. In a circular addressed to all members of the Association they said:

We have no hesitation in advising, in the strongest possible manner, your acceptance of the offer of 6th July, viz. $2\frac{1}{2}$ per cent. and the subjoined conditions. The alternate [sic] proposal is very much worse, as you have to prove before the umpire that you are entitled to anything at all. In the face of South Wales having resumed work on conditions known to you, the visits to Northumberland and Durham, and the fact that the June ascertainment of prices is 6d. per ton lower than March last, we know we are advising you for the best. The only other alternative is to tender notices to terminate contracts,

[1] *Derbyshire Times*, 25 April, 1896.   [2] Arnot, *op. cit.* p. 308.
[3] *Derbyshire Times*, 22 August, 1896.   [4] *Ibid.* 20 March, 1897.
[5] *M.F.G.B.* 6 July, 1898.

and chance the outcome of another struggle equal to the one in 1893, and this, with public opinion and the Press against us. Men, be wise and accept the offer of 6th July, 1898.[1]

After much discussion the offer was accepted by both Derbyshire and the Federation. Towards the end of the year it was announced that Lord James of Hereford, who had been nominated by the Federation with the consent of the employers, had accepted the position of independent chairman to the Board. In doing so, he wrote: 'I must add my satisfaction that in the 11th of your rules of procedure some powers of determination between the different interests are conferred upon the chairman of the Board.'[2]

In periods of rising prices the miners had never experienced much difficulty in securing small increases in wages, and they now entered upon such a period of prosperity in which the new Board worked well. In 1899, in response to a request for an increase of $7\frac{1}{2}$ per cent., they were awarded 5 per cent. in April and a further $2\frac{1}{2}$ per cent. in October. Towards the end of the year a new agreement was drawn up. It provided for the continuance of the Board from 1 January, 1901, until 1 January, 1904. The minimum wage was to remain at its previous level but the maximum was to be raised to 60 per cent. above the 1888 standard. Wages were also to be increased by 5 per cent. from 1 January, 1900, and, for the first time, surface workers were specifically included in the agreement. Harvey spoke strongly in favour of the new agreement at the annual conference of the Federation at Cardiff, in January, 1900: 'The suggested settlement was one of the best the world had ever known and . . . it would redound to the honour of every man who took part in it.'[3] Haslam told the Staveley miners: 'Peace is guaranteed for years to come.'[4]

The boom year of 1900, however, caused some discontent among the miners. They were already receiving increases amounting to 45 per cent. but were unable to claim more until the new maximum came into operation on 1 January, 1901. Speaking at Langwith, in August, 1900, Haslam said: 'There was a general opinion amongst the men that they were not reaping the benefit from the prosperity of the coal trade that they ought, but they were bound to abide honourably with the agreement.'[5] Eventually the employers agreed to give an advance of 15 per cent. in three instalments: one of 5 per cent. in October, which would anticipate the new agreement, and two of 5 per cent. in January and February, 1901. In this way the new maximum of 60 per cent. above the 1888 standard was reached within the first two months of the new

[1] *Derbyshire Times*, 17 September, 1898. [2] *Ibid.* 24 December, 1898.
[3] *M.F.G.B.* 9 January, 1900.
[4] *Derbyshire Times*, 21 July, 1900. [5] *Ibid.* 25 August, 1900.

M

agreement which still had another two years and ten months to run. The price of coal, however, had risen by about 113 per cent. since 1888.[1]

This unsatisfactory aspect of the Conciliation Board agreements led the men to seek their share of the increased profits by demanding improvements in their basic price lists. This was a violation of the agreements, to which the employers rightly objected at a meeting of the Board on 13 February, 1901. The miners' leaders were themselves partly to blame for recommending the acceptance of the agreements. The men argued that there had been changes in working conditions since 1888 and that although the price lists had been agreed upon, yet they were accepted at a time when their bargaining power was weak.[2] Some of the district leaders found themselves in a difficult position. In Derbyshire, there was a particularly bitter dispute at the Blackwell Colliery towards the end of 1900. J. T. Todd, the general manager, wrote to Harvey:

> I am at a loss to understand why you ask for this [a revision of the price list] after your expression made publicly, viz. 'That the men could not, so long as the present agreement existed, get an advance on tonnage prices.' I wish also to point out that the present lists were signed by you in 1891, and since then there has not been any reduction made in the basis prices. . . . I must ask you to honourably carry out the Conciliation Board Agreement with regard to tonnage rates.[3]

III

During 1901 selling prices began to fall and in the following year the employers demanded a reduction in wages of 10 per cent. The miners' leaders argued that the reduction should be postponed on the ground that the men did not benefit to the full extent when the boom was at its height. Eventually it was recommended that there should be two reductions of 5 per cent. in June and August.[4] The matter was referred to the districts and, in Derbyshire, as elsewhere, there was considerable opposition. The men contended that the coal-owners' application was premature. The Staveley Company's miners decided almost unanimously to instruct their delegates to vote against any reduction despite recommendations to the contrary by Haslam and Harvey.[5] Harvey argued that the coal tax, and the wage reductions in Northumberland, Durham and South Wales, made the acceptance of the Board's proposals inevitable. 'It was at such crises as the present', he said, 'that leaders

[1] See Chart 5. For coal prices see Chapter V, Appendix II. For wage rates see Chapter X, Appendix I.
[2] *M.F.G.B.* 13 February, 1901.   [3] *Derbyshire Times*, 1 December, 1900.
[4] *M.F.G.B.* 1 May, 1902.   [5] *Derbyshire Times*, 10 May, 1902.

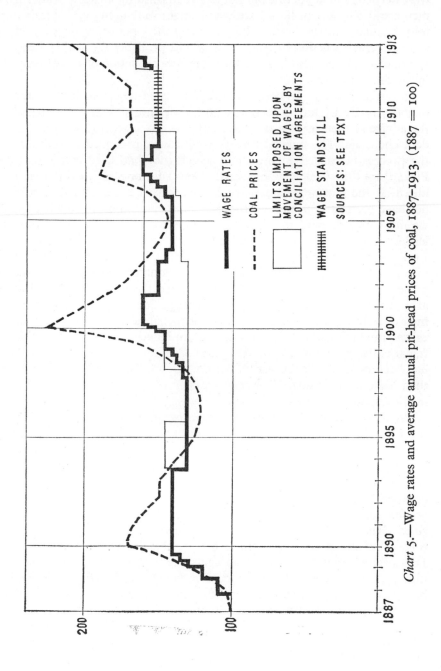

WAGE RATES

COAL PRICES

LIMITS IMPOSED UPON
MOVEMENT OF WAGES BY
CONCILIATION AGREEMENTS

WAGE STANDSTILL

SOURCES: SEE TEXT

Chart 5.—Wage rates and average annual pit-head prices of coal, 1887–1913. (1887 = 100)

were needed, and he for one did not desire to continue to act as leader if men could only accept his advice when wages were going up.'¹ Haslam told the miners at Ilkeston: 'If they rejected the 5 per cent. in June and a 5 per cent. reduction in August, it would probably mean that Lord James of Hereford would award an immediate reduction of 10 per cent. in the present month.'²

Nevertheless, the proposed reductions were rejected by a large majority in Derbyshire. Lancashire and Yorkshire similarly repudiated the advice of their leaders and the matter was referred to the independent chairman. The miners' leaders would have preferred to continue the process of collective bargaining which they had used in the past. Pickard told the Conciliation Board: 'Now I for one, if I had the least idea that the recommendation would not have been accepted, would not have been party to the scheme, because departing from conciliation we must now proceed to arbitration.'³ The worst fears of the miners' leaders were realized when, after a meeting of the Board on 14 June, Lord James awarded a 10 per cent. reduction in wages from the first making-up day in July.⁴ Haslam told the Eckington miners: 'Until the present occasion the Board had never entered the phase of a board of arbitration, and it had been forced into that position by the action of the men in refusing the recommendations of their leaders.'⁵ The reduction caused much discontent. Frank Lee said, in November, 1902: 'Recently remarks had been made that Messrs. Haslam and Harvey and Pickard had been bought over the last reduction. . . . The men should stand by their leaders whose wages had been reduced 10 per cent. the same as the men's wages.'⁶

On 19 November the Board met again to consider an application by the men for an increase of 10 per cent. and a counter-claim by the employers for a further reduction of 5 per cent.⁷ There were many lengthy discussions. The miners' leaders argued that profits rather than selling prices should be taken into account but this was strenuously opposed by the employers. Eventually it was decided that independent accountants should examine the books at selected collieries. Lord James ruled that they should produce details of output, selling prices and wages, but not profits. In coming to a final decision, in April, 1903, James found himself at a disadvantage since both sides refused to give him any further power beyond a casting vote.⁸ He therefore negatived both resolutions and wages remained as they were.

Meanwhile a conciliation board, subject to three months' notice on

¹ *Derbyshire Times*, 10 May, 1902.   ² *Ibid.*
³ *M.F.G.B.* 29 May, 1902.   ⁴ *Ibid.* 14 June, 1902.
⁵ *Derbyshire Times*, 21 June, 1902.   ⁶ *Ibid.* 15 November, 1902.
⁷ *M.F.G.B.* 19 November, 1902.   ⁸ *Ibid.* 28 April, 1903.

either side, had been established in Scotland in 1900 and the formation of another to supersede the sliding scale in South Wales was being discussed. With its own conciliation agreement coming to an end on 1 January, 1904, the Federation was anxious to secure that the other agreements should end at the same time but, in February, 1903, the Welsh coal-owners insisted on a three-year agreement and the plan had to be abandoned. As a result there were changes in the composition of the miners' side of the Conciliation Board for the central coalfields. The Scottish and Welsh members of the Executive Committee of the Federation were removed from the Board and replaced by four delegates from the central coalfields, one of whom was Harvey. Haslam was already on the Board that year as a member of the Executive Committee.

There was no further meeting of the central coalfields' Conciliation Board until 16 October when the owners demanded a reduction in wages of 10 per cent. It was impossible to reach any agreement and the matter was referred to Lord James.[1] At a meeting on 11 November the independent chairman again asked for powers beyond his casting vote. He explained:

But if you confine me to deciding with regard to ten per cent., if I thought that eight per cent. ought to come off, I am bound to say 'No' to your motion, and you do not allow me any opportunity to arrive at any state of wages which I think should exist. There may be objections to that. May I ask you to consider this matter on both sides? Is there any objection to the motion of ten per cent. being taken off—being divided into two fives? I should prefer it if you see no objection to it.

The owners' representatives took the hint and hastily amended their resolution to allow for one or two reductions of 5 per cent. The miners' leaders strongly objected to this procedure and the Board was adjourned for informal discussions on the possibility of renewing the conciliation agreement. Lord James was asked to withhold his casting vote on the owners' amended resolution until 12 December.[2]

On 20 November the employers suggested the renewal of the conciliation agreement for five years, with new rules of procedure. The chairman was to be given the right to refer any question back to the Board 'with or without any expression of his opinion'; meetings were to be held quarterly; there was to be no alteration in wages of more than 5 per cent. at any one time; a selling price was to be agreed upon as proportionate to a certain rate of wages during the life of the Board; and there was to be a maximum of 60 per cent. and a minimum of 35 per cent. on the 1888 wages.[3] These proposals were accepted by the

[1] *M.F.G.B.* 16 October, 1903.
[2] *Ibid.* 11 November, 1903.   [3] *Ibid.* 20 November, 1903.

miners' representatives and recommended to their constituents. The Derbyshire miners again ignored the advice of their leaders, and at a Federation conference, on 10 December, other districts joined them in rejecting the coal-owners' proposals.[1] After a further meeting of the Conciliation Board on 11 December, Lord James was asked to exercise his casting vote which, throughout the negotiations, had been hanging over the miners' heads like the sword of Damocles. James immediately awarded a 5 per cent. reduction, taking effect from the first making-up day in December, which brought wage rates down to 45 per cent. above the 1888 standard.

The Federation conference also approved the continuance of the Conciliation Board for a further three months during which the miners' representatives were given full power to enter into a new agreement 'on the terms as foreshadowed at these Conferences or on such terms as may be agreed upon'.[2] Both the coal-owners and the miners' leaders were anxious to avoid another dispute of the magnitude of the 1893 lock-out but the attitude of some of the men in Derbyshire was far from conciliatory. At a meeting at New Tupton a speaker complained that the union leaders addressed council and school board meetings but very rarely appeared among the miners: 'Leave the lower offices for the working men and leave Messrs. Haslam and Harvey to grapple with the things that are affecting us today. . . . The masters are again trying to crush the miners.'[3] The Clowne miners, who were greatly influenced by Barnet Kenyon, felt it necessary to pass a vote of confidence in their leaders.[4] At the Blackwell and Cotes Park collieries there were strikes of pit boys against the 5 per cent. reduction in wages.[5]

The renewal of the conciliation agreement led to much discussion. The coal-owners clung tenaciously to the proposals which they had elaborated on 20 November, 1903. The miners wanted the new agreement to run for only two years so that it would end at the same time as the South Wales agreement and thereby increase their bargaining power. They were also opposed to the linking of wages with selling prices and demanded a maximum of 65 per cent. and a minimum of 40 per cent. above the 1888 standard.[6] The proposals were discussed at many meetings in Derbyshire. Some lodges, such as Clowne, were prepared to leave the settlement to their leaders. At Creswell, on the other hand, it was resolved: (1) 'That the minimum be 40 per cent. on 1888 prices'; (2) 'That there be no fixed maximum'; (3) 'That the duration of the Board should not extend beyond that of the South Wales

[1] M.F.G.B. 10 December, 1903.   [2] Ibid. 11 December, 1903.
[3] Derbyshire Times, 27 February, 1904.
[4] Ibid. 20 February, 1904.
[5] Ibid. 9 and 23 January, 1904.   [6] M.F.G.B. 27 January, 1904.

Board'.[1] By a Council vote of 318 to 244 (one vote for 50 members) the Derbyshire representatives on the Board were empowered 'to make the best terms possible' but were to oppose the clause linking wages with coal prices.[2]

Eventually it was agreed that the Board should be re-established for three years, from 1 January, 1904, to 1 January, 1907, a year after the termination of the South Wales conciliation agreement. The minimum wage was to be 35 per cent., and the maximum 60 per cent., above 1888 levels. Alterations in wages were not to exceed 5 per cent. at any one time. The owners' proposal giving the independent chairman the power to refer questions back to the Board was also incorporated in the new agreement. They were obliged, however, to modify their views on the methods of wage determination. 'A selling price' was 'to be agreed upon as proportionate to a certain rate of wage' but 'alterations in the selling price' were 'not to be the sole factor for the decision of the Board, but one factor only'.[3] Haslam was well satisfied with the outcome of the negotiations. 'The Federation', he said, 'had accomplished a good thing for the miners.'[4]

IV

During 1904 the price of coal continued to decline. The Conciliation Board was unable to reach any agreement upon a relationship between wages and prices. After an abortive meeting on 22 June, the coal-owners notified their intention of seeking a 5 per cent. reduction in wages.[5] The Board recommended that the reduction should be in two instalments but the miners would not agree and the matter was referred to Lord James who gave his casting vote in favour of the coal-owners' original resolution.[6] 'This is bad news for the men,' said the *Derbyshire Times*, 'for in the present state of trade it will not mean that the pits will be able to turn one hour a week more, and many of the men today are only earning enough to keep their homes together.'[7]

There was no further meeting of the Board for over a year but prices were still falling and short-time working prevailed at most collieries. At the end of the year Haslam told the Pleasley colliers that the membership of the Association had decreased seriously.[8] Again it was argued that the coal-owners and the miners had a common interest in maintaining prices.[9] In January, 1905, A. B. Markham urged the Federation to

[1] *Derbyshire Times*, 23 January, 1904.
[2] *M.F.G.B.* 24 February, 1904.   [3] *Ibid.* 25 February, 1904.
[4] *Derbyshire Times*, 2 April, 1904.   [5] *M.F.G.B.* 22 June, 1904.
[6] *Ibid.* 3 August, 1904.   [7] *Derbyshire Times*, 6 August, 1904.
[8] *Ibid.* 10 December, 1904.   [9] *Ibid.* 6 August, 1904.

bring Northumberland and Durham 'into line' to prevent further price cutting and wage reductions.[1]

On 4 August, 1905, the Conciliation Board met to consider another application for a 5 per cent. reduction in wages.[2] This time the miners' leaders adopted a firmer attitude. Haslam told a meeting of miners at Somercotes: 'The leaders of the men would do all they could to defeat the proposal, and the men could depend upon it, that the only way the masters would get a reduction would be through the decision of Lord James of Hereford.'[3] At the adjourned meeting of the Board, on 27 September, it was reported by the miners' representatives that the men wished to call in the independent chairman.[4] Lord James referred the matter back to the Board and there followed a succession of meetings. The coal-owners offered to withdraw their application if the men would agree not to apply for an increase in wages until after 31 March, 1906. This proposal was rejected by the Derbyshire miners along with those of several other districts and, at a meeting on 2 November, further consideration of the question was deferred until after 31 December, 1905.

'They had had an anxious time', said Haslam, 'and he supposed that they were fit to be abused, blackguarded, maligned and slandered. At the same time they never expected that their actions would meet with the approval of the 25,000 members of their Association. But they did think that Mr. Harvey and himself deserved, as a result of their long service, some little amount of confidence to be placed in them, and the members of the Association should be prepared to defend their characters from aspersions.'[5]

Fortunately for the much-criticized miners' leaders, the owners did not pursue their demand for the 5 per cent. reduction in 1906. Trade was beginning to improve, and miners and coal-owners alike began to look to the future with optimism. From March, 1906, onwards there were many discussions on the new conciliation agreement which would be necessary if the Board was to continue beyond the end of the year. In July the Council of the Derbyshire Miners' Association resolved:

That this Council, realizing that the low selling price of coal prevents miners' wages from being advanced in proportion to the volume of trade done, hereby urges upon the forthcoming conference the desirability of entering into no further agreement unless some method be arrived at which will grapple with the under-selling policy now prevalent, and in no county worse than Derbyshire.[6]

Haslam, speaking at the annual demonstration in August, said:

Once you disband the Conciliation Board, at once you let go the sense of honour and unity it commands on either side and you will leave every collier

---

[1] *Derbyshire Times*, 21 January, 1905.   [2] *M.F.G.B.* 4 August, 1905.
[3] *Derbyshire Times*, 23 September, 1905.   [4] *M.F.G.B.* 27 September, 1905.
[5] *Derbyshire Times*, 11 November, 1905.   [6] *Ibid.* 14 July, 1906.

in the country to do his best to hit you as they [*sic*] choose. Fights here and strikes there will follow, and the whole result will be disastrous.[1]

After the abolition of the coal export duty on 1 November, 1906, the miners' proposals became linked with a demand for a 5 per cent. increase in wages which the owners regarded as a diplomatic move to secure a higher minimum wage.[2] The existing agreement provided for a minimum of 35 per cent. on the 1888 standard but the men asked for 40 per cent. and the abolition of the 60 per cent. maximum. There were also differences of opinion about the life of the agreement. The miners favoured a period of three years: the owners wanted five. Eventually the Conciliation Board reached a compromise. It was proposed that the minimum should be $37\frac{1}{2}$ per cent. and the maximum 65 per cent. and that the new Board should run for five years with provision for terminating the agreement if the eight hours' Bill became law. If these proposals were accepted the owners were willing to grant an increase in wages of $2\frac{1}{2}$ per cent. in January, 1907.[3]

The plan was not received with enthusiasm by the miners. At a meeting at Glapwell, E. Disney, the checkweighman, said:

He was surprised at the Derbyshire Miners' Association officials asking them to accept these terms and in face of the declaration recently made by Mr. Enoch Edwards, M.P., President of the Miners' Federation, that the men would never allow another Conciliation Board to be formed unless the minimum rate of wages was 40 per cent. over 1888 prices. It appeared as if their leaders were betraying them.

Resolutions were carried calling for a 40 per cent. minimum, an unlimited maximum, and an immediate increase in wages of 5 per cent.[4] At a Federation conference, on 3 December, the Conciliation Board's proposals were rejected.[5] Eventually, on 18 December, a settlement was reached. The minimum was raised to $37\frac{1}{2}$ per cent. and the maximum remained at 60 per cent. The new agreement was to run for at least three years from 1 January, 1907, to 31 December, 1909, but could be terminated by six months' notice in the event of any compulsory limitation of the hours of underground labour. After 31 December, 1909, the agreement was to continue, subject to six months' notice from either side. Wages were to be increased by 5 per cent. in January, 1907.[6]

In the period of rising prices which followed there was little difficulty in securing wage increases. In March and September, 1907, there were further advances of 5 per cent. bringing the rate of wages up to 55 per

[1] *Derbyshire Times*, 11 August, 1906.   [2] *Ibid.* 17 November, 1906.
[3] *M.F.G.B.* 13 November, 1906.
[4] *Derbyshire Times*, 24 November, 1 December, 1906.
[5] *M.F.G.B.* 3 December, 1906   [6] *Ibid.* 18 December, 1906.

M*

cent. above the 1888 standard. An application for yet another increase of 5 per cent. was considered by the Board on 15 October and referred to Lord James who eventually gave his casting vote in favour of the miners, 'subject to the increase taking effect from the first making-up day in January, 1908'.

The return of bad trade led to reductions of 5 per cent. in September, 1908, and in March, 1909, the independent chairman being called in on each occasion. An application for a third reduction of 5 per cent. was considered by the Board on 22 July, 1909.[1] Enoch Edwards, who had succeeded Pickard as president of the M.F.G.B. in 1904, warned the Board that any further reduction in wages might mean that the miners would refuse to continue the conciliation agreement. He went on to propose that the employers should withdraw their demand and suggested that when trade improved the miners would forgo any wage increases until the employers had made good their losses.[2] This time Lord James was not consulted. After further discussions the following decision was reached on 3 September:

In consideration of the present application for a reduction of 5 per cent. not being pressed, the Board agree as follows:

(1) No application shall be made for any advance in wages until the selling price exceeds 7s. 10·21d. by such an amount as shall have recouped the owners for the disadvantage they shall have incurred by the payment of the present rate of wages during the period the selling price was less than 7s. 10·21d.

(2) That notice to terminate the Conciliation Board shall not be given until the selling price has recovered to and continued at an amount which the Board, or in case of difference the outside Chairman, shall decide to be sufficient to recoup the owners, as mentioned in Clause 1.[3]

The agreement bound the Federation to an indeterminate period of wage restraint and savoured too much of the sliding scale. Moreover, it was concluded without reference to the districts. On a motion by William Sewell, the Vice-President, the Council of the Derbyshire Miners' Association expressed 'its satisfaction with the agreement' and ratified it but also resolved, on a motion by Morton No. 2 lodge, seconded by Alfreton: 'That before the Conciliation Board be permanently formed for a further length of time, sufficient time for the discussion of its terms be given.'[4] The employers were well pleased with the agreement. Alfred Hewlett, the coal-owners' principal spokesman, said: 'The effect of this is that it keeps the Board alive, and it keeps all other arrangements alive, and we hope it will turn out to be to the benefit of both of us.'[5]

[1] *M.F.G.B.* 22 July, 1909.   [2] *Ibid.* 12 August, 1909.
[3] *Ibid.* 3 September, 1909.
[4] *D.M.A.* 25 September, 1909.   [5] *M.F.G.B.* 3 September, 1909.

The price of coal changed little during the next three years and the miners were unable to claim any percentage increase in wages. Moreover it was not until November, 1911, in the changed conditions brought about by the minimum wage agitation, that the Board held another meeting of any importance.

V

Whilst these national negotiations were going on, the Derbyshire officials had also to deal with the host of day-to-day problems which occupy much of the time of trade union leaders. After the settlement of 1894, which reduced wages by 10 per cent., there was a great deal of unrest among the surface workers and pit boys. Most of these workers had not received the full 40 per cent. increase on 1888 wage rates but were now expected to accept a 10 per cent. reduction along with the colliers. There were strikes of banksmen and boys at a number of collieries.[1] Over a hundred boys were prosecuted by the Derbyshire Silkstone Colliery Company for absenting themselves from work without giving due notice. The claims for damages were eventually withdrawn but each boy had to pay two shillings costs.[2]

In the years which followed there were disputes over boys' wages at practically every colliery in the county. The matter came to a head in the summer of 1902 when there were simultaneous strikes throughout the district. The situation presented difficulties for the Association. It found itself fighting on behalf of a section of labour which was represented in only a very small proportion within its ranks and over which it possessed no adequate control. Nevertheless, action was forced upon the officials because the boys, by their almost general revolt, compelled many pits to stop work and thus threw large numbers of members of the Association upon its 'out-of-work' fund.[3]

The coal-owners argued that it was anomalous for the boys to demand an increase in wages at a time when the miners were accepting a reduction of 10 per cent. in accordance with the decision of the Conciliation Board. The miners' leaders, on the other hand, pointed out that the boys had never had a properly established basic wage and that the owners were trying to take away something which had never been given.[4] The Association decided to ask for a basic wage of 1s. 2d. a day with merit advances of a penny a quarter and the same percentage variations as the miners were receiving. There were several conferences

[1] *Derbyshire Times*, 18 and 25 August, 8 September, 1894.
[2] *Ibid.* 1 September, 1894.
[3] *Ibid.* 23 August, 1902.   [4] *Ibid.* 30 August, 1902.

of owners' representatives and miners' leaders and eventually the following basic scale was agreed upon:

Age	Per day
13	1s. 2d.
14	1s. 4d.
15	1s. 8d.
16	2s. 0d.
17	2s. 4d.
18	2s. 8d.
19	3s. 0d.

This was subject to an addition of 50 per cent. in August, 1902, in accordance with the conciliation agreement. The employers also agreed to issue to the boys weekly pay tickets.[1]

Like the pit boys, the surface workers had never had a recognized basic wage and they had within their ranks a large non-union element which made negotiations difficult for the Federation and the Association. The national agreement of 1899 that the wages of surface men should be governed by the decisions of the Conciliation Board was not easy to enforce locally. In 1910 the National Amalgamated Union of Labour, in conjunction with the Derbyshire Miners' Association, conducted an inquiry into banksmen's wages. A. J. Bailey, an official of the N.A.U.L., told members of his union at a district council meeting in Sheffield:

The evidence they had got from branches . . . proved conclusively that they had some top-men in Derbyshire who were not getting the wage, including all the percentages and advances, that was more than equal to the wage of 1888. In the case of some collieries it was perfectly clear that while small advances had been made on the 1888 basis, nothing like 50 per cent. had been added. At one place, for example, when the basis rate for 1888 was 3s. 6d., the gross wage today was 3s. 7d.[2]

Like the pit boys, the surface workers had to fight for a basic wage throughout the county but it was not until after the 1912 strike that they were able to achieve their objective.

The enginemen and firemen faced similar difficulties because they were not included in the conciliation scheme. With the encouragement of the miners' leaders they had built up their own union which sought to improve wages and conditions and increase the safety of winding operations.[3] These objectives were closely interrelated. The enginemen argued that, in the interests of safety, their hours should be shorter and certain standards of technical proficiency should be required of them by

---

[1] *Derbyshire Times*, 30 August, 1902.
[2] *Ibid.* 14 May, 1910.   [3] See pp. 254-6, 476-7.

law. At the same time the proposed reforms were intended to improve their working conditions and restrict the competition of unskilled labour. The miners had a direct interest in both aspects of this policy. They wanted safe winding by enginemen and firemen who were not likely to throw them out of work by frequent strikes.[1]

The enginemen and firemen had not shared fully the wage increase enjoyed by the miners between 1888 and 1890. In 1890 the average wage for colliery enginemen in Derbyshire was 5s. 6d. for a twelve-hour day, whereas in the north-eastern coalfield the rate was 6s. or 6s. 6d. for an eight-hour day.[2] In January, 1892, there was a general increase in wages in Derbyshire of 10d. a day.[3] When the miners' wages were about to be reduced by 10 per cent. in 1894, Rowarth, the secretary of the Derbyshire and Nottinghamshire Enginemen's and Firemen's Union, said: 'He was in a position to prove that at 30 collieries in Derbyshire their men were entitled to an advance instead of a reduction. At no colliery had their men received the 40 per cent. advance.'[4] In August, 1894, a joint meeting of coal-owners and union representatives at Chesterfield agreed that the wages of enginemen and firemen should not be reduced. Nevertheless, attempts were made to do so by two colliery companies in the Alfreton district: the Blackwell Company and James Oakes and Company.[5] But at the new collieries which were sunk in the 'nineties, where modern and powerful machinery was installed, the enginemen worked only eight hours at a slightly increased wage. In May, 1897, Rowarth reported: 'They had men with 6s. 8d. per day of eight hours and others with 6s. 6d. for 12 hours.'[6]

When the miners received their advance of $2\frac{1}{2}$ per cent. in October, 1898, the Derbyshire Miners' Association and the Enginemen's and Firemen's Union resolved to take joint action to secure some improvement in the wages of enginemen and the introduction of eight-hour shifts. In November 489 of the 600 members of the Enginemen's and Firemen's Union voted in favour of giving in strike notices if the employers persisted in their refusal to negotiate. Haslam presided over a large meeting of the men at Chesterfield and was told that they considered shorter hours to be more important than increased wages. It was resolved:

That the general secretary be requested to write to the secretary of the Coal-Owners' Association reminding him that unless they grant an interview

---

[1] The history of the colliery winders' unions and their relations with the miners' unions have not been adequately investigated. The activities of the Derbyshire and Nottinghamshire Enginemen's and Firemen's Union alone provide sufficient material for a separate study.   [2] *Derbyshire Times*, 25 October, 1890.

[3] *Ibid.* 31 October, 1896; 29 January, 1898.   [4] *Ibid.* 21 July, 1894.

[5] *Ibid.* 15 September, 1894.   [6] *Ibid.* 22 May, 1897.

to consider the hours question, and thus avoid friction, we shall be compelled to take steps to secure our object.[1]

In March, 1899, the men handed in their notices. On 10 March the joint committee of the Enginemen's and Firemen's Union and the Derbyshire Miners' Association met to discuss the situation. A resolution was passed calling upon the employers to meet the joint committee. It concluded:

> If the employers refuse to negotiate, the miners' association's officials will instruct their men to refuse to ride up or down under blackleg enginemen, who may take the place of those on strike, and we trust that no enginemen will make any separate arrangement other than what applies to the whole of the men affected by the Enginemen's Society.[2]

Haslam stated at Grassmoor: 'The Miners' Association of Derbyshire would render their moral help to the men, and financial help as well if necessary. The Association would never allow the miners to be wound up and down the mines by blackleg enginemen.'[3]

In the face of this apparent unity the employers gave way and agreed to meet representatives of the two unions at the Station Hotel, Chester-field, on 13 March. The result was an anti-climax. After a lengthy discussion it was agreed: 'That the notices be adjourned, and that each case be considered on its own merits by the individual owners and the men and their representatives.'[4] Later Haslam explained the reasons for the collapse of the strike:

> He wished to testify that Mr. Rowarth, the enginemen's secretary, had done all that was possible for a man to do under the circumstances, and that the failure, if there had been any, was due to the men themselves. They had no particular settled policy, some winders winding eight hours, and others ten. . . . In his opinion, Mr. Rowarth had been pushed by the men, against his own better judgment, into taking a more or less prestige action. After it was again agreed that notices should be given at all collieries it was found that a number of men had made arrangements of their own apart from the general settlement, while at some collieries no notices at all were served. The owners who met them in conference naturally wanted to know why certain pits were to be laid idle, out of the whole number.[5]

Although the enginemen had failed to obtain an eight-hour day the threatened strike brought some advantages. The employers had at last recognized the union and Rowarth, with the support of the Derbyshire Miners' Association, was able to negotiate substantial wage increases for his members at a large number of collieries.[6] By 1900, the enginemen employed by the Clay Cross Company were earning 7s. 1d. a day.[7]

[1] *Derbyshire Times*, 15 October, 1898. [2] *Ibid.* 11 March, 1899.
[3] *Ibid.* [4] *Ibid.* 18 March, 1899. [5] *Ibid.* 25 March, 1899.
[6] *Ibid.* 6 May, 22 July, 1899. [7] *Ibid.* 3 March, 1900.

The Enginemen's and Firemen's Union began to tackle the problem of non-unionism with determination after the fiasco of 1899. The agitation for the eight-hour day was revived and representation on the national Conciliation Board was demanded. By 1901 the disparities in winders' conditions were increasing. Very few men in the Ripley area received more than 6s. for a twelve-hour day whereas in other parts of the county recent increases had brought enginemen's wages up to 7s. 9d. or 8s. for an eight-hour day.[1] In the following year there were further attempts to reduce wages by the same percentage as that agreed upon for the miners by the Conciliation Board but Rowarth argued that the enginemen had not received the full 60 per cent. increase as the miners had done and ought not to be expected to submit to a 10 per cent. reduction.[2] The enginemen's efforts to secure representation on the Conciliation Board were unavailing but in January, 1907, the employers granted an increase in wages which was to follow the percentage movements of miners' wages with a time lag of two months.[3] In April, 1907, the enginemen secured the formal support of the miners in dealing with non-unionism. It was resolved by the federated board of representatives of the Derbyshire and Nottinghamshire miners' associations and the Enginemen's and Firemen's Union: 'That this meeting . . . agrees to take action in compelling all men working in and about mines to join their respective unions.'[4] In the following October the enginemen and firemen secured an agreement granting an eight-hour day to all winding enginemen raising an average of 450 tons of coal a day, and a ten-hour to all firemen. The enginemen were to forfeit 3d. a day and the firemen 2d.[5]

VI

In addition to the problems of special categories of labour such as the pit boys, surface men and winders, the miners' leaders were constantly dealing with disputes over price lists and changes in the conditions of work. Some of these disputes arose out of the refusal of employers to honour the national agreements. Thus, in 1894, the 200 miners employed at the Gosforth Colliery, near Dronfield, refused to accept a new price list which, with the recognized reduction of 10 per cent., would have reduced their wages by an aggregate of 25 per cent. Non-unionists were persuaded by the management to come from Scotland to work at prices much higher than those normally paid to the Dronfield men. A

[1] *Derbyshire Times*, 2 March, 1901. [2] *Ibid.* 26 July, 1902.
[3] *Ibid.* 5 January, 1907.
[4] *Ibid.* 27 April, 1907. [5] *Ibid.* 17 October, 1908.

number of policemen were posted about the colliery with the result that there were seven prosecutions for intimidation. The Scotsmen eventually offered to return home if the Dronfield men would pay their expenses but Harvey would not agree to this.

'They must have known', he said, 'when promised such an unnatural wage, that there was some reason for such a promise being made, and it was their duty to make enquiries before coming to Dronfield. . . . The names of the men working now would be circulated; they had done something they would never forget.'[1]

At Langwith, in 1897, Harvey told the miners: 'If any union man at Langwith was not paid according to the price list they would take the case into court, and would recover every penny, and do it without costing the men as much as a postage stamp.'[2]

Sometimes the disputes over price lists were the culmination of years of dissatisfaction. In 1906, when the men employed by J. and G. Wells, Ltd., decided to strike, S. Morris, their local leader, said: 'It was not an easy thing for the employers to give back to the men all they had lost through "nibbling" in four or five years.'[3] On this occasion Haslam discussed the difficulties of the older and uneconomic collieries: 'He knew and appreciated the fact that the Eckington Collieries, owing to their unfavourable position geologically, had a hard task in keeping their end up against the newer collieries which had a better coal face. Coal was easily got, and at a considerably less cost.'[4] But the efforts of the union leaders to strike a balance between the difficulties of the coal-owners and the hardships of the miners were not always successful. In 1909 a Tibshelf miner asked:

How would Mr. Haslam and Mr. Harvey and others like to work six days a week and take £1 12s. to keep a wife and four children on, never mind about short time? I think if we have to manage on it they ought to do likewise. Their bread is buttered on both sides, but ours is with lard. If the I.L.P. was in I think things would soon be altered.[5]

Many of the disputes over price lists occurred at the new collieries which were being developed in the 'nineties to exploit the 'top hard' seam. It was important that a good basic wage should be established at the outset. In 1897, the men at the Creswell Colliery preferred to be paid by the day rather than accept the tonnage rates offered by the Bolsover Company. Emerson Bainbridge argued that the colliery was not sufficiently developed for him to offer more than 1s. 4d. a ton. In June the men decided to strike until they received 1s. 5½d. a ton which

---

[1] *Derbyshire Times*, 20 October, 10 and 24 November, 1894.
[2] *Ibid.* 20 March, 1897.   [3] *Ibid.* 22 September, 1906.
[4] *Ibid.*   [5] *Ibid.* 3 July, 1909.

was the rate paid to the men working the same seam at the Bolsover Colliery. 'It would not be just to the other seven pits working the same seam', said Harvey, 'to allow the Creswell men to accept the terms of the Bolsover Company.'[1] The strike ended in August when the employers conceded the Bolsover price list with the proviso that the prices were to be submitted to arbitration in June, 1898.[2]

The situation was complicated by the fact that the Nottinghamshire rates for the men working the 'top hard' seam in the Leen Valley were higher than those prevailing in Derbyshire. Moveover, the new developments were bringing the Derbyshire miners to parts of the county which were close to the Nottinghamshire borders. At the Warsop Main Colliery, where there was a five-month strike over a price list in 1897, the men who were taking up employment were mostly members of the Derbyshire Miners' Association. Warsop is in Nottinghamshire but the miners were reluctant to sever their old connections and presented a petition asking for the lodge to be transferred to the Derbyshire Miners' Association. J. G. Hancock, the Nottinghamshire miners' agent, told the men that the 'top hard' collieries in Derbyshire paid an average of less than 2s. a ton but the average in the Leen Valley for the same seam was 2s. 2d. a ton. 'Would they get this by joining the Derbyshire union?' he asked.[3] Harvey commented:

> The Derbyshire Association was anxious to avoid all friction between the two associations, and they hoped to come to some satisfactory settlement in the interests of the men, whose interests were, after all, paramount. This was a matter which might eventually affect them in that district. There lay the coalfields of the future, and in that district would be the developments of the future. Coalfields on the other sides of the county were now being worked out, and there would be a migration from them. . . . Such being the case, it was surely important that there should be a good understanding as to prices for coal getting.[4]

The most serious dispute over 'top hard' price lists occurred at the Shirebrook Colliery in 1898. The men complained that the roof was bad and that it was impossible to earn a fair wage on the district price. They asked for an increase of 2d. a ton and the removal of the undermanager whose treatment of them had become intolerable. After months of friction the men came out on strike on 25 May. The usual tactics were adopted by the employers. Extra police were drafted into the village and the strikers received notice to leave the Company's houses or pay a fortnight's rent in advance.[5] On 19 June the enginemen and firemen joined the miners and entered into a compact with them

---

[1] *Derbyshire Times*, 3 July, 1897.
[3] *Ibid.* 10 July, 1897.
[4] *Ibid.* 3 July, 1897.

[2] *Ibid.* 21 August, 1897.
[5] *Ibid.* 4 June, 1898.

whereby the miners agreed not to descend the pit under any other winders and the enginemen agreed not to let down any non-unionist miners.[1] On 8 August the surface workers ceased work. Men who came from Glasgow to work at the colliery promptly announced their intention of returning when they discovered that there was a strike in progress. Their expenses were paid by the tradesmen and others in the village.[2]

On 22 August fifty-five miners arrived from South Wales. They were met by a hostile crowd of over a thousand people and were eventually persuaded to return home. The South Wales miners were at the time locked out and receiving financial support from the Federation. Haslam despatched to Lewis Miles, the secretary of the Pontypridd Workmen's Provisional Committee, a telegram in which he stated that the Derbyshire miners were 'furious'.[3] He followed it up with an angry letter:

> Derbyshire Miners' Association, Miners' Offices,
> Saltergate, Chesterfield,
> August 23rd, 1898.
>
> Mr. Lewis Miles,
> Dear Sir,—We have a body of men on strike at the Shirebrook Colliery. I am sorry to say we are troubled with Welsh blacklegs. We have already paid for nine men to return, when, lo! yesterday 55 men turned up. Mr. Harvey has gone with money to pay their fares as they say they would go back if money was found for them; and, as a matter of ordinary practice, whatever it costs to send them away, will be taken out of the donation to Wales this week. One way or another, our men pay about £200 per week to keep the starving poor, and it is black ingratitude for these beggars to come blacklegging. I shall inform Mr. Ashton, and I think if it is not stopped it will be for the Federation as a whole to reconsider its position about granting money at all to South Wales. I do not blame you, but desire that an exposure be made throughout Wales at once of the dastardly conduct of these men. The two Evans are stumping the country, and we are helping all we can, and this is the return we get for it. Set the thing going, and denounce all such men.
>
> Yours, deeply hurt, J. Haslam.

Meanwhile Lupton, the managing director of the Shirebrook Company, had applied to the Board of Trade for the assistance of a conciliator in accordance with the terms of the Conciliation Act, 1896. 'But', said Harvey, 'the moment they accepted conciliation the tyranny had been such as had never been surpassed in any dispute in the county.'[4] In this far from conciliatory atmosphere Lupton and the miners' leaders had several discussions with John Burnett, the conciliator. The price lists were modified and both sides agreed to accept the arbitration of Burnett on the question of the undermanager. The result was that the

[1] *Derbyshire Times*, 25 June, 1898. [2] *Ibid.* 13 August, 1898.
[3] *Ibid.* 27 August, 1898. [4] *Ibid.*

undermanager was suspended for a period and by the end of September all the men were back at work after a protracted stoppage of seventeen weeks.[1] Towards the end of the year it was announced that Lupton had decided to leave the Shirebrook Colliery Company.[2] In November, 1899, Harvey told the Shirebrook miners: 'Reasonable complaints were now listened to and treated fairly.'[3]

VII

Other disputes over price lists centred around changes in the nature of the task rather than changes in the price. In 1895 the men at the Staveley Company's Hollingwood pit were told to use forks instead of shovels when filling their tubs in order to reduce the amount of small coal sent to the surface.[4] Such practices were generally resorted to in times of depression when the market was highly competitive. They increased the profits of the owners at the expense of the miner whose earnings were reduced. By 1910 these methods of reducing labour costs had been developed to a fine art. Lengthy negotiations would follow a proposal by the owners to introduce forks with wider spaces between the prongs or screens and riddles of a larger mesh. At the Markham Colliery, when the management decided to introduce forks with a space of 2 inches between the prongs instead of $1\frac{1}{2}$ inches, the men argued that it would no longer be necessary to continue confiscating tubs which contained an excessive amount of slack but their proposal was rejected.[5] The Clay Cross Company refused to allow the men at their Parkhouse and Black Shale pits to substitute shovel filling for riddle filling unless they accepted a reduction of 5d. a ton on the basic rate.[6] The Bolsover Company went to the length of appointing an official, popularly known as the 'slack bobby', to tour the stalls to ensure that the men were not using shovels to fill their tubs. The activities of the 'slack bobby' resulted in several dismissals, some of them on the flimsiest evidence. The mere sound of a shovel being used in a stall, no matter for what purpose, was sufficient to secure an adverse report to the management.[7]

Confiscations and fines also continued to be used in an attempt to secure the maximum efficiency at the minimum cost. In 1896 an important test case concerning the confiscation of coal was heard before Judge Smyly in the Chesterfield County Court. Marklow, a North

[1] *Derbyshire Times*, 10 September, 1 October, 1898.
[2] *Ibid.* 7 January, 1899.   [3] *Ibid.* 18 November, 1899.
[4] *Ibid.* 18 May, 1895.   [5] *Ibid.* 4 June, 1910.
[6] *Ibid.* 16 July, 1910.   [7] *Ibid.* 25 June, 2 July, 1910.

Wingfield miner, sued the Hardwick Colliery Company for 11s. 3d. in respect of coal taken from tubs sent out of his stall. W. E. Clegg, who represented Marklow and the union, argued that the deductions had been made without the sanction or knowledge of Thomas Hewett, the checkweighman. Smyly gave judgment in favour of the employers with leave to appeal.[1] The case was subsequently heard in the Queen's Bench division before Mr. Justice Cave and Mr. Justice Wills. It turned upon a section of the Coal Mines Regulation Act, 1887, which stated, amongst other things, that deductions could be made in the absence of a checkweighman 'unless the absent checkweigher had reasonable ground to suppose that the weighing or the determination of the deductions, as the case may be, would not be proceeded with'.[2] Atherley Jones, who represented the union, said:

The making of these deductions was not a continuous operation, and the deductions which took place and gave rise to this litigation were made at the time when Hewett was away in bed—at night. . . . What his clients felt was that if this were allowed, this unreasonable thing might occur—the employers might at any moment in the twenty-four hours decide to test a tub of coal, and a man must always be ready to attend such an inspection.

Mr. Justice Wills, in giving judgment, pointed out:

What Mr. Atherley Jones now alleged was that no ascertainment of deductions was to take place unless the person appointed by the men had had a special notice that it would take place at the hour fixed. The Act of Parliament, however, did not say that this was to be so.

Mr. Justice Cave concurred and the appeal was dismissed. When Jones asked leave to appeal, Cave replied: 'Certainly not. There is no bottom in the appeal at all.'[3]

It was evident that the existing legislation provided the men with little or no protection against confiscations in the absence of the checkweighman. Moreover, the Association's case had been weakened by the statement in the Company's contract rules that if the men's representative was not present the work of screening was to go on. When Jones suggested that the employers might be tempted to act unreasonably, Wills had replied: 'There is no fear of their doing that. They would soon have a strike if they did anything of that kind. People must protect themselves when they make such a bargain.'[4] The moral was obvious.

'This matter cannot be allowed to rest where it is,' wrote the officials, 'as unscrupulous Employers can, with such Contract Rules, confiscate the men's coal without the Checkweighman's consent. We are glad that some Contract

---

[1] D.M.A. 31 March, 27 April, 1896; Derbyshire Times, 25 April, 1896.
[2] 50 and 51 Vict. c. 58, Section 13.
[3] Derbyshire Times, 13 June, 1896.   [4] Ibid.

Rules, such as Staveley, and a few others, do stipulate definitely that the person to decide upon the take off shall be the Checkweighman on behalf of the men, and we must insist upon the same principle being adopted at all the Collieries in the County.'[1]

The Association's opposition to unfair confiscation did not mean that it was prepared to condone the malpractices of idle and dishonest workmen. In 1897, when the Blackwell Colliery Company suspended a number of its Alfreton miners until they paid a fine of 10s., Haslam told the men plainly: 'The tubs contained too much dirt.'[2] The checkweighman naturally figured prominently in all such disputes and the union strove unceasingly to have his position more clearly defined by appealing to the courts. In 1896 a checkweighman at the Alfreton Colliery brought an action for the recovery of contributions to the checkweigh fund. The case was heard in the Alfreton County Court before Judge Smyly who ruled that there could be no recovery because the checkweighman had not been elected by ballot in accordance with the law.[3] The Council thereupon urged all members who had not elected their checkweighmen by ballot 'to do it as early as possible, and also to take care that all men receive notice when such ballot will take place so that we may avoid a repetition of what took place at Alfreton'.[4]

The election and removal of checkweighmen sometimes caused serious difficulties. At the Oxcroft Colliery, in 1906, there was a situation 'almost unprecedented in mining history'. There were two checkweighmen sitting in the same box doing the work required to be done by one only. Each claimed to be the rightful occupant. An attempt had been made by the butties to remove the original checkweighman, James Spencer, because they felt that he was not acting in their interests. Without reference to the other underground workers, who regarded Spencer as their champion, the checkweigh committee, which was dominated by the butties, elected a man called Vardy. The Association declared that Vardy had not been elected in accordance with the law which required a ballot of all underground workers who were paid 'according to the actual weight gotten by them of the mineral contracted to be gotten'.[5] It was found impossible to reconcile the opposing factions and eventually the president, secretary and treasurer of the checkweigh fund were taken to the Chesterfield County Court where Judge Lindley awarded £25 18s. 11d. for wages due to Spencer, with power to apply for an injunction.[6]

[1] D.M.A. 23 June, 1896.   [2] Derbyshire Times, 13 March, 1897.
[3] Coal Mines Regulation Act, 1887, Sections 13–14.
[4] D.M.A. 27 April, 1896.
[5] Coal Mines Regulation Act, 1887, Section 12.
[6] Derbyshire Times, 16 June, 1906.

The development of large modern collieries increased the complexities of the checkweighman's task and led to a demand for the installation of automatic weighing machines. In 1904, Frank Welby, an Eckington miner, wrote:

The checkweighmen know it is impossible to weigh and count the tubs correctly with the speed they fly over the machine. We have two- and three-decker cages. The next will be a four-decker, with three tubs on a deck. What man living can weigh nine tubs one after the other correctly. How will it be with twelve tubs in rotation over the same machine, particularly if it is a beam machine, which requires a full stop to honestly weigh each tub of coal. . . . Why not plant down on every pit bank automatic machines, which will count and weigh to perfection? There is a terrible leakage in miners' wages from this cause alone.[1]

Another factor which affected miners' earnings in this period was the use of the safety lamp. The dispute which had begun in the 'eighties continued through the 'nineties and became a matter of increasing importance because the trend of legislation and Home Office orders was all in the direction of abolishing the use of naked lights. At some collieries the men were able to secure small additions of 1d. or 2d. to their tonnage rates where the use of lamps was compulsory but many of the coal-owners refused to make any concessions. A dispute between the South Derbyshire miners and their employers led to an important arbitration case at Nottingham in 1901. One witness said that he would rather have 4d. a ton less with a candle than work with a lamp at his present rate. Josiah Court, the Derbyshire Miners' Association's medical adviser, stated that the eyes of miners had been weakened by the use of safety lamps. In the face of this evidence the arbitrator, Judge Smyly, awarded an increase of 1d. a ton on all coal raised in places where the use of safety lamps was compulsory.[2]

The growing use of machinery also led to many disputes. Most of them centred around the problem of evaluating the work done by the machine in re-adjusting the price list. Sometimes they were settled amicably, and to the satisfaction of the men, as at South Wingfield in 1899.[3] There were, however, strikes at Alfreton, in 1895, over the introduction of a 'holing machine', and at Staveley, in 1897, over an electric cutting machine.[4] When the Clay Cross Company began to mechanize its collieries lengthy negotiations ensued. Throughout 1905 the men were on the verge of striking until, in December, both sides agreed to accept the ruling of an arbitrator. His terms of reference

[1] *Derbyshire Times*, 31 December, 1904.
[2] *Ibid.* 20 April, 11 May, 1901.   [3] *Ibid.* 7 January, 1899.
[4] *Ibid.* 9 November, 1895; 4, 11 and 18 September, 30 October, 1897.

were to decide 'whether the present tonnage price paid for machine-got coal includes the removal of the holing dirt by the workmen, or whether the owners, in addition to the tonnage price paid, are also responsible for removing the said dirt'.[1] The arbitrator appointed by the Board of Trade was Thomas Bell, a Scarborough mining engineer, who gave his decision in favour of the employers. This aroused great dissatisfaction and at a meeting of the Clay Cross miners in March, 1906, it was resolved: 'That Mr. James Haslam write to the arbitrator inviting him to give reasons so as to satisfy us that the decision was arrived at upon the evidence produced at the hearing of the case on 30 January.'[2]

The resistance of the trade unionist to the introduction of machinery is frequently condemned as a stupid restrictive practice stemming the tide of progress. The Derbyshire miners were not unreasonable in this respect. They found that the machines were being credited with more than their fair share of the total amount of work done. The additional tasks which the miners had to perform, after the machines had finished their work, were not being paid for. In connection with a dispute in 1906 at the Alfreton Colliery, where the men had been struggling to maintain adequate rates in the face of growing mechanization for nearly thirteen years, the *Derbyshire Times* commented: 'The men do not object to the machines, but they believe that the advantage should be mutual.'[3] With declining rates of profit, however, it was inevitable that the coal-owners should regard machinery as a means of reducing costs rather than maintaining or increasing wages. In 1907 Frank Hall told the Birchwood miners that the introduction of machinery had resulted in a loss of wages to the miners: 'Machinery had certainly benefited the owners, but it was proved that it adversely affected the miners. . . . Machinery also largely interfered with the average prices on the market.'[4]

The Conciliation Act of 1896, which arose out of the recommendations of the Royal Commission on Labour, gave a considerable impetus to the growth of conciliation and arbitration. Ever since their experiences of the 'seventies the miners' leaders had been opposed to arbitration both nationally and locally. After the legislation of 1896, however, there was a gradual change in their attitude and in Derbyshire the number of arbitration cases increased steadily. They were not always conducted in a healthy atmosphere. In 1903 the Blackwell Company dismissed G. Thorpe and Joseph Severn because they had given evidence before an arbitrator in support of the men at the Alfreton Colliery.[5] Four years later, when another dispute arose, the men rejected the

[1] *Derbyshire Times*, 21 January, 25 November, 2 and 9 December, 1905.
[2] *Ibid.* 3 March, 1906. [3] *Ibid.* 5 May, 1906.
[4] *Ibid.* 31 August, 1907. [5] *Ibid.* 11 April, 1903.

advice of their leaders to resort to arbitration, saying that they had lost all confidence in the management.[1] In 1909 the miners employed by the same company at the A and B Winnings pits agreed to arbitration. G. R. (later Lord) Askwith[2] was appointed by the Board of Trade to act as umpire. The *Derbyshire Times* commented upon his award:

It is largely in favour of the masters and there can be no doubt it will be a great disappointment to the men. To put it in the mildest form, it is questionable whether the men are not in a worse position than they were under the provisional agreement. It is safe to say that Mr. Todd [the colliery manager] offered the men better terms to settle than they have received from the umpire.[3]

In 1901, when the employers' representatives on the national Conciliation Board had complained that the men were attempting to improve their price lists in violation of the agreement, Pickard had argued that such matters should be settled by local conciliation boards.[4] As early as 2 April, 1894, the Derbyshire miners' Executive Committee had resolved: 'That the question of trying to form a Board of Conciliation for this County to deal with local disputes, go before the Lodges.'[5] A month later this decision was confirmed by a Council resolution: 'That this Association is in favour of establishing a Board of Conciliation for the County, for the purpose of settling local disputes.'[6] But it was not until 1907 that the coal-owners were prepared to discuss the matter. Barnet Kenyon told the Loscoe miners:

One great dream of their life had been to obtain a county board of employers' and workmen's representatives, who would be able to discuss all questions affecting the eighty-odd mines in Derbyshire on grounds which would be altogether impartial, and which would not be influenced by personal selfishness. A county board was within sight. The owners had agreed and it was decided that five representatives of workpeople and five representatives of the owners should meet together at an early date to draft rules on which the board should be governed; so that petty differences and serious difficulties might be grappled with and dealt with on absolutely neutral ground.

He concluded: 'The old method of striking is dead and gone. Arbitration and conciliation are becoming the principles of settlement.'[7]

Kenyon was too optimistic. When the employers' and miners' representatives met on 22 April, 1907, no agreement was reached. The miners sought the co-operation of the employers to eliminate non-unionism and demanded a basic wage of 5s. a day for all stallmen. The

[1] *Derbyshire Times*, 16 February, 1907.
[2] Author of *Industrial Problems and Disputes*, (London), 1920.
[3] *Derbyshire Times*, 25 December, 1909.
[4] *M.F.G.B.* 13 February, 1901.   [5] *D.M.A.* 2 April, 1894.
[6] *Ibid.* 1 May, 1894.   [7] *Derbyshire Times*, 30 March, 1907.

employers were unable to agree among themselves on the basic wage and proposed the setting up of two conciliation boards, one of which would have included representation from Nottinghamshire.[1] After much discussion and correspondence the matter fell into abeyance. Thomas Bolton, the Liberal M.P. for North-East Derbyshire, speaking at the miners' annual demonstration in the following August, said: 'He wished it to be understood that it was not the miners but the employers who stood in the way of the formation of a conciliation board for Derbyshire. He could not see why a man in the Ilkeston district was not worth 5s. basis rate as well as a man working at Staveley or elsewhere.'[2] Two years later a further attempt was made to establish county conciliation machinery when a joint committee of coal-owners' and miners' representatives was formed to deal with a strike over price lists at the Blackwell Colliery. The miners' leaders advised the men to give the committee full powers to settle the dispute.[3] The men declined to give their representatives plenary powers and the joint meeting ended in failure.[4] More successful was another *ad hoc* joint committee formed to consider the implementation of the Coal Mines Regulation Act, 1908, which gave the miners the eight-hour day[5] but it was not until 1911 that a county conciliation board was established.[6]

Throughout the period between the 1893 lock-out and the 1912 strike the Association had to continue its struggle for recognition. It was not recognized by the Butterley Company until as late as 1902.[7] The attitude of the employers sometimes led to serious difficulties such as those experienced at Shirebrook in 1898 which resulted in the suspension of the undermanager and the resignation of the managing director.[8] In 1901 Harvey complained about the autocratic treatment of the miners by the Hardwick Colliery Company.[9] At the collieries of the Blackwell Company hardly a year passed without a major dispute.[10] Frank Hall owed his election as a full-time official in 1907 to the experience which he gained in these disputes when he was check-weighman at Alfreton.

Non-unionism also continued to be a problem. It has already been noted that one of the Association's objectives in attempting to establish a county conciliation board was to secure the co-operation of the employers in encouraging the men to join the union. In the absence of a county agreement the policy of eradicating non-unionism colliery by

---

[1] *Derbyshire Times*, 27 April, 15 June, 13 July, 10 August, 1907.
[2] *Ibid.* 10 August, 1907.
[3] *D.M.A.* 8 May, 1909; *Derbyshire Times*, 22 May, 1909.
[4] *Derbyshire Times*, 29 May, 1909.
[5] See below, pp. 384-5.
[6] See Chapter X, pp. 398-9.
[7] *Derbyshire Times*, 22 February, 1902.
[8] See above, pp. 369-71.
[9] *Derbyshire Times*, 23 February, 1901.
[10] *Ibid.* 5 May, 1906.

colliery continued with varying degrees of success. At many collieries there were successful negotiations resulting in the exclusion of all non-union labour. Thus, at the Langwith Colliery, in 1906, H. Ashford, the checkweighman, was able to say: 'The management were with them, and for those who objected their time would be short.'[1] At other collieries the employers remained obdurate. Harvey told the Ilkeston miners:

Ilkeston was the weakest part of the county from the trade union standpoint, and he had a mandate from the Federation of Great Britain to tell non-unionists that their time was up. The pits were all to be balloted in order to test the feeling of the rest of the men with a view to a strike until Ilkeston had been brought into line with the rest of the country.[2]

The opponents of trade unionism were quick to protest against the Association's policy. In 1897 Benjamin Morris, of Blackwell, wrote: 'At the behest of Messrs. Haslam and Harvey and Company non-union men have been compelled to yield up their liberty or be discharged from their employment.'[3] A few years later, in 1902, Haslam put forward the trade unionist's point of view on non-unionism:

There were heaps of men under the Butterley Company that would be nothing but scoundrels. . . . Such men would gather where they had not sown, while they would risk nothing, but take everything upon the risks undertaken by others and accept the benefits to be derived from the honest achievements of those men who were members of the union.[4]

VIII

The agitation for the eight-hour day was conducted as vigorously as ever after the 1893 lock-out. 'Unweariedly at each annual conference', writes Mr. Page Arnot, 'the M.F.G.B. made its routine preparations for what to do if the luck of the ballot brought an Eight Hours' Bill. Each year this took place, with equal regularity, the parliamentary representatives of Durham and Northumberland, Messrs. Burt, Fenwick and John Wilson, could be heard themselves moving its rejection, or speaking against it when coal-owners moved its rejection, in the House of Commons.'[5]

Derbyshire took an active part in the campaign for the shorter working day and adhered closely to the policy of the Federation, organizing innumerable petitions, passing resolutions and lobbying Members of Parliament at the appropriate times. In 1894 the Bill reached the

[1] *Derbyshire Times*, 3 November, 1906.
[2] *Ibid.* 10 November, 1906.
[3] *Ibid.* 6 November, 1897.
[4] *Ibid.* 22 February, 1902.
[5] Arnot, *op. cit.* pp. 266–7.

committee stage but was withdrawn in order to avoid an amendment granting local option. In a speech at Woodthorpe, Harvey attacked the miners' leaders who opposed the Bill:

It seemed an iniquitous thing to see miners' leaders hob-nobbing with the employers to defeat the Bill. Mr. John Wilson's face could be seen beaming with smiles as he was sitting talking with Joseph Chamberlain and Joicey, and the great owners. . . . And yet he knew the defeat of the Bill meant the continuation of one of the most cruel and iniquitous situations of the century —a system under which lads had to work ten and eleven hours to allow the men to work short hours.[1]

The Bill failed to secure even a first reading in the following year but was one of the issues of the general election. Harvey told a joint meeting of the Yorkshire and Derbyshire miners at Whitwell: 'All Lord Salisbury's speeches, all his actions, all his opposition to labour legislation implied that he had no sympathy with the working classes. . . . Lord Salisbury was as great an autocrat as ever lived.'[2] Nevertheless, Salisbury's administration replaced Rosebery's and the prospects of securing the eight-hour day became even gloomier than they had been before the election.

Lack of time prevented a second reading of the Bill on 10 June, 1896, but the following year was one of great activity. The Liberal members for the Derbyshire mining constituencies, now on the opposition benches, began to figure more prominently in the agitation. In April, 1897, petitions in favour of the Eight Hours' Bill from the miners of the North-East Derbyshire division were presented to Parliament by Thomas Bolton.[3] On 5 May the second reading of the Bill was moved by W. Allen and seconded by Sir Walter Foster, Member of Parliament for Ilkeston, but was lost, after a full day's debate, by 227 votes to 186.

Meanwhile discussions were raging in the coalfield on the desirability of the Bill. Benjamin Morris considered that it would interfere with the liberty of the miner to work longer hours: 'Picture to yourself . . . Mr. James Haslam, J.P., sitting on the magistrates' bench when a miner is brought before him charged under the Eight Hours' Bill with the terrible crime of daring to stay at his work a few minutes after the

---

[1] *Derbyshire Times*, 25 August, 1894. In Northumberland and Durham there was only one shift of transit hands (mainly youths) to two of hewers in the double-shift pits, and only two shifts against three in the three-shift pits. The hewers worked a maximum of seven hours bank to bank, but the transit hands worked ten hours. The unions were opposed to the introduction of an eight-hour shift because they feared that there were not enough youths available to work an equal number of shifts with the hewers and that any change in the system would increase the cost of production and make competition in the export market more difficult. They were also opposed to any multiplication of the number of shifts for social and domestic reasons.

[2] *Derbyshire Times*, 6 July, 1895.   [3] *Ibid.* 1 May, 1897.

specified time . . . because he was anxious to do his best for his wife and family.'[1] Emerson Bainbridge was reported to have said that he had tried the eight hours' system in three of his collieries in 1894 with resulting falls in output of 22, 32 and 23½ per cent. respectively.[2]

In 1898, when Cecil W. Norton, M.P. for Newington West, had the opportunity of introducing a Bill he was persuaded by J. A. Jacoby, Member of Parliament for Mid-Derbyshire, to introduce the Eight Hours' Bill but again lack of time prevented the second reading. An intensive campaign followed in 1899 but no further progress was made. In 1900, again largely as a result of the efforts of Jacoby, the Bill was introduced by J. H. Lewis but was defeated on the second reading by 199 votes to 175. The miners' only consolation was that the majority against the Bill had been reduced. In 1901 the Bill passed the second reading by 212 votes to 199 but was talked out in the committee stage. In 1902 it was defeated on the second reading by one vote.

In Derbyshire the 1902 campaign was enlivened by a public debate between Frank Hall and Benjamin Morris at Alfreton[3] but the miners were by now beginning to despair of securing the eight-hour day by legal enactment. A special conference of the Federation at Southport, on 3–4 July, 1902, recommended members to consider the desirability of industrial action 'seeing the Government will not allow a legal eight-hours' day and also that the coal-owners urge on every occasion that the eight-hours' day be got by Trade Union effort'. It was also decided to test the feelings of the men by means of a ballot and to approach the coal-owners in an attempt to reach a settlement.[4] The meeting with the coal-owners, which did not take place until 2 December, 1902, was fruitless.[5] Moreover, although Derbyshire was in favour of a strike, the Federation was reluctant to embark upon another costly industrial conflict in the face of declining trade.[6]

Thereafter there was little progress for three years. In 1903 a number of Members of Parliament, including Bayley and Jacoby, fought for the inclusion of an eight hours' clause in the Mines Regulation Amendment Bill but were defeated by 183 votes to 144. It was not until after the general election of 1906 that the miners' hopes were revived. The Liberals had won 377 seats, a majority of 84 over all other parties combined. Moreover, in the new parliament there were no less than 53 Labour members. Of these 29 were returned under the Labour Representation Committee to sit as an independent party. Of the other 24 a few were ordinary 'Lib-Labs', but most were, like Haslam, officials

---

[1] *Derbyshire Times*, 13 February, 1897.　　　　　　[2] *Ibid*. 22 May, 1897.
[3] *Ibid*. 5 April, 17 May, 14 June, 1902.
[4] *M.F.G.B.* 3–4 July, 1902.　　　　　　　　　[5] *Ibid*. 2 December, 1902.
[6] *Ibid*. 3 December, 1902; *Derbyshire Times*, 21 June, 1902.

of the miners' unions—a body of men not affiliated with the L.R.C. yet representing a powerful working-class interest.[1]

At a special conference of the Federation, on 7 March, the Executive Committee recommended the introduction of a Bill on the lines of the French Mines Act which provided for a gradual reduction in the hours of employment. The new Bill proposed that the working day for miners should not exceed nine hours in 1907, eight and a half in 1908, and eight hours in 1909 and subsequent years. The scheme aroused some opposition, particularly from Yorkshire, but had the support of Derbyshire and was accepted unanimously after a lengthy discussion.[2] On the following day a deputation waited upon Herbert Gladstone, the Home Secretary, who refused to pledge the Government to take up the Bill but promised support for the second reading after which he was prepared to meet a further deputation.[3] On 11 May the Bill was given its second reading without a division.

Meanwhile the Mining Association of Great Britain was organizing petitions against the Bill and informing Members of Parliament of objections to it. The Association contended that the effect of the Bill would be to reduce the time in which men could get coal to about six hours daily; this in turn would affect the earning capacity of the older and less strong men and of men and boys who were paid by the day. It was also argued that the decreased output would cause an increase in the price of coal which would be detrimental to manufacturers and all private consumers. The evidence given before the Royal Commission on Labour in 1891–2 was adduced in support of the view that the miners themselves did not want an eight-hour day and it was urged that the Bill should be delayed until there had been a full investigation of the problem.[4] Gladstone himself, during the debate on the second reading, had spoken in favour of such an investigation and in July, much to the displeasure of the miners, he announced the appointment of a committee of inquiry.

The time had now come when the phrase 'eight hours from bank to bank' had to be considered with more precision. Mr. Rowe has shown that the true average hours from bank to bank must be measured from the first man down to the first man up, or from the middle or last man down to the middle or last man up. 'In other words', he writes, 'one winding time must be added to the hours during which only coal is raised.'[5] In the past the calculation had been made in different ways in different coalfields. In some districts it was usual to exclude both winding times, in which case the measurement was no longer from bank to bank

[1] See Chapter XII.   [2] M.F.G.B. 7 March, 1906.
[3] Ibid. 8 March, 1906; Derbyshire Times, 10 March, 1906.
[4] Derbyshire Times, 12 May, 1906.   [5] Rowe, op. cit. p. 111.

but the average length of time during which coal was daily raised; in other districts both winding times were included, which produced a meaningless result. In 1883 Haslam had defined 'eight hours from bank to bank' as eight hours plus one winding time.[1] The parliamentary return of 1890 had given no exact definition of the phrase 'bank to bank'.[2] The M.F.G.B. inquiry had been equally confused but Ashton had corrected the more serious errors.[3] For the information of the Committee of Inquiry appointed in 1906 the Board of Trade officials collected statistics of 'average hours from bank to bank' but again failed to supply any definition of what they wanted. The Committee assumed that a true eight hours from bank to bank was under consideration and decided, with little justification, that those districts which excluded both winding times would balance those which had included both.

The miners regarded the setting up of the Departmental Committee as an unnecessary delay and expressed their disapproval at the annual conference of the Federation in October, 1906. In the following December the Executive Committee of the M.F.G.B. waited upon the Prime Minister, Sir Henry Campbell-Bannerman, who told them that the Government was 'fully alive' to the 'great importance' of the Eight Hours' Bill. 'It has got to such a stage of public support and of enlightened opinion', he said, 'that it is a matter for the Government, and the Government are going to take it up.'[4] The miners accepted this assurance but decided to introduce their own Bill once again if they had the opportunity. This came early in the following year. The second reading was carried by 273 votes to 33 on 12 April, 1907, and the Bill was then referred to the Standing Committee on Trade. In Committee Herbert Gladstone, the Home Secretary, moved that the Bill should be reported to the House, without amendments, pending the results of the inquiry.

The problems which had to be considered by the Committee of Inquiry were complex. The chief objection to the shorter working day was its probable effects upon coal production and prices. T. Ratcliffe Ellis, the secretary of the Mining Association, told the Committee that if the eight-hour day were introduced the decrease in the annual output of coal from the Midlands alone would be 4,000,000 tons.[5] Such estimates were based upon the false assumption that all miners were working full time. The Committee found that the average theoretical week amounted to 49 hours 53 minutes, and that the introduction of an eight-hour day would reduce this time by 10·27 per cent., resulting in a

---

[1] See Chapter VII, p. 275   [2] *Accounts and Papers*, 1890, LXVIII, 284.
[3] Miners' Federation of Great Britain, *Statistical Report of the Hours Worked at Collieries*, October, 1890.   [4] M.F.G.B. 6 December, 1906.
[5] *Departmental Committee appointed to inquire into the probable economic effect of a limit of eight hours to the working day of coal miners*, 1907, First Report, Part III, Q. 598.

loss of production of 25,783,000 tons on the output of 1906. But the hours actually worked by the miners were found to be 13·36 per cent. less than the theoretical full time.[1] Moreover, it could be argued that the efficiency of the miners would be increased by shorter hours. Against this it was urged that the haulage and winding had to be taken into account. Even if more coal were hewed it did not follow that it could be wound to the surface in a shorter period. Nor would the older collieries be able to bear a further heavy capital outlay on improved winding plant. Double shifts were a possible solution but many of the miners' leaders were opposed to them and there was also the difficulty of securing an adequate labour force.

The Committee issued its report in May, 1907. Meanwhile there had been negotiations between the Government, the miners, the coal-owners and the Labour Party. In August it was announced that the Government would bring in a Bill but that only the first reading would be taken that session. There were further negotiations between the interested parties and the Government. During the latter half of 1908 the Bill went through all its stages and was given the Royal Assent in December.

As it became increasingly obvious that the Bill would become law the coal-owners intensified their campaign against it. Arnold Lupton, the former managing director of the Shirebrook Colliery, in his new role as Member of Parliament for the Sleaford division of Lincolnshire, issued a lengthy pamphlet on the subject.[2] H. Eustace Mitton, of the Butterley Company, contributed an article to *The Times* in which he argued that the shorter hours would mean lower earnings for contractors and for the men they employed.[3] J. P. Houfton, of the Bolsover Company, predicted the closure of many of the older mines.[4] But the miners' leaders received support for their views from the Liberal coal-owners in Parliament. During the debate on the second reading of the Bill, A. B. Markham, who had interests in Derbyshire, Nottinghamshire, Yorkshire and Welsh collieries, said:

It was impossible and indeed ridiculous that any Member of the House should say that the price of coal would increase 2s. or 3s. per ton in consequence of the Bill, because that entirely depended on the law of supply and demand. For example, the supply had only to be a little behind the demand for prices to rise out of all proportion.[5]

[1] *Departmental Committee appointed to inquire into the probable economic effect of a limit of eight hours to the working day of coal miners*, 1907, Final Report, Part I, p. 60.
[2] *Derbyshire Times*, 6 November, 1907.
[3] *The Times Financial and Commercial Supplement*, 28 February, 1908; *Derbyshire Times*, 14 March, 1908.
[4] *Derbyshire Times*, 4 April, 1908.   [5] 191 H.C. Deb. 4s. 1296.

Similarly, Sir Charles McLaren, of the Sheepbridge Company, who had supported the eight-hour day for twenty years, said:

There were a good many collieries in the Midlands to which the passing of the Bill would make a difference of about 2½d. per ton. In others it would make a difference of 3d., 4d., 5d. or 6d. In considerable groups of collieries in North Derbyshire or South Yorkshire they might suffer to the extent of more than 6d. a ton, but the average in any group they might take would certainly not be more than 6d. . . . Every advance of miners' wages of 10 per cent. meant a rise in the price of coal of 4d. or 6d. Every year London coal merchants put up the price of coal by 1s. to their customers in winter and nobody complained . . . yet they had all this outcry and these exaggerated figures because the mining population of the country demanded a measure which would, perhaps, put up the price of house coal by 4d. or 6d. a ton. . . . He thought the statements they had heard were intended for the elections.[1]

The Home Secretary was torn between the wishes of the Conservative coal-owners and manufacturers and those of the miners who now occupied an influential position within the Liberal party. The result of the conflict was a compromise.[2] The Coal Mines Regulation Act of 1908 laid down that 'a workman shall not be below ground in a mine for the purpose of his work, and of going to and from his work, for more than eight hours during any consecutive twenty-four hours'.[3] The Act excluded both winding times. As Mr. Rowe has pointed out: 'It really limited the hours of coal-drawing.'[4] Moreover, the Act provided that the hours of work 'may be extended as respects any mine by the owner, agent, or manager of the mine, on not more than sixty days in any calendar year by not more than one hour a day'.[5] Thomas Ashton reported to the International Miners' Federation, in March, 1909:

The Act is a long way short of what was asked for, but it may be considered a foundation upon which we can now begin to build. It is the first instalment of an eight hours' working day by legal enactment. The agitation will still continue until that which the Federation set out for is obtained, a Mines Act limiting the working hours at not more than eight per day from bank to bank.[6]

The new Coal Mines Regulation Act was due to come into operation on 1 July, 1909, and it became necessary for the employers and the union to reach an agreement on the way in which it was to be implemented.[7] In April, 1909, there was a conference at Derby between nine representatives of the Midland Counties Colliery Owners' Association

[1] 191 H.C. Deb. 4s. 1309–10.   [2] 190 H.C. Deb. 4s. 1345–6.
[3] 8 Edw. VII Ch. 57., Sec. I (i).   [4] Rowe, *op. cit.* p. 115.
[5] 8 Edw. VII Ch. 57, Sec. 3 (i).
[6] International Miners' Federation, *Quarterly Report*, March, 1909.
[7] In Northumberland and Durham the Act did not become effective until 1 January, 1910.

and nine representatives of the Derbyshire Miners' Association. The union representatives were instructed by the Council to ask that all pits should cease work on Saturdays at 12 o'clock and to refuse to work the additional sixty hours a year permitted by the Act.[1] Eventually, at a further conference, on 21 May, the following agreement was reached:

1. HOURS FOR COAL TURNING. It was decided by both sides to recommend that the time for commencing Coal Turning at the individual Collieries shall be left to the Management.

Also in cases where more than one shift in 24 hours is to be worked, the hours of commencing and ceasing to wind coal on the second shift to be left with the Management.

As to turning on Saturday. It was agreed that pits turn Coal for six hours on Saturday, to cease not later than 12.30 p.m. and this to be paid for as three-quarters of a day, or if less than six hours to be worked, payment to be made *pro rata*.

2. EXTENSION OF HOURS TO BE WORKED. The question of the sixty days allowed by the Act (Section 3, Clause 1) was discussed, and at the request of the men was left for further consideration.

3. WAGES OF DAY-MEN AND BOYS UNDERGROUND. The men's Representatives recommend that the Stallmen should not reduce the wages of the Holers and Loaders in the Stalls.

The Owners stated that they were prepared to give the Act a trial, and not ask for reduction during the ensuing six months, but request that the Miners' Association should recommend that all haulage hands should go down first and come up last.

4. AS TO BANKSMEN. The men's Representatives do not object to the Banksmen continuing to work for the same number of hours as at present, at the same rate of wages. They also do not object to extra time being worked by the Banksmen to clear the pit, provided they are paid at the same rate for the overtime.

5. COAL TURNING. It was decided that the Coal Turning shall continue for the eight hours without intermission.

It was distinctly understood that the quarters now paid when the pit works less than six days will be discontinued.[2]

The agreement came into operation with remarkably little friction. Haslam told a special conference of the Federation on 17 June, 1909: 'I may say that I do not expect any great trouble with the employers in Derbyshire, and I may also say that during the negotiations their mannerisms have been of a most courteous character, and they seem as anxious as we are to avoid any difficulty.'[3] There were disputes at some collieries because no time was allowed for 'snap' (i.e. meals) but after a conference between representatives of the owners and the miners at Derby, on 7 July, the owners' representatives decided to recommend to

[1] *D.M.A.* 27 March, 1909.   [2] *Ibid.* 12 June, 1909.   [3] *M.F.G.B.* 17 June, 1909.

N

their Association 'that the pit shall stand fifteen minutes during each shift except on Saturday, when there will be continuous winding'.[1] There were also difficulties at collieries where two shifts were worked. This practice was becoming increasingly prevalent in the new 'top-hard' collieries and was spreading from these to some of the soft coal pits. By 1913 about 15 per cent. of the Derbyshire collieries were working a double-shift system.[2] It was found in July, 1909, that the coal cutters at the Alfreton Colliery were not being given an interval of twenty-four hours between the beginning of one shift and the beginning of the next but when Haslam asked the Inspector of Mines about the legality of this procedure he was told: 'It would be quite legal where a six-hour shift is worked to bring the shift in two hours earlier on the following day, as not more than eight hours would be worked in 24.'[3]

IX

Between 1901 and 1906 the Derbyshire Miners' Association played its part in two other great national movements, the agitation for the repeal of the coal tax and the reversal of the Taff Vale judgment.

The budget proposal of April, 1901, to impose an export duty of a shilling a ton on coal aroused strong opposition from both the miners and their employers. At the public meeting in Chesterfield, convened by the mayor, W. Spooner, at the request of the local colliery owners, Haslam seconded the resolution protesting against the proposal:

He absolutely objected to this tax being placed upon one industry and other industries being allowed to go scot-free. The impost imposed on export coal was quite equal, on the average, to all the advances the miners had received since 1888. If the price of coal were brought down it must bring down wages, and by curtailing the spending power of the people they would curtail the trade of the country.[4]

The matter was taken up by the M.F.G.B. On 29 April a deputation waited upon Hicks-Beach, the Chancellor of the Exchequer, who reiterated the arguments he had used in the House of Commons that the tax would be paid by the foreign consumer rather than by the British coal-owners and miners. The special conference which had been called to discuss the situation did not share the Chancellor's optimism. It was resolved:

That this Conference agrees that those districts that have not considered the question of laying the pits idle, immediately do so by calling Council Meetings during this week, and that a Conference be held next Tuesday to

---

[1] *D.M.A.* 31 July, 1909.　　　　　　　　　　　　　　[2] Rowe, *op. cit.* p. 25.
[3] *D.M.A.* 10 and 31 July, 1909.
[4] *Derbyshire Times*, 27 April, 1901. See Chapter V, pp. 195-6.

finally decide what shall be done; and we also recommend that all miners leave off work unless the tax upon exported coal is withdrawn, and that the date of the stoppage be decided at the adjourned Conference on Tuesday, 7 May.[1]

When the conference re-assembled it was apparent that there would be no strike. Whilst all the districts were opposed to the tax it was only those with a large export trade which felt sufficiently aggrieved to take industrial action. South Wales, exporting 18 million tons a year, Northumberland with 8 million tons, Durham with 6 million and Fifeshire, exporting 65 per cent. of its output, were all in favour of a stoppage but they were outvoted by the inland coalfields. Parrott, a Yorkshire delegate, told the conference that the men had been influenced by the newspapers which had pointed out that they were fighting the employers' battle. Derbyshire was fairly evenly divided, with a majority of only four branches, equal to 400 members, against a strike. Eventually a resolution was proposed by Robert Smillie and seconded by Harvey condemning the tax, repudiating allegations of collusion between the coal-owners and the miners, and calling for a further conference to discuss a general stoppage in the event of any reductions in wages in any districts as a result of the tax.[2]

Thereafter the agitation continued in various forms. Year after year there were resolutions, conferences, deputations and parliamentary questions. At the Derbyshire miners' annual demonstration in July, 1901, James Martin moved a resolution protesting against the coal tax as being 'wrong in principle and against the interests of the coal industry'. He was supported by William Brace, the Welsh miners' leader, who said: 'If, with the employers fighting with them, they could have defeated the tax he would gladly have had their co-operation. Sooner or later, the coal tax question would have to be fought out between the employers and the men.'[3] In 1902, J. P. Houfton, of the Bolsover Company, warned the Creswell miners that they should consider carefully how they voted in the future. 'So far as the Bolsover Colliery Company were concerned', he said, 'last year they sent to Germany over 70,000 tons of coal, and this year, in spite of everything they had done, they had been unable to book a single order for the German market. That meant to the men the difference between working full time and short time.'[4] In the following year, Thomas Bayley, M.P. for Chesterfield, told the Shirebrook miners that 'the coal proprietors would find ways of putting the coal tax on the workers'. *The Derbyshire Times* commented: 'Mr. Bayley is a colliery proprietor and is, therefore, doubtless cognizant of the "ways" in which this can be done.'[5]

[1] *M.F.G.B.* 30 April, 1901.
[3] *Derbyshire Times*, 20 July, 1901.
[4] *Ibid.* 1 February, 1902.
[2] *Ibid.* 6–7 May, 1901.
[5] *Ibid.* 18 July, 1903.

The reductions in wages of 10 per cent. in 1902, 5 per cent. in 1903 and 5 per cent. in 1904 gave some support to the view that the miners were bearing at least part of the burden of the tax. The agitation was reaching a climax in 1905 when Balfour's administration was replaced by Campbell-Bannerman's. The new Chancellor of the Exchequer, H. H. Asquith, was immediately approached by a mass deputation of 105 M.F.G.B. delegates. He told them that he was anxious 'to remove what I believe to be a grievous and unnecessary burden upon one of the greatest industries of the country'. The coal tax was abolished on 1 November, 1906.

The other great campaign of the opening years of the twentieth century, the agitation for the reversal of the Taff Vale judgment, affected not only the miners but the whole of the trade union movement. After the successful dockers' strike of 1889 a new hostility had developed towards the trade unions which found expression in, amongst other things, a succession of adverse judgments against the unions in the Courts. These judgments removed many of the rights which were understood to have been given to the trade unions by the legislation of the 1870's.[1] Before the Taff Vale case it had been taken for granted that the Trade Union Act of 1871 afforded absolute protection to union funds, Parliament having refrained from giving a trade union either the privileges or the burdens of incorporation. But Mr. Justice (after-wards Lord Justice) Farwell, before whom the Taff Vale Railway Company sued the Amalgamated Society of Railway Servants, decided in 1901 that the union was liable to an injunction and could also be sued and mulcted in damages for wrongs done by its agents. His decision was reversed in the Court of Appeal but it was upheld on appeal to the House of Lords.[2] The A.S.R.S. had to pay £23,000 agreed damages, and the total costs came to about £35,000. It was now quite clear that although strikes were legal no trade union could afford to risk the heavy damages which might be claimed under the new interpretation of the law.

At first the attitude of the Derbyshire leaders was one of defiance. At Pilsley, where there was a dispute over a price list in September, 1901, Haslam told the miners:

If the slightest unfair advantage were taken, if unfair tactics were employed by the management, the men's leaders would exercise the liberty, notwith-standing the Taff Vale decision, to come forward at any time and say that in the interests of the men they must advise a certain course to be pursued. They had been compelled to choose between submission to a new regime or a fight.[3]

[1] John Saville, 'Trade Unions and Free Labour: the Background to the Taff Vale Decision', *Essays in Labour History*, (eds. Asa Briggs and John Saville), (London), 1960, pp. 317–50.   [2] [1901] A.C. 426.
[3] *Derbyshire Times*, 14 September, 1901.

But when the full implications of the Taff Vale decision were brought home to Haslam and Harvey by events in the neighbouring county of Yorkshire, they moderated their views considerably.

The Denaby and Cadeby Main case arose out of a particularly bitter strike which lasted from June, 1902, until March, 1903.[1] Large numbers of miners and their families were evicted and there was much distress. At many of the Derbyshire collieries the men paid weekly levies of sixpence in support of the strikers and, in addition, in January, 1903, the Derbyshire Miners' Association decided to grant £100 a week to help the women and children. Harvey and Jarvis were instructed to take the first contribution of £200 to Denaby, to see that it was properly distributed, and to make full inquiries about the situation there.[2] Harvey later recalled 'the awful scenes at Denaby, when women and children were turned out into the street, when he went from tent to tent and chapel to chapel'.[3] The Denaby and Cadeby Main Colliery Company instituted legal proceedings against the Yorkshire Miners' Association, alleging conspiracy and claiming £150,000 in damages.[4] The case was taken up by the M.F.G.B., Rufus Isaacs (afterwards Lord Reading) appearing for the Yorkshire Miners' Association, and Atherley Jones for Pickard and the union officials. Eventually, in 1906, the House of Lords gave judgment in favour of the union.

Whilst the dispute was in progress Haslam and Harvey began to advocate caution. In January, 1903, Harvey told the Clowne miners:

The Taff Vale decision had put weighty and far-reaching responsibility on trade unions, and it meant that in future the men must not do an illegal act—that was to say, they could not spasmodically stop a pit. Picketing must cease, in the case of a strike, and no one must be interfered with.[5] This decision would never have been given but for the harum scarum action on the part of the I.L.P. and socialistic men. It brought before them many object lessons, and they ought to see how it applied from their side. It behoved them to exercise the greatest care in the selection of representatives and officials.[6]

Two months later, Haslam called attention to the need for more discipline. At Tibshelf he said:

There were many examples of late . . . which went to show that if the mob were not allowed to rule, the officials became unpopular. He declined to be 'pushed' by persons who never thought upon the serious consequences of their actions. . . . He did not care for revolutionary measures. . . . At times he

---

[1] Miners' Federation of Great Britain, *The Denaby and Cadeby Main Collieries Ltd. v. The Yorkshire Miners' Association and others, in the King's Bench Division, before Mr. Justice Lawrence and a special jury, 27 January, 1904*, p. 13.

[2] *Derbyshire Times*, 31 January, 1903. [3] *Ibid.* 19 May, 1906.

[4] M.F.G.B., *Report of the Denaby and Cadeby Main case*, p. 13.

[5] Harvey's reference to picketing arises from the case of Lyons v. Wilkins, [1899] I Ch. 256. [6] *Derbyshire Times*, 17 January, 1903.

found himself standing almost alone at their Council meetings. . . . Why were the Denaby men in the wrong? Simply because they ceased work without notices, and without the consent of the Association. If they had gone the right way about it, and got the consent of the Association, it would have paralysed all attempts of persons like Howden of Yorkshire to interfere.[1]

In April, 1904, Haslam told the Blackwell miners:

It was more than his position was worth to stop the colliery illegally. With the object lesson of the Denaby Main question before them he did not propose to pay damages for acting illegally. The miners of Derbyshire were getting to understand that they could not resort to reprisals without taking legal action.[2]

On the other hand, the victory of the Yorkshire Miners' Association in 1906 was greeted with acclamation. Harvey said: 'The Denaby decision was the greatest victory for trades unionism, either in ancient or modern times. What would have become of some of the lesser organizations if they had had to fight that battle? . . . He did not wonder at flags being hung out at Barnsley when the decision was heard. Let them hope it would be a great lesson for the future.' Barnet Kenyon told the Clay Cross miners: 'They could congratulate themselves upon the judgment that had been given in the Denaby Main case. But in the struggle three of the finest leaders had been lost: he referred to the late Messrs. Pickard, Cowey and Parrott.' 'Quite true', interjected a miner. 'It has killed them.'[3]

Meanwhile the political campaign against the Taff Vale judgment was being intensified. It encouraged many of the trade unions to affiliate with the recently formed Labour Representation Committee but the miners' unions continued to hold themselves aloof.[4] Nevertheless, they made the reversal of the Taff Vale judgment a test question for candidates in the general election of 1906. When Haslam was elected to Parliament in that year he found himself sitting with many other Liberal members who were pledged to support such a policy. It was not long before it was implemented by the Trades Disputes Act of 1906.

---

[1] *Derbyshire Times*, 4 April, 1903. W. H. Howden, a member of the Yorkshire Miners' Association, had been granted an injunction prohibiting the union from making strike payments because the strike was not conducted in accordance with the Association's rules. The colliery company paid Howden £4 a week for his part in the affair and all the legal expenses. (M.F.G.B. *Report of the Denaby and Cadeby Main case*, pp. 53, 209–22). Lord Beveridge comments: 'Two points struck me about the case: first the bias, as it appeared to me, shown by the judge against the union; second, that the colliery company, wishing to make the strike impossible, were almost openly financing the nominal plaintiff and were really at the bottom of the action. "Why they don't get sued for maintenance of another's suit I can't say." So I wrote in telling my father about the case.' (*Power and Influence*, (London), 1953, p. 11.)

[2] *Derbyshire Times*, 2 April, 1904.

[3] *Ibid.* 19 May, 1906. Mr. Page Arnot writes of the Yorkshire leaders that the Denaby case 'is generally believed by all who have written or spoken of the period, to have shortened their active lives' (*op. cit.* p. 347).   [4] See Chapter XII.

APPENDIX I

Rules of the Conciliation Board—April, 1894

1. The title of the board shall be 'The Board of Conciliation for the Coal Trade of the Federated Districts'.

2. The board shall determine from time to time, the rate of wages as from February 1st, 1894.

3. The board shall consist of an equal number of coal-owners or coal-owners' representatives elected by the Federated Coal-Owners, and miners or miners' representatives elected by the Miners' Federation of Great Britain —fourteen of each, with a chairman from outside, who shall have a casting vote.

4. The present members of the board are and shall be:

Chairman: The Right Honourable the Lord Shand.
Coal-Owners or Coal-Owners' Representatives: Messrs. A. M. Chambers, David Davy, A. C. Briggs, W. D. Cliff, Alfred Hewlett, Clifford Smith, William Kellett, Richard Pilkington, M. Deacon, Arthur G. Barnes, Walter Salmond, Captain Harrison, Henry Dennis, J. Batey.
Miners or Miners' Representatives: Messrs. B. Pickard, M.P., S. Woods, M.P., E. Edwards, A. Stanley, W. Whitefield, W. Parrott, E. Cowey, J. T. Williams, J. Weir, T. Glover, W. Bailey, J. Haslam, J. Batchelor, J. Wadsworth

of whom Mr. A. M. Chambers shall be president, and Mr. Pickard, M.P., vice-president.

Whenever a vacancy has arisen, from any cause, on the board, except in the office of chairman, such vacancy shall be filled up within one month of its occurrence by the body which appointed the member whose seat has become vacant. Intimation of such appointment shall be at once sent to the secretaries. On the death, resignation, or the removal of the first or any subsequent chairman, the board shall endeavour to elect another chairman, and should they fail, will ask the Speaker for the time being of the House of Commons to nominate one.

5. The meetings of the board shall be held in London, or such other place as the board shall from time to time determine.

6. The constituents of the board, i.e. coal-owners, or coal-owners' representatives, and miners or miners' representatives are for brevity herein referred to as 'the parties'.

7. The parties shall each respectively elect a secretary to represent them in the transaction of the business of the board, and each party shall give written notice thereof to the other party, and both such secretaries shall remain in office until they shall resign or be withdrawn by the parties electing them. The secretaries shall attend all meetings of the board and are entitled to take part in the discussion, but they shall have no power to move or second any resolution or to vote on any question before the board.

8. They shall conjointly convene all meetings of the board and take proper minutes of the board and the proceedings thereof, which shall be transcribed in duplicate books, and each such book shall be signed by the Chairman, president, or vice-president, or other such person, as the case may be, who shall preside at the meeting at which such minutes are read and confirmed. One of such minute books shall be kept by each of the secretaries. The secretaries shall also conduct the correspondence for the respective parties and conjointly for the board.

9. The secretaries shall, on the written application of either of the parties made by the chairman and secretary of either party for an alteration in the rate of wages, or an alteration of these rules or for any of the objects mentioned in Clause 4, call a meeting of the board within twenty-one days at such time and place as may be agreed upon by the secretaries. The application for the meeting shall state clearly the object of the meeting.

10. The president, or in his absence, the vice-president, shall preside at all the meetings at which the chairman is not present as herein provided. In the absence of both president and vice-president, a member of the board shall be elected by the majority to preside at the meeting. The president or vice-president, or other person presiding, shall vote as a representative, but shall not have any casting vote. When the chairman is present he shall preside and have a casting vote.

11. All questions shall, in the first instance, be submitted to and considered by the board, it being the desire and intention of the parties to settle any difficulties or differences which may arise by friendly conference if possible. If the parties on the board cannot agree then the meeting shall be adjourned for a period not exceeding twenty-one days, and the matter in dispute shall be further discussed by the constituents of the two parties, and the chairman shall be summoned by the secretaries to the adjourned meeting when the matter shall be again discussed, and in default of an agreement by the parties on the board, the chairman shall give his casting vote on such matter at that meeting, which shall be final and binding.

12. All questions submitted to the board shall be stated in writing, and may be supported by such verbal, documentary, or other evidence and explanation as the parties may desire, subject to the approval of the board.

13. All votes shall be taken at meetings of the board by show of hands. When at any meeting of the board the parties entitled to vote are unequal in number, all shall have the right of fully entering into the discussion of any matters brought before them; but only an equal number of each shall vote. The withdrawal of the members of whichever body may be in excess to be by lot, unless otherwise arranged.

14. Each party shall pay and defray the expenses of its own representatives and secretary, but the costs and expenses of the chairman, stationery, books, printing, hire of rooms for meeting, shall be borne by the representative parties in equal shares.

CHAPTER X

THE 1912 STRIKE

I

The years since 1900 had been a period of mounting industrial unrest. Wages generally had failed to keep pace with rising prices. Many sections of the trade union movement were becoming disillusioned with the achievements of the Labour Party after its initial success in the 1906 elections. Some of them were influenced by Syndicalism and its doctrine of direct action.[1] The new spirit became conspicuous in the latter half of 1910 when the number and severity of industrial disputes began to increase sharply and the growing reluctance of trade unionists to follow their leaders developed into open criticism and even repudiation. Haslam's protest against indiscipline at the T.U.C., over which he presided in 1910, was in vain.[2] 1911 was a year of strikes and the prelude to the great miners' strike of 1912. The railway strike of 1911 led to scenes of unusual violence in Chesterfield. On the night of 19 August an attempt was made to burn down the railway station, windows were smashed and at least fourteen people were injured. Troops were called in and the Riot Act was read by the mayor, C. P. Markham, before order was restored.[3]

It is not surprising that the miners were infected by the general feeling of unrest. After the meeting of the Conciliation Board on 3 September, 1909, wage rates had been tied more closely than ever to the price of coal which now remained mysteriously steady despite the marked increase in the cost of food and other commodities. Moreover, the miners had another grievance of several years' standing, which was rapidly becoming an important issue: the question of abnormal working places. In discussing the causes which may lead to the earnings of hewers on piece-work falling below the normal, Jevons distinguishes between natural conditions, faults of management and faults of hewers. Natural

[1] G. D. H. Cole, *The World of Labour*, (London), edn. of 1917, pp. 35–38.
[2] *T.U.C. Report*, 1910. See Chapter VI, p. 253.
[3] *Derbyshire Times*, 26 August, 1911.

N*

conditions may give rise to such difficulties as seams which are too thin or too thick for easy working, loose joints in the coal, soft roofs requiring continual attention, bands of stone in or over the coal, excessive amounts of water or gas. Faulty management may lead to excessive numbers of men being put to work in a mine with the result that it is impossible to wind out of the pit all the coal which they could produce. There may be an insufficient stock of tubs, inefficient winding machinery, bad organization of underground traffic, insufficient ventilation, a shortage of timber or rails, or bad conditions of main haulage ways leading to unnecessary jolting of the coal. The hewer may lack skill and knowledge of the coal seams. He may lack physical strength or suffer from ill-health. He may follow a man who has neglected to keep the stall in proper order or he may merely be lazy or satisfied with low earnings.[1]

In most districts, as in Derbyshire, it had for generations been the custom to meet shortages of earnings due to natural conditions, and to some extent where the management was at fault, by making additional payments.[2] Such arrangements were a matter for bargaining between the individual workman and his employer but by the early years of the present century the bargaining was becoming harder. There was a growing need for the employers to reduce their costs[3] and, with the coming of national and district agreements, it became easier to evade or reduce additional payments made to individuals than to challenge the power of the unions.[4] The difficulties of miners working in abnormal places were accentuated by the introduction of the shorter working day which left them with less time at the coal face to make good the reductions in their allowances by working harder. Many of them were working beyond their strength in an attempt to obtain a living wage.

The miners had long been committed to the principle of a general minimum wage rate expressed as a percentage on the 1888 basis. The growing discontent over abnormal places was now leading to a demand for an individual minimum wage for all piece-workers. The movement was at its strongest in South Wales where there was a strong Syndicalist element. For what appear to be ideological reasons Mr. Page Arnot has tended to discount the influence of Syndicalism upon the miners. He writes: 'Indeed, it was not until the artillery of Lenin was brought to bear on it in 1920 that the Syndicalist doctrines were overcome.'[5] But the historian serves no useful purpose by discounting the influence of that which he dislikes. It is true, as Mr. Arnot remarks, that in the conduct of the dispute over the minimum wage 'there was no theoretic

---

[1] Jevons, *op. cit.* pp. 523–5.   [2] See Prologue, p. 29.
[3] See Chapter V, p. 190.
[4] For a full discussion of the effects of this policy on miners' wages see Jevons, *op. cit.* pp. 527–33.
[5] R. P. Arnot, *The Miners: Years of Struggle*, (London), 1953, p. 117.

affirmation of new doctrine' but this does not necessarily mean that the doctrine had little or no influence. Such influences are not susceptible to any precise measurement but it is surely no accident that South Wales became the spearhead of the minimum wage agitation. In the foreword to *The Miners' Next Step*, a pamphlet drawn up by the South Wales Syndicalists and published early in 1912, it is stated: 'Hundreds of men (trade union officials, executive members, and workmen) have given up their time and money to this work.' This may be an exaggeration but when the arguments put forward in the pamphlet are considered in the light of events in the coalfields during this period there can be little doubt that the influence of Syndicalism was at work, in varying degrees, not only in South Wales but also in Derbyshire and the M.F.G.B.

Criticism of the policy of conciliation and its effects upon trade union leadership provide the starting point of the whole argument. Conciliation is condemned because it has not improved wages: 'We can go on like this for centuries securing great principles and legislative reforms, while all the time our pockets grow emptier. This is a fiendish principle that no sane man can countenance.' Conciliation also gives 'the real power of the men' into the hands of a few leaders:

The workmen for a time look up to these men and *when things are going well* they idolise them. The employers respect them. Why? Because they have the men—the real power—in the hollow of their hands. They, the leaders, become 'gentlemen', they become M.P.s, and have considerable social prestige because of this power. . . . *When things go wrong*, and we have shown that they have gone wrong, they deserve to be, and are blamed. What really is blameworthy, is the conciliation policy which demands leaders of this description. . . . First, they are 'trade unionists by trade' and their profession demands certain privileges. The greatest of all these are plenary powers. Now, every inroad the rank and file make on this privilege lessens the power and prestige of the leader. Can we wonder that they try and prevent progress? Progress may arrive at such a point that they would not be able to retain their 'jobs', or their 'jobs' would become so unimportant that from their point of view, they would not be worth retaining. *The leader then has an interest—a vested interest—in stopping progress*. They have therefore in some things an antagonism of interests with the rank and file.

To deal with these shortcomings the writers of the pamphlet advocated 'a united industrial organization, which, recognizing the war of interest between workers and employers, is constructed on fighting lines, allowing for a rapid and simultaneous stopping of wheels throughout the mining industry'. Its constitution was to give 'free and rapid control by the rank and file' and its immediate industrial programme was to secure a minimum wage and a shorter working day.[1] The development

[1] *The Miners' Next Step*, (Tonypandy), 1912.

of such criticism of conciliation and union leadership in Derbyshire has already been noted.[1] With the growth of the minimum wage agitation it was to become greatly intensified.

II

As might be expected, the first serious dispute over abnormal places occurred in South Wales. Dissatisfaction with the 'Abnormal places' clause was one of the principal reasons for the deadlock in the negotiations for a new Conciliation Board in 1910. The matter was referred to a special conference of the M.F.G.B. and, after lengthy negotiations between representatives of the Federation and the Welsh coal-owners, it was decided to advise the Welsh miners to accept the terms of their employers 'as we do not think the points of difference are sufficient to justify either a sectional strike in South Wales or a national struggle, with all the tremendous issues involved'.[2] A few months later there was trouble at the Ely pit of the Naval Colliery Company, which was a subsidiary of the Cambrian Collieries, Ltd. On 1 September over 800 men were locked out because 80 of them refused to accept a price list which, in their opinion, made insufficient allowance for work in abnormal places.[3] The unrest spread from the Rhondda Valley to the Aberdare and Ogmore valleys, and by the end of the year some 30,000 Welsh miners were locked out or on strike. The disturbances at Tonypandy and other places, occasioned by the introduction of non-union labour, led to clashes between the miners and the police and resulted in the intervention of the military.[4]

True to their Syndicalist beliefs, many of the strikers felt that other coalfields should join in the struggle. The Welsh delegates had raised the question of abnormal places at the annual conference of the M.F.G.B. in October, 1910, when it was resolved that 'the miners of Scotland, England and Wales be requested to meet their respective employers and demand a fair living wage to be paid to all miners working in abnormal places'. During the debate Harvey presented a glowing account of the position in Derbyshire:

For years this question has been dealt with in my county, and dealt with somewhat successfully. . . . Now there is not a colliery in my county but what has a price list, and on that price list is a clause, that where men cannot get a day's wage through difficulties, falls, inundation of water, and so forth, they shall be paid a day's wage, that is the day's wage on the price list plus percentage.

[1] See Chapters VI and IX.   [2] *M.F.G.B.* 9 and 30 March, 1910.
[3] *Ibid.* 24 January, 1911.   [4] *Ibid.* 9 November, 1910.

In reply to an interjection from a Lancashire delegate who alleged that these agreements were not in operation, Harvey was forced to admit:

Of course the difficulty there is, is to prove that there are abnormal conditions. . . . Where another difficulty comes in, is the want of backbone in the men to claim their wages, and not be put on one side. . . . You can make prices but you cannot make backbone.[1]

Despite Harvey's assertions, the tension in Derbyshire was increasing. Early in September there was a very disorderly meeting at North Wingfield at which the union leaders were mercilessly criticized. Enoch Edwards, the President of the M.F.G.B., was sufficiently ruffled to remind the men that Parliament had recently passed the Public Meetings Act: 'It was a most serious matter now to interrupt, and he noticed a constable on the outskirts of the crowd.'[2] A few weeks later the exclusion of the Press from the Staveley Company's annual meeting aroused a great deal of comment. Among the workers at Staveley the incident was magnified as the result of a report in the *Sheffield Telegraph* which attributed to C. P. Markham a statement that the labour unrest called for 'drastic action'.[3] The report was widely publicized and 'drastic action' became a catch-phrase.[4] On 15 November there was a large meeting of the Staveley Company's miners at Poolsbrook at which the question of abnormal places was discussed. G. S. Newton, president of the Markham lodge, said:

There were not thirty places in the Markham pit that were getting a day's wage. . . . Ever since the eight hours commenced they knew that the pit was crowded out, and the present complaint was the result. . . . If they were not satisfied with their leaders the same vote that put them in would turn them out. . . . It was for them to make their wishes and wants known.[5]

The difficulties at the Markham Colliery were typical of those at other collieries throughout the country. Since the introduction of the shorter working day, more coal was being turned out but where working conditions had been remunerative the extra men now employed tended to reduce individual earnings. Moreover, there was a shortage of tubs and there were other complaints about faults in the seams which were more difficult to substantiate. The men employed at the eight pits of the Staveley Company decided through their central committee to send a deputation to the management to ask for the recognized day wage of 5s. plus the current additions of 50 per cent. for all piece-workers in abnormal places.[6] The management eventually agreed to prevent

[1] *M.F.G.B.* 6 October, 1910.   [2] *Derbyshire Times*, 10 September, 1910.
[3] *Ibid.* 1 October, 1910.   [4] *Ibid.* 8 October, 1910.
[5] *Ibid.* 19 November, 1910.   [6] *Ibid.*

'overcrowding' in the future and to consider the need for a day wage after examining records of earnings during the following month.[1]

The men's grievances were accentuated by short-time working at some collieries and by the rising cost of living. The *Derbyshire Times*, calling attention to the fact that the Holmewood Colliery was working only three and a half days a week in mid-winter, remarked: 'What is true of Holmewood is true also to a greater or lesser extent in many other districts.'[2] At a miners' meeting at Stonegravels, George Brown declared that there was more friction between employers and workers than there had been fifty years previously: 'It was a deplorable fact that the miners took home today less wages than they did in 1888.'[3] Frank Hall attributed the general unrest throughout the country to rising prices.[4] At a meeting at Brampton, Barnet Kenyon observed: 'Why, our men need "quids" now just as bricklayers need bricks.'[5]

The growing unrest led both the employers and the union leaders to redouble their efforts to establish a county conciliation agreement. In January, 1911, the following proposals were drawn up:

THE MIDLAND COUNTIES COLLIERY OWNERS' ASSOCIATION

Bank Chambers,
London Road, Derby.
30th January, 1911.

Recommendations for the Settlement of Disputes at
Collieries in the County of Derby.

In the case of dispute at any Colliery the matter shall be dealt with in the usual way by the management and representatives of the men employed at the Colliery, together with the checkweighmen, if the men desire it.

Failing an agreement, the matter shall be referred to an informal Committee, consisting of three representatives appointed by the Coal-Owners' Association and three representatives appointed by the Miners' Association, none of whom shall be connected with the Colliery where the dispute arises, but either side may bring anyone to render such assistance as they may require. In the event of this Committee failing to effect a settlement, the matter shall then be referred to a final Board, composed of not more than nine, and not less than seven members on either side. These representatives shall be elected by the respective Associations, and the Board shall elect an independent Chairman, having no connection whatever with the coal trade, and whose decision in all cases of dispute shall be final. The Board to be elected annually, and in case any member of the Board shall cease to serve from any cause whatever, the vacancy shall be filled within one month.[6]

---

[1] *Derbyshire Times*, 26 November, 1910.   [2] *Ibid.*
[3] *Ibid.*   [4] *Ibid.*
[5] *Ibid.* 19 November, 1910.   [6] *D.M.A.* 11 February, 1911.

The Council accepted the principle of establishing a County Board on 11 March, 1911, but the detailed consideration of its rules became entangled with the negotiations on abnormal places and it was not until October, 1911, that full agreement was reached.[1]

Towards the end of 1910 the South Wales Federation appealed to the M.F.G.B. for financial support and a special conference to consider the matter was held in London on 24–26 January, 1911. After much discussion it was decided that the M.F.G.B. should contribute £3,000 a week which was to be raised by a levy of 3d. a member. Ashton and Harvey were instructed to 'assist the South Wales Federation to bring about a satisfactory settlement of the dispute, if possible' and the South Wales Federation was urged to consider the advisability of increasing its monthly contributions.[2] The conference then went on to consider the general question of abnormal places. It was apparent that little progress had been made with the policy recommended by the annual conference in the previous October. Harvey adopted delaying tactics:

I consider this Conference is rather premature. There has not been time from October till now, with a General Election between. . . . I do not know what we can do here today. We can talk it over, but I do not think we could come to any definite policy until we have tried the policy which was set forth at the Conference in Edinburgh.

Harvey was supported by Frank Hall who gave the conference some information about the situation in Derbyshire. The Association had tried to secure a minimum wage of 5s. plus percentages throughout the county but the coal-owners had argued that conditions differed considerably from colliery to colliery and that the existing day wage for contractors ranged from 4s. 6d. to 5s. The employers were prepared to enter into a county agreement on abnormal places if the men were willing to accept a minimum of 4s. 9d. but this offer was rejected. At the Staveley Company's collieries an agreement was reached whereby the men received a basic wage of 5s. if they were unable to earn more whether in normal or abnormal places. Claims had to be based on the average daily earnings over a four-week period and the relevant wage tickets had to be produced. The Association was prepared to support strikes in any stall or pit where the men could not earn at least 4s. 9d. plus the current percentage additions. Hall continued:

I must say, today we have very few collieries which are outside an agreement of this character. . . . Where we get a good colliery there is no difficulty in carrying the clause out; the manager would see it was done without any

[1] D.M.A. 11 March, 8 April, 6 May, 5 August, 23 September, 21 October, 1911.
[2] M.F.G.B. 25 January, 1911.

hesitation at all. But when you get a dying pit where the men have to walk two or three miles, there you get your difficulty. We have a case in point now where they are closing down two pits because we are forcing that Company to carry this particular clause out.[1]

Hall concluded his speech by saying: 'We cannot settle this matter today. . . . Let us go back to our districts and come again to a conference in three months' time and see if we cannot deal with the question, not only of the abnormal places, but as to what shall be paid as a uniform base, right through the Federation.' After further discussion the conference decided that each district should 'immediately press for a minimum wage for all workmen engaged in abnormal places, and that should any district fail within three months, the members of the Federation be recommended to take national action to enforce the same'.[2]

III

The efforts of Ashton and Harvey to settle the Welsh dispute ended in failure. Although D. A. Thomas,[3] the Chairman of the Cambrian Collieries, Ltd., stated that he was prepared to guarantee a minimum wage of 6s. 9d. a day for piece-workers in abnormal places, the miners felt that this assurance was worthless in view of their experiences in the previous two years'.[4] The situation was discussed on 26 April by a special conference of the M.F.G.B. at which Harvey's part in the affair was criticized by F. Barker, a Welsh delegate. He said:

I have a report of some remarks made by Mr. Harvey on the South Wales dispute. Those remarks have caused a good deal of burning indignation in South Wales, and in the district I represent they are very keenly resented indeed, and the men have gone so far as to pass a vote of censure on Mr. Harvey for making use of those observations. . . . There has been a false charge made against the men. They have been charged with doing something unconstitutional. What they have done is in the strictest sense in accordance with the constitution of the Federation. They resent remarks of this character that are being used by the capitalists in order to excite public opinion against the workmen in South Wales.

Harvey replied:

It was the aim, the object, and the desire of the two men who went down to South Wales to assist in the endeavour to find peace. They had no ulterior motives; they could not possibly have; they might have some popularity to

---

[1] *M.F.G.B.* 25 January, 1911. During the early part of 1911 some of the pits in the Eckington district, owned by J. and G. Wells Ltd., were closed because of difficulties over abnormal places. (*Derbyshire Times*, 25 February, 11 and 25 March, 1911.)

[2] *M.F.G.B.* 25 January, 1911.

[3] Later Lord Rhondda.　　　　　　　　　　[4] Cf. Jevons, *op. cit.* p. 538.

lose, but men who are honest can afford to lose popularity rather than sacrifice principles. I think it is wise on my part, and on the part of this Conference, not to take umbrage at what Mr. Barker has said. But I thought silence might be taken as showing there was something I was ashamed of.

After this exchange between the extremist and the moderate the conference decided that the South Wales dispute should be settled by arbitration.[1]

The Welsh coal-owners refused the Federation's offer of arbitration but said that they were willing to resume negotiations. By 15 May, Enoch Edwards, Thomas Ashton, William Abraham and Thomas Richards had agreed, on behalf of the Federation, to a settlement on the basis of a cutting price of 2s. 1·3d. a ton, and the assurance of the allowances being made, with a proviso for reference of any disputes over allowances to a committee of the South Wales Conciliation Board.[2]

At this point the dispute entered upon a new and interesting stage. Enoch Edwards reported to a meeting of the Executive Committee of the Federation, on 25–26 May, that 'Mr. Ashton and himself were not received very graciously' when they attended a meeting of the South Wales Council and reported on the proposed terms of the settlement.[3] Eleven members of the Council voted in favour of accepting the terms and seven against, but four members had left the meeting before the vote was taken. Three of these were representatives from the Cambrian Combine collieries where the men were strongly opposed to the settlement. A manifesto prepared by the Combine representatives was then sent to every lodge in the South Wales coalfield and published in every newspaper. It was followed by a special conference at which the delegates decided unanimously not to accept the terms of the settlement but to press the Federation to take united action to secure a minimum wage for all miners. At a further conference on 12 June this policy was endorsed. Resolutions were passed condemning Ashton for issuing to members of the M.F.G.B. a circular attacking those who 'did not want a settlement' but an extension of the strike to the whole country. Two of the South Wales leaders, Abraham and Hartshorn, were also censured for sending unauthorized letters to newspapers.[4] Jevons writes: 'The group of Rhondda enthusiasts who had stiffened the dispute by their insistence on a guaranteed minimum of 6s. 9d. as a condition of accepting the owners' revised offer of a cutting price of 2s. 1·3d., had during the period of the strike converted the South Wales coalfield to their policy of the minimum wage. In a few months they were to convert the whole country.'[5]

[1] M.F.G.B. 26 April, 1911.   [2] Ibid. 18–19 May, 1911.
[3] Ibid. 25–26 May, 1911.
[4] Ibid. 12 June, 1911.   [5] Jevons, op. cit. pp. 539–40.

But for the moment they seemed defeated. On 13 June the M.F.G.B., at a special conference held at the Westminster Palace Hotel, decided that the settlement of 15 May secured the objects sought by the Caxton Hall conference on 24 April, and that the Federation would no longer take any responsibility for the Cambrian dispute.[1] The conference was one of the most acrimonious in the history of the Federation. The leaders were condemned by two of the Welsh delegates, George Barker and Tom Smith, for departing from the previous decision to enforce arbitration and for accepting assurances which were regarded as worthless. Later in the debate Harvey said:

Leaders, as I understand the word, are not to be panderers: the man who panders will be lost. First know that you are right, and then go on and do right, and the end will be right. It is when you pander to the multitude and you are not willing to reason and deal with these questions on common sense lines, it is there that the danger lies. This will go a long way to save the situation in Wales. It means disruption and disintegration, it means there is no discipline. A wild howling mob could never settle anything, and a mob which does not listen to commonsense ought not to have anything settled for it. We have one down in Wales.

The Welsh delegates were immediately on their feet. 'Will you withdraw "howling mobs"?' said one. 'I, as a Welshman, stand and refuse to be abused', said another. 'We may be wild and irresponsible. Mr. Harvey is old and responsible. I hope he will withdraw the term "howling mob". They are not a howling mob.' Even Hartshorn protested mildly: 'It is a bit insulting.' Eventually, after a polite request from Abraham, Harvey withdrew the offending words.[2]

The conference also considered the general question of payment for work in abnormal places, which had already been discussed at the annual conference in October, 1910, and at the special conference in January, 1911. Some of the districts were able to report progress and others were still negotiating but nowhere was the situation regarded as being entirely satisfactory. As Harvey had done on a previous occasion, Haslam laid the onus upon the men: 'We have to admit that all the men do not get the money that is promised, and we do not forget to tell them they would get more if there was more backbone in them.'[3] The Derbyshire miners' representatives had met the employers in April and had again tried to secure a uniform 5s. basic wage plus percentages. The employers had insisted on preserving the existing differential rate of 4s. 6d. to 5s. They had also sought to include in the agreement two protective clauses which allowed them to remove a man from a stall which was alleged to be abnormal to one which was agreed to be normal, and to withhold

[1] *M.F.G.B.* 13 June, 1911.   [2] *Ibid.*   [3] *Ibid.* 15 June, 1911.

allowances from men who were unable to earn the full wage because of age or infirmity. These terms were unanimously rejected by the Council. Haslam commented:

We should have some trouble with the men in having them moved out of their working place and someone else put in. Our business must be to see that they do not go in those places to test them for the employers. . . . As to old men who are getting practically worn out, I am glad to find there are sons in this bad world with some consideration for an aged father. I do not think it will be so much a matter for the Union as between the son and his father, and the making of such an arrangement as will keep him there at a reasonable wage.[1]

South Wales had submitted a resolution calling for immediate action to secure a minimum wage for all colliery workers but the Business Committee had excluded it from the agenda. When the conference was about to come to a decision on the question of abnormal places the more militant section of the South Wales delegation pressed for a discussion on a general minimum wage. Abraham explained:

I think it is most important that it should be known that our South Wales friends are not here upon the abnormal places question. They have dropped that. I want the Conference to understand South Wales has gone beyond the question of abnormal places. Do you expect us in South Wales to take up abnormal places and not to discuss the minimum wage?

But Enoch Edwards refused to depart from the agenda. 'You could not permit one resolution to be moved from a district to shut others out', he said. After further discussion the conference, by 95 votes to 55, passed its resolution on abnormal places:

That having heard the reports from districts on this question, and seeing that these reports are incomplete and negotiations with the coal owners still proceeding, this Conference be adjourned until the 28th July next, at 10 a.m. to complete the reports and negotiations in the respective districts, and also to decide what action shall be taken.[2]

During the heated debate on the first day of the conference some of the South Wales delegates had complained that their case had not been put fairly before the men in the other coalfields, an allegation which led to a sharp clash with John Wilson, the Durham leader. They now went home temporarily defeated but not dispirited. At a conference on 1 July the South Wales Federation again rejected the May settlement, drew up a manifesto to be sent out to the English and Scottish coalfields, and undertook to send speakers to the various coalfields in support of national action on the question of a guaranteed minimum wage.[3]

[1] *M.F.G.B.* 15 June, 1911.   [2] *Ibid.*   [3] Jevons, *op. cit.* p. 540.

The South Wales delegates who visited Derbyshire, a few weeks later, were well received by the men but not by their leaders. When the delegates called at the offices of the Derbyshire Miners' Association Frank Hall refused to give them a list of the addresses of lodge officials.

'It was most dishonourable and most unfair', said Hall, 'for South Wales miners to send representatives into Derbyshire to disturb our men after they had come to a decision. . . . They were telling the Derbyshire miners tales that were untrue and misleading. . . . We could not possibly assist them to go to our pits in order to undermine the position the Federation had taken up.'[1]

J. Hughes, one of the Welsh delegates, commented:

We have had only one rebuff, and that was at the miners' offices. At every meeting we have attended, on the part of the miners themselves we have had a unanimous opinion expressed that the attitude adopted by the miners' leaders is not the attitude of the Derbyshire miners.[2]

Several lodges invited the Welshmen to address meetings. At Staveley, G. S. Newton, president of the Markham lodge, stated: 'He was not aware that the men had been consulted in Derbyshire as to their action. Their officials had not had instructions from the miners to take the action they had done.' David Bowen, a Welsh delegate, told the meeting: 'If we had done what Mr. Frank Hall told us we should have packed up our traps and gone back to South Wales. We are not going back, however, and when we do we will be sent back by the miners.'[3] When Hughes reported Frank Hall's treatment of the delegation to a meeting at Shirebrook, presided over by John Spencer, there were cries of 'Shame' and 'This is the man we keep'.[4]

The allegations of the Welsh delegates and their Derbyshire supporters were probably true. After the Cambrian Combine strike was taken up by the Federation in January, 1911, there were no resolutions on the subject by the Council of the Derbyshire Miners' Association and the officials appear to have acted quite independently when they attended the various conferences. On 10 April the Executive Committee resolved:

That having fully discussed the South Wales position as explained by Mr. Harvey, and the appeal for South Wales, this Executive decides that assistance given from the County must be done through the Federation, and the Minute Secretary write them to this effect, and also advising them not to send men into our district to collect at our collieries.[5]

At the Staveley meeting the men decided to ask for a ballot on the question of supporting the Welsh dispute but at the Council meeting on

[1] *Derbyshire Times*, 22 July, 1911.
[2] *Ibid.* 29 July, 1911.   [3] *Ibid.* 22 July, 1911.
[4] *Ibid.* 29 July, 1911.   [5] *D.M.A.* 10 April, 1911.

31 July, it was moved by the Swanwick lodge and seconded by the Stanley lodge 'that the Markham No. 1 resolution be not entertained'.[1] At most of the meetings addressed by the Welsh delegates a collection was taken. Harvey came in for a great deal of criticism, particularly from members of the Bolsover I.L.P. who instructed their secretary, J. Thornhill, to obtain full information about Harvey's part in the Cambrian dispute.[2] Thornhill subsequently addressed the Staveley meeting at which a miner alleged: 'Mr. Harvey came back from South Wales, and because he was unable to settle the dispute and was consequently not "the great I am", and could not hand his name down in history as having settled the dispute, he put down his name for stopping the £3,000.' David Bowen, the Welsh delegate, referred to the complaints by Ashton and Harvey that they had been followed through the streets of Tonypandy with shouts of 'We want the 20th rule'.[3] He said: 'At one place some boys, aged fourteen to sixteen, did shout, but had the people of Tonypandy turned out as an unruly mob you would never have seen Mr. Harvey again.' Bowen's words were greeted with laughter and cries of 'No loss'.[4] On 31 July it was resolved:

That this Council desires to express its entire confidence in the Leaders of this Association, and repudiates the action of Welshmen and others in making statements against our Leaders, which are misleading, inaccurate, and calculated to cause dissension amongst our men, and injure our Association. We therefore call upon all our members to remain loyal to the Association and its Leaders.[5]

Judging from the decisions reached by the Council, those who sympathized with the South Wales strikers appear to have been in a fairly small minority. On the other hand, it was not only the officials who were being criticized for failing to express the aspirations of the men but also the delegates to the Council. It was alleged that the Council was dominated by checkweighmen and butties who were conservative in their attitude and unlikely to reflect the true opinions of the rank and file.[6] For these reasons it is not easy to assess the extent of this disaffection but there can be no doubt about its Syndicalist character.

On 7 July the M.F.G.B. stopped its contribution of £3,000 a week towards the support of the 12,000 Cambrian miners still out and the South Wales levy was increased so as partially to fill the gap. The Cambrian men decided to continue the struggle on a much reduced strike pay until 1 September when they were obliged to accept the

---

[1] D.M.A. 31 July, 1911.
[2] Derbyshire Times, 17 June, 1911.
[3] M.F.G.B. 13 June, 1911.
[4] Derbyshire Times, 22 July, 1911.
[5] D.M.A. 31 July, 1911.
[6] See Chapter VI, pp. 225, 227, 264-6.

owners' terms but there is no permanent interest in the final phase of the dispute. The strike had already done its work in the national sense and the movement for dealing with the abnormal places question by national action was now fairly well under way.

At the Federation conference of 28–29 July, held in London, the abnormal places question was again discussed. Haslam reported that an offer had been made by the Derbyshire coal-owners at a meeting at Chesterfield on 21 July but it had not yet been submitted to the men. Its terms were as follows:

Where any difficulty arises such as bunkers, faults, bad roof, water or similar difficulties rendering it impossible for the men to earn a day's wage (unless caused through their own negligence) arrangements shall be made between the manager or undermanager and the stallman as to the compensation to be paid for the difficulty.

Failing an agreement the contractors shall be paid 5s. or 4s. 9d. as at present. Day men and loaders the usual stall rates.

Should a dispute arise as to when a stall is abnormal and the men not earning proper wages, such dispute shall be dealt with by two workmen appointed by the Lodge Committee and two representatives of the Management, who shall inspect the place and come to an agreement if possible.

Failing to agree the dispute shall be settled in the way provided for in the rules of the suggested County Board.

Where wages are not being made in a stall, but are being made in adjoining stalls, conditions of work being the same, then this clause not to apply.

Haslam explained to the conference:

One of our difficulties has been that mentioned by Lancashire, that at times we have been met by the statement that it is not the place but the man that is abnormal. . . . The wages earned by a man before he gets into a difficult place, even if it is only a temporary difficulty, will go a long way to prove that a man has a right to the wage.[1]

Most of the districts were dissatisfied with the terms which had been offered by their employers but there was some disagreement over future policy. Lancashire and Yorkshire were in favour of an immediate strike ballot 'unless the coal-owners agree to a definite payment for all abnormal places of 7s. per day or such payment equal to day-wage coaling rate for each respective county or district in this Federation'.[2] Other districts supported an Executive Committee amendment, which was eventually carried by 82 votes to 54, 'to arrange with the coal-owners of the United Kingdom for a joint meeting to consider the question of paying the district minimum rate of wages for working abnormal places'. If no agreement was reached there was to be a strike ballot.[3]

[1] *M.F.G.B.* 28 July, 1911.   [2] *Ibid.*   [3] *Ibid.* 29 July, 1911.

Before the conference the South Wales Federation had submitted a resolution calling for a national strike 'for the purpose of securing for all colliery workmen a definite guaranteed minimum wage' but Ashton refused to put it on the agenda on the ground that the conference had been called to discuss abnormal places.[1] At the conference the Welsh delegates pressed for the deletion of the words 'abnormal places' from the Executive Committee's amended resolution. Hartshorn said:

> There is no other case in the industrial enterprise of this nation where the onus is on the workmen to prove they have done a fair day's work. We have in our collieries labourers, timberers, repairers and others who are paid without being asked if they have done a fair day's work. It is always assumed that he has done a fair day's work. If the owners can prove that a man has wilfully not done his duty that is another matter; but we say that the collier ought to be treated as being as honest as every other class of workman in this country.[2]

But the Federation was not yet converted to the principle of a general minimum wage. It was difficult for men such as Harvey to accept the policies advocated by the South Wales miners. He told the conference:

> The man who tries to avoid a war and get the conditions he desires through negotiation is a better man than he who tries to get the same conditions through a strike. . . . The principle of payment is being practically recognised and accepted . . . and let me say to our friends, and they can make inquiries about it, that any man at our collieries who works at the coal face, who is short of 7s. 6d. a day, will get it.

'That is what Mr. Brace wants', cried a South Wales delegate.[3]

On 1 August Ashton wrote to Sir Thomas Ratcliffe Ellis, secretary of the Mining Association of Great Britain, suggesting a joint meeting of representatives of his Association and of the M.F.G.B. in order 'to consider the question of a rate of payment for working in abnormal places, and also to consider the low wages paid to day-wage men'.[4] He encountered a difficulty which the Federation had experienced before.[5] Ellis replied that the Mining Association did not deal with questions of wages, and that if there was to be a meeting it must be with representative coal-owners appointed by the different districts.[6] Such a meeting of coal-owners was held in London at the Westminster Palace Hotel on 19 September to consider the M.F.G.B. application. They agreed to meet the miners' representatives but, with the exception of the Yorkshire, Lancashire and Midland owners, they viewed with disfavour the proposal to pay a fixed minimum wage for work in

[1] M.F.G.B. 21 July, 1911.
[2] Ibid. 28 July, 1911.
[3] Ibid.
[4] Ibid. 29–30 September, 1911.
[5] See Chapter VII, pp. 270, 275.
[6] M.F.G.B. 29–30 September, 1911.

abnormal places. The strongest opposition came from the coal-owners of South Wales and Scotland.[1] The Derbyshire miners had already decided, on 5 August, to adopt the report of the officials on the abnormal stall question and 'to give the agreement a trial'.[2]

The joint national meeting of the representatives of the coal-owners' associations and of the M.F.G.B. was held on 29 September. The miners demanded that there should be a definite understanding that whatever was the agreed wage paid when a man was on day-work should be paid to men working in abnormal places. The owners insisted on continuing the practice of paying allowances which took into account not only the character of the abnormal place but also the labour efficiency of the men employed there. They also wanted the negotiations to be referred back to the districts on the ground that it was impossible to fix such allowances on a national basis. The M.F.G.B. was prepared to accept the inevitability of district negotiations but would not agree to the owners' vague formula that wages should be 'commensurate with work performed'.[3] This principle, as Jevons has pointed out, 'could not for a moment be admitted by a responsible trade union, for it contravenes the essential doctrine of the "common rule" which is the very foundation of trade union policy: that for doing the same kind of work all men shall be paid the same rate. . . . Whereas this battle was fought and won by the trade unions of the engineering and building and many other great trades half a century ago, it was only in this abnormal places dispute that it became a dominant question in the coal trade.'[4] It was this fundamental issue which prevented the joint meeting from reaching agreement.

IV

Meanwhile the question of abnormal places was fading into the background and the agitation for a general minimum wage was gathering strength. On 23 September the *Derbyshire Times* asked:

Will there be a miners' strike? . . . If enquiry is made of the miners' leaders the replies received do not give sufficient ground for this belief, but among the rank and file of the miners there is not that deference to the advice given by the leaders there was, and there are to be found many who openly advocate the policy of forcing the hands of their officials, not only on the question of abnormal places, but on that of a minimum wage. . . . Many miners contend, and contend with truth, that their families would be receiving more in strike pay than they have been getting per week during the short time, and point to the accumulated benefits of their association.[5]

[1] Jevons, *op. cit.* pp. 542–3.   [2] *D.M.A.* 5 August, 1911.
[3] *M.F.G.B.* 29 September, 1911.
[4] Jevons, *op. cit.* pp. 544–5.   [5] *Derbyshire Times,* 23 September, 1911.

The movement was particularly strong in the Staveley district. A pit-head meeting at Markham No. 1, on 31 August, resolved unanimously to press for an immediate 5 per cent. advance, another on 1 January, and a minimum wage of 8s. a day.[1] One of the local leaders, with forty years at the coal face, said: 'Whether our leaders are ready to go in for an advance or not, we are ready to push them.'[2]

'There is a growing feeling among the men in this district', reported the *Derbyshire Times*, 'to get men on the Council who are in close touch with the working conditions, and not to rely so much on the check-weighmen. No doubt it has a significant bearing for some men have been "on the top" probably more than a quarter of a century, and the miners contend they are out of touch with the conditions below.'[3] Never-theless, when sufficient pressure was brought to bear on the Council it could be made to move. On 26 August the Warsop Main lodge, seconded by Morton No. 2, succeeded in carrying a resolution: 'That the Executive of the Miners' Federation be instructed by Mr. Haslam to place before the Coal-Owners the question of a minimum wage of 8s. per day for all Stallmen working at the Coal face.'[4] A month later Warsop Main again took the initiative, seconded this time by Bolsover, in securing the adoption of a resolution in favour of raising the question of a minimum wage of 8s. a day at the annual conference of the M.F.G.B.[5]

Similar influences were at work in other districts with the result that the agenda for the annual conference at Southport on 3–6 October, 1911, contained resolutions on the minimum wage from Durham, Yorkshire, Somerset and Lancashire. The Business Committee pro-duced a composite resolution on which there was much discussion. Harvey said: 'I think it meets the situation most admirably.' Eventually it was carried unanimously:

That the Federation take immediate steps to secure an individual Dis-trict Minimum Wage for all men and boys working in mines in the area of the Federation without any reference to the working places being abnormal. In the event of the employers refusing to agree to this then the amended 21st Rule of the Federation be put into operation to demand the same. That a Conference be called on November 14th for the purpose of taking action under Rule 21.[6]

---

[1] *Derbyshire Times*, 2 September, 1911.
[2] *Ibid.* 23 September, 1911.   [3] *Ibid.*
[4] *D.M.A.* 26 August, 1911.   [5] *Ibid.* 23 September, 1911.
[6] *M.F.G.B.* 6 October, 1911. At the 1910 annual conference the rules of the M.F.G.B. were amended and Rule 20, which governed strike action for defensive purposes, became Rule 21. At the 1911 conference Rule 21 was amended as follows: 'That whenever any Federation or District is attacked on the wages question or the conditions of labour or with the approval of the Conference specially called for that purpose has tendered notice to improve the conditions of labour or to obtain an advance in wages a Conference shall be called to consider the advisability of joint action being taken.'

The economic causes underlying the demand for a minimum wage were complex. The much vaunted 'minimum wage' which had been obtained under the national conciliation agreement after the 1893 lock-out had proved to be an illusion. It had been offset by rising prices and by the failure of the Conciliation Board to take into account factors other than the price of coal. According to Frank Hall the growth of mechanization had lowered the cost of production and increased the output of coal year by year but, instead of sharing in these benefits, the miners suffered reductions in their earnings. Before the introduction of machinery two or three contractors would be employed in every stall but under the new conditions the colliery management made a distinction between 'coal getting' and 'loading out'. The machine ousted contractors from their stalls and reduced them to mere 'loaders'. The number of highly-paid, skilled men was greatly reduced and replaced by a cheaper class of labour. Many of the contractors who retained their stalls were unwilling to pay their displaced colleagues an adequate wage for loading. 'The men ought to ask themselves', said Hall, 'whether they as miners were prepared to pay to the men who worked for them the same rate of wages that they were asking the company to pay. He knew that was not carried out honestly amongst their own men.'[1]

Offsetting the advantages accruing to the coal-owners from mechanization were the diminishing returns of an extractive industry. Here again the miners were adversely affected. Under the conciliation agreement wages were still paid on the basis of 1888 prices. But conditions had changed during the twenty-three years the price lists had been in operation. In the older pits the men had further to walk to and from their working places. Many of the better seams which had yielded a fair day's wage had been worked out and the men had been compelled to work thinner ones. These changes in natural conditions together with the introduction of the shorter working day and the problems of 'overcrowding' and abnormal places had all combined to produce a decline in earnings.

In this situation there was a conflict of interest between the contractors and the men who were employed by them. The fear was expressed that the minimum wage might well become the maximum wage. Frank Hall told the Palterton miners:

There were many collieries in the country where the average wage at the coal face was 8s. a day. It would only be a matter of dividing all the money up at these pits; and it would give them 8s. per day all round. Yes, but there were some getting over 8s. a day. They would not want to share with the men getting less.[2]

[1] *Derbyshire Times*, 7 October, 1911. For a full discussion of the effects of the introduction of machinery upon miners' wages see W. D. Stewart, *Mines, Machines and Men*, (London), 1935, pp. 33–41.   [2] *Derbyshire Times*, 7 October, 1911.

Others believed that the adoption of a minimum wage would bring an end to the contract system. 'It was plainly evident', said one miner, 'that if the masters had to guarantee a minimum wage and take the risks of a bad stall, they would take good care to secure the plums of the good stalls.'[1] At Bolsover, where there was strong opposition to the butty system, the men were in favour of a general strike. They were no doubt influenced by Benjamin Lee, the president of the local I.L.P., who had recently returned from Ruskin College. 'The feeling amongst the men at Bolsover', he said, 'is that we must be firm on the subject of an 8s. per day minimum.'[2] An East Derbyshire miner was reported to have said: 'It is only the revolutionaries, the men who having failed to get a stall developed socialistic tendencies, who are shouting out for a strike.'[3] These matters were discussed with great heat at innumerable meetings throughout the county. The union leaders attempted to give the men some guidance through the maze of the conciliation machinery, abnormal places and the minimum wage. Hall confessed that the national Conciliation Board had been a failure because it was based on unsound principles and contended that the employers could well afford to pay higher wages despite the rigidity of the price of coal. He advocated a better conciliation agreement rather than a minimum wage.[4] Barnet Kenyon expressed similar views. He believed that the 8s. minimum wage which was being demanded by Derbyshire, Yorkshire and Notting-hamshire was excessive: 'I ask you, do you think that we can force in this county these enormous advances over and above other coalfields in Britain where the owners have considerably greater advantages in the matter of freightage than those whom we are asking to pay 8s. a day?' He did not believe that the Conciliation Board 'was an ideal body' but 'it could be made capable of bigger things'.[5] But Harvey, speaking on the minimum wage at Staveley, said: 'Nothing else will satisfy us, nothing else shall we accept, believing it to be reasonable. I hope the coal owners will meet us in that spirit and give us what has been so long delayed.'[6]

Despite his bombast, Harvey was united with the other officials in a desire to minimize the influence of the more militant section of the union and to avoid a general strike. At one meeting Frank Hall said: 'The discontent . . . is not of a local character, it is national. . . . I don't want you to be led away by certain men. I can assure you your leaders are most faithful to your interests. I tell you that honestly and fairly.'[7] Barnet Kenyon complained about a leaflet addressed to members of the Association and headed 'Don't trust your leaders'. 'I ask you', he said,

[1] *Derbyshire Times*, 7 October, 1911.
[2] *Ibid.*
[3] *Ibid.*
[4] *Ibid.* 28 October, 1911.
[5] *Ibid.* 21 October, 1911.
[6] *Ibid.* 14 October, 1911.
[7] *Ibid.* 7 October, 1911.

'if you have any grounds on which you should distrust your leaders either central or local. If there are any, send them to your Council meetings and let's have them thrashed out.'[1] At a meeting at Shirebrook he told the men: 'They were living in a Christian country within the four corners of the British Constitution, and before they preached a down tools policy he asked them to look beyond the narrow view of their own personal and class interests.'[2] At a meeting of the Council, on 23 October, Harvey seized the opportunity to condemn the activities of Keir Hardie and George Lansbury:

> By going about the country and inciting men to strike they created responsibilities and left other people to grapple with them. The miners' leaders were fully capable of looking after the interests of the miners, without interference from such irresponsible men who were uttering wild and dangerous statements.[3]

Frank Hall was given the task of preparing a statement on the minimum wage question for presentation to the employers. It began by calling attention to the resolution passed at the annual conference of the Federation on 6 October and continued:[4]

> The application is for a minimum wage for Contractors, Holers, Loaders, and Day Men. (Not necessarily the same wage at every Colliery.)
> Where the 4s. 9d. and 5s. is recognised, as in the Agreement for the Working of Abnormal Places, we ask for 4d. per day to be added to these amounts for Contractors, making a basis [sic] minimum of 5s. 1d. and 5s. 4d.
> Where loading is done by the ton, a day's wage shall be fixed that shall secure to the loader a wage below which it cannot fall. Where filling is done by the day, as at some of our large collieries, 4d. to be added to the base so as to give a general advance of 6d. net.
> The Holers and others to be dealt with in the same way.
> All contracts, and for whatever class of work, a Minimum Wage must be fixed.
> The Federation Resolution also provides for a minimum for datallers and lads after reaching 19 years of age.
> The scale for boys stops at 19, when a boy may be a Corporal or doing some other work. Many such work nights as jobbers without any fixed rate.
> We are asking the Colliery Owners to agree to the general principle of a *Minimum Wage for all Men and Boys over 19 years of age*, with an all-round advance of 4d. per day on the base of the present recognized wage, for the different classes of work in the several districts of the County.
> If the general principle is agreed upon, the details can be worked out at each Colliery by deputation.

[1] *Derbyshire Times,* 14 October, 1911.
[2] *Ibid.* 21 October, 1911.   [3] *Ibid.* 28 October, 1911.
[4] *D.M.A.* 23 October, 1911. It was understood that the rates demanded would be subject to the current additions of 50 per cent.

A National Conference is called for November 14th to hear reports from districts, it being the intention of the Conference, if the reports are not satisfactory, to take action under Rule 21 of the Federation.

The Rule provides for a national stoppage on wages questions.

On 28 October Haslam, Harvey, Kenyon, Hall, Martin and the other members of the Executive Committee met representatives of the Midland Counties Colliery Owners' Association at the Portland Hotel, Chesterfield.[1] Despite the fact that the Association had conceded the principle of differential rates for the older collieries the employers refused to grant a minimum wage of 7s. 7½d. to 8s. a day for contractors. 'We were told we should have to fight for it', said Haslam.[2]

Other districts experienced similar difficulties. The Lancashire and South Wales coal-owners argued that the demand was a breach of the existing conciliation agreements. Early in November, at a quarterly meeting of the English Conciliation Board, the M.F.G.B. raised the question of the minimum wage. According to the rules wages could not be discussed at quarterly meetings but the employers agreed to hold a special conference with the miners' leaders to discuss the minimum wage. 'We felt if we were going to fight this question, as we had all agreed we would,' explained Edwards, 'it was necessary that we should put ourselves right with the people with whom we stood agreed, and at the same time to press our further application for this minimum wage.'[3] The conference was held on 10 November and, after much discussion, the employers accepted the principle of a minimum wage. Edwards stated later:

They were prepared to fix a price for the minimum wage, but some of our people on our side, who had not finished their interviews with their employers, were not anxious to get a fixed rate. They believed they could fix a better rate, but if we could get them to agree . . . to the principle of a general minimum wage . . . then it would be open to each district to build upon it and try to make a better arrangement.[4]

Eventually the coal-owners' representatives made the following offer:

The amended proposal for a minimum wage for coal getters which you have placed before us has had our careful consideration. Whilst we could recommend the adoption of a minimum wage, the matter is beyond our power to decide today. We propose to take it to our districts, and suggest an adjournment to the 6th December, for that purpose. In the meantime the negotiations in regard to abnormal places and boys' and datallers' wages shall be continued in the various districts.

[1] *D.M.A.* 21 October, 1911. [2] *M.F.G.B.* 14 November, 1911.
[3] *Ibid.* [4] *Ibid.*

On the following day the offer was considered by a special Council meeting of the Derbyshire Miners' Association. It was decided, by 64 votes to 8, that the delegates to the forthcoming Federation conference should support a postponement of any decision on the minimum wage until 6 December and that Haslam should ask the Derbyshire coalowners for another meeting.[1]

The results of the negotiations with the employers were reported to the Federation conference on 14 November. There was a considerable difference of opinion as to the value of the assurances given by the employers' representatives on the English Conciliation Board. Lancashire, Somerset, Cumberland, South Wales and Northumberland were all in favour of taking an immediate strike ballot. Yorkshire, Derbyshire, Nottinghamshire, South Derbyshire, Leicestershire, Cleveland, North Wales, Scotland, Durham, the Forest of Dean and the Midland Federation were in favour of continuing negotiations. Haslam said: 'I think my colleagues and myself have every confidence that whatever can be got in any other county can be got in Derbyshire.' Both Haslam and Harvey estimated that 75 per cent. of the men in Derbyshire were already earning more than the 8s. a day which was being demanded.[2]

Harvey referred to the suspicions 'that in certain parts of the Federation' there was a desire to withdraw from the struggle:

Now I want to disabuse the minds of those delegates once and for all, that there is any idea either in Yorkshire or Derbyshire, or under the Conciliation Board known as the English Section, to drop the principle of the minimum wage. . . . I prefer to get what I want by negotiation sooner than by strike, sooner than by bringing disaster on thousands of women and children, and thousands and thousands who have nothing whatever to do with this matter at all. All I am asking for is delay, for time to meet, time to negotiate, time to explain. This is not a sectional question, but must apply to the whole of Great Britain.[3]

The supporters of continued negotiations eventually won the day by 376 votes to 238. After further discussion it was agreed:

That this Conference having heard the Reports from all Districts in reference to a demand for a District Minimum Wage is of opinion that the best course to pursue at the present juncture with a view to attaining that object with the least delay is to negotiate Nationally; and therefore we instruct the Executive Committee of the Federation to formulate a claim for each District. And in order to give effect to this Resolution the Executive Committee, with additional Representatives, meet the Coal-owners of Great Britain at the earliest date and report immediately thereafter to a National Conference,

[1] *D.M.A.* 11 November, 1911.
[2] *M.F.G.B.* 14 November, 1911. This presumably referred only to hewers.
[3] *Ibid.* 15 November, 1911.

but that this Resolution shall not prevent or interfere with the negotiations now being carried on in the various Districts of the Federation. And that this Conference stand adjourned to December 20th to receive the Final Reports.[1]

The *Derbyshire Times* reported that the news was received 'with relief' in Derbyshire and was warm in its praise of the miners' leaders:

The change of feeling in Derbyshire during the last few months has been most marked. The men are realizing that Messrs. Kenyon and Hall have been frankly telling them that the minimum wage will not work in Derbyshire, and there is no class of men that it would hit harder than the stallmen. As their leaders point out, even a 6s. per day minimum in some pits would mean the closing down of these collieries and the throwing out of work of all the men employed. . . . We fail to see why they should be dragged into conflict to meet the wishes of either South Wales or Scotland.[2]

Barnet Kenyon, addressing the Holmewood miners, said: 'He advocated organization rather than the brutal methods of a strike. . . . They had to look at the effects of the dislocation of trade not merely from the point of view of a particular class but all other classes in the community.'[3]

The 'coal-owners of Great Britain', whom the miners' representatives had been instructed to meet, were not so conciliatory as the trade union leaders. They expressed the view that no useful purpose would be served by holding such a meeting. There had been, however, two meetings with the employers of the Conciliation Board area who, in the words of Enoch Edwards, had been 'set down as bits of blacklegs' by the other coal-owners. Walsh, the Lancashire delegate, who reported on these negotiations, stated: 'The people in their own districts had repudiated their suggestions—at least they had not given them any power to put the principle of a minimum wage into effect; they were without authority.'[4] There were lengthy discussions on the 'abnormal man', who by reason of age, infirmity or lack of skill was unable to produce an average day's output of coal, but no agreement was reached. After the second meeting Albert Stanley, of the Midland Federation, was reported to have said: 'It is all a mystery. Really, I do not know where we are but I do know now that we are not likely to meet the owners any more.'[5]

When the adjourned Federation conference re-assembled at the Caxton Hall, in London, on 20 December, and heard of the failure of all national and local negotiations it had no alternative but to make the necessary arrangements for a strike ballot. It was decided that voting should take place on 10–12 January, 1912, and that the result of the

[1] *M.F.G.B.* 15 November, 1911.
[2] *Derbyshire Times*, 18 November, 1911.   [3] *Ibid.* 2 December, 1911.
[4] *M.F.G.B.* 20 December, 1911.   [5] *Derbyshire Times*, 9 December, 1911.

ballot in each district should be sent to the secretary of the Federation not later than 16 January. Each district was also to send in a tabulated statement of its desired minimum wage and to set up, during negotiations, special machinery for dealing with exceptional cases such as old age and infirmity. After John Wilson, the Durham leader, had pointed out that no strike could be called in his district without a two-thirds majority, it was also resolved: 'That in case the ballot results in a two-thirds majority in favour of a national stoppage, notice be given in every district, so as to terminate at the end of February, 1912.'[1]

V

'Are you in favour of giving notice to establish the principle of an individual minimum wage for every man and boy working underground in every district in Great Britain?' was the question which the miners were called upon to answer on 10–12 January, 1912.

'The older miners' leaders', said the *Derbyshire Times*, 'regard the situation seriously, for if the older and wiser heads had their way a settlement would be easy, but the tail is wagging the dog, and the motive power of the tail in this instance, it is feared, has been largely provided by that Socialist element which has been insidiously capturing the miners' lodges of the country for some time. . . . Mr. Haslam regards a minimum wage of a uniform character as impossible, and that is why he thinks, if the ballot goes for a strike, that the coal industry is in for one of the biggest struggles ever known. Such a struggle, if both sides were determined, would result in little less than civil war. . . . Mr. Haslam says he is hopeful of peace. He is not alone.'[2]

Nevertheless, 17,999 Derbyshire miners voted in favour of handing in notices and only 6,816 against. When the special conference of the Federation assembled in Birmingham, on 18 January, it was reported that 445,801 members had voted for the strike and 115,921 against.[3] The two-thirds majority had been easily achieved and the conference decided 'that notices be tendered in every district so as to terminate at the end of February'. It was also agreed that the employers should be informed that the men's representatives were prepared to meet them to continue negotiations either locally or nationally.[4]

Meanwhile the Derbyshire miners' leaders had resumed their attempts to reach a county settlement. In doing so they moderated their demands. On 20 November, 1911, the Executive Committee approved a proposed price list which gave all contractors a minimum wage of 7s. 6d. a day

[1] *M.F.G.B.* 20 December, 1911.   [2] *Derbyshire Times*, 13 January, 1912.
[3] *M.F.G.B.* 18 January, 1912.   [4] *Ibid.* 19 January, 1912.

but eliminated the differential rates for the older collieries.[1] It laid down the following rates:

		s.	d.
Contractors, per day		7	6
Daymen, as at present, but not less than, per day		7	0
Holers, as at present, but not less than, per day		7	0
Loaders, as at present, but not less than, per day		6	0
The above prices to be obtained in machine holed stalls			
Holing machine drivers and timberers, per day		7	6
Other men with machines, per day		6	6
Rippers, chargemen and timberers, per day		7	6
2nd chargemen, when taking full charge, per day		7	6
2nd chargemen, when not taking full charge, per day		7	0
Fillers and gobbers, at not less than, per day		6	0
Able-bodied datallers, per day		6	0
Special arrangements to be made locally for other classes			
Boys' scale, to be extended to 21 years of age, per day		5	6
Pit bottom onsetters, per day		7	6
Assistants, when in charge of bell		7	6
Corporals, as at present but not less than, per day		6	0

On 17 January, 1912, the Executive Committee of the M.F.G.B. sat down to consider this and similar schedules from other districts. In almost every case an advance in wages was being sought. The Committee considered that this was going beyond the terms of the dispute and decided to 'tabulate for each district separately the individual minimum wage for piece-workers, such minimum to be as near as can be ascertained the present rate of wages'.[2] The result was that Derbyshire's differentials of 7s. 1½d. and 7s. 6d. re-appeared in the table of minimum day-wage rates recommended by the Executive Committee. Even so, the Derbyshire coal-owners were now demanding further differential rates which would enable them to pay a minimum wage of 6s. 1½d. to 6s. 6d. in normal, and 7s. 1½d. to 7s. 6d. in abnormal, places.[3]

The fact that some collieries and some coalfields were in a better position to pay higher wages than others was frequently used as an argument against trade union solidarity.[4] In discussing this question trade union leaders and coal-owners sometimes appeared to be stealing each others' clothing. Barnet Kenyon told the Staveley miners that 'it would be impossible for the whole of the coal trade to bear the cost' of a minimum wage of 8s. a day 'if all the profits were pooled'.[5] On the other hand, Sir Arthur Markham, at a Liberal party meeting at Creswell, said that 'if he were a miner, and had done a fair and honest day's work,

[1] *D.M.A.* 20 November, 1911.   [2] *M.F.G.B.* 17 January, 1912.
[3] *D.M.A.* 10 February, 1912.
[4] *Derbyshire Times*, 18 November, 1911.   [5] *Ibid.* 14 October, 1911.

O

and could not get a fair day's wage, he would strike'. He contended that the standard of wages in all mines was fixed by the poorer mines which were working at a loss or a bare margin of profit. 'The worst mines would, therefore, have to work at a loss or shut down. . . . Owing to the enormous development of new pits, the men in the bad mines would readily find work in modern ones.'[1]

But Markham, whose interests were in large, deep, modern mines, omitted to consider the probable effect of this policy upon the wages and conditions of the men employed at the newer pits. Frank Hall commented at Beighton: 'Sir Arthur uttered some truths and also some fallacies. How could they get their minimum by driving a drift through the ranks of the owners? . . . He said something there that was intended to drive a drift into your organization.'[2] At Tibshelf he said:

If the new collieries were not worked on such selfish principles there would not be such ruinous competition between the old and the new pits. The large collieries were setting the prices in the market. . . . They were worked from Monday morning until Sunday night, not six days in some places but actually seven days per week. The time was coming when the miners' organizations would have to grapple with the question.[3]

The minimum rates for hewers recommended by the Executive Committee of the Federation were as follows:

Nottinghamshire	7s. 6d.	South Derbyshire	6s. 6d.
Yorkshire	7s. 6d.	Durham	6s. 1½d.
Derbyshire	7s. 1½d. to 7s. 6d.	North Wales	6s. 0d.
South Wales	7s. 1½d. to 7s. 6d.	Scotland	6s. 0d.
Leicestershire	7s. 2d.	Cleveland	5s. 10d.
Northumberland	6s. 0d. to 7s. 2d.	Forest of Dean	5s. 10d.
Lancashire	7s. 0d.	Bristol	4s. 11d.
Midland Federation	6s. 0d. to 7s. 0d.	Somerset	4s. 11d.
Cumberland	6s. 6d.		

The task of dealing with all the complexities of other grades of underground labour defeated the Executive Committee. It was therefore decided 'that an individual minimum wage for all piece-workers other than colliers be arranged by districts themselves, and to be as near as possible present wages'. Similarly the rates paid to day-wage workers were left to be negotiated locally. It was laid down that no underground adult worker should receive less than 5s. a shift and that boys' wages were not to be less than their present wages with an absolute minimum of 2s. a day.[4]

---

[1] *Derbyshire Times*, 20 January, 1912.
[2] *Ibid.* 27 January, 1912.   [3] *Ibid.* 3 February, 1912.
[4] *M.F.G.B.* 28–30 January, 1912. Somerset, Bristol and the Forest of Dean were exempt from the minima of 5s. and 2s. because their representatives felt that the adoption of such rates would lead to widespread unemployment in those areas.

These proposals were approved by a Federation conference on 1-2 February. On 7 February the miners' representatives met the coal-owners' representatives at the Westminster Palace Hotel but no agreement was reached. The owners were prepared to agree that 'each person in their employment should receive a fair day's pay for a fair day's work' but they were equally convinced that 'the principle of payment in proportion to the amount of work performed is the only one which can be applied successfully in the case of coal getters'. The miners' leaders refused to depart from the principle of an individual minimum wage for all men and boys employed underground but stated that they were willing to meet the coal-owners at any time to discuss the matter further.[1] The failure of the conference did not preclude the continuation of negotiations between the miners and the coal-owners of the English Conciliation Board area who had reached agreement on the principle of the minimum wage but were unable to agree on the details of its implementation. On 10 February the Council of the Derbyshire Miners' Association approved a series of proposals which attempted to define the conditions under which a man might claim the minimum wage. Special provision was made for the aged, the infirm and habitual absentees, and the procedure for settling disputes arising from claims was laid down. The Executive Committee, which drafted the proposals, stated clearly that it did not wish 'that any arrangements should remove the incentive for a man to do a proper day's work'.[2]

Meanwhile preparations were being made by the Association for the strike. The officials were given the power 'to engage what help they think necessary' and the Trustees were authorized 'to sign for the necessary withdrawal of money'. It was also decided that 'notice be given to Corporations, &c., who have money on loan'.[3] By 14 February practically every underground worker in the coalfield, with the exception of those receiving compensation, had handed in his strike notice.[4] The Federation resolution had stated that notices should terminate 'at the end of February, 1912', but there was some confusion, probably increased by the fact that 1912 was a leap year, about the exact day on which work should cease. At most of the Derbyshire collieries notices expired on 26 or 27 February. A Staveley miner complained that 'a strange request' that the men should be allowed to work two further days after the expiration of their notices, had been sent to the coal-owners from the offices of the Derbyshire Miners' Association. This aroused much discontent. At a pit-head meeting at the Ireland Colliery

[1] M.F.G.B. 7 February, 1912.
[2] D.M.A. 10 February, 1912; Derbyshire Times, 17 February, 1912.
[3] D.M.A. 10 February, 1912.
[4] Derbyshire Times, 17 February, 1912; D.M.A. 10 February, 1912.

it was decided that the request, which had been made without consulting the men, should be ignored and James Martin, the President of the Association, was severely criticized for his part in the affair.[1] Barnet Kenyon was likewise censured by the Southgate miners for making a similar arrangement with the Shireoaks Colliery Company.[2]

The employers were also making preparations. The Butterley Company gave its miners notice to quit their houses although it was later stated that this had been done without the authority of the board of directors. Most of the coal and iron firms took the precaution of giving notice to their iron workers that it might be necessary to dispense with their services in the event of a shortage of fuel.[3] The coal-owners gave notice to their surface workers that their contracts would end when the strike began.[4] The *Derbyshire Times* commented:

It is said that neither side desire interference but at a time when every industry in the country is in danger of stoppage through want of coal, light or power, it will be the duty of the Government to step in and find some solution. . . . A month's stoppage of the coal supplies of the country would lead to absolute chaos, not to say anarchy.[5]

The Government, in those years of mounting industrial and international unrest, was well aware of its responsibilities. In 1911 it had appointed an Industrial Council, upon which the miners were represented by Burt and Ashton, to deal with the prevention and settlement of labour disputes. Sir George (later Lord) Askwith, who was well known to the Blackwell miners in the days before he was knighted as a Board of Trade arbitrator, had been made Chairman of the Council with the title of Chief Industrial Commissioner. In February, 1912, he was watching the dispute in the coal industry with 'the closest attention'. It was contrary to the policy of the Board of Trade to intervene as long as the parties to a dispute were negotiating and it seemed to Askwith and to some of the miners' leaders that if the English Conciliation Board area could reach agreement a precedent might be set for other districts. Even so, there would still be the difficulty of bringing the opposing parties together. Askwith writes:

On the very day [February 20] upon which I heard that the miners had finally refused the proposals of the owners in the Federated Area, I suggested to the Industrial Council, specially convened for that day, that in the interests of the community they should consider whether the position should not be clearly put before the Government. . . . The Industrial Council concurred,

---

[1] *Derbyshire Times*, 24 February, 1921.   [2] *Ibid.* 13 April, 1912.
[3] *Ibid.* 24 February, 1912.   [4] *Ibid.* 17 February, 1912.
[5] *Ibid.*

and agreed to the letter which the Prime Minister signed the same day, and sent to the representatives of the coal owners and of the miners.[1]

Asquith's letter stressed the seriousness of the situation and invited representatives of each side to meet him separately on 22 February at the Foreign Office. At these conferences the Prime Minister was accompanied by Lloyd George, Sir Edward Grey and Sydney Buxton (President of the Board of Trade), and Sir H. Llewellyn Smith and Sir George Askwith as chief permanent officials of the Board of Trade. Askwith writes:

There followed the longest series of declamatory speeches and explanations, without any business being done, I have ever heard. The Ministers had no particular plan, and evolved no particular policy ... but seemed to be very interested in hearing for the first time some of the difficulties of the miners' lives and their proposals. Days were consumed in talk, and meanwhile the strike grew more and more near, while the nation waited.[2]

Edwards, Smillie, Abraham and Ashton, the four officials, represented the M.F.G.B. and explained that they could do nothing without the consent of their special conference called for 27 February. Edwards said later: 'We attended the Foreign Office twice, the colliery owners were there in very large numbers, and it did seem a little bit cheeky for the moment that four of us were equal to all the colliery owners of Great Britain.'[3] Meanwhile ninety coal-owners at first, and afterwards a committee, met the Ministers in three sittings.

On 27 February the M.F.G.B. conference agreed to meet Asquith at the Foreign Office at 12 noon that day. After he had addressed the delegates the conference was adjourned and members of the Government met the Executive Committee of the M.F.G.B. When the conference re-assembled on 28 February, Enoch Edwards reported that the Government had made the following proposals:[4]

(1) His Majesty's Government are satisfied, after careful consideration, that there are cases in which underground employees cannot earn a reasonable minimum wage, from causes over which they have no control.

(2) They are further satisfied that the power to earn such a wage should be secured by arrangements suitable to the special circumstances of each district. Adequate safeguards to be provided to protect the employers against abuse.

(3) His Majesty's Government are prepared to confer with the parties as to the best method of giving practical effect to these conclusions, by means of district conferences between the parties, a representative appointed by the Government being present.

[1] Lord Askwith, *Industrial Problems and Disputes*, (London), 1920, pp. 202–3.
[2] *Ibid.* p. 204.
[3] *M.F.G.B.* 27 February, 1912.   [4] *Ibid.* 28 February, 1912.

(4) In the event of any of the conferences failing to arrive at a complete settlement within a reasonable time, the representatives appointed by His Majesty's Government to decide jointly any outstanding points for the purpose of giving effect in that district to the above principles.

In the discussion which followed Harvey denied charges that the Executive Committee had shown weakness, and appealed for unity. He said: 'I think this morning we might direct our attention to the fact that the Prime Minister and the Government have admitted the principle. We are a long way further this morning than we have ever been before, and I do not want us to get at cross purposes now.'[1] The conference was in full agreement with the first and second of the Government's proposals but was not prepared to enter into any further negotiations with the coal-owners to discuss minimum rates other than those already adopted by the Federation. It followed from this decision that the fourth proposal, which smacked of arbitration, was equally unacceptable.

The views of the conference were reported to the Government representatives by the Executive Committee. The coal-owners' representatives had also been considering the proposals. They came back with an acceptance by the Federated Districts, Durham and Cumberland, and a refusal by Scotland, South Wales, Northumberland, and the smaller districts (Forest of Dean, Somerset and Bristol). The employers laid great stress upon the proposed safeguards against abuse but the miners were not prepared to discuss them until the minimum wage had been conceded. 'You are out for the money, Mr. Barker?' said the Prime Minister, and Barker, a member of the South Wales Executive Committee, agreed that he was, and would not go back without it.[2] The day had been one of great activity. The Prime Minister had spent his time between conferences with the coal-owners and miners and visits to the King at Buckingham Palace but little had been achieved.

On 29 February Sir George Askwith succeeded in persuading the coal-owners of Northumberland to accept the first and second of the Government's proposals although they stipulated that they could not consent to pay an individual minimum wage to underground workers 'irrespective of their ability or disposition to earn such a wage'.[3] On the following day the Prime Minister told the House of Commons that, with the exception of South Wales and Scotland, who objected on the grounds of existing agreements, the coal-owners in practically the whole of England and Wales had accepted the proposals, but that the miners would not negotiate rates for coal getters. 'Under these circumstances',

[1] M.F.G.B. 28 February, 1912.
[2] Askwith, op. cit. p. 211.
[3] Ibid. p. 212.

he said, 'it was felt that no useful purpose would be for the moment served in continuing the present conferences between the Government and the parties.'[1]

VI

Meanwhile the strike was already beginning. At most of the collieries in Derbyshire notices expired on 26 and 27 February, and the men without hesitation brought out their tools. The miners in some parts of Leicestershire and Nottinghamshire also finished work on 27 February. By 28 February it was estimated that 115,000 miners were idle. On Friday, 1 March, the number had increased to 803,000. When the last strike notices expired on 2 March there were over a million men out.[2] On the same day the *Derbyshire Times* reported: 'The great coal strike of 1912 has begun and all the miners of Derbyshire have now come out, rendering every pit idle.'[3]

The growth of trade union organization in Derbyshire made the strike an orderly one. There was none of the bitterness and conflict with non-unionists which characterized the 1893 lock-out. A sufficient number of men remained at work to feed the ponies, keep the pumps going, and in some collieries to carry out repairs which were absolutely necessary. The policy of the M.F.G.B. was to allow the mines to be kept in working order on condition that no coal was raised.[4] There was a certain amount of coal picking on pit banks with the permission of colliery managers but it did not assume the proportions of the 'outcropping' during subsequent strikes and there was no disorder.[5] The refusal of some employers to supply allowance coal which was due to the men caused irritation in the Chesterfield district and resulted in what the officials described as 'some unseemly incidents which might have led to violence'. A circular signed by Haslam, Harvey, Hall, Kenyon, Martin and Sewell, stated: 'These are matters that should have been and could have been rectified by your leaders and the owners without resorting to rowdyism. We strongly caution you men against such behaviour. It can do the men's cause no good.'[6] On 9 March the Council authorized Haslam to secure, if necessary, police protection 'for the property and premises of the Association' but it was not required.[7] The officials spent much of their time in London taking part

[1] 34 H.C. Deb. 5s. 1771.   [2] Jevons, *op. cit.* p. 557; Askwith, *op. cit.* p. 213.
[3] *Derbyshire Times*, 2 March, 1912.
[4] *D.M.A.* 9 March, 1912; *M.F.G.B.* 28 February, 1912.
[5] *Derbyshire Times*, 9 March, 1912.
[6] *Ibid.* 2 March, 1912.   [7] *D.M.A.* 9 March, 1912.

in the complicated negotiations for a settlement. Haslam, apologizing for his inability to attend a Council meeting on 9 March, wrote:

I am sorry I cannot be with you as the position becomes more difficult every day, and what the outcome will be nobody knows. Give my greetings to the Delegates, and ask them to stand firm and await consequences with the dignity that becomes men who voluntarily have chosen to fight for the minimum wage.[1]

Meanwhile the miners were amusing themselves. A *Derbyshire Times* reporter, who made a tour of the mining villages, stated that 'wherever he went marbles were of more absorbing interest than anything else. In every street miners were playing, old men of sixty pitting their skill . . . against the pit lads of thirteen and fourteen, and every bit as keen and enthusiastic. The fortunes of the game were followed by scores of interested onlookers. . . . The best of good humour prevails, and the men are quite enjoying their holiday.'[2] The miners at the Swanwick Colliery were entertained by football matches and pit-pony races arranged by their employer, C. R. Palmer Morewood.[3]

The influence of Syndicalism was shown in the attempts at collaboration between trade unions. James Martin, the President of the Derbyshire Miners' Association, speaking at Staveley on 5 March, stated: 'If the topmen are not granted the scale of wages for which they are asking, the miners will not blackleg, and therefore the pits will stand even if the miners' grievances are settled.'[4] Similarly, the railwaymen in the Chesterfield district assured the miners of their 'practical sympathy and support . . . should such be called for by our executive committee to ensure a victory for the working classes', but the officials of the Federation informed the executive of the A.S.R.S. that the railwaymen could best assist the miners by remaining at work.[5] Syndicalism was condemned on all sides. The miners who crowded into the Chesterfield parish church for an intercession service were told by the Bishop of Southwell:

I want you to carry away this thought. There are forces at work today which may oust your leaders, and introduce a system of new leaders; a system which I dare to proclaim is wicked, cruel, and criminal. I mean the system which goes by the name of Syndicalism, the men being used as pawns in the game of war.[6]

---

[1] *D.M.A.* 9 March, 1912.
[2] *Derbyshire Times*, 9 March, 1912.   [3] *Ibid.* 30 March, 1912.
[4] *Ibid.* 9 March, 1912. G. D. H. Cole has called attention to the significance of the increasing interest shown by the M.F.G.B. in the surface workers as a stage in the evolution of industrial unionism. (*World of Labour*, (London), edn. of 1917, pp. 223–6).
[5] *Ibid.* 2 and 9 March, 1912.   [6] *Ibid.* 23 March, 1912.

Harvey considered that the miners had 'turned a deaf ear' to the 'tub-thumping clap-trap' of the Syndicalists and Socialists who had been conducting a rigorous campaign in Derbyshire. He also denounced the pamphlet, *The Miners' Next Step:*

Syndicalism and rabid socialism were no good to the working men. There were statements in the pamphlet which advocated the undermining of the whole of society, and the creating of a state of things too horrible to contemplate. Their policy would take away all incentive to work and make idle men as important as men willing to perform their duties. Syndicalism was an abominable and unclean thing. It should be wiped out completely before it had a chance to do further mischief.[1]

After the first week or two of the strike its effects began to be felt. Railway services were restricted in Derbyshire as in other parts of the country. In Chesterfield the tramway service was restricted and street lighting was reduced. Many of the local engineering works had to close or work short time. Strike payments presented no difficulty to the Derbyshire Miners' Association but those who had allowed their membership to lapse, non-unionists and men thrown out of work because of the shortage of coal, were all in a difficult position. The *Derbyshire Times* reported that distress was widespread in the Chesterfield district:

In the network of drab streets, especially at Brampton, many of the wives and children of the workers are feeling acutely the dire pinch of adversity. Living as many always do literally from hand to mouth, the deadly struggle, brief though it has yet been, has brought sadly too many families almost to the last extremity.[2]

The workhouse was said to be crowded. Soup kitchens were opened and each day there were depressing queues of women and children. It seems unlikely that anyone who was not in desperate need would submit to such indignity but 'to guard against imposition' tickets were issued to 'deserving cases' by the Civic Guild after consultation with relieving officers, miners' representatives and school attendance officers. The main relief centre in Chesterfield was at the Market Hall. Among one group of applicants were four sisters who came hand in hand. 'Where's your tickets?' asked the attendant. 'Please sir, we haven't got any', was the reply, 'but we have had nothing to eat today and we are so hungry.' They were given a meal.[3]

The Sheepbridge Coal and Iron Company established a soup kitchen at Brierley House and issued tickets for groceries and meat to its own workmen who were expected to repay their debts when they resumed

[1] *Derbyshire Times*, 30 March, 1912.   [2] *Ibid.* 23 March, 1912.
[3] *Ibid.*

O*

work.[1] At Ilkeston, towards the end of March, the Mayor, S. Shaw, appealed for £1,000 for his relief fund. He reported to members of the assistance committee that the distress was increasing daily and that he had received over 2,000 applications for relief. 'Nearly all the workmen who are suffering have large families', he said, 'and the average number of children in Ilkeston must be six if not seven per family. I calculate that 10,000 out of the population of 32,000 are in need of help.'[2] At Eckington W. R. Britton, a Methodist minister, co-operated with J. Kiddie, a Wesleyan minister, in arranging daily services for the miners. About 200 attended each service and refreshments, consisting of buns and coffee, were distributed. A similar scheme was in operation at Staveley.[3]

VII

After the failure of the Government's attempt to settle the dispute there were no further negotiations for several days. Meetings of the Industrial Council were held daily from 4 to 7 March but the Executive Committee of the M.F.G.B., which was now directing the strike, declined to treat with it on the grounds that 'negotiations with the Prime Minister and his colleagues are not broken off, and we know of no higher authority than the Government'.[4] On 7 March the Government decided to make a further attempt to break the deadlock and proposed that both parties should 'meet them jointly in conference, without prejudice, with a view to the free discussion of the whole situation'.[5] A special conference of the Federation on 11 March decided to accept the invitation 'with the understanding that the principle of the minimum wage is excluded from the discussion'.[6] The miners did not, however, this time exclude from the discussion the actual figures of the minimum rates, and the method of their determination.

The joint meeting under the chairmanship of the Prime Minister began on 12 March and continued on the two following days. Meanwhile a special conference of the Federation was in session and heard and discussed periodic reports on the negotiations from the Executive Committee. Although the joint meetings discussed a variety of problems associated with the minimum wage neither side was prepared to depart from its previous decision. The coal-owners of the Federated districts

---

[1] *Derbyshire Times*, 23 March, 1912.   [2] *Ibid.* 30 March, 1912.
[3] *Ibid.* For the attitude of the recipients of such forms of charity see George Orwell, *Down and Out in Paris and London*, (London), 1933.
[4] *M.F.G.B.* 5 March, 1912.   [5] *Ibid.* 7 March, 1912.
[6] *Ibid.* 11 March, 1912.

were still willing to grant a minimum wage of the amount asked for by the men, but only for work in abnormal places, and they offered a guaranteed minimum wage under all conditions of a shilling a day less. Owners in other districts continued to offer only a minimum wage for abnormal places. The miners' representatives adhered to the policy laid down by previous conference resolutions and stated clearly that there could be no resumption of work until their schedule of minimum day rates for hewers had been accepted by the owners.[1]

On 15 March the Prime Minister and his colleagues had separate conferences with the representatives of the coal-owners and the miners. It was clear that negotiations were at an end and Asquith announced that the Government intended to introduce a Bill which would provide for the fixing of district minima locally by Joint Boards in each district, consisting of representatives of the coal-owners and the miners, and presided over by an independent chairman, to be selected by the parties themselves, or if necessary, by the Government. The Executive Committee then laid before the Prime Minister and his colleagues five points for their consideration. They were:

(1) No resumption of work until the provisions of the Bill became an Act of Parliament.

(2) A time limit of one month to settle the details after the passing of the Act.

(3) The rates to be paid in each district to be retrospective from the date of resumption of work.

(4) The 5s. for adult workers and the 2s. for boys minimum to be provided for in the Bill.

(5) A minimum rate of wages to be paid to each district: a district to be considered each or any of the seventeen districts of the Federation of Great Britain.[2]

On 9 March the Council of the Derbyshire Miners' Association had resolved 'That no settlement of the present dispute, re the principle of a minimum wage, can be accepted which does not carry with it the payment of the whole of the tabulated rates of wages as already drawn up in our County'.[3] But on 19 March, when the Minimum Wage Bill was introduced in the Commons, Asquith explained that the Cabinet had decided not to include any figures in the Bill.[4] On the following day the M.F.G.B. conference decided that the Bill should specify not only the general minimum wage of 5s. for adults and 2s. for boys but also the schedule of minimum day rates for hewers in each district.[5] Asquith was very firm on the principle that such legislative enactment

---

[1] *M.F.G.B.* 12–14 March, 1912.   [2] *Ibid.* 15 March, 1912.
[3] *D.M.A.* 9 March, 1912.   [4] 35 H.C. Deb. 5s. 1732–3.
[5] *M.F.G.B.* 20 March, 1912.

of wages would be a bad precedent and despite attempts by the miners' M.P.s, with the support of the Labour Party, to secure the desired amendments, the Bill passed through its various stages substantially unaltered. On 26 March the M.F.G.B. conference decided to oppose the Bill on the third reading and to advise the Labour Party to do likewise.[1] This led to a conflict within the party between the trade union wing and the socialist wing. Whilst it was recognized that the Bill was not entirely satisfactory from the miners' point of view it was a legislative measure embodying for the first time the principle of a minimum wage. At a hurried party meeting the trade union wing carried the day but, in spite of the decision, a few Labour members who were in sympathy with the Bill, abstained from voting.[2] The Bill was given its third reading, late that night, by 213 votes to 48, passed quickly through the Lords and received the royal assent on 29 March. Keir Hardie is said to have 'jumped with joy at the result', not because he agreed with all the terms of the Act, but because legislative enactment had at last recognized the minimum wage.[3]

The miners were thoroughly dissatisfied. A special conference which had been in session since 25 March decided after the third reading of the Bill that a ballot of the men should be taken on the question of resuming work. The Executive Committee recommended that no advice should be given to the men but that they should simply be asked: 'Are you in favour of resuming work pending settlement of the minimum rates of wages in the various grades by the District Boards to be appointed under the Mines Minimum Wage Act?' There was almost general agreement that the ballot should be taken but the Executive Committee was sharply criticized for its failure to give a lead. Haslam, who was a member of the Committee, remained silent, but Harvey spoke strongly against the proposed policy. 'All of us have got opinions upon this matter', he said, 'and some of us have been trying to stop destruction. I honestly tell you I am going to try to stop destruction, chaos, defeat, and disgrace.' Eventually it was decided by 98 votes to 31: 'That this Conference does not advise but leaves the ballot paper, as agreed to, to decide for itself.' The ballot papers were to be returned not later than 3 April.[4]

Meanwhile the employers were already trying to persuade the men to return to work. Harvey had been chafing to get back to Derbyshire as early as 26 March when he told the M.F.G.B. conference:

I quite agree that the present time is very unfortunate, that the men who are representing men in districts have to be here at the present time. It is a very serious matter, and when newspapers are circulating reports to the disadvantage of the whole movement, it is important these men should be

---

[1] *M.F.G.B.* 26 March, 1912. [2] *Derbyshire Times*, 30 March, 1912.
[3] Askwith, *op. cit.* p. 215. [4] *M.F.G.B.* 27 March, 1912.

able to speak to the men in the districts, and that they should be amongst the men at the present time.[1]

Early next morning the pickets and the police were astir at the Shipley Colliery where twenty men had returned to work but there was no disorder.[2] Later in the day Barnet Kenyon, who had returned post-haste from London, addressed a mass meeting at Ilkeston and told the men that 'he felt deeply concerned when he saw that there was some serious likelihood of a breach in their ranks in the neighbourhood'. He promised that the Council would make a special grant to relieve the distress in the Ilkeston district and concluded:

If the manager of the Shipley Collieries wishes to keep the peace of this district, he must keep these pits closed down until this matter is settled. . . . If you are going to fight this battle, fight it like Englishmen, but don't be brutal, and don't break the law of the country.[3]

At a meeting at Heanor Frank Hall warned the owners that if they tried to tempt the men to go to work the Association would withdraw the winding men, the enginemen and the stokers.[4] Harvey said:

We trust that our men will take no notice of these . . . appeals. The strike commenced in an orderly fashion and has been carried on so until now under the guidance and instruction of the Miners' Federation. Let it remain orderly.[5]

The Derbyshire miners, along with those in other districts, were bitterly disappointed with the Minimum Wage Act and there were many stormy meetings in the coalfield during the period between the passing of the Act and the announcement of the results of the ballot. The failure of the officials to give a lead was strongly criticized. At a meeting at Creswell one miner said: 'At the outset of the dispute the officials were advising in all directions but now they refuse to advise us one way or the other. We are, in fact, miners without a leader.'[6] Barnet Kenyon was loudly heckled at a meeting in the Chesterfield Market Hall when he suggested that the real issue had been the question of abnormal places rather than the minimum wage. Referring to the demand for the inclusion of schedules in the Bill he said:

I will ask any man how you can put these schedules into the Bill. Tell me how you do it. . . . Never once have you said anything about schedules until just lately. If I were a miner I should vote for a resumption of work, but whatever you do, I swear that we, from your veteran leader old Haslam, down to Frank Hall, will carry out anything and everything you wish to the best of our ability, and will strive to bring about a settlement to the satisfaction of you and your children.[7]

[1] *M.F.G.B.* 26 March, 1912.   [2] *Derbyshire Times*, 30 March, 1912.
[3] *Ibid.*   [4] *Ibid.*   [5] *Ibid.*   [6] *Ibid.* 6 April, 1912.   [7] *Ibid.*

The Staveley miners were opposed to the provisions in the Act for arbitration and pointed to the declaration of James Martin before the Act was passed that they would have 'no arbitration'.[1] Many of the miners could not understand why they should vote for a resumption of work when the Labour Party had voted against the third reading of the Bill.[2]

The impression had been given by the newspapers, including *The Times*, that the Derbyshire miners were indifferent to the strike and were anxious to return to work, but this was not borne out by the results of the ballot. There were only 8,080 votes for a resumption of work and 13,428 against. The *Derbyshire Times* commented:

> In fairness to the Derbyshire leaders it should be said that they have done what they could to induce the men to vote for resumption of work, without actually disobeying the instruction laid down by the Federation, but the men have felt that the appeal to them has been half-hearted. Thousands have refrained from voting, and many cast their vote against the Act to mark their disgust at the poor ending of the strike.[3]

On 4 April the Executive Committee of the Federation met to consider the results of the ballot. All the important coalfields, except South Wales, had voted by considerable majorities against the resumption of work. The South Wales miners, who had originated the movement, had been on strike in large numbers, at one time or another, throughout 1910 and 1911. Their funds were exhausted and they saw in the Minimum Wage Act an opportunity to settle some of their grievances with their employers. The wealthier districts such as Yorkshire, Derbyshire, Lancashire and Durham showed very large majorities against returning to work. In all there were 201,013 votes cast in favour of resuming work and 244,011 against.[4] The Executive Committee was in a dilemma but the moderates, clutching at Wilson's resolution requiring a two-thirds majority to begin the strike, argued that the same majority should be required to continue it.[5] This policy was

---

[1] *Derbyshire Times*, 6 April, 1912.   [2] *Ibid.*   [3] *Ibid.*
[4] The results of the ballot were as follows:—

	For resumption	Against		For resumption	Against
Lancashire and Cheshire	11,334	29,840	Scotland	23,186	30,473
Yorkshire	13,267	43,914	Bristol	772	326
Derbyshire	8,080	13,428	Somerset	2,130	1,220
Nottinghamshire	8,187	8,213	Cleveland	4,919	908
Midland Federation	18,168	11,278	North Wales	7,446	1,190
Cumberland	2,980	4,877	South Derby	1,626	1,090
South Wales	62,538	31,127	Forest of Dean	No ballot	
Durham	24,511	48,828	Leicester	1,195	3,104
Northumberland	10,674	14,195			
			Totals	201,013	244,011

[5] *M.F.G.B.* 4 April, 1912.

recommended to a special conference on 6 April. Whilst the conference was in session the Derbyshire miners' Council resolved, by 53 votes to 24:

That the best interests of the men and the Association will be served in resuming work, if the Federation decides so, seeing that already some counties have broken away and resumed work, and further, we believe unless this course is pursued, serious injury will be done to our Association and Trade Unions in general.[1]

The resolution was immediately telegraphed to Haslam. The Derbyshire delegates had nothing to say at the Federation conference but they now knew how to vote. After some discussion the Executive Committee's resolution was carried by a card vote of 449,500 to 125,000, only Lancashire and Yorkshire voting against it.[2] It ran as follows:

Seeing that there is no provision in the rules or regulations of the Federation to guide this Committee as to the majority required to continue the strike, except the resolution passed at the Conference held December 21st, 1911, that a two-thirds majority was required to declare a national strike, we agree that the same majority be required to continue the strike; and seeing that a two-thirds majority is not in favour of the continuance of the strike, and acting upon that vote, we advise the resumption of work.

The coal-owners were well pleased with this decision. J. T. Todd, the general manager of the Blackwell Colliery Company, told some of his workmen:

My opinion is, and I know a large portion of Derbyshire miners in this district at any rate will agree with me, that there was no reason why we in this county should have been trailed at the heels of other counties. . . . I venture to ask any man in this room whether he would follow the advice of men like Mr. James Haslam, Mr. Harvey, the Rt. Hon. Thomas Burt, Charles Fenwick, John Wilson, Enoch Edwards, Stanley and Ashton, or the advice of men like Hartshorn, of South Wales, and Smillie of Scotland, who are largely responsible for what has taken place.[3]

VIII

The strike ended officially on 9 April, just six weeks after tools were laid down in most of the Derbyshire pits. Large numbers of the men 'signed on' on 9 April and went to work the following morning but a number of collieries were not ready to turn coal. Some pits, with bad roofs, were described as being 'nearly solid' and it was several weeks

[1] *D.M.A.* 6 April, 1912.
[2] *M.F.G.B.* 6 April, 1912.   [3] *Derbyshire Times*, 6 April, 1912.

before they could be opened out again. One unfortunate result of the strike was that some coal-owners refused to employ men who were advancing in years on the ground that they would not be able to afford to pay them the minimum wage.[1]

The criticism of the miners' leaders continued after the men had gone back to work. When Martin and Kenyon tried to address a meeting at Staveley they were greeted with cries of 'Traitors' and 'We have been sold'. 'We have got something now', declared Martin. 'And that's nowt', interjected a miner amidst gales of laughter. Barnet Kenyon was repeatedly booed and could only make himself heard with difficulty.[2] At Bolsover an angry meeting of miners decided to send for Harvey and Hall because they had not been paid by the Association for the two days they did not work before the strike had officially begun. 'We were hoodwinked over the minimum wage question, and now they wish to hoodwink us over our little bit of strike pay', asserted Hadon Kemp. The failure of the officials to appear further infuriated the men. Herbert Waterfall concluded a passionate speech with the words: 'I beg leave to move that we ask our leaders to resign and be done with them.' The resolution was carried by a large majority.[3]

A week later Harvey appeared at Bolsover and explained: 'If Mr. Hall and I had paid the money we should probably have been slaughtered.' Referring to the criticism for lack of leadership he said: 'If you had told the Council you were going to advise the men you would have been howled down. I did the next best thing. I had an interview with the Press, and any man with intelligence would have discovered the meaning I sought to convey.' There were constant interruptions. 'Who is your leader?' asked one miner. 'The coal-owners', retorted another.[4] On 13 April the Council decided to authorize the payment for the two days to the Bolsover men but this did not prevent Barlborough and Seymour lodges from moving that the officials should be asked to resign.[5] Warsop Main lodge made a similar proposal on 4 May.[6]

Much of this ferment must be attributed to Syndicalism which by now had its active exponents in Derbyshire. On 7 November at the Newcastle assizes John Wilson, the Durham miners' leader, brought a successful libel action against George Harvey Wilson, a Chesterfield miner, who had written a pamphlet, *Does John Wilson, M.P. serve the Working Class?* and was described by the plaintiff's counsel as 'belonging to the Syndicalists'. The jury assessed the damages at £200.[7]

Difficulties were also caused by the surface workers. Since the ballot

[1] *Derbyshire Times*, 13 April, 1912.   [2] *Ibid.*   [3] *Ibid.* 20 April, 1912.
[4] *Ibid.* 27 April, 1912.   [5] *D.M.A.* 13 April, 1912.
[6] *Ibid.* 4 May, 1912.   [7] *Derbyshire Times*, 9 November, 1912.

of 1908 the National Amalgamated Union of Labour had been organizing increasing numbers of surface workers in the Derbyshire coalfield until, in 1912, there was a membership of 2,000.[1] During the strike the surface workers had begun to demand a minimum wage for themselves and the miners' return to work depended upon a speedy settlement of this dispute. Without consulting A. J. Bailey, the District Secretary of the N.A.U.L., the Derbyshire Miners' Association had agreed with the coal-owners on a scale for boys employed on pit banks and screens which rose from 1s. a day at 13 years of age to 3s. a day at 22. The scale was subject to the increases and reductions awarded by the Conciliation Board and, in April, 1912, it gave a young man aged 22 a daily wage of 4s. 2½d. This was also to be the minimum daily wage for banksmen and was to apply 'to all persons employed in manipulating Coal on Pit Banks and Screens other than the infirm or physically unfit, such men to be locally arranged for'.[2] The agreement was some improvement on the existing rates paid to surface workers, who were earning from 3s. 4d. to 3s. 8d. a day, but it fell short of their demand for a minimum wage of 4s. 6d. for all adult workers.[3] Bailey complained that he was not a party to the agreement and advised his members not to accept the terms.[4] As a result a number of pits were idle and some 10,000 miners were unable to return to work.

On 13 April the officials of the Derbyshire Miners' Association were instructed by the Council to meet Bailey with a view to getting his men back to work.[5] Bailey was more anxious to secure recognition for his union than to insist on the minimum of 4s. 6d. and eventually an agreement was reached between the N.A.U.L., the Derbyshire Miners' Association and the employers on the basis of the scale previously accepted by the Association. It was becoming increasingly obvious that more attention would have to be paid to the position of the surface workers in the future. Will Thorne, speaking at Tibshelf on 25 April, emphasized the necessity of a working agreement between the N.A.U.L. and the Association.[6] Such an agreement was reached at a joint meeting of the Executive Committee and representatives of the N.A.U.L. on 25 May. A joint committee was established and both unions agreed not to hand in strike notices without consultation.[7] Later in the year the M.F.G.B., at its annual conference, decided to take up the question of banksmen's wages and to demand a minimum wage of 5s. a day for all adult surface workers.[8]

The Minimum Wage Act laid down that minimum wages were to

[1] *Derbyshire Times*, 13 April, 1912. See Chapter VI, p. 256.
[2] *D.M.A.* 30 March, 6 April, 1912.   [3] *Derbyshire Times*, 30 March, 1912.
[4] *Ibid.* 13 April, 1912.   [5] *D.M.A.* 13 April, 1912.
[6] *Derbyshire Times*, 27 April, 1912.
[7] *D.M.A.* 25 May, 1912.   [8] *M.F.G.B.* 2 October, 1912.

be 'an implied term of every contract for the employment of a workman underground in a coal-mine', unless the workman was excluded by the provisions of district rules. These rules were to lay down conditions regarding aged, infirm or partially disabled workmen, emergency interruptions, and the regularity or efficiency of work; and to provide machinery for the settlement of disputes arising out of the existence of a minimum rate. In each district joint boards of miners and coal-owners with an independent chairman were to settle minimum rates of wages and district rules and, in settling any minimum rate, were to 'have regard to the average daily rate of wages paid to the workmen of the class for which the minimum rate is to be settled'. The Act permitted the subdivision or combination of districts and the provision of special minimum rates or special district rules for groups or classes of coal-mines in a district. Minimum rates were subject to variation by agreement or on notice after the lapse of a year. If the joint district board failed to reach agreement on either rates or rules within a specified time the chairman had the power to arbitrate. The Act was to continue in force for three years and no longer, unless Parliament decided otherwise.[1]

The Derbyshire District Joint Board was formally constituted at a meeting at the Victoria Hotel, Nottingham, on 10 April, 1912. It was unanimously resolved that Walter Lindley, a former county court judge for Derbyshire, should be asked to be the chairman of the Board. At the second meeting, at the Portland Hotel, Chesterfield, on 24 April, the Board agreed upon its rules of procedure and began to consider the proposals of the coal-owners and the miners for district rules governing the payment of the minimum wage. The proposals advanced by the Association were those which had been approved by the Council on 10 February. The district rules were not completed until the Board's eighth meeting on 16 May, and then only after a series of interventions by the chairman.

The Board then went on to consider the question of the subdivision of the district. The coal-owners proposed that there should be two districts: the first would cover most of the county, the second would take in the collieries working the profitable top-hard seam. At the ninth meeting, on 20 May, Harvey stated that the Association 'admitted the principle of two Districts for discussion and for fixing the minimum rate, and that in arranging the two districts it is assumed that No. 1 District will include all those collieries where 7s. 1½d. is at present the day-wage rate for contractors brought out of stalls to work for the Company, and the No. 2 District those collieries where the rate is 7s. 6d.'[2] It was now evident that the differential rates, which had been insisted

---

[1] Coal Mines (Minimum Wage) Act, 1912, (2 Geo V c. 2).
[2] *Proceedings of the Derbyshire District Joint Board*, 20 May, 1912.

upon by the employers throughout the dispute, would be preserved. The Board then decided to settle the matter of wage rates and began by reaching agreement on the classification of the various types of labour. At the next meeting, on 3 June, the owners submitted their proposed minima for the various grades of labour in the districts defined as No. 1 and No. 2. There was a lengthy discussion on the minima to be fixed for contractors but no agreement was reached and both sides went away to prepare lists of what they considered to be average wages for the two districts.

On 8 June the Board met to deal with applications for special treatment from some of the smaller collieries but here again full agreement proved to be impossible. The Board had agreed, in accordance with the terms of the Act, that the specified period for settling minimum rates and District Rules should expire on 15 June, 1912. The fifteenth and final meeting of the Board was held on 12 June. By that time, with the assistance of the chairman's casting vote, agreement had been reached on the District Rules, the subdivision of the district, and the classification of the various grades of labour but the actual minimum rates to be paid and the collieries which were to receive special treatment were still unsettled. It was therefore the duty of the chairman to settle these outstanding problems.

On 17 June Lindley's award was published. The minimum rates for contractors were fixed at 6s. 8d. in No. 1 District and 7s. 0d. in No. 2 District. The men had proposed 7s. 1½d. and 7s. 6d. and the owners 6s. 0½d. and 6s. 4½d. Lindley explained:

With a few exceptions the minimum rates are lower than the average daily rates. This in my opinion is right, provided that the minimum rates are fixed at a figure which ensures to every able-bodied workman a fair day's wage (having regard to that average) for a fair day's work, and one for which he might reasonably be asked to work in a pit and incur the difficulties and dangers incidental to such work. For when wages vary as much as they do in this district many workmen are and inevitably must be earning wages below the average and to fix the minimum at the average would, in this district, I am satisfied, throw many out of employment. Moreover, the wages now prevailing are liable to reduction by the Conciliation Board under the terms of agreement which are now in force. Further it must not be forgotten that the minimum rates which I have fixed do not in any way deprive the workmen of any higher wages to which they are entitled under their existing contracts, or prevent a rise in their wages: what they do is to fix, so long as they are in force, a minimum up to which their existing wages (if now below the minimum) must be brought, and below which they cannot fall or be reduced, so long as the workmen comply, as far as lies within their power, with the conditions laid down by the District Rules.[1]

[1] *Coal Mines (Minimum Wage) Act, 1912, Judge Lindley's Award, 17 June, 1912.*

Lindley's award fell short of the men's demands but led to no great dissatisfaction in the county. As Frank Hall pointed out:

> 6s. 8d. per day was not a sum they need be ashamed of, when they remembered that they had had complaints at their Council meetings that many men were working for as little as 3s., 4s., and 5s. per day. . . . If a man made five days per week he would receive no less than 33s. 4d. per week. Wasn't that better than going home with £1 per week? They had had cases where men had gone with that pittance for even five and a half days' work.[1]

There was, however, much discontent over the detailed implementation of the award at the colliery level. On 27 July the Council resolved: 'That Standing Orders be suspended while a discussion takes place on treatment meted out to the men at certain Collieries when claims have been made under the Minimum Wages Award.'[2] On 1 August Harvey told the House of Commons: 'In the great mining counties of Yorkshire and Derbyshire, and those which are producing the greatest quantities of coal and employing the larger numbers of men there is nothing but dissatisfaction, and that dissatisfaction is growing every day.' Some men were being accused of inefficiency and were being dismissed or refused the minimum wage without their inefficiency having been proved before the Joint District Board as required by the Act. Others were being asked to sign certificates contracting out of the Act and were being dismissed for refusing.[3] At some collieries men who claimed the minimum wage were dismissed and replaced by others who were prepared to forgo it.[4] The Clay Cross Company objected to the agreed scale for banksmen and showed its disapproval by stopping their allowance coal. The Butterley Company began to deduct threepence a day as the value of its allowance coal.[5] In January, 1913, Frank Hall stated:

> They had owners in that county who had not paid the minimum wage due to the men for the first week, and there were men that day due to receive money for eight months back. . . . He was sorry to say that there were men in Derbyshire who had not the backbone to make their demands.[6]

Where the men were willing to state a case, regardless of the possibility of victimization, the Association was prepared to take up their grievances through the machinery provided by the District Rules and, if necessary, in the courts. The most important dispute over the payment of the minimum wage was that between Henry Hooley, a holer employed at the Britain Colliery, and the Butterley Company. Hooley claimed the sum of £5 6s. 8d. which represented the difference between his

[1] *Derbyshire Times*, 22 June, 1912.   [2] *D.M.A.* 27 July, 1912.
[3] 41 H.C. Deb. 5s. 2393-7.   [4] *D.M.A.* 23 September, 1912.
[5] *Derbyshire Times*, 11 January, 1913.   [6] *Ibid.*

earnings and the wages he was entitled to under the Minimum Wage Act for the period from April to August, 1912. The Company maintained that the contractor was Hooley's employer and therefore responsible for the payment of the minimum wage. Hooley, with the support of the Association, brought an action against the Butterley Company in the Alfreton county court. The Association found it impossible to get certificates showing that the District Rules had been carried out and the case was dismissed. This cost the Association £260 and delayed further litigation. The Council and the officials were greatly annoyed with H. E. Mitton, of the Butterley Company, for pleading no jurisdiction when the owners' side of the Disputes Committee had refused to grant the necessary certificates, and to show the lodges that it was no fault of the officials some correspondence was published showing how the Butterley Company's employees had been treated. In comparing two letters Frank Hall alleged that certain inconsistencies were deliberate. The documents had been intended for private circulation but a copy found its way into the hands of Mitton who promptly issued a writ for libel.[1]

After the independent chairman of the Disputes Committee had been called in, Hooley obtained the certificates required by the court[2] and the hearing of the case began at Alfreton on 14 March, 1914. Judge Macpherson decided in favour of Hooley. This judgment was affirmed by Mr. Justice Horridge and Mr. Justice Rowlatt in the King's Bench Division but the judgment of the Divisional Court was reversed by Lords Justices Swinfen, Eady, Phillimore and Banks in the Court of Appeal. It was not until the spring of 1916 that the case was finally settled by the House of Lords.[3] Ernest Charles, counsel for the miners, had told the Divisional Court, on 18 November, 1914: 'This question of Mr. Hooley's wages involves . . . hundreds of men who are waiting for a decision in this case. They have not received their minimum wage, either.'[4] When the House of Lords gave judgment in favour of Hooley there was great jubilation. The Council passed resolutions congratulating Bertram Mather, the Association's legal adviser; Frank Hall, who had conducted the case through all its stages; and Henry Hooley 'for the stand made and the help afforded in the matter'. It was recorded in the minutes:

This is a very important matter so far as our members are concerned, deciding as it does that the Colliery Company is responsible for each

[1] D.M.A. 23 May, 1914. The libel action appears to have been settled privately.
[2] Minutes of the Derbyshire Disputes Committee (Minimum Wage Act, 1912), 2 February, 1914.
[3] [1916] 2 A.C. 63.
[4] House of Lords, Hooley v. Butterley Company, (1916), Appendix No. 12, p. 201.

workman's minimum wage. . . . The result means far more to the miners
than ever they anticipated and to the miners of the whole Federation in the
coalfields of Great Britain.[1]

IX

One important result of the 1912 strike was an increase in the price of
coal. On 19 March, when the Minimum Wage Bill was introduced in the
House of Commons, the price of coal in London had reached £2 a ton.[2]
As soon as the immediate problems of the resumption of work had been
settled the miners of the Federated area turned their attention to the
Conciliation Board which had ruled, on 3 September, 1909, that there
were to be no more percentage increases in wages until the owners had
recouped themselves for the disadvantages incurred by forgoing their
demand for a 5 per cent. reduction. The price of coal had now exceeded
the stipulated price of 7s. 10·21d. a ton for some time and the miners
felt that they had a reasonable case for demanding a further increase in
wages. The deaths of Enoch Edwards and Lord James of Hereford, and
the retirement of Alfred Hewlett, the principal spokesman for the coal-
owners, had resulted in important changes in the leading figures of the
Conciliation Board. When the Board met on 20 August, 1912, to consider the miners' claim for a 5 per cent. increase in wages, Harvey and
F. J. Jones, a Yorkshire coal-owner, were the protagonists and Lord
Coleridge was the independent chairman.

Coleridge decided that the agreement of 3 September, 1909, had
expressly suspended the governing rules of the Board which laid down
that the selling price of coal was not to be the sole factor in determining
wages. In order 'to save anything like a catastrophe' he suggested that
the two sides should have further discussions.[3] Eventually there
emerged what amounted to a new conciliation agreement. It was agreed,
on 21 October, 1912:

> That the Conciliation Board be continued until the 31st day of March,
> 1915, determinable thereafter by a three months' notice on either side; with a
> minimum of fifty per cent. above the 1888 rates, and a maximum of sixty-
> five per cent. The procedure regulations of the present Board to apply.

The coal-owners agreed to pay an increase of 5 per cent. from the
third making-up day in October.[4]

The continued rise in the price of coal led to further increases of
5 per cent., under the new agreement, in January and April, 1913,
bringing the miners' wages to the maximum of 65 per cent. above the

[1] *D.M.A.* 1 April, 1916.   [2] Jevons, *op. cit.* p. 560.
[3] *M.F.G.B.* 20 August, 1912.   [4] *Ibid.* 21 October, 1912.

1888 rates.[1] In March, 1913, Frank Hall told the Blackwell miners: 'It was time that the minimum rate of 50 per cent. was merged into the 1888 rates and made the basis of all future advances. . . . The advances of 5 per cent. which they received were misleading to the general public. The 5 per cent. advance was upon rates a quarter of a century old. Really it was not a 5 per cent. advance, but only about $3\frac{1}{3}$ per cent. The question of consolidating the basis must be dealt with.'[2] The misunderstandings caused by percentage increases and reductions on a basic rate was a grievance which had led to much discussion in the 'seventies.[3] It was not to be remedied in its present form until the war years, when rapid increases in coal prices and the cost of living completely outdated the 1888 basis.

Reference has already been made to the fact that formal percentage changes do not necessarily provide an accurate measurement of the wage levels in the mining industry.[4] This can only be done by a comparative study of statistics of average earnings. Such statistical material is extremely scanty. Mr. Rowe, using the census of wages taken by the Board of Trade in 1886, the parliamentary paper on the hours of labour in 1890, and the two schedules of earnings per shift for November, 1913, and June, 1914, which were presented to the Sankey Commission in 1919, has made estimates of wages per shift in 1888 and 1914. He has also compared the figures for 1914 with the 1888 figures adjusted in accordance with the nominal percentage increase. The available statistics have compelled him to consider Derbyshire and Nottinghamshire as an entity, with the following results.[5]

	I Piecework coal-getters	II Coal-getters on day wage	III Haulage hands	IV Timberers rippers, etc.	V Deputies and shot-firers	VI Labourers
1888	5s. 4d.	4s. 6d.	4s. 0d.	4s. 8d.	4s. 5d.	3s. 5d.
1914 (calculated)	8s. 10d.	7s. 5d.	6s. 7d.	7s. 6d.	7s. 3d.	5s. 8d.
1914 (actual)	9s. 10d.	7s. 0d.	6s. 8d.	7s. 0d.	8s. 0d.	5s. 8½d.

Mr. Rowe suggests that the development of the top-hard seams probably accounts for the increased differential enjoyed by the contractors and that the rates of deputies and shot-firers followed in sympathy because such grades were recruited from the ranks of the skilled men. He also points out that the average earnings of pieceworkers in both counties were raised by the agreements for minimum payments in abnormal places. His conclusions would lend support to

[1] M.F.G.B. 6 January, 15 April, 1913. See Appendix I to this chapter.
[2] Derbyshire Times, 8 March, 1913.   [3] See Chapter IV, p. 152.
[4] See pp. 130, 410.   [5] Rowe, op. cit. p. 72.

the view that the miners' unions of Derbyshire and Nottinghamshire
were dominated by the skilled workers during this period. It should be
borne in mind, however, that Mr. Rowe's figures for 1888 are based on
an inquiry which covered only 7·4 per cent. of all underground workers
in the two counties. Moreover, the inclusion of South Derbyshire, where
trade union organization was weak, may have tended to lower the 1888
average more for piece-workers than for other grades.

Whilst an analysis of this kind is useful in so far as it shows changes in
differentials and provides a correct understanding of the difference
between actual and nominal movements of wages over a long period, it
does not, as Mr. Rowe points out, make it possible to correct the nominal
fluctuations year by year.[1] Nor does it permit a detailed account of
movements in real wages. A comparison can be made, however, on the
basis of Mr. Rowe's figures, between real wages in 1888 and 1914.
Using Bowley's cost-of-living index[2] the results are as follows:

	Money wages						Cost of Living	Real wages					
	I	II	III	IV	V	VI		I	II	III	IV	V	VI
1888	100	100	100	100	100	100	100	100	100	100	100	100	100
1914 (calculated)	165	165	165	165	165	165	112	147	147	147	147	147	147
1914 (actual)	184	167	167	150	181	167	112	164	149	149	134	161	149

[1] Rowe, *op. cit.* p. 86.   [2] Bowley, *op. cit.* p. 30.

APPENDIX I

Nominal Movements of Wages, 1888–1913

September, 1888	100	February, 1901	160
October, 1888	110	July, 1902	150
June, 1889	120	December, 1903	145
December, 1889	130	August, 1904	140
March, 1890	135	January, 1907	145
August, 1890	140	May, 1907	150
August, 1894	130	September, 1907	155
October, 1898	132.5	January, 1908	160
April, 1899	137.5	September, 1908	155
October, 1899	140	March, 1909	150
January, 1900	145	October, 1912	155
October, 1900	150	January, 1913	160
January, 1901	155	April, 1913	165

Source: *Minutes of the Miners' Federation of Great Britain*, 1888–1913.

CHAPTER XI

SOCIAL CONDITIONS, WELFARE AND SAFETY

I

The pattern of the Derbyshire miner's life and work, which had developed in the mid-nineteenth century, had the effect of setting him apart from the rest of the community. Similar changes had taken place wherever coal-mining had become a dominant feature of the local economy. The Miners' Eight-Hour Day Committee commented in 1907:

A greater degree of solidarity exists in the class of workers in coal mines, taken as a whole, than appears to exist among those engaged in other industries.... This sense of solidarity is perhaps largely due to the segregation of the mining population in colliery villages, and their comparative isolation from men engaged in other pursuits, to which must be added the circumstance that they all share together in the sum of the actual employment available, a deficiency of trade causing a universal short week's working, and not the dismissal of individual men.[1]

The isolation of the colliery villages prevented other sections of the community from understanding the miner and his problems. A clergyman at a Staveley ruridecanal conference, in 1909, said of the Derbyshire miner: 'He is one of the most difficult men from whom to win real friendship, but when once you have made him your friend he is the truest and best you can find.'[2] To the majority of people, especially those in the non-mining districts, the miner was a curiosity of inferior social status. It was thought amusing when the young Arthur Markham arranged a coal-miners' party at a fashionable London restaurant. The proprietor, in describing Markham's exploit as 'the most original party he had ever catered for', said:

He met twelve miners at the pithead and asked them if they would like to go to London. Of course, they agreed, and he put into the hands of each one

[1] *Departmental Committee appointed to inquire into the Probable Economic Effect of a Limit of Eight Hours to the Working Day of Coal Miners*, (1907), Final Report, (Cd. 3505), p. 45. Cf. Dennis, Henriques and Slaughter, *op. cit.* p. 79.
[2] *Derbyshire Times*, 8 May, 1909.

of them a £10 note and a first-class return ticket. His only stipulation was that they were not to change their clothes or even to wash. So off they went, as black as your hat, and I was asked to see that they had a good dinner—in the restaurant, not in a private room. They thoroughly enjoyed themselves and were the least embarrassed of all the people present.[1]

Similarly, during the 1912 strike, John Marshall, an Alfreton miner, who was reputed to have been the first miner to reach the surface at the first colliery in the country to cease work, accepted a tempting offer from the manager of several London music halls to appear on the stage wearing his pit clothes and carrying his pick and his safety lamp.[2]

Life in the colliery villages continued to be greatly influenced by the paternal rule of the employers, some of whom were beginning to make improvements. The 'model' villages at Bolsover and Creswell, developed in the 'nineties by the Bolsover Colliery Company, were Derbyshire's most notable experiments in miners' housing before the First World War. To modern eyes they are singularly unattractive but they were, in their time, a considerable advance on the ugly, squat rows of back-to-back houses which were hastily thrown up in the older mining centres such as Staveley and Clay Cross in the early nineteenth century. Emerson Bainbridge, the chairman of the Bolsover Company, was largely responsible for the scheme. 'There was no reason', he said, 'why they should not have a village where three things could exist successfully . . . the absence of drunkenness, the absence of gambling, and the absence of bad language.'[3]

Bainbridge drew up the plans for the model village at Bolsover in 1888 and sent them to Sir Richard Webster for revision.[4] Building began in 1891 and by September, 1892, fifty of the houses were occupied.[5] The completed village boasted its own co-operative stores, schools, and a large assembly hall.[6] The experience gained at Bolsover led to the development a few years later of a larger model village at Creswell. The architect was Percy Houfton,[7] who resolved to break away from the traditional rows of houses and follow what was then described as 'the modern principle'. By 1901 the village consisted of 280 two-storied houses built to form two concentric circles.

'The houses vary in design, and the general effect, viewed in perspective, is very pleasing', reported the *Derbyshire Times*. 'Within the inner circle is a large green, which is relieved by shrubberies at intervals. A pretty, artistically designed bandstand occupies a position in the centre. There are also a playground for the children, rustic seats, and each house has its own

[1] *Derbyshire Times*, 7 February, 1931.   [2] *Ibid.* 9 March, 1912.
[3] *Ibid.* 7 April, 1900.   [4] *Ibid.*   [5] *Ibid.* 24 September, 1892.
[6] *Ibid.* 21 December, 1895.
[7] Brother of J. P. Houfton, the general manager of the Bolsover Colliery Company.

flower-garden. The colliery company offer prizes annually for the best laid out flower plot.'[1]

A cricket ground and a clubhouse were provided, and garden allotments could be rented for four shillings a year. There was one shop: a branch of the Bolsover Co-operative Society. The cleansing of the village was done during the night by a special staff, who worked from 10.30 p.m. to 5 a.m. The only blemish on this earthly paradise appears to have been 'an offensive smell', which 'frequently arises from the spot where the sewage is treated'.[2] The houses at Creswell were built at a cost of £200 each and rents therefore tended to be higher than those of the older houses in other parts of the county. This led to a complaint from the miners in 1906.[3]

As a rule the traditional acts of charity performed by the landed aristocracy were forgotten when a colliery company intervened between the landowners and the peasantry but the Duke of Portland, the lessor of the Bolsover Company's collieries, took an unusual interest in the welfare of the miners and the development of the model villages. In 1913 J. P. Houfton told members of the Creswell Colliery cricket club that the Duke, their patron, 'would almost rather entertain a miner than the heir to the Austrian throne . . .'.[4] In 1898 Portland gave a site for a church at Creswell and contributed to the building fund.[5] He also joined with the colliery company to finance the building of schools in the village. The Duchess visited the sick and needy, and maintained in the village a trained nurse who gave her services to the miners and their families free of charge.[6] The Duke of Devonshire, on the other hand, was criticized for his inattention to the welfare of the miners employed on his estates. A speaker at a Liberal meeting at Grassmoor, who was 'quite sure there were houses in Grassmoor that were unfit to live in' asked:

Would it not be better if, instead of having pheasants to be reared and shot on the Chatsworth estates, they had living on these estates some of the healthiest people in England? It would be far more satisfactory to the future Duke of Devonshire and the future King of England to come over and see healthy people than to come for shooting.[7]

Even if they did not improve housing most of the colliery companies continued to provide amenities for the moral well-being of their workmen. Clubs and institutes were an attractive investment. They enabled the companies to control drinking and paid handsome dividends in the

[1] *Derbyshire Times*, 2 November, 1901.   [2] *Ibid.*
[3] *Ibid.* 1 December, 1906.   [4] *Ibid.* 29 November, 1913.
[5] *Ibid.* 26 February, 1898.   [6] *Ibid.* 2 November, 1901.
[7] *Ibid.* 23 April, 1910.

shape of sobriety and more regular attendance at work. Maurice Deacon, of the Sheepbridge Company, in his presidential address to the Chesterfield and Midland Counties Institution of Mining Engineers, in 1899, said: 'The provision of workmen's institutes was an excellent means of counteracting the evil influence and abuse of the public house, and of exercising personal influence upon those who frequented them.'[1] The active trade unionist, however, was wary of the indiscriminate mixing of miners and petty colliery officials which occurred in such institutions, believing that it sometimes led to favouritism and tale-carrying.

The colliery companies watched jealously any attempt to break their monopoly of the licensed premises in the colliery villages. In 1907, when the Worksop and Retford Brewery Company applied unsuccessfully for a new licence at Creswell, the brewery company's solicitor told the county licensing justices:

Among the gentlemen who were opposing the application was Mr. Houfton ... who was in association with the important company who claimed to have proprietary rights to watch over the good of the community amongst which they lived. There was a club they had introduced, and Mr. Houfton was determined, as far as might be, that the application should not succeed.[2]

Many of the coal-owners conducted licensed premises for a profit. The Staveley Company owned the Barrow Hill Hotel which was rented for some years by the Chesterfield Brewery and in 1898 sold privately to Ind Coope and Company for £22,000.[3] The Liberal coal-owners, bound by traditional links with nonconformity and temperance, found their role as publicans embarrassing when they were called upon by the party machine to do battle with the Conservative brewers. In 1905 it was pointed out that Thomas Bolton, the Liberal M.P. for North-East Derbyshire, and a formidable opponent of the Government's Licensing Bill, was a director of the Rhymney Coal and Iron Company which included among its assets a brewery and a number of tied licensed houses.[4]

The building of clubs, chapels and schools provided the colliery owners with an opportunity to display their munificence and to improve the morale of their workmen. With the exception of the attempts of a few pioneers such as Emerson Bainbridge, who had the advantage of making a clean start, little attention appears to have been paid to physical well-being. In the majority of the older colliery villages living conditions were deteriorating rather than improving. Some of the newer villages, which had been hastily built and carelessly planned,

[1] *Derbyshire Times*, 2 September, 1899. [2] *Ibid.* 11 May, 1907.
[3] *Ibid.* 9 April, 1898. [4] *Ibid.* 14 January, 1905.

were almost as bad. The democratization of local government by the creation of county councils in 1888 and the creation of urban and rural district councils in 1894, with the subsequent election to these bodies of miners' representatives, helped to breach the powers of the colliery proprietors and the landowners[1] but little could be done, in the years before the First World War, other than to call attention to the grosser evils.

Overcrowding was one of the most serious problems. In 1898 a doctor, who was called to attend a Clay Cross family, found six children in one bed. The mother, anxious to prevent the spread of infection, had placed three who were suffering from scarlatina at one end of the bed and three who had typhoid fever at the other.[2] At a meeting of the Clay Cross urban district council, in 1907, G. M. Jackson, of the Clay Cross Company, stated that in one house there were fourteen people sleeping in one room. 'Is that a Company's house?' asked Rowarth, the leader of the enginemen's union. 'I do not know', replied Jackson. 'I should be very sorry if it were'.[3] Even at the larger, modern collieries there was a serious shortage of housing. The difficulty was accentuated by the growth of the multiple shift system and the bigger labour force required. 'It was said that in some houses associated with these collieries the beds were never cold', complained Frank Hall, in 1912. 'The houses were overcrowded. Such a system destroyed home comforts and happiness.'[4]

But it was not only in the colliery villages that housing conditions were bad. T. P. O'Connor, the Irish Member of Parliament and the editor of the *Sun*, visited Chesterfield during the 1893 lock-out and wrote:

The starving miners of Chesterfield are of the town, of the slum, slummy —with all the dense overcrowding, the squalid half-filthy interiors that belong to the sombre life of our towns. A large number of miners out on strike live in cottages close to the mines; but some 2,000 or 3,000 live in Chesterfield itself; if 'live' be a proper word to apply to mere worming and burrowing and suffocating in dog holes. I have not the power of giving a description which would bring before your minds anything like an idea of what the dens are like in which some of the colliers of Chesterfield are compelled to live. They are long, narrow, stone runs; they consist of a couple of wretched rooms on the ground floor and a loft on the second floor. The average rent is two shillings a week. There is not even bedding. In many others the beds—if such they can be called—consist of a number of rags on

---

[1] Cf. J. E. Williams, 'Paternalism in Local Government in the Nineteenth Century', *Public Administration*, XXXIII, (1955), pp. 439–46.
[2] *Derbyshire Times*, 5 March, 1898.
[3] *Ibid.* 9 March, 1907.   [4] *Ibid.* 3 February, 1912.

the boards; and often I saw a poor, sick child of tender years lying, pale, silent, affrighted and hungry.[1]

Similarly, the *Westminster Gazette* reported:

There is a part of Chesterfield which goes by the name of 'the dog kennels', and truly it cannot have a more appropriate name. The hovels down either side of these narrow lanes are not fit for human habitation; they are fully as bad as the slums in the worst corners of outcast London . . . some . . . are so low you can hardly stand upright in the rooms.[2]

The 1901 census revealed that 2,384 of the 5,313 houses in Chesterfield had only four rooms or less. There were 19 one-roomed tenements in one of which four persons lived, and 2,008 four-roomed tenements, some of which were occupied by twelve or more persons. There were 143 two-roomed houses, one having nine occupants, and 214 three-roomed houses, in some of which lived nine, ten or eleven persons.[3]

With overcrowding went insanitary conditions. The *Westminster Gazette* commented upon the miners' houses in Chesterfield: 'The women and children live there always, and the wonder is that they do not die like flies during the hot weather, or perish with cold when the nipping cold of autumn and winter enters the cottages through tumble-down walls and doors and windows.'[4] Barwise, the medical officer of health for Derbyshire, reported in 1914 that most of the houses at Clay Cross, which had been built some 75 years previously, had not improved in the interval. Out of the 1,782 houses in the district he estimated that considerably more than half had only two bedrooms. 'It is an exception', he wrote, 'to find a yard paved, or a house with a slopstone, or water laid on to it. Many of the houses have windows partially or entirely fixed.' There were 36 back-to-back houses and 25 others which were considered to be unfit for habitation. In addition there was a much larger group which required considerable structural alterations to make them habitable.

'Nearly all the common yards in the district are unpaved', wrote Barwise, 'and the surface water lies about in puddles which are filled with ashes by the tenants, while within a few yards of most of the houses there are privy middens. The total number of water closets in the district is 273. There is considerable overcrowding, and not a single house which was fit to live in was found vacant.'[5]

Similarly, in 1910, Herbert Peck, the medical officer of health for the Chesterfield Rural District Council, reported: 'The colliery villages,

[1] *Sun*, quoted in *Derbyshire Times*, 28 October, 1893.
[2] *Westminster Gazette*, quoted in *Derbyshire Times*, 30 September, 1893.
[3] Census for 1901.
[4] *Westminster Gazette*, quoted in *Derbyshire Times*, 30 September, 1893.
[5] Report of the Medical Officer of Health for Derbyshire, 1914.

built in parallel blocks with rows of sanitary conveniences between them, are not of a character to elevate the minds of their inhabitants.' He called particular attention to the deplorable housing conditions in certain streets in the colliery villages of Mosborough, Eckington, Grassmoor, Killamarsh, North Wingfield, Stonebroom and Speedwell. The houses were all old, most of them being built before the adoption of building by-laws, and only in Grassmoor had the Public Streets Works Act been employed with advantage. In Renishaw, Eckington, Mosborough, North Wingfield, Staveley and Unstone there was a total of 196 back-to-back houses.[1] Such neglect of housing could not be remedied quickly. The medical officer of health for Derbyshire, commenting on the situation at Clay Cross, in 1914, said:

It is almost impossible to deal with the overcrowding, and for the sanitary authority to make the necessary closing orders if there are no houses for the people to go to. The first thing required is for the district council themselves to erect twenty or thirty houses. Time after time, when enquiring why people were living in the insanitary houses they were, I was told that they would gladly pay more rent if further accommodation could be found.[2]

Epidemics were frequent. From the end of June, 1896, the village of Poolsbrook, owned by the Staveley Company, was stricken with enteric fever. By October over fifty cases had been reported and eight had proved fatal. A deputation from Poolsbrook appeared before the Chesterfield Rural District Council to renew a long-standing complaint about the inadequate water supply. When G. Newton produced a bottle containing a sample of the water used at Poolsbrook a councillor remarked: 'It looks more like coal washings.'[3] A typhoid epidemic at Shirebrook led to a heated discussion on sanitation at a meeting of the Pleasley parish council in 1900. One speaker suggested that Arnold Lupton, who was largely responsible for developing the Shirebrook Colliery, knew nothing about the place. 'I do not suppose', he said, 'that Mr. Lupton expended his capital from any philanthropic motives.'[4]

The state of housing and sanitation was clearly reflected in the vital statistics for the mining villages. In 1910 Herbert Peck compared the death and epidemic death rates for different types of housing. At Barrow Hill, where the houses were built in small blocks with large gardens and a free circulation of air the death rate was 8·1 per thousand, and the epidemic death rate 0·7. The epidemic death rate for the district was 1·54. In 26 back-to-back houses in Palmer Street, Mosborough, deaths occurred at the rate of 40 per thousand and the epidemic diseases rate

[1] Report of the Medical Officer of Health for Chesterfield R.D.C., 1910.
[2] Report of M.O.H. for Derbyshire, 1914.
[3] *Derbyshire Times*, 17 October, 1896.   [4] *Ibid.* 3 February, 1900.

was 16 compared with 12·4 for the remainder of the parish. In 80 houses at Waterloo, North Wingfield, the death rate was 47 per thousand compared with an average for the parish of 9·3. Peck described 170 houses at Speedwell as 'one-doored, built in long rows with long privy middens and coal houses between them. The ground between the houses and out-buildings was garden at one time but has long lost all resemblance to such.' In these dwellings deaths occurred at the rate of 15·6 per thousand, whereas for the rest of the parish it was only 11·9.[1]

In all the colliery districts of Derbyshire the infant mortality rate was high. At Shirebrook, in 1901, it reached the appalling rate of 236·4 per thousand births. At Chesterfield, in the same year, it was 217 and at Blackwell 188·5. In the rural village of Ashbourne the rate was as low as 88 per thousand and the average for the whole of England and Wales was only 151.[2] The medical officer of health for the Blackwell Rural District Council attributed the high infant mortality rate to 'gross neglect in the clothing and feeding'. Such 'parental neglect and in-experience', he said, were 'too often the concomitants of early marriages'.[3] Peck believed that the infant mortality rates were kept up 'by the existence of the privy midden system and the ignorance of mothers'. He advocated, as a speedy remedy, 'the introduction of the water carriage system in urban parts of the district, and the teaching of mothers by health visitors'.[4]

II

Despite the large numbers of houses provided by the colliery companies not all the miners were able to live near their place of work and many of them travelled considerable distances daily in special workmen's trains. John Pendleton's description of one of these trains, in 1894, is worth recalling, if only for its naïvety:

The 'Paddy Mail', that runs from Chesterfield to Staveley, in Derbyshire, is a rich curiosity as a vehicle of locomotion, with its battered carriages and odour of thick twist, stronger than any smell of tobacco that came from the Witch of Endor's pipe, and burly, muscular, shouting, laughing passengers, with faces black as Erebus. . . .

. . . When the train goes out in the darkness of the winter morning a light is placed in the brake van. The illumination is not provided at the cost of the railway company. The members of the 'Candle Club' find the money. The subscription is not a heavy one—only a halfpenny a quarter; and there is a whimsical rule among the toilers that any member thoughtlessly increasing

[1] Report of M.O.H. for Chesterfield R.D.C., 1910.
[2] Report of M.O.H. for Blackwell R.D.C., 1901.
[3] *Ibid.*   [4] Report of M.O.H. for Chesterfield R.D.C., 1910.

P

his subscription shall be fined. Wright of Derby, the noted painter of candle-light pictures, has, in 'The Orrery', given almost dramatic effects of light and shadow on the features of those listening to the philosopher's lecture; but the brake van of the 'Paddy Mail' would afford even a better subject, with its erratic light, its flare and flicker of candle, on the rough faces of the pitmen grouped about the van stove, listening to anecdote or laughing loudly at story or witticism.[1]

To Pendleton the 'Paddy Mail' was a 'comical' and slightly romantic train. To the miners it was a grim reality. In 1907 William Staton asked: 'Is there not a remedy for the icy benches of what is familiarly known as the "Paddy Mail", taking miners from Dronfield to the Grassmoor collieries on the one hand, and Staveley and Glapwell on the other?' He maintained that such a chilly journey, after the warm atmosphere of the mines, 'must be a prolific source from whence bad colds, influenza and other ailments arise'.[2]

The iniquities of the railway companies and the discomforts and unpunctuality of their workmen's trains were fruitful subjects for discussion at many a Council meeting. The union officials were frequently instructed to make representations to the railway companies about the lack of heating and lighting and the failure of the trains to get the men to work on time. In 1892 Harold Cook, a member of the Derbyshire Silkstone lodge, brought an action, with the support of the Association, against the Midland Railway Company for breach of contract. Cook claimed that because the workmen's train from Dronfield was delayed by an accident on 4 November, 1891, he had lost a day's earnings, which he assessed at 6s. 6d. The case went as far as the court of appeal where Lords Justices Lindley, Bowen and Smith upheld the decisions of the county and divisional courts in favour of Cook. Counsel for the railway company said that there were 700 claims for a day's wage ready to be brought forward if Cook succeeded. Lord Justice Lindley replied that the decision must stand but must not be regarded as a test case for more than this particular incident.[3] When a similar case arose in 1910 the Association discovered that the railway company had taken the precaution of printing on the back of its tickets a saving clause relieving it 'from liability for accident or delay or the non-running of the trains . . . except upon proof that such accident, delay or non-running of the trains is due to the wilful misconduct of the Company or their servants'.[4]

Miners who wished to travel in their pit clothes by ordinary trains

[1] J. Pendleton, *Our Railways: Their origin, development, incident and romance*, (London), 1894, I, pp. 34–35, II, p. 215.
[2] *Derbyshire Times*, 9 February, 1907.
[3] *D.M.A.* 5 April, 1892; *Derbyshire Times*, 24 December, 1892.
[4] *D.M.A.* 12 March, 1910.

found that they were prohibited from doing so by the railway companies' by-laws. When two miners were prosecuted for such an offence in 1910 the Association decided to pay the cost of defending them.[1] The case was lost but soon afterwards the Council instructed Frank Hall to ask the railway company to attach a workmen's coach to all trains in the Mansfield district.[2]

The provision of pit-head baths would have obviated some of these difficulties and would have relieved the miners' wives of endless drudgery in houses which often lacked the most rudimentary plumbing and were almost entirely devoid of bathrooms. The idea of pit-head baths originated in Germany. An M.F.G.B. delegation consisting of R. Smillie and A. Onions investigated the social and industrial conditions of the German working classes in 1910. Amongst other things they reported: 'We saw the bathing arrangements for the workmen, which are now to be found in most parts of Germany, wherever the miners' organization is strong enough to insist on their introduction.'[3] In Britain the initiative came from the more enlightened employers. As early as 1904 Emerson Bainbridge said: 'He would be pleased to bring the matter of providing baths at the pits under his control before his co-directors with a view to the adoption of some system such as is now in operation in Germany and Nova Scotia.'[4] The subject of pit-head baths was first discussed by the M.F.G.B. at its annual conference in 1910 when it was resolved: 'That proper washing and changing accommodation be provided at all mines.'[5]

The great difficulty was to persuade many of the miners that pit-head baths were desirable. The miners' leaders advocated legislation on the subject in the Coal Mines Act of 1911 and since they sought to make the provision of baths compulsory they argued that it was only reasonable to make their use compulsory. This aroused great controversy among the miners and those who were opposed to compulsion advanced all manner of reasons for the probable reluctance of miners to use the colliery baths. They argued that the baths might be too hot and they would catch colds; that they would not wish to use baths, or even showers, after others; that they would not wish to use soap and towels provided by the management and might forget to bring their own; that they would have to take their pit clothes home to be washed and repaired; that communal bathing would be immodest; and so on. Stephen Walsh, a Lancashire delegate, remarked: 'The whole question of compulsion is new. I do not object to it. The dirty man ought to be

---

[1] *D.M.A.* 16 April, 1910.
[2] *Derbyshire Times*, 16 April, 1910; *D.M.A.* 4 June, 1910.
[3] Miners' Federation of Great Britain, *Report on the Social and Industrial Conditions of the German Working Classes by R. Smillie and A. Onions*, (1910).
[4] *Derbyshire Times*, 10 September, 1904.   [5] *M.F.G.B.* 5 October, 1910.

compelled to wash himself. All I want is that we shall have our men to consult and be able to say we have them with us.'[1]

The Derbyshire leaders were active in the campaign for compulsory baths. 'The more I think about the question', said Frank Hall, 'the more I realize that it will be a good thing for the men. Daring though the proposal is, I believe the miners will favour it in time.'[2] Some of the men objected to the proposed charge of a penny for the use of the baths. At a meeting held at Heanor to discuss the scheme, a miner told Frank Hall: 'In Germany there is a penny for this and a penny for that, and what do they get when they arrive home? Horse-flesh. That is what we were told by our deputation. . . . We do not want our wages brought down so that we have to eat horses and cats and dogs.'[3] But such men were in a minority and, on 22 April, 1911, the Council gave its support to compulsory baths by sixty votes to nine.[4] Not all the Federation thought likewise and the lack of unity resulted in the abandoning of the principle of compulsion. The Coal Mines Act, 1911, eventually laid down that 'a majority, ascertained by ballot of two-thirds of the workmen employed in any mine' was necessary before the proprietor was required to provide facilities for taking baths and drying clothes.[5]

III

Irregular work and low wages produced much poverty among the Derbyshire miners, some of whom sank to the lowest depths of degradation. In 1909 an Unstone miner's wife was prosecuted for sending her 13-year-old boy to beg in the streets of Chesterfield.[6] A Ripley miner, in 1905, was charged with neglecting his five children. A representative of the N.S.P.C.C. stated:

The woman appeared to be weak and ill. The children were wretchedly clothed, and there was scarcely an ounce of bread in the house. . . . In the bottom rooms of the house were two chairs, a couple of tables, an old sofa without a bottom. Upstairs were a couple of old iron bedsteads, on one of which were a couple of old, dusty mattresses. On the other was a piece of dirty bedding and a single sheet, and in this apology for a bed all those of the family slept.[7]

Four years later the same miner applied to the Association for 'out-of-work' payment.[8]

These were no doubt exceptional cases. The vast majority of the

[1] *M.F.G.B.* 30 March, 1911.   [2] *Ibid.* 25 March, 1911.
[3] *Derbyshire Times*, 8 April, 1911.   [4] *D.M.A.* 22 April, 1911.
[5] 1 and 2 Geo. V. Ch. 50, s. 77 (1).   [6] *Derbyshire Times*, 3 April, 1909.
[7] *Ibid.* 18 February, 1905.   [8] *D.M.A.* 13 November, 1909.

miners and their families struggled to live as decently as they could. A journalist who visited the slums of Chesterfield during the 1893 lock-out reported:

What struck us at Chesterfield, after many days of wandering among the same class of people, was the fact that more homes than we had noticed anywhere else were spotlessly, beautifully clean. The bare, flagged floor, the rickety, wooden chairs, the hearth, the windows, the steps, all showed that the women, in spite of all, had not sat down and folded their arms.[1]

But with large numbers of families living near the subsistence level, with little or no savings, it was inevitable that strikes, unemployment, sickness and accidents should quickly produce the direst poverty.

The growing distress among the miners in the months preceding the 1893 lock-out led to much dissatisfaction with the Poor Law. In May Haslam, who was on his way to the international conference at Brussels, wrote to his fellow members of the Chesterfield Board of Guardians, urging them to authorize the granting of relief to the families of miners who were working only one or two days a week. 'It is not desirable', he said, 'that poor people should break up their homes to go into a workhouse, a course I shall feel bound to advise them to follow if temporary relief is denied them.'[2] On his return Haslam found that his letter to the Guardians had been misunderstood by the miners and that he was accused of 'seeking to put the class he belonged to into the workhouse'. At a meeting at Clay Cross he replied to his critics: 'If he could have his way, he would certainly do something to remedy the grinding unfairness of the parochial law.'[3]

A reporter from the *Clarion* interviewed William Glossop, a large employer in the joinery and cabinet-making trade, and a member of the Chesterfield Borough Council and also of the Board of Guardians. His account of the interview provides a commentary on the attitude of a Chesterfield Poor Law Guardian at a time when some 9,000 miners in the district were working only about two days a week:

'Well, in my belief', began Mr. Glossop, 'there is no exceptional distress in the district. Nothing that would lead me to believe so has come under my notice. Our out-relief returns show an increase of only between £10 and £20 on the corresponding period last year.'

Which goes to show that the miners have not been applying for relief —preferring to do their starving quietly.

'And let me tell you', said Mr. Glossop, fixing a pair of very keen eyes upon me through his spectacles—'and let me tell you, there should be no distress in this country!'

I agreed with alacrity.

[1] *Westminster Gazette*, quoted in *Derbyshire Times*, 30 September, 1893.
[2] *Derbyshire Times*, 27 May, 1893.   [3] *Ibid.* 3 January, 1893.

'If people were only provident and self-reliant'—now I knew what was coming. . . .

With a deepening sense of my insignificance I quitted Mr. Glossop's presence. And I still think the Devil's tail has touched the church in Chesterfield.[1]

The distress of 1893 was greatly intensified by the lock-out. Countless soup kitchens and relief centres were opened throughout the district. One woman, who had 'for some years taken a great and active interest in the management of soup kitchens', sent to the *Derbyshire Times* 'some excellent cheap recipes'. She wrote:

I enclose the recipe and list of what they give at the *crèche* daily to the poor children . . . The favourite dinner is bread and dripping, bread and jam, and cocoa. We have a great deal of dripping given and I am sure that if it were known that broken bread and dripping would be accepted, many people would give it gladly. These pieces of bread can be dipped in water and then (if possible) put in a very cool baker's oven to get crisp through and if put away in a flour bin will keep fresh for weeks. The little bits should be thrown into the soup and boiled with the vegetables, they make an excellent thickening.

The recommended daily menu was as follows: 'Monday, sheep's head soup and bread; Tuesday, plum duff with brown sugar; Wednesday, Irish stew; Thursday, haricot and lentil soup and bread; Friday, bread and dripping, cocoa to drink, jam; Saturday, rice boiled in a bag, with treacle.'[2]

In October, 1893, the Chesterfield Relief Committee reported that there were hundreds of cases of dire poverty in the town. One of the worst examples was that of a stallman, with eleven in the family, receiving 5s. 6d. a week from the Committee.

'As we entered the house', stated members of the Committee, 'the family were at dinner, which consisted of potatoes and salt, not a morsel of bread to be seen. The furniture consisted of two chairs, an old wooden sofa, only made to stand against the wall, more like a plank bed. Some of the family were sitting on the floor, with a pinch of salt in one hand and a potato in the other. . . . We asked what they had for breakfast. The answer was lard and a little bread, the children had just scraped the lard pot out. The poor mother burst into tears during the father's heart-rending description of their poor circumstances.'

Another stallman, with seven in the family, was receiving 3s. 6d. a week. The Relief Committee reported:

There are three children under thirteen years of age, and one child earns eightpence per day, but only working very little, earning last week eightpence

[1] *Clarion*, 3 June, 1893. The last sentence is an allusion to the famous crooked spire of the Chesterfield parish church.
[2] *Derbyshire Times*, 23 September, 1893.

only. This family had to go without food for twenty-four hours the day previous to this visit.[1]

The severe depression in the coal trade of 1904-5 likewise revealed much poverty. The *Derbyshire Times* said of the distress at Clay Cross: 'There is much silent heroism. Very little is known of the acute suffering that some people are undergoing. Children cannot be sent to school because there are no boots for them to go in, and other children faint in the school because they have no food.' The matter was discussed at a meeting of the Clay Cross school managers. The chairman, W. B. M. Jackson, of the Clay Cross Company, raised the question of providing breakfasts for the children out of the rates, in accordance with a Local Government Board order. 'This was not an act of pauperism', he explained, 'and the amount expended on the children could be refunded when the parents got into better positions. They knew the state of trade, how the pits were working a day and a half or two days a week. He did not know how some of them lived at all.' The clerk to the school managers said: 'The teachers found as a rule that the children said least who suffered most.'[2]

In Chesterfield a conference was called by the Trades and Labour Council to discuss the possibility of taking advantage of the Unemployed Workmen Act, 1905, which allowed local authorities to apply to the Local Government Board for permission to establish unemployment committees.[3]

With poverty went debt. Although the truck shops had long ago been abolished the miner continued to rely upon credit when money was scarce. The small shopkeeper, in the colliery village, depended for his very existence upon trade with the miners and was prepared to give credit in bad times in the expectation of sharing in the general prosperity when trade improved. This strange alliance between the miners and the small shopkeepers was most marked during trade disputes when the shopkeepers made common cause with the miners and saw that they did not go hungry. As a result, the great strikes and lock-outs invariably produced a crop of bankruptcies. In 1894 Haslam told the Dronfield miners: 'During the recent strike the tradesmen behaved well towards the men, and it was their bounden duty to deal with these tradesmen until they had paid off their honourable debt.'[4]

The miner who appeared in court for debt generally received scant sympathy but W. F. Woodforde, the county court judge for Derbyshire from 1874, showed great understanding of the problems of the working class, so much so that in 1880 a petition, signed by solicitors, doctors, accountants and tradesmen in Chesterfield, Clay Cross, Alfreton,

---

[1] *Derbyshire Times*, 21 October, 1893.   [2] *Ibid.* 29 July, 1905.
[3] *Ibid.* 4 November, 1905.   [4] *Ibid.* 31 March, 1894.

Belper, Derby, and other parts of the county, was sent to Selborne, the Lord Chancellor. It called attention to 'the conduct and extraordinary decisions' of Woodforde, asked for a full inquiry into his actions and, if necessary, for his removal.[1] At Clay Cross a meeting of miners and a few small shopkeepers decided to organize a counter-petition. Haslam said: 'The action that a section of tradesmen were taking in this matter was mischievous and uncalled for. His Honour was a reasonable and just judge, and considered the position of the working man.'[2] The agitation for Woodforde's removal dropped after Alfred Barnes, the Member of Parliament for Chesterfield, declined to present another petition in 1882[3] but Woodforde continued to be a controversial figure until his retirement in 1889.[4]

The growth of consumers' co-operative societies in the mining villages helped to encourage saving among the better paid workers who did not need to rely on credit. Harvey, addressing members of the Ripley Co-operative Society soon after the end of the 1893 lock-out, said:

He was told that 400 men at Ripley were so provided for out of their own savings through the co-operative system, that today they were solvent after having passed through a very severe ordeal. He was hopeful that the lessons of the last sixteen weeks would give an impetus to the cause of co-operation.[5]

Haslam saw in co-operation an answer to socialism:

It was very desirable, from more standpoints than one, to assimilate capital and labour. . . . There were men propagating socialism from a peculiar standpoint . . . but even the best of them were unable to tell or show how the great change was to come about. In the meantime ordinary people were quietly bringing about the change by working out results for their own good, and the good of the community. . . . When they were all co-operators, when they found the capital and did the work, there would be that complete identity of interest that everyone sensible desired to see between capital and labour.[6]

The colliery companies realized that thrift had a steadying influence upon their workmen and therefore encouraged co-operation. The Staveley Free Labour Society, the company union which had been organized in 1866 to break the strike of that year, established a co-operative society in 1870 with a membership of 40 and a capital of £60. The society grew rapidly and by 1895 was able to open 'extensive and commodious' new premises.[7] Similarly, the Bolsover Colliery Company required that every tenant in the model village of Bolsover should have

[1] *Derbyshire Times*, 28 August, 1880.   [2] *Ibid.* 4 September, 1880.
[3] *Ibid.* 5 August, 1882.   [4] *Ibid.* 28 September, 1889.
[5] *Ibid.* 2 December, 1893.   [6] *Ibid.* 25 April, 1891.
[7] *Ibid.* 9 November, 1895.

at least one share in the Bolsover Co-operative Society. The tenants were not actually required to trade with the society but many of them believed that they would be reported to the colliery management if they failed to do so.[1] Thrift was also encouraged in other ways. In 1899 Maurice Deacon, of the Sheepbridge Company, advocated 'giving the workman the opportunity of purchasing his house on favourable terms by weekly payments'. He also suggested an amendment of the Truck Act to enable the workman to take part payment of his wages in orders for food and clothing upon some shop 'instead of being compelled to wait for the whole of his wages until a pay day, one half of which frequently did not reach the wife and children'.[2]

The disastrous failures of the co-operative collieries of the 'seventies brought an end to the experiments in producers' co-operation as far as the miners were concerned. In the late 'nineties a colliery at Swadlincote was acquired by the Brotherhood Trust and run on co-operative lines. The leading figures in this movement were J. Bruce Wallace, a Congregational minister, and J. C. Kenworthy, who were associated with a number of Tolstoyan communities in England during the latter years of the nineteenth century.[3] The Swadlincote colliery provided coal for a colony at Purleigh but does not appear to have aroused the interest of the Derbyshire miners.

IV

Unemployment, sickness, accidents and old age were all likely to deprive the miner of the chance to earn a living. A fatal accident might leave his family destitute. Despite the gratuitous advice he frequently received it was virtually impossible for the average miner to save sufficient money to guard against all these contingencies. The Miners' Permanent Relief Fund movement, which had the backing of the employers, was started in Northumberland in 1862. By 1879 it had spread to several other parts of the country. The objects of the movement were to raise funds by subscription among the members or by donations from others to cover funeral expenses, to support dependants, to pay accident benefits and to maintain members who were unable to work because of age or infirmity.[4]

In 1877 attempts were already being made to establish branches of

[1] *Derbyshire Times*, 8 December, 1894.   [2] *Ibid.* 2 September, 1899.
[3] W. H. G. Armytage, 'J. C. Kenworthy and Tolstoyan Communities in England', *The American Journal of Economics and Sociology*, Vol. 16, No. 4 (1957), pp. 381–405; W. R. Hughes, 'Bruce Wallace and "Brotherhood" ', *Congregational Quarterly*, October, 1947, pp. 468–71.
[4] *Derbyshire Times*, 11 October, 1879.

P*

the society in Derbyshire. A meeting at Brampton presided over by J. M. Mello, the rector of St. Thomas's, was addressed by H. J. Day, an Anglican clergyman from Barnsley; A. Blythe, secretary of the Northumberland and Durham Relief Fund; William Watson, agent of the West Riding Relief Fund; and John Catchpole, the Derbyshire miners' leader. Catchpole, conscious of the misfortunes of the South Yorkshire Miners' Association, said:

> He thought it would be better to separate the relief principle from the trade principle, have separate rules, and register under the Friendly Societies Act, and to have the funds invested in the hands of gentlemen who were in such a position as would guarantee their safety at all times, and render it impossible for those funds to be applied to any other than their legitimate purposes.[1]

By 1878 the Midland Counties Miners' Permanent Relief Fund was firmly established with 500 members.

In 1883 the Midland District Miners' Fatal Accident Relief Society was established, with the Duke of Devonshire as its president and Alfred Barnes, of the Grassmoor Collieries, as chairman of the board of management. By 1892 the society had over 20,000 members and an income of over £5,000 a year, the colliery proprietors adding $12\frac{1}{2}$ per cent. to the amount contributed by the members.[2] Both the Permanent Relief Fund and the Fatal Accident Society provided for widows and orphans. William Saunders, the secretary of the Fatal Accident Society, raised considerable opposition to a proposal in 1892 by S. Wills, of Newark, to establish a national miners' orphanage.[3] The scheme had the backing of the miners' unions, including the Derbyshire Miners' Association,[4] but Saunders argued that it was unnecessary. On a smaller scale a miners' orphanage at Bolsover was opened by Lord Grey in December, 1901. The site was given by the Duke of Portland and the building, which was planned to accommodate twenty-four boys, was erected largely as a result of the generosity of Emerson Bainbridge.[5]

Despite such voluntary efforts the trade unions, led by the miners and the railwaymen who were both engaged in dangerous occupations, had for years been campaigning for the amendment of the law relating to Employers' Liability. According to common law a person was liable for the results, not only of his own negligence, but also for that of his servant, if acting within the scope of his employment. From 1837, however, it was recognized by the courts that the master was not liable to his servant for the negligence of a fellow-servant in common employment. The trade unions demanded the abolition of the doctrine of

[1] *Derbyshire Times*, 22 September, 1877.   [2] *Ibid.* 15 October, 1892.
[3] *Ibid.*   [4] *D.M.A.* 20 September, 1892.
[5] *Derbyshire Times*, 14 December, 1901.

'common employment' and the placing of the employee upon exactly the same footing for compensation as any member of the public.[1]

As early as 1862 some of the Northumberland miners had raised the cry that the Miners' Permanent Relief Fund was 'a masters' movement'[2] and as time went on such criticism grew. In 1879 a meeting held at Clay Cross, for the purpose of extending the membership of the society, broke up in disorder. S. Smith, a local newsagent, mounted the platform and denounced the Relief Fund and its supporters in the bitterest terms 'asking where the large capitalists were who would support Mr. Macdonald's Compensation Bill, and asking those present if they intended to support a fund which would pay for their own murder'.[3] At another meeting at Wingfield, the Reverend Joseph Hall, the chairman, said: 'The two principal objections made by the men are first, it relieves the masters of their responsibility, and second, the fund is in antagonism to the miners' union.' He went on to argue that the fund did not interfere with any claim which might arise as a result of future legislation.[4]

During the 'seventies the efforts of the trade unions to amend the law met with strong opposition from the great employers of labour of both parties. In 1880, when Henry Broadhurst introduced his Bill, the Sheepbridge Coal and Iron Company petitioned the House of Commons to reject it.

'Your petitioners believe', wrote J. Stores Smith, 'that the principle of such Bill, if carried into law, would be productive of a great injustice to all employers of labour and of injury to the workmen themselves, and would entirely change and overthrow the relations between capital and labour heretofore subsisting, on reliance on the permanence of which their capital has been expended and invested.'[5]

Charles Markham protested:

The paternal system of modern legislation, which attempts to provide for grown up people as if they were children, is creating obstacles in the manufacturing industry which render it more and more difficult to provide labour for the population. . . . The numerous accident and benefit funds which have been created in late years by the mutual co-operation of masters and workmen mark a special part in the social relations of our manufacturing industries.[6]

Broadhurst succeeded in amending the law to the extent that employers became liable for accidents due to the negligence of managers or foremen, or to carrying out an improper order or rule,[7] but the

---

[1] S. and B. Webb, *The History of Trade Unionism*, (London), edn. of 1920, pp. 364–5.
[2] *Derbyshire Times*, 11 October, 1879.   [3] *Ibid.* 24 September, 1879.
[4] *Ibid.* 4 October, 1879.   [5] *Ibid.* 5 June, 1880.
[6] *Ibid.* 17 July, 1880.   [7] 43 and 44 Vic. c. 52.

doctrine of 'common employment', although modified, was by no means abolished. Moreover, many employers began to induce their workmen to contract out of the provisions of the Act. The usual form of contract-ing out was the establishment of a workmen's insurance fund to which the workmen were compelled to subscribe, and to which the employer also contributed. The Clay Cross Company decided to use the Miners' Permanent Relief Fund and to deduct contributions from wages. Haslam described the proposal as a 'despotic attempt to coerce the men'.[1] The Act was silent on the practice of contracting out but the courts decided in 1882, much to the dismay of the trade union leaders, that it was permissible.[2]

In 1883 William Flint, a South Normanton miner, brought an action under the Employers' Liability Act against the Blackwell Colliery Company. In the Alfreton County Court, before Judge Woodforde, Flint claimed £200 for injuries which, he alleged, were due to the negligence of the Company's servants.[3] Woodforde awarded £150 with costs but the Employers' Liability Assurance Corporation, with which the Blackwell Company was insured, insisted that the circum-stances of the accident did not entitle Flint to compensation. Mr. Justice Denman and Mr. Justice Hawkins in the Queen's Bench Division granted an application for a new trial and referred the case back to the County Court.[4] The Derbyshire Miners' Association, despite the paucity of its funds at that time, decided that the issue was of such importance that Flint should be supported in any further litigation. Clegg was consulted and an appeal for subscriptions was launched.[5] In the original hearing it had been proved that as Flint was being lowered into the pit Waterson, an enginewright, had interfered with the winding engine with the result that the cage came very violently in contact with the bottom of the shaft. Flint was in consequence seriously injured and contended that this was caused by Waterson's interference with the machinery, and by the negligence of the engineman, William Brailsford, in allowing Waterson to be in the engine house. When the case was re-heard the court had to decide whether the accident was due to the negligence of Brailsford, who was in a supervisory position, or of Waterson.[6]

Woodforde came reluctantly to the conclusion that Flint had no claim to compensation. In giving judgment he said: 'Here was a man who was employed to let the men down the pit, and there was negligence on his part and on the part of others. Yet, according to the strict letter of the

[1] *Derbyshire Times*, 9 October, 1880.
[2] Griffiths *v.* Earl of Dudley, 9, Queen's Bench Division, 35.
[3] *Derbyshire Times*, 17 February, 1883.
[4] *Ibid*. 17 March, 14 April, 12 May, 1883.
[5] D.M.A. 14 April, 1883.   [6] *Derbyshire Times*, 16 June, 1883.

law he [Woodforde] was not able to protect or grant the injured man any damages. He hoped that the Act might be altered.'[1] The *Derbyshire Times* drew a different conclusion and called the attention of both masters and men to 'the fair and reasonable method' of settling such questions, which was provided by the Miners' Permanent Relief Fund.[2] The trade unions, however, were determined to secure a change in the law. In June, 1883, the Derbyshire miners' leaders wrote:

We are sorry to learn that Messrs. Burt's, Broadhurst's and others' Employers' Liability Amendment Bill has been thrown out, thus showing the necessity there is for unity and energetic action amongst the miners. What has been done in Lancashire, where there are 35,000 workmen compulsorily contracted out of the Act, can be done elsewhere. Men, be up and doing.[3]

Year after year the trade unions continued to demand that the practice of contracting out should be prohibited and that the doctrine of common employment should be completely abolished. Nowhere was the campaign more vigorously conducted than in the miners' unions but it met with little success until the passing of the Workmen's Compensation Act in 1897. Joseph Chamberlain, who was largely responsible for the measure, abandoned the intricacies of the common law about negligence and acted on the principle that the cost of accidents to workmen must be borne by the employer as part of the working costs of his industry.[4] The Act did not apply to seamen, domestic servants and agricultural labourers and there was no prohibition of contracting out.

Despite these shortcomings, the underlying principle of the Workmen's Compensation Act was regarded by many employers as 'revolutionary'. Emerson Bainbridge, addressing a P.S.A. (Pleasant Sunday Afternoon)[5] meeting in his Gainsborough constituency, said: 'The burden on the coal trade would be a very serious one as there must ultimately . . . be a serious rise in prices. . . .'[6] The financial liability was, of course, one against which the industry could conveniently insure. An actuary reported to the Mining Association of Great Britain that 'upon a moderate estimate of the liabilities entailed' the charge per 10,000 men per annum for fatal accident and disablement risks, if the maximum benefit allowance under an appeal were assumed to be the average, would be £14,500, or £1 9s. per annum for each man. Taking into account the fact that most accidents occurred underground, he estimated that the liabilities among the more highly paid workers would amount to £26,500 per 10,000 men per annum or £2 13s. for each man.[7]

---

[1] *Derbyshire Times*, 14 July, 1883.   [2] *Ibid.* 21 July, 1883.
[3] *D.M.A.* 12 June, 1883.
[4] J. L. Garvin, *The Life of Joseph Chamberlain*, (London), 1934, III, pp. 155–9.
[5] Cf. R. C. K. Ensor, *England, 1870–1914*, (Oxford), 1939, p. 528.
[6] *Derbyshire Times*, 29 May, 1897.   [7] *Ibid.*

The miners' leaders welcomed the Act because they believed that it gave to the employers an incentive to make their mines safer. They were not opposed to the continuation of colliery accident funds and the Permanent Relief Fund, which they regarded as a valuable supplement to the new statutory benefits, but expressed their disapproval of employers who evaded their responsibilities by inducing the men to renounce the free benefits of the Act in return for help in maintaining voluntary schemes. Haslam told the Grassmoor miners:

He had taken the trouble to ascertain what the employers had contributed to the funds of the Benefit Society which had its headquarters at Chesterfield. He found that in one year the grand total was £60. Two firms contributed £25 each, another £10, and the rest nothing. They, as leaders of the Derbyshire Association, would do everything in their power to maintain . . . penny accident and permanent relief funds, always providing there was no attempt . . . to steal from the men their birthright by the offer of a mess of pottage.[1]

The Association passed a resolution strongly condemning contracting out at its annual demonstration in 1898 but a few months later Harvey stated:

It seemed that the owners were not so eager as heretofore for their men to enter into any scheme outside the Act. They had now got a scheme of their own—their indemnity fund—a sort of pool, and he was told that the owners had insured their men so as to secure the full amount of £300 in every case of fatal accident. That being so, the owners would profit in some cases.[2]

Many of the claims under the Act were hotly contested by the employers, with the backing of their insurance companies. 'The Workmen's Compensation Act was proving a litigious Act', said Harvey, towards the end of 1898. 'In fact, since it had come into operation they had had nothing but litigation.'[3] The securing of adequate compensation for its members became an increasingly important aspect of the Association's work. In March, 1899, Harvey suggested that the increase in membership was partially due to the fact that the union was prepared to embark upon costly litigation arising out of the Workmen's Compensation Act. 'Men outside the union, who had no funds behind them, stood little chance', he said, 'and in case of fatal accident their dependants were practically helpless.'[4]

The Workmen's Compensation Act did much to remove the hardships caused by deaths and injuries in the mines but the mitigation of the poverty caused by sickness, unemployment and old age still depended upon voluntary efforts. The Derbyshire Miners' Association, in its early days, had firmly set its face against the provision of friendly

---

[1] *Derbyshire Times*, 4 December, 1897.   [2] *Ibid.* 19 November, 1898.
[3] *Ibid.* 3 December, 1898.   [4] *Ibid.* 25 March, 1899.

society benefits but, as time went on, the union turned its attention increasingly to the problem of helping its members in times of difficulty. The first move in this direction was the establishment of the 'out-of-work' fund in 1893.[1]

The Derbyshire Miners' Convalescent Home at Skegness owed its inception to the dubious financial activities of Edward Terah Hooley, a Derbyshire man, who became one of the best-known company promoters of the 'nineties. In less than three years Hooley promoted twenty-six companies with an aggregate nominal capital of £18,600,000, of which £5,000,000 was his gross profit. By 1898 he was a bankrupt for £491,000, and his companies were left in a very difficult position.[2] Hooley's generosity was directed chiefly towards titled and other influential people whose names he wished to obtain as directors but he also established a convalescent home at Skegness for the miners of the Ilkeston district.[3] By January, 1905, the convalescent home had liabilities amounting to £420 and assets valued at £550, and a new governing body was constituted with Barnet Kenyon as its chairman.[4] Kenyon sought to put the home on a sound financial basis by securing the support of colliery owners and miners throughout the county. By 1909 the committee had £120 in hand and a number of colliery companies were providing free coal for the home.[5] In March, 1914, an annual meeting attended by representatives from miners' lodges and subscribing societies was told that a new home would soon be built.[6]

The growing demand for old-age pensions and the reluctance of governments to take any action led the Association to introduce its own scheme in 1906.[7] In the same year the Liberal government, which was to lay the foundations of the 'Welfare State', came into office. Two of its major achievements, the introduction of non-contributory Old-Age Pensions on 1 January, 1909,[8] and the National Insurance Act of 1911, did a little to mitigate the poverty which was still untouched by voluntary action. Part II of the National Insurance Act, which established a compulsory and contributory insurance against unemployment for certain trades, did not apply to the miners.[9] Part I of the Act established a vast contributory scheme to insure the whole of the working population against sickness and brought in the voluntary

---

[1] See Chapter VI, pp. 241–2.   [2] Clapham, *op. cit.* III, pp. 237–8.
[3] *Derbyshire Times*, 20 February, 1909.   [4] *Ibid.* 27 July, 1907.
[5] *Ibid.* 20 February, 1909.   [6] *Ibid.* 14 March, 1914.
[7] See Chapter VI, pp. 242–3.
[8] Men and women over the age of 70 with an income of less than £21 a year were entitled to an Old-Age Pension of 5s. a week. Married couples received 7s. 6d. For incomes between £21 and £31 there was a graduated scale.
[9] The principal industrial groups covered by the scheme were the building and constructional trades, shipbuilding, mechanical engineering, vehicle building and saw milling.

organizations, the friendly societies and the trade unions as 'approved societies' to administer the money benefits for their members. The Derbyshire Miners' Association decided not to become an approved society under the National Insurance Act[1] because, as Harvey explained later, 'theirs was purely a trade union for labour purposes'.[2] The opposition to the Act organized through the British Medical Association led Harvey to criticize the doctors for looking at the scheme from a political standpoint:

I want to say further that they have no right to condemn the trades unions in the future for agitating for more money and they have no right to condemn the people who threaten to strike because they have threatened one. We are getting our eyes opened as to where the strongest trades unions of the day are, and I venture to say that the lawyers and doctors are the strongest trades unions that there are in this country.[3]

V

The gradual reduction of working hours created for the miners, as it did for other sections of the population, 'a vacuum to be filled by recreation'.[4] What had once been an almost endless cycle of working, eating and sleeping was now being broken by slowly increasing periods of leisure. In 1905 Haslam told the Bolsover miners: 'It sometimes seemed to him an unfortunate thing that one could not bring before the eye of the young miners today the history of coalmining. Some young people imagined it had always been "knock off at dinner time on Saturday and cricket and football in the evening", but some of them were old enough to know that in the old days men were practically slaves.'[5]

The amenities of the colliery villages provided little scope for the enjoyment of increasing leisure. The sports and amusements of earlier generations continued to attract the miners and their families. Cricket and football teams, brass bands, flower shows, ambulance and boys' brigades were all fostered by the colliery companies. The provision of clubs and institutes encouraged sobriety but did not eliminate drunkenness. The village of Shirebrook gained much notoriety through its numerous shebeens in the early years of the present century despite the fact that 'time after time the police . . . made big hauls, and the justices . . . imposed exemplary fines'.[6] Gambling was also prevalent. In 1883 fourteen North Wingfield colliers were prosecuted for playing 'pitch and toss'.[7] Rabbit coursing, which combined gambling with the cruel

[1] D.M.A. 8 June, 1912.
[2] Derbyshire Times, 22 June, 1912.   [3] Ibid.
[4] G. Chapman, Culture and Survival, (London), 1940, p. 102.
[5] Derbyshire Times, 10 June, 1905.   [6] Ibid. 4 May, 1901.
[7] Ibid. 16 June, 1883.

spectacle of dogs chasing rabbits in confined spaces, was still popular in the 'nineties. The entrance fee for each dog was 2s. 6d. to which the promoters generally added a sovereign. Such events were held fortnightly in the grounds of public houses, the promoters no doubt recouping themselves by charges for admission and the sale of drinks. The dogs were known by such names as Hewill's Smoker, Dabber's Dinah and Middleton's Luce.[1]

Concerts and teas continued to play an important part in the social life of the colliery villages. Sometimes they were organized by the employers in order to raise funds for the victims of accidents.[2] At Bolsover an 'annual concert and children's conversazione' was given by the pupils attending the colliery schools.[3] More often such gatherings were held in conjunction with trade union lodges, chapels and friendly societies. The main event was generally a meal, provided by the miners' wives, followed by a speech from one of the union leaders and then by singing, recitations and dancing. The tradition of holding annual gatherings of workmen, at which the employers presided, lingered on in the smaller collieries. But already the simple pleasures of earlier generations were giving way to the new commercialized forms of entertainment. In 1902 the proceedings of the annual tea of the Grassmoor lodge were enlivened by 'several selections . . . given by Mr. Farnsworth with his phonograph'.[4]

The same communal feeling which inspired gatherings of this kind also animated the annual colliery outing. The railways, which had by now penetrated to most of the colliery villages, were like a magic carpet spiriting the miners and their families away from their drab surroundings for a day excursion to the El Dorado of the seaside resorts. In 1892 nearly 500 Glapwell miners, with their wives and families, visited Llandudno. 'If the first train from the Glapwell new station may be taken as an augury of its future success', said the *Derbyshire Times*, 'the Midland Railway Company will be repaid for their latest development of the Doe Lea branch.' The special train left Glapwell at two o'clock in the morning and returned at midnight.[5] When the Grassmoor miners visited Scarborough, in 1898, five special trains had to be run from Chesterfield.[6] These excursions were frequently subsidized by the colliery companies. A letter written by the manager of the Mapperley Colliery, in 1907, shows how the fashion was spreading and the spirit in which contributions were sometimes given:

Not to be behind other collieries, the men desire to have a trip to the seaside as early as it can be arranged. The object of the deputation who came to

---

[1] *Derbyshire Times*, 17 March, 1894.   [2] *Ibid*. 6 May, 1893.
[3] *Ibid*. 17 April, 1897.   [4] *Ibid*. 15 November, 1902.
[5] *Ibid*. 30 July, 1892.   [6] *Ibid*. 3 September, 1898.

wait on you was to ask if the Directors would be graciously pleased to assist the men either by a contribution or a guarantee to the Railway Co. for so many tickets. The contribution by the Company need not be much—no sum was mentioned or asked—but a fraction of what was given some years ago by Mr. Checkland would be well received. Supposing 1s. per head. The sum required at such rate would be quite insignificant—a mere bagatelle —say £50 (!)[1]

The way in which the miner spent his leisure and its effects upon his moral well-being continued to be a matter of concern to the union officials. Harvey, presiding at a Primitive Methodist bazaar in 1904, said:

It was no use pandering to working men today, and he would say there, and not in the Press or in letters, that one thing working men had to be told was to keep their mouths from going into pint pots so often as they did. The gambling spirit of the age was an evil that would have to be attended to, and when men would not give themselves so much to pleasure, would not devote all their time to football and other things, but would sit down and think for ten minutes, then there would be no need for public meetings to teach them how to vote, because their common sense would teach them.[2]

In the same year he protested against the 'degrading and demoralizing' cruelty of rabbit coursing.[3]

The influence of religion was beginning to decline and both the established Church and the Nonconformists were alive to the challenge. In 1910 the Bishop of Southwell, in a pastoral letter, wrote:

Our task in this diocese is great. The two counties of Derbyshire and Nottinghamshire contain the vast Midland coalfields. Year by year there is new development. Country villages change suddenly into colliery villages, where churches or mission rooms are needed. In such parishes often times the staff of the clergy is wholly inadequate, and the mass of people, ignorant and unshepherded, are tempted to drift into the ranks of the indifferent or hostile, save where other religious bodies assert their influence.[4]

Methodism continued to have a stronger influence than any of the other sects. In 1904 Harvey said: 'It was a sign of the times that a very large proportion of the men on the Council of the organization with which he was connected were Methodists living in the villages. They were men who would tell the workers their faults.'[5] To Harvey Methodism was a religion of protest against the iniquities of this

[1] Records of the Mapperley Colliery, Letter from G. Spencer to G. H. Blunt, 23 July, 1907.
[2] *Derbyshire Times*, 10 December, 1904.   [3] *Ibid.* 2 July, 1904.
[4] *Ibid.* 30 April, 1910.   [5] *Ibid.* 10 December, 1904.

world rather than a promise of the glories of the next. In 1892 he complained:

There had been too great a chasm between ministers and working men. The latter had to face stern realities and great responsibilities, and to tell them to be honest, knowing them to be inadequately paid, would be to mock them. To be always telling them about another world, and forgetting this, had sickened men. . . . Was not the pew pandered to from the pulpit, and had not the money-bag too often something to do with the selection of the minister?[1]

Again, in 1904, he said:

A man who did not revolt at what was enacted in this country today was unworthy of the name of Nonconformist. . . . Methodism meant more to him than singing himself away to everlasting bliss or talking about golden streets and jasper walls. More important to him was that the streets of Chesterfield should be well paved than that the streets of heaven should be. It was more important to him that the children should wear shoes and clothes than talking about what angels' robes were, that they should have good water to drink than that they should talk about the 'streams that make glad the City of God'. Take care of earth and heaven will take care of itself.[2]

In 1908 Harvey told the Kilburn miners that Nonconformity was a source of strength to the country and that the Speaker of the House of Commons allowed the Nonconformist Members of Parliament to use his room for a weekly prayer meeting. 'But', he added, 'it is as important to vote right as to pray right.'[3]

Harvey was extremely hostile to the established Church. Speaking on the Education Bill, in 1902, he told the Shirland miners: 'There were 9,600 clergymen in receipt of protestant pay and tithe, and who taught Romish doctrines . . . and if they were honest men they would clear out and go to Rome. . . . Ritualism was practised at their very doors, and they didn't know about it.'[4] Harvey's tirades against the Church brought retaliation. In 1896 a writer in the *Derbyshire Times* asked:

Are the local preachers' qualifications about to be revised? I have long been accustomed to Mr. Harvey's 'lightning changes' but from the chairmanship of a threepenny public-house music-hall entertainment, at which a talented lady gives evidence of her skill as a 'Variety Entertainer' and 'American Top-Boot Expert'—whatever that may be—to the pulpit at the Primitive Methodist Chapel seems a larger order.[5]

[1] *Derbyshire Times*, 3 December, 1892.   [2] *Ibid.* 10 December, 1904.
[3] *Ibid.* 26 September, 1908.   [4] *Ibid.* 27 September, 1902.
[5] *Ibid.* 26 September, 1896. The reference was to a smoking concert held by the Grassmoor lodge.

In 1901 Harvey's attack on 'the parson and the squire' at a Creswell hospital demonstration led the vicar of the parish to withdraw his support.[1]

VI

The gaps in the educational system were being slowly filled. The creation of School Boards under the Education Act of 1870, the powers granted to them to pay the fees of necessitous children, and the growth of compulsory attendance all ensured that increasing numbers of miners' children received an elementary education. The Chesterfield School Board began to give free tuition in August, 1872, but only after searching inquiry into the means of the parents. It was common practice for the Clerk to the Board to obtain information from employers about the earnings of workmen who applied for the remission of school fees. In 1880 C. J. Kerslake, the School Board Attendance Officer, instituted a scheme whereby the Clay Cross, Alma and Grassmoor colliery companies compelled every man and boy to pay a penny a week to a school fund. Brass tokens representing the amount of the school fee were then issued to the miners by the colliery companies and accepted from their children by the Chesterfield schools. Kerslake kept a ledger account of the transactions, returning the tokens each month in order to claim a reimbursement for the schools. For the year ending 29 September, 1882, the Grassmoor Colliery Company alone paid out £67 7s. 3d. for school fees. Kerslake wrote: 'Of the sum just named, I do not think, without school checks, five shillings would have been paid by the parents who all plead poverty, but who, in spite of that, would willingly spend four times the amount of school wage in beer. The money would therefore have been lost.'[2]

At a time when education was bedevilled by religious strife there was a marked cleavage between the Nonconformists, who were not so worried about the undenominational religious instruction given by the Board Schools, and the Anglicans and Roman Catholics. The predominance of Nonconformist representatives on the Chesterfield School Board ensured that they were able to shift the burden of paying the fees of necessitous children who were attending denominational schools upon the Board of Guardians. Kerslake's scheme had the advantage of sparing the parents of such children the indignity of appearing before the Guardians but when he appealed to J. Stores Smith for the support of the Sheepbridge Company he met with a refusal. Smith was a Roman

---

[1] *Derbyshire Times*, 16 August, 1902.
[2] W. R. Covell, 'The Chesterfield School Board, 1871–1903'. Unpublished M.A. Thesis, University of Sheffield, (1952).

Catholic member of the School Board who believed, at that time, that indigent parents of Board School children should apply to the Guardians for help in the same way as those whose children attended denominational schools. His refusal to participate in Kerslake's scheme was probably a form of protest against the Board's policy but later he admitted: 'One gross wrong cannot be remedied by creating another.'[1]

The advent of the School Boards made it possible for a few working-class representatives to exercise some control over educational policy. Harvey was elected to the Chesterfield School Board in 1895 and was joined in 1901 by Frederick Hill, a Unitarian plasterer, but they were the only working-class members of the Board during the whole of its existence from 1871 to 1903. Harvey, as a good Primitive Methodist, devoted much of his energy to opposing the inclusion of the Apostles' Creed in the religious training given in Board Schools but it was not until 1897, on the eve of a School Board election, that the Dissenters carried the day.[2] In 1895 he carried his trade union principles into the work of the School Board by submitting a motion calling for the inclusion of a fair wages clause in all of the Board's contracts.[3]

Harvey was strongly opposed, along with other Nonconformists on the School Board, to the Education Bill of 1902, mainly on the ground that it would allow 'Managers of Voluntary Schools to teach Sectarianism, which will be objectionable to Nonconformists and others who will have to pay the Education rate . . .'. 'The Bill', he said, 'may be the voice of Balfour but it is the hands of Salisbury.'[4] Despite the outcry raised by Liberals and Nonconformists throughout the country, the Education Act of 1902 was passed and Haslam and Harvey, who were both by this time borough councillors, became members of the newly formed Chesterfield Education Committee.[5]

For the miner who was too old to have enjoyed the advantages of the improving facilities for elementary education and for the youth who wished to continue his education after leaving school there were growing opportunities to obtain further education. In an age of increasing foreign competition technical efficiency was becoming more important. The Technical Instruction Act, 1889, which empowered local authorities to supply technical and manual instruction, was followed in 1890 by the Local Taxation (Customs and Excise) Act, which allotted annually to county and county borough councils a large variable sum— the Whisky Money—derived from the customs and excise duties, for the provision of secondary and technical education. In 1891 the

[1] Covell, op. cit.   [2] Ibid.
[3] Derbyshire Times, 16 February, 1895.   [4] Covell, op. cit.
[5] Minutes of the Chesterfield Borough Council, 3 April, 1903.

Chesterfield borough council appointed a Technical Instruction Committee, which took over, amongst other duties, the management of the Science and Art classes.[1]

The interest taken by the miners does not appear to have been great. In 1892 only eight out of a total of 301 students attended classes in mining.[2] In the following year the Committee expressed disappointment at this and strongly recommended attendance 'to those miners who wish to get on in the Mining World, and to those who wish to do their work in an efficient manner'.[3] In order to encourage attendance the Committee decided in 1893 to offer exhibitions covering fees and railway fares to qualified mining students who wished to embark on the two-year course leading to a colliery manager's certificate.[4] By 1898, however, there were still only ten mining students out of a total of 402.[5]

The Technical Education Committee of the Derbyshire County Council made similar attempts in other parts of the county to stimulate the interest of the miners. In 1893 it was reported: 'A highly successful series of lectures is being developed at Alfreton for the benefit of mining students. . . .'[6] In 1914 the County Council decided to extend the facilities for mining instruction and to establish centres for advanced study at Chesterfield, Heanor, Belper and Ilkeston.[7] Some miners lacked the inclination, others the ability, to profit from courses of this kind. Many must have lacked the endurance to attend lectures regularly after a gruelling day in the pit but, for the exceptional man, there was the opportunity to rise to the managerial ranks. One of the first miners in Derbyshire to go from the coal face in this way was Jeremiah Rhodes who became certificated manager of the Alfreton and Shirland collieries of the Blackwell Company, retiring in 1909.[8]

The Derbyshire Miners' Association played its part in fostering the growth of technical education. In August, 1891, the Council resolved: 'That we do what we can to assist the County Council Technical Education Committee in the formation of Classes in our Mining Centres, whereby Technical Instruction by lectures and in other ways may be given.'[9] Two months later Haslam and Harvey were authorized to attend meetings of the county council's Technical Education Mining Sub-Committee.[10] Haslam became a member of the Chesterfield Technical Education Committee in 1896, and Harvey in 1898.[11]

[1] Minutes of the Chesterfield Borough Council, 13 October, 1891; Minutes of the Chesterfield Technical Instruction Committee, 21 July, 1892.

[2] Minutes of Chesterfield Technical Instruction Committee, 14 October, 1892.

[3] *Ibid.* 31 October, 1893.   [4] *Ibid.* 11 November, 1895.

[5] *Ibid.* 14 February, 1899.   [6] *Derbyshire Times*, 22 August, 1891.

[7] *Ibid.* 30 May, 1914.   [8] *Ibid.* 22 May, 1909.

[9] *D.M.A.* 25 August, 1891.   [10] *Ibid.* 20 October, 1891.

[11] Chesterfield Borough Council, Minutes of General Purposes Committee, 3 November, 1896; 4 November, 1898.

Harvey used his position to protest against the exclusiveness of the secondary schools of his day by requesting that it should be recorded in the Committee's minutes that he had voted against grants being made to the Grammar School for scientific apparatus and to the Girls' High School for the building of an additional classroom.[1]

Liberal adult education continued to be provided by the University Extension movement which had long since failed to capture the interest of the working class. In 1891 the Cambridge University Extension lectures in Chesterfield were discontinued. 'The movement cannot be made self-supporting in this town', wrote the secretaries, 'as any attempt to accomplish this would (considering the number of students) make the fees prohibitive.'[2] The lectures were revived in 1897 but again there was 'a singular absence amongst the audience of the working class element'.[3] In 1904 Harvey complained:

There was a good deal of attention given to football, cricket and recreation. He did not object to that but he did object to all leisure time being devoted to recreation and none whatever to mental study. He had made enquiries of the Librarian of Chesterfield, and found that educational subjects, philosophy, history, etc., did not form fifty per cent. of the reading at Chesterfield compared with fiction. He hoped the members of that lodge would act as missionaries. It was not necessary for them to go to South Africa. They could start at Shirebrook and he was sure they were needed.[4]

The founding of the Workers' Educational Association by Albert Mansbridge in 1903 and the development of the university tutorial class did much to remedy the defects of the extension movement and to bring about a fruitful and democratic partnership between the trade unions, the co-operative societies and the universities. By 1908 an Oxford tutorial class, on the lines of the prototype established by R. H. Tawney at Rochdale, was flourishing in Chesterfield.[5] In the following year L. V. Gill, one of the pioneers of the W.E.A. in Rochdale, addressed a conference at Chesterfield at which it was decided to form a branch of the W.E.A.[6] In 1909 the Executive Committee of the Derbyshire Miners' Association resolved: 'That the subscription of 4s. for joining the Workers' Educational Association be paid, which includes Entrance Fee and the Monthly Journal.'[7]

The W.E.A. placed in the hands of the working class a powerful

[1] Minutes of Chesterfield Technical Instruction Committee, 27 March, 1902; 30 October, 1902.　　　　　　　　　　　[2] *Derbyshire Times*, 22 August, 1891.

[3] *Ibid.* 19 January, 1901.　　　　　　　　　　　[4] *Ibid.* 2 July, 1904.

[5] *Oxford and Working-Class Education, The Report of a Joint Committee of University and Working-Class Representatives on the relation of the University to Higher Education of Workpeople*, (Oxford), 1908, p. iv.

[6] *Derbyshire Times*, 9 October, 1909.　　　　　[7] *D.M.A.* 13 November, 1909.

instrument for obtaining education of a university character in subjects which were directly relevant to the problems of their day. Inevitably it was criticized on all sides. In connection with the inaugural conference in Chesterfield, Mansbridge had issued a leaflet in which he said: 'The Association has provided the workpeople on their own terms and upon their own conditions the finest teachers in sympathy with Labour that England possesses.' Violet Markham wrote to the chairman: 'I may have misunderstood this sentence, but I cannot read it otherwise than as placing the test of Labour upon your teachers.' Kolthammer, the tutor, explained:

The writer was to some slight degree under a misapprehension ... He did not have to sign any of the thirty-nine articles of the Social Democratic Party or of the Liberals or Conservatives or Church parties. The function of the teacher was not to draw conclusions, but to give facts, to suggest possible explanations, but not to make socialistic speeches.[1]

Many Derbyshire miners were to profit from the education they received in W.E.A. classes. They carried their new-found knowledge, confidence and fluency into their trade union work, local government and politics. There began to emerge a new type of leadership, combining the Nonconformist background of the older leaders with an academic training in economics, politics, history and philosophy, which was to make an important contribution to the social ferment of the years following the First World War. In a society which preferred evolution to revolution it is not surprising that the required training for encroaching upon the preserves of the middle class was to be found in what has been described by the two self-appointed spokesmen of the English middle classes as 'that profoundly middle-class institution, the Workers' Educational Association'.[2]

The revolutionary strand in trade union education was to be found at Ruskin College where the students were among the first Labour intellectuals who responded to the syndicalist teachings which originated in France and in America. Max Beer, who visited the college in 1905, writes: 'I noticed a certain dissatisfaction among some students with the economic teaching of the College professors. The students desired to be taught economics from Marx's *Capital*, particularly the labour theory of value, instead of the Jevonian theory of marginal utility.'[3] The dissatisfied students, led by the Principal, Dennis Hird, eventually formed a separate organization called the Plebs League and finally seceded from the college in 1909. Benjamin Lee, of the Morton No. 2

---

[1] *Derbyshire Times*, 9 October, 1909.
[2] R. Lewis and A. Maude, *The English Middle Classes*, (London), 1949, p. 57.
    Beer, *op. cit.* p. 352.

lodge, was a student at Ruskin during this period of turmoil, his expenses being paid by the Derbyshire Miners' Association.[1] In August, 1908, he reported:

The students have a thorough training to become excellent politicians; but although politics enter so largely in their studies, the work is strictly educational, and the teaching is absolutely impartial. . . . It is a fine field for training trade union officials and political agitators; for moulding social reformers, and giving them that knowledge which will enable them to lift their class higher in the social scale.[2]

The Plebs League, with the support of the South Wales Miners' Federation and the newly formed National Union of Railwaymen, established an institution of their own, the Central Labour College, at first at Oxford, then in London. Out of this movement evolved the National Council of Labour Colleges with which the Derbyshire Miners' Association was later to become affiliated but, in the years before the First World War, the leadership of the Association was thoroughly opposed to an organization which believed that the Labour Party was a feeble and timorous body and that revolution would come through the uncompromising direct action of industrial unions. Indeed, such was the alarm at the news from Ruskin that the Executive Committee resolved, in 1909: 'That the application from T. Mosley, of Williamthorpe lodge, for a year's residence at Ruskin College cannot be entertained, considering the information received about the College.'[3] In the following year the Council decided that as it had already made a grant to Ruskin, it could not make a grant to its rival. An application in 1911 for delegates to the new Labour College conference at Oxford, on 7 August, was 'not entertained'[4] and in 1912 it was decided not to send a representative to the stone-laying ceremony at Ruskin College.[5]

VII

The miner's work continued to be fraught with danger but the rate of fatal accidents in Derbyshire was slowly decreasing. In the five years following the passing of the Coal Mines Act, 1855, the death rate in the Midland inspection district[6] had been one to every 110,096 tons of

[1] D.M.A. 26 September, 21 November, 19 December, 1908.
[2] Derbyshire Times, 29 August, 1908.   [3] D.M.A. 7 August, 1909.
[4] Ibid. 9 April, 5 August, 1911.   [5] Ibid. 27 January, 1912.
[6] The Midland inspection district included Derbyshire, Nottinghamshire, Leicestershire and Warwickshire. In 1910 that part of Derbyshire which is north of the Trent became part of the No. 4 Yorkshire and North Midland district with headquarters at Doncaster. The remainder of Derbyshire became part of the No. 8 Midland and Southern district, which included Staffordshire, Leicestershire, Warwickshire and the rest of England to the south.

coal raised. In the period 1875–9 it was only one to 216,000 tons. Thomas Evans, the district inspector, commented:

I do believe that the legislative enactments which have been passed for the protection of life must have some of the credit. No doubt the higher standards in the class of managers, the persons who have the direction of the mines, the improved state of the machinery, and the better state of discipline of the mines generally, have conduced largely to the lessening of the death-rate of the district.[1]

In 1881 the fatal accident rate fell to one for every 244,643 tons raised, compared with a national average of one for 177,106 tons.[2] By 1908 the Midland district had a death rate of one for 365,545 tons and had held for some years the highest record for safety and the lowest death rate in Great Britain.[3]

Prosecutions of both miners and coal-owners became more frequent as a result of the growth of legislation. In 1881 Evans complained that magistrates were sometimes reluctant to convict and called attention to the difficulty of getting magistrates to sit who were unconnected with collieries.[4]

Derbyshire was fortunate in having only one major colliery disaster during the period 1880–1914. The explosion at the Parkhouse Colliery, at Danesmoor, at 10 o'clock on the morning of 7 November, 1882, causing the deaths of 45 miners, was the worst disaster the county had ever experienced and public opinion was profoundly shocked. The catastrophes of 1861, when 23 men had been drowned at Clay Cross, and of 1871, when 27 lives had been lost in the explosion at Renishaw Park, had occurred at times when trade union organization in the county was weak.[5] The Parkhouse explosion was probably the first serious colliery accident in Derbyshire to be investigated by trade union officials. Haslam, who had been employed at the Parkhouse Colliery before becoming Secretary of the Derbyshire Miners' Association, was allowed to inspect the workings with three other experienced miners.[6] A jury reported:

We are agreed that there has not been any negligence or carelessness on the part of the Clay Cross Company or their officials. We believe proper precautions were taken for the ventilation of the pit. We agree that the explosion occurred by a sudden influx of gas, but no one was to blame for the same.

The jury recommended more frequent examinations of the pit by the deputies and the introduction of safety lamps.[7] A subsequent report by

---

[1] *Reports of H.M. Inspectors of Mines*, 1879. [2] *Ibid.* 1881.
[3] *Ibid.* 1908. See Appendix I to this chapter.
[4] *Reports of H.M. Inspectors of Mines*, 1881. [5] See Chapter II, pp. 70–1.
[6] *Derbyshire Times*, 25 November, 1882. [7] *Ibid.* 2 December, 1882.

Arnold Morley, the Liberal politician, stated that fewer lives would have been lost if fan ventilation had been in use.[1]

On 11 November, 1895, seven men were killed in an explosion at the A Winning pit of the Blackwell Colliery Company. The jury found the explosion was caused 'by an overcharged shot of gunpowder' but that the evidence failed to disclose whether the secondary cause was gas, coal-dust or an admixture of both. Again the management of the colliery was exonerated from any blame.[2] Ten men were injured in another explosion at the Manners Colliery, Ilkeston, on 21 September, 1905.[3]

Explosions were one of the principal sources of danger in mines and increasing attention was paid to their causes. It was impossible to eliminate explosive and combustible gases and dusts in mines but much could be done to minimize their dangers by improved ventilation and the control of dust. Further necessary precautions were the prevention of sparks and the prohibition of naked lights. The dangers of coal-dust were not fully realized until the 'nineties when a Royal Commission was appointed to investigate the matter. The Commissioners recommended that large accumulations of dust should not be allowed to remain in mines; that inspectors should ensure that dust was adequately watered; and that the firing of shots should be carried out between shifts when the majority of men were out of the mine.[4] In 1895 A. H. Stokes, the district inspector of mines, referring to the Blackwell explosion, said: 'Previously a number of them had thought that dust required a certain quantity of gas before gunpowder would set fire to it. Now, however, they had found out that either with gas or without it, dust would fire.'[5]

As early as 1881 Evans, Stokes's predecessor, had recommended further inquiry into the use of Smith and Moore's caustic lime cartridges for breaking down coal.[6] It was reported to the Chesterfield and Derbyshire Institute of Mining and Mechanical Engineers in 1883 that experiments had been made at Clay Cross and that the lime process had been unsuccessful in the hard coal but successful in the soft coal seams, though at a much greater cost than powder.[7] In 1895 Stokes called attention to the inconsistency of prohibiting the use of naked lights and yet allowing shots to be fired by a gunpowder fuse.[8]

The introduction of electricity into the mines was yet another source of danger. Both Robert Smillie and A. B. Markham expressed their

[1] *Derbyshire Times*, 31 March, 1883.   [2] *Ibid.* 30 November, 1895.
[3] *Ibid.* 23 September, 1905.
[4] *R.C. on Explosions from Coal Dust in Mines*, Second Report, 1894.
[5] *Derbyshire Times*, 14 December, 1895.
[6] *Reports of H.M. Inspectors of Mines*, 1881.
[7] *Derbyshire Times*, 21 April, 1883.
[8] *Reports of H.M. Inspectors of Mines*, 1895.

misgivings before a departmental committee which was appointed in 1902 to discuss the safeguards which should accompany the use of electricity[1] but it was not until 1910, when the new Mines Bill was in preparation, that the Derbyshire miners' leaders began to take an active interest in the matter. Harvey insisted: 'Human life . . . must not be sacrificed on the altar of cheapness.'[2] Frank Hall told the Bolsover miners: 'We are against electrical machinery because we believe it constitutes a real danger in our midst.'[3] The explosion at the Cadeby Colliery in Yorkshire in 1912 led Harvey to ask in the House of Commons: 'Has the Home Secretary any knowledge as to whether the explosion was caused by the use of coal-cutting machines, and is he aware whether they are worked by electricity or compressed air. . . ?'[4]

Although deaths from falls of roof continued to be much more numerous than deaths from explosions, they received comparatively little attention. The Mines Regulation Act of 1887, which repealed the Act of 1872, did not do much more than its predecessor to ensure the prevention of such accidents. It required that suitable timber should be provided at the working place and that the distance between props should not exceed six feet 'or such distance as may be ordered by the owner, agent, or manager'. The responsibility for the safety of his working place was still largely the miner's. The *Derbyshire Times* commented in 1888: 'Experience has shown that the miner, knowing that he is only paid for the quantity of mineral that he produces, and, as a rule, being intent on getting as much coal as possible, forgets the danger to which he is exposed because the timbering brings him no money value in return for his labour.'[5]

The invention of safety devices[6] helped to reduce the number of serious winding accidents but the Enginemen's and Firemen's Union, with the support of the Derbyshire Miners' Association, worked unceasingly to secure that enginemen should have adequate qualifications and that winding gear should be properly maintained and inspected. The larger cages and more powerful engines used at the newer collieries encouraged colliery managers to attempt to raise record outputs of coal. Samuel Rowarth told the enginemen and firemen at Glapwell, in 1906, that the men at one colliery had been promised 'a double whisky' if they could break the record, but they had refused to try. 'Do not attempt to break a record of an hour's winding by making so many runs', he said, 'but wait till you get the signal, and then do your level best, and you will find a greater tonnage at the end of the day's

[1] *D.C. on Electricity in Mines*, Evidence of Smillie, Q. 3184; Evidence of Markham, Q. 4273. [2] *Derbyshire Times*, 12 November, 1910.
[3] *Ibid.* 4 March, 1911. [4] 40 H.C. Deb. 5s. 1929.
[5] *Derbyshire Times*, 7 January, 1888. [6] See Chapter V, pp. 206-7.

winding than by jeopardizing the lives of the workmen and destroying property, besides entirely straining your nerves and eyesight.'[1]

The introduction of machinery underground also tended to increase the pace of work and to multiply its dangers. Commenting on the large number of fatal accidents in the county in 1910 James Martin asked: 'What was that due to? It was in great measure due to the dreadful hurry imposed on the men working in the mines.'[2] In 1911 Haslam said: 'He was of the opinion that our mines were being worked on far too extensive a scale. There were too many men in one place, and too many men in the shaft at one time.'[3] Coal-cutting machines were responsible for many accidents. The men who operated them had little knowledge of electricity and although they were forbidden to interfere with the wiring, fuse boxes and switchgear, they sometimes did so, with disastrous consequences.[4] The noise of the machinery prevented the operators from hearing the sounds which indicated to the experienced miner that the roof was unsafe and, in the early days of mechanization, men were sometimes buried by falls.[5]

The miners' leaders were continually pressing for the appointment of more government inspectors of mines. In 1884 Burt and Broadhurst led a deputation which called the attention of Sir William Harcourt to the matter. By 1900, when Haslam served on a deputation which was interviewed by Sir Matthew Ridley, little progress had been made. Ridley replied that no complaints about understaffing had been received from the inspectorate.[6] The question came prominently before the Royal Commission on Mines which was appointed in 1906. Stokes, the inspector for the Midland district, stated in evidence that he needed more assistance.[7] In 1909, at the annual conference of the M.F.G.B., Harvey spoke strongly in support of a resolution calling upon Labour M.P.s and miners' agents to press for the appointment of more inspectors. It was proposed that the additional inspectors should have five years' practical experience at the coal face and that a working miner inspector should be appointed in each inspection district.[8]

The importance of rescue and first aid service was also becoming increasingly apparent. A. H. Stokes, who served as inspector of mines for the Midland district from 1886 to 1909, and before that as assistant inspector, was a great advocate of ambulance training for mine officials and attended the first instruction class in Chesterfield in 1878.[9] In 1883 J. P. Jackson called the attention of members of the Chesterfield and Derbyshire Institute of Mining and Mechanical Engineers to a

[1] *Derbyshire Times*, 20 October, 1906.   [2] *Ibid.* 27 August, 1910.
[3] *Ibid.* 18 February, 1911.   [4] *Ibid.* 12 November, 1910.
[5] *Ibid.* 30 April, 1898.   [6] *Ibid.* 14 April, 1900.
[7] *R.C. on Mines*, First Report, 1907, (Cd. 3548), Evidence of Stokes, Q. 9748.
[8] *M.F.G.B.* 6 October, 1909.   [9] *Derbyshire Times*, 8 May, 1909.

Home Office circular which gave details of the Fleuss breathing apparatus for use in gas-filled mines: 'He did not see why there should be any difficulty in forming a brigade in the same way that fire brigades were established in towns. . . . He thought that a centre might be established . . . . at Chesterfield and a supply of apparatus kept there by proprietors of collieries.'[1] It was not until 1910, however, that the coal-owners of Derbyshire and Nottinghamshire established a miners' rescue station at Mansfield Woodhouse which was one of the first in the country. The site was given by the Duke of Portland and most of the larger collieries agreed to find the money needed for the capital outlay and for the maintenance of the station, contributions being in proportion to the amount of coal produced. Men were sent from the contributing collieries, a few at a time, to be trained in the use of rescue apparatus in special galleries containing varying atmospheres.[2] The scheme was welcomed by the unions. James Martin told the Staveley miners: 'He hoped there were young men in their district who would be ready to qualify themselves by attending mining and ambulance classes.'[3]

The explosion at the Parkhouse Colliery in 1882 gave a great impetus to the introduction of safety lamps despite the opposition of the miners.[4] By 1890 A. H. Stokes was able to attribute the decline in the number of fire-damp explosions to the growing use of Marsaut and Clanny lamps. He wrote:

It has occasionally been publicly stated that the introduction of safety lamps is proving injurious to the miners' eyesight, and I find, when discussing the use of safety lamps with miners' deputations the question of eyesight is frequently brought forward, but the point always appeared to me to be one of sentiment rather than fact.[5]

This statement started a heated controversy in the Press and in medical circles. Josiah Court, the medical adviser to the Derbyshire Miners' Association, undertook voluntarily to investigate the problem. During the winter of 1890–1 he attended a great number of meetings in various parts of the county and examined 573 men working with naked lights, and 524 men working with safety lamps. Each of the 1,097 cases was carefully recorded and, in May, 1891, Court reported:

At the outset I thought the position of the men in working the coal was one of the chief causes of nystagmus, but the enquiry has satisfactorily convinced me that it is *the want of good light* that is the only cause of the mischief.[6]

---

[1] *Derbyshire Times*, 21 April, 1883.　　　　　　　　[2] *Ibid.* 2 July, 1910.
[3] *Ibid.* 27 August, 1910.　　　　　　　　　　　　　[4] See Chapter VII, p. 277.
[5] *Reports of H.M. Inspectors of Mines*, 1889.
[6] W. Batley, ed., *Miners' Diseases: Records of the Researches of Dr. J. Court*, (Sheffield), n.d., p. 18.

Meanwhile Simeon Snell, a Sheffield ophthalmic surgeon, was advancing a counter-theory. He wrote a letter to the *Sheffield Independent* in which he stated:

I am satisfied that any competent investigator approaching the subject with an open mind can arrive at no other conclusion than that the prime cause of the peculiar oscillation of the eyeballs from which miners suffer is the position into which a certain proportion of coal-getters have to throw their eyes whilst at work, and that the lamps exert but a secondary influence. The kind of work is called 'holing'.[1]

Snell repeated this opinion at a meeting of the Sheffield Medical Society on 18 December, 1890, and elaborated his views in the *British Medical Journal*[2] soon after the publication of Court's report. Snell received support for his theories from Dransart, a French doctor, and Neiden, a German.[3] Court continued his researches by visiting Durham and the Forest of Dean and, in July, 1892, read a paper, *Defective Illumination as the Cause of Nystagmus and other Ocular Disorders Observed in Miners*, before the British Medical Association at Nottingham. J. Tatham Thompson, a Cardiff oculist, also read a paper on the same theme.

Court's theory was not generally accepted and the number of cases of miners' nystagmus continued to increase. Between 1908 and 1910 the number of men claiming and obtaining compensation for the disease rose from 460 to 1,618. In 1911 Court wrote to Sir Arthur Markham calling his attention to the matter and pointing out that the received theory was responsible for the increase in the number of compensation cases because it was believed that a miner who had suffered from nystagmus was liable to further attacks:

If the opinions of these expert eye surgeons are allowed to prevail, the disease will be looked upon as a permanent injury and the increase in compensation demanded from the employers will be very great. Furthermore the question as to the cause of the disease ought to be settled.[4]

Markham passed Court's suggestions to the Home Secretary, Reginald McKenna, with excellent results. On 22 February, 1912, J. S. Haldane presented to the Royal Society a paper written by T. Lister Llewellyn, which confirmed Court's conclusion.[5] Haldane wrote to McKenna:

I am sure Dr. Court will be glad to know that Llewellyn's researches, conducted over a number of coalfields, and extending to metalliferous miners, have completely confirmed his conclusions as to the connection between nystagmus and the very bad light given by ordinary safety lamps.[6]

[1] *Sheffield Independent*, 21 November, 1890.
[2] *British Medical Journal*, II, (1891), pp. 61–66.
[3] *Derbyshire Times*, 15 August, 1891.   [4] Batley, *op. cit.* p. 37.
[5] *Proceedings of the Royal Society*, Series B, LXXXV, (1912), pp. 10–27.
[6] Batley, *op. cit.* p. 37.

Court's triumph was complete when he read a paper to the Ophthalmological Congress at Oxford on 19 July, 1912. After hearing and discussing the paper the Congress endorsed Court's views.

Court also gave much attention to another miners' ailment, ankylostomiasis, popularly known as miners' anaemia or worm disease. It appears to have been imported from tropical or sub-tropical countries and was first discovered in England, in 1902, among the Cornish tin-miners, by J. S. Haldane, after an examination of statistics kept by the Miners' Convalescent Hospital at Redruth. When Court heard from Haldane about the new disease he immediately wrote 250 letters to doctors in the South Yorkshire, Nottinghamshire and Derbyshire coalfields but found no trace of ankylostomiasis in the Midland district. He mentioned the matter to Haslam and Harvey who at once saw its extreme importance and asked him to make a report to the Executive Committee of the M.F.G.B. in the spring of 1903. Later in the year Court delivered an address on the disease to the annual conference of the M.F.G.B.[1] He also visited Belgium to carry out investigations in hospitals at Mons and Liège, and did much to advise the Federation on the kind of legislation which was necessary to combat the disease.

The continued efforts of the miners to ensure their safety and welfare led to further government inquiries and Acts of Parliament during the period 1880–1914. The Royal Commission which was set up in 1879, with Thomas Burt as one of its members, to inquire into accidents in mines, issued its final report in 1886. The Commissioners described the dangers of gas and coal-dust and recommended the use of high explosives rather than gunpowder for shot-firing. They also suggested the desirability of first-aid services and rescue stations. The Coal Mines Regulation Act of 1887,[2] which followed the report of the Royal Commission, disclosed a development of the science of mining rather than of legislative policy. Now that the duty of the Government to enforce safe management of the mines was fully recognized, it was natural that each new Mines Act should make compulsory those safety devices and methods which had proved their value in the interval since the last. Thus the principal innovations in 1887 were eight general rules. Other sections of the Act of 1872 were revised and extended. The minimum age of employment underground was raised to 12 and that of winding-enginemen to 22. The system of certification was extended to include second-class certificates for under managers. Nine years later the Coal Mines Regulation Act of 1896 empowered the Home Secretary to issue special rules on such subjects as explosives and safety lamps, and led to a succession of orders regulating the use of explosives in coalmines. An Act of 1900 raised the minimum age for child labour underground to 13.

[1] Batley, *op. cit.* p. 84; *M.F.G.B.* 8 October, 1903.   [2] 50 and 51 Vict. cap. 58.

A GROUP OF DERBYSHIRE MINERS
from the Heanor district, c.1900

The advent of the Liberal government in 1906 led to the appointment of yet another Royal Commission to inquire into the health and safety of miners, and the administration of the Mines Acts. The Federation was represented on the Commission by Abraham, Edwards and Smillie. J. S. Haldane, who had done much useful scientific work to improve conditions in the mines, was also a member. The Royal Commission dealt with many of the problems which had been troubling the miners: the advisability of watering coal-dust; the advantages and disadvantages of various forms of safety lamp; the adequacy of inspection and the investigation of accidents; the qualifications of colliery managers; the prevention of ankylostomiasis; and methods of ventilation.

The work of the Royal Commission resulted in the preparation of a new Coal Mines Bill which, in addition to being a great consolidating measure, was the most comprehensive piece of mining legislation which had ever been considered by Parliament. The provisions of the Bill aroused controversy among the miners and there were many discussions at both the district and the national level before agreement was reached. The policy of the Derbyshire Miners' Association was decided at a special Council meeting on 22 April, 1911, and embodied in the following resolutions:[1]

(1) That this Council is in favour of total exclusion of electricity from our mines except for lighting purposes.

(2) That we favour an amendment to the Bill calling for another shaft when the coal face is two miles from the pit shaft.

(3) That an amendment be supported in favour of the total prohibition of female labour about our mines.

(4) That we are in favour of the age limit for boy labour being as scheduled in the Bill.

(5) That the provision of compulsory baths in the Bill be accepted.

(6) That we favour the five years' practical experience necessary, three of which shall be at the coal face, and that the eyesight test be also applied to the Manager and Undermanager, all having the right of appeal to a specialist, the certificate being sent to the inspector and workmen.

(7) That in the constitution of a jury on a fatal accident inquest, at least one-third of its members shall be men who have been or are practical miners, and that the workmen shall have the power to appoint one of their number to represent them without having to get a majority of the men.

(8) That in the making of special rules to govern this Act, we claim that the miners should have a place on any committee that deals with it.

These far-reaching proposals did not find their way into the Coal Mines Act of 1911. Nevertheless it was an important advance on all previous legislation. The Act laid down an elaborate code of regulations

[1] *D.M.A.* 22 April, 1911.

Q

to govern the certification of managers and undermanagers, and a similar system to control the appointment and qualifications of firemen, examiners and deputies. It provided more fully than ever for the collection by the State of plans and other information from mines. Its detailed safety provisions dealt with ventilation, safety lamps, shafts and winding, haulage, the support of roofs and sides, signalling, machinery, electricity and explosives. The health regulations provided for sanitation, baths and the notification of industrial diseases. The procedure for the reporting and investigation of accidents was overhauled and the provision of ambulance and rescue services was made compulsory. The minimum age for the employment of boys underground was raised to 14. The appointment, power and duties of inspectors were carefully regulated. Perhaps most important of all was the great extension of the principle of administrative supervision made by the section of the Act which allowed the Secretary of State to amend or add to this code of safety rules without recourse to legislation. The transition from the conscientious non-interference of the mid-nineteenth century to the meticulous State supervision of the twentieth century had required sixty years of political and industrial agitation but it was now almost complete.

APPENDIX I

Fatal Accident Rates, 1880–1913

	Underground (Per thousand employed)		Underground and Surface (Per thousand employed)	
	United Kingdom	Midlands[1]	United Kingdom	Midlands[1]
1880	3·1	1·7	2·7	1·5
1881	2·1	1·4	1·9	1·3
1882	2·5	2·4	2·2	2·1
1883	2·2	1·8	2·0	1·6
1884	2·0	1·4	1·8	1·3
1885	2·5	1·5	2·2	1·3
1886	2·0	1·8	1·8	1·6
1887	2·1	1·7	1·8	1·4
1888	1·8	1·3	1·6	1·2
1889	2·0	1·4	1·8	1·3
1890	2·0	1·2	1·8	1·2
1891	1·6	1·1	1·5	1·0
1892	1·6	1·0	1·4	0·9
1893	1·7	1·9	1·5	1·7
1894	1·7	1·0	1·5	0·8
1895	1·6	0·9	1·4	0·9
1896	1·6	1·3	1·4	1·2
1897	1·4	1·0	1·3	0·8
1898	1·3	1·2	1·2	0·9
1899	1·3	0·9	1·2	0·8
1900	1·4	1·0	1·2	0·9
1901	1·4	1·0	1·3	0·9
1902	1·3	1·0	1·2	0·8
1903	1·3	1·0	1·2	1·0
1904	1·3	1·1	1·2	1·0
1905	1·4	1·0	1·3	1·0
1906	1·4	1·1	1·2	1·0
1907	1·4	1·3	1·3	1·0
1908	1·4	1·1	1·3	1·0
1909	1·6	1·3	1·4	1·1
1910	1·9	1·2	1·6	1·0
1911	1·2	1·1	1·1	1·0
1912	1·2	1·4	1·1	0·9
1913	1·7	1·1	1·5	1·0

[1] Includes Yorkshire (East and West Riding), Lincolnshire, Nottinghamshire, Derbyshire, Leicestershire and Warwickshire.

Source: Finlay A. Gibson, *A Compilation of Statistics of the Coal Mining Industry of the United Kingdom*, (Cardiff), 1922, pp. 130–3.

CHAPTER XII

POLITICAL ACTIVITIES[1]

I

Organization, not only for financial, but for political purposes is essential, and . . . the political lever is eminently calculated to raise the order of Labour to a higher level than ever it has stood upon before, if manfully grasped, and persistently and continuously used by the sons of labour for their own elevation.[2]

Thus wrote Haslam in 1883, after hearing the speeches of Charles Bradlaugh, Lloyd Jones, Ben Pickard and John Wilson, at the Derbyshire miners' demonstrations at Ilkeston and Chesterfield. The law relating to coalmining, trade unionism, employers' liability and many other matters, was highly unsatisfactory from the miners' point of view and the miners' leaders, like other trade unionists, were not slow to realize that there was little hope of changing it unless they were prepared to go into politics. The victories of Macdonald and Burt in the general election of 1874 gave the miners the distinction of being the first group of workers to send their own representatives to Parliament.

Thereafter the working-class representatives, particularly those from the mining constituencies, gradually became more numerous and aligned themselves, for want of a distinct party of their own, with the Liberal-Radical element in the House of Commons. The close links between the Liberal politicians and the Nonconformist miners' leaders, which have already been noted, provided a firm basis for a growing tradition of Liberal-Labour politics. Beatrice Webb was appalled by the conservatism of the Derbyshire miners when she attended a meeting of the Council in 1895. The delegates were 'a stupid, stolid lot of men characterized by fair mindedness and kindliness but oh! how dense!' The officials were 'the ordinary good type, hard working, narrow-minded, whiskey drinking, self-complacent persons, excellent speakers

---

[1] Parts of this chapter were originally published as an article, 'The Political Activities of a Trade Union, 1906–1914', *International Review of Social History*, II, (1957), pp. 1–21. I am indebted to the editor for permission to reproduce them here.

[2] *D.M.A.* 4 September, 1883.

on the question of Miners' Trade Unionism and competent negotiators, but stupid, stupid, stupid like the men'.

'Is it', she asked, 'the abnormal quantity of whiskey these good fellows drink—without getting drunk—that deadens their intelligence—or is it brainwork carried on by an uncultivated and untrained mind that exhausts all the intelligence? How can anyone fear anything but unmitigated Conservatism from the English Democracy? The miners' radicalism is largely traditional made up of allegiance to the Party that gave them the vote. Of course there remains the fact that their real interests are on the side of Economic Collectivism, and sooner or later they will, I suppose, perceive it in a dim sort of way. But it will have to be dinned into them—and they will depend exclusively on middle-class leadership for years to come.'[1]

The story of the Barnsley by-election of 1897 is well known.[2] Ben Pickard, the general secretary of the Yorkshire Miners' Association and President of the M.F.G.B. from 1889 to 1904, had pledged his union's support to the Liberal candidate who was a mine-owner prepared to favour the eight-hour day. In opposition the I.L.P. decided to run Pete Curran, an organizer of the Gasworkers' and General Labourers' Union but Pickard did his work so well that Curran was stoned by the miners and mobbed by their women and children. Yet in 1910 when Curran died, leaving four children under ten years of age almost totally unprovided for, the Council of the Derbyshire Miners' Association granted five pounds to his family.[3] This was symptomatic of the changes which had been taking place within the M.F.G.B. between 1897 and 1910.

These changes were largely brought about by the formation, in 1900, of the Labour Representation Committee, later to become the Labour Party. It did not become explicitly socialist until 1918. In February of that year a special conference adopted a new constitution which stated that the ultimate aim of the party was:

To secure for the producers by hand or by brain the full fruits of their industry, and the most equitable distribution thereof that may be possible, upon the basis of common ownership of the means of production and the best obtainable system of popular administration and control of each industry or service.

Before this change, Ramsay MacDonald, writing in 1911, said: 'The Labour Party is not Socialist. It is a union of Socialist and trade union

[1] Beatrice Webb Diaries, quoted in Philip P. Poirier, *The Advent of the Labour Party*, (London), 1958, p. 21 n.

[2] Cf. M. Beer, *A History of British Socialism*, (London), edn. of 1948, II, p. 306; R. P. Arnot, *The Miners*, (London), 1949, pp. 300–2; H. Pelling, *The Origins of the Labour Party, 1880–1900*, (London), 1954, p. 206.

[3] *D.M.A.* 9 April, 1910.

bodies for immediate political work.'[1] The new party was, in many ways *un mariage de convenance* of militant Socialists and Gladstonian Liberal trade union leaders. The 'immediate political work' for which these groups came together was the representation of the working class in Parliament. Of the need for such representation both sides were firmly convinced: the Socialists because they hoped to convert the trade unions to their own way of thinking; the trade union leaders because they were disappointed by the failure of the official Liberal Party constituency caucuses to adopt more working-class candidates.[2]

The organized Socialist groups, in the early days of the L.R.C., were a small but vocal minority. The members of the Independent Labour Party and the Social Democratic Federation took the lead in demanding an examination of the principles on which the party was based. If it was Liberal, there was no need for it, they argued. Its very existence implied that its principles were in some way different from those of Liberalism. If this was so, how did they differ? Eighteen years passed by before the Socialists were able to achieve what they had set out to do but meanwhile it was necessary for the party to have some *raison d'être*. It was argued that if the party was to succeed in sending working-class members to Parliament it must at all costs maintain its independence of the other political parties.[3]

These discussions culminated in a revision of the constitution in 1903 which embodied the so-called 'pledge' of the Labour Members of Parliament to abide by the decisions of the party:

All such candidates shall pledge themselves to accept this constitution, to abide by the decisions of the group in carrying out the aims of this constitution or resign, and to appear before their constituencies under the title of Labour candidates only.

The aims of the party were to secure the election of candidates 'who undertake to form or join a distinct group in Parliament, with its own Whips and its own policy on Labour questions, to abstain strictly from identifying themselves with or promoting the interests of any section of the Liberal or Conservative parties, and not to oppose any other candidate recognised by the Committee'. Nevertheless, it proved difficult for the L.R.C. to ensure that its members maintained an independent political line. Richard Bell, one of the two members representing Labour in the 1900 Parliament, refused to sign the revised constitution in 1904–5 and was expelled from the party. Shackleton and Arthur Henderson were reprimanded in 1904 for appearing in support of a Liberal candidate at a by-election.[4]

---

[1] J. R. MacDonald, *The Socialist Movement*, (London), 1911, p. 235.
[2] Pelling, *op. cit.* pp. 236–7.   [3] Beer, *op. cit.* pp. 335–6.
[4] Minutes, L.R.C. Executive, 30 June, 1904; cited in Pelling, *op. cit.* p. 239.

The opposition of most of the miners' leaders to the new party delayed for several years the affiliation of one of the largest and most powerful trade unions in the country. The discussions about Labour affiliation invariably revolved around methods of organization and sometimes revealed a selfish outlook. In 1899 Pickard wrote:

I should like to ask why we as a Federation should be called upon to join an Association to find money, time, or intellect to focus the weaknesses of other trade unionists to do what you are doing for yourselves, and have done for the last fourteen years. . . . The old National Union, of which some of you were members, agreed nearly thirty years ago to find the returning officer's fees of any candidate who was run in a mining constituency. . . . When the Miners' Federation was formed, most of the old conditions were taken over and acted upon in the new body. . . . It is a well-known fact that the Federation is doing all this; and yet men have the presumption to ask you, in addition to sending members of your own, to assist in preparing schemes to send others outside your Federation.[1]

But in the background were the theoretical issues between Socialism and Liberalism. Thus, when the Scottish Federation sent in a resolution to the M.F.G.B. annual conference in 1897:

That to secure the best conditions of industry and social life it is absolutely necessary that the land, minerals, railways and instruments of wealth production should be owned and controlled by the State for the people.

Yorkshire countered it with an amendment:

That representatives to the Federation Conferences, and all Congresses, act on trade union lines as in the past, and not on socialistic lines.[2]

The Derbyshire Miners' Association played a prominent part in opposing affiliation with the Labour Party. As early as 1899, Harvey argued at the Trades Union Congress for individual self-help by the unions instead of collective action.[3] In the ballot on the affiliation of the M.F.G.B. with the L.R.C. in 1906, Derbyshire rejected affiliation by 11,257 votes to 1,798. (At this time the Association had about 30,000 members.) In a card vote taken at the 1907 annual conference Derbyshire again voted against affiliation. In May, 1908, the M.F.G.B. took another ballot which showed a majority in favour of affiliation. The Derbyshire Association made a gallant bid at the eleventh hour to save the day for Liberalism. It was decided at a Council meeting on 1 August, 1908, by 61 votes to 19, that the following resolution should be sent to the Federation:

That seeing only half the members of the Federation have voted re joining the L.R.C., we therefore consider the question should again be relegated to

---

[1] Miners' Federation of Great Britain, *Annual Report, 1898–9.*
[2] *M.F.G.B.* 5–8 January, 1897. [3] Pelling, *op. cit.* p. 218.

the Districts for a fuller vote on such a vital question and the men again be balloted.[1]

The resolution appeared in a more carefully worded form on the agenda for the annual conference. It was moved by Haslam and seconded by Fred Hall of Yorkshire. The voting was 97,000 for the resolution and 391,000 against.

In 1909 the Miners' Federation of Great Britain, numbering over half a million, joined the ranks of the Labour Party and brought with it fourteen Liberal-Labour Members of Parliament. Until then the revised constitution of the Labour Party had worked fairly well because it had not been too strictly applied. Labour members were left free to vote, in matters of conscience, as they thought right. The organization of the M.F.G.B., ever since its formation in 1889, had been fairly loose and in the matter of political activities the district associations had enjoyed a considerable degree of autonomy. The influx of fourteen miners' M.P.s, who had previously worked closely with the Liberals, presented many problems, which have not, as yet, been fully investigated. The official history of the Miners' Federation[2] is largely concerned with the collective decisions which led to affiliation with the Labour Party and the national events resulting from it. What was happening in the mining constituencies before and after this change of policy is by no means clear. An examination of the political activities of the Derbyshire Miners' Association in this period only becomes intelligible against the background of national events. At the same time it throws new light upon the problems of the Labour Party's attempts to maintain political independence.

II

After the redistribution of seats in 1885 there were four predominantly mining constituencies in Derbyshire: the Chesterfield, North East Derbyshire, Mid-Derbyshire and Ilkeston divisions. Within twenty-five years all of them except Ilkeston were to be represented by miners' leaders. As early as 1885, within five years of the formation of their union, the Derbyshire miners began to seek parliamentary representation. It was resolved in Council:

That strenuous efforts should be made to send a Working Man from one of the Divisions of Derbyshire to the next Parliament, and that the Liberals of the Division agreed upon should make way for such an one, seeing that the labouring classes of the Country are greatly in a majority and have a right to expect this much of direct representation.[3]

[1] D.M.A. 1 August, 1908.   [2] R. P. Arnot, The Miners, (London), 1949.
[3] D.M.A. 17 March, 1885.

This was considered to be necessary in order to make possible a number of radical reforms including 'a thorough change in the Land Laws', the amendment of the Employers' Liability and Mines Acts, support for Broadhurst's Leasehold Bill, the amendment of the Allotments Act, free education, payment of Members of Parliament, the removal of property qualifications to seats on Boards of Guardians, the introduction of stipendiary magistrates ('or open the way to the Bench to all classes') and 'a thousand-and-one things that need attention'. The Pension List was 'an abomination' and 'the swarms of useless sinecure offices' to which 'large salaries' were attached were 'a disgrace to a civilized nation'.[1]

This burst of political activity was linked with the general agitation for the extension of the franchise. The members of the union were informed by their leaders:

> We are in hopes that the Government will introduce a short Bill to give us the Vote earlier than next January should an Election take place before then. It is highly necessary that all new electors see their Overseers in their respective District, and ascertain that their names are on the Register. Don't wait for Agents of any Party to do it for you, do it yourselves. . . . Attend to it men, Register! Register!! Register!!![2]

The extension of the franchise and the election both came before the end of 1885 but the Liberals did not make way for 'a Working Man Member' in any of the Derbyshire constituencies. It was announced that James Haslam would stand for the Chesterfield division without the support of the Liberals. Both the miners and the Liberals were conscious of the danger of splitting the Liberal vote. The committee which had been formed for promoting Haslam's candidature discussed the possibility of arriving at an arrangement with the leaders of the Liberal Party in the division and came to the conclusion that 'the time for any amicable settlement had now gone by'.[3] J. Stores Smith, the general manager of the Sheepbridge Company and one of the Liberal leaders, expressed at a public meeting the hope that 'some arrangements would be come to so that the Liberal Party in the division might present a united front to the enemy. He had nothing to say against the principle of Labour representation but considered that Mr. Barnes had prior claims on the constituency.'[4] The Liberals proposed that the claims of the two candidates should be submitted to an arbitration committee consisting of Sir Charles Dilke, Joseph Chamberlain and others.[5] Haslam's committee rejected this proposal but expressed a willingness 'to consider any reasonable suggestion by which the voice of the people can be taken upon the matter'.[6]

[1] *D.M.A.* 17 March, 1885.
[2] *Ibid.*
[3] *Sheffield Independent*, 22 October, 1885.
[4] *Ibid.* 4 November, 1885.
[5] *Ibid.* 14 November, 1885.
[6] *Ibid.* 12 November, 1885.

Q*

Haslam's campaign as Liberal-Radical candidate for the Chesterfield division was supported by shilling contributions from members of the Association.[1] His programme was ably expounded by Charles Bradlaugh, Annie Besant, Helen Taylor, Joseph Arch, J. A. Jacoby, Edward Cowey, William Brown, Harvey, John Catchpole and Richard Bunting. William Bailey, later to become the leader of the Nottinghamshire miners, was his election agent. As a working man's candidate, Haslam pledged himself to support the miners' cause and to adhere to his election programme on controversial issues. He advocated religious equality, the disestablishment and disendowment of the Church of England, the reform of the House of Lords, the abolition of perpetual pensions, the payment of a fixed allowance to the Royal Family, the removal of property qualifications for candidature to the Boards of Guardians and the magistracy, the payment of Members of Parliament, free trade, free education, arbitration instead of war, and local option on public house licences. For the miners he proposed a revision of the Employers' Liability and Mines Regulations Acts, and changes in the law relating to mining accident inquests so as to reduce the powers of coroners and to ensure that one-third of juries in such cases should be miners. To restrict the flow of cheap labour into the mines, he supported the land reforms advocated by Jesse Collings as an incentive to agricultural workers to remain on the land.[2]

The extension of the franchise had admitted about 6,500 of the 9,000 electors but Haslam obtained only 1,907 votes. Macdona, the Conservative candidate, had 2,136 votes and Alfred Barnes, the Liberal coalowner, was elected with 3,408 votes. Reports received from the various polling districts after the election showed that a number of householders, chiefly Haslam's supporters, had been left off the new register.[3] The *Derbyshire Times* commented: 'One result of the recent elections in Derbyshire is to show the miners that if they chose to look after the register they could return their own men for either North-East Derbyshire, Ilkeston or Chesterfield.'[4]

The split in the Liberal party on the Irish question led to another general election in 1886. The Conservatives decided to support Barnes who proposed to contest the Chesterfield division as a Liberal Unionist.[5] Haslam and Thomas Bayley, a Nottingham coal-owner, were both nominated as Gladstonian Liberal candidates and agreed to accept the decision of the local selection committee. Bayley received 41 votes to Haslam's 35 and was formally adopted. Haslam said: 'He would loyally

---

[1] *D.M.A.* 17 March, 1885.
[2] *Derbyshire Times*, 21 March, 19 and 26 September, 17 October, 1885.
[3] *Ibid.* 5 and 12 December, 1885.
[4] *Ibid.* 5 December, 1885.   [5] *Ibid.* 26 June, 1886.

accept the committee's decision, and do his best to induce all his followers to work heartily for a candidate who would support Mr. Gladstone.'[1] In the election which followed, Barnes defeated Bayley by 3,567 votes to 3,453.

Despite the Corrupt and Illegal Practices Act of 1883, intimidation of electors lingered on. F. C. Corfield, a mining agent of the Butterley Company, was prosecuted for two offences in the Ilkeston division. In one case he was charged with attempting to prevent James Gent, a deputy employed at Butterley Park, from exercising his vote. In another, James Grainger, an old-age pensioner of the Butterley Company, alleged that his pension of 3s. 6d. a week had been stopped because he voted for Sir Walter Foster, the Gladstonian Liberal candidate.[2]

The incursion of the Derbyshire Miners' Association into politics aroused much criticism and some opposition. In 1890 it was announced that a Conservative Miners' Association had been formed, with headquarters at the Rutland Hotel, Ilkeston. The *Derbyshire Times* commented:

No doubt it has been extremely galling to the Conservative miners of Ilkeston to know that they have been subscribing to a union whose leaders —its paid agents—were devoting a portion of their time to addressing meetings, and otherwise assisting to bolster up the cause of local Radical M.P.'s, but we regret that they decided on the course they did. . . . We are still of opinion that Radical miners' unions are a mistake and because the present union has been made political that is an inferior reason in our opinion for the formation of a Conservative miners' union.[3]

Trueman, the secretary of the new association, told his members:

He had no doubt that they would be told that he had been prompted to move in this matter by some of those who provided his salary as registration agent. . . . The idea was entirely his own, and had been put into execution without consulting a single individual who was not now a member of that association.[4]

The Ilkeston Conservative Miners' Association, which was a registered trade union, never had more than one branch. Its membership was as follows:[5]

1892	109	1897	125
1893	153	1898	101
1894	183	1899	91
1895	178	1900	78
1896	148	1901	—

[1] *Derbyshire Times*, 23 June, 1886. [2] *Ibid.* 23 July, 1887.
[3] *Ibid.* 25 January, 1890. [4] *Ibid.* 8 February, 1890.
[5] *Board of Trade (Labour Department) Ninth, Thirteenth and Fourteenth Reports*, 1896, 1900 and 1901, (C.8644, Cd. 773 and Cd. 1348.

It was dissolved in 1901 and is interesting only as a forerunner of the movement for 'non-political' trade unionism which led to the Osborne judgment in 1909 and was to cause serious strife, particularly in the Nottinghamshire and Derbyshire coalfields, in the years following the First World War.

Despite such activities the demand for parliamentary representation continued. The union became affiliated with the Labour Electoral Association and was represented by Haslam and Harvey at the Association's annual conferences. In 1891 the impending retirement of Wardle, the M.P. for South Derbyshire, at the dissolution of the current Parliament, led the Derbyshire Miners' Association to resolve in March: 'That . . . the time has come to again press our claims upon the Liberal Party for a seat to be set aside for a Labour Candidate.' The Association hoped that Bayley would be willing to go to South Derbyshire and that Haslam would be adopted as Liberal candidate for the Chesterfield division,[1] but there was no question of contesting the seat against Bayley. In April Harvey said: 'He knew nothing that would suit the Tories better than a three-cornered fight. They would be only too pleased to bring their man in over two. . . . They did not intend that to be the case.'[2] By October Haslam had to admit, somewhat ruefully: 'The Chesterfield division was not at present to let. . . . While there were plenty of men who said . . . that they would like him to stand, or preferred him to stand, the miners felt that they were under an honourable pledge that Mr. Bayley should stand for the next election.'[3]

Whilst the Association had been negotiating with the Liberals there were discussions in the Council as to whether Haslam's salary should be paid from the funds of the union if at any time he were returned to Parliament. The officials were of the opinion that 'the phase [sic] that has been put in letters in the Press that it is contrary to the Rules, and would be taking the Funds for an improper purpose is all nonsense'.[4] Eventually a ballot was taken but the results were inconclusive. Twelve of the 72 lodges failed to send in returns and others reported that they were unanimously in favour without returning the number of ballot papers given out. Only 8,789 of the union's 18,000 members registered votes. Of these, 5,343 were in favour of paying parliamentary expenses from union funds and 3,446 against. By this time the question of Labour representation had appeared on the agenda for the M.F.G.B. conference which was to be held in January, 1892, and it was decided to postpone any further consideration of the matter until after the conference.[5] Haslam was bitterly disappointed. Referring to an invitation which

[1] *D.M.A.* 10 March, 1891.   [2] *Derbyshire Times*, 11 April, 1891.
[3] *Ibid.* 10 October, 1891.
[4] *D.M.A.* 28 July, 1891.   [5] *Ibid.* 17 November, 1891.

he had received to stand for a mining constituency in another part of the country, he said: 'He was afraid that while there was such narrow-mindedness that the men would not be willing to support a man in one of their own constituencies, they would not have a constituency a hundred miles away.'[1]

The general election of 1892 saw the return of Gladstonian Liberals in all the Derbyshire mining constituencies. Thomas Bayley represented Chesterfield; Sir Walter Foster,[2] Ilkeston; Thomas Dolling Bolton, a solicitor and company director, North-East Derbyshire; and James Alfred Jacoby, a Nottingham lace manufacturer, Mid-Derbyshire. All these men had done much valuable work for the miners and were to do more in the campaign for the eight-hour day. The principal objection to them, from the point of view of the miners' leaders, was that they monopolized a number of safe seats in the mining constituencies.

The miners' leaders, for the time being, had to be content with lesser honours. The long-standing grievance arising from the lack of working-class magistrates was partially remedied in Derbyshire in 1893, by the appointment of Haslam and Harvey to the Chesterfield and Ilkeston Benches respectively. Of Haslam it was said: 'His elevation to the Bench is solely due to the very valuable services he has rendered to Messrs. Bayley, Bolton, Jacoby and Sir W. Foster, without which St. Stephen's would be unknown to them.'[3] In July, 1893, the officials called the attention of the Council to the fact that 'for years, Trades Unions have been contending that workmen should have the right to sit upon all Governing bodies' such as 'the Magisterial Bench, Board of Guardians, School Board, &c.'[4] In the following month the Council decided that any expenses incurred by the officials in performing such duties should be defrayed by the Association.[5] Each year from 1894 both Haslam and Harvey sought election to the Chesterfield Borough Council. Haslam was successful in 1896. Harvey was elected in the following year. 'I look upon this victory as being a working man's victory', he said.[6] Thereafter the miners secured increasing representation on local government and other authorities.

In 1894 Harvey became vice-president of the Labour Electoral Association and of the Chesterfield Trades Council. The Labour Electoral Association worked mainly through the local trades councils and was in opposition to all attempts to secure independent labour representation. Delighted with the failure of Keir Hardie and Tom Mann to split the Liberal vote at Accrington in 1893, Harvey declared:

[1] *Derbyshire Times*, 10 October, 1891.
[2] Created Lord Ilkeston of Ilkeston, 1910.
[3] *Derbyshire Times*, 15 July, 1893.   [4] *D.M.A.* 25 July, 1893.
[5] *Ibid.* 21 August, 1893.   [6] *Derbyshire Times*, 6 November, 1897.

'I am not on a par with the Socialists who deny a fair return for investment.'[1] The feud between Harvey and Hardie became more bitter as the years passed. In 1897 Harvey and Albert Stanley, the leader of the Cannock Chase miners, were invited to address a demonstration of the Derwent Valley Durham Miners' Federation. When they discovered that they were expected to speak from the same platform as Keir Hardie they objected and were promptly told by the organizers of the demonstration that they could return home by the next train, which they did.[2] Hardie later addressed an I.L.P. meeting in Chesterfield and delivered a sharp attack on Harvey in his 'snug little office with rent and coal paid'. He said: 'There were no men in Ayrshire earning ten shillings per week, as there were in Derbyshire, in spite of being led by such a talented leader as Mr. Harvey.' Hardie described his own life as editor of the *Cambrian News:* 'He had a good, comfortable situation, such as Labour leaders dearly loved. He was becoming sleek and fat, like other Labour leaders of whom he had heard and read, and was a member of the School Board.' This he left to work for the miners:

He began to attend the miners' conferences and to fight almost single-handed for an Eight Hours' Bill, and amongst those he had to fight most bitterly was Mr. W. E. Harvey, of Derbyshire. Mr. Harvey's men got converted to his [Hardie's] ideas and Mr. Harvey had to change his opinions or look out for a new job. Naturally, he changed his opinions. One of the Labour leaders from Midlothian was once asked why he changed his opinions to please his followers. . . . His reply was: 'I am the leader, you know, and I must follow the people.'[3]

Harvey, Stanley and Pickard were all criticized for their part in the Derwent Valley affair. Hardie stated that they had taken exception to a speech which he had made at Rothwell, in Yorkshire, on 6 June, 1896. The local *Free Press* had reported Hardie as saying 'that trades unions were not the remedy and that the miners' leaders were backing up a worn-out system'. Pickard had refused to believe that this was a garbled version of the speech. 'The editor of this *Free Press* did all the printing for the Yorkshire Miners' Association', explained Hardie. 'He was Mr. Pickard's election agent, wrote his speeches for him, and saw that they were properly printed in his paper, so he did not wonder at all at Mr. Pickard believing this man.'[4]

The Labour Electoral Association was fighting on two fronts: on the one hand it was pressing the Liberals to make way for more working-class candidates; on the other it was resisting Socialism. Harvey took a keen interest in both aspects of the struggle. In 1894, when there was a dispute over the selection of a Liberal candidate for

[1] *Derbyshire Times*, 30 December, 1893.   [2] *Ibid.* 12 June, 1897.
[3] *Ibid.* 11 September, 1897.   [4] *Ibid.*

the Attercliffe division of Sheffield, Charles Hobson, a trade unionist, was passed over in favour of Batty Langley. Harvey commented: 'He did hope that the Liberal Party would have more sense in the future than to fight their best friend, for the Liberal Party today was composed generally of working men, who were not going to be played with as shuttlecocks.'[1]

Of Pete Curran's intervention as an I.L.P. candidate in the Barnsley by-election of 1897, Harvey said:

> The time had arrived when the doings of these wandering strangers would have to be exposed; and he warned the men of Derbyshire against being misled by these wreckers and snatchers, who had never done, nor would ever do, anything for the alleviation of the masses.[2]

Harvey gave active support to Pickard's campaign against Curran. Tom Shaw, presiding over the annual conference of the Yorkshire I.L.P. Federation, on the day of election, said:

> They had Mr. W. E. Harvey, from his pinnacle of morality, preaching to them, and telling them what they should do, and telling people what class of men the Independent Labour Party consisted of. . . . This Mr. Harvey, who was a paid man for the Derbyshire miners, professed to be free from everything that was bad or corrupt. . . . But there was another miners' agent who was pushing in Barnsley, and who, like Mr. Harvey, was pretty well paid for the work he did. This was Mr. Ben Pickard. Mr. Pickard, who, of course, was a great king, had some hundreds of pounds worth of printing to give out every year in connection with the Miners' Association, and strange to say, this exceedingly pure trades unionist took his printing to a non-union shop.[3]

III

The reluctance of the Liberals to adopt a trade union candidate and of the miners to provide the money necessary for an independent candidature prevented Haslam from contesting any of the Derbyshire seats in the 1886, 1892 and 1895 elections. The miners' decisions were reinforced, after 1893, by the necessity of making good the deficiences in their funds caused by the great lock-out.[4] In 1900, however, the Executive Committee of the Association resolved: 'That the time has come, if ever it will, when the Derbyshire miners should assert themselves and have a Labour representative in Parliament.'[5] A ballot vote was taken but again the proposal for Haslam's candidature was rejected. The *Derbyshire Times* commented:

> Mr. Thomas Bayley's anxiety to see either Mr. Haslam or Mr. Harvey in the House of Commons is now most pathetic. . . . Mr. Bayley wants to see

[1] *Derbyshire Times*, 30 June, 1894.   [2] *Ibid.* 25 September, 1897.
[3] *Ibid.* 9 October, 1897.   [4] See pp. 246-9.   [5] *Derbyshire Times*, 19 May, 1900.

'his friends, Mr. Haslam or Mr. Harvey, in the House of Commons', and he will 'do his utmost, at the very first vacancy they get in a division near, to bring this about'.[1]

Meanwhile discussions were going on in the Federation about the necessity of increasing the financial support given to miners' candidates. The Federation had for many years paid the returning officer's fees for such candidates but it was not until the annual conference of 1901 that Ben Pickard succeeded in pushing through his scheme for the payment of members.[2] Haslam was now in a much stronger position. Moreover, the Liberals could no longer afford to be unco-operative. Since the 1885 election their majority in the Chesterfield division had dwindled from 1,272 to 689 in the 1900 election. In 1886, 1892 and 1895 the figures had been even lower: 114, 180 and 247. A split vote would almost certainly have ensured the return of a Conservative candidate. The time had obviously arrived when the Liberals would have to make way for a 'Working Man Member'. This process was facilitated by the resignation of Thomas Bayley who, a fortnight before the opening of the 1906 election campaign, announced that on the advice of his doctor he was reluctantly 'bringing his association with the division to a close'.[3] There were hurried negotiations between the Liberals and the Derbyshire Miners' Association which led to Haslam's adoption as a Liberal-Labour candidate. Haslam contested this election under the 'Pickard scheme' whereby all the county associations contributed a *per capita* levy of one shilling a year to a central fund from which miners' representatives in Parliament received £350 a year and a first-class railway pass. Haslam obtained 7,254 votes, giving him a majority of 1,664 over his Conservative opponent G. T. Locker-Lampson.

In December, 1906, the death of Thomas Bolton caused a by-election in North-East Derbyshire. Under the Pickard scheme the county associations were allowed one candidate for each 10,000 members and Derbyshire at this time had about 29,000. Here was a chance to send another member to Parliament and Harvey, who had succeeded Haslam as general secretary after the election of 1906, was an obvious choice. The powers of oratory which he had developed in the chapel were in great demand on the political platform[4] and he had already been asked to contest the Handsworth division of Birmingham. The miners of Cannock Chase had also asked him to stand for South Staffordshire but Harvey is reported to have replied: 'No; unless I can go to Parliament to represent the men whose servant I am, I will never go to Parliament at

---

[1] *Derbyshire Times*, 14 July, 1900.   [2] *M.F.G.B.* 2 October, 1901.
[3] *Sheffield Telegraph*, 23 December, 1905. Bayley died on 11 March, 1906, leaving estate to the value of £93,516. (*Derbyshire Times*, 17 March, 2 June, 1906.)
[4] W. Hallam, *Miners' Leaders*, (London), 1894, p. 42.

all.'[1] Some of the Liberals of North-East Derbyshire urged the adoption of Harvey, others favoured the adoption of J. P. Houfton, the general manager of the Bolsover Colliery Company, whilst a third group demanded the adoption of an outsider to obviate the risk of differences between Liberals and Labour.[2]

At a meeting of the Executive Committee of the North-East Derbyshire Central Liberal Council the names of Sir John Bamford Slack and the Hon. Neil Primrose (the second son of Rosebery) were put forward for consideration but Harvey carried the day.[3] Meanwhile the Council of the Derbyshire Miners' Association had adopted Harvey as their candidate subject to a ballot vote of all members.[4] Whilst the ballot was being taken the Conservatives raised the cry 'Your association will cost you more',[5] but when the votes were counted 9,788 members had voted for Harvey and 4,506 against.[6] Nevertheless the suggestion that Harvey would become a financial burden upon the union was not without its influence. Eventually Enoch Edwards and Thomas Ashton, the president and secretary of the M.F.G.B., sent copies of a letter to various lodges in Derbyshire pointing out that 'Mr. Harvey's election will not cost you one penny more than the subscriptions which you now pay under the Parliamentary scheme of the Miners' Federation of Great Britain'. This was later distributed as a leaflet throughout the division together with an addendum, signed by representatives of practically every lodge in the county, which endorsed the contents of the letter from the M.F.G.B. and stated: 'If elected to Parliament Mr. Harvey will continue to live in Chesterfield, and will still work for the Derbyshire Miners' Association.'[7] These statements had the effect of clearing up a misunderstanding which had existed among members of the Glapwell lodge. It was particularly important because two-thirds of the members of this large lodge resided in the North-East division.

The by-election was the first since the mutilation by the House of Lords of the progressive legislation concerning education and plural voting which the Liberals had succeeded in piloting through the Commons. Harvey made the misdoings of the Lords one of the major issues of the election.[8] The Conservatives, on the other hand, described Harvey as 'facing two ways' and 'practically accused him of dishonesty'.[9] Josiah Court, the Association's medical adviser, was in an equally difficult position as a Conservative candidate. Because of his honorary membership of the union it was at first thought that he would not be

[1] *Sheffield Independent*, 26 January, 1907.
[2] *Ibid.* 18 December, 1906.   [3] *Ibid.* 24 December, 1906.
[4] *D.M.A.* 22 December, 1906.   [5] *Sheffield Independent*, 3 January, 1907.
[6] *Ibid.* 7 January, 1907.   [7] *Ibid.* 18 January, 1907.
[8] *Ibid.* 10 January, 1907.   [9] *Ibid.* 17 January, 1907.

willing to oppose Harvey.[1] However, political differences triumphed over personal considerations and at subsequent elections relations between Court and Harvey were to become increasingly acrimonious. Eight days before polling day Harvey retired to his bed with bronchitis and the rest of his campaign was conducted by his supporters.[2] Nevertheless he obtained 6,644 votes which gave him a majority of 729 over Court.

In July, 1909, the death of Sir Alfred Jacoby[3] caused a by-election in Mid-Derbyshire. Jacoby had supported the campaign of the M.F.G.B. for an eight-hour day and was very popular among the miners.[4] After Haslam's success in 1906 Mid-Derbyshire had been unofficially regarded as the next miners' seat[5] but Harvey had now been elected for North-East Derbyshire and the Derbyshire Miners' Association did not wish to put forward another parliamentary candidate. Accordingly, J. G. Hancock, the agent of the Nottinghamshire Miners' Association,[6] was selected to contest Mid-Derbyshire with the support of the Derby-shire miners. Hancock was a typical Liberal-Nonconformist trade union leader of the period. He was a magistrate, a member of the Nottingham City Council and a local preacher in connection with the United Methodist Free Church. He had served on a board of guardians and various educational bodies.[7]

This was the first by-election to be fought by a miner since the M.F.G.B. had become affiliated with the Labour Party and there was some confusion about Hancock's party allegiance. 'Is he a Liberal, is he a Socialist, or is he a mixture of Liberalism and Labour, of the pattern of Mr. Harvey, who has done so little since the North-East miners sent him to Parliament?' asked the *Sheffield Telegraph*.[8] Eventually it became known that Hancock had been officially adopted by the Liberal Associa-tion of the division on the recommendation of the Derbyshire Miners' Association, and the Socialists in the constituency grew restless. At a meeting at Belper, Hancock was asked which side of the House of Commons he would sit on if elected. He replied 'that there were only two sides, and that he should be with the Labour men on the Liberal side'.[9] At Alfreton, where there was a strong I.L.P. organization, about a hundred delegates assembled to hear Hancock's views on labour questions before agreeing unanimously to support his candidature.[10] At another meeting, at Crich, Hancock stated:

---

[1] *Sheffield Independent*, 24 December, 1906.   [2] *Ibid.* 22 January, 1907.
[3] Jacoby was knighted in 1906.   [4] *D.M.A.* 3 July, 1909.
[5] *Sheffield Independent*, 18 December, 1906.
[6] Not 'of the Derbyshire Miners' as stated in G. D. H. Cole, *British Working Class Politics, 1832–1914*, (London), 1941, p. 287.
[7] *Sheffield Independent*, 17 July, 1909.
[8] *Sheffield Telegraph*, 2 July, 1909.
[9] *Ibid.* 5 July, 1909.   [10] *Ibid.* 6 July, 1909.

He had always been actively, not passively associated with the Liberal Party. . . . But circumstances over which he had no control, and for which he was not at all responsible, had compelled him, if he stood at all, to stand as a Labour candidate, and under the constitution of the Labour Representation Committee. He would like to say, however, that that Committee . . . had thoroughly considered the whole of the circumstances under which he and his supporters were placed, and there had been a consideration shown by the L.R.C. so far as that candidature was concerned, that had never been shown in any other case.[1]

In his election manifesto Hancock described himself as 'having been recommended by the Miners' Association to come forward as a candidate under the constitution of the L.R.C. and unanimously adopted as such by the Council of the Mid-Derbyshire Liberal Association'.[2]

Hancock had signed the Labour Party constitution and had expressed his intention of acting with the party in the House of Commons[3] but at the same time he was working very closely with the Liberals. A. B. Markham, the Liberal coal-owner and member for Mansfield, took a great interest in Hancock's campaign. On one occasion he chartered a special train from Manchester to the Duffield district in order to speak for Hancock at three meetings.[4] Both Markham and Hancock attempted to obscure any distinction between Socialism and Liberalism which might have existed in the minds of the electors. At one meeting Markham argued that the L.R.C. was not a socialist body and urged his hearers to vote for Hancock who was a straightforward 'simple-minded' Liberal.[5] At another meeting he said that he did not attach much importance to the term Liberal or Labour. 'Whatever Mr. Hancock's name, he would, if elected, go to Parliament to serve the interests of the constituency, and to carry out the wishes of the electors.'[6] Hancock, in reply to a question at Alfreton, said 'he was a "Socialist according to the Bible" but he was not a Socialist. He was a Labour man associated with the L.R.C.'[7] Amidst such confusion no one was surprised to see Keir Hardie addressing a meeting in support of Hancock and wearing a yellow rosette.[8] The election was important to Hardie because Hancock was the first candidate run by the Miners' Federation under the Labour Party auspices. He stated quite bluntly that 'the Liberals by an act of grace on their part had stood aside, and were lending their support to Mr. Hancock because they preferred a Labour Member in Parliament to a Conservative Tariff Reform member'.[9] As this was one of the first elections since the introduction of Lloyd George's famous budget the

---

[1] *Sheffield Telegraph*, 6 July, 1909.   [2] *Sheffield Independent*, 8 July, 1909.
[3] *M.F.G.B.* 29 June, 1 July, 1909; *Sheffield Telegraph*, 8 July, 1909.
[4] *Sheffield Independent*, 9 July, 1909.   [5] *Sheffield Telegraph*, 6 July, 1909.
[6] *Sheffield Independent*, 7 July, 1909.   [7] *Sheffield Telegraph*, 8 July, 1909.
[8] *Ibid.* 13 July, 1909.   [9] *Sheffield Independent*, 13 July, 1909.

Liberals were anxious to see whether the electors approved these proposals. Hancock received invaluable assistance from the newly formed Budget League.[1]

Hancock was elected by 6,735 votes to the Conservatives' 4,392. Arthur Peters, the national election agent of the Labour Party commented:

> Of course it must be freely admitted that the machinery of the Liberal Party was being used, but as the Liberals readily admit, they recognise that the seat has been handed over to Labour. It is but fair to add that the Liberals have worked hard to win the seat for Labour, and many of their M.P.s have taken an unusually active part in the campaign.[2]

IV

The two general elections of 1910 were conducted under the shadow of the Osborne judgment.[3] After Mr. Justice (later Lord Justice) Farwell's decision in the Chancery Division had been upheld by all three judges in the court of appeal (28 November, 1908) the Executive of the Derbyshire Miners' Association resolved 'that no money should be paid over from the Miners' Federation, until the decision of the House of Lords is known, or at least until the position has been placed before the whole membership of the Federation'.[4] This decision did not prevent the Association from paying the expenses of Haslam and Harvey when they took their places as county magistrates[5] nor did it have the support of the M.F.G.B. The Mid-Derbyshire by-election had been fought with money from the parliamentary fund and Haslam and Harvey continued to receive their salaries from the same source.

Towards the end of 1909 the Association appeared to move into line with national policy and on 20 November the Council recommended, rather belatedly, that Haslam and Harvey should sign the constitution of the Labour Party 'in accordance with the ballot of the Federation'.[6] On 21 December, 1909, the House of Lords delivered its judgment on the Osborne case but this had no marked effect upon the conduct of the Derbyshire elections of January, 1910. Haslam, Harvey and Hancock contested their seats as Labour candidates and, with the support of the Liberals, were all returned. The Chesterfield branch of the Social Democratic Party took the opportunity to protest against Haslam's 'alliance with official Liberalism' as being 'contrary to the best

---

[1] *Sheffield Independent*, 8 July, 1909.   [2] *Ibid.* 17 July, 1909.
[3] Amalgamated Society of Railway Servants *v.* Osborne, [1910] A.C. 87.
[4] *D.M.A.* 9 January, 1909.
[5] *Ibid.* 13 February, 1909.   [6] *Ibid.* 20 November, 1909.

interests of the organized workers who provide the necessary funds, and who have declared for independent political action'.[1] Guy Radford, the Conservative candidate for Chesterfield, complained:

The astuteness of the Socialists in using the Liberals as their tools is nowhere more apparent than in this division, where the former Liberal agent is now agent for Mr. Haslam, and the whole machinery of the so-called 'Liberal' party has been captured, lock, stock, and barrel, by the Socialist wirepullers.[2]

Haslam, on the other hand, admitted openly that he had signed the Labour Party constitution and had received £100 towards his election addresses from Ramsay MacDonald.[3]

Soon after the election C. C. Baggaley, headmaster of Dronfield Grammar School and chairman of the Dronfield Unionist Association, made a speech at a political meeting in which he was reported by the *Sheffield Independent* as having referred to the miners in extremely derogatory terms:

He first warmly commended conscription. One could not help being struck with the number of louts hanging about in our mining villages, he remarked. They used foul language and chewed tobacco. It was a pity that they could not be drilled by a sergeant—perhaps a German drill sergeant for preference. The anaemic, mis-shapen beings that they were now would then have some physique about them. These miners, however, were not without *esprit de corps*. During the recent election they were dragooned and marched to the poll in a body, many against their own opinions.[4]

Baggaley subsequently denied the accuracy of this report but it had by that time aroused the indignation of the miners[5] and Harvey, supported by the *Independent*, made much of it in his political speeches until he received a writ for slander in December, 1910.[6] In March of the following year Baggaley was awarded £375 damages from Harvey and £50 from the *Sheffield Independent*.[7]

Another outcome of the January elections was an action for assault brought by Francis, the Conservative candidate for Mid-Derbyshire, against George Hadley, a member of the Association's Executive Committee. The union was highly critical of what it described as 'the partisan lines' of the magistrates[8] and at a subsequent meeting the Council resolved: 'That this Association is of opinion that a fair proportion of magistrates should be appointed from the working classes, and should be nominated by this Association, this resolution being sent

[1] *Derbyshire Times*, 15 January, 1910.   [2] *Ibid.* 8 January, 1910.
[3] *Sheffield Independent*, 18 January, 1910.   [4] *Ibid.* 5 February, 1910.
[5] *D.M.A.* 12 February, 1910.   [6] *Sheffield Independent*, 6 December, 1910.
[7] *Sheffield Telegraph*, 17 and 20 March, 1911.   [8] *D.M.A.* 12 February, 1910.

to the Lord Chancellor with names.'[1] Haslam suggested a meeting of the Derbyshire M.P.s to take united action on the question.

Before the December elections of 1910 the Association had to face the consequences of the Osborne judgment. On 15 July, 1910, Mr. Justice Joyce, in the Chancery Division, granted to Joseph Fisher, of Huthwaite, a member of the Blackwell lodge, an interim injunction restraining the Derbyshire Miners' Association from administering its funds for parliamentary purposes. Counsel for the Association secured a proviso enabling it to raise voluntary subscriptions from its members but no member was to lose the benefit of the union if he refused to join in any voluntary fund.[2] A similar action had been brought against the Nottinghamshire Miners' Association in respect of Hancock on 10 June, 1910.[3] Harvey was outraged: 'The only thing that troubles me is that they [the capitalists] should find curs amongst us to do their dirty work. I am sorry that Judas Iscariot has left so many relations behind him. But they are not as honest as Judas was because he did go out and hang himself.'[4] Frank Hall, the treasurer of the Association, stated that the injunction was due to ignorance. He had talked to Fisher and discovered that he was 64 years of age, had belonged to the union for twelve years, and yet he had never been to a lodge meeting, and had never before made any complaints. 'He was totally ignorant of the benefits to be derived from the union, and he had stated that had he known what he did now, he would never have taken the action he had.'[5]

The Association immediately set to work to raise money by voluntary subscriptions. A circular was sent out to all lodges asking for a contribution of threepence from each member.[6] Haslam and Barnet Kenyon were appointed secretary and treasurer of the fund so that it could be kept separate from the general funds of the union.[7] The officials addressed a number of mass meetings in an attempt to raise sufficient money to meet their obligations to the M.F.G.B. parliamentary fund. At a meeting at Brampton Frank Hall warned his audience: 'Unless you men subscribe that money which is asked, we shall be unable to further contest the Chesterfield and North-East Derbyshire divisions for parliamentary representation.'[8]

In the December elections of 1910 the Osborne judgment was almost as great an issue as the powers of the House of Lords. The *Sheffield Telegraph* commented:

[1] *D.M.A.* 12 March, 1910.
[2] *Derbyshire Times*, 16 July, 1910; *M.F.G.B.* 24–25 August, 1910.
[3] *Derbyshire Times*, 11 June, 1910; *M.F.G.B.* 8 and 9 June, 1910.
[4] *Derbyshire Times*, 29 July, 1910.   [5] *Ibid.* 19 November, 1910.
[6] *D.M.A.* 27 August, 1910.
[7] *Ibid.* 22 October, 1910.   [8] *Derbyshire Times*, 19 November, 1910.

It is not liberty of political action for the trade unions that the Labour Party wants, but liberty to dip its hands into trades union cash-boxes for the exploitation of its own political designs. Mr. Asquith knows this full well. He probably detests the idea quite as much as we do. But he may have to buy Labour votes, and thus he dare not speak his mind or trust to the guidance of his own judgment. Surely no British Prime Minister in history has cut such a sorry figure as that which Mr. Asquith presents today.[1]

A writer in the *Labour Leader*, on the other hand, was extremely worried about party organization in Derbyshire and some of the other mining constituencies. He argued that the sitting members were mostly opposed to a strengthening of the party organization because they had been returned in the past by Liberal organizations and they preferred to go on relying upon these rather than to create electoral machinery of their own on Labour lines. If there were a vacancy in any of these constituencies the Liberals would attempt to recapture the seat and there would be no Labour organization to oppose them:

> That is a state of affairs which cannot be tolerated, and if these men are to remain in the Labour Party they must conform to the spirit as well as the letter of the constitution. . . . If Messrs. Hall, Wadsworth, Harvey, Haslam, Johnson and Hancock, M.P.s, prefer the Liberals to the I.L.P. well and good, but it must be made quite clear that they cannot have both.[2]

There was a rumour that Harvey intended to stand as a Liberal-Labour candidate until the Bolsover branch of the I.L.P. was active in securing a denial from him before a joint meeting of the branches of the North-East Derbyshire Federation.[3] Eventually, Haslam, Harvey and Hancock all appeared as Labour candidates with the support of the Liberals, although, in the case of Hancock, there was some dissatisfaction among the local Liberals at having to accept a Labour candidate.[4] Haslam even went so far as to advocate a modified form of Socialism: 'Who is afraid of Socialism? I am not. I believe the good common sense of this country would regulate Socialism.'[5] Harvey, on the other hand, felt it necessary to instruct his solicitors to take up the matter of his opponent's description of him as 'Socialist Labour candidate for North-East Derbyshire' because 'it was misleading and could only have been used to try to injure him in his candidature'.[6]

All three of the miners' representatives were re-elected in December, 1910, but after the election the Association began to feel the effects of the Fisher injunction in a number of ways. Money for Harvey's legal

[1] *Sheffield Telegraph*, 23 November, 1910.
[2] *Labour Leader*, quoted in *Sheffield Independent*, 18 November, 1910.
[3] *Derbyshire Times*, 26 November, 1910.
[4] *Sheffield Telegraph*, 25 November, 1910.   [5] *Ibid.* 1 December, 1910.
[6] *Sheffield Independent*, 10 December, 1910.

expenses in the Baggaley case could only be raised by voluntary contribution.[1] Similarly, the union was no longer able to make contributions towards the expenses of those members who became mayors or magistrates.[2] In 1911 it was decided to discontinue the annual demonstration because the union could not consent to 'any payment being made for Railway Fares to a Demonstration, or any other expense connected with a Demonstration'.[3] Various suggestions were made to overcome the disabilities imposed upon the union by the injunction. A resolution that a member should be paid for his magisterial duties 'when the political fund is recouped' was ruled out of order by the chairman and deleted from the minutes of a Council meeting. Another proposal to raise the salaries of officials who were engaged in political work was not acted upon.[4] Meanwhile, in Parliament, Harvey was joining in the campaign for the reversal of the Osborne judgment. He argued in favour of rule by the majority and defended the use of the ballot:

Suggestions have been made that it can be interfered with and manipulated so as to induce the men to do exactly what their leaders desire. Now, in an organization with which I am acquainted we have 40,000 men and to them we sent 40,000 ballot papers. The papers are put into their hands and they record their vote. If that is not a true expression of opinion I do not know what is.[5]

V

By the beginning of 1913 it was becoming obvious to the trade unions that they would not get a complete reversal of the Osborne judgment and they therefore decided to accept the Government's proposals for some regulation of political activity which, within a few months, were embodied in the Trade Union Act, 1913.[6] Meanwhile the Labour Party was working hard to ensure that the ballots which each union would have to take would go in its favour. There was some anxiety about the position in Mid-Derbyshire in view of Hancock's failure to assist in the organization of a Labour Party in the division. On 12 April, 1913, there was a meeting at Alfreton to investigate complaints by the local Labour Party regarding the conduct of Hancock. It was attended by Robert Smillie and W. Straker, of the M.F.G.B., and Arthur Henderson and Arthur Peters represented the Labour Party.[7] Frederick Lee, the local secretary, argued that it was Hancock's first duty to build up

[1] D.M.A. 8 April, 1911.   [2] Ibid. 23 September, 1911; 10 February, 1913.
[3] Ibid. 10 June, 1911.   [4] Ibid. 12 November, 1910.
[5] 41. H. C. Deb. 5s. 3047.
[6] 2 & 3 Geo.V. ch. 30.   [7] M.F.G.B. 23–25 April, 1913.

a Labour Party, but instead he had subscribed £50 to the Liberal agent, attended Liberal Party meetings and voted in Parliament with the Liberal Party. In this he had the support of the Derbyshire miners in the division 'who seemed to regard themselves as the Labour Party'.[1] Hancock denied the charges which were made against him and stated that the Council of the Nottinghamshire Miners' Association had decided against the formation of a Labour Party by forty-eight lodges to two.

Smillie and Straker presented a report of the meeting to the Executive Committee of the M.F.G.B. They expressed surprise at finding that the Derbyshire miners' lodges in the division had held a preliminary meeting, 'and practically made up their minds before hearing the case from the other parties in the meeting':

> Speaking generally, we can only add that it is quite evident, pleasant or otherwise as it may be, that the only political organization in the division behind Mr. Hancock is the Liberal Association, and that the Derbyshire Miners' Lodges in the division have definitely made up their minds not to support a Labour Party organization but on the other hand to support the Liberal Association.[2]

This was described as being 'contrary to all Trade Union principles of loyalty'. The Derbyshire Miners' Association protested against this report on the grounds that 'only six or seven Lodges in the District had credentials sent to attend the meeting while we have 84 Lodges with over 9,000 members in the constituency'. When the ballot was taken in July, 1913, in accordance with the provisions of the new Trade Union Act, there were 539 votes (representing 26,950 members) for the Federation being the unit for the political fund and 314 votes (representing 15,700 members) against.[3]

Meanwhile the death of Haslam had resulted in the adoption of Barnet Kenyon, the Derbyshire miners' agent, as candidate for the Chesterfield division.[4] Kenyon's candidature aroused a storm of controversy. He had been anxious to avoid what he described as 'a wicked three-cornered struggle'[5] and appeared before the electorate as the candidate who had 'received the assent of the two great national executives which stood for Labour and Progress'.[6] In reply to a question at Shirebrook as to whether he could reasonably expect the support of the Labour members who were endeavouring to build up an independent Labour Party, Kenyon replied that he was nominated by his own union, consisting of 39,000 financial members, 'and that nomination had received the approval of Fabians, Social Democrats, members of the I.L.P., the British Socialists and Syndicalists, and the Executive of

[1] M.F.G.B. 23–25 April, 1913.   [2] Ibid.
[3] D.M.A. 2 August, 1913.   [4] Ibid. 3 May, 1 August, 1913.
[5] Sheffield Independent, 6 August, 1913.   [6] Ibid.

the Labour Party'.[1] Harvey, speaking in support of Kenyon, announced that 'the Labour Party were putting all the speakers at their command in order to secure the triumphant return of Mr. Barnet Kenyon'.[2] The Socialists in the constituency, however, were opposed to Kenyon's candidature when they discovered that he was working closely with the Liberals.[3] Objections to the candidature were lodged with the national executive of the Labour Party and a member of the Chesterfield Trades and Labour Council was reported to have said: 'We are prepared to give Ramsay MacDonald a warm time if he comes down.'[4]

The national executive was eventually obliged to withdraw its endorsement of Kenyon's candidature and this decision was accepted by the Executive Committee of the M.F.G.B. Soon after this episode MacDonald explained that the strongly worded letter which he sent to Kenyon 'meant nothing'. G. D. H. Cole commented:

He and his friends of the Labour Party, we are told, did nothing to embarrass Mr. Kenyon, and we are given to understand that he views with enthusiasm the return of a Lib.-Lab. whose chief tenet appears to be an almost theological reverence for the Chancellor of the Exchequer. Very wisely, Mr. MacDonald wishes those Labour members who are pure Liberals to clear out of the Labour Party; the curious thing is that he should seem so anxious to get them elected.[5]

Soon after the Labour Party's formal renunciation of Kenyon, John Scurr, of the Dockers' Union, appeared as a British Socialist candidate. He was supported by George Lansbury who, at that time, was being closely watched by the police.[6] Scurr was described by his supporters as 'this disturber of the peace of the master-class, this cruel critic of genteel and respectable institutions'.[7] The Liberal newspapers did much to discredit Scurr and his followers, 'many of them . . . well-groomed men of means and of culture; men with forty-horsepower motor cars who dashed about the town in a way that wouldn't have disgraced a capitalist millionaire'.[8] Despite the intervention of Scurr the result of the election was very much as had been expected. Scurr received only 583 votes and Kenyon was elected with 7,725 votes, giving a majority of 2,186 over Edward Christie, the Unionist candidate. G. D. H. Cole remarked:

The failure of the B.S.P. and of the 'industrial' Lansburyites shows clearly enough that it is impossible as yet, to build up an independent political force

---

[1] *Sheffield Independent*, 7 August, 1913.   [2] *Ibid.*
[3] *Ibid.* 12 August, 1913.   [4] *Ibid.*
[5] G. D. H. Cole, *The World of Labour*, (London), edn. of 1917, p. 397.
[6] Lansbury, an active supporter of women's suffrage, had just been released from prison, under the so-called 'Cat and Mouse Act', after a hunger-and-thirst strike. (Raymond Postgate, *The Life of George Lansbury*, (London), 1951, pp. 130–1.)
[7] *Sheffield Independent*, 15 August, 1913.   [8] *Ibid.* 20 August, 1913.

outside the Labour Party. The solution lies, then, rather in purging the Labour Party itself, and the Chesterfield by-election gives hope that the process is already beginning.[1]

The Chesterfield by-election of 1913 produced a crisis in the affairs of the M.F.G.B. and of the Labour Party. The refusal of both organizations to endorse Kenyon's candidature meant that they withdrew their financial support and Kenyon was faced, in the middle of his campaign, with the problem of paying election expenses amounting to about £1,750. He later wrote to Frank Hall:

I was allowed to drift on from day to day without any certainty that my expenses would be met. I did my best before and since to get these expenses properly met and I told you that Miss Markham promised me to assist in raising my expenses if I would go out and fight this battle for Labour and Progressive Liberalism.[2]

Support from the Liberals was eventually accepted. According to Sir Arthur Markham, he was visited in London by Harvey and Samuel Short, Kenyon's election agent, and asked to be a guarantor. Harvey, Short, Kenyon, Martin and Hall then made themselves personally responsible to the bank for the election expenses.[3]

At the first Council meeting of the Derbyshire Miners' Association after the election, the affair was discussed at length and a resolution was carried calling for a full investigation into the reasons for the refusal of the executive of the Labour Party to endorse Kenyon's candidature.[4] A further resolution instructed Harvey and Hall to 'consult any legal authority they may consider necessary as to our position with the Miners' Federation, in the event of our disagreeing on Political lines under the Trades Union No. 2 Bill, and that they also consult the Registrar with respect to our becoming a unit under the Bill should it become necessary'.[5] The executives of both the M.F.G.B. and the Labour Party condemned the actions of Kenyon and there were many discussions and much correspondence between these bodies and representatives of the Derbyshire Miners' Association.

At the annual conference of the M.F.G.B. at Scarborough in October, 1913, practically a whole day was taken up by discussion of the Chesterfield election.[6] The principal charges against Kenyon were that he had violated the letter of the Labour Party constitution by describing himself as a 'Labour and Progressive candidate' and its spirit by

[1] Cole, *op. cit.* p. 399.
[2] Derbyshire Miners' Association, Letter from Barnet Kenyon to Frank Hall, 30 April, 1914.
[3] *Derbyshire Times*, 16 May, 1914.   [4] *D.M.A.* 23 August, 1913.
[5] *Ibid.*   [6] *M.F.G.B.* 8 October, 1913.

employing Samuel Short, the former Liberal agent, who was 'in a colliery company, secretary for a colliery company, and . . . on the directorate'.[1] A Yorkshire delegate commented:

Some very peculiar things happened in this election. Mr. House fought a by-election in Houghton-le-Springs not very long ago, and his opponent was Tom Wing, who went to help Barnet Kenyon at Chesterfield. That, in itself, no party could have endorsed that stood for Labour. If they had, then Labour wanted purifying. Then we find the Lord Advocate there, another man who was always prepared to oust Labour on every possible occasion. Ure was sent down to Chesterfield to help this gentleman. Then we find another gentleman, a mine owner, Sir Arthur Markham, helping to get Barnet Kenyon in, a supporter of Mining Legislation, and some of us will be able to say something with regard to this policy of getting Mining Legislation from men of this character.

The conference approved the findings of the Executive Committee and instructed it to request a meeting with the Labour Party executive 'with a view to trying to do something to put matters right in connection with the Chesterfield Election and to ensure Chesterfield in the future being a Labour seat'.[2] This meeting failed to produce a satisfactory settlement with the Derbyshire miners whose Council resolved:

We are desirous of keeping our connection with the Miners' Federation and Labour Party but unless Mr. Kenyon be adopted and the expenses of the last election be paid, we shall be compelled to Ballot our members as to whether we shall sever our connection politically with the Federation.[3]

The Chesterfield election was also discussed at the annual conference of the Labour Party at Glasgow in January, 1914, but as negotiations were still continuing between the Party's executive and the miners' leaders, no decisions were taken. Meanwhile Kenyon made the matter a major issue at meetings in his constituency. 'I will not', he declared, 'have my directions given to me from extraneous organizations unless I should get my instructions to obey from this division and this organization.'[4] Early in February, 1914, the union faced a difficult situation. There had been further discussions and correspondence with the executives of the M.F.G.B. and of the Labour Party, and Kenyon persisted in his refusal to abide by the Party constitution 'except as understood and practised by the late Mr. Haslam'.[5] Frank Hall then had a long talk with Kenyon who eventually agreed to sign the Labour Party constitution unconditionally. Hall wrote to Arthur Henderson, the Party secretary: 'Whatever personal feelings and objections he may have . . . he has

---

[1] See also Chapter VI, pp. 265-6.   [2] M.F.G.B. 8 October, 1913.
[3] D.M.A. 29 December, 1913.   [4] Sheffield Independent, 21 January, 1914.
[5] M.F.G.B. 13-14 January, 1914; D.M.A. 21 January, 1914.

decided to set these aside in order to work for the unity of our own Association and the Miners' Federation.'[1] Kenyon and Hall were then interviewed by the Emergency Committee of the Labour Party Executive. On 11 February Henderson informed Hall that Kenyon had been formally accepted as a member of the Party, 'thereafter taking his place in the Party meeting, and being introduced under Party auspices into the House of Commons yesterday'.[2]

Many Labour Party members were doubtful about Kenyon's sudden conversion. 'He may give his formal adhesion to the Labour Party Constitution', said the *Labour Leader*, 'but he cannot change his convictions in a day.'[3] Others felt that the dispute had been stifled at the Glasgow conference and then settled in a hole and corner fashion to escape criticism and to accommodate the M.F.G.B.[4] On 20 February it was announced in the newspapers that Kenyon had decided to secede from the Labour Party. 'I always had in mind', he said, 'that I was accepting it in the same spirit as Mr. Haslam, my predecessor, who, though he signed the constitution, claimed liberty to address his supporters from any platform, whether Liberal or Labour.'[5] Frank Hall was indignant:

I was with Mr. Kenyon from 7.30 to 11 o'clock last night in London and he did not mention a single word or give a hint of his intentions. The first intimation I had of the change in affairs was when I read it in the newspapers this morning and you can guess my astonishment and amazement. I am ashamed and disgusted over the whole affair. It is nothing but a traitorous thing. I consider Mr. Kenyon has sold the seat and everything else. I have stood abuse, vituperation and calumny and made great sacrifices, and this is the reward of it all.[6]

Kenyon, on the other hand, blandly informed a Co-operative meeting at Clowne: 'In spite of anything that is said, or is going to be said, I am just Barnet Kenyon, nothing more or less. The old principles that I have revered in the past are the same principles that permeate my life tonight.'[7]

The matter was discussed by the Association's Executive Committee, which decided to recommend to Council that 'we cannot see our way clear to advise our members to seek exemption from payment to the Miners' Federation Political Fund, but we do recommend that this Association still continue to pay its levies to the Fund with a view to providing Labour candidates at the forthcoming General Election'.[8]

[1] Derbyshire Miners' Association, Letter from Hall to Henderson, 6 February, 1914.
[2] *Ibid*. Letter from Henderson to Hall, 11 February, 1914.
[3] *Labour Leader*, quoted in *Derbyshire Times*, 14 February, 1914.
[4] *Derbyshire Times*, 14 February, 1914.   [5] *Ibid*. 21 February, 1914.
[6] *Ibid*. 28 February, 1914.   [7] *Ibid*.   [8] *D.M.A.* 23 February, 1914.

This decision was endorsed by the Council, and the Association had at last, after six years, moved into line with the national policy of the M.F.G.B.

Kenyon was not alone in his reluctance to abandon Liberalism. On 25 February he wrote to Frank Hall: 'The majority of the Labour Party itself have assured me that they are going to claim their individual freedom to accept and give help to anybody they think well to do so.' He had discussed with Wilson, Fenwick, Ward, Stanley, Johnson, Thomas, Smith and many other Labour members, the possibility of forming a 'third party' to supersede the Labour Party. Sir Arthur Markham 'and several of the Heads of Departments' had assured Kenyon that his seat would be 'held for Labour' as long as the miners had an official they could put forward as a candidate. 'I hope we may be able to work together', Kenyon told Hall, 'so as to secure your future, if only for the sake of your kindness to me. I will leave no stone unturned to make that possible.'[1]

Hall replied immediately and refused to have anything to do with the proposal. 'There is Labour and Labour', he said. 'The Labour they mean must be of that particular specie that they approve of.' In denouncing Kenyon for his conduct, Hall was not entirely happy about his own part in the affair. He was one of those who had agreed to sign the guarantee for an overdraft on Kenyon's account with Williams Deacon's Bank on the strength of a handsome contribution from Sir Arthur Markham. He reminded Kenyon that it had been agreed that he should continue to fight 'on strictly Labour lines' and that 'you would again announce that your own friends in the Union had rallied to your assistance at a time when your enemies had anticipated your downfall. What a splendid election cry! . . . You were not to be upbraided with receiving Liberal money; it would have spoilt the Election, so said Mr. Short. The solemn question you and I have to ask ourselves is this: Was this a piece of trickery to deceive and delude the electors, or were we deluded and deceived, with the object of putting both of us under an obligation to certain wealthy Liberals? Did they take advantage of our difficulties to put us under bondage?'[2]

The change in the political attitude of the Derbyshire Miners' Association was hastened by the death of Haslam. His influence in the union, as its founder and faithful servant over many years, was immense. He had been elected to Parliament in 1906, before the M.F.G.B. was affiliated with the Labour Party, and he had been allowed a considerable amount of latitude. The secretary of the M.F.G.B. had written to Haslam on many occasions telling him that he was not conforming with

[1] Derbyshire Miners' Association, Letter from Kenyon to Hall, 25 February, 1914.
[2] *Ibid.* Letter from Hall to Kenyon, 26 February, 1914.

the constitution of the Labour Party. The matter had been discussed by the Executive Committee of the Federation and it was only Haslam's age and final illness which had prevented them from reaching a decision.[1] The death of Haslam had not only removed a powerful influence from the Derbyshire Miners' Association but it had also facilitated the enforcement of the constitution by the M.F.G.B.

When, in April, 1914, Harvey also died, the break with the past was almost complete. James Martin, the President of the Association, was nominated as a Labour candidate for North-East Derbyshire and a deputation was sent to meet the Liberal executive of the division to inform them of this decision.[2] There had been previous discussion between the Liberals and the leaders of the union and, on the authority of the Chief Whip, Sir Arthur Markham had stated that if the Derbyshire Miners' Association decided to run a candidate in alliance with the Liberal Party, the Liberals would give the candidate full support and would pay his expenses.[3] The Council had rejected this proposal and the members of the deputation, William Sewell and Frank Lee, were obviously uneasy about their task. They made it clear to the Liberals that Martin would not speak on any Liberal platforms and argued that they were bound by the decision of their Council. Lee stated:

My sympathies are very largely Liberal, and I am belonging to a Trade Union organization, (wisely or unwisely, I am one of its permanent officials) and one can naturally see that if there is to be a National Labour Party, it must be that one of its Trade Union organizations in the County should aspire to belong to that National Party.[4]

He went on to criticize the Labour party constitution: 'Our hope is, that getting inside the movement we shall be able to so broaden that movement, that the Progressive Forces, instead of being divided, shall come together, as one huge phalanx and fight against our common enemy.'[5] Sewell added that Martin would only be a Labour candidate in name. 'In action he will be a good Liberal.'[6]

Violet Markham, who was present at this meeting, writes:

We thought it unfair and ungenerous that Labour should proceed to bite the Liberal hands that fed it, and many of our Lib-Lab. friends were unhappy and embarrassed at the part they were forced to play. But looking back, I can appreciate the political wisdom of this action. The astute leaders of the

[1] *M.F.G.B.* 8 October, 1913.
[2] *D.M.A.* 6 May, 1914.
[3] Derbyshire Miners' Association, Report of a Deputation to the Executive Committee of the North-East Derbyshire Liberal Association, 6 May, 1914, p. 7.
[4] *Ibid.* p. 3.　　　　　　　　　　　　　　　　　　[5] *Ibid.* p. 4.
[6] *Ibid.* p. 12.

Labour Party realised the importance of freeing themselves from any entang-ling alliance of any kind. It was essential to the emergence of a full-blooded Socialist philosophy that all compromises should be eliminated and the vat stand on its own bottom.[1]

Despite the assurances given by Sewell and Lee, the Liberals nomin-ated J. P. Houfton as their candidate and 'Freedom of conscience' became one of the issues of the election. Later, Martin described himself as being committed to the policy of the M.F.G.B. but added: 'There is no more ardent Liberal in the country than I have been, and there is no more ardent Liberal now.'[2] Sir Arthur Markham stated that the Liberal Association 'was informed in effect that, so far as the Labour Party was concerned, Liberalism was extinct and the secretary, Mr. Hall, had written to him "that the consideration of freedom and liberty extended to both their late colleagues, Messrs. Haslam and Harvey, could not, and would not, be extended to others" '.[3]

Another break with the past was the appointment of a new election agent, Bertram Mather, a Chesterfield solicitor. Haslam and Harvey had insisted on retaining the services of Short, despite the objections from the M.F.G.B. and the Labour Party. In order to pay Short's salary and expenses the Executive and the Trustees had agreed to an overdraft on the banking account for the political fund, with Harvey as guarantor. After Harvey's death the bank required repayment of the overdraft, which amounted to £580 5s. 7d. It was decided by the Council that this sum, together with £409 which was owed to Short, should be charged to Harvey's estate.

Martin obtained only 3,669 votes in this election against Houfton's 6,155. G. Harland Bowden, the Unionist candidate, was elected with 6,469 votes. The prophecy of the writer in the Labour Leader had come true.[4] By relying on the dominant personality of Harvey, instead of building up their own electoral machinery, the Derbyshire miners had lost a seat. In the following August their Council resolved to set up a Labour Party in the North-Eastern division.

VI

The political activities of the Derbyshire miners in this period show clearly that the influx of the M.F.G.B. into the ranks of the Labour Party served to increase the difficulties of maintaining an independent political line. Although the Labour Party was normally

[1] Violet Markham, Friendship's Harvest, (London), 1956, p. 19.
[2] Sheffield Independent, 8 May, 1914.
[3] Ibid. 11 May, 1914.   [4] See above, p. 503.

HENRY HICKEN

FRANK HALL

opposed to any form of collaboration with other parties it was, of necessity, obliged to modify its attitude in the face of a large accession of Liberal-Labour M.P.s and their supporters. In the period immediately following the affiliation of the M.F.G.B. Liberal-Labour politics appears to have been a device which commended itself to the Labour Party, to trade union Members of Parliament and to Liberals alike: to the Labour Party because it was able to use the machinery of the Liberal Party for its own purposes; to the trade union Members of Parliament because it represented the easiest way of being re-elected; and to the Liberals because they were struggling to retain the support of the radical element in the electorate. But the kind of situation which arose in connection with the Mid-Derbyshire by-election of 1909 was not accepted for very long. By 1910 the Derbyshire miners' candidates were standing as Labour candidates but still collaborating with the Liberals, and by 1913 both the Labour Party and the Executive Committee of the M.F.G.B. were taking a much firmer line.

This change, in Derbyshire, is largely explained by the disappearance of the old trade union leaders from the political scene. At the same time, the Labour Party was becoming stronger, its organization was becoming much tighter and it was striving increasingly to establish its separate identity even at the risk of losing doubtful seats. By 1914 the Labour Party was well on the road to political independence, despite the number of intransigent Liberals within its ranks, and by 1918 its theoretical position was constitutionally defined.

R

PART III
THE DERBYSHIRE MINERS' ASSOCIATION
1914–44

CHAPTER XIII

THE FIRST WORLD WAR

I

Governmental control of prices and resources was by no means so effective in the First World War as it was in the Second. Throughout the war the coal industry was seriously disturbed by rising costs and a shortage of manpower, equipment and supplies. Sir Richard Redmayne, the technical adviser to the Coal Controller, has likened the system of control which evolved to a house that is constantly being extended 'with the result that . . . the completed building differs materially from what it could have been had all the requirements been known at the commencement of the operation and the house constructed on a pre-conceived and definite plan'.[1]

The outbreak of hostilities in 1914 found the industry entering one of its periodic depressions. The immediate effect of the war was to reduce still further the demand for coal. The loss of overseas markets was felt most acutely in the exporting areas but even in Derbyshire some of the steam-coal pits which had developed a substantial overseas trade had to introduce short-time working.[2] Lord Aberconway told the shareholders of the Sheepbridge Company in September: 'The Baltic was closed so that no coal could go to Russia that way. None could go to Germany, Sweden, or Belgium—all were practically closed markets.'[3] The slackness of the coal trade in the early months of the war was reflected in the average pit-head price which fell from 10s. 2d. a ton in 1913 to 10s. in 1914.

The temporary surplus of coal was of short duration. The lower output due to the enlistment of a large number of miners for naval and military service, the greatly increased requirements of the Admiralty, the stimulus given by the war to the manufacture of armaments, and

---

[1] Sir R. A. S. Redmayne, *The British Coal-mining Industry during the War*, (Oxford), 1923, p. 257.
[2] *Derbyshire Times*, 15 August, 1914.   [3] *Ibid.* 3 October, 1914.

the high prices which were soon being offered for export coal, created a demand which became difficult to meet. The price of coal (more especially the retail price) began to rise sharply. The London retail prices of best Derbyshire coal were as follows:[1]

Date	Price per ton
16 June, 1914	26s. (lowest summer price)
26 September, 1914	27s.
21 November, 1914	28s.
12 December, 1914	29s.
19 December, 1914	30s.
7 January, 1915	31s.
28 January, 1915	32s.
29 January, 1915	33s.
17 February, 1915	35s.

A committee appointed by the Board of Trade recommended on 24 March, 1915, that exports of coal to neutral countries should be restricted and that if prices did not shortly return to a reasonable level, 'the Government should consider a scheme for assuming control of the output of collieries during the continuance of the war'.[2]

In May, 1915, Walter Runciman, the President of the Board of Trade, made voluntary arrangements with the London retail coal merchants whereby they agreed to limit their prices by accepting a maximum margin of profit of 7s. 6d. a ton. The scheme was later extended to some of the larger provincial towns. In the following July the Price of Coal (Limitation) Act laid down that the selling price of any coal at the pit-head was not to exceed by more than 4s. a ton the price of the same kind of coal sold in similar quantities and under similar conditions on the corresponding date in the year ended 30 June, 1914. The Act did not apply to the sale of coal for export but the control of freight rates and the voluntary agreement of the coal-owners helped to restrict the price of coal exported to France and Italy.

The drift of labour from the mines to the armed forces was not at first regarded as a serious matter but the difficulties experienced in meeting the increased demand for coal as the war effort gathered momentum led to the appointment of a Home Office Departmental Committee on 23 February, 1915, 'to inquire into the conditions prevailing in the coal-mining industry with a view to promoting such organization of work between employers and workmen as, having regard to the large number of miners who are enlisting for naval and military service, will secure the necessary production of coal during

[1] Redmayne, *op. cit.* p. 33.   [2] *Ibid.* p. 23.

the war'.[1] On 27 May the Committee reported that in the period to
the end of February, 1915, about 19 per cent. of the total labour force
had left the mines but 50,473 persons had moved into the industry from
other employments. The net reduction in the labour force was 14 per
cent. which was comparable with a 13·5 per cent. reduction in output
in the same period.[2] Although the recruitment of miners for the Forces
continued after the publication of this report, the loss was not so heavy
as in the early months of the war. Nevertheless, the net reduction in the
labour force during the first twelve months amounted to 16 per cent.
The decrease in output was 11 per cent.[3]

The effect of recruitment on output varied as between districts. The
position at the end of 1915 was as follows:[4]

District	Percentage difference in output	Percentage depletion of labour
Scottish Division	− 8·6	−16·5
Northern Division	−10·6	−25·8
York and Midland	+ 0·8	−12·2
Lancashire and North Wales	− 4·0	−14·8
South Wales	− 6·0	−13·4
Midland and Southern	+ 0·4	− 8·9

It has been suggested that the districts which were able to maintain or
slightly increase their output were those with comparatively new collieries and thick seams.[5] Derbyshire's production of coal from 1913 to
1918 compares with the national output as follows.[6]

	Derbyshire Tons	United Kingdom Tons
1913	18,129,424	287,430,473
1914	16,939,286	265,664,393
1915	16,645,131	253,206,081
1916	16,747,857	256,375,366
1917	16,652,208	248,499,240
1918	14,939,053	227,748,654

The possibility of a shortage of pit timber was another immediate
consequence of the outbreak of war. The principal supply, which came
from Russia, was abruptly curtailed. The quantity of pit timber consumed at the collieries of the United Kingdom was equivalent to about
1.7 per cent. of the total weight of coal raised.[7] According to C. P.
Markham, the Staveley Company normally used about 3 cwt. of timber

[1] *Report of Departmental Committee to enquire into conditions prevailing in the Coal-mining Industry due to the war*, 1915. (Cd. 7939.)   [2] *Ibid.*
[3] Redmayne, *op. cit.* p. 15.   [4] *Ibid.* p. 55.   [5] *Ibid.* p. 56.
[6] *Reports of H.M. Inspectors of Mines and Quarries*, 1913–1918.
[7] Redmayne, *op. cit.* p. 136.

for every ton of coal produced.[1] By strict control of the use of timber, the encouragement of home production and the securing of alternative supplies abroad, the Government was able to keep the mines going. Some firms used cast-iron props.

The prices of materials such as timber began to rise sharply as a result of war-time shortages and, since the cost of materials was from one-tenth to one-sixth of the total cost of production, being second only in importance to the cost of labour, the increased charges bore heavily on the coal industry. The average annual declared values of imported pit wood per load rose from £1·32 in 1914 to £4·19 in 1918. Gunpowder and high explosives, also widely used in mining, rose respectively from £2·43 and £4·75 per cwt. in 1914 to £4·77 and £12·92 in 1918. Oats, beans and hay, used for feeding horses and ponies, also increased greatly in price. Steel wire ropes used for haulage increased in price between 1914 and 1918 from 72·2 to 161·6 per cent.; winding ropes from 44·4 to 117·4 per cent.[2]

When labour disputes were added to the war-time difficulties of the coal industry the Government was obliged to take complete control. In return for a pledge by their leaders against strikes the miners had been exempted from the Munitions of War Act, 1915, which established penalties for striking, and specified a method of compulsory arbitration. In July, 1915, however, there was a five-day strike in South Wales followed by a period of industrial unrest. The strategic importance of the 'Admiralty' collieries of South Wales was great and eventually, under the Defence of the Realm Act, the Government made regulations which enabled it to take complete control of the coalfield from 1 December, 1916. It was explained in the House of Commons that this was done in order to eliminate war profits, to avoid industrial disputes, and to secure the best results from the labour of the miners.[3]

Meanwhile the Government had been considering the desirability of taking control of the whole of the coal industry. The matter had first been discussed as early as September, 1915, but it was not until February, 1917, that direct control was finally established under a new department of the Board of Trade.[4] Guy (later Sir Guy) Calthrop, the general manager of the London and North-Western Railway, was appointed Controller of Coal Mines, with Sir Richard Redmayne, the Chief Inspector of Mines, as his technical adviser. An advisory board was set up consisting at first of ten members, five representing the colliery owners and five the miners. The membership of the board was later increased to fourteen.

Before the advent of state control the profits from the coalmines

[1] *Derbyshire Times*, 26 September, 1914.   [2] Redmayne, *op. cit.* pp. 42–43.
[3] 88 H. C. Deb. 5s. 474–5.   [4] Redmayne, *op. cit.* pp. 88–92.

were restricted by the Price of Coal (Limitation) Act and by the war-
time taxation of profits which applied to uncontrolled industrial undertakings generally. In September, 1915, Sir Richard Redmayne had
stated in a memorandum prepared for the Home Secretary: 'No doubt
direct control of the profits would appeal more strongly to the workmen
and conduce in a greater degree to the prevention of labour unrest than
a system of *indirect* control.'[1] Under the system of Government control
the colliery proprietors were given an assurance that they would receive
pre-war profits. It was also agreed that if excess profits were realized,
80 per cent. would pass to the Inland Revenue as Excess Profits duty,
15 per cent. would be retained in a pool from which to meet the
guarantee of pre-war profits to less profitable collieries, and 5 per cent.
would be paid to the companies.

The Controller of Coal Mines was responsible for all aspects of the
industry, including output, distribution, finance, labour, wages, prices,
dividends and the maintenance of essential supplies. Despite controls
the rising costs of labour and materials led to successive modifications of
the permitted maximum prices of coal with the result that the yearly
average selling value at the pit-head rose from 9s. 11d. a ton in 1914 to
12s. 5d. in 1915, 15s. 3d. in 1916, 16s. 7d. in 1917 and 20s. 6d. in 1918.[2]
The average price of best Derbyshire coal at the pit-head increased from
11s. 6d. a ton in August, 1914, to 23s. 3d. in August, 1918. The retail
price rose rather less steeply from 25s. 6d. to 43s. 6d.[3]

II

It has been suggested that while the war had a detrimental effect on the
technical progess of the coal industry, both by slowing down the rate
of new investments and by speeding up capital consumption, it did not
constitute a drawback to the capital or commercial organization of the
industry.[4] The Derbyshire coal-owners did what they could, throughout
the war, to complete existing development projects and to prepare for
new ones. In October, 1914, it was reported that a new company, with
Sir Arthur Markham at its head, was about to be formed to work the
'top hard' seam between Palterton and Heath.[5] In 1915–16 the Hatfield
Main Colliery Company, a Yorkshire firm in which leading members of
the Bolsover Company had personal financial interests, spent £58,050
in sinking shafts to the Barnsley seam of coal.[6] On the eve of the

[1] Redmayne, *op. cit.*, pp. 89–90.   [2] Gibson, *op. cit.* p. 157.
[3] *Coal Industry Commission*, 1919, (Cmd. 361), Appendix 46, p. 73.
[4] A. M. Neuman, *Economic Organization of the British Coal Industry*, (London),
1934, p. 3.
[5] *Derbyshire Times*, 17 October, 1914.   [6] *Ibid.* 8 April, 1916.

R*

armistice it was announced that the Butterley Company expected to begin raising coal from its Bilsthorpe Colliery soon after the war was over and intended to develop another colliery at Ollerton, in conjunction with the Stanton Ironworks Company. The Bolsover Company was planning to sink another pit at Clipstone.[1]

The Sheepbridge Company, through its subsidiaries, continued to develop its Yorkshire collieries at Maltby, Rossington and Firbeck.[2] The Rossington Main Company, with a nominal capital of £500,000, successfully completed its sinking operations in May, 1915, despite the shortage of labour, and was laying down a plant capable of raising from 5,000 to 6,000 tons of coal a day.[3] By June, 1915, some of the leases of the Firbeck coalfield were complete, and the remainder were practically settled. An Act of Parliament authorizing the construction of a railway in connection with the colliery had already been secured.[4] In September, 1916, it was reported that the Sheepbridge Company had taken lease of the lower seams of coal at Glapwell, where for over thirty years only the upper seams had been worked.[5] At the annual general meeting in 1917 Lord Aberconway told the shareholders that the output at the Sheepbridge pits for the year was just over a million tons and, with the addition of the subsidiary companies, the total output was $2\frac{3}{4}$ million tons. 'When they completed Finningley and the other collieries which they were developing,' he said, 'they expected to have an output of something like $4\frac{1}{2}$ million tons, or about the largest output of any colliery company in the Kingdom.'[6] In September, 1917, the Company had just completed the construction of a steel furnace and was 'going into the steel trade on a small scale for the first time'.[7]

Similarly the Staveley Company, which was sinking pits at Palterton and at Edlington, near Doncaster, when the war started, continued to develop them. In 1916 it was reported that the Company, in conjunction with the Bullcroft Main Colliery Company, had acquired a large area of coal near Doncaster and was planning the development of the Markham Main Colliery.[8] New sinkings were also being made at Warsop and plans were being prepared for the sinking of a shaft to the Black Shale Coal in the Staveley works yard.[9] There were also important developments at the engineering works at Chesterfield and a new blast furnace was being constructed at the Devonshire works in 1917.[10]

[1] *Derbyshire Times*, 9 November, 1918.					[2] *Ibid.* 3 October, 1914.
[3] *Ibid.* 17 April, 8 May, 1915.
[4] *Annual Report of the Sheepbridge Company for the year ending 30 June, 1915.*
[5] *Derbyshire Times*, 30 September, 1916.
[6] *Ibid.* 29 September, 1917.					[7] *Ibid.*
[8] *Ibid.* 23 September, 1916.					[9] *Ibid.* 30 September, 1916.
[10] *Annual Report of the Staveley Company for the year ending 30 June, 1917*; *Derbyshire Times*, 2 September, 1916.

The demand for benzol and similar commodities gave a great impetus to the development of by-product plants. 'The soft coal seams which were practically untouched for generations were now of enormous value', said Charles Markham soon after the outbreak of war. The Staveley Company's 150 coke ovens and new concentrated acid plants were then producing weekly about 140 tons of sulphuric acid, 15,000 gallons of benzol and 80 tons of sulphate of ammonia.[1] By May, 1918, the Company had put down, since the outbreak of war, plant for the production of aniline, oil, oleum, hydrochloric and nitric acids, and naphthalene, which were being disposed of in large commercial quantities. Plans were being made to erect a further battery of 60 coke ovens.[2]

The colliery proprietors made frequent complaints about the inroads upon their profits which were made by taxation, price controls, rising costs and a reduced output resulting from the shortage of labour. In September, 1915, Lord Aberconway told the shareholders at the annual meeting of the Sheepbridge Company that 'so far from the colliery companies having made larger profits during the war, they had in nearly every case been lower'.[3] In 1917 Charles Markham complained that the Staveley Company's income tax had risen from £7,710 in 1914 to £80,000 and the average wage bill from £900,000 to £1,200,000. 'On top of that,' he said, 'it should be remembered that the mines were losing from 16 to 35 per cent. all the time. He did not think the shareholders were profiteering to the extent that the working man was profiteering today.'[4]

On the other hand, Aberconway's colleague, Frederick Fowler, in discussing the prospects of trade after the war, said in 1916:

There had been such a disturbance in the labour market caused by the war and the high prices workmen had been receiving—quite properly—and the higher profits colliery companies had been receiving, so contrary to the normal state of things, that they would have difficulty in readjusting matters.[5]

In September, 1918, he told the annual meeting of the Sheepbridge Company: 'They were now on the high tide, and he hoped they would remain there.'[6] Similarly, in the same month, Charles Markham said that the prospects of the Staveley Company 'had never been brighter than at the present time, and he had no hesitation in saying that in years to come they would be "O.K." '.[7]

[1] *Derbyshire Times*, 26 September, 1914.   [2] *Ibid.* 4 May, 1918.
[3] *Ibid.* 2 October, 1915.   [4] *Ibid.* 29 September, 1917.
[5] *Ibid.* 30 September, 1916.
[6] *Ibid.* 28 September, 1918.   [7] *Ibid.*

The prosperity of the coal and iron companies is perhaps more clearly reflected by the dividends paid during the war years:

	Staveley Company Per cent.	Sheepbridge Company Per cent.
1914	12½	15
1915	12½ (+ bonus shares)	15
1916	20	15
1917	15	15
1918	12½	12½ (+ bonus shares)

In 1915 the Staveley Company issued bonus shares to the value of £358,416 from its reserve and undistributed profits, each ordinary shareholder receiving one new share for each three fully paid shares held, and one new share for each four shares, 15s. paid up. At the same time it was decided to increase the nominal capital of the Company to £2,500,000 by the creation of a further 1,302,000 ordinary shares.[1] Similarly, in 1918, the Sheepbridge Company distributed £334,631 in bonus shares at the rate of one for each three shares held.[2]

III

The response of the Derbyshire Miners' Association to the outbreak of war in 1914, unlike that of some of the more militant sections of the Labour movement, was one of resigned acceptance. On a motion by Barnet Kenyon, seconded by Frank Hall, it was resolved:

That this Council regrets the necessity of our intervention as a Nation in this great European War, but hopes for the success of the British Armies and those of our Allies, and that the ultimate end may be a world's lasting peace and good will amongst men and nations. . . . We admire the readiness with which our men have responded to the Nation's Call.[3]

The diminution of the labour force brought about by recruitment led some of the coal-owners to propose that the suspensory clause of the so-called Eight Hours' Act[4] should be operated. A meeting of the Executive Committee of the M.F.G.B. in London, on 2 February, 1915, protested against the proposal as did the Council of the Derbyshire Miners' Association a few days later.[5] The miners disclaimed all responsibility for the high price of coal and pointed out that there had

---

[1] *Annual Report of the Staveley Company for the year ending 30 June, 1915.*
[2] *Annual Report of the Sheepbridge Company for the year ending 30 June, 1918.*
[3] *D.M.A.* 22 August, 1914.   [4] 8 Edw. VII, cap. 57, s. 4.
[5] *M.F.G.B.* 2 February, 1915; *D.M.A.* 8 February, 1915.

been no demand for, or award of, increased wages.[1] In his maiden speech in the House of Commons, in June, 1915, Barnet Kenyon said:

We think that there are better ways than increasing the hours. . . . There is about a third of the county of Nottinghamshire where the miners never work on a Saturday. There is a very large portion of my own county where they do not work on a Saturday. We think that these men would gladly work on a Saturday if the necessity were shown to them.[2]

The miners were represented on the Home Office Departmental Committee, appointed in February, 1915, to inquire into the situation in the mines, by Smillie, Walsh and Hartshorn. Evidence was heard from coal-owners and miners' leaders, including Frank Hall, but the Committee's recommendations appear to have been greatly influenced by the wishes of the miners. The Committee expressed the belief that the Executive of the M.F.G.B. was the body best fitted to deal with absenteeism, that employers and workmen in each district should discuss the desirability of shortening holidays, suspending the Eight Hours' Act, and employing more women on the surface. The possibility of reducing the age limit for the underground employment of boys was rejected and greater economy in the use of coal was suggested. The basis of all the proposals and suggestions made by the Committee was close co-operation between the miners' unions and the employers' associations.[3]

Lord Kitchener's appeal to the miners in 1915 to limit their Easter and Whitsuntide holidays was supported by the Executive of the M.F.G.B. and had already been successful before the Committee's report was published. The Derbyshire and Nottinghamshire miners agreed with their employers in March that all pits in the two counties should be closed on Good Friday and the following day and that work should be resumed on Easter Monday.[4] A similar agreement was reached on the Whitsuntide holiday whereby the miners took only two days instead of the customary four or five.[5]

Such co-operation could not be pushed too far. In April, 1915, the Council protested strongly against the growing amount of Sunday work 'as being unnecessary and an encroachment upon a day which should be free from ordinary labour'.[6] In the following August a number of delegates reported to the council that at their collieries advantage was being taken of the war-time situation to impose conditions upon the men which would not be tolerated in normal times. J. T. Todd, the manager of the

---

[1] *Derbyshire Times*, 13 February, 1915.   [2] 72 H.C. Deb. 5s. 1533.
[3] *Report of Departmental Committee to enquire into conditions prevailing in the Coal-mining Industry due to the war*, 1915, (Cd. 7939), *passim*.
[4] *Derbyshire Times*, 27 March, 1915; *D.M.A.* 10 April, 1915.
[5] *Ibid.* 22 May, 1915.   [6] *D.M.A.* 10 April, 1915.

Blackwell Company, was described as 'taking advantage of the patriotism of the workmen'.[1]

The miners' leaders did all they could to increase output by exhorting the men to greater efforts. J. G. Hancock, speaking for the Mid-Derbyshire Recruiting Committee at Tibshelf, said: 'As a religious man and a life-long member of the Christian Church . . . he would work every Sunday that came, and every other day as well, rather than he would allow those men in the trenches to go short of anything they wanted.' He also warned his audience of the adverse effect of drinking upon the production of war materials.[2] Frank Hall, in June, 1915, stated that there was 5 per cent. of avoidable absenteeism in the collieries of Derbyshire. 'We want every man's labour in this crisis', he said. 'We are in danger, and it is for every man in this country who values liberty and freedom to do his part.'[3]

Early in 1915 the miners began to negotiate the terms of new conciliation agreements. The agreements for the Federated Area, which gave a maximum of 65 per cent. above the 1888 rates and a minimum of 50 per cent., was terminable by three months' notice after 31 March, 1915. The annual conference of the M.F.G.B. had decided as early as 1913:

That steps be taken to create a new standard rate of wages in connection with the various conciliation boards, in place of the present obsolete standards, 1877, 1879, and 1888, by merging into the new standard all bonuses and percentages not less than the existing minimum percentages recognized by the present boards.[4]

Eventually agreement was reached with the coal-owners that the rates enjoyed by the miners in December, 1911, should be consolidated to form a new basis which would be 50 per cent. above the 1888 rates, and that there should be a maximum of $23\frac{1}{2}$ per cent. and a minimum of 10 per cent. on the '1911 standard', as it came to be called, for a period of three years.[5] 'The new Conciliation Board agreement was one of the best they had ever entered into', said Frank Hall. 'It gave them what they had been demanding for a long time. . . . They were sick and tired of the 1888 rate.'[6]

Under the conciliation agreements the miners had always had to justify their demands for wage increases by reference to the state of the coal trade but the steep rise in the cost of living, which occurred whilst the negotiations for the conciliation agreement were in progress, led them to adopt a new policy. In March, 1915, when the average retail prices of food already stood 24 per cent. higher than at the outbreak of war, a M.F.G.B. conference decided to ask for a special and immediate

[1] *Derbyshire Times*, 28 August, 1915; *D.M.A.* 21 August, 1915.
[2] *Ibid.* 3 April, 1915.   [3] *Ibid.* 19 June, 1915.   [4] *M.F.G.B.* 10 October, 1913.
[5] *Ibid.* 22 April, 1915.   [6] *Derbyshire Times*, 19 June, 1915.

increase of 20 per cent. on earnings to meet the high cost of living.[1] The Mining Association of Great Britain refused to hold a joint national meeting with representatives of the M.F.G.B. to discuss the matter, on the usual ground that it did not deal with questions of wages, and recommended district negotiations. The Council of the Derbyshire Miners' Association passed a lengthy resolution regretting the Mining Association's reply and urging the M.F.G.B. 'not to allow any district to make any settlement until all have gained a settlement'.[2] When Walter Runciman, the President of the Board of Trade, met the miners on 21 April he too suggested that they should try district negotiations, but his advice was rejected. The Federation asked the Government to convene a national conference between the two parties. On 29 April Asquith presided over a joint meeting at which no agreement was reached and decided that the dispute should be settled by the conciliation boards and sliding scale committees in the various districts. The decisions were to be made within a week and the advance was to date from 5 May.

The miners' policy of securing a national agreement had been defeated, and nowhere was the full 20 per cent. on earnings conceded. Scotland gained $18\frac{1}{2}$ per cent. on the basic rate, South Wales, $17\frac{1}{2}$ per cent., and Northumberland and Durham, 15 per cent. The Federated Area obtained more than any other district. It was awarded $15\frac{1}{2}$ per cent. which was to be calculated on existing wages and was to be merged into any future advances.[3] Frank Hall thought that the war bonus was a valuable concession because it left existing agreements with the employers intact and would not be taken away until there was a corresponding fall in the cost of living. 'When he saw how the prices of coal advanced by as much as 9s. and 14s. per ton for the best and inferior qualities, he was convinced that they had a right to share these profits—profits which had been taken in the name of patriotism.'[4] The Council passed a resolution complimenting the miners' representatives 'upon the very satisfactory result attained'.[5]

In December, 1915, the miners of the Federated Area obtained an increase of 5 per cent. on the 1911 standard making their wages 15 per cent. above the standard, excluding the war bonus, and 32·05 per cent. above the standard including the war bonus. In March, 1916, a further 5 per cent. was granted which, with the war bonus, brought wages to 37·05 per cent. above the 1911 standard. An increase of $3\frac{1}{3}$ per cent. in June, 1916, raised the level to 40·38 per cent. above the standard. In February, 1917, the war bonus, which then amounted to 13·8 per cent.

[1] M.F.G.B. 17 March, 1915; Labour Gazette.
[2] D.M.A. 10 April, 1915.   [3] Labour Gazette.
[4] Derbyshire Times, 19 June, 1915.   [5] D.M.A. 29 May, 1915.

on current wages, was increased to 18 per cent., making wages 45·5 per cent. above the standard.[1]

No further attempt to put forward a national wage claim was made until after the advent of State control of the mines in 1917, when it could no longer be argued that the matter was one for district negotiations. On 9 June the Council of the Derbyshire Miners' Association discussed the forthcoming claim, which appeared on the agenda for the annual conference of the M.F.G.B., and instructed its delegates to advise the Federation to ask for an advance of 20 per cent.[2] However, when the conference assembled at Glasgow in the following month, the Executive was instructed 'to formulate a minimum demand for a general increase of 25 per cent. on present wages for the whole Federation to meet the high cost of living'.[3] The Coal Controller conceded the principle of a further war bonus to help meet the rise in food prices which were then 102 per cent. higher than at the outbreak of war, but proposed a flat-rate increase of 1s. 3d. a day instead of a percentage increase. A M.F.G.B. special conference on 26 September agreed to accept a flat-rate increase but rejected the offer of 1s. 3d.[4] Eventually it was settled that the increase should be 1s. 6d. a day for all colliery workers of 16 and over, and 9d. a day for those under 16.[5] The agreement, which favoured the lower-paid workers, was the first instance of a flat-rate increase for all grades over all districts.

In June, 1918, the M.F.G.B. decided to ask for another 1s. 6d. a day flat-rate addition to the so-called 'war-wage'.[6] The Coal Controller offered 6d., which the Federation rejected. After the intervention of the Prime Minister the miners' claim was conceded in return for an agreement on Joint Pit Committees which were to be established at all collieries and 'charged with the duty of decreasing voluntary absenteeism and increasing output'. In the same year the M.F.G.B. decided to continue the conciliation agreement for the duration of the war and for six months afterwards. Miners' wages in the Federated Area were then 45·5 per cent. higher than in December, 1911, with the addition of flat-rate increases amounting to 3s. a day.[7]

Other grades of colliery workers shared in the advances won by the miners. By their pre-war agreements the wages of the enginemen and firemen followed the percentage movements of miners' wages automatically. In 1916 the Nottinghamshire Miners' Association successfully negotiated an agreement for improved wage rates for all surfacemen, with the exception of banksmen (i.e. for tradesmen and general labourers). When Derbyshire claimed the same rates the employers refused to pay the increases and the dispute was eventually submitted

[1] *Labour Gazette.*   [2] *D.M.A.* 9 June, 1917.   [3] *M.F.G.B.* 24 July, 1917.
[4] *Ibid.* 26 September, 1917; *D.M.A.* 15 September, 1917.
[5] *Labour Gazette.*   [6] *M.F.G.B.* 5 June, 1918.   [7] *Labour Gazette.*

to arbitration. In March, 1917, the award of W. W. McKenzie, of the Chief Industrial Commissioner's department, gave daily rates ranging from 5s. 6d. to 4s. 2d. to the various grades and was considered by the union to be very satisfactory.[1] Frank Hall claimed 'that the new price list was unique, and that it would meet the case of every man employed in a colliery shop'.[2] A difference of opinion with the coal-owners about the interpretation of the award led to a strike ballot being taken. There were 28,127 votes in favour of a strike and only 2,072 against, but after further negotiations the matter was amicably settled.[3]

The changes in the average earnings per shift for the various classes of colliery workmen in Derbyshire and Nottinghamshire during the war years were as follows:[4]

Class of Workmen	Average Earnings per shift		Percentage increase
	June 1914 s. d.	November 1918 s. d.	
*Underground (Adults)**			
1. Piece work coal getters	9 10·62	17 7·33	78·2
2. Coal getters on day wage	6 10·34	13 8·73	100·1
3. Putters, fillers, hauliers, and trammers	6 9·39	12 8·52	87·4
4. Timbermen, stonemen, brushers and rippers	7 0·27	13 2·94	88·6
5. Deputies, firemen and examiners	8 0·00	15 5·05	89·8
6. Other underground labour	5 8·12	10 10·08	91·0
*Surface (Adults)**			
7. Winding enginemen	8 2·48	14 5·59	76·3
8. Enginemen other than winding enginemen	5 7·31	11 1·43	98·2
9. Stokers and boilermen	5 1·43	10 10·09	111·8
10. Pithead men	5 4·36	10 5·08	94·3
11. Persons on and about screens	4 10·20	9 11·00	104·5
12. Tradesmen, i.e. mechanics, joiners, blacksmiths and other skilled workmen	5 11·10	11 1·40	89·0
13. All other surface labour not included in Forms 7, 8, 9, 10, 11 and 12	4 6·12	8 4·73	86·1
Youths and Boys			
14. Underground	3 6·67	7 4·17	106·6
15. Surface	2 5·82	5 3·32	112·3

* Adults are taken as being over 21 years of age, except in special cases where the rate for adults is applicable to a lower age.

[1] D.M.A. 3 March, 1917; Derbyshire Times, 10 March, 1917.
[2] Derbyshire Times, 17 March, 1917.
[3] Ibid. 18 June, 21 July, 1917; D.M.A. 23 June, 1917.
[4] Coal Industry Commission, 1919, III, (Cmd. 361), Appendix 49, p. 99.

The general effect of the flat-rate increases was to narrow the differentials between the skilled and the unskilled workers. For no grade did the increase in wages keep pace with the increased cost of living. By November, 1918, the average retail prices of food had risen by 133 per cent. and the cost of living, as computed by the Ministry of Labour, by 125 per cent.

The Derbyshire miners played an active part in the general agitation against profiteering and high prices which became particularly bitter in 1917 when the retail prices of food had more than doubled.

'While trade unions had been making sacrifices and helping all they could with recruiting,' said Frank Hall, 'in many cases against their own feelings, because they did not believe in war, what had the other people been doing? Food prices had gone up by leaps and bounds, and the Government, in their attempt to control and regulate, had always been too late.'[1]

Several protests were made by the Council against excessive profits, high prices and the 50 per cent. increase in railway fares.[2] On 18 August, 1917, it was resolved:

That mass meetings be arranged at different centres in the county to lay down a definite policy of protest against the high cost of foodstuffs, believing that the inflated prices now being charged are altogether unjustified and the real cause of much industrial unrest.[3]

IV

The recruitment of miners for the armed forces and its effects upon production continued to be as great a problem throughout the war as the spiral of prices and wages. In November, 1915, Lord Derby launched his scheme whereby miners who offered themselves as recruits would only be accepted on condition that they went back to work in the mines until they were called upon. 'They will be given armlets,' stated a notice posted at the pit-head of every colliery, 'to show that they are willing to obey the call and do whatever will most help their country.'[4] The coalfields were divided into twenty-three recruiting districts, each with a tribunal to advise the recruiting officer. The tribunals consisted of an inspector of mines and two assessors, one representing the employers and one the workmen. Their task was to ascertain which men could be spared from the pits.

After the Government had introduced a Bill, on 5 January, 1916,

---

[1] *Derbyshire Times*, 28 July, 1917.
[2] *D.M.A.* 16 December, 1916; 3 February, 28 April, 1917.
[3] *Ibid.* 18 August, 1917. [4] Quoted in Redmayne, *op. cit.* p. 50

imposing compulsory military service on single men, the Council of the Derbyshire Miners' Association passed a resolution condemning it.[1] The matter was later referred to the lodges which returned 12,283 votes for the Bill, and 26,819 against. Eventually it was resolved:

That this meeting believes that the Military Service Act (1916) is unnecessary and contains a most dangerous principle, viz. compulsion, but believes further opposition of an active character would be misunderstood. We hereby instruct the Executive Committee of the Miners' Federation to keep in touch with its operation and use every endeavour to prevent the principle of compulsion being extended to our workshops, factories, mines, etc.[2]

Under the new Act the local tribunals established under the Derby scheme became Colliery Recruiting Courts.

By July, 1916, 20,000 of the 95,870 miners employed in Nottinghamshire and Derbyshire at the beginning of the war had enlisted voluntarily.[3] But the call for more men for the armed forces was insistent and during 1917 the Government decided to release large numbers from the mines. The co-operation of the M.F.G.B. was sought and there were many discussions among the miners and between their leaders and the representatives of the Government to ensure that there would be a minimum of friction. The Council of the Derbyshire Miners' Association supported the Federation's view that the 'combing-out' procedure should apply to men who had entered the industry since August, 1914, and not August, 1915, as the Government proposed. The officials were instructed 'to obtain some equitable arrangement' whereby consideration would be given to 'the percentage of men already gone from collieries, and the number of lads already gone from . . . families'. The Council also protested, on the ground of safety, against inexperienced men being sent into the pits as substitutes for those who joined the armed forces.[4] Eventually it was agreed that each colliery should have an enlistment quota which would be brought up to the average of the district in which the colliery was situated. The men were to be selected by ballot but the Recruiting Courts, in deciding a man's case, were to have due regard to his family circumstances. Under this scheme 20,000 men were to be enlisted by 9 May, 1917, and another batch of equal number by the end of July.

Early in 1918 the M.F.G.B. had to consider the Government's decision to release another 50,000 men from the mines. A circular letter, signed by Frank Hall, raised the following questions:

(1) Are we to accept the invitation of Sir Auckland Geddes and form joint boards and pit committees unconditionally?

[1] *D.M.A.* 8 January, 1916.
[2] *Ibid.* 5 February, 1916.
[3] *Derbyshire Times,* 22 July, 1916.
[4] *D.M.A.* 16 April, 1917.

(2) If we refuse is it desirable to hand the men over to the military to be drawn upon *ad libitum*?

(3) As a condition in taking part are we to ask for certain terms and conditions? (*a*) Levy on riches to pay for the war? (*b*) Settlement by negotiations on the basis of the Labour Party's war aims—or Mr. Lloyd George's and Mr. Wilson's? (*c*) That representatives of Labour be present and take part in the peace settlement?[1]

A ballot showed that members of the Association were against the withdrawal of a further 50,000 men from the mines but they favoured the use of the Federation machinery if the required number had to be found.[2] Nationally the voting went in the same direction as in Derbyshire but the Government decided to continue with its project. In Derbyshire the men were selected by a ballot organized by the Association at its headquarters.[3]

After the German advance at the end of March a request was made by Sir Auckland Geddes, the Minister of National Service, for yet another 50,000 men from the mines. At the same time France asked for more coal owing to the fall in output from her Pas de Calais mines. It was therefore decided to withdraw only 25,000 men from the mines and also to return 25,000 miners of low medical category from the army. After discussions between the Coal Controller and representatives of the M.F.G.B. it was agreed that further men should be released from the Forces and by the time of the Armistice miners were returning to the pits in increasing numbers.[4]

Absenteeism continued to be a major problem throughout the war, despite constant exhortations from the politicians and trade union leaders. As early as October, 1915, representatives of the Derbyshire and Nottinghamshire miners' associations met representatives of the Coal-Owners' Association at Derby to discuss the question. The union representatives contended that if committees were set up at collieries or a county committee were appointed, matters other than absenteeism should also be discussed in considering ways of increasing output. This was not accepted by the employers and the meeting broke up without reaching any decision.[5] A conference between the Executive Committee of the Mining Association of Great Britain and the M.F.G.B., convened by the Coalmining Organization Committee, recommended on 16 May, 1916, that the question of absenteeism should be referred to the districts 'on the distinct understanding that Committees will at once be set up

---

[1] *D.M.A.* 19 January, 1918; *Derbyshire Times*, 2 February, 1918.
[2] *Ibid.* 18 March, 1918.   [3] *Ibid.* 27 March, 1918.
[4] Redmayne, *op. cit.* p. 196.
[5] *D.M.A.* 11 December, 1915. Cf. *Coal Industry Commission*, 1919, II (Cmd. 360), Evidence of G. D. H. Cole, QQ. 26,001–2.

in each district to devise and put into operation effective machinery to secure the attendance of all workmen employed to the fullest possible extent and to enquire into the circumstances of workmen employed at the mines not being provided with work when they presented themselves at the mine'. After receiving a letter from Ashton, the Secretary of the M.F.G.B, the Council of the Derbyshire Miners' Association decided to send the Executive Committee to meet the coal-owners' representatives to see whether agreement could now be reached under the nationally accepted terms of reference.[1] The meeting was held at Nottingham on 1 June when it was agreed that committees should be set up at every colliery to deal with workmen who were habitual absentees. Difficulties which could not be settled by local committees were to be referred to a county committee.[2]

The committees do not appear to have been very successful. At the end of July, 1916, A. T. H. Barnes, managing director of the Grassmoor Colliery Company, told the Chesterfield Colliery Recruiting Court that at one pit alone 634 shifts had been lost in two weeks. 'They won't work,' he said. 'I should like to fine them as I used to do. They attended a lot better then.'[3] In August, 1916, the Executive Committee of the Association deprecated 'the attitude of men in certain districts' towards the absentee committees and re-affirmed its belief 'that good work can be done in getting the better attendance . . . of those men who are at present not doing their best'.[4] A week later, however, the Council decided that the committees should be suspended until agreement could be reached with the coal-owners on rules of procedure.[5] The rules eventually laid down the methods of dealing with offenders. Local committees were empowered to impose fines up to 5s. The County Committee, which dealt with more serious cases, could institute legal proceedings and, for men of military age, recommend the withdrawal of exemption certificates.[6] In April, 1917, when the Government decided to release 20,000 men from the mines, the Council of the Derbyshire Miners' Association registered its protest by again suspending the absentee committees and demanding that all committee fees paid by the union should be refunded by the Government on the ground that the work done by the committees had been 'in the interests of the nation'.[7]

The re-establishment of absentee committees became necessary in June, 1918, in order to fulfil the terms of the agreement with the Coal Controller when the second flat-rate increase of 1s. 6d. a day was conceded.[8] Nevertheless, the Council did not recommend their re-establish-

[1] D.M.A. 22 May, 1916.   [2] Ibid. 9 June, 1916.
[3] Derbyshire Times, 29 July, 1916.   [4] D.M.A. 12 August, 1916.
[5] Ibid. 19 August, 1916.   [6] Ibid. 24 August, 1916.
[7] Ibid. 14 April, 1917.   [8] See above, p. 528.

ment 'where there is any amount of unnecessary Sunday work being done underground or where there are constant breaches of the Eight Hours' Act'.[1]

V

There were few changes in the officers of the Association during the war years. In February, 1917, while attending the Labour Party Conference at Manchester, James Martin had a sudden attack of colic and pleurisy.[2] He was well enough to preside at the next Council meeting on 3 March but his health continued to be poor. The death of his wife in the following November led Martin, then aged 67, to announce that he was relinquishing many of his official and public appointments, including the presidency of the Derbyshire Miners' Association which he had held for over ten years.[3] At a Council meeting on 6 April, 1918, he was presented with a gold watch and an illuminated address in recognition of his long and faithful service.[4] 'You have left behind a record of work seldom equalled', ran the address. 'Your efforts on behalf of the principles of liberty and freedom, which you hold so dear, have yielded much fruit, and in your retirement you have much to give you satisfaction and peace of mind.'[5]

Martin was succeeded as President, in January, 1918, by William Sewell who had been Vice-President since 1907.[6] Sewell was born at Worksop in 1852 and came into Derbyshire in 1861 to work for J. and G. Wells, Ltd., at their Renishaw Park and Holbrook collieries. At the age of 66 he was still working at the coal face. He had been a member of the Eckington lodge of the South Yorkshire and North Derbyshire Miners' Association in the 'seventies and had played a prominent part in the Derbyshire Miners' Association, helping to form the Holbrook lodge and serving as a delegate to the Council and a member of the Executive Committee for nearly thirty years. Sewell had also been an active member of the Derby and Midland Fatal Accident Society and had given evidence before the Royal Commission on Accidents in Mines. He had been a member of the Eckington parish council since its inception in 1894 and had been four times its chairman. He was a member of the Eckington Burial Board and of the Old-Age Pensions Committee. His name had been repeatedly put forward for the position of county magistrate but he was never selected.[7]

Sewell was succeeded as Vice-President by John Spencer, a check-weighman at the Warsop Main Colliery, but it was not long before

[1] D.M.A. 29 July, 1918. [2] Ibid. 3 February, 1917.
[3] Ibid. 10 November, 1917. [4] Ibid. 6 April, 1918. [5] D.M.A. 13 April, 1918.
[6] Ibid. 5 January, 1918. [7] Derbyshire Times, 12 January, 1918.

Spencer became a full-time official. It will be remembered that no new official was appointed when Harvey died in 1914. Throughout the war Frank Lee had combined the duties of Treasurer and Compensation Agent but in July, 1918, the Executive Committee recommended the appointment of another full-time official to act as Treasurer.[1] In the following October Spencer was elected General Treasurer and Lee was left with the duties of Compensation Agent.[2] The change was probably made to relieve Lee of some of his work so that he would have more time for political activities.[3] The new Vice-President from 1 January, 1919, was Enoch Overton, a Bolsover checkweighman.[4]

John Spencer was born in Norfolk and started work on the land when he was about 8. He came to Derbyshire twelve years later to work at the Markham Colliery, subsequently moving to Glapwell, Pleasley and Warsop. He helped to sink the Warsop Main Colliery and formed there a branch of the Nottinghamshire Miners' Association, which was eventually transferred to the Derbyshire Miners' Association. Spencer was elected checkweighman and delegate to the Council. As General Treasurer of the Association he was to play a prominent part, after the war, in local government. He became a member of the county council and was elected an alderman in 1931. He also became a magistrate for the borough of Chesterfield in 1929 and served on the Town Council from 1933-5. For a long period he was a co-opted member of Chesterfield Education Committee and a governor of several schools in the district.[5]

New rules for the government of the Association came into force on 16 February, 1916. There were no fundamental changes. The qualifying number of members in a lodge for sending a delegate to the Council was raised from twenty to fifty. Voting at Council meetings was to be by show of hands but on matters of importance a card vote could be taken, each delegate having one vote for every fifty members of his lodge. A central audit of lodge accounts was instituted. The miminum amount to be kept in the general fund was raised from £5,000 to £10,000. 'Market men' (i.e. men who work at the coal face but have no fixed task and await instructions at the beginning of each shift) who failed to secure work on six or more consecutive working days were allowed to claim 'out of work' payments. The qualifying period for old-age pensions was raised from twelve to fifteen years. The scales of payments to lodge secretaries and treasurers were revised. The minimum and maximum for secretaries rose from 6s. 6d. and 125s. 6d. a quarter to 9s. 9d. and 188s. 3d., and for treasurers, from 4s. 6d. and 83s. 6d. to 6s. 9d. and 125s. 3d. The current percentages which applied to wages were

---

[1] *D.M.A.* 29 July, 1918.   [2] *Ibid.* 12 October, 1918.   [3] See below, p. 546.
[4] *D.M.A.* 7 December, 1918.   [5] *Derbyshire Times*, 5 February, 1943.

added to these scales. The payment made to members of lodge committees for attendance was raised from 1s. a meeting to 1s. 6d. Perhaps the most important change of all was a new rule which laid down that two-thirds of the members must register a vote by ballot in favour of a general strike or lock-out before it was entered upon or continued.[1]

The membership of the union, which stood at 42,403 at the end of 1914, fell to 33,094 in 1915, largely as a result of recruitment to the armed forces. Thereafter, in common with the rest of the trade union movement, the Association enjoyed a substantial increase in membership, the numbers rising to 43,000 in 1916, 51,444 in 1917, and 52,801 in 1918. The financial reserves rose steadily from £311,926 in 1914 to £454,022 in 1918. The Association continued its policy of distributing its investments between the banks and municipal authorities but in December, 1917, in a belated response to the war-time savings appeals, it decided to invest in Exchequer bonds.[2] By the end of 1918 the union had £50,000 invested in Government securities at $3\frac{1}{2}$ per cent., £290,574 in municipal securities at $5\frac{1}{2}$ per cent., and £105,173 in the banks.

The Association's relations with other unions were greatly influenced by the formation of the Triple Alliance and the impetus which it gave to industrial unionism. The idea had been mooted at the annual conference of the M.F.G.B. in 1913 when the Executive Committee was instructed to 'approach the Executive Committees of other big Trade Unions with a view to co-operative action and the support of each others' demands'.[3] After protracted negotiations the M.F.G.B., the National Union of Railwaymen and the National Transport Workers' Federation reached a tentative agreement for joint action and the first full meeting was held in April, 1916. Another meeting was held in the following December and in June, 1917, the constitution of the Triple Industrial Alliance was formally ratified.

In Derbyshire a meeting was held at Chesterfield on 27 August, 1916, to celebrate the formation of the alliance. The speakers were J. Holmes, a railwayman's leader from Doncaster; Ernest Bevin, who was then the dockers' leader, from Bristol; and Frank Hall.

'The new alliance brought together no fewer than one and a half million workers of this country,' said Hall. 'That was a powerful combination if they cared to put into operation the forces at their command. . . . When approached by Mr. Lloyd George the trades unions agreed to surrender certain privileges, rules and regulations which had taken a century to build up. . . . Had everybody in this country played the same game? (Cries of "No!") The trade unionists ought to have struck their bargain at that time.'[4]

[1] *Rules of the Derbyshire Miners' Association*, 16 February, 1916.
[2] *D.M.A.* 8 December, 1917.   [3] *M.F.G.B.* 9 October, 1913.
[4] *Derbyshire Times*, 2 September, 1916.

At another meeting at Creswell, in July, 1917, he warmly denounced profiteers: 'The conscientious objectors were put in prison but those people who were ten thousand times worse went scot-free.'[1]

The Triple Alliance, with its policy of industrial unionism, had come into conflict with the craft unions such as the Associated Society of Locomotive Engineers and Firemen and the winding enginemen's unions.

'The Enginemen's Union,' said Hall, 'had "downed" a resolution at the forthcoming Trades Union Congress to prevent the Federation from organizing all men who worked in and about the pits. Who had been getting the benefits for the men in and about the pits ? Had there been a single advance in the miners' wages which had not been shared by all the workers in and about their pits ?'[2]

The friction which developed at the national level was reflected in Derbyshire and Nottinghamshire by a disagreement between the miners' associations and the Enginemen's and Firemen's Union. The miners demanded that only winding enginemen should be organized by the enginemen's union but George Annable, who had succeeded Rowarth as secretary, would not agree to this limitation on the activities of his union. After much altercation a working agreement between the three unions was concluded in August, 1918.[3]

Attempts were also made to organize the coke oven and by-product workers. The difficulty with them, as with the enginemen, was that they extended into other industries and the Federation was not prepared to accept as a constituent body any union with members in various industries. In June, 1917, Frank Hall told a meeting of coke oven and by-product workers at Chesterfield: 'By some it was said they had no right to cater for that class of workmen . . . but the development of the coke trade and by-product works was such that the Miners' Federation of Great Britain . . . felt it absolutely necessary that they should organize these men for the sake of themselves and for the sake of the industry as a whole.'[4] Both the winding enginemen and the by-product workers were eventually brought into the M.F.G.B. in special groups but inter-union rivalries were to continue to cause difficulties for many years to come.

Two other groups of colliery workers who received the attention of the miners' unions during the war were the clerks and the deputies. On 13 October, 1917, the Council of the Derbyshire Miners' Association decided to accept colliery clerks as members.[5] In 1916 the National Association of Colliery Deputies discussed the desirability of reaching

[1] *Derbyshire Times*, 28 July, 1917.   [2] *Ibid.*   [3] *D.M.A.* 29 August, 1918.
[4] *Derbyshire Times*, 9 June, 1917.   [5] *D.M.A.* 13 October, 1917.

a working agreement with the Derbyshire Miners' Association. At the annual meeting of secretaries at Derby in November, Gill, the deputies' general secretary, stated that such an agreement would mean that 'there would be no disorganized deputies' and 'there would be no tyranny by deputies towards the miners in order to curry favour with the management'.[1] At a meeting of deputies at Chesterfield in the following month, it was reported that deputies at a Nottinghamshire colliery had been granted an increase in wages on condition that they seceded from their union.[2] There were lengthy negotiations between the Deputies' Association and the Derbyshire Miners' Association but it was not until December, 1918, that the Council gave its approval to the proposed agreement.[3]

Special problems arose in Derbyshire in connection with the lead-miners. The industry, which was of great antiquity but had become uneconomic in the early nineteenth century in the face of Spanish competition, enjoyed a revival of prosperity during the war years. The men employed at the Mill Close lead mine in Darley Dale, and at the Ashover lead-mines, were allowed to join the Association[4] and soon became involved in disputes with their employers. At Mill Close the men objected to a day wage being substituted for piece-work. At Ashover the employers were opposed to their men joining the Association, arguing that they should be members of the National Union of General Workers.[5] There was much unrest among the lead-miners for the remainder of the war and in the years immediately following the armistice. In connection with a dispute at the Mill Close mine the Association asked the Minister of Munitions to intervene. When the employers refused to accept the arbitration award which followed, the Association informed the Coal Controller that it would be necessary to take a strike ballot throughout the coalfield unless a satisfactory settlement was reached.[6] A further intervention of the Minister of Munitions eventually ended the dispute.[7]

VI

Most sections of the community found their usual way of life modified in some degree by the conditions of the war years. The miners were no exception. In common with other workers in the heavy industries they were accustomed to substantial meals and there were complaints about

[1] *Derbyshire Times*, 25 November, 1916.   [2] *Ibid.* 9 December, 1916.
[3] *D.M.A.* 7 December, 1918.   [4] *Ibid.* 19 July, 1917,
[5] *Ibid.* 18 August, 1917; 13 April, 1918; *Derbyshire Times*, 15 September, 1917, 9 March, 1918.
[6] *D.M.A.* 14 September, 1918.   [7] *Ibid.* 24 September, 1918.

the high prices and maldistribution of food.[1] In 1917, when it was proposed that the Government should remedy the shortage of beer, which was said to be having a disastrous effect upon the morale of the workers, there was opposition from the temperance movement. 'Do the miners of Chesterfield and district wish Mr. Kenyon to vote against them having their pint or quart of beer at night after a hard day's toil?' asked one miner. 'Is that what they sent him to Parliament for?'[2] Other grievances were the high prices of pit clothes and the scarcity and high price of tools.[3] Many miners were paying income tax for the first time and felt that it was unjust, that it led to absenteeism, and that the allowances, including those for tools and clothing, were inadequate.[4] There were also demands that the Government old-age pension should be increased to meet the higher cost of living, although a proposal to increase the Association's old-age pensions was rejected.[5] The introduction of the Daylight Saving Act aroused a storm of protest, the miners arguing that they had to get up at 'an unearthly hour in the night'. A meeting of a thousand miners at Mansfield, in April, 1917, discussed the question of the early morning trains and decided to strike if they were not timed to run an hour later.[6] Sunday working, which continued to increase, was described by the Alfreton miners as 'a disgrace to the district'. The working of the stalls on a Sunday was condemned as being 'wholly inexcusable' and all workmen were requested 'to refrain from such work on the Sabbath day as is not absolutely necessary'.[7]

The growing employment of women during the war aroused some misgivings. No women had been employed at Derbyshire collieries, either above or below ground, in the nineteenth century, and the absence of other employment, which is a general feature of colliery districts,[8] meant that most married women stayed in the home. The Derbyshire Miners' Association had taken the lead in demanding an amendment to the Coal Mines Bill of 1911 prohibiting the employment of all women on pit banks but, with the aid of the women suffragists, the proposal had been defeated. As early as 1908 Haslam would quite happily have left to their chosen fate the women who chained themselves to the grille in the House of Commons gallery.[9] In 1911 Robert Smillie remarked: 'University women carry out an agitation and try to prove how nice and

[1] *D.M.A.* 13 October, 1917; 25 May, 26 October, 1918; *Derbyshire Times*, 19 January, 1918.
[2] *Derbyshire Times*, 28 July, 1917.   [3] *D.M.A.* 16 September, 1918.
[4] *Ibid.* 11 November, 1916; 15 September, 8 December, 1917.
[5] *Ibid.* 3 March, 13 October, 1917.
[6] *Ibid.* 31 March, 1917; *Derbyshire Times*, 5 and 19 May, 1917.
[7] *Derbyshire Times*, 15 September, 1917.
[8] Cf. M. P. Fogarty, *Prospects of the Industrial Areas of Great Britain*, (London), 1945, pp. 321, 455–6.   [9] *Derbyshire Times*, 7 November, 1908.

comfortable the work is, but they do not have to earn their livelihood on the pit bank.' Harvey said:

It is surprising to me that in this twentieth century when training for home life is said to be so essential, that we should have factors at work from the cultured part of life trying to keep down the wives and daughters of the workers. . . . I am proud to say . . . that there are counties in England and Wales where there is no such thing as women employed on the pit banks. We long ago believed that was not the place for women. The place for women is the home, in order to make the home happy.[1]

The introduction of women into the engine house, stores and lamp cabin at the Waleswood Colliery in 1916 caused great consternation. The situation was aggravated by the fact that one of the women was doing work formerly done by a disabled man who had been put to heavier work which proved too much for him. A strike was threatened and the women were withdrawn.[2]

Despite their preoccupation with industrial problems arising from the war the miners did not forget the men who were serving in the armed forces. Many colliery companies organized contributory schemes for the financial assistance of the families of soldiers. By the end of 1916 the miners, office staffs and surface workers of the Derbyshire collieries had contributed £124,393. The employers' contributions amounted to £27,286 together with such concessions as free coal and reductions in rent.[3] The miners of Derbyshire and Nottinghamshire also supported the scheme for the provision of motor ambulances launched by Dennis Bayley (afterwards Sir Dennis Reddett Bayley), son of Thomas Bayley, the late Member of Parliament for Chesterfield. The owners agreed to contribute £1 for every 1,000 tons of 1914 output, and the miners sixpence a week for twenty weeks. This joint effort produced £35,000 which provided fifty motor ambulances, four touring cars, three lorries, seven motor-cycles and a repair lorry. The movement spread to other districts and soon the whole mining industry was equipping the British Red Cross Society and the St. John Ambulance Association with vehicles, the total raised being about £500,000.[4]

In 1915 the Derbyshire Miners' Association began to consider plans for the building of a new convalescent home on the sea front at Skegness. Between 1905 and 1914 the subscriptions had increased from £408 to

---

[1] *M.F.G.B.* 3 October, 1911.
[2] *D.M.A.* 4 March, 1 and 29 April, 22 May, 1916; *Derbyshire Times,* 6 May, 1916.
[3] *Derbyshire Times,* 24 March, 1917.
[4] *D.M.A.* 24 July, 21 August, 18 September, 1915; *Derbyshire Times,* 31 July, 16 October, 30 October, 1915; J. R. Raynes, *Coal and Its Conflicts,* (London), 1928, p. 148.

£840 and the number of patients had risen from 93 to 479. The existing home was already inadequate and the needs of miners returning from the trenches at the end of the war were likely to make it more so. Moreover, the lease on the buildings was shortly due to expire. A site was offered by Sir Charles Seely, the Tibshelf coal-owner, who with his brothers J. E. B. Seely[1] and F. E. Seely, agreed to refund half of the purchase price which was £720.[2] In January, 1916, the Council granted a loan at an interest of $2\frac{1}{2}$ per cent. to the Convalescent Home Committee to enable it to buy the land.[3] Plans for a new building at an estimated cost of £10,000 had been prepared by Percy Houfton and in July, 1916, the Council resolved: 'That such amount of money as would be required by the Derbyshire Miners' Convalescent Home Committee be granted at the rate of $2\frac{1}{2}$ per cent. per annum.'[4] It was decided to begin work at the end of the war and, in the meantime, a building fund was started. By May, 1918, it amounted to £1,633.[5]

The miners' keen interest in the safety of mines was given a stimulus in 1915 when George Blythe gave a number of lectures on life-saving at various centres in the county under the auspices of the Association.[6] He alleged that the instructor at the Mansfield Rescue Station had never worked in a mine, that only one of the permanent staff employed there had practical mining experience, and that the breathing apparatus kept at the station was faulty. At Clowne these statements led to the adoption of a lengthy resolution calling upon the Home Secretary to order a full inquiry.[7] Safety lamps were also much discussed during the war years. In August, 1914, the Council gave permission to the Glapwell miners to take a strike ballot because they thought their lamps inadequate.[8] In February, 1916, there was a general complaint about the poor light given by the new double gauze lamps required by the Home Office and the officials were instructed to bring the matter before the Home Secretary and the Chief Inspector of Mines.[9] In the lamp controversy there had been a conflict between safety requirements and economic considerations.[10] In the agitation against the retention of coal in the workings, which developed in 1917, the miner had the best of both worlds. The practice was described by the Council as 'a positive danger and a loss of national wealth' and the M.F.G.B. Executive was requested

---

[1] Born 1868; educated at Harrow and Trinity College, Cambridge; served with Imperial Yeomanry, 1900–1; M.P. 1900; under-secretary for the colonies, 1908–10, for war, 1911; secretary for war, 1912–14; distinguished service in the European War; under-secretary for munitions, 1918, for air, 1919. Created Lord Mottistone, 1933.

[2] *Derbyshire Times*, 1 January, 1916.

[3] *D.M.A.* 8 January, 1916.   [4] *Ibid.* 22 July, 1916.

[5] *Derbyshire Times*, 1 January, 1916; 5 May, 1917; 1 June, 1918.

[6] *D.M.A.* 23 January, 1915.

[7] *Derbyshire Times*, 27 February, 1915.   [8] *D.M.A.* 22 August, 1914.

[9] *Ibid.* 5 February, 1916.   [10] See Chapter IX, p. 374.

to demand the 'removal of forks, screens, and riddles used for the filling of coal, and arrange for the work to be done with shovels'.[1]

It was during the war years that the Workers' Educational Association was able to capture the interest of the Derbyshire miners by discussing problems of post-war reconstruction. As early as 1916 the W.E.A. had secured the permission of the Derbyshire Miners' Association to get in touch with various lodges, and, if possible, establish tutorial classes. In June of that year a trade union conference in the Derbyshire miners' council room was organized by the Chesterfield branch of the W.E.A. Barnet Kenyon, James Martin and representatives of other trade unions assembled to hear G. D. H. Cole speak on 'Trade Union Problems after the War'. He told them:

If labour was to get back all the sacrifices it had made in the national interest there would have to be a better spirit of unity. . . . Demobilization must be done gradually so that every man had his full civil rights back, and labour must safeguard this by insisting that the men kept with the colours should not be used against the industrial movement.[2]

In 1917 there was another W.E.A. conference in Chesterfield to discuss the Fisher Education Bill. It was addressed by J. M. MacTavish, the general secretary of the W.E.A., and W. V. Pearson, a Sheffield clergyman. Barnet Kenyon presided and three other miners' leaders, Martin, Sewell and Hall, were present.[3] In June, 1917, the Association appointed as delegate to the W.E.A. Samuel Sales, who was to play a prominent part in the affairs of the union during the post-war period.[4]

VII

The electoral truce of the war years gave the Derbyshire Miners' Association an opportunity to consolidate its political position after the upheavals of 1913-14. During the early years of the war progress was made with the establishment of Labour electoral machinery in the constituencies. In North-East Derbyshire, on 15 August, 1914, a conference of 150 delegates from trade unions, trades councils, I.L.P. branches and co-operative societies, presided over by Frank Hall, agreed to form a divisional Labour Party. The miners' leaders occupied prominent positions in it. Enoch Overton was elected president; William Sewell a vice-president; and Frank Hall, treasurer. James Martin was chosen as prospective candidate.[5]

---

[1] *D.M.A.* 18 August, 1917.   [2] *Derbyshire Times*, 1 July, 1916.
[3] *Ibid.* 3 November, 1917; *D.M.A.* 13 October, 1917.
[4] *D.M.A.* 23 June, 1917.   [5] *Derbyshire Times*, 22 August, 1914.

Frank Hall and Frank Lee were also taking the lead in organizing a Labour Party in Mid-Derbyshire. Their activities were condemned by the Liberal-Labour supporters of J. G. Hancock. Thomas Spencer, a trustee of the Association, presided over a meeting at Alfreton which resolved: 'That we deprecate the action of Mr. F. Hall and Mr. F. Lee in coming into Mid-Derbyshire to inaugurate an institution which would be a breach of etiquette and a rebuff to the present M.P. for Mid-Derbyshire.'[1] Hancock, who had been told by the M.F.G.B. that his candidature would no longer be supported, told a meeting at Hucknall in February, 1915:

He had always been opposed to three-cornered fights and questioned whether any of them had been necessary. He knew of cases where the Liberals had assisted the Labour candidates, and they would have a free seat so long as they gave occasional reports. . . . He would say to the Nottinghamshire miners: 'Be masters in your own house, and manage your own business.'[2]

Throughout the war the Liberal-Labour M.P.s, Hancock and Kenyon, were active supporters of the national effort. Kenyon told a meeting of Primitive Methodists in October, 1914, that 'he would be in the trenches tomorrow if he had the chance'.[3] So adept did he become at exhorting people to fight, work and save that in 1916 he began a tour of the country, at the request of the Minister of Munitions, to speak to munition workers. By September, 1917, he had addressed well over 150,000 of them and had an impressive collection of inscribed mementos. His proudest possession was said to be a six-pound shell which was made by young women who had formerly been milliners.[4]

There were no by-elections in any of the Derbyshire mining constituencies during the war but by 1917 preparations were already being made for the redistribution of seats which was to accompany the Representation of the People Bill. The Boundary Commissioners' proposals for Derbyshire chiefly affected the Chesterfield, North-East and Mid-Derbyshire divisions, the principal change being a new division carved out of North-East Derbyshire, which was to be called the Bolsover division.[5] Objections to the scheme were heard at Derby on 13 July when the Derbyshire Miners' Association allied itself with the Chesterfield Corporation's proposals, which 'were better than those officially proposed and would make more compact constituencies'.[6] It was estimated that if the Commissioners' proposals were carried there would be 5,997 miners in the North-Eastern division, 14,889 in Chesterfield, and 12,009 in the Bolsover division. Under the Chesterfield proposals the mining vote was more equally divided with 10,000

[1] *Derbyshire Times*, 19 September, 1914.   [2] *Ibid.* 27 February, 1915.
[3] *Ibid.* 31 October, 1914.   [4] *Ibid.* 29 September, 1917.
[5] *Ibid.* 30 June, 1917.   [6] *D.M.A.* 30 June, 1917.

miners in the North-Eastern division, 9,000 in Chesterfield, and 13,000 in the Bolsover division.[1] The Commissioners eventually created eight divisions which they named Ashbourne, Belper, Bolsover, Chesterfield, Clay Cross, High Peak, Ilkeston and Shardlow.[2] The proposals of the Chesterfield Borough Council and the Derbyshire Miners' Association were substantially accepted. The Bolsover division was their suggested North-East Derbyshire division renamed and the Clay Cross division approximated to their proposals for a new constituency.[3] During the committee stage of the Bill the Ashbourne, Shardlow and Bolsover divisions lost their new names and became once again West Derbyshire South Derbyshire and North-East Derbyshire respectively.

Soon after the redistribution of seats the Derbyshire Miners' Association began to consider its plans for the next election. In December, 1917, Derbyshire was allotted two of the forty-three seats which the M.F.G.B. proposed to contest after the war but soon afterwards the number was increased to three.[4] It had been decided as early as October, 1915, when it was thought that the Association would be allowed only one seat, that North-East Derbyshire should be contested[5] but the resignation of James Martin at the end of 1917 meant that a new candidate had to be elected. On 9 February the Council accepted the Executive Committee's recommendation that the matter should be considered by a meeting of the Labour organizations in the division. It was also decided to contest the Chesterfield and Clay Cross divisions in the Labour interest and to refer to the lodges the question of the appointment of an election agent and organizer for the two divisions.[6]

Frank Hall, Frank Lee, James Martin and Henry Hicken were all proposed by the lodges as candidates for the Clay Cross division. When the nominations were considered by the Council on 2 March, 1918, Martin received no votes and Lee withdrew. Hicken, who was to make his mark as a full-time official after the war, asked for an assurance that in the event of his being elected as an M.P. he would be allowed to stand for election as a permanent official of the Association if a vacancy occurred. When the assurance was not forthcoming he also withdrew from the contest. Frank Hall was then unanimously adopted as the Association's nominee for the candidature of the Clay Cross division.[7] Nine nominations were received for the position of organizer and these were referred to the lodges.

Barnet Kenyon's equivocal position in the Chesterfield division continued to cause difficulties. As arrangements for the post-war elections

---

[1] *Derbyshire Times*, 21 July, 1917.　　　　　　　[2] *Ibid.* 6 October, 1917.
[3] *Ibid.*　　　　　　　　　　　[4] *D.M.A.* 8 December, 1917; 5 January, 1918.
[5] *Ibid.* 16 September, 14 October, 1916.
[6] *Ibid.* 9 February, 1918.　　　　　　　[7] *Ibid.* 2 March, 1918.

gathered momentum he gave all the outward and visible signs of adherence to the Labour Party. When the new Labour Party constitution was under consideration at conferences and local meetings he voted in favour of it. At war aims meetings and annual meetings of the Labour Party he gave his support to the official policies. He raised no objections when the Association decided that the Chesterfield division should be contested in the Labour interest. In March, 1918, when a deputation from the Chesterfield Trades and Labour Council met leaders of the Derbyshire Miners' Association to discuss the situation in the division he agreed that a Labour Party should be formed and that meetings should be held. Two months later, however, at a meeting called by the Trades and Labour Council, Kenyon stated that he would not enter 'a three-cornered fight'.[1] This was reported to the Executive Committee of the Association. When Kenyon was questioned by the Committee he stated that because of his advancing years and indifferent health he did not wish to contest the Chesterfield division, even as a Liberal-Labour candidate.[2] Soon afterwards he executed yet another remarkable *volte-face* and let it be known that he intended to stand as a Liberal-Labour candidate with Conservative support.

On 13 April the Council expressed its 'surprise and astonishment' at Kenyon's behaviour:

In doing this, the Council considers that Mr. Kenyon flagrantly flouts the decision of the members. . . . We believe such action on his part must seriously jeopardize the success of his colleagues. In the interests of unity and progress, we trust that he will disavow any such intention, and reconsider his position. After doing so, should he find that he cannot conscientiously stand as our nominee under the auspices of the Labour Party, we strongly urge upon him to again take up his position in the office as a fully paid official of the Association, believing that his ripe experience and knowledge would be of great service to the members generally.[3]

The *Derbyshire Times* suggested that Kenyon was being 'driven out of public life and . . . out of the Miners' Association' by the pacifist element 'because of the prominent part he has taken in the civic and national life of the country, in recruiting, and in his efforts to keep up the spirit and moral character of the nation during this great crisis in the history of the country'.[4] Kenyon himself wrote: 'I disagree with some of those who are taking an active part in the agitation against me today, and whose policy, if followed, would have placed us under Kaiserism for generations.'[5] These allegations were hotly denied by Frank Hall who pointed to the work done by the Association in recruiting. 'If Mr.

[1] *Derbyshire Times*, 4 May, 1918.   [2] *D.M.A.* 26 March, 1918.
[3] *Ibid.* 13 April, 1918.
[4] *Derbyshire Times*, 6 April, 1918.   [5] *Ibid.* 27 April, 1918.

S

Kenyon's policy of dividing the workers is the best,' he wrote, 'after the war conditions will tell. I am quite content to await developments; time is with us.'[1] The Chesterfield Trades and Labour Council censured Kenyon for 'preferring to run under the auspices of the Liberal and Conservative Associations, backed by the capitalist part of the constituency'.[2]

After this episode the Association decided not to nominate a candidate for the Chesterfield division but to concentrate its forces on the Clay Cross and North-East Derbyshire divisions.[3] The appointment of an organizer was deferred and eventually, on 22 June, it was decided that the available funds were not sufficient for the purpose.[4] On 27 April the Council considered the nominations for the candidature for the North-East Derbyshire division. They were Thomas Spencer, Henry Hicken, Enoch Overton, John Spencer and Frank Lee. Hicken and the two Spencers withdrew their nominations on the ground that they did not wish to sever their connection with the Association. Overton was not present. Lee then suggested that the nominations should be held in abeyance and the Executive Committee was asked to consider whether election to Parliament ought to entail exclusion from union elections.[5] Eventually, on the recommendation of the Executive Committee, it was decided that members who were elected to Parliament as nominees of the Association should be allowed to retain their membership and be eligible to occupy any position in the union. If elected as a permanent official, however, such a member would be expected to resign his parliamentary seat.[6] The nominations were then submitted to the lodges, Frank Lee receiving the largest number of votes.[7]

Meanwhile the work of organizing the constituencies was proceeding. On 6 April, 1918, a Labour Party was established in the Clay Cross division and Frank Hall was unanimously adopted as Labour candidate.[8] Frank Lee was adopted by the North-East Derbyshire Labour Party on 1 June, 1918.[9] A campaign was also conducted in the Belper division where, in a veiled reference to Hancock, Frank Hall urged the electors to form a divisional Labour Party and select a 'real Labour candidate'.[10] In August, 1918, F. B. Varley, President of the Nottinghamshire Miners' Association, was formerly adopted by the newly formed Belper Divisional Labour Party.[11] With an eye on the impending enfranchisement of women over 30, the Association sought the aid of a number of women speakers including Margaret Bondfield.[12] Sylvia Pankhurst, who assured the electors of North-East Derbyshire in

[1] *Derbyshire Times*, 4 May, 1918.
[2] *Ibid.* 27 April, 1918.
[3] *D.M.A.* 26 March, 12 October, 1918.
[4] *Ibid.* 27 April, 22 June, 1918.
[5] *Ibid.* 27 April, 1918.
[6] *Ibid.* 6 and 25 May, 1918.
[7] *Ibid.* 25 May, 1918.
[8] *Derbyshire Times*, 13 April, 1918.
[9] *Ibid.* 4 May, 8 June, 1918.
[10] *Ibid.* 1 June, 1918.
[11] *Ibid.* 17 August, 1918.
[12] *D.M.A.* 18 March, 1918.

September, 1918, that the war was 'absolutely a capitalist war—a sordid scramble to get control of the world's raw materials' was fined £50 by the Eckington magistrates under the Defence of the Realm Act.[1]

During 1917 and 1918 an organization known as the British Workers' League became increasingly prominent. Its policy was one of separating the trade unions from the Labour party by the formation of an 'independent' trade union party. In 1917 the Council of the Derbyshire Miners' Association repudiated the programme of the League and instructed its delegates to oppose it at the M.F.G.B. conference at Southport on 18–19 December.[2] A resolution in favour of the League's programme was submitted to the T.U.C. in 1918 by the National Sailors' and Firemen's Union. J. Havelock Wilson, appealing for support, wrote: 'The object of this resolution is to wrest from the pacifists, defeatists, and Bolshevists, who have too long been allowed to masquerade as Labour leaders, the undue influence which they have usurped by intrigue and trickery from their too confiding friends.'[3] Again the Derbyshire Miners' Association decide to oppose the League and to reject Wilson's proposal for a pledge against all dealings with 'the Hun' for six years after the war.[4] 'Anything like an economic boycott would mean preparation for another world struggle', said Frank Lee. 'If they had any faith in the principle of a League of Nations the peoples of Europe ought to come together as nations.'[5] The British Workers' League was not then strong enough to have any direct influence upon the trade union movement. Using more subversive tactics it was to re-appear as the advocate of 'non-political' trade unionism in the post-war years, causing much dissension in the Derbyshire and Nottinghamshire coalfields.[6]

[1] *Derbyshire Times*, 2 November, 1918.
[2] *D.M.A.* 8 December, 1917.
[3] *Derbyshire Times*, 24 August, 1918.
[4] *D.M.A.* 29 August, 1918.
[5] *Derbyshire Times*, 7 September, 1918.
[6] See Chapter XVIII.

CHAPTER XIV

———————

THE COAL INDUSTRY, 1918–39

I

For the British coal industry the First World War was an interlude between a golden age and a time of troubles. The remarkable expansion of output and of the export trade, culminating in the record year of 1913, was never to be surpassed in the inter-war years. But, as Professor Court has pointed out: 'The extraordinary success and activity of that time, the high profits, the overflowing royalties, implanted standards of what was normal and natural in the minds of many colliery owners, managements and royalty owners which were carried over into the post-war period, where they played an important role.'[1] On the other hand, the war-time success of the miners in securing national wage agreements served only to strengthen their determination to resist wage reductions made to meet the needs of competition between the various districts. The conflict between these two standpoints in a period of declining trade was the central feature of industrial relations in the coalfields in the years between 1918 and 1939. The matter soon became a political issue of the highest importance with the result that successive governments intervened, although none was prepared to grant the miners their panacea of nationalization.

Immediately after the war the miners' demands for public ownership of the mines led to the appointment, early in 1919, of the Sankey Commission.[2] Despite the far-reaching recommendations of the Commission the only important ones which were implemented by the Government were those which gave the miners an increase in wages and a reduction of the working day to seven hours exclusive of winding times.[3] The continued rise in the cost of living led to a 20 per cent. increase in wages in May, 1920, and, after a three weeks' strike, another wage increase towards the end of the year. Thus the upward trend of

[1] W. H. B. Court, 'Problems of the British Coal Industry Between the Wars', *Economic History Review*, XV, (1945), p. 3.   [2] See Chapter XVI.
[3] *Coal Industry Commission*, 1919, I (Cmd. 359), pp. vii–viii. For the Miners' Welfare Fund see pp. 617-8, 785-8.

costs in the coal industry, which had been given a great impetus by the First World War, continued during the brief post-war boom. According to Charles Markham the wage bill for the Staveley Company rose from £934,000 in 1914 to £2,428,000 in 1920.[1] Lord Aberconway told the shareholders of the Sheepbridge Company that the cost of producing a ton of coal had risen by 14s. 10d. between 1914 and 1920. Much of this increase was attributable to wages but the prices of materials had also risen sharply.[2]

With increasing costs went declining productivity. The trend had been intensified by the withdrawal of skilled labour from the mines during the war and was not reversed by the return to the industry of a steady flow of demobilized miners. In 1914 the total output per man working at the coal face in the Sheepbridge Company's collieries was 755 tons. By 1919 it had fallen to 688 tons and by 1920 to 561.[3] Taking March, 1915, as 100, the output per unit of labour nationally had fallen to 77·4 by May, 1920.[4] The coal-owners were quick to contrast increased wages with lower productivity and to blame the miners for this situation. Lord Aberconway believed that it was 'entirely the affair of the men at the face'.[5] Charles Markham said: 'The working man refuses to work.'[6]

The higher rates of wages may have been partly responsible for the decline in output per person employed. Many men were working on the minimum wage, which, together with the 'war wage' and the flat rate advance awarded by the Sankey Commission, allowed them to obtain a satisfactory daily wage without resorting to piece-work. Other equally reasonable explanations have been suggested by Sir Richard Redmayne.[7] There was the probability that the miners who were returning from the armed forces had not yet got into their stride after their long absence from the pits. Moreover, the condition of the mines had deteriorated during the war. The pressing need for coal and the greatly reduced labour force had made it necessary to work the most productive seams and areas, leaving the exploitation of the more difficult parts of the mines until more normal times. This, coupled with the difficulty of obtaining plant, retarded the development of the mines. There was also a shortage of transport both below and above ground. It was considered by some mining engineers at the end of the war that it would take five years to put the mines back into a pre-war condition.[8]

The uncertainty about the future control of the industry acted as a check to the much needed capital investment. In 1919 the Sheepbridge

[1] *Derbyshire Times*, 2 October, 1920.
[2] *Ibid.*
[3] *Ibid.*
[4] Redmayne, *op. cit.* p. 236.
[5] *Derbyshire Times*, 2 October, 1920.
[6] *Ibid.*
[7] Redmayne, *op. cit.* pp. 222-3.
[8] *Ibid.* p. 231.

Company decided not to proceed further with the development of the Firbeck and Finningley collieries because of 'the proposed limitation of their profits to 1s. 2d. per ton, and the uncertainty of the coal trade due to government interference'.[1] Lord Aberconway denied the suggestion that this was 'in the nature of a strike of capital'. Maurice Deacon said: 'There was no inducement to sink new pits at heavy capital expenditure. . . . There were nearly 200,000 acres of undeveloped coalfields in the United Kingdom being held up for similar reasons.'[2]

Although the coal-owners complained about high costs and low productivity they were not out of pocket. It is true that profits were restricted under the system of State control of the mines but they were also guaranteed. The national pool, which was created from excess profits, was used to subsidize the uneconomic pits. The war-time policy of the Government had been to obtain the vital supplies of coal regardless of the cost but with successive price increases to meet rising costs, including wages, the national pool was able to show a profit of £170,000,000 at the end of the financial year 1918–19. Most of this accrued from the export trade much to the annoyance of our allies, particularly France and Italy, who felt that they were being shamelessly exploited.[3] In the words of Professor Tawney: 'When prices were high the Government was on velvet. But what would happen when they broke?'[4]

The answer to this question came early in 1921. Already, in December, 1920, it was evident that the boom was coming to an end. Belgium was producing more coal than she did before the war, France was slowly regaining her pre-war position, Germany was beginning to deliver reparations coal and America had captured a considerable portion of the overseas coal trade. In January, 1921, the expenses of the British coal industry exceeded its returns by £4,889,331; in February by £4,536,396. Although 31 August, 1921, had been fixed as the date at which control would cease, the Government hastily decided to rid itself of this financial burden as soon as possible, and ended control on 31 March.[5]

The story of this 'classical example of de-control from fright' has been told in detail by Professor Tawney.[6] The entire wage arrangements of the industry, which had rested on the system of state control and the national pool, immediately collapsed.[7] The employers were anxious to

---

[1] *Annual Report, Sheepbridge Coal and Iron Company, for the year ending 30 June, 1919.* [2] *Derbyshire Times,* 27 September, 1919.

[3] R. H. Tawney, 'The Abolition of Economic Controls, 1918–1921' *Economic History Review,* XIII, (1943), p. 22. [4] *Ibid.* p. 20.

[5] Redmayne, *op. cit.* pp. 244–9. [6] Tawney, *loc. cit.* pp. 21–23.

[7] For a full account of the history of the national pool see G. D. H. Cole, *Labour in the Coal-mining Industry, 1914–1921,* (Oxford), 1923, Chapter IX.

reduce labour costs and resort to district bargaining. The miners demanded national wage arrangements. The result was a national coal lock-out lasting from April to July, 1921, which ended in a compromise. The proceeds of the industry were to be divided between wages and profits in agreed proportions on a district basis and the Government was to grant a temporary subsidy, not exceeding £10,000,000, until 31 September, 1921.[1]

The reduction in wages made possible by this agreement enabled the industry to sell its coal cheaply and to weather the economic storms of the next few years at the expense of the miners and their families and of the new capital growth of the industry.[2] The average selling value of coal tumbled from 34s. 7d. a ton in 1920 to 17s. 8d. in 1922. In Derbyshire it fell even lower, to 17s. 2d. During the same period productivity was still declining and output increased only slightly. The French occupation of the Ruhr in 1923 led to a short-lived improvement in the export trade which raised the national average selling value of coal to 18s. 10d. a ton. The advantages enjoyed by the exporting districts were not immediately felt in the inland coalfields. The value of Derbyshire coal continued to fall to an average of 16s. 9d. a ton, but rose to 17s. 8d. in 1924. Towards the end of 1924 the export trade began to deteriorate. By 1925 the average selling value nationally had fallen to 16s. 4d. a ton and in Derbyshire to 15s. 6d.[3]

The coal-owners again sought to reduce their costs by proposing a reduction of wages and a lengthening of hours. A Court of Inquiry, under the chairmanship of H. P. Macmillan, failed to resolve the deadlock which existed between the coal-owners and the miners. The Government then decided to grant a nine months' subsidy to the industry which would make it possible for the existing minimum wages to be continued, and which allowed for profits up to a maximum of 1s. 3d. a ton in each district. The subsidy was to be paid on a district average basis, and would not allow each individual marginal colliery to make profits. At the same time a Royal Commission was appointed, under the chairmanship of Sir Herbert (later Lord) Samuel, to investigate the whole economic position of the coal industry and to report before the end of April, 1926, when the subsidy was due to expire.[4]

II

The problems facing the Samuel Commission were highly controversial. What were the causes of the decline of the British coal industry?

---

[1] See Chapter XVII.
[3] See Appendix I to this chapter.
[2] Court, *loc. cit.* p. 11.
[4] See Chapter XVIII.

Was it merely due to the general shrinkage of world trade? How far had the situation been aggravated by the economic policies of the Government? Was the substitution of other forms of power having any great influence upon the demand for coal? Were there any inherent defects in the structure of the coal industry itself which added to its misfortunes?

The Commission was quick to recognize that the industry was in the grip of a world-wide depression. In the iron and steel, shipbuilding and engineering trades a great expansion to meet the demands of the war had been followed by a substantial decrease in activity. 'It is only to the revival of these heavy industries,' reported the Commission, 'that the coal-mining industry can look for any substantial increase in the home demand for coal.[1] Similarly, the depression in the British coal export trade was described as being 'in the main, part of a general depression, affecting almost all European coal-producing countries'.[2] The decline in the export trade rightly received special attention. When the overseas demand was low the inland coalfields such as Derbyshire were brought more sharply into competition with the exporting areas which diverted some of their surplus to the home market.[3] Moreover, as Dr. Neuman has shown, the areas producing chiefly for the home market were exposed to even greater fluctuations in their exports than the remaining districts.[4] Between 1913 and 1925 national exports of coal declined by about 22 per cent. Charles Markham told the Commission that the exports of coal from the Staveley Company's collieries decreased by 50 per cent. in the same period.[5] 'It is the export trade rather than the home trade that is the seat of our present troubles,' reported the Commission.[6]

Two aspects of governmental policy which were said to have seriously affected the export trade received scant attention from the Commission. The extent to which the German coal export trade had been assisted by the reparations clauses of the Treaty of Versailles was described as 'obscure', but at the same time the Commission recognized that the depression in the British coal export trade was partly due to 'the competition of foreign countries . . . especially that of Germany'.[7] The return to the gold standard in 1925 which, as Keynes so trenchantly demonstrated, made the coal industry 'above all others a victim of our

[1] R.C. on Coal Industry, 1925, I, Report, p. 12.   [2] Ibid. p. 13.
[3] Cf. A. M. Neuman, Economic Organization of the British Coal Industry, (London), 1934, pp. 57–8.
[4] Ibid. p. 67.
[5] Ibid. II (Part B), Evidence of Charles Markham, p. 539.
[6] Ibid. I, Report, p. 4.
[7] Ibid. pp. 13–14. Cf. G. D. H. Cole, Labour in the Coal-mining Industry, p. 243.

monetary policy'[1] was dismissed as a factor no longer 'of primary importance'.[2]

The substitution of other forms of power for coal was a long-term development. Its origins can be traced to the latter years of the nineteenth century when electricity and oil began to come into use. Even before the First World War the Admiralty had taken the decision to fuel its warships with oil and the Anglo-Persian Oil Company had been formed, with the State holding half its shares.[3] The coal consumption of the Royal Navy declined from 1,700,000 tons in 1913–14 to 110,000 in 1932. In the mercantile marine the number and gross tonnage of steamers fitted for burning oil fuel and of motorships substantially increased in the same period, for the whole world to about 25,000,000 tons, which was equal to 40 per cent. of all tonnage.[4] Oil was also used more widely for heating and in industry. Lignite production was rapidly increasing in Germany. Other substitutes such as hydroelectric power and natural gas were being developed in various parts of the world. Much of this substitution was non-competitive or complementary in its effects and it is difficult to measure statistically the extent to which coal was displaced. Nevertheless the view of the Samuel Commission that the depression in the coal export trade was caused 'partly by the increased use of substitutes' appears to be generally accepted.[5]

Another long-term development of even more importance than substitution was the growth of fuel economy. Sir John Snell, chairman of the Electricity Commission, told the Samuel Commission:

> The whole tendency of development in this country is towards concentration in few and larger stations in which the most modern appliances can be economically adopted, higher steam pressures and larger units of steam raising and generating plant, with the modern refinements in the boiler house which all tend to economy.[6]

In 1920–1 the coal consumption for the generation of electricity was 1·49 tons per million kilowatt hours. By 1934–5 it was estimated that the same amount of electricity could be generated from 0·67 ton of coal. Similar economies were being effected in the production of gas. In 1925 a ton of coal was sufficient to generate 13,600 cubic feet; in 1934 the volume had increased to 15,000 cubic feet. Shortly before the outbreak of the Second World War it was stated that the gas, electricity, iron and steel industries required 31,500,000 tons of coal per

---

[1] J. M. Keynes, *The Economic Consequences of Mr. Churchill*, (London), 1925, p. 22.
[2] *R.C. on Coal Industry*, 1925, I, Report, p. 9.
[3] Ensor, *op. cit.* p. 524.   [4] Neuman, *op. cit.* pp. 69–70.
[5] *R.C. on Coal Industry*, 1925, I, Report, p. 13; Neuman, *op. cit.* pp. 69–73; Jones, Cartwright and Guénault, *op. cit.* p. 22; Court, *loc. cit.* p. 11.
[6] *Ibid.* II (Part A), Evidence of Sir John Snell, p. 225.

S*

annum less than would have been required twenty-five years previously, assuming the existing volume of production in such industries.[1] Fuel economy was being practised with growing success in most of the leading industrial countries of the world.[2]

The extent to which the coal industry was capable of adapting itself to all these changes was the most controversial question of all. The miners' demand for public ownership of the industry, reinforced by the recommendations of the Sankey Commission, continued to be pressed with the utmost vigour. The miners believed that the reduction in costs which would be made possible by an extensive reorganization of the industry would remove the need for any further reductions in wages. The Commission was opposed to the nationalization of the mines and the granting of any further subsidies but was prepared to meet the miners by recommending the acquisition of the minerals by the State on payment of compensation and the amalgamation of many of the existing small units of production. Even so it was felt that the miners ought to accept a reduction in wages by an amount depending upon their willingness to work longer hours.

In the event the General Strike of 1926 supervened, followed by a lengthy coal stoppage. During the course of the dispute the Government introduced legislation permitting a temporary lengthening of the working day to eight hours exclusive of winding times. When work was finally resumed in November, 1926, it was on the basis of district wage agreements, a reduced minimum wage, and longer working hours.[3] 'The solution adopted for the slumping sales and profits of the early 'twenties ... was entirely that suggested by regional competition within the industry,' writes Professor Court. 'It took the form of an attack upon labour costs, to the exclusion of other costs, by the most simple and direct way, the alteration of wages and hours. The way in which this was done embittered the relations of managements and men for the rest of the inter-war years and made extremely difficult the introduction of those other methods of reducing costs which were essential; for these required for their perfect success the intelligent and willing co-operation of the miners.'[4]

III

The symptoms which had appeared at the beginning of the decade became even more pronounced during the world industrial depression of 1929–33. With the exception of a slight increase in 1929 the output

[1] Jones, Cartwright and Guénault, *op. cit.* p. 79.

[2] *Ibid.* pp. 261, 343; Court, *loc. cit.* p. 11.

[3] See Chapter XVIII.

[4] Court, *loc. cit.* p. 10.

of coal nationally and in Derbyshire declined steadily from 1927 to 1933. Thereafter the downward trend was reversed but even in 1938 the outputs of Derbyshire and of the whole country were less than they had been in 1925 and considerably lower than in 1923 which was the most successful year of the inter-war period. Coal prices also continued to be low. Nationally the average selling value fell off sharply from the artificially high figure of 19s. 7d. a ton caused by the 1926 stoppage to 14s. 7d. in 1927 and 12s. 10d. in 1928. By 1930 the average selling value increased to 13s. 8d. a ton, a figure which was not exceeded until 1936–8 when it rose from 14s. 0d. to 16s. 8d. Average selling values in Derbyshire followed a slightly different course, falling from 24s. in 1926 to 14s. 6d. in 1927, and 12s. 5d. in 1928. Thereafter they gradually increased to 13s. 6d. in 1932, declining to 12s. 8d. in 1934, and rising to 15s. 6d. in 1938.[1] Derbyshire's comparative prosperity during the years of world depression is largely explained by the county's small participation in the export trade.

The fall of labour costs after 1925–6 gave the British coal industry a temporary advantage over its foreign rivals but improvements in mining techniques enabled them to retrieve their position in time to face the acutely competitive conditions of the world industrial depression. Meanwhile the British coal-owners were turning their attention to the development of output and price control schemes. It was becoming increasingly apparent to them that the methods of the nineteenth century were no longer successful. The twofold problem which faced the industry was the necessity to stimulate the export trade and to establish a more favourable level of prices for coal consumed in the domestic market. The coal-owners had before them the choice of continuing to produce and sell under conditions of unrestricted competition in the home market and of unorganized competition with foreign producers, or of co-operating with one another so that they might compete more effectively in markets abroad. As early as December, 1925, Frank Hodges, the secretary of the Miners' International Federation, who was already rapidly losing sympathy with the miners' point of view, entered a plea before the Samuel Commission for the introduction of a co-ordinating selling scheme on the lines of the ten German syndicates with the central Reichskohlenverband in command.[2] A few months later Sir Alfred Mond (later Lord Melchett), following the example of Sir George Elliot in 1893, put forward proposals for the establishment of such a scheme in Great Britain.[3] In July, 1926, the Government appointed a Departmental Committee to put forward proposals for

[1] See Appendix I to this chapter.
[2] *R.C. on Coal Industry*, 1925, II (Part B) Evidence of Frank Hodges, p. 512.
[3] 'Central Coal Selling Agencies', *The Economist*, 24 April, 1926, p. 822.

marketing schemes. The Committee recoiled from compulsion but the coal-owner members in a separate report called attention to the need for national co-ordination.[1] The outcome of all this activity was that before the end of 1928 three marketing schemes had come into operation, either fully or partially, in Scotland, South Wales and the Midlands.[2] Of these the Midland counties scheme was by far the most important and effectual.

The Sheepbridge Coal and Iron Company appears to have taken a leading part in establishing the scheme. In June, 1926, Lord Aberconway told the shareholders:

> It is no use everybody sitting on his own cabbage patch and thinking he is going to make a fortune. . . . You have read the report of the Samuel Commission calling attention to the necessity of combination. . . . Now, therefore, in conjunction with several of the largest companies in South Yorkshire, we have proposals for dealing with this question on fair and equal lines. Not only will it help in reducing costs, but it will give us more credit in the money markets and help us with selling prices. Selling prices are the evil we have to deal with today. We are producing more coal, apparently, than the world wants.[3]

In January, 1928, it was reported that a meeting of representatives of the South and West Yorkshire, and Nottinghamshire and Derbyshire coal-owners' associations had met at Sheffield to consider the details of a coal marketing scheme.[4] Soon afterwards the Lancashire and Cheshire Coal-Owners' Association joined in the discussions and by 1 April the Central Collieries Commercial Association had been established. Commonly known as the Five Counties Scheme, it included Cannock Chase, Leicestershire, North Staffordshire and Warwickshire in addition to the five counties already mentioned. The principal objects of the scheme were to regulate output by means of quotas allocated to each colliery and to increase the export of coal. Members were required to pay a levy, not exceeding threepence for each ton of coal raised, to a common fund which was used to subsidize exports.

Output was regulated by two committees. One fixed a basic tonnage for each colliery. The other fixed a monthly quota or general percentage which had to be applied to the basic tonnage of each colliery. Special provisions were made to meet the needs of developing mines. Unraised quotas could be bought and sold through the Quota Committee. A fine of 3s. a ton was imposed on any member who exceeded his quota by more than 1 per cent.

[1] *Report of the Departmental Committee on Co-operative Selling in the Coal Mining Industry*, 1926, (Cmd. 2770), p. 44.
[2] For a full account of these schemes see Jones, Cartwright and Guénault, *op. cit.* Ch. VI.
[3] *Derbyshire Times*, 3 July, 1926.   [4] *Ibid.* 21 January, 1928.

The exporting arrangements were in the hands of a third committee which had to ensure that the coal exporters did not take advantage of the subsidy by continuing to sell in foreign markets at the old price. For the Humber ports a shipping bureau known as the Humber Coal Export Bureau was formed with Arthur Westlake, of the Staveley Company, as export controller.[1] The Bureau consisted of members of the Association who were interested in the export trade. Further, in each port there was a committee consisting of representatives of all the individual coal-owners interested in its trade. Similar arrangements were subsequently made for the Mersey ports. The Bureau was so successful in its handling of the members of the Humber Coal Exporters' Association that it was able to reduce them from independent buyers and sellers of coal to brokers who accepted a percentage commission upon the sale of coal at agreed prices.

The main weakness of the scheme was its failure to exercise any direct control over prices. As early as May, 1928, a sub-committee prepared a scheme for price regulation but it was not accepted, with the result that members were still able to undercut each other. The computation of standard tonnages was also unsatisfactory. Members were allowed to select the output of any one of the previous fifteen years as their basis and naturally chose the year of maximum output. Thus the total basic tonnage was far greater than the effective producing capacity of the collieries covered by the scheme at the time of its introduction. This meant that the Quota Committee had to fix a very restricted percentage from the very beginning. A quota such as 65 or 70 per cent. meant to firms with largely diminished outputs permission to produce at their full capacity, while to the larger and more efficient firms it meant a serious reduction. C. A. (later Sir Cecil) Cochrane, chairman of the Bolsover Company, complained in February, 1929, that great hardship had been inflicted upon the Company because the standard tonnages had been fixed 'upon an altogether fallacious basis'.[2] Sir William Bird, chairman of the Staveley Company, stated in September of the same year that 'prices had been slightly better than they were in 1928, but the curtailment of output under the scheme had obviously increased costs'.[3] In 1929 the Basic Tonnage Committee devised a scheme which took into account both the capacity of a colliery to produce coal and the ability of the owner to sell the coal so produced. Despite such adjustments it proved difficult to reconcile all the conflicting interests.

Another difficulty was that about 10 per cent. of the output of the area covered by the Central Collieries Commercial Association was

[1] *Derbyshire Times*, 5 May, 1928.
[2] *Ibid.* 2 March, 1929.   [3] *Ibid.* 28 September, 1929.

not under its control. The non-associated coal-owners were free to increase their output by working at full capacity and this had to be taken into consideration in fixing quotas. According to C. A. Cochrane, the collieries which remained outside the scheme 'derived most benefit from its existence'. Competition of other areas was an equally serious problem. 'Owing to the forced reduction of output', said Cochrane, 'much of the trade on the east coast and the south coast—which was previously supplied by this district—had passed into the hands of Northumberland and Durham.'[1] Moreover the Association did not reduce output to such an extent as to create a real shortage in that section of the home market in which it enjoyed a partial monopoly. For these reasons the immediate object of the scheme, which had been to raise prices to a more remunerative level, met with failure. In Derbyshire the average selling value of coal rose only slightly, from 12s. 5d. a ton in 1928 to 12s. 11d. in 1929.[2]

On the exporting side the Central Collieries Commercial Association was more successful. Although it controlled an aggregate output of approximately 90,000,000 tons per annum, or more than a third of the total production of the country, only a small proportion of this was exported. During the short time that the scheme was in operation exports accounted for only 3 to 8 per cent. of the total production. This meant that the levy of not more than threepence a ton upon all coal raised in the area enabled the Association to pay a substantial subsidy, which in some cases reached 4s. a ton. It has been estimated that in a predominantly exporting area such as South Wales a levy of threepence a ton would have provided a subsidy of no more than sixpence which would have meant a net advantage of only threepence a ton.[3] The result was that the Association was able, during the first year of its existence, to increase sales abroad from 2·2 million tons to nearly 5 million.[4] Whatever other criticisms they might have made, most coal-owners were prepared to give the scheme credit for improving the export trade. The directors of the Sheepbridge Company reported in September, 1929, that there had been 'a considerable increase in the exports of coal from the Humber ports, which was made possible by the Central Collieries Commercial Association'.[5] C. A. Cochrane also believed that the Association had helped the export trade considerably but added: 'Of course that was not the sole object of the scheme, which was to try to bring back prosperity to Nottinghamshire and Derbyshire

[1] *Derbyshire Times*, 2 March, 1929.
[2] See Appendix I to this chapter.
[3] Jones, Cartwright and Guénault, *op. cit*, pp. 104–5.
[4] Neuman, *op. cit.* p. 164.
[5] *Annual Report of the Sheepbridge Coal and Iron Company for the year ending 30 June, 1929.*

and the surrounding country.'[1] The scheme was severely criticized by producers and exporters in other areas who argued that it spoiled their own market in the Baltic States.

IV

Their experience of the Five Counties Scheme taught the coal-owners some valuable lessons in the successful operation of trade associations. The first need was the creation of similar organizations in other districts. Co-operation between districts was then essential. The over-riding problem was to persuade or compel every producer to join. As early as October, 1928, representatives of the Association met representatives of other districts to discuss the possibilities of developing a national scheme for the marketing of coal.[2] The advent of a Labour Government, pledged to legislate on the coal industry, in June, 1929, resulted in the coal-owners' protracted negotiations becoming merged in the discussions on the Coal Mines Bill. As D. N. Turner, the managing director of the Staveley Company, remarked some years later: 'The Association,[3] evolved purely by the coal-owners, formed the ground work and basis from which the Coal Mines Act of 1930 was constructed.'[4]

Because the Labour Government failed to command a clear majority in the House of Commons the Coal Mines Act of 1930[5] was essentially a political compromise. Instead of nationalization the coal-owners were given what many of them had advocated, a compulsory cartel.[6] The miners were given a shorter working day of seven and a half hours. A Coal Mines Reorganization Commission, which proved to be singularly ineffective, and a Coal Mines National Industrial Board, which never really came to life, were the remaining provisions of the Act. The activities of the Reorganization Commission will be discussed later.[7] Of the miners' shorter working day it need only be said that the increased cost of production was expected to be offset by improvements in the organization of the industry.[8]

By far the most important provision of the Act was Part I which set up machinery regulating the 'production, supply and sale of coal'. It was originally intended as a temporary measure to cushion the financial effect of reduced hours of work and to maintain prices and spread employment while the industry was being reorganized. In the

[1] *Derbyshire Times*, 7 July, 1928.   [2] *Ibid*. 6 October, 1928.
[3] i.e. the Central Collieries Commercial Association.
[4] *Derbyshire Times*, 10 December, 1932.
[5] 20 and 21 Geo. V. c. 34.   [6] Cf. Neuman, *op. cit*. pp. 444-5.
[7] See below, pp. 566-7.   [8] See Chapter XIX, pp. 748-50.

absence of any effective reorganization the scheme continued, with modifications, until the industry was nationalized in 1947. The Act provided for the establishment of central and district organizations. A central council was to regulate the production and sale of coal throughout Great Britain. District executive boards were to perform similar functions within their own regions. The intention of the Act was to make the control of output the sole responsibility of the industry itself. The element of compulsion was provided by giving far-reaching powers to the Board of Trade but these were only to be used if the coal-owners failed to develop their own schemes within the broad framework laid down by the Act. In practice all the bodies set up under the Act, with the exception of the Scottish executive board, were planned by the coal-owners with the co-operation of the Board of Trade.

The central council consisted of representatives of the coal-owners from each district in proportion to its annual output. The council's main tasks were to allocate a maximum output to each district and to impose fines where allocations were exceeded. The district schemes varied in detail but closely resembled each other. The most important functions of the district executive boards were to determine the 'standard tonnage' of each colliery in proportion to its previous output and to impose penalties for failure to comply with the regulations. The boards had also the power to fix minimum prices. Derbyshire became part of the Midland Amalgamated District which included South Yorkshire, West Yorkshire, Nottinghamshire, South Derbyshire and Leicestershire. These were the areas which had formed the nucleus of the old Central Collieries Commercial Association. Neither the miners nor the consumers were represented on the national and regional organizations but provision was made for them to be represented on the central and district committees of investigation which existed for dealing with complaints by consumers against the operation of the scheme.[1]

The primary object of the scheme was to raise prices by regulating output rather than to control prices directly. Its difficulties were similar to those of the Central Collieries Commercial Association. Some of the larger and more efficient collieries were required to work well below capacity, which increased their costs and prevented them from meeting all the demands made by their customers. This in turn meant short time or unemployment for many miners. D. N. Turner of the Staveley Company complained in March, 1931: 'They had plenty of coal to work, the men were anxious to get the coal. They had plenty of orders, yet the Government would not let them turn out more than a strictly

[1] Cf. D. H. Macgregor, 'The Coal Bill and the Cartel', *Economic Journal*, XL, (1930), p. 39.

limited quantity. . . . The tantalizing thing was that while their own miners were working short time when they had orders to keep them in full work, quantities of Polish coal were being imported into this country.'[1] On the other hand the collieries which were less favourably situated in relation to the market had no guarantee that they would be able to sell all the coal which they were permitted to raise under the quota system. Unused quotas were a marketable commodity within districts but not between districts. Thus the uneconomic collieries were kept going and the better collieries were able to reduce their costs by increasing their output, although the reduction in costs was offset by the price which had to be paid for the unused quotas. Some of the larger colliery companies acquired derelict collieries in an attempt to justify an increase in their quotas.[2] The Butterley Company in October, 1932, decided to close its Hartshay Colliery in order to give more tonnage to the other pits and enable them to work on an economic basis.[3]

The control of output soon proved to be ineffective as a means of maintaining prices. District minimum prices were either evaded or were set so low as to be meaningless. The absence of any central price control led to fierce competition between districts, especially when the export market declined and the exporting areas began to undersell on the home market. Sir Cecil Cochrane told the shareholders of the Bolsover Company that in 1923 about 9,855,800 tons, or 57·7 per cent., of the coal sent to London was rail-borne and 7,225,900 tons, or 42·3 per cent., water-borne. By 1931 the proportions were almost exactly reversed, 8,006,900 tons, or 42·79 per cent., being rail-borne and 10,704,700 tons, or 57·21 per cent., water-borne.[4]

The scheme brought forth many criticisms and complaints and some litigation to test the powers of the central and district authorities, but most colliery proprietors were in favour of its modification rather than its abolition. The directors of the Bolsover Company were of the opinion 'that it is exercising a steadying influence on the industry and that it should be continued providing necessary amendments can be secured both in the Act and in the district agreements'.[5] Lord Aberconway told the shareholders of the Sheepbridge Company in 1932: 'In my opinion the Act has helped us. Without it the results would have been disastrous and prices would have fallen to a very low figure. But before real benefits can result, there must be co-ordination between districts and some better method of controlling minimum prices.'[6] D. N. Turner, in a talk to the Chesterfield Rotarians, said: 'The

[1] *Derbyshire Times*, 14 March, 1931. [2] *Ibid.* 18 June, 1932.
[3] *Ibid.* 15 October, 1932. [4] *Ibid.* 25 February, 1933.
[5] *Annual Report of the Bolsover Colliery Company for the year ending 31 December, 1931.* [6] *Derbyshire Times*, 1 October, 1932.

alternative to the regulation of output, which was the return to the condition of free competition, was at this juncture unthinkable.'[1]

In 1935 the scheme was amended. The output of coal for export and inland supply was restricted by separate quotas, which benefited the inland coalfields such as Derbyshire. The central council was authorized to enforce price co-ordination between districts, and to grant separate district allocations for particular classes of coal. These developments were accelerated by the pressure of a miners' wage claim. The ultimate settlement was a compromise in which the miners, the owners, the Government and even some of the consumers all played their parts. The miners accepted, temporarily, an advance less than that for which they asked. In return they were promised that the Government would organize by July, 1936, the marketing of coal in each district by establishing selling agencies and by providing for the central co-ordination of the work of these bodies. The central council was required to issue directions to the districts regarding the terms and conditions for the sale and supply of coal and was empowered to inquire into all complaints made by one district against another.[2] The selling schemes which were to be introduced in every district were to cover every colliery, to prevent all inter-colliery competition and to be so constructed that no evasions could take place.

The object of the introduction of these statutory selling schemes was to enable the price of coal to be increased to meet the higher labour costs resulting from the wage increase and to make possible further wage increases in the future. As an immediate measure to tide the industry over the difficult period between the introduction of higher wages and the coming into operation of the selling schemes many large consumers agreed to a rise in the price of coal even when purchasing under long-term contracts already made. In this way another crisis of the magnitude of the 1926 lock-out was avoided.[3]

The new selling schemes came into operation on 1 August, 1936. They all conformed to the general conditions laid down by the Government but were not similar in structure. There were three main types. In the districts of Lancashire and Cheshire, Shropshire, South Staffordshire and the Forest of Dean systems of complete central selling were adopted. The right of selling coal was transferred from the individual colliery proprietors to an executive board. In the remaining districts, with the exception of the Midland Amalgamated District, there was central control of sales. The colliery owner continued to sell his own coal and seek his own customers, but in each district a sales committee

[1] *Derbyshire Times*, 10 December, 1932.
[2] Previously the central council had power only to inquire into complaints regarding the minimum prices established by any district.   [3] See Chapter XIX, p. 762.

was appointed to issue permits regulating each specific contract. The Midland Amalgamated District, which included Derbyshire, adopted a system which differed both from central selling and from the central control of sales. Even before the introduction of the statutory selling schemes the owners in this district had formed themselves into groups, each of which employed an agent to act for it. This system was continued under the statutory scheme. The 200 coal-owners of the area were divided into eighteen groups. The chairman of the executive board which controlled the scheme was Sir Walter Benton Jones, chairman of the United Steel Companies, Ltd.[1]

It is difficult to estimate the success of the statutory selling schemes for they were introduced at a time when the general industrial recovery and the re-armament programme were leading to a substantial increase in coal consumption. Prices were undoubtedly rising and, perhaps because of that, the schemes appear to have worked fairly smoothly. In Derbyshire the average selling value of coal rose from 14s. od. a ton in 1936 to 15s. 6d. in 1938.[2] In March, 1938, I. W. Lamonby, chairman of the Grassmoor Colliery Company, said the scheme 'had produced a form of co-operation amongst its members which could not be hoped for two years ago, and had in every way more than justified their expectations'.[3]

Nevertheless, the scheme was not without its defects. At the annual meeting of the Sheepbridge Company, in 1938, W. H. McConnell complained that other districts were not co-operating in the export trade. 'Without assistance in some form', he said, 'it was difficult to see how this country could obtain its fair share of the world's export market in view of the policy adopted by other countries for fostering their coal exports by means of direct or indirect subsidies.'[4] Towards the end of the year the central council began to use its powers more extensively. It issued directions to all districts governing the prices of all coal sold on the inland market outside the immediate neighbourhood of the pits or in any area where two or more districts were in competition; railborne and coastwise prices, mainly in respect of sales to London and the South of England; and prices and supplies of coal for export.

The central council had also been given power to enter into agreements with trading organizations and legal entities not only in this

---

[1] *Derbyshire Times*, 14 August, 1936. The members of the board representing Derbyshire and Nottinghamshire were G. M. Jackson (Clay Cross Company), G. C. M. Jackson (Sheepbridge Company), C. A. Lambert (Bolsover Company), C. R. Ellis (Blackwell Colliery Company), F. H. Ellis (Sherwood Colliery Company), E. A. F. Fenwick (New Hucknall Colliery Company), C. M. Humble (James Oakes and Company, Riddings Collieries), and N. D. Todd (Stanton Ironworks Company).

[2] See Appendix I to this chapter.

[3] *Derbyshire Times*, 18 March, 1938.   [4] *Ibid.* 30 September, 1938.

country but also in foreign countries. In 1938 the coal-owners decided, after consultation with the M.F.G.B., that coal exports should be subsidized by a levy on other sales failing the conclusion of an international coal agreement. By 1939 understandings had been reached with Germany and Poland. Together with Great Britain these two countries were responsible for 90 per cent. of the European coal export trade which was the largest in the world. But for the outbreak of the Second World War an international coal agreement might eventually have been reached.[1]

V

The slowness of the British coal industry to adapt itself to the changing conditions of the inter-war years led to an ever closer examination of its structure. As early as 1919 it was widely recognized that there was some need for a re-organization of the industry. Output and productivity were declining. The coal-owners complained that the need to minimize costs prevented them paying adequate wages. The most controversial issue facing the Sankey Commission was not the need for re-organization but the method to be adopted. Sir Richard Redmayne, the Government's principal coal official, stated before the Commission:

In my opinion the present system of individual ownership of collieries is extravagant and wasteful . . . whether viewed from the point of view of the coal-mining industry as a whole or from the national point of view, and I think by thoughtful persons on both sides, both the owners and the workmen, that is pretty generally accepted.[2]

Several other expert witnesses supported Redmayne's view that larger undertakings were desirable.[3] The chairman, Mr. Justice Sankey, and the three government nominees, Arthur Balfour, Sir Arthur Duckham and Sir Thomas Royden, stated in their interim report:

Even upon the evidence already given, the present system of ownership and working in the coal industry stands condemned, and some other system must be substituted for it, either nationalization or a method of unification by national purchase and/or joint control.[4]

The alternatives were posed even more sharply by the M.F.G.B. representatives, Robert Smillie, Frank Hodges, Herbert Smith and Sir Leo Chiozza Money, and by two members of the Commission whose

---

[1] Court, *loc. cit.* p. 17.   [2] *Coal Industry Commission*, 1919, I, Q. 5208.
[3] *Ibid.* Q.Q. 7852–3; II, QQ. 16766–7, 18723, 19795, 20096, 21337, 21355, 26293, 26402–11, 26577.   [4] *Ibid.* I, Interim Report, p. viii.

appointment had been agreed upon between the M.F.G.B. and the Government, R. H. Tawney and Sidney Webb. They reported:

In view of the impossibility of tolerating any unification of all the mines in the hands of a Capitalist Trust we think that, in the interest of the consumers as much as in that of the miners, nationalization ought to be, in principle, at once determined on.[1]

In the absence of nationalization it seemed inevitable that the coal industry should follow the example of other great industries. Already they were resorting to various forms of combination as a protection against the rigours of what was frequently described as 'cut-throat competition'.[2] Sir Richard Redmayne, who was not in favour of nationalization, stated: 'The present system does undoubtedly conduce to cut-throat competition.'[3] To counter this he advocated 'collective production' which would lead to 'enhanced production', 'diminished cost of production', and 'prevention of waste'. These advantages would accrue from combination, he said, because competition would be prevented; the coal-owners would be able to demand lower freight rates; there would be economy of administration; more capital would be available for the development of backward mines; centralized buying of materials would be possible; there would be more harmonious relations between the workmen and the employers; 'vested interest and middlemen' would be largely 'obliterated'; and efficiency would be improved by the greater exchange of technical knowledge and skill.[4]

These were the methods of monopolies, cartels and trusts which successive Governments sought to introduce into the not entirely unwilling coal industry by persuasion or compulsion. Little was done immediately after the publication of the Sankey Report. Even the unanimous recommendation that coal royalties should be nationalized, to make possible more economic methods of working, was ignored. In 1923, however, the Mines (Working Facilities and Support) Act[5] empowered the Railway and Canal Commission to grant orders facilitating or restricting the working of minerals. The movement towards industrial combination was given a greater impetus by the crisis of 1925–6. The Samuel Commission, after hearing a reiteration of the arguments which had been advanced before the Sankey Commission, decided against nationalization but stressed the advantages to be gained by large-scale production:

The amalgamation of many of the present small units of production is both desirable and practicable. This may often be effected from within,

[1] *Coal Industry Commission,* 1919, I, Interim Report, p. xiii.
[2] *Report of Committee on Trusts,* 1919, (Cmd. 9236), p. 16.
[3] *Coal Industry Commission,* 1919, I, Evidence of Redmayne, Q. 5208.
[4] *Ibid.*　　　　　　　　　　　[5] 13 and 14 Geo. V. c. 20.

but in many cases it will only take place if outside assistance is given. Any general measure of compulsory amalgamation, on arbitrary lines, would be mischievous; the action to be taken should be elastic and should enable each case to be treated individually.[1]

The Coal Mines Reorganization Act, 1926, was one of the fruits of the Samuel Commission. It enabled colliery owners to submit to the Board of Trade schemes of total or partial amalgamation to secure greater economy and efficiency in working. A minority of owners unwilling to take part in amalgamation schemes which met with general approval could be brought in compulsorily by 'absorption' schemes subject to ratification by the Railway and Canal Commission. The Act had no substantial results. Little initiative came from the industry and the conditions which had to be satisfied before the Railway and Canal Commission were virtually impossible. All schemes had to be shown to be in the national interest and amalgamation schemes were required to reduce the cost of production or disposal of coal, to do no financial harm to any of the undertakings involved, and to be fair and equitable to all persons concerned.

The process of encouraging amalgamation was carried a stage further in 1930. Part II of the Coal Mines Act of that year established a Coal Mines Reorganization Commission. The five commissioners, appointed by the Board of Trade, were given the task of promoting and assisting amalgamations in accordance with the procedure laid down by the 1926 Act. If the owners proved to be reluctant to draft schemes the Commission itself was authorized to do so. The powers of compulsory amalgamation given to the Commission were considerably restricted by the conditions which still had to be satisfied under the 1926 Act but they were sufficient to arouse strong opposition from the Mining Association. The Commission's failure to secure complete amalgamations led it to attempt to bring about looser forms of combination, including selling syndicates and associations for the control of sales and prices and for the general control of the development of areas. Such schemes were prepared for Durham, South and West Yorkshire, Nottinghamshire and Derbyshire. In May, 1935, the West Yorkshire scheme was rejected by the Railway and Canal Commission on the grounds that there was no financial fusion and no new corporation was established. The *Derbyshire Times* commented: 'Had this scheme succeeded, other schemes would have followed, including Derbyshire, and we should in time have had our smaller collieries closed down and thousands of miners thrown out of work.'[2]

The failure of the Reorganization Commission to make any progress

[1] *R. C. on Coal Industry*, 1925, I, Report, p. 233.
[2] *Derbyshire Times*, 31 May, 1935.

led the Government to suspend its activities in July, 1935, and to review its powers. In the following year the Government introduced a Bill to abolish the conditions imposed upon the Commission by the 1930 Act but it was subsequently withdrawn in the face of extreme opposition from the Mining Association and the Federation of British Industries. It was not until 1938 that any further attempt was made to deal with the problems of re-organization. The Coal Act of that year belatedly implemented the recommendation of the Sankey Commission, and subsequently of the Samuel Commission, that coal royalties should be nationalized. The Act established a Coal Commission in which the nation's coal was to be vested. The transfer was not completed until 1 July, 1942, by which time compensation amounting to £66,450,000 had been paid to the former owners. The Coal Commission also took over the functions of the Reorganization Commission which was abolished. A new procedure was introduced for dealing with compulsory amalgamations. The Commission had first to satisfy the Board of Trade and Parliament (by provisional order procedure) that a proposed amalgamation was desirable on grounds of efficiency: it had then to satisfy the Railway and Canal Commission that the scheme conformed with the requirements of the 1930 Act.

The Coal Commission, under the chairmanship of Sir Ernest Gowers, invited the co-operation of the Mining Association in the setting up of local committees to formulate proposals for reorganization. The Association declined, pointing out that it would be difficult for the members of such committees to initiate proposals for dealing with the property of others, and suggested that the Commission should take the first step by putting forward its own proposals. In June, 1939, the Commission circulated a memorandum, the object of which was 'not to convey decisions but rather to furnish bases for discussion'. There was a wide difference of opinion on the proposals in the various coalmining districts. In Derbyshire it was felt that any drastic action would mean a great increase in unemployment in areas surrounding the smaller and older mines and that it would be better to allow such mines to be worked out or gradually absorbed by voluntary action.[1] The work of the Commission was interrupted by the outbreak of war and little more was heard of it.

VI

The policy of successive Governments for the coal industry during the inter-war years had clearly but one aim: the encouragement or

[1] *Derbyshire Times*, 16 June, 1939.

imposition of combination for both marketing and production. There was much discussion about the desirability of the one form of combination preceding the other. Some argued that the amalgamation of individual undertakings was necessary before cartels and trusts could be created. Others believed that the development of marketing schemes would encourage amalgamation. A third school of thought insisted that the movements for amalgamation and co-operation were to some extent interdependent.[1] By encouraging both lines of development governmental policy left nothing to chance. That the policy was not pursued with more vigour was largely due to the coal-owners themselves.

Dr. Neuman has shown very clearly the disintegrating forces which were at work in the British coal industry during the inter-war years.[2] The scattered nature of the coalfields and the diversity of the markets which they supplied tended to discourage the unified control of either pit-head prices, output, or distribution. Wide differences in the productivity, size, and financial strength of the various units of production meant that integration was likely to lead to great economies for some collieries but not for others. Moreover, restriction of output was not attractive to an industry which tended to reduce its overhead charges by producing larger quantities of coal. 'The British colliery owners . . . were, with few exceptions, champions of cheap production and cheap selling.'[3] Dr. Neuman also calls attention to the diffusion of transport which discouraged co-operative agreements on freight rates such as existed in Germany and the widely dispersed system of royalties which also led to cost disparities (and sometimes prevented the most efficient methods of mine development). The relative lack of mutual dependence between the banks and the pure colliery companies meant that many of the latter were not constrained to reduce their capital to a profitable basis.

On the other hand, as Dr. Neuman has again shown, there were also integrating forces at work.[4] These soon proved to be more powerful than the disintegrating forces. In 1924 there were 2,481 mines belonging to about 1,400 separate undertakings. But of these, in 1923, long before there had been any attempt on the part of the State to encourage combination, 323 undertakings produced 84 per cent. of the country's output of coal.[5] In fostering the development of concentration the State was merely reinforcing a trend which was already very marked. How,

[1] Cf. H. Levy, *Monopolies, Cartels and Trusts in British Industry*, (London), edn. of 1927, p. 313; D. H. Macgregor, 'The Coal Bill and the Cartel', *Economic Journal*, XL, (1930), p. 39.
[2] Neuman, *op. cit.* pp. 47–126.   [3] *Ibid.* p. 53.
[4] *Ibid.* pp. 127–202.
[5] *R. C. on Coal Industry*, 1925, I, Report. p. 47.

then, can the determined opposition of the coal-owners to the activities of the State be explained ? The point of view of the small colliery owner who did not wish to be swallowed up in the process of integration is easy enough to see. The larger units were well satisfied with the amalgamation which was already taking place and of which they were enjoying the benefits. If any further amalgamation were to take place they insisted that it should follow 'natural' lines of development and not be imposed by any form of State interference. In 1937, Sir William Bird, the chairman of the Staveley Company, expressed the opinion that it was better to amalgamate whilst they could choose their associates 'rather than run the risk of having less suitable partners forced upon them'.[1]

The attitude of the larger firms to the smaller ones is well illustrated by the evidence of Charles Markham before the Samuel Commission. As head of one of the largest and most efficient organizations in the country, which on 30 June, 1925, felt strong enough to sever all its connections with trade associations,[2] he was able to say:

I am strongly of opinion that rings and combines are bad for the country, and, with one or two trifling exceptions where we were unable to get out without pecuniary loss, we are not members of any of these trade organizations. We are not members of the Mining Association of Great Britain. In my opinion, all rings are a premium on inefficient management. The combines in the alkali trade which are dominant today work untold harm. For the same reason I consider that amalgamations create monopolies.[3]

When asked by Sir Herbert Samuel if he was aware that two-thirds of the mines employed less than 500 men in each, and produced only 18 per cent. of the output, Markham replied: 'That is so. They want shutting up.'[4] He went on to say: 'Today a colliery is no good at all unless it raises 20,000 tons a week. That is about the minimum at which you can begin to expect a colliery to pay.'[5] When it was pointed out to Markham that his own organization was 'in a sense a combination' he grudgingly admitted: 'I think you might amalgamate some of the small collieries, but I do not think it possible to amalgamate many of the big collieries together. They would be unwieldy.'[6]

The Staveley Company was an early example of vertical integration in the nineteenth century. Even before the First World War its activities extended backwards to ironstone mining and lime quarrying and forwards to ironworks, heavy engineering, by-product plants and even into the chemical industry. The process continued during the inter-war

[1] *Derbyshire Times*, 1 October, 1937.   [2] *Ibid.* 4 July, 1925.
[3] *R. C. on Coal Industry*, 1925, II (Part B), Evidence of Charles Markham, p. 538.
[4] *Ibid.* Q. 9996.   [5] *Ibid.* Q. 9998.   [6] *Ibid.* Q. 9992.

years. New collieries were developed in Derbyshire, Nottinghamshire and Yorkshire. Electricity, generated by new and more powerful engines from waste heat, exhaust steam and blast furnace gases, was supplied to other industrial enterprises and to local authorities. The gas derived from an ever-increasing number of coke ovens was likewise supplied to local authorities. The range of chemical by-products was greatly extended and the salt which was used in their manufacture was produced by the Company itself in Cheshire, much to the displeasure of the 'salt ring', as Markham called it.[1] The engineering firm of Markham and Company became amalgamated with the Staveley Company in 1925. Shortly before his death in 1926 Charles Paxton Markham was head of a vast organization, the chairman and managing director of fifteen companies, joint managing director of one company, and a director of six other companies.[2] The collieries with which he was connected were then raising 10 million tons of coal a year and the ironstone companies one million tons of ore.[3]

Markham was succeeded as chairman of the Staveley Company by Sir William Bird and as managing director by D. N. Turner. Under their guidance further important amalgamations took place. The Company held the whole of the shares in the Yorkshire Main Colliery Company, which in turn held nearly half the shares in the Firbeck Main, and a smaller interest in the Markham Main Colliery Company. It also held half the shares in the Brodsworth Main Colliery Company. These four companies, with the Hickleton and Bullcroft Main colliery companies, all came under the management of William Humble, a director of the Staveley Company, and were already loosely grouped in the Doncaster Collieries Association, Ltd. This was an organization which disposed of coal at a commission of 6d. a ton and bought stores on a 2½ per cent. commission. Its capital was held by the associated colliery companies, profits being returned to them in the form of dividends. Charles Markham explained his attitude towards it before

---

[1] *Derbyshire Times*, 10 January, 1925.

[2] Markham was chairman and managing director of the Staveley Coal and Iron Company, Ltd., the Parkgate Iron and Steel Company, Ltd., the Markham Main Collieries, Ltd., the Bullcroft Main Collieries, Ltd., the Newstead Colliery Company, Ltd., the Yorkshire Main Colliery, Ltd., the British Soda Company, Ltd., the Doncaster Collieries Association, Ltd., the Midland Ironstone Company, the Burton Ironstone Company, Ltd., the Cranford Ironstone Company, Ltd., the Loddington Ironstone Company, Ltd., the Eastwell Iron Ore Company, the Lamport Ironstone Company, Markham and Company (1925), Ltd. He was joint managing director of the Brodsworth Main Colliery Company, Ltd., and director of the Ramcroft Colliery Company, Ltd., the Hickleton Main Colliery Company, Ltd., the Firbeck Main Collieries, Ltd., the Industrial Housing Association, Ltd., The Chesterfield Housing Company, Ltd., the Chesterfield Housing Association, Ltd. (*R.C. on Coal Industry*, 1925, II, (Part B), Evidence of Markham, p. 537.)

[3] *R. C. on Coal Industry*, 1925, II, (Part B), Evidence of Markham, p. 538.

the Samuel Commission: 'It is purely a buying and selling organization. They take over the whole of our coal; they guarantee us the money; we make no bad debts, and we have nothing to do with it.'[1] In 1937 the associated collieries were brought together by a merger company, the Doncaster Amalgamated Collieries, Ltd., in which the Staveley Company was the largest individual shareholder. The chairman of the new company was William Humble.[2]

The other great vertically integrated Derbyshire firm, the Sheepbridge Company, followed a similar pattern of development. Further ironstone mines and limestone quarries were acquired.[3] A new plant for breaking slag and making tar macadam was erected. In 1923, in conjunction with Stokes, Ltd., of Mansfield, the Sheepbridge Company created another subsidiary, the Sheepbridge Stokes Centrifugal Castings, Ltd.[4] In 1927 the Sheepbridge Company's Yorkshire subsidiaries, the Dinnington Main Colliery Company, the Maltby Main Colliery Company, and the Rossington Main Colliery Company (in association with John Brown and Company, of Sheffield), were grouped under the title of the Yorkshire Amalgamated Collieries, Ltd., with another large company, the Denaby and Cadeby Main Collieries, Ltd. The latter was partly controlled by the great coal-shipping and coal-factoring firm of William France, Fenwick & Company, Ltd., which had expanded into coal production, first, with the ownership of the Washington Coal Company, Ltd., in Durham, and, second, into part control of the Denaby and Cadeby Company in 1923.[5] In 1930 the centrifugal castings business of Newton Chambers, the Yorkshire coal and iron firm, was combined with that of the Sheepbridge Stokes Company.[6]

The interconnections between the Staveley and Sheepbridge companies have already been noted.[7] Their joint working of the Newstead and the Firbeck Main collieries was one of the more obvious indications of the close relationship which existed between them. They were also closely tied by interlocking directorates through their various subsidiaries.[8] The result, by the outbreak of the Second World War, was a vast combine of which it is virtually impossible to trace all the

[1] R.C. on Coal Industry, 1925, II, (Part B), Evidence of Markham, Q. 10,303.
[2] Annual Report of the Staveley Coal and Iron Company, Ltd. for the year ending 30 June, 1937.
[3] Annual Report of the Sheepbridge Coal and Iron Company, Ltd. for the year ending 30 June, 1920.
[4] Annual Report of the Sheepbridge Company for the year ending 30 June, 1923.
[5] W. Fox, Coal Combines in Yorkshire, Labour Research Department, (London), 1935, p. 22; Annual Report of the Sheepbridge Company for the year ending 30 June, 1927.
[6] Derbyshire Times, 4 October, 1930.
[7] See pp. 38–41, 201–4.   [8] Cf. Neuman, op. cit. pp. 155–6.

ramifications.[1] Charles Markham played a prominent part in building the organization until his death in 1926. Another dominating figure was the first Baron Aberconway, the son-in-law of H. D. Pochin who was the original founder of both companies and had wide business interests. This historic connection was continued by the second Baron Aberconway who succeeded to the title in 1934. The Aberconways combined directorships of the Sheepbridge Company, the Doncaster Amalgamated Collieries and the Yorkshire Amalgamated Collieries with a variety of other business interests. Their long-standing connection with John Brown and Company, the Sheffield steel firm, could be traced back to the labours of Pochin in the nineteenth century and was reflected in the organization of both the Doncaster Amalgamated Collieries, nominally under the control of the Staveley Company, and of the Yorkshire Amalgamated Collieries, nominally under the control of the Sheepbridge Company. William Humble combined a directorship of the Staveley Company with the chairmanship of the Doncaster Amalgamated Collieries and also had interests in three wagon companies and two finance companies. Sir Henry Stephenson, one of the principal directors of the Sheepbridge Company, had interests in Williams Deacon's Bank, as had E. E. Bird and other important shareholders of the Staveley Company. The soundness of the whole enterprise may perhaps be concluded from the fact that J. M. (later Lord) Keynes had substantial holdings of ordinary and deferred shares in the Yorkshire Amalgamated Collieries.[2]

By 1942 the Staveley-Sheepbridge group had an annual output of 19,650,000 tons of coal which was greater than that of any other colliery combine in the country. Second came the Powell Duffryn group with 15,000,000 tons, and third, the Bolsover Colliery Company.[3] In 1923 the Bolsover Company was producing 11,000 tons of coal a day. The development of the modern electrically operated collieries at Clipstone and at Thoresby, in the heart of the Sherwood Forest, during the 'twenties, increased the Company's output by an additional 6,000 tons a day, making a total output of over 5,000,000 tons a year. By 1942 this had risen to 6,000,000 tons. After the death in 1911 of Emerson Bainbridge, its founder, the Bolsover Company continued to flourish under the guidance of J. P. Houfton as managing director. Houfton retired from this position in 1919 but continued to serve as a director and consulting engineer, and became chairman of the Hatfield Main Colliery Company. He was knighted in 1929 and died soon afterwards,

[1] See Chart 6.
[2] Fox, op. cit. p. 30. £3,000 ord. and 5,750 def. (at 4s.) and £4,500 ord. and 7,000 def. in joint holding. Cf. R. F. Harrod, The Life of John Maynard Keynes, (London), 1951, pp. 299–300.
[3] M. Heinemann, Britain's Coal, (London), 1944, pp. 178, 180.

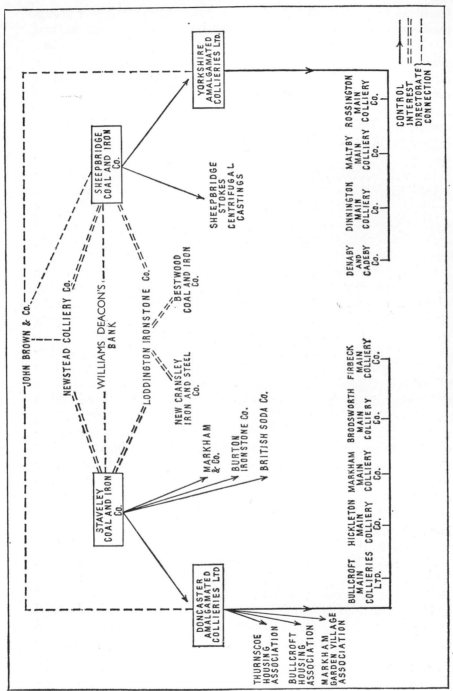

Chart 6.—The Staveley-Sheepbridge Group.

leaving estate worth £88,717.[1] Unlike the Staveley-Sheepbridge group, the Bolsover Company was concerned entirely with the production and sale of coal, and its activities were concentrated upon six large modern collieries in Derbyshire and Nottinghamshire. Apart from a housing company it had no subsidiaries and after the death of Houfton its principal directors had few other colliery interests. Sir Cecil Cochrane had connections with the Blackwell Colliery Company and the Newcastle-upon-Tyne and Gateshead Gas Company. D. A. Stirling had interests in the New Jarrow Steel Company, the British Overseas Bank, the London Life Association, the Westminster Bank and Armstrong-Whitworth securities. In 1936 when the Derbyshire Coalite Company, a subsidiary of Low Temperature Carbonization, Ltd., decided to erect a large 'Coalite' and by-product plant at Bolsover, the Bolsover Colliery Company entered into an agreement to supply the plant with coal and was given the right to nominate two additional directors to the board of the new company.[2]

Changes were also taking place in the medium-sized firms, particularly the family concerns. In 1928, after an association lasting over eighty years, the Barnes family severed their connection with the Grassmoor Collieries which came under the control of a new company with I. W. Lamonby as its chairman.[3] The new company carried out a number of improvements, including the installation of 20 Otto under-jet silica regenerative ovens which were capable of carbonizing 400 tons of coal every 24 hours and did the work of 110 older coke ovens which they replaced.[4] In 1939 the Seely family, who had been interested in coalmining in Derbyshire and Nottinghamshire for nearly eighty years, broke their final link with the industry when their Tibshelf and Birchwood collieries, trading under the name of the Babbington Colliery Company, were absorbed by the Sheepbridge Company.[5] Many of the smaller uneconomic collieries had to close down completely for, as the official historians of the Butterley Company have pointed out: 'An efficient colliery could not be expected to encrust itself with barnacles in the shape of inefficient or expiring concerns. They did not do so, and would not do so.'[6]

Similar developments were taking place throughout the country. The concentration of ownership was proceeding in two ways: by the closing of uneconomic collieries and by amalgamation. Between 1913 and 1938 the number of mines at work in the United Kingdom fell from 3,121 to 2,125. Shortly before the Second World War it was estimated that 80 per cent. of the total output of the country was

---

[1] *Derbyshire Times*, 15 February, 1930. [2] *Ibid.* 1 May, 1936.
[3] *Ibid.* 14 April, 1928. [4] *Ibid.* 16 June, 1934.
[5] *Ibid.* 28 April, 1939. [6] Mottram and Coote, *op. cit.* p. 150.

produced by about 130 undertakings.[1] In Derbyshire, Nottinghamshire and South Yorkshire the Coal Commission found that there were 124 undertakings producing a total output of 62,750,000 tons a year. Two-thirds of the total output was produced by 22 undertakings[2] and 38 per cent. by 7 undertakings. Had the Commission regarded the Staveley and Sheepbridge companies and their subsidiaries as a single undertaking the degree of concentration would have been even higher.

The Commission made no recommendations for the greater part of the area occupied by the twenty-two large concerns 'not because there is no room for reorganization, but because large and small undertakings are so mixed up geographically that more detailed inquiry is necessary before proposals can be made'. On the west of the coalfield were a number of comparatively small concerns, some of which had been acquired by their larger neighbours on the east. For those which were still independent further consolidation was suggested. The largest firms on the west of the coalfield were the Tinsley Park Colliery Company, Ltd., the Nunnery Coal Company, Ltd., Skinner and Holford, Ltd., J. and G. Wells, Ltd., and the Oxcroft Colliery Company, Ltd. For the undertakings in the south-west and south of the coalfield the Commission proposed the creation of three areas. It was recommended that Area I should include the Blackwell Colliery Company, Ltd., the Clay Cross Company, Ltd., and Wingfield Manor Colliery Company, Ltd., the Grassmoor Company, Ltd., the Hardwick Colliery Company, Ltd., the New Hucknall Colliery Company, Ltd., the Pilsley Colliery Company, Ltd., the Pinxton Collieries, Ltd., and the South Normanton Colliery Company, Ltd. In Area II it was suggested that the Butterley Company, Ltd., or Barber, Walker and Company, Ltd., should acquire their smaller neighbours, including James Oakes and Company (Riddings Collieries), Ltd., R. C. A. Palmer Morewood, the Pentrich Colliery Company, Ltd., and J. A. E. Drury Lowe. The principal undertakings included in Area III were the B.A. Collieries, Ltd., the Cossall Colliery Company, Ltd., the Nottingham and Clifton Colliery

---

[1] *Derbyshire Times*, 28 April, 1939; Heinemann, *op. cit.* p. 108.
[2] Amalgamated Denaby Collieries, Ltd; Askern Coal and Iron Company, Ltd.; Barber, Walker & Company, Ltd.; Barnsley Collieries Association; Bolsover Colliery Company, Ltd.; John Brown & Company, Ltd. (Dalton Main Collieries, Ltd.); Butterley Company, Ltd.; Carlton Main Colliery Company, Ltd. (Hatfield Colliery Company, Ltd., Holroyd Coal Company, Ltd.); Doncaster Amalgamated Collieries, Ltd.; Manvers Main Collieries, Ltd.; New Hucknall Colliery Company, Ltd.; New Monckton Collieries, Ltd.; Newstead Colliery Company, Ltd.; Pease and Partners, Ltd. (Thorne Colliery); Sheepbridge Coal and Iron Company, Ltd.; Sherwood Colliery Company, Ltd. (Kiveton Coal Company, Ltd.); Shirebrook Colliery Company, Ltd.; Shireoakes Colliery Company, Ltd.; Stanton Ironworks Company, Ltd.; Staveley Coal and Iron Company, Ltd.; United Steel Companies, Ltd. (Sheffield Coal Company, Ltd., Samuel Fox & Company, Ltd.); Wigan Coal Corporation, Ltd. (Manton Colliery.)

Company, Ltd., the Shipley Collieries, Ltd., the Ilkeston Collieries, Ltd., and the Wollaton Collieries, Ltd.[1]

VII

With improved organization went increased technical efficiency. Mechanization, which had been introduced so slowly into British coal-mines, was given a great impetus by the highly competitive conditions of the late 'twenties and the early 'thirties. The use of coal-cutting machines had increased steadily in the more progressive coalfields ever since their invention in the nineteenth century. Nevertheless, in 1928 only 26 per cent. of the total output of the North Midland inspection division was cut by machines. By 1938 the amount had risen to 79 per cent. Partly for technical reasons the introduction of mechanical con-veyors came even later. In the North Midland division in 1928 only 7 per cent. of the output was mechanically conveyed. By 1938 mechani-cal conveying was as extensive as mechanical cutting, accounting for 78 per cent. of the output. In this respect the North Midland division was well in advance of other areas for in 1938 only 59 per cent. of the country's coal was mechanically cut and 54 per cent. mechanically conveyed.[2]

The principal effect of these developments was to reduce costs by increasing productivity and reducing the demand for labour. The output per man-shift for underground and surface workers in the division increased from 23·52 cwt. in 1928 to 28·41 cwt. in 1938. J. R. Felton, H.M. Inspector of Mines, reported in 1932: 'The chief reason for this increase lies in the extension of mechanical mining, and the concentration of coal getting in smaller areas worked intensively.'[3] The increasing efficiency of labour resulted in a fall in the volume of employment. In Derbyshire 46,713 men were employed underground in 1919. By 1924 the number had risen to 49,879 but thereafter it declined steadily to 32,439 in 1938. Similarly the number of surface workers decreased from 12,251 in 1919 to 9,217 in 1938. Part of this reduction was due to declining trade but most of it was due to mechani-zation. Whilst the output for 1938 was only 1·3 per cent. lower than that for 1919 there was a 31 per cent. reduction in the number of under-ground workers and a 44 per cent. reduction in surface workers.[4]

---

[1] *Derbyshire Times*, 16 June, 1939.
[2] *Reports of H.M. Inspectors of Mines*, 1928–38. Cf. E. C. Rhodes, 'Output, Labour and Machines in the Coal Mining Industry in Great Britain', *Economica*, XII, (1945), pp. 101–10.
[3] *Reports of H.M. Inspectors of Mines*, 1932.
[4] See Appendix II to this chapter.

The development of large modern collieries and the introduction of improved techniques involved a heavy capital outlay. During the 'twenties the Butterley Company was engaged in sinking a new colliery at Ollerton at a cost of £850,000. The total cost of the venture was £1,500,000. In addition there was an expenditure of well over £1,000,000 (equal to about one-third of the Company's issued capital) mostly concentrated into the six or seven years preceding the Second World War. This was exclusive of maintenance and replacement costs. By 1939 about £158,000 had been spent on coal-cutting machinery alone, with the result that in one pit as much as 96 per cent. of the total output was mechanically mined. It has been estimated, on the basis of these figures, that the Butterley Company re-invested in the space of twenty years a sum equal to the whole of its capital.[1]

On the other hand there was some watering of capital. This took place, as Dr. Neuman has shown, during the relatively prosperous period 1919–24, when the projects of the colliery companies seemed profitable to investors.[2] In 1923 the Bolsover Company decided to issue 22,000 ordinary shares at a premium of 5s. a share to existing shareholders, in the proportion of one new share for every ten held.[3] Between 1913 and 1924 the capital reserves (including debenture capital) of the Sheepbridge Company increased from £1,345,000 to £2,112,000 and the valuation of fixed assets (including interests in allied firms) rose from £994,000 to £1,745,000.[4]

During this period profits had been substantial as was shown by the evidence given before the Sankey and Samuel commissions.[5] They were reduced by the deflationary wave which followed and only began to reach their former level during the years immediately preceding the Second World War. By comparison with the high dividends which had been paid in the years before the First World War those which were paid in the 'twenties and 'thirties appeared very unsatisfactory to the coal-owners. Nevertheless, the larger and more efficient organizations were generally able to pay a dividend of 5 per cent. or more except in the years of strikes or extreme financial stringency. The Bolsover Company's dividends only fell below 6 per cent. in 1921 and from 1927 to 1930. The Staveley Company never paid less than 5 per cent. throughout the inter-war years. With the exception of the years 1926, 1928 and 1929 the Sheepbridge Company had a similar record.[6]

---

[1] Butterley Company, Ltd., Coal Mines Nationalization Bill, Report on Development and Past History, April, 1946; Mottram and Coote, *op. cit.* p. 154.

[2] Neuman, *op. cit.* pp. 63, 149, 212.

[3] *Derbyshire Times*, 10 March, 1923. [4] Neuman, *op. cit.* p. 65.

[5] *Coal Industry Commission*, 1919, I, Evidence of A. L. Dickinson, QQ. 22–763; R.C. on Coal Industry, 1925, III, Appendix No. 16, Statement 9, pp. 124–7.

[6] See Appendix III to this chapter.

T

These benefits accrued mainly from the increased use of machinery which large-scale organizations made possible. In 1934 Sir William Bird told the shareholders of the Staveley Company: 'Nearly 95 per cent. of their coal was machine mined. Were it not for this system of working it was doubtful whether they would be able to maintain their place in the coal trade as they had done.'[1] On the other hand many of the smaller concerns could not command sufficient capital for modernization. Speaking in the House of Commons on 11 December, 1935, Herbert Wragg, M.P. for Belper and chairman of the South Leicestershire Colliery Company, stated that he had analysed the results for the previous seven years of 73 public companies engaged in the production of coal. They had paid an average dividend of 2·85 per cent. but 34 of them had paid no dividend at all. Many of them owed bank overdrafts; one to the extent of £1,200,000.[2]

In Derbyshire there were many uneconomic pits, especially in the old exposed coalfield to the west and south of a line running from Chester-field to Nottingham. In this area, which included such centres as Clay Cross, Alfreton, Ripley, Heanor and Ilkeston, many collieries were abandoned during the inter-war years. It was reported in 1945 that the 66 pits still working employed about 40,000 men with an average of 603 per colliery.[3] Since the turn of the century, when the 'top hard' seam began to be fully exploited, new colliery developments had tended to move in an easterly direction towards the older concealed coalfield, bounded on the east roughly by a line drawn from Worksop in the north to Nottingham in the south.[4] In this area, which included part of Nottinghamshire, the collieries were larger and fewer. Although there were over 28,000 miners employed, there were only 26 pits, with an average of 1,070 men in each. Still further east lay the new concealed coalfield, including the greater part of the Sherwood Forest, with the largest and most modern collieries such as the Butterley Company's at Ollerton and the Bolsover Company's at Clipstone and Thoresby. The area contained only eight collieries, with an average of 1,537 men in each and a total of over 12,000 employees.[5]

The Staveley and Sheepbridge Companies had moved even further afield to exploit the highly profitable seams in the Doncaster area. As early as 1921 Charles Markham had stated:

We are losing a lot of money here in Derbyshire. The men are working hard but they are getting too much money compared with the men in other

[1] Derbyshire Times, 28 September, 1934.
[2] 307 H. C. Deb. 5s. 966.
[3] Ministry of Fuel and Power, Regional Survey Report, North Midland Coalfield, (1945), pp. 21–2.   [4] See Chapter V.
[5] Ministry of Fuel and Power, Regional Survey Report, North Midland Coalfield, (1945), p. 22.

parts of the country, and as many of the pits are old, they have to go further for the coal. That sends up the price, and they cannot compete with South Yorkshire.[1]

Referring to Markham's colliery developments in South Yorkshire, the Samuel Commission reported: 'We cannot doubt that what has been successfully achieved in this instance, and in one or two others in different parts of Great Britain, might be imitated in many more.'[2]

Modern mining such as existed in parts of Derbyshire, Nottingham-shire and Yorkshire was not to be found in every coalfield. The Midland district, with its large reserves of coal and many large modern pits, was in a comparatively favourable position during the inter-war years. The older coalfields of Northumberland, Durham, Scotland and South Wales, which had once dominated the export markets, were steadily losing ground. Costs were increasing and productivity was virtually at a standstill. The Reid Committee, in 1945, reported that these areas had 'achieved little or nothing in the way of increased output per man-shift during the 12 years under review'.[3]

These disparities within the coal industry were one of the main reasons for the miners' persistent advocacy of nationalization. They felt, with reason, that their wages were largely determined by the financial position of the inefficient mines, which were great in number yet responsible for a small and ever decreasing proportion of the country's total output of coal. As Mr. Rowe has shown, it was impos-sible under a system of private ownership for the miners 'without sacrificing the first principles of trade unionism' to 'reach the surplus profits of the good pits'.[4] The miners believed that under public ownership profits could be pooled and uniform rates of wages paid throughout the country. The surplus could then be used for a thorough re-organization of the industry. The coal-owners and successive govern-ments believed that it was possible to re-organize the industry and enable it to pay the miner an adequate wage without resorting to nationalization. Whether they were right will never be known for the Second World War brought the mines once again under government control and subsequently they were nationalized. But few would disagree with Professor Court's conclusion 'that the record of the industry between the wars does not afford satisfactory evidence that the change would have been successfully completed under private ownership'.[5]

[1] *Derbyshire Times*, 31 December, 1921.
[2] *R. C. on Coal Industry*, 1925, I, Report, p. 57.
[3] *Ministry of Fuel and Power, Report of the Technical Advisory Committee on Coal-mining*, 1945, (Cmd. 6610), paras. 44, 45.
[4] Rowe, *op. cit.* p. 129.   [5] Court, *loc. cit.* p. 23.

APPENDIX I

Output and the Price of Coal, 1919–1938

	Output		Average Net selling value per ton	
	Derbyshire (exclusive of South Derbyshire) Tons	U.K. Tons	Derbyshire (exclusive of South Derbyshire) s. d.	U.K. s. d.
1919	14,882,429*	229,779,517	—	26 2·97
1920	14,179,075*	229,532,081	—	34 6·97
1921	9,728,657	163,251,181	—	26 2·23
1922	14,213,379	249,606,864	17 2·35	17 7·53
1923	16,065,225	276,000,560	16 9·44	18 9·86
1924	15,602,967	267,118,167	17 8·42	18 10·11
1925	14,724,197	243,176,231	15 5·59	16 4·38
1926	9,164,266	126,278,521	24 0·64	19 6·50
1927	13,744,517	251,232,336	14 6·15	14 7·34
1928	13,093,259	237,471,931	12 5·35	12 10·14
1929	14,198,811	257,906,802	12 11·48	13 5·21
1930	13,787,822	243,881,824	12 11·57	13 7·10
1931	12,645,665	219,458,951	13 5·40	13 5·57
1932	11,877,274	208,733,140	13 5·53	13 3·11
1933	11,238,826	207,112,243	12 11·27	13 0·27
1934	11,797,558	220,726,298	12 8·02	12 10·53
1935	11,978,615	222,248,822	12 8·84	13 0·08
1936	12,471,150	228,448,356	14 0·10	14 0·22
1937	13,807,931	240,409,436	14 7·85	15 2·36
1938	13,014,015	227,015,308	15 6·22	16 7·62

* Including South Derbyshire.

Source: *Reports of H.M. Inspectors of Mines, 1919–1938.*

APPENDIX II

Employment and Productivity, 1919–1938

| | Average Number of Persons Employed (North Derbyshire) | | Mechanization and Output per Man-shift (North Midland Inspection Division) | | |
| | Underground | Above ground | Percentage of total Output produced by machinery | | Output per shift per person employed below and above ground (cwt.) |
			Cut	Conveyed	
1919	46,713	12,251	—	—	—
1920	47,744	12,614	—	—	—
1921	47,241	11,369	—	—	—
1922	47,413	11,348	—	—	—
1923	49,291	11,761	—	—	—
1924	49,879	11,626	—	—	—
1925	47,317	11,184	—	—	—
1926	—	—	—	—	—
1927	45,296	10,592	—	—	—
1928	42,003	10,190	26	7	23·52
1929	42,044	10,079	—	—	24·05
1930	41,769	10,105	35	16	24·20
1931	40,095	9,579	39	23	24·55
1932	38,230	9,281	43	28	24·85
1933	34,962	8,833	52	39	25·98
1934	34,369	8,703	60	50	26·90
1935	33,237	8,716	67	59	27·58
1936	32,209	8,676	73	67	28·03
1937	32,040	9,019	78	74	28·64
1938	32,439	9,217	79	78	28·41

Source: *Reports of H.M. Inspectors of Mines, 1919–1938.*

APPENDIX III

Distributed Profits, 1919–1939

Dividends Paid on Ordinary Shares

	Bolsover Colliery Company, Ltd. per cent.	Staveley Coal and Iron Company, Ltd. per cent.	Sheepbridge Coal and Iron Company, Ltd. per cent.
1919	—	10	10
1920	7·5	11·25	10
1921	3	10	7·5
1922	—	7·5	6
1923	16	10	7·5
1924	14	10	7·5
1925	8	7·5	5
1926	15	5	2·5
1927	2	7·5	7·5
1928	1·5	5	2·5
1929	3·75	5	2·5
1930	2·5	6	5
1931	7	6	5
1932	6	5	5
1933	7	5	5
1934	8	6·5	5
1935	9	8	6·5
1936	9	9	10
1937	10	12·5	10
1938	10	11	12·5
1939	10 (+ bonus of 5%)	10	12·5

Sources: Annual Reports of the Companies.

CHAPTER XV

TRADE UNION ORGANIZATION AND FINANCE, 1918–39

I

During the period from 1880 to 1914 Haslam's and Harvey's long tenure of two of the principal positions in the Association had provided an element of continuity which was resistant to all attempts at violent change. In contrast the much shorter period between the wars was one of rapidly moving events when further links with the past were broken, and new men and new policies emerged. By 1939 Frank Lee was the only permanent official who had held his position in the Association before the First World War.

In February, 1920, the Executive Committee recommended that Lee should become Assistant General and Financial Secretary, that John Spencer should take over Lee's duties as Compensation Agent, and that another official should be appointed to act as Treasurer.[1] This resulted in the election of Henry Hicken whose appointment was confirmed by the Council on 22 May, 1920.[2] Born at North Wingfield in 1882, Hicken left school at the age of 12 and began work as a trammer at the Pilsley Colliery for which he received 10d. a day. He stayed there for twelve years and then, after a year at the Parkhouse Colliery, went to the Williamthorpe Colliery where he became a checkweighman. He was also secretary of the Williamthorpe lodge, which had between 1,700 and 1,800 members. Of his 18 years' experience in the pit, 14 were spent at the coal face.[3] Like the older miners' leaders Hicken had embraced both Liberalism and Methodism but growing to maturity at a time when Socialism and Syndicalism were in the air he soon became influenced by more revolutionary creeds. He gained prominence before the war by his activities on the political platform and in the pulpit. In 1914 he said: 'No one was a more earnest Liberal than I in 1906. And if the Liberals had adhered to their programme I venture

[1] *D.M.A.* 17 February, 1920.
[2] *Ibid.* 22 May, 1920.
[3] *Derbyshire Times,* 7 January, 1928.

to say I should be a Liberal today.'[1] During the war he sought nomination as a prospective Labour candidate but his actions at that time showed that his heart was set on a career as a trade union leader.[2] In 1919 he contested unsuccessfully the presidency of the Association.[3] His sermons and lectures on religious topics[4] no doubt served to win the confidence of some of the more moderate members of the union but after his election as Treasurer in 1920 he soon abandoned the pulpit.[5]

Hicken's powerful oratory, his extreme militancy, his impressive appearance, his long hair, his habit of wearing an immaculate white shirt and collar without a tie (which he was later to continue as an official of the National Coal Board and an O.B.E.), were all characteristics which endeared him to thousands of Derbyshire miners and made him one of the most colourful and dominating personalities in the history of the Association. His election was part of the revolt against the older trade union leader. One writer commented:

> It's no use trying to infuse new life into dead bones. The Kenyon-Hancock type are living in the past. They have not the energy to grasp or wrestle with the gigantic problems that confront us today. That is no doubt the reason why they are held up as ideal Labour leaders by a certain class. The Liberals are satisfied with them. Conservative mine owners sign their nomination forms. They themselves would be quite happy and content if those young rebels would not disturb them from their sleep by talking about economics, social science, capital, wages, etc., things they do not understand.[6]

As a trade union official Hicken was a figure comparable in stature with Haslam and Harvey, and represents a bridge between the old type of leadership and the new. Starting with a background similar to that of the older leaders he was to become one of the *enfants terribles* of the 'twenties, described by the *Derbyshire Times* as 'trying to make our flesh creep with threats of red revolution' and 'revelling in the anticipation of gore and bloodshed'.[7] Later he was to mellow and become a responsible trade union leader whose co-operation was to be sought when the Government took control of the coal industry during the Second World War and when the industry was finally nationalized.

Within eight years of Hicken's election as Treasurer three of the older leaders had disappeared from the scene. Despite his political disaffection Barnet Kenyon had continued to serve as General Agent for which, in accordance with the Association's rule for full-time

[1] *Derbyshire Times* 13 June, 1914.   [2] See Chapter XIII, p. 544.
[3] *D.M.A.* 6 December, 1919.
[4] *Derbyshire Times*, 27 February, 1915.   [5] *Ibid.* 4 March, 1922.
[6] *Ibid.* 5 June, 1920.   [7] *Ibid.* 27 November, 1920.

officials who were elected to Parliament, he received a retaining fee of £100 a year. This was discontinued after the general election of November, 1922, as part of the Association's change of policy regarding parliamentary candidatures in a period of financial stringency, but Kenyon considered that he had been unjustly treated.[1] Thereafter, although still nominally an official who was free to resume full-time work whenever he lost or relinquished his seat in Parliament, Kenyon showed little interest in the affairs of the union. Eventually, on 6 November, 1923, it was resolved by the Executive Committee:

Seeing that Mr. Kenyon has now reached over 70 years of age, and that he does not attend either Council or Executive Committee meetings, neither does he do any work in the offices, it would not be just to continue to place his name amongst the officials at the end of the minutes as being in any way responsible for the policy of the Association. It also recommends that an inclusive figure of £2 per week be given to Mr. Kenyon as a life pension.[2]

This recommendation was endorsed by the Council, and Kenyon was allowed to retain the tenancy of the Association's house in Shaftesbury Avenue at a rent of £30 a year.[3]

Towards the end of 1924 William Sewell, who was then 73, announced that because of his age he did not intend to stand for the presidency for 1925.[4] To celebrate his retirement a dinner was held at the Station Hotel, Chesterfield. In presenting the customary illuminated address and gold watch Frank Hall remarked that it was the first time in the history of the Association that the delegates had dined together. 'It had been suggested on more than one occasion', he said. 'The first time was when the new offices were built, but it was found then that it would not run even to tea.'[5]

Sewell was succeeded by Enoch Overton, who had been Vice-President since 1919. Born at Wrockwardine, in Shropshire, in 1864, Overton came to work at Bolsover when the colliery was being developed. He soon became a prominent figure in the mining community and was elected checkweighman. He was one of the original members of the Bolsover urban district council, a member of the Board of Guardians, and chairman of the Bolsover school managers. He was appointed a magistrate in 1919 and later served on the county magistrates' advisory committee.[6]

The new Vice-President was Samuel Sales. Born at New Tupton, near Chesterfield, in 1880, he began to work in the pit at the age of 11 and was working in a stall at the age of 16. In 1911 he became

[1] See Chapter XXI, pp. 820-1.
[3] *Ibid.* 8 and 20 December, 1923.
[5] *Derbyshire Times*, 10 January, 1925.

[2] *D.M.A.* 6 November, 1923.
[4] *Ibid.* 6 December, 1924.
[6] *Ibid.* 12 March, 1948.

T*

checkweighman at the Grassmoor No. 1 Colliery where he gained the reputation of being a skilful negotiator. Under his guidance the colliery was the first in the county to abolish the butty system and the first to have pithead baths under the Miners' Welfare Scheme. A keen student of economics and logic, he attended W.E.A. classes and summer schools at Oxford.[1] Sales, like Hicken, had a Methodist background, and in 1915 was to be found presiding at one of Hicken's lectures on Martin Luther.[2] In 1920, however, they were both described by a writer to the *Derbyshire Times* as 'extremists', and Hicken was enjoined 'to go to Ireland or to Russia and take his pal Sales with him'.[3]

The death of Frank Hall on 1 December, 1927, severed another link with the past. Hall had been the victim of indifferent health for some time. In 1925 he had a slight seizure whilst attending a Council meeting and, on medical advice, cancelled all his public engagements for a month. The strain of the 1926 stoppage added to his difficulties at a time when rest was desirable.[4] In recording its appreciation of his work the Council commented:

> During his years of office as a permanent official many changes have taken place in the necessary qualifications of a miners' leader, and he fitted himself for these changes by a constant and ever-watchful study of the developments in the industry. He will be greatly missed by this Association and by the Miners' Federation of Great Britain.[5]

Lee and Hicken both contested the general secretaryship which carried no additional salary but greater prestige. Lee had been returned to Parliament as Member for North-East Derbyshire in 1922 and had retained his seat in the 1923 and 1924 general elections. He was apparently not prepared to abandon his parliamentary career to serve as a full-time Assistant Secretary but was prepared to do so if he could become General Secretary of the Association. However, a branch ballot gave Hicken 311 votes to Lee's 247 and he continued to serve as unpaid Assistant Secretary and Member of Parliament for North-East Derbyshire.[6] He lost his seat in the general election of 1931 and was employed as a full-time official until 1935 when he was again returned to Parliament.[7]

Hicken's elevation to the position of General Secretary meant that a new Treasurer had to be elected. Among the twelve candidates nominated by the branches were Joseph Lynch, Oliver Wright, Samuel Sales and Philip Hicken (the brother of Henry). It was decided by the

[1] *Derbyshire Times*, 1 and 8 January, 1937.
[2] *Ibid*. 27 February, 1915.
[3] *Ibid*. 13 November, 1920.
[4] *Ibid*. 10 December, 1927.
[5] *D.M.A.* 3 December, 1927.
[6] *Ibid*. 28 January, 1928.
[7] *Ibid*. 31 October, 1931; 23 November, 1935.

Council that there should be an individual ballot of the members.[1] Lynch, Sales and Wright, with 3,710, 3,168 and 2,154 votes respectively, had a clear majority over the other candidates and were entered for a second ballot.[2] Lynch's success in the first ballot aroused some interest. Since 1912 he had been the chief clerk in the Association's offices but, as a member of the Glapwell lodge, he had served on the Executive Committee since 1921. He had also been active in the Chesterfield Divisional Labour Party. The *Derbyshire Times* commented:

The result . . . clearly indicates that a large number of the miners of Derbyshire have no fear in following the example set by the Durham miners when they appointed to an official position Mr. William Whiteley. . . . Mr. Lynch has gained wide experience on vital questions regarding the industry at the headquarters of the Association in Chesterfield.[3]

Others evidently thought differently, for Lynch complained that rumours had been circulated that he was a member of the Conservative Party and that in one very large district he had sent copies of his election circular to managers, undermanagers and deputies. These allegations he denied publicly and threatened to institute legal proceedings against anyone repeating them.[4] In the second ballot Wright had 6,421 votes; Lynch 6,324; and Sales 3,822.[5] Sales was thus eliminated from the contest and in the final ballot Wright was successful with 9,908 to Lynch's 7,128.[6]

Oliver Wright, who was born at Swanwick in 1881, had been a miner for twenty-eight years. He had been employed by the Butterley Company and since 1920 had been secretary of the Britain lodge and a delegate to the Council. He was also one of the Association's trustees. In the general elections of 1922 and 1923 he had contested the Belper division as a Labour candidate but had been unsuccessful. His health was not good and he had long illnesses during his period of office as Treasurer. He died on 21 January, 1938.[7]

In the election which ensued there were thirteen candidates.[8] Of these Joseph Lynch, Samuel Sales and Harold Neal were successful in the first ballot with 4,765, 1,831 and 1,491 votes respectively.[9] In the second ballot Lynch, with 8,487 votes against Sales's 3,998 and Neal's 2,693, had a clear majority and was declared elected.[10] The appointment of Lynch as Treasurer was a complete departure from the traditions of mining trade unionism. Lynch had never worked in a

[1] *D.M.A.* 28 January, 1928.   [2] *Ibid.* 13 February, 1928.
[3] *Derbyshire Times*, 18 February, 1928.   [4] *Ibid.* 3 March, 1928.
[5] *D.M.A.* 25 February, 1928.   [6] *Ibid.* 24 March, 1928.
[7] *Derbyshire Times*, 17 March, 1928; *D.M.A.* 12 February, 1938.
[8] *D.M.A.* 12 March, 1938.
[9] *Ibid.* 9 April, 1938.   [10] *Ibid.* 7 May, 1938.

mine but had a number of commercial qualifications. He had experience in accountancy, was a Fellow of the Faculty of Teachers in Commerce, and a Member of the Royal Society of Teachers. He had a knowledge of business methods, commercial law, banking, costing, office organization and shorthand. He held several teaching diplomas in commercial subjects and had taken the first and second places respectively in the advanced examinations in commerce of the Royal Society of Arts and of the National Union of Teachers. He had also attended courses in economics at Ruskin College and Nottingham University College and was the author of *Business Methods and Accountancy in Trade Unions*, a book which found its way into many trade union offices.[1] Lynch's unorthodox method of advancement was unlikely to be followed by others for it was stipulated by the Council that his successor, Oscar Cooke, should be a member of the National Union of Clerks.[2]

In October, 1938, Enoch Overton announced his intention of retiring from the presidency. He had held the office for fourteen years, had previously been Vice-President for eleven years, and had been a trustee of the Association for over thirty years.[3] In January, 1939, he was succeeded by Samuel Sales, and Henry White, of Creswell, became Vice-President.[4]

The salaries of the full-time officials continued to be linked with the miners' wages. In 1919 the officials were receiving £16 10s. 0d. a month with percentage additions amounting to £3 17s. 0d. and a war bonus of £7 5s. 3d. By 1939 they were being paid £24 16s. 9d. a month with percentage additions amounting to £2 10s. 1d. and a flat rate addition of 18s.

II

There were few major changes in the Association's rules during the inter-war years although the rules governing contributions and benefits were continually being modified to meet alterations in the union's financial position. The rules were completely re-drafted in 1923 and in their new form came into operation on 1 January, 1924. They reflected the policy of industrial unionism which had been adopted during the war by stating explicitly that the members of the Association 'shall consist of persons employed (manual or clerical) in or about the various mines and by-product works in Derbyshire'. Because of difficulties which had arisen with certain branches on the borders of Yorkshire,[5]

[1] *Derbyshire Times*, 18 March, 1938.
[2] *D.M.A.* 11 June, 30 July, 1938.
[3] *Ibid.* 1 October, 1938.
[4] *Ibid.* 31 December, 1938.
[5] See below, pp. 509-600.

the term 'Derbyshire collieries' was clearly defined as 'all those collieries at which are applicable the Minimum Rates and Rules of the Derbyshire District (exclusive of South Derbyshire) as settled on June 17th, 1912, and varied on September 25th, 1913, with the addition of the West Kiveton section of the Old Kiveton pit, and the Waleswood Collieries'. Among the objects of the Association was included the power to make grants for educational purposes but these were not to exceed £500 a year.[1]

The remaining changes were largely financial. The minimum amount to be held in the general fund was raised to £50,000. The amount which the Council or Executive Committee could grant to other unions without reference to the branches was increased to £10. Revised scales of payment for branch officials were adopted. Secretaries were to receive from 12s. to 251s. and treasurers from 7s. 6d. to 137s. 9d. a quarter according to the size of the branch. Current wage percentages were to be added to these payments as in the past. A new scale determined the maximum percentage of total income which could be used for branch expenses. It ranged from 17 per cent. for the smaller branches to 6 per cent. for the larger ones.[2]

The Association emerged from the First World War with a substantial increase in membership and funds. At the end of 1920 membership reached a peak of 59,035 falling to 51,084 in 1921 and more sharply to 39,455 in 1922 as a result of the 1921 lock-out and the reductions in wages which followed. By 1925 numbers had increased to 43,000 only to be severely diminished by the events of 1926, desertion to the Spencer Union,[3] and the onset of the world economic depression. In 1930 the Association had 18,285 members and in 1933 only 17,215. There was no substantial recovery until 1937, 1938 and 1939 when the figures were 20,210, 20,364 and 21,513 respectively.[4]

The Association's financial reserves had risen to £454,022 in 1918, a figure which was not to be exceeded until 1948. There was a decline in 1919 to £449,406, although membership was still increasing. The swollen membership and the reduction in funds were both due to the return of large numbers of miners from the armed forces. Many ex-servicemen were either temporarily unemployed or displaced men who had been working in the mines during the war. In 1919 the union disbursed £50,700 in unemployment benefits. In addition to this difficulty the Association's funds were being eroded by inflation. Even in nominal values investments per head had fallen from £10·42 in

[1] *Rules of the Derbyshire Miners' Association*, 1 January, 1924.
[2] *Ibid.* The word 'branch' was rapidly superseding the word 'lodge' at this period.
[3] See Chapters XVIII–XIX.
[4] See Appendix I to this chapter.

1915 to £7·88 in 1919. Their real value in that year, in terms of 1914 prices, was only £3·67.[1]

In 1920 unemployment benefits and the three-week strike in October and November swallowed up £21,416 and £201,282 respectively. To meet this expenditure the Association disposed of its National War Bonds, worth £50,000, and drew heavily on the banks. The loans to local authorities were untouched, increasing from £269,427 in 1919 to £274,378 in 1920, but bank deposits fell sharply from £123,620 to £17,075. At the end of the year the total financial reserves were £302,542.

The 1921 lock-out was a more serious matter. Benefits were being paid at the rate of £73,000 a week and the funds were soon exhausted. The final lock-out payments were made on 5 May. The officials, at their own request, were also unpaid until 2 July. By 25 May Parr's Bank, Ltd.[2] had been overdrawn to the extent of £190,000 on the strength of the Association's municipal securities.[3] Unemployment benefits, which had been a serious burden before the lock-out, became an even greater one afterwards and made necessary a further overdraft of £23,000 in July. Loans of £10,000 from the Ripley Co-operative Society and of £15,000 from members and others had enabled the Association to grant loans of 5s. or 10s. with 1s. for each child to its most needy members during the stoppage. These loans amounted to £28,206 and were later included by the Association among its assets although the officials pointed out later: 'We have no authority under the Trade Union Act either to borrow or lend to members. We did both during the strike of 1921, and in doing so put ourselves in an illegal position.'[4]

After the dispute there followed a period of retrenchment. Shortly before the 1920 stoppage the weekly contribution had been raised from sixpence to a shilling and benefits had been increased.[5] Now a levy was imposed and benefits were reduced. At the end of the year the Association's balance sheet showed that £293,132 had been distributed during the lock-out, and unemployment benefits for the year totalled £69,700. The overdraft at the bank had been reduced to £44,765 but municipal securities had dwindled to £54,990. Other liabilities were loans amounting to over £25,000. Including its property, cash in hand, and loans to members the Association was nominally worth about £50,520. However, the bulk of the £28,206 which had been lent to members was never repaid and in January, 1926, the outstanding sum

---

[1] See Chart 7 and Appendix I to this chapter.
[2] i.e. the London County, Westminster and Parr's Bank, Ltd.
[3] *D.M.A.* 25 May, 1921.
[4] *Ibid.* 27 February, 1926.   [5] *Ibid.* 14 June, 1920.

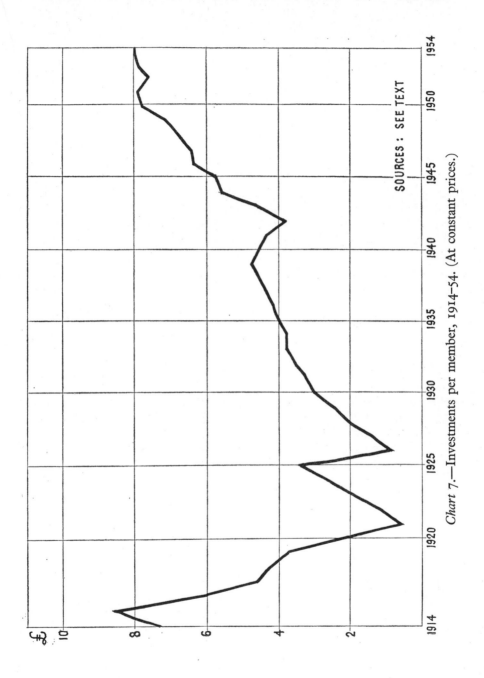

*Chart 7.—*Investments per member, 1914–54. (At constant prices.)

was written off.[1] A further proposal to cancel levies arrears was described by the officials as 'a very dangerous resolution and contrary to the constitution'. They pointed out that the rule relating to levies, if strictly applied, would compel many miners to re-join the Association.[2]

Between 1922 and 1925 the Association's financial position improved steadily. In January, 1923, the entrance fee was reduced from £1 to 10s. in order to encourage recruitment. The bank overdraft was reduced to £4,654 in 1922 and converted into a credit balance of £49,073 in 1923. By 1925 bank deposits had reached £74,208 and loans to local authorities had increased to £142,976. The Association entered the great industrial dispute of 1926 with funds amounting to £250,054, or about £5·8 per head. Within the first six weeks it had paid out, including a grant of £10,000 to the Nottinghamshire Miners' Association, over £161,000. The Westminster Bank had agreed to an overdraft of £110,000 on municipal securities but by 9 July £100,000 of this had been distributed. The Council decided that the remaining £10,000 should be kept in reserve 'for contingencies arising after a settlement is arrived at' and that the payment of all benefits (including old-age pensions) should cease.[3] The officials were again without salaries from early in July until the end of November. Contributions amounting to £69,260 from the M.F.G.B. relief fund enabled further small but diminishing payments to be made. By 20 November the Association had paid out a total of £284,365. It had also made grants to the relief committees in the county from the political fund.[4] At the end of the year the Association had about £139,400 in municipal securities and a bank overdraft of £108,257. Its total reserves amounted to £43,461.

The payment of benefits was quickly resumed after the stoppage, although there were several changes in the rules governing them. By 7 December, 1927, the Association had paid £27,000 in unemployment and victimization benefits and £9,000 in old-age pensions. It was then decided that where a member had received £50 in old-age benefits payment should cease from 3 December. Others were to receive 5s. a

[1] *D.M.A.* 30 January, 1926.

[2] *Ibid.* 27 February, 1926. Rule 34 stated: 'When the accumulated arrears of any member exceed the entrance fee for the time being, such member shall not be allowed to pay off the arrears, but shall re-enter the Union by paying a new entrance fee, and shall not be entitled to benefits until 13 weeks' contributions shall have been paid in accordance with Rule 25.'

[3] *Ibid.* 17 May, 7 July, 1926. According to the 1924 rules (No. 54), strike and lock-out payments were to be at the rate of 3s. a day, with 4d. a day for each child, when the number on strike or locked out was less than 10,000. 'Exceeding this number and in the event of a general strike, the rates of pay for the first two weeks shall be at the rate of 2s. 6d. per day per full member . . . and 4d. per day for each child. Should the dispute continue beyond two weeks the pay shall be at the rate of 1s. 8d. per day per full member . . . and 4d. per day for each child.'

[4] *Ibid.* 15 November, 1926.

week and pay 1s. a week contribution. The last payment to members who had been continuously receiving unemployment or victimization benefits since the stoppage was to be made on 10 December. Others who were then drawing on the funds were to receive 7s. a week and 1s. for each child for a limited number of weeks. From 10 December the unemployment benefit was to be 7s. a week and the victimization benefit 10s. a week.[1] In this period of financial stringency the decision to pay Barnet Kenyon a life pension of £2 a week was rescinded.[2]

By such economies as these the Association slowly improved its financial position despite the depression in trade and the decline in membership. Between 1926 and 1932 the bank overdraft was reduced from £108,257 to £1,172. Nevertheless, the amount being paid in unemployment benefits was still growing, as shown by the following figures:

Unemployment Benefits, 1929–1932

1929	£7,719
1930	£8,978
1931	£18,438
1932	£18,128

In 1933 the bank overdraft increased slightly to £2,299. In April of that year it was decided by the Council that the payment of unemployment benefits should be limited to thirteen weeks in any financial year.[3] Further reductions in benefits, to take effect from 1 January, 1934, were decided upon in October.[4] By the end of 1934 there was a credit balance of £689 at the bank. Municipal securities fell from £139,400 in 1926 to £82,134 in 1933 as part of the principal was repaid, but as soon as the Association had wiped out its overdraft it began to make further loans. £20,000 was invested in the Walthamstow Borough Council in 1934 and from 1936 to 1939 a number of smaller loans were made. By 1939 the municipal securities stood at £126,210 and bank deposits amounted to £27,946. Between 1926 and 1939 the union's financial reserves rose steadily, with the exception of a small decrease in 1933, from £43,461 to £161,823. A great deal of ground had been lost since 1914. Membership had fallen from 42,403 to 21,513, and funds from £311,926 to £161,823. The nominal value of investments per head was about the same in 1939 as in 1914 but their real value had fallen from £7·36 to £4·76.[5]

The inter-war years were abnormal times for the finances of the Association but as far as possible it continued the policy of distributing

---

[1] *D.M.A.* 7 December, 1927.
[3] *Ibid.* 15 April, 1933.
[5] See Chart 7 and Appendix I to this chapter.

[2] *Ibid.* 31 December, 1927.
[4] *Ibid.* 28 October, 1933.

its assets between local authorities and joint-stock banks. In 1919 the union had investments in the boroughs of Chesterfield, Ilkeston, Stepney, Mansfield and Middlesbrough, and in the Watford and Alfreton urban district councils. During the period 1919–39 loans were granted to the boroughs of Chesterfield, Walthamstow, Worksop, Mitcham, Chatham and Walsall, and to the Skegness urban district council and the Easington rural district council. Apart from £50,000 in National War Bonds, which were disposed of in 1920, the remainder of the funds was in the hands of the banks. In 1914 the Association's principal bankers, Crompton and Evans, had been absorbed by Parr's Bank, Ltd. In 1918 Parr's merged with the London County and Westminster Bank, Ltd., to form the London County, Westminster and Parr's Bank, Ltd., which was renamed the Westminster Bank, Ltd., in 1923.[1] Thus from that year the Westminster became the Association's main bank. The smaller accounts with the United Counties Banking Company and the London Joint Stock Bank were closed after the disputes of 1920 and 1921 respectively. Considerable sums had also been deposited with the Co-operative Wholesale Banking Society by 1919 but in 1926 it was found that the Westminster Bank was prepared to allow an overdraft of £110,000 on the union's securities whereas the Co-operative Bank could offer only £100,000.[2]

III

In the flush of post-war prosperity the proposal to appoint a full-time political organizer was revived.[3] In May, 1919, the Executive Committee recommended that an agent should be employed in the Clay Cross and North-East divisions at a starting salary of £250 a year, 'the appointment not being confined to members of our own Association'. Mather was to be retained 'for registration purposes and for general advice' at £50 annually.[4] The Council gave its approval, stipulating that the organizer should have his office on the union's premises, and the position was advertised.[5] Four candidates were selected from over eighty applicants by Sewell and Overton, and on 16 June they were interviewed by the Executive Committee. Alfred W. Hildreth, a Manchester man, was appointed and began his duties on 1 July.[6] In January, 1920, the Executive Committee heard Hildreth's report on his activities, 'expressed its satisfaction with his work', and increased his salary by £50 a year.[7]

[1] T. E. Gregory, *The Westminster Bank through a Century*, (London), 1936, II, opp. p. 302.　　　　　[2] *D.M.A.* 17 May, 1926.
[3] See Chapter XIII, pp. 544, 546.　　　　[4] *D.M.A.* 22 May, 1919.
[5] *Ibid.* 24 May, 1919.　　[6] *Ibid.* 16 June, 1919.　　[7] *Ibid.* 15 January, 1920.

However, Hildreth appears to have felt that his untiring efforts were inadequately rewarded. In March, 1921, the Executive Committee instructed Frank Hall to get 'all possible information from other mining areas as to conditions and payments made to political organizers'. An ominous note appeared on the minutes stating that 'a letter had been received from Mr. Egerton Wake on behalf of the Political Agents' Association'.[1] The 1921 lock-out precluded any possibility of increasing Hildreth's salary. In July, 1922, he reported to the Council that he had accepted 'a more lucrative position' in the north of England, and at his request he was allowed to resign immediately. 'Tributes to Mr. Hildreth's worth as an organizer and platform speaker were paid, regrets for his leaving and hopes of his success in his new sphere expressed, and the President and Vice-President instructed to give testimonials on behalf of the Association.'[2]

The appointment of Hildreth and the election of Hicken as an additional official in the following year increased the pressure on the union's offices. A small concession to the needs of the twentieth-century trade union leader had already been made in November, 1919, when it was decided to have the Association's headquarters wired for electric lighting.[3] In 1920 the Executive Committee expressed the opinion 'that the growth of business transacted at the Head Offices and the large amount of correspondence and actual work entailed, added to by the greatly increased membership, now well over 50,000, has rendered the present office room insufficient'. The officials were instructed 'to seek for land upon which to build a Council Chamber, so that the present Council Chamber can be utilized for office purposes'.[4]

Percy Houfton, the creator of the Bolsover Company's 'model' villages, was consulted. He recommended that Barnet Kenyon's house, which was part of the union's premises, was more suitable for conversion into offices than the Council Chamber. The alternative was to re-build entirely on a new site. The officials began negotiations for the purchase of the old recreation ground in Chesterfield but the price was too high and eventually it was decided, with the approval of the branches, to adopt Houfton's first recommendation and to find another house for Kenyon.[5] The Association already had houses for officials in Tennyson Avenue and in April, 1919, had bought two more in Clarence Road for £1,200.[6] In November, 1920, a house was bought for Kenyon in Shaftesbury Avenue. One of the upper rooms in his former home was converted into a board room for the use of the Executive Committee,

---

[1] D.M.A. 1 March, 1921.
[3] Ibid. 15 November, 1919.
[5] Ibid. 15 September, 9 October, 1920.
[6] Ibid. 1 April, 1919.

[2] Ibid. 29 July, 1922.
[4] Ibid. 30 April, 1920.

and the remainder were made into offices and store rooms.[1] In June, 1923, the Association acquired another house, in Manor Road, for the use of Hicken.

Attempts were made during the inter-war years to revive some of the traditional methods of fostering unity. In 1919 the lodges were asked to state whether they were in favour of holding a county demonstration but the proposal received little support.[2] There was also a movement, following the example of the continental workers, to establish May Day as an annual holiday. At the M.F.G.B. annual conference in 1919, on a Derbyshire motion, it was carried unanimously:

That in view of the greater interest taken in industrial and political questions by the workers generally, a day be set apart in the month of May each year, when all members of the Federation shall take a holiday, and that a central demonstration be arranged in each district to advocate such measures as shall have for their aims the salvation of the workers. The day to be observed and the resolutions to be submitted to the meetings shall be left with the Executive to decide.[3]

In 1920 the officials of the Derbyshire Miners' Association were instructed to make arrangements for the holding of May Day demonstrations at various centres in the county.[4] May Day fell on a Saturday that year and many miners stayed away from the pits. Samuel Sales, presiding over the Chesterfield demonstration in Queen's Park said: 'The day had far gone when they as an association had to have a demonstration to tout for members.'[5]

However, the demonstrations of 1920 were evidently unsuccessful for in the following year the Executive Committee authorized the expenditure of a maximum of £25 each on demonstrations at Ilkeston, North Wingfield, Staveley, Ripley, Creswell, Bolsover, Shirebrook, Killamarsh and South Normanton, but commented: 'Last year's experience taught the Committee that bands and processions were very largely a thing of the past, and they recommended that sports, competitions, or singing contests should take their place.'[6] In the event all expenditure authorized for demonstrations was cancelled during the 1921 stoppage and the inroads which were subsequently made on the Association's funds prevented any further activities of this kind until June, 1928, when Hicken was instructed to arrange area demonstrations in various parts of the county.[7]

In 1933 a resolution from the Glapwell branch calling for the resurrection of the old county demonstration was rejected. Instead the

[1] D.M.A. 6 November, 1919; 4 January, 1921.
[2] Ibid. 21 June, 1919.   [3] M.F.G.B. 18 July, 1919.
[4] D.M.A. 12 April, 1920.   [5] Derbyshire Times, 8 May, 1920.
[6] D.M.A. 15 March, 1921.   [7] Ibid. 16 June, 1928.

Council favoured another gathering of the branch committee members, similar to the one held in St. James's Hall, Chesterfield, in 1932. Such conferences began to be held regularly at various centres in the county and became a useful part of the Association's work. To encourage attendance tea was provided and travelling expenses were paid. The meetings were usually addressed by the officials on matters affecting the coal industry or the organization of the union. In 1935 area meetings of branch committee members were held at Chesterfield, Alfreton, Heanor and Shirebrook so that the officials could 'place all information available as to the probable re-organization of the collieries of the county into complete or partial financial amalgamations, or selling agencies, and the effect such movements are likely to have upon the position of the men'.[1] It was decided in 1936 that only one meeting should be held, at Chesterfield, and that it should be addressed by Ebby Edwards, the Secretary of the M.F.G.B.[2] A conference of branch committees in 1937, addressed by Hicken on the past and future of the Association, was pronounced a great success. The Council expressed the view that such gatherings were preferable to mass demonstrations with processions and decided that Hicken's speech should be published as a pamphlet and distributed to the branches.[3]

Another means of informing members about the activities and policy of the union was the *Derbyshire Worker*, a weekly newspaper aimed at local trade unionists. Early in 1922 it appears to have been in financial difficulties and the Council decided to subsidize it from the political fund on the understanding that the Association should have three to five columns of the paper at its disposal. The union guaranteed to pay for 1,500 copies and the proprietors agreed to distribute them free of charge in nineteen of the most important mining centres.[4] The *Derbyshire Worker*, which was extremely left-wing in outlook, never succeeded in obtaining an adequate readership and the subsidy was soon discontinued.

The nineteenth-century custom of wearing medals was revived in 1924. Branches were left to decide for themselves whether the practice should be adopted and were able to obtain medals from the union's headquarters on condition that all their members were prepared to wear them.[5] In 1934, when the Association was trying to increase its numbers, it decided that a free medal should be distributed to every member.[6]

[1] *D.M.A.* 6 July, 3 August, 1935.   [2] *Ibid.* 26 September, 1936.
[3] *Ibid.* 25 September, 6 November, 1937.
[4] *Ibid.* 20 March, 4 April, 1922. The centres selected were Heanor, Ilkeston, Staveley, Clay Cross, Creswell, Bolsover, Grassmoor, Clowne, Alfreton, Morton, Tupton, Shirebrook, Normanton, Tibshelf, Stanley Common, Shirland, Pilsley, Langwith and Blackwell.
[5] *Ibid.* 21 June, 1924.   [6] *Ibid.* 17 March, 1934.

IV

Problems of organization continued to occupy much of the time of the officials during the inter-war years. On the borders of Yorkshire the union had a lengthy dispute with some of its own members. It was easy for men living near the county boundary to transfer from collieries organized by the Derbyshire Miners' Association to those organized by other unions but many of them were reluctant to abandon the Association. During 1919 there were strikes at Yorkshire and Nottinghamshire collieries and the Association found itself paying strike benefits arising from disputes over which it had no control. The attention of lodge secretaries and members was drawn to the rule which stated that when a member ceased to work at pits where there were branches of the Association his membership automatically came to an end.[1] The Nottinghamshire Miners' Association adopted a similar policy and the difficulties on the Nottinghamshire border were soon resolved. On the Yorkshire border, however, lodge secretaries and committees allowed men to retain their membership of the Derbyshire Miners' Association despite the fact that they were working at pits organized by the Yorkshire Miners' Association.[2]

The Birley Colliery, which was about a hundred yards over the Yorkshire border, had a large number of miners whose homes were in Derbyshire, who had previously worked at Derbyshire pits and were members of the Beighton and Holbrook lodges. In January, 1920, the Council decided that the Birley miners should all be members of the same union and that the officials of the Beighton and Holbrook lodges should consult with the Yorkshire officials as to whether the Birley Colliery should be organized by Yorkshire or Derbyshire.[3] The situation was complicated by the fact that Derbyshire's benefits were higher than Yorkshire's and many of the men were strongly opposed to the suggestion that they should cease to be members of the Derbyshire Association. The negotiations dragged on for almost a year until the Executive Committee finally recommended on 4 January, 1921, that no further contributions should be accepted from men employed at the Birley Colliery after the end of the month.[4] This decision was confirmed by the Council but the secretary of the Holbrook lodge failed to carry out the instruction.[5] After further representations from the Council the last contributions from the Birley miners were accepted on 19 February.

The result was that during the 1921 stoppage a number of men were

[1] *D.M.A.* 29 March, 1919.   [2] *Ibid.* 3 November, 1919.
[3] *Ibid.* 3 January, 1920.
[4] *Ibid.* 4 January, 1921.   [5] *Ibid.* 12 February, 1921.

able to claim that they were still entitled to receive benefits from the Association although they were employed at Yorkshire collieries. Others had left the Derbyshire Association but had not joined the Yorkshire Association and were unable to claim benefits from either union. There were angry scenes at Holbrook when the first lock-out payments were made and about 100 men who had ceased to be members of the Association were turned away without any money. They threatened to prevent any payment being made the following week and a deputation of three was appointed to meet the Executive Committee. On 20 April they stated their case and demanded the payment of benefits for all the men concerned whether they were in arrears with their contributions or not. They also insisted that they should be allowed to continue membership or that there should be a ballot at the Birley pit to decide whether it was to be organized by Derbyshire or Yorkshire. The Executive Committee decided that those who were fully paid up members on 12 February, 1921, should receive benefits but should accept their clearance papers at the end of the lock-out. As an alternative it was suggested that the whole matter should be referred to arbitration under Rule 87 of the Association.[1] The Executive Committee also decided that Charles Smith, secretary of the Holbrook lodge and a trustee of the Association, should resign because 'he was greatly to blame in not carrying out the instruction of the Council meeting and refusing contributions from men working in other counties'.[2]

The Executive Committee subsequently took legal advice and decided not to pay benefits but to pay to each member working at the Birley Colliery £1 as 'returned contributions'.[3] This added to the discontent which was raging at Holbrook and the Council renewed the Executive Committee's previous offer of arbitration. A few weeks later, after further legal advice, this offer was withdrawn and the next move was left to the aggrieved ex-members.[4] Thereafter there was a lull in the struggle. Smith duly resigned at the end of the year 'on account of ill-health and age'.[5] Meanwhile the men who had been expelled from the Association were preparing their campaign under the leadership of

---

[1] D.M.A. 20 April, 1921; Derbyshire Times, 11 June, 1921. Rule 87 stated: 'Any member finding himself aggrieved, or having any complaint against an officer or officers of the lodge, for any action he may have taken in reference to the matter complained of, shall apply to the lodge Committee for redress at its first meeting, and if no satisfaction be obtained, he may lay his case before the next General Branch Meeting, after which, should the case still be dealt with in an unsatisfactory manner, he shall have the power to appeal to the Council or Executive Committee, by giving seven days' notice in writing to the General Secretary of his intention to do so, stating the nature of the grievance at issue, and if the appeal be heard, the decision of the Council or Executive Committee shall be final.'

[2] D.M.A. 20 April, 1921.   [3] Ibid. 30 April, 1921.
[4] Ibid. 25 and 31 May, 1921.   [5] Ibid. 10 December, 1921.

Michael Tierney, of Mosborough. Tierney went to London to lay the men's case before the officials of the M.F.G.B. who said that they could not interfere. Legal advice was then taken. 'The necessary financial backing has been forthcoming,' stated the *Derbyshire Times*, 'and further developments are now awaited.'[1]

An action brought against the Association by Tierney began in the Chancery division on 1 February, 1923.[2] Mr. Justice Sargent held that Tierney's membership was governed by the rules which were in force when he joined the Association in 1902 and granted an injunction restraining the Association from refusing to accept his contributions.[3] Tierney and the others then resumed the payment of their contributions and sought to recover, under Rule 87, the benefits which they considered had wrongfully been withheld from them during the 1921 lock-out. Protracted negotiations ensued. Towards the end of 1924 Arthur Neal, a Sheffield solicitor, was agreed upon as arbitrator and on 27 January, 1925, he began his hearing of the case. He recommended a settlement by agreement rather than by arbitration to prevent further litigation.[4] Eventually his advice was taken and on 12 October, 1925, almost six years after the dispute began, an agreement was signed by Tierney and his solicitor, H. Popplewell, on behalf of the men, and by Hall and Hicken, acting for the Association. All contributions paid since February, 1923, were to be refunded (less the £1 refunded during the 1921 stoppage) and arrangements were to be made for the men to transfer from the Association with clearances which would carry immediate benefit.[5]

Difficulties of a different kind were presented by the lead-miners who had been admitted to the Association during the war as members of the Winster lodge and continued to meet with opposition from their employers. The trouble centre in the years immediately following the war was the Mill Close mine which was the third largest producer of lead ore in the country. On the death of the proprietor, E. M. Wass, in 1887, the previous three years' production had been valued at £127,000. The mine had subsequently been acquired by H. Denman who continued to own it until the end of 1919.[6] In 1918–19 there were four strikes. A fifth occurred in August, 1919, when the management closed a number of workings, transferred non-unionists to the workings of union members and dismissed the union men on the grounds that there was no work for them.[7] Some of the men had worked at Mill Close for many years and objected to being displaced by non-unionists whose

---

[1] *Derbyshire Times*, 18 June, 1921.   [2] *Ibid.* 3 February, 1923.
[3] *Ibid.* 10 February, 1923; *D.M.A.* 3 March, 1923.
[4] *Derbyshire Times*, 31 January, 1925.   [5] *D.M.A.* 10 October, 1925.
[6] *Derbyshire Times*, 31 January, 1920.
[7] This practice was common in coalmining and is not unknown in other occupations.

service in the mine had been much shorter than their own. The result was that eighty-six underground workers, all members of the Derbyshire Miners' Association, were authorized to cease work. The mine was kept going by the early nineteenth century device of employing men who were required to sign a 'document' pledging them not to join the union.[1]

By the end of September the strike was in its eighth week and the Council decided that John Spencer and Henry Hicken should be sent into the Winster district to deal with the matter.[2] On 18 October the Council heard a report of the activities of Spencer, Hicken and the Winster delegate. The situation had been exacerbated by the employment of the non-unionists and three men, one of whom was a member of the Association, were facing charges of assault. The Council considered that the Winster men needed more support and despatched Hicken (who was not yet an official), Samuel Sales, Thomas Kyte, James Randle, William Taylor and Benjamin Lee, 'with plenary powers, for the purpose of creating an atmosphere surrounding the Mill Close mine, which the men who are still continuing to work will find too strong for them to oppose'.[3] Two weeks later the Council decided that the meetings held by Hicken and his party had been useful and that they should continue their efforts in the Winster district for another fortnight if necessary.[4]

The dispute was still unsettled at the beginning of November and Frank Hall was instructed to inform the Minister of Labour that the Executive Committee was seriously considering whether it should recommend a strike ballot of all members of the Association.[5] A week later Barnet Kenyon was asked to question the Minister of Labour in the House of Commons. The Winster men who had been threatened with prosecution for incidents arising out of picketing were assured that they would be defended by the Association. The Executive Committee also considered the question of finding the strikers alternative employment. According to the ancient lead-mining laws of Derbyshire an owner who abandoned his mine could be dispossessed by any claimant who was willing to work it. The Executive Committee therefore decided that a claim should be made to the Barmaster for three of the disused mines nearest to Mill Close. It was also resolved that in the event of the claim being conceded 'some of the men now on strike be placed at these mines to make an examination as to the possibilities of their being profitably worked'.[6]

---

[1] *Derbyshire Times*, 9 August, 1919; *D.M.A.* 9 August, 20 September, 1919.
[2] *D.M.A.* 20 September, 1919.
[3] *Ibid.* 11 October, 1919.
[4] *Ibid.* 25 October, 1919.
[5] *Ibid.* 3 November, 1919.
[6] *Ibid.* 10 November, 1919.

The overhead costs of working such mines were low. The workings were in solid rock, propping was unnecessary and little plant was required. The ore was wound up from the shallow shafts by primitive bucket and windlass arrangements, and the principal expenditure was on explosives and candles. In some mines a small amount of pumping was necessary but most of the workings were drained by gravitation. By 24 January, 1921, the Barmaster had granted the Elton, Placket and Wensley mines to the Association and the Executive Committee had authorized the building of a store for explosives at Winster.[1] Hicken was put in charge of the scheme which was financed by subscriptions from the lodges and, later, by a weekly levy of a penny per member.[2]

Meanwhile the sale of the Mill Close mine by Denman had brought the strike to an end but his successor said that he was unable to find work for the men. On 28 February the Council discussed the future of the co-operative lead-mining scheme. The officials stated:

It has been well understood from the first that no money could be taken for the purpose out of the general funds of the Association, but if that were possible, work could not be found for the whole of the men for a very long time. Considerable development would first have to take place. . . . Most of the members of the Executive Committee were of the opinion that it was not wise to raise any false hopes among the men that the matter could be carried much further.

£1,200 had been subscribed by the lodges for supplementing the men's strike benefit, and £100 for the development fund, but both funds were practically exhausted.[3]

It was decided that part of the balance of £2,000 left over from the war-time ambulance fund should be used to pay for an expert examination of the Raithe mine at Elton.[4] John Saxton, a Sheffield mining engineer, gave a favourable report and on 15 May there was a meeting in the Council Chamber, open to all members of the Association, to consider Hicken's proposals for the formation of a company to keep the lead-mines at work. Eventually the Raithe Lead-Mining Company, Ltd., was registered, with a nominal capital of £7,000 in £1 shares. The first directors were Henry Hicken (chairman); Samuel Sales (secretary); John Spencer; William Harper, of Creswell; John Millward, of Winster; William Harwood, of Elton; and Andrew Nedin, of Winster. 'The mine has been examined by Mr. John Saxton, a mining expert,' they stated, 'and he gives a glowing account of its prospects.' There was some discussion as to whether the balance of the ambulance fund should be invested in the mine but the lodges decided that it

[1] D.M.A. 24 January, 1921.   [2] Ibid. 7 February, 1920.
[3] Ibid. 28 February, 1920.   [4] Ibid. 10 April, 1920.

should go to the Skegness convalescent home.[1] The response of individual members of the Association was equally disappointing. By the end of the year less than £1,000 had been subscribed. In a final appeal to the members of the union Sales pointed out:

We have now arrived at a time when the principle which we maintain is but the natural right of the worker, i.e. control of industry by the worker, has now an opportunity of being put into operation. If we are not prepared to demonstrate our fitness for this important function, then for heaven's sake let us stop our pious platitudes and admit our inferiority in comparison with the other side. . . . We have come to the time when we must either wind up, and as workers admit our inability, or appeal to a wider public, whose only interest will be 'how much profit will it return'.[2]

Lack of capital had brought to an end yet another experiment in co-operative production.

V

The policy of industrial unionism which had been adopted during the war continued to cause difficulties with employers and with other unions. The organization of colliery clerks had been the subject of negotiations between the M.F.G.B. and the National Union of Clerks in 1918. The M.F.G.B. had then expressed the view that colliery clerks should be members of the miners' unions.[3] In March, 1919, the Council of the Derbyshire Miners' Association approved a county scale of wages for colliery clerks and decided that the coal-owners should be asked to accept it.[4] A few weeks later, however, it was pointed out by the officials that many of the clerks were reluctant to join the Association, believing that their employers would prefer them to join the N.U.C. It was therefore decided that instead of attempting to negotiate a county scale which would benefit members and non-members alike, the Association should seek to establish its recognized scale only at those collieries where there was a substantial number of clerical members.[5] Agreements had already been reached with the Staveley and Butterley companies.

In June, 1919, the N.U.C. brought out on strike its members employed by the Butterley Company. The men involved were a very small minority of the Company's clerical staff and were receiving the same rates as the members of the Derbyshire Miners' Association. The action of the N.U.C. was censured by the miners' leaders because there had

---

[1] *Derbyshire Times*, 3 July, 1920; *D.M.A.* 30 April, 19 July, 9 October, 1920.
[2] *D.M.A.* 18 December, 1920.   [3] *M.F.G.B.* 31 October, 1918.
[4] *D.M.A.* 1 March, 1919.   [5] *Ibid.* 29 March, 1919.

been no previous consultation. 'The action is evidently aimed against the Derbyshire Miners' Association,' they said, 'with the purpose of drawing the clerks away from its membership.'[1] The strike was likewise condemned by a joint meeting at Nottingham, on 3 July, of representatives of the Derbyshire and Nottinghamshire miners' associations, the Enginemen's and Firemen's Union and the National Association of Colliery Deputies.[2] Eventually, on 26 July, 1919, at a special meeting of clerks in the Council Chamber, it was decided that a county scale should be prepared and submitted to the employers.[3] On 11 February, 1920, Frank Hall and Frank Lee, with representatives of the clerks, met representatives of the Coal-Owners' Association at Derby. The coal-owners' counter proposals were submitted to another meeting of clerks on 14 February and the officials were empowered to settle the question at the next meeting with the owners.[4]

The outcome of the strike of the members of the N.U.C. employed by the Butterley Company was an inquiry by the Parliamentary Committee of the T.U.C.[5] The N.U.C. had accused members of the Derbyshire Miners' Association of 'blacklegging' but J. B. Williams, E. L. Poulton and F. Bramley, who were appointed to hear the case, reported that no agreement between the N.U.C. and the Butterley Company had ever been ratified, that there had been no previous consultation with the Derbyshire Miners' Association, and that literature containing grave charges against the miners' officials had been freely circulated by the N.U.C. some time before the dispute. 'In view of all the facts', concluded the report, 'we fail to find justification for the charge of blacklegging.'[6]

The agreement which had been concluded between the Derbyshire and Nottinghamshire miners' associations and the National Association of Colliery Deputies was seriously jeopardized early in 1919 when there were a number of strikes of deputies at Swanwick and other places. Their action in stopping work 'without taking into confidence the officials of this Association' was described by the Council on 1 March as being 'in spirit a breach of . . . the agreement' and it was decided that the agreement should be altered so that any future strikes by either union would have to be approved by the joint board of representatives of the Derbyshire and Nottinghamshire miners' associations and the Enginemen's and Firemen's Union.[7] The constitution of the joint board was later amended to permit the representation of the deputies' association but in 1921 the deputies refused to accept the

[1] D.M.A. 21 June, 1919.   [2] Derbyshire Times, 5 July, 1919.
[3] D.M.A. 26 July, 1919.   [4] Ibid. 14 February, 1920.
[5] M.F.G.B. 23 October, 1919.   [6] D.M.A. 16 March, 1920.
[7] Ibid. 1 March, 1919; Derbyshire Times, 8 March, 1919.

decision of the joint board that they should withdraw their labour during the lock-out and passed a resolution 'to continue working to keep the mines safe for the time when work was resumed'. The decision to admit the deputies to the joint board was thereupon rescinded.[1]

Negotiations for the re-admission of the deputies to the joint board were opened in December, 1922, but by June of the following year no agreement had been reached and the Council expressed the view 'that no good purpose would be served' by another meeting with the representatives of the deputies.[2] In July, however, the Council decided that new proposals should be drawn up by the joint board and submitted to the deputies' association.[3] The agreement, which was of the usual kind, stipulated that all deputies, shot-firers, examiners, firemen and overmen should belong to the Deputies' Association or to one of the miners' associations and that the deputies were to 'strictly confine themselves to their statutory duties'. The objects of the agreement were 'to ensure trade union solidarity at the whole of the pits of Nottinghamshire and Derbyshire, and to mutually strive to obtain the maximum prosperity from the industry for the whole of the workers engaged therein'. In the event of a dispute at any colliery leading to a strike or lock-out the question of any of the parties to the agreement continuing to work was to be decided by the Board.[4]

The absorption of the surface workers by the Association gave rise to few difficulties in the inter-war years. A proposal in March, 1919, that they should send their own representatives to the Council meetings was rejected on the ground that if it were allowed 'the clerks and shopmen could very properly ask for the same thing, and the whole Association would be split up into sections instead of working together as a whole'.[5] At a special conference on 18 November, 1921, the representatives of the shopmen and surface workers expressed their confidence in the officials of the Derbyshire Miners' Association and asked that they should address district meetings of surface workers on the necessity of organization. It was also proposed that the Council should arrange quarterly conferences for surface workers and that each branch should make provision for at least one representative of the surface workers to become a member of its committee. The officials observed:

The Conference was certainly a very re-assuring one from every point of view. The delegates expressed themselves very clearly and very intelligently upon the matters discussed. . . . Several complaints were made about the lack of sympathy with the surfacemen in some branches, whilst other delegates quite as strongly said that was not true of their branches, for they had been

[1] D.M.A. 30 April, 1921.   [2] Ibid. 9 December, 1922; 23 June, 1923.
[3] Ibid. 21 July, 1923.
[4] Ibid. 18 August, 15 September, 1923.   [5] Ibid. 1 March, 1919.

shewn the greatest consideration. We would point out that it is desirable that all sections of workers at the mines should be made to feel and recognize that this Association exists for the benefit of all, and that it does not confine its activities to men working down below.[1]

The Council recommended the branches to accept the surface workers' proposal for quarterly conferences but rejected the suggestion that there should be one representative of the surface workers on every branch committee.[2] The question of the appropriate union for craftsmen was again raised in 1938 when their representatives signed an agreement with the M.F.G.B. setting up an advisory committee to deal with grievances about membership. The Council resolved: 'That this Association still continues to hold by its former attitude that all men working at the collieries in Derbyshire should be members of the Derbyshire Miners' Association.'[3]

The attempt to organize the coke-oven and by-product workers ended in failure. In February, 1920, the Executive Committee discussed a letter which had been received from the National Union of Coking and By-product Workers, and instructed Frank Hall to reply 'that it did appear that no good purpose could be served by a meeting for the purpose of discussing the question of forming a federation betwixt the two societies'.[4] After negotiations between the M.F.G.B. and the by-product workers' union had dragged on for over five years, the Federation recommended that all members working on coke ovens and by-product plants should be transferred to the national union. On 28 March, 1925, this recommendation was accepted by the Council of the Derbyshire Miners' Association by 39 votes to 20.[5]

The Derbyshire Miners' Association continued to play a prominent part in the affairs of the M.F.G.B. Frank Hall served on the Executive Committee from 1913 to 1921 and again from 1923 until his death in 1927. Henry Hicken succeeded him in 1928. In 1924, when Frank Hodges was elected to Parliament as Member for Lichfield, the Council wished to nominate Hall for the secretaryship of the M.F.G.B. but he declined. Hicken's name was then put forward but he was not elected, coming at the bottom of the poll with only 12,730 votes, compared with A. J. Cook's 154,659.[6] Thereafter several attempts were made to secure Hicken's election to national office. He was nominated for the vice-presidency of the M.F.G.B. in 1931 and in 1934 and for the presidency in 1930 but on each occasion he was unsuccessful.

[1] *D.M.A.* 18 November, 1921.
[2] *Ibid.* 10 December, 1921, 7 January, 1922.
[3] *Ibid.* 31 December, 1938.   [4] *Ibid.* 4 February, 1920.
[5] *Ibid.* 28 March, 1925.
[6] *Ibid.* 9 February, 1 March, 1924; *M.F.G.B.* 10 April, 1924.

One of the main trends in M.F.G.B. policy throughout the inter-war years, reinforced by the programme of industrial unionism, was towards the creation of a powerful national union to supersede the loose federal structure of the existing organization. As early as 1919 it was suggested at a M.F.G.B. conference that the districts should adopt uniform contributions and strike benefits, arranging their other benefits locally. It was subsequently recommended by the Executive Committee of the Federation that contributions should not be less than a shilling a week to meet the rising cost of living.[1] These proposals led the Association to double weekly contributions and to increase all its benefits in 1920.[2] At a national conference held in London on 10 March to consider the question, Frank Hall suggested that if uniform strike benefits were to be paid they should be at the rate of 25s. a week with 3s. a week for each child. 'We are in a position probably to pay more than most districts', he said, 'because we stand with half a million and have only 49,000 members; we want a free hand, but if it was the decision of this Federation to pay the same strike pay we should fall in.'[3] The general objection to uniform benefits was that they interfered with the autonomy of districts and eventually it was decided to increase contributions from 1 July, 1920, leaving all decisions about benefits to the districts.[4] After the 1921 lock-out the Council instructed its delegates to the annual conference of the M.F.G.B. to oppose the shilling contribution. In this they were supported by other districts but the objection was defeated.[5]

On 4 March, 1922, there appeared on the agenda for a Council meeting a motion: 'That we, the members of the Avenue branch, are in favour of all miners of Great Britain being in one union. The above to be sent in to the M.F.G.B.' The motion was not discussed but was castigated by the officials:

This resolution contains the principle of centralization. It is a delusion to suppose centralization tends to efficiency. It does nothing of the sort. . . . Centralization would tend to multiply officials and delay the work generally. The rank and file would be less in touch with their organization than at the present time. It has been suggested Labour Leaders would oppose 'One big Union', as they would be afraid of losing their jobs; this is nonsensical and could only have been suggested by persons who know nothing of trades' unions and probably never paid a bob into an industrial organization. . . . The Triple Alliance failed because of divergent elements in it. How much more would one great union fail which included the agricultural labourer,

[1] M.F.G.B. 9 January, 1920.
[2] D.M.A. 6 December, 1919; 3 January, 12 and 28 February, 1920.
[3] M.F.G.B. 10 March, 1920.
[4] D.M.A. 16 March, 1920; M.F.G.B. 10 March, 1920.
[5] D.M.A. 5 July, 16 September, 1922; M.F.G.B. 13 April, 28 July, 1922.

municipal workers, etc.? Capture the Parliamentary Machine: through it get control of the principal industries. This power is in your own hands. Why not use it? Do not give Capital a new lease of life by trying to build up one big union. Trades' unions cannot smash the capitalist machinery. Capital is more afraid of Parliament than Trades' unions. To talk otherwise is mere twaddle.[1]

The motion submitted by the Avenue branch was not precise and the officials appear to have been confusing the issue. The impetus which had been given to trade union amalgamation by syndicalism was not yet spent. From the end of the war well into the period of depression powerful new organizations such as the Amalgamated Engineering Union, the Transport and General Workers' Union and the National Union of Building Trade Workers were being created. Heedless of its leaders' outburst the Derbyshire Miners' Council a few months later declared itself in favour of 'one Industrial Union for the whole of the mining industry'.[2] But unlike other groups of workers, the miners failed to unite when conditions were comparatively favourable and were so much the weaker when they had to cope with the problems of the depression.

Despite the protestations of the officials their vested interests were a potent factor in the opposition to any re-organization of the Federation. If they were not afraid of losing their positions they were reluctant to lose their independence, power and prestige. Policies had changed but the autocratic tradition established by Haslam and Harvey lingered on. Moreover, it was possible to argue that a relatively prosperous county such as Derbyshire had little to gain and much to lose by sinking its identity in a large national union.[3] Such opposition to re-organization might have continued without being effectively challenged had it not been for events in Nottinghamshire and, to a lesser extent, in Derbyshire, during and after the stoppage of 1926. The activities of George Spencer and his 'non-political' union are part of the story of the industrial struggles of the inter-war years[4] but they affected organization to the extent of showing the ease with which a substantial part of a district could break away from the Federation. In January, 1927, there was a proposal by the Nottinghamshire miners that the remnants of their association should amalgamate with the Derbyshire Miners' Association which had also suffered from defections to the so-called Spencer Union. There was a meeting of the officials of both associations but no commitments were made.[5] In 1928, when further proposals

---

[1] D.M.A. 4 March, 1922.   [2] Ibid. 16 September, 1922.
[3] Cf. G. B. Baldwin, 'Structural Reform in the British Miners' Union', Quarterly Journal of Economics, LXVII, (1953), pp. 582–4.
[4] See Chapters XVIII–XIX.   [5] D.M.A. 29 January, 1927.

were put forward, the Derbyshire Association set up a special committee to deal with the matter but little progress was made.[1]

The spread of 'non-political' unionism, which had the support of
the coal-owners, to Scotland, Durham, Northumberland, Yorkshire,
Staffordshire and South Wales, became a matter of national importance
to the Federation. The bitter dispute at the Harworth Colliery in
1936–7, when the employers, Barber, Walker and Company, refused
to recognize any but the Spencer Union, almost precipitated a national
strike. As a result of the intervention of the M.F.G.B. it ended instead
with the abolition of the Spencer Union.[2] The leaders of the Federation
were quick to discern the moral of these events. By July, 1937, a
circular suggesting the formation of a national union had been drawn
up by the Secretary and sent to all the districts.[3] Speaking at the annual
conference of the M.F.G.B. in the same month Joseph Jones, the
President, said:

> The events of the past twelve months have made the question of Federa-
> tion reorganization more urgent than ever, and it must now be clear to
> everyone that the form of the organization we have today is in many respects
> out of date and a source of danger to our national unity.[4]

The Derbyshire Miners' Association was prepared to accept
re-organization in principle,[5] but when detailed proposals were circulated
by the Executive Committee of the Federation a year later they were
rejected first by the Council, by 31 votes to 21, and later by the branches,
by 40 votes to 12.[6] The 1938 proposals involved the dissolution of the
existing county associations and the centralization of all their assets
and liabilities. The full-time officials and staffs were to be guaranteed
continued employment. At a Council meeting on 1 October Hicken
pointed out 'several difficulties and objections' to the scheme. In particular, attention was drawn to Rule 91 of the Association which stated,
amongst other things: 'The Union shall not be dissolved if 50 or more
members shall vote against the same.' When the matter was referred
to the branches 18 voted for the scheme and 41 against. Further
proposals were put forward in 1939 but after being submitted to
the branches they were rejected by 35 votes to 23. The attempts to
re-organize the Federation were interrupted by the outbreak of the
Second World War. Before it ended the National Union of Mineworkers was to be born.

---

[1] *D.M.A.* 30 July, 1928.
[3] *D.M.A.* 3 July, 1937.
[5] *D.M.A.* 3 July, 1937.

[2] See Chapter XIX, pp. 764–70.
[4] *M.F.G.B.* 19 July, 1937.
[6] *Ibid.* 11 June, 2 July, 1938.

U

Membership and Funds, 1914–1954

Year	Membership	Total investments £	Investments per head £	Investments per head at constant prices £ (at 1914 prices)
1914	42,403	311,926	7·36	7·36
1915	33,094	344,686	10·42	8·47
1916	43,000	380,813	8·86	6·06
1917	51,444	420,750	8·18	4·64
1918	52,801	454,022	8·60	4·24
1919	57,035	449,406	7·88	3·67
1920	59,035	302,542	5·12	2·05
1921	51,084	50,520	·99	·47
1922	39,455	73,086	1·85	1·01
1923	40,150	135,464	3·37	1·93
1924	43,078	196,794	4·50	2·61
1925	43,000	250,054	5·82	3·31
1926	32,914	43,461	1·32	·77
1927	25,072	53,211	2·12	1·27
1928	19,326	63,658	3·29	1·98
1929	19,114	74,869	3·92	2·39
1930	18,285	85,084	4·65	2·94
1931	19,015	89,344	4·70	3·19
1932	18,300	92,137	5·03	3·49
1933	17,215	88,437	5·14	3·67
1934	18,009	93,725	5·20	3·69
1935	17,449	98,659	5·65	3·95
1936	18,573	109,795	5·91	4·02
1937	20,210	129,645	6·41	4·16
1938	20,364	142,263	6·99	4·48
1939	21,513	161,823	7·52	4·76
1940	22,327	186,262	8·34	4·53
1941	25,287	219,247	8·67	4·36
1942	34,836	265,257	7·61	3·80
1943	34,902	314,625	9·01	4·53
1944	32,417	363,625	11·16	5·55
1945	32,877	376,508	11·45	5·64
1946	31,839	406,543	12·77	6·28
1947	34,290	447,214	13·04	6·39
1948	34,680	484,923	13·99	6·66
1949	34,589	520,139	15·03	7·02
1950	33,327	560,471	16·82	7·73
1951	34,173	612,849	17·93	7·86
1952	36,152	658,655	18·22	7·59
1953	35,417	674,897	19·06	7·81
1954	35,953	708,362	19·70	7·98

Sources: Derbyshire Miners' Association, Account Books and Balance Sheets.
Ministry of Labour: Index of Retail Prices, 1914–1947; Interim Index of Retail Prices, 1947–1954. (The two indices are not strictly comparable but are sufficiently so for the present purpose. Cf. A. L. Bowley, 'Earnings and Prices, 1904, 1914, 1937–8', *Review of Economic Studies*, VIII, (1941), pp. 133–4.)

CHAPTER XVI

THE SANKEY COMMISSION AND ITS AFTERMATH

I

Long before the First World War ended 'reconstruction' was in the air. A weary nation was encouraged to make greater efforts by the assurance of politicians that peace would bring a brave new world. The miners had already formulated an industrial programme of unparalleled optimism. The annual conference of the M.F.G.B. in the summer of 1918 had adopted resolutions calling for a wage increase, a six-hour working day and the nationalization of the mines.

The demand for nationalization, which was to become the crucial issue of the inter-war years, had by that time a fairly long, if not respectable, ancestry. In 1892 two Scottish miners, William Smith and Robert Smillie, managed to steer through the Trades Union Congress resolutions calling for the public ownership of both the mines and the minerals.[1] Keir Hardie, in the following year, introduced a parliamentary Bill which had the same object. In 1894, on a motion by T. Greenall, of Lancashire, seconded by J. Wilson, of Scotland, the M.F.G.B. resolved: 'That in the opinion of this conference the best interests of the nation will be served by the nationalization of the mines of the country.'[2] But the Liberal leadership of the Federation was not in favour of such desperate remedies. 'Every one of you knows my opinion on this question', stated Pickard, in his presidential address. 'I am not a miners' [sic] nationalizer. I don't think that if the mines were nationalized the miners would be a penny better off than they are today.'[3] The Derbyshire miners played little part in the early stages of this campaign. Haslam had been unable to go even so far as those Liberals who were prepared to support the nationalization of mining royalties.[4]

Ten years elapsed before resolutions on the nationalization of mines

[1] *T.U.C. Report*, 1892.
[2] *M.F.G.B.* 19 January, 1894.
[3] *Ibid.* 17 January, 1894.
[4] See Chapter VII, p. 303.

acquired any practical significance. By that time the revolt against the older leaders was gathering force. In 1907 the M.F.G.B. annual conference passed three resolutions on nationalization, one of which came from Derbyshire. Concentrating entirely upon the importance of land nationalization, Harvey moved:

That the Members of Parliament supported by this Federation be instructed to direct the attention of the Government to bring in a Bill for the Nationalization of Land, Mines and Mining Royalties, as we believe that it is only by such reforms that the workers can obtain full value for their labour.[1]

In July, 1912, soon after Robert Smillie became its Acting President, the M.F.G.B. set up a sub-committee to draft a parliamentary Bill for the nationalization of the mines, which was approved by the annual conference in the following October.[2] Keir Hardie's proposals in 1893 had allowed compensation for both mine and royalty owners. The M.F.G.B. Bill excluded compensation for royalties and was therefore unacceptable to the Labour Party. It was presented to the House of Commons in 1913 by the miners' M.P.s, including such strange bedfellows as W. E. Harvey, J. G. Hancock and Keir Hardie.[3] The Bill was not discussed, and the war postponed any further attempts to secure public ownership of the mines. What was new about the demand for nationalization in 1918 was the proposal that there should be 'joint control and administration by the workmen and the State'.

The M.F.G.B. refrained from putting forward any of its demands until after the armistice. Then there was a further delay until the nation had elected a House of Commons which Stanley Baldwin described to his friend Keynes as 'a lot of hard-faced men who look as if they had done very well out of the war'.[4] On 9 January, 1919, the Executive Committee of the M.F.G.B. met Sir Guy Calthrop, the Controller of Coalmines, to discuss the miners' claim for an increase of 30 per cent. upon total earnings (exclusive of 'war wage'). Smillie, now President of the Federation, said:

We base that claim partly on the increased cost of living since we secured the last advance and partly on the fact that the price of coal has increased very considerably, and we think it has increased considerably beyond any increase that has taken place in wages. But we base our claim on a stronger ground and a higher ground than either of these two things. We base it chiefly on the value of the miner's labour, and on the fact that right down through

[1] *M.F.G.B.* 11 October, 1907.   [2] *Ibid.* 3 October, 1912.
[3] Bill 244, (1913).
[4] J. M. Keynes, *The Economic Consequences of the Peace*, (London), 1919, p. 133; D. C. Somervell, *British Politics Since 1900*, (London), edn. of 1953, p. 123.

the ages practically the miner has not been adequately or fairly remunerated for his work, and the families of miners have not had the living conditions which they had a right to expect.[1]

Whilst the Government was considering this claim the M.F.G.B. was discussing the problems of demobilization. The troops were restless and anxious to return to civilian life. There were frequent reports of mutiny and insubordination. On the other hand, the men who had been released from the armed forces were not being absorbed by industry without friction. A special conference of the M.F.G.B., held at South-port on 14–16 January, decided to put forward a number of demobilization demands. They included the release of miners from the armed forces and their reinstatement in the mines they left at the time of enlistment; payment of wages appropriate to their former grade for miners who were unable to perform a normal day's work; training for suitable work, with maintenance allowance, for disabled men; payment of unemployment benefits equivalent to miners' wages for men who were displaced by ex-servicemen; and the use of joint pit and district committees for administering the scheme. It was also resolved:

In order to make easier the realization of these demands we press the Government to amend the Mines' Eight Hours' Act, so that 'six hours' shall be substituted for 'eight hours' in that Act.

Also, for this purpose, and in the interests of miners in particular, and the community in general, we urge the Government to proceed at once to the nationalization of all mines and minerals.[2]

On 31 January representatives of the M.F.G.B. and the Government met to discuss these demands. After Smillie had pointed out that no reply had been given to the wage demand, which had been put forward on 9 January, the Minister of Labour, Sir Robert Horne, gave an assurance that all the questions at issue would be considered by the Cabinet.[3]

In Derbyshire there were a number of disputes arising from reinstatement difficulties. An attempt by the Bolsover Company to dismiss twenty-five men from its Mansfield Colliery to make room for ex-servicemen led to an unofficial strike which, within a few days, had spread to Blackwell, Tibshelf, South Normanton and Pinxton.[4] At a meeting of representatives of the coal-owners and the Derbyshire Miners' Association on 25 January it was agreed that in future ex-servicemen should be found work and that others should not be displaced because of their return. The demobilization proposals of the M.F.G.B. were discussed and it was decided to set up local and district joint

[1] M.F.G.B. 9 January, 1919.
[2] Ibid. 15 January, 1919.
[3] Ibid. 31 January, 1919.
[4] Derbyshire Times, 1 February, 1919.

committees to deal with reinstatement problems in the future. The owners made it clear that they could not take the financial responsibility of employing large numbers of men unremuneratively without authority from the Coal Controller.[1] Speaking about the miners' demands for increased wages and a shorter working day, Frank Lee told a meeting of the Clowne Labour Party:

> While there were many collieries in the county which could afford to pay . . . there were others that could not. . . . The only solution was nationalization under which the profits of the big pits could be pooled with those of the smaller ones.[2]

On 10 February the Government gave its reply to the various claims which had been advanced by the M.F.G.B. To meet the increased cost of living it offered an additional 'war wage' of a shilling a day. The claim for a wage increase irrespective of the cost of living, the demands for a reduction of hours and the nationalization of the mines, were all to be referred to a committee of inquiry which would also consider the position of the coal trade generally. All but one of the demobilization proposals were rejected on the ground that they 'would put the miners in an exceptional position compared with the rest of the citizens of the country'. The Government approved the creation of joint pit committees to administer unemployment benefits and to help the men to find work.[3] These offers were completely unacceptable to the miners. Smillie told the Minister of Labour that they did not come 'within measurable distance' of the Federation's claim. A second special conference at Southport on 12–13 February promptly rejected them, decided to take a strike ballot, and strongly urged the members of the Federation to vote in favour of a stoppage.[4] The ballot paper, which was to be returned by 22 February, read as follows:

1. Application for 30 per cent. increase in wages.
2. Six-hour day.
3. Full maintenance at Trade Union rates of wages for mine workers unemployed through demobilization.
4. Nationalization of mines.
5. The Government having failed to grant any of the above proposals, *are you in favour of a National Strike to secure them?*
   Yes............   No............
   Place a 'X' opposite 'Yes' or 'No' in the space provided for the purpose.

The decisions of the Southport conference were endorsed by the Council of the Derbyshire Miners' Association on 15 February when it

---

[1] *D.M.A.* 4 February, 1919; *Derbyshire Times,* 1 and 8 February, 1919.
[2] *Derbyshire Times,* 1 February, 1919.
[3] *M.F.G.B.* 10 February, 1919.   [4] *Ibid.* 12–13 February, 1919.

was decided that, in the event of a favourable ballot, strike notices should be sent in on Monday, 3 March.[1] The Derbyshire leaders then began a vigorous campaign in the coalfield. At Clowne Frank Hall said:

Vote solidly, stand by your leaders, and success will attend our movement. . . . Your wages have not advanced 300 per cent., but the average selling price of coal has increased beyond 400 per cent., so you are still at least 100 per cent. below the selling price of coal on the 1888 rate.

Of the demand for nationalization he said: 'We are not out for confiscation. We want to give the owners a fair and reasonable return for what they have invested. We don't want a penny of their money.'[2] At Alfreton Frank Lee stated that the Government's dilatoriness was the main factor which had brought the dispute to a head. He did not think they could justify the demand for a 30 per cent. increase in wages either upon the cost of living or the selling price of coal:

But what we are doing is this. We say we are entitled now to eat further into the selling prices of coal than ever before. We believe the coal trade is making enormous profits for somebody but the difficulty is how to get at them. . . . I want to say emphatically as miners we are not prepared to go back to the pre-war basis of living, and we must get more advantage from our services than we have got in the past.[3]

The result of the ballot in Derbyshire was overwhelmingly in favour of a strike by 31,070 votes to 2,403. The national figures were 615,164 for the stoppage and 105,082 against.[4] Meanwhile negotiations had been resumed at the national level. On 21 February the Prime Minister, Lloyd George, invited the Executive Committee of the M.F.G.B. to meet him at 10 Downing Street. He proposed that the miners should delay for a fortnight the expiry of their strike notices, which were dated for 15 March, and should take part in a Commission which would be required to present an interim report by 31 March. Smillie argued that the wages and hours claim should be settled without reference to the Commission but agreed to call a conference to consider the Government's proposals. The announcement of the results of the strike ballot then hastened events. On 24 February a Bill was introduced into the House of Commons to give the Coal Industry Commission full statutory powers to compel the attendance of witnesses, the giving of evidence, and the production of relevant documents. The Labour Party urged the Government to omit wages and hours from the Commission's terms of reference, and to concede these demands without further delay. Eventually, in the Committee stage, under pressure of cogent speeches

[1] *D.M.A.* 15 February, 1919.   [2] *Derbyshire Times*, 22 February, 1919.
[3] *Ibid.*   [4] *M.F.G.B.* 26 February, 1919.

from the mining and other Labour members, Lloyd George agreed that the interim report of the Commission should be published by 20 March.

On 26 February the conference of the M.F.G.B. met to consider whether the miners should participate in the work of the Royal Commission. There was much disagreement for it was recognized by some of the delegates that an adverse report would prejudice the miners' case. On the second day it was resolved unanimously: 'That, providing the Government agree to this Federation having the right of appointment or approval of half the Commission, this conference agrees to take part in this Commission.' It was also decided to postpone the expiry of strike notices until 22 March.[1] The Coal Industry Commission Act stipulated that the Commissioners should consist of 'a chairman, who shall be a judge of the Supreme Court, a vice-chairman, and such other persons as His Majesty may think fit'. After further negotiations it was agreed that the miners should nominate four commissioners directly, and that the other two representatives on the workers' side should be agreed upon between the miners and the Government, but formally nominated by the latter. The employers' side was to be represented by three Government nominees and three coal-owners. By about 1 March the Commission was fully constituted. The Chairman was Mr. Justice Sankey. Robert Smillie, Herbert Smith, Frank Hodges and Sir Leo Chiozza Money were nominated by the Federation. R. H. Tawney and Sidney Webb were agreed upon between the Government and the M.F.G.B. The Government nominees were Arthur Balfour, Sir Arthur Duckham and Sir Thomas Royden. The coal-owners were represented by Evan Williams, R. W. Cooper and J. T. Forgie.

II

Derbyshire played little part in the national events leading to the setting up of the Sankey Commission. The Association was, of course, represented by the usual delegation of the officials and three members chosen by the branches at each of the special conferences but they appear to have confined their activities to voting as instructed by the Council and returning to give their report. Frank Hall, as a member of the Executive Committee of the Federation, was equally inconspicuous. No witnesses from Derbyshire appeared before the Commission during the first stage of the inquiry.

The substance of the evidence given before the Sankey Commission is well known and it is unnecessary to reiterate it here. As the inquiry

[1] *M.F.G.B.* 26–27 February, 1919.

progressed it became increasingly obvious that high prices and low wages had enabled the coal industry to make substantial profits during the war despite its inefficiency and wastefulness. The coal-owners attempted to show that the effect of the miners' claim would be ruinous to the industry but their arguments weakened under the cross-examination of such formidable debaters as R. H. Tawney, Sidney Webb and Sir Leo Chiozza Money. The miners' leaders laid great stress on the human aspect of the claim for a higher standard of living and were able to confront the employers' representatives with detailed examples of conditions in the various coalfields. The *Derbyshire Times*, though generally in sympathy with the coal-owners, commented: 'If they have a case at all it is being very badly set out. Some of them might have been on their trial for murder.'[1]

It was found impossible to produce a unanimous report, and eventually three interim reports were presented. The Majority Report, signed by Smillie, Hodges, Smith, Money, Tawney and Webb, recommended that the miners' claim for a 30 per cent. increase in wages and a six-hour working day (exclusive of winding times), with 'corresponding reductions' in the hours of surface workers, should be granted, and that the demobilization demands should be dealt with 'along with the cases of men in other industries'. The report signed by the three coal-owners' representatives recommended a wage increase of 1s. 6d. a day, a seven-hour working day for underground workers, and an eight-hour day for surface workers. The Sankey Report, signed by the Chairman and the three government nominees, recommended the introduction of a seven-hour day from 16 July, 1919, and, 'subject to the economic position of the industry at the end of 1920', a further reduction to six hours from 13 July, 1921. Surface workers were to have a $46\frac{1}{2}$-hour week, exclusive of meal times, the details to be settled locally. Wages were to be increased by 2s. a day.

Both the Majority Report and the Sankey Report contained preliminary observations on the wider problem of the coal industry, which were to be the subject of the second stage of the inquiry. The Majority Report urged that 'nationalization ought to be, in principle, at once determined on'. The Sankey Report stated that 'the present system of ownership and working in the coal industry stands condemned' and that 'it is in the interests of the country that the colliery worker shall in the future have an effective voice in the direction of the mine'. On social conditions the report commented:

. . . There are houses in some districts which are a reproach to civilization. No judicial language is sufficiently strong or sufficiently severe to apply to their condemnation.

[1] *Derbyshire Times*, 15 March, 1919.

U*

It is a matter for careful consideration whether a 1d. per ton should not be at once collected on coal raised and applied to improve the housing and amenities of each particular colliery district.

A 1d. per ton on our present output means about £1,000,000 a year.[1]

The three reports were presented to Parliament on 20 March when Bonar Law, speaking for the Cabinet in the absence of the Prime Minister, announced that the Government had adopted the Sankey Report 'in the spirit as well as in the letter'.[2] On the following day the M.F.G.B. conference decided to press for a number of amendments to the Sankey proposals including the introduction of the six-hour day from 12 July, 1920, a reduction of surfacemen's hours to 45 a week (inclusive of meal times), a wage increase of 2s. 6d. a day, a revision of piece-work rates to prevent any reduction in earnings, the addition of the wage increase to the sixth shift of a 'bonus turn' (i.e. six shifts for five), and the retrospective payment of the wage increase from 9 January, 1919.[3] The Executive Committee met Bonar Law on 22 March, and again on 25 March, when he stated that the Government could make no substantial change in the terms of the Sankey Report but was prepared to concede the demands relating to piece-work rates, the 'bonus turn' and retrospective payment.[4] The M.F.G.B. conference on 26 March decided to take a ballot on the Government's proposals and recommended their acceptance. The Executive Committee decided that the ballot should be taken on 9–10 April and that the results should be sent to the Secretary by 14 April.[5]

The strike notices had expired on 22 March but the conference held on 21 March had recommended that the men should continue working on day to day contracts. The coalfields were in a ferment. Whilst the Commission was sitting there had been a strike of 38,000 men in Nottinghamshire and sporadic strikes of deputies in Derbyshire.[6] The railwaymen's dispute with the Government, which had reached a critical stage, looked as if it might lead to a national strike and there was much talk among the miners and railwaymen about the Triple Alliance. On the day after the Federation's decision to take a ballot on the Government's proposals, conversations between miners on their way to work and railwaymen at the Chesterfield stations led to an unofficial strike of about 8,000 Derbyshire miners which brought to a standstill twelve pits belonging to the Clay Cross, Grassmoor and Hardwick companies. Hall and Lee, who had just returned from London, attended a meeting, at which Sales presided, and tried in vain to persuade the men to return to work.[7] On the following day E. F. Crosse, the

[1] *Coal Industry Commission*, 1919, I, p. ix.   [2] 113 H.C. Deb. 5s. 2346.
[3] *M.F.G.B.* 21 March, 1919.   [4] *Ibid.* 25 March, 1919.   [5] *Ibid.* 26 March, 1919.
[6] *Derbyshire Times*, 22 and 29 March, 1919.   [7] *Ibid.* 29 March, 1919.

Archdeacon of Chesterfield, called upon the miners to be patient. In the evening a mass meeting was held in the Victoria Picture Palace. 'I will tell you why I want you to work', said Frank Hall. 'You have nothing to lose and everything to gain by going to work.' After much discussion the men accepted his advice.[1]

On 29 March the Council decided to advise the members to accept the Government's offer. Backed by 50,000 copies of a manifesto signed by Smillie and Hodges, the Derbyshire leaders toured the coalfield explaining the Federation's policy.[2]

'If the offer had only included shorter hours and the two shillings advance', said Frank Lee, at Staveley, 'he would have been loth to recommend them to reject it. That was taking the short view of it. What he liked to do was to think of its effect upon the future of the industry. . . . They were getting in this offer the first instalment of their demands.'[3]

The result of the ballot in Derbyshire was 36,559 votes for acceptance of the Government's terms and 3,020 against. The national figures were 693,084 for, and 76,992 against. At a special conference on 16 April the M.F.G.B. decided that all strike notices should be withdrawn.[4]

III

Nationalization was now the only question at issue and the miners firmly believed that the Government's acceptance of the Sankey Report 'in spirit and in letter' implied that serious consideration was going to be given to the re-organization of the coal industry. The Commission began the second stage of its inquiry on 23 April. In the interval Sir Thomas Royden had resigned owing to ill health and had been replaced by Sir Allan Smith, the Chairman of the Engineering Employers' Federation. Soon after the Commission resumed its sittings J. T. Forgie also resigned because of illness and was succeeded by Sir Adam Nimmo, who had previously been adviser to the Coal Controller. The Commission sat for nearly two months and examined 116 witnesses.

The only witness from Derbyshire was H. E. Mitton, of the Butterley Company, who gave evidence on boring development and ancillary work carried out by Pioneer Companies in north Nottinghamshire.[5] G. D. H. Cole, who had been active among the Derbyshire miners as a W.E.A. tutor during the war, referred in his evidence to pit committees at 'certain Derbyshire collieries' which had taken matters other than

[1] *Derbyshire Times*, 29 March, 5 April, 1919.   [2] *D.M.A.* 29 March, 1919.
[3] *Derbyshire Times*, 12 April, 1919.   [4] *M.F.G.B.* 16 April, 1919.
[5] *Coal Industry Commission*, 1919, II, QQ. 17,697–17,827.

absenteeism into their hands and had been 'a very great success'.[1] The Chairman showed considerable interest in these committees and asked Cole to obtain further information from the Derbyshire Miners' Association.[2] A month later, after consultation with the M.F.G.B., Cole was able to tell the Commission no more than his recollections of war-time conversations with Frank Hall and other members of the Association about the working of the pit committees. 'All I know about the matter', he said, 'is that subsequently they broke down upon a disagreement between the owners and the miners as to the matters which were legitimate to come before them.'[3]

Whilst the Commission was in session both the coal-owners and the miners' leaders sought to influence public opinion in their favour. The owners and some sections of the Press were alleging that the higher wages paid to the miners had led to irregular attendance at work and to a determination to do less work; that the miners did not recognize their duty to the nation; and that they should therefore be deprived of the opportunity to participate in the administration of the mines. 'I want you to see that you do not play into their hands', said Frank Hall to the Langwith miners, who had decided not to work on Sunday nights. 'I am no believer in Sunday night work, but if you begin to chop off shifts you are interfering with production unless you can put something else in its place.'[4]

The Staveley Company decided upon an experiment in co-partnership to dissuade its employees from demanding nationalization. When the whole of the Company's capital was converted into 2,500,000 ordinary £1 shares it was announced that Charles Markham had acquired all the preference shares and that he intended to offer them to the staff and workmen as 25,000 ordinary shares at 10s. premium. They would thus be able to take up for 30s. a share which was then worth 38s. in the market. It was decided to hold pit-head meetings to explain the scheme and to ask Frank Hall and A. J. Bailey, of the National Union of General Workers to form a committee with the Company's assistant secretary for the purpose of allotting the shares.[5]

Frank Hall observed that the 25,000 shares would represent so small a proportion of the Company's capital 'that they would not influence the thing one way or the other'. He pointed out that if the shares had been distributed in 1914 the workmen would have received 'a splendid bonus':

As far as I am concerned, the scheme will not interfere with any principle that I hold. I believe, as I think a large number of men do, in the nationalization

[1] *Coal Industry Commission*, 1919, II, Q. 13,206.
[2] *Ibid*. QQ. 13,281–13,282.   [3] *Ibid*. QQ. 25,990–26,004.
[4] *Derbyshire Times*, 21 June, 1919.   [5] *Ibid*. 14 June, 1919.

of the mines, and to suggest that the distribution of one sixty-sixth of the capital of the Company will interfere with that principle is too ridiculous to laugh at. If the Staveley Company want to distribute these shares at less than their market value, a man who refuses to take them is a fool. . . . I have no objection to acting as suggested in the interests of the men, but before I do so I am going to ask Mr. Markham one question, and it is this: whether these shares are going to carry some controlling interest, and whether the Company, having gone so far, will extend to the working men shareholders the right to appoint one of their number on the directorate of the Staveley Company.[1]

Within a week of this speech the Sankey Commission had issued its final reports. Hall wrote immediately to Markham stating that in view of the Commission's recommendations he 'did not see the wisdom of the proposed scheme' and asking that his name should no longer be used in connection with it.[2] Soon afterwards the Council expressed the opinion that the scheme 'is against the general interest of the men, and is only meant for the purpose of counteracting the nationalization of the mines recommended by the Sankey Report'.[3] At the annual meeting of the Staveley Company, in the following September, Charles Markham stated: 'The whole of the shares went like hot cakes. He had hoped to see some little co-operation between capital and labour, but the miners' union turned it down.'[4]

The Sankey Commission had reported by 20 June. Again complete unanimity was impossible but all the four reports which were presented recommended the nationalization of mining royalties and the super-session of the existing wasteful methods of distribution by municipal schemes. The Chairman's report recommended the acceptance of the principle of public ownership. It proposed the immediate introduction of a system of local administration under the supervision of the Coal Controller and nationalization after the scheme had been in operation for three years. Provision was made for workers' representation on local, district and national mining councils but not to the extent that the miners had advocated before the Commission.[5] The six miners' representatives on the Commission were in substantial agreement with the Chairman's recommendations but drew up a separate report in which they objected to the proposed procedure for settling disputes by imposing upon the workers by law a particular form of contract. They also expressed the opinion that all coke and by-product plant attached to collieries should be acquired by the State with the coalmines, demanded an immediate inquiry into allegations that the miners were

[1] *Derbyshire Times*, 21 June, 1919.   [2] *Ibid.* 5 July, 1919.
[3] *D.M.A.* 5 July, 1919.   [4] *Derbyshire Times*, 4 October, 1919.
[5] *Coal Industry Commission*, 1919, II, pp. iv–xiii.

responsible for the decline in output, and suggested that shortages of tubs, waggons and materials should be remedied as soon as possible. Hodges, Smillie and Smith entered a special objection to any compensation of royalty owners.[1]

The coal-owners' representatives and the Government's nominees, with the exception of Duckham, reported that they were not in favour of nationalization. Apart from their recommendations about mining royalties and distribution, the men who signed the report were opposed to any change in the existing system of private ownership other than the setting up of consultative pit committees.[2]

Sir Arthur Duckham, in a separate report, put forward as an alternative to nationalization an elaborate scheme for 'district unification' of collieries, which, he claimed, would make possible more efficient working and control. A Ministry of Mines was to be set up 'to supervise and control all mineral rights throughout Great Britain and to ensure the proper working of all minerals'. A Commission was to be appointed to divide the country into districts where all separate colliery companies were to be amalgamated into statutory companies to be known as District Coal Boards. The shares of each Board were to carry a minimum rate of dividend of 4 per cent. which was to be guaranteed by the Government. Profits in excess of those necessary to pay for depreciation and the guaranteed dividend were to be used to form a reserve fund, subject to the approval of the Minister, and to pay a further 2 per cent. dividend. Of the remaining profits, one-third was to be distributed in further dividends but the other two-thirds was to be used to reduce the price of coal.[3] The scheme appears to have been designed to establish a number of coal trusts, each enjoying a monopoly within its own area.

IV

The publication of these reports lulled the miners into inactivity. Whilst the Chambers of Commerce, the coal-owners and other industrialists were waging a vigorous campaign against nationalization, the miners simply awaited the decision of the Government. In view of Bonar Law's previous assurances, it seemed to them almost certain that the mines would be nationalized. They were awakened to reality by the sudden announcement, on 9 July, that the Government had decided to increase the price of coal by 6s. a ton. Two by-elections in which nationalization of the mines was a major issue were then being fought at Swansea and Bothwell. Frank Hall, Tom Cape and James Winstone

[1] *Coal Industry Commission*, 1919, II, pp. xii–xiv.
[2] *Ibid*. pp. xiv–xxi.   [3] *Ibid*. pp. xxii–xxviii.

had been deputed by the Executive Committee of the Federation to assist the Scottish miners' candidate, John Robertson, in his campaign at Bothwell.[1] Frank Lee commented:

The threatened increase of six shillings per ton on coal is a leap in the dark. No doubt it has for its object the defeat of the scheme for nationalization, also the defeat of the two Labour candidates who are contesting parliamentary by-elections. . . . The statement has been made that the six shillings was to be a sort of subsidy to the men following upon the seven-hour day and the reduction of output. The output could be increased by better facilities being provided for getting the coal out of the pit. Big collieries in Derbyshire are at present working short time through the shortage of trucks.[2]

The miners were further incensed by the difficulties they had encountered over the impending introduction of the shorter working day. Detailed negotiations had been left to the districts. By 12 July there had been five meetings between Derbyshire miners' leaders and representatives of the coal-owners. Agreement had been reached on the hours of banksmen and surfacemen but the appropriate addition to be made to piece-work rates to compensate the underground workers for the loss of an hour remained unsettled.[3] In Lancashire agreement had been reached on an addition of 14·3 per cent. but Sir Evan Jones, who had been appointed Coal Controller in March following the death of Calthrop, had issued a circular, on the instructions of the Government, limiting the amount to be paid in any district to 10 per cent.[4] The difficulty was to find a formula which would satisfy every district. The Government had based its decision on the prediction of the Sankey Commission that there would be a 10 per cent. reduction in output but the working day of miners in counties such as Northumberland and Durham, which was already shorter than the average, was being reduced by anything up to 16 per cent. The miners were prepared to accept the argument that their efficiency was increased, but not to the extent implied by an addition of only 10 per cent. to their piece-work rates.[5] During the negotiations between the Government and the Federation the Yorkshire miners decided to strike, pumpmen were withdrawn and naval ratings were drafted into the coalfield to prevent the mines from being flooded.[6]

The unrest spread to Derbyshire. The Association had originally demanded a 16 per cent. addition to piece-work rates but had later decided to accept 14·3 per cent. as the Lancashire miners had done. On 12 July, at a special Council meeting, several delegates advocated a strike unless the 14·3 per cent. was conceded. Eventually it was

[1] M.F.G.B. 4 July, 1919. [2] Derbyshire Times, 12 July, 1919.
[3] D.M.A. 12 July, 1919. [4] M.F.G.B. 4 July, 1919.
[5] Ibid. 5 July, 1919. [6] Ibid. 23 July, 1919.

resolved: 'That we advise the men to continue working until Friday; failing settlement by that time, the delegates to the Annual Conference at Keswick to be instructed to vote for a national stoppage.'[1] On 15 July Frank Hall told the conference: 'Now, we have kept our men at work, but there will be great difficulty in keeping them at work beyond today. They are only now working on the understanding that this conference is going to do something.'[2] After much discussion the conference decided to ask for the 14·3 per cent. and advised the districts to continue working 'until instructed to the contrary'.[3] It was also decided not to give the pledge requested by Bonar Law, in return for the postponement of the increase in the price of coal, that there should not be any strikes for three months. Instead the Federation offered to co-operate with the Government only if it agreed to nationalize the mines.[4]

On 21 July, the day on which the price of coal was due to go up, 10,000 miners in the Derbyshire coalfield came out on strike despite the advice of their leaders. News of the stoppage spread quickly, and on the following day the number of strikers had increased to over 20,000. Unlike the Yorkshiremen they decided that sufficient men should be left in the pits to keep them safe and in good repair. Many of the men said that they had stopped work in sympathy with the Yorkshire miners. Others objected to the increase in the price of coal. The majority of them were angry because the Government had failed to honour its pledge that the shorter working day would not mean any reduction of wages. In the background was a smouldering discontent over a number of wider issues such as the sending of troops to Russia, the increase in the cost of living, the refusal of the Government to raise the level of exemption from income tax, the continuation of conscription and the use of troops for industrial purposes.[5] Most of these grievances had been ventilated at the annual conference and some of them had been taken up by the Triple Alliance.

Samuel Sales, supported by Hall, Lee and Hicken, presided over a mass meeting at the Victoria Picture Palace, Chesterfield. Lee argued that the men should do 'nothing that would hinder the full realization of the Sankey award—nationalization of the mines'. Hicken said:

If there was anything that would make the gods laugh it was the miners' claim to control their own industry when they could not control themselves. . . . They had got a mean, paltry spirit, and it was not worth a snap of the finger. Arrayed against them were consolidated forces which nothing could disintegrate. . . . They defeated themselves by their miserable arguments and misunderstanding of questions which so vitally affected them. . . . The

[1] D.M.A. 12 July, 1919.   [2] M.F.G.B. 15 July, 1919.
[3] Ibid. 17 July, 1919.   [4] Ibid.   [5] Derbyshire Times, 26 July, 1919.

capitalists had fooled them for the last fifty years, but not to the same extent as they had the last five. If they promised them the kingdom, the moon, they would believe them and call them 'jolly good fellows' and would vie with each other as to who should present the boss with a gold watch when he left.

The men refused to return to work until the question of piece-work rates had been settled and passed a resolution protesting against the increase in the price of coal.[1]

On 24 July, when a sub-committee of the M.F.G.B. Executive Committee met the Coal Controller to continue negotiations on piece-work rates, thirty Derbyshire pits were still idle. On the following day the entire Executive Committee met the Prime Minister and a formula was agreed upon which gave an increase of 14·2 per cent. for the loss of an hour's working time.[2] The news of the agreement was quickly communicated to the Derbyshire miners by their leaders and the strike came to an end.[3] In Yorkshire the men did not return to work until the middle of August.

The miners were still awaiting the Government's decision on the future of the coal industry but it was not until 18 August that Lloyd George made a statement in the House of Commons. He announced that the minerals were to be purchased by the State, that a fund was to be established for improving amenities in the colliery villages, and that 'unification should be promoted by amalgamation in defined areas'. The workers were to be represented on the area governing boards and the scheme was to 'conform to any conditions laid down by the Government for the protection of the general body of coal consumers'.[4] The Government's proposals followed in broad outline the recommendations of Sir Arthur Duckham, although they did not include any explicit statement about the treatment of profits.

The rejection of nationalization aroused a storm of protest from the miners. On 23 August the Council of the Derbyshire Miners' Association passed the following lengthy resolution:

That this meeting . . . regards the attitude taken up by the Prime Minister on behalf of the Government in reference to the second Sankey Report, and

---

[1] *Derbyshire Times*, 26 July, 1919.

[2] M.F.G.B. 25 July, 1919. The formula was as follows:

$$\frac{\text{The reduction in output as calculated over the whole country, viz. } 11 \cdot 1\% \times \text{The reduction in point of time in respect of any given class of workmen in the district in question.}}{47}$$

(The constant 47 was the average reduction in minutes in working time for the whole country.)

[3] *Derbyshire Times*, 26 July, 1919.   [4] 119 H.C. Deb. 5s. 2007.

the Nationalization of Mines, as a distinct breach of faith. The proposal to
set up a commission to enquire into the demands made by the Miners'
Federation of Great Britain came from the Government, and, it was definitely
understood, implied acceptance of the findings of the Commission. If this
was not intended, it can only be a matter of deceiving the workers, or else the
present position must mean a surrender of the Prime Minister to capitalistic
influence since the Commission was established. The Delegates hereby
pledge themselves to use every endeavour in their power both industrially
and politically to defeat the government scheme of Gigantic Trusts in the
Coal Trade, which can only mean the exploiting of the workers and general
public, and using this Great National Industry in the interests of private
owners, and not in the interests of the whole community.[1]

A similar protest was registered by a special conference of the M.F.G.B.
on 3 September. It was decided not to recommend the miners to take
industrial action at that stage but to invite the T.U.C. 'to declare that
the fullest and most effective action be taken to secure that the Government shall adopt the majority policy of the Commission as to the future
governance of the industry'.[2] On 10 September the T.U.C. at Glasgow
decided that the Parliamentary Committee, with representatives of the
M.F.G.B., should interview the Prime Minister and insist upon the
adoption of the majority report. Lloyd George remained inflexible and
in December a special Trades Union Congress launched 'The Mines
for the Nation' campaign.

In Derbyshire it had been decided, on 23 August, to hold mass
meetings throughout the coalfield.[3] Archdeacon Crosse invited Frank
Hall to address the clergy of the archdeaconry on labour problems in
Chesterfield parish church.[4] In a letter to *The Times* Crosse challenged
the 'unfair and unjust charges . . . wildly made against the Miners'
Federation'. 'The miners are a splendid, independent, but, I own, a
difficult race of men,' he wrote, 'and more difficult still will they become
if they are not handled more reasonably, alike by State and public.'[5]
Hildreth, the Association's political organizer, was challenged by a
representative of the coal-owners to take part in a public debate on
nationalization at Bolsover.[6]

There was much talk of 'direct action'. The Triple Alliance had
proposed a strike ballot to secure the abolition of conscription, the
withdrawal of troops from Russia, and the cessation of military intervention in industrial disputes.[7] The Council of the Derbyshire Miners'

---

[1] *D.M.A.* 23 August, 1919.   [2] *M.F.G.B.* 3 September, 1919.
[3] *D.M.A.* 23 August, 1919.
[4] *Derbyshire Times*, 9 August, 1919.   [5] *The Times*, 23 August, 1919.
[6] *Derbyshire Times*, 25 October, 1 November, 1919.
[7] *M.F.G.B.* 23 July, 1919.

Association had advised members to vote in favour of ceasing work if necessary but a special conference of the Triple Alliance, on 4 September, decided not to continue with the plan.[1] Frank Lee told the Staveley District Trades and Labour Council: 'He was the last man in the world to favour the strike, which would upset the commerce of the country, if their objects could be gained by some other method.'[2] The railwaymen's strike at the end of September revived the idea of bringing the Triple Alliance into action. 'I feel that we have a very strong interest in their cause,' said Frank Hall, 'and that sooner or later we shall be in it ... Until we are asked to come in, it is impossible for us to do anything at all, and we can only look on.'[3] Both J. G. Hancock, the Nottinghamshire miners' M.P., and Barnet Kenyon condemned 'direct action' at a meeting at Brimington on 6 October.[4]

'The Mines for the Nation' campaign proved a failure. On 3 January, 1920, the Derbyshire officials complained that 'in many districts the workers are indolent, indifferent, in fact, take no interest in the question'.[5] The general public was equally unmoved. On 9 January the M.F.G.B. Executive Committee decided that the time had come to consider whether a general strike could be used to bring about the nationalization of the mines.[6] After consultation with C. W. Bowerman, secretary of the T.U.C. Parliamentary Committee, it was agreed that there should be a special congress, on 11 March, at which the matter would be discussed. It was to be preceded by a Federation conference on 10 March. In Derbyshire it was decided by 42,095 votes to 4,688 that the delegates to this conference should vote in favour of industrial action being taken to enforce the nationalization of the mines.[7] Opinion in the Federation as a whole, however, was more evenly divided, the voting being 524 for industrial action and 344 against.[8] On the following day the special Trades Union Congress decided by 3,732,000 votes to 1,050,000 not to call a general strike but to concentrate on political rather than industrial action.

V

As their hopes of securing nationalization dwindled, the miners turned their attention increasingly to the question of wages and prices. In 1919 the cost of living was 115 per cent., and in 1920 149 per cent.,

[1] *D.M.A.* 9 August, 1919; *M.F.G.B.* 4 September, 1919.
[2] *Derbyshire Times*, 9 August, 1919.
[3] *Ibid.* 4 October, 1919.   [4] *Ibid.* 11 October, 1919.
[5] *D.M.A.* 3 January, 1920.   [6] *M.F.G.B.* 9 January, 1920.
[7] *D.M.A.* 21 February, 1919.   [8] *M.F.G.B.* 10 March, 1919.

higher than in 1914. The Derbyshire Miners' Association had, for several months, been negotiating with the Coal Controller for a revised minimum wage for contractors of 8s. a day. This was eventually conceded, in April, 1920, by W. H. Stoker, who had been asked to arbitrate. He stipulated that where the inability to earn the minimum wage was due to the shortage of trams, rails and other material, the rate was to be 7s. 9d. There were also corresponding increases for other grades.[1]

On 24 November, 1919, the President of the Board of Trade, Sir Auckland Geddes, had announced in the House of Commons that the price of household coal would be reduced by 10s. a ton from 1 December.[2] Frank Hall told the Alfreton miners: 'This Government after all is either a very foolish Government or a very brainless Government.'[3] The miners' objection to the Government's pricing policy for coal was that it was being directed towards political ends. Moreover they argued that large profits were being derived from the export trade, that the price of industrial coal for home consumers was excessive, that domestic consumers were unable to obtain supplies at the reduced rates, and that the continued high price of coal was having serious effects upon the cost of living. On 8 January, 1920, the Executive Committee of the M.F.G.B. decided to ask the Government either to remedy these economic grievances or to consider an application for an advance in wages 'consequent upon the high cost of living.'[4] The Executive Committee met the Prime Minister and other representatives of the Government at 10 Downing Street on 28 January and 19 February but no agreement was reached.

On 21 February the Council of the Derbyshire Miners' Association decided that an immediate application should be made by the Federation for an increase in wages.[5] The matter was referred to the lodges and on 28 February it was agreed that the Federation should be instructed to demand a flat rate of 1s. 6d. a day and a fortnight's holiday with full pay.[6] At a special conference of the Federation, however, it was decided, on the recommendation of the Executive Committee, to ask for an increase of 3s. a day, dating from 1 March, 1920.[7] Negotiations with the Government were resumed on 18 March when the Executive Committee again met the Prime Minister and presented the Federation's demand, which was based on the increased cost of living, the need for an improved standard of living, and the financial position of the industry.

---

[1] *Derbyshire Times*, 10 April, 1920; *D.M.A.* 12 April, 1920.
[2] 121 H.C. Deb. 5s. 1419.
[3] *Derbyshire Times*, 29 November, 1919.
[4] *M.F.G.B.* 8 January, 1920.   [5] *D.M.A.* 21 February, 1920.
[6] *Ibid.* 28 February, 1920.   [7] *M.F.G.B.* 12 March, 1920.

The miners submitted the following particulars of the effects of their claim:[1]

1. Excluding Sankey Wage

Year	Average wage per worker per shift	Percentage increase of wages over 1914 standard	Percentage increase of cost of living since 1914
	s. d.		
1914	6 5·64	—	—
1918	12 6	93·20	110
1920	15 4·47	137·60	135
(New claim added)			

2. Including Sankey Wage

Year	Average wage per worker per shift	Percentage increase of wages over 1914 standard	Percentage increase of cost of living since 1914
1914	6 5·64	—	—
1918	12 6	93·20	110
1920	14 4·98	122·70	125
(Sankey claim)			
1920	17 3·45	167·19	135
(New claim)			

It was estimated that the total cost of the claim would be £42,912,250 a year and that it would add 3s. 9½d. a ton to the cost of production of coal.

Lloyd George referred the Executive Committee to the new Coal Controller, A. R. Duncan, who had succeeded Sir Evan Jones in October, 1919. Meetings were held on 19 and 23 March but no agreement was reached. There were further meetings with the Prime Minister on 25, 26 and 29 March. The Government's final offer was a 20 per cent. increase on gross earnings, excluding the 'war wage' and the 'Sankey wage', with a guaranteed minimum flat rate increase of 2s. a shift for those over 18 years of age, 1s. for those between 16 and 18, and 9d. for those under 16. It was estimated that the Government's offer would add £36,500,000 to the annual cost of production but the percentage increase was intended to be an incentive to greater output. On 29 March a Federation conference decided to take a strike ballot.[2] The result was reported to a special conference of the M.F.G.B. on 15 April. There were 181,009 votes for acceptance of the Government's offer and 115,874 against. In Derbyshire, where the Council had decided to follow the lead of the national conference and issue no recommendation either for acceptance or rejection, the figures were 25,051 and 14,431 respectively.[3]

No sooner had the miners received their increase in wages than the Government again increased the price of coal. On 10 May, 1920, Sir Robert Horne, the new President of the Board of Trade, told the

[1] M.F.G.B. 18 March, 1920.   [2] Ibid. 29 March, 1920.
[3] Ibid. 15 April, 1920; D.M.A. 30 March, 1920.

House of Commons that there would be an increase of 4s. 2d. a ton on industrial coal and 14s. 2d. on domestic coal.[1] This appeared to the miners and to other observers to be quite unnecessary. As Sir Richard Redmayne has pointed out 'the existing high rate of wages was being met out of the proceeds derived from exported coal, at this time fetching very high prices'.[2] The miners believed that prices were being increased partly to influence public opinion against them and partly in preparation for the ending of state control of the industry, when the inefficient pits would no longer be able to run at a loss. Moreover, the cost of living was continuing to rise sharply. On 24 April the Council of the Derbyshire Miners' Association resolved: 'That in spite of past failures in this direction, all the weight of the Federation should be used with the Government to turn their attention to the urgent necessity for something to be done in the way of reducing the cost of living.'[3] The complaint was general. A deputation of miners' wives attended a meeting of the Executive Council of the South Wales Miners' Federation to urge that the recent wage advances were inadequate to meet the increase in household expenditure.[4]

A special conference of the M.F.G.B. assembled in London on 10 June to discuss the increase in the price of inland coal and to consider whether there should be another wage claim. Robert Smillie argued that either a reduction in the price of coal or an increase in wages would make it impossible for the Government to decontrol the mines. 'I want the miners to prove to Lloyd George,' he said, 'that we are not prepared to allow the coal trade to be decontrolled and each colliery standing on its own legs. This would ruin every step forward for a good many months.' The conference decided to ask for a substantial advance in wages and instructed the Executive Committee to formulate a claim for submission to another conference at an early date.[5]

The Executive Committee considered the situation carefully and decided that it would be better to win the support of public opinion by making a demand for a reduction in the cost of living as part of the Federation's claim. It was decided, on 21 June, to ask for a reduction of 14s. 2d. in the price of household coal and a wage increase of 2s. a day for those over the age of 18, 1s. a day for those between 18 and 16, and 9d. a day for those under 16. These proposals were hotly debated in the districts. Derbyshire was in favour of a percentage rather than a flat rate increase.[6] The Nottinghamshire miners disapproved of the proposal to demand a reduction in the price of coal and advocated a flat rate increase of 4s. a day. At the annual conference of the Federation

[1] 129 H.C. Deb. 5s. 9–10.   [2] Redmayne, *op. cit.* p. 235.
[3] *D.M.A.* 24 April, 1920.   [4] *Derbyshire Times*, 1 May, 1920.
[5] *M.F.G.B.* 10 June, 1920.   [6] *D.M.A.* 17 June, 1920.

in July, after considerable discussion, it was decided by 545 votes to 360 to accept the recommendations of the Executive Committee, Derbyshire voting with the majority.[1] The conference also considered the new Mines Bill. Parts I and III, which established a Department of Mines and a Miners' Welfare Fund, were welcomed by the miners but they objected to Part II, which was designed to implement Sir Arthur Duckham's recommendations and implied a return to district wage agreements. The conference decided 'to refuse to operate the Bill should it become law' and to urge the Labour Party 'to use every means at its disposal to prevent its passage through the House'.[2]

These decisions were endorsed by the Council of the Derbyshire Miners' Association on 19 July.[3] Meetings were held in various parts of the county to protest against the Mines Bill. Frank Hall told the Clay Cross miners that it would mean a reversion to district wage determination and pointed out that the exporting districts were in a far better position than the inland coalfields where there would inevitably be wage reductions.[4] At a mass meeting at Chesterfield John Spencer said: 'The miners were never better off than under the national pool which had been established during the war, and as far as wages were concerned they were not going back to the old greyhound competition and setting one district against another.'[5]

On 26 July Sir Robert Horne, the President of the Board of Trade, gave the Government's reply to the miners' demand for a reduction in the price of coal and an increase in wages. 'The view of the Government is', he said, 'that whatever surplus profits are derived from the sale of coal during the next twelve months should go into the Exchequer.'[6] A special conference of the Federation on 12 August decided almost unanimously to take a strike ballot and to recommend the members to vote for a stoppage.[7] Feeling was running high among the miners' leaders. Hicken declared at South Normanton: 'I am a rebel and the only hope for the working classes is rebellion.' On the other hand W. Holland, a former vice-president of the Nottinghamshire Miners' Association, who was employed by the Bolsover Colliery Company and was later to become active in the British Workers' League, described the threatened strike as a 'huge revolutionary plot' which, if successful, would be 'ten times more serious' than the 1893 lock-out. 'The policy of the Miners' Federation of Great Britain', he said, 'is to make it impossible for colliery owners to run the mines at a profit, by which means nationalization could be, willy-nilly, forced.'[8]

[1] *M.F.G.B.* 7 July, 1920.   [2] *Ibid.*   [3] *D.M.A.* 19 July, 1920.
[4] *Derbyshire Times*, 24 July, 1920.   [5] *Ibid.* 31 July, 1920.
[6] *M.F.G.B.* 26 July, 1920.   [7] *Ibid.* 12 August, 1920.
[8] *Derbyshire Times*, 28 August, 1920.

The Derbyshire miners decided, by 28,352 votes to 11,139, to follow the militant section of their leadership.[1] At a M.F.G.B. conference on 2 September the Secretary reported that 606,782 members had voted for a strike and 238,865 against.[2] It was then agreed that work should cease in all the districts on 25 September, 1920. The Triple Alliance had already declared the miners' demands to be 'reasonable and just' and had appointed a sub-committee to watch events.[3] On 8 September the T.U.C. at Portsmouth also gave its support by passing an emergency resolution.[4]

VI

Despite a further meeting between the Executive Committee of the M.F.G.B. and Sir Robert Horne, on 8 September, the deadlock remained unbroken. Horne had re-stated the Government's views which were, briefly, that the home consumer was already buying coal at or below cost price; that the existing profit on export coal should benefit the country as a whole through the Exchequer; and that any advance in wages should be contingent upon an increase in coal production.[5] The publication by the Board of Trade of its quarterly summary of the financial and other statistics of the coal industry[6] led the miners to change their policy. They had based their claim on an estimated surplus of £66,000,000 but the latest figures suggested that the surplus would be only £33,000,000. On 15 September the Executive Committee of the M.F.G.B. decided to recommend to a special conference that the claim for the reduction in the price of coal should be abandoned. The Government was to be asked to concede the wage claim; to agree that the cost should not be added to the price of home-consumed coal; to appoint 'a competent and representative tribunal' to inquire into the financial position of the industry and determine whether there should be a reduction in the price of domestic coal; and to set up a committee to inquire into the causes of declining output. In return the M.F.G.B. was prepared to accept the Government's proposal for a full inquiry into the wage system of the coal industry.[7] There were further interviews with Horne on 16, 17 and 20 September, but the Government would not agree to the Federation's new proposals.

A M.F.G.B. special conference on 21 September approved the

[1] *D.M.A.* 28 August, 1920.   [2] *M.F.G.B.* 2 September, 1920.
[3] *Ibid.* 31 August, 1 September, 1920.   [4] *T.U.C. Report,* 1920.
[5] *M.F.G.B.* 8 September, 1920.
[6] *Summary of Coal Output, Costs of Production, etc. for three months to June 30, 1920.* (Cmd. 949.)   [7] *M.F.G.B.* 15 September, 1920.

actions of the Executive Committee although there was much criticism of the change of policy. The delegates also expressed the view that 'nothing had emerged during the negotiations ... to justify them in advising the miners to continue work'.[1] On the following day there was a meeting of the Triple Alliance at which J. H. Thomas, the railwaymen's leader, argued that the control of policy should be taken out of the hands of the miners in the event of a sympathetic strike. Havelock Wilson, the secretary of the Sailors' and Firemen's Union, was thoroughly opposed to a stoppage. Eventually it was decided to send a deputation 'to interview the Government and urge further the acceptance by the Government of the miners' claim.'[2] The Prime Minister, who received the deputation, proposed that the dispute should be referred to arbitration or, alternatively, that the miners should accept an increase in wages conditional upon suitable arrangements for higher output.[3]

The M.F.G.B. special conference considered the report of the Triple Alliance deputation on the following day. The Executive Committee was divided and made no recommendation. Smillie advocated arbitration but met with considerable opposition. Derbyshire, along with South Wales, Durham, Scotland, Lancashire, South Derbyshire, Somerset, the Forest of Dean and Kent, voted against Smillie's proposal which was defeated by 545 votes to 360.[4] The miners' rejection of arbitration meant that they lost the support of the transport workers and the railwaymen, both of whom had recently been prevailed upon by their leaders to accept arbitration procedures. At an acrimonious conference of the Triple Alliance later in the day it became apparent that if the Federation decided to carry out its threat to strike on 25 September it would do so alone.[5] On 24 September the miners' leaders again saw the Prime Minister and told him that the miners would cease work on the following day. He asked them to suspend the strike notices for a week to enable them to have discussions with the coal-owners on the possibility of evolving a scheme to increase output. On the recommendation of the Executive Committee the M.F.G.B. conference decided by 134 votes to 31 to accede to the Prime Minister's request. These events were subsequently reported to the Triple Alliance conference. J. H. Thomas and Harry Gosling both expressed their relief. Ernest Bevin commented: 'By God, it has revealed itself to be a paper alliance this week.'[6]

On 25 September the miners' leaders and the coal-owners' representatives began their negotiations. Four days later they reported to the Government that they had failed to reach agreement. At a joint

[1] *M.F.G.B.* 21 September, 1920.   [2] *Ibid.* 22 September, 1920.
[3] *Ibid.*   [4] *Ibid.* 23 September, 1920.
[5] *Ibid.*   [6] *Ibid.* 24 September, 1920.

meeting of the Executive Committee of the M.F.G.B. with representatives of the owners and the Government, on 1 October, Lloyd George suggested that there were four possibilities: a ballot vote on the owners' proposals, arbitration, continued negotiations or a strike. On the same day the M.F.G.B. conference decided, by 530 votes to 401, to accept the recommendation of the Executive Committee that the owners' proposals should be referred to the men. Derbyshire voted with the majority. The strike notices were suspended for a fortnight until 16 October and it was agreed that no recommendation should be made by the conference for acceptance or rejection of the proposals.[1]

The fixing of a datum line from which an increase in output could be calculated was now one of the principal issues in the dispute. The owners had offered a bonus of 1s. a day (with 6d. for youths and 4½d. for boys) if the output in the first fortnight of October increased to the rate of 242 million tons a year; 2s. a day if the rate increased to 250 million tons and higher bonuses for still greater increases in production. The miners had insisted on taking the current output for the third quarter as the datum line. They also demanded an increase of 2s. a shift payable from 14 July and a bonus of 6d. a shift in November if output rose in October to the annual rate of 244 million tons, with a further 6d. a shift for an increase to the rate of 248 million tons in any succeeding month.[2] The owners' final offer may be summarized as follows:[3]

Rate of output of coal, million tons per annum[4]	Over 18		Increase in wages to be given per shift 16–18		Under 16	
	s.	d.	s.	d.	s.	d.
240	1	0		6		4½
244	1	6		9		6¾
248	2	0	1	0		9
252	2	6	1	3		11¼
256	3	0	1	6	1	1½

These proposals were discussed by a special meeting of the Council of the Derbyshire Miners' Association on 4 October. The proceedings which were 'of the liveliest character' lasted for several hours. One delegate described the Council Chamber as a 'chamber of horrors'. After a fierce battle of words the militant section of the Council succeeded in carrying a resolution recommending the members to reject the owners' proposals. Whilst agreeing that output was lower than it should be, the militants argued that the datum line, if accepted, would

[1] *M.F.G.B.* 1 October, 1920.
[2] *Ibid.* 25 September, 1920.
[3] *Ibid.* 1 October, 1920.
[4] The output of coal in 1919 had been 229,779,517 tons.

become a permanent basis for the settlement of wages, whilst the miners would have no effective control over output despite the proposed joint committees.[1] Frank Hall was strongly opposed to a strike but later agreed that the reasons for the decline in output were 'bad management, rotten machinery, re-entrance to the mines of men who have suffered in the war, shortage of steam, etc.'. He pointed out that although Derbyshire's production record was much better than the average for the country, there were collieries near Chesterfield where the men had worked an average of less than three days a week since Christmas 'owing to indifference on the part of the management and defective machinery'. He had little faith in the efficacy of the proposed committees. 'What power', he asked, 'could make the colliery management apply the remedies even if the joint committees prove that they are not doing their best to create output?' The remedy for declining output, he said, was 'real co-operation'.[2]

Some of the more moderate leaders were extremely critical of the policies which were being adopted. Speaking at Northampton, on 3 October, Barnet Kenyon said: 'He stood aghast at the position in the coal trade because it was contrary to everything he had always preached to threaten the nation with dislocation, which would in three weeks leave the national life a wreck.'[3] Thomas Spencer, of Alfreton, one of the Association's trustees, had already been censured for making statements to the Press that the miners' demand for a reduction in the price of coal was 'a false issue and a political move'.[4] On 19 October a meeting of the Executive Committee and the Trustees recorded its regret 'that in a strike crisis like the present, Mr. T. Spencer ... did not attend the meeting'.[5] For different reasons the militant Smillie advised the miners to accept the owners' offer as a temporary measure. In a statement to the Press Association, on 7 October, he said: 'If this course were taken it would give us an opportunity of trying to prove that the mine owner, and not the miner, is mainly responsible for declining output from the mines.'[6]

The result of the ballot in Derbyshire showed that only 10,250 members were in favour of the owners' proposals and 25,919 were against. At a special conference of the M.F.G.B. on 14th October the Secretary reported that there were 181,428 votes for accepting the offer and 635,098 against. It was then resolved: 'That in view of the ballot vote the men be advised to allow the notices to expire, and that a cessation of work take place after Saturday, October 16th, 1920.'[7]

[1] *D.M.A.* 4 October, 1920; *Derbyshire Times*, 9 October, 1920.
[2] *Derbyshire Times*, 9 October, 1920.   [3] *Ibid.*
[4] *D.M.A.* 15 September, 1920.   [5] *Ibid.* 19 October, 1920.
[6] *Derbyshire Times*, 9 October, 1920.   [7] *M.F.G.B.* 14 October, 1920.

Smillie, who had disagreed with Frank Hodges and others on the desirability of a strike, attempted to resign but was eventually persuaded to continue in office.[1]

VII

The 'Datum Line' strike, as it was called, began on Saturday, 16 October. By one o'clock practically every pit in Derbyshire was closed.

'The miners are not demonstrative,' stated the *Derbyshire Times*. 'They handed in their lamps and left the offices as though they were ending the ordinary week's work. Their general opinion was that the strike would soon be over, and they attended football matches and places of amusement just the same as usual.'[2]

Their leaders, however, were prepared for a long struggle. They resolved on 19 October:

That to make the funds of the union last as long as possible during what for the moment appears to be a protracted strike, this Executive Committee recommends to the branches that strike pay to full members be £1 per week and 3s. for each child under working age. . . . The first payment to be made on October 29th.[3]

This recommendation was accepted by the branches and ratified by the Council on 23 October.[4]

At the end of the first week of the strike it was reported: 'As was expected the conduct of the men . . . has been exemplary, and we trust it will remain so. They have beguiled the time in various ways, playing all kinds of sport, gardening, etc.'[5] There were difficulties at some collieries over the misemployment of deputies, pumpmen and enginemen who were allowed to remain at work to keep the pits safe. The miners at the Coppice Colliery complained that the deputies were being given tasks which were ordinarily done by men who were on strike. At the Warsop Colliery, on the other hand, the Staveley Company went so far as to stop the fan and dispense with the services of the enginemen. 'This is absolutely stupid', said Frank Hall. At Barlborough 250 miners, headed by their checkweighman, Solomon Woodhead, marched to the colliery office to protest against the employment of three non-union clerks.[6]

On 21 October there was a dramatic development. A special Delegate Meeting of the National Union of Railwaymen decided to inform the

---

[1] *M.F.G.B.* 15 October, 1920.   [2] *Derbyshire Times*, 23 October, 1920.
[3] *D.M.A.* 19 October, 1920.   [4] *Ibid.* 23 October, 1920.
[5] *Derbyshire Times*, 23 October, 1920.
[6] *Ibid.* 23 October, 1920; *D.M.A.* 23 October, 1920.

Prime Minister that unless the miners' claims were granted or nego-tiations resumed by 23 October the railwaymen would strike. Telegrams were sent out warning members to be prepared to cease work at mid-night on Sunday, 24 October. The Government became alarmed. On Friday, 22 October, the Emergency Powers Bill was introduced into the House of Commons and by Wednesday, 27 October, it had received the Royal Assent. Its introduction provoked a strong protest from a conference of all trade union executives, hastily summoned by the Parliamentary Committee of the T.U.C. Meanwhile Lloyd George had speedily re-opened negotiations with the M.F.G.B. thereby postponing the railwaymen's threatened strike. The miners' leaders had their first meeting with the Prime Minister on Sunday, 24 October. There followed four days of discussion. On 28 October the Executive Com-mittee decided to recommend a ballot on the Government's latest proposals.[1]

As a temporary measure the Government had offered an immediate wage increase of 2s. a shift for adults, 1s. for youths and 9d. for boys. This advance was to be guaranteed until 31 December, 1920. It was to be continued in January, 1921, if the value of export sales for the five weeks ending 18 December, 1920, exceeded the value for the September quarter by a sufficient sum to cover the full wage increase. For every £288,000 less than the amount required there was to be a reduction of 6d., 3d. and $2\frac{1}{4}$d. a shift for adults, youths and boys respectively. For every 6d. reduction in wages the owners were to lose a quarter of the amount by which their profit exceeded the level guaranteed under the Coal Mines (Emergency) Act. Similarly, for every advance of 6d. a shift in wages the owners' profits in excess of their guaranteed standard were to be increased by a quarter.[2] The Government was to guarantee export prices at the level of 72s. a ton. The scheme was to continue until a National Wage Board was established. The owners and workmen were to report to the Government on the permanent scheme not later than 31 March, 1921. Joint production committees were to be formed locally and nationally.

These proposals were printed on the back of each ballot paper and were no doubt incomprehensible to many of the miners. The difficulties of taking the vote when the men were on strike were considerable. The Derbyshire Miners' Association issued ballot papers for each branch to the Council delegates. A special polling station was established in Chesterfield, where members could vote irrespective of their branch, and similar arrangements were made in other parts of the county.[3]

[1] *M.F.G.B.* 28 October, 1920.
[2] Under the Coal Mines (Emergency) Act the owners received one-tenth of the excess profits of the industry.   [3] *D.M.A.* 30 October, 1920.

The Council had decided not to make any recommendation to the branches, members being left to vote 'according to their own convictions', but this did not prevent the officials from addressing mass meetings to 'explain' the proposals. Frank Hall, speaking in the Chesterfield Civic Theatre, on 31 October, said:

There was a sentimental objection to the datum line, which was rather remarkable among hard-headed, thinking men, for they could not have the wages agreement without first having a datum line. By their ballot the men had damned the datum line, and it was now proposed to have the wages on values which depended upon output. . . . They were only 19,136 tons short of output each week for five weeks in November to December last year to secure them an advance of 2s. 6d. per shift, and as there were now an additional 40,000 men in the mines the new proposals were such as he could recommend to them as an honourable settlement.

After his speech Hall had to face a barrage of critical questions. One miner wanted to know why the claim for the reduction of 14s. 2d. in the price of coal was dropped. 'Was it due to the inefficiency of the leaders', he asked, 'in putting forward a claim they could not subsequently justify, or had the Government diddled them?'[1]

Hicken was thoroughly opposed to the acceptance of the Government's terms and addressed a number of meetings arranged by the militant section of the union. At Blackwell, Thomas Kyte, the check-weighman, had a sharp exchange with F. F. Bolstridge, a delegate to the Council, over the right to hold such a meeting. Hicken stated that he would only accept the Government's proposals if they carried with them the control of the pits:

The ballot was damned before we took it because of the two-thirds majority, which is rotten machinery forced upon us to maintain a strike. The Government have out-generalled us and out-manœuvred us and they did it because we stopped too long in the talking shop. . . . Those frauds in high places who recommended us to fight, if they knew they could not maintain a fight or justify its continuance, ought to be shot today. . . . We can starve the Government into subjection now, just the same as they will do to us next March. . . . Every time we went to Downing Street we got weaker, and now the Government have decided that the leaders shall dictate to the rank and file to obey them. I have listened to the hysterical ravings of Thomas and Tillett with scorn—men who were made by the knack of crawling on their bellies and have never done anything else.[2]

Large numbers of miners refrained from voting. In Derbyshire there were 15,917 in favour of the proposed settlement and 12,669 against. The national figures were 338,045 and 346,504 respectively. Despite the

---

[1] *Derbyshire Times*, 6 November, 1920.   [2] *Ibid.*

small majority against the Government's terms it was decided at a special conference on 3 November to abandon the strike in accordance with the Federation's rule requiring a two-thirds majority. The men were instructed to return to work on the following day.[1]

VIII

During the months of unrest at the end of the war the Derbyshire miners' decision to abolish the butty system renewed a controversy which had been raging intermittently for many years. The system was generally favoured by the colliery owners, one of whom wrote in 1879:

It has been proved, from careful experiments, to be considerably cheaper . . . than any other plan . . . as the butty, by his practical knowledge is able to get more work done than the manager, by his utmost exertions, can obtain from the men. The secret is easily explained. The butty is always at hand, and prompt in rendering assistance wherever required in any part of the working over which he has charge, and he is, like a skilful general, always to be found where the difficulties and dangers are greatest, because, as he is well aware, if the work of sending out coal is at a standstill through some trifling impediment, and his men are idle but for a short time, his pocket suffers a proportionate loss.[2]

John Beardsley, of Langley Mill, appears to have been one of the few employers who disliked the scheme. He decided to close his small colliery, employing a hundred men, 'rather than go on any longer with such a rotten system', and produced figures to show that two butties received £4 1s. 8d. for a task which cost them, including their own labour, only £2 13s. 0d.

'Can we wonder,' he asked, 'that these men boast in the public street that they can make the colliery pay on five half days per week? . . . The men who do the hardest work can, under this vexatious system, scarcely get enough to exist upon, while the butty is feasting upon his ill-gotten gains.'[3]

It was this aspect of the butty system which displeased the miners. In 1899 Aaron Bowman, of Sheepbridge, complained:

In some collieries one or two men can have several stalls. They are called bosses. They take over the entire management and sub-let all the work to other men at a reduced figure. The bosses act in a tyrannical way over their employees. They draw all the cash at the office and pay their subordinates the sum agreed upon, which is very small per day in comparison to theirs, yet three-fourths of the men beneath them are really worth half a dozen of such bosses man to man. The bosses carry home £9 to £10 per week, the others perhaps 25s. or 30s.[4]

[1] M.F.G.B. 3 November, 1920.   [2] Ilkeston Pioneer, 29 May, 1879.
[3] Ibid. 22 May, 1879.   [4] Derbyshire Times, 14 January, 1899.

There was much criticism of the butty system in 1909 following the introduction of the shorter working day. This was the period when the leadership of the Association and the domination of the Council by butties and checkweighmen were beginning to be challenged.[1] A Bolsover miner wrote:

As the matter stands at present the men employed by the day have to stand whatever loss (if any) the butty man sustains through the Eight Hours Act coming into force. It would be very interesting if the butty men at Bolsover would allow it to be proved what their weekly earnings were before the Eight Hours and now. . . . Some of the butty men . . . only require a whip, then some of the day men would be working under conditions bordering on slavery. The butty men's greed for gold causes them to lose their better feelings for their fellow workmen, the very men who help to make the butties' weekly wages double what they receive themselves. It is only when every ounce of vitality has been sapped out of his day men that the butty is satisfied.[2]

The growing dissatisfaction with the butty system was discussed at length by a Council meeting on 25 September, 1909, and the officials were instructed to recommend 'a reasonable settlement'.[3] A few days later Solomon Robinson told the Eckington miners: 'We have struck the first nail in the butty man's coffin and in a month that system will be dead.'[4] However, the officials reported:

We are of the opinion that at some collieries in the county there ought to be some changes made, but whatever changes are made, we do not want it to lead to a system of day work, which in our opinion would be disastrous.[5]

On the recommendation of the officials it was decided, on 23 October, 1909:

That this Council recognizes the principle of two day men to each contractor in each stall, and recommends that this principle be sought throughout the county as far as possible, and also insists that stall men shall take their turn in going into vacant or new stalls.[6]

The critics of the butty system appear to have been silenced for a time by this modification but their opposition was renewed during the minimum wage agitation of 1911–12. The war supervened and it was not until 22 June, 1918, that the matter was again raised formally. The Council then instructed the Executive Committee to prepare an alternative scheme to the butty system, 'the principle to be dealt with being some method by which, under certain conditions and qualifications,

[1] See Chapter X, p. 405.   [2] Derbyshire Times, 3 July, 1909.
[3] D.M.A. 25 September, 1909.   [4] Derbyshire Times, 2 October, 1909.
[5] D.M.A. 25 September, 1909.   [6] Ibid. 23 October, 1909.

every man working in the stalls or at the contract shall be a sharer in the total amount of earnings of the stall or contract.'[1] The 'all-throw-in' system, as it came to be called, was accepted by the lodges by 12,276 votes to 4,452.[2] On 9 November, 1918, the Council decided that the coal-owners should be asked to discontinue the butty system at the end of the year.[3] They agreed reluctantly and on 4 January, 1919, it was reported to the Council that the new system was working satisfactorily and it was 'expected that during the coming week the men at all the collieries will have fallen into line'.[4] A few months later the Council declared itself in favour of abolishing the contract system altogether but no further action was taken.[5] The idea has since been canvassed on numerous occasions in Derbyshire and elsewhere, but the tradition of piece-work has a strong hold upon the mining communities and, after more than ten years of nationalization, the question of introducing day wages for every worker is still unsettled.

[1] *D.M.A.* 22 June, 1918.   [2] *Ibid.* 26 October, 1918.
[3] *Ibid.* 9 November, 1918.
[4] *Ibid.* 4 January, 1919.   [5] *Ibid.* 24 May, 1919.

X

CHAPTER XVII

THE 1921 LOCK-OUT

I

At first the agreement reached in November, 1920, worked smoothly. Early in December the Council of the Derbyshire Miners' Association appointed the President, Vice-President, three of the permanent officials, F. F. Bolstridge, A. Trueman, T. Skinner, J. Randle and S. Sales to serve on the county production committee.[1] Towards the end of the month it became known that the national output during the five weeks ending 18 December had reached an average of 5,215,160 tons a week which, when multiplied by the agreed figure of 50, gave an annual rate of 260,758,000 tons. This gave the miners an increase of 1s. 6d. a day from 3 January, 1921, or 3s. 6d. a day more than they had been earning before the 'Datum Line' strike.[2]

The sharp decline in trade at the end of 1920 soon brought more difficulties. The fall in output during the four weeks ending 22 January, 1921, after adjustments had been made for the Christmas and New Year holidays, led to a reduction in wages of 2s. a shift in February.[3] Moreover, Sir Robert Horne, the President of the Board of Trade, had already raised with the M.F.G.B. the question of decontrolling the coal industry. The Federation informed him on 12 January, 1921: 'We cannot acquiesce in any proposal for the decontrol of the coal trade until the coal-owners and ourselves are able to present to the Government a jointly agreed plan for the national control of the industry which will effectively substitute the present arrangements.'[4] During an interview with the miners' leaders on the following day Horne stated:

In the temporary agreement arrived [sic], the Government took the big risk of guaranteeing prices, and they have been hopelessly wrong in their conclusions. As a result of the big decrease in export prices, the industry was now losing money rapidly, and their anticipations were that the surplus pool of profits already accumulated, would, as a result of the wage advances

[1] D.M.A. 3 December, 1920. [2] M.F.G.B. 5 January, 1921.
[3] Ibid. 29 January, 1921. [4] Ibid. 12 January, 1921.

awarded, be exhausted in ten weeks. . . . The Government therefore proposed to decontrol prices and distribution entirely on the 1st March, but to keep on with the pooling of profits for some time longer, say, to take a date at random, until 30th June, 1921. By that time it was hoped the two parties in the industry would have come to their conclusions on the point.[1]

Frank Hall commented: 'The fact of the matter was that the Government had got the trade in a muddle . . . and . . . now did not know how to escape their responsibilities.'[2]

On 23rd February Horne told the miners' leaders that the Government had decided 'to decontrol the coal trade absolutely as at the 31st March'. Smillie pointed out that both the owners and the miners had expected that government control would last until the end of August and that the Government's hasty decision to decontrol the mines was a breach of the pledge given in 1920 when special legislation had been introduced to prolong the war-time control.[3] These matters were discussed by a special conference of the Federation on the following day when it was resolved:

That this conference confirms the attitude of the Executive Committee in protesting against the proposal of the Government to decontrol the coal trade, and declares that the Federation will oppose by every means in its power any such proposal of the Government which is prejudicial to the interests both of the coal trade and the nation generally.[4]

Meanwhile negotiations had been going on between the coal-owners and the M.F.G.B. in order to work out the scheme for the adjustment of wages which was to be submitted to the Government by 31 March, 1921. As a result of the advances which had been authorized during and after the war, the method of calculating miners' wages had become increasingly complicated. To the standard or basic rates had to be added district percentages, dating back to the old conciliation agreements. The war bonus, granted in 1915, was reckoned on basic rates in some districts and upon current wage rates in others. This bonus was increased in 1917. In the same year came the first 'war wage', a flat-rate increase of 1s. 6d. a day. A similar increase was granted in 1918. A further 2s. a day, the so-called 'Sankey wage', was added in 1919 and there was also an adjustment of piece-work rates to compensate for shorter working hours. From March, 1920, to meet the rising cost of living, the Government awarded a 20 per cent. increase which applied to current wage rates less the 'war wage' and the 'Sankey wage'. Where this yielded less than 2s. a shift the difference was to be made up. Finally, in November, 1920, came the agreement which linked a wage

[1] M.F.G.B. 13 January, 1921.   Derbyshire Times, 22 January, 1921.
[3] M.F.G.B. 23 February, 1921.   [4] Ibid. 24 February, 1921.

increase with output. This resulted in an immediate advance of 2s. a day which rose to 3s. 6d. in January, 1921, fell to 1s. 6d. in February and disappeared completely in March.

Both the coal-owners and the M.F.G.B. were anxious to simplify this complex system by consolidating wage rates up to a certain level but could not agree on how it was to be done. The M.F.G.B. put forward two proposals. The first was for a new standard wage of 16s. 5d. a day with the flat rate additions amounting to 5s. The second was for 70 per cent. of the existing wages to be the new 1921 basis, with the remainder as a percentage addition to the basic rate. In February the Executive Committee sent out a questionnaire to ascertain the opinions of the districts on these and other matters affecting wages.

The Council of the Derbyshire Miners' Association decided to reject both of the Executive Committee's proposals on the ground that they did not 'sufficiently guard the continuance of the payment of the War Wage and Sankey under the conditions upon which they were originally granted'. The officials evolved another scheme which kept the 'war wage' and the 'Sankey wage' as separate flat-rate additions but had a lower basic rate and a floating percentage to allow for reductions. The Council expressed the opinion that 'this scheme does provide for the flat rates being kept inviolate until such time as the increased cost of living, for which the War Wage and part of the Sankey were given, shall have fallen below the point at which they were given'.[1] Frank Hall was instructed to send the Derbyshire proposals to Frank Hodges, the Secretary of the M.F.G.B., and to other districts for their consideration.[2] At a special conference of the Federation on 22–23 February the results of the questionnaire were discussed. There were 572,449 votes for flat-rate additions and only 249,160 for percentage additions. Derbyshire had not sent in a reply to the questionnaire nor was the county's proposal considered. The Derbyshire delegates remained silent throughout the proceedings.[3]

The decisions of the M.F.G.B. conference did not meet with the approval of the coal-owners who preferred percentage changes and were unwilling to accept a new 1921 standard with a minimum at over two-thirds of the existing wage rates. Instead they proposed a modified 1914 standard, with a minimum at about half the existing wage rates. There were also differences of opinion of a more fundamental character. The miners demanded the financial unification of the industry under a National Wages Board and the pooling of receipts to enable the more prosperous districts to subsidize the poor ones. The owners insisted that wages must be determined by district boards. On one point, however,

[1] *D.M.A.* 19 February, 1921; *Derbyshire Times*, 19 February, 1921.
[2] *D.M.A.* 12 February, 1921.   [3] *M.F.G.B.* 22–23 February, 1921.

there was agreement. The M.F.G.B. had accepted, with some criticism of co-partnership from militants such as A. J. Cook, the principle of 'the division of surplus income accruing to the industry on the basis of a share to owners and a share to workmen'.[1]

By 25 February the coal-owners and the M.F.G.B. were unable to make any further progress. The Government's decision to decontrol the coal industry had destroyed any possibility of reaching an agreement. Evan Williams, the President of the Mining Association of Great Britain, stated that the coal-owners had been influenced 'to a very considerable extent' by this decision. He explained:

Such decontrol would seriously embarrass the owners and make it impossible for certain districts and collieries to maintain themselves in production. The owners therefore had concluded that they could not agree to the establishment of a National Wages Board, and under no consideration could they agree to the establishment of a national profits pool, as in the absence of financial control the good collieries would have to provide out of their natural profits the means for maintaining the poor collieries in production. . . . The general efficiency of the industry would decline because the incentive to remain efficient or to improve efficiency would disappear once it was established that the skill and energy of the good concerns were to be used to subsidize the inefficiency and indifference of the poor concerns. They therefore could only agree to a proposal to establish District Wages Boards on the lines of the Conciliation Boards in existence before the outbreak of war, with this difference, that whereas the old Conciliation Board's wages were determined nearly exclusively by the price of coal, wages would now be determined by the capacity of the district to pay. They therefore suggested that each district should at once proceed to ascertain the existing financial position, so that it would be known what wages were payable to the workmen after 31st March.[2]

II

By 24 March the Coal Mines (Decontrol) Act had received the Royal Assent. The 'war wage' of 3s. a shift, the 'Sankey wage' of 2s., the 20 per cent. granted in March, 1920, and the increases based on output, which had been granted in November, 1920, had been authorized by the Government. Within a week it was to be absolved from all these responsibilities. Meanwhile the coal-owners in the various districts were giving notice that all contracts of service would end on 31 March. The Derbyshire employers stated:

Following upon the withdrawal of all government directions and orders as from 31st March, 1921, in regard to the payment of war wage, Sankey

[1] *M.F.G.B.* 28 January, 1921.   [2] *Ibid.* 2 March, 1921.

wage and the 20 per cent. advance in March, 1920, the owners are advised to give the above notice. The owners hope, through negotiations with the workmen's representatives, that arrangements shall be made as to the wages which shall be payable on and after 1st April, so as to enable work to be continued without interruption.[1]

On 17 March the Executive Committee of the M.F.G.B. considered the owners' latest proposals. The wages paid in each district in July, 1914, together with the percentage addition for the reduction in hours in 1919, were to be the basic rate. The owners' standard profits in each district were to be 17 per cent. of the aggregate amount paid in basic wages. Any surplus was to be divided between wages and profits in the proportions of 75 per cent. and 25 per cent. respectively. The workmen's share was to be expressed as a percentage upon the standard rate of the district. The effects of the owners' proposals are shown in the following table:[2]

District	(a) Average cost per ton (excluding wages and profits)		(b) Average minimum cost per ton		(c) Average weekly wage at minimum cost		(d) Price of coal per ton (January, 1921)		(e) Proposed average wage (with coal at January, 1921, prices)		(f) Existing average wage	
	s.	d.	s.	d.	s.	d.	s.	d.	s.	d.	s.	d.
Derbyshire, Nottinghamshire and Leicestershire	6	4·29	15	9·74	34	1	30	7·06	97	0	89	1
Yorkshire	7	0·55	17	10·02	35	2	32	5·59	90	9	87	9
Lancashire and North Wales	8	1·31	21	5·27	31	5	33	6·32	64	6	84	10
Durham	8	4·23	19	8·57	32	3	36	7·78	88	10	87	0
Northumberland	8	7·55	19	11·81	31	10	36	10·48	87	9	88	0
Scotland	8	8·23	20	10·22	34	11	33	4·40	76	7	93	2
Midlands	9	2	20	9·63	31	5	31	10·47	66	3	76	10
Cumberland	9	11·11	23	5·27	32	1	32	9·20	57	9	94	9
South Wales	11	1·21	24	6·24	35	5	40	2·25	83	2	103	0
Other Counties	8	0·74	20	6·16	29	7	35	10·61	71	10	81	10
Great Britain	8	6·46	20	3·68	33	8	34	6·51	80	10	90	7

(a) Based on a normal period of four weeks in the September quarter of 1920.

(b) Minimum cost = (a) plus the amount required to pay the miners' basic rate and the owners' standard profit.

Wages were to be related more closely to the profitability of each district. They were to be largely determined by the level of other costs and by the market price of coal, although these factors were to be offset to a certain extent by the adoption of the 1914 standard rate which reflected the relative advantages gained by district bargaining in the years before the war. In low-cost districts such as Derbyshire, Nottinghamshire and Leicestershire the owners' proposals actually gave an increase in wages on the basis of January, 1921, prices. But the price of

[1] *Derbyshire Times*, 19 March, 1921.   [2] M.F.G.B. 17 March, 1921.

coal was falling rapidly. If it had fallen by half, as it had been known to do in the past, the average weekly wage in Derbyshire would have been as low as 34s. 1d., assuming no reduction in the other costs of production. The Federation's proposals, on the other hand, gave Derbyshire an average basic wage of 63s. a week for an average minimum cost price of 23s. 2·64d. a ton.[1] Frank Hall was well aware that if Derbyshire, Nottinghamshire and Leicestershire adopted a selfish attitude they would be playing into the owners' hands:

It may be . . . that we shall seek to resist a reduction in wages in other districts and may be called upon to co-operate with other districts in resisting reductions although we ourselves might not temporarily be threatened with such reductions. . . . The responsibility rests entirely with the Government and the coal-owners, who appear to be one and the same person, for they have one and the same policy.[2]

The intransigence of the coal-owners and the Government, and the increasing deterioration of trade, caused some of the miners' leaders to waver. On 18 March the Executive Committee of the M.F.G.B. recommended to a special conference that the opinion of the districts should be sought 'as to whether or not they are prepared to temporarily abandon the policy of a National Wage Board . . . with a view to establishing a temporary agreement on a district basis for the period of the present abnormal state of trade and prices'.[3] The Council of the Derbyshire Miners' Association decided to take a branch vote on the question and advised the members to reject the Executive Committee's proposals and to continue to press for a National Wages Board with a national pool. It also appointed a committee, consisting of the officials, W. Owen, S. Sales, O. Wright, T. Kyte, F. Haynes, J. Statham and A. Trueman, to discuss with the owners their proposals for the determination of wages in the district.[4]

Frank Hall addressed a number of meetings on the undesirability of 'a strike' although, technically, it was a lock-out which was impending. At Clowne he explained to the miners that the Council resolution recommending the rejection of the owners' terms was not binding upon individual members of the Association:

It is your business to settle this matter and you must take the responsibility upon yourselves. . . . I am not going to prove the justification for a strike. There are larger stocks of coal in the country today than there have ever been before. South Wales will not be able to pay a single penny out-of-work pay for six weeks, Scotland is bankrupt—they were only able to pay a shilling a week during the late strike—and everybody knows the position of Yorkshire.

[1] M.F.G.B. 17 March, 1921.   [2] Derbyshire Times, 19 March, 1921.
[3] M.F.G.B. 18 March, 1921.   [4] D.M.A. 21 March, 1921.

With the exception of Nottinghamshire and Derbyshire there is not a district in the Federation that can support a strike, and in Derbyshire we can only carry on for three or four weeks. . . . I am a man of peace and if I can get what is right for the men by peaceable methods, I shall do so. The conditions and wages of Derbyshire compare more than favourably with those of other counties, and you have done it without a strike. . . . You are asking the owners to pool their profits. That is a stiff proposition. Could you pool your wages without the owners pooling their profits? Yes, and you could do it without a strike. You could surrender 18s. a week and send it into South Wales. You could do it as a voluntary action. Why not?[1]

These were the arguments of the Government and the employers. They were not accepted by the Derbyshire miners who supported the policy recommended by the Council by 761 votes to 270.[2] A member of the Association complained that Hall's speech at Clowne had been 'such a valuable asset to the owners' that one firm had had it typed and posted at the pit-head:

The great lesson Mr. Hall has yet to learn is that he is a paid servant of the Derbyshire Miners' Association and his duty as such is to carry out its policy, and not want to act as dictator. If on principle he finds he cannot conscientiously do this then, instead of trying to cause a division, the alternative is to resign.[3]

At a special conference of the M.F.G.B. on 24 March the voting was 627 to 241 against the Executive Committee's proposals to seek a temporary agreement on a district basis. Herbert Smith, the Yorkshire miners' leader, who had been appointed Acting-President of the M.F.G.B. following the resignation of Robert Smillie earlier in the month, said: 'We have declared war. We are in it.'[4]

On 30 March the Executive Committee of the M.F.G.B. made a final and unsuccessful appeal to the President of the Board of Trade for a government subvention to maintain the wages of the miners. Soon after this interview, instructions were sent to the districts 'that all notices should be allowed to expire regardless of occupation'.[5] This meant that enginemen, pumpmen and others concerned with keeping the pits in working order would take the owners at their word and cease work with everyone else.

'It is fully realized,' said the Derbyshire Times, 'that the order . . . will mean the flooding of many pits and the entire closing down for good, whilst in the case of some of the large Derbyshire and Nottinghamshire pits, where employment is found for several thousand miners, it would take six months to clear them of water ready for work if the pumps stand for a month.'[6]

[1] Derbyshire Times, 26 March, 1921.   [2] D.M.A. 21 March, 1921.
[3] Derbyshire Times, 2 April, 1921.   [4] M.F.G.B. 24 March, 1921.
[5] Ibid. 30 March, 1921.   [6] Derbyshire Times, 2 April, 1921.

At a meeting at Chesterfield on the eve of the lock-out Hicken and Sales urged the need for united action. Sales attacked Frank Hall for his statements to the Press: 'If a leader of a trade union gave an interview that would cause or was likely to cause a division among members of his own association he is using very bad tactics.' Hicken argued that the Government had enjoyed the profits of abnormally good trade and was morally bound to subsidize wages now that trade was abnormally bad:

This fight ought to have taken place before the Sankey Commission. . . . It ought to have taken place when the owners and capitalists generally feared our power and the economic lever we held in our hands. That was at the time when there were glaring headlines in the newspapers that the miners had got a stranglehold upon the community. These same papers today are not telling the public that the owners and the Government have got a stranglehold upon the miners.[1]

III

By 1 April, 1921, the Government had relinquished its control of the coal industry and throughout the country the mines stood idle, many deserted. The Executive Committee of the M.F.G.B. had already, on 31 March, asked the other members of the Triple Alliance to strike in support of the miners. Both the National Union of Railwaymen and the Transport Workers' Federation had asked for time to consider the matter but had issued statements to the Press which showed their sympathy with the miners' cause.[2] The Government again took fright and invoked the recently acquired Emergency Powers Act. A 'state of emergency' was declared, troops were moved into some of the coalfields, all leave was cancelled, reservists were called up and a special 'Defence Force' was created. In Derbyshire there was little disorder but a number of young miners who had seen war service took the opportunity of drawing pay and allowances during the lock-out by joining the Defence Force.[3] At the end of the first week of the dispute the *Derbyshire Times* reported: 'Good feeling has been displayed . . . and in most places the fine weather has enabled large numbers of those out of work to devote their attention to gardening.'[4]

Whilst the Triple Alliance was mobilizing its forces strong pressure was being brought to bear on the Executive Committee of the M.F.G.B. to rescind its decision on the safety and repair workers. There was much propaganda in the Press and in the House of Commons against the

[1] *Derbyshire Times*, 2 April, 1921.   [2] *M.F.G.B.* 31 March, 1921.
[3] *Derbyshire Times*, 16 April, 1921.   [4] *Ibid.* 9 April, 1921.

x*

iniquities of the miners who were prepared to allow pit ponies to be drowned or starved, despite the fact that the Federation had already made it known that workmen would co-operate with the management to bring every pony to the surface.[1] The real issue was, of course, the threat to the mines. The employers did not wish to see their property flooded and ruined. The M.F.G.B. was reluctant to surrender an advantage which might lead to a speedy settlement. On 6 April the Prime Minister wrote to both the M.F.G.B. and the Mining Association proposing a resumption of negotiations but the owners insisted that the enginemen and pumpmen should first return to work. The Prime Minister supported this demand with the result that a deadlock was reached by 8 April.[2]

In Derbyshire some of the miners had taken the matter into their own hands. A meeting of the Bolsover lodge had decided, on 30 March, to allow arrangements to be made to ensure the working of the pumps at the Bolsover Colliery in the event of a stoppage and had sent delegates to Chesterfield to explain the reasons for the decision.[3] In some villages such as Langwith and Shirebrook, where the domestic supplies of electricity and drinking water depended upon the operation of colliery plants, the enginemen decided to remain at work.[4] The Executive Committee of the Association adhered firmly to the policy of withdrawing the pumpmen and enginemen but raised no objection to their work being done by voluntary labour.[5] 'I am not prepared to advise any men to go back to work', said Hicken. 'Let the colliery managers and owners take off their jackets and man the pumps.'[6]

The attitude of the colliery deputies caused some friction. At Nottingham, on 30 March, a meeting of the joint board of the Derbyshire and Nottinghamshire miners' associations, the Enginemen's and Firemen's Union, and the National Association of Colliery Deputies requested the deputies' association to withdraw all its members from every colliery in the two counties. The Council of the National Association of Colliery Deputies met at Chesterfield on the following day and decided 'in the interests of humanity and the miners themselves to instruct its members to continue work to keep the pits and plant in a safe working condition, but not to do anything which would otherwise be done by men or boys locked out'.[7] Samuel Sales complained:

At Grassmoor 90 per cent of the men today acting as blacklegs at the colliery where he was employed had been supplied from the Nonconformist chapel at Grassmoor. That class of men, who outside the ranks of the miners' organization were impotent, were prepared to do any kind of dirty work

[1] *M.F.G.B.* 9 April, 1921.   [2] *Ibid.*
[3] *Derbyshire Times*, 2 April, 1921.   [4] *Ibid.* 9 April, 1921.
[5] *Ibid.*   [6] *Ibid.*   [7] *D.M.A.* 18 April, 1921.

during the present grave crisis to help the employing class. He referred to the deputies, who, although they were making no sacrifice whatever during the struggle, would receive the same benefits as the miners won by fighting.[1]

On 18 April the Council protested 'against Deputies, Enginemen and Firemen, or others whose wages are being attacked, doing any work at the collieries, during the present stoppage, other than that required for the supply of light or water for domestic purposes' and called upon the members 'to do all they can on constitutional lines to stop it'.[2]

At a mass meeting of railwaymen at Chesterfield on 3 April A. Jones, of Hasland, moved a lengthy resolution which ended:

We therefore call upon our executive committee and special general meetings of delegates to accept along with the miners the gauntlet thrown down to them, and thus help to safeguard and secure for organized labour generally their right to a decent standard of life.[3]

Similar resolutions were being passed by meetings of railwaymen and transport workers throughout the country and on 8 April a full conference of the Triple Industrial Alliance decided to issue strike orders taking effect from midnight, 12 April.

After a meeting between the leaders of the other two sections of the Triple Alliance and representatives of the Government, on 9 April, the Executive Committee of the M.F.G.B. sent the following telegram to all districts:

A conference with the owners being opened unconditionally, we urge upon all our members to abstain from all action which will interfere with the measures necessary for securing the safety of the mines, or will necessitate the use of force by the Government.[4]

There was a meeting between representatives of the Government, the Central Committee of the Mining Association of Great Britain, and the Executive Committee of the M.F.G.B. on 11 April at the offices of the Board of Trade. Frank Hodges' statement of the miners' case won expressions of approval from the Executive Committee and also from Lloyd George who said: 'He ought to have gone into another profession. . . . He might have had, perhaps, a more remunerative one.'[5] Hodges was soon to follow this advice but, for the time being, continued to argue the miners' case. There was a further meeting with the representatives of the Government on 12 April.[6] Later in the day there was a third meeting at which the coal-owners' representatives were again present. The terms offered to the miners were substantially the

[1] Derbyshire Times, 9 April, 1921.　　　　[2] D.M.A. 18 April, 1921.
[3] Derbyshire Times, 9 April, 1921.　　　　[4] M.F.G.B. 9 April, 1921.
[5] Ibid. 11 April, 1921.　　　　　　　　　　[6] Ibid. 12 April, 1921.

same as the coal-owners' original proposals with an additional clause which stated that 'the Government will be willing to give assistance, either by loan or otherwise, during a short period, in order to mitigate the rapid reduction in wages in the districts most severely affected'.[1]

The Government's offer was rejected by the Executive Committee of the M.F.G.B. the same evening. Meanwhile the Triple Alliance had issued orders postponing the strike which had originally been planned to start at midnight. On the following day, 13 April, there was a further conference of the Triple Alliance and it was decided that in view of the deadlock the strike should begin at 10 p.m. on 15 April. On the night of 14 April private meetings of Members of Parliament were held in the Committee rooms of the House of Commons. One was addressed by Evan Williams, the Chairman of the Mining Association: another by Frank Hodges. Unfortunately there are no records of either of these meetings. Hodges was freely reported to have said that the M.F.G.B. would be prepared to consider a temporary settlement on a district basis, although he subsequently complained that his statements had been misinterpreted.[2] After receiving reports of Hodges' alleged offer the Prime Minister immediately wrote to the M.F.G.B. proposing a further meeting with the coal-owners. The Executive Committee replied that 'the only condition upon which a temporary settlement can be arrived at is one that must follow the concession of the two principles already made known to you, viz. a National Wage Board and a National Pool'. Hodges, who believed that the Executive Committee was making a mistake in not resuming negotiations, offered his resignation but was persuaded to continue in office.[3]

This episode split the Triple Alliance. The more moderate elements within the N.U.R. and the T.W.F., led by men such as J. H. Thomas, argued, like Hodges, that the M.F.G.B. should accept the Prime Minister's invitation. By the evening of 15 April, the so-called 'Black Friday', the Executive Committee of the M.F.G.B. had been informed by C. T. Cramp, the railwaymen's leader, that the T.W.F., the N.U.R. and the Associated Society of Locomotive Engineers and Firemen were going to call off the strike.[4] This was not the wish of many railwaymen and transport workers throughout the country. On 17 April a mass meeting of railway workers at Chesterfield, presided over by A. Jones, passed a resolution protesting against the action of the executive committees of the N.U.R., the A.S.L.E. & F., and the T.W.F. in cancelling the strike. They refused to accept the explanation 'that the members were not prepared to act spontaneously' and called upon their

[1] *M.F.G.B.* 12 April, 1921.
[2] *Ibid.* 23 April, 1921. Cf. *Derbyshire Times*, 16 April, 1921.
[3] *Ibid.* 15 April, 1921.   [4] *Ibid.*

executive committee to convene a special general meeting 'with a view to the industrial power of the N.U.R. being used in support of the miners in the present struggle'. J. Marchbank, a railwaymen's delegate from Glasgow, told the meeting: 'The miners were just as solid and determined, and the rank and file of the railwaymen were equally determined to support the miners, as they were on March 31st.' At Shirebrook a meeting of miners and railwaymen, presided over by the secretary of the local branch of the N.U.R., passed a resolution approving the action of the miners' leaders and calling upon the responsible officials of the other unions of the Triple Alliance to resign.[1]

The miners' leaders were bitterly disappointed by the collapse of the Alliance but showed little rancour. Sales told the Grassmoor miners: 'I don't want you to go away with any bitterness in your heart towards any sections of the community or the workers because the policy of the coal-owners and the Government has been to divide and conquer.' John Spencer asserted that the rank and file of the railwaymen's and transport workers' unions supported the miners' cause but 'true leadership was lacking in the hour when victory was very near at hand'.[2] J. H. Thomas was held to be largely responsible for the disruption of the Triple Alliance. When he landed in New York on 12 May he was met by hundreds of workers, some of whom carried banners bearing inscriptions such as 'Thomas fleeing from the wrath of England' and 'Judas hung himself after betrayal. Will Thomas follow suit?'[3] During his absence the railwaymen and the transport workers placed an embargo on the movement of coal intended for industrial purposes, which led to a number of minor disputes between Derbyshire railway workers and their employers.[4]

IV

A M.F.G.B. conference on 22 April discussed the failure of the Triple Alliance and recorded its protest 'against the official explanation of the other two sections attributing their defection to the refusal of the Miners' Executive to meet the coal-owners again at the invitation of the Prime Minister'. The resolution continued:

Over and over again, before and after the Triple Alliance had arrived at their decision to strike, it had been quite clear that it was impossible for the Miners' Executive to accept a settlement except on the terms of the concession of the National Wages Board and Pool. The real cause for the sudden,

[1] *Derbyshire Times*, 23 April, 1921.   [2] *Ibid.*
[3] *Ibid.* 14 May, 1921.   [4] *Ibid.* 30 April, 1921.

unexpected and unjustifiable withdrawal of the other two sections of the Alliance must be looked for in the character and structure of the Triple Alliance itself.[1]

On the following day the conference heard Frank Hodges describing how he had been 'crucified' and A. J. Cook arguing 'that Mr. Hodges, as Secretary of the Federation, is not going to defy majority rule . . . I don't care whether it is him or Jesus Christ, he is not going to do it. We don't want any Jimmy Thomases in our Federation.' The delegates, who had already reported that their districts were still strongly in favour of national wage arrangements, then passed a vote of confidence in the Secretary and the Executive Committee.[2]

The conference remained in session from 22 to 28 April. Negotiations were going on throughout this period, the delegates assembling from time to time to hear reports from the Executive Committee. On 28 April the President of the Board of Trade renewed the Government's offer of a subsidy but insisted that there must be district settlements. These terms were rejected by the conference on the same day and the delegates returned to their districts to give their reports.[3]

On 30 April the Council of the Derbyshire Miners' Association heard Frank Hall's report and reaffirmed its decision to resist district settlements. But the situation in the county was becoming increasingly difficult. The last lock-out payments were to be made on 5 May.[4] Many works were being closed because of the shortage of fuel. Distress was increasing. Soup kitchens and relief funds were already being established. The workless miners turned to gardening and other pursuits to occupy their enforced leisure. Sports and races were organized in some colliery villages. Coal-picking and outcrop working became profitable occupations. At Brockwell, near Chesterfield, parties of miners worked in shifts, each party keeping to its own 'stall'. Throughout the day men, women and children were to be seen using lorries, horses and carts, wheelbarrows and even perambulators, to cart away the precious coal. A Newbold coal agent was paying as much as 22s. a ton for the soft outcrop coal obtained from the Brockwell site.[5]

By the middle of May 'outcropping' had reached such large proportions in the Chesterfield and Ilkeston districts that the Association decided to take action. John Spencer and A. W. Hildreth addressed a number of meetings and visited outcrop workings, sometimes seeking the co-operation of the police.[6] Spencer told a newspaper reporter:

One would not say anything about them fetching a bag or a barrowful for their own use, but when it comes to sending hundreds of tons away, there is

[1] *M.F.G.B.* 22 April, 1921. [2] *Ibid.* 23 April, 1921. [3] *Ibid.* 28 April, 1921.
[4] *D.M.A.* 30 April, 1921. [5] *Derbyshire Times*, 16 April, 1921.
[6] *Ibid.* 21 May, 1921; *D.M.A.* 25 May, 1921.

the evil. My contention is that had any of them attempted to do such a thing prior to the lock-out they would have been prosecuted for stealing coal.[1]

Feeling was also running high against the men who were operating colliery engines and pumps. Officials who were keeping essential services going at the Blackwell Company's Sutton Colliery were stoned by four men whose actions were subsequently condemned by the local miners.[2] There was a lively scene at Grassmoor when about a thousand men, women and children, 'with jazz bands and flags', marched to the colliery yard and demanded the withdrawal of the safety men. Frank Hall told a mass meeting at Chesterfield that since the collapse of the Triple Alliance 'there had been a growing feeling that the safety men should be brought out, inasmuch as it was a life and death struggle for the miners'.[3] At Bolsover the pumpmen were withdrawn on 5 May, their places being taken by naval ratings.[4]

The miners were subjected to rhetoric on all sides. Their leaders were extremely active throughout the county in an attempt to stiffen resistance. Sales, who was criticized for driving to the union's offices in his modest two-seater car after urging the men to 'tighten their belts', told the Bolsover miners:

A man who worked hard from morning to night was the man who had the most right to enjoy the luxuries of life, and if his hearers were satisfied to inhale dust while a man who had neither toiled nor spun rolled along in his Rolls Royce, he was not.[5]

Charles Markham complained:

The men were not allowed to come into closer association with their masters, because their leaders would not allow them to think for themselves. . . . If they were going to nationalize he was going to fight against it. . . . He would fight all he was worth for the companies and the shareholders.[6]

Hicken, in characteristic fashion, attacked Markham as 'the uncrowned king of Chesterfield' who had declared that the miners must be reduced to their former status after the war. Of the Government he said:

A more glorious set of imbeciles could not be found outside St. Stephen's. The Government are not the bosses; they have no minds of their own; they are small puppets in the hands of the organizations of the Federation of British Industries.[7]

Archdeacon Crosse, who had already shown his sympathy with the miners in 1919, played a prominent part in the controversy surrounding the 1921 stoppage. In the Lower House of the Convocation of

[1] *Derbyshire Times*, 28 May, 1921.   [2] *Ibid.* 16 April, 1921.
[3] *Ibid.* 23 April, 1921.   [4] *Ibid.* 7 May, 1921.   [5] *Ibid.*
[6] *Ibid.* 30 April, 1921.   [7] *Ibid.* 7 May, 1921.

Canterbury on 27 April a resolution in favour of a National Day of Prayer and Humiliation was carried. During the discussion Crosse said:

The Church was chiefly on the side of the mine-owner in the present dispute and had certainly never taken the stand it ought to have done on the side of those upon whom economic conditions pressed with undue hardship. Miners had greatly advanced in their sense of responsibility. . . . There was no revolutionary motive at their back. They had never had any encouragement from official Christianity. Why not a Day of Sympathy as well as of Prayer and Humiliation?[1]

On 7 May he published in the *Derbyshire Times* an open letter to the miners urging them as 'a temporary measure' to return to work 'in order to put right the unfortunate muddle into which the leaders have landed us, owing to the pressure from a small number of irresponsible extremists'.[2] Two days later, in response to a challenge from the leaders of the Derbyshire Miners' Association, he took part in a public debate with Hall and Lee in the yard of the Vaults Hotel, Chesterfield.[3]

v

The national negotiations were re-opened towards the end of May when the Prime Minister invited the Executive Committee of the M.F.G.B. to meet representatives of the Government and the coal-owners on 27 May. The Government's proposals did not differ substantially from those which it had put forward in April. There was, however, an additional suggestion that if the coal-owners and the miners could not agree on a permanent scheme for the determination of wages the matter should be settled by arbitration.[4] The Executive Committee decided on 28 May that the Government's latest offer should be referred to the districts.[5]

The Government's proposals were considered by the Council of the Derbyshire Miners' Association on 31 May when it was decided that the branches should be recommended to reject them.[6] The meeting was then adjourned until 2 June when the delegates returned with the opinions of their branches. The miners were not prepared to accept proposals for arbitration which ignored their demand for a national wages pool. The Council resolved unanimously:

That the government proposals for settlement of the present dispute be rejected in their entirety, as an unsatisfactory and inefficient method to

[1] *Derbyshire Times*, 30 April, 1921.   [2] *Ibid.* 7 May, 1921.
[3] *Ibid.* 14 May, 1921.   [4] *M.F.G.B.* 27 May, 1921.
[5] *Ibid.* 28 May, 1921.   [6] *D.M.A.* 31 May, 1921.

adopt, in view of the fact that the issues at stake are not proposed to be in the terms of reference, and thus could not decide between the parties.[1]

On a card vote the Council re-affirmed its previous demands for national wages arrangements by 890 votes to 263, the minority supporting an amendment: 'That the Executive Committee of the M.F.G.B. be empowered to call a delegate conference to consider fresh proposals on a wage basis having relation to the cost of living.'[2]

By 3 June all the districts had reported to the Executive Committee of the M.F.G.B. that they were not prepared to accept the Government's proposals.[3] When the Prime Minister was informed of this he replied on 4 June that the Government had nothing further to propose and that the offer of a grant of £10,000,000 to mitigate reductions in wages during the period of the proposed temporary settlement could not stand indefinitely:

Every week during which the strike has lasted has depleted the resources of the nation and has lessened its capacity to afford this assistance to a particular industry. We have, therefore, come to the conclusion that we cannot prolong the offer for more than another fortnight—which should give you sufficient time to take a ballot of your members on the Government suggestions; if you should think that course advisable—or to reach a settlement in some other way.[4]

On 6 June Evan Williams issued an invitation to the Executive Committee to meet the Central Committee of the Mining Association.[5] There is no record of the discussions which followed but on the next day the Executive Committee decided to call a special conference which was to be recommended to authorize a ballot vote on the owners' proposals. Meanwhile the Executive Committee asked the owners to 'further elucidate' their proposals by answering a series of written questions.[6] The special conference, meeting on 10 June, accepted the Executive Committee's recommendation.

The ballot paper was as follows:[7]

Miners' Federation of Great Britain
BALLOT PAPER

Are you in favour of fighting on for the principles of the National Wages Board and National Pool, with loss of Government subsidy of ten million pounds for wages if no settlement by June 18th, 1921?..................
Are you in favour of accepting the Government and owners' terms as set forth on the back of this ballot paper?............................
Please place your 'X' in the space provided for the purpose.
June 10th, 1921   FRANK HODGES, General Secretary

[1] D.M.A. 2 June, 1921.   [2] Ibid.   [3] M.F.G.B. 3 June, 1921.
[4] Ibid. 4 June, 1921.   [5] Ibid. 6 June, 1921.
[6] Ibid. 7 June, 1921.   [7] Ibid. 10 June, 1921.

BACK OF BALLOT PAPER

NOTE.—The Government and owners having definitely rejected the principles of the National Wages Board and the National Pool now offer the terms fully set out below. You are now asked to say whether you will continue the fight for the National Wages Board and the National Pool, or accept the terms offered by the Government and owners. The Government offer of ten million pounds grant in aid of wages referred to below is to be withdrawn on June 18th unless an agreement is arrived at by that date.

TEMPORARY PERIOD

Government offers ten million pounds to prevent large reductions in wages where reductions are necessary.

First reductions not to exceed 2s. per shift for all workers of 16 years and upwards, and 1s. per shift for workers below 16 years.

No further reductions until August 1st.

Further reduction after August 1st to be agreed mutually until Government grant is exhausted.

The temporary agreement will come to an end as soon as Government grant is used up.

PERMANENT SCHEME
OWNERS' PROPOSALS

National Board to fix principles for guidance of districts. Board to be comprised of equal numbers of representatives of both sides with independent chairman.

The parties have already agreed the principle that profits shall only be a fixed percentage of wages paid.

The Board to fix the amount of the percentage of profits to wages.

The Board to fix the amount of the new standard wage.

In this connection the owners have offered as a standard wage the total wages paid in July, 1914, plus district additions to standards, plus the percentages for pieceworkers caused by the reduction of hours from 8 to 7, and a minimum percentage of 20 per cent. added thereto. This minimum percentage to continue until June 30th, 1922.

The Board will also fix the items of cost, which must be taken into account by the district auditors when ascertaining the district revenue.

Wages during permanent scheme to be based upon the capacity of each district to pay.

In the event of a low paid dayworker receiving a wage which does not provide him with a subsistence wage, the District Board will fix a wage which will secure it for that workman.

The decision of the National Board as to the permanent scheme to be binding upon both parties for a period of twelve months and thereafter subject to three months' notice on either side.

The M.F.G.B. estimated that the average wage per shift in Derby-shire, Nottinghamshire and Leicestershire had increased by 163·4 per cent. between July, 1914 and March, 1921, rising from 6s. 6·4d. to 16s. 8·8d. By 1 March, 1921, the cost of living was falling rapidly but was still 141 per cent. higher than in July, 1914. The Mining Association proposed to group Derbyshire, Nottinghamshire, Leicestershire, York-shire, Warwickshire and Cannock Chase. It calculated the average wage per shift in these counties, in March, 1921, as 16s. 9¾d. and estimated that there would be a reduction of 1s. 3¾d., on the basis of the March figures, if the proposed scheme were brought into operation.[1] The miners fully realized that a reduction in wages was inevitable but were not prepared to accept a return to district bargaining with the low basic rates offered by the employers in a time of falling prices and declining trade. Nor were they prepared to accept the argument that their wages had advanced more rapidly than the cost of living for they maintained that they were entitled to an improvement in real wages.

In Derbyshire, as in the other coalfields, there was some hesitance over rejecting the proposals of the Government and the coal-owners. The men had been locked out for eleven weeks and since the cessation of the payment of benefits many families were suffering great hardship. Moreover, tempting offers were being made by employers such as R. C. A. Palmer Morewood, the owner of the Swanwick Collieries, who posted notices saying that he was willing to re-open his pits at a flat reduction of 2s. 6d. a shift pending a national settlement. After John Spencer and a number of local union officials had pointed out to him that a resumption of work at Swanwick 'would probably lead to demonstrations and other undesirable features' Morewood persisted with his scheme and re-opened one of his pits on 3 June. Pickets succeeded in persuading a number of men to return home and even-tually, on 9 June, Morewood decided to withdraw his offer 'owing to the present encouraging state of negotiations between the owners and the Miners' Federation'.[2] Thomas Spencer, of Alfreton, who had criticized the union's policy in 1920, was again advocating a return to work:

He could see no possible excuse for the miners' leaders holding aloof from a round table conference. . . . They had been following what was nothing more than a will-o'-the-wisp, while hundreds and thousands of the miners and their families had been starving and the country going to ruin.[3]

Before the ballot was taken mass meetings were held at various centres in Derbyshire. At Chesterfield Samuel Sales said:

[1] *M.F.G.B.* 10 June, 1921.
[2] *Derbyshire Times*, 4 and 11 June, 1921; *D.M.A.* 2 June, 1921.
[3] *Derbyshire Times*, 11 June, 1921.

Whether Mr. Hall could fully explain the agreement he did not know. Personally, he was unable to do so, and he ventured to say it would need a Philadelphia lawyer to understand it. . . . None of the leaders had lost faith in the ideal for which the fight began, but now, after eleven weeks, the men had the right to say whether the fight should be continued or whether they would accept the owners' offer.

The Executive Committee of the M.F.G.B. had decided not to advise the men how to vote but some of the miners present at the meeting insisted that their leaders were shirking their responsibility. One member stated that the ballot would be 'their downfall', to which Frank Hall replied:

That was the very opposite of democracy. Although they had been out eleven weeks they had never been consulted by a ballot. There had been a considerable amount of criticism in the Press and by individuals that they dare not ballot the men.

Some of the miners asserted that they would abstain from voting and that the ballot was a waste of money.[1] The result was that only about 44 per cent. of the members of the Association voted. Of these, 11,050 were in favour of continuing the struggle and 9,948 were against. The national figures showed a much larger majority of 434,614 to 180,724.[2]

When the result of the ballot was known a deputation from fourteen branches in the Chesterfield district, led by S. Sales, M. Burns and W. Wicks, attended a meeting of the Association's Executive Committee and stated that 'it was necessary that further ways and means of providing funds for the members should be considered, and it would be better to completely exhaust the funds to help to win the present dispute, rather than reserve any amount for men who could not resume work at the same time as the rest when the dispute was over'. It was also suggested that the N.U.R. and the friendly societies should be asked to grant loans and that vouchers for goods should be issued. The Executive Committee assured the deputation that these proposals would be considered but pointed out the difficulty, if not impossibility, of raising loans without adequate security.[3] A few days later Frank Lee told the Whitwell miners:

Our offices are in pawn. We have approached the C.W.S. but I have been badly disappointed with their attitude towards us. We asked for a loan but they wanted 75 per cent. greater security than the money they were prepared to lend us. . . . Parr's Bank, who have stood by us splendidly during the struggle, have advanced us the whole of the money on the loans we had out before the stoppage.[4]

[1] *Derbyshire Times*, 18 June, 1921.   [2] *M.F.G.B.* 17 June, 1921.
[3] *D.M.A.* 18 June, 1921.   [4] *Derbyshire Times*, 25 June, 1921.

VI

It was becoming increasingly obvious that the miners were defeated. By 18 June preliminary work was being done at a number of Derbyshire collieries in preparation for re-opening.[1] During the following week several colliery owners, including R. C. A. Palmer Morewood and the Butterley Company, announced that their pits would re-open and that the men could return to work at a reduction of 1s. 3¾d. a shift. John Spencer and A. W. Hildreth addressed meetings in the Ripley area to dissuade the miners from accepting the Butterley Company's offer. The men at Swanwick decided to await the instructions of the Association and Morewood again had to abandon his attempt to re-open his pits. At Morton G. M. Jackson, of the Clay Cross Company, addressed the men on the owners' proposals. When James Randle, a county councillor and local miners' leader, asked a series of questions he was ordered to leave, the meeting broke up in disorder and Jackson drove away in his car amidst shouts of abuse.[2]

During the last stages of the lock-out the Association redoubled its efforts to bring an end to outcrop workings. The activities of Spencer and Hildreth, in conjunction with the police, had not been very successful. Most 'outcroppers' who had agreed to stop working had, after an interval of a few days, re-started. It was therefore decided that organized parties of miners should visit outcrop workings throughout the county, fill them in and warn the men not to dig any more coal. There was inevitably some violence and disorder. At Hasland a number of carts loaded with coal were overturned. At Grassmoor a midnight raid on the outcrop workings almost resulted in a pitched battle between groups of men armed with picks and shovels. On 19 June some 2,000 miners were summoned by the bellman to an evening meeting in the Chesterfield market place. Hildreth, accompanied by Spencer and Hall, then led the men, marching four abreast, on a tour of the outcrop workings in the Chesterfield district. A number of the workings were filled in but when the demonstrators reached Brierley Wood, near Sheepbridge, they were met by a large body of local police reinforced by contingents from Sheffield. In attempting to disperse the crowd the police drew their truncheons, stones were thrown and a number of men received minor injuries. The *Derbyshire Times* reported: 'Up to the present the military have not been called upon, and it is to be hoped that the necessity for such a course will not arise. There has been no general disorder. . . .'[3]

Meanwhile the Executive Committee of the M.F.G.B. was faced with

---

[1] *Derbyshire Times*, 18 June, 1921.
[2] *Ibid.* 25 June, 1921.   [3] *Ibid.*

a difficult situation. Lloyd George had stated that the Government's offer of financial assistance would be withdrawn after 19 June. An appeal for joint action to the executive committees of other unions affected by wage disputes had brought no results.[1] Frank Hodges told the Labour Party conference at Brighton:

> We who are the leaders of this movement will have to take a great deal of responsibility ourselves, rather than allow this huge mass of the population to go on and on until breaking point comes, and chaos and disorder run where now discipline, good will and solidarity hold the field. . . . It may be that we shall have to bend and bow to the inevitable forces that surround us. . . .[2]

On 24 June 'after a long and protracted discussion' the Executive Committee resolved: 'That we ask the Government and the owners for a meeting with a view to negotiating a satisfactory wages agreement, which we can recommend our members to adopt.'[3] After a week-end at Chequers with the Prime Minister the three officials of the M.F.G.B., Smith, Hodges and Robson, came away with a promise that he would recommend the restoration of the Government's offer of financial assistance to the industry if the Executive Committee would recommend an immediate resumption of work.[4]

On 27 June the Executive Committee met representatives of the Government and the coal-owners at the offices of the Board of Trade. The main points at issue were the ratio of wages to profits and the continuation of the proposed 20 per cent. addition to the standard wages for the duration of the agreement. Eventually agreement was reached. Standard profits were to be equivalent to 17 per cent. of the cost of the standard wages and wages were not to fall below 20 per cent. of the standard in any district.[5] On Tuesday, 28 June, the Executive Committee referred these proposals to the districts and explained:

> The important and responsible step of taking power as a Committee to negotiate a wages settlement, even after the last ballot vote, was the result of our certain knowledge that the National Wages Board, with the National Profits Pool, could not be secured by a continuation of this struggle. Every economic and political factor is dead against us. . . . We, therefore, strongly urge you, with the knowledge of the seriousness of the situation, to accept this agreement, which we have provisionally agreed today, and authorize your Committee to sign the terms by Friday next.[6]

The proposed settlement was accepted by the Council of the Derbyshire Miners' Association on 29 June. Most of the larger districts, with

[1] *M.F.G.B.* 18 June, 1921.   [2] *Derbyshire Times*, 25 June, 1921.
[3] *M.F.G.B.* 24 June, 1921.   [4] *Ibid.* 16 August, 1921.
[5] See Appendix I to this chapter.   [6] *M.F.G.B.* 28 June, 1921.

the exception of Lancashire, reached a similar decision. Bristol, the Forest of Dean, Kent and Somerset were in favour of continuing the struggle. Cumberland was undecided. If a card vote had been taken there would have been 832,840 members in favour of returning to work and 105,820 against.[1] The lock-out was at an end. The news was received quietly in Derbyshire, although the militant section of the union, led by Hicken and Sales, voiced its protest. A meeting of the Grassmoor miners passed a resolution demanding the resignation of the M.F.G.B. Executive Committee because of 'its base betrayal of the rank and file'. The irrepressible Sales declared that Hodges's speech at the Labour Party conference 'revealed to the enemy their weakness' and maintained that no leader was justified in adopting such an attitude without first consulting the rank and file:

Last week-end Hodges, Smith and Robson were parleyvuing at Chequers, the home of the Prime Minister. What passed off nobody knows, but on the Monday morning the three came back to their own executive members. This thing, from my point of view, has been the greatest betrayal of any body of trade unionists in the country.

Hicken stated:

I think we have learned the lesson that is in the past or in the future, we have got to fight. But I hope that we have also learned another lesson—that seeing we have to fight, that we will choose the time and the ground when we have to fight.[2]

VII

The resumption of work marked the beginning rather than the end of the miners' troubles. Some of the immediate problems which confronted them arose from the neglect of many of the pits during the lock-out. The newer collieries in East Derbyshire were able to start turning coal without much delay. At Grassmoor, on the other hand, only 250 men were able to return to work on Monday, 4 July, owing to falls and other difficulties, and it was stated that the colliery would not be fully in operation for a month. Similarly, in the Ripley district, many of the older collieries were in a bad condition. Moreover, the economic climate had completely changed. The Bond's Main, Ford's and Waingroves collieries were said to be permanently closed, as were seams at the Avenue and West Hallam collieries and districts in several other pits. The sharp decline in the iron trade led the proprietors of the Grassmoor Collieries to decide not to re-open their coke ovens. In the Chesterfield district alone between 4,000 and 5,000 miners were unable

---

[1] *M.F.G.B.* 1 July, 1921.   [2] *Derbyshire Times*, 2 July, 1921.

to return to their pits.[1] The Association estimated that at least 15,000 of its members would be unable to resume work immediately.[2]

The employers began to resort to their traditional methods of reducing costs. The Staveley Company refused to re-open any of its pits until the men at the Warsop Colliery agreed to revert to the practice of filling tubs with forks, which had been abolished as a result of trade union pressure in 1919 when there was a heavy demand for coal. The men refused to accept these conditions and the Council described the Company's action as 'a serious and distinct breach of an honourable understanding'.[3] But resistance was difficult. Hicken told the Warsop miners:

> We have had our time and didn't see it, but let it slip by. But now it is the owners' time, and they are going to use it for all they are worth. I would say to you 'keep on fighting', if we had £200,000 in the bank and could pay you £2 a week, but we are bankrupt, and you are starving, and your wives and children are starving.[4]

When Frank Hall reported the dispute to the Executive Committee of the M.F.G.B. it was decided that the Secretary should write to W. A. Lee, the Assistant Secretary of the Mining Association, asking him to advise the Staveley Company to withdraw its proposal.[5] On 14 July T. T. Broad, the Liberal M.P. for the Clay Cross division, asked in the House of Commons: 'Was this refusal to re-open the pits a violation of the settlement of the recent coal stoppage, and victimization of the men, and could the Prime Minister bring some influence to bear upon the directors in order to end this unhappy condition of things?'[6] But the dispute was then almost at an end. Frank Hall met D. N. Turner, the Staveley Company's colliery agent, and agreed that the Warsop men would fill with forks instead of shovels. If, at the end of two months, there was no reduction in the amount of dirt in the coal, the men were to agree to a special scale of deductions from their wages.[7]

The Blackwell Colliery Company attempted to re-introduce the butty system. The owners' acquiescence in its abolition had rested upon their willingness, in a period of prosperity, to pay contractors' minimum rates to all miners working in abnormal stalls. By re-introducing the butty system they could reduce the number of men who were eligible for such payments. In pits where there were many difficult working places the saving would be considerable. The Blackwell Company's men refused to work until a deputation, led by Hall and Lee, had obtained an assurance that every man working at the coal face

[1] *Derbyshire Times*, 9 July, 1921.   [2] *D.M.A.* 7 July, 1921.   [3] *Ibid.*
[4] *Derbyshire Times*, 16 July, 1921.   [5] *M.F.G.B.* 1 July, 1921.
[6] 144 H.C. Deb. 5s. 1456.   [7] *Derbyshire Times*, 23 July, 1921.

would receive the minimum wage if conditions prevented him from earning it at the tonnage rate.[1]

Once begun, the controversies over fork filling and the butty system lasted for several months. The *Derbyshire Times* stated:

Today there is too much slack coming out of the pits and trade cannot absorb it. With by-product plants standing and markets stagnant, while the cotton and textile industries are on short time, the owners do not know what to do with the slack. . . . It is the cost of production of coal which is preventing the iron and steel trades getting on their feet again, and until the latter industries are in full swing there cannot be real prosperity for the nation. . . . The fork system was forcibly abolished when the Miners' Federation was dictator. Unless there is a modification of the war-time policy there will be short time in the pits.[2]

Frank Hall replied:

No miners' leader would defend bad filling. What he is up against is the old method of punishments, viz. fines, dismissals, and deductions from terms. The workmen are in a very anomalous position. Their wages depend upon the amount of coal sent out, hence they have an incentive to send out all the coal possible, and earn the highest possible wage. The more time spent on cleaning out the dirt, the less wages are earned. Take away the incentive by guaranteeing wages, or, in other words, abolish all contracts and cleaner filling will follow.[3]

Representatives of the Midland Coal-Owners' Association invited the leaders of the Derbyshire and Nottinghamshire miners' associations to meet them at Derby, on 21 August, to discuss the question of reducing the amount of slack and dirt in the coal.[4] In the negotiations which followed, the Derbyshire Miners' Association decided to adopt the following principles: if forks were to be used there should be an increase in tonnage rates; if shovels were to be used there should be a decrease in tonnage rates; if screens were to be used the owners should pay for them and no slack should be sent out of the pit; there should be no return to the butty system.[5] The owners wished to revert to fork filling without changing any of the other conditions of employment. The miners argued that this was contrary to the terms of the national settlement. Eventually a deadlock was reached. On 12 October the owners posted notices at collieries throughout Derbyshire and Nottinghamshire stating that from 26 October the old system of filling with screens and forks would be re-introduced.[6]

[1] D.M.A. 7 July, 1921; *Derbyshire Times*, 9 July, 1921.
[2] *Derbyshire Times*, 6 August, 1921.　　　　[3] *Ibid.* 13 August, 1921.
[4] D.M.A. 22 August, 1921.　　　　[5] *Ibid.* 3 September, 1921.
[6] *Ibid.* 13 October, 1921; *Derbyshire Times*, 15 October, 1921.

On 22 October the Council passed a lengthy resolution which ended as follows:

The action of the owners can only lead to reprisals as opportunity presents itself, while at the same time no confidence can be placed in any future agreement. Further, we protest against any change that varies the conditions that existed in March last on which the national settlement was based. The end of this agreement will offer a favourable opportunity to enforce our claim for the conditions of March last, unless the owners in the meantime accept our offer to abide by the scheme agreed to, and we strongly recommend the men on Wednesday morning under no circumstances to use the screen and place the onus on the owners to stop the men from work.[1]

Frank Hall had reported the matter to the Executive Committee of the M.F.G.B.[2] but neither the Federation nor the Association had the strength to resist the demands of the employers. At most Derbyshire collieries the men took the matter into their own hands and made local agreements which enabled them to continue to use shovels. At some pits they accepted a reduction of 1d. a ton: at others they agreed to a reduction in tonnage rates if the amount of dirt exceeded a certain percentage.[3] These settlements showed that the owners, despite their protestations, were not anxious to keep the slack in the pits but wished to reduce their wage costs. In November, 1921, Frank Hall stated: 'So far as this county is concerned there are very few places where the agreement has not been made for the continuance of filling with the shovel.'[4]

No sooner had the question of fork filling been settled than the coal-owners sought to re-introduce the butty system. They argued that the supervision of an experienced collier was necessary if the work was to be done efficiently and safely. Output was lost, they said, because the men in a stall refused to start work until the latecomers had arrived. Another objection to the 'all-throw-in' system was that it placed the experienced or hard-working man on the same level as the inexperienced or lazy man. 'Give the experienced miner the authority of the old butty system', urged one writer, 'and he will weed any slackers out a good deal quicker than the manager can and more effectively.'[5] The miners' leaders argued that the butty system led to favouritism and exploitation.

'The system had been very much abused,' said Frank Hall, 'and at some collieries the men could not get stalls unless they were prepared to pay a certain sum of money. The butties were not always the best and most competent men. . . . There were men in the county who suggested they ought to have a buttying union. . . . The policy of the owners was one of destruction and division.'[6]

[1] D.M.A. 22 October, 1921.   [2] M.F.G.B. 10 October, 1921.
[3] Derbyshire Times, 29 October, 1921.   [4] Ibid. 12 November, 1921.
[5] Ibid. 29 October, 1921.   [6] Ibid. 22 October, 1921.

According to Hicken, 'the owners desired a return to the bad old days, when strong men worked like slaves for the men who could play cricket or football well and who went home with £10 a week when they themselves got 5s., 6s., or 8s. a shift'.[1]

On 6 November William Saunders, the Secretary of the Midland Coal-Owners' Association, informed Frank Hall that the owners had decided, in the case of abnormal stalls, 'to limit henceforward the payment of the contractors' rate to those men only who are recognized by the colliery company as contractors or butties'.[2] The Council decided to take a ballot of all the men working at the coal face. They were to be asked whether they were prepared to accept the coal-owners' proposal and, if so, whether they would continue to share with all the men both in normal and abnormal stalls.[3] 'If this incentive is taken away by making day men of a large number', stated the ballot paper, 'output must go down. It might be in the minds of some persons that by dragooning and slave driving the object might be accomplished. No man with a spark of Christianity and humanity would tolerate such savage, heathenish methods.'[4] Only about 12 per cent. of the men voted in favour of accepting the owners' conditions and 70 per cent. were prepared to continue sharing wages in abnormal stalls even if the new conditions were imposed.[5]

The Association instructed its members to adhere to the 'all-throw-in' system whilst it negotiated with the coal-owners. In January, 1922, a leaflet, headed with biblical and other quotations, was issued by the Council. It stated:

The colliery owners have been trying their utmost to break up the 'all-throw-in' system and take you back to the unequal and disgraceful butty system as it existed in pre-war days. ... The 'all-throw-in' was the longed for relief of every true trade unionist, and whatever colliery managers with the aid of their satellites may do, not one foot of ground will be conceded. The men have set their backs to the wall and will defend the scheme until the time comes when all contract work is abolished.[6]

[1] *Derbyshire Times*, 18 February, 1922.   [2] *Ibid.* 19 November, 1921.
[3] *D.M.A.* 12 November, 1921.   [4] *Derbyshire Times*, 26 November, 1921.   [5] *Ibid.*
[6] *D.M.A.* 7 January, 1922; *Derbyshire Times*, 4 February, 1922. The texts at the head of the leaflet were:
'Every kingdom divided against itself is brought to desolation and every city or house divided against itself shall not stand'—Matthew 12, v. 25.
'All the law is fulfilled in one word even thus: thou shalt love thy neighbour as thyself; but if ye bite and devour one another, take heed that ye be not consumed one of another'—Galatians 5, vv. 14–15.
                    'Whatever freedom for ourselves we claim,
                    We wish all others to enjoy the same:
                    Freedom within our law of sacred might,
                    Trench not on any other's equal right.'
                                        James Thomson.

Meanwhile the Association had been testing the legal validity of the owners' position by taking to court a test case from the Grassmoor Collieries. The action was unsuccessful and Bertram Mather, the union's solicitor, was asked to give his opinion on certain legal aspects of the contract system. He expressed the view that the men were free to decide for themselves how they would share the wages paid for work in a stall. The principal difficulty arose in abnormal stalls.

'It would seem', wrote Mather, 'that the colliery company could, in the event of the stall not making a wage equal to the minimum wage, refuse to make up the wages of all the men to contractors' rates of wages if the colliery company does not recognize these other men as contractors or butties. The company would, however, if the stall were an abnormal one, have to make up the wages of the other men to day wages.'[1]

On 4 March the situation was again discussed by the Council but it was evident that little more could be done than to exhort the men not to return to the butty system.

'The men are masters of the situation so long as they will faithfully carry out the "all-throw-in" ', stated the officials. 'The interests of all workmen are identical. Let cohesion be our policy. Drop the spirit of selfishness. Present a solid front to the employers. This charter of freedom will then stand inviolate.'[2]

But the victory lay with the coal-owners who had again succeeded in lowering their wage costs by paying contractors' minimum rates to a much smaller number of men.

[1] *D.M.A.* 4 March, 1922.   [2] *Ibid.*

APPENDIX I

The Coal Mining Industry Dispute, 1921
Terms of Settlement

1. A National Board shall be constituted forthwith, consisting in equal numbers of persons chosen by the Mining Association of Great Britain and persons chosen by the Miners' Federation of Great Britain.

There shall also be established District Boards, consisting in equal numbers of persons representing owners and workmen in each district.

The National and District Boards shall draw up their own rules of procedure, which shall include a provision for the appointment of an Independent Chairman for each Board.

2. The wages payable in each district shall be expressed in the form of a percentage upon the basis rates prevailing in the district, and shall be periodically adjusted in accordance with the proceeds of the industry as ascertained in such district.

3. The amount of the percentage to be paid in each district during any period shall be determined by the proceeds of the industry in that district during a previous period, as ascertained by returns to be made by the owners, checked by joint test audit of the owners' books carried out by independent accountants appointed by each side.

4. The sum to be applied in each district to the payment of wages above the standard wages as hereinafter defined shall be a sum equal to 83 per cent. of the surplus of such proceeds remaining after deduction therefrom of the amounts of the following items during the period of ascertainment:—

(*a*) the cost of the standard wages;
(*b*) the costs of production other than wages;
(*c*) standard profits equivalent to 17 per cent. of standard wages;

and the share of the surplus applicable to wages shall be expressed as a percentage upon the basis rates prevailing in the district.

Provided that if in any period the ascertained proceeds, after deduction of costs other than wages and the cost of standard wages, prove to have been insufficient to meet the standard profits, the deficiency shall be carried forward as a first charge to be met out of any surplus, ascertained as above, in subsequent periods.

5. If the rates of wages thus determined in any district do not provide a subsistence wage to low paid wage-workers, such additions in the form of allowances per shift worked shall be made for that period to the daily wages of these workers as, in the opinion of the District Board, or, in the event of failure to agree by the parties, in the opinion of the Independent Chairman, may be necessary for the purpose. Such allowances shall be treated as items of cost in the district ascertainments.

6. For the purpose of these periodical adjustments the unit shall be the districts set out in the Schedule hereto, and shall only be varied by the

decision of the District Board or Boards concerned, provided that no variation shall take place prior to 1st February, 1922, in the grouping of any district
unless it is mutually agreed by the representatives of both sides in the district
or districts concerned.

7. The standard wages shall be the district basis rates existing on the
31st March, 1921, plus the district percentages payable in July, 1914 (or the
equivalents in any district in which there has been a subsequent merging into
new standards), plus, in the case of pieceworkers, the percentage additions
which were made consequent upon the reduction of hours from eight to
seven.

8. In no district shall wages be paid at lower rates than standard wages
plus 20 per cent. thereof.

9. The National Board shall forthwith consider what items of cost are to
be included for the purpose of paragraph 4 (b) above, and in the event of
agreement not being arrived at by the 31st July, the matter shall be referred
to the Independent Chairman for decision.

10. The wages payable by the owners up to the 31st August inclusive
shall be based upon the ascertained results of the month of March and the
wages payable during September shall be based upon the ascertained results
of the month of July. The periods of ascertainment thereafter shall be
decided by the National Board.

11. During the 'temporary period', as hereinafter defined, the following
special arrangements shall apply in modification of the general scheme set
out above:—

(a) In calculating the proceeds for March the deduction to be made in
respect of costs other than wages shall be the average of such costs during
January, February, and March.

(b) In any district in which reductions in wages continue to be made after
the first ascertainment, no part of the surplus proceeds shall be assigned to
profits if and in so far as this would have the effect of reducing the wages
below the level in the preceding month.

When in any district there is a break in the continuity of reductions in
wages upon the periodical ascertainments, at that point and thereafter the
general scheme shall apply fully in regard to owners' surplus profits.

(c) The proviso to paragraph 4 regarding the carrying forward of deficiencies in standard profits shall not apply, but any net losses shall be so
carried forward.

(d) The Government will give a grant not exceeding £10,000,000 in subvention of wages.

(e) The subvention shall be available for making such increases to the
wages otherwise payable in any district as may be necessary to prevent the
reductions below the March rates of wages being greater than the following
amounts:—

During July, 2s. a shift for persons of 16 years of age and upwards, and
1s. a shift for persons under 16.

During August, 2s. 6d. and 1s. 3d. respectively.

During September, 3s. and 1s. 6d. respectively, provided that the balance of the subvention is sufficient for this purpose.

(*f*) If any district in which in any month the proceeds available for wages, calculated in accordance with the terms of this settlement, are sufficient to admit of a rate of wages equal to or higher than the rate payable under the maximum reduction for that month, the wages payable by the owners shall be calculated not in terms of basis plus percentage, but on the same basis as during March, less flat rate reductions uniform throughout the district for persons of 16 years of age and upwards, and persons under 16 years of age respectively.

(*g*) In any district in which the wages calculated in accordance with the terms of this settlement are less than the wages payable under the maximum reductions aforesaid, the difference shall be met by the owners in that district during September to the extent of the aggregate net profits realized by them on the district ascertainment for July, and during October to the extent of the aggregate net profits realized by them on the district ascertainments for July and August.

(*h*) The expression 'temporary period' means the period from the date of the resumption of work to the 30th September, 1921.

12. The period of duration of this agreement shall be from the date of resumption of work until the 30th September, 1922, and thereafter until terminated by three months' notice on either side.

13. It is agreed as a principle that every man shall be entitled to return to his place when that place is available for him, and that men temporarily occupying places during the stoppage shall give way to men working in those places before the stoppage.

It is agreed that, on the other hand, there shall be no victimization of men who have been keeping the collieries open, not in the sense that they are to remain at the jobs they filled during the stoppage, but that they shall not be prevented from going back to their own jobs or from working subsequently at the colliery.

For and on behalf of each member of the Central Committee of the Mining Association of Great Britain and for the Mining Association,

> EVAN WILLIAMS, President.
> THOMAS R. RATCLIFFE-ELLIS, Secretary.

For and on behalf of each member of the Executive Committee of the Miners' Federation of Great Britain and for the Miners' Federation,

> HERBERT SMITH, Acting President.
> JAMES ROBSON, Treasurer.
> FRANK HODGES, Secretary.

For and on behalf of His Majesty's Government,

> WILLIAM C. BRIDGEMAN, Secretary for Mines.
> E. A. GOWERS, Under-Secretary for Mines.

Mines Department, July 1st, 1921.

SCHEDULE REFERRED TO

Scotland.

Northumberland.

Durham.

South Wales and Monmouth.

Yorkshire, Nottinghamshire, Derbyshire, Leicestershire, Cannock Chase, and Warwickshire.

Lancashire, North Staffordshire, and Cheshire.

North Wales.

South Staffordshire and Salop.

Cumberland.

Bristol.

Forest of Dean.

Somerset.

Kent.

CHAPTER XVIII

THE ORIGINS AND COURSE OF THE
1926 DISPUTE

I

Immediately after the 1921 lock-out the Derbyshire coal-owners had adopted a policy of reducing costs, largely at the expense of the miners' wages. Their initial successes in the disputes over fork filling and the butty system led them to press for further concessions as trade continued to decline. No economy was too petty to be considered. Early in 1922 there were disputes over reductions in allowance coal with the Staveley and Butterley companies.[1] At the other extreme there were direct attacks on wages. The Staveley Company chose to reduce tonnage rates. In December, 1921, notices were posted at the Hartington and Ireland collieries stating that unless the men accepted reductions in the rates for machine-cut coal the pits would be closed.[2] In February, 1922, the men at one of the Grassmoor collieries were locked out until they accepted a deduction of 20 per cent. from the rates laid down by the Area Wages Board.[3]

It was not long before the owners of the soft-coal pits made a concerted effort to reduce basic rates. During the war, when coal of all descriptions was urgently needed, the same tonnage rates had been paid for both soft and hard coal. The Stoker Award of 1920 had abolished the differentiation, made by the Lindley Award in 1912, between the minimum rates paid in the 'top hard' district and those paid in the remainder of the county.[4] In February, 1922, the owners of the soft-coal pits sought to reduce the basic rates for all grades of labour. They argued that there had been a difference in rates between the two districts before the war and that they could no longer afford to pay the percentage on basic wages given by the Area Wages Board.[5] The

---

[1] *Derbyshire Times,* 14 and 28 January, 1922; *D.M.A.* 4 February, 1922.
[2] *Derbyshire Times,* 24 December, 1921; 7 January, 1922.
[3] *Ibid.* 18 February, 1922.
[4] See pp. 434-5, 628.   [5] *D.M.A.* 11 February, 1922.

Y

Association regarded the owners' proposals as a breach of the 1921 agreement.[1] But resistance was again impossible. The owners had at first proposed that the basic rates should be reduced by 10 per cent. but subsequently moderated their demand to $7\frac{1}{2}$ per cent. They were reported to have stated that if they could not negotiate their claim for $7\frac{1}{2}$ per cent. with the union leaders they would demand 10 per cent. from the men, 'and what is more, they would get it without any trouble at all'.[2] On 29 April the Council empowered the sub-committee which had been handling the negotiations to sign the new Soft Coal Agreement.[3] Basic rates were reduced by $7\frac{1}{2}$ per cent. and provision was made for further reductions in exceptional cases where the owner was able to prove that he was unable to work his colliery economically.[4]

The Staveley Company argued that the Barlborough Colliery was running at a loss of 2s. 8d. a ton and would have to be closed unless the men accepted reductions of 1d. per inch for ripping and 2d. a ton for coal from the deep soft seams in addition to the general reduction of $7\frac{1}{2}$ per cent.[5] The acceptance of these terms would have brought some of the men below the minimum wage and, on the advice of Frank Hall, the local branch of the Association rejected the Company's proposals by 321 votes to 128. However, on Wednesday, 17 May, two days before the pit was due to be closed, Charles Markham received a letter signed by the President and Secretary of the Barlborough branch. It read as follows:[6]

We take the liberty of appealing to you on behalf of the wives and children of our men who are willing to accept your proposals.

We should have done this before now, but we have been held back by our officials at Chesterfield.

We, as a body of men, have not given you any unnecessary trouble, and we think in the kindness of your heart you will not let us suffer for those who have held us up.

At our meeting tomorrow (Thursday), we will pass a resolution, so that the community will know we have complied with your wishes, and justified you in allowing us to work on.

Please think kindly of us at this hard moment of our lives. We shall be glad to come and see you if you will kindly allow us.

Yours respectfully, on behalf of the men,

George P. Scarborough, President.
Solomon Woodhead, Secretary.

[1] *D.M.A.* 25 February, 4 March, 1922.　　　[2] *Derbyshire Times,* 1 April, 1922.
[3] *D.M.A.* 29 April, 1922.
[4] Derbyshire Miners' Association, *Memorandum of Agreement, Derbyshire Collieries, All Seams other than Top Hard Seams, 1 May,* 1922.
[5] *Derbyshire Times,* 29 April, 13 May, 1922.
[6] *Ibid.* 20 May, 1922; *D.M.A.* 27 May, 1922.

Such was the abject condition of some of the men after the 1921 lock-out. Even Markham was touched. 'It is a very humane letter and one you cannot pass over', he said. Frank Hall, on the other hand, described it as 'disgraceful and humiliating'.[1]

The Staveley Company later sent copies of the branch officials' letter to coal merchants with an appeal for orders. Charles Gill, the Corresponding Secretary of the Bristol Miners' Association, received one of these appeals through a local co-operative society with which he was associated and wrote to the Derbyshire Miners' Association complaining that the Bristol miners were being undersold.[2] The Council called upon the branch officials 'to apologize to the Association in writing for the error in tactics made by them' and, on 5 July, decided to accept their letter of explanation.[3]

As wages were reduced by various means, relations between the miners and their employers steadily deteriorated. On 11 May, 1922, the Staveley Company applied to the Mansfield Police Court for the removal of James Edward Iliffe, a checkweighman and secretary of the Warsop Main branch, on the ground that he had impeded the management of the colliery. Iliffe had been a deputy at the Warsop Colliery for about fifteen years and when John Spencer became the Association's compensation agent in 1918 Iliffe had succeeded him as checkweighman. Iliffe's militant behaviour had led the management to forbid him to hold pit-head meetings between 6 a.m. and 7 a.m. when the men were about to descend the shaft. However, on 24 April, Iliffe had called a meeting during the prohibited period to discuss alleged breaches of the Minimum Wage Act and delays in settling compensation claims. The meeting, which led to an unofficial strike of about 2,600 men and boys, was the Staveley Company's immediate complaint, although Walter Stewart, who represented Iliffe in court, stated: 'The Company had taken a long period . . . in trying to get an accumulation of evidence against Iliffe.'[4]

During the proceedings, which lasted for nine hours, Iliffe told the court:

In December, 1919, . . . he received a goose as big as a donkey and returned it. During the lock-out, on two occasions, he was offered money out of the colliery office. The Lord in Heaven knew what he might have received if he had accepted these. He had endeavoured to do his duty honestly and conscientiously as a checkweighman and watch the interests of the men.

The Staveley Company brought forward a number of witnesses who testified that Iliffe had used abusive and inflammatory language on

[1] *Derbyshire Times*, 20 and 27 May, 1922.
[2] *Ibid.* 3 June, 1922; *D.M.A.* 27 May, 1922.
[3] *D.M.A.* 5 July, 1922.   [4] *Derbyshire Times*, 13 May, 1922.

various occasions. Frank Lee stated that a branch secretary of the Association had no right to call upon his men to cease work or to say 'that a matter would not be settled until the wheels stopped'. The court decided to grant the application for Iliffe's removal.[1]

During his dispute with the Staveley Company the unfortunate Iliffe also crossed the path of John Spencer. He told a meeting of miners that Spencer's relations with the Staveley Company had been amicable because he had received a bribe of £2,000. Spencer issued a writ claiming damages for slander but subsequently withdrew it when Iliffe made a public apology. On 27 May the Council resolved: 'That the head officials send out a circular to the branches asking for monetary assistance for getting Mr. Iliffe into some business.'[2]

In this period of low morale the British Workers' League[3] was becoming increasingly active in the Derbyshire and Nottinghamshire coalfields. Its policy was to destroy the miners' confidence in their leaders. It branded all forms of militancy as 'Bolshevism', preached the virtues of 'non-political' trade unionism and advocated industrial peace at any price. There is no evidence to show how the organization was financed. One of its leaders was W. Holland, a former Vice-President of the Nottinghamshire Miners' Association, who had already criticized the policy of the M.F.G.B. during the 1920 stoppage.[4] The local secretary in the Bolsover district was A. J. Heywood, of Carr Vale, who maintained a regular flow of anti trade-union propaganda in the correspondence columns of the *Derbyshire Times*. Some of the most active workers for the League later became prominent in the Spencer Union. A notable example was the Nottinghamshire checkweighman, Joseph Birkin, a former theatre musician, who enlivened the League's meetings with his violin solos.[5]

The League worked hard to recruit the miners who had drifted away from their unions after the lock-out.[6] The membership of the Derbyshire Miners' Association fell from 51,084 in 1921 to 39,455 in 1922.[7] By the end of March, 1923, the supporters of the British Workers' League had organized the Midland Counties Industrial Protection Society with branches at Mansfield, Warsop, Rainworth, Bolsover, Creswell, Rufford and Clipstone. They stated that the society had 'no connection whatever with the British Workers' League, except that it included in its objects constitutionalism, anti-Communism, and working with a view to bring peace in industry'.[8] At a meeting at Mansfield John Spencer and Henry Hicken denounced these activities. 'The new

[1] *Derbyshire Times*, 13 May, 1922.
[2] *D.M.A.* 27 May, 1922; *Derbyshire Times*, 10 June, 1922.
[3] See Chapter XIII, p. 547.   [4] See Chapter XVI, p. 631.
[5] *Derbyshire Times*, 29 July, 1922.   [6] *Ibid.* 20 January, 1923.
[7] See Chapter XV, Appendix I.   [8] *Derbyshire Times*, 31 May, 1923.

organization', said Spencer, 'did not inform them of any policy, except that they advocated passive resistance.' Hicken contended that:

> It was impossible to serve the interests of the workers without entering politics. What their opponents were offering was 'peace, perfect peace' where there was no peace, and contentment where there was no contentment now. Such a proposition was unthinkable.[1]

In May, 1923, the Nottinghamshire Miners' Association invited George Lansbury to address a similar meeting at Mansfield in an attempt to counteract the influence of the Industrial Protection Society. George Spencer, the Nottinghamshire miners' leader, asked: 'Who is at the back of this organization?' A member of the audience replied: 'The Bolsover Colliery Company.'[2]

II

Meanwhile wages were falling steadily. In addition to the attacks which were being made on basic rates, the monthly percentage additions authorized by the Area Wages Boards, under the 1921 agreement, were gradually diminishing. By August, 1922, wages in every one of the thirteen areas had fallen to the minimum. The Eastern District, which included Derbyshire, was one of the more profitable areas and one of the last to reach its minimum. Monthly percentage additions to basic rates in Derbyshire had then fallen from 140·19 in October, 1921, to 32. The average wage per shift for all workers in the Eastern District for November–December, 1922, was 10s. 2·69d., a reduction of 39 per cent. since March, 1921. At the same time the cost of living was falling, but by no means so rapidly as miners' wages. Movements in real wages per shift in the Eastern District were as follows:[3]

	July, 1914	March, 1921	November–December, 1922
Average wage per shift	6s. 7·75d.	17s. 0d.	10s. 2·69d.
Cost-of-living index	100	241	180
Index of real wages per shift	100	106	86

The M.F.G.B. had already made an attempt to bring about an improvement in miners' wages, especially in the less profitable districts. In October, 1921, the Executive Committee had asked the Government to continue its subvention in aid of wages until the balance of the £10,000,000 was exhausted but had met with a refusal.[4] The 1921

---

[1] *Derbyshire Times*, 31 March, 1923.   [2] *Ibid.* 19 May, 1923.
[3] *Ministry of Labour Gazette; M.F.G.B.* 27 March, 1923.
[4] *M.F.G.B.* 19 October, 3 November, 1921.

agreement was terminable on 30 September, 1922, but only Lancashire opposed its renewal. The Derbyshire Miners' Association decided that its delegates to the M.F.G.B. annual conference should support a continuation of the agreement but that the owners' standard profits should be 10 per cent. of the amount required to pay the standard wage and that their share of the surplus should be 15 per cent. instead of 17 per cent.[1] The annual conference adopted the recommendation of the Executive Committee of the M.F.G.B. that the time was 'not opportune' for terminating the agreement and instructed the new Executive Committee to consider means of improving it and, in the meantime, to discuss with the coal-owners and the Government 'plans for rendering immediate assistance to the workmen'.[2] The subsequent negotiations ended in failure on 27 February, 1923.[3] The M.F.G.B. then sought the co-operation of the Labour Party in demanding an amendment of the Minimum Wage Act, 1912,[4] but on 21 June the Bill was defeated on the second reading.

Meanwhile the coal-owners were already proposing that the miners' working day should be lengthened. As early as October, 1922, Charles Markham wrote to *The Times*:

The country demands cheap coal. . . . The colliers now work seven hours from bank to bank. Let them revert to eight hours, thereby working an extra hour a day at the coal face. They will immediately earn more money, and the cost of production will be diminished. It is the only possible solution, to my mind, unless all industries are to be subordinated to the colliers' union.[5]

Frank Hall observed that Markham had not been satisfied to accept the reductions in wages under the 1921 agreement but had attacked the basic rates as well. He also pointed out that the men were not working seven hours from bank to bank, saying:

Mr. Markham has an ulterior motive in advocating a return to eight hours. He knows very well that the 14·17 per cent. paid for the loss of the extra hour would at once be taken off again. . . . If the country is to recover at the sole and entire cost of the miners—well, I hope the country will not recover.[6]

In the months which followed there were lengthy discussions at M.F.G.B. conferences on the operation of the national wages agreement. The Derbyshire miners' leaders were divided. In April, 1923, Frank Hall issued a circular to the branches in which he pointed out that the agreement was 'in no way responsible for the present high cost

---

[1] *D.M.A.* 7 June, 5 July, 1922.   [2] *M.F.G.B.* 20 July, 1922.
[3] *Ibid.* 5 and 19 October, 2 December, 1922; 27 February, 1923.
[4] *Ibid.* 7 March, 1923.
[5] *The Times*, 13 October, 1922.   [6] *Derbyshire Times*, 21 October, 1922.

of living' and that it was 'not altogether responsible' for the low wages the men were receiving because the owners had also reduced the basic rates.[1] Sales, on the other hand, argued that the agreement was the principal cause of low wages and non-unionism:

An industry which could afford to pay £6,000,000 in royalty rents to those who neither toil nor spin ought to be able to pay a living wage to those employed in the industry. The item of 'cost of production other than wages' was being taken advantage of, directors' fees, pensions to officials, suits of clothes and holidays for favourites, etc., all being put in that category. . . . The worst part of the agreement was that it compelled men to think in terms of districts and destroyed the hope of the industry being treated as a unity.[2]

The official policy of the Association continued to favour the mending rather than the ending of the agreement.[3] This was also the policy of the M.F.G.B. In its protracted negotiations with the coal-owners it demanded that the ratio of wages to profits should be 100 : 13 and that the minimum percentage payable on the standard wage should be raised from 20 to 40 per cent. Eventually, on 14 December, 1923, a deadlock was reached and the Executive Committee resolved: 'That we recommend a ballot vote be taken and that the men be advised to vote in favour of terminating the agreement.'[4] This recommendation was endorsed by a special conference on the following day.[5] There was a light poll in Derbyshire, 18,747 miners voting for termination and 5,746 against. The national figures were 510,303 and 114,558 respectively.[6] On 17 January the Executive Committee of the M.F.G.B. gave three months' notice to end the agreement.[7]

Meanwhile there had been a general election which was to result in the formation of the first Labour Government. As Mr. Somervell has pointed out: 'A Labour government cribbed, cabined and confined by an anti-socialist majority of 120 votes could be at worst no more than a harmless experiment.'[8] However, the miners took new heart. An M.F.G.B. conference on 13 March decided to reject the owners' latest proposals that standard profits should be 15 per cent. of standard wages, that the surplus should be divided in the ratio of 87 per cent. to wages and 13 per cent. to profits, and that the general minimum percentage on standard wages should be increased from 20 to 30. It was also decided to urge the Government to amend the Minimum Wage Act.[9] Immediately after the conference the miners' leaders were summoned by MacDonald who explained that the Government was powerless to legislate and expressed the hope that the Federation would reach

[1] *Derbyshire Times*, 14 April, 1923. [2] *Ibid.* 28 April, 1923.
[3] *D.M.A.* 28 April, 1923. [4] *M.F.G.B.* 14 December, 1923.
[5] *Ibid.* 15 December, 1923. *Ibid.* 17 January, 1923. [7] *Ibid.*
[8] Somervell, *op. cit.* p. 147. [9] *M.F.G.B.* 13 March, 1924.

a settlement with the employers.[1] There were further negotiations between the miners' and coal-owners' representatives in which Emanuel Shinwell, the Minister for Mines, took part but no agreement was reached.

At a special conference on 17 March the Federation had to decide whether to accept the employers' terms or a government inquiry. A strike was out of the question but Hicken told the conference:

> I am absolutely convinced in my own mind that you can juggle with figures until heaven gets you (or the other place), but you will never solve the problems confronting the mining industry under private enterprise. I think the more light we can bring to bear upon the anomalies existing in the mining industry the sooner we shall reach the goal after which we are striving. . . . We in Derbyshire stand wholeheartedly for an inquiry into the problems confronting the mining industry. . . . I am with Cook when he says that it is positively unfair, unjust and iniquitous to expect the miner to face the risk and endure the hardships which he has to face and endure for the meagre wages he receives as compared with the wages in other industries where those risks are absent. The miners have been carrying the rest of the community on their backs long enough, and while we have no desire to paralyse the whole of the industries in the country, or put the community to any inconvenience, unless the community is prepared to bring sense and reason to bear on the miners' problems we have no alternative.[2]

The conference decided to recommend the rejection of the owners' proposals and to call for a government inquiry. In the ballot which followed, the voting in Derbyshire was 11,215 for acceptance of the owners' terms and 16,275 against. The national figures were 322,392 and 338,650 respectively.[3]

On 15 April the Minister of Labour, under the Industrial Courts Act, 1919, appointed a Court of Inquiry consisting of Lord Buckmaster (a former Lord Chancellor) as Chairman, Roscoe Brunner (of the firm Brunner, Mond and Company), and A. G. Cameron (Secretary of the Amalgamated Society of Woodworkers). In its report, published on 8 May, 1924, the Court of Inquiry touched upon many of the fundamental difficulties of wage regulation in the coal industry but dismissed the miners' contention that profits should be pooled nationally as 'a political question' with the merits of which 'we are not concerned'.[4] It pointed out that the reduction in miners' wages was 'a fate which has been shared with other unsheltered industries, e.g. agriculture, cotton and engineering'.[5] However, the Court agreed that 'if 1914 were taken

---

[1] *M.F.G.B.* 26 March, 1924.   [2] *Ibid.* 28 March, 1924.
[3] *Ibid.* 10 April, 1924.
[4] *Report by a Court of Inquiry Concerning the Wages Position in the Coal Mining Industry, 1924,* (Cmd. 2129), p. 14.   [5] *Ibid.* p. 12.

as a measure of the proper wages to be paid to those engaged in the mining industry, practically every class of day-wage worker is, in terms of real wages, worse off today than he was then. In some cases this deficiency is most marked.'[1] The wages of some piece-workers were also found to be less than the equivalent of their pre-war earnings. The Court accepted the miners' contention that the 1921 agreement, while giving certain workmen wages less than the equivalent of pre-war profits, allowed certain owners profits 'substantially in excess of pre-war profits'.[2] It expressed the view that the resumption of negotiations between the employers and the workmen 'might not be unprofitable'.[3]

Negotiations with the coal-owners were resumed on 13 May. Four days later the proposed terms of settlement were published. Standard profits were to be at the rate of 15 per cent. of the amount paid in standard wages, the surplus was to be divided in the proportions of 88 per cent. to wages and 12 per cent. to profits, and the general minimum percentage on standard wages was to be increased from 20 to $33\frac{1}{3}$. In no district were the wages of any adult day-wage workmen to fall below 40 per cent. above the standard wages of the lowest paid class of day-wage workmen in the district. The subsistence wages which were being paid in some of the poorer districts, in accordance with Clause 5 of the 1921 agreement, were to be increased by one-eighth. Only one-third of the surplus accruing from any one ascertainment period was to be used to make good previous deficiencies in standard profits, any balance of the deficiency being carried forward. The M.F.G.B. estimated that the increase in the minimum percentage would raise the average standard wage in the Eastern District from 7s. 9·39d. to 8s. 9·84d. and that the other concessions would yield an additional 3·97d. a shift. It was also estimated that the cumulative effect of these changes in the Eastern District would be an increase of 4·68 per cent. on basic rates. The estimated increase in some of the poorer districts was much higher: in Lancashire it was 14·66 per cent.[4] On 29 May an M.F.G.B. conference decided, by a card vote of 473 to 311, to accept the coal-owners' terms. The agreement was to last for twelve months and was subject to a month's notice on either side.[5]

III

The negotiations for an improved wage agreement brought the coal industry once again under the close scrutiny of the politicians. On

---

[1] *Report by a Court of Inquiry Concerning the Wages Position in the Coal Mining Industry, 1924*, (Cmd. 2129), p. 12.
[2] *Ibid.* p. 15.   [3] *Ibid.* p. 14.
[4] *M.F.G.B.* 17 May, 1924.   [5] *Ibid.* 29 May, 1924.

Y*

19 July, soon after the publication of *Coal and Power*,[1] Lloyd George addressed a meeting of 8,000 people in Chesterfield. It was compared with the famous Rosebery meeting of 16 December, 1901, which had been planned by Arthur and Violet Markham, Samuel Short and William Jacques (the editor of the *Derbyshire Courier*), to rally the forces of Liberalism throughout the country.[2]

'Will today's meeting be a case of history repeating itself?' asked the *Derbyshire Times*. 'The Liberal Party is as much in want of a policy and a leader as in 1901. . . . The significant publication on the eve of the meeting of . . . *Coal and Power* gives colour to the suggestion that he [Lloyd George] has a policy for the miners and round that policy he is about to frame one for his party which he hopes may be acceptable to the country.'[3]

If this was the purpose of the Chesterfield meeting it was a complete failure, as indeed was *Coal and Power*. The Report, with its proposals for the nationalization of mining royalties, amalgamation of mines, and statutory joint consultation between employers and workers, was no more than a variation of the watered-down Duckham proposals which Lloyd George had first advanced after the publication of the Sankey Report. It pleased neither the coal-owners nor the miners.[4]

It was not long before wages resumed their downward trend. Wage rates in the Eastern District had stood at 58·47 per cent. above the basis when the 1921 agreement came to an end in March, 1924. The modified agreement had brought them as high as 79·83 per cent. above the basis in July, but by October they had fallen to 52·53 per cent., only 5·86 per cent. above the new minimum. The owners had already rejected the Derbyshire miners' application for a subsistence wage for the lowest paid workers.

'It was a remarkable thing and a disgrace to the area', said Frank Hall, 'that while Derbyshire owners had been doing very much better than owners in any other district where men had been on the minimum, the lower paid men in Derbyshire were at least 1s. a day worse off than either South Wales, Lancashire, Cheshire or North Staffordshire.'[5]

A. J. Cook, who had succeeded Hodges as Secretary of the M.F.G.B. in April, told the Staveley miners on 19 November:

The average wage for the adult worker last year was 10s. 9d. a day, and he had averaged four-and-a-half days a week. What were they going to do about it? . . . Next June they would need a new agreement and were going

[1] *Coal and Power, The Report of an Enquiry Presided over by the Right Hon. D. Lloyd George, O.M., M.P.*, (London), 1924.
[2] Cf. Violet Markham, *Friendship's Harvest*, (London), 1956, pp. 16–17; G. M. Trevelyan, *Grey of Fallodon*, (London), 1937, pp. 76, 80–81.
[3] *Derbyshire Times*, 19 July, 1924.
[4] *Ibid.* 26 July, 2 August, 1924.   [5] *Ibid.* 22 November, 1924.

to fight for it. Success would depend upon every district being inside the Federation.[1]

Attempts were being made by some of the employers to crush trade unionism completely. A. J. Cook's speech at Staveley was part of a week's programme of similar meetings intended to stiffen resistance.[2] In October, 1924, the manager of the Dowell pit interviewed a number of miners and suggested that they would receive better treatment if they abandoned their union. He also stated that the Staveley Company wished to make Dowell its first non-union pit. After the Association had protested, the Company decided to take a ballot to discover the views of the men on the matter. Hicken, who went to the colliery to inquire into the situation, was ordered off the premises by a policeman. Frank Hall wrote to D. N. Turner:

> Has it ever occurred to you that you are indulging in something which might have happened 40 or 50 years ago? You appear to be living in the dark ages. Indeed, there is an interesting book in existence regarding what was at that time to be the breaking of the union, when a bullock was roasted to celebrate the occasion. I could put you on to this interesting little volume; you could, I am sure, get one or two wrinkles.[3]

On 6 November, 1924, the Council decided to take a strike ballot at all the soft-coal pits in view of the owners' persistence in refusing to give back the $7\frac{1}{2}$ per cent. which the men had conceded in 1922. There were 12,966 votes in favour of a strike and 2,955 against.[4] When the owners were informed of this decision they offered to restore the $7\frac{1}{2}$ per cent. in the event of a successful joint application to the Eastern Area Board by the workmen's representatives and the owners of the soft-coal pits in Derbyshire and Nottinghamshire. The Council decided that these proposals would mean the destruction of the Area Wages Board set up by the national agreement, that the owners of the hard-coal pits would never consent to such changes, and that the proposals were impracticable 'and calculated to split up the men and the owners in the county, as well as create friction as between colliery company and colliery company'. It was agreed that notice should be given that work would cease on 27 January, 1925.[5] About 20,000 men were affected.[6]

Frank Hall alleged that the Midland coal-owners had not co-operated in providing the necessary information for the wage ascertainments. 'One of the owners', he said, 'had refused to make any returns until

[1] *Derbyshire Times*, 22 November, 1924.
[2] *D.M.A.* 11 October, 8 November, 1924.
[3] *Derbyshire Times*, 22 November, 1924. Cf. Comte de Paris, *Trade Unions of England*, (London), 1869, pp. 132–3. See Chapter III, p. 113.
[4] *D.M.A.* 3 January, 1925.
[5] *Ibid.* 10 January, 1925.   [6] *Derbyshire Times*, 3 January, 1925.

the beginning of 1923, and one of the largest coal-owners, the Staveley
Coal and Iron Company, had not made a single return during the whole
of the period.'[1] Hall's statement about the Staveley Company was
subsequently confirmed by Charles Markham himself, in evidence
before the Samuel Commission. 'Is it playing the game to belong to
an association, and pay wages on the ascertainments from the worst
pits and keep your best pits out?' asked Herbert Smith. 'Rather',
replied Markham.[2] Hall argued that the workmen's representatives and
their accountants should be allowed to investigate the owners' claim
that they could not afford to restore the $7\frac{1}{2}$ per cent. 'We have no
intention of letting these people off', he said.[3]

However, the miners were not ready for another stoppage. The men
in the Alfreton district were particularly apathetic despite the determined efforts of Hicken and Sales to arouse enthusiasm. Frank Hall
complained:

> The owners have brought a great deal of pressure to bear on certain classes
> of workers; in fact, undue influence and threats have been used. The notices
> which have been posted up and the action of the companies generally is a most
> disgraceful piece of business. One company posted up notices that coal face
> men would not be affected, whereas it is well known that these men were
> reduced from 8s. make-up in abnormal places to 7s. 8d. . . . All this has been
> done to split and divide the men.[4]

Large numbers of them failed to hand in their strike notices. On 24
January, 1925, the Council decided that all notices should be withdrawn
on the ground that 'the moment is not opportune for ceasing work to
enforce the claim'. In a lengthy resolution the Council regretted that
the owners had not justified their position, deplored the amount of
pressure and intimidation used against the men, and declared that the
claim would be put forward again at a suitable time.[5]

Another defeat followed at the end of March. In November, 1924,
the Association had decided to press for a subsistence wage for Derbyshire through the Area Wages Board.[6] After lengthy negotiations the
matter was referred to arbitration, Judge Staveley Hill being the independent chairman. He awarded increases of up to 6d. a shift to give a
subsistence wage of 8s. 9d. The miners were greatly dissatisfied. 'The
owners were in a better position in the Eastern Area than in any other
district,' said Frank Hall, 'yet the independent chairman has given the

[1] *Derbyshire Times*, 17 January, 1925.
[2] *R.C. on Coal Industry*, 1925, II, Part B, Evidence of Markham, QQ. 10,233,
10,242.
[3] *Derbyshire Times*, 17 January, 1925.   [4] *Ibid.*
[5] *D.M.A.* 24 January, 1925.   [6] *Ibid.* 8 November, 1924.

least allowance for a minimum wage. . . . It appears that wages are paid in an inverse ratio to profits.'[1]

Meanwhile another national crisis in the coal industry was developing. MacDonald's government had been ousted in October, 1924, and had been succeeded by Baldwin's. On 28 November the coal-owners had written to the M.F.G.B. suggesting 'that in view of the extremely serious condition of the coal industry at the present time it would be useful if a small sub-committee of representatives of the Miners' Federation and the Mining Association could be appointed to consider the position of the industry, the causes thereof and possible remedies'.[2] A meeting of the Executive Committee of the M.F.G.B. with the coal-owners' representatives on 29 January, 1925, led to a series of talks which lasted until the end of June. The owners concentrated on markets and production but the miners' representatives insisted on discussing a number of other matters which affected their wages under the profit-sharing system. The burden of the miners' case, prepared with the help of the Labour Research Department, was subsequently published in a pamphlet entitled *The Economic Position of the Coal Industry*.

The miners viewed the industry against the background of general world depression and called attention to the declining consumption of coal, the growing use of other sources of power including lignite, and the harmful effects of reparations coal upon British exports. They were not satisfied that all items of capital expenditure were excluded from the ascertainments. They demanded that the workmen should 'share in the results of the industry in the widest sense' by which they meant the inclusion in the ascertainments of the profits accruing from coking and by-product plants, electric power plant, selling agencies, railway wagons, brickworks, quarries, farms and all the other ancillary activities of colliery companies. Closely related to this question was the demand to discuss the effects of 'multiple ownership' upon wages. The miners asserted that the vertically-integrated firms were able to transfer coal to their iron works, coke ovens and other industrial enterprises at low prices. 'The owners of collieries have such varied and complex interests', they said, 'that a loss in one department may be more than offset by a profit in another.'[3] The capitalization and administration of the industry, and the organization of production and distribution were also sharply criticized. Eventually the discussions turned to the desirability of reducing wages and increasing hours. On 18 June the

---

[1] *Derbyshire Times*, 28 March, 1925.   [2] *M.F.G.B.* 10 December, 1924.

[3] Miners' Federation of Great Britain, *The Economic Position of the Coal Industry*, May, 1925, p. 25. For a full discussion of the workings of the profit-sharing system in the coal industry see A. G. Pool, *Wage Policy in Relation to Industrial Fluctuations*, (London), 1938, pp. 189–243.

owners stated that they intended to give notice to end the existing wages agreement and that in their view a return to the eight-hour day was essential. The joint discussions broke down on 23 June when the miners' leaders made it clear that the workmen would not agree to longer hours or lower wages but would press for increased wages which would be 'at least commensurate with the increase in the cost of living'.[1] On 30 June the Mining Association gave formal notice that it wished to end the wages agreement on 31 July, 1925.

On 1 July the Mining Association sent to the M.F.G.B. its proposals for a new wages agreement. They involved a radical modification of the principles of the 1921 and 1924 agreements. The whole of the proceeds of the industry, after deducting costs of production other than wages, was to be divided between wages and profits in the proportion of 87 to 13. The men's share, after deducting any special subsistence allowances, was to be expressed as a percentage on their basic rates. The minimum percentage addition to basic rates, which had been the vital part of the previous agreements, was to disappear. Professor Pool comments: 'Such a scheme implied that as long as the proceeds of the industry enabled any wages at all to be paid, the owners as a whole would continue to draw some profits, since there was no minimum wage payable as a first charge on the proceeds. It put wages and profits on precisely the same footing as equal sharers in all the fluctuations of the industry.'[2]

The miners were not prepared to abandon the principle of the minimum wage which had been endorsed as recently as 1924 by the Buckmaster Inquiry. Nor were they willing to accept the reductions in wages and the increases in profits which the proposals entailed. The M.F.G.B. estimated that if the owners' offer had been in operation during the nine months ending 31 March, 1925, the sum of £11,565,478 would have been deducted from the wage bill of £111,206,709 and added to the owners' profits which amounted to £3,323,441. Under the 1924 agreement the percentage addition to basic rates in the Eastern District in July, 1925, was 46·67. Under the owners' proposals it would have been 37·59. The average wage per man-shift would have fallen from 10s. 9·62d. to 10s. 1·64d. The earnings of a day-wage worker at the coal face in Derbyshire would have been reduced from 11s. 8¾d. to 11s. od. a shift, and those of a labourer employed on the surface, from 8s. 8½d. to 7s. 4d. Taking July, 1914, as 100, average earnings per man-shift in the Eastern District would have fallen from 163·01 in May, 1925, to 152·53, although the cost of living stood at 173. Real earnings would have been 12 per cent. lower than in July, 1914.[3] A special

[1] M.F.G.B. 19 June, 1925. [2] Pool, op. cit. p. 204.
[3] Miners' Federation of Great Britain, The Coal Crisis, 22 July, 1925, pp. 9–15.

conference of the M.F.G.B. on 3 July decided unanimously to reject the owners' proposals.[1]

IV

The M.F.G.B. refused to enter into any further discussions with the coal-owners until they withdrew their notices, despite the requests of Evan Williams, the Chairman of the Mining Association, and of W. C. Bridgeman, the First Lord of the Admiralty, who was nominated by the Government to act as mediator. On 13 July the Minister of Labour, Sir Arthur Steel-Maitland, appointed a Court of Inquiry consisting of H. P. Macmillan as Chairman, W. Sherwood (a trade union official) and Sir Josiah (later Lord) Stamp, 'to inquire into the causes and circumstances of the dispute in the coal mining industry and to report thereon'. News of this move reached the M.F.G.B. during its annual conference which was being held at Scarborough. It was immediately decided not to accept any Court of Inquiry 'that has for its object the ascertainment of whether mine workers' wages can be reduced or their hours extended, as these questions were fully discussed at the last inquiry'. The conference reaffirmed the willingness of the M.F.G.B. to meet the coal-owners as soon as they withdrew their notices.[2] The Federation subsequently declined all invitations to give evidence.

The Court therefore conducted its inquiry without the assistance of the M.F.G.B. After hearing the evidence of the Mining Association it issued, on 28 July, a report which was not unfavourable to the miners. Evan Williams had admitted that the Minimum Wage Act 'applied in effect to only a limited number of the workers, it was really negligible as a basis of regulation of wages in the industry'. The Court reported: 'We are satisfied on one point, that the workers are justified in claiming that any wages agreement which they can be asked to accept should provide for a minimum wage.' It also stated fairly the miners' point of view:

They concern themselves not with the economic wage, but with what they term a 'living wage'. They represent that unless they receive a remuneration for their labour which at least represents what they received before the war equated to the present cost of living, they cannot carry on the lives of themselves and their families any more than the owners can carry on their collieries if they have to pay more than an economic price for labour.

Sir Josiah Stamp added a special note on the effects of the return to the gold standard. He concluded: 'I do not think the state of affairs in the coal industry in the last few months must be regarded as the

[1] *M.F.G.B.* 3 July, 1925.   [2] *Ibid.* 15 July, 1925.

necessary result either of normal trade movements or the present agreement. Currency policy has aggravated the evil.'[1]

Meanwhile preparations were being made for a stoppage of work. On 23 July the T.U.C. assumed full responsibility for conducting the dispute. It was agreed that the Prime Minister, Stanley Baldwin, should be asked to bring about an unconditional meeting between representatives of the M.F.G.B. and the Mining Association.[2] In Derbyshire a special meeting of the Council on 9 July had given the delegates to the annual conference at Scarborough plenary powers to deal with any counter-proposals which might be advanced by the M.F.G.B. and arrangements had been made for realizing the Association's securities. Circulars had been sent to the branches reminding them of the decision 'that no district or pit must enter into any negotiations for, or accept any settlement of, the present wages dispute other than that arrived at by the national executive of the M.F.G.B.'[3] This proved to be a necessary precaution because the Staveley Company, which had withdrawn from the Mining Association and was not a party to the national agreement, decided not to issue notices. The men at one of the Company's pits had approached the management about continuing to work and had been told that they could do so without any reduction in wages. The Association subsequently intervened and the men agreed to abide by the decisions of the M.F.G.B.[4] By 25 July most of the Derbyshire coal-owners had issued notices terminating all existing contracts of employment on 31 July. The Council endorsed recommendations by the Executive Committee of the M.F.G.B. that the owners' notices should be accepted and that the necessary safety men should be allowed to continue working provided their rates of wages and conditions of employment were not less favourable than those obtaining before 31 July.[5]

The last week of July was one of mounting tension. Negotiations were going on almost continuously between the Government, the T.U.C., the Mining Association and the M.F.G.B. The negotiations with Baldwin were at first discouraging. He was firmly opposed to the granting of a subsidy.[6] On 30 July the miners' leaders reported to a

---

[1] *Report by a Court of Inquiry concerning the Coal Mining Industry Dispute*, 1925.
[2] *M.F.G.B.* 23 July, 1925.   [3] *D.M.A.* 9 July, 1925.
[4] *Derbyshire Times*, 25 July, 1925.   [5] *D.M.A.* 25 July, 1925.
[6] *M.F.G.B.* 19 August, 1925. Baldwin's attitude to the minimum wage is shown in a speech made at Birmingham on 5 March, 1925: 'If you fix on paper minimum standards of pay it does not follow that those standards will, in fact, apply to all men in the industry. What often results is the stoppage of the marginal factory or the marginal coal-pit, or you may find that some of them near the margin will have to go on short time, and you often find that many men are thrown out of employment.' Stanley Baldwin, *On England, and Other Addresses*, (Harmondsworth) edn. of 1937, pp. 45–46.

special conference of trade union executives that Baldwin had asserted that not only the miners but 'all workers in this country have got to take reductions in wages to help put industry on its feet'.[1] This aroused indignation and the conference at once empowered the T.U.C. to issue strike notices if necessary and to give financial support to the strikers. The same evening instructions were issued for an embargo on coal movements to be put into force at midnight on 31 July. This move forced the Government's hand. After hasty negotiations with the miners' leaders and the coal-owners, Baldwin met the special committee of the T.U.C. and the Executive Committee of the M.F.G.B. on Friday, 31 July, and explained that the owners had agreed to suspend their notices, that the Government had decided to hold an inquiry, and that a subsidy would be granted to maintain existing rates of wages until 1 May, 1926. These proposals were accepted and the districts were instructed to continue work as usual.[2]

V

Red Friday, as it was called, was represented by the Labour Press as a great victory. The miners took a more realistic view of the situation. Early in August Smith and Cook were the principal speakers at a Labour Party demonstration held at Renishaw Park, the home of the Sitwell family who turned out in force to hear the speeches. Oliver Baldwin, the Prime Minister's Labour son, was also present and was loudly cheered. Cook said:

The crisis was not yet over. The fight was only just begun. An armistice had been declared, but they must make no mistake about it, the issues during the next nine months were far greater than a mere wage issue. They had got to concentrate on their interests in this industry. It was theirs—it was going to be theirs.[3]

Mr. D. C. Somervell dismisses the view of 'some left-wing writers' that the real purpose of the settlement was to give the Government time to prepare for a general strike as 'great nonsense'.[4] However, on 8 August, 1925, a provincial Conservative newspaper, the *Derbyshire Times*, was able to report:

The reason the Cabinet settled the coal crisis by giving the subsidy is stated to be that they agreed that . . . if such an issue should ever be brought

[1] Cf. *M.F.G.B.* 19 August, 1925; *Daily Herald*, 31 July, 1925; G. D. H. Cole and R. Postgate, *The Common People*, (London), edn. of 1949, pp. 577–8. The accuracy of this report was denied by Baldwin several months later.
[2] *M.F.G.B.* 31 July, 1925.   [3] *Derbyshire Times*, 8 August, 1925.
[4] D. C. Somervell, *British Politics since 1900*, (London), edn. of 1953, p. 175.

to a head public opinion would have to be educated into a state of prepared-
ness to accept the consequences.[1]

The utterances of two of the more ebullient members of the cabinet,
Sir William Joynson-Hicks and Winston Churchill, lent colour to such
reports.[2] Baldwin himself, when asked some years later by his bio-
grapher, Mr. G. M. Young, why he gave the subsidy, replied: 'We
were not ready.'[3]

The coal-owners, free from the restraints of political discretion, were
even more forthright. Lord Londonderry stated: 'Whatever it may
cost in blood and treasure we shall find that the trade unions will be
smashed from top to bottom.'[4] Charles Markham told the Chesterfield
Rotary Club, on 26 September: 'That this trouble is going to finish
without bloodshed I do not believe.'[5] He was later asked by Herbert
Smith, before the Samuel Commission: 'Do you know that men are
"doing time" for saying less than that?' He replied: 'Oh, yes.'[6]

Both the Government and the coal-owners made good use of their
nine months' respite. Frank Hall, who welcomed the prospect of a
peaceful solution to the problems of the industry, said:

The settlement for the moment is certainly in favour of the owners, who
are taking every advantage in re-opening collieries, and it is their intention
to get out of the subsidy as much as possible, without regard to its limitations.[7]

The claiming of the subsidy involved the completion of the ascertainment returns, which the Staveley Company had previously ignored.
The following exchanges between Herbert Smith and Charles Markham were heard by the Samuel Commission:

When the subvention comes along, what happens then?—I take everything
that is going.
So that you do supply your ascertainments now?—It is worth my while
now.
And there is no agreement by Act of Parliament now to compel you to do
it?—No.
But you do it because you say, 'I am going to have my share'?—It is
money for nothing.
Out of the nation?—Yes.

[1] *Derbyshire Times*, 8 August, 1925.
[2] *The Times*, 3 August, 1925; 187 H.C. Deb. 5s. 1684–5; 189 H.C. Deb. 5s. 733.
[3] G. M. Young, *Stanley Baldwin*, (London), 1952, p. 99.
[4] Quoted in W. Hannington, *Unemployed Struggles, 1919–1936*, (London), 1936,
p. 135.
[5] *R.C. on Coal Industry*, 1925, II, Part B. Evidence of Markham, QQ. 10,319 –
10,320.
[6] *Ibid*. Q. 11,590.　　　　　　　　　　[7] *Derbyshire Times*, 15 August, 1925.

That will be patriotic, is it not ?—Yes. It is your unions that force these things.[1]

Whilst the coal-owners were building up, at reduced cost, stocks of coal which they would be able to sell at scarcity prices, the Government was making preparations for the maintenance of public order, supplies and essential services. In this work it soon had the support of an unofficial movement, the Organization for the Maintenance of Supplies, which announced its existence in the newspapers on 25 September, 1925. The O.M.S. (as it came to be called) appealed for volunteers to maintain supplies and services in the event of a general strike and stressed that it was non-political and had no aggressive or provocative aims.[2] On 1 October it received the public blessing of Joynson-Hicks who stated that the promoters of the O.M.S. had consulted him some weeks previously about the desirability of their scheme.[3] On the eve of the General Strike the O.M.S. was handed over to the Government. It was joined by leading members of the British Fascists, said to have been financed by a Central Council of Economic Leagues, which included some 500 industrial firms and was directed by a triumvirate consisting of Rear-Admiral Armstrong, Allan N. Smith and Evan Williams, the coal-owner.[4]

The Government's plans were less spectacular but of greater maturity. The possibility of a general strike, even of revolution, had haunted the minds of British statesmen ever since the armistice. The Supply and Transport Service, designed to meet war-time emergencies, had been kept in existence until 1921. It had been reinforced in 1920 by the Emergency Powers Act. One of Baldwin's first acts as Prime Minister in 1923 was to direct that the Supply and Transport Service should be reviewed by a committee of all the departments concerned. 'So quietly was the weapon forged which three years later was to defeat the General Strike', writes Mr. G. M. Young.[5] The development of these plans was given a stimulus by the railway strike during the Labour interregnum. They finally came to fruition after Red Friday under the supervision of the Permanent Under-Secretary to the Home Office, John Anderson (later Lord Waverley).[6]

By November, 1925, the Ministry of Health had issued Circular 636 to local authorities. It explained that in the event of a stoppage the country was to be divided into areas under the supervision of Civil

---

[1] R.C. on Coal Industry, 1925, II. Part B. Evidence of Markham, QQ. 10,245–10,250.

[2] The Times, 25 September, 1925.   [3] Ibid. 1 October, 1925.

[4] W. H. Crook, The General Strike, (Chapel Hill, University of North Carolina Press), 1931, pp. 301–2.   [5] Young, op. cit. pp. 59, 110.

[6] J. Symons, The General Strike, (London), 1957, p. 25.

Commissioners. Local authorities were to co-operate with these Commissioners in the control of road transport, food and fuel supplies. The Commissioners were to be responsible for the maintenance of law and order and were to be given extensive powers under the emergency regulations. Lord Winterton, one of the Commissioners, writes:

> We were given further instructions in the event of a complete breakdown, to take drastic action of a comprehensive character. Since there was happily no need to carry out these instructions, it might be a breach of the Official Secrets Act to state their nature. . . .[1]

For the most part these preparations were made unobtrusively, although former Labour ministers could not have been entirely unaware of them. It was left to the Labour member for Lincoln, R. A. Taylor, to raise the matter in the House of Commons. On 19 November, he complained that town clerks were receiving letters marked 'Secret', asking them to co-operate with the Government in various ways.[2]

All that remained to be done was to ensure that the promised inquiry into the coal industry would not be a repetition of the Sankey Commission, which had been described by the coal-owners as 'a circus'.[3] The Government had insisted that neither the coal-owners nor the miners should be represented on the Royal Commission and accordingly, on 5 September, had appointed Sir Herbert Samuel as Chairman, Sir Herbert Lawrence, Sir William Beveridge and Kenneth Lee. The miners objected that capital was heavily represented and labour not at all. 'It is true it is not directly representative of the Mining Association,' stated a pamphlet published by the Labour Research Department, 'but it is difficult to imagine any small body of persons more completely representative of capitalist interest, and more completely trained in approaching matters from the capitalist standpoint.'[4]

Mr. Somervell, despite his Panglossian attitude to the Samuel Commission, writes: 'The Government used the respite to very much better purpose than the T.U.C. who hoped for the best and did nothing, and when the "class-war" came, entered it unprepared.'[5] The T.U.C. did nothing because most union leaders did not believe in the class-war which the Government and its supporters seemed to regard as inevitable. The coal-owners fostered the impression that the miners were dominated by 'Bolshevists'. Charles Markham told the Samuel Commission: 'The whole of the miners today have got into the hands of the Bolshevists, and we feel very strongly that the hard things that are said about the

---

[1] Earl Winterton, *Orders of the Day*, (London), 1953, p. 136.
[2] 188 H.C. Deb. 5s. 553.   [3] *M.F.G.B.* 19 August, 1925.
[4] *The Coal Crisis: Facts from the Samuel Commission, 1925–26*, Foreword by Herbert Smith, Labour Research Dept., 1926.
[5] Somervell, *op. cit.* p. 175.

coal-mining industry are not warranted.'[1] In a letter to *The Times* the Archdeacon of Chesterfield criticized the propaganda of the Mining Association of Great Britain: 'The general implication of the pamphlets is that trade unions as a whole are dominated by disloyal revolutionists, a charge which is both false and unfair, and the result can only be to embitter the general body of trade union members.'[2]

There were, of course, in many unions left-wing groups which were advocating extreme measures. The Minority Movement, which had been founded by A. J. Cook and other South Wales miners' leaders, urged that Workers' Defence Corps should be formed in opposition to the O.M.S. and the Fascists but the idea was condemned by both the General Council of the T.U.C. and the Labour Party.[3] Revolution was out of the question. There were many influential leaders in the Labour movement to whom even strikes were anathema. Ramsay MacDonald asserted in the spring of 1925: 'No greater calamity could come over the country than that there should be raised a great block of unions on the one side and capital on the other engaged in a suicidal fight in industry.[4] J. H. Thomas, who has been described as 'the greatest buffoon the Labour movement has known'[5] and was invariably depicted in evening or court dress by David Low, was happier as a social climber than as an organizer of strikes. Lack of enthusiasm prevented the General Council of the T.U.C., of which Thomas was a member, from producing any plan of campaign. Attempts were made to revive the idea of the Industrial Alliance but it proved impossible to reconcile speedy action with the autonomy of the individual unions. After some prodding by the M.F.G.B., the Industrial Committee of the T.U.C., which had been set up to deal with the July, 1925, crisis, issued a statement of policy on 19 February, 1926, declaring that 'there was to be no reduction in wages, no increase in working hours, and no interference with the principle of national agreements'. This was the sum total of the preparations for the General Strike.

Amidst all this inertia A. J. Cook was completely frustrated. His feverish efforts to rouse the T.U.C. and the Industrial Alliance met with failure. He toured the country inspiring the miners by his militant and sometimes violent speeches but many of his proposals had not the slightest chance of acceptance by the Labour movement as a whole. He was particularly anxious to ensure that the strikers would not be beaten by hunger. When he suggested that the co-operative societies would be 'the victualling movement for the fighting forces of labour', the secretary

[1] *R.C. on Coal Industry*, 1925, II, Part B. Q. 10,003.
[2] *The Times*, 1 October, 1925.   [3] Crook, *op. cit.* p. 326.
[4] J. Murray, *The General Strike of 1926*, (London), 1951, p. 70.
[5] Symons, *op. cit.* p. 6.

of the Co-operative Union denied that any such arrangement had been made and said that it was a pity Cook could not be muzzled.[1] When Cook told a T.U.C. meeting that his mother-in-law had been taking in an extra tin of salmon for weeks past, Thomas sneered: 'By God! A British revolution based on a tin of salmon.'[2] Many thought Cook to be misguided but few doubted his sincerity. 'Not a penny off the pay, not a second on the day', was his slogan. For thousands of miners he was the hero of the hour.

During this uneasy truce the Derbyshire miners had to face many difficulties. In September, 1925, there was a strike at the Grassmoor collieries against a further reduction of basic rates.[3] Non-unionism, which had become a serious problem at the Bolsover Company's pits, led the joint board of the Derbyshire and Nottinghamshire miners' associations to take a strike ballot in October. There were 3,261 votes in favour of a strike and 381 against, but only a small proportion of the men voted.[4] When Sales advised a meeting of the Bolsover Company's men at Mansfield to hand in their notices one miner said: 'Tell us how we are going to beat the Company, not how we are going to be starved to death.'[5] By the end of November the men still refused to strike. It was estimated that about half of the Bolsover Company's miners were non-unionists. The Derbyshire and Nottinghamshire associations asked the Company to co-operate by dismissing twenty non-unionists each week. 'The miners embrace men of all political faiths,' said Houfton, a director of the Company, 'and it is not surprising that many men withdraw their membership. The remedy is to make the unions non-political.'[6]

In December there was a strike at the Blackwell Company's collieries arising from the dismissal of a number of men who were alleged to have persistently sent out too much slack. The difficulty was settled by Hicken who said: 'We are highly satisfied. We have obtained more than a hundred per cent. of what we asked for.'[7] The stocking of coal had led to a brief period of comparative prosperity of which the owners wished to take full advantage. When, in February, 1926, coal was struck at the Staveley Company's new Markham No. 1 Colliery, it was found that there was a shortage of labour. Frank Hall told J. Hunter, the Company's agent, that there were no unemployed miners in the area.[8] The Company decided to bring in 117 unemployed miners from Durham but they refused to stay. Many of them had not worked for years and could not easily adapt themselves to conditions in Derbyshire. In

[1] Crook, *op. cit.* p. 314.
[2] J. H. Thomas, *My Story*, (London), 1937, pp. 105–6.
[3] *Derbyshire Times*, 19 and 26 September, 1925.   [4] *Ibid.* 17 October, 1925.
[5] *Ibid.* 21 November, 1925.   [6] *Ibid.* 28 November, 1925.
[7] *Ibid.* 19 December, 1925.   [8] *Ibid.* 13 February, 1926.

particular they objected to the butty system. Some of the men who decided to return to Durham said that others who were thinking of coming to Derbyshire would change their minds when they heard that the butty system operated.[1]

Meanwhile the Samuel Commission was industriously amassing its three volumes of evidence and statistical material. It covered much old ground. All the arguments which had been used before the Sankey Commission were reiterated by the miners and the coal-owners. The only important new evidence was that relating to the decline of the industry since 1919. Apart from Frank Hall, who represented the M.F.G.B., Charles Markham was the only other witness from Derbyshire. His views on the state of the industry have already been discussed.[2] In addition he made some trenchant comments on the miners' unions:

> Their primary objects at the present day seem to be political rather than industrial. In the Staveley area, it is a long time since any of the principal officials of the Derbyshire Miners' Association worked underground, and consequently they know nothing of present-day conditions. Their information is therefore gained from the local extremists who prompt them.

At the same time he blamed some of the miners' leaders for doing 'everything in their power to ferment trouble and discontent . . . solely with the idea of getting power and control for themselves and of bringing stagnation to industry'. Markham advocated the limitation of union funds, the settlement of all disputes at the colliery level, changes in the law relating to political funds and stricter control of union ballots.[3] He also favoured a re-introduction of the so-called eight-hour day, an increase in the difference between the wages of skilled and unskilled workers, the abolition of the minimum wage legislation of 1912, and a return to the butty system.[4]

VI

The Report of the Samuel Commission was published on 10 March, 1926. The miners had not expected the Commission to recommend nationalization and were not disappointed on that score. Some of the Commission's proposals for the re-organization of the industry[5] appeared to offer the possibility of improvement, but only in the distant future. 'To bring any of these measures of re-organization into effect', stated the Report, 'must need a period of months; to bring all of them

---

[1] *Derbyshire Times*, 20 February, 1926.   [2] See Chapter XIV, p. 569.
[3] *R.C. on Coal Industry*, 1925, II, (Part B), Evidence of Markham, p. 539.
[4] *Ibid.* p. 540.   [5] See Chapter XIV, p. 554.

into full operation must need years. . . . Meantime the hard economic conditions of the moment remain to be faced.'[1] On the immediate problem of wages and hours, which had precipitated the crisis of July, 1925, the recommendations of the Commissioners were even more unsatisfactory. They were completely opposed to the continuation of any government subsidy:

> If the present hours are to be retained, we think a revision of the 'minimum percentage addition to standard rates of wages', fixed in 1924 at a time of temporary prosperity, is indispensable. A disaster is impending over the industry, and the immediate reduction of working costs that can be effected in this way, and in this way alone, is essential to save it. . . . Should the miners freely prefer some extension of hours with a less reduction of wages, Parliament would no doubt be prepared to authorize it. We trust, however, that this will not occur.

The Commissioners recognized the desirability of continuing national wage agreements but considered it essential 'that there should be, as there always has been hitherto, considerable variation in the rates of wages in the several districts'.[2] Several months later, the Executive Committee of the M.F.G.B. summed up the miners' objections to these proposals: 'The principle of the Royal Commission's Report—stripped of its flummery—was that the workers should pay for the inefficiency of the mineowners.'[3]

In the negotiations which followed the publication of the Report it soon became clear that the owners favoured not only wage reductions and district settlements but also the longer working day.[4] In many districts they began to post notices to end all existing contracts of employment on 30 April when the government subsidy would cease. The Midland Coal-Owners' Association decided not to issue notices but to continue working on existing contracts. The Staveley Company and other employers who were not members of the coal-owners' association adopted the same policy. The Derbyshire miners' Executive Committee discussed the situation on 17 April and decided 'that the Association must act with the Federation whatever attitude was adopted by the coal-owners in the district'.[5] The policy of the Midland coal-owners made matters difficult for the union officials, as many of the men were reluctant to strike. The Staveley Company posted at its collieries a notice which asked: 'If you give in your notices you know when you

[1] R.C. on Coal Industry, 1925, I, Report, p. 235.   [2] Ibid. p. 236.
[3] Miners' Federation of Great Britain, Statement on the occasion of the Conference of Trade Union Executive Committees held to receive the Report of the General Council of the T.U.C. on the work entrusted to them in the General Strike, 12 January, 1927, p. 10.   [4] M.F.G.B. 25 and 31 March, 1, 8, 9, and 13 April, 1926.
[5] D.M.A. 17 April, 1926.

will get out, but do you know when you will come back?'[1] Most of the men at the Bolsover Company's collieries in Nottinghamshire failed to hand in their notices with the exception of those at the Rufford Colliery which was described by the *Derbyshire Times* as 'the centre of all the Red propaganda in the Mansfield district'.[2]

After the Industrial Committee of the T.U.C. had, on 14 April, publicly reiterated its intention of giving the miners 'the fullest support',[3] the Prime Minister said he would try to persuade the owners to resume negotiations on a national basis. His efforts ended in failure at a joint meeting of the miners' and owners' representatives on 22 April. On the following day, at the request of the Industrial Committee, he made another attempt. The coal-owners' response was to draw up a series of wage offers based on an eight-hour day which were rejected by the M.F.G.B. at a joint meeting on 28 April.[4] On Friday, 30 April, when many of the miners were already locked out, the coal-owners withdrew their opposition to a national wage agreement and put forward proposals which entailed a reversion to the wages of 1921 and the re-introduction of the 'eight-hour' day. Despite the advice of the Samuel Commission the Government stated that it was prepared to introduce temporary legislation permitting the extra hour to be worked without the permanent removal of the seven-hour Act from the Statute Book.[5] The M.F.G.B. immediately rejected these proposals on the grounds that it was not prepared to accept any reductions in wages as a preliminary to the re-organization of the industry, that the lengthening of hours was contrary to the recommendations of the Royal Commission, and that the existing working day was long enough to supply all the coal for which a market could be found.[6] The Industrial Committee then attempted to secure a temporary withdrawal of the owners' notices by the continuation of the subsidy for a short period. The Government continued to insist on the acceptance of wage reductions as a necessary preliminary to any settlement and the negotiations broke down.

At noon, on Saturday 1 May, a conference of trade union executives accepted proposals for the co-ordination of policy, which meant that they surrendered their powers to the General Council. Only the Sailors' and Firemen's Union, led by Havelock Wilson, dissented. Ernest Bevin made it clear that the proposals had not been printed

[1] *Derbyshire Times*, 24 April, 1926.   [2] *Ibid.*
[3] *M.F.G.B.* 14 April, 1926.   [4] *Ibid.* 28 April, 1926.
[5] The public had already been prepared for this proposal by a confidential notice, issued to the Press from the Conservative and Unionist Central Office on 26 April, stating that 'it is desirable to concentrate attention upon the question of hours rather than upon the reduction in wages'. D. H. Robertson, 'A Narrative of the General Strike of 1926', *Economic Journal*, XXXVI, (1926), p. 378n.
[6] *M.F.G.B.* 30 April, 1926.

until after the General Council had heard that the Emergency Powers Act had been invoked. Indeed, such had been the reluctance of the General Council to prepare for a strike that, as Bevin stated some months later, it did not begin to draft any plans until 27 April.[1]

The strike was to begin at midnight on Monday, 3–4 May. Notices were sent out by the unions immediately after the meeting on Saturday, 1 May. Even at the eleventh hour negotiations continued in an effort to find a general formula which would permit a temporary settlement. But, as Laski has commented: 'It is impossible not to feel that during the evening of 2 May the diehards in the Tory Government were bringing pressure to bear upon Mr. Baldwin to break off negotiations.'[2] The *Daily Mail* incident was the *casus belli*. The machine men, despite the blandishments of their union leader, George Isaacs, refused to print a leading article describing all who sympathized actively with the miners as revolutionaries. The Government was not prepared to continue negotiations without a repudiation of this 'gross interference with the freedom of the Press' and 'an immediate and unconditional withdrawal of the instructions for a general strike'.[3] In the words of Mr. Kingsley Martin: 'The T.U.C. stood as a combatant in a war which had been forced upon it and which it feared to win.'[4] Keynes, in a statement to the *Chicago Daily News* correspondent in London, subsequently described Baldwin's handling of the situation as 'fatal blundering'.[5]

VII

On Tuesday, 4 May, trade unionists throughout the country answered the call of the General Council of the T.U.C. to strike in support of the miners' cause. The *British Worker*, published by the General Council at the offices of the *Daily Herald*, reported:

The workers' response has exceeded all expectations. . . . All the essential industries and all the transport services have been brought to a standstill. The only exception is that the distribution of milk and food has been permitted to continue. The Trades Union General Council is not making war on the people. It is anxious that the ordinary members of the public shall not be penalized for the unpatriotic conduct of the mine owners and the Government.[6]

[1] T.U.C. *The Mining Crisis and the National Strike, 1926, Official Reports*, (1927), p. 138A.
[2] H. J. Laski, 'The Coal Strike and Beyond', *The Nation*, (New York), 26 May, 1926, p. 579.
[3] M.F.G.B. 1–12 May, 1926, *Report of Events leading up to, and during the General Strike, and the conclusion thereof.*
[4] Kingsley Martin, *The British Public and the General Strike*, (London), 1926, p. 58.
[5] *British Worker*, 9 May, 1926.   [6] *Ibid.* 5 May, 1926.

On the other hand the *British Gazette*, edited by Winston Churchill and published at the offices of the *Morning Post* by His Majesty's Stationery Office, stated:

The great strike began yesterday. There are already many signs, however, that it is by no means so complete as its promoters hoped.[1]

These were the opening salvos in the propaganda battle which was to play such an important part in the General Strike. The Government through its official newspaper and the B.B.C. consistently minimized the effects of the strike, put out reports that men were returning to work, and represented the strikers as a lawless mob who were challenging the constitution and holding the country to ransom. The *British Worker* was at pains to demonstrate the solidarity of the strikers and to emphasize that they were not revolutionaries. As a reply to the perverted patriotism of Government supporters some of the strikers wore their war medals.[2]

Most of the miners had been locked out since 30 April. For the Derbyshire miners it was a sympathetic strike rather than a lock-out. The majority of them ceased work on 30 April before their strike notices had actually expired, thereby enabling the colliery owners and the Press to argue that they had broken their contracts.[3] Most of the Chesterfield engineering works attempted to continue working and Bryan Donkin, Ltd., was stated to be working full time on 10 May.[4] The Sheepbridge Company, anticipating transport difficulties, closed its works on 3 May before the strike began. After the first week of the strike the Staveley Company decided to close its Devonshire Works and damp down its blast furnaces.[5]

The Government's plans for the emergency were quickly brought into operation. Derbyshire, with Nottinghamshire, Lincolnshire, Leicestershire, Northamptonshire and Rutland, formed the North Midland Division under the control of Captain H. Douglas King, M.P., the Civil Commissioner, with headquarters at Nottingham. The local authorities, many of them Labour-controlled, willingly assumed the responsibilities imposed upon them by the Ministry of Health and the Civil Commissioner. At a special meeting of the Chesterfield Borough Council the Mayor, H. Cropper, said:

They represented the whole of the ratepayers of the Borough, and their position as such should be entirely neutral. . . . They were acting on specific instructions from the Government, the skeleton organization for which,

[1] *British Gazette*, 5 May, 1926. Baldwin is reported to have said to a colleague: 'Don't forget the cleverest thing I ever did. I put Winston in a corner and told him to edit the *British Gazette*.' (Young, *op. cit.* p. 116.)

[2] *British Worker*, 7 May, 1926.   [3] *Derbyshire Times*, 15 May, 1926.

[4] *British Gazette*, 12 May, 1926.   [5] *Derbyshire Times*, 8 May, 1926.

curiously enough, was set up by the Labour Government under the premier-
ship of Mr. Ramsay MacDonald when the country was threatened with a
strike.[1]

The local authorities were responsible for the distribution of food and
fuel and for recruiting volunteers to maintain essential services. By
7 May only 4,000 volunteers had been enrolled in the whole of the
North Midland Division.[2] The Ilkeston Borough Council rationed food
and coal supplies, asked for reports of cases of profiteering, and arranged
for centres to be opened for the feeding of necessitous children.[3]

Public transport was virtually at a standstill. The *British Worker*
reported: 'There has been an almost total suspension of rail, bus and
tramway services at Ilkeston. Private bus proprietors attempted to run
the usual service to Nottingham, but were stopped there and returned
empty, passengers having to walk back.'[4] At all Chesterfield Corporation's
bus stops messages were chalked on the pavements in such terms as:
'Please do not ride on the buses. Blackleg labour. Thank you.' Joseph
Lynch wrote to the *Derbyshire Times* complaining that the untrained
drivers were a danger to the public. He concluded: 'I would like to
know what our Labour members of the Council will have to say about
this matter.' At Clowne privately owned buses were stoned and the
skeleton service which had been arranged by the proprietors had to be
discontinued.[5] By 7 May only 5 per cent. of the clerks and $2\frac{1}{2}$ per cent.
of the traffic grades had reported for duty at the London and North-
Eastern Railway Company's stations and depots in the North Midland
Division. The *British Gazette* reported the running of only two trains
in the whole Division.[6] Many old motor-cars, sometimes held together
by wire or string, were to be seen on the Derbyshire roads. Motor-
cycles and bicycles became increasingly popular. Lorries with various
printed labels such as 'All food supplies' or 'Urgent medical supplies'
made their appearance on the streets of Chesterfield.[7]

Local strike committees were busily engaged picketing the roads and
factories in an attempt to prevent the movement of vehicles or the
carrying out of work unauthorized by the T.U.C. The Ilkeston committee appears to have been particularly active and, at the beginning of
the strike, sent in a daily report to the *British Worker*. On 7 May it
stated: 'Stoppage is proceeding in most orderly fashion with determination to stand fast until victory is won for the miners.'[8] On the following
day: 'All workers solid.'[9] At Ripley there was a federated board at work

[1] *Derbyshire Times*, 8 May, 1926.   [2] *British Gazette*, 7 May, 1926.
[3] *British Worker*, 5 and 8 May, 1926.   [4] *Ibid.* 5 May, 1926.
[5] *Derbyshire Times*, 8 May, 1926.   [6] *British Gazette*, 7 May, 1926.
[7] *Derbyshire Times*, 8 May, 1926.
[8] *British Worker*, 7 May, 1926.   [9] *Ibid.* 8 May, 1926.

to ensure that the safety men employed at the pits were trade unionists and that they confined themselves to their own duties. The board issued permits to all authorized safety men. John Spencer advised the men in the Ripley area to carry out the instructions of the board and to keep the peace.[1]

Most of the national newspapers were able to improvise emergency issues and some of the provincial papers, such as the weekly *Derbyshire Times*, printed by non-union labour, appeared in their usual format. Nevertheless, newspapers were scarce and not even the combined circulations of the *British Gazette* and the *British Worker* were able to make good the deficiency. In any case the difficulties of distribution were formidable. The *Derbyshire Times* reported: 'Belper is completely isolated so far as news is concerned. Not a single paper of any description was on sale after Tuesday, and this absence of news gave birth to some extravagant rumours.'[2] Many of the strike committees produced cyclostyled news sheets. The *Sheffield Forward* had a representative in Chesterfield who telephoned news about the miners.[3] Another strike bulletin was the *Derbyshire Chronicle*, published by Albert Vincent Williams, a Mosborough miner, who was also a part-time organizer for the Labour Party. Williams duplicated his closely typewritten sheets in a room rented by the local Trades Council at the Chesterfield Miners' Welfare Hall. They were sold on the streets at a halfpenny a copy. The news was brought in by twelve despatch riders who toured the county.[4]

The third issue of the *Derbyshire Chronicle*, published on 10 May, 1926, led to the prosecution of Williams under the emergency regulations. He was charged with 'committing an act calculated to cause mutiny, sedition or dissatisfaction among members of H.M. Forces and among members of the civilian population' by printing and publishing his paper. The passage complained of read as follows:

The whole life of London, the hub of British Capitalism, is gradually being brought to a standstill. Troops stationed in Hyde Park refused to act against the workers. The Welsh Guards likewise took up the same course of action. Blood is thicker than water, as the trite saying goes. The ruling class can don our class in soldiers' clothes but the working-class heart pulsates beneath.

S. Walker, the Deputy Town Clerk, stated in the Chesterfield police court on 11 May that Williams 'held strong Communist views' and had come to Chesterfield 'with the avowed intention of creating strike disturbances in what had hitherto been a peaceful area'. A. F. Day, employed in the office of the borough surveyor, had bought a copy of

---

[1] *Derbyshire Times*, 8 May, 1926.   [2] *Ibid.*
[3] Symons, *op. cit.* p. 174.   [4] *Derbyshire Times*, 15 May, 1926.

the *Derbyshire Chronicle* which was subsequently passed on to Colonel Little, the military intelligence officer for the area. Little denied the accuracy of the reports about the troops. Williams, who pleaded not guilty, stated that he had received the information from a Member of Parliament and had published it in good faith. The Mayor, H. Cropper, who presided, said that Williams's publication was likely to be 'seriously believed and taken notice of by hundreds and possibly thousands of people'. The magistrates considered that 'justice would not be met' except by sentencing Williams to two months' imprisonment with hard labour and fining him five pounds.[1]

A week later two other miners, Joseph Hugh Fretwell, of Pinxton, and Arthur Wilkinson, of South Normanton, appeared before the Alfreton magistrates on charges of exhibiting or possessing the offending publication. They were bound over for six months.[2]

Despite the fears of the authorities there was little disorder in Derbyshire. At Ilkeston the strike committee reported that the police assisted rather than interfered with them.[3] The Chesterfield police wisely decided to prohibit all outcrop working from the start of the strike.[4] The *British Worker* reported on 8 May: 'Miners at Clay Cross have located an outcrop seam, and all sorts of vehicles, including an icecream barrow, convey the coal to the miners' homes.'[5] There was coal picking at Staveley and Eckington but outcrop working did not become widespread until the General Strike was over. The T.U.C.'s appeal for orderly conduct was backed by local leaders.[6] On 12 May the *British Gazette* reported: 'Derbyshire is quiet and there are plenty of special constables.'[7] Arrangements were quickly made to keep the strikers occupied and amused. Many cinemas offered free or cheap seats.[8] The Mayor of Chesterfield suggested that 'it was in the public interest that provision of recreation and sport and music should be made by the Parks Committee'. He also appealed to cinema proprietors to allow their premises to be used for Sunday evening concerts. The Miners' Welfare Adult Education Joint Committee arranged short talks, lectures and concerts at various centres in Derbyshire and Nottinghamshire.[9]

Meanwhile little was being done nationally to ease the tension. Many churchmen were becoming uneasy about the moral aspects of the situation. Before the strike Archdeacon Crosse had delivered, in the Chesterfield parish church, a sermon based on Baldwin's message: 'Remember peace on earth comes to men of good will. Keep steady!'

[1] *Derbyshire Times*, 15 May, 1926.　　[2] *Ibid.* 22 May, 1926.
[3] Symons, *op. cit.* p. 110.　　[4] *Derbyshire Times*, 8 May, 1926.
[5] *British Worker*, 8 May, 1926.
[6] *Derbyshire Times*, 8 May, 1926.　　[7] *British Gazette*, 12 May, 1926.
[8] *British Worker*, 8 May, 1926.　　[9] *Derbyshire Times*, 8 May, 1926.

After roundly asserting that 'the whole history of the mining industry was too disgraceful for words' Crosse asked: 'Did they wonder that men were saying things? Did they wonder that men sometimes acted with extravagance? Did they know that they were their brethren and were the best and truest and bravest of men?'[1] On 7 May a meeting of leaders of the Christian Churches, presided over by the Archbishop of Canterbury, issued an appeal for the resumption of negotiations, suggesting that there should occur 'simultaneously and concurrently' a cessation of the General Strike, a renewal by the Government of its offer of financial assistance for a short, indefinite period, and a withdrawal of the coal-owners' notices. The Government at first refused to allow these proposals to be published by the *British Gazette* and the B.B.C. but they appeared in *The Times* and the *British Worker* on 8 May.[2]

The Government continued to treat the strikers as potential revolutionaries. On 8 May the *British Gazette* notified all ranks of the armed forces 'that any action which they may find it necessary to take in an honest endeavour to aid the Civil Power will receive both now and afterwards, the full support of His Majesty's Government'. The King wrote through his secretary to the War Office: 'His Majesty cannot help thinking that this is an unfortunate announcement.'[3] The *British Worker* stated on 10 May: 'The idea of representing a strike which arose entirely out of industrial conditions and had entirely industrial aims as a revolutionary movement was mainly Mr. Churchill's. It is a melodramatic "stunt" on Sidney Street lines.'[4]

The Government was assisted in its efforts to portray the strike as a challenge to constitutional government by Sir John Simon who argued in the House of Commons on 6 May that the strike was not a trade dispute within the meaning of the Trade Disputes Act, 1906, and was therefore illegal. 'Every trade union leader who has advised and promoted this course of action is liable in damages to the uttermost farthing of his personal possessions', he said.[5] On 10 May veiled threats that the Government was considering the arrest of certain trade union leaders appeared in the *British Gazette*. Simon's opinions were reinforced by Mr. Justice Astbury's *obiter dictum* on 11 May. In granting an injunction to the National Sailors' and Firemen's Union to restrain the officials of its Tower Hill Branch from calling upon members to strike, he said: 'The so-called general strike called by the Trades Union

[1] *Derbyshire Times*, 8 May, 1926.
[2] *The Times*, 8 May, 1926; *British Worker*, 8 May, 1926.
[3] Symons, *op. cit.* p. 159.   [4] *British Worker*, 10 May, 1926.
[5] Cf. Sir John Simon. *Three Speeches on the General Strike*, (London), 1926, p. 5. Section 3 of the Trades Dispute Act, 1906, provides that 'an act done by a person in contemplation or furtherance of a trade dispute shall not be actionable on the ground only that it induces some other person to break a contract of employment'.

Congress is illegal and contrary to law, and those persons inciting or taking part in it are not protected by the Trade Disputes Act of 1906.'[1] The alleged illegality of the General Strike was first challenged by Sir Henry Slesser in the House of Commons on 10 May and has since been shown by many eminent legal authorities, notably Professor A. L. Goodhart, to be quite unfounded.[2] Nevertheless, at the time, the combined efforts of Simon and Astbury were sufficient to alarm some of the union leaders.

Meanwhile, on Thursday, 6 May, Sir Herbert Samuel, who had been to Italy to recover from his labours as Chairman of the Royal Commission, travelled post-haste to London. The circumstances of his return are, as Sir Dennis Robertson has remarked, 'the most carefully guarded secret of the strike'.[3] Soon afterwards J. H. Thomas agreed to put him in touch with the Negotiating Committee of the T.U.C. On Friday, 7 May, and the three following days, Samuel met the Committee in the Bryanston Square house of Thomas's friend, the South African mining magnate, Sir Abe Bailey.[4] The meetings were kept secret and not even the miners' leaders knew of them until Saturday, 8 May.[5] Thomas appears to have been the only parliamentary Labour leader who took part in these discussions although, according to J. R. Clynes he, Snowden, Henderson and MacDonald were also busy behind the scenes.[6] Meanwhile Thomas was entering into even more exclusive negotiations. On Saturday, 8 May, he attended a luncheon party at Wimborne House in Arlington Street. There Lord Wimborne and his wife had assembled the coal-owners Lord Londonderry and Lord Gainford, Lord Reading, Osbert Sitwell, J. A. Spender and Mrs. Snowden. Thomas blandly informed them that the miners were now inclined to accept the Samuel Report.[7] On the following day he told a public meeting at Hammersmith: 'I have never disguised and do not disguise now that I have never been in favour of the principle of the general strike.'[8] Later that evening he was driven from his home to Arlington Street by Baldwin's secretary, Selwyn Davies. Thomas had further discussions with Wimborne followed by a meeting with Wimborne and Reading at 8.45 on Monday morning, again arranged by Selwyn Davies.[9]

It is doubtful whether the activities of Thomas and the Wimborne

[1] Simon, *op. cit.* p. 68.
[2] A. L. Goodhart, 'The legality of the General Strike in England', *Yale Law Journal*, XXXVI, (1927).
[3] D. H. Robertson, 'A Narrative of the General Strike of 1926', *Economic Journal*, XXXVI (1926) p. 390.   [4] Thomas, *op. cit.* p. 107.
[5] T.U.C. *The Mining Crisis and the National Strike, 1926, Official Reports*, (1927), p. 161A.   [6] J. R. Clynes, *Memoirs, 1924–37*, (London), 1937, p. 76.
[7] Osbert Sitwell, *Laughter in the Next Room*, (London), 1949, p. 226.
[8] *British Gazette*, 11 May, 1926.   [9] Sitwell, *op. cit.* pp. 228–33.

House group had any practical results other than to gratify Thomas's passion for social climbing and to indicate to the Government the attitude of members of the General Council. The important negotiations were those conducted by Sir Herbert Samuel. On Sunday, 9 May, the miners' leaders received their first official intimation of these negotiations and were presented with the initial draft of the famous Samuel memorandum which was promptly rejected. On the following day Smith, Richardson and Cook were invited to take part in the discussions and that evening the General Council and the Executive Committee of the M.F.G.B. met to consider a modified draft of the memorandum. The General Council regarded it as 'a satisfactory basis for drawing up proposals for the purpose of re-opening negotiations in the mining industry' but it was still unacceptable to the miners.[1]

The difficulty arose from the fact that the General Council, in its anxiety to end the General Strike, had misrepresented the miners' position. Samuel wrote to Baldwin on Tuesday, 11 May:

The T.U.C. were deceiving themselves when they informed me that there was no longer an absolute veto upon any kind of reduction in any circumstances. My clear view is that the veto remains exactly the same now as it was throughout the negotiations.[2]

Samuel's proposals for a settlement had all been within the framework of the Report of the Royal Commission which, of course, implied eventual reductions in wages. The miners' leaders asserted, as they had done throughout the dispute, that they would not accept reductions in wages. This, they said, was the reason for the General Strike and there had been no changes which justified a return to work. Moreover, even if they accepted Samuel's proposals, he was not an official spokesman and they had no guarantee that the Government would implement them.

On Tuesday, 11 May, Sir Herbert Samuel dictated a lengthy letter to the Prime Minister describing the difficulties of the negotiations. The letter was never sent, for within two hours of its dictation Samuel received a message from the T.U.C. that the strike was to end regardless of the wishes of the miners.[3] The members of the General Council felt that they could not be 'tied to a mere slogan'. This fact was not generally known at the time. The General Council did not wish its desertion of the miners' cause to split the unity of the Labour movement and therefore continued to press the miners' leaders to accept the Samuel

---

[1] T.U.C. *The Mining Crisis and the National Strike, 1926, Official Reports,* (1927), p. 77A.　　　　　　　　　　　　　　[2] Quoted in Symons, *op. cit.* p. 200.
[3] Symons, *op. cit.* pp. 202–3; J. Bowle, *Viscount Samuel, A biography,* (London), 1957, p. 253.

Z

memorandum. There were lengthy meetings until midnight on Tuesday, 11 May.[1] Further appeals were made to the miners on the following day by Ernest Bevin and A. A. Purcell who had been responsible for the organization of the strike. Herbert Smith accused the General Council of entering into negotiations and agreements without the miners' knowledge and declared that the rank and file had more enthusiasm for the strike than their leaders.[2] Shortly after noon Arthur Pugh and his colleagues arrived at Downing Street to tell the Prime Minister that the strike was over. It was an unconditional surrender. The Samuel memorandum was not even mentioned and individual unions were left to make their own arrangements with the employers for the safeguarding of their members' interests.

In the recriminations between the General Council and the M.F.G.B. which followed the General Strike, the miners' leaders complained that they had been confronted with an ultimatum on the night of Tuesday, 11 May. This was hotly denied by members of the General Council. George Hicks said that the final decision to call off the strike had not been made until 'well after midnight'. According to Citrine the General Council 'definitely and finally made up their minds' about ten minutes before they went to see Baldwin.[3] Mr. Symons writes: 'There is an overwhelming weight of evidence that the decision had been reached by 9.30 on Tuesday night.'[4] The miners had been sacrificed in the interests of industrial peace.

Much harm had been done to their cause by the suggestion that the country was on the verge of revolution. Nothing could have been further from the truth. The Labour movement, politically and industrially, was completely unprepared for the General Strike, much less for a revolutionary civil war. The 'General Strike' itself was, in fact, only a partial strike. The weak and distressed answers of Thomas and other members of the Labour Front Bench to the assertions of government spokesmen showed their complete lack of understanding of the situation they had helped to create. 'The Labour leaders most opposed to the idea of a general strike', writes Mr. Symons, 'were those who most feared its success: they were afraid that it would destroy British civilization—by which they meant, among other things, the civilization that allowed respectable leaders to argue peacefully about ways of changing that civilization.'[5] Lloyd George, who had faced the much more revolutionary years of 1919–20, proved to be more perceptive than the Labour leaders. 'I know a great many of the people responsible', he

[1] T.U.C. *The Mining Crisis and the National Strike, 1926, Official Reports,* (1927), p. 147A.
[2] *Ibid.* p. 149A.
[3] *Ibid.* pp. 136A, 168A.
[4] Symons, *op. cit.* p. 205.
[5] *Ibid.* p. 51.

assured the Commons. 'They are as little revolutionary as any Member of this House. They have fought the rebellious ones in their own party.'[1]

VIII

For the miners the General Strike was the unfortunate prelude to a much longer and more desperate struggle. On Wednesday, 12 May, A. J. Cook had instructed the districts not to resume work pending the decision of a national conference. When the delegates assembled in London on Friday, 14 May, they heard that the Government was preparing its proposals for the settlement of the dispute in the coal industry. These proposals, which were received by Herbert Smith on the following day, were much less favourable than even the Samuel memorandum. The Samuel proposals, in their final form, had provided for a temporary subsidy to enable the men to resume work at the previous rates, a National Wages Board to administer the eventual reductions in wages, an assurance that the industry would be re-organized on the lines suggested by the Royal Commission before any revision of wages, and an agreement that the wages of the lowest paid men would not be adversely affected. The miners' main objection to these proposals had been the eventual reductions in wages which, they argued, would be unnecessary if the industry were re-organized. The Baldwin proposals did not allow for any return to the *status quo* for the purpose of further negotiations. A subsidy of only £3,000,000 was to be granted to enable the miners to return to work at a reduction of 10 per cent. in minimum wages for three weeks. Meanwhile a National Wages Board was to frame a national wages and hours agreement which would inevitably lead to further wage reductions after the withdrawal of the subsidy. The wages of the lowest paid men were no longer to be guaranteed if they exceeded 45s. a week. In return for these concessions the Government gave an assurance that it intended to introduce a number of Bills to give effect to the recommendations of the Royal Commission for the re-organization of the industry. But nothing was to be done without first consulting the Coal Advisory Committee of the Secretary for Mines.[2]

The Government's proposals were rejected by the adjourned M.F.G.B. conference on 20 May.[3] They also proved to be unpopular with the coal-owners who, on the following day, issued a statement demanding an eight-hour day and 'freedom from political interference'. It was now apparent that there would be no speedy settlement of the dispute. By the end of May the Government had made its preparations

[1] 195 H.C. Deb. 5s. 84.
[2] *M.F.G.B.* 15 and 20 May, 1926.   [3] *Ibid.*

by arranging for the importation of foreign coal, restricting the allowance of coal for domestic purposes, and proclaiming once again a state of emergency. The M.F.G.B. also prepared by seeking aid from the other trade unions but the time was not propitious.[1]

In Derbyshire and Nottinghamshire, after the eventful days of the General Strike, the employers again reminded the miners that they were not locked out. Their reminders fell upon deaf ears as far as Derbyshire was concerned but in Nottinghamshire the union's funds were already practically exhausted and there was much talk of returning to work. Frank Varley, the Nottinghamshire leader, told the Mansfield miners on 16 May: 'Temporarily, at any rate, we have got to agree with the enemy while we are in the gate with him.' It was stated at a meeting of the Council of the Nottinghamshire Miners' Association, on 17 May, that even if the union's assets were mortgaged to the full there would only be enough money for half a week's strike payments.[2] On the same day, at a special meeting of the Derbyshire miners' Council, the Langley delegate proposed that £10,000 should be granted to the Nottingham-shire Miners' Association for the relief of its members.[3] The grant, which was approved by an overwhelming majority of the Derbyshire branches, enabled the Nottinghamshire Miners' Association to distribute one week's strike payments. 'It was one of the noblest actions ever performed,' wrote J. G. Hancock, 'and you may rest assured that it will never be forgotten or cease to be appreciated by us all.'[4]

Meanwhile the distress was increasing in both counties. Towards the end of May the Mansfield Board of Guardians stated that about a fifth of the population of the Union was receiving out-relief. In Chesterfield, where the guardians had to deal with about 5,000 cases of distress among miners, the overworked clerks were unable to cope with the situation. Hungry men who had walked long distances were fainting as they waited for hours in the queues.[5]

Some of the employers tried to take advantage of the situation by now offering to re-open their pits on less favourable terms than they had put forward at the beginning of the strike. The Staveley Company posted notices at all its collieries and in prominent places in the mining towns and villages, stating that the men could return to work at their former rates with a minimum daily wage of 7s. 8d. for a period of three months. Thereafter wage rates were to be determined by the district ascertainments. The length of the working day was to be increased to $7\frac{1}{2}$ hours and the 14·17 per cent. addition to piece-work rates was to be halved. Similar proposals were posted at the Shipley Collieries in

---

[1] M.F.G.B. 9 June, 1926.   [2] Derbyshire Times, 22 May, 1926.
[3] D.M.A. 17 May, 1926.
[4] Ibid. 21 June, 1926.   [5] Derbyshire Times, 29 May, 1926.

the Ilkeston and Heanor district. Deputies plied the miners with drinks in public houses in the Warsop and Staveley districts in an attempt to persuade them to return to work. At Mansfield Woodhouse they had a hostile reception. 'This is a rather low down game which will not take on in these days', said Frank Hall. 'The men are not to be bribed with a pint of ale. . . . Yet it is a great pity that anything should be done that would lead to a breach of the peace.'[1] Mass meetings at Shirebrook and Staveley passed resolutions rejecting the Staveley Company's offer. D. N. Turner, the general manager, commented: 'I think Mr. Hall agrees with some of our proposals, but does not like to say so openly.'[2]

Whatever his beliefs, Frank Hall stood loyally by the Federation's policy in all his public utterances. But others were already sowing the seeds of disunity. Thomas Spencer, a consistent advocate of moderation for several years, was quick to follow the lead of Hodges who, as secretary of the International Miners' Federation, had been touring the country putting forward the employers' point of view. Spencer, who had been a trustee of the Derbyshire Miners' Association for many years, was a Liberal-Labour trade unionist of the old school. Born at Alfreton in 1865, he had played an active part in local government and claimed to be the first working-class magistrate in Derbyshire. An ardent Primitive Methodist, he had been a local preacher since the early age of 17.[3] Like J. H. Thomas he was a snob. 'He was . . . a life member of the Henley Regatta Club', we are told. 'On several occasions he had the honour of meeting members of the Royal Family, and twice he attended the Lord Mayor of London's Banquet.'[4]

Spencer's open criticism of M.F.G.B. policy after the General Strike led to much dissatisfaction among the miners. 'Let us make the best terms we can in the present circumstances,' he urged, 'and get back to work as soon as possible.' On 1 June Frank Hall wrote to Spencer accusing him of 'stabbing the leaders in the back'. He concluded: 'I am going to raise the question of your trusteeship at the next Council meeting.'[5] On 21 June the Council decided to ask Spencer to resign.[6] When he ignored this request the branches were asked to vote for or against his removal according to rule.[7] On 6 September it was reported to the Council that 71 of the 72 branches had voted in favour of Spencer's ceasing to be a trustee.[8]

---

[1] *Derbyshire Times*, 5 June, 1926.   [2] *Ibid.*
[3] *Alfreton and Belper Journal*, 20 January, 1922.
[4] *Derbyshire Times*, 17 January, 1927.
[5] *Ibid.* 5 June, 1926.   [6] *D.M.A.* 21 June, 1926.
[7] Rule 17 stated: 'They [the trustees], or any of them, may be removed by a vote of the Council, confirmed by a vote of the branches, who shall vote according to numbers.'
[8] *D.M.A.* 6 September, 1926.

Spencer was doubtless familiar with the rules of the Association but he chose to represent his dismissal as further evidence of the 'undemocratic' nature of the miners' unions. The action of the Council, he said, was *ultra vires* and ought to have been confirmed by a ballot vote of all the members.[1] Frank Hodges, who was soon to be well rewarded for his efforts to disunite the miners,[2] wrote to Spencer:

You have dared to criticize the policy of Smith and Cook in the conduct of the present dispute. . . . You have been cruelly frank and now the dumb have been invoked to speak against you, but they have not. It is only claimed that they have so spoken. Oh Democracy! what baseness has been committed in thy name! . . . You have seen before your very eyes the steady accumulation of human misery. You have seen golden opportunities come and go, which, had they been seized by a competent leadership, would long since have led to an honourable and just peace.[3]

For a man who claimed to be impoverished as a result of the stoppage, Thomas Spencer went to remarkable lengths to justify his case. Taking his cue from Hodges's letter, which ended 'You may make what use you like of this', he had extracts from it printed and distributed throughout the county, and in October brought a High Court action against the officials of the Association for their alleged non-compliance with the rules. The Council passed a lengthy resolution condemning Hodges's behaviour and recording 'its utter lack of confidence in him as International Secretary'.[4] The legal dispute dragged on until May, 1927, when it was reported that Spencer had withdrawn his case and agreed to pay all expenses, the Association paying taxed costs amounting to only £12 0s. 9d.[5]

The arguments of Hodges and his followers were identical with those of the coal-owners. In a letter to *The Times* Charles Markham stated:

The miners' unions have got into the hands of the Socialist members of South Wales and Scotland, where undoubtedly wages are very much lower than in the Midlands. . . . If the ballot were secret, taken in a constitutional manner, the men would go back to work immediately. The outcome of this would inevitably lead to a dissolution of the Miners' Federation and the reversion to district settlements. Neither Mr. Smith nor Mr. Cook dares face a secret ballot. . . .[6]

Captain Charles Waterhouse, a former Conservative candidate for North-East Derbyshire, wrote:

A prolonged strike in the East Midlands cannot conceivably help these depressed areas which are inherently doomed to suffer either a considerable

[1] *Derbyshire Times*, 18 September, 1926.
[2] See R. P. Arnot, *The Miners: Years of Struggle*, (London), 1953, pp. 522–3.
[3] Thomas Spencer's papers: Letter from Hodges to Spencer, 15 September, 1926.
[4] *D.M.A.* 25 September, 1926.
[5] *Ibid.* 21 May, 1927.   [6] *The Times*, 5 June, 1926.

decrease in rates of wages or an area of widespread, possibly of permanent unemployment. . . . Let them follow the lead of their own men, of Varley and of Mr. Spencer. . . . If they wish to follow the lead outside Derbyshire, let them turn to Frank Hodges. . . .[1]

Such appeals to the selfishness of the Derbyshire miners at first met with little response. They were not prepared to be divided, for they feared that they would subsequently be ruled. They were well aware of the economic facts of the situation but believed that it was preferable to try to change them rather than abandon the basic principles of trade unionism. At Mansfield Woodhouse, on 6 June, Frank Hall commented on Markham's letter. 'I can tell him', he said, 'that if a ballot were taken at any pit under his company . . . there would be a very large majority in favour of rejecting the Markham terms.' At Killamarsh, on 8 June, a meeting of 350 miners passed resolutions condemning the actions of Frank Varley and Thomas Spencer.[2]

During June the Government announced a programme of legislation which did little to allay the suspicions of the miners. Priority was to be given to a Bill permitting a lengthening of the working day in coal-mines to eight hours exclusive of winding times. This was to be followed by measures for the re-organization of the industry. There was to be legislation to facilitate amalgamations and the development of new mines, to double the mineral rights duty for the purpose of financing such amenities as pit-head baths, and to restrict employment for men over 18 years of age to those already working in the mines. In the autumn session the Government also planned to amend the law relating to trade unions. Frank Hall commented:

The declaration of policy by the Prime Minister consisted of the most astonishing proposals and it is quite evident that he has taken up the owners' cause as advocate-general of the Mining Association. . . . This suicidal race for trade will put the owners and miners in a worse position than they find themselves today. . . . I can only conceive that it was the intention of the Government to place a weapon in the hands of the coal-owners to be used against the workmen and to increase their profits. . . . The men are saying: 'Sold again'. . . . Selling agencies, nationalization of minerals, municipal selling and amalgamations appear now to be quite unimportant matters to the Government, whilst the Commission regarded these proposals as essential to the future wellbeing of the industry.[3]

The decision to lengthen the working day, despite the advice of the Samuel Commission, was particularly resented by the miners. Their leaders had on many occasions argued that reductions in wages were preferable to the longer working day, a change which would be difficult

[1] *Derbyshire Times*, 12 June, 1926.   [2] *Ibid.*   [3] *Ibid.* 19 June, 1926.

to reverse. In the face of this threat the quarrel between the T.U.C. and the M.F.G.B. was temporarily buried and a joint appeal for unity was issued. The Council of the Derbyshire Miners' Association decided not to meet the coal-owners to discuss their proposed new wages agreement.[1] The Government's Bill, which suspended for five years the seven-hour day and made an eight-hour day permissible, was given its third reading on 1 July. On the following day the General Council of the T.U.C. issued a manifesto denouncing the Government's action and calling for financial support for the miners but declined to impose a levy on the affiliated unions or to place an embargo on the movement of coal.

Meanwhile some of the Derbyshire coal-owners were attempting to re-open their collieries. On 23 June a number of men resumed work at the Staveley Company's Markham No. 2 Colliery on the terms which had been offered earlier in the month. There were some hostile demonstrations by the strikers. 'It is regrettable', said Frank Hall, 'that the owners should act in such a way as to tempt the men and women to do anything which could be regarded as a breach of the emergency regulations.'[2] On the following Sunday, 27 June, the Association held a large demonstration at Staveley. The miners and their families marched in contingents from the surrounding villages to form a procession of over 5,000, headed by a brass band. The men carried their lodge banners and many of the women had placards bearing slogans. Speeches were made by Frank Lee, Frank Hall, John Spencer, Henry Hicken and a number of local officials. Resolutions calling for solidarity were carried unanimously.[3] R. C. A. Palmer Morewood, the owner of the Swanwick Collieries, and G. M. Jackson, the managing director of the Clay Cross Company, soon followed the example of the Staveley Company. John Spencer told the Eckington miners on 1 July: 'The men who had returned to work ought to be persuaded to come out again. . . . They must not, however, use any methods that were not fair or constitutional. There must be no breaches of the law.' A. V. Williams, who had been released from prison that day, was received with applause when he appeared at the meeting.[4]

On 6 July, two days before the Eight Hours' Bill received the Royal Assent, notices were posted at most of the Derbyshire and Nottinghamshire collieries stating that the men could return to work at their former rates until the end of September. Thereafter wages were to be governed by the district ascertainments with a minimum of 32 per cent. upon basic rates. The men were to work an eight-hour day and piece-workers were to surrender the percentage addition which had been granted on

[1] D.M.A. 21 June, 1926.   [2] Derbyshire Times, 26 June, 1926.
[3] Ibid. 3 July, 1926.   [4] Ibid.

the introduction of the seven-hour day.[1] The majority of the miners rejected these offers.

IX

As the distress in the coalfields increased, the leaders of the churches grew more critical of the attitude of the Government and the coal-owners. Speaking at Sheffield, the Archbishop of York, Cosmo Lang, said:

I entirely understand the position of the miners who say: 'We cannot pledge ourselves beforehand to reductions in the rates of wages or on the matter of hours unless and until we know what is to happen about these proposals on wide reconstruction.' I cannot but think, as a purely dis-interested outsider, that it would have been far more hopeful and a more generous attitude on the part of the owners if they had said: 'Come, now, let us reason together.'[2]

On 15 July, after a joint meeting with representatives of all the Christian churches, the Executive Committee of the M.F.G.B. accepted a memorandum which proposed an immediate resumption of work with wages and hours as they were before the dispute. The Government was to grant a subsidy for a period not exceeding four months, under a scheme to be prepared by the Samuel Commission, to enable a national settlement to be reached. The Commissioners were also to prepare Bills for the re-organization of the industry, which the Government was to introduce as speedily as possible. If, at the end of the four months, agreement were still not reached, there was to be a Joint Board to appoint an Independent Chairman, whose award was to be accepted.[3] On 19 July these proposals were submitted to the Prime Minister who promptly rejected them on the ground that no subsidy could be granted.

At a special conference of the M.F.G.B., on 30 July, the Executive Committee was criticized for supporting the memorandum and the matter was referred to the districts.[4] Derbyshire decided by 33,050 votes to 6,700 to accept the proposals.[5] Frank Hall explained to the *Derbyshire Times*:

Already Derbyshire had made an enormous sacrifice in coming out in support of the other districts, particularly the export districts, and it was not to be understood that Derbyshire would agree to a national minimum based on the worst economic district. By accepting the Report they were

---

[1] *Derbyshire Times*, 10 July, 1926.
[3] *M.F.G.B.* 29 June, 15 July, 1926.
[4] *Ibid.* 30 July, 1926.

[2] *Ibid.* 12 June, 1926.
[5] *D.M.A.* 3 August, 1926.

Z*

bound to accept what the Commissioners described as a variable minimum, that was to say a different minimum from district to district, having some relation to economic conditions.[1]

However, at a M.F.G.B. conference on 16 August the combined forces of Yorkshire, South Wales, Lancashire, Cumberland and the Forest of Dean resulted in the rejection of the 'Bishops' Memorandum' by 367,650 votes to 333,036.[2]

The position in Derbyshire was becoming increasingly difficult. The last strike payments had been made in mid-July and the miners and their families were now relying for their subsistence upon the poor law authorities, various charities and the M.F.G.B. strike relief fund. Outcrop working was becoming more prevalent and the offers of the coal-owners were tempting some of the men to return to the pits. On 12 July the Council decided by 41 votes to 21 to ask the Executive Committee of the M.F.G.B. to consider the advisability of taking a ballot on the acceptance of the eight-hour day.[3] John Spencer reported to the M.F.G.B. conference on 30 July that the majority of the Derbyshire miners were still standing by the Federation's policy but that about 250 men were back at work at the Markham No. 2 Colliery, about 100 at the Oxcroft Colliery, and another 130 or so at various small mines. Complaining of 'the subtle manner in which these men have been got at by house to house visitation', Spencer said:

I think I can say it has been a question of bitter and stout. There has been a certain amount of bribery to get some of these men back to work. . . . We have picketed. We have had the E.P.A. to deal with, and we have a number of our men at the present time doing three months in gaol for trying to stop this.[4]

When Spencer gave his report to the next M.F.G.B. conference on 16 August the situation was even worse:

Coal-owners in Derbyshire have opened their pits. Various offers have been made. . . . It is not true, as reported in the *Sunday Worker* yesterday, that Derbyshire has met the coal-owners . . . to discuss arrangements. I am here to deny that. We have not yet met the coal-owners and we don't intend meeting the coal-owners or doing anything behind the back of the Miners' Federation.

According to Frank Hall 1,793 men had returned to the pits. There were also at work 1,601 'outcroppers' and 1,302 safety men and deputies.[5] Other districts, notably Nottinghamshire and Warwickshire,

[1] *Derbyshire Times*, 7 August, 1926.   [2] *M.F.G.B.* 16 August, 1926.
[3] *D.M.A.* 12 July, 1926.
[4] *M.F.G.B.* 30 July, 1926.   [5] *Ibid.* 16 August, 1926.

were experiencing similar difficulties and, after much discussion, it was decided by 428 votes to 360 to empower the Executive Committee to open negotiations with the coal-owners and the Government for a settlement of the dispute.[1]

The efforts of the Derbyshire and Nottinghamshire coal-owners to persuade the men to return to work were intensified during August. The most important move in this direction was that made by the Bolsover Colliery Company. On 19 August a hundred delegates from all the Company's pits met the directors at Edwinstowe to discuss terms for the resumption of work, which were similar to those offered by the Staveley Company. Previous rates were to be guaranteed for seven months. The men were to work a $7\frac{1}{2}$-hour day and the additional percentage paid to piece-workers was to be halved. The Company agreed to adhere to the $7\frac{1}{2}$-hour day regardless of any national settlement on the basis of an eight-hour day. Arrears of rent were not to be deducted during the first month of the new agreement and a loan of a pound after two days' work was offered to those in need of money.[2] The Grassmoor, Clay Cross and Sheepbridge companies all stated that they were willing to re-open their pits on the basis of a $7\frac{1}{2}$-hour day.

In an effort to prevent a wholesale drift back to work, A. J. Cook, accompanied by the Derbyshire officials, toured the county. He had already scandalized the district by a speech made in Nottinghamshire soon after Charles Markham's death, in which he had stated that Markham had offered to find him another job or capitalize his income for twenty years if he would advocate the eight-hour day.[3] (*Nihil de mortuis nisi bonum.*) On 24 August he was given a great reception by an audience of over 4,000 at Chesterfield. After singing *England Arise!* and *The Red Flag* they listened to Cook for nearly two hours. He advised Derbyshire and Nottinghamshire to stand firm:

No two counties had a greater chance to make good . . . but they could not make good unless there was a national agreement with a national minimum as high as possible and a seven-hour day to stop cheap coal being produced in other districts to flood the market. . . . Derbyshire had a glorious name and they should not let it be thrown at them that Mr. Hall, Mr. Spencer and their colleagues had to get up and apologize for blacklegs at a British conference.

At the end of the meeting Cook was carried from the hall shoulder high.[4]

Wherever he went in Derbyshire Cook was given the same hearty reception. Towards the end of his remarkable campaign he was

---

[1] *M.F.G.B.* 17 August, 1926.   [2] *Derbyshire Times,* 21 August, 1926.
[3] *Ibid.* 17 July, 1926.   [4] *Ibid.* 28 August, 1926.

practically exhausted and at Bolsover an appeal had to be made to the crowd to allow him to walk quietly to his car because of his physical condition. Cook's oratory filled many Derbyshire miners with renewed enthusiasm. 'The result was', stated the *Derbyshire Times*, 'that many men were kept from continuing or going to work. A considerable amount of feeling has been engendered in the dispute during the past few days, which up to this time has been absent.'[1] It was later alleged in the Chesterfield police court that Cook had incited the miners to violence.[2]

Until the end of August there was little disorder in Derbyshire. When Henry Webb, a Communist party organizer, was prosecuted at Chesterfield on 22 July for a speech made at Shirebrook, the chairman of the bench stated that the case was the first under the emergency regulations in the county. 'The conduct of the miners in Derbyshire up to now has been exemplary', he said.[3] A similar case arose at Clay Cross on 6 August when C. E. Mason, of Bakewell, was charged with 'making a speech calculated or likely to cause disaffection among the civil population'. When Mason was bound over by the magistrates, Samuel Sales and E. Marsden offered themselves as surety and were applauded by the miners in the court. The demonstrations against the outcrop workers were also mostly of a peaceful character. At Shirland a procession of 3,000 people, headed by jazz bands and miners carrying their lodge banners, heard speeches by Sales, Spencer, Hicken and Hall. Sales said that he did not believe in violence but thought passive resistance was the most powerful weapon of all. Hall asked the miners 'not to interfere with the Shirland Colliery or the outcrop workers'.[4]

The disorder at the end of August was largely provoked by the Home Secretary, Joynson-Hicks, who announced that every man who wished to return to work would be protected. Large reinforcements of police were sent into Derbyshire from Manchester and other centres. Enoch Overton, who was a magistrate, said:

He hoped that the police drafted into Bolsover during the past few days would be cleared out and the situation left to him to deal with. In that event he was prepared to guarantee that there would be no trouble, for he felt perfectly sure if he told the men to keep quiet they would respect his wishes.[5]

Frank Hall, who was an equally level-headed leader, stated:

We have had many obstacles and difficulties put in our way owing to the action of the coal-owners in demanding that there shall be sent into the district a number of police. It is hard to tell the exact numbers, but they

---

[1] *Derbyshire Times*, 28 August, 1926. [2] *Ibid.* 11 September, 1926.
[3] *Ibid.* 24 July, 1926.
[4] *Ibid.* [5] *Ibid.* 28 August, 1926.

must amount to several hundreds, possibly thousands, throughout the county. . . . I am surprised to know what took place without any aggravation or incitement at Holmewood on Wednesday, and also at Doe Lea, where I am informed the police bludgeoned the civilian population. . . . Martial law has not been proclaimed. Why men and women were driven into their houses I am at a loss to understand. . . . Not only have the police been ferocious, but their language and their threats are of the most abominable character.[1]

The police began to interfere with the rights of the trade unionists to picket the collieries. At Grassmoor they removed one of the Association's notice boards on the ground that it gave inaccurate information about the colliery.

'What have the police to do with the figures issued by either the colliery company or by the miners' offices?' asked Frank Hall. 'What business is it of theirs? Are they acting under instructions? And if so, whose instructions? We hear extraordinary accounts of them being used to knock men up and tell them what time to go to work, and of meeting men in the street and asking them what they are doing as they are not at work. Why should they be interfering with the liberties of the people to walk in the streets?'[2]

A Heath woman was fined 40s. for 'attempting to prevent men from working at the Holmewood Colliery' by chalking on the road: 'Don't be a scab!' Four Staveley miners were fined £5 each for 'taking action likely to restrict the supply of fuel' by intimidating a man who had returned to work.[3]

Prosecutions for 'violent and seditious speeches' also became increasingly numerous. John Davis, a Welsh miners' leader from the Rhondda Valley, was sentenced at Chesterfield to two months' imprisonment for making a speech 'calculated to cause disaffection'. An electrical engineer and an Indian journalist who came from London to address the Clay Cross and Alfreton miners were prosecuted for similar offences.[4] The Association decided to make itself responsible for the defence and payment of costs in all prosecutions in Derbyshire under the emergency regulations whether the accused were members of the union or not.[5] The Council also discussed the behaviour of the police. Several cases of 'prosecution for very frivolous charges' were mentioned and complaints were made about 'bad language' and 'interference with the legitimate procedure of picketing'. The advice of Arthur Neal, the Sheffield solicitor, had been sought. He commented:

If last Wednesday's cases are a sample, they are taking actions on most frivolous grounds, on the *ex parte* statements of men who are working. . . .

[1] *Derbyshire Times*, 28 August, 1926.   [2] *Ibid.* 11 September, 1926.
[3] *Ibid.* 4 September, 1926.
[4] *Ibid.* 25 September, 1926.   [5] *D.M.A.* 25 September, 1926.

I think strong representations should be made to the Chief Constable and support in this action should be got, if possible, from prominent members of the County Council.[1]

When the emergency regulations came before the House of Commons for renewal at the end of September there was the usual acrimonious debate. Joynson-Hicks stated that the increase in the number of prosecutions during the previous month had been greatest in Nottinghamshire, Derbyshire, Staffordshire and Warwickshire, where the return to work was most marked. In Nottinghamshire, where the number of men at work had increased from about 600 on 22 August to 17,678 on 24 September, there had been 20 prosecutions, as compared with none in the previous month. In Derbyshire, where the number at work had risen from 6,000 to over 20,000 the number of prosecutions had gone up from 4 to 131.[2]

X

Meanwhile the Executive Committee of the M.F.G.B. was carrying out its instructions to re-open negotiations with the coal-owners and the Government. The owners insisted on district settlements and refused to negotiate on the basis of a national agreement.[3] On 31 August, in a debate on the mining situation in the House of Commons, Churchill made it clear that the Government would take no further action. The coal-owners' spokesmen re-emphasized their rejection of national negotiations. A speech by George Spencer, the Nottinghamshire miners' leader, gave the coal-owners much encouragement. Herbert Wragg, the Member for Belper, complimenting Spencer on his 'very moderate speech', said: 'Had he been in control of the negotiations on behalf of the Miners' Federation from the beginning there would have been no stoppage, or if there had been a stoppage, it would have been over months ago.'[4]

The position in Nottinghamshire was already causing some concern. On the day Spencer made his speech in the House of Commons the Executive Committee of the M.F.G.B. considered a request from the Nottinghamshire Miners' Association, presented by Frank Varley, for permission to meet the owners locally and discuss possible terms of settlement. Herbert Smith ruled the question out of order on the ground that it was 'directly contrary to the Federation policy'.[5] At a special conference of the M.F.G.B. on 2 September it was reported by W. Carter that there were between 7,000 and 8,000 men, including safety men, at work in Nottinghamshire. At the Bolsover Company's

---

[1] *D.M.A.* 25 September, 1926.　　　　　　　　[2] 199 H.C. Deb. 5s. 411–12.
[3] *M.F.G.B.* 19 and 26 August, 1926.
[4] 199 H.C. Deb. 5s. 184.　　　　　　　　　　[5] *M.F.G.B.* 2 September, 1926.

three pits between 6,000 and 7,000 men (about 65 per cent. of the required labour force) were back at work. Carter stated:

After the meetings took place, some three or four of the collieries imported police, and charges are being made of a wholesale character; men brought to the courts on the most trivial offences; there is almost a state of terror in these particular districts.[1]

John Spencer gave a more heartening account of the efforts which had been made to maintain solidarity in Derbyshire:

We got to work, however, as officials, as lodge committees and lodge officials and no men could have worked harder, more nobly, or more faithfully. We also started a rousing campaign right through the county; friends from Wales, Yorkshire, friends of the I.L.P. came along and helped us, and I am pleased to say that through our efforts, we absolutely stopped any rot setting in so far as the Derbyshire miners were concerned. They were telling us (the coal-owners), on the Friday and Saturday, after our conference on the Wednesday, when the men were signing on, that 20 Cooks would not stop the rot in Nottinghamshire and Derbyshire. Well, I am pleased to say with the assistance we gave Mr. Cook, one Cook stopped the rot so far as Derbyshire is concerned. I am bound to say if I understand the psychology of the men, they are more determined today than ever in the history of the struggle. So far as we are concerned, we have at the coal face today, right through the county, about 3,400 at work—not the 8, 9, 10 or 15,000 as reported in the Press. We have 3,400 who ought not to be at work—coal face men. That is our position. Now our greatest weakness is the Bolsover Colliery Company. They have been the villains of the piece, and of course, we have had to put in the strongest efforts there. . . . We are up against a very serious position in helping our men having regard to what is happening in the Mansfield and in some parts of the Nottinghamshire coalfield.[2]

The conference decided that the Executive Committee should continue its efforts to negotiate a national settlement. On the following day the Federation wrote to Winston Churchill asking him to arrange a joint meeting with the Mining Association. 'We are prepared', stated the letter, 'to enter into negotiations for a new national agreement with a view to a reduction in labour costs to meet the immediate necessities of the industry.'[3] When Churchill met representatives of the Mining Association, on 6 September, Evan Williams reminded them that the Government had urged the owners to offer relatively high terms in certain districts in order to bring about 'a breakaway, piecemeal, district by district'. A national agreement, he said, was incompatible with this policy.[4] The Prime Minister then formulated proposals for

[1] *M.F.G.B.* 2 September, 1926.   [2] *Ibid.*   [3] *Ibid.* 3 September, 1926.
[4] Miners' Federation of Great Britain, *The Coal Situation, Note of a Meeting between His Majesty's Ministers and the Mining Association*, 6 September, 1926, pp. 14–15.

district settlements 'with national supervision' which were sent to the M.F.G.B. on 17 September. Provisional settlements were to be reached in each district after which the Government would set up a statutory National Arbitration Tribunal to confirm or modify the local agreements at the request of either party where there was any increase in hours.[1]

On 21 September the Executive Committee rejected these proposals on the ground that they involved 'the entire surrender of the principle of national negotiations and agreements, a principle which the Commission stated (Report, pages 152-3) to be essential'.[2] At nine o'clock that night the miners' leaders were summoned to Downing Street where they told the Prime Minister that they would recommend an immediate resumption of work temporarily at wages prevailing under the 1921 agreement and that they were prepared to submit the terms of a national wages agreement to an independent tribunal, which should also consider putting into effect the recommendations of the Samuel Commission.[3] Three days later the Prime Minister replied that the miners' proposals did not 'afford the means of reaching an early or lasting settlement of the present dispute'.[4]

At a M.F.G.B. conference on 29 September it was decided to refer the Executive Committee's report of these negotiations and the Government's proposals to the districts. John Spencer reported that 10,100 men had returned to work in Derbyshire:

There is no denying the fact that the position in our county has gradually become worse. It is very regrettable. At some collieries where our own coal face men are standing as solid as a rock with the Federation, from outlying districts they are coming in buses, char-a-bancs, and other conveyances to such an extent that some of the collieries have actually got their full complement of men and just about to turn double shifts as they had been doing prior to the stoppage. Not only that, another regrettable thing is this, these unscrupulous men who have come into the pits have also appointed their own checkweighmen, and the men who have been checkweighmen there as long as 30 years and over—well—we don't know what their position will be in the future. . . . I am sorry to have to report on behalf of our county this morning that our men are dribbling back. That is our position.

W. Carter stated that the situation in Nottinghamshire was even worse. At a Council meeting on 25 September it had been reported that there were 13,000 men at work. 'Since then', said Carter, 'we have not had the Derbyshire dribble but the Notts. deluge. I can say with some certainty that so far as Notts. is concerned it would not be an incorrect

[1] Miners' Federation of Great Britain, *The Coal Situation, Note of a Meeting between His Majesty's Ministers and the Mining Association*, 6 September, 1926, p. 28.
[2] *Ibid.* p. 29.   [3] *Ibid.* p. 30.   [4] *Ibid.* p. 31.

computation to say there were 16,000 to 17,000 at work.' George Spencer recommended the acceptance of the Government's proposals:

Now if we are going to fight on, does anyone think for one moment that we are going to succeed in achieving our original object? Is there any man in this conference who thinks that? I think we had better face realities, and what are we going to gain by prolonging this struggle for another fortnight or three weeks?[1]

The Derbyshire miners also favoured the acceptance of the Government's proposals, although they advocated two important amendments:

(1) That any district irrespective of whether the old hours are worked or not, be free to apply to the National Tribunal.

(2) That all questions in the provisional agreements—hours, wages, ratio, or any matter dealt with in such agreement—be open to be dealt with in any appeal to the Tribunal.

The Council decided by 51 votes to 22 to recommend this policy to the branches. It was adopted by 25,800 votes to 12,200.[2] Derbyshire and Leicestershire were the only districts supporting the acceptance of the Government's proposals at the adjourned M.F.G.B. conference on 7 September. A militant resolution from South Wales calling for a return to 'the *status quo* conditions' was carried by 589 to 199, with Scotland, Derbyshire, Nottinghamshire, Leicestershire and the small counties voting against it. The South Wales resolution enumerated the methods by which its objective was to be achieved. Safety men were to be withdrawn; efforts were to be made to secure an embargo on all imported coal and to bring an end to outcrop working; a special congress of the trade unions was to be asked to arrange a levy in support of the miners; and there was to be an intensive propaganda campaign. On the recommendation of the Executive Committee these proposals were referred to the districts.[3]

The conference also discussed the situation in Nottinghamshire. It had been reported in the *Nottingham Evening Post* on 6 October that George Spencer had negotiated with the employers for a resumption of work at the Digby Colliery. Spencer was summoned to attend the conference on the following day to give an explanation. He showed a certain pride in his achievement. 'I don't regret it', he said, 'and I do not plead extenuating circumstances. I believe I did the best day's work in my life for these men, and you can pass your sentence.' A. J. Cook replied:

I hope this conference will treat Mr. Spencer as they would treat a blackleg. Mr. Spencer is a blackleg of the worst order. A conscious blackleg. I want

[1] *M.F.G.B.* 29 September, 1926.
[2] *D.M.A.* 1 and 9 October, 1926.
[3] *M.F.G.B.* 7 October, 1926.

to say here that Notts. has been more responsible for the present position we are in, and Mr. Spencer is more responsible for Notts. than any other district in the coalfield. That is the opinion of Derbyshire, and the opinion of everyone else. While we are fighting, Mr. Spencer is prepared to accept a reduction, and advocated a district agreement in his own district.

By an almost unanimous vote Spencer was ordered to leave the conference and his expulsion from the union and suspension as a miners' Member of Parliament were referred to the Nottinghamshire Miners' Association.[1]

A. J. Cook spent the following week-end in Derbyshire. 'I ought to have been at the Labour Party conference in Margate,' he said, 'but I have no heart to attend while my own men are not true.' Everywhere he appealed to the men not to work. At Ripley he asserted: 'The names of Hodges and Spencer stink in the nostrils of honest men.' At Staveley he complained about the 'bribery and corruption' of the employers who had 'even scab recruiting agencies'. At Clay Cross he told the men that neither he nor Herbert Smith would ever agree to terms which meant longer hours in the mining industry. 'I will sweep the roads first', he said. John Spencer told the Alfreton miners: 'No man could have worked harder than Mr. Cook to stem the tide. On Monday he was at it for 15 hours.' The miners gave Cook a hearty reception. The men from Shirebrook and Langwith marched in procession to Warsop, headed by a jazz band, in order to hear his speech.[2]

From Derbyshire Cook went into Nottinghamshire. On Tuesday, 12 October, he was reported to have held 'a hastily arranged conference in a wayside inn with members of the Nottinghamshire Miners' Association'. Frank Varley was present and the meeting was said to have been 'of a lively character'. Speaking later at Old Basford, Cook said: 'I understand the Government are going to proscribe this area. I have been informed, I do not know with what truth, that if on Thursday the Federation's policy is to continue to fight, they are talking about declaring martial law in Derbyshire, Nottinghamshire and the Midlands.' At Selston he declared: 'In Nottinghamshire you are like a lot of sheep without a shepherd. Every man's hand is against everybody else, because there has not been here as there has been in other districts, a straight, honest lead given.'[3]

The Derbyshire miners decided, by 28,300 votes to 2,650, to support the South Wales proposals for the continuation of the struggle.[4] The policy was also endorsed nationally by 460,150 votes to 284,336.[5] On 15 October the Executive Committee of the M.F.G.B. agreed, as part of the propaganda campaign, to hold its future meetings in the coalfields.

[1] M.F.G.B. 8 October, 1926.   [2] Derbyshire Times, 16 October, 1926.
[3] Ibid.   [4] Ibid.   [5] M.F.G.B. 13 October, 1926.

The next meeting of the Committee, on 19 October, was held at the offices of the Nottinghamshire Miners' Association. Frank Varley, who after his initial vacillation had decided to stand by the Federation's policy, reported that twenty-five members of the Council had been suspended for resuming work. The Executive Committee interviewed the recalcitrant delegates in an attempt to persuade them to be loyal to the Federation. Meetings were arranged throughout the county and also in Derbyshire.[1] Speaking at Chesterfield, on 20 October, Herbert Smith said: 'Derbyshire helped to build this Federation up, and I am not going to let you pull it down.'[2]

Meanwhile the Nottinghamshire and Derbyshire coal-owners were doing their utmost to induce the miners to accept their terms. Early in October J. P. Houfton, of the Bolsover Company, stated that he hoped the Nottinghamshire and Derbyshire officials would soon negotiate district settlements. He said: 'In the very forefront of these agreements will be: "It is hereby agreed that no man who has returned to work pending the district settlement shall be victimized."' Houfton was willing to embody in a five- or seven-year agreement the terms which the Company was then offering and to introduce a scheme for pensions at 65.[3] Frank Hall commented:

The longer hours, the reduction in the minima, the increase in the ratio in the owners' favour of £2 out of every £100, besides the reduction of the subsistence wage, give the owners conditions which never in the history of the industry have they enjoyed. . . . There are no less than 11,000 men employed by the Bolsover Colliery Company. The half-hour a day extra which the men are asked to work without remuneration is equal to the employment of 700 men without wages.[4]

Houfton himself stated, on 3 November, that the 8,740 men who had returned to work at the Company's five pits were, with the longer working day, producing as much coal as when between 10,000 and 11,000 men were at work. 'They were today saving the wages of 1,000 men,' he said. 'The men who had not gone back they did not want, and when a general settlement took place they would not allow the leaders to insist upon these men going back to their old jobs.'[5]

At the M.F.G.B. conference on 4 November W. Carter reported that about half of the Nottinghamshire miners, some 40,000 men and boys, had returned to work. George Spencer and his followers were already negotiating a district settlement for Nottinghamshire. Carter told the conference:

We know, so far as the owners are concerned, that they are giving every possible assistance to this unofficial body to enter into a district settlement.

[1] *M.F.G.B.* 19 October, 1926.   [2] *Derbyshire Times*, 23 October, 1926.
[3] *Ibid.* 16 October, 1926.   [4] *Ibid.* 23 October, 1926.   [5] *Ibid.* 6 November, 1926.

. . . Now our Council meeting passed a resolution, so far as the nature of the activities of the unofficial body was concerned with respect to any agreement, that we absolutely repudiated it. What do we find? We find that we have men who have been loyal and true to the Federation, who are still on the altar of sacrifice, and have wives and children practically starving, and we have men who have got their cards from the employer saying that they have done, so far as that pit is concerned.[1]

When Frank Varley and his colleagues tried to negotiate with the Bolsover Company they were told that they did not represent the miners since the majority of them had gone back to work. 'Nobody knows where Mr. Frank Varley is', said Houfton. 'I don't think Mr. Varley knows himself. If ever there was a man who represented workmen, and a great constituency like Mansfield, and has wobbled as he has, I have yet to meet him.'[2]

Towards the end of November the Spencer group signed a five-year agreement with the Nottinghamshire coal-owners. Ramsay MacDonald was reported to have sent his congratulations to George Spencer 'on the efforts he has put forward to secure district settlements'.[3] On 22 November, thirty-nine delegates from Nottinghamshire and Derbyshire pits met at the Victoria Hotel, Nottingham, and decided to form the Nottinghamshire and District Miners' Industrial Union. B. Smith was elected Chairman; W. Crans, Vice-Chairman; and R. Gascoyne, Secretary. 'After a lengthy discussion', state the minutes, 'Mr. G. A. Spencer was elected as leader of the men at work represented.'[4] This nebulous definition of Spencer's position in the new union had the advantage of enabling him to assert that he had not organized the union but had been invited to become its leader. The meeting decided to ask the coal-owners in the district covered by the agreement to deduct a shilling a week from wages. Half of this contribution was to be used for superannuation purposes. It was also agreed 'that no funds be used for any political purposes whatsoever'.[5] Spencer's expulsion from the M.F.G.B. and the Labour Party did not prevent him from continuing to represent Broxtowe in the House of Commons. However, as 'leader' of a 'non-political' union he now spoke from the Liberal benches.[6]

As the men drifted back to work the operation of the emergency regulations became more stringent than ever. Frank Lee complained that policemen had been present at the miners' branch meetings at Bolsover and other places.[7] Shapurji Saklatvala, the Parsee Communist M.P. for North Battersea, was told by the Alfreton police that all

---

[1] *M.F.G.B.* 4 November, 1926.   [2] *Derbyshire Times*, 6 November, 1926.
[3] *Ibid.* 20 November, 1926.
[4] Minutes of the Nottinghamshire and District Miners' Industrial Union, 22 November, 1926.   [5] *Ibid.*
[6] *Derbyshire Times*, 7 May, 1927.   [7] *Ibid.* 23 October, 1926.

public meetings in the district were banned.[1] Tom Mullins was likewise prohibited from speaking at Clowne and Frank Lee raised the
matter in the House of Commons. Joynson-Hicks stated that the
speech was considered by the police 'as likely to cause disaffection'.
Asked by another member if he did not think that his own speeches
caused disaffection, Joynson-Hicks replied, amidst laughter: 'Honestly,
I do not think they do.'[2] There were further exchanges with Joynson-
Hicks after A. V. Williams was prohibited from speaking at Ripley on
17 November. Joynson-Hicks justified the action of the police by
stating that Williams had been prosecuted during the General Strike
'for issuing one of those lying bulletins, which are well known to hon.
Members'.[3]

When David Kirkwood and James Maxton visited Derbyshire they
both came into conflict with the police. Maxton, who was prohibited
from speaking at Staveley, described the action of the police as 'deliberate
interference with freedom of speech'.[4] Kirkwood appeared in court
at Eckington on 15 November to face various charges under the
emergency regulations. He was accompanied by Maxton, Neil
MacLean, Campbell Stephen and Tom Johnson, all Clydeside M.P.s,
and by Saklatvala. Kirkwood asked for an adjournment on the ground
that 'great constitutional principles' were involved. When the irrepressible Maxton was ordered to be silent, Kirkwood remarked gravely:
'That was Mr. James Maxton, M.P., addressing you.' Maxton was
eventually told to leave the court. After the case had been adjourned
the politicians were greeted outside the court by a crowd singing *The
Red Flag*. At the railway station the police were held back by the throng
while Kirkwood delivered a farewell speech. 'The general working-
class movement of Great Britain is turned towards Derbyshire', he
said. 'Therefore, my comrades, be of good cheer. We shall win in the
end.'[5] A week later Kirkwood returned to Eckington where he was
fined £25. There were again disturbances outside the court and several
people were arrested.[6]

XI

The Federation was fighting the last stages of what was now a hopeless
battle. The response of the transport unions to the request for an
embargo on the movement of coal had been discouraging. The T.U.C.
had declined to impose a compulsory levy in support of the miners
but had recommended a voluntary contribution of a penny a day by

---

[1] *Derbyshire Times*, 13 November, 1926.   [2] 199 H.C. Deb. 5s. 1932–3.
[3] 200 H.C. Deb. 5s. 516.   [4] *Derbyshire Times*, 20 November, 1926.
[5] *Ibid.*   [6] *Ibid.* 27 November, 1926.

each member of the affiliated unions. The General Council had been negotiating with the Government in an attempt to bring the dispute to an end on the basis of district settlements made in accordance with 'certain agreed national principles'. The M.F.G.B. conference of 4–5 November empowered the Executive Committee to take part in those negotiations. A further conference, which was in session from 10 to 13 November, considered the Government's proposals and authorized the Executive Committee 'to continue the negotiations with the Government unfettered'.[1]

On 12 November the Government's latest proposals were considered. They included an immediate resumption of work by means of district settlements, 'the hours to be worked not being excluded from the district negotiations'. The owners in every district except Northumberland, Durham, Cumberland and North Wales were willing to pay temporarily a general district percentage on basic rates not less than that prevailing on 30 April. The men were to be reinstated 'as opportunity offers without prejudice to the men at present at work'. Permanent district agreements were to be regarded as 'standard' agreements if they provided for a district board with an independent chairman, ascertainments, a ratio of wages to profits of between 87 : 13 and 85 : 15, a minimum of 20 per cent. above the standard wage, and payment of subsistence wages at the previous rates. Such agreements were to be for three years. The Government agreed to establish a national arbitral authority for a period of six months to consider appeals by either party to all agreements which were not 'standard' provided that they were based on a longer working day.[2]

The delegates to the special conference were dismayed by these unfavourable terms. For over six months they had resisted district agreements, the longer working day and lower wages. All these undesirable changes would inevitably follow their acceptance of the Government's proposals. The conference asked for further explanations. The Government's replies were not encouraging. On the other hand, the M.F.G.B. was obviously beaten. The men had been virtually starved into submission and were drifting back to work in varying proportions in every district. South Wales, with 129,000 miners, had only 6,000 at work. Durham had 3,018 at work out of 120,000; Northumberland, 6,000 out of 56,000. At the other extreme were counties like Leicestershire with 6,700 at work out of 7,000; Nottinghamshire with 44,000 out of 51,000; and Derbyshire with 36,000 out of 47,000. The conference decided, by 432 to 352, to recommend the acceptance of the Government's proposals.[3]

---

[1] *M.F.G.B.* 10 November, 1926.
[2] *Ibid.* 12 November, 1926.　　　　　[3] *Ibid.* 10–13 November, 1926.

Derbyshire decided to accept the proposals, for the position in the county was becoming daily more serious. A number of delegates had been suspended for resuming work, several branches were unrepresented on the Council, and there were fears that if the dispute continued, the Association would disintegrate as the Nottinghamshire Miners' Association had done. When the M.F.G.B. conference assembled on 19 November it was reported that the proposed settlement had been rejected by 480,806 votes to 313,200. After much discussion the conference saved its face by recommending the districts to open negotiations with the owners and instructing the Executive Committee to formulate general principles for the guidance of the districts in their negotiations. No district was to enter into a final settlement until a further conference had received reports of all the negotiations.[1]

On the following day the Executive Committee's guiding principles were approved by the conference. They were as follows:

1. The method of ascertaining the district percentage on basis rates to be as provided by the National Wages Agreement of 1924.
2. The ratio of division of net proceeds to be 87 : 13.
3. The minimum percentage to be provided of not less than 20 per cent. upon the standard wages prevailing on April 30th, 1926.
4. The payment of April, 1926, subsistence wages to low paid day-wage men.
5. All agreements to be terminable by one month's notice from either side.
6. Districts to endeavour to effect the complete reinstatement of all men and boys employed at April 30th, 1926, on the lines provided by Clause 13 of the National Wages Agreement of 1921.[2]

On his return to Derbyshire Frank Hall made a joint application with W. Carter, of the Nottinghamshire Miners' Association, to the Midland Counties Colliery Owners' Association for a meeting to consider the arrangements for a district agreement embracing the two counties. The owners stated that they were not prepared to meet Carter or any other official of the Nottinghamshire Miners' Association and that they regarded George Spencer as the representative of the Nottinghamshire miners. They agreed to meet the Derbyshire officials separately. The Council of the Derbyshire Miners' Association decided to accept the invitation and also to issue a circular condemning the Spencer agreement. Meetings between the coal-owners' representatives and the miners' leaders began on 25 November at the Midland Hotel, Derby.[3] By 27 November an agreement had been drafted which, in the words of the official statement issued after the meeting, 'shall follow exactly the terms embodied in the agreement made between the Nottinghamshire

[1] M.F.G.B. 19 November, 1926.   [2] Ibid. 20 November, 1926.
[3] D.M.A. 23 November, 1926; Derbyshire Times, 27 November, 1926.

and District Colliery Owners and representatives of the workmen
working at Notts. and district collieries, dated November 20th, 1926'.
The Derbyshire miners had been obliged to accept the Spencer agreement. It was signed on 29 November. 'Our conversation ended very
pleasantly,' said Frank Hall, 'and I was presented with a gold-mounted
fountain pen by Mr. H. E. Mitton.'[1]

The Derbyshire delegates to the M.F.G.B. conference on 26 November were unable to report on their new agreement as the negotiations
had not been completed. Most of the districts complained bitterly
about the terms which had been imposed upon them by the coal-
owners. It was recorded:

> That this conference expresses its indignation at the terms offered by the
> coal-owners in the several districts, and invites the attention of the Cabinet
> to the action of the employers in Notts., Bristol, Leicester, Kent, in refusing
> to meet the accredited representatives of our members.

Frank Varley said of the Spencer group:

> They represent nobody but themselves except such men as were from the
> Bolsover Collieries. I am not sure there were not 12 men in the 30 represent-
> ing three collieries only. We can only say that they were some of the lick-
> spittles who hang round the colliery.[2]

The conference gave no formal recognition that the dispute was at an
end since the matter was now in the hands of the districts but within
a few days every district had capitulated. The Derbyshire officials
instructed the men to return to work immediately after the signing of
the new agreement.[3]

The agreement came into operation on 1 December and was for a
period of five years, after which it was terminable by six months'
notice. The length of the working day was increased from 7 to $7\frac{1}{2}$ hours
($5\frac{1}{2}$ hours on Saturdays) and the addition to the wages of piece-workers
was reduced to 7 per cent. Surface workers were given a $46\frac{1}{2}$-hour
week. The ratio of wages to profits was 85 : 15 instead of 87 : 13. The
minimum percentage addition to the basic rates was reduced from
46·67 (which was equivalent to $33\frac{1}{3}$ per cent. on 'standard' wages) to
38 (which was still above the 20 per cent. on 'standard' wages recommended by the M.F.G.B.). The immediate effect of the agreement was
to increase wage rates from the previous minimum of 46·67 per cent.
on basic rates (where they had stood before the General Strike) to
90 per cent. Thereafter they were to fall to 80 per cent. in January,
1927, 70 per cent. in March, and 60 per cent. in June. From September,

---

[1] *Derbyshire Times*, 4 December, 1926.
[2] *M.F.G.B.* 26 November, 1926.   [3] *D.M.A.* 30 November, 1926.

1927, by which time it was evidently thought that the post-strike boom would have completely subsided, wages were to depend upon the condition of the industry as shown by the district ascertainments, which were to begin in May, 1927. The agreement also embodied an alteration in the system of recoupment. Previously the recoupment clauses had allowed for deficiencies in the profits fund to be made good from subsequent surpluses. Now deficiencies were not to be carried forward beyond 30 April in any year.[1] On 30 November the Council of the Derbyshire Miners' Association resolved:

> That we express our disappointment with the Agreement which has been entered into by the Officials and Deputation, which provides for a longer working day with a less ratio and a reduced minimum, as we have always been led to believe by the Owners that in a District Settlement Derbyshire would be able to improve their position, and that they had everything to gain by a District Settlement, whereas this agreement does not provide for these favourable conditions indicated by the Coal Owners.[2]

Thus ended the greatest dispute the British coal industry had ever experienced. There was much sympathy with the miners who had been hopelessly defeated. The *Manchester Guardian*, the *Daily News* and other responsible newspapers accused Baldwin and the Government of bad faith, and of deliberately choosing a fight to the finish. The funds of the miners' unions were exhausted. Trade unions and labour movements in all parts of the world had contributed to the M.F.G.B. Relief Fund a total of £1,813,680. Of this, £1,161,459 had been contributed by the Russian trade unions, a fact which led to allegations that the dispute was being financed by 'Soviet gold'. However, when it is remembered that the M.F.G.B. had some 785,000 members, it will be seen that the Russian contribution did not go very far towards financing a seven-month dispute. The miners and their families suffered serious privations because they believed that important principles were at stake. The funds of the Derbyshire Miners' Association were exhausted by mid-July and for the remaining four-and-a-half months the 35,000 to 11,000 strikers and their families were supported by a contribution of £69,260 from the M.F.G.B. Relief Fund. Poverty and the combined forces of the coal-owners and the Government had proved too much for the miners.

A. J. Cook believed that the strike had failed for other reasons. He told the Yorkshire miners:

> They were forced, through circumstances over which they had no control, to go back, not because the employers or the Government had beaten them, but because the men in Nottinghamshire and Derbyshire and the Midlands

[1] See Appendix I to this chapter.   [2] *D.M.A.* 30 November, 1926.

had gone back. That had been the canker that had been eating at the heart of the Federation. . . . They had been forced to retreat because the rank and file of the trade union had not recognized as it ought to have done, all that was involved in the struggle.[1]

Nottinghamshire and Derbyshire had the misfortune to be the areas in which the coal-owners were able to offer comparatively favourable terms in order to break the strike. In George Spencer the Nottingham-shire employers had found a willing tool. The Derbyshire leaders had shown greater integrity but had been able to do little to stiffen the resistance of the rank and file. The beginning of the drift back to work had coincided with the exhaustion of the Association's funds. The defection of Nottinghamshire and Derbyshire undoubtedly hastened the end of the dispute but even if there had been no partial resumption of work the scales were already heavily weighted against the M.F.G.B. The trade union movement as a whole, still recovering from the fiasco of the General Strike, was either reluctant or unable to help the miners. The Government and the coal-owners became increasingly determined to enforce district settlements. In these circumstances it is difficult to see how the dispute could have ended successfully for the miners.

[1] *Derbyshire Times*, 4 December, 1926.

APPENDIX I

The Derbyshire Agreement, 1926

Agreement made between the Colliery Owners of the Derbyshire District (exclusive of South Derbyshire) and Representatives of the Workmen working at the Collieries in the Derbyshire District (exclusive of South Derbyshire)

1. A District Wages Board (hereinafter called 'the Board') shall be constituted consisting in equal numbers of persons chosen by the coal-owners in the district and persons who are employed or have been employed at Collieries in the District chosen by the workmen employed at Collieries in the District. The Board shall draw up its own rules of procedure which shall include a provision for the appointment of an independent Chairman.

2. The wages payable in the District during any period shall be expressed in the form of a percentage of the basis rates then prevailing and shall be periodically adjusted in accordance with the results of the industry as ascertained in the District.

3. The amount of the percentage to be paid in the District during any period shall be determined by the results of the industry in the District during a previous period (hereinafter called the period of ascertainment) as ascertained by returns to be made by the owners, checked by joint test audit of the owners' books carried out by independent firms of Accountants appointed by each side.

4. Subject to the provisions of Clause 8 hereof, in order to determine the percentage payable in the district in accordance with Clause 3, 85 (eighty-five) per cent. of the difference between the proceeds and the costs of production other than wages in the District during the period of ascertainment shall be taken. From the amount so determined shall be deducted the amount paid during the like period as allowances under Clause 6, and the balance so remaining shall be expressed as a percentage of the wages paid at basis rates during the period of ascertainment.

5. Wages in the District shall not be paid at lower rates than basis rates plus 38 (thirty-eight) per cent. thereof.

6. To any adult able-bodied day wage workmen whose rate per shift, after adding district percentage, is less than 8/9 (eight shillings and ninepence), a subsistence wage shall be paid sufficient to bring him up to 8/9 (eight shillings and ninepence) provided that the maximum addition in any instance shall not exceed 6d. (sixpence) per shift. This wage applies only to ordinary working time.

Provided also that no adult able-bodied day wage workman shall be paid a gross rate, including the subsistence wage, of less than 7/11 (seven shillings and elevenpence) per shift on his ordinary working time, not including overtime.

7. The hours of work per shift for manipulators of coal above and below ground shall be half an hour longer than those in operation in the District

above and below ground respectively on April 30th, 1926. The percentage payable to piece-workers shall be 7 (seven) per cent., in place of 14·17 per cent.

8. If the amount of the ascertained proceeds in respect of any period of ascertainment is less than the sum of the amounts of (1) costs other than wages, (2) the cost of wages at the minimum rates as provided for in Clause 5, and of allowances paid during such period under Clause 6, and (3) an amount equal to 15/85ths (fifteen-eighty-fifths) of the cost of such wages and allowances, the deficiency shall be carried forward and dealt with in subsequent periods of ascertainment according to the following method so as to secure effective recoupment thereof:

In any ascertainment in which the amount of the proceeds is greater than the amount required to meet (1) costs other than wages, (2) the cost of wages at the minimum provided for in Clause 5, and of allowances paid during the period of ascertainment under Clause 6 hereof, and (3) an amount equal to 15/85ths (fifteen-eighty-fifths) of the cost of such wages and allowances, the balance shall be applied so far as may be necessary to make good any deficiency brought forward from previous ascertainments. Of that part of the balance which remains after meeting the deficiency, 85 (eighty-five) per cent. shall be applied to wages. If there be no balance available for meeting a deficiency or if the deficiency brought forward exceeds the balance, the deficiency or such portion thereof as remains shall be again carried forward to be made good in a subsequent period or periods according to the above method.

Provided that no deficiency shall be carried forward for recoupment purposes beyond the 30th April in any year.

The first ascertainment period shall be May, June and July, 1927.

9. The District shall comprise the Derbyshire District (exclusive of South Derbyshire) and shall only be varied by the decision of the Board.

10. In ascertaining the proceeds, wages and costs of production other than wages, the Accountants shall follow the principles set out in the Schedule hereto, and any amendment or addition to such principles which may hereafter be adopted by the Board.

11. The basis rates payable by the owners for the months of December, 1926, and until the end of August, 1927, shall carry percentages as follows:

90 (ninety) per cent. on basis rates for December, 1926.
80 (eighty) per cent. on basis rates for January and February, 1927.
70 (seventy) per cent. on basis rates for March, April and May, 1927.
60 (sixty) per cent. on basis rates for June, July and August, 1927.

The wages payable by the owners for the month of September, 1927, shall be based upon the ascertained results of the months of May, June and July, 1927, those for the month of October upon the ascertained results of the months of June, July and August, and so on, unless and until the periods of ascertainment thereafter are varied by the Board.

12. The period of the duration of this agreement shall be to the 31st December, 1931, and thereafter until terminated by 6 (six) months' notice on either side given on the first day of any month following.

Dated this 29th day of November, 1926.

(Signed) For and on behalf of THE COAL OWNERS of the Derbyshire District (exclusive of South Derbyshire)—	(Signed) For and on behalf of THE WORKMEN working at Collieries in the Derbyshire District (exclusive of South Derbyshire)—
H. EUSTACE MITTON G. M. JACKSON F. CHAMBERS G. NICHOLSON JNO. T. TODD HUBERT O. BISHOP J. W. LAMONBY ALFRED HEWLETT GEO. SPENCER L. WARD WALTERS	FRANK HALL JOHN SPENCER HENRY HICKEN ROBERT A. BAILEY JOSEPH E. KIRK THOS. EDWARDS OLIVER WRIGHT THOMAS KYTE

Witness to all the foregoing signatures—
WILLIAM SAUNDERS,
Regent Buildings,
London Road,
Derby.

CHAPTER XIX

WAGES, DISPUTES AND INDUSTRIAL POLICY,
1927–39

I

The years following the 1926 stoppage were some of the worst the miners had ever experienced. The higher wage rates which they received for the first few months in no way corresponded with the temporary sharp increase in the price of coal. As the trade returned to normal wages were gradually reduced in accordance with the terms of the settlement until, in September, 1927, they were regulated by the district ascertainments. Then the miners had to face the harsh realities of the state of the coal industry and its effect upon their wages as a result of the new agreement. Wages in Derbyshire dropped immediately to the miminum and were to remain there, or only slightly above, throughout the years of economic depression. Indeed the only redeeming feature of the agreement was that the minimum was fixed at a point which prevented wage rates from falling to the starvation level dictated by the district ascertainments. In September, 1927, the ascertained percentage addition to basic rates was only 16·17. It was to fall even lower. Month after month the employers had to make good the difference between the ascertained percentage and the minimum percentage. Year after year the deficiencies in standard profits had to be wiped off the books.

The coal-owners' insistence on district settlements and the longer working day had served only to aggravate the problems of the coal industry. The reduction in costs, which they had achieved at the expense of the miners, enabled them to reduce their prices and engage once more in internecine competition. Keynes held the longer working day as a temporary policy for aiding existing over-production to be 'half-witted'.[1] The Samuel Commission had shown that the extension of hours would result in an increased output of 30 million tons of coal

[1] J. M. Keynes, 'The Need of Peace by Negotiation', *New Republic*, 19 May, 1926, p. 395, cited in Crook, *op. cit.* p. 344n.

for which a market was not likely to be found, or else the unemployment of 130,000 more miners, which would throw the cost of their keep upon the nation.[1] Frank Hall told the Chesterfield Rotary Club:

I think that the owners made a terrible blunder in seeking to recoup themselves out of wages. They ought to have increased prices, and followed the example of the railway companies, who, when they were unable to pay dividends and had to fall back on reserves, increased the cost of carriage in this country, and did not seek to recoup themselves out of the wages of the railwaymen.[2]

Taking into account the variations in hours and ratios, Hall estimated that the new minimum rates in Derbyshire were equivalent to a reduction of $17\frac{1}{2}$ per cent. on the basic rates.[3] Moreover, short time and unemployment were widespread. In March, 1927, the Staveley Company introduced a system whereby the men worked one week in two. J. Hunter, the Company's colliery agent, explained: 'The new working arrangements would allow the men to obtain unemployment pay for the week they were not at work. If they had been put on three days a week they would not have been eligible for the unemployment benefit.'[4] Two months later, when the seasonal decline in trade had started, the *Derbyshire Times* reported: 'Men are only working as a rule about two days a week in Derbyshire, and in many cases the miners are actually shorter of money than they were during the strike.'[5] Nor was there much improvement in the following winter. In November Frank Hall stated:

The average wage in Derbyshire is 10s. 7·12d. per day, but as the pits are only working on an average approximately $3\frac{1}{2}$ days per week, the average wage for all workers is only 37s. a week. When taking out rent, national insurance, unemployment insurance, and other stoppages at the colliery, amounting to from 10s. to 12s., it reduces the average wage to between 25s. and 27s. per week. Pits work for three days a week, and if the men go to work on the fourth day and make less than a shift, they are deprived of their unemployment insurance, so that the position of the miner is far worse than it was at the beginning of 1926.[6]

In addition to bad trade and under-employment the miners had to face other difficulties. Victimization after the 1926 stoppage was not easily resisted. Well-known trade unionists who had been prominent in the dispute were told when they returned to the pits that other men had taken their places. The Bolsover Company employed a number of miners who came from the Shropshire coalfield during the stoppage.[7] Frank Hall stated towards the end of December: 'There are a few men,

[1] *R.C. on Coal Industry*, 1925, I, Report, pp. 173–4.
[2] *Derbyshire Times*, 12 February, 1927.   [3] *Ibid.* 4 December, 1926.
[4] *Ibid.* 26 March, 1927.   [5] *Ibid.* 7 May, 1927.
[6] *Ibid.* 5 November, 1927.   [7] *Ibid.* 27 November, 1926.

who, in the eyes of the companies, have made themselves a little too conspicuous and their activities have not been approved by the companies.'[1] On 3 January, 1927, it was reported to the Council that 948 men in the county were still without employment.[2]

II

The situation was complicated by the existence of the Spencer union. By the beginning of 1927 the Nottinghamshire and District Miners' Industrial Union had framed its rules and was rapidly expanding. On 8 March, 1927, it was decided that Spencer should be given a ten-year contract as 'agent' at a salary of £400 a year, to be increased to £800 'on the expiration of his office as M.P.'[3] B. Smith and R. Gascoyne continued to act as President and Secretary respectively; and W. Evans, H. Cooper, J. Birkin, J. Shaw, J. France, J. Cobley and N. Buxton were the first members of the Executive Committee. Later Thomas Spencer, who had been removed from his position as a trustee of the Derbyshire Miners' Association, also became a member. J. G. Hancock, the former Nottinghamshire miners' leader and Liberal-Labour member for Mid-Derbyshire, became the Treasurer in September, 1927.[4] The activities of Birkin in the British Workers' League have already been noted.[5] He became a magistrate early in 1927.[6] Horace Cooper later became Secretary of the union in succession to Gascoyne. To all these men 'non-political' unionism meant company unionism.

The employers, who had agreed to recognize only the Spencer union, discovered after taking legal advice that they could not deduct contributions from wages, as originally proposed, without violating the Truck Act. It was therefore agreed that the new union would have to make its own collections in the usual way.[7] The pension scheme, however, was quickly established. The Nottinghamshire coal-owners granted £10,000 in December, 1926, 'as a nucleus to start the fund' and agreed to consider the imposition of a levy on tonnage for its future maintenance.[8] In April, 1927, the coal-owners made a further grant of £2,500 and promised to review the position at the end of three months.[9]

The strife between the Spencer union and the Nottinghamshire and Derbyshire miners' associations was bitter. The Nottinghamshire

---

[1] *Derbyshire Times*, 25 December, 1926.   [2] *D.M.A.* 3 January, 1927.
[3] Minutes of the Nottinghamshire and District Miners' Industrial Union, 8 March, 1927.
[4] *Derbyshire Times*, 17 September, 1927.   [5] See Chapter XVIII, p. 676.
[6] Minutes of the Nottinghamshire and District Miners' Industrial Union, 19 April, 1927.   [7] *Ibid.* 13 and 18 December, 1926.
[8] *Ibid.* 18 December, 1926.   [9] *Ibid.* 4 April, 1927.

Miners' Association was virtually suppressed because of the refusal of the coal-owners to recognize it or allow it any facilities at the collieries. In Derbyshire the miners' leaders worked hard to prevent the contagion from crossing the county boundary. Samuel Sales presided over a meeting of the Pinxton miners on 29 November, 1926, at which W. Carter, the Secretary of the Nottinghamshire Miners' Association, sharply criticized Spencer's activities:

Mr. George Spencer is not a negotiator but a dictator. He has turned his back on all his principles, if he had any. He has now fallen into a trap, and is saying he doesn't believe in political action. . . . Mr. Spencer has signed away your freedom and queered the pitch for others. He has got his fountain pen, but the owners have got £700,000 more than they ought to have.[1]

At Alfreton a branch of the new union was soon established by Thomas Spencer.[2] The movement spread to a number of collieries in Derbyshire. Some of the miners on the Yorkshire borders, at Beighton, Birley and Waleswood, also declared their allegiance to George Spencer.[3] Wherever the new union became strongly organized the employers refused to negotiate with the Derbyshire Miners' Association.

The most serious difficulties occurred at the collieries of the Bolsover Company. T. Harper, E. Lenthall and W. Johnson became the leading exponents of 'non-political' unionism at Bolsover and Creswell and, with the aid of the management, quickly recruited a large following. In April, 1927, A. J. Cook paid a special visit to Bolsover as part of a campaign for strengthening the Derbyshire Miners' Association in the area. Referring to the Spencer union, he said: 'Without the patronage of the Bolsover Company the organization could not last a week.'[4]

Disputes over the reinstatement of checkweighmen lasted for many months. During the stoppage the men who had returned to work had elected their own checkweighmen and many trade union checkweighmen lost their positions. The problem was particularly acute at the Bolsover Company's pits in Nottinghamshire and Derbyshire where there had been an early resumption of work. In June, 1927, J. H. Williamson, a miner at the Company's Rufford pit, in Nottinghamshire, was granted an injunction by Mr. Justice Russell in the Chancery division, restraining Thomas Brown from acting as checkweighman on the ground that he had not been properly elected. The ballot was held to be illegal because it had been conducted in such a way as to prevent the miners from voting for a man who was not employed at the colliery.[5] When a strong agitation developed at Tibshelf for the removal of the checkweighmen who had been elected during the stoppage, they promptly

[1] *Derbyshire Times*, 4 December, 1926.
[2] *Ibid.* 11 December, 1926, 8 January, 1927.   [3] *Ibid.* 12 March, 1927.
[4] *Ibid.* 16 April, 1927.   [5] *Ibid.* 18 June, 1927.

became agents for the Spencer union in an attempt to safeguard their positions. The colliery management refused to allow the Derbyshire Miners' Association any facilities for collecting contributions.[1]

In addition to such guerrilla tactics there was a steady propaganda warfare between the rival unions. Before the end of the stoppage the Derbyshire Miners' Association had issued a leaflet condemning the Spencer agreement which it was eventually obliged to accept. Soon afterwards Frank Hall published the text of a letter, which he had sent to Spencer, complaining about the infiltration of the new union at Bolsover and Cresswell:

A 'non-political' union; what a grotesque idea! As the head of a 'non-political' union, your sincerity and consistency should have taught you to first strip yourself of all political associations. . . . What can you do in the men's interests that the Derbyshire Miners' Association cannot do? You have failed in the past to build up a healthy and active organization in Nottinghamshire. April last found you and your men, I am sorry to say, stranded. The Derbyshire Miners' Association generously handed you £10,000. You were then fulsome in your appreciation. How soon you have forgotten.[2]

Spencer was quick to point out that the Derbyshire leaders had signed an agreement similar to his own. 'I give you fair warning', he wrote, 'that now I am a free agent . . . I shall undertake to conduct the business and organize any pit in Derbyshire that cares to associate with my organization.'[3] Frank Hall responded with another lengthy letter which ended: 'My advice to you is, while "free" be honest, and chuck it.'[4] In May, 1927, at a meeting of the Industrial Peace Conference at Mansfield, J. P. Houfton complained of a 'scurrilous pamphlet', issued by the Derbyshire Miners' Association, which asserted that the Spencer union was subsidized by the Bolsover Colliery Company.[5]

The recriminations between the two unions resulted in a lawsuit. Richard Gascoyne, the Secretary of the Spencer Union, stated at a public meeting that Frank Hall had worked in collusion with Frank Varley to bring about a Nottinghamshire and Derbyshire settlement during the 1926 stoppage. Gascoyne said:

In the third week of the strike Mr. Hall said to Mr. Varley: 'If you will work with me for a Notts. and Derbyshire agreement we will give your Association £20,000.' Mr. Varley spoke to me about this offer and I urged him to accept it. Mr. Hall, however, made his proposal without consulting his colleagues, Messrs. Hicken and Spencer, and when he returned to Chesterfield he got a good wigging, but the Notts. Association received £10,000 on account.

[1] *D.M.A.* 18 June, 1927.   [2] *Derbyshire Times,* 11 December, 1926.
[3] *Ibid.* 18 December, 1926.
[4] *Ibid.* 25 December, 1926.   [5] *Ibid.* 4 June, 1927.

Frank Hall reported Gascoyne's speech to the Council of the Derby-shire Miners' Association and was given authority to bring an action against him for slander.[1] The case was due to be heard at the Leeds Assizes on 28 July before Mr. Justice Talbot. An impressive array of witnesses from Nottinghamshire and Derbyshire assembled in the court. They included two Members of Parliament, George Spencer and Frank Varley; J. G. Hancock, the former Nottinghamshire miners' M.P.; John Spencer and Henry Hicken. At the last minute Gascoyne decided to withdraw his allegations. Willoughby Jardine, K.C., who appeared for Frank Hall, told the court:

> If the words are unreservedly withdrawn I have nothing more to say. My clients are content to have no damages as long as the statement is made publicly that the reflection which has been cast on Mr. Hall is without foundation, and is withdrawn.[2]

III

Trade unionism of the Spencer variety was not peculiar to Notting-hamshire and Derbyshire although these were the counties in which it first made its appearance. 'It was not local in its creation', Horace Cooper told the Creswell miners, 'it was national. In South Wales— Mr. Cook's home—there were 151 branches, while the movement had spread to Scotland, Northumberland, Durham, Leicestershire, and Cannock Chase.'[3] The miners' 'non-political' unions were part of a much wider movement which had as its object the disruption of the trade unions. There was a close alliance between the miners' 'non-political' unions and the Industrial Peace Union, founded by J. A. Seddon, the former leader of the shop assistants' union and an ex-president of the T.U.C., and Havelock Wilson, the leader of the seamen's union which was soon to be expelled from the T.U.C. The Industrial Peace Union provided opportunities for employers and renegade trade union leaders to indulge in mutual admiration and advocate a harmonious coexistence which apparently depended upon the willingness of the miners and others to accept reductions in wages. Seddon and Wilson addressed meetings of the miners' 'non-political' unions in various parts of the country. Both spoke at Cresswell in December, 1927, when J. P. Houfton described Wilson as 'a man for whom I have the highest regard and esteem, not to say affection'.[4]

Another faithful ally of the movement was the Economic League.

[1] *D.M.A.* 26 March, 1927.
[2] *Derbyshire Times*, 30 July, 1927; *D.M.A.* 13 August, 1927.
[3] *Derbyshire Times*, 2 July, 1927.   [4] *Ibid.* 10 December, 1927.

During June, 1927, the League's 'Flying Squad' made its appearance in Nottinghamshire and Derbyshire and conducted an intensive campaign lasting for eight days, during which it was estimated that 20,000 people had been addressed. Taking as its slogan 'Every man is a capitalist' the League advised the miners to rid their unions of politics and listen to the appeals for co-operation and goodwill instead of indulging in class warfare.[1]

For a movement which professed to be non-political the miners' Industrial Unions and their allies devoted an inordinate amount of attention to politics. 'Communists, atheists, Bolsheviks and men who were traitors to their country and to their class and were spies and the tools of Russia have dragged men time after time into strikes', declared J. G. Hancock.[2] 'How can they support a ship that has been weakened beyond repair by the folly and weakness of leaders who have tried to bring about revolution?' asked Joseph Birkin.[3] George Spencer told the Northumberland Miners' Non-Political Trade Union: 'It would be less than useless to accept the philosophy of Communism—that they must decide the whole of the economic structure by lock-outs and strikes before they could win a higher standard of living for the working people.'[4] There were many such outbursts. All uses of trade union power, whether political or industrial, were branded as communistic and were therefore taboo. A. J. Cook, the Minority Movement and the Communists were represented as tyrants who dominated the trade unions. The appeals for peace in industry, which formed a prominent part of the 'non-political' movement's policy, were appeals for peace at any price.

The campaign was fundamentally dishonest and was aimed at producing a compliant trade union movement in a time of economic depression. The attacks upon Communism were used as a cloak to attack militancy of any kind. These facts were recognized by the T.U.C. which at that time was as busily engaged in fighting Communism as the 'non-political' unions. The General Council eventually intervened in the struggle in Nottinghamshire. Ben Turner, A. Hayday, A. B. Swales, G. Hicks and Walter Citrine met representatives of the Nottinghamshire owners in March, 1928, and tried in vain to secure an agreement that the men should be free to join whichever union they wished.[5] The tyranny of the employers proved to be as great as that of A. J. Cook. George Spencer complained: 'The T.U.C. who had turned war on the Communists ought to support the new union instead of crushing it. . . . The only reason they were not with the Industrial Union was that there

[1] *Derbyshire Times*, 18 June, 1927.   [2] *Ibid.* 26 October, 1929.
[3] *Ibid.* 5 January, 1929.
[4] *Ibid.* 13 August, 1927.   [5] *Ibid.* 24 March, 1928.

were no politics in their organization. That was their only offence.'[1] Oliver Wright, the Treasurer of the Derbyshire Miners' Association, was equally dissatisfied for different reasons. He told the T.U.C. at Belfast in 1929:

The General Council were placing too much of the blame for the disruption of trade unionism upon the shoulders of the Communist Party and the Minority Movement. . . . He was not a member of the Communist Party, and he did not agree with their policy, but it was not the Communist Party who were responsible for the Spencer Union. It was the betrayal of the workers by the General Council in 1926 which was responsible for the break away. The trade union movement ought to pursue a bolder and more militant policy and ought not to collaborate with the employers.[2]

This reaction against the movement for 'peace in industry' resulted from the behaviour of the Derbyshire coal-owners. In February, 1927, Frank Hall stated:

I am among those who want peace in industry. We have nothing to gain from disputes; we always lose. There is no doubt a great deal of prejudice against the mining community and always the feeling if we have a dispute that we are up against the country and the community in general. That has never entered the miners' heads at all. What they are seeking is a decent living wage.[3]

But the attitude of some of the employers soon led the miners to believe that peace was to be observed only by the trade unions. In May, 1927, the Shipley Colliery Company decide to close its No. 1 pit and dismissed 800 men without giving any reason. Another of the Company's pits was working the same seam full time.

'The reason for working one colliery full time and starving the other is the difference in the price list,' said Frank Hall. 'Our disappointment is that the owners of this colliery have made no explanation whatever as to the reason they gave the men notice. . . . I suppose this is the coal owners' idea of contributing to peace in the industry. I wonder what would be said if a body of men, without approaching the companies, were to decide to give notice without any explanation . . . to the owners, who, we are told, are so anxious to work amicably and co-operate with the men?'

The *Derbyshire Times*, generally in sympathy with the coal-owners, commented: 'The day has gone by when men could be treated in this cavalier fashion. . . . Action such as that causes friction and ill-feeling in the industry.'[4]

The root of the trouble at Shipley was the Spencer Union. Frank Hall told members of the Council:

[1] *Derbyshire Times*, 28 April, 1928. [2] *Ibid.* 7 September, 1929.
[3] *Ibid.* 21 May, 1927. [4] *Ibid.*

There never was a time in the history of trade unionism when it was more necessary for branches under the same company to work together. This is illustrated from what is now taking place under the Shipley Colliery Company but I am glad to say that the branches under the Company are now pulling themselves together and holding joint meetings. It is essential that this should be done under all Companies, indeed it is necessary if for no other purpose than propaganda to try to get the men back into the union and also to put up the strongest defence against Spencerism.[1]

Later the Association complained to the Midland Counties Colliery Owners' Association that the Shipley Company was breaking the Soft Coal Agreement at its Coppice Pit. Robert Chaytor, of the Shipley Company, wrote to Saunders, the secretary of the coal-owners' association:

We are not having any nonsense. Our idea is to close it, or work it on the terms of the Woodside Pit. It would have paid us to have closed it as the coal trade is today, but at the request of a large number of men, whom Mr. Frank Hall does not represent, we left the pit open. The men that Mr. Frank Hall does represent need not come. You can tell him this. This is my last word on the matter.[2]

Other colliery companies were equally unco-operative. The Bolsover Company, which recognized only the Spencer union, refused to allow the Association facilities for conducting a pit-head ballot to enable the men to decide whether they wished to be included in the Derbyshire wage ascertainments.[3] The Staveley Company declined to sign the District Agreement, without giving any reason, with the result that its profits were once again excluded from the district ascertainments.[4] Many companies refused to allow the Association to collect contributions on the colliery premises. By the end of 1927 active trade unionists were still being denied employment. It is therefore not surprising that the Derbyshire miners received the news of the Mond-Turner talks with indignation. On 31 December, 1927, the Council passed a resolution protesting against the acceptance by the T.U.C. of the employers' invitation to confer on peace in industry 'when we have men in our own industry still out of work through being victimized'.[5]

Another aftermath of the General Strike, the Trade Disputes and Trade Unions Act of 1927,[6] said by the Liberal Lord Reading 'to offer no single ray of light for the British working man',[7] aroused much opposition from the Derbyshire miners and the whole of the Labour movement. Frank Lee pointed out that the General Strike had provided an excuse for introducing a Bill similar to others which had been

[1] *D.M.A.* 18 June, 1927.
[2] *Ibid.* 23 June, 1927.
[3] *Derbyshire Times*, 6 August, 1927.
[4] *D.M.A.* 18 June, 1927.
[5] *Ibid.* 31 December, 1927.
[6] 17 and 18 Geo. V. c. 22.
[7] Symons, *op. cit.* p. 226.

brought forward on several occasions since the end of the war. Protesting against the prohibition of sympathetic strikes, he said: 'No one wanted to strike for the sake of striking, but the strike was the working man's only weapon. If that was taken away from him he would lose his bargaining power.'[1] Frank Hall asked why it was necessary to bring in new legislation when the Government had already pronounced that the General Strike was illegal.[2] George Spencer, on the other hand, spoke in support of the Bill in the House of Commons. He said:

Unless something is done on the lines of this Bill to protect trade unionism against those who are working assiduously against it, in a comparatively few years it will be the men who are behind the revolutionary movement who will be directing its policy and not the moderate men who are at the head of it at present.[3]

His speech was well received by the opponents of trade unionism and was later published as a pamphlet by the Anti-Socialist and Anti-Communist Union.[4] 'Public opinion was undoubtedly influenced by the courageous action of Mr. G. A. Spencer', writes Lord Winterton.[5] Frank Varley, who also spoke in the debate and could by no stretch of the imagination be described as a revolutionary, called the action of Spencer and his followers 'a dirty thing'.[6] Despite the opposition of practically the whole of the trade union movement and the Labour Party the Bill quickly became law as a result of the Government's determined use of the closure.

IV

Meanwhile the coal industry showed no sign of recovering from its persistent depression and conditions in the Derbyshire coalfield became more desperate. Short time became the rule, more collieries were closed and large numbers of miners found themselves unemployed. In November, 1927, the Grassmoor Colliery Company alone dismissed about 500 men. Frank Hall commented:

Three days a week, with stoppages, means that in many cases there is not sufficient to live on. It has come to my notice today that in one case five men went to work without anything to eat. The distress in this district is worse than ever it has been in its history.[7]

Samuel Sales told a *Derbyshire Times* reporter:

It is no use thinking of living in terms of 1913 to 1914. We are living in 1927, and we have to face the hard economic fact that the world is producing

[1] *Derbyshire Times*, 7 May, 1927. [2] *Ibid.* 9 April, 1927.
[3] 205 H.C. Deb. 5s. 1418.
[4] *The Trade Unions Bill Vindicated by a Labour M.P.*, Anti-Socialist and Anti-Communist Union, (London), 1927. [5] Winterton, *op. cit.* p. 143.
[6] 205 H.C. Deb. 5s. 1707. [7] *Derbyshire Times*, 19 November, 1927.

more coal than it can consume. . . . At the present nobody seems to care what conditions the miners are working under so long as the nation is getting cheap coal.[1]

The situation became even worse in 1928 when the price of coal reached its lowest point in the inter-war years.[2] In March Hicken told the Carr Vale miners: 'Before Christmas this year between 5,000 and 7,000 men now working would be permanently unemployed in Derbyshire.' The county was spared the extreme poverty and unemployment which prevailed in the depressed areas but conditions were sufficiently bad, as they were in all the coalfields, to arouse violent protests.

'Private enterprise could not solve the problems confronting the mining industry,' said Hicken. 'Private enterprise had failed, and while the miners were waiting for something the owners had promised them, they and their wives and children were starving. . . . The present was not the time for despair, for hanging their harps on the weeping willow tree. It was the time for girding their loins for another struggle.'[3]

Oliver Wright expressed similar views:

He had been told that he had to be fair and impartial and take no part in politics, and that every miners' trade union should be built up on the basis of co-operation and peace in industry. He wished it were possible to accept such a rosy picture . . . but he was a stark realist as well as an idealist. He knew what a hell of a life it was today in the pits of Derbyshire and what a desperate struggle it was for miners to exist. . . . It was all very fine for the mine owners to talk about industrial peace when they had one foot on the miner's neck and the other on his mouth. It was the peace of the graveyard they were furthering; the contentment of the slave with his slavery. The miners should not be misled by talk of industrial peace and stabilization. There could be no stabilization under a capitalist system.[4]

The attempts of the employers to set their house in order were regarded by the miners' leaders as quite inadequate. When Sales, towards the end of 1927, suggested that central selling agencies might help to improve conditions in the coal industry, he was immediately taken to task by Joseph Lynch, who asserted: 'Mr. Sales has shouted out from scores of platforms: "Nationalization of the mines is the only remedy," and it is feared by those who feel most strongly about it that this can only come about out of the death throes of the present system.'[5] The Five Counties Scheme was received with little enthusiasm. Frank Lee thought that it had 'certain defects'.[6] Hicken pointed to its obvious weakness: its failure to prevent inter-regional competition.[7]

---

[1] *Derbyshire Times*, 26 November, 1927.   [2] See Chapter XIV, Appendix I.
[3] *Derbyshire Times*, 31 March, 1928.   [4] *Ibid.*   [5] *Ibid.* 3 December, 1927.
[6] *Ibid.* 15 June, 1929.   [7] *Ibid.* 14 September, 1929.

After the resounding defeat of 1926 the M.F.G.B. was weak and disunited. District settlements had made many of the miners' leaders more parochial in their outlook. Industrial action, nationally or locally, was temporarily out of the question. The miners pinned their faith once more upon political action. After explaining to the Clay Cross miners the provisions of the Trade Disputes and Trade Unions Act, Sales said:

The extension of hours was made possible only by the use of the political machine and the same machine will have to be used for the purpose of reducing them. Frankly, I see no wisdom in having strikes to remedy injustices if these same injustices can be remedied by putting crosses on ballot papers.[1]

As Mr. Page Arnot has pointed out: 'To a certain extent, though under greatly changed conditions, they were turning to the same type of activity as, forty and fifty years earlier, had been the main function of the defunct Miners' National Union. They were sending deputations to Ministers, asking for legislative enactments, or keeping watch on how existing legislation was administered in an endeavour to get some amelioration of harsh conditions.'[2]

This policy proved to be singularly unsuccessful under the Baldwin Government but the General Election of 1929 gave the miners renewed hope. Hicken emphasized its importance to them and urged the Council delegates to use their influence in their branches to secure the election of Labour candidates.[3] Before the election the M.F.G.B. took the precaution of obtaining pledges from the Labour Party. On 26 March the miners' leaders met the officials of the Parliamentary Labour Party. MacDonald stated that in the first session of Parliament the Government would not be able to deal with the question of nationalization but would tackle some of the immediate problems confronting the industry and affecting the welfare of the men. He proposed to repeal the legislation permitting the eight-hour day and to regulate the supply of labour in the mines by raising the school-leaving age, suspending the recruitment of adult labour from outside the industry, and providing a superannuation allowance for mine-workers at the age of 60. A. J. Cook reported:

The question of hours in particular was an outstanding question and one on which they desired to know the views of the Federation. . . . The Federation representatives said that while the Federation stood for the repeal of the present Act, it desired that future legislation should provide for a seven-and-a-half hour day bank to bank.

Eventually it was agreed that the Party's election manifesto, *Labour and the Nation*, should state: 'The disastrous Act by which the Tory

[1] *Derbyshire Times*, 24 December, 1927.
[2] R. P. Arnot, *The Miners: Years of Struggle*, (London), 1953, pp. 541–2.
[3] *D.M.A.* 18 May, 1929.

AA*

Government added an hour to the working day of the miners must be at once repealed.'[1]

In the event Ramsay MacDonald was obliged to form another minority government which enabled him to live in the world of compromise he loved so well. The miners' leaders realized that nationalization would now be improbable, if not impossible, and decided to bring the question of working hours to the fore as the most urgent of all the promised reforms. The agreements in Nottinghamshire and Derbyshire would last until the end of 1931 but in most districts they were due to expire at the end of 1929. The miners wanted to make sure of the shorter working day before they began negotiations for new agreements. This proved to be more difficult than they had been led to believe. As A. J. Cook told the miners at Chesterfield, in October, 1929: 'To put an hour on the day was one thing, but to take it off another.'[2]

Since the miners were not anticipating any reduction in wages, the Government had to consider whether the already flagging coal industry could bear the additional cost which would result from the shorter working day. The coal-owners asserted that they would have to claim a reduction in wages of up to 20 per cent. or close some of the pits. Mac-Donald was not anxious to precipitate industrial strife or add to the growing numbers of unemployed. 'You may, by forcing the issue, immediately bring us down', he told the miners' leaders.[3] With these considerations in mind, the Government decided that there could be no reduction in hours without some reorganization of the coal industry. The Government's proposals, after many consultations with the M.F.G.B. and the Mining Association, were eventually embodied in the Coal Mines Bill, which was introduced into the House of Commons in December, 1929. There followed a protracted struggle which lasted for more than six months and took eighty-eight divisions. The Government, in fighting the Conservatives and the House of Lords, had to carry with it both the Liberals and the M.F.G.B. The Executive Committee of the Derbyshire Miners' Association was 'considerably disturbed by newspaper suggestions that, should the Coal Bill be defeated at the third reading, the Government would not consider it of sufficient importance to merit an appeal to the country, but would continue to remain in office'. Hicken was instructed to write to Cook requesting that 'such pressure be brought to bear on the Government as will avoid what . . . would be a tragedy'.[4]

The Government had decided, with the approval of the M.F.G.B., that the Bill should reduce the length of the working day by half an

---

[1] *M.F.G.B.* 12 April, 1929.
[2] *Derbyshire Times*, 12 October, 1929.
[3] *M.F.G.B.* 23 July, 1929.   [4] *D.M.A.* 15 March, 1930.

hour 'as a first instalment'.[1] The Mining Association, which had stead-fastly refused to negotiate with the M.F.G.B. since the 1926 stoppage despite Cook's taunts about 'peace in industry', now invited the miners' leaders to discuss the possibility of adopting a 'spread-over' system whereby the men would work a 90-hour fortnight or a 45-hour week instead of a rigid 7½-hour day. The officials of the M.F.G.B. reported:

If these proposals were accepted it would mean that, in all probability, the workmen in those districts where an eight-hour day is now in operation, would find that, despite the Bill, they would still be working an eight-hour day on every day on which work was available to them. In short, the proposal negated the whole principle of the shorter working day; and if accepted, would not only defeat all the efforts made by the Federation for a shorter working day but also defeat the purpose of the Bill, which, to a great extent, was framed for the definite purpose of providing a shorter working day without any reduction in wages.[2]

Nevertheless, when the Bill went to the Lords it was amended to permit the spread-over of hours by arrangement between the owners and the workmen.

The Government had to compromise on a number of issues in con-nection with its proposals for reorganization before the Bill became law, but gradually a large measure of agreement was reached. At length the permissive spread-over of hours remained the only matter in dispute. The Lords, where the coal-owners' interests were very strongly repre-sented, obstinately insisted on the spread-over but now modified their amendment so that the spread-over would operate by an order of the Board of Trade, on the application of the parties concerned in any district. The M.F.G.B. continued firmly to oppose the proposal. The Government was faced with the dilemma of abandoning the Bill altogether or coming to terms with the Lords. On 15 July William Graham, the President of the Board of Trade, told the M.F.G.B. officials that the Government was considering a proposal to table an amendment to the Lords amendment, which would provide that the spread-over of hours in any district could not become operative without the approval of the Mining Association and the M.F.G.B. Rather than sacrifice the Bill, the Executive Committee of the M.F.G.B. reluctantly agreed to the Government's proposal.[3] The amendment was accepted by Parliament and on 1 August, 1930, the Coal Mines Bill received the Royal Assent. The Executive Committee of the M.F.G.B reported: 'This amendment has placed a powerful weapon in the hands of our organization; it has also placed us in a position of great responsibility.'[4]

[1] M.F.G.B. 5 November, 1929.   [2] Ibid. 10 April, 1930.
[3] Ibid. 16–17 July, 1930.
[4] Miners' Federation of Great Britain, Report of the Executive Committee for the year ending June, 1930, p. 87.

The Coal Mines Act as a whole fell short of the miners' expectations but was nevertheless regarded as an important advance. The Executive Committee commented:

The Bill has been described as 'the work of the Labour Government, and the contribution of the Government to the reorganization of the industry and to the solution of its economic difficulties'. Such a description is likely to cause considerable misconception as to its nature and origin. Part I expands and makes compulsory upon all districts certain schemes for the regulation of output and sale, and endeavours to co-ordinate those schemes under national authority. But the schemes in their inception are the work of certain groups of coal-owners, and their main principles were operating in certain parts of the country before the present Bill was introduced (e.g. under the Five Counties Scheme).

The extension of these schemes to all districts and their co-ordination by a national authority is nevertheless a work of great importance, and has been urged by the Federation ever since such schemes were first initiated in the districts. The importance and effect of Part I should not, therefore, be underrated, and to the main principles thereof . . . we give unqualified support, although the methods of applying the principles provided by the Bill do not conform to our views and policy. But the constructive parts of the Bill by no means represent the full extent of the contribution which a majority Labour Government would make to the reorganization of the industry.[1]

Frank Lee told the Eckington miners: 'Imperfect as this Bill is, unsocialistic as it may be, going in the wrong direction as it may appear to be, I believe it will give us a bigger say in the trade, it will tend to stabilize the industry and organize the trade. It is leading in the right direction.'[2]

Part III of the Coal Mines Act, which regulated the hours of work, was due to come into operation on 1 December, 1930. Its immediate effect was to abrogate all district agreements based on a working day of more than $7\frac{1}{2}$ hours. The Derbyshire, Nottinghamshire and Yorkshire agreements were the only ones unaffected by the change. The employers in other districts attempted to enforce reductions in wages or to enforce the spread-over without securing the consent of the workmen.[3] A national strike, which had the support of Derbyshire and Yorkshire, was imminent but when the M.F.G.B. complained to the Government about the contravention of the law the response was discouraging. MacDonald pointed out:

As you say there are about 210,000 people at present working on the spread-over, it is an utterly impractical proposition to think of prosecution. . . . The position has to be legalized and if prosecution is impossible and

[1] Miners' Federation of Great Britain, *Report of the Executive Committee for the year ending June, 1930*, p. 88.
[2] *Derbyshire Times*, 15 March, 1930.   [3] *M.F.G.B.* 19 November, 1930.

ridiculous we have one alternative only left, that is, to amend Section 14 of the Act so as to remove the veto. . . . We do not want to do that. . . . Therefore, we would say to the Miners' Federation: That the Federation give the industry a chance to get its reorganization scheme of the Mines Act working effectively by approving spread-over applications for a temporary period— say, three months—subject to no reduction in wages and without prejudice to the position of those districts not affected by the Act or those who have arrived at settlements in accordance with the provisions of the Mines Act.[1]

At an adjourned M.F.G.B. conference on 4 December the delegates considered the Prime Minister's proposal. 'We are not in a position to say "yea" or "nay" ', said Hicken. 'We left here after carrying that resolution a week ago where we had overwhelmingly turned down the suggestion of a spread-over, that under the Act the spread-over was dead. We called our Council meeting to deal with this situation on Monday. On the Saturday morning we got our newspapers and saw that far from being dead the spread-over was operating apparently with the authority of the Minister of Mines.'[2] The conference decided to refer the matter to the districts. By 271 votes to 265 the M.F.G.B. adopted the Prime Minister's suggestion, Derbyshire voting with the majority.[3] The Scottish miners, who refused to accept the spread-over system, were locked out for a week. 'Orders for coal poured into this district,' stated the Derbyshire Times, 'and many sidings standing full of coal were cleared.'[4]

The employers' insistence upon the spread-over was bound up with their desire for greater flexibility in operations as a result of the growth of mechanization. Practically every district, whether troubled by the spread-over system or not, was experiencing a pressure to work longer hours. The coal-owners were consistently evading the law by abusing the emergency clause of the 1908 Act. Men employed on coal-cutting machines and conveyors were being retained in the pit, after the statutory limit, either to complete the 'cut' of coal or to move conveyors in readiness for the next shift.[5] The miners argued that where such practices occurred regularly the colliery management was at fault in not organizing the work properly. It was cheaper for the employers to impose excessive overtime than to work a multi-shift system in a time of depression, but for the miners it meant long hours and more unemployment. Samuel Sales urged the M.F.G.B. annual conference in 1930 to demand for the miners the right to prosecute employers for such breaches of the law.

We have a colliery in Derbyshire where the men are being compelled to stop to turn a cut out. For weeks and weeks it has taken place, at least eleven

[1] M.F.G.B. 3 December, 1930.   [2] Ibid. 4 December, 1930.
[3] Ibid. 16 December, 1930.
[4] Derbyshire Times, 27 December, 1930.   [5] M.F.G.B. 11 September, 1930.

hours per day to turn this cut out, and yet men have been compelled to stop eleven hours a day. When we got a few men to stand and refuse to work the eleven hours a day, those men were given notice to leave their employment. Steps were taken to remedy this and we gathered sufficient evidence to prove our case. We had men who were prepared to stand the consequences of their action by giving evidence in a Court of Law. Yet in spite of this evidence being given to the inspector he refused to prosecute.[1]

The problem was complicated, as were most problems in Derbyshire, by the existence of the Spencer union. John Spencer told the conference:

Practically all our coalfield is free from this, but cases arise where we have one part of our coalfield which touches Notts., where you have got the Industrial Union in power. We have had the cream of the Trades Union Congress, the cream of the Labour Party, we have had the best men in the Federation come to assist us. We have admired their help, but in spite of their advice, in spite of the amount of enthusiasm whilst the meetings were carried on, the men filtered back, hunted victims of the tyranny meted out by the colliery managers and Spencerism in the shape of the Industrial Union. The men have not been courageous enough to put all the trade union spirit into this abuse that we would like. Where we have men who refuse at two or three pits which touch Notts. to work these longer hours, they are given their cards. They are scrapped from the pit. They are pursued in the county courts or the police courts, with the sacking of their homes, and when they appeal to the Labour Exchange they are vetoed there. I have also been with them, and the employer puts in a statement that the reason these men are stopped is not the true reason but because they would not work over seven and a half hours. It is put down in the present courts as insubordination if men will not work ten and twelve hours at a stretch.[2]

V

The immediate effect of the compulsory restriction of output, which came into operation on 1 January, 1931, was to create further short-time working and unemployment. On 23 December, 1930, the Swanwick Colliery Company took the precaution of giving the men notice that they would be required to work on day to day contracts.[3] Early in January, 1931, the Oxcroft Colliery Company dismissed 120 men.[4] In March the Bolsover Colliery Company dispensed with a whole shift, thereby displacing about 500 men. These and many similar occurrences led the *Derbyshire Times* to comment: 'The Coal Mines Act recently passed by the present Government has done little up to now but throw men

[1] *M.F.G.B.* 15 August, 1930.   [2] *Ibid.* 14 August, 1930.
[3] *Derbyshire Times*, 27 December, 1930.   [4] *Ibid.* 10 January, 1931.

out of employment.'[1] An official of the Derbyshire Miners' Association explained how the quota system affected the employment of miners:

There were various arrangements at collieries. For instance, at some collieries only one shift per day was being turned, or, again, the men were engaged alternate weeks. The men either had other jobs or the gap was bridged by benefit received through the employment exchanges.[2]

The Coal Mines Act was criticized on all sides. 'When governments interfere with industry we generally find that the result is more un-employment', stated the *Derbyshire Times*. 'This is certainly the case with the socialistic Coal Mines Act, and one wonders what the end is going to be so far as the Derbyshire coalfield is concerned.'[3] W. H. Sales, the son of the Vice-President of the Derbyshire Miners' Association, asserted:

Miners are not, I think, going to be hoodwinked into believing this Act is for their good, just because it was introduced by a Labour Government. We read a lot about the 'dole', a big budget deficit, and yet hear our own representatives introducing this mad Act which has caused the wholesale dumping of men on the 'dole'.[4]

The miners' leaders loyally defended the scheme. 'The quota system is not intended to create a coal famine', said one official, but 'to prevent huge accumulations of stocks which might be produced and put on the market as "spot lots". . . . The quota provides for as much as the nation requires for internal and export trade.'[5] Samuel Sales, fortified by infor-mation gleaned from the *Social Democrat*, laid the blame on the Mid-land coal-owners for mishandling their quotas and causing a shortage of coal. He also accused them of delaying the fixing of minimum prices, 'the result being that they were able to enter markets at cut-throat prices (just the thing the Act aimed at preventing) undercutting Durham, Northumberland and other districts which had played the game by fixing reasonable minimum prices.'[6] In June, 1931, A. J. Cook told a M.F.G.B. conference:

It is true that up to the present little or no advantage has accrued to the miners from these schemes. Nevertheless, they are slowly but surely being improved in the light of the experience gained by their operation. In the future we may expect a considerable advance towards unification through the experience of these schemes.[7]

The Coal Mines Act came into operation at a most difficult time. The industry had suffered from a persistent depression for years, mainly due to permanent influences but intensified by currency policy and reparations. On top of this came the world depression heralded by the New York Stock Exchange crisis of 1929. Recovery from this

[1] *Derbyshire Times*, 7 March, 1931.   [2] *Ibid*. 14 March, 1931.
[3] *Ibid*. 7 March, 1931.   [4] *Ibid*. 28 March, 1931.   [5] *Ibid*. 14 March, 1931.
[6] *Ibid*. 18 April, 1931; cf. T. Smith, 'The Recent Coal Shortage—Who was responsible?', *Social Democrat*, April, 1931, p. 1.   [7] M.F.G.B. 23 June, 1931.

essentially cyclical depression was then delayed by the British financial crisis of 1931 and the suspension of the gold standard. The exporting areas suffered most. The average monthly tonnage of coal exported fell from 4,573,289 in 1930 to 3,504,676 in the first quarter of 1931. The average value of exported coal fell from 16s. 8d. to 16s. 1d. a ton in the same period. Average earnings per shift in Durham had fallen from 9s. 11·35d. in 1926 to 7s. 7·62d. in 1931, a reduction of 20·5 per cent. In the Eastern division (which included Derbyshire) they had fallen by only 8 per cent. from 10s. 10·50d. to 10s. 0·16d. Wages in the exporting areas also lagged far behind the cost of living. In Northumberland average earnings per shift in March, 1931, were only 23 per cent. higher than in June, 1914, whereas the cost of living was 47 per cent. greater. In Derbyshire, on the other hand, average earnings per shift were 57 per cent. higher than before the war.[1]

These statistics of average earnings per shift do not, of course, reflect the loss of earnings caused by short-time working, a factor which offset to some extent the apparently better position of the inland districts, as shown by the following table:

Average Number of Days Worked per Week by the Collieries[2]

District	1927	1928	1929	1930	1931 (First 5 months)
Northumberland	5·01	5·12	5·43	4·96	5·47
Durham	4·94	5·02	5·31	5·04	5·00
Cumberland and West-morland	5·12	4·95	5·36	5·33	5·49
S. Yorkshire	4·71	4·60	5·04	4·75	4·76
W. Yorkshire	4·30	4·15	4·47	4·26	4·77
Lancashire and Cheshire	4·23	4·09	4·31	4·31	5·09
Derbyshire	4·25	4·10	4·45	4·28	4·44
Notts. and Leics.	4·29	4·22	4·50	4·23	4·69
Warwicks.	5·40	5·06	5·35	5·09	5·65
N. Staffs.	4·82	4·24	4·60	4·53	5·23
S. Staffs., Worcs. and Salop	5·05	4·59	4·83	4·63	5·35
Glos. and Somerset	4·62	4·37	5·04	5·06	5·37
Kent	5·33	5·31	5·47	5·39	5·44
N. Wales	5·42	5·25	5·49	5·25	5·72
S. Wales and Mon.	5·17	5·40	5·64	5·39	5·73
Scotland	5·09	5·22	5·38	5·13	4·92
Great Britain	4·81	4·78	5·08	4·85	5·11

[1] *Ministry of Labour Gazette.*
[2] Miners' Federation of Great Britain, *The Coal Crisis,* 1931, p. 3.

The position of Derbyshire, in comparison with the other districts, is therefore more accurately reflected by statistics of earnings over a period:

Miners' Average Annual Earnings, 1927–30[1]

District	1927			1928			1929			1930		
	£	s.	d.	£	s.	d.	£	s.	d.	£	s.	d.
Northumberland	109	2	7	97	3	5	100	1	0	96	3	11
Durham	115	12	9	104	0	10	106	6	8	103	12	2
Lancs., Cheshire and N. Staffs.	113	8	5	103	10	1	108	9	6	108	9	6
Yorkshire	124	17	8	112	13	2	119	8	0	115	9	0
North Derbyshire and Notts.	127	13	6	112	19	5	119	18	9	117	0	11
S. Derbyshire, Leics., Cannock Chase and Warwicks.	127	8	11	110	0	5	115	1	0	113	11	7
S. Wales and Mon.	123	13	11	126	2	0	128	7	8	124	13	0
Other districts	117	3	10	110	11	3	115	9	10	115	18	11
Scotland	136	5	5	135	9	6	135	19	6	134	2	8
Great Britain	122	11	3	113	15	9	118	4	7	115	12	2

Such averages, inflated by the comparatively high earnings of the better-paid miners, tend to obscure the position of vast numbers of men whose earnings were below the average. In Northumberland and Durham the subsistence wage was 6s. 9½d. a day. In Derbyshire and Nottinghamshire the men received an allowance of 6d. a shift subject to a maximum of 8s. 9d. and a minimum of 7s. 11d.

The question of hours came to the fore once again during 1931. The Coal Mines Act of 1930 had stated: 'During the continuance of the Coal Mines Act, 1926, section three of the Coal Mines Regulation Act, 1908, shall have effect as if for the words "one hour" there were therein substituted the words "half an hour".'[2] The 1926 Act was due to expire in July, 1931, and, in the absence of new legislation, the 1919 Act, which gave the miners the seven-hour day, would have again become operative. The owners made it clear to the Government that the industry could not be carried on with a seven-hour day and that further legislation was imperative. The M.F.G.B., on the other hand, pressed the Government to introduce a new Minimum Wage Act. The Government would not consider wages unless the miners were prepared to discuss them in relation to hours. The coal-owners, who had persistently refused

[1] Miners' Federation of Great Britain, *The Coal Crisis*, 1931, p. 3.
[2] 20 and 21 Geo. V. c. 34, s. 14 (1).

to enter into national negotiations on wages since 1926, responded with alacrity when the Government suggested that their representatives should meet the miners' leaders to discuss wages in relation to hours. During these discussions the owners proposed an unlimited extension of the legislation permitting the $7\frac{1}{2}$-hour day, with guaranteed wages for a limited period. The Federation countered this with a demand for some agreed national machinery for the determination of wages. The owners refused to consider national wage negotiations and the Government was not prepared to resort to compulsion. The Federation then renounced its claim for a return to the seven-hour day and compromised on its claim for a legal minimum wage but failed to reach a settlement. The Government was called upon to act. It did not grant the miners' claim for a restoration of the seven-hour day with a legal minimum to increase wages but adopted the compromise the Federation had already made in an attempt to reach a settlement. The Coal Mines Act, 1931, continued the statutory limit of $7\frac{1}{2}$ hours for a further twelve months or until the coming into operation of an Act to ratify the Geneva Convention of 18 June, 1931 (if this occurred within the twelve months).[1]

In the absence of a national wages agreement the Derbyshire Miners' Association began negotiations with the coal-owners for a new district agreement to supersede the 1926 agreement, which after 31 December, 1931, was subject to six months' notice. The owners put forward a claim for a lower minimum percentage but this was successfully resisted.[2] On 15 December the new agreement was signed. It was merely a renewal of the 1926 agreement for another year with the addition of a proviso 'that if and whenever the permitted hours of work for underground workers shall, by the operation of any statutory enactment or otherwise, be reduced below $7\frac{1}{2}$ per shift, this agreement shall forthwith terminate and cease to have effect'.[3]

Before the end of 1931 the Labour Government was replaced by the so-called National Government. The only member of the new Government who had taken part in the hours and wages discussions with the M.F.G.B. earlier in the year was the Prime Minister, Ramsay MacDonald. Immediately after the general election the coal-owners submitted a memorandum to the Government, asking it not to ratify the Geneva Convention. The owners' case, which stressed the fact that certain articles of the Convention could not be applied to British mines, was used by the Government to frustrate its early ratification. The M.F.G.B. was not consulted. As the 1931 Act regulating the hours of

[1] Miners' Federation of Great Britain, *Hours of work in British Coal Mines*, 1 October, 1937. The Geneva Convention, if ratified, would have restricted the daily hours of work for miners to $7\frac{1}{4}$.   [2] *D.M.A.* 21 November, 1931.

[3] Derbyshire Miners' Association, *Agreement made between the Colliery Owners of the Derbyshire District and Representatives of the Workmen, 15 December, 1931.*

labour expired on 8 July, 1932, further legislation was required. The Mining Association again agreed to meet the M.F.G.B. to discuss the question of hours. On 7 April, 1932, there was a very unsatisfactory meeting between representatives of the two organizations at which the coal-owners simply asserted that they wanted a continuation of the $7\frac{1}{2}$-hour day and refused to discuss wages. After the deadlock had been reported to the Government there was a further meeting on 29 April at which the owners proposed an unlimited extension of the $7\frac{1}{2}$-hour day, subject to the ratification of the Geneva Convention, and offered to guarantee wages for a year. The M.F.G.B. insisted that such a guarantee should be unlimited or, alternatively, that the twelve-month guarantee should be followed by the setting up of national machinery to regulate district changes in wages. On 25 May Walter Runciman informed the M.F.G.B. that the Government intended to introduce a Bill to continue indefinitely (subject to the ratification of the Geneva Convention) the $7\frac{1}{2}$-hour day.

The *Colliery Guardian* commented:

We think the Government, in escaping from the toils of a time-limit, has met the situation in a rational way, which will commend itself to the general body of coal-owners. The $7\frac{1}{2}$-hour day is to be continued indefinitely, or until the Geneva Hours Convention is ratified by all the Powers; as far as can be seen at present . . . this is a contingency that need not cause many sleepless nights.[1]

Ebby Edwards, who had succeeded A. J. Cook as Secretary of the M.F.G.B., described the 1932 Act as

the greatest piece of partisan and class legislation ever introduced against the miners by any government. It reflected in its entirety only what the owners desired; it embodied their proposals without modification. . . . We hear much of continuity of government policy; here was a case in which the Prime Minister was the same personality in a changed government, yet what a dishonourable record.[2]

Towards the end of 1932 the Derbyshire coal-owners stated that they would not give notice to end the 1931 agreement but that they wished the miners to consider whether an agreement should not be for a longer period than twelve months and whether the minimum percentage should not be 38 per cent. as in the existing agreement, but 32 per cent. as in Yorkshire.[3] The coal-owners had already discussed with the Association the desirability of including in the ascertainments the expenses of operating the marketing scheme established under the Coal Mines Act,

[1] *Colliery Guardian*, 27 May, 1932.
[2] Miners' Federation of Great Britain, *Hours of Work in British Coal Mines*, 1 October, 1937, p. 25.　　　　　　　　　[3] *D.M.A.* 31 December, 1932.

1930.[1] On 6 February, 1933, the District Wages Board agreed that an additional clause should be added to the agreement:

The proceeds are also to include any sums received under the provisions of the Midland (Amalgamated) District (Coal Mines) Scheme, 1930, and costs of production are also to include payments and expenses in connection with the Midland (Amalgamated) District (Coal Mines) Scheme, 1930, other than penalties thereunder or costs of individual appeals for increased Standard Tonnage.

The conclusion of an entirely new agreement for a longer period, as suggested by the coal-owners, was delayed by the Federation's campaign for national machinery for the regulation of wages and conditions. The Government was being urged to legislate but the Mining Association persistently refused to discuss the matter. On 18 March the Council of the Derbyshire Miners' Association endorsed a resolution, passed by a national conference, inviting the districts 'to give power to the Executive Committee to call upon all affiliated district organizations to terminate their agreements simultaneously, unless guarantees satisfactory to the National Executive are obtained before July, 1933'.[2] The guarantees were not forthcoming but there was no strike. District agreements and economic depression had, for the time being, destroyed the unity of the Federation and sapped its strength. On 1 June, 1933, Oliver Wright advised an M.F.G.B. Conference to recognize defeat:

We have an invitation to negotiate a wages agreement which would give us one of the best wages agreements in the country. I contend that if districts can make arrangements for high wage rates there is no danger to the other districts. There is nothing for other districts to fear. I want the conference to face facts. Districts ought not to be tied.[3]

Wright was not allowed to forget these remarks. Samuel Middup, a leading figure in the Spencer union at the Newstead Colliery, taunted the Derbyshire leaders with their eagerness to secure an agreement on the same terms as that obtained by the Spencer union. Wright replied:

My speech was not in favour of district agreements as against a national agreement, but only in the nature of advice to the M.F.G.B. conference that we had to make the best of a bad job. We had tried to get a national agreement and had failed, because the Government refused to implement its pledges given to the M.F.G.B., the owners could not be persuaded to voluntarily agree, and in the Notts. district we were up against the splitting tactics of men like Mr. Middup, who had already signed district agreements.[4]

On 18 July the officials of the Derbyshire Miners' Association signed a new district agreement which was to last for five years and was

---

[1] *D.M.A.* 23 July, 31 December, 1932.   [2] *Ibid.* 18 March, 1933.
[3] *M.F.G.B.* 1 June, 1933.   [4] *Derbyshire Times,* 7 October, 1933.

thereafter terminable by three months' notice. The owners' demand for a lower minimum percentage was again successfully resisted. The terms of the new agreement were exactly the same as those of the 1931 agreement. There was an additional proviso that if 'in the opinion of either party any change of circumstances or conditions in the coal industry should react to the disadvantage of this district as compared with any other district or districts' the agreement could be revised. Disputes arising from this proviso were to be referred to arbitration in accordance with the Arbitration Act, 1889.[1]

Towards the end of 1933 the M.F.G.B. began a campaign for increased membership. In Derbyshire numbers had dwindled from 43,000 in 1925 to 17,215 as a result of low wages, unemployment and secession to the Spencer union.[2] In October, 1933, W. Burke, the Secretary of the Shirebrook Branch, who presided over a meeting addressed by Ebby Edwards, told the miners: 'Prior to 1921 there was not throughout all the country a better organized area than Derbyshire, and he was sorry to have to confess that at the present time they were probably one of the worst.' Edwards said:

As far as the amount of the contribution was concerned, all he would say was that they could only have a 'Woolworth's Union' for 'a tanner', or, in other words, out of nothing, nothing comes. If a Derbyshire miner was not paying his contribution he was a cad.[3]

Throughout 1934 the Derbyshire Miners' Association made great efforts to remedy the situation and by the end of the year membership had risen slightly to 18,009.

The miners' leaders had not lost faith in the efficacy of the marketing schemes established by the Coal Mines Act of 1930 but they were severely critical of the behaviour of the coal-owners. In October, 1934, Joseph Jones, the President of the M.F.G.B., told the Alfreton miners:

Under this Act the owners had absolute power to fix their own prices, but in spite of this provision they continued to squander the resources of their industry. . . . Colliery owners desirous of honestly operating the Act had been penalized in the shape of loss of trade. The Act had been wantonly and shamefully evaded. In some cases coal owners were driven to commit these evasions in self-defence.[4]

This had already been admitted by some of the coal-owners themselves. John Hunter, the general manager of the Staveley Company, had complained earlier in the year that minimum prices had not been observed:

Certain piratical and selfish coal owners had taken up an attitude inimical

---

[1] Derbyshire Miners' Association, *Agreement made between the Colliery Owners of the Derbyshire District and Representatives of the Workmen, 18 July, 1933.*
[2] See Chapter XV, Appendix I.
[3] *Derbyshire Times,* 28 October, 1933.   [4] *Ibid.* 26 October, 1934.

to the fulfilment of the provisions of the Act, and then started to blame each other for disregarding its machinery. . . . The Staveley Company held off for some considerable time, but was eventually forced, in order to hold its trade, to follow suit, the only alternative being to suffer loss of trade.[1]

Apart from 1921 and 1926, when there were major disputes, 1933 was the year of lowest output, both nationally and in Derbyshire, in the inter-war period. Coal prices continued to fall but not quite as quickly as general prices, measured by the Ministry of Labour cost-of-living index. Between 1927 and 1933 the cost of living fell by about 16 per cent. The output and price of coal in Derbyshire fell by 22 per cent. and 11 per cent. respectively.[2] By the beginning of 1933 the district ascertainment of additions to the miners' basic rates stood at 5·9 per cent. above the minimum, the highest point reached since the 1926 stoppage. Restriction of output, price control, increased mechanization and other economies were beginning to produce results. The gains accruing to the miners from slightly more favourable ascertainments were still offset by short-time working. The average number of days worked per week by the Derbyshire collieries fell from 4·28 in 1930 to 3·72 in 1933, although these figures do not necessarily imply that all the men employed worked every day the mines were open. The level of employment, measured by the number of days worked per week by the pits, improved only very slightly in 1934, rising to 3·76, but fell to 3·58 in 1935.[3] As output increased slightly between 1933 and 1935 the price of coal continued to fall.[4]

VI

The miners were beginning to despair of securing any marked improvement in their standard of living. Hicken had said, in 1932:

We are attempting to distribute twentieth-century wealth through the eighteenth-century distributing machine. Yesterday we could not have what we wanted because we could not produce enough; today we cannot have what we want because there is too much. Demand was once ahead of supplies; now the position is reversed, but the abundance is not being distributed.[5]

All the attempts of the M.F.G.B. to secure national machinery for the regulation of wages had ended in failure. The Minimum Wage Bill, sponsored in 1934 by Thomas Cape, the miners' M.P. for Workington, met with a similar fate. When the branches of the Derbyshire Miners' Association sent resolutions to their local Members of Parliament

---

[1] *Derbyshire Times*, 13 January, 1934.   [2] See Chapter XIV, Appendix I.
[3] *Ministry of Labour Gazette.*
[4] See Chapter XIV, Appendix I.   [5] *Derbyshire Times*, 15 October, 1932.

asking them to support the Bill it was reported to the Council that 'replies had been forwarded from the Members for Chesterfield, North-East Derbyshire and Belper, all of a non-committal character'.[1]

In 1935 the annual conference of the M.F.G.B. decided to launch a campaign for a flat-rate increase in wages of 2s. a day for adults and 1s. for boys. Elaborate plans were made in every district for meetings and other forms of publicity. Hicken was given the task of supervising the campaign in Derbyshire and it was decided, amongst other things, 'that Labour Parties, Co-operative Guilds, and any organization of social, political, or religious character' should be invited to help.[2] At a meeting at Ripley, presided over by Joseph Kitts, Hicken said:

There would be no need for a strike if justice were done but if indifference on the part of the coal-owners of the country led them to it they would sit up and take notice and see what line to adopt.

Oliver Wright declared:

The Derbyshire miners did not agree with the owners that there was not enough money in the industry to warrant an increase in wages, nor with the idea that the pit-head prices reflected the true economic state of the industry. During the past few years Derbyshire owners had made a profit of ninepence a ton, yet sixpence a ton was considered to be a good profit before the war.[3]

There were many such speeches as the campaign progressed. During September thirty meetings were held in the county. Help was given by various sections of the Labour movement. The Council of the Derby Diocesan Union of the Church of England Men's Society also associated itself with the miners in their demand for better wages.[4] The miners and their supporters argued that wages had lagged behind the cost of living for many years and had declined relatively to those in other trades; that productivity was increasing as a result of the growth of mechanization; that large profits were being reaped from by-product plants and other ancillary enterprises; and that the shares of colliery companies were increasing in value.

On 18 October a special conference of the M.F.G.B. decided to take a ballot on the question: 'Are you in favour of authorizing the Executive Committee to press the claim for an advance of 2s. a shift for adults and 1s. a shift for youths, even to the extent of tendering your notice, if necessary, to enforce the claim?'[5] The Derbyshire miners, by 15,292 votes to 1,059, declared themselves in favour of a strike if it should be necessary. The national figures were 409,351 for, and 29,215 against: an overwhelming majority of 93 per cent. On 22 November the miners'

[1] D.M.A. 20 January, 1934.
[2] Ibid. 10 August, 1935.
[3] Derbyshire Times, 13 September, 1935.
[4] Ibid. 25 October, 1935.
[5] M.F.G.B. 18 October, 1935.

leaders reported the result of the ballot to the Secretary for Mines. They also decided to confer with the General Council of the T.U.C. 'with regard to implementing the resolution passed by the Congress in September'. In that resolution the Congress had pledged itself to give the miners 'the maximum assistance' in their efforts to raise their wages. A member of the Executive Committee of the M.F.G.B. said:

We shall do our best to avoid a strike. We do not want it, nor do the men in the coalfields want it; but they are becoming dispirited, and unless something is done there is nothing but a strike in front of us.[1]

Samuel Sales told a *Derbyshire Times* reporter that nobody wanted a strike:

The country cannot afford it, but it is as well to remind the country that the miners cannot afford to go on as at present. . . . For anyone to argue that the ballot meant 2s. a day increase or a strike, is misrepresenting the feelings of the men. Some improvement on the present conditions must be guaranteed, however, if a stoppage is to be avoided. I would suggest that if the men could be given an immediate advance of 1s. per day with a guarantee that the first charge upon any results accruing from selling agencies would be devoted to making this up to 2s. per day it would be something the men would consider before running the risk and suffering of a general stoppage.[2]

Sales was immediately taken to task by a miner who asserted: 'It would be far better if Mr. Sales would not prejudice the course of negotiations by rushing into print at such an awkward time. But it seems that his desire to be in the limelight is greater than his good judgment.'[3]

Meanwhile national negotiations were taking place. After receiving the M.F.G.B. deputation on 27 November the Secretary for Mines had discussions with representatives of the Mining Association and eventually arranged a meeting between them and the miners' leaders. No agreement was reached. On the eve of the M.F.G.B. conference, called for 18 December to decide on future action, there was a further meeting between the two sides at which the owners' representatives stated that the response to their requests for increases in price under existing contracts had not been as satisfactory as they hoped. They offered, however, an advance in wages in each district as from 1 January, 1936, the amount and method of payment to be determined locally. The miners' leaders expressed their dissatisfaction but, in order to preserve as far as possible the national character of the negotiations, they asked that the district offers should be conveyed to them as representatives of the Federation. At the M.F.G.B. Conference on 18–19

[1] *Derbyshire Times*, 22 November, 1935.
[2] *Ibid.* 6 December, 1935.　　　　　[3] *Ibid.* 13 December, 1935.

December it was decided by 278,000 to 28,000 that notices to cease work at midnight on 26 January, 1936, should be tendered unless wage proposals satisfactory to the Executive Committee were obtained in the meantime. The Government had already informed the M.F.G.B. that there could be no subsidy or loan from public funds for the purpose of increasing wages in the industry.[1]

The problem was complicated by the differences in prosperity between the various districts. The owners did not want a national settlement, but, on the other hand, the employers in the more prosperous areas did not want to see any settlement which would increase the competitive power of the poorer regions. C. R. Ellis, of the Blackwell Company, told the miners:

A national agreement would have to be fixed on a basis of the worst district in the country, because the worst district could not possibly pay day rates of the existing highest district. . . . Would they agree to any pooling scheme with wages regulated under a national basis system? Would they approve of a scheme whereby the efforts of their labour would go to swell the exchequer of another district? In this coalfield they were in a fortunate position.[2]

Samuel Sales argued: 'Until we are able to get some form of unification of the industry the most prosperous districts will get off with paying less wages than they would otherwise have to pay.'[3]

The Staveley Company, untrammelled by any trade association, was able to take the lead. On 30 December it posted notices at its collieries informing the men that from 1 January, 1936, until such time as a county settlement was reached, the wages of men of 18 years and over would be increased by 9d. a day and those of boys by 4d. 'The Staveley Coal and Iron Company have for some time past been in sympathy with the claims put forward on behalf of the workmen', read the notice, 'and they hope that the above increase will still further improve the good relationship that already exists between them.'[4] In Nottinghamshire the Spencer union quickly settled for an increase of 1s. a day for men over 18 and 6d. for boys.

On 8 January, 1936, the owners' representatives placed before the miners' leaders particulars of their offers of increases in wages which ranged between 1s. and 5d. a day in the various districts. These offers were not accepted but a further meeting was arranged for 23 January and the Executive Committee of the M.F.G.B. agreed to postpone the handing in of notices to cease work. At the meeting on 23 January amended offers of increased wages were considered. The owners'

[1] *M.F.G.B.* 18-19 December, 1935.   [2] *Derbyshire Times*, 20 December, 1935.
[3] *Ibid.* 6 December, 1935.   [4] *Ibid.* 3 January, 1936.

representatives also stated that the coal-owners in all districts had accepted the principle of co-operating with the M.F.G.B. in setting up a joint standing committee 'for the consideration of all questions of common interest and of general application to the industry, not excluding general principles applicable to the determination of wages by district agreements'. The Secretary for Mines had already given the miners an assurance, after consultation with the coal-owners, that schemes for district selling agencies with central co-ordination would be established not later than 1 July, 1936. Many large consumers had agreed to a rise in the price of coal, even when purchasing under long-term contracts already made, and the coal-owners were thus helped to finance the increase in wages until the selling agencies were established. The general public showed a great deal of sympathy with both the coal-owners and the miners. The *Iron and Coal Trades Review* commented: 'Nobody is entitled to obtain supplies of a commodity at less than the cost of production and a fair price should cover a fair profit as well as a fair wage.'[1]

In the face of these developments the M.F.G.B. decided to compromise. At a national conference on 24 January, 1936, it was decided, by 360,000 votes to 112,000, to accept the following recommendation of the Executive Committee:

The Executive Committee of the Mineworkers' Federation cannot regard the offers made by the coal-owners as satisfactory, as they are unfair in their incidence and do not afford the miners the standard of living to which they are justly entitled. But in view of the undertaking which is being given by the representative body of coal-owners that a National Joint Standing Consultative Committee shall be set up for the consideration of all questions of common interest and general application to the industry, not excluding general principles applicable to the determination of wages by district agreements, it recommends that the present offers be accepted as an instalment of the further improvement which will be rendered possible by the proposed selling agreements.

In making this recommendation the Executive Committee are strongly influenced by the desirability of avoiding industrial disturbance in the present circumstances of the nation and by the keenest desire to prevent loss and injury to the public who have so loyally supported the miners' claim.[2]

The effect of the district settlements was to give the miners increases ranging from 6d. to 1s. a day from 1 January, 1936, according to the ability of the coalfields to pay. The Derbyshire coal-owners had offered 9d. a day for workers over 21 and 4d. for others but later followed the

---

[1] *Iron and Coal Trades Review*, 17 January, 1936, p. 84.
[2] M.F.G.B. 24 January, 1936. The phrase 'the present circumstances of the nation' refers to the period of national mourning following the death of King George V.

example of the Staveley Company in granting the full increase to all workers of 18 and over. The increase was limited to six shifts per week and was not to apply to overtime or week-end work.[1] The miners employed by the Bolsover Colliery Company received an increase of 1s. a day (6d. for boys) in accordance with the Spencer union's agreement in Nottinghamshire.

VII

The friction between the Derbyshire Miners' Association and the Spencer union had continued, unabated, since 1926. On 20 January, 1937, ten years after the secession had occurred, Oliver Wright told a M.F.G.B. conference:

We have been terribly handicapped in our activities in the Derbyshire Miners' Association since 1926, and we have had to swallow a good deal because of the danger of opposition, and probably from that point of view we have not been able to take the active part in this Federation that we should like to have taken. Two of our largest collieries in Derbyshire have been in exactly the same position as Notts. since 1926. I refer to Bolsover and Creswell. There have been several occasions since 1926 when we should have had a strike at our Bolsover Colliery. The men were quite ready to strike, but we had to damp down their enthusiasm, because we knew in the circumstances we were absolutely impotent at the other Derbyshire colliery that came under Spencer, and we also knew that at the four or five other Bolsover Company's pits in Nottinghamshire there was no hope of getting any support from there. So that we know what Spencerism means, and we have felt all the time that it could only be defeated on a national basis.[2]

Nevertheless, the Association had scored minor victories. In 1931 the Bolsover Colliery Company had negotiated new price lists with the officials of the Spencer union. The agreements were repudiated by a large number of the men who had returned to the Derbyshire Miners' Association and argued that the Spencer union did not represent them.[3] The Company retaliated by giving notice that all contracts of employment would be terminated and those who wished to do so would be able to sign contracts embodying the new price lists. The members of the Association then insisted that since all the men at the colliery had been given new contracts they had the right to elect new checkweighmen. The Company, by various means, prevented the elections from taking place and the matter was taken to court by the Association. The Company was found guilty of illegal interference in the appointment of checkweighers and was obliged to allow the men to call meetings for

[1] *D.M.A.* 27 January, 1936. [2] *M.F.G.B.* 20 January, 1937.
[3] *Derbyshire Times,* 21 February, 1931.

the necessary nominations and elections. The Council recorded its thanks 'to those men at Bolsover who have been standing the brunt of the intimidation, and have been making a stand for the rights of the men to nominate and elect their own checkweighers, with complete freedom from pressure by the Colliery Company'.[1] In the ballot which ensued members of the Association held the first seven places. The three men who were finally elected were A. Gilberthorpe, T. Groves and J. T. Tighe.[2]

The opposition to the Spencer union reached a climax in 1936. In August of that year two boys employed at the Harworth Colliery of Barber, Walker and Company were assaulted by colliery officials. Despite the fact that the majority of the men were members of the Nottinghamshire Miners' Association the colliery manager refused to meet their leaders to discuss the matter, saying that he would negotiate only with the Industrial Union. Early in September there was a dispute over working conditions. Two men employed on one of the conveyor units were dismissed for taking 'snap' time (i.e. a break for a meal) without authority from the management. In sympathy with these men most of the other miners stopped work on 3 September. The colliery manager refused to discuss the matter until the men returned to work and when they had complied with his wishes he insisted on punishing the alleged ringleaders. To this end he drew up a document which, he said, they must sign before he would reinstate them. This inflamed the feelings of the men who decided to take a strike ballot. It was supervised by the local postmaster—an entirely independent person—and resulted in 785 votes being cast in favour of giving notices and 136 votes against.

At this stage the M.F.G.B. intervened at the request of the Nottinghamshire Miners' Association. 'We determined', reported the Executive Committee, 'to prosecute this matter not only with the object of securing justice for the men at Harworth, but for the even bigger and wider purpose of winning back freedom of organization and recognition of our Association in Nottingham[shire] generally.'[3] The M.F.G.B. advised the men to remain at work and attempted, without success, to negotiate with the colliery company. On 7 October the Federation asked the Secretary for Mines to intervene but he replied, on 23 October, that the owners of the colliery had told him 'that they do not consider the trouble is of such a nature as to lend itself to arbitration by an outside body'.[4] The Federation then arranged a secret ballot, again supervised by disinterested persons, in which the men were asked to state which

[1] D.M.A. 29 June, 1931.
[2] Ibid. 8 August, 1931; Derbyshire Times, 15 August, 1931.
[3] Miners' Federation of Great Britain, Annual Report of the Executive Committee, 1936–7. [4] M.F.G.B. 20 January, 1937.

union they wished to represent them. There were 1,175 votes for the Nottinghamshire Miners' Association and only 145 for the Industrial Union.

The Federation decided that notices should be handed in on 23 November if the owners persisted in their refusal to negotiate. In the meantime there was a further dispute at the colliery, over the right to appoint checkweighmen, which resulted in an immediate cessation of work. On this issue the men were morally right but technically wrong and the Federation advised them to return to work and deal with the matter in accordance with the law. At this point the management refused to take any of the men back unless they joined the Industrial Union. The M.F.G.B. once again pressed the Government to intervene and in January, 1937, an industrial officer of the Mines Department interviewed representatives of the Company. The management then agreed not to make membership of the Industrial Union a condition of re-employment, but at the same time utterly refused to recognize the Federation or to discuss any grievances of the men except with representatives of the Industrial Union.[1]

The stoppage at Harworth displayed all the worst features of disputes in the coal industry. The employers, Barber, Walker and Company, practically owned the village of Bircotes where many of the men lived. Apart from the power of eviction, the colliery company controlled so much of the activity of the village as to make it extremely difficult for the miners to carry on their propaganda and their communal life. The church, the parish hall and the Salvation Army hut were all built on ground belonging to the Company and the miners were constantly refused facilities for public meetings. Between 100 and 150 police were drafted into the district from all parts of the county at an estimated average extra charge on police funds of £120 a week. Their arrival served only to exacerbate the situation and led to many unfortunate incidents. The worst disorders occurred when the men still employed in the pits, popularly known as the 'Chain Gang', were marched to and from their work under a strong police escort. At such times the main road running past the colliery entrance was closed by police cordons. Heavy penalties were inflicted upon a number of the strikers as a result of their conflicts with the police.[2]

Serious allegations were made to the National Council for Civil Liberties about the high-handed actions of the police. There were a large number of complaints that they had exceeded their authority in

[1] Miners' Federation of Great Britain, *Annual Report of the Executive Committee, 1936–7*.
[2] *The Harworth Colliery Strike. A Report to the Executive Committee of the National Council for Civil Liberties by the Secretary of the Council*, March, 1937.

ordering law-abiding men and women not to be seen in the streets at certain times. It was alleged that persons going to keep appointments, or even to buy fish and chips, were not allowed to pass the police cordons. The police were accused of using bad language and differentiating between those who were connected with the dispute and the families of the men who were still at work. There were complaints that the police were interfering with pickets, and abusing their powers of search and detention; that summonses were being issued ordering men to appear in court twelve or thirty-six hours later for offences committed as much as a month previously; that local magistrates, consciously or unconsciously, were favouring the owners in their judgments.

Ronald Kidd, the Secretary of the National Council for Civil Liberties, who investigated these complaints, concluded that they were justified. He reported:

It is impossible to avoid the belief that the owners have abused their position to deny to their employees their civil rights of freedom of association and freedom of assembly, both of which are essential for political life in general, and in particular for the peaceful settlement of industrial disputes.

It is unfortunate that so much of the public administration of the County is in the hands of those whose economic interests coincide with the interests of the owners rather than with the interests of the men who are dependent on the owners for their livelihood.

Whatever the cause, there can be no reasonable doubt, I think, that there have been serious irregularities in the conduct of the police during the dispute and this, coupled with the attitude and composition of the local Bench and with the method of serving summonses and making charges, has led to a feeling throughout the district that the general administration of law and order in the County is being used in a manner which must do infinite harm to a belief in the traditions of public administration and justice.[1]

On 20 January, 1937, after the stoppage had lasted for two months, the Executive Committee of the M.F.G.B. convened a special conference to consider the situation. Arthur Horner, the South Wales delegate, moved a resolution empowering the Executive Committee 'to take a ballot vote of the entire coalfields upon the question of enforcing freedom of organization and trades union recognition for those so organized' and to approach the General Council of the T.U.C. 'in order to enlist the support of the whole trade union movement'. Oliver Wright said:

I think Derbyshire can welcome this resolution more than any other district in the Federation, with the exception of Notts., because right down from 1926 we in Derbyshire along with our Notts. comrades have suffered from this poison of non-political trades unionism. The difference between the two counties has only been a question of degree. I was very pleased to

[1] *The Harworth Colliery Strike. A Report to the Executive Committee of the National Council for Civil Liberties by the Secretary of the Council*, March, 1937.

hear Mr. Horner say that this resolution from the Executive is not a matter of bluff, because I would like to impress upon this conference that if once we enter into this struggle with Spencerism we have either to completely smash Spencer and non-political trade unionism in the coalfields of Great Britain, or Spencer will emerge stronger than ever, and our next position is going to be worse than our present position.[1]

The resolution was carried unanimously.

The decision of the conference was immediately reported to the Secretary for Mines and the General Council of the T.U.C. The Executive Committee had thought for some time that an amalgamation of the two unions in Nottinghamshire would be the best solution to the problem and readily accepted an invitation from the Secretary for Mines to meet representatives of the Industrial Union under his chairmanship. Heads of proposals were drawn up for the fusion of the two unions but the negotiations were discontinued when it was found that, even with the aid of the Secretary for Mines and his industrial officers, it was impossible to obtain any assurances from Barber, Walker and Company that there would be no victimization at Harworth. When the Executive Committee gave its report to a special conference on 1–2 April there was strong opposition to the conditions insisted upon by the Industrial Union for the proposed amalgamation. The Derbyshire delegates were divided. Sales told the Executive Committee:

I submit that this agreement which you are asking Notts. to accept gives them nothing at all. There is not one single redeeming feature in it. This has come as a result of ten years' struggling. The whole terms are dictated terms. Terms dictated by Spencer himself.

He suggested as an alternative that the Derbyshire and Yorkshire associations should absorb those parts of Nottinghamshire which were nearest to their boundaries and that the officials of the Nottinghamshire Miners' Association should become part of the new organizations. When J. A. Hall, a Yorkshire delegate, asked whether this proposal represented the views of Derbyshire, Frank Hall replied: 'No.'[2]

On the following day the Executive Committee, sensing the feelings of the conference, recommended the adoption of a resolution rejecting Spencer's terms, deploring the absence of any satisfactory assurance regarding the reinstatement of the Harworth men, and calling for a ballot 'with the object of securing recognition of the Mineworkers' Federation of Great Britain and adequate assurances to prevent victimization at Harworth Colliery'. Frank Lee argued that recognition was not enough:

I can see no hope for our Notts. people unless fusion is arrived at in Notts. There you have got the best paying coalfield in Great Britain. You have got

[1] *M.F.G.B.* 20 January, 1937. [2] *Ibid.* 1 April, 1937.

the greatest output, and the owners can afford to give better terms under the ascertainment. Spencer is getting all the credit for it. They are saying: 'See what Spencer has done, the other Association cannot do anything for us.' I cannot, therefore, see any hope unless you get something in addition to this ballot, some idea of fusion. This resolution states that these terms are un-reasonable and unacceptable. I agree. I would like to see something in addi-tion to this ballot vote, that the door shall not be closed with regard to terms on which we might get fusion with Spencer.

Despite the fact that the President assured Lee that this was made clear in the mover's speech the Derbyshire delegates voted against the resolu-tion which was carried by 503 to 32.[1]

In the ballot which followed on 15–16 April Derbyshire supported the tendering of strike notices by 21,309 votes to 3,902. The national figures were 444,546 for a strike and 61,445 against. On 20 April the Executive Committee of the M.F.G.B. appointed J. Gilliland, J. A. Hall, Arthur Horner and James (later Sir James) Bowman to act with the officials as a negotiating sub-committee. On the same day the sub-committee met a representative of the Mines Department and asked him to make two requests to the Nottinghamshire owners: first, that they should grant direct recognition to the Federation, and second, that the question of victimization at Harworth should be disposed of by drawing lots to fill the vacant places. The owners refused to give direct recognition but were prepared to adopt the procedure recommended for reinstating the men if the Federation would accept Spencer's proposals for the fusion of the two unions. In the discussions which followed at the Mines Department the Nottinghamshire coal-owners and the Industrial Union acted together. The Federation sought unsuccessfully a modification of Spencer's proposals and eventually decided to recommend to a national conference that the two unions should be left to negotiate for 'a reasonable period'. In the event of agreement being reached the M.F.G.B. was to approve it and accept the method of reinstatement at Harworth which had been arranged between the owners and the Mines Department.

The national conference rejected the Executive Committee's recom-mendation and decided that notices should be handed in to expire simultaneously in every district on 22 May. Early in May the dispute was debated in the House of Commons and Baldwin, whose Premier-ship was rapidly coming to an end, made one of his characteristic appeals for industrial peace. Soon afterwards Crookshank, the Secretary for Mines, suggested to the M.F.G.B. that the question of the amalgama-tion of the two unions should be referred to arbitration. This was rejected

[1] *M.F.G.B.* 2 April, 1937. Leicestershire, Somerset and the Forest of Dean added their 7 votes to Derbyshire's 25.

by the miners' leaders who advanced a counter-proposal for a suspension of the strike notices provided an early conference of the Nottinghamshire colliery owners, the Industrial Union and the M.F.G.B. could be arranged. The owners would only accept this invitation subject to the acceptance by the M.F.G.B. of the principles of amalgamation and arbitration and the Executive Committee then made final arrangements for the strike to begin on 29 May.

The Secretary for Mines asked whether the M.F.G.B. would accept the principle of amalgamation if satisfactory terms could be arranged. The officials of the M.F.G.B. now had to decide whether they could sustain the claim for direct recognition, or whether it would not be wiser to concentrate on the principle of fusion, which, since the conference of 1-2 April, had been recognized as the secondary method of settlement. There was no time for consultation with the Executive Committee so they decided to accept amalgamation. This enabled the negotiating sub-committee of the M.F.G.B. to meet the Nottinghamshire owners and the Industrial Union's representatives and to discuss terms of amalgamation under a neutral chairman, John (later Sir John) Forster, on 24 May and the following days. By midday on 26 May the negotiating committee was able to present to the Executive Committee provisional terms of settlement which were ratified by a national conference on the following day.

A new organization, the Nottinghamshire and District Miners' Federated Union, was created, with George Spencer as President and his trusted follower, Horace Cooper, as Financial Secretary and Treasurer. Val Coleman and W. Bayliss, former officials of the Nottinghamshire Miners' Association, became General Secretary and Agent respectively. J. G. Hancock was also to be given the opportunity of becoming an agent and, if he declined, the vacancy was to be filled by another representative of the Industrial Union. Clause 7 of the settlement laid down that the rules of the new union should conform with the rules and constitution of the M.F.G.B. and be in strict accordance with the provisions of the Trade Disputes and Trade Unions Act, 1927. Spencerism, if not destroyed, was at least firmly fettered.

On 29 May the Council of the Derbyshire Miners' Association decided to ask the Secretary of the M.F.G.B. to remind the negotiating committee that the union's original boundaries in Derbyshire should be observed in the new agreement, and that members of the Industrial Union who were working inside the original boundaries should be transferred to the Derbyshire Miners' Association as soon as possible.[1] However, the Bolsover and Creswell collieries, which had been the strongholds of the Industrial Union in Derbyshire, continued to be

[1] D.M.A. 29 May, 1937.

organized from Nottinghamshire. A small number of men remained loyal to the Derbyshire Miners' Association, most of them in order to qualify for their old-age pensions, but no branch meetings were held and there were no negotiations with the employers. In January, 1944, Bolsover and Creswell ceased to exist as branches. The Creswell members were transferred to the Whitwell branch and the Bolsover branch became a collecting station connected with one of the Markham branches. Benjamin Lee, one of the Bolsover veterans, was appointed collector, for which he received a small fee.[1]

VIII

The upward trend of the trade cycle and the re-armament programme led to a marked improvement in the coal trade in 1936–7. The average selling value of coal in Derbyshire rose from 12s. 8·84d. per ton in 1935 to 14s. 0·10d. in 1936 and 14s. 7·85d. in 1937. In 1938 it was to rise even more steeply to 15s. 6·22d. Output increased from 11,978,615 tons in 1935 to 13,807,931 in 1937, falling to 13,014,015 in 1938.[2] Miners' wages showed a corresponding improvement. By June, 1937, they averaged almost 13s. a shift in Derbyshire.[3] The employers were ready to make concessions and the Association was quick to seize its opportunity. In August Hicken proposed the opening of negotiations for a new wage agreement and holidays with pay.[4] By 19 November the negotiations had been successfully completed.[5]

The main purpose of the new wages agreement was to smooth out the violent fluctuations in wages which sometimes occurred as a result of the ascertainments. The monthly ascertainments were based on a period of twelve months instead of three and the basic rates were consolidated. The new basic rate was equal to the sum of the basic rates existing at 30 November, 1937, plus 38 per cent. and, where applicable, the subsistence allowances. In addition the flat-rate increase of 9d., granted in 1936, was continued. The agreement came into operation on 1 December, 1937, and was to last until 30 June, 1943, subject to the usual qualifications regarding changes in the hours of work or the conditions in the district.[6] The agreement favoured the lower-paid workers by stabilizing their wages. Under the old system a small percentage addition was of little advantage to the lower paid men. Moreover the time lag between the ascertainments and the payment of the percentage determined by them meant that the men were often receiving

[1] D.M.A. 15 January, 1944.   [2] See Chapter XIV, Appendix I.
[3] Ministry of Labour Gazette.   [4] D.M.A. 28 August, 1937.
[5] Ibid. 20 November, 1937.
[6] Derbyshire Miners' Association, Agreement made between the Colliery Owners of the Derbyshire District and Representatives of the Workmen, 19 November, 1937.

low rates when they were working good time and high rates when they were working short time. Under the new system the men received approximately the same percentage throughout the year whether working good time or bad. Hicken estimated that if the new system had been in operation during the period 1936–7 the average ascertainment would have been 48 per cent. instead of fluctuating between the minimum of 38 per cent. and 66 per cent. as it had done. 'It is one of the biggest steps forward in the history of the organization', he said. 'It simplifies the whole question of ascertainments, will necessitate less clerical work, and will rule out misunderstanding.'[1] When the scheme came into operation the lowest grades had an immediate increase of 4d. a shift, making their daily earnings 9s. The first ascertainment gave an addition of 4·17 per cent. to the new basic rates for December. But for the new arrangements wages for the month would have been at the former minimum. The movement for holidays with pay in 1936–7, which had the support of the T.U.C., was the subject of a government inquiry presided over by Lord Amulree. W. A. Lee, the Secretary of the Mining Association, told the Committee that his Association viewed the idea sympathetically but was strongly opposed to any legislation because of wide differences in economic conditions in the districts.[2] Derbyshire and Nottinghamshire were sufficiently prosperous to bear the cost of holidays with pay and were the first coalfields in the country to make the concession. In June, 1936, the Bolsover Company started a scheme for summer gifts to workmen, closing the pits for a week and giving £3 to married men over 21, £2 to other married men, £1 10s. to single men over 18, and £1 to boys.[3] The Derbyshire agreement, which was signed at the same time as the new wages agreement, provided allowances of £3 for married men and widowers, £1 10s. for single men, and £1 for boys under 18. It was estimated that the scheme would cost over £100,000 a year. The fund was to be established as part of the monthly ascertainment machinery, owners and men subscribing to it in the proportion of 15:85. The employers' contribution was to be treated as a cost of production other than wages.

After years of low wages, short time and unemployment the position of the miners was beginning to improve. During 1938 earnings continued to rise but already the drums of war were rumbling in the distance. During the next few years there were to be profound changes in the wages and conditions of the miners and, from the melting-pot of the Second World War, a national union and a nationalized industry were to emerge.

[1] *Derbyshire Times*, 12 November, 1937.
[2] *D.C. on Holidays with Pay*, 1938, Evidence of W. A. Lee, pp. 285–94.
[3] *Derbyshire Times*, 5 November, 1937.

CHAPTER XX

SOCIAL CONDITIONS, WELFARE AND SAFETY,
1918–39

I

Poverty was the greatest social evil of the inter-war years. The areas which were highly specialized and dependent on the basic industries suffered most. There was probably more distress among the miners than in any other section of the community. Wage rates, which in many cases were already inadequate, lagged behind the cost of living from 1921 onwards.[1] The onset of the world economic depression brought wage rates ahead of the cost of living in the more prosperous areas such as Derbyshire after 1929, but this gain was offset by short-time working.[2] Real earnings per week in 1929 were already lower than in 1914.

A rough index of the level of employment in Derbyshire throughout the period is provided by the statistics of the average number of days worked per week by the mines.[3] In 1923, the peak year, it was 5·56. By 1933 it had fallen to 3·72, a reduction of 34 per cent. For most miners the reduction would be even greater because the policy of spreading employment during the depression meant that they were unable to work every day the mines were open. This reduction in earning capacity of more than 34 per cent. between 1923 and 1933 was aggravated by falling wage rates but offset to some extent by a 20 per cent. reduction in the cost of living. Between 1933 and 1939 conditions improved. As wage rates increased slightly, the average number of days worked per week increased by 17 per cent. from 3·72 to 4·36 but these gains were almost counterbalanced by a 12 per cent. increase in the cost of living. By the outbreak of war miners' earnings were still below the level which they had reached in the years immediately before the 1921 lock-out. In addition to short-time working there was much unemployment. The closing of collieries and the advance of mechanization led to a sharp contraction in the volume of employment during the inter-war years.[4]

[1] See Chapter XVIII. [2] See Chapter XIX, pp. 751-3.
[3] See Appendix I to this chapter. [4] See Chapter XIV, p. 576.

Between 1924 and 1939 the total number of wage earners on the books of the Derbyshire collieries fell by 32 per cent. from 66,211 to 44,723.[1]

The miners' attitude to the frictional unemployment following the First World War has already been noted.[2] The Bishop of Southwell attributed the poverty of the miners at this time to 'moral failure'.[3] However, within two years there was to be a degree of unemployment against which the savings of even the most abstemious were of no avail. By the end of 1921 there were nearly two million unemployed out of a total of twelve million insured workers. Frank Lee told the Eckington miners: 'The question we are all most concerned about at the present time is unemployment. It has always been the bogy of the working man, who, in his prosperous time, feels in the near future he might be out of a job.'[4]

The unemployment rate in 1921 was probably greater than had ever before been experienced.[5] It was to rise even higher in 1931–3. Until 1939 the number of unemployed hardly ever fell below a million. The advent of mass unemployment of this character called for both palliatives and remedies. Relief funds were quickly organized in 1921 to deal with the worst cases of distress. In Chesterfield the Borough Welfare Committee appealed for second-hand boots, clothing and toys in order to brighten the Christmas of the unemployed.[6] The Derbyshire Miners' Association did much useful work in representing unemployed members who wished to appeal to the Courts of Referees, established under the unemployment insurance legislation.[7] In April, 1922, the Council expressed the view 'that Unemployment Insurance should be national in its application to all industries, and that benefits should be paid through recognized trade unions'.[8]

The miners were then trying to formulate a scheme, based on the continuation of the Sankey levy of a penny a ton on coal, which would give them pensions at 60. Apart from the obvious advantage of providing for old age, the scheme had the additional virtue of reducing unemployment by facilitating earlier retirement. A Derbyshire resolution calling for the provision of a superannuation fund was accepted in principle by the annual conference of the M.F.G.B. in 1923.[9] Later, detailed proposals outlined in the *Derbyshire Times* by Samuel Sales won the approval of Frank Hodges who wrote: 'I am fully in agreement with the proposals. . . . You can always rely upon me to give

[1] See Appendix I to this chapter.
[2] See Chapter XVI, pp. 613-14.
[3] *Derbyshire Times*, 16 August, 1919.
[4] *Ibid.* 5 March, 1921.
[5] Cf. Lord Beveridge, *Full Employment in a Free Society*, (London), 1944, pp. 72–3.
[6] *Derbyshire Times*, 3 December, 1921.
[7] D.M.A. 7 July, 10 December, 1921.
[8] *Ibid.* 4 April, 1922.
[9] M.F.G.B. 13 July, 1923.

you whatever assistance is necessary to help you to further the idea.'[1]

The Derbyshire Miners' Association was extremely critical of the Government's failure to create more employment. In January, 1921, the Council protested 'against the ineffectiveness of the Government in coping with the unemployment problem' and urged 'that they should adopt the policy advocated by the Labour Party, or that more active measures for the purpose of providing work should be taken, rather than dividing the amount of work available amongst all workmen, which is simply feeding the dog with a bite from its own tail'.[2] The Labour Party's policy was explained to the Eckington miners by Frank Lee, in March, 1921:

Unemployment insurance would not provide a remedy. What they suggested instead of doles was that they should find them work. If they had ridden with him in the car that night they would have thought new roads would not be out of place. Even in Eckington more houses were needed. . . . These were things among others, such as reclamation of land, the planting of trees, and settling men in smallholdings, which were embodied in the Labour Party's policy in dealing with temporary unemployment.[3]

It was not long before unsympathetic employers began to raise the familiar cry of the inter-war years that the unemployed did not want work. Charles Markham told the Samuel Commission: 'I am strongly of the opinion that doles are pernicious. The majority of the men who are receiving the dole have no desire to work again. Some of them are as well off as others who are working under present day conditions.'[4] If this statement was correct it implied a very low standard of living for some of those who were at work. But Markham was an unreliable witness. His allegation before the Samuel Commission that men who had been sent from the Employment Exchange had asked his manager not to find them work was challenged by Sir William (later Lord) Beveridge. Markham then modified his statement and said that the men had refused work. 'In which case they would not get benefit, would they?' said Beveridge. Inquiries into this incident, made at the request of the Commission, showed that four of the nine men referred to by Markham were sent by the Employment Exchange, one of whom was engaged. The reasons given by the colliery officials for not engaging the other three did not indicate that the men had shown unwillingness to accept work, nor did they disclose any other grounds of disqualification for benefit. The other five men were not sent by the Exchange and were not in fact

[1] *Derbyshire Times*, 29 December, 1923; 19 January, 1924.
[2] *D.M.A.* 5 January, 1921.   [3] *Derbyshire Times*, 5 March, 1921.
[4] *R.C. on Coal Industry*, 1925, II, Part B. Evidence of Markham, p. 541.

drawing unemployment benefit.[1] The moral and physical deterioration of those who were unemployed for long periods is well known. Dr. Morris Robb has shown that unemployment sometimes led to severe psychic illnesses in which the patient was 'incapable of facing the strain of competitive industry, even if he should be fortunate enough to have a job offered to him'.[2] Such cases were exceptional and required special treatment rather than vilification. The majority of unemployed went to great lengths to find work.[3]

The poverty among the miners was revealed and intensified by the great industrial disputes of the inter-war years. During the 1921 stoppage many of them fell into debt. The M.F.G.B. argued that since the men were locked out they were entitled to unemployment benefit but the Minister of Labour insisted that the stoppage was a trade dispute within the meaning of the Unemployment Insurance Act, 1920. Test cases brought before the Courts of Referees in each district were unsuccessful. When the payment of union benefits ceased the men appealed to the Boards of Guardians for loans which they were later unable or unwilling to repay. It was reported to the Chesterfield Board of Guardians in October, 1922, that it would take over fifty-eight years for the loans to be wiped off at the existing rate of repayment.[4]

The longer dispute of 1926 caused even greater hardship. Joseph Kitts, later to become one of the officials of the union, describes how the miners of Somercotes made arrangements to care for the children:

We fed them at four centres. I was responsible for cadging. I used to write to Cadbury's, Fry's, Marsden's and other firms and get two-hundred-weight bags of sugar, chests of tea, etc. Then we went round the local butchers and got beasts' heads to make soup. At one time we were feeding about 1,200 children a day, giving them two solid meals. I was also responsible for seeing that certain teams of men went coal picking to supply the chapel schoolrooms with fuel. We had some little miners' lamps and used to stand collecting in Derby market. The farmers there used to call us names. Several of us went to Leicester and obtained about 300 pairs of boots. We also had two marches to the Belper workhouse to force the issue with the Board of Guardians. We collected sufficient money to take three bus-loads of children. We went to stay and made them feed us.[5]

Similar conditions prevailed in every mining village in Derbyshire and throughout the country. Again the miners received from the Boards of Guardians loans which they had to repay from their much reduced

[1] R.C. on Coal Industry, 1925, II, Part B. Evidence of Markham, QQ. 11,269–11,276.
[2] Morris Robb, 'The Psychology of the Unemployed from the Medical Point of View,' (H. L. Beales and R. S. Lambert, eds., Memoirs of the Unemployed, (London), 1934, pp. 276–7).   [3] Cf. Beveridge, op. cit. pp. 242–3.
[4] Derbyshire Times, 7 October, 1922   [5] Statement by Joseph Kitts.

incomes after the stoppage. The coal-owners were generally well represented on the Boards and did not fail to point out the 'injustice' of
allowing the miners to evade repayment. Arrangements were sometimes
made for deductions from wages.[1] In March, 1928, the Belper Board of
Guardians took legal proceedings against eighteen miners in the Riddings and Somercotes district who agreed to deductions from their
wages of 1s. a week until the loans were repaid.[2]

The men who failed to secure work after the 1926 dispute were in an
even worse plight. In July, 1927, a member of the Bolsover Urban
District Council urged that an appeal should be made to the Bolsover
Company and other firms in the district to reinstate the men who had
been unemployed since the stoppage.[3] A Warsop miner who had moved
to Manton in search of work told the Warsop Board of Guardians:

> My children have no clothing and no snap [i.e. food]. I have six children,
> the eldest being 12 years and the youngest 7 years, and my wages, after
> deducting stoppages and after working for four days are 26s., sometimes
> only 24s. I have nothing to eat in the house. I have had nothing near my lips
> this morning except cold water. The youngest child has no rags to its back;
> neither has its mother. Two of my children are unable to go to school today
> because they have no boots to their feet.[4]

The relieving officer said that if they granted relief they would have
200 similar cases immediately. The unfortunate miner was eventually
awarded 10s. a week, 'the relief to be on loan and in kind'.

II

Towards the end of 1927 unemployment began to increase. The
Chesterfield Corporation appointed a special committee to deal with
the matter and decided to send a deputation to the Minister of Labour.[5]
1928 was a year of great distress in the coalfields. In the House of Commons in May, Frank Lee raised the question of unemployment in
Derbyshire and asked the Minister of Health and the Minister of
Labour whether the Government would be prepared to make grants to
local authorities to enable them to employ men on road and quarry
work but was told that there were no funds available.[6] In August the
Prime Minister appealed to employers to give preference to men and
boys from the depressed mining areas. In October, in reply to a resolution sent to him by the M.F.G.B, the Home Secretary stated that the
Government was 'gravely anxious' about the position of the coal

[1] *Derbyshire Times*, 10 March, 1928.   [2] *Ibid*. 24 March, 1928.
[3] *Ibid*. 2 July, 1927.   [4] *Ibid*. 10 September, 1927.
[5] *Ibid*. 3 and 17 December, 1927.   [6] 217 H.C. Deb. 5s. 1709–10.

industry but added that it was 'perfectly certain' that there were 200,000 men who could never be employed again in the industry and who would have to find work elsewhere, either in this or some other country.

The situation was made worse by the fact that an increasing number of miners had exhausted their statutory unemployment benefits. The unemployment statistics ceased to give a true picture of the growing poverty in the country for there was a steadily widening gap between the official figures of insured persons 'unemployed' and the total numbers actually out of work. The exporting districts of Northumberland, Durham and South Wales were the most seriously affected. In the absence of effective action by the Government, relief funds were started. The Lord Mayor of the City of London made his appeal for Northumberland, Durham and South Wales in April. In the autumn the M.F.G.B. launched the Miners' National Distress Fund. This was given wide publicity and met with an excellent response. The *Daily Mail* played a prominent part in the campaign. Footwear, clothing, blankets, food and cash came pouring into the headquarters of the miners' unions in time for Christmas, 1928. The offices of the Derbyshire Miners' Association 'presented something of the appearance of a large grocery and provisions store' with the officials unpacking cases of goods for allocation to the different areas. 'There are far more justifiable claims than we can ever hope to meet', said Hicken.[1] Local committees were appointed to distribute the goods.[2] Help was also given by the Society of Friends.[3]

The Council of the Derbyshire Miners' Association expressed its dissatisfaction that the county had not been included in the Lord Mayor's appeal and decided to press Derbyshire's claim for assistance.[4] When the scheme was extended to cover Yorkshire and Nottinghamshire the *Derbyshire Times* commented: 'Derbyshire has not so far been looked upon as a distressed area. As a whole it is not, but there are some bad patches—as bad as anything in the other areas.'[5] The committee charged with the administration of the Lord Mayor's fund eventually gave its approval to the inclusion of certain parts of Derbyshire and the Mayors of Chesterfield and Ilkeston took the lead in forming local committees. The Government had already promised to grant a pound for every pound of voluntary subscriptions to the fund. Unemployment in Derbyshire was worst in the older parts of the coalfield where the uneconomic pits were concentrated. Some of the newer collieries were working full time but the managements preferred to employ the younger men. In these areas the incidence of unemployment was greatest among

[1] *Derbyshire Times*, 22 December, 1928.   [2] *D.M.A.* 13 October, 1928.
[3] *Ibid.* 3 November, 1928.
[4] *Ibid.* 29 December, 1928.   [5] *Derbyshire Times*, 12 January, 1929.

BB*

miners between the ages of 50 and 60 and surface labourers. The demand for young hewers and coal-face workers was said to exceed the supply.[1]

The National Unemployed Workers' Committee Movement, founded by the Communist Party in 1921, became increasingly active in Derbyshire as the world economic depression deepened. It was a revolutionary organization intended to hold the unemployed together, prevent them blacklegging during strikes and give them legal advice about benefits. In April, 1930, about eighty marchers, who were on their way to a May Day demonstration in Hyde Park, arrived in Chesterfield carrying banners and singing the *Internationale*. They were joined by a local contingent whose banner read: 'Chesterfield Branch, N.U.W.M. Task work must be abolished.' One of the leaders said that their object was 'to protest against a system of society which condemns thousands of men to unemployment, and also against the Labour Government for not taking steps to ease the situation'.[2] This policy evidently did not commend itself to the Council of the Derbyshire Miners' Association which had already decided that members of the N.U.W.M. should not be allowed to hold office in the union.[3] In 1933, when Hicken brought before the delegates an application from the N.U.W.M. for assistance in organizing another of its many marches, it was resolved:

That this Council can take no further responsibility for assistance for these marches of unemployed workers, having on two former occasions provided food and lodgings. Sympathy has been greatly alienated by the attitude of the marchers to the trade union movement in general, and the Derbyshire Miners' Association in particular.[4]

Complaints about the administration of the Unemployment Insurance Acts led to the setting up of the Morris Committee in 1929. In September the M.F.G.B. submitted a lengthy memorandum to the Committee, calling attention to the unsympathetic attitude of many of the Courts of Referees and the difficulties encountered by the miners in proving, in accordance with the law, that they were 'genuinely seeking work but unable to obtain employment.' Early in 1930 the Labour Government repealed the 'genuinely seeking work' clause and put the onus upon the authorities to prove that the applicant for benefit had refused a suitable offer of employment. In April, 1931, Oliver Wright was able to report to the Council of the Derbyshire Miners' Association that the amount of money gained from successful appeals to the Courts of Referees on behalf of members 'ran into thousands of pounds'.[5]

[1] *Derbyshire Times*, 2 March, 1929.   [2] *Ibid.* 19 April, 1930.
[3] *D.M.A.* 4 January, 1930.
[4] *Ibid.* 23 September, 1933.   [5] *Ibid.* 18 April, 1931.

The financial crisis of 1931 led to serious cuts in government expenditure at a time when unemployment was increasing rapidly. The publication, in June, of the Interim Report of the Holman Gregory Commission, which recommended economies in the Unemployment Insurance Scheme, aroused a strong protest from the Council. It assured the Government 'of its emphatic and active opposition to any change at this time in any general application of the Act' and demanded 'an all-in Insurance Act comprising all the industrial workers in the country'.[1] The recommendations of the Holman Gregory Commission were followed in July by the Report of the May Committee which also advocated, amongst other things, drastic cuts in unemployment benefit. The result was the hated Family Means Test (called by its supporters a 'needs test') administered by the public assistance authorities. Its operation was watched closely by the Derbyshire Miners' Association and was the subject of many complaints.[2] The peak year for unemployment was 1932 when 21·9 per cent. of the insured population were without work. The Association arranged a scheme which enabled members to buy second-hand clothing.[3]

The hardships of many of the miners and their families are well illustrated by a statement written by the wife of a Derbyshire miner in 1933. After twenty years in the pit her husband had lost his job in 1926 and had then worked as a navvy for five years. When all road work was stopped in 1931 he became unemployed. The benefits paid to him by the Public Assistance Committee had gradually been reduced until he was receiving only 2s. 6d. a week. But for his unmarried son who lived with him and contributed 20s. a week he would have been destitute. The mother wrote:

He pays me his money regularly and ungrudgingly but he does not realize that it is only enough to keep *him*. I can barely find rent and rates and coal and gas money out of what remains when I have bought enough food for him for the week. There is little food for us; for this reason we never have our meals together. I buy a shilling's worth of meat a week for my son, half-a-pound of bacon, and I make him a milk pudding sometimes. I can only have half a pint of milk a day and that has to be enough for everything. If my son were to know that his father and I have bread-and-butter and tea for every meal he would not eat what I put before him and that would not do. He must eat it if he is to work. I rely on him for rent and coal money. (We pay 5s. a week rent and £6 a year rates.) . . .

. . . My children cannot help us, although the Public Assistance man thinks they can. But I know they cannot. My married son has a young family and he is a poor thing himself, with asthma and bronchitis to torment him all through the winter. Both of my daughters' husbands are on short time, and

[1] *D.M.A.* 20 June, 1931.   [2] *Ibid.* 21 November, 1931; 23 January, 1932.
[3] *Ibid.* 16 April, 11 June, 1932.

they have children of their own to feed and clothe. It is left to my youngest
son to keep us in a house of our own. . . .

. . . We would both rather be dead than go on like this; but there is no
prospect of change if my husband does not begin to work again. He has
been out of work so long now that I do not think he will get his Old Age
Pension when he is sixty-five, for he will not have enough stamps on his
Health Insurance cards. . . . That will be our greatest disappointment, for
our Old Age Pension would put us into comfort again. At present we are
miserable for want of the bare necessities of a decent life, and the visits of
the Public Assistance man every month are to be dreaded. He asks so many
questions and is so strict; and yet there is nothing we can tell him that he
cannot see for himself. . . . Our dependence on our youngest son is terrible
for us both. If there is a harder case than mine then it is indeed bad.[1]

Despite the gradual reduction in the numbers of unemployed after
1932 there were still well over a million without work in 1939. Men
such as the unemployed Derbyshire miner mentioned above, who was
62 in 1933, had little hope of finding work and were still at the
mercy of the Public Assistance Committees. The Unemployment Act,
1934, based largely on the recommendations contained in the Final
Report of the Holman Gregory Commission, issued in December,
1932, aroused further discontent. Part II of the Act created the
Unemployment Assistance Board, of which Violet Markham was a
member, as a central authority to administer the scheme. The Board,
with its local advisory committees, relieved the public assistance
authorities of the task of supervising transitional payments to those
who had exhausted their statutory unemployment benefits.

In February, 1935, the Council of the Derbyshire Miners' Association protested against the treatment of the unemployed under the new
Act and called for 'more generous scales of benefit and for more local
autonomy in the administration of the regulations'. It also protested
against the appointment by the Minister of Labour of the chairman of
the Chesterfield Area Board and of the vice-chairman of the Ilkeston
Area Board on the grounds that they were actively associated with
party politics, which was a disqualification under the Act.[2] In May, 1936,
Frank Lee asked the Minister of Labour in the House of Commons:

Whether he is aware that resentment is felt owing to the fact that officials
at the Employment Exchanges in the Ripley and Alfreton districts in Derbyshire, when new applications for statutory benefit are being made, put questions to married men with dependants regarding the amount they allow
their wives for household expenses and how much they keep for themselves
and afterwards spend on drink, tobacco, etc.[3]

[1] H. L. Beales and R. S. Lambert, eds., *Memoirs of the Unemployed*, (London),
1934, pp. 214–19.   [2] *D.M.A.* 19 January, 16 February, 1935.
[3] 312 H.C. Deb. 5s. 1348; *D.M.A.* 9 May, 1936.

The Family Means Test, described by the Council as 'a humiliating inquisition into every portion of the family income',[1] was also criticized by Alfred Holland, the Labour M.P. for Clay Cross. He told the miners:

> Old Scrooge was a generous person compared with the Minister of Labour. The Unemployment Assistance Board had been responsible for the breaking up of thousands of the best homes in the land as a result of the Means Test.[2]

III

In addition to unemployment and poverty the miners continued to suffer from a lack of decent housing and other amenities, although conditions were slowly improving. In Derbyshire, where the coal industry was comparatively young, the houses described by the Sankey Report as 'a reproach to our civilization' were not so numerous as in other districts. Nevertheless, they were still to be found in the older colliery villages. Some of them were visited by R. A. Scott-James, who contributed an Appendix on housing conditions to the Lloyd George report, *Coal and Power*, in 1924. He wrote:

> Old Poolsbrook, for example, is a gloomy and unsightly area, with its forbidding houses in parallel lines. Some condemned, but still inhabited, dwellings at Seymour are worse.
> Speedwell, also, is a relic from a bad period of what Mr. Aldridge has called the 'Black Century' of housing. It affords an example of the kind of house which ought never to have been built, which ought to be scrapped, but which, as it cannot yet be scrapped in view of the shortage, has been substantially amended by the landlords in an attempt to alleviate bad conditions.[3]

Indeed, the real problem in Derbyshire in the inter-war years was not so much the badness as the shortage of houses. In December, 1921, the Chairman of the Clowne Rural District Council stated: 'People were coming to them in tears, begging and praying for somewhere to live. Only a week ago he had brought to his notice a case of a mother and a little child who had been sleeping on the hearthrug for six weeks and it was not an isolated case.' Another councillor reported that there were similar conditions at Cresswell. In one house childbirth had taken place in a room where other children were sleeping.[4] Scott-James reported in 1924:

> Everywhere the cry among the miners and their families is for houses. 'We have been for six years in lodgings waiting for a house', said a woman

---

[1] *D.M.A.* 29 August, 1936.   [2] *Derbyshire Times*, 7 August, 1936.
[3] *Coal and Power, The Report of an Enquiry presided over by D. Lloyd George*, (London), 1924, pp. 126–7.   [4] *Derbyshire Times*, 17 December, 1921.

who had a husband and two children, and had at last found one. 'We have been sharing four rooms with another family', said a mother of three children, 'and the worst of it is Mrs. —— and I don't get on very well.' They have filled up all the houses in the ugly mining town of Staveley. They have over-flowed into the equally ugly town of Brimington. Barrow Hill has not a room to spare.[1]

The publication of this report inspired the *Derbyshire Times* to make its own investigations in Killamarsh, Halfway, Mosborough and Staveley. It reported:

Shocking overcrowding is quite general. The first thing that struck our representative in every part of the district was the difficulty experienced, particularly in the poorer quarters, in finding a house which did not shelter at least two families under very cramped conditions. . . . Many of the unfortunate people were living under the most appalling conditions imaginable— conditions which few people would credit existed in England unless they came in actual personal contact with them. . . . How some of the people would exist were it not that the men are on different shifts does not bear thinking of. As it is, in some cases they go to bed in relays.

In Barber's row, Killamarsh, eighty-six people lived in a row of eight houses, none of which had more than two bedrooms. The position at Staveley was described as 'a disgrace to civilization'.[2]

Conditions were equally bad in other parts of the county. In 1926, as a result of a survey conducted by the Clay Cross Labour Party, it was reported that 200 married couples were living in lodgings. Examples were given of some of the most notable cases of overcrowding. A house with only two bedrooms and an attic was occupied by two families: a total of eleven people. In another house thirteen people occupied two bedrooms, each about eight feet square.[3] Ten years later, when the Church Assembly considered a report of the Social and Industrial Commission on the Coal Trade, S. J. Bartle, of Chesterfield, asserted: 'The houses of many miners were nothing more than hovels. He believed no class of workmen were herded together so much in what should be lovely country villages as the miners.'[4]

The attitude of the coal-owners to housing played an important part in determining the rate of improvement. The building programmes of local authorities were not always popular because of the added burden to the rates. In 1922 H. Stevenson, the general manager of the Pinxton Collieries, Ltd., announced his intention of seeking election to the Blackwell Rural District Council in order to put a stop to the building of fifty houses at a cost of nearly £1,000 each. 'Put the rents at 9s. 6d. per week and rates at 5s. 2d. per week', he said. 'What man can afford to

[1] *Coal and Power*, p. 127.   [2] *Derbyshire Times*, 29 November, 1924.
[3] *Ibid.* 13 March, 1926.   [4] *Ibid.* 19 June, 1936.

pay that sum while the pits are making three and three-and-a-half days per week? Where is the money coming from? . . . The Pinxton Collieries, Ltd., pay roughly half the rates in the parish, and I am fighting for those who pay the rates.'[1]

The larger colliery companies were able to arrange their own housing schemes. In 1922 members of the Staveley-Sheepbridge group and some of their associates formed the Industrial Housing Association with a nominal capital of £1,000,000. The chairman was Lord Aberconway and the directors included Sir William Bird, Maurice Deacon, William Humble, W. H. McConnell and Charles Markham. H. D. McLaren and Sir Charles Ellis were also on the board, representing the Tredegar Iron and Coal Company and John Brown and Company respectively. No dividend was to be paid on the ordinary share capital and the directors were to receive no fees. The balance of the capital required was to be raised by mortgages on the houses erected, and by debenture issue upon the uncalled capital held by the colliery companies in the Association. The object of the scheme was to provide houses at important collieries in South Yorkshire, Derbyshire and Wales, and to let them at moderate rents.[2]

The Industrial Housing Association's plan to build two thousand houses in the Staveley district brought it into conflict with the Chesterfield Rural District Council which refused to approve the scheme because some of the houses were to have only one door and because the arrangements for drainage and water supply were not satisfactory.[3] Charles Markham was severely critical of the Council, which, he alleged, was dominated by 'a lot of old farmers'. He wrote:

The water supply at Netherthorpe, Hartington and Staveley is absolutely inadequate and has been so for an indefinite number of years—long prior to the war. If you write and complain no notice is taken of you. . . . Here we have a local authority supposed to look after water, drainage, and the welfare of the community, and when you find them absolutely inoperative, slothful and neglectful of their duties I can only refer to the words of Jackie Fisher: 'Sack the lot.'[4]

The difficulties encountered by Staveley led to a movement for obtaining urban powers, or amalgamating with Chesterfield.[5] By 1924, as a result of Markham's energetic agitation, conditions began to improve. Scott-James reported:

On the slope of the hill . . . with Staveley coal and iron works dominating the intermediate space, is growing up a large, new, well-planned town. The

[1] *Derbyshire Times*, 11 March, 1922.
[2] *Ibid.* 22 July, 1922. Cf. P. H. White, 'Some Aspects of Urban Development by Colliery Companies, 1919–1936', *The Manchester School of Economic and Social Studies*, XXIII, (1955), pp. 275–6.   [3] *Derbyshire Times*, 4 and 18 August, 1923.
[4] *Ibid.* 22 September, 1923.   [5] *Ibid.* 6 and 27 October, 1923.

houses are being constructed in blocks of two or four, with gardens behind and in front; and each has generally an entrance hall, a living room, a scullery, a w.c., a bath-room and a larder on the ground floor, three bedrooms with cupboards upstairs, and a handy substantial coal-house at the back. Some of them are supplied with hot water from the colliery.[1]

Other colliery owners also began to take a greater interest in housing. In 1926 H. E. Mitton, of the Butterley Company, told members of the Nottinghamshire Mining Students' Association:

Disgraceful housing conditions and an utter lack of interest in their employees' welfare was a discredit to many owners of large commercial undertakings. . . . Happily, however, in recent years, an entirely different state of affairs had been brought about in the mining world.[2]

J. and G. Wells, Ltd., decided in 1927 to build 600 houses at Killamarsh in connection with the development of the new Westthorpe Colliery.[3] The economic depression brought to a halt many schemes for the building of houses by both colliery companies and local authorities. In 1928 the Bolsover Company decided to abandon its plan to build more houses at Cresswell because of the condition of the coal trade.[4] The miners' leaders worked hard to prevent local authorities from following the example of the coal-owners. Samuel Sales was successful in convincing the Chesterfield Rural District Council in 1931 that it was undesirable to abandon its Tupton housing scheme.[5]

Many of the miners still had to travel long distances to their work and the feud between the Derbyshire Miners' Association and the railway companies continued in the years following the First World War. There were numerous complaints from the miners about the discomforts and unpunctualities of the workmen's trains. Their irritation was increased as railway rates rose. By 1922 workmen's fares in Derbyshire had increased by as much as 200 per cent. on certain routes.[6] Delegates from branches affected by the running of workmen's trains attended a special meeting at Chesterfield on 6 May, 1922. They complained that the increase in fares was being continued although wages had been reduced; that the full weekly fare was charged when the men were working short time; that the heating and lighting of the trains were inadequate; and that the conditions printed on the tickets, which compelled the holders to relieve the companies from liability for accident or delay, were unreasonable.[7]

Repeated efforts were made by the Association to remedy these

[1] Coal and Power, p. 127.
[2] Derbyshire Times, 6 November, 1926.
[3] Ibid. 5 February, 1927.
[4] Ibid. 29 September, 20 October, 1928.
[5] Ibid. 28 November, 1931.
[6] M.F.G.B. 6 March, 1923.
[7] D.M.A. 6 May, 1922.

grievances but correspondence produced no result, and the railway companies refused to receive a deputation. Other districts were experiencing similar difficulties and the matter was eventually taken up by the M.F.G.B. In March, 1923, the Executive Committee met representatives of all the railway companies and asked that miners' railway fares should not be more than 50 per cent. above the pre-war rates. This was refused but the companies promised that their local agents would consider applications for reductions where the existing charges were thought to be exceptionally heavy.[1]

IV

Amenities in the mining villages were considerably improved as a result of the Sankey Commission's recommendation that there should be a welfare levy of a penny a ton on coal output. The levy was first imposed for a period of five years by the Mining Industry Act, 1920, and subsequently continued. It was augmented in 1927 by a levy of a shilling in the pound on coal royalties. The output levy was reduced to a halfpenny a ton in 1934 but restored to a penny a ton in 1939. The fund thus created was administered by the Miners' Welfare Committee, appointed by the Board of Trade, consisting of representatives of colliery owners and mine-workers with some independent members. Hicken was appointed to the Committee in 1938. In the following year the Committee was replaced by the Miners' Welfare Commission which was of a similar composition. Pit-head baths, institutes, canteens, recreation grounds, health services and educational activities were all supported by the scheme. Allocations from the fund were intended to assist in defraying capital expenditure. Maintenance costs were to come largely from voluntary sources. Local authorities were allowed to participate in the schemes.

The Miners' Welfare Committee was assisted by county and district committees. The Derbyshire committee consisted of the miners' leaders, Hall, Lee, Spencer and Hicken; and J. Bayley (Bolsover Colliery Company), J. T. Todd (Blackwell Colliery Company), E. J. Fox (Stanton Coal and Iron Company) and G. Spencer (Mapperley Colliery Company). After the first meeting on 11 November, 1921, the Council decided to send circulars to the branches explaining the scheme and instructing them to call meetings and formulate proposals for submission to the Committee.[2] There were many misunderstandings about the purposes and working of the Miners' Welfare Fund and the

[1] Miners' Federation of Great Britain, *Report of the Executive Committee for the year ending 30 June, 1923.*   [2] *D.M.A.* 12 November, 1921.

miners' leaders had to spend much time in explaining it and urging the men to take advantage of it. Frank Lee told a miners' meeting:

One suggestion was that they should establish pit-head restaurants and send to the men at the coal face a supply of mutton chops and beefsteak. Another suggestion was that a supply of fresh drinking water should be sent down the mine. Personally, he was glad that the idea of public libraries and reading rooms seemed to be acceptable to the men.[1]

The employers favoured schemes which would relieve them of existing expenditure, such as grants for ambulance brigades and equipment or for the development of miners' institutes. L. Henton, the manager of the Cresswell Colliery, stated at a meeting called to discuss the local welfare scheme: 'They had as many institutions as any colliery village in the country, but their upkeep involved a tremendous amount of money, and he was hoping that their financial difficulties in this respect could be somewhat overcome by the quota they would receive under the scheme.'[2] The majority of the colliery institutes were quickly handed over to local welfare committees which became responsible for their maintenance. Several of the colliery companies arranged to deduct a penny a week from each man's wages in order to carry out the welfare schemes. Frank Hall told the Council on 21 July, 1923:

There are certain objections to this being done privately. The money will get into the hands of the coal-owners, who will disburse it as they think well, and men will be called upon to pay, who live some distance from the colliery and who will not be able to claim the proportion that they pay to the scheme, and therefore the district in which they live will be deprived of their payments. Otherwise they will be called upon to pay twice.

To avoid these difficulties he proposed that the men should pay their contributions into a county fund which could then be distributed in the same proportion as the grants from the Welfare Fund, thereby giving each district an assured income.[3]

The branches supported Hall's proposal by 41 votes to 24 but when the matter was raised with the coal-owners nearly a year later they suggested that no decision should be taken until it was known whether the welfare levy was to be continued beyond the original five years.[4] Towards the end of 1924 the Mining Association agreed with the Executive Committee of the M.F.G.B. to make a joint application to the Mines Department for the continuation of the levy for another five years. Output in Derbyshire had been greater than was expected with the result that the £3 per head allowed for the various welfare schemes

[1] *Derbyshire Times*, 25 March, 1922.   [2] *Ibid.*
[3] *D.M.A.* 21 July, 1923.   [4] *Ibid.* 18 August, 1923; 19 July, 1924.

left a substantial surplus. It was therefore decided to distribute a further 10s. per head to enable schemes to be completed. 'Those districts who hurry up will get first attention', stated the officials. 'There will now be ample funds to carry out further welfare schemes.'[1]

In January, 1925, the officials once again reminded the delegates of the possibilities of the Miners' Welfare Scheme:

We have been astonished at the indifference of our members in that they do not take a more active part in the Welfare Schemes which have been adopted in the different districts of the county. Gradually this Welfare money is getting into the hands of the coal-owners. . . . There is also an inclination to place these schemes in the hands of the local authorities, parish or urban district councils. In each case they have been a failure, while at the same time it is handing over the control of the scheme to a foreign body.

The renewal of the levy for another five years led the officials to urge members to greater activity. Most of the Derbyshire schemes in the first five years had been concerned with the development of institutes and recreational facilities. The officials now suggested that the institutes should be provided with books not only for technical instruction but 'other works, not novels in particular, but on all social questions'. Pit-head baths, a new convalescent home and old-age pensions were other possibilities which the miners were asked to consider.[2]

Perhaps the greatest achievement of the Miners' Welfare Scheme was the provision of pit-head baths. Their introduction was delayed by the heavy capital outlay involved and the lack of enthusiasm of many of the miners. Frank Lee told the Staveley miners in June, 1924: 'He hoped to see the day when there would be pit-head baths at every colliery. . . . Unfortunately many of the younger men still retained the old belief that if they washed their backs twice a week they were weakening them.'[3] A month later the Council decide to send a circular to the branches 'with a view to educating the members in favour of pit-head baths'.[4] But it was not until 7 December, 1929, that the first pit-head baths in Derbyshire were opened by Ben Turner, the Minister of Mines. They were at the Grassmoor Colliery and were largely the result of the efforts of Samuel Sales. The cost of construction, estimated at nearly £15,000, was borne by the Miners' Welfare Fund. The colliery company provided the necessary land, water and fuel. The men contributed 2d. a week towards the cost of maintenance.[5] The scheme was a great success. Sales reported: 'The demand for the use of the baths exceeded all our

[1] *D.M.A.* 6 December, 1924. [2] *Ibid.* 3 January, 1925.
[3] *Derbyshire Times*, 7 June, 1924. [4] *D.M.A.* 19 July, 1924.
[5] *Ibid.* 30 November, 1929; *Derbyshire Times*, 26 May, 2 June, 24 November, 1928; 14 December, 1929.

expectations.'[1] Other collieries followed the example of Grassmoor. Baths at Langwith, costing £21,000, were opened by Frank Lee on 12 September, 1931.[2] Baths at Shirebrook and Wingfield Manor were opened in 1932, and at Whitwell in 1933. By 1936 ten collieries in Derbyshire had taken advantage of the scheme and several others were planning to do so.[3]

V

The miners' demand for greater leisure continued to meet with resistance from the coal-owners during the inter-war years. The seven-hour day was regarded by many of them as the ruination of the industry and they were not content until a longer working day had been re-introduced. The miners' campaign for an annual holiday with pay, in which Derbyshire played a prominent part,[4] also met with opposition. One Derbyshire coal-owner commented in 1922:

Could anything be more absurd in these terribly difficult days than the proposal to grant a fortnight's holiday with full pay? . . . Will Mr. Frank Hodges or any other miners' leader say what cost it would add to the production of coal in the year?[5]

By 1937, however, as a result of the general movement for holidays with pay, some of the coal-owners were taking a more enlightened view of the matter. The Bolsover Colliery Company began its scheme of closing the pits for a week during the summer and giving the miners 'gifts' to enable them to enjoy a holiday.[6] Because these payments were regarded as gifts the men were also able to draw unemployment benefit, although the practice was frowned upon by the Minister of Labour.[7] When the Derbyshire Miners' Association negotiated its holiday scheme in 1937 it was hoped that the Minister would approve arrangements similar to those made by the Bolsover Company.[8] However, when the scheme started in the summer of 1938 a number of test cases were brought before the Courts of Referees. Some were successful and others were not. The Association argued that the scheme was for holiday *savings* since the men contributed 85 per cent. of the money and on 30 July the Council decided that in future 'in all circulars the Association shall not write of "Holidays with Pay" but of the "Holidays Saving Scheme".'[9]

[1] *Derbyshire Times*, 14 December, 1929.   [2] *Ibid.* 19 September, 1931.
[3] *Ibid.* 3 July, 1936.   [4] *D.M.A.* 4 February, 1919.
[5] *Derbyshire Times*, 11 February, 1922.   [6] See Chapter XIX, p. 771.
[7] *D.C. on Holidays with Pay*, 1938, Report, p. 46.
[8] See Chapter XIX, p. 771.   [9] *D.M.A.* 30 July, 1938.

An appeal was made to the Umpire who ruled that the men were receiving deferred wages and were not entitled to unemployment benefits.[1]

When the delegates assembled for a Council meeting on 24 September, 1938, there were resolutions from five branches calling for the ending of the Holidays Saving Scheme in view of the Umpire's decision. Three others favoured a protest in the House of Commons and an attempt to get the decision reversed. After a long discussion the matter was referred to the next Council meeting.[2] Meanwhile a branch vote was taken and the officials consulted Sir Stafford Cripps. On 22 October it was reported that 30 branches had voted in favour of continuing the scheme and 28 against. In view of the smallness of the majority it was decided that the officials should arrange meetings to explain the scheme to the men.[3] The meetings had the desired effect for, on 14 January, 1939, it was reported that 42 branches were now in favour of the scheme and 18 against.[4] In the following month the Council adopted, by 43 votes to 8, the recommendations of the Executive Committee that the scheme should be continued and that the holiday payments in 1940 and succeeding years should be £4 to married men, £3 to single men over 18, and £1 10s. to single men under 18. These increased payments were made possible because contributions for 1940 would be derived from the proceeds of a full year whereas for 1938 and 1939 they were derived from the proceeds of only 16 months.[5] In April, 1939, the Council decided that the Association should pay unemployment benefits to members during their holiday week.[6]

An integral part of the holiday scheme was the building of a holiday centre at Skegness. This was made possible by a grant of £40,000 from the Miners' Welfare Fund and by various contributions from the coal-owners. The Derbyshire Miners' Holiday Centre was officially opened by Sir Frederick Sykes, the Chairman of the Miners' Welfare Central Committee, on 20 May, 1939.[7] It was capable of accommodating nearly a thousand visitors, A man and his wife were able to have a week's holiday at the centre for 33s. Children over four years of age could be taken at a cost of 8s. 6d. a week. The miners and their families were accommodated in small chalets overlooking the sea and meals were served in a large dining hall at very low prices. Special arrangements were made with the railway companies for cheap fares from Derbyshire to Skegness.[8] The scheme, which was the first of its kind in the country, owed much to the inspiration of Hicken and enabled many miners and their families to have a week's holiday by the sea for the first time

[1] *Derbyshire Times*, 24 September, 1938.   [2] *D.M.A.* 23 September, 1938.
[3] *Ibid.* 22 October, 1938.   [4] *Ibid.* 14 January, 1939.
[5] *Ibid.* 28 January, 11 February, 1939.   [6] *Ibid.* 8 April, 1939.
[7] *Ibid.* 3 June, 1939.   [8] *Derbyshire Times*, 5 and 12 May, 1939.

in their lives. At the opening ceremony Sir Frederick Sykes said: 'I do not think there is any other non-profit making camp of the kind in the country. It is a pioneer venture which is being watched with close interest.'[1]

In other ways facilities for entertainment and recreation were increasing. The coming of the cinema to the mining villages helped the miners and their families to escape from the monotony of their surroundings into the sometimes tawdry but infinitely more exciting world created by the film industry. Charles Markham felt that this escapism was carried to extremes. He complained to the Samuel Commission: 'An ordinary collier's house will not spend less than 5s. per week in attending the "films".'[2] He based his assertion on the fact that the night shift men in Staveley were to be seen queuing outside the cinema before 10 o'clock in the morning and suggested that many of the children were suffering from nystagmus as a result of spending too much time watching films.[3] Herbert Smith protested that since the price of admission was as low as 2d. for children Markham's estimate of 5s. a week was an exaggeration 'to bias the mind of the public and to lead the public to think that the miner, when he earns his money, is spending it frivolously'.[4] 'I put it to you', said Smith, 'that this is not a fair statement to put in your précis, and it is not correct. And I put it to you that you spend more in one night when you go to see a play than the miner spends in a month.'[5]

Sports of various kinds continued to be fostered in the mining villages by the coal-owners and, later, by the Miners' Welfare Scheme. In 1922 H. Cropper told a Chesterfield football club: 'One of the reasons why this country would never witness a political or social revolution or upheaval was because the average Englishman was . . . immersed in sport. . . . This was far better than hanging and slouching around street corners arguing about Socialism and Bolshevism.'[6] A similar view was expressed by D. N. Turner, of the Staveley Company, in 1935: 'Cricket taught people more than just how to use a bat and ball. It taught them to play cricket through life, in everything they did. Generally the best sportsman was the best workman and the most useful citizen in the end.'[7] The trade union leaders, on the other hand, saw in the encouragement of welfare work for sports an opportunity to strengthen their own organization. In 1929 Hicken reported to the Council:

We are doing our utmost to co-ordinate miners' interests in sports of all kinds. . . . Social amenities to mining communities in the past have been

[1] *Derbyshire Times*, 26 May, 1939.
[2] *R.C. on Coal Industry*, 1925, II, Part B. Evidence of Markham, p. 540.
[3] *Ibid*. QQ. 11,454, 11,457.   [4] *Ibid*. Q. 11,454.   [5] *Ibid*. Q. 11,463.
[6] *Derbyshire Times*, 14 January, 1922.   [7] *Ibid*. 29 November, 1935.

very sadly neglected as compared with the social amenities within reach of other classes of workers. We now have an opportunity of wiping out this invidious comparison. . . . From the point of view of our Association, Welfares are of great importance; if we come in and do our utmost to foster the movement, then it is obvious that their influence can be used to our advantage. . . . From the point of view of organization alone we cannot afford to ignore this most important movement.[1]

The spiritual values of sport tended to be overlooked by the coalowners where absenteeism was involved. D. N. Turner told the Chesterfield Rotary Club, in 1923: 'Today all coal-owners were troubled by the irregularity with which men attended their work, especially on cup-tie days, race meetings and local feast times.'[2] Charles Markham stated in evidence before the Samuel Commission:

I find that far too much time is taken by the colliers in holidays. The average time worked by colliers when trade is good is only about 230 days to the year. They have their local feasts at which they usually take several days' holiday, and it is impossible to work the pits at these times. I also find that a considerable amount of time off is taken by the colliers to go to race meetings and for other voluntary reasons. This, to my mind, is one of the greatest set-backs to trade in the country.[3]

The miners continued to take an active interest in education. In 1921 the Council of the Derbyshire Miners' Association passed two lengthy resolutions calling attention to the educational deficiencies of the county. The 'failure of the education authorities to provide efficient educational services for the children of the working classes' was attributed to a shortage of teachers arising from an inadequate salary scale. A protest was also made against 'any suspension of provisions under the 1918 Education Act by Ministers of the Crown and government departments without consulting the people and Parliament'.[4] In 1928 the Association expressed the opinion 'that the children of the workers, in these times, cannot receive their share of secondary school education' and requested the Derbyshire Education Committee to reduce 'the present heavy £10 fee' and to increase the number of free places to at least 75 per cent.[5]

Conditions in the schools left much to be desired. Overcrowding was a serious problem. A member of the Staveley parish council complained in 1926 that a number of children had to sit on the floor for their lessons. 'In the Hollingwood district there are children who cannot go to school', he said. 'Both Brimington and Barrow Hill schools are packed and children have been turned away from them. . . . I have supplied the teachers

[1] D.M.A. 30 November, 1929.   [2] Derbyshire Times, 24 February, 1923.
[3] R.C. on Coal Industry, 1925, II, Part B. Evidence of Markham, p. 540.
[4] D.M.A. 26 February, 1921.   [5] Ibid. 13 October, 1928.

with sugar bags with which to make mats to put on the floor for children to sit on.'[1] In 1929 Jack Lees, the Labour member for Belper, was told by the President of the Board of Education, in reply to a Parliamentary question, that the average number of children per class in the Derbyshire elementary schools was thirty-five.[2]

During the inter-war years adult education played an increasingly prominent part in the lives of the more thoughtful and intelligent miners. The Derbyshire Miners' Association continued its affiliation with the Workers' Educational Association with Sales as its delegate.[3] In 1920 Sales and Hildreth attended a W.E.A. conference in Chesterfield to discuss the report of the Adult Education Committee of the Ministry of Reconstruction. 'Labour was going to rule,' said Sales, 'and they would require knowledge, for power without knowledge would lead to chaos.' Another delegate complained:

> The W.E.A. should keep in close touch with the trade union organizations. At present they were running a series of lectures on art, and he ventured to state that they were not being attended by one out of a thousand of the working class of Chesterfield. The lectures were being attended by the middle class. They were organizing it into a middle class organization instead of a Workers' Educational Association.[4]

Early in 1921 the officials of the Derbyshire Miners' Association prepared an educational scheme which was to operate in co-operation with the W.E.A., Ruskin College and its offshoot, the Central Labour College. A reference library was to be provided at the union's headquarters.

'To be able to benefit under this scheme,' stated the officials, 'members must have shown themselves interested in trade union matters generally, and especially in our own Association. It is not intended to confer special benefits upon individual members so much as to spread the desire and facilities for education in industrial history and economics amongst as large a number of the members of the Association throughout the county as possible.'[5]

In 1924 the Council accepted the principles embodied in the 'Ten Points' put forward by the National Council of Labour Colleges and agreed to co-operate in its work.[6] There were complaints in 1927 by the Secretary of the Chesterfield branch of the W.E.A. that members were transferring their allegiance to the propagandist N.C.L.C.[7] The Derbyshire Miners' Association continued to support both organizations and left the miners to decide which they preferred. The W.E.A. provided a forum for discussing many problems affecting the miners in the

[1] *Derbyshire Times*, 17 April, 1926.   [2] 230 H.C. Deb. 5s. 1477.
[3] *D.M.A.* 6 August, 1919; 17 June, 1920.
[4] *Derbyshire Times*, 7 February, 1920.   [5] *D.M.A.* 5 January, 1921.
[6] *Ibid.* 15 September, 1924.   [7] *Derbyshire Times*, 26 February, 1927.

inter-war years. Hicken sometimes took part in debates and discussions on such subjects as nationalization and, in 1932, was one of the principal speakers in a conference called to protest against the economies in education.[1] During the depression the minds of many miners were kept occupied by adult classes. In 1932 the Chesterfield Borough Welfare Committee heard details of a scheme organized by the Lincoln branch of the W.E.A., the first of its kind in the country, for the rehabilitation of the unemployed.[2]

The creation of the Miners' Welfare Fund made more money available for activities of this kind. In 1924, on the initiative of Robert Peers, Professor of Adult Education in the University College of Nottingham, the Miners' Welfare Joint Adult Education Committee was set up to arrange extra-mural classes for the miners of Nottinghamshire and Derbyshire. The Committee also offered scholarships to enable miners to attend lectures at the College for two days a week. By 1939, when the outbreak of war interrupted the scheme, some eighty men had attended these courses, some for two sessions. Some of them continued their formal studies with the aid of further scholarships and obtained university degrees. One became a university lecturer, others have risen to positions of importance in the nationalized coal industry and the trade union movement.[3] H. W. Wynn and Hugo Street were to become full-time officials of the Derbyshire Area of the National Union of Mineworkers. W. H. Sales, the son of the Vice-President of the Derbyshire Miners' Association, was awarded a Miners' Welfare Scholarship which took him to the London School of Economics in 1927.[4] He was later to become a member of the National Coal Board.

Scholarships were also available for miners' children, and the miner's son at Oxford gradually ceased to be regarded as a curiosity. Technical education and research were likewise fostered by the Miners' Welfare Committee. Grants were made to local authorities for the building of mining and technical colleges. The Chesterfield Technical College was financed by the scheme. In 1932 the building of a new Mining Department for the University of Sheffield was completed at a cost of £29,152, of which £19,210 was contributed from the Miners' Welfare Fund.[5]

As the horizons of the miners widened, the arts also began to flourish. In 1927 Frederick C. Boden published his *Pithead Poems*, with a preface by Sir Arthur Quiller-Couch.[6] The son of a railway goods porter, Boden was born at Chesterfield in 1903. He left school at the age of 13 and went into the pit. Later he secured night work at the pit-head which

[1] *Derbyshire Times*, 17 December, 1932.　　　　[2] *Ibid.* 12 November, 1932.
[3] A. H. Thornton, 'Day-Release for Liberal Studies'; *Adult Education*, XXIX, (1956), p. 197.　　　　[4] *Derbyshire Times*, 25 June, 1927.
[5] *Mines Department, Miners' Welfare Fund, Eleventh Report*, 1932, p. 65.
[6] F. C. Boden, *Pithead Poems*, (London), 1927.

enabled him to read poetry and philosophy during the day. Eventually he began to write. His work attracted the attention of Guy N. Pocock, who showed some of it to his friend Quiller-Couch. H. N. Brailsford, the editor of the *New Leader*, also became interested. Soon after the publication of *Pithead Poems*, through the good offices of Robert Bridges, the Poet Laureate, and other eminent literary figures, Boden was transferred from the pit to the University College of Exeter, where he graduated in philosophy. In his second book of verse, *Out of the Coalfields*, published in 1929, Boden writes of his new-found peace:

> Now out of utter darkness I have passed,
>   Out of the wretched days that were my life,
>   And under sunny skies I've found at last
>   Calm after storm and quiet after strife.[1]

When asked what he wanted to do in life, Boden told Pocock: 'The suffering and ignorance I see about me make my heart ache. I hope to be something of a comforter—something of a saviour.'[2] In 1932 Boden published his first novel, *Miner*, which was largely autobiographical, followed by *Flo* in 1933 and *Derbyshire Tragedy* in 1935.

VI

Despite the safety devices and the stricter legislation which had been introduced before the First World War, coalmining was still a dangerous trade. During the inter-war years the underground death rate averaged about one per thousand.[3] The Derbyshire Miners' Association, like the other miners' unions, continued to pay the greatest attention to developments which might lead to accidents or help to prevent them. Evasions and breaches of the Mines Acts were not allowed to pass without protest. In 1919 the Executive Committee decided to draw the attention of the Inspector of Mines to the failure of a deputy at the Oxcroft Colliery to inspect the whole of his district before allowing the men to work in the mine.[4] Similarly, in 1924, the Association informed the Inspector of Mines of certain breaches of the law in connection with the length of the working day.[5]

Falls of roof were still one of the principal dangers accounting for nearly half of all fatal accidents. The introduction of steel props in the Butterley Company's pits led to a threatened strike in May, 1920. The men contended that the steel props were not as safe as wooden ones

---

[1] F. C. Boden, *Out of the Coalfields*, (London), 1929, p. 71.
[2] F. C. Boden, *Pithead Poems*, (London), 1927, p. vii.
[3] *Reports of H.M. Inspectors of Mines*, 1919–39.
[4] *D.M.A.* 10 November, 1919.   [5] *Ibid.* 16 August, 1924.

(which would creak to give warning of roof movements), and much more difficult to handle.[1] Like many 'safety' disputes this was really a wages issue since more work was involved in using the new props. 'They had found great difficulty in proving the new steel prop was unsafe,' said Frank Lee, 'and it was stated there had not been a single accident yet in setting one.'[2] In June a similar dispute arose at Bolsover.[3] But steel props and arches had come to stay. In 1926 the Inspector of Mines reported that after the long stoppage roads and faces thus supported had stood firmer and required less attention than those supported by timber.[4] In 1930 he stated that during the previous two years not a single accident had been reported as resulting from a fall on a roadway supported by steel arches.[5] By 1933 there were 140,358 steel props in use in the North Midland Division.[6]

The dangers of withdrawing props from the 'goaf' or 'wastes' after work had been completed were gradually reduced by the introduction of various safety devices. In 1923, J. Allcock, of the Bolsover Colliery, demonstrated to the Council an apparatus of his own design. 'We have no need to impress upon members the usefulness of such an apparatus'. stated the officials, 'and the necessity for one that will make it more safe, and protect the lives of our men.'[7] In 1926 the Inspector of Mines appealed for a more extensive use of the Sylvester appliance for withdrawing props instead of the ring and chain, and for the use of safety appliances instead of the pick or axe to loosen props.[8]

There were great improvements in the design of safety lamps during the inter-war years. In 1919 the Association supplied information to the Home Office committee appointed to consider the whole question of miners' lamps.[9] Experiments were made in Derbyshire in 1922 by J. Davis and Son, Ltd., of Derby, in conjunction with G. Dearle, of Hasland, to produce a safety lamp without side pillars and other obstructions to the free distribution of light.[10] Electric lamps became increasingly portable and efficient and began to be more widely used. In 1924 the Council decided that where electric lamps were introduced the men should not be expected to concede the $1\frac{1}{2}$d. a ton which had been awarded to contractors working with safety lamps in the 1890's.[11] Frank Hall advised the men at the Hartshay Colliery to revert to the use of candles at their own expense rather than use the electric lamps provided free by the colliery company, if they were not paid the $1\frac{1}{2}$d. a

[1] D.M.A. 16 March, 12 April, 22 May, 1920.
[2] Derbyshire Times, 24 July, 1920.   [3] D.M.A. 17 June, 17 July, 1920.
[4] Reports of H.M. Inspectors of Mines, 1926.   [5] Ibid. 1930.
[6] Ibid. 1933.   [7] D.M.A. 15 September, 13 October, 1923.
[8] Reports of H.M. Inspectors of Mines, 1926.
[9] D.M.A. 20 September, 11 October, 1919.
[10] Derbyshire Times, 15 April, 1922.   [11] D.M.A. 19 July, 1924.

ton. 'I think if you were to do so, in spite of what Mr. Bircumshaw may say,' he wrote, 'I think you would find that he would again insist on the electric lamps, and that might be the means by which you might get the $1\frac{1}{2}$d. a ton.' In November the officials stated: 'The owners are contending that the electric lamps are quite as good as candles—they are nothing of the sort. We hope, however, that where electric lamps have been introduced, every attempt will be made to resist the encroachments on present tonnage rates.'[1] The miners' case was weak. Electric lamps, like steel props, had come to stay. J. R. Felton, the Inspector of Mines, reported in 1924, that there had been an increase in the use of electric lamps and that it was likely to continue.[2] Ten years later he commented on the improvement in safety brought about by the greater use of high candle power electric hand lamps.[3]

The growing use of electric lamps meant that the miners were unable to detect gas as they could with their flame safety lamps. In 1930 Hicken reported to the Council that experiments were being made with the Ringrose lamp gas detector.[4] At that time the M.F.G.B. was beginning its campaign for the compulsory use of gas detectors in every colliery. The Ringrose lamp, which normally gave a white light, showed a red light in the presence of gas. Since it operated automatically it was testing continuously and did not require the skill and knowledge necessary for testing the atmosphere with a flame lamp. In 1934 it was given a trial by the Staveley Company at the Markham Collieries. The Derbyshire Miners' Association watched the experiments with great interest, and Lee and Hicken were invited to visit the collieries and see the lamp in operation. Frank Lee stated that the colliery officials and the men were pleased with the results of the tests:

The officials recognized that the lamp did not relieve them of any part of their duties, and that their examination should not be any the less thorough because of it. It was realized that the lamp must act as a sentinel on duty in the absence of the deputy, and as an improved substitute for the oil lamp.[5]

Towards the end of 1936 Hicken was appointed a member of the Fire-damp Detector Committee set up by the Mines Department.[6]

The Association was always ready to co-operate with any of the government departments in the matter of safety. In 1930 Frank Lee was appointed a member of the Safety in Mines Research Board. The Board was originally appointed by the Secretary for Mines, in 1921, to direct the work which had been begun by the Mining Association with the assistance, later, of the Home Office. The Miners' Welfare Fund

---

[1] *D.M.A.* 8 November, 1924.   [2] *Reports of H.M. Inspectors of Mines*, 1924.
[3] *Ibid.* 1933.   [4] *D.M.A.* 25 October, 1930.
[5] *Ibid.* 9 June, 24 November, 1934; *Derbyshire Times*, 28 April, 1934.
[6] *D.M.A.* 28 December, 1936.

made possible the establishment of new experimental stations. The Home Office station at Eskmeals, in Cumberland, where explosive tests had been carried out, was abandoned as being too remote and, in 1926, a new research centre was opened at Buxton.[1] There was also a smaller experimental station at Sheffield.

Co-operation with the employers was rather more difficult, for the question of safety was often linked with wages and conditions. In 1923, when the Mines Department issued a circular asking employers and workmen to co-operate in a 'Safety First' movement, the Council dutifully resolved: 'That the General Secretary be instructed to fix a meeting with the owners for the purpose of discussing the question and ascertaining the scope of the movement.'[2] When the Staveley Company proposed the setting up of 'Safety First' committees at its collieries in 1925 the Council instructed Frank Hall to obtain full information about the scheme before accepting the Company's invitation to co-operate.[3] 'There is nothing behind the movement', said D. N. Turner. 'The object is purely and simply to try and prevent accidents.'[4] As time went on these suspicions were broken down. In 1935 the Bolsover Company appointed a safety officer and introduced a number of safety measures such as the provision, free of charge, of protective helmets and gloves.[5] In 1936 the Staveley Company also appointed a safety officer[6] and, gradually, other companies began to follow the example of these pioneers.

A number of colliery explosions in Derbyshire and other parts of the country in the 1930's called attention to the dangers of electrical equipment in mines and the need for adequate gas detectors. At 2 a.m. on Sunday, 19 November, 1933, there was a disaster in the Deep Hard Seam at the Grassmoor Colliery in which fourteen men were killed and eight injured.[7]

'Nothing so disastrous has occurred in the coalfield during the last fifty years,' asserted the Council, 'and the whole neighbourhood has been violently shocked to realize such a calamity was possible. . . . This meeting calls upon the Government to hasten their enquiry into the effectiveness of certain gas detectors and alarms which are now available, and which, if put into operation, would appear to be one method of reducing risk.'[8]

Hicken, Lee and Mather represented the Association at the inquiry into the causes of the explosion which was conducted by Sir Henry Walker,

---

[1] *Derbyshire Times*, 4 June, 1927.   [2] *D.M.A.* 13 April, 1923.
[3] *Ibid.* 5 December, 1925; 2 January, 1926.
[4] *Derbyshire Times*, 16 January, 1926.
[5] *Ibid.* 20 September, 1935.   [6] *Ibid.* 14 February, 1936.
[7] *Mines Department, Explosion at Grassmoor Colliery, Derbyshire, Report by Sir Henry Walker*, 1934, (Cmd. 4550).   [8] *D.M.A.* 25 November, 1933.

the Chief Inspector of Mines. Evidence was given by W. H. Macmillan, the Professor of Mining in the University College of Nottingham, and by J. R. Felton, the District Inspector of Mines. Both subscribed to the theory that the explosion was caused by a broken electric cap-lamp. E. Dunn, who was one of the M.F.G.B. representatives, asked: 'Are the whole of the circumstances of this case ordered and made to fit this theory?' Hicken remarked: 'I suggest that the thread upon which you hang your opinion is a very delicate one.'[1]

On 23 April, 1934, a sub-committee of the Council endorsed the main finding of Sir Henry Walker, which followed the lines of the evidence submitted by Macmillan and Felton. However, Walker also called attention to the fact that there had been contraventions of the Coal Mines Act, 1911, and the Explosives in Coal Mines Order. The sub-committee therefore asked the Secretary of the M.F.G.B. to arrange for the matter to be raised in the House of Commons.[2] The owners and the manager of the colliery were later prosecuted for employing more than ten men in a part of a mine which had only one means of egress to the surface and for unlawfully storing explosives in the pit.[3] Another sequel to the Grassmoor explosion was that from 1 January, 1933, the manufacturers of approved electric cap-lamps were required to fit covers of unsplinterable glass if the lamps were not protected by a safety device which automatically switched off the current on the breakage of the cover-glass.[4]

At 2.45 p.m. on 21 January, 1937, there was an explosion at the Staveley Company's Markham No. 1 pit, in which nine men were killed. At the time of the explosion Hicken was at the coal face in the Warsop Main Colliery with the Firedamp Detector Committee. He at once went across to the Markham Colliery and, with the Inspector of Mines and other officials, investigated the condition of the part of the pit in which the explosion had occurred.[5] At the inquest the cause of the explosion was said to have been a flame which escaped from a coal-cutting machine box due to the faulty replacement of a covering plate. 'The jury are satisfied', stated the verdict, 'that every precaution and provision have been and are taken by the Staveley Coal and Iron Company to ensure the safety of the men working in the mine.'[6] The Inspector of Mines commented in his report on the explosion:

Incidentally, the 'Ringrose' detectors here were set to operate at two per cent. of firedamp. At this setting the detector does not meet with the requirements

---

[1] *Derbyshire Times*, 23 December, 1933.   [2] *D.M.A.* 23 April, 1934.
[3] *Derbyshire Times*, 19 May, 21 July, 1934.
[4] *Mines Department, Explosion at Grassmoor Colliery, Derbyshire*, 1934, (Cmd. 4550), p. 26.
[5] *D.M.A.* 13 February, 1937.   [6] *Derbyshire Times*, 26 February, 1937.

of the General Regulation 132 (v), nor provide the means for compliance with Section 60 (2) of the Coal Mines Act, 1911; to do so it must be set to function at $1\frac{1}{4}$ per cent., failing which a flame lamp must also be provided.[1]

Within a month of the Markham disaster seven men were killed and four injured (one of whom subsequently died) in an explosion in the Waterloo seam of the South Normanton Colliery Company's Winterbank pit. The explosion occurred at 9 p.m. on Monday, 15 February and caused surprise as well as sorrow for the pit had always been regarded as being 'safe' for naked lights, which had been abandoned only two years previously.[2] Although in Derbyshire, the colliery was organized by the Nottinghamshire union. Speaking in the debate on the Gresford colliery explosion, in the House of Commons, George Ridley, the Labour member for Clay Cross, referred to South Normanton:

I had never quite realized before, and I think that the House as a whole cannot realize, the long shadow which is cast by a mining disaster. Its disastrous consequences are not limited to death or physical disablement; they extend themselves even to mental disablement and distress. I visited in the course of the day, a man in the middle thirties, a normal, healthy, virile man who had, 48 hours before, been within 50 yards of the disaster. In that 48 hours he had succumbed, a nervous wreck, conscious for the first time in his mining life of what fear in the presence of death really meant. . . . The shadow cast itself not only upon a man in the immediate vicinity of the disaster, but I could feel it in the whole of that mining constituency. There was a new nervousness, a new apprehension of what it meant to be in the presence of such an emergency. . . . Until the desperate necessity of making a profit out of the industry is lifted, no matter what precautionary methods are employed, we shall in this House not be able to discharge our social obligations under the existing situation.[3]

In the following July, when twenty-seven men lost their lives in an explosion at the Brymbo Colliery, in North Staffordshire, the Council of the D.M.A. noted 'with dismay . . . the frequent occurrences of these awful calamities'.[4]

The worst disaster of all in Derbyshire was in the district of the Markham colliery where the nine men had been killed in 1937. The explosion occurred at 5.45 a.m. on 10 May, 1938, when over 100 men were trapped underground; seventy-nine were killed and thirty-eight injured. The men were preparing to leave the pit after completing the night shift. Had the explosion happened half an hour later, the loss of life would have been heavier, for the 250 men comprising the day shift

[1] *Mines Department, Explosion at Markham Colliery, Derbyshire, Report by J. R. Felton*, 1937, (Cmd. 5456), p. 18.
[2] *Derbyshire Times*, 19 February, 1937.
[3] 320 H.C. Deb. 5s. 1924–7.   [4] *D.M.A.* 3 July, 1937.

would have been involved.[1] The Council of the Derbyshire Miners'
Association expressed its dismay 'at the recurrence of such disasters,
for it had considered that researches of science and experiments carried
out in certain directions had made it well nigh impossible for explosions
to carry over large areas'. The Council questioned whether stone dusting
was as effective as it was thought to be for limiting the area of explosions
in collieries. It was decided to engage Sir Stafford Cripps to represent
the Association at the inquiry.[2] Samuel Sales who, with two other
members of the union, examined the pit some days after the explosion,
told the Council: 'The Company treated them very kindly. . . . They
could not point to anything wrong for which the Company could be
made responsible.'[3]

The public inquiry opened at Chesterfield on 27 June before P. E.
Sandlands, K.C., the Recorder of Leicester, with F. M. Wynne, the
Chief Inspector of Mines, as assessor. It was the first time an Independent Commissioner had conducted an inquiry of this kind. Nearly all
the men giving evidence described the pit as having a good reputation
for ventilation and safety precautions. Many witnesses were called to
testify that stone dusting was carried out extensively and systematically.
It was stated that the explosions had been caused by some runaway
tubs which had broken an electric joint box and caused a short circuit.
The spark had ignited the coal-dust thrown up from the tubs.[4] Cripps
suggested that the electric cable used in the pit was unreliable and
'completely out of date' but a representative of the manufacturers gave
evidence to the contrary. 'You are the makers of this cable and naturally
anxious to stand up for it', said Cripps. 'Haven't some of the larger
cities had this cable removed because of the trouble it caused?' Cripps
eventually left the case in the hands of his junior and, after eleven days'
sitting, the inquiry came to an end.[5] In his report Sandlands accepted
the theory of the runaway tubs. He attributed no blame but made a
number of recommendations including the provision of covers for tubs
carrying coal-dust, proper attention to tub-catches and better protection
for electric joint boxes.[6] The miners' leaders appear to have been satisfied with these findings for they made no comment upon them.

VII

The dangers of the miner's work led him to take a keen interest in workmen's compensation and medical services. In 1919 Frank Hall was one

[1] *Derbyshire Times*, 20 May, 1938.   [2] *D.M.A.* 16 May, 1938.
[3] *Ibid.* 4 June, 1938.   [4] *Derbyshire Times*, 1 July, 1938.
[5] *Ibid.* 8 and 29 July, 1938.   [6] *Ibid.* 21 October, 1938.

of the three M.F.G.B. representatives who gave evidence before the Holman Gregory Committee, appointed by the Home Secretary to inquire into the question of workmen's compensation, and to report upon the desirability of establishing a system of accident insurance under the control and supervision of the State.[1] Hall told the Committee that instead of receiving 50 per cent. of his average weekly earnings up to £1 a week an injured man should receive 100 per cent. 'The trade should carry full liability', he said, 'and pay the weekly amount equal to the average weekly earnings of the person injured during the twelve months prior to the accident.'[2] On 7 July, 1920, the Holman Gregory Committee issued its report in which it recommended the payment of compensation amounting to 66⅔ per cent. of average weekly earnings subject to a maximum of £3. For partial incapacity two-thirds of the difference between former and existing earnings was recommended. In December the Council protested against 'the delay on the part of the Government to pass a measure containing the suggested increases in compensation payments made by the Holman Gregory Report'.[3]

Compensation cases raised many technical difficulties. The rights of the partially incapacitated members of the union had to be carefully safeguarded in strikes and lock-outs.[4] The law regarding the notification of accidents had to be strictly observed.[5] The delays, difficulties and expense involved in settling compensation claims through the County Courts were notorious.

'For months members are being deprived of their just claims,' stated Frank Lee, 'causing much hardship and irritation. County Court procedure does require changes making it easier and quicker in its methods. At present, no ordinary workman without the backing of some organization has much, if any, chance of getting an equal fight with his employer or insurance company through the Court.'[6]

In 1922 Lee proposed that the Association should take advantage of Section 11, Clause 16 of the Compensation Act which gave the Secretary of State power to confer on any committee representative of an employer and his workmen all the powers conferred by the Act upon the County Courts. Such a scheme had been operated by the Durham miners since 1907. On 4 March the Council decided to consult the owners about the matter[7] but no further progress was made.

Although the Workmen's Compensation Act, 1923, brought about some improvements, the miners' leaders were still dissatisfied. Frank Lee condemned the principle which, he said, had been followed in the

[1] M.F.G.B. 13 August, 1919. [2] Derbyshire Times, 20 September, 1919.
[3] D.M.A. 4 December, 1920. [4] Ibid. 18 December, 1920.
[5] Derbyshire Times, 15 March, 1921.
[6] Ibid. 4 February, 1922. [7] Ibid. 4 March, 1922.

new Act, 'that the man must not receive anything like the same amount for compensation as he did while at work'. John Spencer complained: 'The system under which the legislature . . . had framed the Bill was extraordinarily like that of a Chinese puzzle.' Both Spencer and Lee were in favour of a simplification of the law based on more generous provisions.[1] The annual conference of the M.F.G.B in 1924 accepted a resolution, moved by John Spencer, expressing disappointment with the 1923 Act and instructing the Executive Committee to press for payment of compensation on the day of the accident, an increase in the weekly compensation to not less than two-thirds of the average earnings, the payment of the full difference in wages to partially incapacitated workmen, and the placing of an obligation upon the employer to find light work for all their injured workmen who were capable of doing it. 'I am afraid', said Spencer, 'that the present Act of 1923, with the exception of one improvement, namely, in the case of fatal accidents, has been reactionary rather than progressive.'[2]

In 1932 the complexities of compensation law were commented upon by Judge Turner, who had acted in Derbyshire during the 'twenties':

In this class of work one has to be careful. In the North, where the trades unions take up the claims, their officials know the work, and there is none of the trouble we get with people having to select their own solicitors, who may not be acquainted with the class of work. In this respect trade unions are the best thing for any workman to be in. It is very peculiar work, and the one underlying principle of it is to get it done at once, and not run up a case for costs.[3]

In 1938 Frank Lee introduced into the House of Commons as a private member's Bill, the Employers' Liability Bill which was designed to make employers liable to their workmen for injuries caused by the negligence of fellow workers. Lee received strong support from Ridley, the member for Clay Cross, but neither was able to show how the legal difficulties involved in the doctrine of common employment could be overcome. The Bill was rejected by 142 to 122 on the second reading.[4]

The miners' health and industrial diseases continued to receive the attention of Josiah Court whose knighthood in 1920 was warmly approved by the Derbyshire miners.[5] In 1924 Court carried out investigations at the Warsop colliery into the effects of working in a high temperature. He confirmed the findings of J. S. Haldane and other research workers that the addition of a little salt to the men's drinking water enabled them to withstand the fatigue which invariably resulted from working in hot districts in the mine.[6] Court was then already 84 years of age and

[1] *Derbyshire Times*, 15 March, 1924.   [2] *M.F.G.B.* 11 July, 1924.
[3] *D.M.A.* 19 March, 1932.   [4] 332 H.C. Deb. 5s. 2273–2358.
[5] *D.M.A.* 3 January, 1920.   [6] *Derbyshire Times*, 22 November, 1924.

although he was still to remain active for some years his researches in the interests of the miners were virtually at an end. The Council paid a lengthy tribute to his work when he died early in 1938.[1]

Court's discovery that nystagmus was caused by inadequate light gave an impetus to the attempts to improve the miner's safety lamp but for many years technical developments lagged behind medical knowledge. A Chesterfield ophthalmic surgeon stated in 1922 that 50 per cent. of miners suffered from nystagmus to a certain degree, although it did not become apparent to them until they were attacked by dizziness or other head complaints.[2] In the same year, W. C. Bridgeman, the Secretary for Mines, told the Derbyshire Mining Students' Association that nystagmus was the worst of the occupational diseases affecting the miners.[3] Every year about 6,000 miners in Great Britain became incapable of working at the coal face as a result of nystagmus and had to receive compensation. In 1935 the Government appointed a committee to inquire into the operation of the Workmen's Compensation Act in relation to men affected by the disease.

The miners made their own provision for medical services by contributing to their colliery 'field clubs' and also to the hospitals. Most of the employers also made donations to the hospitals. Rising costs in the period following the First World War meant that the miners had to provide more money. In 1920 the Chesterfield branch of the British Medical Association asked the unions to convene a meeting of representatives of the colliery field clubs to consider an application for increased contributions.[4] The hospitals were also in financial difficulties and the miners were asked to raise their weekly contributions from 2d. to 3d.[5] In the following year the Council decided to submit to the annual conference of the M.F.G.B a resolution: 'That the whole of the general hospitals in the country be taken over, and conducted by the State.'[6]

The Association also had to consider how to implement the plans which it had made during the war for the building of a new convalescent home at Skegness. The cost of building the home had originally been estimated at £9,000 but rising prices meant that £16,000 or £17,000 was now needed. Various attempts were made to raise the money. In 1919 the officials suggested that the war-time relief funds should be continued for a short period and that the proceeds should be diverted to the building fund.[7] When the ambulances provided under Sir Dennis Bayley's scheme returned from the battlefields it was first suggested that they should be allocated to collieries but when it was realized that

[1] D.M.A. 12 February, 1938.   [2] Derbyshire Times, 11 February, 1922.
[3] Derbyshire Times, 4 March, 1922.
[4] D.M.A. 4 and 12 February, 1920; Derbyshire Times, 1 May, 1920.
[5] D.M.A. 17 June, 1920.   [6] Ibid. 30 March, 1921.   [7] Ibid. 1 March, 1919.

they were in very bad condition it was decided to sell them and devote the balance of the fund to the convalescent home.[1] After much discussion about a suitable memorial for members of the Association who had been killed during the war it was agreed that the entire cost of building the new convalescent home should be borne by the funds of the Association.[2] In 1923 the fines imposed by the absentee committees during the war were paid into the building fund.[3]

The industrial strife of the post-war period and the continuing rise in building costs made it impossible for the Association to realize its ambition for a number of years. Meanwhile the existing home was quite inadequate and the lease was due to expire in 1926. The decision to continue the Miners' Welfare Scheme for a further five years at last made the project possible. 'If we have to go on with our convalescent home', wrote Frank Hall, early in 1925, 'there is no reason why we should not tap the fund with this object in view. A grant of £25,000 for the county would be a very small amount, and it is a question as to whether or not it should be supplemented with a fund for the endowment of the same so as to give future security to the Home.'[4] Gradually the scheme became more ambitious. The Miners' Welfare Committee granted £60,000 to pay for the building and £50,000 as an endowment. The maintenance fund thus created was still insufficient. Help was given by the coal-owners, and the miners themselves agreed to contribute a penny a week, which was to be equally divided between the convalescent home and the other welfare schemes in the county.[5]

The new convalescent home, designed by Percy Houfton who died before it was completed, provided accommodation for 120 men and 30 women. It was officially opened on 10 March, 1928, by Lord Chelmsford, who said:

> You in Derbyshire have for a great number of years been spending the main bulk of your Welfare Fund on recreational facilities. I do not criticize that, but it is to be remembered that the Welfare Fund is meant to be an all-round fund and to be utilized for the benefit of those who are ill as well as those who enjoy good health. I therefore welcome this fine home. . . . I think you have done the right thing because one of the greatest factors in recuperation is a complete change of air and scenery.[6]

[1] D.M.A. 26 April, 3 May, 10 November, 1919; 19 July, 15 September, 9 October, 1920.
[2] Ibid. 22 May, 21 June, 26 July, 1919.   [3] Derbyshire Times, 6 October, 1923.
[4] D.M.A. 3 January, 1925.
[5] Ibid. 17 September, 1927.   [6] Derbyshire Times, 17 March, 1928.

APPENDIX I

Employment in Coal Mines, 1922–1939

| | Total Number of Wage Earners on Colliery Books | | Average Number of Days Worked per Week by the Mines. a | |
	Derbyshire	Great Britain	Derbyshire	Great Britain
1922	62,365	1,095,186	5·02	5·17
1923	63,392	1,137,926	5·56	5·00
1924	66,211	1,171,896	5·27	5·26
1925	64,204	1,086,103	5·04	5·02
1926	b	b	b	b
1927	60,057	999,941	4·26	4·80
1928	55,459	923,092	4·02	4·68
1929	55,544	932,330	4·48	4·73
1930	54,948	916,809	4·28	5·09
1931	53,020	848,455	4·12	4·85
1932	50,866	802,705	3·81	4·50
1933	47,005	790,868	3·72	4·56
1934	46,402	774,866	3·76	4·80
1935	44,928	758,587	3·58	3·91
1936	44,307	756,232	4·05	5·02
1937	44,187	777,791	4·38	5·26
1938	44,737	781,865	4·11	4·97
1939 c	44,723	771,950	4·36	5·18

a   The figures in these columns show the average number of days (allowance being made for short time) on which coal was got from the mines included in the returns. It is not necessarily implied that all the persons worked every day the mines were open. Mines not working are omitted in computing the average number of days worked.

b   National stoppage.

c   Average of eight months.

Source: *Ministry of Labour Gazette.*

CHAPTER XXI

POLITICAL ACTIVITIES, 1918–39

I

Despite the 'political immorality'[1] of Lloyd George's so-called 'coupon election', the sudden dissolution of Parliament, ten days after the Armistice, did not find the Derbyshire Miners' Association unprepared. Plans had already been made, before the end of the war, for Frank Hall and Frank Lee to contest the Clay Cross and North-East Derbyshire divisions respectively. The wooing of the female electorate, who would be included in the new registers, had already begun.[2] Ignoring the appeals of J. R. Clynes and Will Thorne, the Labour Party decided to eschew the coalition and fight independently. The 'coupon', the letter signed by Lloyd George and Bonar Law and sent to coalition candidates, proved to be all important. The voters were much less prepared for Lloyd George's onslaught than the party machines. 'Hang the Kaiser', 'Make Germany pay', and 'Homes for Heroes' were irresistible, if deceptive, slogans.

In North-East Derbyshire there were four candidates, three of whom claimed to be coalitionists. The Marquis of Hartington was the official coalition candidate. Harland Bowden, who had been disowned by the local Conservative caucus during the war,[3] appeared as an Independent candidate prepared to support the coalition. The Liberals argued that the party truce had been broken because they had not been consulted about the adoption of Hartington and decided to put forward their own candidate who would also be a coalitionist. J. P. Houfton, who had been the prospective candidate, decided not to stand.[4] Eventually the Liberals secured the services of Stanley Holmes, an accountant, described by the *Derbyshire Times* as 'a carpet-bagger from London', who proclaimed that he was a supporter of the coalition. Frank Lee

---

[1] Cf. J. M. Keynes, *The Economic Consequences of the Peace*, (New York), edn. of 1920, p. 137.
[2] See pp. 546–7.   [3] *Derbyshire Times*, 1 July, 1916; 12 and 19 May, 1917.
[4] *Ibid*. 16 November, 1918.

was the only candidate who offered an alternative policy.[1] The *Derbyshire Times* commented:

The old-fashioned Liberal Party are perhaps in the most anomalous position. For years they have been hanging on to the skirts of Labour. Now Labour disowns them very bitterly, and we see in North-East Derbyshire, for instance, their leaders trying to invoke the shades of Gladstone and Bright to help them. Truly some people have learned nothing.[2]

Lee, who obtained 5,560 votes, was only narrowly defeated by Holmes, with 6,117. Bowden and Hartington followed with 5,067 and 2,738 respectively. 'Mr. Lee is so estimable an official of the Miners' Association', stated the *Derbyshire Times*, 'that had he cut himself clear from the official Labour Party, and boldly declared for an "out and out" policy so far as Germany was concerned, he would have won.'[3]

In the Clay Cross division Frank Hall had a straight fight against T. T. Broad, a former Sheffield Nonconformist minister, who was a Liberal coalitionist. Hall, like Lee, put forward the official Labour Party programme.[4] Broad's fearless advocacy of the 'make the Germans pay' policy was more popular. He was elected by 7,987 votes to Hall's 6,766. 'Mr. Hall went under because of his after the war policy', commented the *Derbyshire Times*. 'Had he trodden in the patriotic steps of Mr. B. Kenyon and Mr. J. G. Hancock, he would have been M.P. for the Clay Cross division to-day.'[5]

In the Belper division J. G. Hancock, the Nottinghamshire miners' leader, was returned unopposed as a Liberal coalition candidate. It was rumoured that his colleague, Frank Varley, might contest the seat as a Labour candidate.[6] Later Varley stated that he was not standing for the Belper division because he lacked financial support. 'The Derbyshire Miners' Association would have given me moral support', he said, 'but whilst pronouncing the benediction they have forgotten to take up the collection, and without money it is impossible to cover a straggling constituency like Belper.'[7] Barnet Kenyon, the other recalcitrant miners' leader, was likewise returned unopposed as a Liberal coalition candidate for Chesterfield, but not without protest. A Labour Party meeting resolved: 'That this conference emphatically protests against Mr. Barnet Kenyon holding the ring in the division for the Tory and Liberal parties, and resolves to leave no stone unturned to remove him from his false position as a so-called Labour candidate.'[8] Kenyon made much of the work he had done during the war for service men and their relatives.[9] The Conservative *Derbyshire Times* gave Kenyon and

[1] *Derbyshire Times*, 23 November, 1918.   [2] *Ibid*. 30 November, 1918.
[3] *Ibid*. 4 January, 1919.   [4] *Ibid*. 16 November, 1918.
[5] *Ibid*. 4 January, 1919.   [6] *Ibid*. 16 November, 1918.
[7] *Ibid*. 23 November, 1918.   [8] *Ibid*. 30 November, 1918.   [9] *Ibid*.

Hancock full support: 'They have just cause for pride that after a life-time of service to the miners this compliment of an unopposed return should be paid to them by the "capitalists" and that the pacifist element of Labour dare not risk a fight with them.'[1]

Apart from Lee and Hall, and J. H. Thomas in Derby, the only other Labour candidate in Derbyshire was G. H. Oliver who contested the Ilkeston division. He was defeated by J. E. B. Seely (later Lord Mottistone) by 9,660 votes to 8,062. Lloyd George had swept the country. With the exception of J. H. Thomas, all the Derbyshire members were coalitionists. On the Derbyshire registers there were 257,609 electors of whom 40,234 were serving in the armed forces. As in other parts of the country, only about 50 per cent. of the resident electors took the trouble to vote. The women were reported to have polled in greater proportion than the men in almost every district of Derbyshire.[2] On spurious issues the 'hard faced men' had won the election. 'It provided Great Britain,' writes Mr. Somervell, 'during four years which were to be packed full of industrial crises and social problems, with the wealthiest, the stupidest and the least representative House of Commons since the Great Reform Bill of 1832.'[3]

II

Labour's defeat in the general election stimulated the Derbyshire Miners' Association to greater activity. In January, 1919, the Council reminded members that it was prepared to pay the expenses of any Labour candidate who had a reasonable chance of success in the county council elections.[4] Eleven nominations were received, six of which were approved by the Executive Committee.[5] Three of the recognized candidates were elected, together with three other members of the Association.[6] All were eligible for expense allowances when attending meetings of the county council. The miners' leaders were also busy strengthening Labour Party organization.[7] In June, 1919, A. W. Hildreth was appointed to act as political organizer.[8]

Meanwhile rising prices were leading the M.F.G.B. to consider the state of the political fund. At the annual conference in July, 1919, it was decided that the yearly political levy should be increased from 1s. to 2s. per member.[9] This enabled the Federation to double the amount which it returned to the districts for local representation and propaganda

---

[1] *Derbyshire Times*, 7 December, 1918.　　[2] *Ibid.* 21 December, 1918.
[3] Somervell, *op. cit.* p. 123.　　[4] *D.M.A.* 18 January, 1919.
[5] *Ibid.* 3 February, 1919.　　[6] *Ibid.* 22 March, 1919.
[7] *Ibid.* 19 April, 1919.　[8] See Chapter XV, p. 594.　[9] *M.F.G.B.* 18 July, 1919.

work. The salaries of the Federation M.P.s were also becoming inadequate. They had been fixed at £350 a year nearly twenty years previously and when payment of members was introduced in 1911 the miners' M.P.s had handed their annual salary of £400 to the Federation and continued to receive their usual payment of £350 a year. The increased political levy enabled the Federation to raise its parliamentary representatives' salaries to £600 a year from 1 October, 1919.[1] These changes led the Derbyshire Miners' Association to reconsider the position of officials in the event of their election as Members of Parliament.[2] The Executive Committee had already recommended that the Association should put forward only two candidates at the next general election.[3] On 3 November, 1919, the Council decided that Hall and Lee should again contest the Clay Cross and North-East divisions respectively. If elected they were to receive a retaining fee of £100 a year and if they lost their seats at a subsequent election they would be allowed to resume their duties as full-time officials.[4]

A week later the Executive Committee made detailed recommendations on the payment for loss of wages of members who were elected to local government authorities and Boards of Guardians. Each candidate was to be a nominee of the local Labour Party and his nomination was to be endorsed by the Association. The union reserved the right to limit the number of candidates to whom support would be given. No candidature was to be endorsed for more than one position and payments were to be made from the political fund of the Association. For county and borough council election expenses a maximum of £5 was to be allowed. For urban and rural district council elections and Board of Guardian elections the maximum was to be £2 10s. Recognized candidates who were elected were to be compensated for loss of wages through attending meetings. They were to receive 75 per cent. of the amount paid to delegates for attending meetings of the Council of the Association.[5]

Early in 1920 the Executive Committee decided that Barnet Kenyon's political position should be clarified. Hildreth, Sewell and Overton were instructed to interview him,[6] but found him evasive. The Executive Committee then submitted the following questions to Kenyon 'as an agent of the Association':

(a) Are you willing to at once ally yourself with the Parliamentary Labour Party in accordance with the political policy of this Association as members of the Miners' Federation of Great Britain and publicly announce the same?

(b) If your reply to question (a) is in the negative, are you prepared to

[1] *M.F.G.B.* 22 October, 1919.   [2] *D.M.A.* 25 October, 1919.
[3] *Ibid.* 10 October, 1919.   [4] *Ibid.* 3 November, 1919.
[5] *Ibid.* 10 November, 1919.   [6] *Ibid.* 15 January, 1920.
CC*

retire from your candidature for the Chesterfield Division for the next election and publicly announce your retirement, so as to clear the way for a miners' candidate on direct Labour lines?

The answers to these questions were to be 'direct, and in writing' and to be returned to Hildreth not later than 3 February.[1]

Kenyon replied: 'Much as I regret it, I have no alternative but to answer your two questions, "A" and "B", in the negative, as I purpose continuing my political life along the lines I have always pursued.' He then received a lengthy letter signed by every member of the Executive Committee except the permanent officials. It called attention to his vacillations and evasions in the past, to his collaboration with Holmes and Broad 'whom your two colleagues have been by ballot selected to oppose on direct Labour lines', and to his failure to conform with the political policy of the Association. 'Ours is the only mining county in the kingdom', stated the Executive Committee, 'in which a Miners' Agent is sitting in Parliament as a member of a Capitalist Party, and supporting Capitalist employers in the constituency. We are not satisfied in believing that we in Derbyshire are right and all the other miners of the kingdom are wrong.' Kenyon remained unrepentant. 'I have nothing to add to my last letter to you', he wrote. 'The whole thing is most painful to me. My public life is what our Organization has largely made it, and I have determined to do nothing which would cause dissension or division and the weakening of its great influence for good to its members.'[2]

The Executive Committee again discussed the situation on 12 February. Since the M.F.G.B. allotted one candidate to each 15,000 members, the Association, with its 49,000 members, was entitled to three candidates. It was therefore decided to recommend the nomination of a Labour candidate for the Chesterfield division.[3] Meanwhile Oliver Wright, who was then a miner at the Butterley Company's Britain Colliery, had been selected by the Belper Divisional Labour Party to fight J. G. Hancock at the next election.[4] On hearing that the Association was now to support candidates in three divisions, a number of branches in the Belper district advanced the claims of their own constituency.[5] By 35,233 votes to 19,062 the branches decided in favour of contesting Chesterfield.[6] Before nominations were requested the Executive Committee again interviewed Kenyon who asserted 'that he had already defined his position, and could not recede from it. If his health permitted he would fight the next election in the Chesterfield division

[1] D.M.A. 24 January, 1920.   [2] Ibid. 4 February, 1920.
[3] Ibid. 12 February, 1920.   [4] Derbyshire Times, 7 February, 1920.
[5] D.M.A. 16 March, 1920.   [6] Ibid. 24 April, 1920.

as a Liberal.'[1] Spencer, Sales, Hicken and Lee were all nominated by the branches as possible candidates for the Chesterfield division. Hicken and Lee withdrew and the branches were then asked to choose between Spencer and Sales.[2] There were 625 votes for Spencer and only 320 for Sales.[3]

When the Association sought the co-operation of the Chesterfield Labour Party it encountered difficulties. In October, 1920, Hall was instructed to write to the Secretary asking why there had been 'such delay in calling the necessary meeting for the adoption of a parliamentary candidate for the division in view of the fact that nominations were asked for several months ago'.[4] A few weeks later the Council expressed its dissatisfaction that the Chesterfield Labour Party had made no further move and threatened to raise the matter with the National Secretary if the meeting was not held within a month.[5] On 9 November the Executive Committee of the Chesterfield Labour Party resolved that the two letters from the Derbyshire Miners' Association should 'lie on the table'. H. Varley, who moved the resolution, remarked: 'We are the people to settle this thing, and we are not going to be dictated to by the miners.' John Spencer, who was at the meeting, reported this to the other officials, and, with Hall and Hildreth, interviewed Henry Wilde, the chairman of the Labour Party, on the following day. Wilde denied that the resolution meant that the letters were to be ignored and stated that the selection of a candidate had been delayed by the municipal elections and that the Executive Committee was not satisfied with the quality of the local candidates. 'They would rather have an outsider like Mr. Tawney', he said. Wilde himself was a prospective candidate, but on the advice of Egerton Wake, the Labour Party's national agent, would have withdrawn in favour of R. H. Tawney. Wilde asserted that Chesterfield was not a miners' constituency. 'His attitude throughout', reported the officials, 'was that of the leader of a number of trades unions and individual Labour Party members banded together in opposition to any step the Miners' Association might take.'[6]

The meeting for the selection of a candidate was eventually held on 18 December, 1920. Hall, Spencer and Hildreth were present but delegates from affiliated miners' lodges were not invited. H. Drinkwater, a member of the national executive of the Labour Party, who was present as a result of the complaints of the Derbyshire Miners' Association, protested that the meeting was not properly constituted and

[1] D.M.A. 3 May, 1920.   [2] Ibid. 22 May, 1920.   [3] Ibid. 17 June, 1920.
[4] Ibid. 9 October, 1920.   [5] Ibid. 6 November, 1920.
[6] Derbyshire Miners' Association, 'Report of an Interview between Mr. H. Wilde, and Mr. Frank Hall and Mr. Hildreth—John Spencer present part of the time—10 November, 1920'.

no further business was done.[1] The disunity of the Chesterfield Labour Party continued to prevent the selection of a candidate for many months. The difficulties of the party were increased by friction with the Chesterfield Co-operative Society over the municipal elections. In April, 1921, the co-operative society decided to end its affiliation with the Labour Party. 'By introducing politics into our society they were shaking the very foundation of the movement', protested one co-operator. 'The men who laid the foundations of the co-operative movement were all Chartists and Christian Socialists fighting for political ends, the emancipation of the working classes', asserted Hildreth.[2]

On 30 April, 1921, R. H. Tawney was again considered as a possible candidate by the Executive Committee of the Chesterfield Labour Party.[3] When the situation was discussed at the next Council meeting, John Spencer stated that he could no longer allow his name to be put forward as a candidate by the Derbyshire Miners' Association.[4] At a further meeting of the management committee of the Chesterfield Labour Party on 11 June, 1921, Spencer and Wilde withdrew their nominations and the nomination of H. Cropper was ruled out of order on the ground that it had been made six months too late. Frank Hall, seconded by John Spencer, then moved: 'That it be an instruction to the executive council of the party to consider suitable outside candidates and report to this committee such names as they believe will consolidate the party in this constituency, and win the seat for Labour.' This was carried by 26 votes to 23.[5]

The selection of an outside candidate caused further difficulties. It proved impossible to secure the services of Tawney, and Egerton Wake was then asked to submit a list of other suitable candidates. 'Having regard to their financial status', reported the *Derbyshire Times*, 'the local Labour Party, we are informed, are anxious to secure a candidate who is in a position to pay his own expenses.'[6] On 11 November, Harold Laski, addressing the Chesterfield Labour Party, expressed doubts that Labour was 'fit to govern' and emphasized the point that 'a seat in the House of Commons should not be regarded as an old-age pension for the trades union official'.[7] Meanwhile the Derbyshire Miners' Association had decided, on 13 October, that only the Clay Cross and North-East Derbyshire divisions should be contested by its nominees at the next general election.[8]

[1] *Derbyshire Times*, 26 December, 1920.   [2] *Ibid.* 16 April, 1921.
[3] *Ibid.* 7 May, 1921.   [4] *D.M.A.* 25 May, 1921.
[5] *Derbyshire Times*, 18 June, 1921.   [6] *Ibid.* 8 October, 1921.
[7] *Ibid.* 19 November, 1921.   [8] *D.M.A.* 13 October, 1921.

III

The 1921 lock-out turned the thoughts of the miners away from political action. In December, 1921, Hall and Lee warned the Council of the possibility of an early general election and suggested that the branches should be consulted as to whether they were still in favour of officials being allowed to retain their connection with the Association if elected to Parliament.[1] Only 17 branches continued to support the policy of paying a retaining fee, 44 were opposed to Members of Parliament holding any official position in the union, and 20 did not bother to vote. The matter was discussed at great length by the Council. 'The delegates made it perfectly plain', reported Hall, 'that they did not want their officials in the present state of the coal trade, and of the Association generally, to go to Parliament, but to give their undivided attention to the Association.' Hall and Lee thereupon announced that they could no longer be candidates for the Clay Cross and North-East Derbyshire divisions, and Spencer and Hicken said that they could not accept nomination. It was then decided to take a ballot vote of the members to ascertain whether they were in favour of contesting the two seats at the next election. To save the expense of a further ballot, nominations were also requested.[2]

Frank Hall commented:

This is a change of policy which we, as officials, cannot possibly accept. We who are standing for Labour are not disposed to accept less than was paid to Messrs. Haslam and Harvey when conditions were much more favourable than they are today. We had no alternative but to withdraw our candidatures as we believe the vote was a reactionary one and certainly one against our principles.

The *Derbyshire Times* took a different view. 'In their decision to separate business from politics', it stated, 'we think the miners have chosen wisely.'[3] Hildreth, who was likely to be dismissed if the miners decided to forgo all political activities, stated that he was not concerned so much about his own position as 'that the miners of Derbyshire should do the right thing and toe the line politically along with the rest of the miners in the United Kingdom'. He asserted that the whole question had been completely mishandled. The decision to pay the officials a retaining fee of £100 a year had been reaffirmed as recently as 3 November, 1919. Their salaries as Members of Parliament would have been no financial burden on the Association.

'There was no reason why, under the present conditions, they should have been asked again to reaffirm that decision', said Hildreth. 'When it was put to

[1] *D.M.A.* 10 December, 1921.
[2] *Ibid.* 7 January, 1922.   [3] *Derbyshire Times*, 14 January, 1922.

them, however, they were not given sufficient data on which to record their decision. In fact, one sentence in the meagre explanation that was given was to the effect that "you know all the circumstances".[1]

The branches eventually decided to contest the Clay Cross and North-East Derbyshire divisions. Enoch Overton was nominated for both divisions but declined to stand. Thomas Spencer, a most unlikely Labour candidate, was nominated for the Clay Cross division. He obtained 2,703 votes to Samuel Sales's 2,197 and J. Price's 1,874.[2] Spencer and Sales, along with three other candidates, J. Randle (a local miners' leader), C. Brown and J. R. Renshaw, were interviewed by the Clay Cross Labour Party on 4 February. J. R. Renshaw, pastor of the Baptist Church at Clay Cross, was adopted.[3]

The withdrawal of Enoch Overton meant that there were no nominees for the candidature of the North-East Derbyshire division. On 25 February a deputation, none of whom was a miner, from the Divisional Labour Party, met the officials of the Derbyshire Miners' Association and urged that the constituency should be fought by a miners' nominee. They argued that the chances of success were considerable, that North-East Derbyshire was essentially a mining constituency and that it was important not to waste the effort which had already been expended there.[4] The Belper division was also pressing its claims. On 4 March the Council asked the branches to decide whether Belper should be substituted for one or other of the constituencies already selected. 'It is understood', stated the officials, 'that if this is accepted, it will be necessary, to put the matter in order, to ask for nominations for a candidate, though it will be remembered that for some time Mr. O. Wright has been the accepted candidate of the local Labour Party.'[5]

Before the branches had made their decisions there was another change of policy. The publication of the auditors' report on the political fund was accompanied by a note which stated:

£1,291 has actually been spent and all we can see for it is a heap of ruins in the two constituencies where the bulk of the money has been spent. . . . If this political department is to be carried on it will be necessary to reorganize it. The question is certain to arise as to the need for a separate department having regard to the position in both the Clay Cross and North East divisions. It is quite obvious things are much worse today than in 1918 and '19. Any resolution with regard to this must be sent in for the agenda.[6]

The result of this reconsideration of the political work of the Association was a Council resolution on 4 April, carried by 55 votes to 18:

[1] *Derbyshire Times*, 14 January, 1922.   [2] *D.M.A.* 4 February, 1922.
[3] *Derbyshire Times*, 11 February, 1922.   [4] *D.M.A.* 25 February, 1922.
[5] *Ibid.* 4 March, 1922.   [6] *Ibid.*

That in the event of any permanent official being elected to Parliament as the nominee of the Association he shall not be expected to sever his connection with the Association, but shall retain tenancy of house with coal, light, etc. as at present, but with no retaining fee. In the event of non-success at a future election, he shall go back to his work as an official.

In view of this decision the whole question of candidates and constituencies was referred to the Executive Committee.[1] On 29 April the Council accepted the Executive Committee's recommendation that the North-East and Belper divisions should be contested by nominees of the Association. Frank Lee was to be the nominee for North-East Derbyshire and Oliver Wright for Belper, although he had not been nominated by the branches in the usual way. 'This is done', it was explained, 'out of consideration for the fact that Mr. Wright has for some time been the official candidate of the local Labour Party, and is not to be taken as a precedent.'[2]

IV

By the autumn of 1922 the Conservatives were becoming disgruntled with the coalition. They decided, at the famous Carlton Club meeting, on 17 October, to fight the next general election as an independent party. Lloyd George at once resigned and was succeeded by Bonar Law who immediately sought a dissolution. Once again the Derbyshire Miners' Association found itself fairly well prepared for the election. Although Hildreth had resigned and, for reasons of economy, had not been replaced, the party machinery had been gradually strengthened in the two constituencies which were to be contested by the union's nominees. On 11 November the Council called upon all the workers in the county to vote for the Labour candidates 'and help forward the emancipation of the workers from the tyranny and oppression of Capital'. The delegates strongly condemned 'the scurrilous and lying methods adopted by those candidates who are opposing Labour and supporting the capitalist system and the coal-owners' candidates'. 'The coal-owners', they asserted, 'have refused to carry out almost every agreement, national and local; have imposed reductions in wages outside agreements and placed compensation men in a precarious position, thus placing the wife and family with the man in a state of semi-starvation.'[3]

The dissolution of Parliament found the Chesterfield Divisional Labour Party still unable to agree on a suitable candidate. M. B. Shipsey, a Birmingham doctor, was invited to address a meeting with a view to

[1] *D.M.A.* 4 April, 1922.
[2] *Ibid.* 26 and 29 April, 1922.   [3] *Ibid.* 11 November, 1922.

his adoption but failed to appear.[1] Then there were negotiations with
Fred Richards, the President of the Boot and Shoe Operatives. At the
last minute it was decided not to contest the seat.[2] Once again, with the
support of the Conservatives, Barnet Kenyon, describing himself as 'a
Radical with national views', was unopposed.[3] In the Ilkeston division
there was a three-cornered fight between J. E. B. Seely, a Lloyd
Georgian Liberal; W. M. Freeman, a Conservative; and G. H. Oliver,
the Labour candidate. Oliver had begun life as an engineer and had
been employed by Rolls-Royce, Ltd. at Derby. Although he was not an
official miners' candidate, he had the support of the Derbyshire Miners'
Association and won the election. The voting was, Oliver, 9,342; Seely,
8,348; and Freeman 5,841.

In the Clay Cross division there had been a change in the Labour
candidature. Renshaw had withdrawn in August because there were no
funds to support his campaign and shortly before the election Charles
Duncan, Secretary of the General Workers' Union, was adopted.
Duncan had been sponsored by the Engineers as an L.R.C. candidate
at Barrow-in-Furness in 1906. As a result of the Liberal-Labour
electoral pact of 1903 Ramsay MacDonald had worked against Duncan's
candidature. Neither MacDonald nor Keir Hardie was impressed by
Duncan. MacDonald was reported to have said privately that Duncan
was being run in the Conservative interest and with Conservative
money. The pressure of the Engineers and the local members of the
L.R.C. had ensured Duncan's adoption.[4] He had eventually been
elected with official Liberal support and he had held the seat until 1918.
At Clay Cross Duncan had the support of the Derbyshire Miners'
Association. He was adopted on the motion of Samuel Sales, with
John Spencer presiding.[5]

T. T. Broad, who had rarely been seen in the Clay Cross division
after his election in 1918, had been repudiated by the local Liberal
Association on 24 July, 1920.[6] Shortly before the 1922 election he was
flirting with the Labour Party but it is not clear who made the first
advance. On 10 November Frank Hall asserted:

Mr. Broad began as a Liberal and had ended as a Tory because he got
the Tory vote. What do you think? Three weeks ago he went to Mr. Frank
Hodges and asked him how he could get inside the Labour Party. . . . What
do you think of the hypocrisy of politics?[7]

Broad gave a different account of the affair. He stated that he had met
Frank Hodges and Thomas Spencer in the Station Hotel, Chesterfield,

[1] *Derbyshire Times*, 3 June, 1922.   [2] *Ibid.* 4 November, 1922.   [3] *Ibid.*
[4] Philip P. Poirier, *The Advent of the Labour Party*, (London), 1958, p. 253.
[5] *Derbyshire Times*, 4 November, 1922.
[6] *Ibid.* 26 November, 1921.   [7] *Ibid.* 11 November, 1922.

'last week'. Hodges said to him: 'You have made a mistake. You ought to have taken my advice and joined us.' On the basis of this scrap of conversation Broad argued that he had been urged to join the Labour Party and that Hodges's report to the local Labour leaders that he had sought admission could not therefore be true.[1] Hodges and Spencer were both masters of misrepresentation and intrigue, and were opposed to Socialism. It is likely that they would favour the adoption of Broad as a Labour candidate rather than risk the adoption of a convinced Socialist. Broad eventually appeared as a 'National Liberal'. The official Liberal candidate was C. F. G. Masterman who formerly sat for West Ham and South-West Bethnal Green. In Asquith's administration he had served as Parliamentary Secretary to the Local Government Board, Under-Secretary to the Home Office, Financial Secretary to the Treasury, and Chancellor of the Duchy of Lancaster. Duncan was elected with 13,206 votes to Masterman's 6,294 and Broad's 3,294.

There were only two candidates in the Belper division. Hancock, like Kenyon, proclaimed himself a National Liberal and had the support of both the Liberals and the Conservatives. Oliver Wright, the miners' nominee, was the official Labour candidate. At the formal adoption meeting, it was reported, 'the "Red Flag" was sung for the first time in Belper'.[2] The campaign was vigorous. The Association was doubly anxious to win the seat for it wished not only to secure a victory for Labour but also to oust Hancock. Hicken, described as 'this firebrand from North Wingfield', delivered some characteristic speeches. Speaking of the policy of the coalition Government he said:

To hell with such a policy. . . . If you believe in a policy like that then on the judgment day I hope to stand face to face with you when called upon to give an account of your stewardship, and I hope the most withering, blistering flames of hell will consume you.

The *Derbyshire Times* commented:

We have mild mannered miners' leaders like Mr. Lee now openly avowing complete adherence to the socialistic Labour proposals and we have men, who in time of peace occupied the pulpits of some of our local chapels, preaching fire, brimstone and whatnot in their advocacy of the doctrines of Bolshevism. . . . What a delightful gentleman to follow! Lenin and Trotsky and the Bolshevist crowd would take him to their hearts as a true disciple.[3]

Whether Hicken's oratory contributed to Wright's defeat, as the *Derbyshire Times* predicted, will never be known. In the reorganization of the constituencies in 1918 the Belper division had lost mining areas

[1] *Derbyshire Times*, 11 November, 1922.
[2] *Ibid.* 4 November, 1922.   [3] *Ibid.* 11 November, 1922.

such as South Normanton and Pinxton, and had gained the Conservative stronghold of Repton. Hancock defeated Wright by 12,494 votes to 7,942.

In North-East Derbyshire the Marquis of Hartington and Harland Bowden had both withdrawn in favour of Charles Waterhouse who was the official Conservative candidate. Stanley Holmes, an Asquithian Liberal, had therefore to defend his seat against Lee and Waterhouse. Lee was helped in his campaign by Frank Hodges who addressed meetings at Whitwell and Staveley. The problems of the coal industry were much discussed. Holmes propounded a scheme for the repayment of the British war debt to America by means of coal, which completely ignored the fact that America was looking for markets for her own coal. Waterhouse told the Shuttlewood miners:

> I stand before you today as a frank supporter of trades unionism. . . . Keep your unions industrial, and I will give you my backing both in Parliament and out of Parliament, and you may depend upon it that no Conservative Government will infringe on the industrial rights of those unions.[1]

The election in the North-East Derbyshire division became a matter of national interest as the result of a dispute over the counting of the votes. The counting began at 10 a.m. on Thursday, 16 November. At about three o'clock in the afternoon it was announced that Lee had a majority of 14. The original figures were Lee, 9,385; Holmes, 9,371; and Waterhouse, 8,881. Holmes then demanded a recount which reduced Lee's majority to two. On the strength of this result he demanded another recount, which gave Lee a majority of three. Holmes still refused to accept Lee's majority as final and insisted on yet another recount. It was then eight o'clock and the enumerators were growing tired and confused. Reports were circulated about ten o'clock that Holmes had a majority of 201 on the third recount. Later his majority was stated to be 1,000. The results of the fifth and sixth recounts were stated to be indecisive and were not officially announced. At 1 a.m. on Friday, 17 November, it was decided to abandon the counting until 10 a.m. Several of the clerks refused to continue with the work and others were provided by a Chesterfield accountant and by the Staveley Coal and Iron Company. After two counts they arrived at the following result: Lee, 9,357; Holmes, 9,352; Waterhouse, 8,879. There were 115 spoilt ballot papers, making a total of 27,703. Lee had a majority of five but the Returning Officer pointed out that 27,708 ballot papers had been issued and that five were now missing.[2]

In accordance with the Parliamentary Elections Act, 1868, Holmes then presented a petition in the King's Bench division against the

[1] *Derbyshire Times*, 11 November, 1922.   [2] *Ibid.* 25 November, 1922.

return of Frank Lee as member for North-East Derbyshire. He alleged that H. R. Cleaver, the Returning Officer, had permitted a number of irregularities in the counting of the votes, stated that five ballot papers had been mislaid, and asked that Lee's election should be declared void.[1] The case was to be heard by Mr. Justice Avory and Mr. Justice Sankey who, on 19 January, 1923, ordered that the ballot papers should be inspected and recounted by the Master of the Counterfoils.[2] On 29 January, at the Royal Courts of Justice, Master Jelf began his examination of the ballot papers in the presence of Lee and Holmes and their legal advisers. The petition was heard by Avory and Sankey on 17 April. Lee was represented by Henry (later Sir Henry) Slesser and Arthur Henderson: Holmes by Willoughby Williams and Cyril Asquith. It was stated that after the election result had been finally declared three of the missing papers had been discovered. The fact that a number of the ballot papers did not bear the official stamp of the Returning Officer, or were stamped so faintly as to be doubtful, led to much discussion.[3] Eventually the judges ruled that Lee had 9,359 votes and Holmes, 9,344. The petition was dismissed and Holmes was ordered to pay Lee's costs. 'Having regard to the errors made, which may have led to the presentation of the petition', said Avory, 'the Returning Officer must pay his own costs.'[4]

After several months of uncertainty, Lee's election as M.P. for North-East Derbyshire was at last confirmed. It was the first seat to be won by a representative of the Association since its affiliation with the Labour Party. Soon afterwards Holmes announced that he had no intention of standing for North-East Derbyshire at the next election.[5] In May Lee asked the Home Secretary in the House of Commons whether he would see that more satisfactory stamps were provided for use in polling stations but was told by Locker-Lampson, the Under-Secretary, two months later, 'that the instruments, assuming they were used with ordinary care, could not have been responsible for the absence of the official mark on ballot papers'.[6]

Another sequel to the 1922 election was a further dispute with Barnet Kenyon. The Council resolution calling upon the workers in the county to vote for the Labour candidates and criticizing the coal-owners had been issued as an election manifesto signed by all the officials. Soon after the election the Conservative agent wrote to the *Derbyshire Times*:

I am informed by Mr. Kenyon that the .... resolution was not signed by him and that his name was used without his permission. Also that

[1] *Derbyshire Times*, 16 December, 1922.   [2] *Ibid.* 20 January, 1923.
[3] *Ibid.* 21 April, 1923.   [4] *Ibid.* 28 April, 1923.
[5] *Ibid.* 5 May, 1923.   [6] 163 H.C. Deb. 5s. 1419; 166 H.C. Deb. 5s. 438.

he had written to colliery owners to the effect that he did not identify himself with the statements contained in such a resolution. As the manifesto was widely circulated, this Association consider that it is due to the Unionists of the Chesterfield division who supported Mr. Kenyon that they should be informed of the circumstances.[1]

The union replied that as Kenyon was an official his name was automatically appended to any document of this kind.[2]

On 6 January, 1923, Kenyon read a prepared statement to the Council in which he protested that the resolution of 4 April, 1922, concerning the position of officials who were elected to Parliament meant that he was being driven out of the Association. He then left the meeting before anyone could reply. He had already made political capital out of the situation in various speeches by asserting that 'there was only one thing more they could do, so far as he could see, and that was to take his house from him'. On 11 January Kenyon wrote to Thomas Spencer:

I see now they have coupled you with me. My lad has sent me a cutting from a London evening paper with our photo's in the centre, setting forth clearly that we are both to be sacked, but, I sacked myself last Saturday. I am fed up with the whole thing. I enclose you a copy of my final address to them.[3]

Kenyon was summoned to a meeting of the Executive Committee on 18 January to hear a formal statement in reply to his allegations. It was pointed out to him that he was in the same position as any other official who was a Member of Parliament and that he could not expect to continue to receive the £100 retaining fee; that the Association had left him free to express his opinion on any political platform despite considerable provocation; and that there was no intention of depriving him of his house. Kenyon said that he had no objection to the publication of the Executive Committee's statement and that he would accept the conditions laid down by the April resolution.[4]

Kenyon attended only one more Council meeting, on 3 February. According to Sales he had gone there with the intention of resigning. There had been a number of letters in the local newspapers attacking the other officials for their 'unfair' treatment of Kenyon. When these letters were discussed by the Council Sales said 'that it seemed

[1] *Derbyshire Times*, 9 December, 1922.
[2] *D.M.A.* 9 December, 1922; *Derbyshire Times*, 16 December, 1922.
[3] The Papers of Thomas Spencer: Letter from Kenyon to Spencer, 11 January, 1923.
[4] *D.M.A.* 13 January, 1923. According to Sales it was Kenyon's supporters who voted against the payment of the retaining fee. (*Derbyshire Times*, 10 February, 1923.)

strange . . . that while all these bitter and lying remarks were being made about Messrs. Hall and Lee, Mr. Kenyon kept quiet when a few words from him stating the truth would put an end to the correspondence'.[1] After a heated discussion Kenyon left the Council Chamber vowing that he would never enter it again, but he did not formally resign. Sales pointed out that Kenyon still enjoyed the concession of his house, light and fuel:

> Furthermore, if he considers his parliamentary duties are too much for him then he has the option of returning to the Derbyshire Miners' Association offices on full-time official's salary. As Mr. Frank Hall so kindly put it to him: 'Come when you like, Barnet, all the help I can give you I will give willingly. If you can't attend every day, it won't matter. Come when you can, and if you don't feel like work, come and have a smoke. While ever you live you will always be assured of the full official salary equal to any other official.'[2]

However, Kenyon's persistent refusal to attend Council and Executive Committee meetings led to a decision, towards the end of the year, that he should cease to be an official and be given a life pension of £2 a week. He was allowed to retain the tenancy of his house at a nominal rent.[3]

V

The dust of battle from the previous election had barely settled in Derbyshire before Parliament was again dissolved. Baldwin, who had succeeded Bonar Law in May, 1923, believed that the best remedy for the growing unemployment was a protective tariff. Prevented from carrying out his policy by Bonar Law's election pledge that no such tariff would be introduced, he decided in the autumn to appeal to the electorate. The defence of free trade brought the Liberals together again and in all the mining constituencies in Derbyshire there were three-cornered fights between Conservatives, Liberals and Labour.

There had been much speculation about Barnet Kenyon's intentions but in July he had denied the rumour 'which seems to be sedulously propagated every few months' that he intended to resign his seat.[4] The Chesterfield Divisional Labour Party had decided to put forward a candidate in opposition to Kenyon and meetings had been addressed by Hugh Dalton and Gilbert Dale.[5] Baldwin announced the dissolution on

[1] *Derbyshire Times*, 10 February, 1923.   [2] *Ibid.*
[3] *D.M.A.* 6 and 10 November, 8 December, 1923. See Chapter XV, p. 585.
[4] *Derbyshire Times*, 28 July, 1923.   [5] *Ibid.* 3 November, 1923.

10 November. On the following day Dalton visited Chesterfield. He quotes from his diary:

> November 11th. To Chesterfield. Spend the night with Frank Hall. . . .
> He advises me against calling on Kenyon at his house since Mrs. K. will be there and will make trouble. He suggests I should see K. at House of Commons which reassembles (for the last time before its dissolution) on Tuesday the 13th.
> November 12th. See Wake in afternoon. Horrified at news from Chesterfield. Says: 'We are running straight into a cul-de-sac.' Arrange to lunch with Wedgwood at the House next day, and ask him to find out K's intentions, if he can.
> November 13th. . . . Wedgwood says he has spoken to K. who intends to stand again. . . . I decide that Chesterfield is off, and begin to look elsewhere.[1]

Eventually George (later Sir George) Benson was adopted as the Labour candidate for Chesterfield at a meeting held in the Miners' Offices on 17 November. After being educated by the Society of Friends, Benson had joined his father's land and estate agency in Manchester, and later succeeded to the senior position in the firm. He had been a member of the I.L.P. for eighteen years, and was also its national treasurer, a position his father had held for twenty years. In the 1922 election George Benson had been the Labour candidate at Altrincham. The Conservatives, who had been waiting to see whether Kenyon would be opposed, then adopted A. B. Colton Fox, a Yorkshire farmer, who had hitherto taken no part in public affairs. He had local connections, being related to one of the partners in a Sheffield firm of solicitors and, by marriage, to one of the directors of the Chesterfield Brewery Company.[2]

Kenyon, who was the official Liberal candidate, made numerous references to his disputes with the Derbyshire Miners' Association in order to win public sympathy. He complained, probably with justice, that his salary of £400 a year, which he received as a Member of Parliament, was quite inadequate to meet all his expenses. He was careful to mention the cost of typing 'hundreds of letters' in cases which he had taken up on behalf of war widows and orphans. He also had people who wanted to see him at the House of Commons—'and many of them were thirsty'. 'When they wanted to charge me with an enormous salary,' he said, 'when my poor wife for those lads in the trenches agreed to manage on £2 per week. . . .' He had no need to say more for his speech was lost in applause. He omitted to point out that his penurious existence was of his own choosing. By becoming an approved

---

[1] Hugh Dalton, *Memoirs: Call Back Yesterday*, (London), 1953, pp. 138-9.
[2] *Derbyshire Times*, 24 November, 1923.

miners' candidate he could have increased his salary and had a railway season ticket to London. If his conscience prevented him from joining the Labour Party he had the alternative of returning to the miners' offices as a full-time official. H. Varley, one of the Labour leaders, denied allegations made in a Chesterfield chapel 'that the Labour Party was trying to throw the old man on the scrap heap'. Frank Hall stated that the Association's books were open for examination by any accountant in the town.[1]

Trivial and rather sordid issues of this kind are sometimes an influential factor in local elections, although national history is largely written in terms of party political issues. These were not entirely neglected in the Chesterfield election. Kenyon was particularly critical of the Labour Party's proposed capital levy.[2] Despite a vigorous effort on the part of Benson and his supporters, Kenyon was again the victor. The voting was: Kenyon, 12,164; Benson, 6,198; and Fox, 5,554.

In the Ilkeston division G. H. Oliver was opposed by W. M. Freeman, the Conservative candidate, and T. W. Casey, the Liberal. Oliver retained his seat, with 9,191 votes, against Freeman's 6,566 and Casey's 6,112. There was also a Labour victory in the Clay Cross division. The Conservative candidate was J. Sherwood Kelly, a former Lieutenant-Colonel who had been awarded the Victoria Cross during the war. He had ended his distinguished military career, when in command of troops in Russia, by advocating the withdrawal of the British forces and exposing what he described as the Winston Churchill 'gamble'.[3]

F. C. Thornborough, the Liberal candidate, had been president of the Young Liberals' League and had been defeated in the Morpeth by-election of June, 1923, by Robert Smillie. Charles Duncan was again the Labour candidate although, according to Mr. Kingsley Martin, Harold Laski wrote to his friend Firuski: 'Arthur Henderson . . . wanted me to run for Clay Cross which Labour eventually won by six thousand; but with Tawney ill I thought it my job to work in his place as he couldn't be there, and after a fight I got out of it.'[4] In one of his speeches Duncan said that some comment had been made about his visiting the constituency only once since he was elected but his reply was that he had come into the division every time the Labour Party had asked him. 'You should not need asking', interjected a member of the audience.[5] Nevertheless, Duncan retained his seat. He had 11,939 votes to Kelly's 4,881 and Thornborough's 4,488.

[1] *Derbyshire Times*, 1 December, 1923.   [2] *Ibid.* 24 November, 1923.
[3] Cf. Raymond Postgate, *George Lansbury*, (London), 1951, pp. 194–5.
[4] Kingsley Martin, *Harold Laski*, (London), 1953, p. 60.
[5] *Derbyshire Times*, 24 November, 1923.

The Derbyshire Miners' Association again put forward Frank Lee and Oliver Wright for the North-East Derbyshire and Belper constituencies respectively.[1] In Belper Herbert Wragg, a coal-owner, was the Conservative candidate and J. G. Hancock the Liberal. Hancock was more extreme in his condemnation of the Labour Party than Wragg:

I have seen many disorderly scenes at pit gates but the most disorderly scene I ever witnessed was in the House of Commons when a dozen wild men, irresponsible men, who respect or acknowledge no leader, created pandemonium and caused the sitting to be suspended. Such men openly boast that they want another Russia, a Russian revolution. The wild men boss trade unions today. The extremists rule the unions. They have spoilt them and practically ruined them.[2]

With speeches of this kind Hancock not only lost his seat but came at the bottom of the poll with only 6,178 votes. Oliver Wright had 7,284 and Wragg was elected with 9,662.

In North-East Derbyshire Charles Waterhouse was the Conservative candidate and Philip Guedalla, the Liberal. Protection and the problems of the coal industry were the main subjects discussed by the candidates. 'My objection to nationalizing the coal industry', said Guedalla, 'is that it does not take the workers an inch further along the road that they want to go. If you put "G.R." and the Lion and the Unicorn on the colliery gates they will just be regarded as part of the machinery.'[3] Despite formidable opposition Lee was again elected. The voting was: Lee, 10,971; Waterhouse, 8,768; and Guedalla, 8,080.

The Council of the Derbyshire Miners' Association was well pleased with the results of the election.[4] In addition to the Labour victories in Derbyshire, Frank Varley, the Nottinghamshire miners' leader, had been elected in the Mansfield division. The 1923 election resulted in the formation of the first Labour Government. The Conservatives, with 257 seats, had obviously been defeated on the issue of protection, although they were still the largest party in the House. Labour had 192 seats and the Liberals, 157. Baldwin decided not to resign until Parliament met. His Government fell within the first week on an amendment to the Address and MacDonald, as leader of the larger of the two opposition parties, became Prime Minister. Frank Lee told some of his supporters at Staveley: 'It may be that they would be disappointed by what was going to happen during the next twelve months, and they might find that 192 members in the House of Commons had not the power that they thought they would have.'[5]

---

[1] *D.M.A.* 6 November, 1923. [2] *Derbyshire Times*, 8 December, 1923.
[3] *Ibid.* 24 November, 1923.
[4] *D.M.A.* 8 December, 1923. [5] *Derbyshire Times*, 5 January, 1924.

VI

Yet another general election in the near future appeared inevitable. Its timing largely depended upon the Liberals who, like the Labour Party, did not want it to come indecently early. Barnet Kenyon, who had been criticized for supporting the Liberal amendment to the Address which defeated the Baldwin Government, assured the League of Young Liberals at Chesterfield: 'We can either make or unmake governments but we do not want to disrupt the peace of the Government again just yet . . . The country cannot afford the money which a general election costs.'[1] Frank Hall told the Bolsover Labour Party: 'The longer they remained in office the better would their chances be of retaining the reins of government when the next appeal was made to the country.'[2] The temporary alliance between the Liberal and Labour parties was an uneasy one. Neither could be sure of the other's intentions. The Conservatives were equally uncertain how long the alliance would last. The result was that all three parties lost no time in making their preparations for the next election.

The immediate cause of the Labour Government's downfall was the Campbell case. The Attorney-General, Sir Patrick Hastings, had decided to prosecute J. R. Campbell, editor of the communist *Workers' Weekly*, on the grounds that he had published an article urging soldiers to disobey orders rather than open fire on strikers, but the prosecution was suddenly withdrawn. The opposition parties alleged that improper pressure had been brought to bear on the Attorney-General and demanded a full inquiry. MacDonald refused, the Government was defeated, and Parliament was dissolved on 9 October, 1924. Kenyon thought it necessary to explain why he did not take part in the fateful division:

I stood there ready to do my duty at 11.10 p.m. My train—I leave by the last train possible—went at 11.30 p.m. I have never failed once in my life in stopping to the last minute until this night, but when I saw the confusion, the fog and the nastiness, I could not possibly stop amongst it. Therefore, I left them to it.[3]

Kenyon was again the Liberal candidate for Chesterfield. The Conservatives decided not to oppose him but later resolved:

That we as Unionists do not support Mr. Barnet Kenyon either by vote or influence unless we receive from him the written guarantee that he will support our interests in the House of Commons, and that on no account will he be allowed to support the Socialist Government as he did after the last election.[4]

[1] *Derbyshire Times*, 9 February, 1924.   [2] *Ibid.* 26 April, 1924.
[3] *Ibid.* 18 October, 1924.   [4] *Ibid.*

Kenyon, whose support of the Labour Government had been no more than was necessary to satisfy the Liberal Whips, readily complied with the Conservatives' request. In January, 1924, Minnie Pallister, a Labour Party organizer, had told a Chesterfield meeting: 'By careful organization Chesterfield could be won for Labour within the next year or two.'[1] But Kenyon, with the support of two political parties and of large numbers of Liberal miners, was difficult to remove. Asquith was reported to have said: 'Barnet Kenyon may stay in Parliament until the doctors order him out.'[2] George Benson complained that the Conservatives and Liberals were 'using Mr. Barnet Kenyon as a cat's-paw and drawing upon the well known and well deserved sympathy Chesterfield had for Mr. Kenyon to defeat Labour'.[3] Labour was defeated by 13,971 votes to 9,206.

In the Ilkeston division both the Conservatives and the Liberals put forward new candidates. The Conservative candidate H. V. A. M. (later Sir Victor) Raikes, received 9,203 votes and the Liberal, Lady Barlow, 4,320. G. H. Oliver, with 11,011 votes, again retained his seat. Charles Duncan's success at Clay Cross in 1923 had led the Conservative Party to make greater efforts. Previously there had been no party organization in the division but shortly after the election an agent had been appointed to remedy this deficiency.[4] Sherwood Kelly was again the Conservative candidate. The Liberals decided not to split the vote. Despite all these precautions Duncan was elected with 14,618 votes to Kelly's 8,069.

There were important changes in the Belper division. Hancock had decided after his defeat in 1923 not to contest the seat again and the Liberals tried to find another candidate. Sir Charles Seely was invited to stand but refused and eventually the Liberals decided not to adopt a candidate.[5] The Labour Party was growing dissatisfied with Oliver Wright, who had lost ground, and began to look for another candidate. On 2 February three nominations were considered: Hugh Dalton; Montague Lyons, a young Nottingham barrister; and Alfred Varley, a local Labour leader from Wirksworth. Oliver Wright had also been nominated but stated that he was prepared to withdraw and work for Dalton. It was unanimously decided to ask Dalton to become the prospective candidate.[6] He asked for time to consider the matter but eventually decided not to commit himself. On 29 March the Council of the Derbyshire Miners' Association expressed its willingness 'to consider finding a miners' candidate to contest the Belper division if it is found that there is a unanimous request from the Divisional Labour Party'.[7] A month later the branches were asked to send in nominations

[1] *Derbyshire Times*, 12 January, 1924. [2] *Ibid.* 18 October, 1924.
[3] *Ibid.*   [4] *Ibid.*   [5] *Ibid.* 16 August, 1924.
[6] *Ibid.* 9 February, 1924.   [7] *Ibid.* 23 February, 1924.

and the officials were asked to state their position. 'We know of none better qualified to bring together the scattered forces in the constituency than Mr. Hall, your General Secretary, could he get the unanimous support of the Council and Branches', they asserted. 'The effect of such effort with Mr. Hall as the candidate would reflect itself in our industrial organization and guarantee greater efficiency.'[1]

Hall and Wright were both nominated by the branches but Hall decided to withdraw because of his wife's indifferent health and suggested that Hicken's name should be put forward.[2] When the matter was again referred to the branches there were 391 votes for Wright and 326 for Hicken. 'Twenty per cent. of the branches failed to record any vote, which is regrettable', reported the officials.[3] By 9 August, when the Belper Divisional Party met to select its candidate, Montague Lyons had withdrawn and the choice was between Wright and Jack Lees. By 65 votes to 37 Lees was adopted. He had worked in the Northumberland mines for eighteen years before winning a scholarship to Ruskin College. His education there had been cut short by the war, after which he was appointed political agent to the Northumberland Miners' Association. Until 1905 Lees had been a Liberal but in that year he came under the influence of J. Bruce Glasier. He joined the I.L.P. and, as well as being chairman of the Newcastle branch, had played a prominent part in the national organization.[4]

In an election in which the Zinoviev letter played a prominent part, accusations of Communism were bandied about freely. G. H. Strutt, the Belper Conservative leader, said: 'They did not know Mr. Lees' views, whether he was a genuine Labour man or whether he belonged to the Communist Party. He asked his audience, as one that believed in genuine Labour men, to support Mr. Wragg.'[5] Evelyn G. Corkery, the Secretary of the Women's Conservative Association was convinced that Lees was a Communist because he was 'a nominee of the I.L.P. and not the Miners' Association' and 'had been known to stand on the same platform as Mrs. Besant, whose writings and speeches have caused so much trouble in India'.[6] Herbert Wragg, the Conservative candidate, defeated Lees by 14,766 votes to 10,618 but Labour had gained ground.

Frank Lee was again the miners' candidate for North-East Derbyshire.[7] G. Harland Bowden reappeared as the official Conservative candidate and Philip Guedalla as the Liberal. Bowden raised the Communist bogy: 'I say Communists are the end of the Socialist tail and

[1] D.M.A. 26 April, 1924.   [2] Ibid. 24 May, 1924.
[3] Ibid. 21 June, 1924.   [4] Derbyshire Times, 16 August, 1924.
[5] Ibid. 4 October, 1924.
[6] Ibid. 11 October, 1924.   [7] D.M.A. 11 October, 1924.

are the end of the tail that wags the dog. I will fight with my last breath against Socialism because it means Communism and Russian rule.'[1] Despite such tactics Frank Lee was re-elected with 13,420 votes to Bowden's 9,914 and Guedalla's 6,529.

The election was a national victory for the Conservatives, who secured 413 seats. Labour had 151 and the Liberals only 40. In Derbyshire, however, the Labour Party had not only succeeded in holding its three seats but had also gained more votes in the Chesterfield and Belper divisions. 'This is considered to show an increased interest in the Labour Party', stated the officials, 'and that Derbyshire is coming more and more into line with the other mining areas in the country.'[2] The election results were a reflection of the increasing efficiency of Labour Party organization in the county. It even extended to a few Socialist Sunday Schools which were sharply criticized by the Bishop of Southwell soon after the election: 'On the night of the poll, a crowd of young men marched up and down a Derbyshire village shouting out blasphemous and filthy hymns. . . . The Sunday school was a place to implant into the minds of the young things that were pure, wholesome and noble.'[3]

VII

Soon after the 1924 election the miners had to turn their attention increasingly to industrial problems. The 1926 stoppage sadly depleted their funds. The Derbyshire Miners' Association made grants from its political fund to various relief funds in the county with the result that, in March, 1927, the Council decided to suspend the payment of affiliation fees to local Labour parties until more money had accumulated.[4] Moreover, although the Labour Party in Derbyshire was growing steadily stronger, largely as a result of the activities of the Association in the mining constituencies, the actual task of representing the miners in Parliament was falling to men who were rapidly becoming professional politicians. After the 1924 election Frank Lee was the only candidate put forward by the Association until after the Second World War. This trend became more marked as a result of the legislation following the General Strike. The Trade Disputes and Trade Unions Act of 1927, which, amongst other things, introduced 'contracting in' instead of 'contracting out' for payment of the political levy, increased the difficulties of building up the political fund.[5] In November, 1928, the

[1] *Derbyshire Times*, 18 October, 1924.   [2] *D.M.A.* 8 November, 1924.
[3] *Derbyshire Times*, 22 November, 1924.
[4] *D.M.A.* 26 March, 1927.   [5] See Appendix I to this chapter.

Executive Committee of the Association recommended that the payment of affiliation fees to local Labour parties should be discontinued. Branches were urged to make a further attempt before the end of the year 'to secure a 100 per cent. signing of political cards. . . . In view of an early general election, this is very urgent and necessary.'[1] By 23 March, 1929, only 14,000 members had agreed to pay the political levy and less than 9,000 contributions had actually been received at the union's offices. The total membership had by that time fallen to 19,326.

Meanwhile the M.F.G.B. had been obliged to revise its political rules to comply with the law and to make economies in its expenditure on political activities. The salaries of Members of Parliament had been reduced and it had been decided that the districts should be entitled to one parliamentary candidate for each 10,000 political members.[2] Thus when the Baldwin Government's term of office came to an end in 1929 the Derbyshire Miners' Association was entitled to only one candidate and Frank Lee was again nominated for North-East Derbyshire.[3]

Guedalla had given up the unequal struggle and had been succeeded as the prospective Liberal candidate by a local man, C. O. Foster, of Dronfield.[4] Foster later withdrew and on 6 April, 1929, H. A. Briggs, a Sheffield railway spring-fitter, was adopted. There were three changes in the prospective Conservative candidature. Harland Bowden died in October, 1927, and was succeeded by A. T. W. Taylor, who soon withdrew.[5] In March, 1928, Norman Winning, a barrister, was adopted. He was followed, in November, by R. E. Samuelson, a young London business man. On the eve of his election campaign Frank Lee was suffering from quinsy, and Hicken and Wright addressed meetings in his support. Unemployment and the Trade Disputes and Trade Unions Act were the principal issues of the election. At a meeting at Whitwell Samuelson alleged that Frank Lee had been opposed to the 1926 stoppage from the start, that he had therefore failed to come forward and give the miners a lead, and that he had been defeated in the election for the position of General Secretary in 1928 because of his attitude during the stoppage.[6] These charges quickly brought Lee from his sick-bed. 'I stood by the men throughout the stoppage', he declared. 'I spoke throughout the country, addressing meetings in London and the agricultural counties of the south of England. I should like to know what Mr. Samuelson himself was doing throughout the stoppage.'[7] Lee's illness did not prevent him from increasing his majority considerably. The voting was: Lee, 21,633; Samuelson, 9,167; and Briggs, 8,861.

[1] D.M.A. 12 November, 1928.   [2] M.F.G.B. 20 December, 1928.
[3] D.M.A. 23 March, 1929.   [4] Derbyshire Times, 19 September, 1925.
[5] Ibid. 21 January, 1928.   [6] Ibid. 25 May, 1929.   [7] Ibid.

In the Chesterfield division relations between the Derbyshire Miners' Association and the Labour Party continued to be unsatisfactory. H. Cropper had been practically disowned by the party since 1923 when, in connection with his proposed candidature, he had stated that he was not in favour of either the nationalization of the mines or the capital levy. In 1925 he became Mayor of Chesterfield and conformed with the unwritten law which required abstention from party politics until early in 1926 when he stated publicly that he was no longer a member of the Labour Party:

I have always taken the attitude that the political side of the Labour movement, which has a definite mission to fulfil, has been dominated by the purely I.L.P. section of the party with their wretched adherence to the doctrinarian opinions of Karl Marx. Some people considered that I was never a Labour man, even when I spoke on a Labour platform.

At about the same time H. Varley, the brother of Frank Varley, the Nottinghamshire miners' leader, also left the Labour Party. He had been the leader of the Labour group of the Chesterfield borough council but had abandoned his political activities after becoming a publican. 'The Labour Party is dominated by the Derbyshire Miners' Association,' he said, 'and really that is the cause of the trouble . . . Both Alderman Cropper and I refused . . . to take instructions from the Derbyshire Miners' Association.'[1]

Further confusion was created in the division by Barnet Kenyon's announcement that he did not intend to stand at the next general election. It was soon rumoured that Cropper would be the next Liberal candidate. Frank Lee, speaking in support of George Benson, in October, 1926, explained that this was the first time he had been on a Labour platform in Chesterfield:

Mr. Barnet Kenyon and he had been very close friends. Neither had agreed with the other's politics, but there had been a tacit understanding, and so long as both were in the field neither would go into the other's constituency and speak against him. . . . He did not know who would oppose Mr. Benson. He understood the Conservative Party were going to get someone who would be acceptable to the Liberals also.[2]

On 21 December the executive committee of the Chesterfield Conservative and Unionist Association resolved: 'That in the event of Alderman H. Cropper standing as independent candidate for the division, this committee pledges itself to give him the wholehearted support of the Chesterfield Divisional Conservative and Unionist Association.'[3] However, when it was announced soon afterwards that Cropper was to

[1] *Derbyshire Times*, 27 February, 1926.   [2] *Ibid.* 9 October, 1926.
[3] *Ibid.* 25 December, 1926.

be the prospective Liberal candidate the Conservatives quickly withdrew their support.[1] Cropper resigned in April, 1928, on private and
domestic grounds, but in February, 1929, again decided to stand as
Liberal candidate for the Chesterfield division.[2]

T. J. Gooding, of Leicester, was adopted as Conservative candidate
in April, 1927, but resigned in March, 1928, owing to ill health. He was
succeeded by R. J. E. Conant, a Rutland farmer.[3] George Benson was
once again the Labour candidate but, like Frank Lee, he was ill and
unable to conduct the early part of his campaign. J. H. Harvey, who
had been asked to withdraw from Daventry in order to allow Speaker
Fitzroy to be returned unopposed, deputized for Benson.[4] This time
the Labour Party was successful. The voting was: Benson, 20,296;
Conant, 9,915; and Cropper, 7,329.

There were also three-cornered fights in the Ilkeston and Belper
divisions. G. H. Oliver, who in 1927 had been called to the bar and
was now in practice, retained his seat with 20,202 votes. The Liberal
candidate, J. V. Shaw, a former Ilkeston doctor, had 7,766 votes and
the Conservative, H. V. A. M. Raikes, 6,258. Jack Lees won a victory
for Labour in the Belper division with 15,958 votes to Herbert Wragg's
13,003. The Liberal candidate, T. Scott Anderson, the managing
director of the Peak Chert Mines Company, Bakewell, had 8,149 votes.
Charles Duncan had a straight fight in the Clay Cross division. The
Conservative candidate was Montague Lyons who, in 1924, had been
considered as a possible Labour candidate for the Chesterfield division.
Along with George Spencer he had addressed meetings advocating the
introduction of protective tariffs, especially for the iron and steel
trades.[5] Duncan defeated Lyons by 24,480 votes to 6,055.

The 1929 election, in which the 'flappers' voted for the first time,
resulted in the formation of the second Labour Government. The
Labour Party, with 290 seats, was now the largest party in the House
but did not obtain a clear majority. The Conservatives and the Liberals
had 260 and 60 seats respectively. In Derbyshire every mining constituency had been won by Labour. The Council of the Derbyshire
Miners' Association expressed 'its complete satisfaction' and congratulated the successful candidates and also the members 'who have rallied
round the Banner of Labour, and shown by their votes at the Ballot
Box what they think of the Industrial Policy of the last Government
in the passing of the Trade Disputes Act, and the Miners' Eight
Hours' Act'. The Council also called for the repeal of 'these iniquitous
measures'.[6]

[1] *Derbyshire Times*, 5 February, 1926.
[2] *Ibid.* 21 April, 1928; 23 February, 1929.   [3] *Ibid.* 19 May, 1928.
[4] *Ibid.* 25 May, 1929.   [5] *Ibid.* 18 May, 1929.   [6] *D.M.A.* 15 June, 1929.

The Labour Government was unable to repeal the Trade Disputes Act without the support of the Liberals and the financing of political activities continued to be difficult because union members were reluctant to pay the political levy. A special committee, appointed by the Derbyshire Miners' Council to investigate the position of the political fund, reported in June, 1930: 'In view of our straitened circumstances and very much lessened income, far from being able to expand our financial assistance, we are compelled to face up to a restriction of same.' The committee recommended a number of economies in the allowances made to members serving on local authorities and the appointment of a sub-committee 'to inspect and inquire into all items of income and expenditure of the political fund at least once every six months'. Hicken, W. Hardy and H. White were appointed to carry out these duties.[1]

The controversy which had surrounded Barnet Kenyon since 1913 had a brief revival in 1930. Kenyon, who was then 79 years of age, had been in retirement since the 1929 election. His 'life pension' had been discontinued by the Association after the 1926 stoppage.[2] On 15 January, Violet Markham suggested an appeal for subscriptions 'as a testimonial to our veteran ex-member', and the *Derbyshire Times* opened its Barnet Kenyon Shilling Fund.[3] A statement that the Association had refused to give any assistance because of Kenyon's 'refusal to sign the Labour Ticket', aroused the indignation of Hicken:

Since 1913, up to January, 1925, Mr. Kenyon has received in cash assistance from the Derbyshire Miners' Association, no less than £2,250. . . . In addition to these cash payments, perquisites amounting, at a very conservative estimate, to £53 6s. per year, or over the period to £586 6s. have been received from the Derbyshire Miners' Association. . . . We can only hope that the sympathies of the general public will deal as generously with Mr. Kenyon through this shilling fund as to raise a total in his support approximately as grand as the £2,836 6s. od. contributed to Mr. Kenyon by the Derbyshire Miners' Association during those years, during which he was engaged practically the whole of his time in his parliamentary duties.[4]

On 20 February Kenyon died and the controversy came to an end. The Association paid the tribute which customarily marked the death of an official. In moving a resolution of sympathy John Spencer said: 'Although perhaps Mr. Barnet Kenyon and the Derbyshire Miners' Association did not always see eye to eye with regard to politics, death, the great healer, had swept those differences away.'[5] The officials attended the funeral, as did the Duke of Devonshire.

[1] *D.M.A.* 14 June, 1930. See Appendix I to this chapter.
[2] See Chapter XV, p. 593.   [3] *Derbyshire Times*, 18 January, 1930.
[4] *Ibid.* 1 February, 1930. The Barnet Kenyon Shilling Fund raised only £783 10s. 6d. (*Derbyshire Times*, 12 October, 1934.)
[5] *Ibid.* 1 March, 1930; *D.M.A.* 22 February, 1930.

VIII

After two years of ineffectual rule the minority Labour Government was brought down by the financial crisis of 1931. In August MacDonald offered to resign but, since he was in favour of economies, was persuaded by the King to form a 'National' Government, much to the disgust of the bulk of the Labour Party. On 2 September Hicken reported to the Derbyshire Miners' Council the results of the discussions of the M.F.G.B. Executive Committee on the political situation. Lee reported on the meetings of the Parliamentary Labour Party, the Executive Committee of the Labour Party and the General Council of the T.U.C. The Council then approved 'the Miners' Federation Executive Committee's opposition to the National Government in their attempt to economize at the expense of the poorer class of the nation' and instructed the miners' M.P.s 'to support without fail the policy adopted by the T.U.C. and the Labour Party'.[1]

In October MacDonald appealed to the country. The Government wanted a mandate to save the nation from financial ruin. Upon this decision, said MacDonald, 'depends how the tables and cupboards of the working-class families are to be stocked'. The Derbyshire Miners' Association found itself ill-prepared for the election. On 10 October the Council decided that 'in view of the position of the Political Fund ... no contribution can be made towards the expenses of fighting in any of the Derbyshire divisions'.[2] In all the Derbyshire mining constituencies except the North-East division, there was a straight fight between Labour and National candidates. In the Chesterfield division R. J. E. Conant defeated George Benson by 23,026 votes to 17,046. In the Belper division Herbert Wragg ousted Jack Lees by 23,361 votes to 15,450. In the Ilkeston division A. J. Flint, a National Labour candidate, defeated G. H. Oliver by 17,587 votes to 17,585. In the Clay Cross division Philip Hicken, the brother of the General Secretary of the Derbyshire Miners' Association, who was then unemployed, announced his intention of standing as a Communist candidate, if he could raise the necessary £150 deposit. He had played a prominent part in the National Unemployed Workers' Movement and, in support of his proposed candidature, Wal Hannington was to have addressed a meeting at Clay Cross but was prevented from doing so by his imprisonment in Winchester Jail.[3] The pennies of the unemployed proved to be insufficient to finance Hicken's candidature, although he registered his protest against 'the sham nature of British democracy' by attempting

[1] *D.M.A.* 2 September, 1931.   [2] *Ibid.* 10 October, 1931.
[3] *Derbyshire Times*, 17 October, 1931.

DD

to hand in his nomination papers without the deposit.[1] Charles Duncan thus had a straight fight with Jacob Weinberg, a young Nottingham lace manufacturer, defeating him by 21,163 votes to 11,611.

Frank Lee contested North-East Derbyshire as a M.F.G.B. candidate and was opposed by J. B. Whyte, a London consulting engineer, who was the National Conservative candidate, and A. V. Williams, one of Sir Oswald Mosley's New Party candidates. Williams had had an eventful career as a left-wing propagandist in Derbyshire, being imprisoned during the General Strike for his journalistic activities.[2] He had worked as a miner, but, because of his political views, it was not always easy for him to find employment and at various times he had turned to other occupations. In the early 'twenties he had been a furniture dealer. At the time of the 1931 election he was a travelling draper. The New Party, Mosley's protest against the lack of militancy in the Labour Party, had close connections with North-East Derbyshire, for it had been launched by a demonstration at Renishaw Park, the home of the Sitwells, in the previous August. People had assembled from Chesterfield, Nottingham, Leicester and as far afield as Newcastle and other parts of the north of England. They had heard Mosley deliver a scathing attack on the Labour Party in which he charged it with cowardice and incompetence, and described Snowden as 'the flunkey of the bondholder and the banker'.[3] The two dozen New Party candidates, including Mosley himself, were all defeated in the 1931 election and Mosley soon afterwards re-appeared as the leader of the British Fascists. He stated at Bolsover that he had left the Labour Party because 'they had let down the working class'.[4] When Frank Lee was asked about Mosley he said that he had made up his mind at the opening of his campaign to say nothing about the New Party. 'However,' he continued, 'the whole point about Sir Oswald was, that unless he could be right at the top of the tree he would be nowhere, and because the Labour Party had not done exactly as he had wished, he had left them.'[5] Whyte, the National Conservative candidate, defeated Lee by 20,719 votes to 19,385. Williams, with 689 votes, lost his deposit.

Labour had been thoroughly defeated: 558 National Government candidates were elected against 56 for the Labour opposition. In Derbyshire Charles Duncan was the only Labour member to retain his seat. G. H. Oliver later described the election as 'a gigantic fraud' and accused MacDonald of asking for 'the Tory programme absolutely' instead of 'a true mandate'.[6]

Early in 1933 Philip Hicken appeared before the Chesterfield

[1] *Derbyshire Times*, 24 October, 1931.
[2] See Chapter XVIII, pp. 701–2.
[3] *Derbyshire Times*, 8 August, 1931.
[4] *Ibid.* 24 October, 1931.
[5] *Ibid.* 17 October, 1931.
[6] *Ibid.* 26 March, 1932.

magistrates charged with 'disturbing the public peace and inciting persons to commit the offence of wilful damage and larceny'. At a meeting of the National Unemployed Workers' Movement, at Staveley, Hicken had said: 'The law says you shall starve. We are being denied things when the shops are full. Winter is coming, and the unemployed are supplied with no food; the shop windows have the answer.' This was regarded as 'a direct incitement to people to help themselves to things from the shops'. Hicken refused to be bound over for twelve months and elected to serve three months' imprisonment.[1] Following the intervention of the trustees and officials of the Association, Hicken gave notice of his intention to appeal and was released from prison on bail.[2] Despite the Association's opposition to the National Unemployed Workers' Movement, the Council approved the action of the trustees and officials and passed a lengthy resolution protesting 'against the action of the authorities in bringing into operation this Act of Edward III' and calling for its repeal.[3]

In April Sir Stafford Cripps represented Hicken at the Derby Quarter Sessions. The appeal was unsuccessful but Hicken had by that time only one week to serve in prison.[4] The legal expenses amounted to £995 and there followed a lengthy controversy over the Association's right to use its political fund for such purposes. On 29 July R. J. E. Conant, the member for Chesterfield, asked the Minister of Labour in the House of Commons whether he would institute an inquiry into the matter.[5] He also published a letter in the *Derbyshire Times* calling upon the Association to justify the expenditure.[6] Oliver Wright replied:

The questions put to the officials of the Derbyshire Miners' Association by Mr. Conant, in respect of the financial transactions of the Association, savour of impertinence. If he asked questions in the public Press about the affairs of the employers' associations he would be promptly told to mind his own business. . . . We are fighting not for persons but for principles. We profoundly disagree with the Communist policy, but we demand fair play and freedom of speech for all our members, irrespective of political opinions. . . . Perhaps Mr. Conant does not know that no prosecutions have taken place under this inadequate law since the appeal. Previously men were being thrown into prison all over the country. The appeal cost approximately £1,000. More shame that we had to spend it in the interests of justice.[7]

Whilst this controversy was going on the Association was preparing to contest a by-election in the Clay Cross division, caused by the death of

[1] *Derbyshire Times*, 14 January, 1933.
[2] *D.M.A.* 21 January, 1933; *Derbyshire Times*, 21 January, 1933.
[3] *Ibid.*   [4] *Derbyshire Times*, 8 April, 1933; *D.M.A.* 15 April, 1933.
[5] 280 H.C. Deb. 5s. 2771–2.
[6] *Derbyshire Times*, 5 August, 1933.   [7] *Ibid.* 12 August, 1933.

Charles Duncan on 7 July. There was no shortage of candidates for many of the Labour leaders who had been defeated in 1931 were still scrambling for safe seats. There was a struggle between the National Executive Committee of the Labour Party, which was anxious to find a seat for Arthur Henderson, and Ernest Bevin, who argued that the Transport and General Workers' Union had a prescriptive right to nominate a candidate for Clay Cross because of Duncan's long association with the union. Bevin's candidate was Ben Smith, a former M.P. for Rotherham and ex-Labour Whip, who had been Treasurer of the Household in the second Labour Government. Other names which were put forward from London were those of J. R. Clynes, Alfred Short, Emanuel Shinwell and A. V. Alexander. The National Union of Railwaymen instructed its branches to support the nomination of P. G. Barstow, one of its national officials.[1] With such a galaxy of talent before it, the Clay Cross Divisional Labour Party completely overlooked the Derbyshire Miners' Association. On 15 July the Council had a long and heated discussion on the situation in the Clay Cross division and Henry Hicken was instructed to write to the Labour Party protesting against 'the injustice meted out to us in ignoring our right to make nomination for the vacancy'. It was also decided to call for nominations from the branches and, in the event of an unsatisfactory reply from the Labour Party, to consider the possibility of running a miners' candidate in opposition to the official Labour candidate.[2] Henry Hicken, Frank Lee and Samuel Sales were nominated by the branches. Hicken immediately withdrew, and Lee decided to remain loyal to North-East Derbyshire. Sales thus became the Association's nominee. He was not an official M.F.G.B. candidate but the Executive Committee agreed to guarantee £500 for his election expenses, about £400 of which was expected to be recovered from the Labour Party by-election fund if Sales were adopted. The Clay Cross Divisional Labour Party had already responded to the Association's protest by calling for nominations from all its affiliated organizations.[3]

At a selection committee meeting held in the division, on 29 July, four nominations were considered. The voting was as follows:

A. Henderson (National Executive)	50
S. Sales (D.M.A.)	16
B. Smith (T. & G.W.U.)	14
P. G. Barstow (N.U.R.)	7

Sales subsequently stated that the Association would have withdrawn its nomination if the other unions had agreed to do the same and that

[1] *Derbyshire Times*, 15 July, 1933.
[2] *D.M.A.* 15 July, 1933; *Derbyshire Times*, 22 July, 1933.
[3] *D.M.A.* 19 July, 1933.

Henderson would have full support of the miners.[1] He told the Council: 'The prestige of the Derbyshire Miners' Association has been enhanced by what has happened. . . . I believe that by the action taken now, the Clay Cross Parliamentary Division has been marked out as a Miners' Association constituency.'[2] The Conservative candidate was John Moores, the managing director of Littlewoods, the Liverpool mail order company, now better known as one of the major football pool promoters. It was rumoured that Philip Hicken would contest the seat for the Communist Party[3] but eventually the National Secretary, Harry Pollitt, appeared as a candidate. Henderson had an easy victory. He was supported by such speakers as Ebby Edwards, Arthur Greenwood, Ellen Wilkinson, and Harold Laski. 'Great Britain has been conquered twice in history,' asserted Laski, 'once by William the Norman and once by Montagu Norman.'[4] The voting was: Henderson, 21,931; Moores, 6,293; Pollitt, 3,434. Pollitt forfeited his deposit.

IX

In the summer of 1935 MacDonald resigned the premiership because of ill health and was succeeded by Baldwin. Soon afterwards there was a general election in which the principal issue was the Government's rearmament programme. Parliament was dissolved on 25 October. Five days earlier Arthur Henderson had died in a London nursing home. Again it was necessary to find a Labour candidate for the Clay Cross division. The Labour Party informed the Derbyshire Miners' Association that there were five possible candidates: Ernest Bevin and J. E. Edmunds, of the Transport and General Workers' Union; A. Holland, of the National Union of Distributive and Allied Workers; R. H. Tawney, then Professor of Economic History at the London School of Economics; and Henry Hicken. The Council, after a lengthy discussion, decided to rescind all previous resolutions dealing with the position of officials who might be elected to Parliament. Hicken and Lee were nominated to stand for Clay Cross and North-East Derbyshire respectively and, if elected, were to continue to hold office in the Association without salaries. Lee was to continue to be the official M.F.G.B. candidate and Hicken's parliamentary salary was to be supplemented from the political fund in the event of his election.[5]

Bevin and Tawney stated that they did not wish their names to go

[1] *Derbyshire Times*, 5 August, 1933.   [2] *D.M.A.* 5 August, 1933.
[3] *Derbyshire Times*, 5 August, 1933.
[4] *Ibid.* 2 September, 1933.   [5] *D.M.A.* 23 October, 1935.

before the selection committee and on 23 October Alfred Holland, a member of the Derbyshire County Council and a co-operative employee, was adopted. The Executive Committee of the Derbyshire Miners' Association expressed its regret that Hicken had not been selected and Lee was instructed to write to the secretaries of the branches in the Clay Cross division, asking how many delegates attended the meeting of the selection committee and for whom they voted.[1] It was discovered that only 17 delegates had attended.[2] Holland succeeded in holding the seat for Labour with 24,590 votes. His Conservative opponent, Bridget Jackson, the 26-year-old daughter of G. M. Jackson, the coal-owner, obtained 8,391 votes.

Frank Lee had two opponents in North-East Derbyshire. The Conservative candidate was H. B. Trevor Cox, the son of a director of the Edison Swan Electrical Company. At the last minute A. T. Marwood, a Nottingham commercial traveller, was adopted as an opposition Liberal candidate. Frank Lee, who was helped in his campaign by George Lansbury, regained the seat for Labour. The voting was: Lee, 25,382; Cox, 15,802; Marwood, 3,186. In the Chesterfield division George Benson defeated R. J. E. Conant by 21,439 votes to 16,555. An opposition Liberal candidate, R. G. Hill, obtained 4,069 votes. Jack Lees was narrowly defeated in a straight fight in the Belper division by Herbert Wragg, the voting being: Wragg, 20,078; Lees, 19,250. In the Ilkeston division a fleet of cars bearing the slogan 'Mark 'em for Markham' advertised the presence of Sir Charles Markham (the son of Sir Arthur) as the National Government candidate. G. H. Oliver defeated him by 23,851 votes to 13,250 and thus recaptured the division for Labour. Of the five mining constituencies, four were again in the hands of Labour, but, despite the efforts of the Derbyshire Miners' Association, only one was represented in Parliament by a miners' leader.

In 1936 there was another by-election in the Clay Cross division as a result of the unexpected death, in September, of Alfred Holland. Again the Association was ignored by the local Labour Party. On 26 September the Council had asked the branches to decide whether the seat should be contested, if possible, by a nominee of the Association. On the same day the selection committee met and drew up a list of six possible candidates. They were George Dallas, of the Transport and General Workers' Union; George Ridley, of the Railway Clerks' Association; Hugh Gaitskell, then a lecturer at University College, London; Thomas Bennison, a Clay Cross schoolmaster; J. W. Clements, of North Wingfield; and R. H. Lewis, of Langwith. The announcement that these nominees would be interviewed on 10 October had an adverse effect on the Association's branch vote. Only 19 were in

[1] *D.M.A.* 26 October, 1935.   [2] *Ibid.* 23 November, 1935.

favour of contesting the seat and 35 against. After a heated discussion a resolution was passed:

That this Council meeting of the Derbyshire Miners' Association strongly protests against the method of adoption by the Executive Committee of the Clay Cross Divisional Labour Party, of a candidate for the forthcoming Parliamentary by-election, and considers that the Emergency Rule for selection of candidates in by-elections should not have applied in circumstances like the present, when there was sufficient time to obtain nominations from all the affiliated bodies in the division by invitation.

The Council decided 'to take no financial responsibility of any kind for the contest'.[1] George Ridley was eventually adopted. He defeated Bridget Jackson, the National candidate, by 24,290 votes to 8,042.

As the Second World War approached, the Association turned its attention increasingly to international affairs, largely under the guidance of Hicken. Grants were made to the International Peace Campaign, the League of Nations, the Council for Peace and Friendship with Russia, and the International Brigade fighting in the Spanish civil war. German, Italian and Japanese aggression was condemned and the foreign policy of the British Government was frequently criticized. Scarcely a month passed without a Council resolution on one or other of these topics. The opposition of the Labour Party to the Popular Front Movement led to many protests from the Derbyshire miners. When Sir Stafford Cripps was expelled from the Party the Council supported the Executive Committee of the M.F.G.B. in urging that he should be given a hearing at the Labour Party conference.[2] The introduction of the Military Training Bill, in 1939, was strongly condemned. 'Not sufficient change in the international situation has arisen', declared the Council, 'to justify the breaking of a Prime Minister's pledge, more than once given in Parliament and on outside platforms, and it is going to be impossible to secure world peace if the pledges and statements of public men cannot be trusted. It is feared that conscription will also be detrimental to trade unionism and industry generally.'[3]

But the catastrophe was now close at hand. In July, 1939, the Council protested vainly against the delay in concluding the proposed pact with Russia.[4] Even after the signing of the Russo-German pact the Association urged the Government to send a responsible minister to Moscow, 'with full powers to act'. On 26 August, 1939, it was resolved:

That this Council even at this late hour, and in spite of the immediate peril of war in Europe, is of the belief that there is nothing in dispute between

[1] *D.M.A.* 30 September, 1936.   [2] *Ibid.* 8 April, 1939.
[3] *Ibid.* 6 May, 1939.   [4] *Ibid.* 29 July, 1939.

the countries of Europe that could not be more satisfactorily settled by conference between nations concerned or by reference to a board of representatives of unaffected countries, than by the arbitrament of war. It calls
upon all responsible powers to seriously consider the destruction of millions
of pounds' worth of property and much more valuable still, the millions of
lives that would be blighted or lost, in a war which might well destroy civilization, and to use their best efforts to maintain peace.[1]

When the Council next met, Britain was at war.

[1] *D.M.A.* 26 August, 1939.

APPENDIX I

Derbyshire Miners' Association Political Fund, 1920–1936

	Total £	Expenditure £	Balance £
1920	10,040	1,858	8,182
1921	10,205	1,291	8,914
1922	—	—	—
1923	—	—	—
1924 (October)			
1925	10,224	10,216	8
1926			
1927 (March)			
1927 (December)	1,562	1,311	251
1928	1,978	487	1,491
1929	2,556	707	1,849
1930	2,401	580	1,821
1931	2,384	565	1,819
1932	2,486	536	1,950
1933	2,478	521	1,957
1934	2,356	644	1,712
1935	3,908	2,330	1,578
1936	2,359	572	1,787

Source: Derbyshire Miners' Association, Reports of the Auditors of the Political Fund.

DD*

CHAPTER XXII

THE SECOND WORLD WAR

I

The demands of the Second World War imposed upon the depressed and contracting coal industry a strain which it was scarcely able to bear. The estimated requirements were of the order of 260 to 270 million tons of coal a year. The annual capacity of the industry was reckoned to be about 243 million tons with the existing labour force and 285 million tons if additional workers could be found. Output in 1937 had been only 240 million tons and had declined in the following year to 227 million. Throughout the war the estimated capacity of 243 million tons a year was never realized. The highest output was in 1940 when the mines turned out 224 million tons. Thereafter production declined steadily until the end of the war, reaching 183 million tons in 1945. Fortunately for the nation the requirements were over-estimated but the margin between actual requirements and output was sufficiently narrow to cause grave concern at various times during the war.[1]

Although the Government was armed with extensive powers under the Defence Regulations, political considerations dictated that it should adopt a form of indirect control of the coal industry if it was to avoid such problems as had arisen during and after the First World War. Part of the machinery for indirect control was ready to hand in the statutory price-controlling mechanism which had developed since the Coal Mines Act of 1930. The supply and distribution of coal was controlled by officers of the Mines Department. In each of the seventeen coalfields was a Coal Supplies Officer. The Midland district, with the largest output in the country, had two such officers. In each of the twelve regions into which the country was divided for the purposes of civil defence there was a Divisional Coal Officer. In each of the five great coal-shipping districts, and in London, there was a Coal Export Officer. In order to maintain the necessary link between the Government and the selling agencies the chairmen of the District Executive Boards of the

[1] W. H. B. Court, *Coal*, (London), 1951, pp. 29–34.

colliery owners became the Coal Supplies Officers, their salaries being paid not by the Mines Department but by the Boards.[1] The pit-head price of coal was not to be advanced without the consent of the Mines Department. Fuel Overseers, appointed by the local authorities, enforced coal rationing.

Apart from the increase in the cost of living, the immediate impact of the war upon the miner was slight. Until June, 1940, the movement of mining labour was entirely free, although Frank Lee complained in the House of Commons, on 29 September, 1939, that some Derbyshire colliery managers were telling their workmen that they were not allowed to move from one mine to another.[2] Between August, 1939, and June, 1940, more than half of the 65,000 men who left the industry joined the forces. In the same period about 60,000 men entered the industry.[3] On 23 September, 1939, Hicken reported to the Council that the Joint Standing Consultative Committee of the Coal Industry had discussed possible methods of meeting the Mining Department's estimated increase in demand of between 20 and 40 million tons of coal a year 'remembering that there are now 27,000 less persons in the industry'.[4] But the expected heavy demands for coal did not immediately materialize. British war production was slow in getting under way. The months following September, 1939, were described by some as the period of 'phoney' war. The dislocation of transport, caused mainly by the cutting off of the great coastwise movement of coal to London and the South of England, led to a shortage of railway wagons at some of the Derbyshire collieries.[5]

Meanwhile the Joint Standing Consultative Committee, which had been established in 1936,[6] was being put to the test on the issue of wages. In September, 1939, the M.F.G.B. put forward a claim for a flat rate increase of 1s. a shift for men and 6d. for boys to meet the higher cost of living. The owners offered increases of 8d. and 4d. a shift, subject to a maximum of six shifts per week. 'For ascertainment purposes', stated the owners' proposals, 'the advances shall be termed a War Bonus, and shall be merged in any rise of wages that may hereafter be accorded by the district ascertainments owing to increased proceeds.' The Derbyshire Miners' Association decided, by 289 votes to 168, to accept the offer. A national conference, on 27 October, reached the same decision by 342,000 to 253,000.[7] In accepting the offer the Council had stipulated that the increase should apply to men receiving compensation. The Derbyshire coal-owners eventually agreed that men on full compensation

[1] Court, *op. cit.* pp. 40–43. [2] 351 H.C. Deb. 5s. 1612.
[3] Court, *op. cit.* p. 132. [4] *D.M.A.* 23 September, 1939.
[5] *Ibid.* 18 November, 1939. [6] See Chapter XIX, pp. 761–2.
[7] *D.M.A.* 21 October, 1939; *M.F.G.B.* 27 October, 1939.

and those on partial compensation but not working should be granted the increase.[1]

The failure of the owners in some coalfields to make this concession was the source of much discontent. The miners also objected to the limitation of the payment of war bonus increases to six shifts per week at a time when they were being called upon to work overtime. The M.F.G.B. was unable to secure any satisfaction on either of these points. On the general question of wages the Federation argued that there should be an agreed formula which would allow the cost-of-living adjustments to be made periodically.[2]

When the Joint Standing Consultative Committee met on 20 December the cost-of-living index had risen by 18 points since the outbreak of war. The miners' leaders therefore urged that while the discussions on a suitable formula for cost-of-living adjustments to wages should continue, the immediate business for the meeting was to consider the amount of the flat-rate advance which was to operate from 1 January, 1940. The owners offered an additional 4d. a shift for adults and 2d. for boys for the period 1 January–31 March, 1940. The Federation representatives demanded an additional 7d. a shift for adults and 3½d. for boys. An interview with the Secretary for Mines failed to improve matters. These negotiations were reported, on 29 December, to a national conference of the M.F.G.B. which decided to reject the owners' offer.[3] Eventually a formula was evolved for the automatic adjustment of wages. It was agreed:

That 0·7d. per shift be the variation in the flat-rate war additions to the shift wage of the adult worker corresponding to a variation of one point in the cost-of-living index number, subject to three-monthly reviews, and that there should be no change in the flat rates unless the index figures vary by not less than 5 points.

On 25 January, 1940, a national conference recommended the acceptance of this formula.[4] An additional 5d. a shift for adults and 2½d. for boys was granted to cover the period 1 January–31 March. The new agreement was signed on 20 March and came into operation on 1 April.

The growth of mechanical mining meant that increasing numbers of men were called upon to work on Saturday afternoons to complete the cycle of operations so that coal turning could be resumed normally on the Monday day-shifts. Although they were paid overtime rates they were denied the cost-of-living increases. Early in March the Derbyshire

---

[1] *D.M.A.* 18 November, 30 December, 1939.
[2] Miners' Federation of Great Britain, *Wages and the Cost of Living*, 29 December, 1939, pp. 3–5.
[3] *Ibid.* pp. 9–10.   [4] *M.F.G.B.* 25 January, 1940.

Miners' Association reached an agreement with the owners that these men should receive the increases, subject to the maximum of six shifts in one week.[1]

II

In the spring of 1940, for strategic, political and financial reasons it became important to increase the production of coal to meet the heavy export programme, particularly to France.[2] The Coal Production Council, consisting of representatives of the colliery owners and the miners, and officials of the Mines Department, was hastily set up at the beginning of April under the chairmanship of Lord Portal. On 4 May Hicken, reporting the results of one of the Production Council's meetings, told the Derbyshire miners' delegates that county production committees were soon to be formed.[3] It was later decided that the District Wages Board should act as the Coal Production Committee for the county.[4] The Committee occasionally held joint meetings with the Nottinghamshire Committee to consult with O. V. Smithson, the Coal Production Adviser for the East Midlands and Yorkshire, who was appointed in June, 1940. The Derbyshire Miners' Association agreed to the formation of pit production committees subject to the approval of the Council.[5]

The German military successes in the Low Countries in May led to further urgent appeals for increased production. The Minister of Mines addressed a meeting of the Executive Committee of the M.F.G.B. Ernest Bevin, the new Minister of Labour, appealed for co-operation at a special meeting of the Executive Committees of Trade Unions called by the T.U.C. On 29 May the Council of the Derbyshire Miners' Association held an emergency meeting at which it endorsed 'the action of the General Council of the T.U.C. in giving its full support to the necessary measures that must be taken to protect our people'. It was also resolved: 'That this Council undertakes to co-operate with the Colliery Owners and the Government to the best of its ability to increase the output of coal in the county, demanded by the Government as fundamentally necessary to the winning of the war.' Mass meetings were arranged at various centres in the county to call attention to the need for greater output.[6]

The production drive encountered some resistance. The miners were not prepared to make more than what they thought to be their fair

[1] *D.M.A.* 18 November, 1939, 9 March, 1940. [2] Court, *op. cit.* pp. 78–9.
[3] *D.M.A.* 4 May, 1940. [4] *Ibid.* 29 May, 1940.
[5] *Ibid.* 8 June, 1940. [6] *Ibid.* 29 May, 1940.

share of sacrifices. At the emergency meeting on 29 May the Council called attention to the need 'to ensure the maintenance of the hard-won liberties of the workmen' and advised members 'to retain wherever possible the $7\frac{1}{2}$-hour working day and the six-day week.'[1] In March, 1940, T. E. B. Young, the general manager of the Bolsover Company, had announced that he had promised the Mines Department that output would be increased by 10 per cent.[2] Soon afterwards the Bolsover miners were asked to pledge themselves to work as regularly as possible and 'to surrender by arrangement such recognized holidays as may reasonably be required'.[3] On 6 April the Council of the Derbyshire Miners' Association recommended 'that in the interests of the miners' health and well being' the usual holidays with pay should be taken at each pit in Derbyshire.[4] Early in June, however, the Coal Production Committee for the county decided that no summer holiday should be taken at any colliery but that a week-end holiday might be taken later in the year if circumstances permitted.[5] The decision was approved by the Council on the understanding that colliery officials should be expected to forgo their usual holidays.[6] As a price for their co-operation the Derbyshire miners also demanded that the employers should make membership of the Association a condition of employment.[7]

The production committees spent much of their time dealing with absenteeism. In July, 1940, a Chesterfield miner, who had defied the resolution of one of these committees, appeared before the magistrates. It was probably the first case of its kind in the district. The Sheepbridge Company complained that the man had worked only 13 shifts out of 29 and was awarded 2 guineas damages for breach of contract and costs.[8] Members of the Association began to refuse to continue their contributions on the ground that their officials were working with the production committees. On 24 August the Council decided to ask the owners to deal with absenteeism themselves. 'In the event of no action being taken by the owners', stated the resolution, 'the Association will take no further notice of the Committees, either of the district or local.'[9]

Meanwhile the fall of France had temporarily transformed the situation in the coal industry. The disappearance of the French demand meant that there was now a surplus of coal. The exporting districts of Northumberland, Durham and South Wales had lost one of their traditional markets. The Council of the Derbyshire Miners' Association discussed the matter at length on 27 July. Hicken reported that the

---

[1] *D.M.A.* 29 May, 1940.   [2] *Derbyshire Times*, 15 March, 1940.
[3] *Ibid.* 22 March, 1940.   [4] *D.M.A.* 6 April, 1940.
[5] *Derbyshire Times*, 7 June, 1940.   [6] *D.M.A.* 8 June, 1940.
[7] *Ibid.* 4 May, 8 June, 1940. See below, pp. 869–70.
[8] *Derbyshire Times*, 2 August, 1940.   [9] *D.M.A.* 24 August, 1940.

proposed pooling of orders 'would have a detrimental effect upon the Yorkshire, Nottinghamshire and Derbyshire pits and would mean perhaps three or four working days per week all round'. Nevertheless the Council was in favour of the pooling of orders to keep all the pits in production 'which may become the more necessary in view of the possible danger occasioned by air raids, etc.' It was also agreed that if, because of short time, men were to be taken from the pits to other work of national importance, those of military age who had recently entered the industry should be 'the first to go'.[1] The Mines Department's proposal to bring coal from Northumberland and Durham to Lancashire so that it could be supplied through the Lancashire Associated Collieries aroused much opposition from the owners and the miners in the area covered by the Midland Amalgamated Collieries which also supplied parts of Lancashire.[2]

On 4 June the Undertakings (Restriction on Engagement) Order[3] had been applied to coalmining to prevent labour from moving to better paid jobs on aerodrome construction and in munitions factories. With miners unemployed as a result of the disorganization of the export trade the Order was soon relaxed. From 5 July miners who had returned to the industry during the war, and were now unemployed, were permitted to take up other work. An attempt was made to raise the age of reservation for miners to 30 but the Ministry of Labour tribunals, consisting of representatives of owners and miners, which were set up in each district, reported (with the exception of Northumberland) that they were unable to recommend the release of any miners for the Forces.[4] In December, 1940, Hicken stated:

The short-time working . . . in the Derbyshire coalfield is due to dislocation of transport, and if that difficulty were overcome, Derbyshire collieries would be able to work six days a week. Far from there being redundancy of men there would be employment available for many more men. . . . Take away the young men and replace them with men over 30 from other counties who are not used to thin seams, and what happens? I am satisfied output per manshift would come down by 50 per cent. The cost of production would inevitably increase, and reduced wages and discontent among the men would follow.[5]

III

After the fall of France the Government embarked upon an extensive programme of coal stocking. The major problems of the winter of 1940–1 arose from difficulties of transport and distribution. By the

[1] D.M.A. 27 June, 1940.
[2] Ibid. 21 September, 1940.
[3] S.R. & O., 1940, No. 877.
[4] Court, op. cit. pp. 136–7.
[5] Derbyshire Times, 13 December, 1940.

spring of 1941, however, output was declining seriously. There was much condemnation of absenteeism but, as Professor Court has shown, it was not the principal cause of falling output.[1] He writes: 'There is no need to depreciate the importance of the habitual absentees as a social and industrial problem; they reflected many discontents, old and new, and many features of mining life. Neither was the acrid absenteeism controversy unimportant, as a symptom of habits of mind both in the industry and outside it. But the habitual absentees were not the determining force in creating the great coal-production problem of the middle years of the war.'[2] The most important cause of falling output in the first two years of the war was the decline in the number of face-shifts. The change in the balance of shifts was brought about by the movement of colliery manpower to the Forces and the new munition industries in the early part of the war, and the annual wastage through deaths and retirements among an ageing labour force. The sharp fall in the birth-rate among the mining population in the years of industrial unrest and low earnings between 1924 and 1927, coupled with the failure of mining wages and conditions to attract boys into the industry, meant that the number of new entrants was far smaller than the annual wastage. The fall in the total number of workers entailed a reduction in the number of face workers in order to provide the essential labour for such overhead services as haulage, surface work, winding, maintenance and repair.

Derbyshire, along with the other more productive coalfields, was able to retain its labour more easily than some districts.[3] Indeed there was a slight influx of labour from other industries. In February, 1941, there were 2,323 men from Derbyshire collieries serving with the Forces. Most of them were Territorials or reservists who had been called up at the outbreak of war. Nevertheless between September, 1939, and December, 1940, the number of men employed in Derbyshire pits rose slightly from 38,617 to 38,752. Attempts to transfer unemployed miners from other districts were not successful. A number of Durham miners were brought to a colliery near Chesterfield but it was found that they were not accustomed to working in thin seams, and their output was only half that of the local men. Hicken stated, in February, 1941: 'Delegates from all parts of the county frequently call attention to the fact that non-miners are being introduced into the collieries in their districts. . . . Doubtless some were actuated by the fact that mining is to a great extent a reserved occupation.'[4]

On 27 March, 1941, a conference of owners' and workers' representatives was addressed by the Lord President of the Council, Sir John

[1] Court, *op. cit.* pp. 111–14.   [2] *Ibid.* p. 127.
[3] *Ibid.* p. 122.   [4] *Derbyshire Times*, 21 February, 1941.

Anderson, who stressed the urgent need for the production of at least an additional 25 million tons of coal by the end of the summer. At subsequent meetings the desirability of extending the working day to eight hours and methods of reducing absenteeism were discussed. Eventually the Government decided to apply the Essential Work Order. These developments were reported to the Council of the Derbyshire Miners' Association by Hicken on 29 and 31 March and 12 April but no decisions were taken. On 15 May the Minister of Labour and National Service made the Essential Work (Coalmining Industry) Order[1] under the Defence Regulations. The order prohibited the free taking on and dismissal of men by the employers; it gave the miner a guaranteed wage, whether short time was being worked or not, although not during an industrial dispute; and it gave the National Service Officer power to deal with persistent absenteeism.

The introduction of the guaranteed wage gave the M.F.G.B. an opportunity to draw attention to the need for improving wages. An increase of a shilling a shift was given to men and sixpence to boys on condition that they attended for work every day of the week. The attendance bonus led to many disputes as to whether or not men had qualified for it. The Derbyshire Miners' Association accepted the offer on the understanding 'that such matters as availability for work and other conditions are largely questions for the local Pit Production Committees to decide upon'.[2] The M.F.G.B. argued that the bonus should be a reward for good rather than perfect attendance. Eventually the President of the Board of Trade, Sir Andrew Duncan, intervened and from 1 September, 1941, the bonus became a straightforward flat-rate increase in wages.

The Essential Work Order, although the most important, was only one aspect of the production drive of 1941. The Coal Production Council became active again and on 3 March the Council of the Derbyshire Miners' Association recommended to the branches that where pit production committees had lapsed they should be re-established.[3] Towards the end of the year these committees were given the right to report persistent absentees to the National Service Officer by amendments of the Essential Work Order.[4] On 11 June the Association adopted a recommendation by the District Wages Board (which was also the county Coal Production Committee) that the miners should forgo their usual week's holiday for the duration of the war and that it should be left to the colliery management 'to decide upon such holidays as have been customary at local Feasts, etc.'[5]

[1] S.R. & O., 1941, No. 707.
[2] D.M.A. 11 June, 1941.
[3] Ibid. 3 May, 1941.
[4] S.R. & O., 1941, Nos. 2008 and 2096.
[5] D.M.A. 11 June, 1941.

In the same month, when the German attack upon Russia opened a new phase of the war, the efforts to increase production were intensified, now with the support of the extreme Left of the trade union movement. In September an appeal on behalf of the Derbyshire Coal Production Committee, signed by G. M. Jackson and Henry Hicken, called for greater output. 'Coal will win the war, or lose it!' they stated. 'Coal provides "the tools with which to finish the job"! Russia *needs* these tools to fight our battle!'[1] Hicken and others addressed mass meetings at most of the collieries in the county. Various attempts were made to recruit additional labour for the mines. A broadcast appeal by the Ministry of Labour and National Service, on 23 June, for the return of 50,000 ex-miners to the coal industry met with a disappointing response. A few days later an embargo was placed on further recruiting from the industry for the forces. In July all men under 60 years of age who had more than six months' experience in the industry since 1 January, 1935, were required to register but there were many difficulties in transferring them back to the mines. The Council of the Derbyshire Miners' Association expressed the opinion that the only method by which production could be increased was by bringing back from the forces men who had previously worked at the coal face. 'It does not consider', continued the resolution, 'that men not accustomed to coalface work with present machinery could add to the output. They would only increase costs of production and lower the output per man.'[2]

By April, 1942, when the first few men were being released to the mines from the Army, the manpower situation was improving. The proportion of face-shifts to all shifts worked was higher than at any time since October, 1940.[3] But output continued to fall. The cause was now to be found in the decline in the output per man-shift at the face. It had remained fairly steady in the first two years of the war but showed a serious falling off in the autumn of 1941. Professor Court estimates that this factor was responsible for about four-fifths of the decline in the output per shift in the industry between the latter months of 1941 and the summer of 1942. The other one-fifth was due to the effects of absenteeism.

There were, of course, important variations in local conditions. Durham, Cannock Chase, North Wales, South Staffordshire and Worcestershire, Forest of Dean, Bristol, South Wales and Scotland had all shown a steady decline in output per man-shift at the face since 1938, despite the mechanization which had taken place in most of these fields. Productivity was also declining in Yorkshire but it was still high. Nottinghamshire, Derbyshire, Leicestershire, Somerset and

[1] *Derbyshire Times*, 26 September, 1941.
[2] *D.M.A.* 26 July, 1941.   [3] Court, *op. cit.* p. 145.

Shropshire were areas of increasing productivity. The Lancashire and Cheshire field showed an increase in output between 1938 and 1941 but thereafter productivity declined. Fortunately for the war effort the more productive districts such as Derbyshire, Nottinghamshire and Yorkshire were providing in 1942 a greater proportion of the total national coal output than they did in 1938, as the following table shows:

Percentage of National Coal Output Mined in Six Districts[1]

High Productivity Districts

	1938	1942 (January–June)
	Per cent.	Per cent.
Yorkshire	18·67	20·58
Nottinghamshire	6·81	8·78
North Derbyshire	5·73	7·23
	31·21	36·59

Low Productivity Districts

	Per cent.	Per cent.
Durham	13·84	12·27
South Wales	15·55	13·20
Scotland	13·34	12·99
	42·73	38·46

The output in every coalfield would doubtless have been greater had it not been for the fatigue of the miners. By the end of 1941 the strain of a week of $5\frac{1}{2}$ shifts or more since the fall of France was beginning to make itself felt by the ageing labour force employed in the mines. Moreover the men complained that food rationing denied them an adequate diet for the heavy work required in the pits.[2] As early as February, 1941, the Council of the Derbyshire Miners' Association instructed the officials to urge the Minister of Food to introduce 'a more equitable system' of rationing.[3] Another factor influencing output was the recruitment from other industries of men who required time to adapt themselves physically to mining conditions. Industrial disputes were a serious matter in some districts but Derbyshire was fairly peaceful. A strike at the Ramcroft Colliery in January, 1941, led the Council to draw the attention of members to the fact that 'the scheme for settlements of disputes during the war provides for

---

[1] Court, *op. cit.* p. 121. [2] See below, p. 862.
[3] *D.M.A.* 15 February, 1941.

grievances to be placed before the County Coal Production Committee, and to arbitration if necessary'.[1]

By the spring of 1942 a growing dissatisfaction with wages was also contributing to the general unrest of the miners. Since the outbreak of war cost-of-living increases had been awarded as follows:

	Per shift
1 November, 1939	8d.
1 January, 1940	5d.
1 April, 1940	4d.
1 October, 1940	5d.
1 January, 1941	6d.
1 July, 1941	4d.

In addition the miners had received the attendance bonus of 1s. 0d. a shift on 1 June, 1941, which, after 1 September, had become an ordinary flat-rate increase. These advances, together with the longer working week, caused the average weekly earnings of adult miners to rise from £3 0s. 10d. in 1938 to £4 11s. 1d. in the first quarter of 1942. Earnings per shift rose from 12s. 4d. to 17s. 0d. in the same period.[2] The stabilization of the cost-of-living index by subsidies meant that the miners received no more automatic flat-rate increases. Moreover, the results of the district ascertainments were such that percentage additions to basic rates began to fall. As a result of war-time conditions output and prices were not rising substantially but industrial costs other than wages were increasing rapidly. The disposal proceeds therefore showed a tendency to fall.

IV

Declining output and the discontent of the miners led the War Cabinet in April, 1942, to appoint a committee under the chairmanship of the Lord President of the Council to make recommendations on the reorganization of the industry. In January the M.F.G.B. had already discussed the desirability of pressing the Government to implement the *Plan for the Coal Industry* which had been adopted by the T.U.C. and the Labour Party in 1936. An alternative proposal was that there should be 'some greater national control of the mining industry with labour representation within the present structure of the industry'. The Derbyshire miners were in favour of public ownership but were willing to accept the alternative proposal as 'a temporary expedient'.[3] The M.F.G.B. representatives in their evidence before the Lord President's Committee strongly advocated nationalization.

[1] *D.M.A.* 11 January, 1941.
[2] 380 H.C. Deb. 5s. 785.　　　　[3] *D.M.A.* 17 January, 1942.

As a result of the recommendations of the Committee, in June, 1942, the general direction of coalmining operations, although not the day-to-day working of the mines, was assumed by the Government. The experience of war had proved that direct control was necessary in order to meet the problems which arose. Gwilym Lloyd George was appointed Minister of Fuel and Power, with Lord Hyndley as Controller-General to assist him. Hyndley was succeeded at the beginning of 1944 by Hubert (later Sir Hubert) Houldsworth who had been chairman of the district committee for the Midland (Amalgamated) District under the schemes initiated by the Coal Mines Act of 1930 and as such had become a Coal Supplies Officer for the Midland area on the outbreak of war. Between 1942 and 1944 Houldsworth was Regional Controller for the Minister of Fuel and Power in South and West Yorkshire. The Coal Division of the new Ministry had four Directorates responsible for production, labour, services and finance respectively. The first Production Director was T. E. B. Young, of the Bolsover Colliery Company. He resigned on 31 January, 1943, and was succeeded by C. C. (later Sir Charles) Reid.[1] The Regional Organization was divided into eight coal-producing regions and four non-coal-producing regions. Each coal-producing region had a Regional Controller who was assisted by Assistant Production Directors and Technical Advisers, a Regional Labour Director and a Services Director. F. Raymond Evershed, a King's Counsel, became the Regional Controller for Nottinghamshire, Derbyshire and Leicestershire. H. Watson Smith, the managing director of the Hardwick Colliery Company, became the Regional Production Director and Henry Hicken the Regional Labour Director.[2]

National and Regional Coal Boards were created to advise the Controller-General and the Regional Controllers. The National Coal Board, under the chairmanship of the Minister and the vice-chairmanship of the Controller-General, consisted of representatives of the Regional Boards, pit managers and technicians, the coal distributive trades and the consumers. The Regional Boards consisted of representatives of the colliery companies, miners, managers and technical staff. The two vice-chairmen, who represented the owners and the miners respectively, were *ex officio* members of the National Coal Board. The Regional Boards were more active than the National Board and were able to make use of local knowledge.[3] The creation of these bodies secured for the miners a voice, however small, in the running of the industry. Joseph Lynch and Joseph Kitts, two of the full-time officials of the Derbyshire Miners' Association, were elected by the branches to serve on the Regional Board.[4] Other prominent members of the Association,

[1] Court, *op. cit.* p. 206.   [2] *Derbyshire Times*, 7 and 21 August, 1942.
[3] Court, *op. cit.* p. 208.   [4] *D.M.A.* 1, 22 and 25 August, 1942.

such as Leonard Haywood, president of the Morton No. 1 branch, and J. S. Mugglestone, secretary of the Langwith branch, became Regional Investigation Officers.[1]

On 5 June, two days after it had published its plans for the tighter control of the coal industry, the Government appointed a Board of Inquiry, under the chairmanship of Lord Greene, the Master of the Rolls, to go first into the wage issue and then into the whole question of the machinery for the negotiation of mining wages and conditions of work. The M.F.G.B. had already put before the Joint Standing Consultative Committee a claim for a uniform national minimum wage of 85s. to come into effect at the age of 18; 4s. a shift increase for all workers over 18 years and 2s. a shift increase for boys. The miners argued that their wages had virtually reached a standstill, that wages in the Royal Ordnance factories and elsewhere were much higher, and that the miners were tied to the pits. The owners were opposed to any increase in wages which did not provide incentives to better attendance and greater output. The Board recommended an unconditional flat-rate increase of 2s. 6d. a shift for all adult workers over the age of 21 and all underground workers between 18 and 21; additions ranging from 1s. 3d. to 2s. 3d. a shift for underground workers under 18, and from 9d. to 2s. 3d. a shift for surface workers under the age of 21. The percentage additions to basic rates under the district ascertainment system were not to fall below the level which they had then reached.[2] In Derbyshire the percentage was stabilized at 4·61. The Board also recommended a national minimum wage of 83s. a week for adult underground workers and 78s. for adult surface workers.[3] To encourage increased production the Board recommended the payment of an output bonus. The Government accepted the principles and asked the Board to work out the details. The scheme adopted provided for a computation of bonus by a monthly comparison of the output of each district with a 'standard output', calculated from past performance. Bonus payments of 3d. a shift were made in accordance with a sliding scale for every complete 1 per cent. by which the output exceeded the standard output.

The Board then went on to complete the second part of its task. On 1 May, 1943, as a result of its recommendations, a new National Conciliation Scheme was introduced. A National Board was set up in two parts: a Negotiating Committee consisting of eleven representatives of the miners and eleven of the owners; and a National Reference Tribunal of three permanent members, appointed by the Master of the Rolls, sitting with four assessors (two chosen from each side of the

[1] Derbyshire Times, 18 September, 2 October, 1942.
[2] Report of the Board of Investigation into the Immediate Wages Issue in the Coalmining Industry, (1942), paras. 7, 8 and 13.   [3] Ibid. paras. 9–10.

Negotiating Committee) with no voting rights. The Reference Tribunal was given power to deal with all 'national questions' on which the Negotiating Committee was unable to reach agreement. Lord Porter became the chairman of the Tribunal. The new scheme also provided for district conciliation machinery, on a model drawn up by the Board, with details of the conditions under which questions were to be referred from the district to the national level.

A further consequence of the Greene Award was the development of a greater degree of national financial pooling between the districts. The cost of the Award, estimated at £23,500,000 a year, was met by increasing the price of coal and imposing a levy of 5s. a ton, to be paid into the Coal Charges Account controlled by the Ministry of Fuel and Power, from which individual collieries were reimbursed. The Coal Charges Account had evolved as a result of the need for controlling prices and costs.[1] As the war progressed it became an increasingly important part of the financial machinery of the coal industry. The national wage standards, and consequently negotiating machinery, were entirely dependent upon it. The needs of war had given the miners the methods of wage determination which they had been demanding for over twenty years. The Government had willy-nilly become more and more concerned not only with the technical details and the labour relations of the industry but also with the finance of coalmining, including just those questions of profits and wages which indirect control had been designed to avoid.

The output bonus scheme devised by the Greene Board was not very successful. In the later months of 1942 a fair number of the twenty-five districts into which the country was divided for the purposes of the scheme earned bonus on additional production, but from January of the following year only a few of the more productive fields continued to do so. In June, 1943, North Derbyshire was the first of the coalfields in the country to win an output bonus of 6d. a shift, an event which led the Minister of Fuel and Power to send his congratulations to the miners. Nottinghamshire, Leicestershire and South Derbyshire, the remainder of the North Midland Region, were the only other districts to exceed the target figure, qualifying for a bonus of 3d. a shift.[2] The failure of the district scheme in other parts of the country led the M.F.G.B. to put forward alternative proposals for payment of the bonus on a pit basis, which were opposed by the Derbyshire Miners' Association.[3]

Against an overall picture of falling productivity the North Midland

[1] For a full account of the evolution of the Coal Charges Account see Court, *op. cit.* pp. 193–8, 333–51.
[2] *Derbyshire Times*, 4 June, 1943.   [3] *D.M.A.* 19 December, 1942.

Region, with its large reserves of unworked coal, its modern methods of business organization and mining technique and its high degree of mechanization, continued to increase its productivity per man until 1942. Between 1940 and 1942 its share of the total coal output of the country rose from 16¾ per cent. to 18½ per cent.[1] The output and number of men employed in the Region during the war years were as follows:[2]

	Output Saleable Tons	Average Number of Wage Earners on Colliery Books
1938	32,180,300	98,692
1939	34,682,000	99,050
1940	37,530,900	99,266
1941	37,724,500	97,548
1942	38,094,700	98,334
1943	36,946,400	97,768
1944	35,659,600	99,089

Output rose steadily from the high, but not exceptional, 1938 figure to a peak in 1942, when in spite of a decline of ·36 per cent. in manpower, the output was 18·38 per cent. above the 1938 level.

As a result of the operation of the Coal Charges Account the low-cost districts subsidized the high-cost ones. North Derbyshire, Nottinghamshire, South Derbyshire and Leicestershire (i.e. the North Midland Region), together with Warwickshire, were the five districts with the highest output per shift in the country. They contributed consistently to the Account and drew little from it in the way of assistance to necessitous undertakings. During 1945 the assisted undertakings in the North Midland Region and Yorkshire accounted for only 5 per cent. of the output. Apart from South Staffordshire, with 2 per cent., it was the lowest proportion in the country. In Northumberland 25 per cent. of the output was produced by assisted undertakings and in Lancashire and Cheshire, 17 per cent. In some of the smaller districts the percentage was much higher.[3]

v

Labour unrest in the coalfields and the continued decline in national productivity led to a further crisis in the industry in 1943. The Minister of Fuel and Power submitted to the M.F.G.B. three proposals for increasing coal production. They were the working of a twelve-day fortnight by pits which were then working only eleven days a fortnight; the clearing of faces each day; and in certain contingencies the working of one Sunday in four. The M.F.G.B. was not convinced that these

[1] *Derbyshire Times*, 30 October, 1942.
[2] *Ministry of Fuel and Power, North Midland Coalfield, Regional Survey Report,* (1945), p. 15.
[3] Court, *op. cit.* pp. 347–8.

changes were sufficient and, on 7 October, addressed a memorandum to the Minister suggesting more fundamental and, to the miners, more desirable ways of dealing with the situation. The miners' leaders condemned the dual control of the industry which had been in operation since 1942, and advocated that the Government should take over full financial and operational control:

From the information we have at our disposal, it is obvious that the men are very concerned with the possibilities of the future, particularly the post-war period. It is useless to tell men who have experienced years and years of hardships brought about by under-employment, unemployment and intolerable working conditions that their experience following the last war will not be repeated. They require something far more concrete.[1]

The miners' post-war programme included legislation governing hours of work,[2] Government control of the disposal and price of coal, the continuation of the guaranteed week and national minima, the erection of pit-head baths and canteens at all collieries, a comprehensive workmen's compensation scheme, further safety measures and the extension of scientific research on coal utilization. The M.F.G.B. also demanded that the national minimum wage should be raised to £6 a week for adult underground workers and £5 10s. od. a week for adult surface workers; that the award for youths made by the new National Reference Tribunal in October, 1943, after the Government had announced its intention of conscripting youths for the pits, should be reviewed; and that piece rates should be adjusted to take into account any new minimum that might be granted.[3] The Federation had already submitted a claim to the National Conciliation Board for a national agreement giving holidays with pay.

In submitting these proposals to the Minister the M.F.G.B. expressed the view that the problems of the industry could not be wholly solved under private ownership. The revival of the demand for nationalization touched off a lively debate in the House of Commons on 12 October. The Minister assured the House that Government control was to continue after the war until Parliament decided the future of the industry. On the following day the Prime Minister averted what looked like the beginning of a political crisis for the coalition Government by re-emphasizing this assurance and by stating that he would gladly authorize the Minister of Fuel and Power to open discussions with the miners' leaders on the post-war period so that 'the uncertainty and harassing fears [for the future] shall be as far as possible allayed'.[4]

[1] M.F.G.B. 7 October, 1943.
[2] On a Derbyshire motion the M.F.G.B. annual conference had decided to demand a 6½-hour day for the post-war period. (M.F.G.B. 21 July, 1943.)
[3] M.F.G.B. 7 October, 1943.   [4] 392 H.C. Deb. 5s. 932.

Little progress was made with these discussions for the Minister soon had to concentrate his attention on the wage issue. Although he had refused to promise that coal prices would be raised to meet any award that might be made, the M.F.G.B. had submitted its claim for higher miminum wages to the National Reference Tribunal, under the chairmanship of Lord Porter. The Tribunal awarded a minimum rate of £5 a week to adult underground workers and £4 10s. od. to surface men. It also awarded substantial increases in the minimum rates for youths. The claim for a revision of piece rates was rejected on the ground that it would be inconsistent with the granting of what was merely a minimum wage. The Tribunal regarded the award as a temporary expedient and hoped that it might give time for a general overhaul of the wage structure of the industry.[1] The Porter Award aggravated rather than soothed the discontent in the coalfields. In the poorer paid districts, such as South Wales, the minimum rates were raised to a level which upset the lower wage rates actually being paid. Men whose rates had previously been different found themselves receiving the same rates. Existing wage rates in the better paid districts such as Derbyshire, Nottinghamshire and Yorkshire remained largely unaffected. On 5 February the Council of the Derbyshire Miners' Association authorized the officials to attend a meeting in Nottingham with the officials of the neighbouring county associations of Nottinghamshire, Yorkshire, Leicestershire, South Derbyshire and Warwickshire, to discuss 'the anomalies created by the Porter Award'.[2]

In South Wales and other districts new piece rates were negotiated despite the Minister's refusal to finance them from the Coal Charges Account. The Government was anxious that any further change in the wage structure of the industry should ensure increased output. The negotiations which had been going on since 1942 to devise an improved bonus system had so far been unsuccessful. The effect of flat-rate additions to miners' wages was to reduce the proportion of the piece-worker's wage which was dependent on his personal efforts and to lessen the ratio which his wage conventionally bore to the earnings of the day-wage man. The discontent in the coalfields over the Porter Award was diminished and the problem of relating wages more closely to output was solved by a National Wages Agreement which was accepted by the M.F.G.B. on 13 April, 1944.[3] The existing ascertainment agreements were suspended, current percentage additions being merged in the day wages or piece rates payable under the new agreement. For piece-workers all existing flat-rate additions, except the cost-of-living

[1] National Conciliation Board for the Coal-mining Industry, National Reference Tribunal, Fourth Award, 22 January, 1944.
[2] D.M.A. 5 February, 1944.   [3] M.F.G.B. 13 April, 1944.

bonus of 2s. 8d. a shift, were merged into the piece-work rates by the addition of an appropriate percentage.[1] Day-wage workers continued to receive the flat-rate increases. The output bonus scheme was discontinued, special consideration being given to wages in districts which had regularly earned a bonus. The agreement was to operate until 31 December, 1947, after which date it was subject to six months' notice.

The closer relation of wages to output achieved by the absorption of the flat-rate increases into the piece-work rates went some way towards restoring the wage differential between the piece-worker and the day-wage man which had been upset in some districts by the Porter Award. In Derbyshire the basic daily wage was 10s. 7d. to which was added the current ascertained percentage, fixed at 4·61 after the Greene Award, making 11s. 0·85d. the effective district minimum rate. To this were added the war bonuses, totalling 2s. 8d. a day, and the flat-rate increases, amounting to 4s. 3d. a day making 17s. 11·85d. in all. For piece-workers the flat-rate increases of 4s. 3d. a day, expressed as a percentage of the effective district minimum rate, gave an addition of 38 per cent. to the tonnage rate. The effect of the new agreement is perhaps best illustrated by taking a specific example. A miner producing eight tons of coal a shift at 2s. 3d. a ton found that his earnings increased from 27s. 0·76d. to 30s. 6·4d.[2] Between 1938 and the second quarter of 1944 the average weekly cash earnings of miners rose from £2 15s. 9d. to £6 0s. 0d. and the weekly value of allowances in kind from 2s. 2d. to 4s. 0d.[3] The greatest single advance in this upward trend came about as a result of the Greene Award in 1942. The Porter Award and the National Wages Agreement brought further important gains. The improvement in miners' wages during the war was substantial both from the point of view of purchasing power and from the point of view of comparison with other industries, as the following table shows:[4]

Year	Cost-of-living index figure (Dec., 1924 = 100)	Average wage rates (all industries) (Dec., 1924 = 100)	Coal	Engineering Fitters	Railways	Cotton
1939	88	106	109	119	96	92
1940	104	119	126	128	106	113
1941	110	128	129	134	112	122
1942	111	138	172	143	123	124
1943	110	144	172	154	129	135
1944	112	154·5	208	161	136	143·5
1945	112·5	164	222	169	148·5	158
1946	112·5	177	227	179	148·5	169

[1] i.e. the percentage which the flat-rate allowances, other than the cost-of-living allowance, bore to the effective district minimum shift rate.

[2] D.M.A. 11 March, 1944.　　　　　　　　　[3] 403 H.C. Deb. 5s. 2221.

[4] The London and Cambridge Economic Service Memorandum, No. 50, May, 1947, quoted in Court, op. cit. p. 328.

Other advances gained from the National Reference Tribunal early in 1944 were payment for overtime at time rates plus one-third, and for week-end work at double time, and payment for a week's holiday at a rate based on the weekly average earnings of all workers. Security for the future, at least until the end of 1947, was assured by the National Wages Agreement. The miner had become one of the best paid workers in British industry. As such he excited a certain amount of envy and much ill-founded criticism. In particular, he was reproached with the rising price of coal. The more obvious anomalies arising from the Porter Award had been adjusted by drawing upon the Coal Charges Account but the bulk of the cost of the 1944 wage concessions was met by increasing the price of coal by 4s. a ton from 1 August. By May, 1945, the average retail price of 'Derby Brights' to London consumers had risen to 77s. 9d. a ton, compared with 51s. 6d. in 1938.[1] Moreover, for reasons which have already been discussed, output continued to decline. On 14 October, 1944, the Council of the Derbyshire Miners' Association protested against a statement made by the Minister of Fuel and Power that absenteeism was solely responsible for the reduction in output. 'Whilst not condoning absenteeism', stated the resolution, '. . . this Association is of the opinion that other causes, over which the men have no control, are also contributory factors to the loss in output.'[2]

Opencast mining, which developed rapidly towards the end of the war, did not commend itself to the miners as a method of increasing coal production. It was criticized by one of their former leaders, Harold Neal, when he made his maiden speech in the House of Commons as member for the Clay Cross division, in July, 1944:

I am credibly informed that the men engaged on these outcrop workings —'sunshine pits' the miners call them—are earning three times the wages of men who go into the deep pits and undergo the dangers they are called upon to face. The whole scheme is ill-conceived and ill-considered and is calculated to lower the morale of mining communities more than any other operation which the Minister has introduced.[3]

The appointment of the Technical Advisory Committee on Coal-Mining in September, 1944, led to further protests by the Derbyshire Miners' Association because the Minister of Fuel and Power had not invited representatives of the M.F.G.B. to join the Committee.[4] From the managerial side Derbyshire was well represented for John Hunter, of the Doncaster Amalgamated Collieries and formerly of Staveley, and H. Watson Smith, of the Hardwick Colliery Company, were two of the six members of the committee, which had Charles Reid, the Ministry's Production Director, as chairman. The Reid Committee's

---

[1] 410 H.C. Deb. 5s. 1229.   [2] D.M.A. 14 October, 1944.
[3] 401 H.C. Deb. 5s. 1964.   [4] D.M.A. 14 October, 1944.

terms of reference were: 'To examine the present technique of coal production from coal-face to wagon and to advise what technical changes are necessary in order to bring the industry to a state of full technical efficiency.' The Reid Report,[1] published in March, 1945, is a landmark in the economic history of the coal industry. It showed clearly one of the most important causes of the declining productivity of the mines. Despite the growth of intensive mechanized mining in the 'twenties and 'thirties the British coal industry compared with the continental fields was more technically backward than ever it had been. Technical reorganization and the elimination of uneconomic units were impossible without important changes in the structure of the industry. The need for improved industrial relations was also recognized. 'The problem of securing full co-operation between employers and workers is the most difficult and urgent task the industry has to face', stated the Committee. 'Unless this problem is solved, the value of our technical recommendations will be greatly reduced.' The Report ended with the words: 'But there is no time to be lost.'

Cutting, conveying, and loading are the three main stages which can be distinguished in the development of mechanization in the coal industry. In all countries the power-loader came late, owing to the technical difficulties involved. Later still came the combined cutter and loader, a machine without practical importance in Great Britain before the Second World War. The Bolsover Colliery Company played an important part in demonstrating the advantages of modern machinery. In June, 1944, a Meco-Moore power cutter and loader was installed at the Company's Clipstone Colliery. It was described by Douglas Hay, formerly Professor of Mining in the University of Sheffield, as 'the first really successful attempt to modernize the loading of coal by power'. Experiments showed that the machine could be used in British mines in seams not less that 4 feet thick. By July, 1945, the output of three of these machines at Clipstone averaged 6,600 tons a day, equal to 44 per cent. of the output of the pit.[2] The Reid Report and the innovations introduced by efficient organizations such as the Bolsover Colliery Company set the pattern for the future development of the coal industry under state ownership and control.

VI

In addition to their industrial efforts the Derbyshire miners contributed to the war effort in a variety of other ways. Soon after the outbreak of

[1] *Coal Mining: Report of the Technical Advisory Committee*, 1945, (Cmd. 6610).
[2] *Derbyshire Times*, 23 June, 1944; 20 July, 1945.

war the Council decided to nominate Hicken to serve on the local panel of the Ministry of Information.[1] In December, 1940, Hicken and Sales were appointed members of the District Tribunal which dealt with the recruitment of miners to the Forces.[2] Some miners, such as A. Wilcox, a member of the Executive Committee, left the pits to do other work of national importance. In August, 1941, Wilcox was appointed by the Mines Department as a Labour Supply Officer for Derbyshire, Nottinghamshire and Leicestershire.[3] The Association gave its support to numerous voluntary war-time activities. In June, 1940, as the result of an appeal through the M.F.G.B., £1,000 was granted to provide two ambulances for the Anglo-French Ambulance Corps.[4] Many of the miners enrolled in the colliery demolition and rescue squads which were placed at the disposal of the civil defence authorities.[5] They were also urged by the Council to support the 'Dig for Victory' campaign and 'do their utmost by cultivating gardens and allotments'.[6] In April, 1941, the Association decided to offer its Council Chamber and other suitable rooms to the Chesterfield billeting officer 'to be used for temporary evacuation should they be required on account of invasion or air-raid damage'.[7]

The miners shared the war-time inconveniences of fire-watching and restricted transport services with the rest of the civilian population. Food and clothes rationing, however, aroused some opposition. The miners' complaints about the inadequacy of their diet and its effect upon output have already been noted. They argued in 1941 that it was unfair that those who could afford to patronize restaurants could still obtain their full ration of food, whilst miners, who needed greater sustenance, were limited to ordinary rations. In particular they called attention to the smallness of the meat and cheese rations.[8] The miners' demands for increased rations gave a great impetus to the provision of colliery canteens, which in 1941 became compulsory under the Essential Work Order. Progress was at first slow. As late as September, 1942, the Ministry of Fuel and Power reported that special efforts were needed to raise the standard of nutrition in the coalfields. The Miners' Welfare Commission assumed the initial capital outlay on building the canteens, which were then managed on a non-profit basis by committees of employers and workers. Many of the Derbyshire collieries had canteens which provided hot drinks and snacks and where canteens did not exist they were quickly improvised. In November, 1941, it was announced that the first colliery canteen in the country for the provision

[1] D.M.A. 7 October, 1939.   [2] Ibid. 28 December, 1940.
[3] Ibid. 9 August, 1941.   [4] Ibid. 4 May, 8 June, 1940.
[5] Ibid. 8 February, 1941.   [6] Ibid. 15 February, 1941.
[7] Ibid. 12 April, 1941.   [8] Derbyshire Times, 21 February, 1941.

of full meals was to be erected at the Grassmoor Colliery. One of the initiators of the scheme was Samuel Sales who had done much in the inter-war years to ensure that Grassmoor was the first colliery in the county to have pit-head baths.[1] The canteens were not used as much as was expected. In continuing to advocate increased rations for miners, to be consumed in their own homes, the M.F.G.B. pointed out that the nature of the miner's work prevented him from making use of the canteen during his shift and that after the shift transport arrangements often allowed no time for a meal when men had long distances to travel. Moreover, the M.F.G.B. stated that 'the most precious experience of the mineworker is to eat one hot meal a day in his own home *following* the completion of his shift'.[2] Nevertheless, the colliery canteen, as a result of the war, became an accepted part of the daily routine for many miners, particularly the unmarried ones.

Clothes rationing also caused some discontent. In June, 1941, the Council of the Derbyshire Miners' Association decided to 'press for the right to obtain working clothes for miners without the use of coupons'.[3] The matter was taken up by the M.F.G.B. and later in the year the Board of Trade agreed to grant underground workers a supplementary annual allowance of sixty coupons in addition to the normal allowance of sixty-six.

Similarly, when it became necessary to enforce strict rationing of coal, the miners insisted on retaining their usual allowance. In June, 1942, the Derbyshire Miners' Association called upon the M.F.G.B. to ask the Government to give special consideration to the position of the miners, 'having regard to the inferior quality of miners' allowance coal, their need for a greater amount than the ordinary householder, and that it is a perquisite of their occupation'.[4] The possibility of compensating miners financially for surrendering their allowance coal was considered but the Government decided that the difficulties of arranging retail distribution in the colliery villages and the dangers of aggravating industrial unrest were too great to make the withdrawal of allowance coal worth while. In May, 1943, it became illegal for miners to sell coal supplied to them free or at a reduced rate.[5]

The Derbyshire miners continued to show an interest in social welfare during the war. In March, 1942, the Council discussed a resolution from the Whitwell branch calling for a national superannuation scheme for all miners.[6] The policy was later adopted by the M.F.G.B.[7] Towards the end of 1942 the publication of the Beveridge Report was welcomed

[1] *Derbyshire Times*, 28 November, 1941. See Chapter XX, p. 787.
[2] *M.F.G.B.* 7 October, 1943.   [3] *D.M.A.* 28 June, 1941.
[4] *Ibid.* 30 June, 1942.   [5] S.R. & O., No. 702, 13 May, 1943.
[6] *D.M.A.* 7 March, 1942.   [7] *Ibid.* 14 November, 1942.

by the Council and steps were taken to publicize its recommendations.[1] The Association also devoted much energy during the war to finding suitable accommodation to replace the Convalescent Home, at Skegness, which was taken over by the Government on 1 September, 1939, for use as a military hospital for the duration of the war.[2] In May, 1942, the Council instructed the Executive Committee to consider a proposal that a temporary convalescent home should be established.[3] A number of resorts on the north-west coast, including Grange-over-Sands, Southport and St. Anne's-on-Sea, were visited by the officials and the Executive Committee in the early part of 1943.[4] In May the Association acquired the Russell Hotel at Blackpool. The Charity Commissioners agreed to the use of the accumulated contributions of the members for the initial capital outlay and to the use of the endowment fund of the Skegness Home for the maintenance of the temporary premises during the war. The Blackpool Convalescent Home was officially opened on 10 July, 1943, with Benjamin Lee, the veteran Bolsover miners' leader, as its manager.[5] In the following year additional accommodation was made available by the acquisition of an adjacent building, the Hood Hotel.[6]

There were no major colliery disasters in Derbyshire during the war but the accident rate in the North Midland Division rose sharply. In 1938 the number of killed and injured per thousand persons employed below ground was 243. By 1943 it was 384.[7] The increase was largely due to the increased tempo of work in the mines, the growth of mechanization and the influx of inexperienced labour. An important advance towards safer conditions was made in 1941 when the Joint Standing Consultative Committee of the Coal Industry reached agreement on the subject of workmen's inspectors of mines. On 26 April the Executive Committee of the Association recommended the appointment of one full-time inspector holding a first-class certificate of competency under the Coal Mines Act, 1911, at a salary of £350 a year, with travelling expenses. Each branch was asked to appoint not less than two or more than four miners with a minimum of ten years' experience of underground work to act as local inspectors and in turn accompany the full-time inspector when the mine was being examined.[8] It was not until 1 May, 1943, however, that W. Morrison, of Bowhill, Cardenden, Fife, was appointed as workmen's inspector. By this time the salary offered had been increased to £450 a year, rising by annual increments of £10 to £500.[9]

[1] D.M.A. 19 December, 1942.　　　　　　　[2] Ibid. 23 September, 1939.
[3] Ibid. 30 May, 1942.　　　[4] Ibid. 6 and 16 February, 6 March, 1 May, 1943.
[5] Ibid. 29 May, 26 June, 1943.　　　　　　[6] Ibid. 12 February, 1944.
[7] Ibid. 13 November, 1944.
[8] Ibid. 26 April, 1941.　　　　　　[9] Ibid. 6 January, 1 May, 1943.

VII

There were a number of changes in the Association's leadership during the war years. For reasons which will be explained later it was decided in June, 1941, to appoint an additional official.[1] Of the twelve nominees, four obtained a sufficient number of votes to qualify for the second ballot. They were Samuel Sales (Grassmoor No. 2), with 3,025 votes; A. Wilcox (Warsop Main), 2,074; Joseph Kitts (Ripley), 2,069; and Harold Neal (Shipley Low Main), 1,642.[2] Sales and Kitts qualified for the third ballot with 5,747 and 4,737 votes respectively.[3] Kitts was finally elected with 9,863 votes to Sales's 6,809.[4]

Born at Somercotes in 1894, Joseph Kitts came of a mining family. His grandfather, father and uncles had a total of 600 years' service with the Babbington Colliery Company. Kitts started work at the Company's Birchwood Colliery at the age of 14 and, on his father's instructions, joined the Derbyshire Miners' Association on his first pay day. He became a member of the branch committee in 1920 and played an active part in the lock-out of the following year. In 1923 he became a delegate to the Council. His position was made difficult by the fact that his father was a deputy and his uncle an under-manager. After the 1926 dispute Kitts was victimized but through the good offices of his wife's relatives eventually found employment at the Ripley Colliery. Since the Birchwood miners were reluctant to take an active part in trade union affairs because of the attitude of the management, Kitts continued to be their delegate, although employed at Ripley. In 1928 he became delegate for the Ripley branch. He also played an active part in local politics and was for a number of years chairman of the Alfreton I.L.P. and secretary of the Somercotes and Riddings Labour Party. From 1927 until he moved to Chesterfield to take up his position as a full-time union official, Kitts was a member of the Alfreton urban district council and had held office as its chairman and vice-chairman.[5]

On 21 December, 1941, shortly before Kitts was elected, Frank Lee died. He was then 74 years of age and had been in poor health since the spring of 1940 when he had a serious operation. 'Mr. Lee has laboured indefatigably in the interest of those whom he served,' stated the Executive Committee, 'and has left behind him the imprint of a benignity, sincerity and wholeheartedness that will go down in the history of the Association as unique, and that may well be emulated by

[1] D.M.A. 20 and 31 May, 28 June, 1941.
[2] Ibid. 18 October, 1941.   [3] Ibid. 15 November, 1941.
[4] Ibid. 27 December, 1941.
[5] Derbyshire Times, 2 January, 1942. Also private information.

EE

those who are privileged to follow in his footsteps.'[1] Although Kitts had been elected as an additional official he now took over the duties of Lee and no further appointment was made.[2] Henry White, the Association's Vice-President, succeeded Lee as member for the North-East Derbyshire division[3] and Harold Neal became the new Vice-President.[4]

Hicken's appointment as Regional Labour Director by the Ministry of Fuel and Power in August, 1942, led to further changes. Hicken suggested that the Council might either accept his resignation or grant him leave of absence.[5] The Council recommended leave of absence by 36 votes to 18 but when the matter was referred to the branches they decided by 32 to 22 that Hicken should resign.[6] Among some of the men there was the uneasy feeling that their popular leader had 'gone over to the other side'. Joseph Lynch was appointed Acting General Secretary pending the election of a new official.[7] Of the twelve nominees Harold Neal (Shipley Low Main), Herbert Gallagher (Markham No. 3), and H. W. Wynn (Coppice No. 3), qualified for the second ballot with 4,604, 2,988 and 2,287 votes respectively.[8] Neal, with 8,208 votes, and Wynn, with 6,666, were both successful in the second ballot[9] but Neal alleged that more votes had been cast at Wynn's branch and at the Coppice No. 1 branch than there were men on the colliery books.[10] He also criticized Wynn because of his membership of the Communist Party. 'My candidature is not being sponsored by any outside political organization', he wrote. 'My passion for increased production did not begin with the entry of Russia into the European conflict. . . . I am strongly opposed to the funds of your Association being used for Communist propaganda.'[11] Subsequent investigations by the Council showed Neal's allegations to be unfounded.[12] Wynn defeated him in the final ballot by 11,906 votes to 8,492.[13] After the election Lynch was appointed General and Financial Secretary; Kitts, Assistant Secretary and Treasurer; and Wynn, Agent and Organizer.[14]

Herbert William Wynn, the son of a railway signalman, was born in 1901 and began work at the age of 13, at the Moor Green pit of the Eastwood Collieries. Because of the prominent part he played in the 1926 dispute he was told that he would never be employed in a Nottinghamshire pit again. In December, 1927, he found work at the Shipley Company's Coppice pit. After many years underground, mainly at the

[1] D.M.A. 24 December, 1941.   [2] Ibid. 28 January, 1942. See below, p. 868.
[3] See below, p. 872.   [4] D.M.A. 9 May, 1942.
[5] Ibid. 1 August, 1942.   [6] Ibid. 22 August, 1942.
[7] Ibid. 4 and 22 August, 1942.   [8] Ibid. 17 October, 1942.
[9] Ibid. 14 November, 1942.   [10] Derbyshire Times, 4 December, 1942.
[11] Ibid. 27 November, 1942.
[12] D.M.A. 19 December, 1942; Derbyshire Times, 4 December, 1942.
[13] D.M.A. 19 December, 1942.   [14] Ibid. 6 January, 1943.

coal face, he was elected checkweighman in 1940. Although Wynn was an active and militant trade unionist at the branch level his early upbringing and his subsequent educational[1] and political interests helped to make him also one of the left-wing intellectuals of the Labour movement. A forceful speaker and a good organizer, he soon held various offices in the Ilkeston Divisional Party, including that of vice-president. He was also chairman of the Heanor District Labour Party. From 1927 to 1930 he was a member of the Derbyshire County Council. In 1929, because of his disagreement with the policy of the Labour Party during MacDonald's premiership, Wynn joined the Communist Party, eventually becoming Chairman of the Chesterfield branch and Chairman of the East Midland District Committee. He was perhaps better known to many Derbyshire miners at the time of his election for the part he played in the 'Aid for Russia' campaign during the war than he was for his trade union activities.[2]

Soon after Wynn's election the death of John Spencer, on 28 January, 1943, at the age of 75, created yet another vacancy in the ranks of the officials. Kitts took over Spencer's work as Compensation Agent, Wynn became the Treasurer, and nominations were requested for the position of Agent.[3] Of the seventeen competitors in the first ballot, H. Neal, H. Gallagher, T. Hunt and H. Street were successful with 3,314, 2,984 2,093 and 1,583 votes respectively.[4] Hunt and Street were eliminated in the second ballot and Gallagher defeated Neal in the final ballot by 10,906 votes to 10,652.[5] Herbert Gallagher's success was unprecedented. He was the first member of the Association to be elected a full-time official who was not a member of the Council. Born at Danesmoor in 1902, he had worked at various collieries in Derbyshire. He had been unemployed for nine years after being dismissed in 1930 from the Glapwell Colliery where he was secretary of the checkweigh society. After the outbreak of war he had found work at the Markham No. 3 Colliery.[6]

In the annual election for the presidency at the end of 1943 Samuel Sales was defeated by Hugo Street. This was another unusual occurrence for, although in theory the presidency was not a permanent position, in practice no president had been defeated since 1906. Sales ceased to play a prominent part in the affairs of the union and eventually became interested in 'Moral Rearmament'. In September, 1946, he told the European Assembly for Moral Rearmament, at Caux: 'Higher wages alone are not going to solve the problems of the mining industry. There

[1] See Chapter XX, p. 793.
[2] *Derbyshire Times*, 5 June, 27 November, 1942; 19 December, 1947. Also private information.
[3] *D.M.A.* 16 February, 6 March, 1943.   [4] *Ibid.* 1 May, 1943.
[5] *Ibid.* 29 May, 26 June, 1943.   [6] *Derbyshire Times*, 13 September, 1946.

are miners here from all over Britain. Our job is to go back into the coal-fields carrying the spirit of Moral Rearmament. That spirit alone is the key to the coal problem.'[1]

Hugo Street, a much younger man than Sales, was born at Church Gresley in 1901. He began work as a boy at the Warsop Main Colliery and became a member of the Association in 1916. By 1927 he was the branch secretary and, with only 380 members out of the 2,000 men employed at the colliery, succeeded in persuading the management not to encourage the formation of a branch of the Spencer union. He was elected a delegate to the Council in 1941. Street had been secretary of various accident, hospital and benevolent funds at Warsop and Staveley. He had also taken an active part in local politics, serving on the Shire-brook parish council, the Derbyshire County Council, the Clay Cross, and later the Bolsover constituency Labour parties. At the time of his election he was president of the Shirebrook Trades Council.[2]

Harold Neal's election as M.P. for the Clay Cross division in April, 1944[3] led to the election of Samuel Greenough as Vice-President of the Association in the following June.[4] Greenough had worked at the Wingfield Manor Colliery for over forty years and was a check-weighman, secretary of his branch, and a delegate to the Council. He had been active in local government and was a magistrate.[5]

On 26 August, 1939, the Council had instructed the Trustees and the Executive Committee to 'consider the increase of all benefits paid by the Association, salaries to Branch Officials and Head Officials in ratio to work done'.[6] As far as the full-time officials were concerned, their salaries were already linked to miners' wages by custom if not by rule. The Council accepted the Executive Committee's recommendation that the officials 'would be better served by adopting a superannuation or pension fund than by a present increase in salary'.[7] The question of the officials' salaries was raised again in May, 1941, when the Executive Committee recommended that there should be no increase but that an additional official should be appointed.[8] This decision led to the appointment of Joseph Kitts but the vacancy created by Lee's death in the meantime was not filled.[9] Nothing was done about adopting a super-annuation scheme until March, 1942, when the Association decided to make arrangements for the older officials to receive a pension of £3 a week at the age of 65 on a non-contributory basis. Kitts, who had recently been appointed, and all future officials were to contribute half

---

[1] *Derbyshire Times*, 13 September, 1946.
[2] *Ibid.* 17 December, 1943. Also private information.
[3] See below, p. 873.   [4] *D.M.A.* 24 June, 1944.
[5] *Derbyshire Times*, 30 June, 1944.   [6] *D.M.A.* 26 August, 1939.
[7] *Ibid.* 30 September, 7 October, 18 November, 1939.
[8] *Ibid.* 3 and 20 May, 1941.   [9] See above, p. 866.

the cost of their pensions.[1] As a corollary of the superannuation scheme the officials were required to resign at the age of 65.[2] By the end of 1944 the officials were receiving a salary of £38 7s. 3d. a month with a war bonus of £3 4s. od. From September, 1942, a number of attempts were made in the Council to carry a resolution requiring the officials to seek re-election every five years but the proposal met with little support.[3] In September, 1943, the annual payments made to the President and the Vice-President were increased to £10 and £5 respectively.[4] In November, 1939, the remuneration of branch secretaries was increased by 15 per cent.[5]

There were also increases in the benefits paid to members of the Association. From 21 October, 1939, old-age payments were raised from 20s. a month to 24s. with a maximum payment of fifty months. Unemployment benefit was increased from 5s. to 6s. a week.[6] Old age payments were further increased to 30s. a month in October, 1942, but a proposal to introduce a life pension was rejected.[7]

The price which the Derbyshire coal-owners had to pay for the miners' war-time co-operation was to give some assistance in strengthening trade union organization. On 19 October, 1940, the Council had a long discussion on the question of non-unionism when it was proposed, amongst other things, that wage rates and conditions negotiated by the Association should not be paid to non-unionists.[8] No decision was reached but a month later it was decided to hold area conferences to discuss methods of dealing with non-unionism and to issue a circular urging the branches to increase their membership.[9] By April, 1941, the recruiting campaign had resulted in an increase in membership of only 5,782.[10] In the autumn of 1941 the miners' representatives suggested to the County Wages Board that the war advances should be paid to members of the Association only.[11] This proposal was not acceptable to the owners but by February, 1942, they had agreed in principle to the deduction of union contributions from wages subject to a written authorization from each workman. The union was to pay a commission of 4 per cent. on all contributions collected in this way. The officials were empowered to sign an agreement on these lines provided that the owners promised to deal with the minority who refused to consent to the deduction of contributions at the colliery office by withholding their 'attendance bonus' of 1s. a shift.[12] The owners gave a verbal assurance that

[1] D.M.A. 28 January, 21 February, 7 March, 1942.   [2] Ibid. 16 March, 1943.
[3] Ibid. 19 September, 1942; 9 January, 26 June, 11 December, 1943.
[4] Ibid. 27 September, 1943.
[5] Ibid. 18 November, 1939.   [6] Ibid. 21 October, 1939.
[7] Ibid. 24 October, 1942.   [8] Ibid. 19 October, 1940.
[9] Ibid. 16 November, 1940.   [10] Ibid. 19 April, 1941.
[11] Ibid. 20 September, 1941.   [12] Ibid. 7 and 21 February, 1942.

they would do so if the Association would indemnify them against any legal action which might arise. After the signing of the agreement the branches became responsible for seeing that the men completed the necessary authorization forms for the employers.[1] The first deductions from wages were made in July, 1942.[2] The agreement was intended to be a war-time measure only.

By the end of June a considerable number of men had not signed the authorization forms and it was decided to allow a further month to elapse before taking any action against them.[3] Early in August the Association pressed the owners to implement their verbal promise to withhold the 'attendance bonus' from non-unionists.[4] At a meeting of the Wages Board on 7 August it was agreed that legal advice should be taken on possible methods of dealing with men who refused to sign the authorization forms.[5] Meanwhile the owners agreed to interview all such men in an attempt to obtain their consent to the deduction of contributions.[6] Many of those who refused to participate in the scheme were staunch members of the union who preferred to pay their contributions in the usual way. About 80 per cent. of the members had given their consent by September, 1942. The Registrar of Friendly Societies replied to a member who sent him a letter of complaint:

This method of payment of contributions is not novel and on present information I do not know what principle may be said to be involved in payment by deduction rather than direct to the Association. I should have thought it would save trouble and work on both sides.[7]

In January, 1943, the Council discussed the desirability of taking strike action to enforce membership of the Association but decided to await legal advice.[8] It was later discovered that the employers could not legally withhold the 'attendance bonus' from non-unionists and the matter was quietly dropped.

One consequence of the deduction of union contributions from wages was a decline in the importance of the branch treasurer. It was necessary to retain the office for the collection of contributions from members who refused to adopt the new procedure but, in November, 1942, the remuneration of branch treasurers was reduced by 50 per cent. and that of branch secretaries increased by 15 per cent. to compensate them for their additional duties. A month later it was also decided to increase the payments made to branch presidents by 50 per cent.[9] Although the Association was unsuccessful in its attempts to enforce a 'closed shop', the new

[1] D.M.A. 7 March, 1942.
[2] Ibid. 9 May, 1942.
[3] Ibid. 30 June, 1942.
[4] Ibid. 4 August, 1942.
[5] Ibid. 8 August, 1942.
[6] Ibid. 19 September, 1942.
[7] Ibid. 20 October, 1942.
[8] Ibid. 9 January, 1943.
[9] Ibid. 24 October, 14 November, 19 December, 1942.

method of collecting contributions appears to have increased the membership considerably. The improvement in earnings and the influx of labour brought about by the war probably accounted for the small increase in numbers from 21,513 in 1939 to 22,327 in 1940. The membership campaign of 1941 increased the total to 25,287. In 1942, when payment of contributions through the colliery office was introduced, membership rose sharply to 34,836. Thereafter there was a slight increase in 1943 to 34,902 followed by a decline to 32,417 in 1944.[1]

The growth of membership led to a substantial increase in the union's funds which rose from £161,823 in 1939 to £363,625 in 1944. Although in April, 1940, the union decided to protest against 'any system of national compulsory saving'[2] it was prepared to support the war effort by its own investment policy. Indeed, apart from loans of £20,000 to the Borough of Fulham and £8,000 to the Shirebrook parish council, and a deposit of £20,000 with the Co-operative Wholesale Society, the bulk of the Association's war-time investments were in Government securities. In August, 1940, the Council authorized a loan to the Treasury of £5,000 free of interest.[3] A year later a further loan of £15,000 was made, again free of interest.[4] Thereafter from £20,000 to £40,000 was invested in 3 per cent. savings bonds each year. In 1943 the officials were empowered to distribute the sum of £20,000 to the various districts in the county which were arranging 'Wings for Victory' weeks. The miners were also urged to save. In 1944, after meeting representatives of the National War Savings Committee, the Executive Committee of the M.F.G.B. recommended the districts 'to render every possible assistance with a view to savings among employees in the coalmining industry being increased'.[5]

VIII

During the war the electoral truce between the major political parties enabled a vacant seat to be filled without contest by a representative of the party to which the last occupant had belonged. This arrangement did not prevent independent candidates or members of the minor parties from standing for election. A general election was prevented by prolonging the life of Parliament. Similarly, in local government, all contests were suspended, vacancies were filled by co-option, and councillors enjoyed an indefinite term of service.

When a vacancy occurred in the Mansfield division, early in 1941, as

[1] See Chapter XV, Appendix I.
[3] *Ibid*. 24 August, 1940.
[5] *M.F.G.B.* 8 June, 1944.

[2] *D.M.A.* 6 April, 1940.
[4] *Ibid*. 9 and 13 August, 1941.

a result of the death of Charles Brown, the Derbyshire Miners' Association decided to put forward a candidate. A. Wilcox, J. Mugglestone and Henry Hicken were nominated by the branches but Hicken withdrew. When the matter was again referred to the branches Wilcox received 194 votes and Mugglestone only 23.[1] Wilcox was a checkweighman at the Warsop Colliery and a member of the Nottinghamshire County Council. His nomination was submitted to the Mansfield Divisional Labour Party but he was not adopted.

Later in the year the death of Frank Lee created a vacancy in the North-East Derbyshire division. Henry White, the Association's Vice-President since 1939, was nominated as a M.F.G.B. candidate.[2] There was the usual manœuvring in London to secure the adoption of an outside candidate. I. O. Thomas, a member of the N.U.R. head office staff and, since 1938, a prospective Labour candidate in the Wrekin division of Shropshire, was nominated by a number of local branches of the N.U.R.[3] T. Fallows was nominated by the Staveley branch of the National Union of Public Employees. There were also four local candidates nominated by various branches of the divisional Labour Party.[4] The miners' candidate carried the day and was returned unopposed. White, who was then 51 years of age, had been one of the pioneers of the North-East Derbyshire Labour Party and had been its President and Vice-President for several years before becoming Frank Lee's political agent in 1935. He had served on the Creswell parish council for 21 years, the Clowne rural district council for 11 years and the Derbyshire County Council for 9 years. For 14 years he had been a member of the Executive Committee of the Derbyshire Miners' Association and for 12 years a delegate to the Council.[5] When White was elected to Parliament the Council decided that he should relinquish the position of Vice-President but be permitted to retain his membership of the Association. He was to have access to all Council meetings and be allowed to take part in any discussion involving political issues.[6]

The death of George Ridley, the Labour member for Clay Cross, caused another parliamentary vacancy early in 1944. The Association again decided to put forward a candidate. H. Bostock, H. Neal, S. Sales and H. Street were nominated by the branches. Neal was eventually successful with 348 votes to Street's 254.[7] In addition to Neal there were eight other nominees: D. T. Jones, of the National Union of Railwaymen; Thomas Scollan, of the National Union of Distributive

[1] D.M.A. 11 January, 8 and 15 February, 8 March, 1941.
[2] Ibid. 10 January, 7 February, 1942.   [3] Derbyshire Times, 30 January, 1942.
[4] Ibid. 6 February, 1942.
[5] D.M.A. 21 February, 1942; Derbyshire Times, 20 February, 6 March, 1942.
[6] D.M.A. 21 February, 1942.   [7] Ibid. 8 and 15 January, 5 February, 1944.

and Allied Workers; W. J. C. Webber, of the Railway Clerks' Association; E. F. M. Durbin, the Socialist economist, then personal assistant to the Deputy Prime Minister, nominated by the Clay Cross Divisional Executive; and four local nominees, including T. M. Bennison, a retired schoolmaster, who had for many years played a prominent part in the Clay Cross Labour Party.[1] Neal was adopted but was not returned unopposed. It had been rumoured that there were to be four other candidates, including D. Craven Griffith, a Board of Trade official who was secretary of the North Midland Prices Regulating Committee, and C. J. Taylor, a Carlisle chemist.[2] However, the candidates who were finally nominated were Philip Hicken and William Douglas Home. Hicken, who had now found employment as a railway shunter, described himself as an Anti-Fascist candidate. Home, who accused Neal of 'trying to slide into Parliament under the skirts of Mr. Churchill', appeared as an Atlantic-Charter candidate. He had 'left the army to denounce the politicians' and 'had no party attachments' but 'stood between Liberal and Labour, with a slight leaning to Labour'.[3] Neal was elected with 13,693 votes to Hicken's 2,336 and Home's 1,911.

Neal, who had been Vice-President of the Association since May, 1942, relinquished his office as his predecessor, Henry White, had done and was accorded the same right of attending meetings of the Council.[4] Harold Neal was 46 years of age at the time of his election to Parliament. He had been a branch official since he was 20 and had also been a delegate to the Council and a member of the Executive Committee of the Association. After twenty years' experience of working underground he had been a checkweighman at the Shipley Colliery for over four years.

IX

The early years of the war made such great demands on the time and attention of the miners' leaders that their interest was temporarily diverted from the difficult question of the reorganization of the M.F.G.B. But the war also led to a growth of national negotiations which revealed an immediate practical need for structural reform. The Greene Award, which conceded the principle of a national minimum wage, was perhaps one of the strongest influences in bringing about the creation of a national union. James Bowman, the Vice-President of the M.F.G.B., told the annual conference in 1942:

It is impossible for us to be continuously demanding national control for

[1] *Derbyshire Times*, 10 March, 1944.   [2] *Ibid.* 24 March, 1944.
[3] *Ibid.* 7 April, 1944.   [4] *D.M.A.* 6 May, 1944.
EE*

this, national direction for that, and at the same time allowing to reserve to ourselves the right to continue as we have continued for so many years on a basis of district organization . . . for I say to you here and now, and I say it with studied assurance, that the Mineworkers' Federation as it is constituted today is not fitted to meet the responsibilities which face it in the immediate future.[1]

The Executive Committee's recommendation that there should be a single union for mineworkers was accepted by the delegates and during the following year the Reorganization Sub-Committee drafted its proposals, meeting representatives from every district.

These proposals were submitted by the Executive Committee to the annual conference of the M.F.G.B. in 1943. They were similar to the 1938 proposals: a compromise between district autonomy and complete unification. The union's industrial work, including the handling of compensation cases, was to be completely centralized but there was to be no interference with the traditional friendly society functions of the district unions. The conference accepted the Executive Committee's proposals and referred them to the districts.

A special conference at Nottingham on 16–18 August, 1944, considered the amendments proposed by the districts. Derbyshire had supported the policy of reorganization at every stage and submitted few amendments to the draft constitution. The most important one provided for the election of area officials by the 'exhaustive' system, which had long been used in Derbyshire, but the proposed single transferable vote system carried the day.[2] The question of amalgamating neighbouring districts led to some discussion. A Yorkshire amendment provided for the creation of nine geographical areas which involved, among other things, the amalgamation of the Derbyshire and South Derbyshire associations. The conference decided that there should be no immediate amalgamations but that the Executive Committee should have the power to recommend them, subject to the approval of a national conference. The introduction of the compulsory retirement of officials at the age of 65 did not affect Derbyshire since the Association had already adopted such a rule in 1943. The Executive Committee's proposal that every district union should pay into the new national union £1 for each member aroused fears that the officials in some districts would suffer reductions in salaries under the new financial arrangements. Derbyshire supported a Scottish amendment that the capitation fee should be reduced by half but the Executive's original proposal was adopted. Mr. G. B. Baldwin comments: 'More than anything else, this action showed that by 1944 delegates really meant business in their desire to

---

[1] *M.F.G.B.* 20 July, 1942.
[2] *D.M.A.* 18 March, 1944; *M.F.G.B.* 17 August, 1944.

form "one mineworkers' organization".[1] Another controversial issue was the amount per member which should be regularly paid to the national organization by the districts. In effect this was determined by the lowest contribution then being collected by any district, which was found to be 6d. a week. Since the Derbyshire miners were already contributing 1s. a week the agreed 4½d. *per capita* payment left the district with a fairly wide margin of financial safety. In addition to maintaining its unemployment and old-age benefits Derbyshire was in a position to supplement the national union's strike benefit of 10s. a week by a further £1.

Reorganization, carried out on these lines, gave neither uniform contributions nor benefits. It created a new legal and financial relationship between the affiliated unions and the central organization but did not interfere with the number or internal structure of the component parts. The old district unions became administrative areas of a single National Union of Mineworkers, and the salaries of Area officials were now paid from bank accounts controlled by the national body. Of the 21 Areas, 15 were geographical and 6 were occupational, catering for winders, craftsmen and electrical power workers. The new union had control over all questions of industrial policy, including strike action, which needed a two-thirds majority on a national vote. The President and Secretary of the N.U.M. were full-time officials. The Vice-President was a part-time official elected biennially by the national conference. District autonomy was preserved in such matters as the retention of real property, individual registration under the laws governing trade unions, the election of Area officials and the nomination of representatives to serve on the national Executive Committee.

The rules agreed upon by the Nottingham conference were submitted to a ballot vote of the membership in October, 1944. In Derbyshire they were approved by 21,629 votes to 854.[2] Nationally there were 430,630 members in favour of the new rules and 39,666 against. On 1 January, 1945, after sixty-five years' existence, the Derbyshire Miners' Association became the Derbyshire Area of the National Union of Mineworkers.

[1] G. B. Baldwin, 'Structural Reform in the British Miners' Union', *Quarterly Journal of Economics*, LXVII, (1953), p. 595.
[2] *D.M.A.* 13 November, 1944.

EPILOGUE

EPILOGUE

I

The end of the war in Europe led to a general election and the advent of a Labour Government with, for the first time in history, a handsome majority over all other parties. War-time experience had confirmed, if confirmation were needed, that the complete reorganization of the coal industry could no longer be delayed. The post-war boom, the export drive and the policy of full employment were all likely to make increasingly heavy demands upon the mines. Greater output was to become more necessary than ever before. The new Government was pledged to an extensive programme of nationalization, with the coal industry high on the list of priorities. This combination of circumstances resulted in the passing of the Coal Industry Nationalization Act, 1946, which established the National Coal Board, transferred the assets, rights and liabilities of the industry to the Board, and provided for the payment of compensation to the former colliery owners. On 1 January, 1947, the primary vesting date, the blue and white N.C.B. flags fluttered above the headstocks of the collieries and the miners' long campaign for nationalization was at an end.

North and South Derbyshire, with Nottinghamshire and Leicester-shire, became the East Midlands Division, one of the nine regional divisions created by the National Coal Board, following, with some modifications, the regional system established by the Ministry of Fuel and Power during the war. The East Midlands Division was sub-divided into eight Areas, which became the basic units for commercial management. Employers and workmen were appointed to positions of responsibility in the new organization. Sir Eric Young, a former managing director of the Bolsover Colliery Company, was one of the original full-time members of the National Coal Board. The East Mid-lands Division, under the chairmanship of Sir Hubert Houldsworth, had H. Watson Smith, formerly of the Hardwick Colliery Company, as its Production Director and Henry Hicken as its Labour Director. In 1948 Hicken was appointed O.B.E. H. Buck, the South Derbyshire Miners' agent , and W. H. Sales, the son of the former President of the Derbyshire Miners' Association, became Deputy Divisional Labour Directors. Sales was later to become the Labour Relations Member of the National Board. At the Area and pit levels of the Division the process was repeated. Many well-known colliery managers occupied prominent positions. Former trade union leaders such as A. Wilcox and J. Mugglestone became Area or Colliery Labour Officers.

On vesting day the East Midlands Division took over about 120 pits varying widely in size and efficiency, and five major coking and by-product plants. Twelve brickworks, two pipeworks, six waterworks, 18,350 houses, 112 farms and more than 14,300 acres of land, all formerly owned by colliery companies, had also to be brought within the organization. To reorganize and develop the vast coal resources of the Division a heavy programme of capital investment was required. The original *Plan for Coal*, published in October, 1950, envisaged an average annual output of 47·3 million saleable tons for the East Midlands Division between 1960 and 1965. The figure for capital investment was put at £84,000,000. *Investing in Coal*, published in April, 1956, revised those estimates and gave the Division the task of producing 52·7 million saleable tons by 1965. It was expected that the Division's entire capital expenditure programme for the fifteen years 1950–65 would amount to £191,000,000, the bulk of the sum being spent in the first ten years of the period.

Further mechanization was one of the industry's greatest needs. Power-loading techniques, such as those used in the Meco-Moore machine, were introduced extensively. Machines such as the 'Gloster Getter', evolved by W. V. Sheppard, formerly of the Bolsover Colliery Company, almost doubled output per man-shift and made possible the development of continuous longwall mining.[1] Between 1947 and 1956 power-loaded tonnage in the East Midlands Division increased from 2,742,571 tons to 9,629,980. The advance in coal-face mechanization was greatly assisted by the development and increasing use of armoured, flexible chain conveyors in place of the conventional belt conveyor; and the wide use of hydraulic props, special types of roof bar and new types of chocks. Underground haulage was also improved by replacing rope haulage by conveyor belts, and, to some extent, by locomotive haulage. Between 1949 and 1956 the mileage of conveyor belt haulage in the Division increased from 340 to 500 and that of rope haulage decreased

[1] See W. V. Sheppard, 'Continuous Longwall Mining. Experiment at Bolsover Colliery', *Colliery Guardian*, 22 February, 1951, p. 255; J. N. Booth, 'The Bolsover System of Mining', *Sheffield University Mining Magazine*, 1951, pp. 40–59.

from 196 to 55. By 1956 very nearly 100 per cent. of the Division's output of coal was mechanically cut and conveyed, and a programme for the provision of a central workshop in each area for the maintenance and repair of mechanical equipment was well under way. Central workshops were in operation in two areas, a third was under construction, two more were in an advanced stage of planning and another was in the early planning stage.

The five carbonization plants which the Board took over in 1947 produced in the first year of nationalization 630,800 tons of coke, mainly for domestic and industrial use. The Grassmoor and Hardwick plants were both extended and, along with the Harworth plant, were kept in operation. In November, 1956, the new Avenue Carbonization and Chemical Plant at Wingerworth, near Chesterfield, came into operation. The plant was designed to produce 500,000 tons of solid smokeless fuel and more than 5,000 million cubic feet of gas a year. By 1956 the Division's output of coke had already risen to 886,800 tons, the amount of gas sold had more than doubled, and there had been large increases in the whole range of the main carbonization by-products.

The saleable output of the East Midlands Division increased yearly from 1946. In 1956 the total was 46,266,739 tons, about 42 per cent. higher than the 1946 figure. The East Midlands was then the biggest coal-producing Division in the country, producing more than 22 per cent. of the entire national deep-mined output. Productivity increased substantially. Between 1946 and 1956 output per man-shift for all workers increased by 27 per cent. to 36·9 cwt., which was by far the highest in the country. The yearly output of each wage earner increased from 358 tons in 1946 to 454 tons in 1956, about 170 tons above the national average. Mechanization was largely responsible for the improved productivity of face workers whose output per man-shift in 1956 was 94·8 cwt. compared with 81·74 cwt. in 1946, and the 1956 national average of about 66·75 cwt. Except for the years 1950 and 1951, the number of men employed in the Division increased steadily between 1946 and 1956, but output increased at a higher rate. The greater efficiency of the industry made possible an important redistribution of manpower. While surface labour declined from 22,450 to 20,450, coal-face manpower rose from 36,190 to 45,038.

During the first ten years of nationalization the annual profits of collieries of the East Midlands Division, before charging interest on capital after depreciation, were as follows:

Year	Profit of Collieries £	Per ton saleable s. d.
1947	7,510,621	4 4·0
1948	14,501,366	7 9·3

Year	Profit of Collieries £	Per ton saleable s. d.
1949	15,546,716	7 11·8
1950	13,620,508	6 9·9
1951	17,086,820	7 11·6
1952	13,106,303	5 11·2
1953	15,909,214	7 2·0
1954	15,710,526	6 11·0
1955	16,970,253	7 5·0
1956	21,877,339	9 6·2

II

The advent of nationalization ensured the continuation of national wage negotiations. By an agreement made in December, 1946, the National Coal Board adopted the collective agreements made previously between the National Union of Mineworkers and the Mining Association and between their constituent district bodies. This agreement also removed the ban on application for changes in piece-work rates at pit level but continued the ban on alterations in day-wage rates in the districts. The energies of the N.C.B. in wage negotiations were directed towards giving the necessary incentives to better attendance and increased output. The Five-Day Week Agreement of 18 April, 1947, gave uniformity to the length of the working week and shift, reduced the working week to five shifts, without loss of earnings, and introduced an attendance qualification whereby six shift payments were made for five shifts worked. The bonus to day-wage workers amounted to payment for a normal shift's work; for piece-workers it was equivalent to 16 per cent. of earnings. From 1947 to 1954 there were six general increases in adult day rates embodied in national agreements (subject to ceilings in some cases). The main provisions were as follows:

Effective date of agreement	Minimum Weekly Wage Surface £ s. d.	Underground £ s. d.	Increase per shift Surface s. d.	Underground s. d.	
November, 1947	5 0 0	5 15 0	1 8	2 6	
October, 1950	5 5 0	6 0 0	6	6	(i)
January, 1951	5 10 0	6 7 0	10	1 2	
November, 1951	6 1 6	7 0 6	1 11	2 3	(ii)
February, 1953	6 7 6	7 6 6	1 0	1 0	
January, 1954	6 15 0	7 15 0	1 3	1 5	

Notes: (i) The War Addition of 2s. 8d. per shift for day-wage men was also merged into the day-wage rate: for piece-workers it was continued as a flat rate.

(ii) Piece-workers, who apart from a very few work underground, also received the increase. The flat rate of 2s. 8d. was increased to 4s. 11d. per shift for underground piece-workers.

These agreements broadly followed the same pattern. National minimum rates were raised; day-wage rates were usually increased by equivalent amounts and national juvenile rates for age were either increased by the same amounts or else in some agreed proportion; national rates for craftsmen (in two grades) were established and a national scale for winding enginemen. The net effect of these changes was to reduce the range of variations in day-wage rates and increasing numbers of day-wage men came on to the national minima or national rates.

An important feature of the agreement which operated from November, 1951, was that a joint committee of the N.C.B. and the N.U.M. was set up to consider the possibility of achieving 'a more rational wage structure with greater uniformity in wages and emoluments for similar work and effort'. Over 6,000 local job names were examined and reduced to about 400 agreed occupations with a precise description of the tasks performed. The 400 occupations were then classified under grades for daily paid underground workers, surface workers and craftsmen. National standard rates were fixed for each grade, and for each age for juveniles under 21, by the Revision of the Wages Structure Agreement, dated April, 1955. A new wages structure for piece-workers proved to be a more formidable task which still remains to be completed.

A thorough discussion of wages in the coal industry since nationalization necessarily lies beyond the scope of this concluding chapter. Mr. K. J. W. Alexander, in a careful analysis,[1] gives the following details of earnings and hours in mining and manufacturing industry, 1947–54:

	Retail Prices	Coalmining			Manufacturing Industry		Wage rate of adult male manual workers
		Day-wage rate	Average earnings	Average hours	Average earnings	Average hours	
1947 (a)	100	100	100	100	100	100	100
(b)	100	114	115	102	104	100	102
1948 (a)	106	114	122	101	107	101	106
(b)	108	114	125	104	111	101	107
1949 (a)	109	114	122	98	112	101	109
(b)	112	114	129	103	115	101	109
1950 (a)	113	114	127	100	117	102	110
(b)	114	119	136	104	121	103	111
1951 (a)	121	126	142	104	128	103	118
(b)	129	126	159	106	133	103	122
1952 (a)	135	140	155	101	139	103	128
(b)	138	140	171	103	143	103	131

[1] K. J. W. Alexander, 'Wages in Coal-mining Since Nationalization', *Oxford Economic Papers*, N.S. VIII, (1956), pp. 164–80.

	Retail Prices	Coalmining			Manufacturing Industry		Wage rate of adult male manual workers
		Day-wage rate	Average earnings	Average hours	Average earnings	Average hours	
1953 (a)	141	146	164	98	149	103	135
(b)	140	146	177	104	152	104	136
1954 (a)	141	151	175	100	159	104	141
(b)	144	151	186	104	165	105	143

Notes: Coalmining. The index of day-wage rates is a weighted one for adult male workers underground and on the surface. The index for average earnings is based on the figures given in the *Quarterly Statistical Statement* of the costs of production, etc., of collieries published by the N.C.B., the figures used are for adult males and include the value of allowances in kind. The index for average hours is based on the figures for average numbers of shifts worked given in N.C.B. annual reports.

Manufacturing Industry. The earnings and hours indices are calculated from the figures for adult males in the twice yearly inquiry made by the Ministry of Labour.

Wage Rates of Adult Male Manual Workers, from *Ministry of Labour Gazette*.

In addition to agreements governing national wage increases there were also a number of agreements introducing uniform conditions of service. They dealt with such matters as a guaranteed wage, annual and statutory holidays, extensions of hours, compensations for redundancy, supplementary injuries, fatal accidents and pensions.

Industrial relations in the East Midlands Division after nationalization were good. During the first nine years the combined loss through disputes was only 302,400 tons, less than two days' output in 1955. In 1956 this record was marred by an under-officials' dispute but even then the loss of 205,600 saleable tonnage represented less than $1\frac{1}{2}$ days' output. During the complete decade, 1947–56, the Division lost through disputes little more than half a week's output, less than 4 per cent. of the tonnage lost through disputes in the whole industry.

III

The membership of the Derbyshire Area of the N.U.M. fluctuated between 32,000 and 36,000 from 1945 to 1954. Total investments increased fairly steadily from £376,508 to £708,362. Investments per head rose from £11·45 to £19·7 but much of this apparent advance was offset by inflation. Allowing for changes in prices, investments per head had fallen in value from £7·36 in 1914 to £5·64 in 1945 and had risen to £7·98 in 1954.[1] In other words, as a result of the disputes of the inter-war years and the inflation of the post-war years, the union was no more powerful financially in 1954 than it had been forty years earlier. Rising costs and the increasing financial demands of the central

[1] See Chapter XV, Appendix I.

organization led the Derbyshire Area to increase its weekly contribution to 1s. 6d. in 1957.

There were further changes in the union's leadership after the war. Towards the end of 1945 the Council called upon Herbert Gallagher to resign. He was succeeded as Agent in March, 1946, by Hugo Street, the union's President. Samuel Greenough, the new President, was succeeded as Vice-President by Michael Kane. The retirement of Joseph Lynch led to the election of another new official towards the end of 1947. Kane, who had a long record of active trade union work and had been imprisoned for the part he had played in the Harworth dispute in 1937, was successful in the ballot. On a branch vote H. W. Wynn was elected Area Secretary in succession to Lynch. Hugo Street took over Wynn's duties as Area Treasurer and Kane became the new Agent. J. Boam succeeded Kane as Vice-President but resigned in October, 1951, when he took up an appointment with the N.C.B.

H. E. Parkin then became Vice-President, and at the end of 1952 when Greenough retired, was elected President. Born at Waingroves in 1908, Herbert Parkin began work at the Hartshay Colliery in 1922. When the pit was closed in 1931 he moved to the Butterley Company's New Langley Colliery. He played a prominent part in resisting the Company's attempts to impose a form of butty system when mechanical conveyors were introduced and thereafter became increasingly active in the union. In 1937 he was elected to the checkweigh committee and the branch committee. In 1941 he became a delegate to the Council and in 1948 President of his branch. A leading member of his local Labour Party, Parkin was elected to the Heanor urban district council in 1946 and was its Vice-Chairman in 1951. He was succeeded as Vice-President of the union by J. Patilla, of Morton. In 1954 F. Peacock of Swanwick succeeded Patilla, who was nominated for the presidency and the vice-presidency but withdrew from both elections.

Apart from the additions of electric lighting, telephones and central heating the union's headquarters had remained practically unchanged since they were opened in 1893. In 1954–5 the Council Chamber was completely transformed. The old half-tiled walls and dadoes were covered with wooden panelling, the ceiling was lowered and fitted with fluorescent lighting, new window frames were installed, and the room was provided with carpets, curtains and new seating accommodation.

As if to symbolize the change from the nineteenth to the twentieth century the old banner of the Derbyshire Miners' Association which had adorned the wall behind the platform was replaced by a plaque depicting modern mining scenes and bearing the inscription 'N.U.M., Derbyshire Area'. Two smaller rooms adjoining the Council Chamber were converted into an Executive Committee Room.

Another post-war innovation was the publication of a monthly union journal, *The Derbyshire Miner*. The first issue appeared in March, 1957, and within a few months the journal, sold at twopence, had reached a circulation of between 7,000 and 8,000.

Harold Neal and Henry White continued to represent the Clay Cross and North-East Derbyshire divisions after the war. In the 1945 election Neal defeated his Conservative opponent, W. P. Bull, by 27,538 votes to 6,021, and White defeated R. E. Warlow by 35,795 votes to 18,789. George Benson and G. H. Oliver, the veterans of the Chesterfield and Ilkeston divisions, were both re-elected. Herbert Wragg, who was knighted in 1944, decided not to contest the Belper division and George A. Brown, the Labour candidate, was elected. Following the redistribution of seats, Neal became the member for the new Bolsover division in 1950. White, Benson, Oliver and Brown all retained their seats in the other mining constituencies. There was no change in the 1951 and 1955 elections. In 1958 George Benson was knighted for his work in connection with penal reform.

After the Hungarian uprising of October, 1956, H. W. Wynn resigned from the Communist Party. His growing dissatisfaction with its organization and policies had been greatly increased by Khrushchev's speech at the twentieth Congress of the Communist Party of the Soviet Union in the previous February. After an absence of twenty-seven years Wynn rejoined the Labour Party but showed himself broadly in sympathy with the outlook of such journals as the *New Reasoner*, the *Universities and Left Review* and the short-lived *Forum*.

IV

Despite the great increase in output and the growth of mechanization in the East Midlands Division after nationalization, there was a considerable reduction in the accident rates. In 1946 the number of fatal and serious accidents was 434, compared with 248 in 1956. The rate of such accidents for each million tons of output was reduced from 12·4 in 1946 to 5·4 in 1956. The number of fatal accidents fell from 76 to 36 in the same period. Much valuable work was done by the safety organization at Divisional, Area and colliery levels, which was set up by the Board in the first year of nationalization. The most serious disaster in the Division was at the Creswell Colliery, in September, 1950, when 80 men lost their lives as a result of a fire involving a belt conveyor. 'Blood is on coal today as it has always been', commented Arthur Horner, the General Secretary of the N.U.M. 'Let those who criticize the miners and the cost of coal now realize the price of its getting.'[1]

The N.C.B. was specifically required by Parliament to pay attention to the safety, health and welfare of its employees. These functions were exercised jointly with the Miners' Welfare Commission through the National Miners' Welfare Joint Council until 1952 when colliery welfare became the sole responsibility of the Board and social welfare became the responsibility of the new Coal Industry Social Welfare Organization, in which the Board and its employees acted as joint managers. C.I.S.W.O. thus continued the tradition of the old Miners' Welfare Commission, although relieved of some of the latter's responsibilities. Financed by grants from the Board, C.I.S.W.O. worked through a central Council and nine Divisional Welfare Committees.

These schemes resulted in further advances in the welfare of the miners and their families. At the collieries in the East Midlands Division considerable sums were spent to improve feeding and bathing facilities at the surface. By 1956 there were 95 canteens in the Division. At 45 of them a full hot meals service was provided. Many pit-head baths and medical centres were built. By 1956 the baths in the Division served more than 99 per cent. of the manpower and others were being built. The Board then employed 10 medical officers, 70 state-registered nurses and more than 250 full- or part-time attendants at 69 medical centres.

Under the social welfare scheme the provision and extension of halls, community centres and recreation grounds continued. C.I.S.W.O. began to organize and encourage a wide variety of sporting, musical and other activities. Divisional competitions became an important feature of the work. The Derbyshire Miners' Holiday Centre at Skegness was requisitioned for military purposes during the war but proved to be more popular than ever when it was reopened. An outbreak of fire in October, 1949, destroyed the central buildings and a new dining hall, kitchens and concert hall were erected at a cost of about £80,000. When this work was completed there followed a steady programme of improvement and extension. The post-war years also saw the development of another holiday centre, on a smaller scale, at Rhyl.

The Miners' Welfare Scholarship Schemes continued to be administered by C.I.S.W.O. but the special course for miners, revived in 1947 by the University College of Nottingham, lapsed temporarily under the new arrangements. Mindful of his own experiences as a student in the inter-war years, H. W. Wynn discussed with K. J. W. Alexander, a lecturer in economics in the University of Sheffield, the possibilities of devising a new educational scheme for the Derbyshire miners. By 1952 arrangements had been made for selected students to attend courses in

[1] *Derbyshire Times*, 29 September, 1950.

economic and industrial problems held at the union's headquarters. Extra-mural lecturers were provided by the University of Sheffield, the teaching costs being grant-aided by the Ministry of Education. As the scheme developed, the courses were extended to three sessions, each of twenty-four weeks. In the first year the students attended for one day a week and in the second and third for two days. About twenty miners were admitted each year. The union gave them an allowance for meals and travelling expenses, and shared with the N.C.B. the cost of compensating them for absence from work.[1] Soon afterwards a similar scheme was developed by the University of Nottingham to cater for the Nottinghamshire miners and the many Derbyshire miners who live within its extra-mural area.[2]

In addition to the improvement in conditions which the miner enjoyed in his industry he shared, with the rest of the community, the benefits of greater social security. There were also further improvements in housing. In 1945 it was estimated by the Derbyshire local authorities that there was a shortage of at least 1,800 houses for miners. Of the existing miners' houses large numbers fell below the requirements of the Ministry of Health because they provided inadequate accommodation or were without bathrooms, hot water systems or proper sanitation.[3] Much was done to remedy these deficiencies both by the local authorities and by the N.C.B. In 1952 the Derbyshire miners raised objections to the N.C.B. housing, because it was let on service tenancies, and expressed a preference for local authority housing schemes.

The lives of many miners were completely transformed in the years following the war. Motoring, television and holidays abroad all came within the realms of possibility for the better paid worker. In some cases he was able to move into a new house. The younger man was able to indulge in 'contemporary' furnishing. But the social revolution was not so swift nor so universal as was popularly imagined. There were still miners' families living in dismal and unsatisfactory houses. There were still poorly paid men, such as surface workers, striving to bring up families on less than £10 a week.

It must be the task of some future historian to examine in detail the events which have been baldly described in this concluding chapter. At the time of writing (November, 1958) the coal industry is again facing grave difficulties. The growing use of oil, economies in coal consumption and a trade recession have all combined to reduce the

[1] J. E. Williams, 'An Experiment in Trade Union Education', *Adult Education*, XXVII, (1954), pp. 113–24.
[2] A. H. Thornton, 'Day-Release for Liberal Studies', *Adult Education*, XXIX, (1956), pp. 197–204.
[3] *Ministry of Fuel and Power, North Midland Coalfield, Regional Survey Report*, (1945), p. 37.

demand for coal for the first time since the war. The future historian will know how these difficulties were overcome and will be able to see the whole development of the industry since 1947 in perspective. Whether he will see fit to write a regional history is a matter for speculation. In the past the differing economic conditions in the various coalfields were the key to the understanding of the industry's history and the attitude of the miners' unions. The miners hoped that nationalization would eliminate the differences as far as wages and conditions were concerned. The extent to which this is achieved in the future will largely determine the utility of investigating the history of trade unionism in particular coalfields.

BIBLIOGRAPHY

I. PRIMARY AUTHORITIES: MANUSCRIPT

(1) Records of the Derbyshire Miners' Association: Minutes of Council and Executive Committee meetings, 1886–1891, 1893–1896, 1908–1926, (typescript after 1926); Derbyshire Miners' Conference Minute Book, 1887–1890; account books, letter books, reports of deputations, miscellaneous documents.
>   (At the offices of the National Union of Mineworkers, Derbyshire Area, Chesterfield.)

(2) Minutes of the Nottinghamshire and District Miners' Industrial Union.
>   (By courtesy of Mr. A. R. Griffin.)

(3) The Papers of Thomas Spencer.
>   (By courtesy of Mrs. F. Wilson.)

(4) The Mundella–Leader Correspondence.
>   (At the Sheffield University Library.)

(5) The Records of the Shipley and Mapperley collieries. Butterley Company, Ltd., Coal Mines Nationalization Bill, Report on Development and Past History, April, 1946 (typescript).
>   (By courtesy of officials of the National Coal Board, East Midlands Division, No. 5 Area.)

(6) Minutes of the Chesterfield Borough Council.
>   (At the Town Hall, Chesterfield.)

(7) Annual Returns submitted to the Chief Registrar of Friendly Societies.

II. PRIMARY AUTHORITIES: PRINTED

(1) *Trade Union Records*

(a) The Derbyshire Miners' Association: Minutes of Council and Executive Committee meetings, 1880–1888, 1890–1896, 1909, 1911–1934; balance sheets, circulars, rule books, colliery price lists and agreements.
>   (At the offices of the National Union of Mineworkers, Derbyshire Area, Chesterfield.)

(b) The South Yorkshire Miners' Association: Minutes, 1858–1880; balance sheets, circulars and other miscellaneous documents.
>   (At the offices of the National Union of Mineworkers, Yorkshire Area, Barnsley.)

(c) Miners' Federation of Great Britain: Minutes, circulars, reports and balance sheets, 1889–1944.

(d) T.U.C. Reports.

(e) Leaflet issued by the United Society of Brushmakers, 1867.
>   (By courtesy of Mr. Arthur Horner.)

(2) *Parliamentary Papers and other Official Publications*

Select Committee on the State of the Coal Trade, 1830.

Children's Employment Commission, 1842.

Reports of H.M. Inspectors of Mines and Quarries, 1856–1938.

Royal Commission to Enquire into Trades Unions and other Associations, 1867–1869.

Select Committee on Railway Companies' Amalgamations, 1872.

Select Committee on the Causes of the Present Dearness and Scarcity of Coal, 1873.

Royal Commission on the Master and Servant Act, 1867, and the Criminal Law Amendment Act, 1871, (1874).

Select Committee on Railway Rates and Fares, 1882.

Royal Commission on the Depression of Trade, 1886.

Board of Trade, Accounts and Papers, LXVIII, 1890.

Royal Commission on Mining Royalties, 1891.

Royal Commission on Labour, 1892.

Select Committee on Railway Rates and Charges, 1893–1894.

Royal Commission on Explosions from Coal Dust in Mines, 1894.

Board of Trade, Reports on Trade Unions, 1896–1910.

Departmental Committee on Electricity in Mines, 1904.

Departmental Committee appointed to inquire into the probable economic effect of a limit of eight hours to the working day of coalminers, 1907.

Departmental Committee appointed to inquire into conditions prevailing in the coalmining industry due to the war, 1915.

Coal Industry Commission, 1919.

Report of Committee on Trusts, 1919.

Report by a Court of Inquiry Concerning the Wage Position in the Coalmining Industry, 1924.

Report by a Court of Inquiry Concerning the Coalmining Industry Dispute, 1925.

Royal Commission on the Coal Industry, 1925.

Departmental Committee on Co-operative Selling in the Coalmining Industry, 1926.

Mines Department, Miners' Welfare Fund, Annual Reports.

Mines Department, Explosion at Grassmoor Colliery, Derbyshire, Report by Sir Henry Walker, 1934.

Mines Department, Explosion at Markham Colliery, Derbyshire, Report by J. R. Felton, 1937.

Departmental Committee on Holidays with Pay, 1937.

Report of the Board of Investigation into the Immediate Wages Issue in the Coalmining Industry, 1942.

National Conciliation Board for the Coalmining Industry, National Reference Tribunal Awards.

Ministry of Fuel and Power, North Midland Coalfield, Regional Survey Report, 1945.

Parliamentary Debates, Fourth and Fifth Series.

Ministry of Labour Gazette.

(3) *Newspapers and Periodicals*

(a) Local: *Alfreton and Belper Journal, Derbyshire Chronicle, Derbyshire Courier, Derbyshire Times, Ilkeston Pioneer, Sheffield and Rotherham Independent, Sheffield Telegraph.*

(b) National: *The Beehive, British Gazette, British Worker, Clarion, Chambers's Journal, Colliery Guardian, Daily Chronicle, Daily Herald, Daily Telegraph, The Economist, Iron and Coal Trades Review, Sun, The Times, Westminster Gazette.*

(4) *Autobiographies and Memoirs*

Lord Beveridge, *Power and Influence*, London, Hodder & Stoughton, 1953.

Clynes, J. R., *Memoirs: 1924–37*, London, Hutchinson, 1937.

Dalton, Hugh, *Memoirs: Call Back Yesterday*, London, Muller, 1953.

Markham, Violet, *Friendship's Harvest*, London, Reinhardt, 1956.

Metcalfe, F. J., *Colliers and I: or Thirty Years' Work among Derbyshire Colliers*, Manchester, Ashworth, 1903.

Sitwell, Osbert, *Laughter in the Next Room*, London, Macmillan, 1949.

Thomas, J. H., *My Story*, London, Hutchinson, 1937.

Earl Winterton, *Orders of the Day*, London, Cassell, 1953.

(5) *Other authorities largely or partly primary in nature*

Lord Aberconway, *The Basic Industries of Great Britain*, London, Benn, 1927.

Anti-Socialist and Anti-Communist Union, *The Trade Unions Bill Vindicated by a Labour M.P.*, London, 1927.

Lord Askwith, *Industrial Problems and Disputes*, London, Murray, 1920.

Earl Baldwin, *On England, And Other Addresses*, Harmondsworth, Penguin, edn. of 1937.

Batley, W., ed., *Miners' Diseases: Records of the Researches of Dr. J. Court*, Sheffield, *Sheffield Daily Telegraph*, n.d.

Beales, H. L., and Lambert, R. S., eds., *Memoirs of the Unemployed*, London, Gollancz, 1934.

Boden, F. C., *Pithead Poems*, London, Dent, 1927.

Bolsover Colliery Company, *Annual Reports*.

Cole, G. D. H., *The World of Labour*, London, Bell, edn. of 1917.

Curr, John, *The Coal Viewer and Engine Builder's Practical Companion*, Sheffield, Printed for the author by Mortholl, 1797.

Engels, F., *The Condition of the Working Class in England in 1844*, London, Allen & Unwin, edn. of 1892.

Farey, J., *General View of the Agriculture and Minerals of Derbyshire*, London, Board of Agriculture, 1811–1817, 3 vols.

Glover, Stephen, *A History of the County of Derby*, Derby, Mozley, 1829, 2 vols.

Hallam, W., *Miners' Leaders*, London, Bemrose, 1894.

Hannington, W., *Unemployed Struggles, 1919–1936*, London, Lawrence & Wishart, 1936.

Houghton, John, *A Collection for the Improvement of Husbandry and Trade*, ed. Richard Bradley, London, 1727–8, 4 vols.

Kidd, R., *The Harworth Colliery Strike: A Report to the Executive Committee of the National Council for Civil Liberties*, London, 1937.

Kiddier, W., *The Old Trade Unions from Unprinted Records of the Brushmakers*, London, Pitman, 1930.

Kynder, P., 'Historie of Derbyshire', *The Reliquary*, (Old Series) XXII, 1881–1882.

MacDonald, J. R., *The Socialist Movement*, London, Butterworth, 1911.

Management of Collieries: Colliers, Their Oppression and Complaints, How are they to be remedied? Lincoln, 1864. (Anonymous pamphlet.)

Martin, Kingsley, *Harold Laski*, London, Gollancz, 1953.

Morris, C., ed., *The Journeys of Celia Fiennes*, London, Cresset, 1947.

Nettleship, R. L., ed., *The Works of Thomas Hill Green*, London, Longmans, 1911, 3 vols.

Oxford and Working-Class Education: The Report of a Joint Committee of University and Working-Class Representatives on the Relation of the University to the Higher Education of Workpeople, Oxford University Press, 1908.

Comte de Paris, *Trade Unions of England*, London, Smith, Elder & Co., 1869.

Pendleton, J., *Our Railways: Their Origin, Development, Incident and Romance*, London, Cassell, 1894, 2 vols.

Pilkington, James, *A View of the Present State of Derbyshire*, Derby, Drewry, 1789, 2 vols.

Porter, G. R., *The Progress of the Nation*, London, Murray, edn. of 1851.

Postgate, R., *The Life of George Lansbury*, London, Longmans, 1951.

Proceedings of the Royal Society.

Report of the M.O.H. for Chesterfield, 1914.

Report of the M.O.H. for Chesterfield R.D.C., 1910.

Report of the M.O.H. for Derbyshire, 1914.

Reports of the Non-Union Meetings held by Workpeople Employed by the Staveley Coal and Iron Company in Vindication of the Freedom and Liberty of Labour, Chesterfield, 1867. (Manchester Municipal Reference Library.)

Sheepbridge Coal and Iron Company, *Annual Reports*.

Simon, Sir John, *Three Speeches on the General Strike*, London, Macmillan, 1926.

Staveley Coal and Iron Company, *Annual Reports*.

Symons, J., *The General Strike*, London, Cresset, 1957.

The Miners' Next Step, Tonypandy, Davies, 1912.

Transactions of the Chesterfield and Derbyshire Institute of Mining, Civil and Mechanical Engineers.

Transactions of the Institute of Mechanical Engineers.

White's History, Gazetteer and Directory of the County of Derby, Sheffield, 1857.

III. SECONDARY AUTHORITIES

(1) *Books, Articles and Pamphlets*

A Hundred Years of Enterprise (published by the Clay Cross Company), 1937.

Alexander, K. J. W., 'Wages in Coal-mining Since Nationalization', *Oxford Economic Papers*, N.S., VIII, 1956.

Allen, G. C., *British Industries and their Organization*, London, Longmans, edn. of 1952.

Allen, G. C., *The Industrial Development of Birmingham and the Black Country, 1860–1927*, London, Allen & Unwin, 1929.

Allen, V. L., *Power in Trade Unions*, London, Longmans, 1954.

Armytage, W. H. G., *A. J. Mundella, 1825–1897: The Liberal Background to the Labour Movement*, London, Benn, 1951.

Armytage, W. H. G., 'J. C. Kenworthy and Tolstoyan Communities in England', *The American Journal of Economics and Sociology*, Vol. 16, 1957.

Armytage, W. H. G., 'The Railway Rates Question and the Fall of the Third Gladstone Ministry', *English Historical Review*, LXV, 1950.

Arnot, R. P., *The Miners*, London, Allen & Unwin, 1949.

Arnot, R. P., *The Miners: Years of Struggle*, London, Allen & Unwin, 1953.

Ashton, T. S., 'The Coal-Miners of the Eighteenth Century', *Economic History*, I, 1928.

Ashton, T. S., *An Economic History of England: The Eighteenth Century*, London, Methuen, 1955.

Ashton, T. S., and Sykes, J., *The Coal Industry of the Eighteenth Century*, Manchester University Press, 1929.

Baldwin, G. B., 'Structural Reform in the British Miners' Union', *Quarterly Journal of Economics*, LXVII, 1953.

Beales, H. L., 'The "Great Depression" in Industry and Trade', *Economic History Review*, V, 1934.

Beer, M., *A History of British Socialism*, London, Allen & Unwin, edn. of 1940.

Lord Beveridge, *Full Employment in a Free Society*, London, Allen & Unwin, 1944.

Booth, J. N., 'The Bolsover System of Mining', *Sheffield University Mining Magazine*, 1951.

Bowle, J., *Viscount Samuel, A Biography*, London, Gollancz, 1957.

Bowley, A. L., *Wages and Income in the United Kingdom since 1860*, Cambridge, 1937.

Bowley, A. L., *Wages in the United Kingdom*, London, Clay, 1900.

Boyd, R. N., *Coal Pits and Pitmen*, London, Whittaker, 1892.

Briggs, A., and Saville, J., eds., *Essays in Labour History*, London, Macmillan, 1960.

Brown, E. H. Phelps, and Handfield-Jones, S. J., 'The Climacteric of the 1890's: A Study in the Expanding Economy', *Oxford Economic Papers*, IV, 1952.

Bulman, H. F., and Redmayne, R. A. S., *Colliery Working and Management*, London, Technical Press, edn. of 1906.

Burnham, T. H., and Hoskins, G. O., *Iron and Steel in Britain, 1870–1930*, London, Allen & Unwin, 1943.

Cadbury, G., and Dobbs, S. P., *Canals and Inland Waterways*, London, Pitman, 1929.

Chapman, G., *Culture and Survival*, London, Cape, 1940.

Clapham, J. H., *Economic History of Modern Britain*, Cambridge University Press, 1926–1938, 3 vols.

Cole, G. D. H., *Attempts at General Union, 1818–1834*, London, Macmillan, 1953.

Cole, G. D. H., *British Working Class Politics, 1832–1914*, London, Routledge, 1941.

Cole, G. D. H., and Postgate, R., *The Common People*, London, Methuen, edn. of 1949.

Coppock, D. J., 'The Climacteric of the 1890's: A Critical Note', *The Manchester School of Economic and Social Studies*, XXIV, 1956.

Court, W. H. B., *Coal*, London, H.M.S.O. and Longmans, 1951.

Court, W. H. B., *The Rise of the Midland Industries, 1600–1838*, Oxford University Press, 1938.

Court, W. H. B., 'Problems of the British Coal Industry Between the Wars', *Economic History Review*, XV, 1945.

Crook, W. H., *The General Strike*, Chapel Hill, University of North Carolina Press, 1931.

Daniels, G. W., and Ashton, T. S., 'The Records of a Derbyshire Colliery, 1763–1779', *Economic History Review*, II, 1929.

Dennis, N., Henriques, F., and Slaughter, C., *Coal is Our Life*, London, Eyre & Spottiswoode, 1956.

Ensor, R. C. K., *England, 1870–1914*, Oxford University Press, 1939.

Fane, W. D., 'Melbourne Castle and Park', *Journal of the Derbyshire Archaeological Society*, XI, 1889.

Firth, J. B., *Highways and Byways in Derbyshire*, London, Macmillan, 1908.

Fogarty, M. P., *Prospects of the Industrial Areas of Great Britain*, London, Methuen, 1945.

Fox, W., *Coal Combines in Yorkshire*, Labour Research Department, 1935.

Galloway, R. L., *Annals of Coal-mining*, London, Colliery Guardian Co., 1907, 2 vols.

Garvin, J. L., *The Life of Joseph Chamberlain*, London, Macmillan, 1934, 3 vols.

Gibson, F. A., *A Compilation of Statistics of the Coal-mining Industry of the United Kingdom*, Cardiff, Western Mail, 1922.

Gibson, Walcot, *Coal in Great Britain*, London, Arnold, edn. of 1927.

Goldstein, J., *The Government of British Trade Unions*, London, Allen & Unwin, 1952.

Goodhart, A. L., 'The Legality of the General Strike of 1926', *Yale Law Journal*, XXXVI, 1927.

Gore, C., *A New Commentary on Holy Scripture*, London, S.P.C.K., 1937.

Grant, Sir Allan, *Steel and Ships, The History of John Brown's*, London, Michael Joseph, 1950.

Green, H., 'The Southern Portion of the Nottinghamshire and Derbyshire Coalfield and the Development of Transport before 1850', *Journal of the Derbyshire Archaeological Society*, LVI, 1935.

Gregory, T. E., *The Westminster Bank through a Century*, Oxford University Press, 1936, 2 vols.

Grinling, C. H., *The Great Northern Railway*, London, Methuen, 1898.

Griffin, A. R., *The Miners of Nottinghamshire*, Nottingham, N.U.M., Nottinghamshire Area, 1956.

Hammond, J. L. and B., *The Town Labourer*, London, Longmans, 1917.

Hardy, S. M., 'The Development of Coal-mining in a North Derbyshire Village, 1635–1860', *University of Birmingham Historical Journal*, V, 1957.

Harrod, R. F., *The Life of John Maynard Keynes*, London, Macmillan, 1951.

Heinemann, M., *Britain's Coal*, London, Gollancz, 1944.

Hobsbawm, E. J., *Primitive Rebels*, Manchester University Press, 1959.

Hobsbawm, E. J., 'The British Standard of Living, 1790–1850', *Economic History Review*, X, 1957.

Hughes, W. R., 'Bruce Wallace and "Brotherhood"', *Congregational Quarterly*, October, 1947.

Jevons, H. S., *The British Coal Trade*, London, Kegan Paul, 1915.

Johnson, R., 'An Ancient Swanwick Coal Mine', *Journal of the Derbyshire Archaeological Society*, LXXIII, 1953.

Jones, J. H., Cartwright, G., and Guénault, P. H., *The Coal-mining Industry*, London, Pitman, 1939.

Keynes, J. M., *The Economic Consequences of the Peace*, London, Macmillan, 1919.

Keynes, J. M., *The Economic Consequences of Mr. Churchill*, London, Macmillan, 1925.

Keynes, J. M., 'The Need of Peace by Negotiation', *New Republic*, 19 May, 1926.

Laski, H. J., 'The Coal Strike and Beyond', *The Nation*, 26 May, 1926.

Lewis, R., and Maude, A., *The English Middle Classes*, London, Phoenix, 1949.

Levy, H., *Monopolies, Cartels and Trusts in British Industry*, London, Macmillan, edn. of 1927.

Macgregor, D. H., 'The Coal Bill and the Cartel', *Economic Journal*, XL, 1930.

Macrosty, H. W., *The Trust Movement in British Industry*, London, Longmans, 1907.

McCormick, B., and Williams, J. E., 'The Miners and the Eight-Hour Day, 1863–1910', *Economic History Review*, XII, 1959.

Martin, Kingsley, *The British Public and the General Strike*, London, Hogarth, 1926.

Masters, D., *The Plimsoll Line*, London, Cassell, 1955.

Mottram, R. H., and Coote, C., *Through Five Generations*, London, Faber, 1950.

Murray, Gilbert, *Four Stages of Greek Religion*, New York, Columbia University Press, 1912.

Murray, John, *The General Strike of 1926*, London, Lawrence & Wishart, 1951.

Musson, A. E., 'The Great Depression in Britain, 1873–1896', *Journal of Economic History*, XIX, 1959.

Nef, J. U., *The Rise of the British Coal Industry*, London, Routledge, 1932, 2 vols.

Neuman, A. M., *Economic Organization of the British Coal Industry*, London, Routledge, 1934.

Peers, Robert, *Adult Education in Practice*, London, Macmillan, 1934.

Pelling, Henry, *The Origins of the Labour Party, 1880–1900*, London, Macmillan, 1954.

Poirier, Philip P., *The Advent of the Labour Party*, London, Allen & Unwin, 1958.

Pollard, Sidney, *A History of Labour in Sheffield*, Liverpool University Press, 1959.

Pool, A. G., *Wage Policy in Relation to Industrial Fluctuations*, London, Macmillan, 1938.

Potter, Eric, 'Through the Butterley Country in Search of Outram's Railway', *Ad Rem* (House magazine of the Butterley Company), No. 5, 1953.

Raynes, J. R., *Coal and Its Conflicts*, London, Benn, 1928.

Redmayne, Sir R. A. S., *The British Coal-mining Industry during the War*, Oxford University Press, 1923.

Rhodes, E. C., 'Output, Labour and Machines in the Coal-mining Industry in Great Britain', *Economica*, XII, 1945.

Robertson, D. H., 'A Narrative of the General Strike of 1926', *Economic Journal*, XXXVI, 1926.

Rostow, W. W., *British Economy of the Nineteenth Century*, Oxford University Press, 1948.

Rowe, J. W. F., *Wages in the Coal Industry*, London, King, 1923.

Saville, J., ed., *Democracy and the Labour Movement*, London, Lawrence & Wishart, 1954.

Sheppard, W. V., 'Continuous Longwall Mining: Experiment at Bolsover Colliery', *Colliery Guardian*, 22 February, 1951.

Sires, R. V., 'The Beginnings of British Legislation for Old-Age Pensions', *Journal of Economic History*, XIV, 1954.

Smiles, Samuel, *Life of George Stephenson*, London, Murray, edn. of 1858.

Somervell, D. C., *British Politics Since 1900*, London, Dakers, edn. of 1953.

Stainton, J. H., *The Making of Sheffield*, Sheffield, Weston, 1924.

Stewart, W. D., *Mines, Machines and Men*, London, King, 1935.

Stretton, C. E., *History of the Midland Railway*, London, Methuen, 1901.

Sweezy, P. M., *Monopoly and Competition in the British Coal Trade*, Harvard University Press, 1938.

Tate, G., *London Trades Council, 1860–1950*, London, Lawrence & Wishart, 1950.

FF

Tawney, R. H., 'The Abolition of Economic Controls, 1918–1921', *Economic History Review*, XIII, 1943.

The Staveley Story (Published by the Staveley Coal and Iron Company, Ltd.), n.d.

Thornton, A. H., 'Day-Release for Liberal Studies', *Adult Education*, XXIX, 1956.

Trevelyan, G. M., *Grey of Falloden*, London, Longmans, 1937.

Trueman, Sir Arthur, ed., *The Coalfields of Great Britain*, London, Arnold, 1954.

Victoria County History, Derbyshire, London, Constable, 1907, 2 vols.

Wearmouth, R. F., *Methodism and the Struggle of the Working Classes, 1850–1900*, Leicester, Backus, 1954.

Webb, Sidney, *The Story of the Durham Miners*, London, Labour Publishing Co., 1921.

Webb, Sidney and Beatrice, *Industrial Democracy*, London, Longmans, edn. of 1911.

Webb, Sidney and Beatrice, *The History of Trade Unionism*, London, Longmans, edn. of 1920.

Welbourne, E., *The Miners' Unions of Northumberland and Durham*, Cambridge University Press, 1923.

West, Julius, *A History of the Chartist Movement*, London, Constable, 1920.

White, P. H., 'Some Aspects of Urban Development by Colliery Companies, 1919–1925', *The Manchester School of Economic and Social Studies*, XXIII, 1955.

Williams, F. S., *The Midland Railway*, London, Bemrose, edn. of 1878.

Williams, J. E., 'An Experiment in Trade Union Education', *Adult Education*, XXVII, 1954.

Williams, J. E., 'Paternalism in Local Government in the Nineteenth Century', *Public Administration*, XXXIII, 1955.

Williams, J. E., 'The Political Activities of a Trade Union, 1906–1914', *International Review of Social History*, II, 1957.

(2) *Unpublished Works*

Covell, W. R., 'The Chesterfield School Board, 1871–1903', M.A. thesis, University of Sheffield, 1952.

Stevenson, P. J., 'Trade Unionism among the Derbyshire Coal-miners, 1866–1894'. B.A. dissertation, University of Birmingham, 1954.

INDEX

FF*

GEORGE ALLEN & UNWIN LTD
London: 40 Museum Street, W.C.1

Auckland: 24 Wyndham Street
Bombay: 15 Graham Road, Ballard Estate, Bombay 1
Buenos Aires: Escritorio 454–459, Florida 165
Calcutta: 17 Chittaranjan Avenue, Calcutta 13
Cape Town: 109 Long Street
Hong Kong: F1/12 Mirador Mansions, Kowloon
Karachi: Karachi Chambers, McLeod Road
Madras: Mohan Mansion, 38c Mount Road, Madras 6
Mexico: Villalongin 32–10, Piso, Mexico 5, D.F.
New Delhi: 13–14 Ajmeri Gate Extension, New Delhi 1
São Paulo: Avenida 9 de Julho 1138–Ap. 51
Singapore: 36c Prinsep Street, Singapore 7
Sydney, N.S.W.: Bradbury House, 55 York Street
Toronto: 91 Wellington Street West

by R. Page Arnot

THE MINERS

A HISTORY OF THE MINERS' FEDERATION
OF GREAT BRITAIN 1889–1910

'Mr Page Arnot has written a very good book, and the Mine-workers' Federation is to be congratulated on its choice of him to do its official history.'
Manchester Guardian

'Here is something finer than the bare chronicles of a trade union. It is a piece of history that lives as the men lived who wrought the deeds and endured the hardships, who shared the hopes, and shaded the events that compose the story of the coalfields.'
Times Literary Supplement

'A thorough scholarly job. Part of its worth is the skill with which he assembles the best that others have said and written on this subject. He has compiled a reference book with much in it to interest the general student of social history, but above all a book for the miners themselves.'
Tribune

Sm. Royal 8vo. 25s. net

THE MINERS: YEARS OF STRUGGLE

FROM 1910 ONWARDS

'This is a book of outstanding importance. In nothing is it more impressive than its study of miners' strategy and tactics in particular and trade union strategy and tactics in general. . . . The greatness of Robert Smillie, the solid sterling qualities of Herbert Smith, the brilliant, wayward personality of A. J. Cook—these are imprinted on the reader's mind by a book which, in its class, has not many superiors.'
Birmingham Post

'For Mr Arnot there can be only commendation for a masterly achievement. Another might have written a different history from the same facts, but none could have written one more absorbingly interesting.'
Sheffield Telegraph

'A graphic, lucidly arranged, and admirably documented record of a phase in the class struggle in which the miners were the spearhead.'
New Statesman and Nation

Sm. Royal 8vo. 35s. net

by R. Page Arnot

THE MINERS IN CRISIS AND WAR
FROM 1930 ONWARDS

In this third volume of the history of the Miners' Federation of Great Britain, the author, R. Page Arnot, drawing on original sources placed at his disposal, tells the story of two sharply contrasting periods, of world crisis and of world war.

The story begins with the Miners' Federation fallen upon evil days, diminished in numbers, shorn of its former powers of national wage negotiation, divided in counsel and almost whelmed beneath the seismic waves of world economic crisis. Unemployment prevailed, greater than at any time before. They looked to Ramsay MacDonald and his second Labour Government for legislative remedies. The sudden collapse of the cabinet, the formation of the four-party coalition, and the rout of the Labour Party in 1931 shattered these hopes.

The climb from the economic abyss of the early 'thirties is made against a sombre background of the spread of fascism and the approach of war. The tensions are expressed in dramatic exchanges between Prime Ministers and miners' leaders.

Then, during the war, the British coal industry and its workers encounter a series of rapid changes, both for better and for worse. The whole main purpose of their trade unions, to maintain and improve the standard of life, is conditioned by the six-year war to such an extent that all come to be merged in a single national union a few months before victory. Thus, in circumstances utterly unforeseen, the old Miners' Federation, now once more built up in its numbers and in its powers—and its original purpose fulfilled at last—comes to an end after an existence of fifty-five years.

Sm. Royal 8vo. 42s. net

GEORGE ALLEN AND UNWIN LTD

2